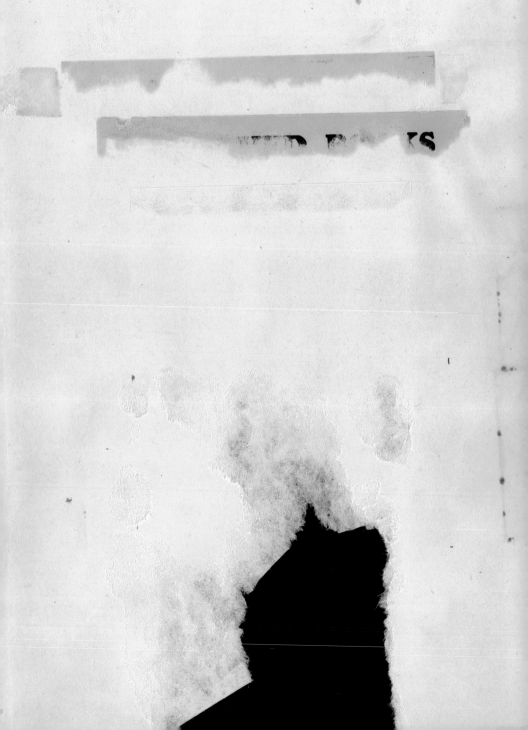

MAN *and the* STATE

Modern Political Ideas

Books *by* WILLIAM EBENSTEIN

FASCIST ITALY

THE LAW OF PUBLIC HOUSING

THE NAZI STATE

THE PURE THEORY OF LAW

THE GERMAN RECORD
A Political Portrait

MAN AND THE STATE
Modern Political Ideas

MAN *and the* STATE

Modern Political Ideas

edited by WILLIAM EBENSTEIN

Associate Professor of Politics

Princeton University

RINEHART & COMPANY, INC.

Publishers   *New York*

Ⓡ

To

JOHN M. GAUS

PREFACE

THE twentieth century has seen more world wars and revolutions than any other period in history. Conflicts between, and within, nations are over power and advantage; but they also express profound cleavages of ideas and creeds. In fact, the experience of both world wars has taught us that ideas are more resilient than the toughest aggregates of material power.

The purpose of this book is to present the major ideas that have animated the political thinking of the Western world in the modern age. The most direct way of acquainting oneself with the statements of great ideas is to go back to the great writers themselves. This is the method employed in the present book. However, I have prefaced each chapter of selections from original sources with a short introductory essay of my own. Its purpose is to explain the nature of the problem dealt with as well as to place the writers and their ideas in the proper historical setting and perspective. Selected bibliographies at the end of the book contain, in many cases, additional important works as well as critical studies.

As to the organization of this book: it has seemed to me that the customary chronological approach to the study of political ideas in terms of individual men is too impressionistic and biographical in character. Nor do I think that an intelligent understanding can best be attained by an arrangement under countries, because important ideas express the needs and responses of an age rather than of any one particular country. As a consequence, I have adopted the method of using *great issues* as the focus of attention and organization.

Part I, "The Foundations of Democracy," attempts to explore democracy as a way of life rather than as a governmental system. Democracy is not only institutions: it is men—and if the quality of the men who compose it is lacking, the hope of democratic survival will be dim.

Part II offers representative selections from modern "Antidemocratic Thought." The eruption of irrational, demonic forces in national and international politics has shaken our former confidence in the inevitability of democratic progress, and has demonstrated anew how fragile are the foundations of civilized living. The tradition of antidemocratic thinking is much older than Nazism and Fascism; while antidemocratic ideas and attitudes have been historically more deeply rooted in some countries than in others, no one can deny that all nations, even the most firmly democratic ones, have had their share of foes of free government and human fellowship based on equality.

Part III deals with "Capitalism, Socialism, Planning." Economic crises of unprecedented severity, unemployment, the concentration of wealth and income have all contributed to reawaken the awareness that economic and political problems are inseparably linked, and that, specifically, no body politic can be sound and healthy if it suffers from economic strangulation. Traditional ideologies of property and economic organization are being challenged by revolutionary Marxism on the one hand and by democratic socialism on the other.

Finally, Part IV, "From Nationalism to World Order," takes up the most urgent issue that confronts mankind. It examines such sources of international friction as nationalism, imperialism, racialism, and the concept of sovereignty. Positively, it shows how the British Commonwealth and the Soviet Union have sought to form political organizations in which several nations are associated in a wider framework than that of national sovereignty. As a nation of nations, the United States has a great part to play in the development of international government and administration, and this is why the last chapter of the book draws so heavily on American sources of inspiration.

In selecting the contributions that make up the main body of this volume I have not clung slavishly to well-known names. The first consideration has been readability and freshness of thought and expression. In several cases, I myself have translated materials hitherto unavailable in English, and in a few instances I have slightly revised older translations. The headings of the chapters and of most of the selections are my own.

My warm thanks are due to Professors Grayson L. Kirk of Columbia University and Alpheus T. Mason of Princeton University for friendly advice and helpful comments.

W. E.

Princeton University
July, 1947

CONTENTS

Part I: The Foundations of Democracy

Part II: *Antidemocratic Thought*

Part IV: From Nationalism to World Order

CHAPTER XIV. NATIONALISM: PEACEFUL OR AGGRESSIVE?   551

CHAPTER XV. RACE: SENSE AND NONSENSE   593

Chapter I

THE RIGHT TO REBEL

ONE of the stereotypes that will die, if at all, a slow death is the "conservative Englishman." The English could not be really conservative even if they tried.

In the sixteenth century they were the first (and only) major nation to break away from the authority of the Roman Church—then as now a pillar of conservatism in theology and politics. The other great nations of that era of religious revolt, the Spanish, French, and Italians, extirpated the seeds of protest with hot iron, if necessary. The Germans could not, as on other occasions, make up their minds how to save their souls. This first major revolution in the life of the English people is so important because, more perhaps than any other event in their history, it made English nationality conscious of itself. As elsewhere, war and nationalism were closely linked, and the English struggle against the Roman Church and its loyal monarchies, Spain and France, sharpened the awareness of the English that they were a people with a destiny of their own.

In the seventeenth century the English scored no better on conservative respectability. To cut off one king's head and to exile another monarch in one century is not a bad record, however one interprets the ideal of radical democracy. Since that time the British have not been so spectacular—they did not have to be. Try as they may, they can never hope to regain their "political innocence."

The "Glorious Revolution" of 1688 established, once and for all, the principle of parliamentary sovereignty in England. Twice in forty years the will of the people had triumphed over the will of the king.

In 1690 John Locke published *Two Treatises of Government,* in which he formulated, clearly and briefly, the classical theory of representative government. What makes the *Two Treatises* remarkable is that they are more than an *apologia* for the revolution of 1688. Unlike most political writers, Locke was able to perceive what lay behind the events of his own age. In particular, he insisted that popular consent was the sole legitimate basis of government, and that revolution was, under predictable circumstances, a natural and justifiable remedy in defending liberty. Before Locke, respectable people had abhorred rebellion as a form of sporadic, untamed, mob violence, illegitimate in origin and incapable of achieving any moral good. To impose upon power

3

the necessity of justifying its very existence, not by reference to divine grace, nor to tradition, nor to sheer force, but through the freely given consent of the people who alone were to judge their rulers, was one of the most revolutionary and potentially most civilizing acts of the human mind. When Locke declared the arbitrary autocrat an outcast and the people in rebellion against him as the defenders of the law, he gave new meanings to the words "law" and "rebellion." His insistence that there is a law higher than the formally proclaimed law of a community has led to the conception, so widespread in the English-speaking world, that obedience to the law is a high, but not, as in Germany and Japan, the highest civic virtue.

Opponents of the democratic solution of the problem of government, from Hobbes to Hitler, have charged that making political rule dependent upon the consent of the ruled "lays a ferment for frequent rebellion," as Locke puts it. To this grave accusation, Locke himself adduces several answers which are included below. The perspective of experience since 1690 supplies the most effective reply to the charge that democracy contains within itself seeds of anarchy and rebellion: the British and American systems of government, based upon recognition of the right to rebel, have proved themselves the most stable and successful political societies the world has ever seen. Paradoxically, where the right of revolution has been rejected in the name of order and stability, the political results have been putsches, blood purges, conspiracies, and violent swings from one extreme to another—the political record, specifically, of Germany and, to a lesser extent, of Japan. Neither Italian Fascism nor German Nazism, both extolling the principle of order, have been good propaganda for that creed. Mussolini's ouster in 1943, and his subsequent assassination, occurred under circumstances which suggest that Fascism was not all stability; the anti-Hitler plot of July 20, 1944, revealed that Prussian officers of the highest military rank had conspired to assassinate their beloved war leader. Stable as Nazism may have been throughout most of its career, there was always an element of plain murder in it— and that, again, was no better than a touch of anarchy or lawlessness would have been.

If Locke was the intellectual father of the British political system of the last two and a half centuries, his influence on American political thinking has been even more massive. To the extent that ideas and doctrines can be said to have affected political acts and institutions in the United States, Locke has influenced American political life more than any other writer, American or foreign. In fact, Locke has become more typically American than British, as time has gone by, especially in his economic views.

By committing themselves to Locke's theories of government, the British themselves supplied the case for the American Revolution, and, as can be seen from the text of the Declaration of Independence, the chief ideas and their wording were almost pure Locke. As a consequence, the main elements of the American political system, the inviolability of property, limited governmental powers, and the inalienable rights of the individual, are all contained in Locke. Writing in an expanding commercial society, his ideas also fitted the needs of a dynamic pioneer country. Above all, Locke's defense of the right to rebel seemed to the authors of the American Revolution eminently reasonable.

The most forceful expression of the right to revolution is to be found in a letter by the author of the Declaration of Independence. In a letter (dated November 13, 1787) to Colonel William Stephen Smith, Jefferson refers to Shays' insurrection in 1786, a minor revolt in Massachusetts, which seemed to prove to fearful souls that the government of the United States was producing more anarchy than peace. Jefferson adds general observations on the issue of rebellion. His thought that the "tree of liberty must be refreshed from time to time with the blood of patriots and tyrants" is probably as shocking to legitimists now as it was in 1787.

This Lockean-Jeffersonian theory of revolution has been vigorously reaffirmed in our own time by Harold J. Laski. His political thought has sprung from the rich heritage of the liberal faith, and his socialism is but an enlargement of his liberalism from the purely political into the economic and social aspects of life. His defense of the democratic socialist movements against the inroads of revolutionary communism, resumed by him with renewed vigor after the end of the Second World War, is inconsistent with the attempt to build up Harold J. Laski into a gauleiter or commissar. While no yogi, he never embraced the creed of the commissar.

During the years 1933–1939, when Nazism and Fascism grew stronger and stronger, unchecked by weak and divided democracies, Laski, like many other liberals, became intellectually moody and a bit pessimistic as to the ability of the capitalist democracies to survive the ordeal of Fascism. In this period he accepted some of the points of the Marxian analysis of history; his *State in Theory and Practice,* published in 1935, is the book which best represents that phase in his development. But even then, the main assumptions of his political theory were in the grand tradition set by Locke, and not in the deviation set by Marx. "The roots of valid law are, and can only be," says Laski, "within the individual conscience." This is pure Locke, and not even impure Marx or Lenin. To the charge that such a view, "by justifying refusal to obey, opens the door to anarchy, the answer is that the accusation is true." This, again, is a leading idea expressed by Laski in words that can be found almost identically in Locke.

In fact, Laski outdoes Locke: whereas Locke restricts the right to rebel to the injured *majority,* Laski goes further: he sees in history many examples of minorities and even single men revolting against intolerable iniquities, and he is therefore driven to the conclusion that, in the last resort, the *individual* will have to decide for himself whether he will bow to established law and order, or whether he will feel compelled, by an inner impulse of irrepressible intensity, to rebel.

The Constitution of the United States, wisely recognizing that the individual will accept social compulsion only up to a point, also adheres to this conception which goes beyond Locke, by declaring that some rights of the individual are inalienable.

Whatever the social and economic system that may exist at a particular time—be it early or advanced capitalism, rural economy or urban industry, pioneering conditions or an old established society, New Deal or Labor Party socialism—the right to rebel remains the great tradition of British and American politics. Rebelliousness, too, can, paradoxically, grow into tradition: the tradition of the dignity of man and of his unbreakable spirit.

―――――――――――――――――――――――――――

1. Democracy, Revolution, and the Threat of Anarchy *

JOHN LOCKE

―――――――――――――――――――――――――――

Perhaps it will be said that, the people being ignorant and always discontented, to lay the foundation of government in the unsteady opinion and uncertain humor of the people is to expose it to certain ruin; and no government will be able long to subsist if the people may set up a new legislative whenever they take offense at the old one. To this I answer: Quite the contrary. People are not so easily got out of their old forms as some are apt to suggest. They are hardly to be prevailed with to amend the acknowledged faults in the frame they have been accustomed to. And if there be any original defects, or adventitious ones introduced by time or corruption, it is not an easy thing to get them changed, even when all the world sees there is an opportunity for it. This slowness and aversion in the people to quit their old constitutions has, in the many revolutions which have been seen in this kingdom, in this and former ages still kept us to, or after some interval of fruitless attempts still brought us back again to, our old legislative of Kings, Lords, and Commons. And whatever provocations have made the crown be taken from some of our princes' heads, they never carried the people so far as to place it in another line.

But it will be said, this hypothesis lays a ferment for frequent rebellion. To which I answer:

First, no more than any other hypothesis. For when the people are made miserable, and find themselves exposed to the ill-usage of arbitrary power,

* From John Locke, *Two Treatises of Government* (1690).

cry up their governors as much as you will for sons of Jupiter, let them be sacred and divine, descended, or authorized from heaven, give them out for whom or what you please, the same will happen. The people generally ill-treated, and contrary to right, will be ready upon any occasion to ease themselves of a burden that sits heavy upon them. They will wish and seek for the opportunity, which in the change, weakness, and accidents of human affairs seldom delays long to offer itself. He must have lived but a little while in the world who has not seen examples of this in his time, and he must have read very little who cannot produce examples of it in all sorts of governments in the world.

Secondly, I answer, such revolutions happen not upon every little misman-agement in public affairs. Great mistakes in the ruling part, many wrong and inconvenient laws, and all the slips of human frailty will be borne by the people without mutiny or murmur. But if a long train of abuses, pre-varications and artifices, all tending the same way, make the design visible to the people—and they cannot but feel what they lie under, and see whither they are going—it is not to be wondered that they should then rouse themselves and endeavor to put the rule into such hands which may secure to them the ends for which government was at first erected, and without which ancient names and specious forms are so far from being better that they are much worse than the state of nature or pure anarchy; the inconveniences being all as great and as near, but the remedy farther off and more difficult.

Thirdly, I answer that this power in the people of providing for their safety anew by a new legislative when their legislators have acted contrary to their trust by invading their property, is the best fence against rebellion, and the probablest means to hinder it. For rebellion being an opposition, not to persons, but authority, which if founded only in the constitutions and laws of the government, those whoever they be who by force break through, and by force justify their violations of them, are truly and properly rebels. For when men by entering into society and civil government have excluded force, and introduced laws for the preservation of property, peace, and unity amongst themselves, those who set up force again in opposition to the laws do *rebellare*—that is, bring back again the state of war—and are properly rebels; which they who are in power (by the pretense they have to authority, the temptation of force they have in their hands, and the flattery of those about them) being likeliest to do, the properest way to prevent the evil is to show them the danger and injustice of it who are under the greatest temptation to run into it.

In both the forementioned cases, when either the legislative is changed or the legislators act contrary to the end for which they were constituted, those who are guilty are guilty of rebellion. For if anyone by force takes away the established legislative of any society, and the laws by them made pursuant to their trust, he thereby takes away the umpirage which everyone had consented to for a peaceable decision of all their controversies, and a bar to the state of war amongst them. They who remove or change the legislative, take away this decisive power, which nobody can have by the appointment and consent of the people, and so destroying the authority which the people did, and nobody else can, set up; and introducing a power which the people hath not authorized, actually introduce a state of war which is that of force without authority. And thus by removing the legislative established by the society (in whose decisions the people acquiesced and united as to that of their own will), they untie the knot and expose the people anew to the state of war. And if those who by force take away the legislative are rebels, the legislators themselves, as has been shown, can be no less esteemed so, when they who were set up for the protection and preservation of the people, their liberties and properties, shall by force invade and endeavor to take them away; and so they, putting themselves into a state of war with those who made them the protectors and guardians of their peace, are properly and with the greatest aggravation *rebellantes* (rebels).

But if they who say it lays a foundation for rebellion mean that it may occasion civil wars or intestine broils, to tell the people they are absolved from obedience when illegal attempts are made upon their liberties or properties, and may oppose the unlawful violence of those who were their magistrates when they invade their properties contrary to the trust put in them and that therefore this doctrine is not to be allowed, being so destructive to the peace of the world: they may as well say upon the same ground that honest men may not oppose robbers or pirates because this may occasion disorder or bloodshed. If any mischief come in such cases, it is not to be charged upon him who defends his own right, but on him that invades his neighbor's. If the innocent honest man must quietly quit all he has for peace's sake to him who will lay violent hands upon it, I desire it may be considered what a kind of peace there will be in the world which consists only in violence and rapine, and which is to be maintained only for the benefit of robbers and oppressors. Who would not think it an admirable peace betwixt the mighty and the mean when the lamb without resistance yielded his throat to be torn by the imperious wolf? Polyphemus's den gives us a perfect pattern of such a peace and such a government, wherein Ulysses and his companions had nothing to do but quietly to suffer themselves to be devoured. And no doubt Ulysses, who was a prudent man, preached up passive obedience, and exhorted them to a quiet submission by representing to them of what concernment peace was to mankind, and by showing the inconveniences which might happen if they should offer to resist Polyphemus, who had now the power over them.

The end of government is the good of mankind, and which is best for mankind, that the people should be always exposed to the boundless will of tyranny, or that the rulers should be sometimes liable to be opposed when they grow exorbitant in the use of their power, and employ it for the destruction and not the preservation of the properties of their people?

Nor let anyone say that mischief can arise from hence as often as it shall please a busy head or turbulent spirit to desire the alteration of the government. It is true such men may stir whenever they please, but it will be only to their own just ruin and perdition. For till the mischief be grown general, and the ill designs of the rulers become visible, or their attempts sensible to the greater part, the people, who are more disposed to suffer than right themselves by resistance, are not apt to stir. The examples of particular injustice or oppression of here and there an unfortunate man moves them not. But if they universally have a persuasion grounded upon manifest evidence that designs are carrying on against their liberties, and the general course and tendency of things cannot but give them strong suspicions of the evil intention of their governors, who is to be blamed for it? Who can help it if they, who might avoid it, bring themselves into this suspicion? Are the people to be blamed if they have the sense of rational creatures, and can think of things no otherwise than as they find and feel them? And is it not rather their fault who put things in such a posture that they would not have them thought as they are? I grant that the pride, ambition, and turbulency of private men have sometimes caused great disorders in commonwealths, and factions have been fatal to states and kingdoms. But whether the mischief hath oftener begun in the people's wantonness, and a desire to cast off the lawful authority of their rulers, or in the rulers' insolence and endeavors to get and exercise an arbitrary power over their people, whether oppression or disobedience gave the first rise to the disorder, I leave it to impartial history to determine. This I am sure, whoever, either ruler or subject, by force goes about to invade the rights of either prince or people, and lays the foundation for overturning the constitution and frame of any just government, he is guilty of the greatest crime I think a man is capable of, being to answer for all those mischiefs of blood, rapine, and desolation, which the breaking to pieces of governments bring on a country; and he who does it is justly to be esteemed the common enemy and pest of mankind, and is to be treated accordingly.

2. Declaration of Independence *

When, in the Course of human events, it becomes necessary for one people to dissolve the political bonds which have connected them with another, and

---

* From the *Declaration of Independence* (1776).

to assume, among the Powers of the earth the separate and equal station to which the Laws of Nature and of Nature's God entitle them, a decent respect to the opinions of mankind requires that they should declare the causes which impel them to the separation.

We hold these truths to be self-evident, that all men are created equal, that they are endowed by their Creator with certain unalienable Rights, that among these, are Life, Liberty, and the pursuit of Happiness. That, to secure these rights, Governments are instituted among Men, deriving their just Powers from the consent of the governed. That, whenever any form of Government becomes destructive of these ends, it is the Right of the People to alter or to abolish it, and to institute new Government, laying its foundation on such Principles, and organizing its Powers in such form as to them shall seem most likely to effect their Safety and Happiness. Prudence, indeed, will dictate that Government's long established should not be changed for light and transient causes; and, accordingly, all experience hath shewn, that mankind are more disposed to suffer, while evils are sufferable, than to right themselves by abolishing the forms to which they are accustomed. But, when a long train of abuses and usurpations, pursuing invariably the same Object, evinces a design to reduce them under absolute Despotism, it is their right, it is their duty, to throw off such Government, and to provide new Guards for their future Security. Such has been the patient sufferance of these Colonies; and such is now the necessity which constrains them to alter their former Systems of Government.

~~~~~~

3. Rebellion and Liberty *

THOMAS JEFFERSON

~~~~~~

The British ministry have so long hired their gazetteers to repeat and model into every form lies about our being in anarchy, that the world has at length believed them, the English nation has believed them, the ministers themselves have come to believe them, and what is more wonderful, we have believed them ourselves. Yet where does this anarchy exist? Where did it ever exist, except in the single instance of Massachusetts? And can history produce an instance of rebellion so honourably conducted? I say nothing of

* From a letter to Colonel William Stephens Smith (November 13, 1787).

its motives. They were founded in ignorance, not wickedness. God forbid we should ever be twenty years without such a rebellion. The people cannot be all, and always, well informed. The part which is wrong will be discontented in proportion to the importance of the facts they misconceive. If they remain quiet under such misconceptions it is a lethargy, the forerunner of death to the public liberty. We have had thirteen states independent for eleven years. There has been one rebellion. That comes to one rebellion in a century and a half, for each state. What country before ever existed a century and a half without a rebellion? And what country can preserve its liberties if their rulers are not warned from time to time that their people preserve the spirit of resistance? Let them take arms. The remedy is to set them right as to facts, pardon and pacify them. What signify a few lives lost in a century or two? The tree of liberty must be refreshed from time to time with the blood of patriots and tyrants. It is its natural manure.

4. Challenge to Authority *

HAROLD J. LASKI

There is, outside the purely formal realm, no obligation to obey the actual state. Our obedience is, and can only be, a function of our judgment upon its performance. That judgment, moreover, is never one which each citizen can make upon the same postulates, intellectual or emotional. What he decides will be the product of the place he occupies in the state, and the relation of that place to his view of what he ought to attain. He may be wrong in the view he takes; but he has never any rational alternative to action in the light of his own certainties. Upon this attitude there hinges a view of law the implications of which are important. It regards the validity of law as unrelated to the source from which it comes. Law becomes law as it goes into application; it is made law by being accepted. That is not to say that accepted law is right law; for law may be accepted by the might which is behind it. We have, in fact, to distinguish between three different senses in which the idea of law can be used. There is the formal juristic sense, which is no more than an announcement, ultimately dependent upon the sovereign authority, of the will to enforce certain decisions. There is the political sense, in which the formal announcement is validated by the acceptance of it by those to whom it applies. There is, finally, the ethical sense in which the decision announced ought to be obeyed, because it is morally right that what it proposes should be done.

Now it is clear that in the first two of these three senses the citizen has no inherent duty to obey. Few people would seriously claim that the juristic sense is always to be equated with the ethical; certainly, to take an obvious example, no Quaker could admit that a state whose government ordered its citizens to make war had, for this purpose, a title to their obedience. Nor can it, I think, be seriously claimed, either, that the political and ethical senses are identical; the commands of the Hitlerite state on June 30, 1934, were law in the sense that they went into effective operation, and were accepted by the population over whom it ruled; but most people in a position to make an independent judgment would, I suggest, regard them as ethically outrageous. Might, however profound, does not make right; effective operation of law still leaves undecided the question of ethical adequacy.

Neither formal competence, then, nor political power can confer a just title to obedience. With what are we left? Only, I think, with the insistence that law to be ethically valid must conform with the requirements of the system of rights the purposes of which the state exists to maintain. And since law is a command seeking to control my behaviour in some particular way, I must judge that conformity for myself as the test of its ethical adequacy. The roots of valid law, that is, are, and can only be, within the individual conscience. I make law legal, so to say, by giving to its operation the consent of my conscience.

If it is said that such a view, by justifying refusal to obey, opens the door to anarchy, the answer is that the accusation is true. But it is not a serious accusation. In the life of states the door to anarchy is always open because men are never willing to admit the unconditional conference of power. If, further, it be said that the individual conscience is at least as likely to be wrong as the consciences of those who rule the state, the answer, again, is that while this may be true, the citizen who yields his conviction on the ground that he may be mistaken will soon cease, in any meaning sense, to be a citizen at all. There is no way of making a state active in the fulfilment of its function except the knowledge that men will refuse to obey its commands where they regard them as a violation of that function. That was the truth that Pericles saw when he told the citizens of Athens that the secret of liberty was courage. Unless men are prepared to act by the insights they have, even when these insights are erroneous, they are bound to become no more than the passive recipients of orders to whose moral quality they are indifferent. When they do that, they poison the foundations of the state. For they then cease to be moral beings in any sense of the word that has meaning. They associate truth and justice and right automatically with the possession of physical power. No people prepared in that fashion to abdicate its humanity is likely to be long capable of creative achievement. For so to abdicate the duty of moral judgment is to sell oneself into slavery.

It is said that the individual is powerless, and that he wastes his energy by acting upon his judgment. But there are at least two answers to this view. A moral obligation is not less compelling because it may end in failure. To adopt that canon of effort is to accept the view that justice is the will of the stronger—a doctrine against which, as I have pointed out, the whole history of humanity is a protest. And to argue, secondly, that the individual is powerless is, on the record, quite untrue. He is powerless only when his perceptions are so completely unshared that he fails to arouse any note of response among his fellow-citizens; and he has always to remember that the shift of events may cause them to be shared at a later stage. The early Christians must have appeared singularly futile to their own generation when they challenged the majesty of Rome; but their steadfastness conquered the Western world. Luther's recalcitrance must have appeared akin to madness to a church which remembered its successful emergence from the stresses of the Conciliar revolt; but he changed the history of the world by his courage. Even so liberal a mind as Emerson could write of the American abolitionists that they were "narrow, self-pleasing, conceited men, and affect us as the insane do"; [1] but it was hardly a generation afterwards that so respectable an observer as Oliver Wendell Holmes, not given to extreme views, could say of his friend's judgment that "it would have taken a long time to get rid of slavery if some of Emerson's teachings had been accepted as the whole gospel of liberty." [2]

History, indeed, abounds with such instances. The individual who protests against the law he deems unjust is far less alone than he is likely to imagine. He is acting in a mental climate in which the experience borne in upon him is likely to be shared by others; and the gesture he makes may awaken others to the understanding of their obligations. No one who looks back upon their history can doubt that the suffragettes who, for eight years, defied the law awakened the British government to a sense that their claims were serious in a way that altered the whole perspective of those claims. No one can doubt either that the unbreakable will of Lenin was central to the success of the Bolshevik Revolution in 1917. That we must fight for our philosophy if we believe in it, seems to me the inescapable implication of the record.

Against this view two considerations are urged, in both of which there is, unquestionably, considerable force. It is said that to challenge the government is to weaken the authority of all law, and that to do so is to open the flood-gates to chaos. It was the sense of this danger which made T. H. Green, who admitted, in the last resort, the right to revolution, insist that we

[1] Quoted in V. F. Calverton, *The Liberalism of American Literature* (1932), p. 330.
[2] *Ibid.*, p. 331.

must approach the state in fear and trembling. But it is surely not less important to realise that respect for law must always mean respect for what the law does; and if the individual, whether alone or in concert with others, judges what the law does to be ethically intolerable, he must act upon the basis of his judgment. To decide otherwise is to argue that the highest duty of the individual is to maintain order, without regard to the quality of the order that is maintained. I do not find this argument compatible with the notion of the individual as a moral being.

It is said, secondly, that this view admits the right of any doctrine to support itself by force, if it can. Men have only to announce that they are moved by some profound conviction to be justified in using violence to attain their ends. Such an attitude, it is argued, is utterly destructive of the foundations of social well-being.

But the answer is surely that no doctrine, however evil, moves to the use of force unless it is rooted in profound grievance which it sees no other way to remedy. We may believe the Bolshevik Revolution to have been wholly evil; but it is clear that the previous conditions of the Russian state alone account for its origin and methods. We may argue, with the Communists, that Hitler has been no more than the agent of finance-capitalism in Germany; [1] but it is also clear that his victory was built upon the profound grievances of millions of Germans who saw no adequate redress for them in the habits of the Weimar republic. The truth is that men in general are so accustomed to obey that their departure from the normal canons of political behaviour is always an index to grave disease in the state. They have, as Burke said, "no interest in disorder; where they do wrong it is their error and not their crime." We need not argue that a doctrine which arms itself is wise or right to do so. But, on the facts, we have to argue that no doctrine ever does successfully arm itself unless the government it attacks has failed to deal with the grievances it expresses in a reasonable way.

That is, I think, apparent in the history of most revolutions. Certainly the student of the English civil wars, of the revolutions of France and of Russia, will note as not the least remarkable of their features, the patient efforts of the common people to await reform before they turned to violence. And in any society violence is unlikely if the conviction is widespread that the state is seriously attempting to fulfil its obligations. Violence comes when the facts persuade men to believe that the bona-fides of their rulers is no longer to be trusted.

[1] Cf. E. Henri, *Hitler Over Europe* (1933).

Chapter II

FREEDOM

IMPORTANT as the right of revolution is, especially in the Anglo-American view of government, there must be something else, if life is to be not only interesting, but also happy. Liberty and the pursuit of happiness go together, because each depends on the other.

Friedrich Schiller, the great German poet, sang that "freedom is only in the land of dreams." Others have agreed with Schiller that at best freedom is an illusion, and at worst, licence and anarchy. Where there has been no solid experience of freedom, liberty has often been confused, even by great minds like Goethe, with submission to laws—physical laws of nature or political laws of society.

The Greeks showed their genius of originality in matters political when they defined liberty essentially as the right to participate in public affairs. Only beasts or gods lived, according to Aristotle, outside the confines of the sheltering city; thoughtful Greek statesmen, like Pericles, refused to apply the concept of liberty to the arbitrary rule of the tyrant or to the individual outside of the social group, facing the universe in his pitiable loneliness. As true "political animals" (Aristotle), the Greeks could not think of freedom as a purely individual affair, unrelated to the quality of a person as a member of his organized political community.

With the triumph of Christianity, and its emphasis on the individual soul and its relations to God, Western man lost, for good or bad, the unconscious, almost naïve, sense of total integration into the social group. The very duality of the individual versus the state (one of the key issues of all modern political philosophy) presupposes the concepts of individual and state. Both are historically, post-Renaissance ideas. The modern concept of the individual was born in the great revolutionary movements of the sixteenth century—economic individualism as capitalism, religious individualism as Protestantism, and cultural individualism as scientific learning. Likewise, the modern national state is only a product of the last four centuries (in Germany and Italy, of only two or three generations).

In the changed circumstances, economic and political, of the modern state, the concept of liberty tended to assume, more and more, the negative emphasis of the *absence of restraint* rather than the positive stress on participation in public affairs. In the English-speaking nations this view of liberty was especially current from the eighteenth to the late nineteenth century, and its full force is far from spent.

French political thought has never quite followed this Anglo-American tradition, possibly because the economic individualism of capitalism never flourished in France with the same thoroughness as in England and America. Jean Jacques Rousseau's *Social Contract,* published twenty-seven years before the French Revolution, has been one of the most influential books in history. The opening sentence, "Man is born free; and everywhere he is in chains," proclaims the voice of a fearless challenger who had the intellectual gift to think clearly, as well as the artistic genius to express his mind dramatically and imaginatively. Outside the English-speaking countries, Rousseau has had more popular philosophical appeal than any other political writer of the last two centuries (with the possible exception of Karl Marx). The young Continental European or Latin American discovers the world of liberty through Rousseau rather than through Locke and John Stuart Mill. In the Soviet Union, too, Rousseau's works have been more widely printed and read since 1917 than those of any other non-Russian political writer before Karl Marx.

Rousseau's theory of the social contract is one of the most ingenious doctrinal attempts to base political obligation on *consent*. Whether Rousseau was in possession of all the anthropological facts in describing the "state of nature" is immaterial, when compared with the timeless moral truths that he expressed about the nature of the state. What makes *The Social Contract* one of the most complex and baffling documents is the fact that democrats, as well as some Nazis, Fascists and Communists, have seen in it the rays of their particular light. Rousseau's central idea of the "general will" has frequently attracted the totalitarian mentality. Some of this confusion is due, perhaps, to Rousseau's failure to distinguish clearly the "general will" from the "will of all." Yet Rousseau is one of the few eighteenth-century libertarian writers who managed to go beyond individualism unlimited, who captured the spirit of "We, the people. . . ." Without this spirit of communal solidarity, democratic institutions are bound to lead from selfish individual interest and group greed to social chaos and dissolution. To say, as Rousseau did, that "the general will considers only the common interest," while "the will of all takes private interests into account, and is no more than a sum of particular wills," is a statement of the problem rather than its solution. Still, the statement is important enough. Difficult as it may be to define what the public interest is in a concrete issue, thoughtful citizens in a working democracy are aware that some practical way must be found to transcend purely private, or group, interests. In labor relations boards, e.g., we have long accepted the principle that in addition to representatives of labor and capital, the public view must be reflected by a "public member," who has the most complex task of defending what is the "general will" or interest of the whole community rather than of a particular group.

As the Western world, including Britain and the other English-speaking democracies, becomes more conscious of society and its responsibilities toward the individual, Rousseau will appear less strange to erstwhile readers of Locke and Mill. Also, Rousseau's stress on the small political unit as the only one suited to real and direct democracy may acquire new significance, the more we seek to discover the means by which we can create small geographical and functional areas of self-government within the overly impersonal and anonymous methods of modern large-scale technology and government.

Turning from Rousseau to John Stuart Mill's essay *On Liberty* (1859), we move from brilliance to balance, from the general to the specific, from glittering *esprit* to superb common sense. With the Periclean funeral address and Lincoln's Gettysburg Address, *On Liberty* possibly ranks as the greatest testimony of the liberal faith. Liberalism as a way of life rather than as a set of governmental procedures—this is the spirit captured by John Stuart Mill in his immortal essay.

When does freedom become "licence"? Are there any limits at all to freedom of thought and (if the latter is not to remain a monologue or communion with the cosmos) freedom of speech, including all the other freedoms of communication? Although the Constitution of the United States expressly protects freedom of speech, two-thirds of the American people believed, according to a public-opinion poll in the summer of 1946, that some opinions (especially if opposed to the basic doctrines of "Americanism") should not be permitted freedom of expression. Only one-third held firm that there should be no limitation of freedom of speech in the United States, even for those who hold views contrary to the established form of government. Of the forty-eight states of the Union, thirty-three have passed "sedition" or "criminal syndicalism" laws, mostly in the immediate years following the First World War; under them, men have been sentenced to long prison terms for selling, or even merely possessing, so-called "radical" books or pamphlets.

One of the most famous cases dealing with freedom of opinion is *Abrams v. United States* (1919). On August 23, 1918, an obscure anarchist, named Abrams, distributed some leaflets in a poor section of New York, in which he attacked the United States government for sending troops and munitions to Russia to fight the Bolshevik government that had been established in November, 1917. Abrams was charged with violation of the Espionage Act of 1918, specifically with having hindered the war effort of the United States against Germany, by publishing leaflets intending to cause strikes and revolts. Abrams, aged twenty-nine, was sentenced to twenty years' imprisonment by a federal district court. His four codefendants, also completely unknown Socialist and anarchist youths, received prison terms ranging from three to twenty years. In 1919 the case came to the Supreme Court, and seven out of the nine judges upheld the sentence of the lower court. Mr. Justice Holmes wrote the dissenting opinion, in which Mr. Justice Brandeis concurred. Holmes denied that society has the right to punish opinions unless they "so imminently threaten immediate interference with the lawful and pressing purposes of the law that an immediate check is required to save the country." Holmes had expressed the nature of this test in even sharper terms in *Schenck* v. *United States* (1919): "The question in every case is whether the words used are used in such circumstances and are of such a nature as to create a clear and present danger that they will bring about the substantive evils that Congress has a right to prevent. It is a question of proximity and degree." Holmes thus denied that words are punishable because they might incite to violence in an undefined future. In the *Abrams* case the test of "imminent threat" seemed to indicate to Holmes that Abrams was unjustly punished: "Now nobody can suppose that the surreptitious publishing of a silly leaflet by an unknown man, without more, would present any immediate danger that its opinions would hinder the success of the government arms or have any appreciable tendency to do so." Far from being pro-German, Abrams had bitterly denounced German militarism in his leaflets. Holmes finally asserted this: "In this case sentences of twenty years imprisonment have been imposed for the publishing of two leaflets that I believe the defendants had as much right to publish as the Government has to publish the Constitution of the United States now vainly invoked by them." As time went on, more and more people realized the folly of the Anglo-French-American-Japanese expedition to Russia in 1918; in 1929 Secretary of War Newton D. Baker wrote that "the expedition was nonsense from the beginning."

Democracies, it seems, therefore, are not immune from the danger of oppressing freedom of opinion and speech in the name of patriotism, loyalty to democratic institutions, and fear of nonconformity. This is why Mill's warning is perennially timely that no society is "completely free" in which "absolute freedom of opinion and sentiment on all subjects, practical or speculative, scientific, moral or theological" does not exist "absolute and unqualified." And those who justify the right of the majority to persecute dissenters on the ground that majorities are right should reflect on Mill's warning that "ages are no more infallible than individuals."

Max Eastman's discussion of what has happened to American freedom (in his essay "Political Liberty," included in *Freedom in the Modern World,* edited by Horace M. Kallen) amply bears out Mill's anxieties as to what can happen to freedom under intolerant majorities. When Eastman published his essay in 1928, he was described by his editor, Horace M. Kallen, as a "notable apostle of communism, the friend of Trotsky, and a critic of the present regime in Russia." In the meantime, Eastman has risen in the world of freedom by becoming a "roving editor" of *The Reader's Digest*. He is still "a critic of the present regime in Russia," but, as roving editor of *The Reader's Digest,* no longer a "notable apostle of communism."

It is one of the merits of John Dewey to have broadened the Anglo-American tradition of philosophical pragmatism by applying methods of scientific inquiry to the solution of social problems. There is hardly a province of American life in which his influence has not been seminal: in particular, Dewey has taught us that wrong answers are more often than not the result of bad questions, and he has always sought to replace meaningless generalities and abstractions by concrete issues. Whereas the orthodox point of view maintains that individual freedom and collective organization are irreconcilable, Dewey holds that "there is no effective or objective freedom without organization," although he is willing to concede that "organization may become a hindrance to freedom," especially if it becomes "over-organization." Therefore, abstract theory cannot settle this issue, and "the relation of individual freedom to organization is seen to be an experimental affair." Dewey's faith in reason and intelligence as guides through the labyrinth of conflict and passion is more needed today than ever before. The world has become less rational than it was a generation or two ago, and the attack upon scientific thinking has been increasing in violence and dogmatism.

Dewey's "instrumentalist" approach to the problem of freedom, theoretical and practical, is supported by Bronislaw Malinowski's *Freedom and Civilization* (published in 1944, two years after the author's death). Malinowski was one of the most distinguished anthropologists of his time. His best known work is the *Sexual Life of the Savages*. His analysis of freedom in *Freedom and Civilization* is founded on a lifetime study of the fundamentals of human culture and civilization, from the natives of the Trobriand Islands in the south Pacific to the natives of the British Isles in the north Atlantic, among whom he spent most of his life. "The concept of freedom," Malinowski says, "can only be defined with reference to human beings organized and endowed with cultural motives, implements and values, which *ipso facto* implies the existence of law, an economic system and political organization —in short, a cultural system."

One of the most original interpretations of the deviations and aberrations of modern man from the path of freedom to the road of self-enslavement is to be found in *Escape from Freedom* (1941), by Erich Fromm. Strongly influenced by the teachings of Freud, Fromm finds psychoanalysis too individualistic in its stress on the problems of satisfaction or frustration of instinctual needs. "The key problem of psychology," Fromm writes, "is that of the specific kind of relatedness of the individual toward the world." Long before modern psychology, writers and poets saw in the loneliness of man one of the main driving forces of his existence. Fromm summarizes the political, economic, and cultural causes that make modern man feel small and helpless amidst the bigness in which he finds himself. His analysis of masochism and sadism as escape mechanisms from personal insecurity deserves the closest attention, as it explains one of the mainsprings of the dynamics of fascist mass movements, both of submissive followers and authoritarian leaders. But Fromm's study goes beyond the critique of fascist perversions of liberty, and shows the meaning of positive freedom in the realization of the self as the "full affirmation of the uniqueness of the individual."

An entirely different approach to the political problem of the human personality will be found in Jacques Maritain's *Rights of Man and Natural Law* (1943). Within the world organization of the Roman Catholic Church, France has always had the reputation of following the most liberal interpretation of religious faith, just as Spain has been the home of uncompromising fanaticism. Within that French tradition, no Catholic writer has achieved higher fame in recent times than Maritain. He is in the great tradition of political speculation, firmly inaugurated by Plato, that man's politics is based, in the last resort, on man's nature. To a deeply religious thinker like Maritain, politics is but a branch of theology. The laws governing human conduct must be based upon natural law as expressing the very nature of man, and "only when the Gospel has penetrated to the very depth of human substance will natural law appear in its flower and its perfection."

Perhaps the only concept born in the Second World War which will permanently enrich the language of liberty is President Franklin D. Roosevelt's idea of the "Four Freedoms." He used this term in a message to Congress on the State of the Union, which he delivered on January 6, 1941. The outlook for democracy was not too promising in those dark days, when Britain held the fortress of freedom, fighting alone with her back to the wall. President Roosevelt felt, with deep conviction, that freedom on the American continent would be mortally imperiled, were the Axis to overcome the last defender of freedom in Europe. He realized that freedom, to survive, could not be the privilege of only one country, just as freedom within a nation could not be founded on the privileged few. His "Four Freedoms"—freedom of speech and religion, and freedom from want and fear—express this meaning of freedom, clearly stated and appealing to all men who love liberty. "This is no vision of a distant millennium," the President said; "it is a definite basis for a kind of world attainable in our time and generation."

1. Freedom and the General Will *

JEAN JACQUES ROUSSEAU

Man is born free; and everywhere he is in chains. One thinks himself the master of others, and still remains a greater slave than they. How did this change come about? I do not know. What can make it legitimate? That question I think I can answer.

If I took into account only force, and the effects derived from it, I should say: "As long as a people is compelled to obey, and obeys, it does well; as soon as it can shake off the yoke, and shakes it off, it does still better, for, regaining its liberty by the same right as took it away, either it is justified in resuming it, or there was no justification for those who took it away." But the social order is a sacred right which is the basis of all other rights. Nevertheless, this right does not come from nature, and must therefore be founded on conventions.

The strongest is never strong enough to be always the master, unless he transforms strength into right, and obedience into duty. Hence the right of the strongest, which, though to all seeming meant ironically, is really laid down as a fundamental principle. But are we never to have an explanation of this phrase? Force is a physical power, and I fail to see what moral effect it can have. To yield to force is an act of necessity, not of will—at the most, an act of prudence. In what sense can it be a duty?

Suppose for a moment that this so-called "right" exists. I maintain that the sole result is a mass of inexplicable nonsense. For, if force creates right, the effect changes with the cause: every force that is greater than the first succeeds to its right. As soon as it is possible to disobey with impunity, disobedience is legitimate; and, the strongest being always in the right, the only thing that matters is to act so as to become the strongest. But what kind of right is that which perishes when force fails? If we must obey perforce, there is no need to obey because we ought; and if we are not forced to obey, we are under no obligation to do so. Clearly, the word "right" adds nothing to force: in this connection, it means absolutely nothing.

Obey the powers that be. If this means yield to force, it is a good precept, but superfluous: I can answer for its never being violated. All power comes from God, I admit; but so does all sickness: does that mean that we are

* From Jean Jacques Rousseau, *The Social Contract* (1762; Everyman's Library, E. P. Dutton & Co., Inc., 1938). By permission.

forbidden to call in the doctor? A brigand surprises me at the edge of a wood: must I not merely surrender my purse on compulsion; but, even if I could withhold it, am I in conscience bound to give it up? For certainly the pistol he holds is also a power.

Let us then admit that force does not create right, and that we are obliged to obey only legitimate powers.

Since no man has a natural authority over his fellow, and force creates no right, we must conclude that conventions form the basis of all legitimate authority among men.

If an individual, says Grotius, can alienate his liberty and make himself the slave of a master, why could not a whole people do the same and make itself subject to a king? There are in this passage plenty of ambiguous words which would need explaining; but let us confine ourselves to the word *alienate*. To alienate is to give or to sell. Now, a man who becomes the slave of another does not give himself; he sells himself, at the least for his subsistence: but for what does a people sell itself? A king is so far from furnishing his subjects with their subsistence that he gets his own only from them; and, according to Rabelais, kings do not live on nothing. Do subjects then give their persons on condition that the king takes their goods also? I fail to see what they have left to preserve.

It will be said that the despot assures his subjects civil tranquillity. Granted; but what do they gain, if the wars his ambition brings down upon them, his insatiable avidity, and the vexatious conduct of his ministers press harder on them than their own dissensions would have done? What do they gain, if the very tranquillity they enjoy is one of their miseries? Tranquillity is found also in dungeons; but is that enough to make them desirable places to live in? The Greeks imprisoned in the cave of the Cyclops lived there very tranquilly, while they were awaiting their turn to be devoured.

To say that a man gives himself gratuitously, is to say what is absurd and inconceivable; such an act is null and illegitimate, from the mere fact that he who does it is out of his mind. To say the same of a whole people is to suppose a people of madmen; and madness creates no right.

Even if each man could alienate himself, he could not alienate his children: they are born men and free; their liberty belongs to them, and no one but they has the right to dispose of it. Before they come to years of discretion, the father can, in their name, lay down conditions for their preservation and well-being, but he cannot give them irrevocably and without conditions: such a gift is contrary to the ends of nature, and exceeds the rights of paternity. It would therefore be necessary, in order to legitimise an arbitrary government, that in every generation the people should be in a position to accept or reject it; but, were this so, the government would be no longer arbitrary.

To renounce liberty is to renounce being a man, to surrender the rights of humanity and even its duties. For him who renounces everything no indemnity is possible. Such a renunciation is incompatible with man's nature; to remove all liberty from his will is to remove all morality from his acts. Finally, it is an empty and contradictory convention that sets up, on the one side, absolute authority, and, on the other, unlimited obedience. Is it not clear that we can be under no obligation to a person from whom we have the right to exact everything? Does not this condition alone, in the absence of equivalence or exchange, in itself involve the nullity of the act? For what right can my slave have against me, when all that he has belongs to me, and, his right being mine, this right of mine against myself is a phrase devoid of meaning?

The passage from the state of nature to the civil state produces a very remarkable change in man, by substituting justice for instinct in his conduct, and giving his actions the morality they had formerly lacked. Then only, when the voice of duty takes the place of physical impulses and right of appetite, does man, who so far had considered only himself, find that he is forced to act on different principles, and to consult his reason before listening to his inclinations. Although, in this state, he deprives himself of some advantages which he got from nature, he gains in return others so great, his faculties are so stimulated and developed, his ideas so extended, his feelings so ennobled, and his whole soul so uplifted, that, did not the abuses of this new condition often degrade him below that which he left, he would be bound to bless continually the happy moment which took him from it for ever, and, instead of a stupid and unimaginative animal, made him an intelligent being and a man.

Let us draw up the whole account in terms easily commensurable. What man loses by the social contract is his natural liberty and an unlimited right to everything he tries to get and succeeds in getting; what he gains is civil liberty and the proprietorship of all he possesses. If we are to avoid mistakes in weighing one against the other, we must clearly distinguish natural liberty, which is bounded only by the strength of the individual, from civil liberty, which is limited by the general will; and possession, which is merely the effect of force or the right of the first occupier, from property, which can be founded only on a positive title.

We might, over and above all this, add, to what man acquires in the civil state, moral liberty, which alone makes him truly master of himself; for the mere impulse of appetite is slavery, while obedience to a law which we prescribe to ourselves is liberty.

The general will is always right and tends to the public advantage; but it does not follow that the deliberations of the people are always equally correct. Our will is always for our own good, but we do not always see what that is; the people is never corrupted, but it is often deceived, and on such occasions only does it seem to will what is bad.

There is often a great deal of difference between the will of all and the general will; the latter considers only the common interest, while the former takes private interest into account, and is no more than a sum of particular wills: but take away from these same wills the pluses and minuses that cancel one another, and the general will remains as the sum of the differences.

If, when the people, being furnished with adequate information, held its deliberations, the citizens had no communication one with another, the grand total of the small differences would always give the general will, and the decision would always be good. But when factions arise, and partial associations are formed at the expense of the great association, the will of each of these associations becomes general in relation to its members, while it remains particular in relation to the State: it may then be said that there are no longer as many votes as there are men, but only as many as there are associations. The differences become less numerous and give a less general result. Lastly, when one of these associations is so great as to prevail over all the rest, the result is no longer a sum of small differences, but a single difference; in this case there is no longer a general will, and the opinion which prevails is purely particular.

It is therefore essential, if the general will is to be able to express itself, that there should be no partial society within the State, and that each citizen should think only his own thoughts.

As nature has set bounds to the stature of a well-made man, and, outside those limits, makes nothing but giants or dwarfs, similarly, for the constitution of a State to be at its best, it is possible to fix limits that will make it neither too large for good government, nor too small for self-maintenance. In every body politic there is a *maximum* strength which it cannot exceed and which it only loses by increasing in size. Every extension of the social tie means its relaxation; and, generally speaking, a small State is stronger in proportion than a great one.

A thousand arguments could be advanced in favour of this principle. First, long distances make administration more difficult, just as a weight becomes heavier at the end of a longer lever. Administration therefore becomes more and more burdensome as the distance grows greater; for, in the first place, each city has its own, which is paid for by the people: each district its own, still paid for by the people: then comes each province, and then the great governments, satrapies, and vice-royalties, always costing more the higher you go, and always at the expense of the unfortunate people. Last of all comes the supreme administration, which eclipses all the rest. All these overcharges are a continual drain upon the subjects; so far from being better governed by all these different orders, they are worse governed than if there were only a single authority over them. In the meantime, there scarce remain resources enough to meet emergencies; and, when recourse must be had to these, the State is always on the eve of destruction.

This is not all; not only has the government less vigour and promptitude for securing the observance of the laws, preventing nuisances, correcting abuses, and guarding against seditious undertakings begun in distant places; the people has less affection for its rulers, whom it never sees, for its country, which, to its eyes, seems like the world, and for its fellow-citizens, most of whom are unknown to it. The same laws cannot suit so many diverse provinces with different customs, situated in the most various climates, and incapable of enduring a uniform government. Different laws lead only to trouble and confusion among peoples which, living under the same rulers and in constant communication one with another, intermingle and intermarry, and, coming under the sway of new customs, never know if they can call their very patrimony their own. Talent is buried, virtue unknown and vice unpunished, among such a multitude of men who do not know one another, gathered together in one place at the seat of the central administration. The leaders, overwhelmed with business, see nothing for themselves; the State is governed by clerks. Finally, the measures which have to be taken to maintain the general authority, which all these distant officials wish to escape or to impose upon, absorb all the energy of the public, so that there is none left for the happiness of the people. There is hardly enough to defend it when need arises, and thus a body which is too big for its constitution gives way and falls crushed under its own weight.

The better the constitution of a State is, the more do public affairs encroach on private in the minds of the citizens. Private affairs are even of much less importance, because the aggregate of the common happiness furnishes a greater proportion of that of each individual, so that there is less for him to seek in particular cares. In a well-ordered city every man flies to the assemblies: under a bad government no one cares to stir a step to get to them, because no one is interested in what happens there, because it is foreseen that the general will will not prevail, and lastly because domestic cares are all-absorbing. Good laws lead to the making of better ones; bad ones bring about worse. As soon as any man says of the affairs of the State: *What does it matter to me?* the State may be given up for lost.

Those who distinguish civil from theological intolerance are, to my mind, mistaken. The two forms are inseparable. It is impossible to live at peace with those we regard as damned; to love them would be to hate God who punishes them: we positively must either reclaim or torment them. Wherever theological intolerance is admitted, it must inevitably have some civil effect; and as soon as it has such an effect, the Sovereign is no longer Sovereign even in the temporal sphere: thenceforth priests are the real masters, and kings only their ministers.

Now that there is and can be no longer an exclusive national religion, tolerance should be given to all religions that tolerate others, so long as their dogmas contain nothing contrary to the duties of citizenship. But whoever dares to say: *Outside the Church is no salvation,* ought to be driven from the State, unless the State is the Church, and the prince the pontiff. Such a dogma is good only in a theocratic government; in any other, it is fatal.

2. Freedom of Opinion—Limited or Unlimited? *

JOHN STUART MILL

Speaking generally, it is not, in constitutional countries, to be apprehended, that the government, whether completely responsible to the people or not, will often attempt to control the expression of opinion, except when in doing so it makes itself the organ of the general intolerance of the public. Let us suppose, therefore, that the government is entirely at one with the people, and never thinks of exerting any power of coercion unless in agreement with what it conceives to be their voice. But I deny the right of the people to exercise such coercion, either by themselves or by their government. The power itself is illegitimate. It is as noxious, or more noxious, when exerted in accordance with public opinion, than when in opposition to it. If all mankind minus one, were of one opinion, and only one person were of the contrary opinion, mankind would be no more justified in silencing that one person, than he, if he had the power, would be justified in silencing mankind. Were an opinion a personal possession of no value except to the owner; if to be obstructed in the enjoyment of it were simply a private injury, it would make some difference whether the injury was inflicted only on a few persons or on many. But the peculiar evil of silencing the expression of an opinion is, that it is robbing the human race; posterity as well as the existing generation; those who dissent from the opinion, still more than those who hold it. If the opinion is right, they are deprived of the opportunity of exchanging error for truth; if wrong, they lose, what is almost as great a benefit, the clearer perception and livelier impression of truth, produced by its collision with error.

* From John Stuart Mill, *On Liberty* (1859).

It is necessary to consider separately these two hypotheses, each of which has a distinct branch of the argument corresponding to it. We can never be sure that the opinion we are endeavouring to stifle is a false opinion; and if we were sure, stifling it would be an evil still.

First: the opinion which it is attempted to suppress by authority may possibly be true. Those who desire to suppress it, of course deny its truth; but they are not infallible. They have no authority to decide the question for all mankind, and exclude every other person from the means of judging. To refuse a hearing to an opinion, because they are sure that it is false, is to assume that their certainty is the same thing as absolute certainty. All silencing of discussion is an assumption of infallibility. Its condemnation may be allowed to rest on this common argument, not the worse for being common.

Unfortunately for the good sense of mankind, the fact of their fallibility is far from carrying the weight in their practical judgement, which is always allowed to it in theory; for while every one well knows himself to be fallible, few think it necessary to take any precautions against their own fallibility, or admit the supposition that any opinion, of which they feel very certain, may be one of the examples of the error to which they acknowledge themselves to be liable. Absolute princes, or others who are accustomed to unlimited deference, usually feel this complete confidence in their own opinions on nearly all subjects. People more happily situated, who sometimes hear their opinions disputed, and are not wholly unused to be set right when they are wrong, place the same unbounded reliance only on such of their opinions as are shared by all who surround them, or to whom they habitually defer: for in proportion to a man's want of confidence in his own solitary judgement, does he usually repose, with implicit trust, on the infallibility of 'the world' in general. And the world, to each individual, means the part of it with which he comes in contact; his party, his sect, his church, his class of society: the man may be called, by comparison, almost liberal and large-minded to whom it means anything so comprehensive as his own country or his own age. Nor is his faith in this collective authority at all shaken by his being aware that other ages, countries, sects, churches, classes, and parties have thought, and even now think, the exact reverse. He devolves upon his own world the responsibility of being in the right against the dissentient worlds of other people; and it never troubles him that mere accident has decided which of these numerous worlds is the object of his reliance, and that the same causes which make him a Churchman in London, would have made him a Buddhist or a Confucian in Pekin. Yet it is as evident in itself, as any amount of argument can make it, that ages are no more infallible than individuals; every age having held many opinions which subsequent ages have deemed not only false but absurd; and it is as certain that many opinions, now general, will be rejected by future ages, as it is that many, once general, are rejected by the present.

The objection likely to be made to this argument would probably take some such form as the following. There is no greater assumption of infallibility in forbidding the propagation of error, than in any other thing which is done by public authority on its own judgement and responsibility. Judgement is given to men that they may use it. Because it may be used erroneously, are men to be told that they ought not to use it at all? To prohibit what they think pernicious, is not claiming exemption from error, but fulfilling the duty incumbent on them, although fallible, of acting on their conscientious conviction. If we were never to act on our opinions, because those opinions may be wrong, we should leave all our interests uncared for, and all our duties unperformed. An objection which applies to all conduct, can be no valid objection to any conduct in particular. It is the duty of governments, and of individuals, to form the truest opinions they can: to form them carefully, and never impose them upon others unless they are quite sure of being right. But when they are sure (such reasoners may say), it is not conscientiousness but cowardice to shrink from acting on their opinions, and allow doctrines which they honestly think dangerous to the welfare of mankind, either in this life or in another, to be scattered abroad without restraint, because other people, in less enlightened times, have persecuted opinions now believed to be true. Let us take care, it may be said, not to make the same mistake: but governments and nations have made mistakes in other things, which are not denied to be fit subjects for the exercise of their authority: they have laid on bad taxes, made unjust wars. Ought we therefore to lay on no taxes, and, under whatever provocation, make no wars? Men, and governments, must act to the best of their ability. There is no such thing as absolute certainty, but there is assurance sufficient for the purposes of human life. We may, and must, assume our opinion to be true for the guidance of our own conduct: and it is assuming no more when we forbid bad men to pervert society by the propagation of opinions which we regard as false and pernicious.

I answer, that it is assuming very much more. There is the greatest difference between presuming an opinion to be true, because, with every opportunity for contesting it, it has not been refuted, and assuming its truth for the purpose of not permitting its refutation. Complete liberty of contradicting and disproving our opinion, is the very condition which justifies us in assuming its truth for purposes of action; and on no other terms can a being with human facilities have any rational assurance of being right.

When we consider either the history of opinion, or the ordinary conduct of human life, to what is it to be ascribed that the one and the other are no worse than they are? Not certainly to the inherent force of the human understanding; for, on any matter not self-evident, there are ninety-nine persons totally incapable of judging of it, for one who is capable; and the capacity of the hundredth person is only comparative; for the majority of the eminent men of every past generation held many opinions now known to be erroneous, and did or approved numerous things which no one will now justify. Why is it, then, that there is on the whole a preponderance among mankind of rational opinions and rational conduct? If there really is this preponderance—which there must be unless human affairs are, and have always been, in an almost desperate state—it is owing to a quality of the human mind, the source of everything respectable in man either as an intellectual or as a moral being, namely, that his errors are corrigible. He is capable of rectifying his mistakes, by discussion and experience. Not by experience alone. There must be discussion, to show how experience is to be interpreted. Wrong opinions and practices gradually yield to fact and argument: but facts and arguments, to produce any effect on the mind, must be brought before it. Very few facts are able to tell their own story, without comments to bring out their meaning. The whole strength and value, then, of human judgement, depending on the one property, that it can be set right when it is wrong, reliance can be placed on it only when the means of setting it right are kept constantly at hand. In the case of any person whose judgement is really deserving of confidence, how has it become so? Because he has kept his mind open to criticism of his opinions and conduct. Because it has been his practice to listen to all that could be said against him; to profit by as much of it as was just, and expound to himself, and upon occasion to others, the fallacy of what was fallacious. Because he has felt, that the only way in which a human being can make some approach to knowing the whole of a subject, is by hearing what can be said about it by persons of every variety of opinion, and studying all modes in which it can be looked at by every character of mind. No wise man ever acquired his wisdom in any mode but this; nor is it in the nature of human intellect to become wise in any other manner. The steady habit of correcting and completing his own opinion by collating it with those of others, so far from causing doubt and hesitation in carrying it into practice, is the only stable foundation for a just reliance on it: for, being cognisant of all that can, at least obviously, be said against him, and having taken up his position against all gainsayers—knowing that he has sought for objections and difficulties, instead of avoiding them, and has shut out no light which can be thrown upon the subject from any quarter—he has a right to think his judgement better than that of any person, or any multitude, who have not gone through a similar process.

It is not too much to require that what the wisest of mankind, those who are best entitled to trust their own judgement, find necessary to warrant their relying on it, should be submitted to by that miscellaneous collection of a few wise and many foolish individuals, called the public. The most intolerant of churches, the Roman Catholic Church, even at the canonization of a saint, admits, and listens patiently to, a 'devil's advocate.' The holiest of men, it appears, cannot be admitted to posthumous honours, until all that the devil could say against him is known and weighed. If even the Newtonian philosophy were not permitted to be questioned, mankind could not feel as complete assurance of its truth as they now do. The beliefs which we have most warrant for, have no safeguard to rest on, but a standing invitation to the whole world to prove them unfounded. If the challenge is not accepted, or is accepted and the attempt fails, we are far enough from certainty still; but we have done the best that the existing state of human reason admits of; we have neglected nothing that could give the truth a chance of reaching us: if the lists are kept open, we may hope that if there be a better truth, it will be found when the human mind is capable of receiving it; and in the meantime we may rely on having attained such approach to truth, as is possible in our own day. This is the amount of certainty attainable by a fallible being, and this the sole way of attaining it.

Strange it is, that men should admit the validity of the arguments for free discussion, but object to their being 'pushed to an extreme'; not seeing that unless the reasons are good for an extreme case, they are not good for any case. Strange that they should imagine that they are not assuming infallibility, when they acknowledge that there should be free discussion on all subjects which can possibly be doubtful, but think that some particular principle or doctrine should be forbidden to be questioned because it is so certain, that is, because they are certain that it is certain. To call any proposition certain, while there is any one who would deny its certainty if permitted, but who is not permitted, is to assume that we ourselves, and those who agree with us, are the judges of certainty, and judges without hearing the other side.

In the present age—which has been described as 'destitute of faith, but terrified at scepticism'—in which people feel sure, not so much that their opinions are true, as that they should not know what to do without them—the claims of an opinion to be protected from public attack are rested not so much on its truth, as on its importance to society. There are, it is alleged, certain beliefs, so useful, not to say indispensable to well-being, that it is as much the duty of government to uphold those beliefs, as to protect any other of the interests of society. In a case of such necessity, and so directly in the line of their duty, something less than infallibility may, it is maintained, warrant, and even bind, governments, to act on their own opinion, confined by the general opinion of mankind. It is also often argued, and still oftener thought, that none but bad men would desire to weaken these salutary beliefs; and there can be nothing wrong, it is thought, in restraining bad men, and prohibiting what only such men would wish to practise. This mode of thinking makes the justification of restraints on discussion not a question of the truth of doctrines, but of their usefulness; and flatters itself by that means of escape the responsibility of claiming to be an infallible judge of opinions. But those who thus satisfy themselves, do not perceive that the assumption of infallibility is merely shifted from one point to another. The usefulness of an opinion is itself matter of opinion: as disputable, as open to discussion, and requiring discussion as much, as the opinion itself. There is the same need of an infallible judge of opinions to decide an opinion to be noxious, as to decide it to be false, unless the opinion condemned has full opportunity of defending itself. And it will not do to say that the heretic may be allowed to maintain the utility or harmlessness of his opinion, though forbidden to maintain its truth. The truth of an opinion is part of its utility. If we would know whether or not it is desirable that a proposition should be believed, is it possible to exclude the consideration of whether or not it is true? In the opinion, not of bad men, but of the best men, no belief which is contrary to truth can be really useful: and can you prevent such men from urging that plea, when they are charged with culpability for denying some doctrine which they are told is useful, but which they believe to be false? Those who are on the side of received opinions, never fail to take all possible advantage of this plea; you do not find them handling the question of utility as if it could be completely abstracted from that of truth: on the contrary, it is, above all, because their doctrine is the 'truth,' that the knowledge or the belief of it is held to be so indispensable. There can be no fair discussion of the question of usefulness, when an argument so vital may be employed on one side, but not on the other. And in point of fact, when law or public feeling do not permit the truth of an opinion to be disputed, they are just as little tolerant of a denial of its usefulness. The utmost they allow is an extenuation of its absolute necessity, or of the positive guilt of rejecting it.

In order more fully to illustrate the mischief of denying a hearing to opinions because we, in our own judgement, have condemned them, it will be desirable to fix down the discussion to a concrete case; and I choose, by preference, the cases which are least favourable to me—in which the argument against freedom of opinion, both on the score of truth and on that of utility, is considered the strongest. Let the opinions impugned be the belief in a God and in a future state, or any of the commonly received doctrines of morality. To fight the battle on such ground, gives a great advantage to an unfair antagonist; since he will be sure to say (and many who have no desire to be unfair will say it internally), Are these the doctrines which you do not deem sufficiently certain to be taken under the protection of law? Is the belief in a God one of the opinions, to feel sure of which, you hold to be assuming infallibility? But I must be permitted to observe, that it is not the feeling sure of a doctrine (be it what it may) which I call an assumption of infallibility. It is the undertaking to decide the question *for others*, without allowing them to hear what can be said on the contrary side. And I denounce and reprobate this pretension not the less, if put forth on the side of my most solemn convictions. However positive any one's persuasion may be, not only of the falsity but of the pernicious consequences—not only of the pernicious consequences, but (to adopt expressions which I altogether condemn) the immorality and impiety of an opinion; yet if, in pursuance of that private judgement, though backed by the public judgement of his country or his contemporaries, he prevents the opinion from being heard in its defence, he assumes infallibility. And so far from the assumption being less objectionable or less dangerous because the opinion is called immoral or impious, this is the case of all others in which it is most fatal. These are exactly the occasions on which the men of one generation commit those dreadful mistakes, which excite the astonishment and horror of posterity. It is among such that we find the instances memorable in history, when the arm of the law has been employed to root out the best men and the noblest doctrines; with deplorable success as to the men, though some of the doctrines have survived to be (as if in mockery) invoked, in defence of similar conduct towards those who dissent from *them,* or from their received interpretation.

Mankind can hardly be too often reminded, that there was once a man named Socrates, between whom and the legal authorities and public opinion of his time, there took place a memorable collision. Born in an age and country abounding in individual greatness, this man has been handed down to us by those who best knew both him and the age, as the most virtuous man in it; while *we* know him as the head and prototype of all subsequent teachers of virtue, the source equally of the lofty inspiration of Plato and the judicious utilitarianism of Aristotle, '*i maëstri di color che sanno,*' the two headsprings of ethical as of all other philosophy. This acknowledged master of all the eminent thinkers who have since lived—whose fame, still growing after two thousand years, all but outweighs the whole remainder of the names which make his native city illustrious—was put to death by his countrymen, after a judicial conviction, for impiety and immorality. Impiety, in denying the gods recognized by the State; indeed his accuser asserted (see the *Apologia*) that he believed in no gods at all. Immorality, in being, by his doctrines and instructions, a 'corrupter of youth.' Of these charges the tribunal, there is every ground for believing, honestly found him guilty, and condemned the man who probably of all then born had deserved best of mankind, to be put to death as a criminal.

The initiation of all wise or noble things, comes and must come from individuals; generally at first from some one individual. The honour and glory of the average man is that he is capable of following that initiative; that he can respond internally to wise and noble things, and be led to them with his eyes open. I am not countenancing the sort of 'hero-worship' which applauds the strong man of genius for forcibly seizing on the government of the world and making it do his bidding in spite of itself. All he can claim is freedom to point out the way. The power of compelling others into it, is not only inconsistent with the freedom and development of all the rest, but corrupting to the strong man himself. It does seem, however, that when the opinions of masses of merely average men are everywhere become or becoming the dominant power, the counterpoise and corrective to that tendency would be the more and more pronounced individuality of those who stand on the higher eminences of thought. It is these circumstances most especially, that exceptional individuals, instead of being deterred, should be encouraged in acting differently from the mass. In other times there was no advantage in their doing so, unless they acted not only differently, but better. In this age, the mere example of nonconformity, the mere refusal to bend the knee to custom, is itself a service. Precisely because the tyranny of opinion is such as to make eccentricity a reproach, it is desirable, in order to break through that tyranny, that people should be eccentric. Eccentricity has always abounded when and where strength of character has abounded; and the amount of eccentricity in a society has generally been proportional to the amount of genius, mental vigour, and moral courage which it contained. That so few now dare to be eccentric marks the chief danger of the time.

I have said that it is important to give the freest scope possible to uncustomary things, in order that it may in time appear which of these are fit to be converted into customs. But independence of action, and disregard of custom, are not solely deserving of encouragement for the chance they afford that better modes of action, and customs more worthy of general adoption, may be struck out; nor is it only persons of decided mental superiority who have a just claim to carry on their lives in their own way. There is no reason that all human existence should be constructed on some one or some small number of patterns. If a person possesses any tolerable amount of common sense and experience, his own mode of laying out his existence is the best, not because it is the best in itself, but because it is his own mode. Human beings are not like sheep; and even sheep are not undistinguishably alike. A man cannot get a coat or a pair of boots to fit him, unless they are either made to his measure, or he has a whole warehouseful to choose from: and is it easier to fit him with a life than with a coat, or are human beings more like one another in their whole physical and spiritual conformation than in the shape of their feet? If it were only that people have diversities of taste, that is reason enough for not attempting to shape them all after one model. But different persons also require different conditions for their spiritual development; and can no more exist healthily in the same moral, than all the variety of plants can in the same physical, atmosphere and climate. The same things which are helps to one person towards the cultivation of his higher nature, are hindrances to another. The same mode of life is a healthy excitement to one, keeping all his faculties of action and enjoyment in their best order, while to another it is a distracting burthen, which suspends or crushes all internal life. Such are the differences among human beings in their sources of pleasure, their susceptibilities of pain, and the operation on them of different physical and moral agencies, that unless there is a corresponding diversity in their modes of life, they neither obtain their fair share of happiness, nor grow up to the mental, moral and aesthetic stature of which their nature is capable. Why then should tolerance, as far as the public sentiment is concerned, extend only to tastes and modes of life which extort acquiescence by the multitude of their adherents? Nowhere (except in some monastic institutions) is diversity of taste entirely unrecognized; a person may, without blame, either like or dislike rowing, or smoking, or music, or athletic exercises, or chess, or cards, or study, because both those who like each of these things, and those who dislike them, are too numerous to be put down. But the man, and still more the woman, who can be accused either of doing 'what nobody does,' or of not doing 'what everybody does,' is the subject of as much depreciatory remark as if he or she had committed some grave moral delinquency. Persons require to possess a title, or some other badge of rank, or of the consideration of people of rank, to be able to indulge somewhat in the luxury of doing as they like without detriment to their estimation. To indulge somewhat, I repeat: for whoever allow themselves much of that indulgence, incur the risk of something worse than disparaging speeches—they are in peril of a commission de lunatico, and of having their property taken from them and given to their relations.

A theory which maintains that truth may justifiably be persecuted because persecution cannot possibly do it any harm, cannot be charged with being intentionally hostile to the reception of new truths; but we cannot commend the generosity of its dealing with the persons to whom mankind are indebted for them. To discover to the world something which deeply concerns it, and of which it was previously ignorant; to prove to it that it had been mistaken on some vital point of temporal or spiritual interest, is as important a service as a human being can render to his fellow creatures, and in certain cases, as in those of the early Christians and of the Reformers, those who think with Dr. Johnson believe it to have been the most precious gift which could be bestowed on mankind. That the authors of such splendid benefits should be requited by martyrdom; that their reward should be to be dealt with as the vilest of criminals, is not, upon this theory, a deplorable error and misfortune, for which humanity should mourn in sackcloth and ashes, but the normal and justifiable state of things. The propounder of a new truth, according to this doctrine, should stand, as stood, in the legislation of the Locrians, the proposer of a new law, with a halter round his neck, to be instantly tightened if the public assembly did not, on hearing his reasons, then and there adopt his proposition. People who defend this mode of treating benefactors, cannot be supposed to set much value on the benefit; and I believe this view of the subject is mostly confined to the sort of persons who think that new truths may have been desirable once, but that we have had enough of them now.

But, indeed, the dictum that truth always triumphs over persecution, is one of those pleasant falsehoods which men repeat after one another till they pass into commonplaces, but which all experience refutes. History teems with instances of truth put down by persecution. If not suppressed for ever, it may be thrown back for centuries. To speak only of religious opinions: the Reformation broke out at least twenty times before Luther, and was put down. Arnold of Brescia was put down. Fra Dolcino was put down. Savonarola was put down. The Albigeois were put down. The Vaudois were put down. The Lollards were put down. The Hussites were put down. Even after the era of Luther, wherever persecution was persisted in, it was successful. In Spain, Italy, Flanders, the Austrian empire, Protestantism was rooted out; and, most likely, would have been so in England, had Queen Mary lived, or Queen Elizabeth died. Persecution has always succeeded, save where the heretics were too strong a party to be effectually persecuted. No reasonable person can doubt that Christianity might have been extirpated in the Roman Empire. It spread, and became predominant, because the persecutions were only occasional, lasting but a short time, and separated by long intervals of almost undisturbed propagandism. It is a piece of idle sentimentality that truth, merely as truth, has any inherent power denied to error, of prevailing against the dungeon and the stake. Men are not more zealous for truth than they often are for error, and a sufficient application of legal or even of social penalties will generally succeed in stopping the propagation of either. The real advantage which truth has, consists in this, that when an opinion is true, it may be extinguished once, twice, or many times, but in the course of ages there will generally be found persons to rediscover it, until some one of its reappearances falls on a time when from favourable circumstances it escapes persecution until it has made such head as to withstand all subsequent attempt to suppress it.

The despotism of custom is everywhere the standing hindrance to human advancement, being in unceasing antagonism to that disposition to aim at something better than customary, which is called, according to circumstances, the spirit of liberty, or that of progress or improvement. The spirit of improvement is not always a spirit of liberty, for it may aim at forcing improvements on an unwilling people; and the spirit of liberty, in so far as it resists such attempts, may ally itself locally and temporarily with the opponents of improvement; but the only unfailing and permanent source of improvement is liberty, since by it there are as many possible independent centres of improvement as there are individuals. The progressive principle, however, in either shape, whether as the love of liberty or of improvement, is antagonistic to the sways of Custom, involving at least emancipation from that yoke; and the contest between the two constitutes the chief interest of the history of mankind. The greater part of the world has, properly speaking, no history, because the despotism of Custom is complete.

We have now recognized the necessity to the mental well-being of mankind (on which all their other well-being depends) of freedom of opinion, and freedom of the expression of opinion, on four distinct grounds; which we will now briefly recapitulate.

First, if any opinion is compelled to silence, that opinion may, for ought we can certainly know, be true. To deny this is to assume our own infallibility.

Secondly, though the silenced opinion be an error, it may, and very commonly does, contain a portion of truth; and since the general or prevailing opinion on any subject is rarely or never the whole truth, it is only by the collision of adverse opinions that the remainder of the truth has any chance of being supplied.

Thirdly, even if the received opinion be not only true, but the whole truth; unless it is suffered to be, and actually is, vigorously and earnestly contested, it will, by most of those who receive it, be held in the manner of a prejudice, with little comprehension or feeling of its rational grounds. And not only this, but, fourthly, the meaning of the doctrine itself will be in danger of being lost, or enfeebled, and deprived of its vital effect on the character and conduct: the dogma becoming a mere formal profession, inefficacious for good, but cumbering the ground, and preventing the growth of any real and heartfelt conviction, from reason or personal experience.

The worth of a State, in the long run, is the worth of the individuals composing it; and a State which postpones the interests of *their* mental expansion and elevation, to a little more of administrative skill, or of that semblance of it which practice gives, in the details of business; a State which dwarfs its men, in order that they may be more docile instruments in its hands even for beneficial purposes—will find that with small men no great thing can really be accomplished; and that the perfection of machinery to which it has sacrificed everything, will in the end avail it nothing, for want of the vital power which, in order that the machine might work more smoothly, it has preferred to banish.

3. The Logic of Persecution *

MR. JUSTICE HOLMES

Persecution for the expression of opinions seem to me perfectly logical. If you have no doubt of your premises or your power and want a certain result with all your heart you naturally express your wishes in law and sweep away all opposition. To allow opposition by speech seems to indicate that you think speech impotent, as when a man says that he has squared the circle, or that you do not care wholeheartedly for the result, or that you doubt either your power or your premises.

But when men have realized that time has upset many fighting faiths, they may come to believe even more than they believe the very foundations of their own conduct that the ultimate good desired is better reached by free trade in ideas—that the best test of truth is the power of the thought to get itself accepted in the competition of the market, and that truth is the only ground upon which their wishes safely can be carried out. That, at any rate, is the theory of our Constitution. It is an experiment, as all life is an experiment. Every year if not every day we have to wager our salvation upon some prophecy based upon imperfect knowledge. While that experiment is part of our system I think that we should be eternally vigilant against attempts to check the expression of opinions that we loathe and believe to be fraught with death, unless they so imminently threaten immediate interference with the lawful and pressing purposes of the law that an immediate check is required to save the country.

4. Freedom in America †

MAX EASTMAN

Freedom lived a great life in America. I imagine there have been few times in history when the common man was more independent of dictation

---

* *Abrams* v. *United States*, 250 U.S. 616 (1919) (dissenting opinion).

† From "Political Liberty" by Max Eastman, reprinted from *Freedom in the Modern World*, edited by H. M. Kallen. Copyright, 1928, by Coward-McCann, Inc. By permission.

from the state than he was in the early history of this country—especially before they began to protect his liberties with the Constitution of the United States. "All men were created free and equal," "Life, liberty and the pursuit of happiness," "Give me liberty or give me death," those were the thoughts in men's minds in those days. And even after they nailed down the twelve articles of the Constitution, the spirit of liberty survived to a degree that is now difficult to imagine. Difficult to imagine a President of the United States casually remarking, as Thomas Jefferson did, that "A little rebellion now and then is a good thing—pray God we may never be twenty years without a rebellion!" Can you imagine Calvin Coolidge pausing for a moment in his arduous task of preventing the embattled farmers of Nicaragua from shooting into the profits of the United Fruit Company, pausing to say a few kind words for rebellion? All the time that Thomas Jefferson used to spend loving liberty, Cal Coolidge spends worrying about prosperity—about efficiency. You might describe the entire ideological history of this country as a gradual extirpation from the public mind of the ideal of liberty, and all that is associated with it—the liberty complex, as we say now—and its replacement by the complex of national efficiency.

You can realize how far this process has gone, if you will remember that in the year 1805 an American citizen by the name of Joseph Dennie was arrested and indicted for sedition. He was described as "a factious and seditious person of wicked mind and unquiet and turbulent disposition." (How much better English they wrote in those days, too!) And among the principal charges against him was this: that he had written and published statements "intending to condemn the principle of revolution." Just think of that—indicted for sedition in the United States of America—and moreover, if you will believe it, in the city of Philadelphia,—for condemning the principle of revolution! That is how things really were in those days.

A good deal of that spirit survived until the Civil War. It still lived in the mind of Abraham Lincoln, who asserted, you remember, the "revolutionary right" of a people to overthrow their government if they don't like it. And it lived again with a pale academical flicker in the mind that Woodrow Wilson had before he went to war. I remember clipping with considerable gratification from the pages of the *New Republic* the following passage from Woodrow Wilson's pre-war writings:

"We have forgotten the very principles of our origin, if we have forgotten how to object, how to resist, how to agitate, how to pull down and build up, even to the extent of revolutionary practices if it be necessary. . . ."

About two years after he made this remark and I clipped it from the *New Republic* with such happy gratification, Woodrow Wilson was spending the funds of the United States government in a peculiarly obstinate effort to send me and my political friends to the penitentiary, not for indulging in revolutionary practices but for making semi-revolutionary remarks.

Our entry into the World War marked the final and complete eradication of the liberty complex from the mind of the American people, its replacement by the complex of national efficiency. Since that date anybody who raises a serious question about the "principles of origin" of the American republic is regarded as un-American. Anybody who touches on the more fundamental rights of Anglo-Saxon citizens as they were laid down in Magna Charta is regarded as quixotic. Anybody who breathes a word of the right of revolution is criminally insane—or criminally syndicalist, which amounts to the same thing. You can't read the Declaration of Independence to a body of striking workers without getting arrested for inciting them to riot. A man's house is no longer his castle, except in the sense that if he is going to protect it against unlawful entry from the state's agents he has got to have a moat, a portcullis and a body of men-at-arms in the cellar. He has got to have either that or a large roll of bills in the bank. And just who are these dry-agents who transgress so conscientiously and so profitably all the fundamental rights of Anglo-Saxons that were laid down, as was thought, for all time in the Great Charter of King John? What motive in our body politic do they represent? From what new principle or dominating interest in the public mind do they derive the sanction for these irresponsible invasions of a domain heretofore presided over by an individual intelligence? From the ideal of national efficiency. From that goal, and that purpose of life, and from no other source.

Sacco and Vanzetti were burned to death without a judicial trial—that is the plain truth of the matter, for they were condemned with an obscene epithet before the consideration of the evidence by the judge who tried them —they were burned to death without trial within two miles of Bunker Hill for talking to the people of Massachusetts in extreme language about liberty. But that is not all their crime. You can talk in extreme language about liberty, if you choose the time and place and the audience. But they talked to the working people, and they talked about *industrial* liberty. Such talk holds a menace to the smooth operation of the machinery of our economic life. It holds a menace to our national efficiency. That is why they were burned to death with the consent of the vast majority of the population of Massachusetts. And such old-fashioned New Englanders as Edna St. Vincent Millay, who stood up in Boston Common and attempted to say a word in favor of the old ideals—of liberty and equal justice—were arrested for what? For *loitering!* There you have in a single picture the whole change of trend and color, and of the basic intention of the public mind of America in its short century and a half of life. We have abandoned our first love, human liberty, and we are in love with industrial efficiency and the business prosperity of the nation.

It is interesting to understand the causes of this. Virgil said that a man is happy who understands the causes of things. And I don't think he meant merely because that understanding gives him power to change them. He meant that it is fun. It gives us a feeling of superiority to things to understand them. This feeling of superiority is about the only consolation left for those who used to love liberty, and who now mourn her loss. They can write books about the rise of American civilization, and explain just why it is that American civilization has fallen so low, and that gives them a kind of spiritual elevation over the tragical facts, which are nothing more imposing after all than just plain economics of ways of doing business.

I don't intend to go into the economic explanation of the decline of American civilization. It is enough to remind you of it. But in so far as it was a decline and disappearance of liberty, I should like to make in the process a distinction which I consider significant. In the first place we ought not to talk about liberty, but about liberties. And then we ought to divide these liberties which are gradually but so obviously disappearing with the growth of our machine civilization into two classes. First, those liberties whose disappearance is an inevitable consequence of the growing complexity of the industrial machine, and its increasingly social or cooperative mode of operation. The relation between what one person or one group is doing, and what another person or group is doing, becomes continually more close and more complicated in this machine age. And thus it follows by an almost mathematical necessity that the liberties of each individual and each group grow less. All society is coming to be more and more like a big business house or factory. And to the extent that this is true all society has to be run on schedule and by a boss. A great number of liberties are thus automatically and irremediably lost.

For instance, I have to wait until a man in a blue uniform with brass buttons up and down his belly holds up his hand and beckons to me, before I can walk across the street in my own home town. That doesn't accord very well with the phraseology of the Declaration of Independence either. But I don't believe even the most fanatical lover of liberty would feel inclined to revolt against the tyranny of the traffic policeman. Not on Forty-second Street. He would only make it absolutely certain that he was going to die under the wheels of a truck or a taxi-cab—whereas if he obeys the policeman he has at least one chance in ten of surviving. I believe that if all our lost liberties were gathered together and tabulated, we should find that an astonishingly large number belong in the same class with these liberties we have lost to the traffic policeman. They are lost because they are absolutely incompatible with a modern machine civilization. We must either kiss these liberties a gallant good-bye, or break the machines. There is no other choice.

But there is another class of liberties that are dead or dying, not because they are incompatible with the machine and factory system, but because they are incompatible with the wage system. There are restraints and regimentations which arise, not from the social or cooperative way in which our industrial machines are operated, but from the anti-social and uncooperative way in which they are owned. It is fairly easy to explain to any sound-minded men that if a group of people are going to cooperate in producing something, there must be one boss and the rest must submit themselves to his orders. But when it comes to dividing up what they have produced, it is not so easy to make them see that a very small group, composed mainly of those who were standing on the side-lines cheering and encouraging the work, should take the lion's share, and that the vast majority of those who were actually doing the work should content themselves with the mean, cheap and contemptible handful of crumbs which we describe as a "living wage."

There are a good many things, such as insurance and the distribution of stock-holdings, which mitigate the rigor of this wage system or class system of producing wealth. But they are superficial. Five per cent of the people own 65 per cent of the wealth and 65 per cent of the people own little or nothing but the hands with which they work. The wealth is increasing all the time, and the *proportion* which goes to the toiling masses is not increasing. And yet these masses are becoming more and more educated, more and more thoughtful of their interests, more and more aware of the economic situation as a whole. And besides that there are always a lot of us disreputable agitators going around telling them how bad it is, and there always will be. It is quite obvious that for the successful and efficient operation of such a system, the liberties of these masses and of the agitators who go among them must be pretty closely cropped down and killed. To put it in short language: the working classes must be kept in order.

I do not pretend that these two necessities of our economic system exhaust the causes of the disappearance of liberty and the ideal of liberty from America. There are other causes. America is suppressing the free expression of sex, because she is for the first time confronting in her conscious mind the realities of sexual life, and she is frightened by them. That accounts for the absurdities of the movie censorship, the padlocking of New York's most intelligent theaters, and the rigid prohibition of love-stories in Boston. In these respects we are actually becoming more free, and that is the reason why the censorship is so absurdly and, in fact, pathologically exaggerated. Boston is an hysterical old maid going into convulsions at the mere literary reminder of the existence of her own bare skin. These convulsions will soon pass off, and we shall find that the process marked by this hysteria has been wholly a process of liberation. In fact, I think we are on the verge of a revival of faith in nature, a revival of the straightforward, affirmative living of life as we were made to live it, such as characterized the Elizabethan era. We are not exactly on the verge of it, but we are approaching it. This country is going to have its youth, you may be sure of that. And when grown-up people wake up and find out that they were old all the time that they ought to have been young, and then start in to make up for it, you might as well clear away the furniture and get out. That is what is going to happen in America.

A similar thing is going to happen, and is happening, in my judgment, in the sphere of religious opinion. The back provinces are passing laws against the theory of evolution, not because they are becoming more orthodox and intolerant than they were, but because they are just beginning to hear about evolution. They are just waking up to the fact that some people honestly believe that monkeys played a serious and even a passionate part in the creation of man. They would have passed these same laws any time in the last hundred and fifty years, if they had had any cause to dream that anybody had such a reverent thought about monkeys. The fact that these laws are being passed is the first streak of the dawn of an age of enlightenment. Just as the burning at the stake of Giordano Bruno was a sign and signal for the great rebirth of knowledge and the pagan faith in life that we call the Renaissance—so in its more modern and more ludicrous way, the monkey trial in Tennessee was a sign of the rapid and victorious march of science and free thought over these medieval United States. Of that I feel quite sure. And I think it would be wiser to worry about what we are going to put in the emotional place of orthodox religion when it is all gone than to worry lest these ridiculous and provincial resistance-hysterias are going to stop the victorious march of science.

We are going to have free thought about God and the earth and the universe in these states. It is an inevitable consequence of our prosperity and our mechanical achievements. And we are going to have free art and poetry too, freedom in love and in the experience of life for those who have wealth enough to attain it. All the signs point that way—and these exaggerated repressions which are almost as futile as they are exaggerated, point that way most of all.

But we are not going to have freedom to act in ways that throw out of gear the gigantic social and industrial machine upon which our civilization is founded. In that respect we are going to be more and more regimented and repressed as time goes on. That is why I say that the problem of liberty, so far as it is a real and deep and tragic problem, is merely this problem of how a group of free people can constitute a factory and operate a machine. And the answer is, that if you take freedom in any extreme or realistic sense, they can't. We have lost half of our liberties to the imperious demands of the belt and the traveling crane, and we can't do anything about that.

The other half we have lost to the way these instruments are owned, and it does seem as though we might do something about that. It is neither humane nor practical for a comparatively small class of people to own all this precious machinery, as well as the earth under it, and to enjoy the profits of the general toil at the expense of the rest. It entails a continual repression at home and a continual search for new markets and consequent preparation for imperialist wars abroad. In these wars and preparation for wars whatever little remnants of liberty we might have left, are lost. Therefore the problem of reviving liberty or saving what little of it we can, reduces itself to the problem of getting rid of the wage system, or the class system, of owning our vast social and industrial machine and distributing its profits. It does seem as though if we put our minds to it, and our muscles, we might be able to accomplish that supremely wise and beautiful task.

5. Measuring Freedom: The Control of the Future *

JOHN DEWEY

The place of natural fact and law in morals brings us to the problem of freedom. We are told that seriously to import empirical facts into morals is equivalent to an abrogation of freedom. Facts and laws mean necessity we are told. The way to freedom is to turn our back upon them and take flight to a separate ideal realm. Even if the fight could be successfully accomplished, the efficacy of the prescription may be doubted. For we need freedom in and among actual events, not apart from them. It is to be hoped therefore that there remains an alternative; that the road to freedom may be found in that knowledge of facts which enables us to employ them in connection with desires and aims. A physician or engineer is free in his thought and his action in the degree in which he knows what he deals with. Possibly we find here the key to any freedom.

What men have esteemed and fought for in the name of liberty is varied and complex—but certainly it has never been a metaphysical freedom of will. It seems to contain three elements of importance, though on their face not all of them are directly compatible with one another. (i) It includes efficiency in action, ability to carry out plans, the absence of cramping and thwarting obstacles. (ii) It also includes capacity to vary plans, to change the course of action, to experience novelties. And again (iii) it signifies the power of desire and choice to be factors in events.

Few men would purchase even a high amount of efficient action along

---

* From John Dewey, *Human Nature and Conduct*. Copyright, 1922, by Henry Holt and Company. By permission.

definite lines at the price of monotony, or if success in action were bought by all abandonment of personal preference. They would probably feel that a more precious freedom was possessed in a life of ill-assured objective achievement that contained undertaking of risks, adventuring in new fields, a pitting of personal choice against the odds of events, and a mixture of success and failures, provided choice had a career. The slave is a man who executes the wish of others, one doomed to act along lines predetermined to regularity. Those who have defined freedom as ability to act have unconsciously assumed that this ability is exercised in accord with desire, and that its operation introduces the agent into fields previously unexplored. Hence the conception of freedom as involving three factors.

Yet efficiency in execution cannot be ignored. To say that a man is free to choose to walk while the only walk he can take will lead him over a precipice is to strain words as well as facts. Intelligence is the key to freedom in act. We are likely to be able to go ahead prosperously in the degree in which we have consulted conditions and formed a plan which enlists their consenting cooperation. The gratuitous help of unforeseen circumstance we cannot afford to despise. Luck, bad if not good, will always be with us. But it has a way of favoring the intelligent and showing its back to the stupid. And the gifts of fortune when they come are fleeting except when they are made taut by intelligent adaptation of conditions. In neutral and adverse circumstances, study and foresight are the only roads to unimpeded action. Insistence upon a metaphysical freedom of will is generally at its most strident pitch with those who despise knowledge of matters-of-fact. They pay for their contempt by halting and confined action. Glorification of freedom in general at the expense of positive abilities in particular has often characterized the official creed of historic liberalism. Its outward sign is the separation of politics and law from economics. Much of what is called the "individualism" of the early nineteenth century has in truth little to do with the nature of individuals. It goes back to a metaphysics which held that harmony between man and nature can be taken for granted, if once certain artificial restrictions upon man are removed. Hence it neglected the necessity of studying and regulating industrial conditions so that a nominal freedom can be made an actuality. Find a man who believes that all men need is freedom *from* oppressive legal and political measures, and you have found a man who, unless he is merely obstinately maintaining his own private privileges, carries at the back of his head some heritage of the metaphysical doctrine of free-will, plus an optimistic confidence in natural harmony. He needs a philosophy that recognizes the objective character of freedom and its dependence upon a congruity of environment with human wants, an agreement which can be obtained only by profound thought and unremitting application. For freedom as a fact depends upon conditions of work which are socially and scientifically buttressed. Since industry covers the most pervasive relations of man with his environment, freedom is unreal which does not have as its basis an economic command of environment.

I have no desire to add another to the cheap and easy solutions which exist of the seeming conflict between freedom and organization. It is reasonably obvious that organization may become a hindrance to freedom; it does not take us far to say that the trouble lies not in organization but in over-organization. At the same time, it must be admitted that there is no effective or objective freedom without organization. It is easy to criticize the contract theory of the state which states that individuals surrender some at least of their natural liberties in order to make secure as civil liberties what they retain. Nevertheless there is some truth in the idea of surrender and exchange. A certain natural freedom is possessed by man. That is to say, in some respects harmony exists between a man's energies and his surroundings such that the latter support and execute his purposes. In so far he is free: without such a basic natural support, conscious contrivances of legislation, administration and deliberate human institution of social arrangements cannot take place. In this sense natural freedom is prior to political freedom and is its condition. But we cannot trust wholly to a freedom thus procured. It is at the mercy of accident. Conscious agreements among men must supplement and in some degree supplant freedom of action which is the gift of nature. In order to arrive at these agreements, individuals have to make concessions. They must consent to curtailment of some natural liberties in order that any of them may be rendered secure and enduring. They must, in short, enter into an organization with other human beings so that the activities of others may be permanently counted upon to assure regularity of action and far-reaching scope of plans and courses of action. The procedure is not, in so far, unlike surrendering a portion of one's income in order to buy insurance against future contingencies, and thus to render the future course of life more equably secure. It would be folly to maintain that there is no sacrifice; we can however contend that the sacrifice is a reasonable one, justified by results.

Viewed in this light, the relation of individual freedom to organization is seen to be an experimental affair. It is not capable of being settled by abstract theory. Take the question of labor unions and the closed or open shop. It is folly to fancy that no restrictions and surrenders of prior free-doms and possibilities of future freedoms are involved in the extension of this particular form of organization. But to condemn such organization on the theoretical ground that a restriction of liberty is entailed is to adopt a position which would have been fatal to every advance step in civilization, and to every net gain in effective freedom. Every such question is to be judged not on the basis of antecedent theory but on the basis of concrete consequences. The question is of the balance of freedom and security achieved, as compared with practicable alternatives. Even the question of the point where membership in an organization ceases to be a voluntary matter and becomes coercive or required, is also an experimental matter, a thing to be decided by scientifically conducted study of consequences, of pros and cons. It is definitely an affair of specific detail, not of wholesale theory. It is equally amusing to see one man denouncing on grounds of pure theory the coercion of workers by a labor union while he avails himself of the increased power due to corporate action in business and praises the coercion of the political state; and to see another man denouncing the latter as pure tyranny, while lauding the power of industrial labor organizations. The position of one or the other may be justified in particular cases, but justification is due to results in practice, not to general theory.

Organization tends, however, to become rigid and to limit freedom. In addition to security and energy in action, novelty, risk, change are ingredients of the freedom which men desire. Variety is more than the spice of life; it is largely of its essence, making a difference between the free and the enslaved. Invariant virtue appears to be as mechanical as uninterrupted vice, for true excellence changes with conditions. Unless character rises to overcome some new difficulty or conquer some temptation from an unexpected quarter we suspect its grain is only a veneer. Choice is an element in freedom and there can be no choice without unrealized and precarious possibilities. It is this demand for genuine contingency which is caricatured in the orthodox doctrine of a freedom of indifference, a power to choose this way or that apart from any habit or impulse, without even a desire on the part of will to show off. Such an indetermination of choice is not desired by the lover of either reason or excitement. The theory of arbitrary free choice represents indeterminateness of conditions grasped in a vague and lazy fashion and hardened into a desirable attribute of will. Under the title of freedom men prize such uncertainty of conditions as give deliberation and choice an opportunity. But uncertainty of volition which is more than a reflection of uncertainty of conditions is the mark of a person who has acquired imbecility of character through permanent weakening of his springs of action.

Whether or not indeterminateness, uncertainty, actually exists in the world is a difficult question. It is easier to think of the world as fixed, settled once for all, and man as accumulating all the uncertainty there is in his will and all the doubt there is in his intellect. The rise of natural science has facilitated this dualistic partitioning, making nature wholly fixed and mind wholly open and empty. Fortunately for us we do not have to settle the question. A hypothetical answer is enough. *If* the world is already done and done for, if its character is entirely achieved so that its behavior is like that of a man lost in routine, then the only freedom for which man can hope is one of efficiency in overt action. But *if* change is genuine, if accounts are still in process of making, and if objective uncertainty is the stimulus to reflection, then variation in action, novelty and experiment, have a true meaning. In any case the question is an objective one. It concerns not man in isolation from the world but man in his connection with it. A world that is at points and times indeterminate enough to call out deliberation and to give play to choice to shape its future is a world in which will is free, not because it is inherently vacillating and unstable, but because deliberation and choice are determining and stabilizing factors.

Upon an empirical view, uncertainty, doubt, hesitation, contingency and novelty, genuine change which is not mere disguised repetition, are facts. Only deductive reasoning from certain fixed premisses creates a bias in favor of complete determination and finality. To say that these things exist only in human experience and not in the world, and exist there only because of our "finitude" is dangerously like paying ourselves with words. Empirically the life of man seems in these respects as in others to express a culmination of facts in nature. To admit ignorance and uncertainty in man while denying them to nature involves a curious dualism. Variability, initiative, innovation, departure from routine, experimentation are empirically the manifestation of a genuine nisus in things. At all events it is these things that are precious to us under the name of freedom. It is their elimination from the life of a slave which makes his life servile, intolerable to the freeman who has once been on his own, no matter what his animal comfort and security. A free man would rather take his chance in an open world than be guaranteed in a closed world.

These considerations give point to the third factor in love of freedom: the desire to have desire count as a factor, a force. Even if will chooses unaccountably, even if it be a capricious impulse, it does not follow that there are real alternatives, genuine possibilities, open in the future. What we want is possibilities open in the *world* not in the will, except as will or deliberate activity reflects the world. To foresee future objective alternatives and to be able by deliberation to choose one of them and thereby weight its chances in the struggle for future existence, measures our freedom. It is assumed sometimes that if it can be shown that deliberation determines choice and deliberation is determined by character and conditions, there is no freedom. This is like saying that because a flower comes from root and stem it cannot bear fruit. The question is not what are the antecedents of deliberation and choice, but what are their consequences. What do they do that is distinctive? The answer is that they give us all the control of future possibilities which is open to us. And this control is the crux of our freedom. Without it, we are pushed from behind. With it we walk in the light.

The doctrine that knowledge, intelligence rather than will, constitutes freedom is not new. It has been preached by moralists of many a school. All rationalists have identified freedom with action emancipated by insight into truth. But insight into necessity has by them been substituted for foresight of possibilities. Tolstoi for example expressed the idea of Spinoza and Hegel when he said that the ox is a slave as long as he refused to recognize the yoke and chafes under it, while if he identifies himself with its necessity and draws willingly instead of rebelliously, he is free. But as long as the yoke is a yoke it is impossible that voluntary identification with it should occur. Conscious submission is then either fatalistic submissiveness or cowardice. The ox accepts in fact not the yoke but the stall and the hay to which the yoke is a necessary incident. But if the ox foresees the consequences of the use of the yoke, if he anticipates the possibility of harvest, and identifies himself not with the yoke but with the realization of its possibilities, he acts freely, voluntarily. He hasn't accepted a necessity as unavoidable; he has welcomed a possibility as a desirability.

Perception of necessary law plays, indeed, a part. But no amount of insight into necessity brings with it, as such, anything but a consciousness of necessity. Freedom is the "truth of necessity" only when we use one "necessity" to alter another. When we use the law to foresee consequences and to consider how they may be averted or secured, then freedom begins. Employing knowledge of law in order to submit to it without further action constitutes fatalism, no matter how it be dressed up. Thus we recur to our main contention. Morality depends upon events, not upon commands and ideals alien to nature. But intelligence treats events as moving, as fraught with possibilities, not as ended, final. In forecasting their possibilities, the distinction between better and worse arises. Human desire and ability cooperates with this or that natural force according as this or that eventuality is judged better. We do not use the present to control the future. We use the foresight of the future to refine and expand present activity. In this use of desire, deliberation and choice, freedom is actualized.

~~~~~~

6. *An Anthropologist Looks at Freedom* *

BRONISLAW MALINOWSKI

~~~~~~

Freedom is a quality of the cultural process as a whole and it is a quality which cannot be predicated with reference to any specific aspect of the process, nor yet to any partial phase thereof. The distinctions of political, legal, or economic freedom introduce some confusion and are impossible

* From Bronislaw Malinowski, *Freedom and Civilization* (Roy Publishers). Copyright, 1944, by Anna Valetta Malinowska. By permission.

simply because political power, economic pressure, and legal restraint are fundamentally interrelated. Within the framework of a concrete situation we may isolate things legal, as when a policeman arrests an individual *in flagrante delicto* of speeding, trespassing, of "committing a nuisance." Even then, in the real world in which we live, it is important to know whether the policeman will accept a substantial bribe, in which case economic and legal factors intertwine; or whether the arrestee is a Senator, a Lord, or a higher police officer, perhaps even a member of the Gestapo, in which politics override law and make economics unnecessary. If, however, we consider freedom with reference to the working of human culture as a whole, or with reference to the cultural constitution of a particular society, we shall be able to define the concept in a manner which precludes any ambiguities and solves more of the quibbles, contentions and uncertainties.

I submit that the real difficulty is due to the fact that no definition in terms of individual psychology or individual behavior can be given, because all individual freedoms, as all aspects of individual action, are related to the actions of others. They are also related in this to the instrumentalities necessary for action, that is, to systems of organization, to techniques, to mechanism, and also to words, that is, to speech, thought, deliberation and agreement.

In other words, freedom is an attribute of organized and instrumentally implemented phases of human action. Its great emotional potency is due to the fact that human life and indeed the pursuit of happiness depend upon the nature and the efficiency of those means which culture gives man in his struggle with the environment, with other human beings, and with Destiny herself. Hence unless we refer freedom to the techniques and technicalities of culture, and unless we understand it in terms of anthropological analysis, we shall never be able to establish the real semantic criteria in the distinction between legitimate and illegitimate uses of this word. Freedom is a symbol which stands for a sublime and powerful ideal. The same symbol, however, may become a dangerous weapon in the hands of the enemies of freedom.

We can predicate freedom with reference to three integrally related phases or aspects of human action. First of all we can speak about the freedom of conscience, of thought or purpose; about the freedom of speech, of the press, of the written word. All these are what might be called the freedom of framing the purpose, individual or social. The second phase about which freedom can be predicated is human action. Lastly, since human action is always purposeful and anticipatory of results, we also predicate freedom with reference to the results or the fruits of human endeavor. In this sense freedom is closely related to prosperity; to the effective exercise of political influence, that is, democracy; and to such fundamental rights as *habeas corpus,* freedom of worship, and the freedom of reaping the benefits of arts, recreation and all public amenities. All this already implies the definition of the term.

Freedom can be defined as the conditions necessary and sufficient for the formation of a purpose, its translation into effective action through organized cultural instrumentalities, and the full enjoyment of the results of such activity. The concept of freedom therefore can only be defined with reference to human beings organized and endowed with cultural motives, implements and values, which *ipso facto* implies the existence of law, an economic system and political organization—in short, a cultural system.

Our definition of freedom is composed of three links: purpose, which is embodied in the charter of an institution; instrumentalities, which include the men who work, the tools they use and the rules by which their work is carried to its conclusion; and result or effect, which is the function of the institution. The essential nature of freedom thus conceived is pragmatic. Freedom comes into being when the activities of organized behavior follow human choice and planning. Freedom is determined by the results of action as well as by its prerequisites. The individual's freedom consists in his ability to choose the goal, to find the road, and to reap the rewards of his efforts and endeavors. Those men are free who are able to decide what to do, where to go, or what to build. All claims for freedom remain idle and irrelevant unless planning and aiming can be translated into an effective execution through well-implemented and well-organized behavior. The determining conditions of freedom are therefore to be found in the manner in which a society is organized; in the way in which the instrumentalites are made accessible; and in the guarantees which safeguard all the rewards of planned and purposeful action and insure their equitable distribution.

Any definition in terms only of choices, of maturing and deciding on motives, or even of thought begs the question whether a decision however mature, wise, just or ethical can be effectively carried through. Definitions in terms of mere instruments, mechanical, social or spiritual, beg the question of purpose and result; for the freedom of instrumentalities is in the hands of those by whom the instrumentalities are used and controlled, individually or collectively, and is dependent on whose purpose is carried out, on who enjoys the results and how the results affect others. Sorcery in a primitive culture and a machine gun in our higher civilization give man the freedom to kill. They imply also the freedom of other people to be killed. This example shows not only that our definition is a minimum one as regards its scope and comprehensiveness, but that it must always be supplemented with regard to co-ordination or relating of purposes and ends. Definitions of freedom only in terms of results achieved, of the enjoyment of a higher standard of living, prosperity, ambition, exercise of powers, and pursuit of happiness in general beg the serious question referring to both purposes and instruments. The freedom of the abuse of power and parasitic enjoyment of wealth in complete idleness implies instruments of exploitation, enslavement and subjection of others. Such freedom is probably enjoyed most fully by Mr. Schickelgruber, the few remaining Oriental despots and perhaps a couple of war profiteers.

Our insistence therefore is on choice, or the formation of a purpose; on instrumentalities or the means to the end, and on enjoyment, or the end achieved and controlled. Only when freedom of thought or of inspiration becomes embodied in an active performance does it become relevant to the student of organized behavior, that is, of culture. The freedom which we need to understand is that powerful force which moves men to deeds, which inspires martyrdom and heroism, which precipitates revolutions and mobilizes nations into wars. Hence we insist on considering freedom only insofar as it refers to action, that is, to a decision which through full scope of being implemented becomes a reality of human behavior.

Clearly, since freedom of action means the conditions sufficient and necessary for the mastery of all circumstances inherent in the execution of purpose, freedom means power. Yet since freedom also means absence of restraint, it implies for every individual a condition of not being submitted to the power of others. It is evident therefore that the element of power, of efficiency, of ability to overcome obstacles, must be regarded as indispensable in any definition of freedom. Without some order—and order always implies a residue of authority if not coercion—freedom means anarchy. Thus submission to laws as well as the power to enforce laws and rules are indispensable in human behavior. It is equally evident that the real plus or minus of freedom is dependent on this legitimate use or on the abuse of power. When the work and effort of carrying out a task are imposed on the members of the group, and the advantages of this enterprise are enjoyed only by those who are in authority in the group, we have an abuse of power, through the differential distribution of advantage and effort respectively; and with it, a denial of freedom to those who have done the work.

It is clear from this that we shall need to throw some light on the nature of the rules, norms of conduct, and sanctioned laws which bind co-operating groups, in order to differentiate between tyranny and order, between dictatorship and democracy; in short, between a culture based on the arbitrary use of violence as its main principle, as opposed to a community in which the laws originate from spontaneous and bilateral agreements, while some of the rules have to be accepted simply because they are technical rules of concerted and implemented behavior, or laws which are guarantees of existence and of the exercise of culture. We shall also be able to show that cultures differ as regards the quota of freedom which they give, and we shall see that this largely depends upon the integral constitution of a culture, or as we shall call it, on its charter. Cultures organized for the pursuit of collective violence; cultures economically founded on slavery; cultures chronically or occasionally facing crises, especially war crises, imply a type of constitution where freedom does not flourish.

~~~~~~

7. Escape from Freedom *

ERICH FROMM

~~~~~~

The insignificance of the individual in our era concerns not only his role as a businessman, employee, or manual laborer, but also his role as a customer. A drastic change has occurred in the role of the customer in the last decades. The customer who went into a retail store owned by an independent businessman was sure to get personal attention: his individual purchase was important to the owner of the store; he was received like somebody who mattered, his wishes were studied; the very act of buying gave him a feeling of importance and dignity. How different is the relationship of a customer to a department store. He is impressed by the vastness of the building, the number of employees, the profusion of commodities displayed; all this makes him feel small and unimportant by comparison. As an individual he is of no importance to the department store. He is important as "a" customer; the store does not want to lose him, because this would indicate that there was something wrong and it might mean that the store would lose other customers for the same reason. As an abstract customer he is important; as a concrete customer he is utterly unimportant. There is nobody who is glad about his coming, nobody who is particularly concerned about his wishes. The act of buying has become similar to going to the post office and buying stamps.

This situation is still more emphasized by the methods of modern advertising. The sales talk of the old-fashioned businessman was essentially rational. He knew his merchandise, he knew the needs of the customer, and on the basis of this knowledge he tried to sell. To be sure, his sales talk was not entirely objective and he used persuasion as much as he could; yet, in order to be efficient, it had to be a rather rational and sensible kind of talk. A vast sector of modern advertising is different; it does not appeal to reason but to emotion; like any other kind of hypnoid suggestion, it tries to impress its objects emotionally and then make them submit intellectually.

* From Erich Fromm, *Escape from Freedom* (Rinehart & Company, Inc.). Copyright, 1941, by Erich Fromm. By permission.

This type of advertising impresses the customer by all sorts of means: by repetition of the same formula again and again; by the influence of an authoritative image, like that of a society lady or of a famous boxer, who smokes a certain brand of cigarette; by attracting the customer and at the same time weakening his critical abilities by the sex appeal of a pretty girl; by terrorizing him with the threat of "b.o." or "halitosis"; or yet again by stimulating daydreams about a sudden change in one's whole course of life brought about by buying a certain shirt or soap. All these methods are essentially irrational; they have nothing to do with the qualities of the merchandise, and they smother and kill the critical capacities of the customer like an opiate or outright hypnosis. They give him a certain satisfaction by their daydreaming qualities just as the movies do, but at the same time they increase his feeling of smallness and powerlessness.

As a matter of fact, these methods of dulling the capacity for critical thinking are more dangerous to our democracy than many of the open attacks against it, and more immoral—in terms of human integrity—than the indecent literature, publication of which we punish. The consumer movement has attempted to restore the customer's critical ability, dignity, and sense of significance, and thus operates in a direction similar to the trade-union movement. So far, however, its scope has not grown beyond modest beginnings.

What holds true in the economic sphere is also true in the political sphere. In the early days of democracy there were various kinds of arrangements in which the individual would concretely and actively participate in voting for a certain decision or for a certain candidate for office. The questions to be decided were familiar to him, as were the candidates; the act of voting, often done in a meeting of the whole population of a town, had a quality of concreteness in which the individual really counted. Today the voter is confronted by mammoth parties which are just as distant and impressive as the mammoth organizations of industry. The issues are complicated and made still more so by all sorts of methods to befog them. The voter may see something of his candidate around election time; but since the days of the radio, he is not likely to see him so often, thus losing one of the last means of sizing up "his" candidate. Actually he is offered a choice between two or three candidates by the party machines; but these candidates are not of "his" choosing, he and they know little of each other, and their relationship is as abstract as most other relationships have become.

Like the effect of advertising upon the customer, the methods of political propaganda tend to increase the feeling of insignificance of the individual voter. Repetition of slogans and emphasis on factors which have nothing to do with the issue at stake numb his critical capacities. The clear and rational appeal to his thinking are rather the exception than the rule in political propaganda—even in democratic countries. Confronted with the power and size of the parties as demonstrated in their propaganda, the individual voter cannot help feeling small and of little significance.

All this does not mean that advertising and political propaganda overtly stress the individual's insignificance. Quite the contrary; they flatter the individual by making him appear important, and by pretending that they appeal to his critical judgment, to his sense of discrimination. But these pretenses are essentially a method to dull the individual's suspicions and to help him fool himself as to the individual character of his decision. I need scarcely point out that the propaganda of which I have been speaking is not wholly irrational, and that there are differences in the weight of rational factors in the propaganda of different parties and candidates respectively.

Other factors have added to the growing powerlessness of the individual. The economic and political scene is more complex and vaster than it used to be; the individual has less ability to look through it. The threats which he is confronted with have grown in dimensions too. A structural unemployment of many millions has increased the sense of insecurity. Although the support of the unemployed by public means has done much to counteract the results of unemployment, not only economically but also psychologically, the fact remains that for the vast majority of people the burden of being unemployed is very hard to bear psychologically and the dread of it overshadows their whole life. To have a job—regardless of what kind of a job it is—seems to many all they could want of life and something they should be grateful for. Unemployment has also increased the threat of old age. In many jobs only the young and even inexperienced person who is still adaptable is wanted; that means, those who can still be molded without difficulty into the little cogs which are required in that particular setup.

The threat of war has also added to the feeling of individual powerlessness. To be sure, there were wars in the nineteenth century too. But since the last war the possibilities of destruction have increased so tremendously —the range of people to be affected by war has grown to such an extent as to comprise everybody without any exception—that the threat of war has become a nightmare which, though it may not be conscious to many people before their nation is actually involved in the war, has overshadowed their lives and increased their feeling of fright and individual powerlessness.

The "style" of the whole period corresponds to the picture I have sketched. Vastness of cities in which the individual is lost, buildings that are as high as mountains, constant acoustic bombardment by the radio, big headlines changing three times a day and leaving one no choice to decide what is important, shows in which one hundred girls demonstrate their ability with clocklike precision to eliminate the individual and act like a powerful though smooth machine, the beating rhythm of jazz—these and many other details are expressions of a constellation in which the individual is confronted by uncontrollable dimensions in comparison with which he is a small particle. All he can do is to fall in step like a marching soldier or a worker on the endless belt. He can act; but the sense of independence, significance, has gone.

The extent to which the average person in America is filled with the same sense of fear and insignificance seems to find a telling expression in the fact of the popularity of the Mickey Mouse pictures. There the one theme—in so many variations—is always this: something little is persecuted and endangered by something overwhelmingly strong, which threatens to kill or swallow the little thing. The little thing runs away and eventually succeeds in escaping or even in harming the enemy. People would not be ready to look continually at the many variations of this one theme unless it touched upon something very close to their own emotional life. Apparently the little thing threatened by a powerful, hostile enemy is the spectator himself; that is how *he* feels and that is the situation with which he can identify himself. But of course, unless there were a happy ending there would be no continuous attraction. As it is, the spectator lives through all his own fears and feelings of smallness and at the end gets the comforting feeling that, in spite of all, he will be saved and will even conquer the strong one. However—and this is the significant and sad part of this "happy end"—his salvation lies mostly in his ability to run away and in the unforeseen accidents which make it impossible for the monster to catch him.

The position in which the individual finds himself in our period had already been foreseen by visionary thinkers in the nineteenth century. Kierkegaard describes the helpless individual torn and tormented by doubts, overwhelmed by the feeling of aloneness and insignificance. Nietzsche visualizes the approaching nihilism which was to become manifest in Nazism and paints a picture of a "superman" as the negation of the insignificant, directionless individual he saw in reality. The theme of the powerlessness of man has found a most precise expression in Franz Kafka's work. In his *Castle* he describes the man who wants to get in touch with the mysterious inhabitants of a castle, who are supposed to tell him what to do and show him his place in the world. All his life consists in his frantic effort to get into touch with them, but he never succeeds and is left alone with a sense of utter futility and helplessness.

The feeling of isolation and powerlessness has been beautifully expressed in the following passage by Julian Green: "I knew that we counted little in comparison with the universe, I knew that we were nothing; but to be so immeasurably nothing seems in some way both to overwhelm and at the same time to reassure. Those figures, those dimensions beyond the range of human thought, are utterly overpowering. Is there anything whatsoever to which we can cling? Amid that chaos of illusions into which we are cast headlong, there is one thing that stands out as true, and that is—love. All the rest is nothingness, an empty void. We peer down into a huge dark abyss. And we are afraid." [1]

However, this feeling of individual isolation and powerlessness as it has been expressed by these writers and as it is felt by many so-called neurotic people, is nothing the average normal person is aware of. It is too frightening for that. It is covered over by the daily routine of his activities, by the assurance and approval he finds in his private or social relations, by success in business, by any number of distractions, by "having fun," "making contacts," "going places." But whistling in the dark does not bring light. Aloneness, fear, and bewilderment remain; people cannot stand it for ever. They cannot go on bearing the burden of "freedom from"; they must try to escape from freedom altogether unless they can progress from negative to positive freedom. The principal social avenues of escape in our time are the submission to a leader, as has happened in Fascist countries, and the compulsive conforming as is prevalent in our own democracy.

The first mechanism of escape from freedom I am going to deal with is the tendency to give up the independence of one's own individual self and to fuse one's self with somebody or something outside of oneself in order to acquire the strength which the individual self is lacking. Or, to put it in different words, to seek for new, "secondary bonds" as a substitute for the primary bonds which have been lost.

The more distinct forms of this mechanism are to be found in the striving for submission and domination, or, as we would rather put it, in the masochistic and sadistic strivings as they exist in varying degrees in normal and neurotic persons respectively. We shall first describe these tendencies and then try to show that both of them are an escape from an unbearable aloneness.

The most frequent forms in which masochistic strivings appear are feelings of inferiority, powerlessness, individual insignificance. The analysis of persons who are obsessed by these feelings shows that, while they consciously complain about these feelings and want to get rid of them, unconsciously some power within themselves drives them to feel inferior or insignificant. Their feelings are more than realizations of actual shortcomings and weaknesses (although they are usually rationalized as though they were); these persons show a tendency to belittle themselves, to make themselves weak, and not to master things. Quite regularly these people show a marked dependence on powers outside of themselves, on other people, or institutions, or nature. They tend not to assert themselves, not to do what they want, but to submit to the factual or alleged orders of these outside forces. Often they

[1] Julian Green, *Personal Record, 1928–1939,* translated by J. Godefroi, Harper & Brothers, New York, 1939.

are quite incapable of experiencing the feeling "I want" or "I am." Life, as a whole, is felt by them as something overwhelmingly powerful, which they cannot master or control.

In the more extreme cases—and there are many—one finds besides these tendencies to belittle oneself and to submit to outside forces a tendency to hurt oneself and to make oneself suffer.

This tendency can assume various forms. We find that there are people who indulge in self-accusation and self-criticism which even their worst enemies would scarcely bring against them. There are others, such as certain compulsive neurotics, who tend to torture themselves with compulsory rites and thoughts. In a certain type of neurotic personality, we find a tendency to become physically ill, and to wait, consciously or unconsciously, for an illness as if it were a gift of the gods. Often they incur accidents which would not have happened had there not been at work an unconscious tendency to incur them. These tendencies directed against themselves are often revealed in still less overt or dramatic forms. For instance, there are persons who are incapable of answering questions in an examination when the answers are very well known to them at the time of the examination and even afterwards. There are others who say things which antagonize those whom they love or on whom they are dependent, although actually they feel friendly toward them and did not intend to say those things. With such people, it almost seems as if they were following advice given them by an enemy to behave in such a way as to be most detrimental to themselves.

The masochistic trends are often felt as plainly pathological or irrational. More frequently they are rationalized. Masochistic dependency is conceived as love or loyalty, inferiority feelings as an adequate expression of actual shortcomings, and one's suffering as being entirely due to unchangeable circumstances.

Besides these masochistic trends, the very opposite of them, namely, *sadistic* tendencies, are regularly to be found in the same kind of characters. They vary in strength, are more or less conscious, yet they are never missing. We find three kinds of sadistic tendencies, more or less closely knit together. One is to make others dependent on oneself and to have absolute and unrestricted power over them, so as to make of them nothing but instruments, "clay in the potter's hand." Another consists of the impulse not only to rule over others in this absolute fashion, but to exploit them, to use them, to steal from them, to disembowel them, and, so to speak, to incorporate anything eatable in them. This desire can refer to material things as well as to immaterial ones, such as the emotional or intellectual qualities a person has to offer. A third kind of sadistic tendency is the wish to make others suffer or to see them suffer. This suffering can be physical, but more often it is mental suffering. Its aim is to hurt actively, to humiliate, embarrass others, or to see them in embarrassing and humiliating situations.

Sadistic tendencies for obvious reasons are usually less conscious and more rationalized than the socially more harmless masochistic trends. Often they are entirely covered up by reaction formations of overgoodness or overconcern for others. Some of the most frequent rationalizations are the following: "I rule over you because I know what is best for you, and in your own interest you should follow me without opposition." Or, "I am so wonderful and unique, that I have a right to expect that other people become dependent on me." Another rationalization which often covers the exploiting tendencies is: "I have done so much for you, and now I am entitled to take from you what I want." The more aggressive kind of sadistic impulses finds its most frequent rationalization in two forms: "I have been hurt by others and my wish to hurt them is nothing but retaliation," or "By striking first I am defending myself or my friends against the danger of being hurt."

There is one factor in the relationship of the sadistic person to the object of his sadism which is often neglected and therefore deserves especial emphasis here: his dependence on the object of his sadism.

While the masochistic person's dependence is obvious, our expectation with regard to the sadistic person is just the reverse: he seems so strong and domineering, and the object of his sadism so weak and submissive, that it is difficult to think of the strong one as being dependent on the one over whom he rules. And yet close analysis shows that this is true. The sadist needs the person over whom he rules, he needs him very badly, since his own feeling of strength is rooted in the fact that he is the master over some one. This dependence may be entirely unconscious. Thus, for example, a man may treat his wife very sadistically and tell her repeatedly that she can leave the house any day and that he would be only too glad if she did. Often she will be so crushed that she will not dare to make an attempt to leave, and therefore they both will continue to believe that what he says is true. But if she musters up enough courage to declare that she will leave him, something quite unexpected to both of them may happen: he will become desperate, break down, and beg her not to leave him; he will say he cannot live without her, and will declare how much he loves her and so on. Usually, being afraid of asserting herself anyhow, she will be prone to believe him, change her decision and stay. At this point the play starts again. He resumes his old behavior, she finds it increasingly difficult to stay with him, explodes again, he breaks down again, she stays, and so on and on many times.

I come now to the main question: What is the root of both the masochistic perversion and masochistic character traits respectively? Furthermore, what is the common root of both the masochistic *and* the sadistic strivings?

The direction in which the answer lies has already been suggested in the beginning of this chapter. Both the masochistic and sadistic strivings tend to help the individual to escape his unbearable feeling of aloneness and powerlessness. Psychoanalytic and other empirical observations of masochistic persons give ample evidence (which I cannot quote here without transcending the scope of this book) that they are filled with a terror of aloneness and insignificance. Frequently this feeling is not conscious; often it is covered by compensatory feelings of eminence and perfection. However, if one only penetrates deeply enough into the unconscious dynamics of such a person, one finds these feelings without fail. The individual finds himself "free" in the negative sense, that is, alone with his self and confronting an alienated, hostile world. In this situation, to quote a telling description of Dostoevski, in *The Brothers Karamazov,* he has "no more pressing need than the one to find somebody to whom he can surrender, as quickly as possible, that gift of freedom which he, the unfortunate creature, was born with." The frightened individual seeks for somebody or something to tie his self to; he cannot bear to be his own individual self any longer, and he tries frantically to get rid of it and to feel security again by the elimination of this burden: the self.

Masochism is one way toward this goal. The different forms which the masochistic strivings assume have one aim: *to get rid of the individual self, to lose oneself; to get rid of the burden of freedom.* This aim is obvious in those masochistic strivings in which the individual seeks to submit to a person or power which he feels as being overwhelmingly strong. (Incidentally, the conviction of superior strength of another person is always to be understood in relative terms. It can be based either upon the actual strength of the other person, or upon a conviction of one's own utter insignificance and powerlessness. In the latter event a mouse or a leaf can assume threatening features.) In other forms of masochistic strivings the essential aim is the same. In the masochistic feeling of smallness we find a tendency which serves to increase the original feeling of insignificance. How is this to be understood? Can we assume that by making a fear worse one is trying to remedy it? Indeed, this is what the masochistic person does. As long as I struggle between my desire to be independent and strong and my feeling of insignificance or powerlessness I am caught in a tormenting conflict. If I succeed in reducing my individual self to nothing, if I can overcome the awareness of my separateness as an individual, I may save myself from this conflict. To feel utterly small and helpless is one way toward this aim; to be overwhelmed by pain and agony another; to be overcome by the effects of intoxication still another. The phantasy of suicide is the last hope if all other means have not succeeded in bringing relief from the burden of aloneness.

Under certain conditions these masochistic strivings are relatively successful. If the individual finds cultural patterns that satisfy these masochistic strivings (like the submission under the "leader" in Fascist ideology), he gains some security by finding himself united with millions of others who share these feelings. Yet even in these cases, the masochistic "solution" is no more of a solution than neurotic manifestations ever are: the individual succeeds in eliminating the conspicuous suffering but not in removing the underlying conflict and the silent unhappiness. When the masochistic striving does not find a cultural pattern or when it quantitatively exceeds the average amount of masochism in the individual's social group, the masochistic solution does not even solve anything in relative terms. It springs from an unbearable situation, tends to overcome it, and leaves the individual caught in new suffering. If human behavior were always rational and purposeful, masochism would be as inexplicable as neurotic manifestations in general are. This, however, is what the study of emotional and mental disturbances has taught us: that human behavior can be motivated by strivings which are caused by anxiety or some other unbearable state of mind, that these strivings tend to overcome this emotional state and yet merely cover up its most visible manifestations, or not even these. Neurotic manifestations resemble the irrational behavior in a panic. Thus a man, trapped in a fire, stands at the window of his room and shouts for help, forgetting entirely that no one can hear him and that he could still escape by the staircase which will also be aflame in a few minutes. He shouts because he wants to be saved, and for the moment this behavior appears to be a step on the way to being saved—and yet it will end in complete catastrophe. In the same way the masochistic strivings are caused by the desire to get rid of the individual self with all its shortcomings, conflicts, risks, doubts, and unbearable aloneless, but they only succeed in removing the most noticeable pain or they even lead to greater suffering. The irrationality of masochism, as of all other neurotic manifestations, consists in the ultimate futility of the means adopted to solve an untenable emotional situation.

These considerations refer to an important difference between neurotic and rational activity. In the latter the *result* corresponds to the *motivation* of an activity—one acts in order to attain a certain result. In neurotic strivings one acts from a compulsion which has essentially a negative character: to escape an unbearable situation. The strivings tend in a direction which only fictitiously is a solution. Actually the result is contradictory to what the person wants to attain; the compulsion to get rid of an unbearable feeling was so strong that the person was unable to choose a line of action that could be a solution in any other but a fictitious sense.

The implication of this for masochism is that the individual is driven by an unbearable feeling of aloneness and insignificance. He then attempts to overcome it by getting rid of his self (as a psychological, not as a physiological entity); his way to achieve this is to belittle himself, to suffer, to make himself utterly insignificant. But pain and suffering are not what he wants; pain and suffering are the price he pays for an aim which he compulsively tries to attain. The price is dear. He has to pay more and more and, like a peon, he only gets into greater debts without ever getting what he has paid for: inner peace and tranquillity.

I have spoken of the masochistic perversion because it proves beyond doubt that suffering can be something sought for. However, in the masochistic perversion as little as in moral masochism suffering is not the real aim; in both cases it is the means to an aim: forgetting one's self. The difference between the perversion and masochistic character traits lies essentially in the following: In the perversion the trend to get rid of one's self is expressed through the medium of the body and linked up with sexual feelings. While in moral masochism, the masochistic trends get hold of the whole person and tend to destroy all the aims which the ego consciously tries to achieve, in the perversion the masochistic strivings are more or less restricted to the physical realm; moreover by their amalgamation with sex they participate in the release of the tension occurring in the sexual sphere and thus find some direct release.

The annihilation of the individual self and the attempt to overcome thereby the unbearable feeling of powerlessness are only one side of the masochistic strivings. The other side is the attempt to become a part of a bigger and more powerful whole outside of oneself, to submerge and participate in it. This power can be a person, an institution, God, the nation, conscience, or a psychic compulsion. By becoming part of a power which is felt as unshakably strong, eternal, and glamorous, one participates in its strength and glory. One surrenders one's own self and renounces all strength and pride connected with it, one loses one's integrity as an individual and surrenders freedom; but one gains a new security and a new pride in the participation in the power in which one submerges. One gains also the security against the torture of doubt. The masochistic person, whether his master is an authority outside of himself or whether he has internalized the master as conscience or a psychic compulsion, is saved from making decisions, saved from the final responsibility for the fate of his self, and thereby saved from the doubt of what decision to make. He is also saved from the doubt of what the meaning of his life is or who "he" is. These questions are answered by the relationship to the power to which he has attached himself. The meaning of his life and the identity of his self are determined by the greater whole into which the self has submerged.

But what about ourselves? Is our own democracy threatened only by Fascism beyond the Atlantic or by the "fifth column" in our own ranks? If that were the case, the situation would be serious but not critical. But although foreign and internal threats of Fascism must be taken seriously, there is no greater mistake and no graver danger than not to see that in our own society we are faced with the same phenomenon that is fertile soil for the rise of Fascism anywhere: the insignificance and powerlessness of the individual.

This statement challenges the conventional belief that by freeing the individual from all external restraints modern democracy has achieved true individualism. We are proud that we are not subject to any external authority, that we are free to express our thoughts and feelings, and we take it for granted that this freedom almost automatically guarantees our individuality. *The right to express our thoughts,* however, *means something only if we are able to have thoughts of our own;* freedom from external authority is a lasting gain only if the inner psychological conditions are such that we are able to establish our own individuality. Have we achieved that aim, or are we at least approaching it? This book deals with the human factor; its task, therefore, is to analyze this very question critically. In discussing the two aspects of freedom for modern man, we have pointed out the economic conditions that make for increasing isolation and powerlessness of the individual in our era; in discussing the psychological results we have shown that this powerlessness leads either to the kind of escape that we find in the authoritarian character, or else to a compulsive conforming in the process of which the isolated individual becomes an automaton, loses his self, and yet at the same time consciously conceives of himself as free and subject only to himself.

It is important to consider how our culture fosters this tendency to conform, even though there is space for only a few outstanding examples. The suppression of spontaneous feelings, and thereby of the development of genuine individuality, starts very early, as a matter of fact, with the earliest training of a child. This is not to say that training must inevitably lead to suppression of spontaneity if the real aim of education is to further the inner independence and individuality of the child, its growth and integrity. The restrictions which such a kind of education may have to impose upon the growing child are only transitory measures that really support the process of growth and expansion. In our culture, however, education too often results in the elimination of spontaneity and in the substitution of original psychic acts by superimposed feelings, thoughts, and wishes. (By original I do not mean, let me repeat, that an idea has not been thought before by someone else, but that it originates in the individual, that it is the result of his own activity and in this sense is *his* thought.) To choose one illustration somewhat arbitrarily, one of the earliest suppressions of *feelings* concerns hostility and dislike. To start with, most children have a certain measure of hostility and rebelliousness as a result of their conflicts with a surrounding world that tends to block their expansiveness and to which, as the weaker opponent, they usually have to yield. It is one of the essential aims of the educational process to eliminate this antagonistic reaction. The methods are different; they vary from threats and punishments, which frighten the child, to the subtler methods of bribery or "explanations," which confuse the child and make him give up his hostility. The child starts with giving up the very feeling itself. Together with that, he is taught to suppress the awareness of hostility and insincerity in others; sometimes this is not entirely easy, since children have a capacity for noticing such negative qualities in others without being so easily deceived by words as adults usually are. They still dislike somebody "for no good reason"—except the very good one that they feel the hostility, or insincerity, radiating from that person. This reaction is soon discouraged; it does not take long for the child to reach the "maturity" of the average adult and to lose the sense of discrimination between a decent person and a scoundrel, as long as the latter has not committed some flagrant act.

On the other hand, early in his education, the child is taught to have feelings that are not at all "his"; particularly is he taught to like people, to be uncritically friendly to them, and to smile. What education may not have accomplished is usually done by social pressure in later life. If you do not smile you are judged lacking in a "pleasing personality"—and you need to have a pleasing personality if you want to sell your services, whether as a waitress, a salesman, or a physician. Only those at the bottom of the social pyramid, who sell nothing but their physical labor, and those at the very top do not need to be particularly "pleasant." Friendliness, cheerfulness, and everything that a smile is supposed to express, become automatically responses which one turns on and off like an electric switch.[1]

What then is the meaning of freedom for modern man?

He has become free from the external bonds that would prevent him from doing and thinking as he sees fit. He would be free to act according to his own will, if he knew what he wanted, thought, and felt. But he does not know. He conforms to anonymous authorities and adopts a self which is not his. The more he does this, the more powerless he feels, the more he is forced to conform. In spite of a veneer of optimism and initiative, modern man is overcome by a profound feeling of powerlessness which makes him gaze toward approaching catastrophes as though he were paralyzed.

Looked at superficially, people appear to function well enough in economic and social life; yet it would be dangerous to overlook the deep-seated unhappiness behind that comforting veneer. If life loses its meaning because it is not lived, man becomes desperate. People do not die quietly from physical starvation; they do not die quietly from psychic starvation either. If we look only at the economic needs as far as the "normal" person is concerned, if we do not see the unconscious suffering of the average automatized person, then we fail to see the danger that threatens our culture from its human

[1] As one telling illustration of the commercialization of friendliness I should like to cite *Fortune*'s report on "The Howard Johnson Restaurants." (*Fortune,* September, 1940, p. 96.) Johnson employs a force of "shoppers" who go from restaurant to restaurant to watch for lapses. "Since everything is cooked on the premises according to standard recipes and measurements issued by the home office, the inspector knows how large a portion of steak he should receive and how the vegetable should taste. He also knows how long it should take for the dinner to be served and he knows the exact degree of friendliness that should be shown by the hostess and the waitress."

basis: the readiness to accept any ideology and any leader, if only he promises excitement and offers a political structure and symbols which allegedly
give meaning and order to an individual's life. The despair of the human
automaton is fertile soil for the political purposes of Fascism.

Does our analysis lend itself to the conclusion that there is an inevitable
circle that leads from freedom into new dependence? Does freedom from all
primary ties make the individual so alone and isolated that inevitably he
must escape into new bondage? Are *independence* and *freedom* identical
with *isolation* and fear? Or is there a state of positive freedom in which the
individual exists as an independent self and yet is not isolated but united
with the world, with other men, and nature?

We believe that there is a positive answer, that the process of growing
freedom does not constitute a vicious circle, and that man can be free and
yet not alone, critical and yet not filled with doubts, independent and yet an
integral part of mankind. This freedom man can attain by the realization of
his self, by being himself. What is realization of the self? Idealistic philosophers have believed that self-realization can be achieved by intellectual insight alone. They have insisted upon splitting human personality, so that
man's nature may be suppressed and guarded by his reason. The result of
this split, however, has been that not only the emotional life of man but also
his intellectual faculties have been crippled. Reason, by becoming a guard
set to watch its prisoner, nature, has become a prisoner itself; and thus both
sides of human personality, reason and emotion, were crippled. We believe
that the realization of the self is accomplished not only by an act of thinking
but also by the realization of man's total personality, by the active expression
of his emotional and intellectual potentialities. These potentialities are present
in everybody; they become real only to the extent to which they are expressed. In other words, *positive freedom consists in the spontaneous activity
of the total, integrated personality.*

We approach here one of the most difficult problems of psychology: the
problem of spontaneity. An attempt to discuss this problem adequately would
require another volume. However, on the basis of what we have said so far,
it is possible to arrive at an understanding of the essential quality of spontaneous activity by means of contrast. Spontaneous activity is not compulsive
activity, to which the individual is driven by his isolation and powerlessness;
it is not the activity of the automaton, which is the uncritical adoption of
patterns suggested from the outside. Spontaneous activity is free activity of
the self and implies, psychologically, what the Latin root of the word, *sponte,*
means literally: of one's free will. By activity we do not mean "doing something," but the quality of creative activity that can operate in one's emotional,
intellectual, and sensuous experiences and in one's will as well. One premise
for this spontaneity is the acceptance of the total personality and the elimina-

tion of the split between "reason" and "nature"; for only if man does not repress essential parts of his self, only if he has become transparent to himself, and only if the different spheres of life have reached a fundamental integration, is spontaneous activity possible.

While spontaneity is a relatively rare phenomenon in our culture, we are not entirely devoid of it. In order to help in the understanding of this point, I should like to remind the reader of some instances where we all catch a glimpse of spontaneity.

In the first place, we know of individuals who are—or have been—spontaneous, whose thinking, feeling, and acting were the expression of their selves, and not of an automaton. These individuals are mostly known to us as artists. As a matter of fact, the artist can be defined as an individual who can express himself spontaneously. If this were the definition of an artist—Balzac defined him just in that way—then certain philosophers and scientists have to be called artists too, while others are as different from them as an old-fashioned photographer from a creative painter. There are other individuals who, though lacking the ability—or perhaps merely the training—for expressing themselves in an objective medium as the artist does, possess the same spontaneity. The position of the artist is vulnerable, though, for it is really only the successful artist whose individuality or spontaneity is respected; if he does not succeed in selling his art, he remains to his contemporaries a crank, a "neurotic." The artist in this matter is in a similar position to that of the revolutionary throughout history. The successful revolutionary is a statesman, the unsuccessful one a criminal.

Small children offer another instance of spontaneity. They have an ability to feel and think that which is really *theirs;* this spontaneity shows in what they say and think, in the feelings that are expressed in their faces. If one asks what makes for the attraction small children have for most people I believe that, aside from sentimental and conventional reasons, the answer must be that it is this very quality of spontaneity. It appeals profoundly to everyone who is not so dead himself that he has lost the ability to perceive it. As a matter of fact, there is nothing more attractive and convincing than spontaneity whether it is to be found in a child, in an artist, or in those individuals who cannot thus be grouped according to age or profession.

Most of us can observe at least moments of our own spontaneity which are at the same time moments of genuine happiness. Whether it be the fresh and spontaneous perception of a landscape, or the dawning of some truth as the result of our thinking, or a sensuous pleasure that is not stereotyped, or the welling up of love for another person—in these moments we all know what a spontaneous act is and may have some vision of what human life could be if these experiences were not such rare and uncultivated occurrences.

Why is spontaneous activity the answer to the problem of freedom? We have said that negative freedom by itself makes the individual an isolated being, whose relationship to the world is distant and distrustful and whose self is weak and constantly threatened. Spontaneous activity is the one way in which man can overcome the terror of aloneness without sacrificing the integrity of his self; for in the spontaneous realization of the self man unites himself anew with the world—with man, nature, and himself. Love is the foremost component of such spontaneity; not love as the dissolution of the self in another person, not love as the possession of another person, but love as spontaneous affirmation of others, as the union of the individual with others on the basis of the preservation of the individual self. The dynamic quality of love lies in this very polarity: that it springs from the need of overcoming separateness, that it leads to oneness—and yet that individuality is not eliminated. Work is the other component; not work as a compulsive activity in order to escape aloneness, not work as a relationship to nature which is partly one of dominating her, partly one of worship of and enslavement by the very products of man's hands, but work as creation in which man becomes one with nature in the act of creation. What holds true of love and work holds true of all spontaneous action, whether it be the realization of sensuous pleasure or participation in the political life of the community. It affirms the individuality of the self and at the same time it unites the self with man and nature. The basic dichotomy that is inherent in freedom— the birth of individuality and the pain of aloneness—is dissolved on a higher plane by man's spontaneous action.

In all spontaneous activity the individual embraces the world. Not only does his individual self remain intact; it becomes stronger and more solidified. *For the self is as strong as it is active.* There is no genuine strength in *possession* as such, neither of material property nor of mental qualities like emotions or thoughts. There is also no strength in use and manipulation of objects; what we use is not ours simply because we use it. Ours is only that to which we are genuinely related by our creative activity, be it a person or an inanimate object. Only those qualities that result from our spontaneous activity give strength to the self and thereby form the basis of its integrity. The inability to act spontaneously, to express what one genuinely feels and thinks, and the resulting necessity to present a pseudo self to others and oneself, are the root of the feeling of inferiority and weakness. Whether or not we are aware of it, there is nothing of which we are more ashamed than of not being ourselves, and there is nothing that gives us greater pride and happiness than to think, to feel, and to say what is ours.

This implies that what matters is the activity as such, the process and not the result. In our culture the emphasis is just the reverse. We produce not for a concrete satisfaction but for the abstract purpose of selling our commodity; we feel that we can acquire everything material or immaterial by buying it, and thus things become ours independently of any creative effort of our own in relation to them. In the same way we regard our personal qualities and the result of our efforts as commodities that can be sold for money, prestige, and power. The emphasis thus shifts from the present satisfaction of creative activity to the value of the finished product. Thereby man misses the only satisfaction that can give him real happiness—the experience of the activity of the present moment—and chases after a phantom that leaves him disappointed as soon as he believes he has caught it—the illusory happiness called success.

If the individual realizes his self by spontaneous activity and thus relates himself to the world, he ceases to be an isloated atom; he and the world become part of one structuralized whole; he has his rightful place, and thereby his doubt concerning himself and the meaning of life disappears. This doubt sprang from his separateness and from the thwarting of life; when he can live, neither compulsively nor automatically but spontaneously, the doubt disappears. He is aware of himself as an active and creative individual and recognizes that *there is only one meaning of life: the act of living itself.*

If the individual overcomes the basic doubt concerning himself and his place in life, if he is related to the world by embracing it in the act of spontaneous living, he gains strength as an individual and he gains security. This security, however, differs from the security that characterizes the preindividualist state in the same way in which the new relatedness to the world differs from that of the primary ties. The new security is not rooted in the protection which the individual has from a higher power outside of himself; neither is it a security in which the tragic quality of life is eliminated. The new security is dynamic; it is not based on protection, but on man's spontaneous activity. It is the security acquired each moment by man's spontaneous activity. It is the security that only freedom can give, that needs no illusions because it has eliminated those conditions that necessitate illusions.

Positive freedom as the realization of the self implies the full affirmation of the uniqueness of the individual. Men are born equal but they are also born different. The basis of this difference is the inherited equipment, physiological and mental, with which they start life, to which is added the particular constellation of circumstances and experiences that they meet with. This individual basis of the personality is as little identical with any other as two organisms are ever identical physically. The genuine growth of the self is always a growth on this particular basis; it is an organic growth, the unfolding of a nucleus that is peculiar for this one person and only for him. The development of the automaton, in contrast, is not an organic growth. The growth of the basis of the self is blocked and a pseudo self is superimposed upon this self, which is—as we have seen—essentially the incorporation of extraneous patterns of thinking and feeling. Organic growth is possible only under the condition of supreme respect for the peculiarity of the self of other persons as well as of our own self. This respect for and cultivation of the uniqueness of the self is the most valuable achievement of human culture and it is this very achievement that is in danger today.

The uniqueness of the self in no way contradicts the principle of equality. The thesis that men are born equal implies that they all share the same fundamental human qualities, that they share the basic fate of human beings, that they all have the same inalienable claim on freedom and happiness. It furthermore means that their relationship is one of solidarity, not one of domination-submission. What the concept of equality does not mean is that all men are alike. Such a concept of equality is derived from the role that the individual plays in his economic activities today. In the relation the man who buys and the one who sells, the concrete differences of personality are eliminated. In this situation only one thing matters, that the one has something to sell and the other has money to buy it. In economic life one man is not different from another; as real persons they are, and the cultivation of their uniqueness is the essence of individuality.

Positive freedom also implies the principle that there is no higher power than this unique individual self, that man is the center and purpose of his life; that the growth and realization of man's individuality is an end that can never be subordinated to purposes which are supposed to have greater dignity. This interpretation may arouse serious objections. Does it not postulate unbridled egotism? Is it not the negation of the idea of sacrifice for an ideal? Would its acceptance not lead to anarchy? These questions have actually already been answered, partly explicitly, partly implicitly, during our previous discussion. However, they are too important for us not to make another attempt to clarify the answers and to avoid misunderstanding.

To say that man should not be subject to anything higher than himself does not deny the dignity of ideals. On the contrary, it is the strongest affirmation of ideals. It forces us, however, to a critical analysis of what an ideal is. One is generally apt today to assume that an ideal is any aim whose achievement does not imply material gain, anything for which a person is ready to sacrifice egotistical ends. This is a purely psychological—and for that matter relativistic—concept of an ideal. From this subjectivist viewpoint a Fascist, who is driven by the desire to subordinate himself to a higher power and at the same time to overpower other people, has an ideal just as much as the man who fights for human equality and freedom. On this basis the problem of ideals can never be solved.

We must recognize the difference between genuine and fictitious ideals, which is just as fundamental a difference as that between truth and falsehood. All genuine ideals have one thing in common: they express the desire for something which is not yet accomplished but which is desirable for the purposes of the growth and happiness of the individual.[1] We may not al-

[1] Cf. Max Otto, *The Human Enterprise*, T. S. Croft, New York, 1940. Chaps. IV and V.

ways know what serves this end, we may disagree about the function of this or that ideal in terms of human development, but this is no reason for a relativism which says that we cannot know what furthers life or what blocks it. We are not always sure which food is healthy and which is not, yet we do not conclude that we have no way whatsoever of recognizing poison. In the same way we can know, if we want to, what is poisonous for mental life. We know that poverty, intimidation, isolation, are directed *against* life; that everything that serves freedom and furthers the courage and strength to be oneself is *for* life. What is good or bad for man is not a metaphysical question, but an empirical one that can be answered on the basis of an analysis of man's nature and the effect which certain conditions have on him.

But what about "ideals" like those of the Fascists which are definitely directed against life? How can we understand the fact that men are following these false ideals as fervently as others are following true ideals? The answer to this question is provided by certain psychological considerations. The phenomenon of masochism shows us that men can be drawn to the experiencing of suffering or submission. There is no doubt that suffering submission, or suicide is the antithesis of positive aims of living. Yet these aims can be subjectively experienced as gratifying and attractive. This attraction to what is harmful in life is the phenomenon which more than any other deserves the name of a pathological perversion. Many psychologists have assumed that the experience of pleasure and the avoidance of pain is the only legitimate principle guiding human action; but dynamic psychology can show that the subjective experience of pleasure is not a sufficient criterion for the value of certain behavior in terms of human happiness. The analysis of masochistic phenomena is a case in point. Such analysis shows that the sensation of pleasure can be the result of a pathological perversion and proves as little about the objective meaning of the experience as the sweet taste of a poison would prove about its function for the organism.[1] We thus come to define a genuine ideal as any aim which furthers the growth, freedom, and happiness of the self, and to define as fictitious ideals those compulsive and irrational aims which subjectively are attractive experiences (like the drive for submission), but which actually are harmful to life. Once we accept this definition, it follows that a genuine ideal is not some veiled force superior to the individual, but that it is the articulate expression of utmost affirmation of the self. Any ideal which is in contrast to such affirmation proves by this very fact that it is not an ideal but a pathological sin.

[1] The question discussed here leads to a point of great significance which I want at least to mention: that problems of ethics can be clarified by dynamic psychology. Psychologists will only be helpful in this direction when they can see the relevance of moral problems for the understanding of personality. Any psychology, including Freud's, which treats such problems in terms of the pleasure principle, fails to understand one important sector of personality and leaves the field to dogmatic and unempirical doctrines of morality. The analysis of self-love, masochistic sacrifice, and ideals as offered in this book provides illustrations for this field of psychology and ethics that warrant further development.

From here we come to another question, that of sacrifice. Does our definition of freedom as nonsubmission to any *higher* power exclude sacrifices, including the sacrifice of one's life?

This is a particularly important question today, when Fascism proclaims self-sacrifice as the highest virtue and impresses many people with its idealistic character. The answer to this question follows logically from what has been said so far. There are two entirely different types of sacrifice. It is one of the tragic facts of life that the demands of our physical self and the aims of our mental self can conflict; that actually we may have to sacrifice our physical self in order to assert the integrity of our spiritual self. This sacrifice will never lose its tragic quality. Death is never sweet, not even if it is suffered for the highest ideal. It remains unspeakably bitter, and still it can be the utmost assertion of our individuality. Such sacrifice is fundamentally different from the "sacrifice" which Fascism preaches. There, sacrifice is not the highest price man may have to pay to assert his self, but it is an aim in itself. This masochistic sacrifice sees the fulfillment of life in its very negation, in the annihilation of the self. It is only the supreme expression of what Fascism aims at in all its ramifications—the annihilation of the individual self and its utter submission to a higher power. It is the perversion of true sacrifice as much as suicide is the utmost perversion of life. True sacrifice presupposes an uncompromising wish for spiritual integrity. The sacrifice of those who have lost it only covers up their moral bankruptcy.

One last objection is to be met: If individuals are allowed to act freely in the sense of spontaneity, if they acknowledge no higher authority than themselves, will anarchy be the inevitable result? In so far as the word anarchy stands for heedless egotism and destructiveness, the determining factor depends upon one's understanding of human nature. I can only refer to what has been pointed out in the chapter dealing with mechanisms of escape: that man is neither good nor bad; that life has an inherent tendency to grow, to expand, to express potentialities; that if life is thwarted, if the individual is isolated and overcome by doubt or a feeling of aloneness and powerlessness, then he is driven to destructiveness and craving for power or submission. If human freedom is established as *freedom to,* if man can realize his self fully and uncompromisingly, the fundamental cause for his asocial drives will have disappeared and only a sick and abnormal individual will be dangerous. This freedom has never been realized in the history of mankind, yet it has been an ideal to which mankind has stuck even if it was often expressed in abstruse and irrational forms. There is no reason to wonder why the record of history shows so much cruelty and destructiveness. If there is anything to be surprised at—and encouraged by—I believe it is the fact that the human race, in spite of all that has happened to men, has retained—and actually developed—such qualities of dignity, courage, decency, and kindness as we find them throughout history and in countless individuals today.

8. Natural Law and Human Rights *

JACQUES MARITAIN

The idea of natural law is a heritage of Christian and classical thought. It does not go back to the philosophy of the eighteenth century, which more or less deformed it, but rather to Grotius, and before him to Suarez and Francisco de Vitoria; and further back to St. Thomas Aquinas; and still further back to St. Augustine and the Church Fathers and St. Paul; and even further back to Cicero, to the Stoics, to the great moralists of antiquity and its great poets, particularly Sophocles. Antigone is the eternal heroine of natural law, which the Ancients called *the unwritten law,* and this is the name most befitting it.

Since I have not space here to discuss nonsense (you can always find very intelligent philosophers to defend it most brilliantly) I am taking it for granted that you admit that there is a human nature, and that this human nature is the same in all men. I am taking it for granted that you also admit that man is a being gifted with intelligence, and who, as such, acts with an understanding of what he is doing, and therefore with the power to determine for himself the ends which he pursues. On the other hand, possessed of a nature, being constituted in a given, determinate fashion, man obviously possesses ends which correspond to his natural constitution and which are the same for all—as all pianos, for instance, whatever their particular type and in whatever spot they may be, have as their end the production of certain attuned sounds. If they don't produce these sounds they must be tuned, or discarded as worthless. But since man is endowed with intelligence and determines his own ends, it is up to him to put himself in tune with the ends necessarily demanded by his nature. This means that there is, by very virtue of human nature, *an order or a disposition which human reason can discover and according to which the human will must act in order to attune itself to the necessary ends of the human being. The unwritten law, or natural law, is nothing more than that.*

The great philosophers of antiquity knew, Christian thinkers know even better, that nature comes from God, and that the unwritten law comes from the eternal law which is Creative Wisdom itself. That is why the idea of natural law or the unwritten law was linked for them to a sentiment of natural piety, to that profound and sacred respect unforgettably expressed by

* From Jacques Maritain, *The Rights of Man and Natural Law* (Charles Scribner's Sons, 1943). By permission.

Antigone. Because they understand the real principle of this law, belief in it is firmer and more unshakable in those who believe in God than in the others. Belief in human nature and in the freedom of the human being, however, is in itself sufficient to convince us that there is an unwritten law, and to assure us that natural law is something as real in the moral realm as the laws of growth and senescence in the physical.

The law and knowledge of the law are two different things. The man who does not know the law (so long as this ignorance itself does not spring from some failing) is not responsible before the law. And knowing that there is a law does not necessarily mean knowing what that law is. It is because this very simple distinction is forgotten that many perplexities have arisen concerning the unwritten law. It is written, they say, in the heart of man. True, but in the hidden depths, as hidden from us as our own heart. This metaphor itself has been responsible for a great deal of damage, causing natural law to be represented as a ready-made code rolled up within the conscience of each one of us, which each one of us has only to unroll, and of which all men should naturally have an equal knowledge.

Natural law is not a written law. Men know it with greater or less difficulty, and in different degrees, running the risk of error here as elsewhere. The only practical knowledge all men have naturally and infallibly in common is that we must do good and avoid evil. This is the preamble and the principle of natural law; it is not the law itself. Natural law is the ensemble of things to do and not to do which follow therefrom in *necessary* fashion, and *from the simple fact that man is man,* nothing else being taken into account. That every sort of error and deviation is possible in the determination of these things merely proves that our sight is weak and that innumerable accidents can corrupt our judgment. Montaigne maliciously remarked that, among certain peoples, incest and thievery were considered virtuous acts. Pascal was scandalized by this. We are scandalized by the fact that cruelty, denunciation of parents, the lie for the service of the party, the murder of old or sick people should be considered virtuous actions by young people educated according to Nazi methods. All this proves nothing against natural law, any more than a mistake in addition proves anything against arithmetic, or the mistakes of certain primitive peoples, for whom the stars were holes in the tent which covered the world, prove anything against astronomy.

Natural law is an unwritten law. Man's knowledge of it has increased little by little as man's moral conscience has developed. The latter was at first in a twilight state.[1] Anthropologists have taught us within what structures of tribal life and in the midst of what half-awakened magic it was primitively formed. This proves merely that the idea of natural law, at first immersed in rites and mythology, differentiated itself only slowly, as slowly even as the

---

[1] Cf. Raissa Maritain, *La Conscience Morale et l'État de Nature,* New York, 1942.

idea of nature; and that the knowledge men have had of the unwritten law has passed through more diverse forms and stages than certain philosophers or theologians have believed. The knowledge which our own moral conscience has of this law is doubtless itself still imperfect, and very likely it will continue to develop and to become more refined as long as humanity exists. Only when the Gospel has penetrated to the very depth of human substance will natural law appear in its flower and its perfection.

We must now consider the fact that natural law and the light of moral conscience within us do not prescribe merely things to be done and not to be done; they also recognize rights, in particular, rights linked to the very nature of man. The human person possesses rights because of the very fact that it is a person, a whole, master of itself and of its acts, and which consequently is not merely a means to an end, but an end, an end which must be treated as such. The dignity of the human person? The expression means nothing if it does not signify that by virtue of natural law, the human person has the right to be respected, is the subject of rights, possesses rights. There are things which are owed to man because of the very fact that he is man. The notion of right and the notion of moral obligation are correlative. They are both founded on the freedom proper to spiritual agents. If man is morally bound to the things which are necessary to the fulfillment of his destiny, obviously, then, he has the right to fulfill his destiny; and if he has the right to fulfill his destiny he has the right to the things necessary for this purpose. The notion of right is even more profound than that of moral obligation, for God has sovereign right over creatures and He has no moral obligation towards them (although He owes it to Himself to give them that which is required by their nature).

The true philosophy of the rights of the human person is therefore based upon the idea of natural law. The same natural law which lays down our most fundamental duties, and by virtue of which every law is binding, is the very law which assigns to us our fundamental rights. It is because we are enmeshed in the universal order, in the laws and regulations of the cosmos and of the immense family of created natures (and finally in the order of creative wisdom), and it is because we have at the same time the privilege of sharing in spiritual nature, that we possess rights vis-à-vis other men and all the assemblage of creatures. In the last analysis, as every creature acts only by virtue of its Principle, which is the Pure Act; as every authority worthy of the name (that is to say, just) is binding in conscience only by virtue of the Principle of beings, which is pure Wisdom; so too every right possessed by man is possessed only by virtue of the right possessed by God, which is pure Justice, to see the order of His wisdom in beings respected, obeyed and loved by every intelligence.

Another altogether opposite philosophy has sought to base the rights of the human person on the claim that man is subject to no law other than that of his will and his freedom, and that he must "obey only himself," as Jean-Jacques Rousseau put it, because every measure or regulation springing from the world of nature (and finally from creative wisdom) would destroy at one and the same time his autonomy and his dignity. This philosophy built no solid foundation for the rights of the human person, because nothing can be founded on illusion; it compromised and squandered these rights, because it led men to conceive them as rights in themselves divine, hence infinite, escaping every objective measure, denying every limitation imposed upon the claims of the ego, and ultimately expressing the absolute independence of the human subject and a so-called absolute right—which supposedly pertains to everything in the human subject by the mere fact that it is in him—to unfold one's cherished possibilities at the expense of all other beings. When men thus instructed clashed on all sides with the impossible, they came to believe in the bankruptcy of the rights of the human person. Some have turned against these rights with an enslaver's fury; some have continued to invoke them, while in their inmost conscience they are weighed down by a temptation to scepticism which is one of the most alarming symptoms of the present crisis. A kind of intellectual and moral revolution is required of us, in order to re-establish on the basis of a true philosophy our faith in the dignity of man and in his rights, and in order to rediscover the authentic sources of this faith.

The consciousness of the dignity of the person and of the rights of the person remained implicit in pagan antiquity, over which the law of slavery cast its shadow. It was the message of the Gospel which suddenly awakened this consciousness, in a divine and transcendent form, revealing to men that they are called upon to be the sons and heirs of God in the Kingdom of God. Under the evangelical impulse, this same awakening was little by little to spread forth, with regard to the requirements of natural law, over the realm of man's life here on earth, and of the terrestrial city.

9. *The Four Freedoms* *

FRANKLIN D. ROOSEVELT

I address you, the Members of the Seventy-Seventh Congress, at a moment unprecedented in the history of the Union. I use the word "unprecedented,"

* *Message to Congress on the State of the Union* (January 6, 1941).

because at no previous time has American security been as seriously threatened from without as it is today.

Since the permanent formation of our government under the Constitution, in 1789, most of the periods of crisis in our history have related to our domestic affairs. Fortunately, only one of these—the four year War between the States—ever threatened our national unity. Today, thank God, one hundred and thirty million Americans, in forty-eight States, have forgotten points of the compass in our national unity.

It is true that prior to 1914 the United States often had been disturbed by events in other Continents. We had even engaged in two wars with European nations and in a number of undeclared wars in the West Indies, in the Mediterranean and in the Pacific for the maintenance of American rights and for the principles of peaceful commerce. In no case, however, had a serious threat been raised against our national safety or our independence.

What I seek to convey is the historic truth that the United States as a nation has at all times maintained opposition to any attempt to lock us in behind an ancient Chinese wall while the procession of civilization went past. Today, thinking of our children and their children, we oppose enforced isolation for ourselves or for any part of the Americas.

That determination of ours was proved, for example, during the quarter century of wars following the French Revolution.

While the Napoleonic struggles did threaten interests of the United States because of the French foothold in the West Indies and in Louisiana, and while we engaged in the War of 1812 to vindicate our right to peaceful trade, it is, nevertheless, clear that neither France nor Great Britain nor any other nation was aiming at domination of the whole world.

In like fashion from 1815 to 1914—99 years—no single war in Europe or in Asia constituted a real threat against our future or against the future of any other American nation.

Except in the Maximilian interlude in Mexico, no foreign power sought to establish itself in this Hemisphere; and the strength of the British fleet in the Atlantic has been a friendly strength. It is still a friendly strength.

Even when the World War broke out in 1914, it seemed to contain only small threat of danger to our own American future. But, as time went on, the American people began to visualize what the downfall of democratic nations might mean to our own democracy.

We need not over-emphasize imperfections in the Peace of Versailles. We need not harp on failure of the democracies to deal with problems of world reconstruction. We should remember that the Peace of 1919 was far less unjust than the kind of "pacification" which began even before Munich, and which is being carried on under the new order of tyranny that seeks to spread over every continent today. The American people have unalterably set their faces against that tyranny.

Every realist knows that the democratic way of life is at this moment being directly assailed in every part of the world—assailed either by arms, or by secret spreading of poisonous propaganda by those who seek to destroy unity and promote discord in nations still at peace.

During sixteen months this assault has blotted out the whole pattern of democratic life in an appalling number of independent nations, great and small. The assailants are still on the march, threatening other nations, great and small.

Therefore, as your President, performing my constitutional duty to "give to the Congress information of the state of the Union," I find it necessary to report that the future and the safety of our country and of our democracy are overwhelmingly involved in events far beyond our borders.

Armed defense of democratic existence is now being gallantly waged in four continents. If that defense fails, all the population and all the resources of Europe, Asia, Africa, and Australasia will be dominated by the conquerors. The total of those populations and their resources greatly exceeds the sum total of the population and resources of the whole of the Western Hemisphere—many times over.

In times like these it is immature—and incidentally untrue—for anybody to brag that an unprepared America, single-handed, and with one hand tied behind its back, can hold off the whole world.

No realistic American can expect from a dictator's peace international generosity, or return of true independence, or world disarmament, or freedom of expression, or freedom of religion—or even good business.

Such a peace would bring no security for us or for our neighbors. "Those, who would give up essential liberty to purchase a little temporary safety, deserve neither liberty nor safety."

As a nation we may take pride in the fact that we are soft-hearted; but we cannot afford to be soft-headed.

We must always be wary of those who with sounding brass and a tinkling cymbal preach the "ism" of appeasement.

We must especially beware of that small group of selfish men who would clip the wings of the American eagle in order to feather their own nests.

I have recently pointed out how quickly the tempo of modern warfare could bring into our very midst the physical attack which we must expect if the dictator nations win the war.

There is much loose talk of our immunity from immediate and direct invasion from across the seas. Obviously, as long as the British Navy retains its power, no such danger exists. Even if there were no British Navy, it is not probable that any enemy would be stupid enough to attack us by landing troops in the United States from across thousands of miles of ocean, until it had acquired strategic bases from which to operate.

But we learn much from the lessons of the past years in Europe—particularly the lesson of Norway, whose essential seaports were captured by treachery and surprise built up over a series of years.

The first phase of the invasion of this Hemisphere would not be the landing of regular troops. The necessary strategic points would be occupied by secret agents and their dupes—and great numbers of them are already here, and in Latin America.

As long as the aggressor nations maintain the offensive, they—not we—will choose the time and the place and the method of their attack.

That is why the future of all American Republics is today in serious danger.

That is why this Annual Message to the Congress is unique in our history. That is why every member of the Executive branch of the government and every member of the Congress face great responsibility—and great accountability.

The need of the moment is that our actions and our policy should be devoted primarily—almost exclusively—to meeting this foreign peril. For all our domestic problems are now a part of the great emergency.

Just as our national policy in internal affairs has been based upon a decent respect for the rights and dignity of all our fellow-men within our gates, so our national policy in foreign affairs has been based on a decent respect for the rights and dignity of all nations, large and small. And the justice of morality must and will win in the end.

Our national policy is this:

First, by an impressive expression of the public will and without regard to partisanship, we are committed to all-inclusive national defense.

Second, by an impressive expression of the public will and without regard to partisanship, we are committed to full support of all those resolute peoples, everywhere, who are resisting aggression and are thereby keeping war away from our Hemisphere. By this support, we express our determination that the democratic cause shall prevail; and we strengthen the defense and security of our own nation.

Third, by an impressive expression of the public will and without regard to partisanship, we are committed to the proposition that principles of morality and considerations for our own security will never permit us to acquiesce in a peace dictated by aggressors and sponsored by appeasers. We know that enduring peace cannot be bought at the cost of other people's freedom.

In the recent national election there was no substantial difference between the two great parties in respect to that national policy. No issue was fought out on this line before the American electorate. Today, it is abundantly evident that American citizens everywhere are demanding and supporting speedy and complete action in recognition of obvious danger.

Therefore, the immediate need is a swift and driving increase in our armament production.

Leaders of industry and labor have responded to our summons. Goals of speed have been set. In some cases these goals are being reached ahead of time; in some cases we are on schedule; in other cases there are slight but not serious delays; and in some cases—and I am sorry to say very important cases—we are all concerned by the slowness of the accomplishment of our plans.

The Army and Navy, however, have made substantial progress during the past year. Actual experience is improving and speeding up our methods of production with every passing day. And today's best is not good enough for tomorrow.

I am not satisfied with the progress thus far made. The men in charge of the program represent the best in training, ability, and patriotism. They are not satisfied with the progress thus far made. None of us will be satisfied until the job is done.

No matter whether the original goal was set too high or too low, our objective is quicker and better results.

To give two illustrations:

We are behind schedule in turning out finished airplanes; we are working day and night to solve the innumerable problems and to catch up.

We are ahead of schedule in building warships; but we are working to get even further ahead of schedule.

To change the whole nation from a basis of peace time production of implements of peace to a basis of war time production of implements of war is no small task. And the greatest difficulty comes at the beginning of the program, when new tools and plant facilities and new assembly lines and ship ways must first be constructed before the actual matériel begins to flow steadily and speedily from them.

The Congress, of course, must rightly keep itself informed at all times of the progress of the program. However, there is certain information, as the Congress itself will readily recognize, which, in the interests of our own security and those of the nations we are supporting, must of needs be kept in confidence.

New circumstances are constantly begetting new needs for our safety. I shall ask this Congress for greatly increased new appropriations and authorizations to carry on what we have begun.

I also ask this Congress for authority and for funds sufficient to manufacture additional munitions and war supplies of many kinds, to be turned over to those nations which are now in actual war with aggressor nations.

Our most useful and immediate role is to act as an arsenal for them as well as for ourselves. They do not need man power. They do need billions of dollars' worth of the weapons of defense.

The time is near when they will not be able to pay for them in ready cash. We cannot, and will not, tell them they must surrender, merely because of present inability to pay for the weapons which we know they must have.

I do not recommend that we make them a loan of dollars with which to pay for these weapons—a loan to be repaid in dollars.

I recommend that we make it possible for those nations to continue to obtain war materials in the United States, fitting their orders into our own program. Nearly all of their matériel would, if the time ever came, be useful for our own defense.

Taking counsel of expert military and naval authorities, considering what is best for our own security, we are free to decide how much should be kept here and how much should be sent abroad to our friends who by their determined and heroic resistance are giving us time in which to make ready our own defense.

For what we sent abroad, we shall be repaid, within a reasonable time following the close of hostilities, in similar materials, or, at our option, in other goods of many kinds which they can produce and which we need.

Let us say to the democracies: "We Americans are vitally concerned in your defense of freedom. We are putting forth our energies, our resources and our organizing powers to give you the strength to regain and maintain a free world. We shall send you, in ever-increasing numbers, ships, planes, tanks, guns. This is our purpose and our pledge."

In fulfillment of this purpose we will not be intimidated by the threats of dictators that they will regard as a breach of international law and as an act of war our aid to the democracies which dare to resist their aggression. Such aid is not an act of war, even if a dictator should unilaterally proclaim it so to be.

When the dictators are ready to make war upon us, they will not wait for an act of war on our part. They did not wait for Norway or Belgium or the Netherlands to commit an act of war.

Their only interest is in a new one-way international law, which lacks mutuality in its observance, and, therefore, becomes an instrument of oppression.

The happiness of future generations of Americans may well depend upon how effective and how immediate we can make our aid felt. No one can tell the exact character of the emergency situations that we may be called upon to meet. The Nation's hands must not be tied when the Nation's life is in danger.

We must all prepare to make the sacrifices that the emergency—as serious as war itself—demands. Whatever stands in the way of speed and efficiency in defense preparations must give way to the national need.

A free nation has the right to expect full cooperation from all groups. A free nation has the right to look to the leaders of business, of labor, and of agriculture to take the lead in stimulating effort, not among other groups but within their own groups.

The best way of dealing with the few slackers or trouble makers in our midst is, first, to shame them by patriotic example, and, if that fails, to use the sovereignty of government to save government.

As men do not live by bread alone, they do not fight by armaments alone. Those who man our defenses, and those behind them who build our defenses, must have the stamina and courage which come from an unshakeable belief in the manner of life which they are defending. The mighty action which we are calling for cannot be based on a disregard of all things worth fighting for.

The Nation takes great satisfaction and much strength from the things which have been done to make its people conscious of their individual stake in the preservation of democratic life in America. Those things have toughened the fibre of our people, have renewed their faith and strengthened their devotion to the institutions we make ready to protect.

Certainly this is no time to stop thinking about the social and economic problems which are the root cause of the social revolution which is today a supreme factor in the world.

There is nothing mysterious about the foundations of a healthy and strong democracy. The basic things expected by our people of their political and economic systems are simple. They are:

Equality of opportunity for youth and for others.

Jobs for those who can work.

Security for those who need it.

The ending of special privilege for the few.

The preservation of civil liberties for all.

The enjoyment of the fruits of scientific progress in a wider and constantly rising standard of living.

These are the simple and basic things that must never be lost sight of in the turmoil and unbelievable complexity of our modern world. The inner and abiding strength of our economic and political systems is dependent upon the degree to which they fulfill these expectations.

Many subjects connected with our social economy call for immediate improvement.

As examples:

We should bring more citizens under the coverage of old age pensions and unemployment insurance.

We should widen the opportunities for adequate medical care.

We should plan a better system by which persons deserving or needing gainful employment may obtain it.

I have called for personal sacrifice. I am assured of the willingness of almost all Americans to respond to that call.

A part of the sacrifice means the payment of more money in taxes. In my budget message I recommend that a greater portion of this great defense program be paid for from taxation than we are paying today. No person should try, or be allowed, to get rich out of this program; and the principle of tax payments in accordance with ability to pay should be constantly before our eyes to guide our legislation.

If the Congress maintains these principles, the voters, putting patriotism ahead of pocketbooks, will give you their applause.

In the future days, which we seek to make secure, we look forward to a world founded upon four essential human freedoms.

The first is freedom of speech and expression—everywhere in the world.

The second is freedom of every person to worship God in his own way —everywhere in the world.

The third is freedom from want—which, translated into world terms, means economic understandings which will secure to every nation a healthy peace time life for its inhabitants—everywhere in the world.

The fourth is freedom from fear—which, translated into world terms, means a world-wide reduction of armaments to such a point and in such a thorough fashion that no nation will be in a position to commit an act of physical aggression against any neighbor—anywhere in the world.

That is no vision of a distant millennium. It is a definite basis for a kind of world attainable in our time and generation. That kind of world is the very antithesis of the so-called new order of tyranny which the dictators seek to create with the crash of a bomb.

To that new order we oppose the greater conception—the moral order. A good society is able to face schemes of world domination and foreign revolutions alike without fear.

Since the beginning of our American history we have been engaged in change—in a perpetual peaceful revolution—a revolution which goes on steadily, quietly adjusting itself to changing conditions—without the concentration camp or the quick-lime in the ditch. The world order which we seek is the cooperation of free countries, working together in a friendly civilized society.

This nation has placed its destiny in the hands and heads and hearts of its millions of free men and women; and its faith in freedom under the guidance of God. Freedom means the supremacy of human rights everywhere. Our support goes to those who struggle to gain those rights or keep them. Our strength is in our unity of purpose.

To that high concept there can be no end save victory.

Chapter III

LIBERTY AND EQUALITY

SOLUTIONS of historical problems are never final, because as long as the world persists in imperfection, the very solution creates new problems. Out-and-outers, like absolute pacifists, anarchists, religious fanatics, uncompromising believers in vegetarianism, nudism, and other radical approaches to man's material and spiritual woes, are to be envied for the peace of mind which they derive from their faith that a single formula will solve complex issues for all time. I have known one or two Socialists naïve enough to think that, once the means of production were nationalized, crime (a typical product of capitalist injustice) would disappear, even the *crime passionel*. Come the revolution—and men will become angels, or something very close to it. Yet all historical experience shows that problems are the product, not only of unsolved troubles, but also of apparently solved ones. As we can glimpse only a part of the truth in any given situation, we can never quite catch up with our failures.

The second half of the eighteenth century was one of the few brief spells when men thought they had found the key to heaven. The architects of the popular revolutions in England, America, and France could be well satisfied with their accomplishments. The old, prerevolutionary order was defeated, never to return to life again in those nations. Absolute monarchy—the devil of the drama—was extirpated altogether, or else reduced to harmless social decoration. The old ruling classes had to concede first place to the rising new middle and commercial classes. Liberty! Who could deny that freedom was firmly established for all time, when the people were governing themselves in freely elected assemblies, without privileges of caste or creed?

In the United States the problem of race equality was first to test the meaning of equality to millions of American citizens. On June 26, 1857, Lincoln made an address in Springfield, Illinois, in which he discussed some of the implications of the Dred Scott decision of the Supreme Court, which held that Negroes could not sue in United States courts, and that Congress could not prohibit slavery in the territories. Lincoln stressed the fact that equality does not mean identity; equality must be understood, not as describing a condition that is, but as postulating a condition that ought to exist, a right. Of such rights, life, liberty, and the pursuit of happiness were singled out by the authors of the Declaration of Independence.

As the optimistic eighteenth century was followed by the more sceptical nineteenth century, the problems created by the newly won liberties became increasingly manifest. As often happens when freedom is unregulated by a sense of social responsibility, crass inequality, especially of wealth and income, was the direct result. More and more, freedom meant the opportunity to enrich oneself—at the expense of one's own health and ethical standards, and even more so at the expense of one's employees, and of the community as a whole. To many, political liberty appeared as a device of social and economic inequality. Those who had hoped that political freedom, enjoyed by all, would automatically lead to genuine equality, were alarmed by the growing inequalities, based mainly on differences of property, among citizens formally equal before the law. In its majestic respect for the ideal of equality, the law forbids, as Anatole France once put it, the rich as well as the poor to steal bread and sleep under bridges.

The relations between liberty and equality, the conditions under which both ideas can be transformed from empty abstractions into living reality, are examined below more extensively by Harold J. Laski, Sidney and Beatrice Webb, and R. H. Tawney. "Liberty and Equality" is the subject of the fourth chapter of Laski's *Grammar of Politics,* first published in 1925, and generally recognized as the outstanding general treatise on politics of the past two generations. It is Laski's most ambitious work, and destined to become a classic in the field of political literature. In the tradition of humanistic liberalism, Laski opens his analysis with the definition of liberty as "the eager maintenance of that atmosphere in which men have the opportunity to be their best selves." If this be socialism, it is not of the Marxian or Leninist kind. The "life of spiritual enrichment" is the sole test which determines when restraint is justified and when it turns evil. After an examination of the "safeguards of liberty," Laski discusses the central problem of the relationships of liberty and equality. He rejects the view of two outstanding liberals of the nineteenth century, de Tocqueville and Lord Acton, that liberty and equality are "antithetic," and ascribes their "drastic conclusion" to the mistaken conception of equality as "identity of treatment." Laski does not find equality incompatible with men's differences: "The meaning, ultimately, of equality surely lies in the fact that the very differences in the nature of men require mechanisms for the expression of their wills that give to each its due hearing." Absence of special privileges and adequate opportunities open to all are the two primary conditions of equality. In particular, Laski stresses educational opportunity: its lack inflicts not only cruel injustice on the individual, but causes waste of talent and ability to the detriment of society as a whole.

In the context of modern civilization, Laski argues, social and economic inequality is the most serious obstacle to freedom. "There are men in every community whose power is built upon not what they are or do, but upon the possessions they embody." Analyzing the influence of wealth in government, education, communication of news and ideas, and religion, Laski arrives at the conclusion, perceived by thinkers as diverse as Aristotle and Madison, that "political equality, therefore, is never real unless it is accompanied by virtual economic equality." To Laski equality in economic power means not only approximate equality of wealth: he is even more concerned about the authoritarianism in industrial relations, as "unconstitutional" as political power used to be, before it was tamed by self-rule of the governed.

Unlike most political philosophers, Laski also examines the *international* aspects of the concepts of liberty and equality. Although the law of nations may assume equality of states, "even the most genial fictions of law cannot make a small State equal to a great one." How can equality, then, be achieved? As long as war is a recognized institution, equality is well-nigh impossible. "Concepts like freedom are devoid of meaning as long as a State is free to force its solution upon a neighbor." On the other hand, Laski does not believe that a stable international order can be built upon purely political and legal foundations alone, and he strongly advocates the development of social and economic international control on a functional basis. Freedom and social control are complementary, for individuals as well as for States: "Just as, that is, no individual can find freedom outside the common rules of his society, so, also, no State can find freedom save by accepting limitations of its sovereignty by the will formed by the common decision of a society of States." Those who oppose rational settlement of disputes between states by claiming that certain types of disputes (especially where "honor" or prestige is involved) are non-justiciable, are reminded by Laski that "states, like men, never protest their honour loudly unless they have a bad case to argue."

Another major analysis of the relations of liberty and equality is the third chapter of Sidney and Beatrice Webb's *The Decay of Capitalist Civilization* (1923). Few partnerships have left their imprint on modern social thought and action as has that of Sidney and Beatrice Webb. Their name is best known in connection with the Fabian Society, founded in 1884. Sidney Webb was one of the first members, joining it in its first year; after his marriage to Beatrice in 1892, "the Webbs" became a household word in English life. Their pioneering studies on poor law, trade unionism, and local government, were the intellectual mainsprings of a movement of reform such as England had not witnessed since the early nineteenth century. Under the primary influence of the Webbs, Fabianism successfully avoided the double pitfall of small political groups (the Fabian membership never exceeded a few thousand): uncompromising dogmatism, or excessive expediency. Although limited in numbers, Fabianism was by no means a small coterie of idol worshipers attached to Sidney and Beatrice Webb. In the 1945 parliamentary elections, resulting in a Labor victory, 229 out of 394 Labor members belonged to the Fabian Society: in the Government the proportion was even higher, 45 out of 62.

Another institution which owes its existence and reputation more to the Webbs than to anyone else is the London School of Economics and Political Science. Its foundation in 1895 was the effort of several men and women, but the Webbs were more identified with it than any other name. Sidney Webb saw the school through its first difficult years, from finding financial support to doing the daily chores of detail administration. The school started out with eight students, and in forty years rose to over three thousand. Lord (then Sir William) Beveridge was one of its directors, and its faculty has included enough creative scholars to earn for it a unique reputation in the world. In the Labor government which came into office in 1945, the Prime Minister, Mr. Attlee, the Chancellor of the Exchequer, Mr. Dalton, and several other members, were former teachers of the school. The number of graduates of the school, both in Parliament and in the Labor government, is legion.

Among all the works bequeathed to England by the Webbs, none are a greater tribute to their genius, brought to full fruition by indefatigable industry, than the Fabian Society and the London School of Economics and Political Science. The Webbs believed in reason rather than in deceit, in facts rather than in propaganda, in peaceful evolution rather than in revolutionary catastrophes. If the England they left behind was a happier one than the one they knew in their youth, the change was due to them as much as to anyone of their generation.

In *Equality* (1931), R. H. Tawney dissects the anatomy of a society built on the "religion of inequality." His illustrations are mainly drawn from the British experience, although Tawney also gives due consideration to conditions in the United States. What Tawney deplores is not the inequality of talent and ability, "but of the social and economic environment." Tawney, like Lincoln and Laski, realizes that equality does not mean identity: "The more anxiously, indeed, a society endeavours to secure equality of consideration for all its members, the greater will be the differentiation of treatment which, when once their common human needs have been met, it accords to the special needs of different groups and individuals among them." Tawney sees the "chief enemy of the life of the spirit" in the "idolatry of wealth, with its worship of pecuniary success." If economic equality, therefore, is pre-eminently on the list of social agenda of real urgency, this is necessary, "not because such wealth is the most important of man's treasures, but to prove that it is not."

1. The Meaning of Equality *

ABRAHAM LINCOLN

I think the authors of that notable instrument [the Declaration of Independence], intended to include *all* men, but they did not intend to declare all men equal *in all respects*. They did not mean to say all were equal in color, size, intellect, moral developments, or social capacity. They defined with tolerable distinctness in what respects they did consider all men created equal—equal with "certain inalienable rights, among which are life, liberty, and the pursuit of happiness." This they said, and this they meant. They did not mean to assert the obvious untruth that all were then actually enjoying that equality, nor yet that they were about to confer it immediately upon them. In fact, they had no power to confer such a boon. They meant simply to declare the right, so that enforcement of it might follow as fast as circumstances should permit.

They meant to set up a standard maxim for free society, which should be familiar to all, and revered by all; constantly looked to, constantly labored for, and even though never perfectly attained, constantly approximated, and thereby constantly spreading and deepening its influence and augmenting the happiness and value of life to all people of all colors everywhere. The assertion that "all men are created equal" was of no practical use in effecting our separation from Great Britain; and it was placed in the Declaration not for that, but for future use. Its authors meant it to be—as, thank God, it is now proving itself—a stumbling block to all those who in after times might seek to turn a free people back into the hateful paths of despotism. They knew the proneness of prosperity to breed tyrants, and they meant when such should reappear in this fair land and commence their vocation, they should find left for them at least one hard nut to crack.

* From an address delivered at Springfield, June 26, 1857.

2. *Liberty and Equality* *

HAROLD J. LASKI

THE NATURE OF LIBERTY

By liberty I mean the eager maintenance of that atmosphere in which men have the opportunity to be their best selves. Liberty, therefore, is a product of rights. A State built upon the conditions essential to the full development of our faculties will confer freedom upon its citizens. It will enable them to contribute their peculiar and intimate experience to the common stock. It will offer security that the decisions of the government are built upon the widest knowledge open to its members. It will prevent that frustration of creative impulse which destroys the special character of men. Without rights there cannot be liberty, because, without rights, men are the subjects of law unrelated to the needs of personality.

Liberty means absence of restraint; it is essentially a negative thing. But regulation, obviously enough, is the consequence of gregariousness; for we cannot live together without common rules. What is important is that the rules made should embody an experience I can follow and, in general, accept. I shall not feel that my liberty is endangered when I am prohibited from committing murder. My creative impulses do not suffer frustration when I am bidden to drive on a given side of the road. I am reasonably restrained when the law ordains that I must educate my children. Historic experience has evolved for us rules of convenience which promote right living; and to compel obedience to them is a justifiable limitation of freedom. To permit such compulsion is to invade liberty; but it is not necessarily to destroy the end liberty seeks to serve.

That is not, of course, to argue that every such prohibition is justified merely because it is made by an authority legally competent to issue it. Governments may in fact invade liberty even while they claim to be acting in the common interest. The exclusion of Nonconformists from full political privilege was an invasion of liberty. The restriction of the franchise to the owners of property was an invasion of liberty. The Combination Acts of 1799–1800 destroyed the liberty of working men. They could not realise their best selves because they could not unite in the effort to translate their experience into terms of statute. It is, in other words, essential to freedom that the prohibitions issued should be built upon the wills of those whom

* From Harold J. Laski, *A Grammar of Politics* (Yale University Press, 1925). By permission.

they affect. I must be able to feel that my will has access to avenues through which it can impress itself upon the holders of power. If I have the sense that the orders issued are beyond my scrutiny or criticism, I shall be, in a vital sense, unfree.

Liberty, therefore, is not merely obedience to a rule. My self is too distinct from other selves to accept a given order as good unless I feel that my will is embodied in its substance. I shall, of course, be compelled to endure irksome restraints. I must fill up income-tax returns; I must light the lamps upon my own motor-car at a set time. But no normal person will regard restrictions of this kind as so unrelated to his will as to constitute coercion of it. Where restraint becomes an invasion of liberty is where the given prohibition acts so as to destroy that harmony of impulses which comes when a man knows that he is doing something it is worth while to do. Restraint is felt as evil when it frustrates the life of spiritual enrichment. What each of us desires in life is room for our personal initiative in the things that add to our moral stature. What is destructive of our freedom is a system of prohibitions which limits the initiative there implied. And it is important that the initiative be a continuous one. The minds of citizens must be active minds. They must be given the habit of thought. They must be given the avenues through which thought can act. They must be accustomed to the exercise of will and conscience if they are to be alert to the duties implied in their function as citizens. Liberty consists in nothing so much as the encouragement of the will based on the instructed conscience of humble men.

In such a background, we cannot accept Mill's famous attempt to define the limits of State interference. All conduct is social conduct in the sense that whatever I do has results upon me as a member of society. There are certain freedoms I must have in order to be more than an inert recipient of orders; there is an atmosphere about those freedoms of quick vigilance without which they cannot be maintained. Liberty thus involves in its nature restraints, because the separate freedoms I use are not freedoms to destroy the freedoms of those with whom I live. My freedoms are avenues of choice through which I may, as I deem fit, construct for myself my own course of conduct. And the freedoms I must possess to enjoy a general liberty are those which, in their sum, will constitute the path through which my best self is capable of attainment. That is not to say it will be attained. It is to say only that I alone can make that best self, and that without those freedoms I have not the means of manufacture at my disposal.

Freedoms are therefore opportunities which history has shown to be essential to the development of personality. And freedoms are inseparable from rights because, otherwise, their realisation is hedged about with an uncertainty which destroys their quality. If, for example, my utterance of opinion is followed by persecution, I shall, in general, cease to express my mind. I shall cease, in fact, to be a citizen; and the state for me ceases to have meaning. For if I cannot embody my experience in its will, it ceases, sooner or later, to assume that I have a will at all. Nothing, therefore, is so likely to maintain a condition of liberty as the knowledge that the invasion of rights will result in protest, and, if need be, resistance. Liberty is nothing if it is not the organised and conscious power to resist in the last resort. The implied threat of contingent anarchy is a safeguard against the abuse of government.

I have set liberty here in the context of opportunity, and, in its turn, opportunity in the context of the State. That is the only atmosphere in which it admits of organisation. We can create channels; we cannot force men to take advantage of those channels. We can, further, create channels only in limited number. A man may feel that all that he cares for in life depends upon success in love; we can remove the barriers of caste or race or religion which, in the past, have barred his access to that love. But we cannot guarantee to him that his plea will be successful. The avenues which organisation can create are always limited by the fact that the most intimate realisation of oneself is personal and built upon isolations which evade social control.

Yet the social control is important. If, in the last resort, the State cannot make me happy, certainly it can, if it so will, compel unhappiness. It can invade my private life in wanton fashion. It can degrade me as a political unit in a fashion which distinguishes me from other citizens. It can protect an economic order which "implicates," in William James' phrase, unfreedom. None of these things is, of course, a genuinely separate category; at most the distinction is one of convenience. For liberty is a definite whole, because the life I lead is a totality in which I strive to realise a whole personality as harmonious. Yet each of these aspects is sufficiently clear to warrant a separate word.

But it must first be urged that in this context State-action is action by government. It means the maintenance of rules which affect my liberty. Those rules will be issued by persons, and, normally, those persons will be the government. Theories which seek to differentiate between State and government almost always ignore the substance of the administrative act. Rights withheld mean rights which the holders of power withhold. To say that in a democratic theory the mass of citizens are the holders of power is to miss the vital fact that the people, in the pressure of daily affairs, cannot exercise that power in detail in States of the modern size. They may have influence and opinion; but these are not the power of government. It is the cumulative force of administrative acts which are the heart of the modern State. The principles behind these acts are, of course, of prime importance. But principles may be invalidated by the method of their application; and it is governments which have the actual administration of them.

Liberty, therefore, is never real unless the government can be called to account; and it should always be called to account when it invades rights. It will always invade them unless its organisation prevents it from being weighted in some special interest. The three aspects of liberty I have noted are always relative to this situation. By private liberty, for example, I mean the opportunity to exercise freedom of choice in those areas of life where the results of my effort mainly affect me in that isolation by which, at least ultimately, I am always surrounded. Religion is a good instance of this aspect. I am not truly free to decide without hindrance upon my creed unless there is not merely no penalty on any form of religious faith, but, also, no advantage of a political kind attached to one form rather than another. When the government of England denied public employment to Dissenters it invaded private liberty. It did not directly punish; but, at least, it offered special benefit to an alternative faith. When France repealed the Edict of Nantes it invaded private liberty; for the honourable profession of religious conviction involved political outlawry.

These are simple instances. In the complex modern State invasions of private liberty may be more subtle. Private liberty may be denied when the poor citizen is unable to secure adequate legal protection in the Courts of Justice. A divorce law, for example, which gives the rich access to its facilities but, broadly, makes them difficult, if not impossible, for the poor, invades their private freedom. So does the demand for excessive bail; so, too, when the poor prisoner, with inadequate counsel, confronts the legal ability at the command of government. Private liberty is thus that aspect of which the substance is mainly personal to a man's self. It is the opportunity to be fully himself in the private relations of life. It is the chance practically to avail himself of the safeguards evolved for the maintenance of those relations.

Political liberty means the power to be active in affairs of State. It means that I can let my mind play freely about the substance of public business. I must be able without hindrance to add my special experience to the general sum of experience. I must find no barriers that are not general barriers in the way of access to positions of authority. I must be able to announce my opinion and to concert with others in the announcement of opinion. For political liberty to be real, two conditions are essential. I must be educated to the point where I can express what I want in a way that is intelligible to others. Anyone who has seen the dumb inarticulateness of the poor will realise the urgency of education in this regard. Nothing is more striking than the way in which our educational systems train the children of rich or well-born men to habits of authority while the children of the poor are trained to habits of deference. Such a division of attitude can never produce political freedom, because a class trained to govern will exert its power because it is conscious of it, while a class trained to deference will not fulfill its wants because it does not know how to formulate its demands. Combination in the period of experience will, of course, as with trade unions, do something to restore the balance; but it will never fully compensate for the defect of early training. For the inculcation of deferential habits will never produce a free people. It is only when men have learned that they themselves make and work institutions that they can learn to adjust them to their needs.

The second condition of political liberty is the provision of an honest and straightforward supply of news. Those who are to decide must have truthful material upon which to decide. Their judgment must not be thwarted by the presentation of a biased case. We have learned, especially of late years, that this is no easy matter. A statesman can sometimes be made what the press chooses to make him. A policy may be represented as entirely good or bad by the skilful omission of relevant facts. Our civilisation has stimulated the creation of agencies which live deliberately on the falsification of news. It would, indeed, not be very wide of the mark to argue that much of what had been achieved by the art of education in the nineteenth century had been frustrated by the art of propaganda in the twentieth. The problem is made more complex than in the past by the area over which our judgment must pass. We have no leisure to survey that area with comprehensive accuracy. We must, very largely, take our facts on trust. But if the facts are deliberately perverted, our judgment will be unrelated to the truth. A people without reliable news is, sooner or later, a people without the basis of freedom. For to exercise one's judgment in a miasma of distortion is, ultimately, to go disastrously astray.

By economic liberty I mean security and the opportunity to find reasonable significance in the earning of one's daily bread. I must, that is, be free from the constant fear of unemployment and insufficiency which, perhaps more than any other inadequacies, sap the whole strength of personality. I must be safeguarded against the wants of to-morrow. I must know that I can build a home, and make that home a means of self-expression. I must be able to make my personality flow through my effort as a producer of services, and find in that effort the capacity of enrichment. For, otherwise, I become a stunted and shrunken being in that aspect of myself which lends colour and texture to all that I am. Either I must, in this sense, be free, or I become one of those half-souls who are found in the slums and prisons as the casualties of civilisation. Nor is this all. I must be more than the recipient of orders which I must obey unthinkingly because my labour is only a commodity bought and sold in the market, like coal and boots and chairs. Without these freedoms, or, at least, an access to them, men are hardly less truly slaves than when they were exposed for purchase and sale.

Economic liberty, therefore, implies democracy in industry. That means two things. It means that industrial government is subject to the system of rights which obtain for men as citizens, and it means that industrial direction must be of a character that makes it the rule of laws by co-operation and not by compulsion. Obviously, the character of those laws must depend upon the needs of production. Those needs leave less room for spontaneity than is true either of private or of political liberty. A man is entitled to be original about his politics or his religion; he is not entitled to be original when he is working with others, say, in a nitro-glycerine factory. But he is entitled to co-operate in the setting of the standards by which he is judged industrially and in the application of those standards. Otherwise, he lives at the behest of other men. His initiative becomes not the free expression of his own individuality, but a routine made from without and enforced upon him by fear of starvation. A system built upon fear is always fatal to the release of the creative faculties, and it is therefore incompatible with liberty.

THE SAFEGUARDS OF LIBERTY

Freedom, therefore, will not be achieved for the mass of men save under special guarantees. It can never, firstly, exist in the presence of special privilege. Unless I enjoy the same access to power as others, I live in an atmosphere of contingent frustration. It does not matter that I shall probably not desire to take full advantage of that access. Its denial will mean that I accept an allotted station as a permanent condition of my life; and that, in its turn, is fatal to the spontaneity that is of the essence of freedom. Anyone who has seen the political inertia of English rural life will have realised how slow to mature is the plant of initiative. The English agricultural labourer lived for so long in an atmosphere of frustrated impulse that, when he was raised to the status of citizenship, he rarely, in general, knew how to take advantage of his opportunities. The genius of a Joseph Arch might stir him into angry and sudden revolt against intolerable conditions, but he was too habituated to uncritical inertia to persist when opposition came. So, too, the endurance of oppression by negro slaves was the outcome of their wonted subjection to a régime of privilege. They lost the habit of creativeness. They became, in fact, those "animate tools" which Aristotle described as the characteristic of the natural slave. Men who see others selected to govern by a principle other than their own choice tend, over a period, to believe that these have come to govern by nature. They will lose both the will and the power to act for themselves. They will learn to think that institutions made by their ancestors are the necessary foundations of the State. They will think it their duty to accept where, in truth, it is their duty to inquire. Whenever men accept, their habits, sooner or later, come to be formed at the will of others. They lose the ability to realise their own good. Their personality lies at the disposal of others whose action is not instinct, at least inherently, with a desire for the good of all; for those who desire the good of all begin by the abolition of special privilege.

Nor must we omit here the influence of such privilege upon those who possess it. They are free in the sense that they can build their own system of restraints. But their restraints will be manipulated for their own advantage. They will come to regard those outside their own circle as inferior beings. They will insist that their subordination is part of a natural order. They will even argue, like the slave-owners of the South, that exclusion from privilege is a benefit to those so excluded. They will discover special virtues in themselves, as when Macaulay argued that the middle class is "the natural representative of the human race." They will tend to identify demands for the admission to power of the unemancipated as the very definition of evil. They will part with their power, too often, only at the point of the sword; for voluntary abdication from special privilege has been the exception, and not the rule, in history. They will therefore seek at all costs to maintain their authority; and that will mean, most often, the further depression of the unfree. So Lord Sidmouth passed the Six Acts lest inconvenient criticism be made of an effete political régime. And the reaction from such policy will, as in France and Russia, tend to be proportionately violent to the degree of repression it has encountered. Special privilege is incompatible with freedom because the latter quality belongs to all alike in their character as human beings. We cannot differentiate between men until we have shown those excluded from a share in power that their exclusion is in their own interest. There seems no reason to suppose that the demonstration can be made.

Nor, secondly, can there be liberty where the rights of some depend upon the pleasure of others. Our common rules must bind those who exercise power as well as those who are the subjects of power. No groups of men must be in a position to encroach upon my enjoyment of the rights which attach to me as a citizen. That is not the case to-day. My livelihood may be destroyed by the whim of an employer. The meaning of my wage-standard may be injured by the cornering of the market in some essential commodity. The whole quality of my citizenship may be impaired by the manner in which the wealth of the community is distributed; and while I seem to enjoy political freedom, the absence of economic freedom may, in fact, render illusory my hope of a harmony of impulses. At every point, therefore, where the action of a man or group of men may impinge upon the exercise of rights a control is wanted which will frustrate their power so to impinge. That control, I submit, is, above all, a matter for the State, because it is upon the plane of citizenship that the undifferentiated interests of men come most clearly into view. State control means, in daily fact, control by government. It therefore follows that the action of all men who, by what they do, have the fate of others in their hands, is set in the perspective of limitation by the power of authority.

This, it should be added, does not necessarily mean intervention by the government at every turn and twist of individual life. It means the planning

of the principles of social action. It means the absence from social organisation of those uncertainties which result in social loss and are deliberately
planned by individuals. We cannot abolish the uncertainties due to such
natural phenomena as earthquakes; but we can at least destroy the uncertainty that comes when, say, the Standard Oil Trust drives competitors out
of the field by making an agreement for differential rates with the Pennsylvania Railroad.[1] We can at least prevent the dismissal of teachers from
their posts because some utterance has proved displeasing to the trustees
they serve.[2] Our principles of control are general principles; but because
their application will need to be as various as the problems they indicate,
they will, as a rule, require decentralised administration.

All this is to assume, thirdly, that the incidence of State action is unbiased.
In a full sense, doubtless, we cannot achieve that ideal. In any society the
varied personalities of which it is composed, the weight of the different interests involved, the degrees of effort men will make, the amount of knowledge
they will possess, are certain to bend its authority in the support of some special interest. The most we can do for the maintenance of freedom is to seek
that system which will minimise the bias involved. That is why rights
assume so vast an importance; they are the guarantee of a minimum bias.
They give us what assurance we may have that the State power will not be
perverted to the use of some few. But it is important to insist that it is
bound to suffer perversion unless men are unceasingly vigilant about its
exercise. Those who consented to the passage in 1917 of the American
Espionage Act did not realise that it would become the parent of similar
legislation destined to protect the most powerful industrial autocracy in the
world from criticism of its foundations. Those who voted in the House of
Commons for the Restoration of Order in Ireland, October 1920, can hardly
have expected that it would be used to deprive British citizens of the ordinary resource of justice.[3] Obviously, few things are more urgent than the
scrutiny of the problem of liberty in the terms that are most likely to prevent
the operation of that bias. A citizen-body that is quick to resent its presence,
and willing, in the last resort, to compel its repudiation, has the most obvious
guarantee that it will be minimised. But even such a body of citizens as
that of ancient Athens, to whom, as Pericles said in the great Funeral
Speech, "the secret of liberty is courage," will have need of the channels
through which courage may flow to its appointed purpose.

LIBERTY AND EQUALITY

Those channels converge towards the concept of equality. No idea is more
difficult in the whole realm of political science. To minds so ardent for

[1] Cf. H. D. Lloyd, *Wealth against Commonwealth,* pp. 87 ff.
[2] Cf. Lightner Witmer, *The Nearing Case,* and, in general, Upton Sinclair, *The Goose Step.*
[3] Though, of course, *Rex* v. *O'Brien* fortunately prevented the fulfillment of the Home
Secretary's desire.

liberty as Tocqueville and Lord Acton liberty and equality were antithetic things. It is a drastic conclusion. But it turns, in the case of both men, upon a misunderstanding of what equality implies. Equality does not mean identity of treatment. There can be no ultimate identity of treatment so long as men are different in want and capacity and need. The purpose of society would be frustrated at the outset if the nature of a mathematician met an identical response with that to the nature of a bricklayer. Equality does not even imply identity of reward for effort so long as the difference in reward does not enable me, by its magnitude, to invade the rights of others.

Equality, broadly, is a coherence of ideas each one of which needs special examination. Undoubtedly, it implies fundamentally a certain levelling process. It means that no man shall be so placed in society that he can over-reach his neighbour to the extent which constitutes a denial of the latter's citizenship. It means that my realisation of my best self must involve as its logical result the realisation by others of their best selves. It means such an ordering of social forces as will balance a share in the toil of living with a share in its gain also. It means that my share in that gain must be adequate for the purposes of citizenship. It implies that even if my voice be weighed as less weighty than that of another, it must yet receive consideration in the decisions that are made. The meaning, ultimately, of equality surely lies in the fact that the very differences in the nature of men require mechanisms for the expression of their wills that give to each its due hearing. The power, in fact, of the ideal of equality lies in the historical evidence that so far in the record of the State the wills of men have been unequally answered. Their freedom, where it has been gained, has accordingly been built upon the unfreedom of others. Inequality, in a word, means the rule of limited numbers because it secures freedom only to those whose will is secure of respect. They will dominate the State and use its power for their own purposes. They will make the fulfillment of their private desires the criterion of public good.

Equality, therefore, means first of all the absence of special privilege. I have already discussed the general meaning of that phrase. In the penumbra of equality, it means, in the political sphere, that my will, as a factor in the counting of heads, is equal to the will of any other. It means that I can move forward to any office in the State for which men are prepared to choose me. It means that I am not to find that there are persons in the State whose authority is qualitatively different from my own. Whatever rights inhere in another by virtue of his being a citizen must inhere, and to the same extent, in me also. There is no justification in such a view for the existence of an hereditary second chamber. For, obviously, in the second generation of such an assembly men exercise political authority not in virtue of their own qualities, but by reason of parental accident. So, also, no office that carries with it power can ever be rightly regarded as an incorporeal hereditament, for that is to associate important functions with qualities other than fitness for their performance. The exclusion of any man, or body of men, from access to the avenues of authority is always, that is to say, a denial of their freedom.

Equality means, in the second place, that adequate opportunities are laid open to all. By adequate opportunities we cannot imply equal opportunities in a sense that implies identity of original chance. The native endowments of men are by no means equal. Children who are brought up in an atmosphere where things of the mind are accounted highly are bound to start the race of life with advantages no legislation can secure. Parental character will inevitably affect profoundly the quality of the children whom it touches. So long, therefore, as the family endures—and there seems little reason to anticipate or to desire its disappearance—the varying environments it will create make the notion of equal opportunities a fantastic one.

But that is not to say that the opportunities created may not be adequate. We can at least see first that all men are given such training as seems, in the light of experience, most likely to develop their faculties to the full. We can at least surround those circumstances with the physical media without which the training of the mind can hardly be successful. We can, where we discover talent, at least make it certain that it does not perish for want of encouragement. These conditions do not exist to-day. Children who come hungry to school cannot, on the average, profit by education in like degree to those who are well fed. The student who is trying to do his work in a room which serves for the various tasks of life cannot find that essential isolation without which the habit of thought can rarely be cultivated. The boy or girl who has to assume that at fourteen they are bound to pass into the industrial world rarely acquires that frame of mind which searches with eagerness for the cultivation of intelligence. In the modern world, broadly speaking, opportunity is a matter of parental circumstance. Boys of a certain social status may assume that they will pass from the secondary school to the university. Boys whose parents are, broadly, manual workers will in the vast majority of cases be inevitably destined to manual work also. There is no reason to decry either the value or the dignity of manual work; but there is every reason to examine the social adequacy of a system which does not at every point associate the best training available with those whose qualities most fit them to benefit by that training. We do not want—possibly we cannot afford—to prolong the period of education unduly. But no State has established conditions of reasonable adequacy until the period of education is sufficiently long, first, to ensure that the citizen knows how to use his mind, and second, that those of special capacity are given that further training which prevents the wastage of their talent.

No one can deny that this wastage to-day is enormous. Any student of the results of adult education in Europe will have realised how great is the reservoir of talent we leave unused until it is too late. The sacrifices to-day involved when the average manual worker seeks the adequate education of his children are sacrifices we have no right to demand. Often enough, the training of one child is built upon the conviction of others to a life of unremitting toil. The circumstances which those who live by intellectual work know to be essential to its performance are, as a matter of definition almost, denied to the vast majority of the population. And since citizenship is largely a matter of the use of trained intelligence, it is obvious, accordingly, that its substance is denied to all save a fraction of the community. Our business, therefore, is to assure such an education to all as will make every vocation, however humble, one that does not debar those who follow it from the life of intelligence. That certainly means an extension of the period within which the earning of one's living is impossible. It means also that even after the earning period has commenced there are full opportunities for the devotion of leisure to intellectual ends. It means, thirdly, that those who devote themselves to the business of teaching represent the best minds at the service of the community. In the modern State the teacher has a responsibility far greater than that which devolves upon any other citizens; and unless he teaches from a full mind and a full heart he cannot release the forces which education has in leash.

Nothing in all this denies the probability that mental qualities are inherited and that, other things being equal, the children of able parents will be abler than the children of average parents. But it does deny the equation, characteristic of the modern State, between ability and material position. The average trade-union leader cannot afford to send his sons to the university; but the ability of the average trade-union leader is probably not inferior to that of the average banker or the average bishop. Where, that is to say, the inequalities of our system are not due to natural causes, there is a clear case for their remedy. Nor can we hope to discover the existence of capacity unless our system provides for its discovery. It may do so to-day in the case of the rich; assuredly it does not do so in the case of the poor. And it is urgent to remember that, important as nature may be, it requires an adequate nurture if it is to function satisfactorily. The present inequalities are not referable to principle. We have therefore to define the outlines of such a system as build the inequalities we admit upon the needs of society. At present they most largely arise from the impact of the property system upon the structure of the State. But what is reflected by the property system is less ability to serve the community than ability to gain economic power without reference to the quality of wants supplied.

The provision of adequate opportunity is, therefore, one of the basic conditions of equality, and it is mainly founded upon the training we offer to citizens. For the power that ultimately counts in society is the power to utilise knowledge; and disparities of education result, above all, in disparities in the ability to use that power. I am not pleading for equality of function. I am pleading only for the obvious truth that without education a man is not so circumstanced that he knows how to make the best of himself and that therefore, for him, the purpose of society is, *ab initio,* frustrated. Once men are in the situation where they can know themselves, the use they make of their opportunities becomes subject to principles of which equality is only one.

But if we agree, as I have argued earlier, that a democratic State regards its members as equally entitled to happiness, it follows that such differences as exist must not be differences inexplicable in terms of reason. Distinctions of wealth or status must be distinctions to which all men can attain and they must be required by the common welfare. If a State permits the existence of an hereditary aristocracy it must be because it is capable of proof that an hereditary aristocracy multiplies the chances of each man's realising his best self. If we are to have an economic system in which the luxury of a few is paralleled by the misery of the many, it must be because the common welfare requires that luxury. In each case the proposition is open to historical disproof. An hereditary aristocracy is bound, sooner or later, to use its political power to general disadvantage, unless, like the peerage of France, it has ceased to be anything but a faded memory. A State divided into a small number of rich and a large number of poor will always develop a government manipulated by the rich to protect the amenities represented by their property. It therefore follows that the inequalities of any social system are justified only as it can be demonstrated that the level of service they procure is obviously higher because of their existence. It is obvious that a general must have larger powers than a private because, thereby, the purpose of an army is more likely to be fulfilled. It is obvious that a statesman in office must be so remunerated that he is not oppressed by narrow material cares; and that might well involve placing him in a higher financial rank than a bootmaker or a shop assistant. In each case the measure of difference is conceived in social terms. It is set in a principle which is demonstrably rational. It is fitting the circumstances of function to the environment of which it has need.

Such a view admits, at least as a matter of theory, of fairly simple statement in institutional terms. The urgent claims of all must be met before we can meet the particular claims of some. The differences in the social or economic position of men can only be admitted after a minimum basis of civilisation is attained by the community as a whole. That minimum basis must admit of my realising the implications of personality. Above that level, the advantages of the situation I occupy must be advantages necessary to the performance of a social function. The advantages I enjoy must be the result of my own effort, because they are the return to me for my own services, and I am clearly not entitled to enjoy them as the result of someone else's services. One man is not entitled to a house of twenty rooms until all people are adequately housed; and one man, even in that environment, is not entitled to a house of twenty rooms because his father was a great advocate or a large industrialist. The things that are due to me are the rights I must enjoy in order to be a citizen, and the differential advantages which society adjudges inherent in the particular occupation I follow. We may, in other words, have Belgravias, if their existence is a necessary condition of social welfare; but we are not entitled to have Belgravias until we have secured the impossibility of Poplar's existence.

If all this is true, equality is most largely a problem in proportions. There is an aspect in which the things without which life is meaningless must be accessible to all without distinction in degree or kind. All men must eat and drink and obtain shelter. But those needs are, in their turn, proportionate to what they do. My wants are my claims to find a harmony of impulses. I do not want the same harmony if I am a miner as I shall want if I am a surgeon. But the system which obtains must not satisfy the claims of the surgeon at the expense of the miner's claims. My urgent needs are not less urgent than the needs of any other person, and they are entitled to equal satisfaction. Once urgency is satisfied superfluity becomes a problem of so fixing the return to service that each man can perform his function with the maximum return to society as a whole.

In this aspect, the problem of proportions is largely an economic problem. It is a question of the methods we use to determine the claim of each citizen upon the social dividend, and of the environment which surrounds the application of those methods. There have been famous answers to this problem. We have been told that response should be made in terms of need, or in terms of contribution; it has been insisted that identity of response is alone adequate. Of these solutions that which would reward me by what I do for society is certainly the least satisfactory. For it is impossible in any genuine way to measure service. We cannot say what Newton or Lister, Shakespeare or Robert Owen were "worth" to their fellow-citizens. We cannot measure the contribution of a banker against the contribution of a bricklayer. Often enough, as in the case of Galilee, for example, we may not be able to see how vast in truth the contribution is. Nor, it may be argued, is the communistic solution adequate. For, in the first place, there is no total identity of needs between men; nor is their effort so equal as to merit an identical return. The communistic principle is adequate up to the point where human urgencies are in question; it is not adequate after that point. And it is adequate only so far as its application wins the result of a deliberate effort on the part of those whose needs are satisfied to do work of civic quality. And since to do work of civic quality involves differentiation of function, it is, I think, clear that when the primary needs of all men are met, the differences they encounter must be differences their function requires; requirement involving always the context of social benefit.

But this, it will be argued, is to assume sufficiency. It implies that there is in fact enough to go round, whereas we know that the productivity of men does not suffice for their wants. What we ought rather to do is to allow the free play of capacity to win response to its need and let those prosper who show the power to triumph in the race. The answer involved in this attitude is far less simple than it seems. If the State exists for social good, "capacity" can only mean capacity to add to social good. It is not in the least certain that the exercise of talent in a society like our own does in fact result in social benefit. Capacity, in short, must run in the leading-strings of principle. It must be excited to the end our institutions have in view. And since that end is the achievement of happiness for each individual, it seems obvious that we must, if the margin be insufficient, suffer equally by its insufficiencies. We can never, therefore, as a matter of principle, justify the existence of differences until the point is reached when the primary claims of men win a full response. I have no right to cake if my neighbour, because of that right, is compelled to go without bread. Any social organisation from which this basis is absent by denying equality denies all that gives meaning to the personality of men.

Equality, therefore, involves up to the margin of sufficiency identity of response to primary needs. And that is what is meant by justice. We are rendering to each man his own by giving him what enables him to be a man. We are, of course, therein protecting the weak and limiting the power of the strong. We so act because the common welfare includes the welfare of the weak as well as of the strong. Grant, as we may well grant, that this involves a payment by society to men and women who limp after its vanguard, the quality of the State depends on its regarding their lives as worth preserving. To act otherwise is to regard them not as persons, but as instruments. It is to deny that their personality constitutes a claim. It is deliberately to weight institutions against a section of the community. If they are to harmonise their impulses in the effort after happiness, such bias is inadmissible. For it is utilising their service not for their own well-being, but for the well-being of others. That is essentially the definition of slavery.

It is no answer to this view to urge that it bases social organisation upon a principle hitherto inoperative in history. The decay of previous systems has been most largely based on the fact that it was inoperative. Men have seen institutions pass, or have co-operated to destroy institutions, precisely because they did not see in them the forces which sought response to what made them men. Nor are we seeking to compel all citizens to win from life an identical response. We seek identity only up to the level where the facts insist upon identity. We argue that some will not starve quietly if others have abundance. We urge that the conference of knowledge upon some while others are excluded from its benefits is, in fact, their exclusion from the purpose of the State. And no other principle, as a working system, will effect the results the State has in view. For immediately we admit privilege within the area of equal need, it will use every weapon at its disposal to multiply its access to special benefits. The history of privileges is not a history of voluntary abdication in terms of social welfare; it is rather the history of a careful limitation of the idea of social welfare to those who enjoy the opportunity it offers. It is only, as a consequence, by making identity the basis of our institutions, and differences an answer to the necessities of social functions that we can make our society call into play the individuality of men.

I shall inquire later into the principles upon which those differences may be organised. Here it is immediately important to insist on certain conditions upon which alone that basis of identity may be maintained. A first essential is approximate equality of wealth. I do not mean by that the absence of varying rates of payment for effort. I mean only that the rates of payment shall not so differ that merely in virtue of those differences men can exert an unequal pressure upon the fabric of institutions.

That unequal pressure obviously exists to-day. There are men in every community whose power is built not upon what they are or do, but upon the possessions they embody. The influence they exercise is not a tribute to themselves but an offering to their wealth. They act by owning. They command the service of others to the performance of functions built upon a private will not necessarily relevant to the social welfare. They can direct the flow of production into channels notable only for their wastefulness. They can dominate the supply of news, and so influence to their own ends the working of political institutions. They can adjust the economic power of the community to purposes fatal to the welfare of those who have nothing but their labour to sell. The desire, for instance, of the great ironmasters of France to dominate the heavy industries of Europe may well send the next generation to die on the battlefield. Where there are great inequalities of fortune, there is always inequality of treatment. It is only when no man merely by virtue of his possessions can influence the course of affairs that the equal interest of men in the results of the political process can secure validation. The surest way to that end is to prevent those disparities of wealth which permit the owners of fortune to manipulate unfairly the mechanisms of power.

Broadly, I am urging that great inequalities of wealth make impossible the attainment of freedom. It means the dictation of the physical and mental circumstances which surround the less fortunate. It means the control of the engines of government to their detriment. The influence of the great corporations upon the legislative system of the United States is only a supreme example of that control. Hardly less deleterious is the way in which it controls the intellectual environment it encounters. It is able to weight the educational system in its interest. It is able, by the rewards it offers, to affect the propertyless brain-worker to its service. Since the judiciary will be largely selected from its paid advocates, legal decisions will largely reflect the lessons of its experience. Even the Churches will preach a gospel which is permeated by their dependence upon the support of the wealthy.

Political equality, therefore, is never real unless it is accompanied by virtual economic equality; political power, otherwise, is bound to be the handmaid of economic power. The recognition of this dependence is in the main due to the explanation of historic evolution, and it is, indeed, almost as old as the birth of scientific politics. Aristotle pointed out the equation between democracy and the rule of the poor, between oligarchy and the rule of the rich. The struggle to remedy economic disparity is the key to Roman history; it is at the root of English agrarian discontent. It underlies the sermons of John Ball, the *Utopia* of More, the *Oceana* of Harrington. The early history of socialism is most largely the record of a perception that the concentration of property other than labour-power in a few hands is fatal to the purpose of the State. It was that perception which Marx, in the *Communist Manifesto,* made the foundation of the most formidable political philosophy in the modern world. For though the materialistic interpretation of history is an over-emphasis of one link in the chain of causation, it is the link most intimately related to the experience of ordinary men. It is overwhelmingly right in its insistence that either the State must dominate property, or property will dominate the State.

For, as Madison wrote,[1] "the only durable source of faction is property." But it is obvious that to base the differences between men on a contest for economic wealth is to destroy the possibility of a well-ordered commonwealth. It is to excite all the qualities in men—envy, arrogance, hatred, vanity —which prevent the emergence of social unity. It is to emphasise a competition based on their separation, instead of a competition based on their mutual interest. As soon as we postulate approximate equality of wealth, our methods of social organisation enable us to respond to men's needs in terms of the substance of those needs. We are the more bound to this effort immediately we admit the logic of universal suffrage. For to confide to the mass of men the control of ultimate political power is broadly to admit that the agencies of the State must be utilised to respond to their needs. They involve, if they are to be satisfied, such a distribution of influence over authority as will balance fairly the incidence of its results among the members of society. It means, that is, that I must adjust my scale of wants to social welfare as that is organised in terms of a valuation which equally weights the

[1] *The Federalist,* No. X.

primary needs of citizens; and that valuation remains ineffective if my power is a function not of my personality, but of my property.

But virtual equality in economic power means more than approximate equality of wealth. It means that the authority which exerts that power must be subject to the rules of democratic governance. It means the abrogation of unfettered and irresponsible will in the industrial world. It involves building decisions on principles which can be explained, and the relation of those principles to the service any given industry is seeking to render. The authority of a medical officer who orders the isolation of an infected house is intelligible; he is relating his powers to the preservation of public health. But the authority of an employer is not intelligible except in terms of self-interested motives. His demands cannot be scrutinised. They are not relevant to the well-being of his servants. If a worker refuses to adulterate the product made by an employer, he may suffer dismissal. He may be penalised if he refuses to falsify his accounts, even when the sufferer by that falsification is the public revenue the burden of which he himself partially bears. There is, that is to say, all the difference in the world between an authority which grows naturally out of functions which are set consistently in a public context, and an authority which, equally consistently, is the outcome of private and irresponsible will.

The existence of this latter type is fatal to the civic implications of equality. It poisons industrial relations. It makes the position of master and servant one of waiting upon the threshold of war. Above all, it is intolerable wherever the function involved is one where continuity of service is essential to the life of the community. That industries like coal and electric power, transport and banking, the supply of meat and the provision of houses, should be left to the hazards of private enterprise will appear as unthinkable to a future generation as it is unthinkable to our own that the army of the State should be left to private hands. They must be subject to rules as rigorous as those which govern medicine, simply because they are not less vital to the national life. That does not mean direct operation by government as the inevitable alternative. It means the planning of constitutions for essential industries; and the possible types of constitutions are as various in industry as elsewhere.

I shall discuss in a later chapter the forms such constitutions may usefully take. Here it is enough to emphasise the urgency to freedom of making the relationship between men in industry one in which no will affected by decisions is regarded as significant. That does not mean that all wills are to be weighed equally; all men, obviously, are not equally entitled to give orders. But it does imply that those who exercise authority can, like the minister in office, or the trade union official, be called to account for the orders they issue. My freedom is not hampered if I have the sense that I have access to the source of authority. The members of a trade union feel "free" because they are governed by men made by, and responsible to, themselves. That cannot be the case where authority, as in modern industry, is unconstitutional in its nature. The inequalities of status, the power which results from status, are unrelated to the interests of personality. The worker is involved in a hierarchy in which he has no spiritual recognition. The university teacher, the doctor, the lawyer, are all of them involved in hierarchies; but these breed equality because they are established by co-operation. Their members feel that they contribute to the definition of their working lives. We cannot secure professional standards in industry until room is found there also for principles which destroy the present irresponsible autocracy.

THE INTERNATIONAL ASPECT

So far, I have discussed conceptions of liberty and equality as though they raised problems soluble within the confines of a single State. But in fact the issues go far beyond that territorial limitation. World co-operation, as I argued earlier, has advanced to the point where we must legislate for civilisation as a whole. We have, therefore, in matters of common world concern, to apply methods which affect the Bantu in Africa and the Melanesian in the Pacific as well as the Englishman and the Frenchman. What do liberty and equality mean in the presence of such complexities? The Dutchman in Java finds his freedom in the application of all his powers to an intense labour for wealth built upon a supply of native workers. The Javanese means by freedom such spasmodic effort as will give him the food he wants, and, otherwise, leave him to lie out in the enjoyment of the sun. How are these different wants to be reconciled? How are we to assure, for instance, equality of treatment between black and white in tropical Africa, when the fact from which we start is that of unequal power? How are we to ensure in a conference of European States that the interests of Switzerland will be considered equally with the interests of England, or Russia, or France?

Until the Peace of Versailles, the common method was to assume the equality of States in international law, and to leave each State free to discover, by what means it would, its own salvation; and force resided in the background as the sanction most likely to secure the ultimate solution. But it is obvious that, for example, Nicaragua and the United States, Venezuela and England, cannot really, in vital matters, bargain on equal terms. Even the most genial fictions of law cannot make a small State equal to a great one.

The possibility of equal consideration and, consequently, of freedom, depends upon two things. It depends first upon the outlawry of war. Concepts like freedom are devoid of meaning so long as a State is free to force its solution upon its neighbour. But the outlawry of war depends, in its turn, upon the building of international institutions which are capable of mobilising the authority of the world against any belligerent. That will be the outcome only of a proof that international institutions can be built which take the problems which give rise to war on to a plane of discussion where they can be analysed in terms of reason. Such institutions will not, I think, be discovered by counting each State as equal in voting power to every other State. It will be impossible to make a league of States effective by the maintenance of that fiction. The solution rather lies in choosing the subjects of international control and finding a method of proportional representation for their governance. There will emerge, for instance, the view that only Englishmen can choose the Prime Minister of England, but that the size of the British Navy is a matter for international determination. France may settle the foreign languages to be taught in her schools, but the character of her foreign loans will be settled by international consent. Each State will be entitled to bargain, to criticise, to object; but when the decision is given against her, she will be compelled to give way. Equality, then, will mean (1) that the method of discussion gives full weight to the facts each State puts forward, (2) that the use of force is ruled out from consideration. Freedom will mean that without the ambit of international control each State is entitled to decide its own life. Just as, that is, no individual can find freedom outside the common rules of his society, so, also, no State can find freedom save by accepting limitation of its sovereignty by the will formed by the common decision of a society of States.

That this habit of rational settlement will be slow in growth needs no emphasis. At the moment I am concerned only to argue that the solution lies in conceiving of the world as a federal State, the members of which do not possess equal voting power. The problem, I suggest, is one of starting a tradition of inquiry and judgment, and finding the appropriate institutions for the range of questions such a federal State will have to administer. When once a great State accepts a verdict given against her we shall at least have begun the exploration of such a tradition. When once a great subject —the protection of the native races, for example—is administered with competence by an international authority we shall have begun the building of a belief in its possibilities. Freedom will come to mean only self-determination in the things peculiar to a given State; outside that sphere it will mean freedom to state a case and not the right to begin war. Equality will mean that the solutions adopted—say in access to raw materials—seek the statistical measurement of need in one range of problems with assurance of response to it; in another it will mean the protection afforded by the presence in an international organisation of other States whose representatives assist in the making of decisions.

The more these issues are brought before international authorities, the more they will be found susceptible of such treatment. The responsibility of Serbia for the assassination of Serajevo was a subject obviously capable of intellectual inquiry. The action of Austria settled nothing about the facts;

she used her power and her prestige to make judgment impossible. Had
Serbia, upon investigation, been found guilty, punishment could have been
assessed in a way which would have made equality real, in that both States,
though unequal in power, would have been equally bound by a body external to them both. If she was innocent, a world-war, which involved the destruction of Austria-Hungary, was a heavy price to pay for a mistaken notion
of prestige.

Those, in truth, who talk of non-justiciable disputes do sorry service to
civilisation. They speak in terms of a historic condition which no longer fits
the facts of the world. To suggest that a nation is humiliated by being proved
in error is as wise as to suggest that trial by battle is likely to result in justice.
A power, indeed, which urges its prestige as a means of evading international jurisdiction is fairly certain to be wrong. The prestige of England was
not diminished when she submitted the *Alabama* incident to arbitration;
what lowered her prestige was the administrative carelessness in permitting
the incident to occur. States, like men, never protest their honour loudly
unless unless they have a bad case to argue. And if it be said that this is to
over-rationalise a problem in which the exercise of reason is inadmissible,
the answer is that our choice is between the deliberate adoption of reason
and an anarchy which, by the weapons at its disposal, is like to make civilisation itself a legend buried beneath the ruins of its discoveries.

The situation is somewhat different in the case of subject-peoples. No institutions can give genuine equality to a discussion between a European race
and, say, the Bushmen of Australia. The problem here is rather the discovery
of principles which, when applied, will enable the backward races to draw
from life such means of happiness as they desire; adding thereto the benefits
that scientific discovery will enable us to confer upon them. We must, it
seems clear, prohibit slavery, and human sacrifice and tribal warfare. We
must reserve for them the lands of which they have need. We must prohibit
all forced labour save where it is devoted to such public matters as the making of roads. We must utilize the tribal organisation for all the purposes to
which it seems obviously suited. We must prevent such traffic—that, for instance, in drink—as we know to be destructive of native morale. We must
allow no traders to make contracts with the native save under supervision
of officials, and that the more particularly when natural resources are in
question. Above all, it is essential that those who enter the public service
among these subject-peoples should be fully trained in that knowledge which
can only be real when the results of anthropological science are behind it. It
is no use sending out a man to Africa who has not already learned the true
method of approach to its problems. He will not learn it from the European
society there. He will only learn it adequately from the native himself if he
has been given beforehand that point of view which is the clue to its sympathetic interpretation. Most native customs, weird as they are to the Euro-

pean mind, have their roots deep in the tribal consciousness. To adjust them forcibly to a point of view the native finds inexplicable is to destroy for him all that gives his life its meaning. The result is a psychological *malaise* which ruins his happiness.

Nor can we allow any State the full control of territory mandated to it. What it does there, the method and the results of its administration, it must answer for to an international organisation. That involves, I think, something more than the issue of a report by the mandatory power. It means some such institution as the presence of an international minister at the capital of the territory who will watch the interests of the natives in the same way, for example, as the French Ambassador watches the interests of Frenchmen in London. He will be entitled to inspect and to report. His word will carry weight against the pronouncement of the mandatory power. He will be able to suspend projected action, to warn, and to encourage. He ought, it is clear, only in rare cases to be of the same nationality as the power in actual control. Only when, for example, South Africa knows that there is independent authority to report upon its activities will the suppression of an *émeute* like that of the Bondelwarts rebellion become definitely impossible.

This is, of course, frankly to abandon the meaning of freedom and equality in the sense those terms possess in the context of Western civilisation. On any realistic analysis, it is necessary to abandon them. The formulation by the native of his wants deserves all the response we can give; but it must be admitted that the clash of backward and advanced civilisations means that the wants formulated must be met by special considerations. There is, I think, more likelihood that the Zulu or the Hottentot will achieve what he will regard as a full life under such conditions of protection as those outlined than if we proceed upon the basis that he is being made ready for Western institutions. What Graham Wallas has called "the optimistic ethnology of Exeter Hall" is the most fatal attitude in which to approach these questions. It destroys all that has meaning for the native by denying, at the outset, all that gives colour and substance to the life he knows. It seeks to prepare him for another life in which, in general, it is unlikely that he will find meaning. His freedom, therefore, must be relative to his peculiar situation. It must mean all that he can be given without the destruction of the basic Western ideal. It means, above all, his protection against what has too often been the result of those ideals in operation.

LIBERTY AND GOVERNMENT

This view of liberty and equality lays cardinal importance upon the powers of government and the mechanisms by which they may be made to respond to the wills of those affected. I do not argue that the action of legislation can make men free and equal; but unless some such conditions exist as those here urged, it is certain enough that the effect of legislation will be to keep the majority unfree and unequal. To make the personality of the ordinary man creative, it is necessary to build the conditions within which creativeness is possible. That can only happen when ordinary men are made to feel significant, and this, in the absence of liberty and equality, we cannot hope to achieve. Where there is in a community the absence of those factors which make the interests of men so differently considered, there is likely to be the means at hand for the development of personality. The enforcement of equality by the State has the great merit of promoting freedom by preventing the private person from the exercise of force for his own ends. By force I do not necessarily mean physical violence, but the use of a differential advantage to hinder another from the opportunity to be the best he can.

But it is also important to remember that whatever adds to the power of government is always attended by contingent danger. The individual in the modern State tends to feel impotent before the vast administrative machine by which he is confronted. It seems to have absorbed all initiative towards a single centre and to have deprived him of the power to make, or to share in making, responsible decisions. That is a real difficulty. In relieving the individual from the power of his fellow, we may well seem to subject him to a collective power under which he seems hardly more free than before. That was the danger which made Rousseau insistent that liberty is the product of the small State only, and to find in a modern Athens the area within which alone democratic initiative is possible.

We cannot adopt that view because the nature of modern economic organisation makes it impossible to return to the city-State. But in States of the modern size the mere achievement of equality would be harmful without the maximum decentralization. That is the solution to the paradox by which Rousseau was haunted. It solves the dread of constraint by making men in wider numbers the authors of the power to which they are subjected, and, through that authority, the utilisation of power to liberate the creative energy which is in them. Ultimately, at least, any laws save those which men make for themselves are devoid of meaning. But to make laws for themselves at all adequately, they must have the instruction to judge what laws they ought to make and the character to operate those laws. Someone, doubtless, they will have to trust; the artist will have no desire to scrutinise each act of the policeman. But they must be so intimately a part of the system as to know that they can trust with safety or, if there is abuse of confidence, to be able to apply pressure to its correction. In that sense, liberty is the organisation of resistance to abuse; and the chief safeguard against the emergence of abuse is such a wide distribution of power as makes certain and effective the onset of refusal to obey.

But the utmost that the action of government can achieve will be worthless save in so far as its action is paralleled by effort on the part of individual men. Ultimately, each one of us has sufficient of the Athanasius in him to make it certain that the true liberty we build is for ourselves. The State is built so certainly upon the character of men that they can only mould it to their desire by consistent devotion to its activities. If men are indifferent or careless, if they are satisfied to withdraw from the arena, not the most ingenious mechanisms can ultimately prevent abuse of power. That was the meaning of Thoreau's great sentence that "under a government which imprisons any unjustly, the true place for a just man is also prison." [1] Men must learn that the actions of the State are their own. They must learn that they will realise justice only to the degree that they bend their efforts to the making of justice. Every man is essential to the State if he has a mind and will. Every man can make that State responsive to the things he needs only by making his knowledge of life accessible as a basis for its actions. He can be free, ultimately, only by willing to be free. No State will be governed by that reason which alone guarantees him significance save as he makes his mind a part of its possessions.

But if the individual is thus, in concert with his fellows, the author of his own freedom, he cannot exert himself to build it save as he is prepared for that constructiveness. He must know what it means to find himself before he seeks the adventure. That is no easy task in a world encumbered by its traditions. There is never likely to be an enlightened State until there is respect for individuality; but, also, there will not be respect for individuality until there is an enlightened State. It is only the emphasis upon equality which will break this vicious circle. When the source of power is found outside of property, authority is balanced upon a principle which bases prestige on service. At that stage, the effort of statesmanship is the elevation of the common man. A society which seeks to protect acquisition is replaced by a society which seeks to protect the spiritual heritage of the race. We cannot assure ourselves of an entrance to that heritage, but at least we can discover the pathway to the goal.

[1] Thoreau, *On the Duty of Civil Disobedience.*

〜〜

3. *Inequality and Personal Freedom* *

SIDNEY AND BEATRICE WEBB

〜〜

There is another inequality in the capitalist state, which is perhaps more intensely resented by the modern artisan, and is more difficult to bring to

* From Sidney and Beatrice Webb, *The Decay of Capitalist Civilization* (Harcourt, Brace and Company, 1923). By permission.

the comprehension of the governing class than the inequality of income; namely, the disparity in personal freedom. Freedom is, of course, an elusive term, with various and conflicting meanings. To some simple minds freedom appears only a negation of slavery. To them any one is free who is not the chattel of some other person. The shipwrecked mariner on a barren island and the destitute vagrant wandering among property owners protected by an all-powerful police, are "free men," seeing that they "call no man master." But this sort of freedom is little more than freedom to die. In the modern industrial community, in which no man is able to produce for himself all that he needs for life, personal freedom is necessarily bound up with the ability to obtain commodities and services produced by other persons. Translated into the terms of daily life, personal freedom means, in fact, the power of the individual to buy sufficient food, shelter and clothing to keep his body in good health, and to gain access to sufficient teaching and books to develop his mind from its infantile state. Moreover, as we cannot regard as a free man any one with none but vegetative experiences, freedom involves the command at some time, of at least some money to spend on holidays and travel, on social intercourse and recreation, on placing one's self in a position to enjoy nature and art. We can, in fact, best define personal freedom as the possession of opportunity to develop our faculties and satisfy our desires. Professor Graham Wallas suggests the definition of "the possibility of continuous initiative." In this sense freedom is a relative term. It is only the very rich man who has freedom to consume all that he desires of the services and commodities produced by other persons, and also the freedom to abstain from all personal toil that would stand in the way of his "continuous initiative," and stop it by absorbing his energy and his time. Any poor man has a very limited freedom. To the propertyless wage-earner freedom may mean nothing more than the freedom, by dint of perpetual toil, to continue to exist on the very brink of starvation. Hence inequality in income in itself entails inequality in personal freedom.

"EQUAL BEFORE THE LAW"

We have grown so accustomed, under the reign of capitalism, to the grossest disparity in personal freedom among nominally free citizens, that we fail to recognize how gross and how cruel is the inequality even where we profess to have adopted equality as a principle. Both Britain and America are proud of having made all men equal before the law. Yet no one can even ask for justice in the law-courts without paying fees which (though the statesmen and the wealthy refuse to credit the fact) do, in actual practice, prevent the great mass of the population from obtaining legal redress for the wrongs that are constantly being done to them. The very object with which the legal tribunals are established is to give men security for their personal freedom—to prevent this being impaired by assaults, thefts, extortions, defalcations and failure to fulfill contracts and pay debts. In every city of Britain and America the vast majority of the population never appear as plaintiffs in the civil courts, not because they are not assaulted and robbed, cheated and denied payment of what is due to them—every one must know that these evils happen much more frequently and, at one time or another, much nearer universally, to the poor and friendless than to the rich—but because they cannot afford, out of their scanty earnings, even the court fee, let alone that of the lawyer. But the disparity in personal freedom between the rich and the poor is seen most glaringly when the one and the other are charged in the criminal court with an offense against the law. The rich man, except in extreme cases such as murder, practically always receives a summons; the poor man is still often, for the same offense, peremptorily arrested, as was formerly always the case, and taken to prison to await trial. On a remand, the rich man easily procures bail, whilst quite a large proportion of propertyless defendants find themselves returned to the prison cells, a procedure which, coupled with their lack of means, does not, to say the least, facilitate their hunting up of witnesses who might prove their innocence, or their obtaining help in their defense. It is needless to recount the further advantages of the rich man in engaging the ablest lawyers and expert witnesses; in obtaining a change of venue, and successive remands, or in dragging the case from court to court. When sentence is imposed, it is, in the vast majority of cases, a pecuniary fine, which means practically nothing to the rich man, while to the poor man it may spell ruin for himself, his little business and his household. To the average police magistrate or clerk to the justices, it is quite a matter of course that a positive majority of those whom they sentence to small fines go to prison for one, two or six weeks, in default of payment. Ruinous as prison is known to be to the family of the prisoner as well as to the prisoner himself, the poor are sent to prison, in the United States as in Britain, by thousands every year, merely because they cannot immediately produce the few shillings or dollars that they are fined for minor offenses, which rich men commit daily with practical impunity. No inequality in personal freedom could be more scandalous than this practical inequality of rich and poor before the law courts, which characterizes every capitalist community, and which, though known to every judge and every practicing lawyer for a century, has remained unredressed.[1]

THE PSYCHOLOGICAL REACTION

But all this springs directly from the disparity in incomes, a material interpretation of personal freedom which does not exhaust the question. There is a psychological aspect of personal freedom which arises merely from the relation between one man and another. Even when the wage-earner is getting what he calls "good money" and steady work, he resents the fact that

[1] See *The Law and the Poor*, by E. A. Parry, 1914.

he, like the machine with which he works, is bought as an instrument of production; *that his daily life is dealt with as a means to another's end.* Why should he and his class always obey orders, and another, and a much smaller class, always give them? It is this concentration of the function of command in one individual, or in one class, with the correlative concentration of the obligation to obey in other individuals of another class, which constitutes the deepest chasm between the nation of the rich and the nation of the poor. In one of his novels Mr. Galsworthy vividly describes the contrast between the daily life of the English country house and the daily life of the laborer's cottage. The rich man, and his wife and children, get up in the morning at any time they please; they eat what they like; they "work" and they play when they like and how they like; their whole day is controlled by the promptings of their own instinct or impulse, or is determined by their own reason or will. From morning till night they are perpetually doing what is pleasant to them. They fulfill their personality, and they exercise what Professor Graham Wallas rightly calls their "continuous initiative," by giving, day in day out, year in year out, orders to other people. The laborer and his family are always obeying orders; getting up by order, working by order, in the way they are ordered, leaving off work by order, occupying one cottage rather than another by order of the farmer, being ejected from home by order of the landowner, attending school by order, sometimes even going to church by order; relying for medical attendance on the "order" of the Poor Law Relieving Officer, and in some cases ordered into the workhouse to end a life which, under the British Constitution, has always been legally and politically that of a freeman. From morning till night—save in rare hours of "expansion" usually expiated painfully—the "working class" find themselves doing what is irksome or unpleasant to them. What is called in Britain the governing class (which includes a great many more persons than are engaged in political government), is, typically, the class that passes its life in giving orders. What are called the "lower classes" are those that live by obeying orders.

WHEN AUTHORITY IS ACCEPTABLE

Now let no one imagine that these lower classes, or the socialists who champion them, or indeed any persons with common sense, object to one man exercising authority over another. What is resented in the capitalist organization of industry is both the number and the kind of the orders given by the rich to the poor, by the owners of land and capital to the persons who gain their livelihood by using these instruments of production. The authority of the capitalist and the landlord has invidious characteristics. It is continuous over the lives of the individuals who are ordered; it is irresponsible and cannot be called to account; it is not in any way reciprocal; it does not involve the selection of the person in command for his capacity to exercise authority either wisely or in the public interest; above all, it is designed to promote, not the good of the whole community, but the personal pleasure or private gain of the person who gives the order. No one but an anarchist objects to the authority of the policeman regulating the traffic in the crowded street; to the authority of the sanitary inspector compelling the occupier of the house to connect his domestic pipe with the main drain; to the authority of the Medical Officer of Health enforcing the isolation of an infectious person; or even to the demand note of the tax-collector. No one resents the commands of the railway guard—"take your seats" or "all change here." All these orders are given in respect of particular occasions in the citizen's life, and by persons assumed to be selected for their fitness for the duty of giving these particular orders. The persons exercising command are themselves under orders; they are responsible to superior authority; and they may be called to account for bad manners or for "exceeding their powers." Moreover, their orders are, in the best sense, disinterested, and have no connection with their personal gain or convenience. We may complain that the official is going beyond his function or is unmannerly in his methods. We may object to the policy of the national executive, or deplore the legislation enacted by Parliament. But in obeying these orders all men are equal before the law; and all men have the same right of appeal to the superior authority. Finally, in political democracy, the persons who are subejct to the authority are exactly the persons who have created it; and they can, if and when they choose, sweep it away. In their capacity of citizen-electors they may exercise collectively, through the Parliament and the government of the day, an ultimate control over the stream of orders they are called upon as individuals to obey.

In this connection it is interesting to notice the socialist interpretation of a phrase much in vogue in the twentieth century. We often hear at labor meetings of the desirability of a man "controlling his own working life." But this does not mean that each man or woman is to be free to work at starvation wages, or for excessive hours, or under the most unpleasant conditions. This is the freedom demanded for the worker by the capitalist. Against it the socialists and the organized workers have carried on a war of attrition for a century, the victories in that war being factory laws, mines and railway regulation laws, minimum wage laws, and the like. What the insurgent worker means by "the worker's control over his own life" is, on the contrary, the sort of control exercised by means of his trade union, through an executive council and officials, whom he and his fellows have elected, and can depose. These agents of the workers stand or fall, paradoxical as it may sound to those who still ignorantly regard trade unions as tyrannies, according to their ability to maintain and increase the personal freedom of the persons who elect them. The revolt of the workers is not against authority as such, but against the continuous and irresponsible authority of the profit-making employer. Where is the warrant, he asks, for the power of the owners of factories and mines, land and machinery to dictate the daily life and the weekly expenditure of hundreds of their fellowmen, and even, at their pleasure, to withdraw from them the means of life itself? This power is not derived from popular election. It has no relation to the ascertained merit or capacity of those who wield it. It is, in many cases, not even accompanied by any consciousness of responsibility for the moral or material well-being of those over whom it is exercised. Not only is there no necessary connection between the particular orders which the workers find themselves compelled to obey, and the security or prosperity of the commonwealth: there is often a great and patent contradiction, orders to adulterate and cheat being quite common. From the standpoint of labor the authority of the capitalist and landlord is used for a corrupt end—to promote the pecuniary gain of the person in command.

DICTATION AS TO ENVIRONMENT

Few persons who have not deliberately analyzed the way in which the wage-system is organized have any adequate conception of the continuity and the dictatorial character of the stream of orders by which the workman is called upon to direct his life. But this stream of orders is not the only way in which the property-owning class directs the daily life of those who are dependent on their toil. Even more dangerous, because more subtle, and less obviously an outcome of the inequality in wealth, is the power possessed by the propertied class to determine, for many years at a stretch, what shall be the physical and mental environment, not only of the manual laborer, but of all the local inhabitants. The most striking manifestation of this power is the steadily increasing "industrializing" of a countryside, ending in the creation of an urban slum area, by the continuous pollution of the water and the atmosphere, the destruction of vegetation, the creation of nuisances, the erection of "back to back" dwellings, in row after row of mean streets. The devastation wrought in this way, in some of the most fertile and most beautiful parts of England and Scotland, as also in the United States, is, as we now know, comparable only to that effected by a long-drawn-out modern war. In peace times the community as a whole fails to realize, in time, the catastrophe that is being caused by the private ownership of land and capital in the establishment and growth of an industrial center. By the time that the evil is recognized, the health and happiness of whole generations have been vitally affected. Belated statutes and tardy by-laws may then, at best, lessen the pollution, abate the darkening of the atmosphere by noxious gases and coal smoke, perhaps even save the last surviving vegetation. But nothing can bring back the lives the dictatorship of the capitalist has wasted. The leisured rich are able to escape from the noise, the gloom, the dirt, the smoke, the smells that their power has created; but the wage-earners, the industrial brain-workers, and all their retinue of professional men and shopkeepers find themselves compelled to dwell, and to rear their families, in the graceless conditions unconsciously determined for them by the industrial and financial organizers in their pursuit of private gain. When the city dweller escapes into the still unspoilt countryside on a scanty holiday, it comes as a new insult to find himself and his children barred from the pleasant park, excluded from the forest, and warned off the mountain and the moor by the property rights of the very class of persons who have rendered his place of abode abhorrent to him. In the end he is forced in self-defense to form a perverse habit of liking grimy streets, blackened skies, and the deafening clatter of drayhorses' shoes on stone sets, on the principle that if you cannot have what you like you must like what you have.

DICTATION OF THE MENTAL ENVIRONMENT

Nor is even this unconscious determination by the property-owning class of the material environment of the mass of the community, for the sake of its own private gain, the worst form taken by the inequality in personal freedom. It has been reserved to our own time for the profit-making capitalist to determine also the mental environment. Who can estimate the effect on the mind of the incessantly reiterated advertisements that hem us in on every side? It is, moreover, the capitalist who directs the character of the recreation afforded to the mass of people. It is the brewery company and the distillery that give us the public house; other capitalists, controlling the music hall and the cinematograph, may say, with Fletcher of Saltoun, that they care not who makes the laws as long as they provide the songs and films. But the most glaring instance of the capitalist direction of our mentality, and perhaps, ultimately, the most pernicious, is the modern system of ownership of the newspaper press. Here we have even a double capitalist control, first by the millionaire proprietors of whole series of journals, daily, weekly, and monthly under autocratic control, and secondly, by the great dispensers of lucrative advertisements to these journals. The combination of the colossal expense involved in the successful conduct of a modern daily newspaper, and the natural reluctance of the wealthy advertisers to support any publication adverse to the system, if not even to the particular business, by which they obtain their own fortunes, have made it almost impossible for the property-less wage-earners, even in cooperation with each other, to establish, either in Britain or the United States, any organ of their own at all comparable in circulation and influence with those of the millionaire proprietors. Thus, the mass of the population is quite unable to protect itself against the stream of suggestion, biased information, and corruptly selected news that is poured on them by the giant circulation of the press.[1]

[1] For accounts of the manner and extent to which the newspaper press, and behind it the possessors of wealth, now control the mental environment, as well as the local and central

Lastly, we have the control insidiously exercised by the owners and organizers of the instruments of production, by means of their wealth, over the working of municipal government and parliamentary institutions.

DICTATION IN GOVERNMENT

Of this control, the direct power of the proprietors of the newspaper press —which, in Britain, goes far to make a Prime Minister, and in the United States not only to elect a President but also to select his chief ministers—is only the most obvious example. The influence, not only upon elections and legislatures, but also upon national and municipal executives, of the great financial, shipping, manufacturing, and trading amalgamations and combinations, in which the power of wealth is cast defiantly into the scale as the sword of Brennus, has, in recent decades, become notorious and scandalous. It is, we suggest, to the suspicion, followed by the detection of this far-reaching coercive guidance of national and local government by the property-owners and profit-makers, large and small, more than to any other cause, that is to be ascribed the sudden and rapid decay of the confidence of the wage-earning class in these institutions, manifested not in this country alone, but throughout the Continent of Europe and North America. Unfortunately, one invidious feature of the Great War, so far as the United Kingdom is concerned, has been the extension of a similar capitalist control to the national executive, in ways not previously open. The temporary handing over of various government departments to leading representatives of the business interests concerned, and the shameless use of the influence thus acquired for the promotion of the private profits of those branches of business, represents, so it is felt by the British workman, the final degradation of the state to be the handmaid and accomplice of the profiteer.

THE BRAIN-WORKERS IN CAPITALIST SERVICE

This control of the physical and mental environment, which, in a capitalistic society, the property-owning class progressively and almost automatically accomplishes (for all those effects are mere incidents in the pursuit of private gain, and are no more consciously aimed at than the devastation caused by the trampling of a herd in pursuit of food), brings into prominence the instrument of its far-reaching dominance. The deep-seated intolerance by the more ignorant manual workers of the very existence of the profes-

---

government of the United States and Britain, the student should consult *The Press and the Organization of Society,* by Norman Angell, 1922; and *Liberty and the News,* 1920, and *Public Opinion,* 1922, both by Walter Lippmann, himself the editor of a great New York newspaper; the more lurid descriptions given from personal experience as journalists, on the one hand, by Hilaire Belloc in *The Free Press,* 1918, and' by Upton Sinclair in *The Brass Check,* 1919; and, incidentally, in the technical account of how a modern newspaper is run, by G. B. Dibblee in *The Newspaper,* 1913 (London), and by John La P. Given in *Making a Newspaper,* 1913 (New York).

sional brain-workers is not due solely to the difficulty a navvy finds in believing that a man who sits in a comfortable chair by a cheerful fire in a carefully sound-proofed room is doing any work at all, much less work that will leave him hungry and exhausted in three or four hours. Many wage-workers are sufficiently educated to know better; and others are employed in occupations quite as sedentary and even less apparently active than those of the financier or mathematician. Their share in the prejudice is explained, if not justified, by the fact that the brain-workers, in every capitalist state, find themselves attracted, and economically compelled, to take service under the property-owners. Historically the professions emerge as the hirelings of the governing class for the time being. In the modern industrial system they naturally serve the proprietors of the instruments of production, who alone can insure to the vast majority of them a secure and ample livelihood, with some prospect of climbing up to the eminence of "living by owning." The lawyers, the engineers, the architects, the men of financial and administrative ability, the civil servants, the authors and journalists, the teachers of the schools beyond the elementary grade, the whole class of managers, the inventors, even the artists and the men of science—not altogether excluding, in spite of their long charitable service of the poor, the medical profession and the ministers of religion, nor yet, for all their devotion to the children of the masses, even the elementary school teachers—are almost inevitably retained, consciously or unconsciously, in the maintenance and defense of the existing social order, in which the private ownership of the instruments of production is the corner-stone. Is it surprising that the manual workers of the world should be tempted to regard, not science, art or religion (as is often ignorantly asserted), but the brain-workers who have been trained under the capitalist system, and enlisted in its service, as being as much the "enemies of the people" as the "idle rich"? But this is not all. The brain-workers themselves, especially those who are poorly paid and socially segregated, are beginning to rebel openly against this all-pervading coercive guidance of national policy and national culture by wealthy men and a wealthy class. As school teachers, as municipal officials, as civil servants, as scientific workers, as journalists and editors, sometimes even (notably in the United States as under the German Empire) as university lecturers and professors, they find their freedom of thought and expression strangled by the fear of dismissal, or at any rate by that of losing all chance of promotion, should they dare to oppose not merely the political party or the pecuniary interests of influential patrons, but even the current principles of social organizations to which nearly all rich men cling. Moreover, the majority of the situations of authority and affluence are still habitually reserved, in most countries, either by administrative devices or through personal influence, for persons who have qualified as brain-workers though belonging to the class of those who live by owning or organizing the instruments of production, irrespective of their inferiority of attainments or inability to render, in the posts to which they are assigned, the highest service to the community. It is here that we find the fundamental cause of the prevailing unrest in all countries in practically all the brain-working professions, leading in many cases to the adherence of the younger professionals to the socialist movement, and nowadays even inclining some of the professional organizations to make common cause with the trade unions and the labor and socialist parties in resisting the dominance of the property-owners.

WHY LIBERALISM DECAYED

We may suggest that the foregoing analysis incidentally reveals the root-cause of the universal failure of the political parties styled Liberal, which were so typical of the advanced thought of European nations during the nineteenth century—notably at the zenith of unrestrained capitalism—to retain, in the twentieth century, their hold of a wage-earning class that has become conscious of its citizenship. To the political Liberals, personal freedom actually meant the personal power of the man of property; just as political progress meant the abolition of feudal, ecclesiastical and syndicalist restrictions upon the right of the property-owner, small as well as large, to do what he liked "with his own"—his own land and capital no less than his own personality. Down to the present day the unrepentant Liberal refuses to recognize—cannot even be made to understand—that, in the modern industrial state, a man who is divorced from the instruments of production cannot, as we have shown, even live his own life, let alone do what he likes with his own personality. Even to the political Liberal who is not a capitalist, such as the young barrister or doctor, artist or author, the conception that the laborers' engagement for hire is of the nature of "wage-slavery" is unintelligible. To him it seems, on the contrary, that the typical engagement for hire of the propertyless professional, "calling no man master" but earning his livelihood by fees from a succession of clients, upon no one of whom is he specially dependent, constitutes the very perfection of honorable service which is perfect freedom. What even this highly educated Liberal fails to understand is that, whatever may once have been the case, the industrial revolution has made anything like the freedom of professional life impossible for the artisan or the factory operative, the laborer or the clerk. The fact that the ordinary manual worker or minor clerical employee has not the ownership, and, therefore, not the control of the instruments of production, or of the complicated industrial or financial organization by which he can earn a livelihood, and cannot support himself on a succession of fees from a multitude of clients, compels him, whether or not he desires this, to obtain his food by placing himself under a master whom he cannot call to account; whose orders he has to obey; whose interests he has to serve; who, in fact, possesses him and uses him, during the greater part of his waking life, for ends which are not his own. He cannot choose where he will live, and in what environment his children will grow up. He finds himself restricted in the amusements and even in the literature to which he has access, to that which it suits the pecuniary interests of the capitalist class to supply. He finds, as it seems to him, nearly every professional brain-worker retained against him and his class. And through this control over his working life and his leisure hours, over his physical and mental environment, the propertyless worker, by hand or by brain—though conscious that he and his fellows constitute a majority of the electorate—discover that even with the widest suffrage he is unable, in fact, to control the government of his state. Accordingly, once he has been admitted to voting citizenship, the liberty which Liberalism offers him seems a hypocritical pretense. He finds in the creed of Liberalism no comprehension either of the nature of the servitude in which the capitalist system has engulfed the great bulk of every industrial community, or of the need for an application to industrial organization of the first principles of democracy. Now this comprehension is the very atmosphere of socialism. The socialist is out to destroy the dictatorship of the capitalist. And as that dictatorship is the grievance which the worker is never allowed to forget for a single working day from his cradle to his grave he naturally turns to socialism the moment he begins to connect politics with his personal affairs and perceives that his vote is an instrument of political power.

~~~~~~

4. The Religion of Inequality *

R. H. TAWNEY

~~~~~~

Discoursing some fifty years ago on the text, "Choose equality and flee greed," Mathew Arnold observed that in England inequality is almost a religion, and remarked on the incompatibility of that attitude with the spirit of humanity, and sense of the dignity of man as man, which are the marks of a truly civilized society. "On the one side, in fact, inequality harms by pampering; on the other by vulgarizing and depressing. A system founded on it is against nature, and, in the long run, breaks down."

Much has changed since Arnold wrote, and not least what he called the Religion of Inequality. The temper which evoked his criticism, the temper

* From R. H. Tawney, *Equality* (George Allen and Unwin, 1931). By permission.

which regarded violent contrasts between the circumstances and opportunities of different classes with respectful enthusiasm, as a phenomenon, not
merely inevitable, but admirable and exhilarating, if not wholly unknown,
is no longer general. Few politicians to-day would dwell, with Mr. Lowe, on
the English tradition of inequality as a pearl beyond price, to be jealously
guarded against the profane. Few educationalists would seek, with Thring,
the founder of the Headmasters' Conference and one of the most influential
figures in the educational world of his day, to assuage the apprehension felt
by the rich at the extension of education by arguing that "the law of labour"
compels the majority of children to work for wages at the age of ten, and
that "it is not possible that a class which is compelled to leave off training
at ten years of age can oust, by superior intelligence, a class which is able to
spend four years more in acquiring skill." Few political thinkers would
find, with Bagehot, the secret of English political institutions in the fact
that they have been created by a deferential people; or write, as Erskine May
wrote in his *Democracy in Europe,* of the demoralization of French society,
and the paralysis of the French intellect, by the attachment of France to the
blood-stained chimera of social equality; or declare, with the melancholy
assurance of Lecky, that liberty and equality are irreconcilable enemies, of
which the latter can triumph only at the expense of the former. When
Taine published his *Notes sur l'Angleterre* in 1872, he could describe it, by
contrast with France, as still haunted by the ghost of the feudal spirit, a
country governed by 100,000 to 120,000 families, with an income (*quantum
mutatus!*) of one thousand pounds a year and upwards, in which "the lord
provides for the needs of his dependent, and the dependent is proud of his
lord." It is improbable that, if he analysed the English scene today, even the
relentless exigencies of historical antithesis would lead him to regard it as
gilded with quite the same halo of haughty benevolence and submissive
gratitude.

Institutions which have died as creeds sometimes continue, nevertheless,
to survive as habits. If the cult of inequality as a principle and an ideal has
declined with the decline of the aristocratic society of which it was the accompaniment, it is less certain, perhaps, that the loss of its sentimental cre-
dentials has so far impaired its practical influence as to empty Arnold's words
of all their significance. It is true, no doubt, that, were he writing to-day, his
emphasis and illustrations would be different. No doubt he would be less
impressed by inequality as a cause of active irritation and confusion. No
doubt he would say less of great landed estates, and more of finance; less
of the territorial aristocracy and the social system represented by it, and
more of fortunes which, however interesting their origin, are not associated
with historic names; less of the effects of entail and settlement in preventing
the wider distribution of property in land, and more of the economic forces,
in his day unforeseen, which have led to a progressive concentration of the

control of capital; less of the English reverence for birth, and more of the English worship of money and economic power. But, if he could be induced to study the statistical evidence accumulated since he wrote, it is possible that he would hail it, with one of his ironical smiles, as an unanticipated confirmation of conclusions to which, unaided by the apparatus of science, he had found his way, and, while noting with interest the inequalities which had fallen, would feel even greater astonishment at those which had survived. Observing the heightened tension between political democracy and a social system marked by sharp disparities of circumstance and education, and of the opportunities which circumstance and education confer, he would find, it may be suspected, in the history of the two generations since his essay appeared, and, in particular, in that of the last decade, a more impressive proof of the justice of his diagnosis than it falls to the lot of most prophets to receive. "A system founded on inequality is against nature, and, in the long run, breaks down."

Men are rarely conscious of the quality of the air they breathe. It is natural that a later generation of Englishmen, if they admit that such criticisms may not have been without significance for the age to which they were addressed, should deny, nevertheless, that they are relevant to their own. On a question of the kind, where the sentiments of all of us are involved, we are none of us reliable witnesses. The course of wisdom, therefore, is to consult observers belonging to other nations, who are accustomed to a somewhat different social climate and tradition from our own, and who are less practised, perhaps, in the art of not letting the left side of their brain know what the right side thinks.

It is obvious, again, that the word "Equality" possesses more than one meaning, and that the controversies surrounding it arise partly, at least, because the same term is employed with different connotations. Thus it may either purport to state a fact, or convey the expression of an ethical judgment. On the one hand, it may affirm that men are, on the whole, very similar in their natural endowments of character and intelligence. On the other hand, it may assert that, while they differ profoundly as individuals in capacity and character, they are equally entitled as human beings to consideration and respect, and that the well-being of a society is likely to be increased if it so plans its organization that, whether their powers are great or small, all its members may be equally enabled to make the best of such powers as they possess.

If made in the first sense, the assertion of human equality is clearly untenable. It is a piece of mythology against which irresistible evidence has been accumulated by biologists and psychologists. In the light of the data presented—to mention only two recent examples—in such works as Dr. Burt's admirable studies of the distribution of educational abilities among school-children, or the Report of the Mental Deficiency Committee, the fact that, quite apart from differences of environment and opportunity, individuals differ widely in their natural endowments, and in their capacity to develop them by education, is not open to question. There is some reason for holding, for instance, that, while eighty per cent of children at the age of ten fall within a range of about three mental years, the most backward may have a mental age of five, while the most gifted may have one of as much as fifteen.

The acceptance of that conclusion, nevertheless, makes a somewhat smaller breach in equalitarian doctrines than is sometimes supposed, for such doctrines have rarely been based on a denial of it. It is true, of course, that the psychological and political theory of the age between 1750 and 1850—the theory, for example, of thinkers so different as Helvétius and Adam Smith at the beginning of the period, and Mill and Proudhon at the end of it—greatly underestimated the significance of inherited qualities, and greatly overestimated the plasticity of human nature. It may be doubted, however, whether it was quite that order of ideas which inspired the historical affirmations of human equality, even in the age when such ideas were still in fashion.

It is difficult for even the most sanguine of assemblies to retain for more than one meeting the belief that Providence has bestowed an equal measure of intelligence upon all its members. When the Americans declared it to be a self-evident truth that all men are created equal, they were thinking less, perhaps, of the admirable racial qualities of the inhabitants of the New World than of their political and economic relations with the Old, and would have remained unconvinced that those relations should continue even in the face of proofs of biological inferiority. When the French, whose attachment to the equalitarian idea roused the same horror a century and a quarter ago as that of the Russians does to-day, and who have had more success than the Russians in disseminating it, set that idea side by side with liberty and fraternity as the motto of a new world, they did not mean that all men are equally intelligent or equally virtuous, any more than that they are equally tall or equally fat, but that the unity of their national life should no longer be torn to pieces by obsolete property rights and meaningless juristic distinctions. When Arnold, who was an inspector of schools as well as a poet, and who, whatever his failings, was not prone to demagogy, wrote "choose equality," he did not suggest, it may be suspected, that all children appeared to him to be equally clever, but that a nation acts unwisely in stressing heavily distinctions based on birth or money.

Few men have been more acutely sensitive than Mill to the importance of encouraging the widest possible diversities of mind and taste. In arguing that "the best state for human nature is that in which, while no one is poor, no one desires to be richer," and urging that social policy should be directed to increasing equality, he did not intend to convey that it should suppress varieties of individual genius and character, but that it was only in a society marked by a large measure of economic equality that such varieties were likely to find their full expression and due meed of appreciation. Theologians have not, as a rule, been disposed to ignore the fact that there are diversities of gifts and degree above degree. When they tell us that all men are equal in the eyes of God, what they mean, it is to be presumed, is what Jeremy Taylor, when he wrote, in a book to-day too little read, that "if a man be exalted by reason of any excellence in his soul, he may please to remember that all souls are equal, and their differing operations are because their instrument is in better tune, their body is more healthful or better tempered; which is no more praise to him than it is that he was born in Italy." It is the truth expressed in the parable of the prodigal son, which clever people, like deans, sometimes seem to forget, but which it is specially necessary, perhaps, for such people to remember—the truth that it is absurd and degrading for men to make much of their intellectual and moral superiority to each other, and still more of their superiority in the arts which bring wealth and power, because, judged by their place in any universal scheme, they are all infinitely great or infinitely small. And, when observers from the dominions, or from foreign countries, are struck by inequality as one of the special and outstanding characteristics of English social life, they do not mean that in other countries differences of personal quality are less important than in England. They mean, on the contrary, that they are more important, and that in England they tend to be obscured or obliterated behind differences of property and income, and the whole elaborate façade of a society that, compared with their own, seems stratified and hierarchical.

The equality which all these thinkers emphasize as desirable is not equality of capacity or attainment, but of circumstances, and institutions, and manner of life. The inequality which they deplore is not inequality of personal gifts, but of the social and economic environment. They are concerned, not with a biological phenomenon, but with a spiritual relation and the conduct to be based on it. Their view, in short, is that, because men are men, social institutions—property rights, and the organization of industry, and the system of public health and education—should be planned, as far as is possible, to emphasize and strengthen, not the class differences which divide, but the common humanity which unites them.

Such a view of the life which is proper to human beings may, of course, be criticized, as it often has been. But to suppose that it can be criticized effectively by pointing to the width of the intellectual and moral differences which distinguish individuals from each other is a solecism, an *ignoratio elenchi*. It is true, of course, that such differences are important, and that the advance of psychology has enabled them to be measured with a new precision, with results which are valuable in making possible both a closer adaptation of educational methods to individual needs and a more intelligent selection of varying aptitudes for different tasks. But to recognize a specific difference is one thing; to pass a general judgement of superiority or inferiority, still more to favour the first and neglect the second, is quite another. The nightingale, it has been remarked, was placed in the fourth class at the fowl show. Which of a number of varying individuals is to be judged superior to the rest depends upon the criterion which is applied, and the criterion is a matter of ethical judgment, which will, if it is prudent, be tentative and provisional, since men's estimates of the relative desirability of initiative, decision, common sense, imagination, humility and sympathy appear, unfortunately, to differ, and the failures and fools—the Socrates and St. Francis—of one age are the sages and saints of another. Society would not be the worse, perhaps, if idiots like Dostoievsky's were somewhat less uncommon, and the condemnation passed on those who offend one of these little ones was not limited to offenders against children whose mental ratio is in excess of eighty-five.

It is true, again, that human beings have, except as regards certain elementary, though still sadly neglected, matters of health and development, different requirements, and that these different requirements can be met satisfactorily only by varying forms of provision. It is to be achieved, not by treating different needs in the same way, but by devoting equal care to ensuring that they are met in the different ways most appropriate to them, as is done by a doctor who prescribes different regimens for different constitutions, or a teacher who develops different types of intelligence by different curricula. The more anxiously, indeed, a society endeavours to secure equality for all its members, the greater will be the differentiation of treatment which, when once their common human needs have been met, it accords to the special needs of different groups and individuals among them.

It is true, however, that, while inequality is easy, since it demands no more than to float with the current, equality is difficult, for it involves swimming against it. It is true that, like all other goods, whether economic or spiritual, it has its price and its burdens. It involves material sacrifices by some, and a not less painful surrender of sentimental claims by others, and, on the part of all, sufficient self-control and public spirit, sufficient respect for themselves and appreciation of their neighbours, to prefer what Wordsworth called "joy in widest commonalty spread"—a high standard of general well-being and a wide diffusion of the means of culture and civilization—to the temper that is on the watch to snatch opportunities for personal advancement, or stands stiffly on established rights, even when rights are wrong. It implies the disinterestedness needed to expose dear, respectable absurdities to the light of reason, and the patience to endure the toil of thought which alone can supersede them. The last great equalitarian movement, in its nobler, which was also its more successful, version, sought to create a society free from mean-ingless privilege and capricious class divisions by emancipating the individ-ual from legal fetters. In the industrial civilization, which has been that movement's heir, such a society is to be attained, if attained at all, by de-liberate organization and collective effort. It must so plan the lines of its industrial structure that authority is associated, not with property, but with function, and rest on conscious consent, not on the power of wealth. It must so distribute its resources that an ever larger proportion of the surplus, which, thanks to science and invention, modern industry yields, is employed not for private gratification, but for the common advantage.

If the means are complex, the end is simple. When the false gods depart, there is some hope, at least, of the arrival of the true. The reason for equaliz-ing, as means and opportunity allow, the externals of life is not that the scaffolding is more important than the shrine, or that economic interests, for all their clamour and insistence, possess the unique and portentous sig-nificance which the fashionable philosophy of the age is accustomed to ascribe to them. It is not, as austere critics assert, to pamper the gross bodily appetites of an envious multitude, but to free the spirit of all.

In the currency of the soul, as in that of states, spurious coin drives out good. Its stamp is different in different generations, but in our own it is familiar. The chief enemy of the life of the spirit, whether in art, culture, and religion, or in the simple human associations which are the common vehicle of its revelation to ordinary men, is itself a religion. It is, as everyone knows, the idolatry of wealth, with its worship of pecuniary success, and its reverence for the arts, however trivial or unamiable in themselves, by which success is achieved, and its strong sense of the sanctity of possessions and weak sense of the dignity of human beings, and its consequent emphasis, not on the common interests which unite men, but on the accidents of property, and circumstance, and economic condition, which separate and divide them. The cult has strange antics of devotion, and singular observances, and a rit-ual sometimes comic, sometimes cruel, sometimes both. It causes its devotees to admire what is not admirable, while despising what is, and to seek hap-piness where it cannot be found, not where it can. It is not favourable to simplicity of life, for it makes much of display; or to sincerity of mind, for it burns incense to sham; or to a just and sensitive taste, for its criteria are those of quantity and mass; or to harmonious relations between human beings, for it labours hard, and with success, to multiply discords. But, with all its crudities and extravagances, the creed rests on reality. It draws its strength from the truth that, as the world is to-day, wealth opens the gates of opportunity, and poverty, save for fortunate exceptions, still commonly closes them.

So it is not sufficient to exorcize the demon with pious conjurations. It is necessary to destroy the hard pediment of fact, on which his power reposes.

Though the ideal of an equal distribution of material wealth may continue to elude us, it is necessary, nevertheless, to make haste towards it, not because such wealth is the most important of man's treasures, but to prove that it is not. *Sint temporalia in usu, aeterna in desiderio.* It is possible that the ultimate goods of human life, which belong to the realm where to divide is not to take away, may more easily be attained, when its instruments and means are less greedily grasped and more freely shared.

Chapter IV

CHARACTER AND WISDOM IN DEMOCRATIC POLITICS

THE political history of the world since 1918 has taught us what common sense should have taught us before: that political decency is a matter not only of politics, but also of—decency. After Germany and her allies were defeated in 1918, there was the general hope, and faith, among the victors that the removal of That Bad Man, Kaiser Wilhelm II, would inaugurate a new Germany, living in peace and democracy. The Weimar Constitution was one of the most perfect political charters ever devised; to have been successful it needed only one minor detail—a people that really wanted democracy rather than Hindenburg, Hitler, Hugenberg, and von Papen. Democracy cannot be a success with too many decent fools and clever criminals around. Regardless of which of these two groups is in the majority, the final result is almost invariably the same.

The glory of the democratic faith is its optimism, its insistence that men are malleable, and its liberating creed that man is not a prisoner of fact, but its creator. The danger and weakness of the democratic attitude is its unhistorical disregard for unpleasant facts, its tendency to confuse the Ought with the Is.

Because democratic societies have developed certain institutions, such as parliaments, and have established certain freedoms, such as those of opinion, press, and association, many well-meaning practicing politicians, as well as students of politics, have fallen into the error of confusing cause with effect. The United States and Great Britain are not democracies because they have popularly elected representative assemblies and free newspapers, but they have parliamentary institutions and a free press because they are democratic societies. Democracy is more than a system of government. The key to the understanding of politics lies in the *nonpolitical* aspects of society. Life is richer than politics. What determines the political habits of a nation is to be found less in the proceedings of constitution-making assemblies than in the day-to-day proceedings of husband and wife, parent and child, clergyman and parishioner, teacher and pupil, officer and soldier, and employer and employee.

This is why denazification and deshintoization are so difficult. To denazify party headquarters, town halls, and parliaments is one thing. To denazify the kitchen and parlor, the classroom and church is a proposition of a different order.

If President Wilson had paid due attention to John Stuart Mill's *Representative Government* (1861), his easy optimism about the outlook of democracy in Germany would have given way to a more realistic appraisal of what was possible under the circumstances, and what was likely to happen. As yet it is too early to say whether the successors of Wilson and Lloyd George have taken Mill more seriously. Mill expresses the central idea of his approach to the problem of representative government in a few words that are now even timelier than in 1861: "If we ask ourselves on what causes and conditions good government in all its senses, from the humblest to the most exalted, depends, we find that the principal of them, the one which transcends all others, is the qualities of the human beings composing the society over which the government is exercised." Long before Mill, Plato had expressed this thought in similar phrases: "Do you imagine that constitutions grow at random 'from stone to stone,' and not from those characters of the men in the cities which preponderate and draw the rest of the city after them?"

Barbara Wootton's essay on "Public and Private Honesty," (*The Political Quarterly,* July-September, 1945) discusses the problem of character and politics from the angle of public honesty. The experience recorded in the essay is mostly English. This is of particular interest to Americans concerned with the raising of public standards in the United States. In the last hundred years standards of public conduct have been substantially higher in Britain than in the United States. Yet British politics in the eighteenth century was as corrupt as could be. What happened in nineteenth-century England was not a change of national character; it was the victory of long and arduous efforts of reformers over those who liked to think of corrupt politics and administration as colorful and picturesque. If it could be done in England, more integrity in American public affairs will be possible, too.

But Mrs. Wootton's essay is important for another reason: the more the modern state assumes new activities, the vaster the possible scale of public dishonesty becomes, and the greater the need for higher standards. If a capitalist society can get along with a good deal of bribery, nepotism, and corruption, a socialist society simply cannot stay afloat in a seat of dishonesty. The opportunities to sin are too abundant then. Prerevolutionary Russia was one of the most corrupt empires in the world; yet the Soviet regime has been noted for the personal integrity of the leaders. Compared with Goering and his castles and picture galleries, compared with Mussolini and his castles and mistresses, the private lives of Lenin and Stalin (and Trotsky), as of the other outstanding Bolshevik leaders, were ultra-Puritan and of Victorian bourgeois solidity. As to public corruption (the Latin Americans have a better term: "administrative irregularity"), the Soviets solved the problem by simply liquidating corruptionists as saboteurs and enemies of the state. This method is quite effective, but not likely to be adopted in the United States, where the British experience in this respect is of more practical relevance. The more the government of the United States, local, state, and federal, moves into new orbits of activity, the more imperative will be the reappraisal of public standards of integrity.

Jacob Klatzkin's *In Praise of Wisdom* (1943) is his first major work presented in an English version. His main contributions have been in the study of Hebrew philosophy, and he is thoroughly steeped in the long tradition of Hebrew thought, from Biblical and Talmudic lore to the present day. Written in Hebrew, *In Praise of Wisdom* gives a summary of Klatzkin's ideas on man, man lonely in his solitude, and man associated with others in fellowship or slavery.

Josiah C. (later Lord) Wedgwood was one of those men to whom England owes her political greatness. Born in a business family of world-wide renown, he dedicated himself to public service via a political career. In Parliament he rose high: he became a "good House of Commons man" rather than a party wheel horse. His socialism was the product of an alliance of aristocracy and militant democracy. Author of many books, his last book, *Testament to Democracy* (1942), gives an insight into the spirit of British freedom. During the Spanish civil war, Wedgwood felt angered over the active support of the Fascist rebels by the Roman Catholic hierarchy (in Britain and elsewhere), as much as he was dismayed by the silence and apathy of the liberals. Wedgwood did not belong to the generation of Englishmen who defined a liberal as a man who treads firmly on thin air, and he felt compelled to speak up. His letter to the *Sunday Times* (London, August 18, 1937) is important beyond the immediate issue of the Spanish civil war. What he attacks in his letter is more than appeasement of Franco and his cohorts in Vatican City, Berlin, New York, and London. What he challenges is the lack of moral courage without which democracy becomes anemic and incapable to resist attacks upon its very life.

This is exactly what happened to France in 1940. Her military defeat in that year was not nearly so tragic as the intellectual confusion and spiritual surrender symbolized by the word "collaboration." *La grande épreuve des démocraties* ("The Great Ordeal of the Democracies"), by Julien Benda, carries a preface, dated January, 1941, and the work was published in New York (in French) in 1942. It has not been translated into English so far, but it should be, because it analyzes with clear and ruthless logic the shortcomings of democracy, alleged and real. Benda showed unusual moral courage when he wrote and published his work under circumstances which might easily have cost him his life, not to speak of his liberty. The purity and nobility of his courage is fully equaled by the strength of his reasoning.

What Benda exposes, in particular, is the danger of destroying democracy by carrying certain democratic principles, such as individualism, equality, love of peace, to their absurd and suicidal extremes. "Individualist imperialism" leads to social dissolution from within, just as surely as the doctrine of "peace at any price" leads to annihilation from without.

Democracy seeks to tame the beast in man. But if members of a democratic society become tamed to the point where they no longer possess the capacity to act and survive as an effectively organized group, their civilized conduct will be replaced by the savagery of their conquerors. How to combine the sweetness of reasoning with the control of force—this always remains the dilemma of democracy.

Salvador de Madariaga's *Anarchy or Hierarchy* (1937) is based, like Benda's work, on an unusual political experience: in Spain, where Madariaga spent most of his early life, he could observe what happens to a country with a weak liberal tradition. In England, where he has made his home in Oxford for many years, he has had the opportunity of studying politics in a country with the strongest liberal tradition in Europe. What fits Madariaga to discuss problems of democracy is also his grasp of practical affairs, acquired as Spanish Ambassador in some of the world's great capitals, including Washington. During the civil war of 1936–1939, started by General Franco, and completed by German and Italian troops and armaments, Madariaga was one of the Spaniards who maintained neutrality between the Republicans and the Fascists. Only a few weeks after the outbreak of the civil war he left Spain, and eventually settled again in Oxford. The two main points that Madariaga makes in *Anarchy or Hierarchy* are, first, that democracy can not subsist, in practice, if the citizens pursue individual and group aims to the exclusion of the public interest; second, and this is Madariaga's major concern, "liberal democracies are dependent on leadership even more so perhaps than other more authoritarian forms of government." Madariaga touches one of the sorest wounds of sick democracies when he stresses the need for responsible and strong leadership. There is always a deep prejudice in democracies, even in comparatively healthy ones, against great leaders; both Lincoln and Franklin D. Roosevelt were calumniated as dictators, Caesars, and mad tyrants. One of the most dangerous tendencies in a democracy, always present, is for the public to lend a friendly ear to those demagogues who tell the audience exactly what it wishes to hear, and to shun those true leaders who dare speak the truth, unpleasant as it may seem at the time. Ultimately it is a question of character, whether there are enough leaders in a democratic society who have the capacity and courage to lead, rather than to follow, the people, and whether the people possess enough judgment and integrity to recognize these qualities in their leaders. Writing in 1937, Madariaga foresaw with prophetic accuracy that the crisis of leadership in democracy would lead to serious consequences: "The collapse of democratic institutions which threatens the world will, to a great extent, be due to the cowardliness of leaders, in itself a consequence of their feeling of their own failure as leaders."

Spanish problems of government reappeared in Hispanic America both before and after Independence. None understood the relations between politics and personal integrity more clearly than Simon Bolivar. He saw in ignorance, tyranny, and vice the "triple yoke" which was the real oppressor of the Hispanic-American peoples. Having liberated his fellow-countrymen, he addressed the Congress of Venezuela, in 1819, on the political problems that faced the peoples of Venezuela as well as of the other freed new nations of Hispanic America. His sense of caution and moderation has been more than justified by subsequent constitutional developments. His preference for the English, rather than the French or American governmental system may have been based on unfeasible assumptions, but Bolivar was realistic enough to know that the political future of Hispanic America had to be planned in accordance with the human qualities and historical materials available. One of the great emancipators of all human history, he combined the capacity for quick and decisive action with the broad culture and wisdom of the gentleman scholar.

The last two discussions in this chapter deal with the place of the expert in government. *The Limitations of the Expert* by Harold J. Laski is "Fabian Tract" No. 235, and was published in 1931. We live in an age in which the expert is not only idolized, but *expects* to be idolized. Those who want to see the expert relegated to his proper place, with his wings duly clipped, will find *The Limitations of the Expert* of lasting value. The wresting of military control from the experts, the military, was one of the great achievements of Parliament in England, and involved the cost of a civil war. In the United States, the expert (especially the successful businessman) has held greater sway than in England, and this difference is apparent in a first glance at both countries—it pervades the structure of politics at the top (selection of ministers) as well as at the bottom (entrance examinations for the civil service). Germany has long believed in the expert (*Fachmann* or *Sachverständiger*), in military as in other matters, thus putting intellect above common sense, and knowledge above understanding.

The problem of the expert becomes particularly acute in the complex modern world, and the plain man, the charge runs, "is simply obsolete in a world he has never been trained to understand." However, the citizen cannot be relieved of his duty of judgment, after all the relevant facts have been brought to his attention. The expert can supply the citizen and ruler with the raw materials that may enter the final decision, but he cannot think *for* the citizen or ruler. Without utilizing the *expertise* of the specialist, a democracy may suffer from ignorance. By allowing experts (military, bureaucratic, propagandistic, or economic) to run society, democracy may soon find itself transformed into an arrogant tyranny. "We must ceaselessly remember," Laski concludes, "that no body of experts is wise enough, or good enough, to be charged with the destiny of mankind." Opposed to this democratic conception of the place of the expert is the idea of Frederick Engels, e.g., who expresses the typically Marxist illusion that in the classless socialist society domination of man over man would be replaced by "administration of things." In such a Utopian world, when all political problems—who tells whom what to do—will be eliminated, the expert will have a field day. In the Soviet Union, in the meantime, administrative problems have been raised to political ones, instead of the latter's being demoted to the lower status of the former.

The problem of knowledge as distinct from wisdom is further examined by A. D. (now Lord) Lindsay in his *Modern Democratic State* (first volume published in 1943). Since the publication of Laski's *Grammar of Politics* in 1925, Lindsay's work is the first notable general treatise on politics. In typically British fashion, Lindsay is little infatuated with the experts. They "do not like being told that the shoes they so beautifully make do not fit. They are apt to blame it on the distorted and misshapen toes of the people who have to wear their shoes." However, Lindsay warns against the argument that "ordinary plain people have a certain wisdom which is denied to the expert," because "an expert is not necessarily a fool." And he stresses the idea that the expert is a specialist: "that what is wanted for conduct is all-round experience of people and things." Those who believe that because specialized knowledge may lead to narrowness no knowledge will produce breadth of view, are reminded by Lindsay that "sound judgment" or "common sense" are not the "products of ignorance." Summing up the process through which a person develops wisdom, Lindsay concludes as follows: "Knowledge of the common life and its possibilities; understanding of the things which produce in it bitterness and thwart men's activities are the wisdom most wanted for politics."

Lindsay draws special attention to the fact that, in a country like Britain (or the United States), modern industrialism has robbed many people of their independence and condemned them to "specialized and narrow lives." The great danger of modern society is that of being turned by totalitarian propagandists and manipulators into a crowd, mass, or mob. The antidote to this challenge has been supplied, according to Lindsay, by industrialism itself in the form of the working-class movement. "If we consider what gives that movement its vitality, we see that it creates innumerable centres of discussion." Just as totalitarianism depends on the suppression of free discussion, "the key to democracy is the potency of discussion. A good discussion can draw out wisdom which is attainable in no other way." This may explain why the suppression of a free working-class movement has always been a top priority on the agenda of Fascism.

1. Government of Gentlemen, for Gentlemen, by Gentlemen*

JOHN STUART MILL

But there are also cases in which, though not averse to a form of government—possibly even desiring it—a people may be unwilling or unable to fulfil its conditions. They may be incapable of fulfilling such of them as are necessary to keep the government even in nominal existence. Thus a people may prefer a free government, but if, from indolence, or carelessness, or cowardice, or want of public spirit, they are unequal to the exertions necessary for preserving it; if they will not fight for it when it is directly attacked; if they can be deluded by the artifices used to cheat them out of it; if by momentary discouragement, or temporary panic, or a fit of enthusiasm for an individual, they can be induced to lay their liberties at the feet even of a great man, or trust him with powers which enable him to subvert their institutions; in all these cases they are more or less unfit for liberty: and though it may be for their good to have had it even for a short time, they are unlikely long to enjoy it. Again, a people may be unwilling or unable to fulfil the duties which a particular form of government requires of them. A rude people, though in some degree alive to the benefits of civilized society, may be unable to practise the forbearances which it demands: their passions may be too violent, or their personal pride too exacting, to forego private conflict, and leave to the laws the avenging of their real or supposed wrongs. In such a case, a civilized government, to be really advantageous to them, will require to be in a considerable degree despotic: to be one over which they do not themselves exercise control, and which imposes a great amount of forcible restraint upon their actions. Again, a people must be considered unfit for more than a limited and qualified freedom, who will not co-operate actively with the law and the public authorities, in the repression of evil-doers. A people who are more disposed to shelter a criminal than to apprehend him; who, like the Hindoos, will perjure themselves to screen the man who has robbed them, rather than take trouble or expose themselves to vindictiveness by giving evidence against him; who, like some nations of Europe down to a recent date, if a man poniards another in the public street, pass by on the other side, because it is the business of the police to look to the matter, and it is safer not to interfere in what does not concern them; a people who are revolted by an execution, but not shocked at an assassination

* From John Stuart Mill, *Representative Government* (1861).

—require that the public authorities should be armed with much sterner powers of repression than elsewhere, since the first indispensable requisites of civilized life have nothing else to rest on. These deplorable states of feeling, in any people who have emerged from savage life, are, no doubt, usually the consequence of previous bad government, which has taught them to regard the law as made for other ends than their good, and its administrators as worse enemies than those who openly violate it. But however little blame may be due to those in whom these mental habits have grown up, and however the habits may be ultimately conquerable by better government, yet while they exist, a people so disposed cannot be governed with as little power exercised over them, as a people whose sympathies are on the side of the law, and who are willing to give active assistance in its enforcement. Again, representative institutions are of little value, and may be a mere instrument of tyranny or intrigue, when the generality of electors are not sufficiently interested in their own government to give their vote, or if they vote at all, do not bestow their suffrages on public grounds, but sell them for money, or vote at the beck of some one who has control over them or whom for private reasons they desire to propitiate. Popular election thus practised, instead of a security against misgovernment, is but an additional wheel in its machinery. Besides these moral hindrances, mechanical difficulties are often an insuperable impediment to forms of government. In the ancient world, though there might be, and often was, great individual or local independence, there could be nothing like a regulated popular government, beyond the bounds of a single city-community; because there did not exist the physical conditions for the formation and propagation of a public opinion, except among those who could be brought together to discuss public matters in the same agora. This obstacle is generally thought to have ceased by the adoption of the representative system. But to surmount it completely, required the press, and even the newspaper press, the real equivalent, though not in all respects an adequate one, of the Pnyx and the Forum. There have been states of society in which even a monarchy of any great territorial extent could not subsist, but unavoidably broke up into petty principalities, either mutually independent, or held together by a loose tie like the feudal: because the machinery of authority was not perfect enough to carry orders into effect at a great distance from the person of the ruler. He depended mainly upon voluntary fidelity for the obedience even of his army, nor did there exist the means of making the people pay an amount of taxes sufficient for keeping up the force necessary to compel obedience throughout a large territory. In these and all similar cases, it must be understood that the amount of the hindrance may be either greater or less. It may be so great as to make the form of government work very ill, without absolutely precluding its existence, or hindering it from being practically preferable to any other which can be had. This last question mainly depends upon a consideration which we have not yet arrived at—the tendencies of different forms of government to promote Progress.

If we ask ourselves on what causes and conditions good government in all its senses, from the humblest to the most exalted, depends, we find that the principal of them, the one which transcends all others, is the qualities of the human beings composing the society over which the government is exercised. We may take, as a first instance, the administration of justice; with the more propriety, since there is no part of public business in which the mere machinery, the rules and contrivances for conducting the details of the operation, are of such vital consequence. Yet even these yield in importance to the qualities of the human agents employed. Of what efficacy are rules of procedure in securing the ends of justice, if the moral condition of the people is such that the witnesses generally lie, and the judges and their subordinates take bribes? Again, how can institutions provide a good municipal administration, if there exists such indifference to the subject, that those who would administer honestly and capably cannot be induced to serve, and the duties are left to those who undertake them because they have some private interest to be promoted? Of what avail is the most broadly popular representative system if the electors do not care to choose the best member of parliament, but choose him who will spend most money to be elected? How can a representative assembly work for good, if its members can be bought, or if their excitability of temperament, uncorrected by public discipline or private self-control, makes them incapable of calm deliberation, and they resort to manual violence on the floor of the House, or shoot at one another with rifles? How, again, can government, or any joint concern, be carried on in a tolerable manner by people so envious, that if one among them seems likely to succeed in anything, those who ought to co-operate with him form a tacit combination to make him fail? Whenever the general disposition of the people is such, that each individual regards those only of his interests which are selfish, and does not dwell on, or concern himself for, his share of the general interest, in such a state of things good government is impossible. The influence of defects of intelligence in obstructing all the elements of good government requires no illustration. Government consists of acts done by human beings: and if the agents, or those who choose the agents, or those to whom the agents are responsible, or the lookers-on whose opinion ought to influence and check all these, are mere masses of ignorance, stupidity, and baleful prejudice, every operation of government will go wrong: while, in proportion as the men rise above this standard, so will the government improve in quality; up to the point of excellence, attainable but nowhere attained, where the officers of government, themselves persons of superior virtue and intellect, are surrounded by the atmosphere of a virtuous and enlightened public opinion.

The first element of good government, therefore, being the virtue and intelligence of the human beings composing the community, the most important point of excellence which any form of government can possess is to promote the virtue and intelligence of the people themselves. The first question in respect to any political institutions is, how far they tend to foster in the members of the community the various desirable qualities, moral and intellectual; or rather (following Bentham's more complete classification) moral, intellectual, and active. The government which does this the best, has every likelihood of being the best in all other respects, since it is on these qualities, so far as they exist in the people, that all possibility of goodness in the practical operations of the government depends.

We may consider, then, as one criterion of the goodness of a government, the degree in which it tends to increase the sum of good qualities in the governed, collectively and individually; since, besides that their well-being is the sole object of government, their good qualities supply the moving force which works the machinery. This leaves, as the other constituent element of the merit of a government, the quality of the machinery itself; that is, the degree in which it is adapted to take advantage of the amount of good qualities which may at any time exist, and make them instrumental to the right purposes. Let us again take the subject of judicature as an example and illustration. The judicial system being given, the goodness of the administration of justice is in the compound ratio of the worth of the men composing the tribunals, and the worth of the public opinion which influences or controls them. But all the difference between a good and a bad system of judicature lies in the contrivances adopted for bringing whatever moral and intellectual worth exists in the community to bear upon the administration of justice, and making it duly operative on the result. The arrangements for rendering the choice of the judges such as to obtain the highest average of virtue and intelligence; the salutary forms of procedure; the publicity which allows observation and criticism of whatever is amiss; the liberty of discussion and censure through the press; the mode of taking evidence, according as it is well or ill adapted to elicit truth; the facilities, whatever be their amount, for obtaining access to the tribunals; the arrangements for detecting crimes and apprehending offenders;—all these things are not the power, but the machinery for bringing the power into contact with the obstacle: and the machinery has no action of itself, but without it the power, let it be ever so ample, would be wasted and of no effect. A similar distinction exists in regard to the constitution of the executive departments of administration. Their machinery is good, when the proper tests are prescribed for the qualifications of officers, the proper rules for their promotion; when the business is conveniently distributed among those who are to transact it, a convenient and methodical order established for its transaction, a correct and intelligible record kept of it after being transacted; when each individual knows for what he is responsible, and is known to others as responsible for it; when the best-contrived checks are provided against negligence, favouritism, or jobbery, in any of the acts of the department. But political checks will no more act of themselves, than a bridle will direct a horse without a rider. If the checking functionaries are as corrupt or as negligent as those whom they ought to check, and if the public, the mainspring of the whole checking, are too ignorant, too passive, or too careless and inattentive, to do their part, little benefit will be derived from the best administrative apparatus. Yet a good apparatus is always preferable to a bad. It enables such insufficient moving or checking power as exists, to act at the greatest advantage; and without it, no amount of moving or checking power would be sufficient. Publicity, for instance, is no impediment to evil nor stimulus to good if the public will not look at what is done; but without publicity, how could they either check or encourage what they were not permitted to see? The ideally perfect constitution of a public office is that in which the interest of the functionary is entirely coincident with his duty. No mere system will make it so, but still less can it be made so without a system, aptly devised for the purpose.

What we have said of the arrangements for the detailed administration of the government, is still more evidently true of its general constitution. All government which aims at being good is an organization of some part of the good qualities existing in the individual members of the community, for the conduct of its collective affairs. A representative constitution is a means of bringing the general standard of intelligence and honesty existing in the community, and the individual intellect and virtue of its wisest members, more directly to bear upon the government, and investing them with greater influence in it, than they would in general have under any other mode of organization; though, under any, such influence as they do have is the source of all good that there is in the government, and the hindrance of every evil that there is not. The greater the amount of these good qualities which the institutions of a country succeed in organizing, and the better the mode of organization, the better will be the government.

2. Public and Private Honesty [*]

BARBARA WOOTTON

It is chastening to reflect how wide is the gap, even amongst the relatively public-spirited, between standards of honesty in personal, and in public, rela-

[*] *The Political Quarterly*, Vol. XVI (July–September, 1945). By permission.

tionships. The reflection is also apt, since the growth of public enterprise is bound to make severe demands upon private integrity.

Naturally, exact and measurable information on this subject is not easily come by; a Gallup poll on methods of cheating the public authorities would be hardly likely to elicit the truth! What comes to light from everyday observation of one's own and one's neighbour's behaviour, and from the admissions of candid friends (and still more candid casual acquaintances) is no scientifically selected sample. I have, however, done my best to get such evidence as one person can, and am much indebted to many collaborators in this task, who must for obvious reasons remain anonymous. And since most of us like to put a good face on our own actions, and to keep quiet about those which are too difficult to dress up, the casual observer is likely to get on the whole a flattering, rather than an unflattering, view of what is going on.

Naturally, one can never be sure to what extent honesty is due to fear of being found out. It is certainly possible to prevent a great deal of cheating and theft by Act of Parliament, and still more by acts of magistrates. There is plenty of evidence, beside the growth of larcenies in the blackout, to suggest that many of us would be a good deal more dishonest than we are, if we were more often convinced that there was absolutely *no* risk of being found out. Ultimately, however, as everybody knows well enough, the law itself rests on social codes the maintenance of which is the personal responsibility of individual men and women: deterrence by itself (especially the relatively mild deterrence of contemporary English law!) is an unstable sanction. I have therefore tried as far as possible to confine my examples to cases in which the subject is at least himself convinced that he is safe from detection; since these alone reveal, without distortion, the content of prevailing codes.

Now it will, I think, be admitted that in the personal relationships of ordinary people very high standards of financial honesty are common. If Mrs. Jones has done some shopping for her neighbour and is not absolutely certain, when it comes to settling up, whether the total was 6s. 6d. or 7s. 6d., it would be at least very usual for her to mention the lower figure: the principle of giving the other party the benefit of any doubt in transactions between personal friends and acquaintances is surely fairly well established. How many of us have reached a similar standard in our dealings with anonymous public authorities, except in the special case in which we happen to occupy some position of trust (e.g., as treasurer of a society)? Consider the test case of income tax. Pay as you earn notwithstanding, there are still plenty of opportunities for underestimating income for income tax purposes: there may be some genuine element of doubt or there may be odd sums (e.g., casual fees) which can conveniently be forgotten. Of all those who would unhesitatingly give the benefit of any doubt in a personal transaction to the other party, what proportion apply the same code to their dealings with the Inland Revenue Commissioners? I have heard the practice of understatement in this connection justified on the grounds, first, that the income tax rates are fixed on the assumption that a certain proportion of income will escape assessment, and that therefore anyone who is scrupulously honest will actually be paying more than his due or expected share; and, second, that the Inland Revenue authorities equally weight the scales in their own favour in any case of doubt. An analogy is suggested here with the case of the friend who habitually forgets to repay money which he has borrowed from you: in such circumstances even the most scrupulous might take the view that it would be legitimate to keep quiet, if on one occasion his forgetting took the form of repaying a debt twice over. But the presumption that the revenue authorities themselves expect to cheat and be cheated carries implications as to standards of public honesty which are worth pondering. Or is it just a case of what the psychologists call projection?

Into many minor dishonesties against public authorities there enters, indeed, a peculiar pride. I know people who in larger matters live up to a very high standard of social duty, but always make a point of using again a postage stamp which has escaped the cancellation mark in coming through the post; and this is not because their economic position is such that a penny or two saved is a matter of any consequence. Some small tricks with railway tickets also fall into the same class. There is a sense of achievement in these little frauds, a satisfaction in victory in a battle of wits in which the other party is felt to have the greater initial advantage. The source of this pride lies in the assumption that the normal relationship of the parties is one of combat, not co-operation. In ordinary personal relationships the presumption is just the opposite. One would not take a stamp from somebody else's desk in his absence, unless it was known that the owner would expect and approve such an action, in which case nobody would think himself particularly clever for taking it.

In these matters language is, as often, a significant index of social attitude. Throughout this article I have deliberately used terms like "stealing" and "cheating" to describe the peculations of public and private relations alike; but it is the former for which popular speech is most ready to coin euphemistic synonyms. One "scrounges" or "wins" primarily from public bodies or corporate persons, not from private individuals.

Whether the motive is one of simple indifference or (more or less playful) opposition, it is of some significance to consider what are the limits of its range. In general this seems to be a question of the width of moral horizons; and these differ notably with different people, perhaps with different social classes, although, without such a scientific inquiry which, as I have already suggested, is hardly practicable, one can make only guesses about this. The narrowest horizon embraces only one's immediate circle of friends and acquaintances: after all, even honour among thieves is proverbial. Civilized life would hardly be possible if most of us were not morally more long-sighted than this. But it is possible, and indeed common, for moral responsibility to reach much further than this, without attaining the wide range which the successful socialist state must eventually demand. One standard, which appears to be fairly general, keeps private and public codes of honesty in step just so far as they relate to persons who can be named or at least identified, but allows them to diverge thereafter, the public code sometimes coming to a dead stop at this point.

The principle holds all along the line. It is morally easier to steal an umbrella left behind if you have not seen the passenger who left it. It is easier to steal soldiers' blankets from a depot than a blanket from a soldier. Again, if a shop assistant makes a mistake in change, the reason for pointing this out is often said to be the fact that, otherwise, she would have to make the loss good herself. Indeed, the influence of personal relationships on public honesty is strong enough to be sometimes quite irrational. A passenger is more inclined to get off a bus without paying the fare if the conductor is disagreeable than if he is generally affable. The anonymity of the corporate body is a better cloak for the public's attempts to defraud it than for the shortcomings of its own agents towards that public: as witness the passenger who was heard to assert that, *because* he had been given two farthings in place of sixpences in change in the dark on another bus "I must somehow get a shilling off the company."

Anonymity itself is indeed merely one aspect of remoteness. The observant will find other kinds of remoteness which affect standards of honesty. For instance: it is at least in some cases easier to be dishonest about raw materials than about finished articles, which have a more personal quality. One contributor has suggested that if you are knitting for the Red Cross it would be shocking to help yourself to any of the garments made; but you might be inclined to take a different view of occasionally converting a little of the wool supplied to your own use, *especially if you had had it in stock a long time*.

The curious thing about these codes is that, although they clearly govern a wide range of behaviour, they are generally unquotable in self-defence. Ordinarily, the man who occasionally defrauds the railway or pilfers from public stores to which he has access will, if challenged (and I am referring here to friendly discussion, not to legal proceedings into which different considerations enter), either frankly admit that no justification can be offered, or suggest that it is the fact that the losses are trivial to the loser which mitigates the offence. Naturally this is a particularly tempting line for those who are themselves short of money. "If I can avoid paying my fare without being found out, I do so, because they can afford it better than I can." This defence is, however, a rationalization, for, in the ordinary case, the resistance to stealing even a few shillings from a known person who is well enough off not to suffer noticeably from such a loss is much stronger. And it is not just that the risk of detection is generally greater, or thought to be greater, in thefts from individuals. If it comes to a conviction, there are few who would not rather be found guilty of avoiding a railway fare than of theft from even a well-to-do neighbour.

Sometimes, however, other influences are at work besides this factor of remoteness. Private standards of judgment as to the reasonableness or unreasonableness of charges or regulations may be used to justify some, while they condemn other, evasions. For instance: to use a season ticket between two points by a route for which it is not valid is generally thought to be much less dishonest than to attempt to use the ticket for a longer distance than that for which it is issued, on the ground that if you have paid for the right to travel from A to B it is not the railway's business to dictate by which way you should go. Similarly, people have little compunction about trying to break their journeys on through tickets; and perhaps the widespread practice of trying to defraud the customs is evidence of the prevalence of Free Trade opinions. Sometimes, however, the standard of private reasonableness comes into conflict with the code which demands strict honesty towards persons. A customer who feels that he has been overcharged is less likely than one who thinks he has paid a fair price to point out a mistake in change in his own favour, even though he knows that the shop assistant will have to make up the loss herself.

With the introduction of rationing, old codes have to be adapted, or new ones invented, for dealing in the new coinage of coupons, points and so forth. Here a number of interesting points emerge. First and foremost, rationing has made the well-to-do feel for the first time the normal and chronic temptations of the poor. Since rations are usually equal for all, and generally well below the normal consumption of the relatively prosperous, certain dishonesties now become attractive to those who could afford to take a very high moral line before. If you are not very short of money it is no great hardship to call a Post Office clerk's attention to the fact that she has given you five 2½ d. stamps instead of four: it is not so easy to do the same if you have inadvertently been given twopence halfpenny worth of butter (which is a whole week's ration) over your share; or to refrain from buying the ration a second time if the shop has for some reason forgotten to mark your book; or to keep quiet if too few points are cut out when you are buying "pointed" goods. There are those who confess that in such cases the strength of the temptation prevails, though they would be strictly honourable over any mistake in money. Moreover, there is another reason which may weaken the conscience on these occasions. A great part of the English public is brought up with a peculiar sense of the sanctity of money: a child might be forgiven for stealing sweets from a counter, but actually to take money from a till marks him as a real thief. Since we mostly have not learned to think of points and coupons as money, the same associations are not evoked by them, and there are correspondingly less powerful resistances to overcome.

As against all this, however, there is one extremely strong pull the other way: that is the very firm and widespread public conviction that rationing is both necessary and, on the whole, fair, and that in consequence it is much more anti-social to be unscrupulous about rations than to be careless to your own advantage about money. One might think nothing of acquiring or using a stamp illegitimately, or even take a certain pride in doing so; but two ounces of butter (for the same money value) would be a different matter—quite outside the pale. Where this feeling is strong, it will triumph over the limited horizons which, as we have seen, are apt to restrict monetary honesty. Under this code even the rights of the community, of the unknown, command respect; for cheating about rations does not ordinarily deprive any known and nameable person of anything. This notable advance on widely prevailing standards of financial honesty is significant and encouraging, though it is not so certain that the differentiation between rations and money is equally logical. Actually, on any *one* occasion on which any *one* person uses an opportunity to get more than his share of rationed goods, it is fairly certain that no other person is actually deprived: the shops have a margin for visitors and emergencies which will cover occasional mistakes as well. Nor does it get us any further to say that, if large numbers cheat habitually, the system would break down and others would have to go short. For in the first place there are adequate safeguards to prevent this, so that the hypothesis is unreal: and, in the second place, exactly the same is true of financial dishonesty. Indeed, it has already been suggested (as a *defence* of cheating!) that we do in fact suffer from one another's dishonesties towards the income tax, rates being higher than they need be if complete integrity were the rule.

The higher sense of social responsibility about rations is, I think, itself partly the obverse of the greater strength of the temptation. Whatever your income, you would feel acutely the loss of any of your own rations: and therefore you also feel acutely how wrong it would be to help yourself to the portions intended for others. But the real root of the matter is surely the wholehearted acceptance of the purpose of the rationing laws. The limitation on consumption is consciously recognized as necessary to the war effort, and acceptance of the share-and-share-alike principle is equally conscious and popular. What is the reason why we do not feel the same about the taxes? They, too, impose restrictions on consumption that are necessary for the war and its aftermath; and they represent the government's interpretation of an equitable, though not of course, an equal, distribution of burdens. Is it that we reject this concept of equity? Or is it just that taxation, unlike rationing, has too long been used for purposes upon the merits of which a democracy may legitimately disagree? If taxation had only been invented as a war weapon, should we have felt the same about both taxes and rations?

While new responses have been evoked by the new situation created by rationing, these in their turn interact with traditional attitudes transferred from the field of financial obligations and temptations. Once more the personal factor has a significant part to play. The fact that the loss cannot fall upon the shop assistant is one of the reasons why it is easier to take advantage of mistakes in rations or points, than of slips about money. I have an extreme case of this from X, who records that on one occasion when her grocer accidentally gave her double rations she was about to go off with the booty when she realized that she had only been charged in money for the legitimate amount; she, *therefore,* pointed out the error, lest the assistant should have to make up the deficit on the money accounts. I have met also other refinements, based upon the same principle. Some people's moral horizons extend beyond the shop assistant to the shop, but come to an end there. The more knowledgeable of these will take advantage of mistakes over their soap ration, but not over points, on the ground that points are cut out of the ration book and must be surrendered by the shop for goods sold. If the retailer takes too few from a customer, he will be short; whereas, since the soap ration is merely crossed off, the shopkeeper cannot possibly be asked for evidence of sales to customers, or lose by his failure to mark a particular book.

Again, private standards of reasonableness make their mark on codes. Some of the regulations, especially those relating to clothing, appear rather silly: at least the reason for them is not generally understood. Such is the rule which forbids the offer of loose coupons in a shop, but permits the same coupons to be dropped, addressed to the same shop, into a pillar-box at the door. Observance of this rule is, I think, almost entirely maintained by fear of detection. It seems rather absurd, also, that while the use of another person's clothing book (outside a not very well defined family circle) is apparently illegal, shops may display rationed goods labelled as "attractive gifts," without any prevarication at all. On this issue, the Ministry of Food has adopted a more liberal attitude than the Board of Trade in frankly conceding to those who wish to do so the right to give away their rations. The right to give, however, almost necessarily implies the right to barter; for if A may give some of his rations to B, B in his turn can hardly be prevented from giving some of his to A. And the right to barter immediately suggests the right to sell for money. Here divergent standards make their appearance. In general, there is, I think, a tendency to be more lax about illegal transactions in clothing coupons than over parallel offences against the food rationing laws. This distinction presumably derives from a sense that the rationing of clothes is a less socially urgent matter than the strictly equalitarian distribution of foods; support for the *purpose* of the restriction is relatively lukewarm. Indeed, I have heard a considered defence of the illegal purchase of clothing coupons from those who would firmly condemn the sale of food rations or points. The logical arguments used were, however, in principle, equally applicable, though the user would not himself apply them, in either case. If A wants 5s. towards the purchase of such unrationed goods as salmon, beer, cocoa, or a day in the country, more than he wants a title to buy clothes, and B wants stockings more than she wants five shillings, it is arguable that the sale of some of A's clothing coupons to B would be to their mutual advantage. But if this argument is good, may it not also be used in the case in which A's desire for money with which to buy unrationed goods exceeds his desire for butter or milk or cheese, while B's preferences are exactly opposite? I am not, of course, here concerned with the merits of the principle which forbids the sale of titles to rations: the point is that there are people who will accept this standard in some cases and reject it in others. These examples are, however, more tricky than those previously quoted, for illegal transactions in coupons (though apparently widespread) are fraught with risks that are much greater and plainer than those attaching to tacit acceptance of the benefit of genuine mistakes. People who regard such transactions as socially justified will therefore refrain from taking part in them for fear of the consequences; and we are thus driven off the solid evidence of behaviour on to the slippery ground of verbal opinions.

I will add only one further example of a sophisticated defence of dishonesty in regard to clothes rationing. A person who accidentally found a book which contained unused coupons, but on which no owner's name had been entered, excused converting them to his own use on the ground that this could neither deprive any other person, nor divert resources from the war effort to the manufacture of unnecessary clothing. The rightful owner's position was unaffected, whatever happened, since there was no clue by which he could be traced. His book was irretrievably lost anyway, and he might or might not be successful in a claim for replacement; but if the claim was successful, it was improbable that the Board of Trade would be sufficiently well informed to feel obliged to make a corresponding increase in production! The action, it was admitted, was illegal and properly prohibited by law: it was morally indefensible on the ground that it was an infringement of regulations admittedly designed for the common good. It was a plain case of stealing by finding, but apparently caused no injury to anybody or anything except the moral standards of the person responsible for it. There is, however, one subtle difference between stealing an (unnamed) ration book by finding and a similar theft of money. A person who loses money in the street is extremely unlikely to be able to recover his loss; but a similar loss of a food ration book can always, and of a clothing-book sometimes, be made good by application for replacement. Conceivably, knowledge of this fact may have affected the standards of the finder.

Some of the implications of this case reappear in certain attitudes towards petrol rationing. In the days when there was (and presumably when there is again) a basic ration, it was illegal for an owner to give or sell coupons which he did not propose to use himself to any other motorist. But I have heard such transfers defended on the ground that, since the total number of coupons issued was limited and could not be increased by this or any other practice, it was immaterial whether any part of the available supply was used by A or by B. This is obviously a rather shaky defence, since if A's coupons were unused, stocks would last longer, and imports could be correspondingly reduced. But be this as it may, it is the implied principle which is interesting. Honesty towards a private person would forbid stealing his coupons: but honesty towards the public was not felt to forbid voluntary redistribution of shares, so long as the community did not have to bear the burden of increased total consumption.

In so far as an approximation of at least the best public to the best private standards of honesty is an essential condition for successful socialism, a special responsibility in these matters may well lie upon socialists: a responsibility both personally to observe, and by any means in their power to foster the general observance by others, of the standards which a socialist state will necessarily demand. Here, as so often, no doubt half the battle is to recognize that the job has to be done; and to give at least as much attention to this barrier to social progress as to others which are readier material for rhetoric on the one hand, or subtle intellectual analysis on the other. Unhappily, from one point of view the circumstances are particularly inopportune. The greater part of a whole generation has spent anything up to six years in service in the Forces; and this is, by general consent, hardly the environment in which high standards of precise public honesty thrive most profusely. It is significant how prominent in Service slang are the politer synonyms for stealing and cheating, if indeed they do not commonly have their origin there. There will be real leeway to make up here, and socialists might well bestir themselves about it, for, the magnificent virtues of the battlefield notwithstanding, army habits are hardly the ideal foundation for the civic character of a socialist people.

Nevertheless, it is astonishing how standards change; and the example of the Civil Service may be quoted here to our encouragement. The financial vagaries of Mr. Pepys and his colleagues are now so remote from reality as to rank as sheer entertainment. Hardly less comic, but much more recent, are the Civil Servants who at the end of the eighteenth century could only afford to retire, if they could nominate to their posts successors willing to pay anything up to half-salary as a life-pension to these patrons and predecessors. In the past century we have well and truly learned the lesson that the road to socialism, or indeed to social reform, is blocked at an early stage if Civil Servants are recruited by patronage and supplement their incomes by bribes. The task of the next generation is perhaps to teach a somewhat similar lesson, not to our servants, but to ourselves. A certain section of upper middle class Victorian society did, I think, succeed in inculcating into their offspring standards of private and public integrity which were as near synchronizing as any have ever been. Things move faster now. What those few could do by family tradition, intelligent public education (intelligent, that is, in both purpose and method) could surely achieve for the much larger numbers now concerned.

It is clear enough that the limitations of moral horizons, and the disproportionate influence of direct personal contacts, are the most serious obstacles. This is, of course, only one facet (and happily one of the least formidable) of a hydra-headed problem, of what to the democratically-minded is the most fundamental, and the most intractable of all the social problems of our time—the problem of the growing gap between the range of mutual dependence, and the limits of ordinary personal experience. Technical invention, which is so often credited with unifying the world, is responsible less for unification than for widening that gap. In the world of aeroplanes and radio, thousands even of Londoners never cross the boundaries of their metropolitan boroughs for weeks at a time. They thought Mr. Chamberlain was right to refer to Czechoslovakia as a remote and unknown country in 1938, although he had flown nearly there and back in a matter of hours. If they have since suffered bitterly enough for the limitation of their vision, the hard fact remains that in 1945 Czechoslovakia is no nearer to the people of, say, Fulham than it was in 1938, nor are they appreciably more knowledgeable about it. No one supposes that any individual who is particularly scrupulous about his income-tax is necessarily also particularly sensitive to the fate of the Czechs or the Chinese. But it is not fanciful to suggest that there is a common element in both attitudes.

~~~~~~

3. Power and Slavery*

JACOB KLATZKIN

~~~~~~

Some say: Power is the only reality. Hence, all moral laws that are intended for the protection of the weak create unreal and imaginary values.

However, if we examine the character of dominant power, we discover that often it is itself a mythical thing, owing its existence to imagination. In essence, it is a psychological phenomenon; all the reality it has is illusory in character.

*From Jacob Klatzkin, *In Praise of Wisdom* (L. B. Fischer, 1943). By permission.

We see one person ruling a people, dictating to an entire nation. Multitudes of human beings serve him with fear. Whom do they fear? In actual power the slaves are immeasurably superior to their master. But each slave sees himself as an individual against his fellow-slaves. If they are impelled to rebel, they are afraid of each other. Sometimes one of them does rebel; then his fellows are forced to punish that one, though in their hearts they wish or scheme to do as he has done.

It is not the ruler whom they fear, but the host of slaves who do his bidding. In other words, they fear themselves. Their weakness is a fiction, an error, a slave's error.

The ruler derives his power from the fact that he adds the power of others to his own. He does this through obliterating from the consciousness of his slaves the fact of their common interests. The multitude sees itself as individuals opposed to each other. Each enslaved creature regards himself as enslaved by the community of his fellow-slaves. It is through this common error, the error of many, that the power of one is upheld.

The many come back into their proper power the moment they see through this secret of mutual fear. The abolition of error in the hearts of slaves marks the end of the fictitious power of tyranny.

The emancipation of slaves is, first of all, their liberation from this small error. All great revolutions are really the correction of an error, a trifling error in the minds of the enslaved.

4. Toleration and Cowardice *

JOSIAH C. WEDGWOOD

SIR,—The Lord Chancellor writes to tell me that I am intolerant. Lord Macmillan, whom I admire so much, tells the whole British people the virtues of toleration. And now the Fascist chorus join in!

"Britons! Mind your own business!" is the Mosley slogan. We who smashed the slave trade and freed the slaves are now to be tolerant and put expediency before justice. Gladstone, denouncing King Bomba's Neapolitan prisons, or Bulgarian and Armenian atrocities, was immorally intolerant. Palmerston, jeering at Marshal Haynau's Austria and welcoming Kossuth, should have held his tongue. Let pogroms in Poland go; let Scottsboro flour-

* *The Sunday Times* (London, August 18, 1937). By permission.

ish; silence about Dreyfus and Ferrer, about Matteotti and concentration camps. "Judgment Day" should be banned by the censor. It is not safe—let us be tolerant!

Parliament stopped the Tsar coming to England before the war, and Mannerheim since. Now we are to welcome Goering and make a "gentleman's" agreement with Mussolini by sacrificing Abyssinia and dropping the mandate for Palestine. We are to tolerate cruelty, injustice and tyranny, as long as it is abroad, because it is wrong to be intolerant and safer to be quiet.

The Catholic Archbishop of Westminster dares to speak of the Spanish insurrection as a crusade. May we not dare to speak of it as a crusade against the poor? Must the Deans of Canterbury and of Chichester be silent on their faith? Must liberals be silent on their faith when attacked, because it is wrong to be intolerant? Or, because it is unsafe to speak the truth?

It is not unsafe. Our position was won in the nineteenth century, for we secured the respect of the world by standing up to evil and taking the risks like men. Now we are losing that respect, and so losing our strength and our friends. Nor is it even virtuous to condone tyranny and to be silent about wrongs done to others. Pray tolerate my view that we should not even tolerate error. Toleration is the vice of the old, but I hope to die still utterly intolerant, for I am quite sure that the toleration preached to-day is cowardice. Still, whosoever would seek to save his life shall lose it.

~~~~~~

5. *When Democracy Destroys Itself* *

JULIEN BENDA

~~~~~~

The abuse of the principle of individualism lies in the tendency of the citizen to see himself only as an individual, with the rights which democracy confers upon him, and not as a member of a collective group which imposes upon him duties which are the necessary corollary of those rights. One could also say that this tendency leads the citizen to see in freedom only its material benefits, the personal expansion which it permits, but not the self-denials which it demands of each member of the whole so that the latter may preserve its liberty.

The abuse of the individualist principle is manifest, first of all, in the rela-

* From Julien Benda, *La grande épreuve des démocraties* (Editions de la Maison Française, New York, 1942). By permission. Translated by William Ebenstein.

tions of citizens among themselves. It consists in acting entirely according to one's own pleasure without troubling about the effects on one's fellow citizens. It consists in the shameless scoffing at rules, the purpose of which is precisely the protection of mutual interests. This conduct has been called by a French philosopher (Ernest Seillière) *individualist imperialism;* it makes the common life intolerable for those who, by contrast, respect the rights of others, and leads to hatred of democracy on the part of those who, otherwise, would quite naturally adhere to it.

The relations of the individual to the state are characterized, in the attitude of abused individualism, by the evasion of governmental authority, rendering the latter impotent insofar as it interferes with personal convenience. The majority of those delinquents explain their evasions from due behavior on the ground that the public authority which demands from them obedience "is not worthy of it." One has the feeling that such persons would obey authorities no more if they held them worthy of respect, and that their law is to resist authority, *regardless of its character*. Needless to say, the adoption of this outlook by citizens of a state leads it to straight ruination on the day in which it has to defend itself. In this way, the abuse of individualism has only to wait for the nation being at war to assure its disintegration.

The exaltation of the family spirit is often advocated as a remedy for the anti-national individualism of the individual. But this overlooks the possible selfishness of the family. It comes out, for example, when the public treasury is defrauded in order to protect the family estate, or when one hides one's children from military service in wartime. It may also be said that the egotism of the family is even more dangerous insofar as it is glorified whereas personal selfishness is ignominious.

Some people insist that the individualism which refuses the vital sacrifices for the nation is inscribed in the nature of man, in his organic egotism, and that democracy, therefore, fatally contains it. These learned persons seem to forget, to mention only the modern period, Switzerland of the fifteenth century, the Netherlands of the seventeenth, with their acceptance of personal sufferings for the independence of the whole: they seem to forget England of 1914 and 1939, the United States of 1917, the members of which knew, perhaps after too much patient endurance, how to decree the ordeals which the welfare of the nation, occasionally only its honor, required.

Under the democratic regime, the individual conceives life to be in some way happy, or, at least, potentially happy. Such a mode of living appears to him as the norm, and therefore war, with its privations, seems to him the end of an ordered world, especially since it means to him a very cruel break with his normal life. This distinguishes him profoundly from the citizen of a military state: being continually in a sort of continuous state of war, the latter knows already in peace-time the essential conditions which will be imposed upon him in time of war. The citizen of a democracy possesses, in this, a privilege which results in his inclination to desire peace regardless of its cost, even if that desire goes against the security of the nation. The menaced democracies must triumph over this instinct, and only if they win through this ordeal, will they survive. They must deserve the honor conferred by Pericles upon an ancient democracy some twenty centuries ago, when the great patriot said in his funeral address in honor of his fellow-citizens fallen for their state: "Those have a right to the palm of courage who, knowing better than others the blessings of peace, did not refuse the sufferings of war."

Another road by which individualism can lead straight to the destruction of the collectivity, is to permit citizens to struggle against each other in the name of clan or party. It is evident that if citizens are unable to restrain themselves from such actions at the very hour at which a predatory foreign power thrusts itself upon the nation, the latter will be certain to perish, at least as a free society. And I say nothing of the case of a party which opens the gates of the nation to that power, so that it annihilates the opposing party, and which hates the latter more than the alien invader.

The capacity of citizens in a democracy to put their class interests above those of the nation appears in another fact: *to be ruled, in matters of foreign policy, solely by considerations of domestic policies.* Those citizens will seek an alliance with this country, or be firm with another, not in accordance with national interests, but because the regimes of those countries seem to serve better their own party interests. Of this, a nation of Western Europe has given a telling example in the last ten years.

According to some, a democratic state must abstain, by reason of its very nature, from any war, whether of defense or conquest, and from any action, and be it of simple dignity, likely to lead to war: in short, it must pursue, in international relations, the policy of *peace at any price.* This is the doctrine of *integral pacifism.*

Those who adhere to this view do not always openly declare themselves. They are embarrassed to admit that they oppose defensive warfare just as much as one of conquest, and therefore claim that what is represented to them as defensive war is in reality offensive, that it is wanted by politicians or industrialists interested in having people kill each other, and that no state harbors any harmful schemes as far as they are concerned. . . . Very often they refuse to accept the logical consequence of their position, which is to consent to being molested by an aggressor from morning to evening to the end of their days without any attempt to resist such aggression. I once asked one of them: "Do you think that the Greeks did well in standing up to

Xerxes rather than become his slaves?" He remained silent, although he was bound to say that they acted wrongly, were he faithful to his belief. Some time ago a citizen of a great democracy publicly proclaimed: "With the policy of our head of government, war will kill one of my four sons!" One could have replied to him that with his policy all four ran the risk of becoming slaves one day. I believe that, as a matter of sentiment, he preferred that possibility; but he would not have dared to admit it, not even to himself.

Others, of course, speak frankly and subscribe to that doctrine, formulated some years ago by certain French socialists: "Servitude rather than war!" Or they follow another doctrine, expressed by other thinkers of the same country: "Nothing justifies, in our eyes, war." Both groups act, by the way, in the same manner.

The error of integral pacifism stems from the belief that the supreme democratic value is *human life,* whereas in reality it is *human freedom,* without which life is worthless. Democracy therefore admits and sanctifies the sacrifice of life in order to safeguard liberty for its children. No one will deny that democracy has proved many times in history that this is its true law. . . . In any case, if the integral pacifists follow their ideas logically, they must condemn the French revolutionaries who consented to shed human blood for the conquest of their liberties, as well as the Americans of the eighteenth century who preferred war to continued enslavement to European masters. Some of these "thinkers" admit, perhaps, this degrading view. But the question then arises how they can still present themselves as democrats.

One would like to have these moralists meditate on a word of a statesman whom they could hardly challenge as lacking in democracy: "If we remain one people, under an efficient government, the period is not far off, when we may defy material injury from external annoyance; when we may take such an attitude as will cause the neutrality, we may at any time resolve upon, to be scrupulously respected; when belligerent nations, under the impossibility of making acquisitions upon us, will not lightly hazard the giving us provocation; when we may choose peace or war, as our interest, guided by justice, shall counsel." (Farewell Address of Washington to the people of the United States, September 17, 1796.) We see that to choose war did not seem to this democrat necessarily incompatible with justice. One may object that war has become different from what it was in 1796. However, the question of principle remains the same.

Is it necessary to state specifically that, to accept war, to resign oneself to war, has nothing to do with *wanting* war, *desiring* war? The integral pacifists practise this confusion daily by accusing as "warmongers" and "spillers of blood" those who admit that the interests of their nation may force war upon it. The misfortune is that this confusion bears fruit with many people. It is certain that a public speaker can rally all the support and crush his adversaries by simply crying: "These people here want war!" The audience does not try to find out whether this war is imposed from abroad, in accordance with national security. Conversely, it does not care to reflect upon the nature of the peace that the pacifists propose, whether it is shameful for the nation and deadly for its future. If political demagoguery consists in seeking popularity by flattering the passions of the people, with complete contempt for national interests, then demagogues have found, in our day, a new form of flattering their cult by crying: "Peace must be saved!"

Democrats who are opposed to intervention in other states base this attitude on the desire to "save the peace." The truth is that with their inaction they encourage the activities of aggressive governments which end up by committing an act which the democrats cannot submit to, and which leads to war. Thus, the failure to act in 1908 led to the war of 1914, and the "pacifists" of the Ethiopian, Rhineland and Austrian issues led to the war of 1939.

By the very essence of its existence democracy implies intervention in a foreign state if its head violates justice in the relations with his own people. He who mocks at the Rights of Man within his own nation has no reason to act differently abroad, and it is no coincidence that the rulers of autocratic states are unfailingly those who trouble the peace of the world. If democracy has failed to intervene on many an occasion in these latter times, this failure is not due, as some claim, to the democratic principle (during the nineteenth century such abstention would have been a reason for shame), but solely to the cult of doing nothing—which cult is not inscribed in any of the statutes of democracy. If, as some retort, this abstention is due to the democratic principle of liberty, the answer is, that that principle has never decreed the liberty of evil!

6. *The Failure of Democratic Leadership* *

SALVADOR DE MADARIAGA

Nowhere perhaps is the contrast between principles and assumptions more striking than in what concerns democracy. The principle of democracy rests

* From Salvador de Madariaga, *Anarchy or Hierarchy* (1937). By permission of The Macmillan Company, publishers.

on the vision of a society of enlightened citizens who postpone their lower and more immediate interests to their higher interests, identical with those of the community. Democracy presupposes, therefore, a well-educated mass of citizens, well-educated morally and politically even more so than in other ways. And once the existence of such a mass of citizens is granted, the case for democracy is unanswerable. A truly noble sight. Here is a nation in which every man and woman, whether city merchant, shopkeeper, civil servant, domestic servant, field labourer, landowner, member of the liberal professions, or financier, is fully aware of his duties to the State; adequate agencies of information convey to every individual the objective facts which he must know about the coming budget, current legislation, trade relations, the cost of living, the proposed treaty with a powerful nation; the citizens, high or low, study the facts carefully in order to form an opinion on them, and thus be able to judge of the services to the nation of the particular representative they have helped to choose; when their taxes are asked of them, they scrupulously fill up their schedules and punctually pay the sums claimed on their own showing; while, by frequent gatherings with their co-citizens, they keep alive a constant discussion of the affairs of the State. In such a happy democracy the problems of public life are always solved in peace and according to reason, for public opinion is well-meaning and well-informed, while parliament and government are well chosen and well watched over. Every citizen performs his duties to the full and claims no more than his strict rights. Education prepares the co-operation of the coming citizens under the best auspices. Defence is adequate, and never seeks either foreign aggression or internal tyranny. Foreign affairs are conducted with cordial dignity. All is well in the best of worlds.

But what has that to do with democracy "as she is lived"? That such an Arcadia may be in front of us, that we aim at it, is that a reason for assuming that the methods of government which would be possible under it can be applied in our day? The confusion between democracy as a goal and democracy as a method is one of the most tragic mistakes of our times. It is, of course, but natural that government *by* the people should have been fought for and obtained as the only guarantee of government *for* the people. But if and when experience has shown that government *by* the people means not only a bad government and a bad guarantee of government *for* the people, but also a road leading astray from the true way towards government *by* the people, what is there left to say for it? The fact is that not one of the assumptions of the democratic principle resists the wear and tear of daily political life; that the average inhabitant is a bad citizen, unable to see in the collective interest his own higher interest, ill-formed, caught in a mesh of prejudices of class or of religious or political creed, selfish, though at times capable of sacrifice, sluggish, though at times capable of sudden flares of political enthusiasm, usually due to partisanship, hardly ever to citizenship.

In these conditions the principle of democracy applied in all its implications leads to the very negation of what it seeks to attain. The interests of the community are lost in the dust of personal and party strife, and would-be democracy remains for ever in sight of the promised land, for ever unable to attain it precisely because, in its impatience, it has mistaken the road for the end of the journey.

Behind this misconception there lurks a deeper one. Democracy rests on the idea of the sovereignty of the people. But what is the people? In the eyes of the theorists, who have reflected upon it, it is the nation organized for collective life, with an adequate distribution of labour and responsibility amongst its several institutions. In the eyes of the average man "the people," in the phrase "the sovereignty of the people," means 15 million votes against 14 million. The difference is bound to appeal to the thoughtful as a political problem of the utmost gravity.

Of all the ways and practices of liberal democracies, that which has been the most effective in bringing them to their present position of discredit is the failure of leaders actually to lead. Despite appearances, liberal democracies are dependent on leadership even more so perhaps than other more authoritarian forms of government; for, in authoritarian systems, the springs of authority are more firmly established at all the levels of the political organization, while, in liberal democracies, their natural tendency to weaken the springs of political authority must be counterbalanced by a higher level of personal and moral authority on the part of their leaders. Now, liberal-democratic leaders can hardly be said to have shown the courage and self-control which are necessary for the acquisition of moral authority.

At the outset it may be said that, through the operation of the set of the current axioms and postulates on liberty, equality, democracy, capitalism, and labour which we have endeavoured to analyse above, liberal-democratic leaders have seldom had a sufficiently clear perception of the organic nature of the State and, even when they have had it, they have often lacked the courage to say so and to act accordingly. Steeped in the prejudices of the day, they have accepted in all its disastrous implications the statistical conception of democracy, i.e. the view that numbers of votes, no matter by whom, how, or on what occasion given, decide the issues before the community.

This numerical or *statistical* conception of the State has had for its initial effect a total reversal of the current of power, through a literal interpretation of the doctrine of the sovereignty of the people. Leaving comfortably asleep on their library shelves all that the best authors have to say on this subject, all their nicely balanced *buts* and *notwithstandings,* politicians go before their electorates and loudly proclaim them sovereign. To them they submit the most abstruse problems of finance, the most delicate questions of foreign policy or of national defence; or else, keeping a discreet silence on these, the real issues, they catch their vote and the delgation of sovereignty which it implies by appealing to their passions, their petty interests, or their taste for drink. Thus a competition downwards becomes the law of political life, and thoughts on government have to be gauged to the minimum intellectual size of the electorate.

This observation holds equally good when from the sphere of political action we pass to that of political thought. Nothing is more striking than the gravitation of intellectuals towards one or other of the two poles of attraction which, between them, dominate the century—either they become servants of capitalism or servants of labour. The phenomenon is more striking with the intellectual servants of labour. Capitalism, after all, in so far as it claims free individual initiative, would seem to be more akin to the individualistic character of the intellectual; there is a *prima facie* similarity of tendency between capitalism and intellectualism. Capitalistic enterprise is not unlike intellectual creation, and it may be that they are but different forms of the same energy. At any rate, many are the capitalists in whom the urge forward is due, not to any material ambition, but to a creative impulse. Nevertheless, the obvious evils of unfettered capitalism in the nineteenth, and perhaps even more so in the twentieth century should have led intellectual leaders to a more cautious and critical attitude with regard to capitalism. As for social-istic-minded intellectuals, if their initial impulse may be explained as a gen-erous and human protest against the thraldom to which capitalism had reduced the working classes, it is hardly possible to approve whole-heartedly their surrender of all the duties and dignity of mental leadership, their acceptance of the utterly inadequate doctrine of class struggle, their dema-gogic flattery of the power, importance and virtues of the working classes, and their passive acquiescence, and even active collaboration, in the contempt for intellectual work which is a subconscious but only too real and active a feeling among the masses.

Few are those among intellectuals who have known how to remain free critics of both socialism and capitalism; who, convinced that classical capi-talism has had its historical day and must give place to other forms of social and industrial life, are nevertheless aware of the incapacity of the working classes to provide the adequate solution for this delicate problem, not merely because they are not competent enough, but because they are not objective enough, not sufficiently able to disentangle the interest of the nation from their own class interest.

The failure of intellectual and political leaders has been, in part, the inevitable result of the liberal democratic ferments and misconceptions which typify collective life in the nineteenth and twentieth centuries; but it can also be traced to the corrupting effect of power in an epoch of wealth and prosperity during which, moreover, the traditional springs of ethics had given way while new ones had not, have not yet, been evolved. The inherent immorality of our age need not be considered as particularly worse than that of other periods of history; but the enormous expansion of wealth, which is a specific feature of the industrial era, no doubt developed the appetite and capacity for enjoyment in all classes, particularly in the leading ones, with the obvious result that leaders lost much of their moral authority by becoming the prey of power-lust, for the sake of the other pleasures which go with power.

The collapse of democratic institutions which threatens the world will, to a great extent, be due to the cowardliness of leaders, in itself a consequence of their feeling of their own failure as leaders. A leader, conscious of his own value from the point of view both of ethics and of competence, dares lead, he dares precede and form public opinion. But our democratic leaders have gloried in the idea that they have an ear to the ground. Mr. Coolidge went so far as to assert with the blunt frankness which characterized him, that a President who would imagine that he had the right to precede and lead, instead of following, public opinion would be a traitor to American institutions. Far from me to suggest that the upright and taciturn New Englander was corrupt; but when Calvin Coolidge uttered that thought he was, as he so often was, the passive mouthpiece of a state of opinion current in the leading classes, and that state of opinion came to be formed in them by the general conviction of their unworthiness, a conviction arrived at by the rulers themselves, who, of course, had their reasons for so acquiescing in the general verdict. Now, though inequality is at the basis of all reasonable organizations of collective life, without which specialization and hierarchy are unthinkable, the principle of equality, which is antagonistic to it, must also be satisfied, and this principle demands that inequality should be continuously justified by competence and merit. A true democracy must exact from its leaders an ever renewed proof of their capacity to lead. Unfortunately, our liberal-democratic leaders have not always been able to provide such a proof, and, what is worse, they have often thought that they would be excused from producing it by giving up their right and their duty to lead.

The consequences of this social phenomenon could hardly be exaggerated. We know that the axioms and postulates on which liberal democracies have lived for a century have been evolved with an almost complete disregard for the all-important role of hierarchy. To such natural tendencies the moral bankruptcy of leaders came to give a formidable impetus. Attacked both from below and from above, the pyramid of social and political authority crumbles down rapidly. This process of disintegration is one of the diseases which threatens to destroy altogether the liberal-democratic system in the nations which still remain faithful to it.

7. The Triple Yoke *

SIMON BOLIVAR

The people of America having been held under the triple yoke of ignorance, tyranny and vice, have not been in a position to acquire either knowledge, power or virtue. Disciples of such pernicious masters, the lessons we have received and the examples we have studied, are most destructive. We have been governed more by deception than by force, and we have been degraded more by vice than by superstition. Slavery is the offspring of Darkness; an ignorant people is a blind tool, turned to its own destruction; ambition and intrigue exploit the credulity and inexperience of men foreign to all political, economical or civil knowledge; mere illusions are accepted as reality, license is taken for liberty, treachery for patriotism, revenge for justice. Even as a sturdy blind man who, relying on the feeling of his own strength, walks along with the assurance of the most wideawake man and, striking against all kinds of obstacles, can not steady his steps.

A perverted people, should it attain its liberty, is bound to lose this very soon, because it would be useless to try to impress upon such people that happiness lies in the practice of righteousness; that the reign of law is more powerful than the reign of tyrants, who are more inflexible, and all ought to submit to the wholesome severity of the law; that good morals, and not force, are the pillars of the law and that the exercise of justice is the exercise of liberty. Thus, Legislators, your task is the more laborious because you are to deal with men misled by the illusions of error, and by civil incentives. Liberty, says Rousseau, is a succulent food, but difficult to digest. Our feeble fellow-citizens will have to strengthen their mind much before they will be ready to assimilate such wholesome nourishment. Their limbs made numb by their fetters, their eyesight weakened in the darkness of their dungeons and their forces wasted away through their foul servitude, will they be capable of marching with a firm step towards the august temple of Liberty? Will they be capable of coming close to it, and admiring the light it sheds, and of breathing freely its pure air?

Consider well your decision, Legislators. Do not forget that you are about to lay the foundations of a new people, which may some day rise to the heights that Nature has marked out for it, provided you make those foundations proportionate to the lofty place which that people is to fill. If your

* From an address by Simon Bolivar to the Congress of Venezuela (1819).

selection be not made under the guidance of the Guardian Angel of Venezuela, who must inspire you with wisdom to choose the nature and form of government that you are to adopt for the welfare of the people; if you should fail in this, I warn you, the end of our venture would be slavery.

The annals of past ages display before you thousands of governments. Recall to mind the nations which have shone most highly on the earth and you will be grieved to see that almost the entire world has been, and still is, a victim of bad government. You will find many systems of governing men, but all are calculated to oppress them, and if the habit of seeing the human race, led by shepherds of peoples, did not dull the horror of such a revolting sight, we would be astonished to see our social species grazing on the surface of the globe, even as lowly herds destined to feed their cruel drivers.

Nature, in truth, endows us at birth with the instinctive desire for liberty; but whether because of negligence, or because of an inclination inherent in humanity, it remains still under the bonds imposed on it. And as we see it in such a state of debasement we seem to have reason to be persuaded that the majority of men hold as a truth the humiliating principle that it is harder to maintain the balance of liberty than to endure the weight of tyranny. Would to God that this principle, contrary to the morals of Nature, were false! Would to God that this principle were not sanctioned by the indolence of man as regards his most sacred rights!

Many ancient and modern nations have cast off oppression; but those which have been able to enjoy a few precious moments of liberty are most rare, as they soon relapsed into their old political vices; because it is the people more often than the government, that bring on tyranny. The habit of suffering domination makes them insensible to the charms of honor and national prosperity, and leads them to look with indolence upon the bliss of living in the midst of liberty, under the protection of laws framed by their own free will. The history of the world proclaims this awful truth!

Only democracy, in my opinion, is susceptible of absolute freedom. But where is there a democratic government that has united at the same time power, prosperity and permanence? Have we not seen, on the contrary, aristocracy, monarchy, rearing great and powerful empires for centuries and centuries? What government is there older than that of China? What republic has exceeded in duration that of Sparta, that of Venice? The Roman Empire, did it not conquer the world? Does not France count fourteen centuries of monarchy? Who is greater than England? These nations, however, have been, or still are, aristocracies and monarchies.

Notwithstanding such bitter reflections, I am filled with unbounded joy because of the great strides made by our republic since entering upon its noble career. Loving that which is most useful, animated by what is most just and aspiring to what is most perfect, Venezuela in separating from the Spanish Nation has recovered her independence, her freedom, her equality, her national sovereignty. In becoming a democratic republic, she proscribed monarchy, distinctions, nobility, franchises and privileges; she declared the rights of man, the liberty of action, of thought, of speech, of writing. These preeminently liberal acts will never be sufficiently admired for the sincerity by which they are inspired. The first Congress of Venezuela has impressed upon the annals of our legislation with indelible characters the majesty of the people, so fittingly expressed in the consummation of the social act best calculated to develop the happiness of a Nation.

8. The Limitations of the Expert*

HAROLD J. LASKI

I.

The day of the plain man has passed. No criticism of democracy is more fashionable in our time than that which lays emphasis upon his incompetence. This is, we are told, a big and complex world, about which we have to find our way at our peril. The plain man is too ignorant and too uninterested to be able to judge the adequacy of the answers suggested to our problems. As in medicine we go to a doctor, or in bridge-building to an engineer, so in matters of social policy we should go to an expert in social questions. He alone, we are told with increasing emphasis, can find his way about the labyrinthine intricacies of modern life. He alone knows how to find the facts and determine what they mean. The plain man is simply obsolete in a world he has never been trained to understand. Either we must trust the making of fundamental decisions to experts, or there will be a breakdown in the machinery of government.

Now much of this scepticism is a natural and justifiable reaction from the facile and romantic optimism of the nineteenth century. Jefferson in America, Bentham in England did too easily assume not only an inherent rightness in the opinions of the multitude but also an instinctive wisdom in its choices. They did tend to think that social problems could be easily understood and that public interest in their solution would be widespread and passionate. From their philosophy was born the dangerous inference that any man, without training in affairs, could hope usefully to control their operation. They did not see that merely to formulate rightly the nature of a

* *Fabian Tract* No. 235 (1931). By permission of Harold J. Laski and The Fabian Society.

social problem is far more difficult than to formulate rightly a problem in physics or chemistry. No one assumes that the plain man is entitled to an opinion about the ether or vitamins or the historicity of the Donation of Constantine. Why should it be assumed that he has competence about the rates of taxation, or the validity of tariff-schedules, or the principles of a penal code? Here, as in the fields of pure and applied science, his well-being, it is argued, depends essentially upon accepting the advice of the disinterested expert. The more elbow-room the latter possesses, the more likely we are to arrive at adequate decisions.

No one, I think, could seriously deny to-day that in fact none of our social problems are capable of wise resolution without formulation of its content by an expert mind. A Congressman at Washington, a Member of Parliament at Westminster cannot hope to understand the policy necessary to a proper understanding of Soviet Russia merely by the light of nature. The facts must be gathered by men who have been trained to a special knowledge of the new Russia, and the possible inferences from those facts must be set out by them. The plain man cannot plan a town, or devise a drainage system, or decide upon the wisdom of compulsory vaccination without aid and knowledge at every turn from men who have specialised in those themes. He will make grave mistakes about them, possibly even fatal mistakes. He will not know what to look for; he may easily miss the significance of what he is told. That the contours of any subject must be defined by the expert before the plain man can see its full significance will, I believe, be obvious to anyone who has reflected upon the social process in the modern world.

II.

But it is one thing to urge the need for expert consultation at every stage in making policy; it is another thing, and a very different thing, to insist that the expert's judgment must be final. For special knowledge and the highly trained mind produce their own limitations which, in the realm of statesmanship, are of decisive importance. *Expertise,* it may be argued, sacrifices the insight of common sense to intensity of experience. It breeds an inability to accept new views from the very depth of its preoccupation with its own conclusions. It too often fails to see round its subject. It sees its results out of perspective by making them the centre of relevance to which all other results must be related. Too often, also, it lacks humility; and this breeds in its possessors a failure in proportion which makes them fail to see the obvious which is before their very noses. It has, also, a certain caste-spirit about it, so that experts tend to neglect all evidence which does not come from those who belong to their own ranks. Above all, perhaps, and this most urgently where human problems are concerned, the expert fails to see that every judgment he makes not purely factual in nature brings with it a scheme of values which has no special validity about it. He tends to confuse the importance of his facts with the importance of what he proposes to do about them.

Each one of these views needs illustration, if we are to see the relation of *expertise* to statesmanship in proper perspective. The expert, I suggest, sacrifices the insight of common sense to the intensity of his experience. No one can read the writings of Mr. F. W. Taylor, the efficiency-engineer, without seeing that his concentration upon the problem of reaching the maximum output of pig-iron per man per day made him come to see the labourer simply as a machine for the production of pig-iron. He forgot the complexities of human nature, the fact that the subject of his experiments had a will of his own whose consent was essential to effective success. Business men prophesied the rapid break-down of the Russian experiment because it had eliminated that profit-making motive which experience had taught them was at the root of Western civilization. But they failed to see that Russia might call into play new motives and new emotions not less powerful, even if different in their operation, from the old. The economic experts of the early nineteenth century were fairly unanimous in insisting that the limitation of the hours of labour must necessarily result in a decrease of prosperity. They lacked the common sense to see that a prohibition upon one avenue of profit would necessarily lead to so intense an exploration of others as to provide a more than adequate compensation for the effort they deplored.

The expert, again, dislikes the appearance of novel views. Here, perhaps, the experience of science is most suggestive since the possibility of proof in this realm avoids the chief difficulties of human material. Everyone knows of the difficulties encountered by Jenner in his effort to convince his medical contemporaries of the importance of vaccination. The Royal Society refused to print one of Joule's most seminal papers. The opposition of men like Sir Richard Owen and Adam Sedgwick to Darwin resembled nothing so much as that of Rome to Galileo. Not even so great a surgeon as Simpson could see merit in Lister's discovery of antiseptic treatment. The opposition to Pasteur among medical men was so vehement that he declared regretfully that he did not know he had so many enemies. Lacroix and Poisson reported to the French Academy of Sciences that Galois' work on the theory of groups, which Cayley later put among the great mathematical achievements of the nineteenth century, was quite unintelligible. Everyone knows how biologists and physicists failed to perceive for long years the significance of Gregor Mendel and Willard Gibbs.

These are instances from realms where, in almost every case, measurable proof of truth was immediately obtainable; and, in each case, novelty of outlook was fatal to a perception of its importance. In social matters, where the problem of measurement is infinitely more difficult, the expert is entitled to far less assurance. He can hardly claim that any of his fundamental questions have been so formulated that he can be sure that the answer is capable of a certainly right interpretation. The student of race, for instance, is wise only if he admits that his knowledge of his subject is mainly a measure of his ignorance of its boundaries. The student of eugenics can do little more than insist that certain hereditary traits, deaf-mutism, for example, or haemophilia, make breeding from the stocks tainted by them undesirable; he cannot tell us what fitness means nor show us how to breed the qualities upon which racial adequacy depends. It would be folly to say that we are destined never to know the laws which govern life; but, equally certainly, it would be folly to argue that our knowledge is sufficient to justify any expert, in any realm of social importance, claiming finality for his outlook.

He too often, also, fails to see his results in their proper perspective. Anyone who examines the conclusions built, for example, upon the use of intelligence tests will see that this is the case. For until we know exactly how much of the ability to answer the questions used as their foundation is related to differentiated home environment, how effectively, that is, the experiment is really pure, they cannot tell us anything. Yet the psychologists who accept their results have built upon them vast and glittering generalisations as, for instance, about the inferior mental quality of the Italian immigrant in America; as though a little common sense would not make us suspect conclusions indicating mental inferiority in the people which produced Dante and Petrarch, Vico and Machiavelli. Generalisations of this kind are merely arrogant; and their failure to see, as experts, the *a priori* dubiety of their results, obviously raises grave issues about their competence to pronounce upon policy.

Vital, too, and dangerous, is the expert's caste-spirit. The inability of doctors to see light from without is notorious; and a reforming lawyer is at least as strange a spectacle as one prepared to welcome criticism of his profession from men who do not practise it. There is, in fact, no expert group which does not tend to deny that truth may possibly be found outside the boundary of its private Pyrenees. Yet, clearly enough, to accept its dicta as final, without examination of their implications, would be to accept grave error as truth in almost every department of social effort. Every expert's conclusion is a philosophy of the second best until it has been examined in terms of a scheme of values not special to the subject matter of which he is an exponent.

Everyone knows, for example, that admirals invariably fail to judge naval policy in adequate terms; and in Great Britain, at any rate, the great military organisers, men like Cardwell and Haldane, have had to pursue their task in face of organised opposition from the professional soldier. The Duke of Wellington was never brought to see the advantage of the breech-loading rifle, and the history of the tank in the last war is largely a history of civilian enterprise the value of which the professional soldier was brought to see only with difficulty.

The expert, in fact, simply by reason of his immersion in a routine, tends to lack flexibility of mind once he approaches the margins of his special theme. He is incapable of rapid adaptation of novel situations. He unduly discounts experience which does not tally with his own. He is hostile to views which are not set out in terms he has been accustomed to handle. No man is so adept at realising difficulties within the field that he knows; but, also, few are so incapable of meeting situations outside that field. Specialism seems to breed a horror of unwonted experiment, a weakness in achieving adaptability, both of which make the expert of dubious value when he is in supreme command of a situation.

This is, perhaps, above all because the expert rarely understands the plain man. What he knows, he knows so thoroughly that he is impatient with men to whom it has to be explained. Because he practises a mystery, he tends to assume that, within his allotted field, men must accept without question the conclusions at which he has arrived. He too often lacks that emollient quality which makes him see that conclusions to which men assent are far better than conclusions which they are bidden, without persuasion, to decline at their peril. Everyone knows how easily human personality becomes a unit in a statistical table for the bureaucrat; and there must be few who have not sometimes sympathised with the poor man's indignation at the social worker. People like Jane Addams, who can retain, amid their labours, a sense of the permanent humanity of the poor are rare enough to become notable figures in contemporary life.

The expert, in fact, tends to develop a certain condescension towards the plain man which goes far towards the invalidation of his *expertise*. Men in India who have become accustomed to the exercise of power, cannot believe, without an imaginative effort of which few of them are capable, that the Indian is entitled to his own ideas of how he should be governed. Civil servants tend easily to think that Members of Parliament or Congress are an ignorant impediment to their labours. Professional historians, who cultivate some minute fragment of an epoch's history, cannot appreciate the superb incursions of a brilliant amateur like Mr. H. G. Wells. It has taken professional economists more than a generation to realise that the trade unions have a contribution to make to the understanding of industrial phenomena without which their own interpretation is painfully incomplete.

There is, in fact, not less in the expert's mind than in that of the plain man what Mr. Justice Holmes has termed an "inarticulate major premise" quite fundamental to his work. I have known an expert in the British Foreign Office whose advice upon China was built upon the assumption that the Chinese have a different human nature from that of the Englishmen; and what was, in fact, an obvious private prejudice was, for him, the equally obvious outcome of a special experience which could not brook contradiction. Judges of the Supreme Court have had no difficulty in making the Fourteenth Amendment the embodiment of the *laissez-faire* philosophy of the nineteenth century; and few of them have realised that they were simply making the law express their unconscious dislike of governmental experiment. The history of trade-union law in England is largely an attempt, of course mainly unconscious, by judicial experts to disguise their dislike of working-men's organisation in terms of a mythology to which the convenient name of "public policy" could be attached. The attitude of the British High Command to the death penalty, of lawyers like Lord Eldon to the relaxation of penal severity, of business men to secrecy in finance, of statesmen to proposals for institutional reconstruction are all revelations of the expert's dislike of abandoning premises which, because he has grown accustomed to them, he tends to equate with the inevitable foundations of truth.

The expert tends, that is to say, to make his subject the measure of life, instead of making life the measure of his subject. The result, only too often, is an inability to discriminate, a confusion of learning with wisdom. "The fixed person for the fixed duties," Professor Whitehead has written, "who in older societies was such a godsend, in the future will be a public danger. In a sense, indeed, the more expert such fixed persons are, the more dangerous they are likely to be. For your great chemist, or doctor, or engineer, or mathematician is not an expert about life; he is precisely an expert in chemistry or medicine, engineering or mathematics. And the more highly expert he is, the more profoundly he is immersed in his routine, the less he is likely to know of the life about him. He cannot afford the time or the energy to give to life what his subject demands from him. He restrains his best intellectual effort within the routine about which he is a specialist. He does not co-ordinate his knowledge of a part with an attempt at wisdom about the whole.

This can be seen from many angles. Lord Kelvin was a great physicist, and his discoveries in cable-laying were of supreme importance to its development; but when he sought to act as a director of a cable-laying company, his complete inability to judge men resulted in serious financial loss. Faraday was obviously one of the half-dozen outstanding physicists of modern times; but in the field of theological belief, he retained convictions which no man of common sense could accept. Mr. Henry Ford is obviously a business man of genius; but, equally obviously, his table talk upon themes outside his special sphere reveals a mentality which is mediocre in the extreme. Charles Babbage rendered immense service to the development of statistical science; but when he came to judge one of Tennyson's most famous poems he missed its beauty through an over-vivid sense of its failure to conform to the revelations of the census returns.

The expert, in short, remains expert upon the condition that he does not seek to co-ordinate his specialism with the total sum of human knowledge. The moment that he seeks that co-ordination he ceases to be an expert. A doctor, a lawyer, an engineer who sought to act in terms of his specialism as President or Prime Minister would inevitably fail; to succeed, he must cease to be an expert. The wisdom that is needed for the direction of affairs is not an expert technic but a balanced equilibrium. It is a knowledge of how to use men, a faculty of judgment about the practicability of principles. It consists not in the possession of specialised knowledge, but in a power to utilise its results at the right moment, and in the right direction.

III.

My point may, perhaps, be made by saying that *expertise* consists in such an analytic comprehension of a special realm of facts that the power to see that realm in the perspective of totality is lost. Such analytic comprehension is purchased at the cost of the kind of wisdom essential to the conduct of affairs. The doctor tends to think of men as patients; the teacher sees them as pupils; the statistician as units in a table. Bankers too often fail to realise that there is humanity even in men who have no cheque-books; Marxian socialists see sinister economic motive in the simplest expressions of the universal appetite for power. To live differently is to think differently; and to live as an expert in a small division of human knowledge is to make its principles commensurate with the ultimate deposit of historic experience. Not in that way does wisdom come.

Because a man is an expert on medieval French history, that does not make him the best judge of the disposition of the Saar Valley in 1919. Because a man is a brilliant prison doctor, that does not make him the person who ought to determine the principles of a penal code. The skill of the great soldier does not entitle him to decide upon the scale of military armament; just as no anthropologist, simply as an anthropologist, would be a fitting governor for a colonial territory peopled by native races. To decide wisely, problems must be looked at from an eminence. Intensity of vision destroys the sense of proportion. There is no illusion quite so fatal to good government as that of the man who makes his expert insight the measure of social need. We do not get progress in naval disarmament when admirals confer. We do not get legal progress from meetings of Bar associations. Congresses of teachers seem rarely to provide the means of educational advance. The knowledge of what can be done with the results obtained in special disciplines seems to require a type of co-ordinating mind to which the expert, as such, is simply irrelevant.

This may be looked at from two points of view. "Political heads of departments are necessary," said Sir William Harcourt, "to tell the civil service what the public will not stand." That is, indeed, an essential picture of the place of the expert in public affairs. He is an invaluable servant and an impossible master. He can explain the consequences of a proposed policy, indicate its wisdom, measure its danger. He can point out possibilities in a proposed line of action. But it is of the essence of public wisdom to take the final initiative out of his hands.

For any political system in which a wide initiative belongs to the expert is bound to develop the vices of bureaucracy. It will lack insight into the movement and temper of the public mind. It will push its private nostrums in disregard of public wants. It will become self-satisfied and self-complacent. It will mistake its technical results for social wisdom, and it will fail to see the limits within which its measures are capable of effective application. For the expert, by definition, lacks contact with the plain man. He not only does not know what the plain man is thinking; he rarely knows how to discover his thoughts—He has dwelt so austerely in his laboratory or his study that the content of the average mind is a closed book to him. He is at a loss how to manipulate the opinions and prejudices which he encounters. He has never learned the art of persuading men into acceptance of a thing they only half understand. He is remote from the substance of their lives. Their interests and hopes and fears have never been the counters with which he has played. He does not realise that, for them, his technical formulae do not carry conviction because they are, as formulae, incapable of translation into terms of popular speech. For the plain man, he is remote, abstract, alien. It is only the juxtaposition of the statesman between the expert and the public which makes specialist conclusions capable of application.

That, indeed, is the statesman's basic task. He represents, at his best, supreme common sense in relation to *expertise*. He indicates the limits of the possible. He measures what can be done in terms of the material at his disposal. A man who has been for long years in public affairs learns the art of handling men so as to utilise their talents without participating in their experience. He discovers how to persuade antagonistic views. He finds how to make decisions without giving reasons for them. He can judge almost by intuition the probable results of giving legislative effect to a principle. He comes to office able to co-ordinate varied aspects of *expertise* into something which looks like a coherent programme. He learns to take risks, to trust to sub-conscious insight instead of remaining dependent upon reasoned analysis. The expert's training is, as a rule, fatal to these habits which are essential to the leadership of a multitude. That is why, for example, the teacher and the scholar are rarely a success in politics. For they have little experience of the need for rapid decision; and their type of mental discipline leads them to consider truth in general rather than the truth of popular discussion. They have not been trained to the business of convincing the plain man, and modern government is impossible to those who do not possess this art.

Nothing, indeed, is more remarkable in a great public department than to watch a really first-rate public man drive his team of expert officials. He knows far less than they do of the affairs of the Department. He has to guess at every stage the validity of their conclusions. On occasion, he must either choose between alternatives which seem equally balanced or decide upon a policy of which his officials disapprove. Not seldom, he must quicken their doubts into certainties, not seldom, also, he must persuade them into paths they have thus far refused to tread. The whole difference between a great Minister and a poor one lies in his ability to utilise his officials as instruments. His success depends upon weaving a policy from the discrete threads of their *expertise*. He must discover certain large principles of policy and employ them in finding the conditions of its successful operation. He must have the power to see things in a big way, to simplify, to co-ordinate, to generalise. Anyone who knows the work of Lord Haldane at the British War Office from 1906 to 1911, or of Mr. Arthur Henderson as Foreign Secretary in the last eighteen months, can understand the relation between the statesman and his expert which makes, and which alone can make, for successful administration.

Its essence, as a relation, is that the ultimate decisions are made by the amateur and not by the specialist. It is that fact which gives them coherence and proportion. A cabinet of experts would never devise a great policy. Either their competing specialisms would clash, if their *expertise* was various in kind, or its perspective would be futile because it was similar. The amateur brings to them the relevance of the outer world and the knowledge of men. He disposes of private idiosyncrasy and technical prejudice. In convincing the non-specialist Minister that a policy propounded is either right or wrong, the expert is already half-way to convincing the public of his plans; and if he fails in that effort to convince, the chances are that his plans are, for the environment he seeks to control, inadequate or mistaken. For politics by its nature is not a philosophy of technical ideals, but an art of the immediately practical. And the statesman is pivotal to its organisation because he acts as the broker of ideas without whom no bridges can be built between the expert and the multitude. It is no accident, but an inherent quality of his character, that the expert distrusts his fellow-specialist when the latter can reach that multitude. For him the gift of popular explanation is a proof of failure in the grasp of the discipline. His intensity of gaze makes him suspect the man who can state the elements of his mystery in general terms. He knows too much of minutiae to be comfortable upon the heights of generalisation.

Nor must we neglect the other aspect of the matter. "The guest," said Aristotle with his homely wisdom, "will judge better of a feast than the cook." However much we may rely upon the expert in formulating the materials for decision, what ultimately matters is the judgment passed upon the results of policy by those who are to live by them. Things done by government must not only appear right to the expert; their consequences must seem right to the plain and average man. And there is no way known of discovering his judgment save by deliberately seeking it. This, after all, is the really final test of government; for, at least over any considerable period, we cannot maintain a social policy which runs counter to the wishes of the multitude.

It is not the least of our dangers that we tend, from our sense of the complexity of affairs, to underestimate both the relevance and the significance of those wishes. We are so impressed by the plain man's ignorance that we tend to think his views may be put aside as unimportant. Not a little of the literature upon the art of government to-day is built upon the supposition that the plain man has no longer any place in social economy. We know, for example, that he does not understand the technicalities of the gold-standard. It is clear that it would be folly to consult him upon matters like the proper area for the generation of electricity supply, or the amount that it is wise for a government to spend in testing the action of pavements under changing temperatures and variations of load. But the inference from a knowledge that the plain man is ignorant of technical detail and, broadly speaking, uninterested in the methods by which its results are attained, is certainly not the conclusion that the expert can be left to make his own decisions.

For the results of the gold standard are written plain in the life of the average man. The consequences of an inefficient electricity supply are apparent to him every day. It is his motorcar which uses the roads, and he makes up his mind about the quality of the road service with which he is provided. Every degree by which he is separated from consultation about decisions is a weakening of the governmental process. Neither goodwill in the expert nor efficiency in the performance of his function ever compensates in a state for failure to elicit the interest of the plain man in what is being done. For the nature of the result is largely unknown save as he reports his judgment upon it; and only as he reports that judgment can the expert determine in what direction his plans must move. Every failure in consultation, moreover, separates the mind of the governors from those who are governed; this is the most fertile source of misunderstanding in the state. It is the real root of the impermanence of autocracies which fail from their inability to plumb the minds of those by whose opinions, ultimately, they must live.

The importance of the plain man's judgment is, in short, the foundation upon which the expert, if he is to be successful, must seek to build. It is out of that judgment, in its massive totality, that every society forms its schemes of values. The limits of possible action in society are always set by that scheme. What can be done is not what the expert thinks ought to be done. What can be done is what the plain man's scheme of values permits him to consider as just. His likes and dislikes, his indifference and his inertia, circumscribe at every stage the possibilities of administration. That is why a great expert like Sir Arthur Salter has always insisted upon the importance of advisory committees in the process of government. He has seen that the more closely the public is related to the work of *expertise,* the more likely is that work to be successful. For the relation of proximity of itself produces conviction. The public learns confidence, on the one hand, and the expert learns proportion on the other. Confidence in government is the secret of stability, and a sense of proportion in the expert is the safeguard against bureaucracy.

At no time in modern history was it more important than now that we should scrutinise the claims of the expert more critically; at no time, also, was it more important that he himself should be sceptical about his claims. Scientific invention has given us a material power of which the possible malignancy is at least as great as its contingent benefits. The danger which confronts us is the quite fatal one that, by the increase of complexity in civilisation, we may come to forget the humanity of men. A mental climate so perverted as this would demonstrate at a stroke the fragility of our social institutions. For it would reveal an abyss between rulers and subjects which no amount of technical ingenuity could bridge. The material power that our experts multiply brings with it no system of values. It can only be given a system related to the lives of ordinary people to the degree that they are associated with its use. To exclude them from a share in its direction is quite certainly to exclude them also from a share in its benefits; for no men have been able in the history of past societies exclusively to exercise its authority without employing it ultimately for their own ends. Government by experts would, however ardent their original zeal for the public welfare, mean after a time government in the interest of experts. Of that the outcome would be either stagnation, on the one hand, or social antagonism, on the other.

IV.

Our business, in the years which lie ahead, is clearly to safeguard ourselves against this prospect. We must ceaselessly remember that no body of experts is wise enough, or good enough, to be charged with the destiny of mankind. Just because they are experts, the whole of life is, for them, in constant danger of being sacrificed to a part; and they are saved from disaster only by the need of deference to the plain man's common sense. It is, I believe, upon the perpetuation of this deference that our safety very largely depends.

But it will be no easy thing to perpetuate it. The expert, to-day, is accustomed to a veneration not very different from that of the priest in primitive societies; for the plain man he, like the priest, exercises a mystery into which the uninitiated cannot enter. To strike a balance between necessary respect and sceptical attack is a difficult task. The experience of the expert is so different, his approach to life so dissimilar, that expert and plain man are often impatient of each other's values. Until we can somehow harmonise them, our feet will be near to the abyss.

Nor must we forget that to attain such harmony immense changes in our social habits will be necessary. We shall have to revolutionise our educational methods. We shall have to reconstruct the whole fabric of our institutions. For the first time, perhaps, in the history of mankind, we shall have, as a civilisation, deliberately to determine what kind of life we desire to live. We must so determine it remembering that the success of our effort will depend upon harnessing to its fortunes the profounder idealism of ordinary men and women. We shall appeal to that idealism only as we give it knowledge and persuade it that the end we seek is one in which it, too, can hope to share.

9. *Democracy and the Expert* *

A. D. LINDSAY

DEMOCRATIC SOCIETY AND DEMOCRATIC GOVERNMENT

The task of the government of a democratic society implies a wisdom and understanding of the complicated life of modern societies very far removed from the simple 'horse sense' which is sufficient for the running of small and simple democracies. It is clear that a modern state can do its job only with a lot of expert help, expert statesmen, expert administrators. We must nowadays go on and say 'expert economists and expert scientists.' Perhaps we must go further and say 'expert sociologists.'

That is clear enough. What is not so clear is where the ordinary plain man comes in. What is the justification of submitting the expert work of all these superior people to the control of the ordinary voter? We recognize that the man in the street cannot, in the strict sense of the word, govern a modern state. The ordinary person has not the knowledge, the judgement, or the skill to deal with the intricate problems which modern government involves. The primitive democracy of a Swiss commune or of a New England township in the eighteenth century was quite different. The things which the community had to get done in those simple societies were within the competence of most members of the community and open to the judgement of

* From A. D. Lindsay, *The Modern Democratic State,* I (Oxford University Press, 1943). By permission.

all. Readers of *Coniston,* that admirable political novel in which the American Winston Churchill describes the corruption of simple New Hampshire democracy by the coming of the boss, will remember the society he depicts— hard-headed, sensible, decent farmers, good judges of men and of horses. The select men whom they elect to govern them are well known to them all. They have nothing to do about which their electors cannot form a sound and shrewd judgement.

To ignore the immense difference between such a society and the society of the modern democratic state is to court disaster. Where are the simple and familiar issues on which shrewd if unlearned men may judge? Where, perhaps it may be asked, in our great urban populations are the hard-headed, shrewd, independent men to judge soundly on any issues?

We all recognize that expert and technical knowledge must come from specialists—that the ordinary man or woman is not capable of judging the detail of legislative proposals. We say that the public decides upon broad issues. That is what the working of modern democracy is supposed to imply. An election makes clear that the public insists, for example, that something pretty drastic must be done about unemployment, or that the United States should support Great Britain by all measures 'short of war,' and so on. One party rather than another gets into power because the public broadly approves of its programme more than the programme of its rivals and judges well of its capacity to carry out its programme. The public is not supposed to have any views as to how that programme should be carried out but it is supposed to have decided that it prefers the main lines of one party's programme to another's.

What does this imply? Does democracy assume that ordinary men and women are better judges on broad issues than experts or than educated people? We can only take this line if we hold that 'broad issues' demand not knowledge or skill or special training but 'common sense' or sound judgement and that 'common sense' is the possession of the ordinary man.

This is the stumbling-stone of democratic theory. On this subject men seem to hold opposing views which cannot be reconciled. Think of the way in which some people talk with conviction of the mob or the herd or the vulgar. Think of the long tradition of denunciation from Thucydides downwards of the folly and fickleness and weakness of the masses. Think, on the other hand, of the continual appreciation in democratic literature of the good sense and sound judgement of the common man—the often expressed conviction that there is something in the 'plain man' or in 'the man in the street' which makes his judgement often more worth while than that of many superior persons.

There must be something to be said for both sides in such a controversy. It is worth while to attempt some disentangling.

Let us begin by noting that there are arguments for democratic control which do not assume that men and women are or ought to be given votes only because of the soundness of their judgement. We may summarize the two arguments in the two statements: 'Only the wearer knows where the shoe pinches' and 'We count heads to save the trouble of breaking them.'

THE 'SHOES PINCHING' ARGUMENT

Let us begin with the argument about shoes pinching. If we start with the statement I have described as the authentic note of democracy, 'The poorest he that is in England has a life to live as the richest he,' if we remember that the end of democratic government is to minister to the common life of society, to remove the disharmonies that trouble it, then clearly a knowledge and understanding of that common life is a large part of the knowledge essential to the statesman. But the common life is the life lived by all members of the society. It cannot be fully known and appreciated from outside. It can only be known by those who live it. Its disharmonies are suffered and felt by individuals. It is their shoes that pinch and they only who can tell where they pinch. No doubt the ordinary voter has the vaguest ideas as to what legislative or administrative reform will stop the pinching of his shoes. That is no more his business and no more within his capacity than it is the ordinary customer's business to make shoes. He may think, and often does think, that his shoes are pinching only because of the gross ignorance or perhaps because of the corrupt and evil intentions of his government; he may think the making of governmental shoes which ease his feet to be a much simpler business than it is; he may listen too easily to charlatans who promise to make the most beautiful shoes for the lowest possible price. But for all that, only he, the ordinary man, can tell whether the shoes pinch and where; and without that knowledge the wisest statesman cannot make good laws. It is sadly instructive to find what a gap there always is between the account even the best administrations give of the effect of their regulations and the account you get from those to whom the regulations apply. The official account tells what ought to happen if men and women behaved and felt as decent respectable officials assume that they think and feel. What is actually happening is often quite different.

The argument about shoes pinching is the argument which justifies adult suffrage. If government needs for its task an understanding of the common life it exists to serve, it must have access to all the aspects of that common life. All classes in society must be able to express their grievances. The qualification for voting is not wisdom or good sense but enough independence of mind to be able to state grievances. This does not seem a difficult qualification, but oppressed people are not always prepared to stand up for themselves or even always to think that there is anything wrong in what happens to them. They do not always accept the teaching of 'certain revolutionary maniacs' referred to by the Rev. Mr. Twist 'who teach the people that the convenience of man, and not the will of God, has consigned them to labour and privation.' They vote as 'their betters' or their employers or their bosses tell them. To give more of them votes in a society where these conditions exist is to give more power into the hands of those who can manage and exploit them. So in some societies to give votes to women would only mean to give more power into the hands of the men who could deliver their votes. To be an independent person, to be ready to stand up for your rights, to be able to express your grievances and demand that something should be done about them, demand qualities of character and mind which are not always forthcoming, as organizers and defenders of the downtrodden and oppressed often learn sadly to their cost.

LIMITATIONS OF THIS ARGUMENT

However weighty this argument about 'shoes pinching' may be, it does not seem necessarily to involve the control of government by public opinion. It does involve that government should be sensitive and accessible to public opinion, but that is not necessarily the same thing. The safeguarding of the right of petition has little to do with democracy. It is an old tradition of kingly rule that the humblest member of the public should have access to the king to state his grievances. That is the mark of the good Eastern king from Solomon to Haroun al Rashid. The administration of government always gives opportunities for petty tyranny. The member of parliament who asks a question on behalf of one of his constituents who has a complaint against the administration is fulfilling a very old function which existed in undemocratic days. Why should the argument about shoes pinching imply the control of government by the ordinary voter?

The answer is that experts do not like being told that the shoes they so beautifully make do not fit. They are apt to blame it on the distorted and misshapen toes of the people who have to wear their shoes. Unless there is power behind the expression of grievances, the grievances are apt to be neglected. The very way in which the stories talk about the good king who takes pains to find out what his subjects really think implies that most kings do not do so. Solomons or Harouns al Rashid do not grow on every bush. Contrast the very great care which is officially taken in the army to encourage and listen to complaints with what the men say about it. There may be the most regular machinery by which men can express their grievances, the most frequent opportunities to respond to the questions 'Any complaints?'; but the rank and file will remain convinced that, if they complain, nothing will be done, but the sergeant-major will have it out of them somehow. Men will continue to talk and think quite differently about getting their grievances redressed through their member of parliament who wants their votes on the one hand and through their superior officer over whom they have no power on the other.

On this theory what happens in parliamentary democracy is that the people vote for a government on the understanding that it will remedy their grievances, deal with what is most manifestly wrong, and that they judge and they alone can judge whether the grievances are remedied. The vote at a general election is primarily a judgement on results: the people say, 'Our shoes are still pinching and we shall try another shoemaker, thank you': or, 'Yes, you have made our feet so much more comfortable that we shall let you go on and see if you can do still better.' Of course what happens is not so simple as that. The verdict of the electors is not just on results: it is to some extent an assent to this or that proposal for the future; but broadly speaking an election is an expression of approval or disapproval of what has happened. This is of course strictly in accordance with the 'where the shoe pinches' theory. It does not imply any more than the theory does that the electorate are particularly intelligent: that their judgement as to what ought to be done is at all out of the ordinary. It does imply that, as the end of government is to promote the free life of all its citizens, all citizens must have their say as to how that free life is actually being hindered and how far the work of government is actually removing those hindrances.

But it will also be clear that this argument has its limitations. It does not meet anything like all the claims made for democratic government. It does not even support the claim that the general public can decide broad issues. It would not, for example, justify the democratic control of foreign policy. Foreign policy involves a judgement as to how the internal life of the country is to be preserved from danger from abroad. If we assume that the democratic voter is only concerned to be allowed to 'live his own life,' to be freed from hindrances to it, but that he has not the necessary knowledge to know what means should be taken to ensure that end, it follows that the ordinary man or woman has on the argument of 'the shoe pinching' no particular competence to control foreign policy. Is he then to leave foreign policy entirely to 'his betters'?

No democrat would assent. Let us see why.

WHAT PEOPLE ARE PREPARED TO DO

Errors in foreign policy may mean that a country is faced with the threat of war which may involve, unless that threat is met in one way or another, the destruction of all in its life which its people hold dear. But there are only two conceivable ways in which a threat of war can be met, and both involve the severest sacrifices falling on the ordinary men and women in the country. One of the ways of course is to meet the threat of war by accepting its challenge and resisting it. The other has never been tried but it is advocated by Mr. Gandhi and extreme pacifists. It is to meet the threat of war by passive resistance. Let us first consider the second.

Passive resistance to invasion which would prevent the invader from destroying the soul of a country demands a heroism and goodness in the population of a kind which no people has ever yet shown. If a sincere pacifist statesman, say Mr. Gandhi in power in India, committed his country to this alternative by making the other alternative impossible, he might produce the most horrible disaster. If his people were not really prepared to act up to his principles, and he had incapacitated them from acting up to their own, the result would be disaster indeed. No statesman has a right to commit his country to action unless he has reason to believe that the people will respond to the challenge which that action involves.

The same point is obvious when we consider the conditions in which alone a democratic statesman can commit his country to war. If it be true that free men fight better than other men for what they hold dear, it is also true that they fight worse than others for what they do not hold dear. It is possible, as Nazi Germany has shown, for a government to get such control over the minds and wills of a people and to have imposed such discipline upon them, that they, the government, can make up their mind about what they intend the nation to do and then make their people ready to undergo almost any sacrifice in obedience to their will. But a democratic people is not disciplined in that way. Its government can never go much beyond what their people are prepared to do. It is therefore quite essential that its government should know what that is. No statesman can pursue a foreign policy of appeasement unless he knows how much his people will stand. No statesman can pursue a policy which may end in resistance to aggression unless he knows for what his people are prepared to fight. The weakness of British foreign policy in the period between the two wars was largely due to the fact that, because of the bad working of the democratic machinery or of faulty leadership or of a combination of both, British statesmen did not have this essential knowledge to guide them in their conduct of foreign policy. Britain found herself in a new position. The development of air power had made her vulnerable as she had never been before. The existence of the League of Nations meant the adoption of a new attitude to foreign policy. The spread of pacifism and semi-pacifism further confused the issue. Before the last war a foreign minister could say with confidence, that the British people would go a very long way to preserve peace but there were certain things which they would not stand, and he could have said what those things were. After the war that could no longer be said, and this had a disastrous effect on the conduct of foreign policy.

This need of knowledge of what people are prepared to do is not confined to foreign policy. In a democratic society at least, laws, if they are to be successful, must rest largely upon consent. The force behind government can do something, but not very much. If laws are to be effectively obeyed, their demands cannot go much beyond what people are prepared to do. Successful law-making therefore demands an understanding of the ways and the willingness of ordinary people. That understanding can, to some extent, be got without voting or the ordinary processes of democratic machinery. But in so far as democratic machinery produces the expert representative, it is probably as reliable a way as can be devised of ensuring that this necessary knowledge is in the hands of government and that the government pay attention to it.

It is important to notice that though 'what people are prepared to do' is a matter of fact, it is fact of an odd kind. For any one who reflects on it knows that what people are prepared to do depends on the varying tone of their societies and that that tone depends on leadership, inspiration, and imponderables of that kind. What people are prepared to do is not a distinct fact, to be discovered in its distinct existence by scientific analysis. Indeed we may say in general about all the argument of these last few pages that we shall go wrong if we think of 'the pinching of shoes' and 'what people are prepared to do' as distinct facts, existing separately and there to be discovered. They are that to some extent but not altogether. In a small meeting the process of discovering what needs to be done and what people are prepared to do is also a process of getting people prepared to do something. Something of the same is true in the elaborate democratic processes which culminate in men and women recording their votes in the polling booths. They are, or at least ought to be, processes of discussion, discussion carried on in the most multifarious ways as it is in a healthy society, by means of the press, of clubs and societies of all kinds: in public-houses and in W.E.A. classes as well as, indeed more than, at political meetings. The process of discovering the sense of the meeting is also a process of making the sense of the meeting. So to some extent at least with a nation at large.

We shall come back to this point later. Meanwhile let us consider how far towards democracy these two arguments take us. They assert that government needs for its task knowledge which cannot be got by ordinary learning but is provided normally by the democratic machinery. That would not necessarily imply control. If the knowledge could be got in another way, presumably on this argument the democratic machinery would not be necessary. Mass observation may claim to be a scientific process of discovering accurately what is now a rather clumsy by-product of elections. There is no reason why Hitler or any other autocrat should not use such a process. It is part of any government's job to know these facts about its people even when its main purpose is to understand how to exploit them to serve its own evil ambitions.

These arguments only imply democracy when we remember that men in power need often to be compelled to serve the true purposes of government. Expert shoemakers, as we saw, do not always like to be told that their shoes are at fault. Men who have control over executive and administrative power easily forget that they are only servants and that their power has only value as an instrument. Hence all the democratic devices to ensure that government shall attend to the purposes for which it exists, shall be made to do something about the grievances and wishes of the ordinary people it is meant to serve. Hence the necessity for responsible government—for arrangements which make the government somehow responsible to the ordinary people as contrasted with the most elaborate arrangements for advising an irresponsible government, for seeing that government has the necessary information without compelling it to act on that information. If the theory of all this were properly put into practice it would mean that the government were given a free hand to deal with means. The purpose of the control exercised by the ordinary voters is to see that those means—the technical skill of the administrative are used to right ends.

THE WISDOM OF THE PLAIN MAN

This leads to a third argument for democracy where it is assumed that ordinary plain people have a certain wisdom is denied to the expert, and that therefore they are the best judges of ends if not of means.

This argument can easily be so put as to be absurd. An expert is not necessarily a fool. It may be and often is true that experts are apt to give their minds an almost complete holiday outside their own special sphere. Who does not know the distinguished scientist who thinks that his scientific attainments in one sphere justify his making the most surprising generalizations in matters of which he has no knowledge? But knowledge even in a restricted sphere cannot be a greater handicap to sound judgement than ignorance in all spheres. Yet we are not wrong when we pray to be delivered from the clever ass and it is on the whole true that for a certain kind of practical wisdom—very important in politics—we do not naturally go to the scientific expert. That does not mean that we go instead to the most ignorant man we can find or to just any one. We go to some one who has learnt wisdom from life.

It is an old story that wisdom in conduct is not learnt from books or technical study, but from experience and character. We know what we mean when we talk of men or women of 'sound judgement' or of 'common sense.' We distinguish them from the expert whom we rather distrust. We should defend this attitude by saying that the expert is a specialist: that what is wanted for conduct is all-round experience of people and things. 'Sound judgement' or 'common sense' are not the products of ignorance. They are produced by experience of a certain kind, by responsibility, by a varied acquaintance with men and things and by an all-round experience. The expert or specialist on the other hand has probably paid for his expert knowledge by having had to undergo a long training which has removed him from the ordinary rough-and-tumble of life. He has probably not had to check his judgements by practical experience. He has perhaps not had to pay for his mistakes. He has become 'academic' in the bad sense of that term.

If we think about the men and women whose judgement on practical affairs and on conduct we respect, we should certainly agree that academic education did not seem to be very important in their production. We should say that some of them were learned and some not, some rich, some poor. They have no special training or accomplishment. That is why we contrast the one-sidedness of the expert with the good sense or common sense of the *ordinary* man and why democrats think that the proposals of the expert should be improved by the ordinary man.

There clearly is something in this, but we must be careful. 'Common sense' it is sometimes said, 'is one of the rarest of qualities.' The word 'common' is used in New England as a term of uncommon praise. It means, I think, much what the word 'plain' means in the north of England or Scotland. We were proud as children when some one described our mother as 'the plainest woman I have ever set eyes on,' though we used the ambiguity of the remark as a weapon to tease her. 'Plain' meant, as I think, 'common' means, that she had no pretensions and no pomposity; that she took people as she found them, and entirely disregarded their external attributes, their rank or class or anything else. Such an attitude of mind, receptive and humble, is essential to the true understanding of men and of life. It is found in all sorts of people who may have no other particular accomplishments and are therefore regarded as ordinary. But in reality such people are neither common nor ordinary.

The democrat who stands up for the good sense and sound judgement of 'the ordinary man' against the pronouncements and dicta of superior persons is really thinking of the good sense and sound judgement he has found— not by any manner of means in everybody—but in some humble, simple persons. This is really the secularized version of the Puritans' government by the elect. What is the difference, I once heard asked in a discussion, between government by the *élite* and government by the elect? The answer was: 'The *élite* are people you choose; the elect are those whom God chooses.' The untheological version of this would be to say that if you talk of *élite* you mean people characterized by some clearly marked and almost measurable quality—skill, training, birth, and so on; if you talk of the elect you mean men who have nothing of this about them but are nevertheless remarkable.

Practicable wisdom, the democrat would say, shows itself in the most unexpected places. You must be prepared for it wherever it turns up, and you must not imagine you can, by any training or planning, produce it to order. The democratic leader turns up. He is recognized by his fellows and carries them with him. He has the power of calling out the best in ordinary people. Because he shares the life and experience of ordinary men and women he knows, almost unconsciously, 'where the shoe pinches' and 'what people are prepared to do,' and because he shares the ordinary responsibilities of life, he has an all-round experience and is saved from the narrowness of the specialist. Knowledge of the common life and its possibilities; understanding of the things which produce in it bitterness and thwart men's activities are the wisdom most wanted for politics. The state will be wisely directed if the final control is in the hands of 'ordinary' men—men not specialized in their vocation or training—who have 'common sense' and 'sound judgement.' But those men are, in favourable circumstances, the men to whom others listen, and who furnish the real if informal leadership in a community. The great mass of really ordinary people will follow them, and to give power to everybody by means of universal suffrage is to give power to them.

This view still implies a judgement about the mass of ordinary men and women. It implies their power of recognizing 'sound judgement' and 'common sense' in their fellows; in being able to judge a man and ready to approve the natural leader and reject the charlatan. That they do not always do so is notorious. What is important to discover is whether we can say anything about the conditions favourable to the mass of men and women in society judging men well or ill.

DISCUSSION

The argument for democratic as contrasted with expert leadership is that political wisdom needs more than anything else an understanding of the common life; and that that wisdom is given not by expert knowledge but by a practical experience of life. If the defect of the expert is his onesidedness, the merit of the practical man of common-sense judgement will be his all-round experience. The simple agricultural societies where democracy flourishes and seems native to the soil produce naturally men of common sense and sound judgement, appraisers alike of men and horses. The men whom we readily think of as men of sound judgement though unlearned have often had that kind of training. The part played by the village cobbler or blacksmith in the democratic life of a village has often been noticed. The inhabitants of a natural democracy like the New England township described in Mr. Winston Churchill's *Coniston* are independent, accustomed to act on their own, and to make judgements within the scope of their experience.

Modern industrialism has taken away from the great mass of men in an industrialized community their independence. It has condemned very many of them to specialized and narrow lives. Their lives are far more specialized and far narrower than the lives of the experts whom our democratic argument has been putting in their place, and they are without the expert's skill or knowledge or his partial independence. Where under such conditions are the common-sense qualities and sound judgement of the ordinary man to be found? How can we keep a modern industrial society from becoming not a community but a mob, not a society of persons capable of judging for themselves, discussing and criticizing from their experience of life the proposals put before them, but a mass played upon by the clever people at the top? These, nowadays, armed with new psychological techniques, claim to be able to manipulate those masses to their will, make them believe what the rulers want, hate what the rulers want, and even fight and die for what the rulers want.

For the real issue between the democrats and the anti-democrats is that democrats think of a society where men can and do act as responsible persons. The anti-democrats talk of the mob, or the herd, or the crowd. What these latter say of mobs or herds or crowds is as true as what the democrats say of the sound sense of the ordinary man who acts and thinks as an individual. No one can read a book like Ortega y Gasset's *The Revolt of the Masses* without recognizing the strength of the forces in modern society which go to the making of men into masses or crowds; or without seeing that, if they prevail, mass democracy must produce, as it has in so many countries produced, totalitarianism. That is the greatest of the challenges to democracy. But modern industrialism has supplied an antidote in the working-class movement. If we consider what gives that movement its vitality, we see that it creates innumerable centres of discussion. Trade union branches, co-operative guild meetings, W.E.A. classes and discussion groups of all kinds provide conditions as far removed as possible from those that produce a mob. The key to democracy is the potency of discussion. A good discussion can draw out wisdom which is attainable in no other way. The success of anti-democratic totalitarian techniques has depended on the suppression of discussion. If the freedom of discussion is safeguarded and fostered, there is no necessity for the most urbanized of committees becoming a mob. Those of us who have seen anything of the spread of discussion in England during the war, in the Army, in A.R.P. posts, in shelters, in all kinds of places where people come together have seen something of how in discussion the 'plain' man can come into his own.

~~~~~~~~~~~~~~~~~~~~~~ Part II ~~~~~~~~~~~~~~~~~~~~~~~

ANTIDEMOCRATIC THOUGHT

~~~~~~

The Politics of Pessimism

The Idol State

The Cry for the Leader

Fascism: Government by Force and Lies

Chapter V

THE POLITICS OF PESSIMISM

FUNDAMENTAL political attitudes reach below the level of conscious and articulate expression, and stem from one's whole personality. Typical structures of personality are reflected in correspondingly typical approaches to politics: a general inclination to look at the world optimistically leads to a radically different political temper from that of the habitual pessimist. Democracy, anarchy, individualism, and socialism are varied expressions of an essentially optimistic faith: that man is perfectible; that progress is possible and within practical reach; that the burden of history can be overcome by the liberating and uplifting force of reason; and that, finally, the range of human possibilities has hardly been perceived. Conversely, the pessimist sees man as incapable of progressive perfectibility, denies the very idea of progress as a criterion of human development, and is impressed with the helplessness of reason and principles in the face of historically evolved reality. Where the optimist tends to look into the *future* in the thought of what *might* happen, the pessimist turns his eyes backward into the *past* and is overawed by what *has* happened. Few political writers have been pure pessimists or pure optimists; nevertheless, most have tended to stress an approach to politics that is predominantly optimistic or preponderantly pessimistic.

The philosophers of political pessimism have always sought to justify their general point of view by declaring themselves the only true "realists," as contrasted with the illusionary and Utopian wishful thinking of the optimists. The first clearly formulated theory of politics from such a "realistic" and profoundly pessimistic starting point was Machiavelli's *The Prince* (1513). The whole pre-Machiavellian tradition of political speculation had concerned itself primarily with the purposes and aims of the state. Machiavelli was the first writer of the modern age who was interested in political means and techniques rather than in political ideals and objectives. Before him, political power was assumed to be a means itself—a means in the service of a higher end, such as justice, faith in God, or freedom. Machiavelli reversed this whole tradition of classical antiquity and of the Middle Ages by postulating power as the end to be sought and maintained, and confining himself to an analysis of the means that are best suited to the conquest and retention of political power. He thus separated the age-old connection between morals and politics, and made politics amoral, if not immoral. This Machiavellian hypothesis of the autonomous validity of politics as a separate and distinct sphere of life has been one of the most revolutionary events in the intellectual history of the West. Much that is labeled "Machiavellian" can hardly be attributed to Machiavelli himself. He was much less Machiavellian than most of his admirers or, despite their verbal protestations, many of his detractors. Yet, although the meaning of an idea may have been originally different from the effects it eventually produced, there is, in a deeper sense, a connection between meaning and effect.

Machiavelli's pessimism is reflected in his conviction that moral considerations may be laudable in themselves, but that the practical statesman cannot afford the luxury of living up to them: "For how we live is so far removed from how we ought to live, that he who abandons what is done for what ought to be done, will rather learn to bring about his own ruin than his preservation." In the struggle between political rulers, Machiavelli says, "there are two methods of fighting, the one by law, the other by force: the first method is that of men, the second of beasts; but as the first method is often insufficient, one must have recourse to the second. It is therefore necessary for a prince to know well how to use both the beast and the man." Specifically, the ruler must imitate the fox and the lion, "for the lion cannot protect himself from traps, and the fox cannot defend himself from wolves." Should a ruler keep faith? Machiavelli admits that everybody knows how "laudable" it is for a ruler to do so. However, in the world of actual politics such laudable intentions may be irreconcilable with expediency and interest: "Therefore, a prudent ruler ought not to keep faith when by doing so it would be against his interest, and when the reasons which made him bind himself no longer exist. If men were all good, this precept would not be a good one; but as they are bad, and would not observe their faith with you, so you are not bound to keep faith with them." Machiavelli thus takes an essentially pessimistic view of human nature. Political methods of the Renaissance were hardly known for their humanitarian mellowness; death by poison or the silent dagger—not to speak of bribery and coercion—was a mere technical detail in the execution of a political program. Leaders of the churches acted in as unholy and ruthless a fashion as mundane rulers, with the result that it was not unnatural for Machiavelli, as for many of his contemporaries, to become permeated with a mood of skepticism, not to say pessimism and outright cynicism. Unlike Fascist and Nazi ideologists later on, Machiavelli never praised immorality for its own sake, nor did he raise nihilism to the pinnacle of worldly wisdom. Prudence and moderation saved him from such extremism, as much as lack of these qualities doomed some of the later would-be Machiavellis to disaster. In particular, Mussolini might have pondered over Machiavelli's warning that, in planning aggressive warfare, "a prince ought never to make common cause with one more powerful than himself."

While Machiavelli was not antidemocratic in the sense that he was opposed to democratic forms of government on principle (in *The Discourses,* published in 1521, he sympathetically discussed republicanism), the general temper of *The Prince,* in particular, is imbued with psychological and intellectual elements that do not fit into the democratic way of life. Like other "realists" after him, he identified all too readily certain methods and techniques of naked power politics with the whole of political reality, and thus failed to grasp that ideas and ideals, too, can, if properly mobilized, become potent facts, even decisive weapons, in the struggles for political survival. History is a vast graveyard filled with the corpses of great realists like Napoleon, William II, Hitler, and Mussolini, to mention but a few notorious realists of recent record.

Thomas Hobbes was, like Machiavelli, the child of an age of struggle, discord, and civil war. His *Leviathan* (1651) is evidence of the quest for a theory of the state that could guarantee peace and security for its members. These may not be the highest aims for a society in normal times, but the *Leviathan* was published in the early part of Cromwell's stern rule, only two years after the English had beheaded their king. When there is no peace, peace seems the greatest end.

In the fashion of his time, Hobbes starts out with a description of the state of nature, and how men live in it. He finds three principal causes of quarrel: competition, diffidence, and glory. This state of nature is, according to Hobbes, a continual war or threat of war of every man against every man. Force and fraud, "the two cardinal virtues" in war, flourish in that atmosphere of perpetual fear and strife. There is no "mine" and "thine," there are no arts, no letters, no amenities of civilized living, and, "which is worst of all," there is "continual fear and danger of violent death; and the life of man, solitary, poor, nasty, brutish, and short." This pessimistic account of man's character and conduct in the state of nature is in sharp contrast with Locke's conception. Locke insists that in the state of nature, too, men are guided by reason and are obliged to abide by the rules of natural law, whereas Hobbes denies all that, because the "notions of right and wrong, justice and injustice" have no place in a condition that knows no law nor a common power to enforce it.

Locke, like Hobbes, urged the necessity of civil government to be set up by a joint compact; but whereas Locke assumed that men ordinarily abide by reasonable and decent standards of conduct, so that the state is required only for the "marginal" cases of violations of law and reason, Hobbes considered strife and war the rule rather than the exception in uncontrolled human intercourse. This is why Hobbes advocated the sovereign state, strong and unassailable against enemies from within or without, while Locke was satisfied with a state that could best justify itself by making itself as unnecessary as possible.

The sovereign power in the Hobbesian state is "incommunicable and inseparable." Hobbes attacked any institution that could weaken the omnipotence of the state, such as the division of power, the principle of mixed government, liberty of the subject, or the right of the individual to challenge the wisdom or legality of the sovereign's actions. To strengthen his authority, the sovereign should not permit the growth of groups and associations that intervene between the individual and the state. In one special chapter Hobbes listed a catalog of the causes that weaken or tend to the dissolution of the state. In it, he attacked with particular irony and vehemence the "poisonous doctrine" that "every private man is judge of good and evil actions," and that "whatsoever a man does against his conscience, is sin." Against these "seditious doctrines" Hobbes demanded unqualified obedience of the subject.

One important aspect of Hobbes' political thought is his doctrine of the relationships between natural and civil law. Since the Stoics, the conception has never died out in the Western tradition of law and government that civil (or positive) law is derived from, and inferior to, a higher law, a "law behind the law"—the law of nature. In the Bible, too, the law of the kings and princes is held to be subordinate, and responsible, to the law of God. This Stoic-Jewish-Christian approach to the validity of civil law has had civilizing effects on the Western world, because it has always reminded rulers that there is still a higher law above their edicts and commands, be that higher law founded on reason or divine revelation. By contrast, Hobbes is opposed to carrying the search for the validity of the law beyond the formal source of the legal sovereign. There can be, according to Hobbes, no unjust law, no law that is wrong, because laws "are the rules of just and unjust." As to the relations between natural law and civil law, Hobbes maintained that they "contain each other." Specifically, the law of nature is not really law at all, but only "qualities that dispose men to peace and obedience." Hobbes lists equity, justice, gratitude, and "other moral virtues" as the laws of nature. But these qualities are not true law, because, before the state is established, there is no authority to decide finally which idea of the law is binding. In practice, therefore, the law of nature is, according to Hobbes, nothing but a set of general principles of the civil law; the main formal difference is the fact that the civil law is written, whereas the law of nature is unwritten. Thus Hobbes sought to sweep away the doctrine of natural law from the theory of the state; with the insight of genius he correctly foresaw the revolutionary implications of natural law ideas as they became manifest only a century later in the American and French revolutions. Locke, too, admitted the revolutionary possibilities of the doctrine of natural law, but, unlike Hobbes, he was not too frightened by that prospect.

The complex character of Hobbes' political ideas puzzled critics and commentators from the most varied camps. The conservatives who believed in legitimate monarchy abhorred the fact that Hobbes was little interested in the divine right of monarchs and was solely concerned with the pragmatic issue of *effective* government, regardless of the source of authority. Conservatives of a religious observance charged Hobbes with atheism, because he subordinated the church, like all other associations, to the sovereign state. Morally neutral, Hobbes believed that tyrants should be punished by God but not by their subjects, and he enjoined all true believers to follow Christ into martyrdom, if their conscience conflicted with the commands of the sovereign. Finally, Hobbes has consistently encountered opposition among the advocates of parliamentary government and limited governmental authority. Since the last group developed into the dominant tradition in England and the United States, there has been no Hobbesian school in English and American political thought.

By contrast, Hobbes' influence in Germany and, under Fascism, in Italy has been very considerable. As a spokesman for the "strong state" he has always appealed to the traditional German schools of political thought, as well as to the more recent representatives of Italian Fascism. Yet the attempt to claim Hobbes as one of the precursors of Nazism and Fascism is more untenable than would appear from a cursory glance at some key phrases in the *Leviathan*. First, government is set up, according to Hobbes, by compact among the ruled. This contractual foundation alone is anathema to the Nazi or Fascist: in their political mythology, the origin and foundation of the state is to be sought in the *Volksgeist,* the people's spirit, rather than in deliberate creation. The Nazis and Fascists attack the contractual theory of the state, because contract implies mutuality of some sort, and, more important still, there can be no contract without consent. Democracy is government by consent. Second, Hobbes assigns to the state a prosaic business: to maintain order and security for the body of citizens. By contrast, the aim of the Nazi or Fascist state is the glory of the German master race, or the revival of the Roman empire. Third, the Hobbesian state is *authoritarian,* whereas the Nazi or Fascist state is *totalitarian*. Authority in the Hobbesian state is mostly concentrated in the political sphere, and in it alone. The sovereign will normally permit his subjects "the liberty to buy and sell, and otherwise contract with one another, to choose their own abode, their own diet, their own trade of life, and institute their children as they themselves think fit; and the like." The Hobbesian assumption of economic *laissez faire* hardly fits into the Nazi-Fascist pattern of a rigidly planned economy. Similarly, the Hobbesian freedom to bring up one's children was hardly reflected in the "Hitler-Youth" in Germany or the "Balilla" youth organization in Fascist Italy. The Nazi-Fascist state is totalitarian, inasmuch as it seeks to regulate and control man's life, by force if necessary, in all its aspects. Fourth, Hobbes recognizes that the sovereign may be one man, or "an assembly of men," whereas Nazism and Fascism support the dogma of the leadership principle. Hobbes preferred monarchy for practical reasons, but he was free from the mystical dogmatism that endowed Nazi and Fascist leaders with alleged charismatic and prophetic gifts. The Hobbesian sovereign is a top administrator and lawgiver, but not a top rabble rouser, spellbinder, or Fuehrer. Fifth, Hobbes recognizes that war is one of the two main reasons (the first being the danger of internal disorder) why men are driven to set up a state. But whenever he speaks of war, it is *defensive war* only, and there is no glorification of war, let alone of aggressive war, in the *Leviathan*. By contrast, Nazis and Fascists have looked upon war as something highly *desirable,* and on expansive, imperialist war as the highest form of national life. Also, Hobbes, the English bourgeois, prefers "commodious living" to the Nazi-Fascist doctrine of "living dangerously." Finally, the Hobbesian state does not completely swallow the individual: "A man cannot lay down the right of resisting them that assault him by force to take away his life." Since the purpose of political society is the preservation and protection of man's life, Hobbes recognizes the inalienable right of the individual to resist when his life is at stake, because "man by nature chooses the lesser evil, which is danger of death in resisting, rather than the greater, which is certain and present death in not resisting." For a long time, this Hobbesian caveat seemed unimportant, because the sanctity of human life was universally accepted. But when millions of people were put to death in gas chambers and concentration camps by a state, the Hobbesian stress on the integrity of human life acquired new meaning.

All this should not create the impression that Hobbes was a democrat in disguise. He was not. But the Hobbesian state is neither the modern democratic state nor the Nazi-Fascist state; it can be found in modern times in countries that possess social and economic conditions not too dissimilar from seventeenth-century England—some nations in Latin America, Southeastern Europe, and Asia. The dictatorships in Latin America in the nineteenth and twentieth centuries, such as that of General Porfirio Diaz in Mexico, approximated very closely to the Hobbesian state: society was still in a precapitalist or, at best, early capitalist phase. Economic *laissez faire* was mingled in such countries with a strong political power, possibly a dictatorship. But that dictatorship was authoritarian, and not totalitarian. In cultural, educational, and social matters it was often very lenient. By comparison with an advanced democracy, the Hobbesian state may appear dictatorial enough. By comparison with twentieth-century totalitarianism of the Nazi-Fascist kind, it is a vision of refined political civilization.

What detracts from the effective impact of Machiavelli and Hobbes is that their basically pessimistic views about the nature of man, especially the common man, are almost too coldly scientific and analytically objective. In the works of Edmund Burke, particularly in his later writing, antidemocratic political pessimism is couched in thought and language that are an arresting mixture of poetry, philosophy, and religious mysticism, all suffused with a penetrating sense of practical wisdom. No wonder, then, that Burke's statement of his political creed, particularly as expressed in his *Reflections on the Revolution in France* (1790), should have remained, to this day, the bible of conservatives and moderate antidemocrats. Burke denied the validity of the pivotal tenet of democracy: that only the governed have the right to determine who is to govern, and, secondly, that all votes are, politically, equal. He opposed this democratic method as an "arithmetic" devoid of practical meaning, and thought of representation in terms of historic interests, such as the Lords, the Commons, the monarchy, the Established Church, rather than in terms of the individual. There is something medieval in his idea that man is politically significant, not as an individual citizen, but solely as a member of a group to which he belongs socially or economically. This theory of corporate representation was also supported by Hegel, and found its perverted expression more recently in the "corporate state" of the Nazi-Fascist type.

Burke was liberal enough not to desire the oppression of persons of low station in life, like hairdressers and working tallow chandlers, provided they stayed in their place: "Such descriptions of men ought not to suffer oppression from the state; but the state suffers oppression, if such as they, either individually or collectively, are permitted to rule." Because of his firm conviction that wealth and aristocracy were the repositories of political wisdom and experience, he stubbornly ridiculed those who saw in the "rotten boroughs" and in stringent suffrage qualifications impediments to parliamentary government. The system of representation, that he advocated, and that brought England near the brink of revolution, was adjudged by Burke to be "adequate to all the purposes for which a representation of the people can be desired or devised." In the field of religion, too, he believed in a preferred position for one church, the Established Church, and suspected radical democrats of atheistic leanings; he saw in religion a force that taught men to look at nature and society with a sense of awe and reverence rather than with inquisitive analytical curiosity.

The faith of the French revolutionaries in the creative potentialities of reason provoked Burke to scathing denunciations of the revolutionaries as metaphysicians and ruthless logicians. By stressing the value of historical experience as well as the claims of circumstance, Burke sought to delimit more narrowly the boundaries within which reason could operate freely. He was skeptical about innovations unless "models and patterns of approved utility" were before the eyes of the reformers. In the French Revolution he saw only the violence and terror incidental to civil war, but failed to see its constructive aims and achievements. By constantly referring to the past, Burke sought to convince his contemporaries that France before 1789 was an ably and justly governed country, and that radical change would therefore be disastrous. In this, he idealized the past as much as he feared the future.

"Prescription" and "inheritance" are two key words that appear often in Burke's writings. Both connote the idea of continuity, of slow growth, and both stress the evolutionary aspect of political institutions rather than the problem of their moral and ethical worth. Specifically, he applied these two terms to the issue of property (dealt with more fully below in Chapter IX), the inequalities of which he candidly associated with political and social inequalities. While Burke never reached the Hegelian sanctification of the existing ("What is rational is actual and what is actual is rational"), his strong sense of the past, combined with his religious mysticism, especially in his later years, tended to endow the existing with value solely because it exists. In his cautious attitude toward reason, in his exaltation of feeling and imagination, he exercised a lasting influence on conservative thought in England and the United States, as well as on the great exponents of anti-democratic thought in Germany and France, such as Hegel and De Maistre.

Yet, when all is said and done, no reader of the *Reflections* can escape the impact of a mature and imaginative mind: "The nature of man is intricate; the objects of society are of the greatest possible complexity: and therefore no simple disposition or direction of power can be suitable either to man's nature, or to the quality of his affairs." Bismarck defined politics as "the art of the possible," and this is one of the guiding principles of Burke's thinking on politics. Whether one accepts the basic tenets of his political philosophy or not, one finds on almost every page of the *Reflections* epigrammatic and aphoristic gems of wisdom and observation, which make the work a perpetual source of inspiration even for those who feel more optimistic about the possibilities of democracy than Burke did.

~~~~~~

1. The Lion and the Fox *

NICCOLÒ MACHIAVELLI

~~~~~~

OF THE THINGS FOR WHICH MEN, AND ESPECIALLY PRINCES, ARE PRAISED OR BLAMED

It now remains to be seen what are the methods and rules for a prince as regards his subjects and friends. And as I know that many have written

* From Niccolò Machiavelli, *The Prince* (1513). Modern Library edition. By permission of Random House, publishers.

of this, I fear that my writing about it may be deemed presumptuous, differing as I do, especially in this matter, from the opinions of others. But my intention being to write something of use to those who understand, it appears to me more proper to go to the real truth of the matter than to its imagination; and many have imagined republics and principalities which have never been seen or known to exist in reality; for how we live is so far removed from how we ought to live, that he who abandons what is done for what ought to be done, will rather learn to bring about his own ruin than his preservation. A man who wishes to make a profession of goodness in everything must necessarily come to grief among so many who are not good. Therefore it is necessary for a prince, who wishes to maintain himself, to learn how not to be good, and to use this knowledge and not use it, according to the necessity of the case.

Leaving on one side, then, those things which concern only an imaginary prince, and speaking of those that are real, I state that all men, and especially princes, who are placed at a greater height, are reputed for certain qualities which bring them either praise or blame. Thus one is considered liberal, another *misero* or miserly (using a Tuscan term, seeing that *avaro* with us still means one who is rapaciously acquisitive and *misero* one who makes grudging use of his own); one a free giver, another rapacious; one cruel, another merciful; one a breaker of his word, another trustworthy; one effeminate and pusillanimous, another fierce and high-spirited; one humane, another haughty; one lascivious, another chaste; one frank, another astute; one hard, another easy; one serious, another frivolous; one religious, another an unbeliever, and so on. I know that every one will admit that it would be highly praiseworthy in a prince to possess all the above-named qualities that are reputed good, but as they cannot all be possessed or observed, human conditions not permitting of it, it is necessary that he should be prudent enough to avoid the scandal of those vices which would lose him the state, and guard himself if possible against those which will not lose it him, but if not able to, he can indulge them with less scruple. And yet he must not mind incurring the scandal of those vices, without which it would be difficult to save the state, for if one considers well, it will be found that some things which seem virtues would, if followed, lead to one's ruin, and some others which appear vices result in one's greater security and wellbeing.

OF LIBERALITY AND NIGGARDLINESS

Beginning now with the first qualities above named, I say that it would be well to be considered liberal; nevertheless liberality such as the world understands it will injure you, because if used virtuously and in the proper way, it will not be known, and you will incur the disgrace of the contrary vice. But one who wishes to obtain the reputation of liberality among men must not omit every kind of sumptuous display, and to such an extent that a prince of this character will consume by such means all his resources, and will be at last compelled, if he wishes to maintain his name for liberality, to impose heavy taxes on his people, become extortionate, and do everything possible to obtain money. This will make his subjects begin to hate him, and he will be little esteemed being poor, so that having by this liberality injured many and benefited but few, he will feel the first little disturbance and be endangered by every peril. If he recognizes this and wishes to change his system, he incurs at once the charge of niggardliness.

A prince, therefore, not being able to exercise this virtue of liberality without risk if it be known, must not, if he be prudent, object to be called miserly. In course of time he will be thought more liberal, when it is seen that by his parsimony his revenue is sufficient, that he can defend himself against those who make war on him, and undertake enterprises without burdening his people, so that he is really liberal to all those from whom he does not take, who are infinite in number, and niggardly to all to whom he does not give, who are few. In our times we have seen nothing great done except by those who have been esteemed niggardly; the others have all been ruined. Pope Julius II, although he had made use of a reputation for liberality in order to attain the papacy, did not seek to retain it afterwards, so that he might be able to wage war. The present King of France has carried on so many wars without imposing an extraordinary tax, because his extra expenses were covered by the parsimony he had so long practised. The present King of Spain, if he had been thought liberal, would not have engaged in and been successful in so many enterprises.

For these reasons a prince must care little for the reputation of being a miser, if he wishes to avoid robbing his subjects, if he wishes to be able to defend himself, to avoid becoming poor and contemptible, and not to be forced to become rapacious; this niggardliness is one of those vices which enable him to reign. If it is said that Cæsar attained the empire through liberality, and that many others have reached the highest positions through being liberal or being thought so, I would reply that you are either a prince already or else on the way to become one. In the first case, this liberality is harmful; in the second, it is certainly necessary to be considered liberal. Cæsar was one of those who wished to attain the mastery over Rome, but if after attaining it he had lived and had not moderated his expenses, he would have destroyed that empire. And should any one reply that there have been many princes, who have done great things with their armies, who have been thought extremely liberal, I would answer by saying that the prince may either spend his own wealth and that of his subjects or the wealth of others. In the first case he must be sparing, but for the rest he must not neglect to be very liberal. The liberality is very necessary to a prince who marches with his armies, and lives by plunder, sack and ransom, and is dealing with the wealth of others, for without it he would not be followed by his soldiers. And you may be very generous indeed with what is not the property of yourself or your subjects, as were Cyrus, Cæsar, and Alexander; for spending the wealth of others will not diminish your reputation, but increase it, only spending your own resources will injure you. There is nothing which destroys itself so much as liberality, for by using it you lose the power of using it, and become either poor and despicable, or, to escape poverty, rapacious and hated. And of all things that a prince must guard against, the most important are being despicable or hated, and liberality will lead you to one or other of these conditions. It is, therefore, wiser to have the name of a miser, which produces disgrace without hatred, than to incur of necessity the name of being rapacious, which produces both disgrace and hatred.

OF CRUELTY AND CLEMENCY, AND WHETHER IT IS BETTER TO BE LOVED OR FEARED

Proceeding to the other qualities before named, I say that every prince must desire to be considered merciful and not cruel. He must, however, take care not to misuse this mercifulness. Cesare Borgia was considered cruel, but his cruelty had brought order to the Romagna, united it, and reduced it to peace and fealty. If this is considered well, it will be seen that he was really much more merciful than the Florentine people, who, to avoid the name of cruelty, allowed Pistoia to be destroyed. A prince, therefore, must not mind incurring the charge of cruelty for the purpose of keeping his subjects united and faithful; for, with a very few examples, he will be more merciful than those who, from excess of tenderness, allow disorders to arise, from whence spring bloodshed and rapine; for these as a rule injure the whole community, while the executions carried out by the prince injure only individuals. And of all princes, it is impossible for a new prince to escape the reputation of cruelty, new states being always full of dangers. Wherefore Virgil through the mouth of Dido says:

> Res dura, et regni novitas me talia cogunt
> Moliri, et late fines custode tueri.

Nevertheless, he must be cautious in believing and acting, and must not be afraid of his own shadow, and must proceed in a temperate manner with prudence and humanity, so that too much confidence does not render him incautious, and too much diffidence does not render him intolerant.

From this arises the question whether it is better to be loved more than feared, or feared more than loved. The reply is, that one ought to be both feared and loved, but as it is difficult for the two to go together, it is much safer to be feared than loved, if one of the two has to be wanting. For it may be said of men in general that they are ungrateful, voluble, dissemblers, anxious to avoid danger, and covetous of gain; as long as you benefit them, they are entirely yours; they offer you their blood, their goods, their life, and their children, as I have before said, when the necessity is remote; but when it approaches, they revolt. And the prince who has relied solely on their words, without making other preparations, is ruined; for the friendship which is gained by purchase and not through grandeur and nobility of spirit is bought but not secured, and at a pinch is not to be expended in your service. And men have less scruple in offending one who makes himself loved than one who makes himself feared; for love is held by a chain of obligation which, men being selfish, is broken whenever it serves their purpose; but fear is maintained by a dread of punishment which never fails.

Still, a prince should make himself feared in such a way that if he does not gain love, he at any rate avoids hatred; for fear and the absence of hatred may well go together, and will be always attained by one who abstains from interfering with the property of his citizens and subjects or with their women. And when he is obliged to take the life of any one, let him do so when there is a proper justification and manifest reason for it; but above all he must abstain from taking the property of others, for men forget more easily the death of their father than the loss of their patrimony. Then also pretexts for seizing property are never wanting, and one who begins to live by rapine will always find some reason for taking the goods of others, whereas causes for taking life are rarer and more fleeting.

But when the prince is with his army and has a large number of soldiers under his control, then it is extremely necessary that he should not mind being thought cruel; for without this reputation he could not keep an army united or disposed to any duty. Among the noteworthy actions of Hannibal is numbered this, that although he had an enormous army, composed of men of all nations and fighting in foreign countries, there never arose any dissension either among them or against the prince, either in good fortune or in bad. This could not be due to anything but his inhuman cruelty, which together with his infinite other virtues, made him always venerated and terrible in the sight of his soldiers, and without it his other virtues would not have sufficed to produce that effect. Thoughtless writers admire on the one hand his actions, and on the other blame the principal cause of them.

And that it is true that his other virtues would not have sufficed may be seen from the case of Scipio (famous not only in regard to his own times, but all times of which memory remains), whose armies rebelled against him in Spain, which arose from nothing but his excessive kindness, which allowed more licence to the soldiers than was consonant with military discipline. He was reproached with this in the senate by Fabius Maximus, who called him a corrupter of the Roman militia. Locri having been destroyed by one of Scipio's officers was not revenged by him, nor was the insolence of that officer punished, simply by reason of his easy nature; so much so, that some one wishing to excuse him in the senate, said that there were many men who knew rather how not to err, than how to correct the errors of others. This disposition would in time have tarnished the fame and glory of Scipio had he persevered in it under the empire, but living under the rule of the senate this harmful quality was not only concealed but became a glory to him.

I conclude, therefore, with regard to being feared and loved, that men love at their own free will, but fear at the will of the prince, and that a wise prince must rely on what is in his power and not on what is in the power of others, and he must only contrive to avoid incurring hatred, as has been explained.

IN WHAT WAY PRINCES MUST KEEP FAITH

How laudable it is for a prince to keep good faith and live with integrity, and not with astuteness, every one knows. Still the experience of our times shows those princes to have done great things who have had little regard for good faith, and have been able by astuteness to confuse men's brains, and who have ultimately overcome those who have made loyalty their foundation.

You must know, then, that there are two methods of fighting, the one by law, the other by force: the first method is that of men, the second of beasts; but as the first method is often insufficient, one must have recourse to the second. It is therefore necessary for a prince to know well how to use both the beast and the man. This was covertly taught to rulers by ancient writers, who relate how Achilles and many others of those ancient princes were given to Chiron the centaur to be brought up and educated under his discipline. The parable of this semi-animal, semi-human teacher is meant to indicate that a prince must know how to use both natures, and that the one without the other is not durable.

A prince being thus obliged to know well how to act as a beast must imitate the fox and the lion, for the lion cannot protect himself from traps, and the fox cannot defend himself from wolves. One must therefore be a fox to recognise traps, and a lion to frighten wolves. Those that wish to be only lions do not understand this. Therefore, a prudent ruler ought not to keep faith when by so doing it would be against his interest, and when the reasons which made him bind himself no longer exist. If men were all good, this precept would not be a good one; but as they are bad, and would not observe their faith with you, so you are not bound to keep faith with them. Nor have legitimate grounds ever failed a prince who wished to show colourable excuse for the non-fulfilment of his promise. Of this one could furnish an infinite number of modern examples, and show how many times peace has been broken, and how many promises rendered worthless, by the faithlessness of princes, and those that have been best able to imitate the fox have succeeded best. But it is necessary to be able to disguise this character well, and to be a great feigner and dissembler; and men are so simple and so ready to obey present necessities, that one who deceives will always find those who allow themselves to be deceived.

I will only mention one modern instance. Alexander VI did nothing else but deceive men, he thought of nothing else, and found the occasion for it; no man was ever more able to give assurances, or affirmed things with stronger oaths, and no man observed them less; however, he always succeeded in his deceptions, as he well knew this aspect of things.

It is not, therefore, necessary for a prince to have all the above-named qualities, but it is very necessary to seem to have them. I would even be bold to say that to possess them and always to observe them is dangerous, but to appear to possess them is useful. Thus it is well to seem merciful, faithful, humane, sincere, religious, and also to be so; but you must have the mind so disposed that when it is needful to be otherwise you may be able to change to the opposite qualities. And it must be understood that a prince, and especially a new prince, cannot observe all those things which are considered good in men, being often obliged, in order to maintain the state, to act against faith, against charity, against humanity, and against religion. And, therefore, he must have a mind disposed to adapt itself according to the wind, and as the variations of fortune dictate, and, as I said before, not deviate from what is good, if possible, but be able to do evil if constrained.

A prince must take great care that nothing goes out of his mouth which is not full of the above-named five qualities, and, to see and hear him, he should seem to be all mercy, faith, integrity, humanity, and religion. And nothing is more necessary than to seem to have this last quality, for men in general judge more by the eyes than by the hands, for every one can see, but very few have to feel. Everybody sees what you appear to be, few feel what you are, and those few will not dare to oppose themselves to the many, who have the majesty of the state to defend them; and in the actions of men, and especially of princes, from which there is no appeal, the end justifies the means. Let a prince therefore aim at conquering and maintaining the state, and the means will always be judged honourable and praised by every one, for the vulgar is always taken by appearances and the issue of the event; and the world consists only of the vulgar, and the few who are not vulgar are isolated when the many have a rallying point in the prince. A certain prince of the present time, whom it is well not to name, never does anything but preach peace and good faith, but he is really a great enemy to both, and either of them, had he observed them, would have lost him state or reputation on many occasions.

HOW A PRINCE MUST ACT IN ORDER TO GAIN A REPUTATION

Nothing causes a prince to be so much esteemed as great enterprises and giving proof of prowess. We have in our own day Ferdinand, King of Aragon, the present King of Spain. He may almost be termed a new prince, because from a weak king he has become for fame and glory the first king in Christendom, and if you regard his actions you will find them all very great and some of them extraordinary. At the beginning of his reign he assailed Granada, and that enterprise was the foundation of his state. At first he did it at his leisure and without fear of being interfered with; he kept the minds of the barons of Castile occupied in this enterprise, so that thinking only of that war they did not think of making innovations, and he thus acquired reputation and power over them without their being aware of it. He was able with the money of the Church and the people to maintain his armies, and by that long war to lay the foundations of his military power, which afterwards has made him famous. Besides this, to be able to undertake greater enterprises, and always under the pretext of religion, he had recourse to a pious cruelty, driving out the Moors from his kingdom and despoiling them. No more miserable or unusual example can be found. He also attacked Africa under the same pretext, undertook his Italian enterprise, and has lately attacked France; so that he has continually contrived great things, which have kept his subjects' minds uncertain and astonished, and occupied in watching their result. And these actions have arisen one out of the other, so that they have left no time for men to settle down and act against him.

It is also very profitable for a prince to give some outstanding example of his greatness in the internal administration, like those related of Messer Bernabò of Milan. When it happens that some one does something extraordinary, either good or evil, in civil life, he must find such means of rewarding or punishing him which will be much talked about. And above all a prince must endeavour in every action to obtain fame for being great and excellent.

A prince is further esteemed when he is a true friend or a true enemy, when, that is, he declares himself without reserve in favour of some one or against another. This policy is always more useful than remaining neutral. For if two neighbouring powers come to blows, they are either such that if one wins, you will have to fear the victor, or else not. In either of these two cases it will be better for you to declare yourself openly and make war, because in the first case if you do not declare yourself, you will fall a prey to the victor, to the pleasure and satisfaction of the one who has been defeated, and you will have no reason nor anything to defend you and nobody to receive you. For, whoever wins will not desire friends whom he suspects and who do not help him when in trouble, and whoever loses will not receive you as you did not take up arms to venture yourself in his cause.

Antiochus went to Greece, being sent by the Ætolians to expel the Romans. He sent orators to the Achaeians who were friends of the Romans to encourage them to remain neutral; on the other hand the Romans persuaded them to take up arms on their side. The matter was brought before the council of the Achaeians for deliberation, where the ambassador of Antiochus sought to persuade them to remain neutral, to which the Roman ambassador replied: 'As to what is said that is best and most useful for your state not to meddle in our war, nothing is further from the truth; for if you do not meddle in it you will become, without any favour or any reputation, the prize of the victor.'

And it will always happen that the one who is not your friend will want you to remain neutral, and the one who is your friend will require you to declare yourself by taking arms. Irresolute princes, to avoid present dangers, usually follow the way of neutrality and are mostly ruined by it. But when the prince declares himself frankly in favour of one side, if the one to whom you adhere conquers, even if he is powerful and you remain at his discretion, he is under an obligation to you and friendship has been established, and men are never so dishonest as to oppress you with such a patent ingratitude. Moreover, victories are never so prosperous that the victor does not need to have some scruples, especially as to justice. But if your ally loses, you are sheltered by him, and so long as he can, he will assist you; you become the companion of a fortune which may rise again. In the second case, when those who fight are such that you have nothing to fear from the victor, it is still more prudent on your part to adhere to one; for you go to the ruin of one with the help of him who ought to save him if he were wise, and if he conquers he rests at your discretion, and it is impossible that he should not conquer with your help.

And here it should be noted that a prince ought never to make common cause with one more powerful than himself to injure another, unless necessity forces him to it, as before said; for if he wins you rest in his power, and princes must avoid as much as possible being under the will and pleasure of others. The Venetians united with France against the Duke of Milan, although they could have avoided that alliance, and from it resulted their own ruin. But when one cannot avoid it, as happened in the case of the Florentines when the Pope and Spain went with their armies to attack Lombardy, then the prince ought to join for the above reasons. Let no state believe that it can always follow a safe policy, rather let it think that all are doubtful. This is found in the nature of things, that one never tries to avoid one difficulty without running into another, but prudence consists in being able to know the nature of the difficulties, and taking the least harmful as good.

A prince must also show himself a lover of merit, give preferment to the able, and honour those who excel in every art. Moreover he must encourage his citizens to follow their callings quietly, whether in commerce, or agriculture, or any other trade that men follow, so that this one shall not refrain from improving his possessions through fear that they may be taken from him, and that one from starting a trade for fear of taxes; but he should offer rewards to whoever does these things, and to whoever seeks in any way to improve his city or state. Besides this, he ought, at convenient seasons of the year, to keep the people occupied with festivals and shows; and as every city is divided either into guilds or into classes, he ought to pay attention to all these groups, mingle with them from time to time, and give them an example of his humanity and munificence, always upholding, however, the majesty of his dignity, which must never be allowed to fail in anything whatever.

2. *The Sovereign State* *

THOMAS HOBBES

Nature has made men so equal in the faculties of the body and mind, as that though there be found one man sometimes manifestly stronger in body, or of quicker mind than another, yet when all is reckoned together, the difference between man and man is not so considerable, as that one man can thereupon claim to himself any benefit to which another may not pretend as well as he. For as to the strength of body, the weakest has strength enough to kill the strongest, either by secret machination, or by confederacy with others that are in the same danger with himself.

And as to the faculties of the mind, setting aside the arts grounded upon words, and especially that skill of proceeding upon general and infallible rules, called science, which very few have, and but in few things, as being not a native faculty, born with us, nor attained, as prudence, while we look after somewhat else, I find yet a greater equality among men than that of strength. For prudence is but experience, which equal time equally bestows on all men in those things they equally apply themselves unto. That which may perhaps make such equality incredible is but a vain conceit of one's own wisdom, which almost all men think they have in a greater degree than the vulgar; that is, than all men but themselves, and a few others, whom by fame, or for concurring with themselves, they approve. For such is the nature of men, that howsoever they may acknowledge many others to be more witty, or more eloquent, or more learned, yet they will hardly believe there be many so wise as themselves; for they see their own wit at hand, and other men's at a distance. But this proves rather that men are in that point

* From Thomas Hobbes, *Leviathan* (1651). Spelling and punctuation have been modified for this selection.

equal, than unequal. For there is not ordinarily a greater sign of the equal distribution of any thing, than that every man is contented with his share.

From this equality of ability arises equality of hope in the attaining of our ends. And therefore if any two men desire the same thing, which nevertheless they cannot both enjoy, they become enemies; and in the way to their end, which is principally their own conservation, and sometimes their delectation only, endeavour to destroy or subdue one another. And from hence it comes to pass, that where an invader has no more to fear, than another man's single power, if one plant, sow, build, or possess a convenient seat, others may probably be expected to come prepared with forces united, to dispossess and deprive him, not only of the fruit of his labour, but also of his life, or liberty. And the invader again is in the like danger of another.

And from this diffidence of one another, there is no way for any man to secure himself, so reasonable, as anticipation; that is, by force, or wiles, to master the persons of all men he can, so long, till he sees no other power great enough to endanger him; and this is no more than his own conservation requires, and is generally allowed. Also because there be some that, taking pleasure in contemplating their own power in the acts of conquest, which they pursue farther than their security requires, if others, that otherwise would be glad to be at ease within modest bounds, should not by invasion increase their power, they would not be able, long time, by standing only on their defence, to subsist. And by consequence, such augmentation of dominion over men being necessary to a man's conservation, it ought to be allowed him.

Again, men have no pleasure, but on the contrary a great deal of grief, in keeping company where there is no power able to over-awe them all. For every man looks that his companion should value him, at the same rate he sets upon himself; and upon all signs of contempt, or undervaluing, naturally endeavours, as far as he dares (which, among them that have no common power to keep them in quiet, is far enough to make them destroy each other), to extort a greater value from his contemners, by damage; and from others, by the example.

So that in the nature of man, we find three principal causes of quarrel. First, competition; secondly, diffidence; thirdly, glory.

The first makes men invade for gain; the second, for safety; and the third, for reputation. The first use violence, to make themselves masters of other men's persons, wives, children, and cattle; the second, to defend them; the third, for trifles, as a word, a smile, a different opinion, and any other sign of undervalue, either direct in their persons, or by reflection in their kindred, their friends, their nation, their profession, or their name.

Hereby it is manifest that, during the time men live without a common power to keep them all in awe, they are in that condition which is called war; and such a war, as is of every man against every man. For war consists not in battle only, or the act of fighting, but in a tract of time, wherein the will to contend by battle is sufficiently known; and therefore the notion of *time* is to be considered in the nature of war, as it is in the nature of weather. For as the nature of foul weather lies not in a shower or two or rain, but in an inclination thereto of many days together, so the nature of war consists not in actual fighting, but in the known disposition thereto, during all the time there is no assurance to the contrary. All other time is peace.

Whatsoever therefore is consequent to a time of war, where every man is enemy to every man, the same is consequent to the time wherein men live without other security than what their own strength, and their own invention, shall furnish them withal. In such condition, there is no place for industry, because the fruit thereof is uncertain; and consequently no culture of the earth; no navigation, nor use of the commodities that may be imported by sea; no commodious building; no instrument of moving, and removing, such things as require much force; no knowledge of the face of the earth; no account of time; no arts; no letters; no society, and which is worst of all, continual fear, and danger of violent death; and the life of man, solitary, poor, nasty, brutish, and short.

It may seem strange to some man that has not well weighted these things that nature should thus dissociate, and render men apt to invade, and destroy one another; and he may therefore, not trusting to this inference, made from the passions, desire perhaps to have the same confirmed by experience. Let him therefore consider with himself: when taking a journey, he arms himself, and seeks to go well accompanied; when going to sleep, he locks his doors; when even in his house he locks his chests; and this when he knows there be laws, and public officers, armed, to revenge all injuries shall be done him; what opinion he has of his fellow-subjects, when he rides armed; of his fellow citizens, when he locks his doors; and of his children, and servants, when he locks his chests. Does he not there as much accuse mankind by his actions as I do by my words? But neither of us accuse man's nature in it. The desire, and other passions of man, are in themselves no sin. No more are the actions that proceed from those passions, till they know a law that forbids them, which till laws be made they cannot know, nor can any law be made till they have agreed upon the person that shall make it.

It may peradventure be thought there was never such a time, nor condition of war, as this; and I believe it was never generally so, over all the world; but there are many places where they live so now. For the savage people in many places of America, except the government of small families, the concord whereof depends on natural lust, have no government at all, and live at this day in that brutish manner, as I said before. Howsoever, it may be perceived what manner of life there would be, where there were no common power to fear, by the manner of life, which men that have formerly lived under a peaceful government used to degenerate into in civil war.

But though there had never been any time wherein particular men were in a condition of war one against another, yet in all times, kings, and persons of sovereign authority, because of their independency, are in continual jealousies, and in the state and posture of gladiators, having their weapons pointing, and their eyes fixed on one another; that is, their forts, garrisons, and guns upon the frontiers of their kingdoms, and continual spies upon their neighbours, which is a posture of war. But because they uphold thereby the industry of their subjects, there does not follow from it that misery which accompanies the liberty of particular men.

To this war of every man against every man, this also is consequent: that nothing can be unjust. The notions of right and wrong, justice and injustice have there no place. Where there is no common power, there is no law: where no law, no injustice. Force and fraud are in war the two cardinal virtues. Justice and injustice are none of the faculties neither of the body nor mind. If they were they might be in a man that were alone in the world, as well as his senses, and passions. They are qualities that relate to men in society, not in solitude. It is consequent also to the same condition that there be no propriety, no dominion, no *mine* and *thine* distinct, but only that to be every man's that he can get, and for so long as he can keep it. And thus much for the ill condition which man by mere nature is actually placed in, though with a possibility to come out of it, consisting partly in the passions, partly in his reason.

The passions that incline men to peace are fear of death, desire of such things as are necessary to commodious living, and a hope by their industry to obtain them. And reason suggests convenient articles of peace, upon which men may be drawn to agreement. These articles are they which otherwise are called the laws of nature.

A covenant not to defend myself from force, by force, is always void. For, as I have showed before, no man can transfer, or lay down, his right to save himself from death, wounds, and imprisonment, the avoiding whereof is the only end of laying down any right; and therefore the promise of not resisting force, in no covenant transfers any right, nor is obliging. For though a man may covenant thus, *unless I do so, or so, kill me,* he cannot covenant thus, *unless I do so, or so, I will not resist you when you come to kill me.* For man by nature chooses the lesser evil, which is danger of death in resisting, rather than the greater, which is certain and present death in not resisting. And this is granted to be true by all men, in that they lead criminals to execution and prison with armed men, notwithstanding that such criminals have consented to the law by which they are condemned.

The final cause, end, or design of men who naturally love liberty and dominion over others, in the introduction of that restraint upon themselves in which we see them live in commonwealths, is the foresight of their own preservation and of a more contented life thereby; that is to say, of getting themselves out from that miserable condition of war which is necessarily consequent, as has been shown, to the natural passions of men, when there is no visible power to keep them in awe, and tie them by fear of punishment to the performance of their covenants and observation of the laws of nature.

For the laws of nature, as *justice, equity, modesty, mercy,* and, in sum, *doing to others, as we would be done to,* of themselves, without the terror of some power to cause them to be observed, are contrary to our natural passions that carry us to partiality, pride, revenge, and the like. And covenants, without the sword, are but words, and of no strength to secure a man at all. Therefore notwithstanding the laws of nature (which everyone has then kept, when he has the will to keep them, when he can do it safely), if there be no power erected, or not great enough for our security, every man will, and may, lawfully rely on his strength and art for caution against all other men. And in all places where men have lived by small families, to rob and spoil one another has been a trade, and so far from being reputed against the law of nature, that the greater spoils they gained, the greater was their honour; and men observed no other laws therein, but the laws of honour, that is, to abstain from cruelty, leaving to men their lives, and instruments of husbandry. And as small families did then, so now do cities and kingdoms, which are but greater families, for their own security, enlarge their dominions upon all pretences of danger and fear of invasion or assistance that may be given to invaders, and endeavour as much as they can to subdue or weaken their neighbours, by open force and secret arts, for want of other caution, justly; and are remembered for it, in after ages with honour.

It is true that certain living creatures, as bees and ants, live sociably one with another, which are therefore by Aristotle numbered among political creatures, and yet have no other direction than their particular judgments and appetites, nor speech whereby one of them can signify to another what he thinks expedient for the common benefit; and therefore some man may perhaps desire to know why mankind cannot do the same. To which I answer:

First, that men are continually in competition for honour and dignity, which these creatures are not; and consequently among men there arises on that ground envy and hatred, and finally war; but among these not so.

Secondly, that among these creatures the common good differs not from the private; and being by nature inclined to their private, they procure thereby the common benefit. But man, whose joy consists in comparing himself with other men, can relish nothing but what is eminent.

Thirdly, that these creatures, having not, as man, the use of reason, do not see, nor think they see, any fault in the administration of their common business, whereas among men there are very many that think themselves wiser and abler to govern the public better than the rest; and these strive to reform and innovate, one this way, one that way, and thereby bring it into distraction and civil war.

Fourthly, that these creatures, though they have some use of voice in making known to one another their desires and other affections, yet they want that art of words by which some men can represent to others that which is good, in the likeness of evil; and evil, in the likeness of good; and augment or diminish the apparent greatness of good and evil, discontenting men and troubling their peace at their pleasure.

Fifthly, irrational creatures cannot distinguish between *injury* and *damage*, and therefore, as long as they be at ease, they are not offended with their fellows: whereas man is then most troublesome, when he is most at ease, for then it is that he loves to show his wisdom, and control the actions of them that govern the commonwealth.

Lastly, the agreement of these creatures is natural; that of men is by covenant only, which is artificial; and therefore it is no wonder if there be somewhat else required, besides covenant, to make their agreement constant and lasting, which is a common power to keep them in awe, and to direct their actions to the common benefit.

The only way to erect such a common power, as may be able to defend them from the invasion of foreigners and the injuries of one another, and thereby secure them in such sort as that by their own industry and by the fruits of the earth they may nourish themselves and live contentedly, is to confer all their power and strength upon one man, or upon one assembly of men, that may reduce all their wills, by plurality of voices, unto one will: which is as much as to say, to appoint one man, or assembly of men, to bear their persons, and every one to own and acknowledge himself to be the author of whatsoever he that so bears their person shall act, or cause to be acted, in those things which concern the common peace and safety, and therein to submit their wills, every one to his will, and their judgments to his judgment. This is more than consent, or concord; it is a real unity of them all, in one and the same person, made by the covenant of every man with every man, in such manner as if every man should say to every man, *I authorize and give up my right of governing myself, to this man, or to this assembly of men, on this condition, that thou give up thy right to him, and authorize all his actions in like manner.* This done, the multitude so united in one person is called a Commonwealth, in Latin, *civitas*. This is the generation of the great *Leviathan,* or rather, to speak more reverently, of that *mortal god* to which we owe, under the *immortal God,* our peace and defence. For by this authority, given him by every particular man in the commonwealth, he has the use of so much power and strength conferred on him that by terror thereof he is enabled to form the wills of them all, to peace at home, and mutual aid against their enemies abroad. And in him consists the essence of the commonwealth; which, to define it, is *one person, of whose acts a great multitude, by mutual covenants one with another, have made themselves every one the author, to the end he may use the strength and means of them all, as he shall think expedient, for their peace and common defence.*

And he that carries this person is called Sovereign, and said to have *sovereign power;* and every one besides, his subject.

The attaining to this sovereign power is by two ways. One, by natural force, as when a man makes his children to submit themselves and their children to his government, as being able to destroy them if they refuse, or by war subdues his enemies to his will, giving them their lives on that condition. The other is when men agree among themselves to submit to some man, or assembly of men, voluntarily, on confidence to be protected by him against all others. This latter may be called a political commonwealth, or commonwealth by *institution;* and the former, a commonwealth by *acquisition.*

The law of nature and the civil law contain each other, and are of equal extent. For the laws of nature, which consist in equity, justice, gratitude, and other moral virtues on these depending in the condition of mere nature, as I have said before, are not properly laws, but qualities that dispose men to peace and obedience. When a commonwealth is once settled, then are they actually laws, and not before, as being then the commands of the commonwealth, and therefore also civil laws: for it is the sovereign power that obliges men to obey them. For in the differences of private men to declare what is equity, what is justice, and what is moral virtue, and to make them binding, there is need of the ordinances of sovereign power, and punishments to be ordained for such as shall break them, which ordinances are therefore part of the civil law. The law of nature therefore is a part of the civil law in all commonwealths of the world. Reciprocally also, the civil law is a part of the dictates of nature. For justice, that is to say, performance of covenant, and giving to every man his own, is a dictate of the law of nature. But every subject in a commonwealth has covenanted to obey the civil law, either one with another, as when they assemble to make a common representative, or with the representative itself one by one, when subdued by the sword they promise obedience that they may receive life; and therefore obedience to the civil law is part also of the law of nature. Civil and natural law are not different kinds, but different parts of law; whereof one part being written, is called civil, the other unwritten, natural. But the right of nature, that is, the natural liberty of man, may by the civil law be abridged and restrained: nay, the end of making laws is no other but such restraint, without the which there cannot possibly be any peace. And law was brought into the world for nothing else but to limit the natural liberty of particular men in such manner, as they might not hurt, but assist, one another and join together against a common enemy.

Though nothing can be immortal which mortals make, yet, if men had the use of reason they pretend to, their commonwealths might be secured at least from perishing by internal diseases. For by the nature of their institution they are designed to live as long as mankind, or as the laws of nature, or as justice itself which gives them life. Therefore when they come to be dissolved, not by external violence but intestine disorder, the fault is not in men, as they are the *matter,* but as they are the *makers* and orderers of them. For men, as they become at last weary of irregular jostling and hewing one another, and desire with all their hearts to conform themselves into one firm and lasting edifice, so for want, both of the art of making fit laws to square their actions by, and also of humility and patience to suffer the rude and cumbersome points of their present greatness to be taken off, they cannot without the help of a very able architect be compiled into any other than a crazy building, such as hardly lasting out their own time must assuredly fall upon the heads of their posterity.

Among the *infirmities* therefore of a commonwealth, I will reckon in the first place those that arise from an imperfect institution, and resemble the diseases of a natural body which proceed from a defectuous procreation.

Of which this is one, *that a man, to obtain a kingdom, is sometimes content with less power than to the peace and defence of the commonwealth is necessarily required.* From whence it comes to pass that when the exercise of the power laid by is for the public safety to be resumed, it has the resemblance of an unjust act, which disposes great numbers of men, when occasion is presented, to rebel, in the same manner as the bodies of children, gotten by diseased parents, are subject either to untimely death or, to purge the ill quality derived from their vicious conception, breaking out into biles and scabs. And when kings deny themselves some such necessary power, it is not always, though sometimes, out of ignorance of what is necessary to the office they undertake, but many times out of a hope to recover the same again at their pleasure. Wherein they reason not well, because such as will hold them to their promises shall be maintained against them by foreign commonwealths, who in order to the good of their own subjects let slip few occasions to *weaken* the estate of their neighbours. So was Thomas Becket, archbishop of Canterbury, supported against Henry the Second by the Pope, the subjection of ecclesiastics to the commonwealth having been dispensed with by William the Conqueror at his reception, when he took an oath not to infringe the liberty of the church. And so were the barons, whose power was by William Rufus, to have their help in transferring the succession from his elder brother to himself, increased to a degree inconsistent with the sovereign power, maintained in their rebellion against king John, by the French.

Nor does this happen in monarchy only. For whereas the style of the ancient Roman commonwealth was *The Senate and People of Rome,* neither senate nor people pretended to the whole power, which first caused the seditions of Tiberius Gracchus, Caius Gracchus, Lucius Saturninus, and others, and afterwards the wars between the senate and the people, under Marius and Sylla; and again under Pompey and Caesar, to the extinction of their democracy, and the setting up of monarchy.

The people of Athens bound themselves but from one only action, which was that no man on pain of death should propound the renewing of the war for the island of Salamis; and yet thereby, if Solon had not caused to be given out he was mad, and afterwards in gesture and habit of a madman, and in verse, propounded it to the people that flocked about him, they had had an enemy perpetually in readiness, even at the gates of their city; such damage, or shifts, are all commonwealths forced to that have their power never so little limited.

In the second place, I observe the *diseases* of a commonwealth that proceed from the poison of seditious doctrines, whereof one is *that every private man is judge of good and evil actions.* This is true in the condition of mere nature, where there are no civil laws, and also under civil government in such cases as are not determined by the law. But otherwise, it is manifest that the measure of good and evil actions is the civil law, and the judge the legislator who is always representative of the commonwealth. From this false doctrine, men are disposed to debate with themselves and dispute the commands of the commonwealth, and afterwards to obey or disobey them, as in their private judgments they shall think fit; whereby the commonwealth is distracted and *weakened.*

Another doctrine repugnant to civil society is that *whatsoever a man does against his conscience is sin,* and it depends on the presumption of making himself judge of good and evil. For a man's conscience and his judgment is the same thing, and as the judgment, so also the conscience may be erroneous. Therefore, though he that is subject to no civil law sins in all he does against his conscience, because he has no other rule to follow but his own reason, yet it is not so with him that lives in a commonwealth, because the law is the public conscience, by which he has already undertaken to be guided. Otherwise in such diversity as there is of private consciences, which are but private opinions, the commonwealth must needs be distracted, and no man dare to obey the sovereign power further than it shall seem good in his own eyes.

It has been also commonly taught that *faith and sanctity are not to be attained by study and reason, but by supernatural inspiration or infusion.* Which granted, I see not why any man should render a reason of his faith; or why every Christian should not be also a prophet; or why any man should take the law of his country, rather than his own inspiration, for the rule of his action. And thus we fall again in the fault of taking upon us to judge of good and evil, or to make judges of it such private men as pretend to be supernaturally inspired, to the dissolution of all civil government. Faith comes by hearing, and hearing by those accidents which guide us into the presence of them that speak to us; which accidents are all contrived by God Almighty, and yet are not supernatural, but only, for the great number of them that concur to every effect, unobservable. Faith and sanctity are indeed not very frequent; but yet they are not miracles, but brought to pass by education, discipline, correction, and other natural ways by which God works them in his elect, at such times as he thinks fit. And these three opinions, pernicious to peace and government, have in this part of the world proceeded chiefly from the tongues and pens of unlearned divines, who, joining the words of Holy Scripture together otherwise than is agreeable to reason, do what they can to make men think that sanctity and natural reason cannot stand together.

A fourth opinion, repugnant to the nature of a commonwealth, is this, *that he that has the sovereign power is subject to the civil laws.* It is true that sovereigns are all subject to the laws of nature, because such laws be divine and cannot by any man, or commonwealth, be abrogated. But to those laws which the sovereign himself, that is, which the commonwealth makes, he is not subject. For to be subject to laws is to be subject to the commonwealth, that is, to the sovereign representative, that is to himself; which is not subjection, but freedom from the laws. Which error, because it sets the laws above the sovereign, sets also a judge above him, and a power to punish him; which is to make a new sovereign; and again for the same reason a third, to punish the second; and so continually without end, to the confusion and dissolution of the commonwealth.

A fifth doctrine, that tends to the dissolution of a commonwealth, is *that every private man has an absolute propriety in his goods, such as excludes the right of the sovereign.* Every man has indeed a propriety that excludes the right of every other subject; and he has it only from the sovereign power, without the protection whereof, every other man should have equal right to the same. But if the right of the sovereign also be excluded, he cannot perform the office they have put him into, which is to defend them both from foreign enemies and from the injuries of one another; and consequently there is no longer a commonwealth.

And if the propriety of subjects excludes not the right of the sovereign representative to their goods, much less to their offices of judicature, or execution, in which they represent the sovereign himself.

There is a sixth doctrine, plainly and directly against the essence of a commonwealth; and it is this, *that the sovereign power may be divided.* For what is it to divide the power of a commonwealth, but to dissolve it; for powers divided mutually destroy each other. And for these doctrines men are chiefly beholding to some of those that, making profession of the laws, endeavour to make them depend upon their own learning and not upon the legislative power.

As there have been doctors that hold there be three souls in a man, so there be also that think there may be more souls, that is, more sovereigns than one, in a commonwealth, and set up a *supremacy* against the *sovereignty, canons* against *laws,* and a *ghostly authority* against the *civil;* working on men's minds with words and distinctions that of themselves signify nothing, but betray by their obscurity that there walks, as some think, invisibly another kingdom, as it were a kingdom of fairies, in the dark. Now seeing it is manifest that the civil power and the power of the commonwealth is the same thing, and that supremacy and the power of making canons and granting faculties implies a commonwealth, it follows that where one is sovereign, another supreme, where one can make laws, and another make canons, there must needs be two commonwealths, of one and the same subjects, which is a kingdom divided in itself and cannot stand. For notwithstanding the insignificant distinction of *temporal* and *ghostly,* they are still two kingdoms, and every subject is subject to two masters. For seeing the *ghostly* power challenges the right to declare what is sin, it challenges by consequence to declare what is law, sin being nothing but the transgression of the law; and again, the civil power challenging to declare what is law, every subject must obey two masters, who both will have their commands be observed as law; which is impossible. Or, if it be but one kingdom, either the *civil,* which is the power of the commonwealth, must be subordinate to the *ghostly,* and then there is no sovereignty but the *ghostly;* or the *ghostly* must be subordinate to the *temporal,* and then there is no *supremacy* but the *temporal.* When therefore these two powers oppose one another, the commonwealth cannot but be in great danger of civil war and dissolution. For the *civil* authority being more visible, and standing in the clearer light of natural reason, cannot choose but draw to it in all times a very considerable part of the people; and the *spiritual,* though it stand in the darkness of School distinctions and hard words, yet, because the fear of darkness and ghosts is greater than other fears, cannot want a party sufficient to trouble, and sometimes to destroy, a commonwealth. And this is a disease which not unfitly may be compared to the epilepsy, or falling sickness, which the Jews took to be one kind of possession by spirits in the body natural. For as in this disease, there is an unnatural spirit, or wind, in the head that obstructs the roots of the nerves and, moving them violently, takes away the motion which naturally they should have from the power of the soul in the brain, and thereby causes violent and irregular motions, which men call convulsions, in the parts; insomuch as he that is seized therewith falls down sometimes into the water, and sometimes into the fire, as a man deprived of his senses; so also in the body politic, when the spiritual power moves the members of a commonwealth by the terror of punishments and hope of rewards, which are the nerves of it, otherwise than by the civil power, which is the soul of the commonwealth, they ought to be moved; and by strange and hard words suffocates their understanding, it must needs thereby distract the people, and either overwhelm the commonwealth with oppression, or cast it into the fire of a civil war.

Sometimes also in the merely civil government there be more than one soul, as when the power of levying money, which is the nutritive faculty, has depended on a general assembly; the power of conduct and command, which is the motive faculty, on one man; and the power of making laws, which is the rational faculty, on the accidental consent, not only of those two, but also of a third; this endangers the commonwealth, sometimes for want of consent to good laws, but most often for want of such nourishment as is necessary to life and motion. For although few perceive that such government is not government, but division of the commonwealth into three factions, and call it mixed monarchy, yet the truth is that it is not one independent commonwealth but three independent factions, nor one representative person, but three. In the kingdom of God, there may be three persons independent, without breach of unity in God that reigns; but where men reign that be subject to diversity of opinions, it cannot be so. And therefore if the king bear the person of the people, and the general assembly bear also the person of the people, and another assembly bear the person of a part of the people, they are not one person, nor one sovereign, but three persons, and three sovereigns.

~~~~~~

3. Politics, History, Religion *

<div align="right">EDMUND BURKE</div>

~~~~~~

You will observe, that from Magna Charta to the Declaration of Right, it has been the uniform policy of our constitution to claim and assert our liberties, as an *entailed inheritance* derived to us from our forefathers, and to be transmitted to our posterity; as an estate specially belonging to the people of this kingdom, without any reference whatever to any other more general or

---

* From Edmund Burke, *Reflections on the Revolution in France* (1790).

prior right. By this means our constitution preserves an unity in so great a diversity of its parts. We have an inheritable crown; an inheritable peerage; and a House of Commons and a people inheriting privileges, franchises, and liberties, from a long line of ancestors.

The policy appears to me to be the result of profound reflection; or rather the happy effect of following nature, which is wisdom without reflection, and above it. A spirit of innovation is generally the result of a selfish temper, and confined views. People will not look forward to posterity, who never look backward to their ancestors. Besides, the people of England well know, that the idea of inheritance furnishes a sure principle of conservation, and a sure principle of transmission; without at all excluding a principle of improvement. It leaves acquisition free; but it secures what it acquires. Whatever advantages are obtained by a state proceeding on these maxims, are locked fast as in a sort of family settlement; grasped as in a kind of mortmain for ever. By a constitutional policy working after the pattern of nature, we receive, we hold, we transmit our government and our privileges, in the same manner in which we enjoy and transmit our property and our lives. The institutions of policy, the goods of fortune, the gifts of Providence, are handed down to us, and from us, in the same course and order. Our political system is placed in a just correspondence and symmetry with the order of the world, and with the mode of existence decreed to a permanent body composed of transitory parts; wherein, by the disposition of a stupendous wisdom, moulding together the great mysterious incorporation of the human race, the whole, at one time, is never old, or middle-aged, or young, but, in a condition of unchangeable consistency, moves on through the varied tenor of perpetual decay, fall, renovation, and progression. Thus, by preserving the method of nature in the conduct of the state, in what we improve, we are never wholly new; in what we retain, we are never wholly obsolete. By adhering in this manner and on those principles to our forefathers, we are guided not by the superstition of antiquarians, but by the spirit of philosophic analogy. In this choice of inheritance we have given to our frame of polity the image of a relation in blood; binding up the constitution of our country with our dearest domestic ties; adopting our fundamental laws into the bosom of our family affections, keeping inseparable and cherishing with the warmth of all their combined and mutually reflected charities, our state, our hearths, our sepulchres, and our altars.

Through the same plan of a conformity to nature in our artificial institutions, and by calling in the aid of her unerring and powerful instincts, to fortify the fallible and feeble contrivances of our reason, we have derived several other, and those no small benefits, from considering our liberties in the light of an inheritance. Always acting as if in the presence of canonized forefathers, the spirit of freedom, leading in itself to misrule and excess, is tempered with an awful gravity. This idea of a liberal descent inspires us with a sense of habitual native dignity, which prevents that upstart insolence almost inevitably adhering to and disgracing those who are the first acquirers of any distinction. By this means our liberty becomes a noble freedom. It carries an imposing and majestic aspect. It has a pedigree and illustrating ancestors. It has its bearings and its ensigns armorial. It has its gallery of portraits; its monumental inscriptions; its records, evidences, and titles. We procure reverence to our civil institutions on the principle upon which nature teaches us to revere individual men; on account of their age, and on account of those from whom they are descended. All your sophisters cannot produce anything better adapted to preserve a rational and manly freedom than the course that we have pursued, who have chosen our nature rather than our speculations, our breasts rather than our inventions, for the great conservatories and magazines of our rights and privileges.

France, by the perfidy of her leaders, has utterly disgraced the tone of lenient counsel in the cabinets of princes, and disarmed it of its most potent topics. She has sanctified the dark, suspicious maxims of tyrannous distrust; and taught kings to tremble at (what will hereafter be called) the delusive plausibilities of moral politicians. Sovereigns will consider those, who advise them to place an unlimited confidence in their people, as subverters of their thrones; as traitors who aim at their destruction, by leading their easy good-nature, under specious pretences, to admit combinations of bold and faithless men into a participation of their power. This alone (if there were nothing else) is an irreparable calamity to you and to mankind. Remember that your parliament of Paris told your king, that, in calling the states together, he had nothing to fear but the prodigal excess of their zeal in providing for the support of the throne. It is right that these men should hide their heads. It is right that they should bear their part in the ruin which their counsel has brought on their sovereign and their country. Such sanguine declarations tend to lull authority asleep; to encourage it rashly to engage in perilous adventures of untried policy; to neglect those provisions, preparations and precautions, which distinguish benevolence from imbecility; and without which no man can answer for the salutary effect of any abstract plan of government or of freedom. For want of these, they have seen the medicine of the state corrupted into its poison. They have seen the French rebel against a mild and lawful monarch, with more fury, outrage, and insult, than ever any people has been known to rise against the most illegal usurper, or the most sanguinary tyrant. Their resistance was made to concession; their revolt was from protection; their blow was aimed at a hand holding out graces, favours, and immunities.

This was unnatural. The rest is in order. They have found their punishment in their success. Laws overturned; tribunals subverted; industry without vigour; commerce expiring; the revenue unpaid, yet the people impoverished; a church pillaged, and a state not relieved; civil and military anarchy made the constitution of the kingdom; everything human and divine sacrificed to the idol of public credit, and national bankruptcy the consequence; and, to crown all, the paper securities of new, precarious, tottering power, the discredited paper securities of impoverished fraud, and beggared rapine, held out as a currency for the support of the empire, in lieu of the two great recognized species that represent the lasting, conventional credit of mankind, which disappeared and hid themselves in the earth from whence they came, when the principle of property, whose creatures and representatives they are, was systematically subverted.

Were all these dreadful things necessary? Were they the inevitable results of the desperate struggle of determined patriots, compelled to wade through blood and tumult, to the quiet shore of a tranquil and prosperous liberty? No! nothing like it. The fresh ruins of France, which shock our feelings wherever we can turn our eyes, are not the devastation of civil war; they are the sad but instructive monuments of rash and ignorant counsel in time of profound peace. They are the display of inconsiderate and presumptuous, because unresisted and irresistible authority. The persons who have thus squandered away the precious treasure of their crimes, the persons who have made this prodigal and wild waste of public evils (the last stake reserved for the ultimate ransom of the state) have met in their progress with little, or rather with no opposition at all. Their whole march was more like a triumphal procession, than the progress of a war. Their pioneers have gone before them, and demolished and laid everything level at their feet. Not one drop of *their* blood have they shed in the cause of the country they have ruined. They have made no sacrifices to their projects of greater consequence than their shoebuckles, whilst they were imprisoning their king, murdering their fellow-citizens, and bathing in tears, and plunging in poverty and distress, thousands of worthy men and worthy families. Their cruelty has not even been the base result of fear. It has been the effect of their sense of perfect safety, in authorizing treasons, robberies, rapes, assassinations, slaughters, and burnings, throughout their harassed land. But the cause of all was plain from the beginning.

This unforced choice, this fond election of evil, would appear perfectly unaccountable, if we did not consider the composition of the National Assembly; I do not mean its formal constitution, which, as it now stands, is exceptional enough, but the materials of which, in a great measure, it is composed, which is of ten thousand times greater consequence than all the formalities in the world. If we were to know nothing of this assembly but by its title and function, no colours could paint to the imagination anything more venerable. In that light the mind of an inquirer, subdued by such an awful image as that of the virtue and wisdom of a whole people collected into one focus, would pause and hesitate in condemning things even of the very worst aspect. Instead of blamable, they would appear only mysterious. But no name, no power, no function, no artificial institution whatsoever, can make the men of whom any system of authority is composed, any other than God, and nature, and education, and their habits of life have made them. Capacities beyond these the people have not to give. Virtue and wisdom may be the objects of their choice; but their choice confers neither the one nor the other on those upon whom they lay their ordaining hands. They have not the engagement of nature, they have not the promise of revelation for any such powers.

After I had read over the list of the persons and descriptions elected into the *Tiers État,* nothing which they afterwards did could appear astonishing. Among them, indeed, I saw some of known rank; some of shining talents; but of any practical experience in the state, not one man was to be found. The best were only men of theory. But whatever the distinguished few may have been, it is the substance and mass of the body which constitutes its character, and must finally determine its direction. In all bodies, those who will lead, must also, in a considerable degree, follow. They must conform their propositions to the taste, talent, and disposition, of those whom they wish to conduct: therefore, if an assembly is viciously or feebly composed in a very great part of it, nothing but such a supreme degree of virtue as very rarely appears in the world, and for that reason cannot enter into calculation, will prevent the men of talents disseminated through it from becoming only the expert instruments of absurd projects! If, what is the more likely event, instead of that unusual degree of virtue, they should be actuated by sinister ambition, and a lust of meretricious glory, then the feeble part of the assembly, to whom at first they conform, becomes in its turn the dupe and instrument of their designs. In this political traffic, the leaders will be obliged to bow to the ignorance of their followers, and the followers to become subservient to the worst designs of their leaders.

To secure any degree of sobriety in the propositions made by the leaders in any public assembly, they ought to respect, in some degree perhaps to fear, those whom they conduct. To be led any otherwise than blindly, the followers must be qualified, if not for actors, at least for judges; they must also be judges of natural weight and authority. Nothing can secure a steady and moderate conduct in such assemblies, but that the body of them should be respectably composed, in point of condition in life, of permanent property, of education, and of such habits as enlarge and liberalize the understanding.

In the calling of the states-general of France, the first thing that struck me, was a great departure from the ancient course. I found the representation for the third estate composed of six hundred persons. They were equal in number to the representatives of both the other orders. If the orders were to act separately, the number would not, beyond the consideration of the expense, be of much moment. But when it became apparent that the orders were to be melted down into one, the policy and necessary effect of this numerous representation became obvious. A very small desertion from either of the two other orders must throw the power of both into the hands of the third. In fact, the whole power of the state was soon resolved into that body. Its due composition became therefore of infinitely the greater importance.

Judge, sir, of my surprise, when I found that a very great proportion of the assembly (a majority, I believe, of the members who attended) was composed of practitioners in the law. It was composed, not of distinguished magistrates, who had given pledges to their country of their science, prudence, and integrity; not of leading advocates, the glory of the bar; not of renowned professors in universities;—but for the far greater part, as it must in such a number, of the inferior, unlearned, mechanical, merely instrumental members of the profession. There were distinguished exceptions; but the general composition was of obscure provincial advocates, of stewards of petty local jurisdictions, country attorneys, notaries, and the whole train of the ministers of municipal litigation, the fomenters and conductors of the petty war of village vexation. From the moment I read the list, I saw distinctly, and very nearly as it has happened, all that was to follow.

The degree of estimation in which any profession is held becomes the standard of the estimation in which the professors hold themselves. Whatever the personal merits of many individual lawyers might have been, and in many it was undoubtedly very considerable, in that military kingdom no part of the profession had been much regarded, except the highest of all, who often united to their professional offices great family splendour, and were invested with great power and authority. These certainly were highly respected, and even with no small degree of awe. The next rank was not much esteemed; the mechanical part was in a very low degree of repute.

Whenever the supreme authority is vested in a body so composed, it must evidently produce the consequence of supreme authority placed in the hands of men not taught habitually to respect themselves; who had no previous fortune in character at stake; who could not be expected to bear with moderation, or to conduct with discretion, a power, which they themselves, more than any others, must be surprised to find in their hands. Who could flatter himself that these men, suddenly, and, as it were, by enchantment, snatched from the humblest rank of subordination, would not be intoxicated with their unprepared greatness? Who could conceive that men, who are habitually meddling, daring, subtle, active, of litigious dispositions, and unquiet minds, would easily fall back into their old condition of obscure contention, and laborious, low, and unprofitable chicane? Who could doubt but that, at any expense to the state, of which they understood nothing, they must pursue their private interests, which they understood but too well? It was not an event depending on chance or contingency. It was inevitable; it was necessary; it was planted in the nature of things. They must *join* (if their capacity did not permit them to *lead*) in any project which could procure to them a *litigious constitution;* which could lay open to them those innumerable lucrative jobs, which follow in the train of all great convulsions and revolutions in the state, and particularly in all great and violent permutations of property. Was it to be expected that they would attend to the stability of property, whose existence had always depended upon whatever rendered property questionable, ambiguous, and insecure? Their objects would be enlarged with their elevation, but their disposition and habits, and mode of accomplishing their designs, must remain the same.

Well! but these men were to be tempered and restrained by other descriptions, of more sober minds, and more enlarged understandings. Were they then to be awed by the super-eminent authority and awful dignity of a handful of country clowns, who have seats in that assembly, some of whom are said not to be able to read and write? and by not a greater number of traders, who, though somewhat more instructed, and more conspicuous in the order of society, had never known anything beyond their counting-house? No! both these descriptions were more formed to be overborne and swayed by the intrigues and artifices of lawyers, than to become their counterpoise. With such a dangerous disproportion, the whole must needs be governed by them. To the faculty of law was joined a pretty considerable proportion of the faculty of medicine. This faculty had not, any more than that of the law, possessed in France its just estimation. Its professors, therefore, must have the qualities of men not habituated to sentiments of dignity. But supposing they had ranked as they ought to do, and as with us they do actually, the sides of sick-beds are not the academies for forming statesmen and legislators. Then came the dealers in stocks and funds, who must be eager, at any expense, to change their ideal paper wealth for the more solid substance of land. To these were joined men of other descriptions, from whom as little knowledge of, or attention to, the interests of a great state was to be expected, and as little regard to the stability of any institution; men formed to be instruments, not controls. Such in general was the composition of the *Tiers État* in the National Assembly; in which was scarcely to be perceived the slightest traces of what we call the natural landed interest of the country.

The Chancellor of France, at the opening of the states, said, in a tone of oratorical flourish, that all occupations were honourable. If he meant only that no honest employment was disgraceful, he would not have gone beyond the truth. But in asserting that anything is honourable, we imply some distinction in its favour. The occupation of a hair-dresser, or of a working tallow-chandler, cannot be a matter of honour to any person—to say nothing of a number of other more servile employments. Such descriptions of men ought not to suffer oppression from the state; but the state suffers oppression, if such as they, either individually or collectively, are permitted to rule. In this you think you are combating prejudice, but you are at war with nature.[1]

I see that your example is held out to shame us. I know that we are supposed a dull, sluggish race, rendered passive by finding our situation tolerable, and prevented by a mediocrity of freedom from ever attaining to its full perfection. Your leaders in France began by affecting to admire, almost to adore, the British constitution; but, as they advanced, they came to look upon it with a sovereign contempt. The friends of your National Assembly amongst us have full as mean an opinion of what was formerly thought the glory of their country. The Revolution Society has discovered that the English nation is not free. They are convinced that the inequality in our representation is a 'defect in our constitution *so gross and palpable,* as to make it excellent chiefly in *form and theory.'* [2] That a representation in the legislature of a kingdom is not only the basis of all constitutional liberty in it, but of *'all legitimate government;* that without it a *government* is nothing but an *usurpation';*—that 'when the representation is *partial,* the kingdom possesses liberty only *partially;* and if extremely partial, it gives only a *semblance;* and if not only extremely partial, but corruptly chosen, it becomes a *nuisance.'* Dr. Price considers this inadequacy of representation as our *fundamental grievance;* and though, as to the corruption of this semblance of representation, he hopes it is not yet arrived to its full perfection of depravity, he fears that 'nothing will be done towards gaining for us this *essential blessing,* until some *great abuse of power* again provokes our resentment, or some *great calamity* again alarms our fears, or perhaps till the acquisition of a *pure and equal representation by other countries,* whilst we are *mocked* with the *shadow,* kindles our shame.' To this he subjoins a note in these words. 'A representation chosen chiefly by the treasury, and a *few* thousands of the *dregs* of the people, who are generally paid for their votes.'

You will smile here at the consistency of those democratists, who, when they are not on their guard, treat the humbler part of the community with the greatest contempt, whilst, at the same time, they pretend to make them

---

[1] Ecclesiasticus, chap. xxxviii. ver. 24, 25. 'The wisdom of a learned man cometh by opportunity of leisure: and he that hath little business shall become wise.'—'How can he get wisdom that holdeth the plough, and that glorieth in the goad; that driveth oxen; and is occupied in their labours; and whose talk is of bullocks?'

Ver. 27. 'So every carpenter and work-master that laboureth night and day,' &c.

Ver. 33. 'They shall not be sought for in public counsel, nor sit high in the congregation: they shall not sit on the judge's seat, nor understand the sentence of judgment: they cannot declare justice and judgment, and they shall not be found where parables are spoken.'

Ver. 34. 'But they will maintain the state of the world.'

I do not determine whether this book be canonical, as the Gallican Church (till lately) has considered it, or apocryphal, as here it is taken. I am sure it contains a great deal of sense and truth.

[2] 'Discourse on the Love of our Country,' 3rd edit. p. 39.

the depositories of all power. It would require a long discourse to point out
to you the many fallacies that lurk in the generality and equivocal nature of
the terms 'inadequate representation.' I shall only say here, in justice to that
old-fashioned constitution, under which we have long prospered, that our
representation has been found perfectly adequate to all the purposes for
which a representation of the people can be desired or devised. I defy the
enemies of our constitution to show the contrary. To detail the particulars in
which it is found so well to promote its ends, would demand a treatise on
our practical constitution. I state here the doctrine of the revolutionists, only
that you and others may see, what an opinion these gentlemen entertain of
the constitution of their country, and why they seem to think that some great
abuse of power, or some great calamity, as giving a chance for the blessing
of a constitution according to their ideas, would be much palliated to their
feelings; you see *why they* are so much enamoured of your fair and equal
representation, which being once obtained the same effects might follow.
You see they consider our House of Commons as only 'a semblance,' 'a form,'
'a theory,' 'a shadow,' 'a mockery,' perhaps 'a nuisance.'

These gentlemen value themselves on being systematic; and not without
reason. They must therefore look on this gross and palpable defect of representation, this fundamental grievance (so they call it) as a thing not only
vicious in itself, but as rendering our whole government absolutely *illegitimate,* and not at all better than a downright *usurpation.* Another revolution,
to get rid of this illegitimate and usurped government, would of course be
perfectly justifiable, if not absolutely necessary. Indeed their principle, if you
observe it with any attention, goes much further than to an alteration in the
election of the House of Commons; for, if popular representation, or choice,
is necessary to the *legitimacy* of all government, the House of Lords is, at
one stroke, bastardized and corrupted in blood. That House is no representative of the people at all, even in 'semblance or in form.' The case of the
crown is altogether as bad. In vain the crown may endeavour to screen itself
against these gentlemen by the authority of the establishment made on the
Revolution. The Revolution which is resorted to for a title, on their system,
wants a title itself. The Revolution is built, according to their theory, upon
a basis not more solid than our present formalities, as it was made by a
House of Lords, not representing anyone but themselves; and by a House of
Commons exactly such as the present, that is, as they term it, by a mere
'shadow and mockery of representation.'

Something they must destroy, or they seem to themselves to exist for no
purpose. One set is for destroying the civil power through the ecclesiastical;
another for demolishing the ecclesiastical through the civil. They are aware
that the worst consequences might happen to the public in accomplishing
this double ruin of church and state; but they are so heated with their theories, that they give more than hints, that this ruin, with all the mischiefs that

must lead to it and attend it, and which to themselves appear quite certain, would not be unacceptable to them, or very remote from their wishes. A man amongst them of great authority, and certainly of great talents, speaking of a supposed alliance between church and state, says, 'perhaps *we must wait for the fall of the civil powers* before this most unnatural alliance be broken. Calamitous no doubt will that time be. But what convulsion in the political world ought to be a subject of lamentation, if it be attended with so desirable an effect?' You see with what a steady eye these gentlemen are prepared to view the greatest calamities which can befall their country.

It is no wonder therefore, that with these ideas of everything in their constitution and government at home, either in church or state, as illegitimate and usurped, or, at best as a vain mockery, they look abroad with an eager and passionate enthusiasm. Whilst they are possessed by these notions, it is vain to talk to them of the practice of their ancestors, the fundamental laws of their country, the fixed form of a constitution, whose merits are confirmed by the solid test of long experience, and an increasing public strength and national prosperity. They despise experience as the wisdom of unlettered men; and as for the rest, they have wrought under ground a mine that will blow up, at one grand explosion, all examples of antiquity, all precedents, charters, and acts of parliament. They have 'the rights of men.' Against these there can be no prescription; against these no argument is binding: these admit no temperament, and no compromise: anything withheld from their full demand is so much of fraud and injustice. Against these their rights of men let no government look for security in the length of its continuance, or in the justice and lenity of its administration. The objections of these speculatists, if its forms do not quadrate with their theories, are as valid against such an old and beneficent government, as against the most violent tyranny, or the greenest usurpation. They are always at issue with governments, not on a question of abuse, but a question of competency, and a question of title. I have nothing to say to the clumsy subtlety of their political metaphysics. Let them be their amusement in the schools.—'*Illa se jactet in aula—Æolus, et clauso ventorum carcere regnet.*'—But let them not break prison to burst like a *Levanter,* to sweep the earth with their hurricane, and to break up the fountains of the great deep to overwhelm us.

Far am I from denying in theory, full as far is my heart from withholding in practice (if I were of power to give or to withhold) the *real* rights of men. In denying their false claims of right, I do not mean to injure those which are real, and are such as their pretended rights would totally destroy. If civil society be made for the advantage of man, all the advantages for which it is made become his right. It is an institution of beneficence; and law itself is only beneficence; acting by a rule. Men have a right to live by that rule; they have a right to do justice; as between their fellows, whether their fellows are in politic function or in ordinary occupation. They have a right to the fruits of their industry; and to the means of making their industry fruitful. They have a right to the acquisitions of their parents; to the nourishment and improvement of their offspring; to instruction in life, and to consolation in death. Whatever each man can separately do, without trespassing upon others, he has a right to do for himself; and he has a right to a fair portion of all which society, with all its combinations of skill and force, can do in his favour. In this partnership all men have equal rights; but not to equal things. He that has but five shillings in the partnership, has as good a right to it as he that has five hundred pounds has to his larger proportion. But he has not a right to an equal dividend in the product of the joint stock; and as to the share of power, authority, and direction which each individual ought to have in the management of the state, that I must deny to be amongst the direct original rights of man in civil society; for I have in my contemplation the civil social man, and no other. It is a thing to be settled by convention.

If civil society be the offspring of convention, that convention must be its law. That convention must limit and modify all the descriptions of constitution which are formed under it. Every sort of legislature, judicial, or executory power, are its creatures. They can have no being in any other state of things; and how can any man claim, under the conventions of civil society, rights which do not so much as suppose its existence?—rights which are absolutely repugnant to it? One of the first motives to civil society, and which becomes one of its fundamental rules, is, *that no man should be judge in his own cause.* By this each person has at once divested himself of the first fundamental right of uncovenanted man, that is, to judge for himself and to assert his own cause. He abdicates all right to be his own governor. He inclusively, in a great measure abandons the right of self-defence, the first law of nature. Men cannot enjoy the rights of an uncivil and of a civil state together. That he may obtain justice, he gives up his right of determining what it is in points the most essential to him. That he may secure some liberty, he makes a surrender in trust of the whole of it.

Government is not made in virtue of natural rights, which may and do exist in total independence of it; and exist in much greater clearness, and in a much greater degree of abstract perfection; but their abstract perfection is their practical defect. By having a right to everything, they want everything. Government is a contrivance of human wisdom to provide for human *wants.* Men have a right that these wants should be provided for by this wisdom. Among these wants is to be reckoned the want, out of civil society, of a sufficient restraint upon their passions. Society requires not only that the passions of individuals should be subjected, but that even in the mass and body, as well as in the individuals, the inclinations of men should frequently be thwarted, their will controlled, and their passions brought into subjection. This can only be done *by a power out of themselves;* and not, in the exercise of its function, subject to that will and to those passions which it is its office to bridle and subdue. In this sense the restraints on men, as well as their liberties, are to be reckoned among their rights. But as the liberties and the restrictions vary with times and circumstances, and admit of infinite modifications, they cannot be settled upon any abstract rule; and nothing is so foolish as to discuss them upon that principle.

The moment you abate anything from the full rights of men, each to govern himself, and suffer any artificial, positive limitation upon those rights, from that moment the whole organization of government becomes a consideration of convenience. This it is which makes the constitution of a state, and the due distribution of its powers, a matter of the most delicate and complicated skill. It requires a deep knowledge of human nature and human necessities, and of the things which facilitate or obstruct the various ends, which are to be pursued by the mechanism of civil institutions. The state is to have recruits to its strength, and remedies to its distempers. What is the use of discussing a man's abstract right to food or medicine? The question is upon the method of procuring and administering them. In that deliberation I shall always advise to call in the aid of the farmer and the physician, rather than the professor of metaphysics.

The science of constructing a commonwealth, or renovating it, or reforming it, is, like every other experimental science, not to be taught *a priori*. Nor is it a short experience that can instruct us in that practical science; because the real effects of moral causes are not always immediate; but that which in the first instance is prejudicial may be excellent in its remoter operation; and its excellence may arise even from the ill effects it produces in the beginning. The reverse also happens; and very plausible schemes, with very pleasing commencements, have often shameful and lamentable conclusions. In states there are often some obscure and almost latent causes, things which appear at first view of little moment, on which a very great part of its prosperity or adversity may most essentially depend. The science of government being therefore so practical in itself, and intended for such practical purposes, a matter which requires experience, and even more experience than any person can gain in his whole life, however sagacious and observing he may be, it is with infinite caution that any man ought to venture upon pulling down an edifice, which has answered in any tolerable degree for ages the common purposes of society, or on building it up again, without having models and patterns of approved utility before his eyes.

These metaphysic rights entering into common life, like rays of light which pierce into a dense medium, are, by the laws of nature, refracted from their straight line. Indeed, in the gross and complicated mass of human passions and concerns, the primitive rights of men undergo such a variety of refractions and reflections, that it becomes absurd to talk of them as if they continued in the simplicity of their original direction. The nature of man is intricate; the objects of society are of the greatest possible complexity: and therefore no simple disposition or direction of power can be suitable either to man's nature, or to the quality of his affairs. When I hear the simplicity of contrivance aimed at and boasted of in any new political constitutions, I am at no loss to decide that the artificers are grossly ignorant of their trade, or totally negligent of their duty. The simple governments are fundamentally defective, to say no worse of them. If you were to contemplate society in but one point of view, all these simple modes of polity are infinitely captivating. In effect each would answer its single end much more perfectly than the more complex is able to attain all its complex purposes. But it is better that the whole should be imperfectly and anomalously answered, than that, while some parts are provided for with great exactness, others might be totally neglected, or perhaps materially injured, by the over-care of a favourite member.

The pretended rights of these theorists are all extremes: and in proportion as they are metaphysically true, they are morally and politically false. The rights of men are in a sort of *middle,* incapable of definition, but not impossible to be discerned. The rights of men in governments are their advantages; and these are often in balances between differences of good; in compromises between good and evil, and sometimes between evil and evil. Political reason is a computing principle; adding, subtracting, multiplying, and dividing, morally, and not metaphysically or mathematically, true moral denominations.

We know, and, what is better, we feel inwardly, that religion is the basis of civil society, and the source of all good, and of all comfort.[1] In England we are so convinced of this, that there is no rust of superstition, with which the accumulated absurdity of the human mind might have crusted it over in the course of ages, that ninety-nine in a hundred of the people of England would not prefer to impiety. We shall never be such fools as to call in an enemy to the substance of any system to remove its corruptions, to supply its defects, or to perfect its construction. If our religious tenets should ever want a further elucidation, we shall not call on atheism to explain them. We shall not light up our temple from that unhallowed fire. It will be illuminated with other lights. It will be perfumed with other incense, than the infectious stuff which is imported by the smugglers of adulterated metaphysics. If our ecclesiastical establishment should want a revision, it is not avarice or rapacity, public or private, that we shall employ for the audit, or

---

[1] Sit igitur hoc ab initio persuasum civibus, dominos esse omnium rerum ac moderatores, deos; eaque, quæ gerantur, eorum geri vi, ditione, ac numine; eosdemque optime de genere hominum mereri; et qualis quisque sit, quid agat, quid in se admittat, qua mente qua pietate colat religiones intueri: piorum et impiorum habere rationem. His enim rebus imbutæ mentes haud sane abhorrebunt ab utili et a vera sententia.' Cic. de Legibus, i. 2.

receipt, or application of its consecrated revenue. Violently condemning neither the Greek nor the Armenian, nor, since heats are subsided, the Roman system of religion, we prefer the Protestant; not because we think it has less of the Christian religion in it, but because, in our judgment, it has more. We are Protestants, not from indifference, but from zeal.

We know, and it is our pride to know, that man is by his constitution a religious animal; that atheism is against, not only our reason, but our instincts; and that it cannot prevail long. But if, in the moment of riot, and in a drunken delirium from the hot spirit drawn out of the alembic of hell, which in France is now so furiously boiling, we should uncover our nakedness, by throwing off that Christian religion which has hitherto been our boast and comfort, and one great source of civilization amongst us, and among many other nations, we are apprehensive (being well aware that the mind will not endure a void) that some uncouth, pernicious and degrading superstition might take place of it.

For that reason, before we take from our establishment the natural, human means of estimation, and give it up to contempt, as you have done, and in doing it have incurred the penalties you well deserve to suffer, we desire that some other may be presented to us in the place of it. We shall then form our judgment.

On these ideas, instead of quarrelling with establishments, as some do, who have made a philosophy and a religion of their hostility to such institutions, we cleave closely to them. We are resolved to keep an established church, and established monarchy, an established aristocracy, and an established democracy, each in the degree it exists, and in no greater. I shall show you presently how much of each of these we possess.

It has been the misfortune (not as these gentlemen think it, the glory) of this age, that everything is to be discussed, as if the constitution of our country were to be always a subject rather of altercation than enjoyment. For this reason, as well as for the satisfaction of those among you (if any such you have among you) who may wish to profit of examples, I venture to trouble you with a few thoughts upon each of these establishments. I do not think they were unwise in ancient Rome, who, when they wished to new-model their laws, set commissioners to examine the best constituted republics within their reach.

First, I beg leave to speak of our church establishment, which is the first of our prejudices, not a prejudice destitute of reason, but involving in it profound and extensive wisdom. I speak of it first. It is first, and last, and midst in our minds. For, taking ground on that religious system, of which we are now in possession, we continue to act on the early received, and uniformly continued sense of mankind. That sense not only, like a wise architect, hath built up the august fabric of states, but like a provident proprietor, to preserve the structure from profanation and ruin, as a sacred temple, purged from all the impurities of fraud, and violence, and injustice, and tyranny, hath solemnly and for ever consecrated the commonwealth, and all that officiate in it. This consecration is made, that all who administer in the government of men, in which they stand in the person of God Himself, should have high and worthy notions of their function and destination; that their hope should be full of immortality; that they should not look to the paltry pelf of the moment, nor to the temporary and transient praise of the vulgar, but to a solid, permanent existence, in the permanent part of their nature, and to a permanent fame and glory, in the example they leave as a rich inheritance to the world.

Such sublime principles ought to be infused into persons of exalted situations; and religious establishments provided, that may continually revive and enforce them. Every sort of moral, every sort of civil, every sort of politic institution, aiding the rational and natural ties that connect the human understanding and affections to the divine, are not more than necessary, in order to build up that wonderful structure, Man; whose prerogative it is, to be in a great degree a creature of his own making; and who, when made as he ought to be made, is destined to hold no trivial place in the creation. But whenever man is put over men, as the better nature ought ever to preside, in that case more particularly, he should as nearly as possible be approximated to his perfection.

The consecration of the state, by a state religious establishment, is necessary also to operate with a wholesome awe upon free citizens; because, in order to secure their freedom, they must enjoy some determinate portion of power. To them therefore a religion connected with the state, and with their duty towards it, becomes even more necessary than in such societies, where the people, by the terms of their subjection, are confined to private sentiments, and the management of their own family concerns. All persons possessing any portion of power ought to be strongly and awfully impressed with an idea that they act in trust; and that they are to account for their conduct in that trust to the one great Master, Author and Founder of society.

This principle ought even to be more strongly impressed upon the minds of those who compose the collective sovereignty, than upon those of single princes. Without instruments, these princes can do nothing. Whoever uses instruments, in finding helps, finds also impediments. Their power is therefore by no means complete; nor are they safe in extreme abuse. Such persons, however elevated by flattery, arrogance, and self-opinion, must be sensible that, whether covered or not by positive law, in some way or other they are accountable even here for the abuse of their trust. If they are not cut off by a rebellion of their people, they may be strangled by the very janissaries kept for their security against all other rebellion. Thus we have seen the King of France sold by his soldiers for an increase of pay. But where popular authority is absolute and unrestrained, the people have an infinitely greater,

because a far better founded confidence in their own power. They are themselves, in a great measure, their own instruments. They are nearer to their
objects. Besides, they are less under responsibility to one of the greatest controlling powers on earth, the sense of fame and estimation. The share of
infamy, that is likely to fall to the lot of each individual in public acts, is
small indeed; the operation of opinion being in the inverse ratio to the number of those who abuse power. Their own approbation of their own acts has
to them the appearance of a public judgment in their favour. A perfect democracy is therefore the most shameless thing in the world. As it is the
most shameless, it is also the most fearless. No man apprehends in his person
that he can be made subject to punishment. Certainly the people at large
never ought: for as all punishments are for example towards the conservation
of the people at large, the people at large can never become the subject of
punishments by any human hand. It is therefore of infinite importance that
they should not be suffered to imagine that their will, any more than that of
kings, is the standard of right and wrong. They ought to be persuaded that
they are full as little entitled, and far less qualified, with safety to themselves,
to use any arbitrary power whatsoever; that therefore they are not, under a
false show of liberty, but, in truth, to exercise an unnatural, inverted domination, tyrannically to exact from those who officiate in the state, not an
entire devotion to their interest, which is their right, but an abject submission
to their occasional will; extinguishing thereby, in all those who serve them,
all moral principle, all sense of dignity, all use of judgment, and all consistency of character; whilst by the very same process they give themselves
up a proper, a suitable, but a most contemptible prey to the servile ambition
of popular sycophants, or courtly flatterers.

When the people have emptied themselves of all the lust of selfish will,
which without religion it is utterly impossible they ever should, when they
are conscious that they exercise, and exercise perhaps in a higher link of the
order of delegation, the power, which to be legitimate must be according to
that eternal, immutable law, in which will and reason are the same, they will
be more careful how they place power in base and incapable hands. In their
nomination to office, they will not appoint to the exercise of authority, as to
a pitiful job, but as to a holy function; not according to their sordid, selfish
interest, nor to their wanton caprice, nor to their arbitrary will; but they will
confer that power (which any man may well tremble to give or to receive)
on those only in whom they may discern that predominant proportion of
active virtue and wisdom, taken together and fitted to the charge, such as,
in the great and inevitable mixed mass of human imperfections and infirmities, is to be found.

When they are habitually convinced that no evil can be acceptable, either
in the act or the permission, to him whose essence is good, they will be better
able to extirpate out of the minds of all magistrates, civil, ecclesiastical, or

military, anything that bears the least resemblance to a proud and lawless domination.

But one of the first and most leading principles on which the commonwealth and the laws are consecrated, is lest the temporary possessors and life-renters in it, unmindful of what they have received from their ancestors, or of what is due to their posterity, should act as if they were the entire masters; that they should not think it amongst their rights to cut off the entail or commit waste on the inheritance, by destroying at their pleasure the whole original fabric of their society; hazarding to leave to those who come after them a ruin instead of a habitation—and teaching these successors as little to respect their contrivances, as they had themselves respected the institutions of their forefathers. By this unprincipled facility of changing the state as often, and as much, and in as many ways, as there are floating fancies or fashions, the whole chain and continuity of the commonwealth would be broken. No one generation could link with the other. Men would become little better than the flies of a summer.

And first of all, the science of jurisprudence, the pride of human intellect, which, with all its defects, redundancies, and errors, is the collected reason of ages, combining the principles of original justice with the infinite variety of human concerns, as a heap of old exploded errors, would be no longer studied. Personal self-sufficiency and arrogance (the certain attendants upon all those who have never experienced a wisdom greater than their own) would usurp the tribunal. Of course no certain laws, establishing invariable grounds of hope and fear, would keep the actions of men in a certain course, or direct them to a certain end. Nothing stable in the modes of holding property, or exercising function, could form a solid ground on which any parent could speculate in the education of his offspring, or in a choice for their future establishment in the world. No principles would be early worked into the habits. As soon as the most able instructor had completed his laborious course of institution, instead of sending forth his pupil, accomplished in a virtuous discipline, fitted to procure him attention and respect, in his place in society, he would find everything altered; and that he had turned out a poor creature to the contempt and derision of the world, ignorant of the true grounds of estimation. Who would insure a tender and delicate sense of honour to beat almost with the first pulses of the heart, when no man could know what would be the test of honour in a nation, continually varying the standard of its coin? No part of life would retain its acquisitions. Barbarism with regard to science and literature, unskilfulness with regard to arts and manufactures, would infallibly succeed to the want of a steady education and settled principle; and thus the commonwealth itself would, in a few generations, crumble away, be disconnected into the dust and powder of individuality, and at length dispersed to all the winds of heaven.

To avoid therefore the evils of inconstancy and versatility, ten thousand times worse than those of obstinacy and the blindest prejudice, we have consecrated the state, that no man should approach to look into its defects or corruptions but with due caution; that he should never dream of beginning its reformation by its subversion; that he should approach to the faults of the state as to the wounds of a father, with pious awe, and trembling solicitude. By this wise prejudice we are taught to look with horror on those children of their country, who are prompt rashly to hack that aged parent in pieces, and put him into the kettle of magicians, in hopes that by their poisonous weeds, and wild incantations, they may regenerate the paternal constitution, and renovate their father's life.

Society is indeed a contract. Subordinate contracts for objects of mere occasional interest may be dissolved at pleasure—but the state ought not to be considered nothing better than a partnership agreement in a trade of pepper and coffee, calico or tobacco, or some other such low concern, to be taken up for a little temporary interest, and to be dissolved by the fancy of the parties. It is to be looked on with other reverence; because it is not a partnership in things subservient only to the gross animal existence of a temporary and perishable nature. It is a partnership in all science; a partnership in all art; a partnership in every virtue, and in all perfection. As the ends of such a partnership cannot be obtained in many generations, it becomes a partnership not only between those who are living, but between those who are living, those who are dead, and those who are to be born. Each contract of each particular state is but a clause in the great primeval contract of eternal society, linking the lower with the higher natures, connecting the visible and invisible world, according to a fixed compact sanctioned by the inviolable oath which holds all physical and all moral natures, each in their appointed place. This law is not subject to the will of those, who by an obligation above them, and infinitely superior, are bound to submit their will to that law. The municipal corporations of that universal kingdom are not morally at liberty at their pleasure, and on their speculations of a contingent improvement wholly to separate and tear asunder the bands of their subordinate community, and to dissolve it into an unsocial, uncivil, unconnected chaos of elementary principles. It is the first and supreme necessity only, a necessity that is not chosen, but chooses, a necessity paramount to deliberation, that admits no discussion, and demands no evidence, which alone can justify a resort to anarchy. This necessity is no exception to the rule; because this necessity itself is a part too of that moral and physical disposition of things, to which man must be obedient by consent of force: but if that which is only submission to necessity should be made the object of choice, the law is broken, nature is disobeyed, and the rebellious are outlawed, cast forth, and exiled, from this world of reason, and order, and peace, and virtue, and fruitful penitence, into the antagonist world of madness, discord, vice, confusion, and unavailing sorrow.

I do not know under what description to class the present ruling authority in France. It affects to be pure democracy, though I think it in a direct train of becoming shortly a mischievous and ignoble oligarchy. But for the present I admit it to be a contrivance of the nature and effect of what it pretends to. I reprobate no form of government merely upon abstract principles. There may be situations in which the purely democratic form will become necessary. There may be some (very few, and very particularly circumstanced) where it would be clearly desirable. This I do not take to be the case of France, or of any other great country. Until now, we have seen no examples of considerable democracies. The ancients were better acquainted with them. Not being wholly unread in the authors, who had seen the most of those constitutions, and who best understood them, I cannot help concurring with their opinion, that an absolute democracy, no more than absolute monarchy, is to be reckoned among the legitimate forms of government. They think it rather the corruption and degeneracy, than the sound constitution of a republic. If I recollect rightly, Aristotle observes, that a democracy has many striking points of resemblance with tyranny. Of this I am certain, that in a democracy, the majority of the citizens is capable of exercising the most cruel oppressions upon the minority, whenever strong divisions prevail in that kind of polity, as they often must; and that oppression of the minority will extend to far greater numbers, and will be carried on with much greater fury, than can almost ever be apprehended from the dominion of a single sceptre. In such a popular persecution, individual sufferers are in a much more deplorable condition than in any other. Under a cruel prince they have the balmy compassion of mankind to assuage the smart of their wounds; they have the plaudits of the people to animate their generous constancy under their sufferings; but those who are subjected to wrong under multitudes, are deprived of all external consolation. They seem deserted by mankind, overpowered by a conspiracy of their whole species.

All this violent cry against the nobility I take to be a mere work of art. To be honoured and even privileged by the laws, opinions, and inveterate usages of our country, growing out of the prejudice of ages, has nothing to provoke horror and indignation in any man. Even to be too tenacious of those privileges is not absolutely a crime. The strong struggle in every individual to preserve possession of what he has found to belong to him, and to distinguish him, is one of the securities against injustice and despotism implanted in our nature. It operates as an instinct to secure property, and to preserve communities in a settled state. What is there to shock in this? Nobility is a graceful ornament to the civil order. It is the Corinthian capital of polished society. *Omnes boni nobilitati semper favemus,* was the saying of a wise and good man. It is, indeed, one sign of a liberal and benevolent mind to incline to it with some sort of partial propensity. He feels no ennobling principle in his own heart, who wishes to level all the artificial institutions which have been adopted for giving a body to opinion and permanence to fugitive esteem. It is a sour, malignant, envious disposition, without taste for the reality, or for any image or representation of virtue, that sees with joy the unmerited fall of what had long flourished in splendour and in honour. I do not like to see anything destroyed; any void produced in society; any ruin on the face of the land. It was therefore with no disappointment or dissatisfaction that my inquiries and observations did not present to me any incorrigible vices in the noblesse of France, or any abuse which could not be removed by a reform very short of abolition. Your noblesse did not deserve punishment; but to degrade is to punish.

With us the king and the lords are several and joint securities for the equality of each district, each province, each city. When did you hear in Great Britain of any province suffering from the inequality of its representation; what district from having no representation at all? Not only our monarchy and our peerage secure the equality on which our unity depends, but it is the spirit of the House of Commons itself. The very inequality of representation, which is so foolishly complained of, is perhaps the very thing which prevents us from thinking or acting as members for districts. Cornwall elects as many members as all Scotland. But is Cornwall better taken care of than Scotland? Few trouble their heads about any of your bases, out of some giddy clubs.

The body of the people must not find the principles of natural subordination by art rooted out of their minds. They must respect that property of which they cannot partake. They must labour to obtain what by labour can be obtained; and when they find, as they commonly do, the success disproportioned to the endeavour, they must be taught their consolation in the final proportions of eternal justice. Of this consolation whoever deprives them deadens their industry, and strikes at the root of all acquisition as of all conservation. He that does this is the cruel oppressor, the merciless enemy of the poor and wretched; at the same time that by his wicked speculations he exposes the fruits of successful industry, and the accumulations of fortune, to the plunder of the negligent, the disappointed, and the unprosperous.

Chapter VI

THE IDOL STATE

THE indestructible reality of the individual stands in the center of the Western democratic theory of politics. Compared with the majesty of the individual, state, society, and government are but pale artifacts, devices to enable the individual to be most himself. By contrast, the antidemocratic theory of politics puts the state into the pivotal position of social reality, and within the shadow of its frightful power the individual leads but a timid and dependent existence.

If so many of the voices of democracy heard in the first part of this book have been English and American, history rather than accidental selection has been responsible. Similarly, it will be found in this part of the book that antidemocratic political thought, although represented in all countries, was the specific contribution of German writers and philosophers. With her long and consistent antidemocratic experience, Germany was peculiarly equipped to give clear and systematic expression to antidemocratic ideas. The heavy German representation among antidemocratic writers is based on a double consideration: first, nowhere else has the antidemocratic theory of politics been so firmly entrenched as the *orthodox national tradition* (with the democrats always being looked upon as intellectually alien) and, secondly, antidemocratic writers in all countries have long felt a special kinship with the dominant German movements of thought. If Germans feel uneasy about their place in the political thinking of the world, they ought to ponder the French saying, *que messieurs les assassins commencent.*

In the German intellectual tradition, Hegel's system of philosophy towers over the rest in more than one way. Hegel's work encompasses philosophy, metaphysics, religion, art, ethics, history, and politics. In its range alone, his work is unique in Germany, and possibly in the whole world. Furthermore, his ideas are considered by most Germans themselves as the most typically representative, more German than those of any other major philosopher, not barring Kant. Kant's political philosophy often reflected a vision of what his fellow countrymen *should* think. Hegel's philosophy was more a mirror of what they actually *did* think. Hegel's position in German thought was so powerful that even the most ferocious attack against the orthodox German tradition, Karl Marx's ideas, sprang very largely from Hegelian assumptions.

Hegel's *Philosophy of Law* ("Philosophie des Rechts"), published in 1821, contains the best statement of his political ideas. In it he expresses his conception of freedom, natural and social, which provides the key to an understanding of his political thought. Hegel starts with the assertion that "people grant that it is nature as it is which philosophy has to bring within its ken." What knowledge has to investigate in nature, Hegel argues, is its "eternal harmony" and "inherent rationality." He attacks those who believe that the ethical world—actualized in the state—should be approached differently from nature, the physical world. Just as reason becomes "actual" in nature, Hegel says, so it does in the state. In both instances, the observer does not, and cannot, *make* the laws expressing reason, but can merely understand them. There is no "chance and caprice" in rationality as it may be apprehended in either the world of nature or in the ethical world—the state. Because some philosophers of the state have followed the principle that every thinker is authorized "to take his own road," political philosophy has earned for itself all kinds of "scorn and discredit," Hegel observes. This has led to the worst kind of scorn, viz., that "everyone is convinced that his mere birthright puts him in a position to pass judgment on philosophy in general and to condemn it." Since philosophy in Germany is "in the service of the state," Hegel accords to the state the right to defend itself against those who "indulge in subjective feeling and particular conviction," from which evil follows "the ruin of public order and the law of the land." This encouragement to persecute freedom of thought came from Hegel at a moment when antiliberal, authoritarian government in Prussia had become more ruthless than ever before. The Prussian absolute state—thus can philosophy prostitute itself—appeared to Hegel as the historically most perfect realization of political rationality. "What is rational is actual and what is actual is rational"—this most famous Hegelian phrase has been interpreted, like an ambiguous Biblical passage, in many ways. Whatever the meaning of that phrase as Hegel himself thought it, the impact (historical and psychological, and not hypothetical and logical) has been entirely in one direction: to sanctify the existing as the good. Hegel himself might have refused to accept the proposition that, because Hitler was actual, he was rational, but the historical effect of Hegel was to strengthen the tradition of servility to the existing, which has characterized German political life and thought.

The intimate inner connection between Hegelianism and militarism is evident in Hegel's idea that "in duty the individual finds his liberation." This concept of freedom is the product of a society which honors militarism as *the* way of life, as becomes evident in Hegel's further statement that "self-sacrifice" is the "real existence of one's freedom." This philosophy can be safely taught to members of an army (or Nazi party) without amendment. Hegel also considers this readiness to sacrifice oneself for the state as the "intrinsic worth of courage." The courage of resistance is unknown to Hegel.

Where Locke sees the indestructible essence of man in his act of resisting, Hegel sees man's fulfillment in obedience. Life, liberty, and the pursuit of happiness are thus the exact opposites of the Hegelian concepts of citizenship of self-sacrifice, duty, and discipline.

If the individual is nothing in Hegel's world, the state is all. In his *Philosophy of History,* published posthumously in 1837 (six years after his death), Hegel defines the state as "the realization of Freedom"; the state "exists for its own sake." As to the relation between state and individual, Hegel says that "all the worth which the human being possesses—all spiritual reality, he possesses only through the State." Only through the state does the individual partake of morality. Hegel's state idolatry reaches its peak in the famous sentence, "The State is the Divine Idea as it exists on Earth." In the state, Reason becomes actual and objective, and the individual finds all his spiritual reality through the state. On the basis of this assumption, when "the subjective will of man submits to laws, the contradiction between Liberty and Necessity vanishes."

Who is to determine the law? Hegel takes up this question in both his *Philosophy of Law* and *Philosophy of History.* He attacks the doctrine that "all should participate in the business of the state" as a "ridiculous notion." To permit all individuals to share in public decisions, because all concerns of the state are the concerns of its members, is "tantamount to a proposal to put the democratic element without any rational form into the organism of the state." Hegel anticipates the corporate organization of the twentieth century fascist state by his emphasis that the individual should be politically articulate only as a member of a social class, group, society, or corporation, and not just as a citizen *qua* citizen, as in the liberal democracies.

The fundamental law of the state is in its constitution. Hegel opposes the Western idea of the constitution as an instrument of government, a charter and compact consciously framed for desired ends. The constitution, Hegel says, "should not be regarded as something made, even though it has come into being in time. It must be treated rather as something simply existent in and by itself, as divine therefore, and constant, and so as exalted above the sphere of things that are made." Since the state is "the march of God through the world," the constitution of the state is not something to be tampered with by ordinary mortals.

Going back into the history of the state, Hegel finds that its origin "involves imperious lordship on the one hand, instinctive submission on the other." This leadership principle (later extolled as one of the central dogmas of Nazism) is also stressed by Hegel in his discussion of the merits of the different types of political organization—democracy, aristocracy, and monarchy. The advantage of the monarchical form of government lies in the fact that leadership is always clearly present, whereas in the aristocracies, and even more in democracies, leaders *may* rise to the top. Because of his preference for monarchy, Hegel is not overly partisan in favor of "sovereignty of the people," especially if that term implies opposition to the sovereignty of the monarch. "So opposed to the sovereignty of the monarch, the sovereignty of the people is one of the confused notions based on the wild idea of the 'people.' Taken without its monarch and the articulation of the whole which is the indispensable and direct concomitant of monarchy, the people is a formless mass and no longer a state." The Western concept that the people are the state is described by Hegel as a "perversity" and a "ruse."

Few writers popularized Hegel's main ideas as skillfully as Heinrich von Treitschke. One of the leading German historians in the nineteenth century, Treitschke was typical of a whole generation: in his youth he was a strong supporter of the liberal revolution of 1848, but later on he became the leading admirer of Bismarckian *Machtpolitik*. *Macht* (power) became the central concept of his thinking, as applied to both domestic and foreign policy. In his hatred of England and his contempt for the United States he anticipated the Nazis, as also in his attitudes toward Catholics, Socialists, and democracy in general. Openly anti-Semitic at a time when respectable people in Europe did not dare to admit such bias, Treitschke planted the seeds of Maidanek and Oswiecim in Germany's intellectual leaders. Treitschke was not only a brilliant writer, but one of the most popular lecturers of his time. His classes at the University of Berlin were more than academic exercises; society women attended them as a "must" social event of the season.

Shortly after his death in 1896, his lectures on *Politics* were published in two volumes (1897-1898). On the central issue of all Western political thinking, the relation of the individual to the state, including the right to resist authority, Treitschke is unequivocal: "There must be no question of subjects having the right to oppose a sovereignty which in their opinion is not moral." After 1848, several hundred thousands of Germans left their fatherland for the freedom of America; "it is foolish to admire them for this." Treitschke takes a dim view of democracy in general, and of particular democracies like the United States or Switzerland. "The Presidents of the United States, with a few exceptions, have never been men of great ability, because these are not of the stuff to make head against the flood of slander which envy lets loose over them. There will always be natures of too rare a quality for the common herd to understand." The dominant note of democracy, according to Treitschke, is mediocrity, in politics as well as in the arts and sciences. His faith in inequality makes him say that "where the foundation of slavery is lacking, that is to say in all modern Democracies, one may expect to find a dominant note of political mediocrity."

The unity of German thought emerges from the fact that the opponents of the predominant authoritarian tradition do not diverge from its fundamentals so much as it may appear to them. In the thirty years preceding his death in 1923, Ernst Troeltsch was one of Germany's most distinguished liberal scholars, his main work having been dedicated to the study of the social doctrines of the Christian churches. His profound democratic sentiment made him enter active political life after the First World War. In 1919 he was elected to the Prussian Diet, and he served as parliamentary undersecretary to the Prussian minister of education. Troeltsch's intellectual integrity was tested in the First World War and, unlike most of his colleagues, he stood the test of crisis remarkably well. In 1916 he published a hitherto untranslated essay on "The German Idea of Freedom." In it Troeltsch shows the historical reasons that account for the basically different conceptions of liberty in the English-speaking countries and France on the one side and in Germany on the other. In Germany, too, "liberty is the key word," but it has a meaning of its own. Troeltsch re-emphasizes the German conception of liberty, as interpreted by philosophers like Hegel or poets like Goethe, in the following way: "Liberty as creative participation in the formation of state authority means to us, not the bringing forth of governmental will out of individual wills, not control of the mandatory by the principal, but the free, conscious and dutiful dedication of oneself to the whole, as it has been molded by history, state and nation." In this interpretation of freedom by a great German liberal, the essential elements of the antidemocratic Hegelian philosophy are not only present, but freely recognized. In this conception the state is an organic whole, beyond the scrutiny of the individual, who finds his fulfillment as a citizen in free and dutiful dedication to the whole. Troeltsch refrains from Hegel's inhuman crudity, that only in self-sacrifice for the state does the individual find his true freedom, but he accepts what is the core of Hegelian thought on this issue. Whereas the Western idea of freedom stresses the opportunity of citizens to control and unseat the government, the Germans virtually identify state and government, both assuming an existence of their own, different from, and superior to, that of individuals. In the Western approach to politics, loyalty to the state is not impaired by opposition to the government—as the latter is only an instrument in the service of the former. Finally, and this point is of supreme importance, the Western idea of liberty inevitably leads to equality, and the one is unreal to the extent that the other is unfulfilled. According to Troeltsch, by contrast, "liberty is not equality, but service of the individual in his station organically due to him." This is, again, an echo of the Hegelian position that man counts politically, not as a citizen *qua* citizen, but as a member of a social class, group, or society. One of Troeltsch's most interesting observations, which ought to invite a good deal of pondering, is his comment that the German spirit of service and self-dedication to the whole is reflected in "two expressions of life so contrary to one another as the German army and the socialist party." German references to Frederick the Great as the "first German socialist," and the phenomenon of "military socialism" or "Prussian socialism," culminating in "National Socialism" of the Hitler-

Himmler variety, demonstrates how the idea of socialism, essentially a philosophy of happiness and individual fulfillment, was transformed, on German soil, into a service philosophy of a society perpetually geared for war.

~~~~~~

1. Freedom in Nature and Society*

G. W. F. HEGEL

~~~~~~

At the present time, the idea that freedom of thought, and of mind generally, evinces itself only in divergence from, indeed in hostility to, what is publicly recognized, might seem to be most firmly rooted in connection with the state, and it is chiefly for this reason that a philosophy of the state might seem essentially to have the task of discovering and promulgating still another theory, and a special and original one at that. In examining this idea and the activity in conformity with it, we might suppose that no state or constitution had ever existed in the world at all or was even in being at the present time, but that nowadays—and this 'nowadays' lasts for ever—we had to start all over again from the beginning, and that the ethical world had just been waiting for such present-day projects, proofs, and investigations. So far as nature is concerned, people grant that it is nature as it is which philosophy has to bring within its ken, that the philosopher's stone lies concealed somewhere, somewhere within nature itself, that nature is inherently rational and that what knowledge has to investigate and grasp in concepts is this actual reason in it; not the formations and accidents evident to the superficial observer, but nature's eternal harmony, its harmony however, in the sense of the law and essence immanent within it. The ethical world, on the other hand, the state (i.e. reason as it actualizes itself in the element of self-consciousness), is not allowed to enjoy the good fortune which springs from the fact that it is reason which has achieved power and mastery within that element and which maintains itself and has its home there. The universe of mind is supposed rather to be left to the mercy of chance and caprice, to be God-forsaken, and the result is that if the ethical world is Godless, truth lies outside it, and at the same time, since even so reason is supposed to be in it as well, truth becomes nothing but a problem. But it is this also that is to authorize, nay to oblige, every thinker to take his own road, though not

* From G. W. F. Hegel, *Philosophy of Law* (1821; translated by T. M. Knox as *Philosophy of Right*, Oxford University Press, 1942). By permission.

in search of the philosopher's stone, for he is saved this search by the philoso-
phizing of our contemporaries, and everyone nowadays is assured that he
has this stone in his grasp as his birthright. Now admittedly it is the case
that those who live their lives in the state as it actually exists here and now
and find satisfaction there for their knowledge and volition (and of these
there are many, more in fact than think or know it, because ultimately this
is the position of everybody), or those at any rate who consciously find their
satisfaction in the state, laugh at these operations and affirmations and regard
them as an empty game, sometimes rather funny, sometimes rather serious,
now amusing, now dangerous. Thus this restless activity of empty reflection,
together with its popularity and the welcome it has received, would be a
thing on its own, developing in privacy in its own way, were it not that it is
philosophy itself which has earned all kinds of scorn and discredit by its
indulgence in this occupation. The worst of these kinds of scorn is this, that,
as I said just now, everyone is convinced that his mere birthright puts him in
a position to pass judgement on philosophy in general and to condemn it.
No other art or science is subjected to this last degree of scorn, to the supposition that we are masters of it without ado.

At the present time, the pettifoggery of caprice has usurped the name of
philosophy and succeeded in giving a wide public the opinion that such
triflings are philosophy. The result of this is that it has now become almost
a disgrace to go on speaking in philosophical terms about the nature of the
state, and law-abiding men cannot be blamed if they become impatient so
soon as they hear mention of a philosophical science of the state. Still less is it
a matter of surprise that governments have at last directed their attention to
this kind of philosophy, since, apart from anything else, philosophy with us
is not, as it was with the Greeks for instance, pursued in private like an art
but has an existence in the open, in contact with the public, and especially,
or even only, in the service of the state. Governments have proved their trust
in their scholars who have made philosophy their chosen field by leaving
entirely to them the construction and contents of philosophy—though here
and there, if you like, it may not have been so much confidence that has
been shown as indifference to learning itself, and professorial chairs of
philosophy have been retained only as a tradition (in France, for instance,
to the best of my knowledge, chairs of metaphysics at least have been allowed
to lapse). Their confidence, however, has very often been ill repaid, or
alternatively, if you preferred to see indifference, you would have to regard
the result, the decay of thorough knowledge, as the penalty of this indifference. Prima facie, superficiality seems to be extremely accommodating, one
might say, at least in relation to public peace and order, because it fails to
touch or even to guess at the substance of the things; no action, or at least
no police action, would thus have been taken against it in the first instance,

hċd it not been that there still existed in the state a need for a deeper education and insight, a need which the state required philosophical science to satisfy. On the other hand, superficial thinking about the ethical order, about right and duty in general, starts automatically from the maxims which constitute superficiality in this sphere, i.e. from the principles of the Sophists which are so clearly outlined for our information in Plato. What is right these principles locate in subjective aims and opinions, in subjective feeling and particular conviction, and from them there follows the ruin of the inner ethical life and a good conscience, of love and right dealing between private persons, no less than the ruin of public order and the law of the land. The significance which such phenomena must acquire for government is not likely to suffer any diminution as a result of the pretentiousness which has used that very grant of confidence and the authority of a professorial chair to support the demand that the state should uphold and give scope to what corrupts the ultimate source of achievement, namely universal principles, and so even to the defiance of the state as if such defiance were what it deserved. 'If God gives a man an office, he also gives him brains' is an old joke which in these days surely no one will take wholly in earnest.

What is rational is actual and what is actual is rational. On this conviction the plain man like the philosopher takes his stand, and from it philosophy starts in its study of the universe of mind as well as the universe of nature. If reflection, feeling, or whatever form subjective consciousness may take, looks upon the present as something vacuous and looks beyond it with the eyes of superior wisdom, it finds itself in a vacuum, and because it is actual only in the present, it is itself mere vacuity. If on the other hand the Idea passes for 'only an Idea,' for something represented in an opinion, philosophy rejects such a view and shows that nothing is actual except the Idea. Once that is granted, the great thing is to apprehend in the show of the temporal and transient the substance which is immanent and the eternal which is present. For since rationality (which is synonomous with the Idea) enters upon external existence simultaneously with its actualization, it emerges with an infinite wealth of forms, shapes and appearances. Around its heart it throws a motley covering with which consciousness is at home to begin with, a covering which the concept has first to penetrate before it can find the inward pulse and feel it still beating in the outward appearances. But the infinite variety of circumstance which is developed in this externality by the light of the essence glinting in it—this endless material and its organization—this is not the subject matter of philosophy.

It is the fact that the ethical order is the system of these specific determinations of the Idea which constitutes its rationality. Hence the ethical order is freedom or the absolute will as what is objective, a circle of necessity whose moments are the ethical powers which regulate the life of individuals. To these powers individuals are related as accidents to substance, and it is in individuals that these powers are represented, have the shape of appearance, and become actualized.

The bond of duty can appear as a restriction only on indeterminate subjectivity or abstract freedom, and on the impulses either of the natural will or of the moral will which determines its indeterminate good arbitrarily. The truth is, however, that in duty the individual finds his liberation; first, liberation from dependence on mere natural impulse and from the depression which as a particular subject he cannot escape in his moral reflections on what ought to be and what might be; secondly, liberation from the indeterminate subjectivity which, never reaching reality or the objective determinacy of action, remains self-enclosed and devoid of actuality. In duty the individual acquires his substantive freedom.

Virtue is the ethical order reflected in the individual character so far as that character is determined by its natural endowment. When virtue displays itself solely as the individual's simple conformity with the duties of the station to which he belongs, it is rectitude.

But when individuals are simply identified with the actual order, ethical life (*das Sittliche*) appears as their general mode of conduct, i.e. as custom (*Sitte*), while the habitual practice of ethical living appears as a second nature which, put in the place of the initial, purely natural will, is the soul of custom permeating it through and through, the significance and the actuality of its existence. It is mind living and present as a world, and the substance of mind thus exists now for the first time as mind.

In this way the ethical substantial order has attained its right, and its right its validity. That is to say, the self-will of the individual has vanished together with his private conscience which had claimed independence and opposed itself to the ethical substance. For, when his character is ethical, he recognizes as the end which moves him to act the universal which is itself unmoved but is disclosed in its specific determinations as rationality actualized. He knows that his own dignity and the whole stability of his particular ends are grounded in this same universal, and it is therein that he actually attains these. Subjectivity is itself the absolute form and existent actuality of the substantial order and the distinction between subject on the one hand and substance on the other, as the object, end, and controlling power of the subject, is the same as, and has vanished directly along with, the distinction between them in form.

The state is the actuality of concrete freedom. But concrete freedom consists in this, that personal individuality and its particular interests not only achieve their complete development and gain explicit recognition for their right (as they do in the sphere of the family and civil society) but, for one thing, they also pass over of their own accord into the interest of the universal, and, for another thing, they know and will the universal; they even recognize it as their own substantive mind; they take it as their end and aim and are active in its pursuit. The result is that the universal does not prevail or achieve completion except along with particular interests and through the co-operation of particular knowing and willing; and individuals likewise do not live as private persons for their own ends alone, but in the very act of willing these they will the universal in the light of the universal and their activity is consciously aimed at none but the universal end. The principle of modern states has prodigious strength and depth because it allows the principle of subjectivity to progress to its culmination in the extreme of self-subsistent personal particularity, and yet at the same time brings it back to the substantive unity and so maintains this unity in the principle of subjectivity itself.

In contrast with the spheres of private rights and private welfare (the family and civil society), the state is from one point of view an external necessity and their higher authority; its nature is such that their laws and interests are subordinate to it and dependent on it. On the other hand, however, it is the end immanent within them, and its strength lies in the unity of its own universal end and aim with the particular interest of individuals, in the fact that individuals have duties to the state in proportion as they have rights against it.

To hold that every single person should share in deliberating and deciding on political matters of general concern on the ground that all individuals are members of the state, that its concerns are their concerns, and that it is their right that what is done should be done with their knowledge and volition, is tantamount to a proposal to put the democratic element without any rational form into the organism of the state, although it is only in virtue of the possession of such a form that the state is an organism at all. This idea comes readily to mind because it does not go beyond the abstraction of "being a member of the state," and it is superficial thinking which clings to abstractions. The rational consideration of a topic, the consciousness of the Idea, is concrete and to that extent coincides with a genuine practical sense. Such a sense is itself nothing but the sense of rationality on the Idea, though it is not to be confused with mere business routine or the horizon of a restricted sphere. The concrete state is the whole, articulated into its particular groups. The member of a state is a member of such a group, i.e. of a social class, and it is only as characterized in this objective way that he comes under consideration when we are dealing with the state. His mere character as universal implies that he is at one and the same time both a private person and also a thinking consciousness, a will which wills the universal. This consciousness and will, however, lose their emptiness and acquire a content and a living actuality only when they are filled with particularity, and particularity means determinacy as particular and a particular class-status; or, to put the matter otherwise, abstract individuality is a generic essence, but has its immanent universal actuality as the generic essence next higher in the scale. Hence the single person attains his actual and living destiny for universality only when he becomes a member of a Corporation, a society, &c., and thereby it becomes open to him on the strength of his skill, to enter any class for which he is qualified, the class of civil servants included.

Another presupposition of the idea that all should participate in the business of the state is that everyone is at home in this business—a ridiculous notion, however commonly we may hear it sponsored. Still, in public opinion a field is open to everyone where he can express his purely personal political opinions and make them count.

Since the laws and institutions of the ethical order make up the concept of freedom, they are the substance or universal essence of individuals, who are thus related to them as accidents only. Whether the individual exists or not is all one to the objective ethical order. It alone is permanent and is the power regulating the life of individuals. Thus the ethical order has been represented by mankind as eternal justice, as gods absolutely existent, in contrast with which the empty business of individuals is only a game of see-saw.

Duty is a restriction only on the self-will of subjectivity. It stands in the way only of that abstract good to which subjectivity adheres. When we say: "We want to be free," the primary meaning of the words is simply: "We want abstract freedom," and every institution and every organ of the state passes as a restriction on freedom of that kind. Thus duty is not a restriction on freedom, but only on freedom in the abstract, i.e. on unfreedom. Duty is the attainment of our essence, the winning of positive freedom.

The intrinsic worth of courage as a disposition of mind is to be found in the genuine, absolute, final end, the sovereignty of the state. The work of courage is to actualize this final end, and the means to this end is the sacrifice of personal actuality. This form of experience thus contains the harshness of extreme contradictions; a self-sacrifice which yet is the real existence of one's freedom; the maximum self-subsistence of individuality, yet only a cog playing its part in the mechanism of an external organization; absolute obedience, renunciation of personal opinions and reasonings, in fact complete *absence* of mind, coupled with the most intense and comprehensive *presence* of mind and decision in the moment of acting; the most hostile and so most personal action against individuals, coupled with an attitude of complete indifference or even liking towards them as individuals.

2. The State Divine*

G. W. F. HEGEL

Subjective volition—Passion—is that which sets men in activity, that which effects "practical" realization. The Idea is the inner spring of action; the State is the actually existing, realized moral life. For it is the Unity of the universal, essential Will, with that of the individual; and this is "Morality." The Individual living in this unity has a moral life; possesses a value that consists in this substantiality alone. Sophocles in his Antigone, says, "The divine commands are not of yesterday, nor of to-day; no, they have an infinite existence, and no one could say whence they came." The laws of morality are not accidental, but are the essentially Rational. It is the very object of the State that what is essential in the practical activity of men, and in their dispositions, should be duly recognized; that it should have a manifest existence, and maintain its position. It is the absolute interest of Reason that this moral Whole should exist; and herein lies the justification and merit of heroes who have founded states,—however rude these may have been. In the history of the World, only those peoples can come under our notice which form a state. For it must be understood that this latter is the realization of Freedom, *i.e.* of the absolute final aim, and that it exists for its own sake. It must further be understood that all the worth which the human being possesses—all spiritual reality, he possesses only through the State. For his spiritual reality consists in this, that his own essence—Reason—is objectively present to him, that it possesses objective immediate existence for him. Thus only is he fully conscious; thus only is he a partaker of morality —of a just and moral social and political life. For Truth is the Unity of the universal and subjective Will; and the Universal is to be found in the State, in its laws, its universal and rational arrangements. The State is the Divine Idea as it exists on Earth. We have in it, therefore, the object of History in a more definite shape than before; that in which Freedom obtains objectivity, and lives in the enjoyment of this objectivity. For Law is the objectivity of Spirit; volition in its true form. Only that will which obeys law, is free; for it obeys itself—it is independent and so free. When the State or our country constitutes a community of existence; when the subjective will of man submits to laws,—the contradiction between Liberty and Necessity vanishes. The

Rational has necessary existence, as being the reality and substance of things, and we are free in recognizing it as law, and following it as the substance of our own being. The objective and the subjective will are then reconciled, and present one identical homogeneous whole. For the morality (*Sittlichkeit*) of the State is not of that ethical (*moralische*) reflective kind, in which one's own conviction bears sway; this latter is rather the peculiarity of the modern time, while the true antique morality is based on the principle of abiding by one's duty (to the state at large). An Athenian citizen did what was required of him, as it were from instinct: but if I reflect on the object of my activity, I must have the consciousness that my will has been called into exercise. But morality is Duty—substantial Right—a "*second* nature" as it has been justly called; for the *first* nature of man is his primary merely animal existence.

The development *in extenso* of the Idea of the State belongs to the Philosophy of Jurisprudence; but it must be observed that in the theories of our time various errors are current respecting it, which pass for established truths, and have become fixed prejudices. We will mention only a few of them, giving prominence to such as have a reference to the object of our history.

The error which first meets us is the direct contradictory of our principle that the state presents the realization of Freedom; the opinion, viz., that man is free by *nature,* but that in *society,* in the State—to which nevertheless he is irresistibly impelled—he must limit this natural freedom. That man is free by Nature is quite correct in one sense; viz., that he is so according to the Idea of Humanity; but we imply thereby that he is such only in virtue of his destiny—that he has an undeveloped power to become such; for the "Nature" of an object is exactly synonymous with its "Idea." But the view in question imports more than this. When man is spoken of as "free by Nature," the mode of his existence as well as his destiny is implied. His merely natural and primary condition is intended. In this sense a "state of Nature" is assumed in which mankind at large are in the possession of their natural rights with the unconstrained exercise and enjoyment of their freedom. This assumption is not indeed raised to the dignity of the historical fact; it would indeed be difficult, were the attempt seriously made, to point out any such condition as actually existing, or as having ever occurred. Examples of a savage state of life can be pointed out, but they are marked by brutal passions and deeds of violence; while, however rude and simple their conditions, they involve social arrangements which (to use the common phrase) *restrain* freedom. That assumption is one of those nebulous images which theory produces; an idea which it cannot avoid originating, but which it fathers upon real existence, without sufficient historical justification.

What we find such a state of Nature to be in actual experience, answers exactly to the Idea of a *merely* natural condition. Freedom as the *ideal* of that which is original and natural, does not exist *as original and natural*. Rather must it be first sought out and won; and that by an incalculable medial discipline of the intellectual and moral powers. The state of Nature is, therefore, predominantly that of injustice and violence, of untamed natural impulses, of inhuman deeds and feelings. Limitation is certainly produced by Society and the State, but it is a limitation of the mere brute emotions and rude instincts; as also, in a more advanced stage of culture, of the premeditated self-will of caprice and passion. This kind of constraint is part of the instrumentality by which only, the consciousness of Freedom and the desire for its attainment, in its true—that is Rational and Ideal form—can be obtained. To the Ideal of Freedom, Law and Morality are indispensably requisite; and they are in and for themselves, universal existences, objects and aims; which are discovered only by the activity of thought, separating itself from the merely sensuous, and developing itself, in opposition thereto; and which must, on the other hand, be introduced into and incorporated with the originally sensuous will, and that contrarily to its natural inclination. The perpetually recurring misapprehension of Freedom consists in regarding that term only in its *formal,* subjective sense, abstracted from its essential objects and aims; thus a constraint put upon impulse, desire, passion—pertaining to the particular individual as such—a limitation of caprice and self-will is regarded as a fettering of Freedom. We should on the contrary look upon such limitation as the indispensable proviso of emancipation. Society and the State are the very conditions in which Freedom is realized.

If the principle of regard for the individual will is recognized as the only basis of political liberty, viz., that nothing should be done by or for the State to which all the members of the body politic have not given their sanction, we have, properly speaking, no *Constitution*. The only arrangement that would be necessary, would be, first, a centre having no *will* of its own, but which should take into consideration what appeared to be the necessities of the State; and, secondly, a contrivance for calling the members of the State together, for taking the votes, and for performing the arithmetical operations of reckoning and comparing the number of votes for the different propositions, and thereby deciding upon them. The State is an *abstraction,* having even its generic existence in its citizens; but it is an actuality, and its simply generic existence must embody itself in individual will and activity. The want of government and political administration in general is felt; this necessitates the selection and separation from the rest of those who have to take the helm in political affairs, to decide concerning them, and to give orders to other citizens, with a view to the execution of their plans. If *e.g.* even the people in a Democracy resolve on a war, a general must head the army. It is only by a Constitution that the *abstraction*—the State—attains life and reality; but this involves the distinction beween those who command

and those who obey.—Yet obedience seems inconsistent with liberty, and those who command appear to do the very opposite of that which the fundamental idea of the State, viz. that of Freedom, requires. It is, however, urged that,—though the distinction between commanding and obeying is absolutely necessary, because affairs could not go on without it—and indeed this seems only a compulsory limitation, external to and even contravening freedom in the abstract—the constitution should be at least so framed, that the citizens may obey as little as possible, and the smallest modicum of free volition be left to the commands of the superiors;—that the substance of that for which subordination is necessary, even in its most important bearings, should be decided and resolved on by the People—by the will of many or of all the citizens; though it is supposed to be thereby provided that the State should be possessed of vigour and strength as a reality—an individual unity.—The primary consideration is, then, the distinction between the governing and the governed, and political constitutions in the abstract have been rightly divided into Monarchy, Aristocracy, and Democracy; which gives occasion, however, to the remark that Monarchy itself must be further divided into Despotism and Monarchy proper; that in all the divisions to which the leading Idea gives rise, only the generic character is to be made prominent,—it being not intended thereby that the particular category under review should be exhausted as a Form, Order, or Kind in its *concrete* development. But especially it must be observed, that the above-mentioned divisions admit of a multitude of particular modifications,—not only such as lie within the limits of those classes themselves,—but also such as are mixtures of several of these essentially distinct classes, and which are consequently misshapen, unstable, and inconsistent forms. In such a collision, the concerning question is, what is the *best constitution;* that is, by what arrangement, organization, or mechanism of the power of the State its object can be most surely attained. This object may indeed be variously understood; for instance, as the calm enjoyment of life on the part of the citizens, or as Universal Happiness. Such aims have suggested the so-called Ideals of Constitutions, and,—as a particular branch of the subject,—Ideals of the Education of Princes (Fénelon), or of the governing body—the aristocracy at large (Plato); for the chief point they treat of is the condition of those subjects who stand at the head of affairs; and in these Ideals the concrete details of political organization are not at all considered. The inquiry into the best constitution is frequently treated as if not only the theory were an affair of subjective independent conviction, but as if the introduction of a constitution recognized as the best,—or as superior to others,—could be the result of a resolve adopted in this theoretical manner; as if the form of a constitution were a matter of free choice, determined by nothing else but reflection. Of this artless fashion was that deliberation,—not indeed of the Persian *people,* but of the Persian *grandees,* who had conspired to overthrow the pseudo-Smerdis and the Magi, after their undertaking had succeeded, and when there was no scion of the royal family living,— as to what constitution they should introduce into Persia; and Herodotus gives an equally naive account of this deliberation.

In the present day, the Constitution of a country and people is not represented as so entirely dependent on free and deliberate choice. The fundamental but abstractly (and therefore imperfectly) entertained conception of Freedom, has resulted in the Republic being very generally regarded—in *theory*—as the only just and true political constitution. Many even, who occupy elevated official positions under monarchical constitutions—so far from being opposed to this idea—are actually its supporters; only they see that such a constitution, though the best, cannot be realized under all circumstances; and that—while men are what they are—we must be satisfied with less freedom; the monarchical constitution—under the given circumstances, and the present moral condition of the people—being even regarded as the most advantageous. In this view also, the necessity of a particular constitution is made to depend on the condition of the people in such a way as if the latter were non-essential and accidental. This representation is founded on the distinction which the reflective understanding makes between an idea and the corresponding reality; holding to an abstract and consequently untrue idea; not grasping it in its completeness, or—which is virtually, though not in point of form, the same,—not taking a concrete view of a people and a state. We shall have to show further on, that the constitution adopted by a people makes one substance—one spirit—with its religion, its art and philosophy, or, at least, with its conceptions and thoughts—its culture generally; not to expatiate upon the additional influences, *ab extra,* of climate, of neighbours, of its place in the World. A State is an individual totality, of which you cannot select any particular side, although a supremely important one, such as its political constitution; and deliberate and decide respecting it in that isolated form. Not only is that constitution most intimately connected with and dependent on those other spiritual forces; but the form of the entire moral and intellectual individuality—comprising all the forces it embodies—is only a step in the development of the grand Whole,—with its place preappointed in the process; a fact which gives the highest sanction to the constitution in question, and establishes its absolute necessity.—The origin of a state involves imperious lordship on the one hand, instinctive submission on the other. But even obedience—lordly power, and the fear inspired by a ruler—in itself implies some degree of voluntary connection. Even in barbarous states this is the case; it is not the isolated will of individuals that prevails; individual pretensions are relinquished, and the general will is the essential bond of political union. This unity of the general and the particular is the Idea itself, manifesting itself as a *state,* and which subsequently undergoes further development within itself. The abstract yet necessitated process in the development of truly independent states is as follows:—They begin with regal power, whether of patriarchal or military origin. In the next phase, particularity and individuality assert themselves in the form of Aristocracy and Democracy. Lastly, we have the subjection of these separate interests to a single power; but which can be absolutely none other than one outside of which those spheres have an independent position, viz. the Monarchical. Two phases of royalty, therefore, must be distinguished,—a primary and a secondary one. This process is necessitated, so that the form of government assigned to a particular stage of development *must* present itself: it is therefore no matter of choice, but is that form which is adapted to the spirit of the people.

In a Constitution the main feature of interest is the self development of the *rational*, that is, the *political* condition of a people; the setting free of the successive elements of the Idea: so that the several powers in the State manifest themselves as separate,—attain their appropriate and special perfection,—and yet in this independent condition, work together for one object, and are held together by it—*i.e.* form an organic whole. The State is thus the embodiment of rational freedom, realizing and recognizing itself in an objective form. For its objectivity consists in this,—that its successive stages are not merely ideal, but are present in an appropriate reality; and that in their separate and several workings, they are absolutely merged in that agency by which the totality—the soul—the individuate unity—is produced, and of which it is the result.

The State is the Idea of Spirit in the external manifestation of human Will and its Freedom. It is to the State, therefore, that change in the aspect of History indissolubly attaches itself; and the successive phases of the Idea manifest themselves in it as distinct political *principles*. The Constitutions under which World-Historical peoples have reached their culmination, are peculiar to them; and therefore do not present a generally applicable political basis. Were it otherwise, the differences of similar constitutions would consist only in a peculiar method of expanding and developing that generic basis; whereas they really originate in diversity of principle. From the comparison therefore of the political institutions of the ancient World-Historical peoples, it so happens, that for the most recent principle of a Constitution—for the principle of our own times—nothing (so to speak) can be learned. In science and art it is quite otherwise; *e.g.,* the ancient philosophy is so decidedly the basis of the modern, that it is inevitably contained in the latter, and constitutes its basis. In this case the relation is that of a continuous development of the same structure, whose foundation-stone, walls, and roof have remained what they were. In Art, the Greek itself, in its original form, furnishes us the best models. But in regard to political constitution, it is quite otherwise: here the Ancient and the Modern have not their essential principle in common. Abstract definitions and dogmas respecting just government,—importing that intelligence and virtue ought to bear sway—are, indeed, common to both. But nothing is so absurd as to look to Greeks, Romans, or Orientals, for models for the political arrangements of our time. From the East may be derived beautiful pictures of a patriarchal condition, of paternal government, and of devotion to it on the part of peoples; from Greeks and Romans, descriptions of popular liberty. Among the latter we find the idea of a Free Constitution admitting all the citizens to a share in deliberations and resolves respecting the affairs and laws of the Commonwealth. In our times, too, this is its general acceptation; only with this modification, that—since our states are so large, and there are so many of "the Many," the latter,—direct action being impossible,—should by the indirect method of elective substitution express their concurrence with resolves affecting the common weal; that is, that for legislative purposes generally, the people should be represented by deputies. The so-called Representative Constitution is that form of government with which we connect the idea of a free constitution; and this notion has become a rooted prejudice. On this theory People and Government are separated. But there is a perversity in this antithesis; an ill-intentioned *ruse* designed to insinuate that the People are the totality of the State. Besides, the basis of this view is the principle of isolated individuality—the absolute validity of the subjective will—a dogma which we have already investigated. The great point is, that Freedom in its Ideal conception has not subjective will and caprice for its principle, but the recognition of the universal will; and that the process by which Freedom is realized is the free development of its successive stages. The subjective will is a merely formal determination—a *carte blanche*—not including what it is that is willed. Only the *rational* will is that universal principle which independently determines and unfolds its own being, and develops its successive elemental phases as organic members. Of this Gothic-cathedral architecture the ancients knew nothing.

3. Sovereignty: Monarchical or Popular? *

G. W. F. HEGEL

The state is the actuality of the ethical Idea. It is ethical mind *qua* the substantial will manifest and revealed to itself, knowing and thinking itself, ac-

* From G. W. F. Hegel, *Philosophy of Law* (1821; translated by T. M. Knox as *Philosophy of Right*, Oxford University Press, 1942). By permission.

complishing what it knows and in so far as it knows it. The state exists immediately in custom, mediately in individual self-consciousness, knowledge, and activity, while self-consciousness in virtue of its sentiment towards the state finds in the state, as its essence and the end and product of its activity, its substantive freedom.

The *Penates* are inward gods, gods of the underworld; the mind of a nation (Athens for instance) is the divine, knowing and willing itself. Family piety is feeling, ethical behaviour directed by feeling; political virtue is the willing of the absolute end in terms of thought.

The state is absolutely rational inasmuch as it is the actuality of the substantial will which it possesses in the particular self-consciousness once that consciousness has been raised to consciousness of its universality. This substantial unity is an absolute unmoved end in itself, in which freedom comes into its supreme right. On the other hand this final end has supreme right against the individual, whose supreme duty is to be a member of the state.

If the state is confused with civil society, and if its specific end is laid down as the security and protection of property and personal freedom, then the interest of the individuals as such becomes the ultimate end of their association, and it follows that membership of the state is something optional. But the state's relation to the individual is quite different from this. Since the state is mind objectified, it is only as one of its members that the individual himself has objectivity, genuine individuality, and an ethical life. Unification pure and simple is the true content and aim of the individual, and the individual's destiny is the living of a universal life. His further particular satisfaction, activity, and mode of conduct have this substantive and universally valid life as their starting point and their result.

Rationality, taken generally and in the abstract, consists in the thoroughgoing unity of the universal and the single. Rationality, concrete in the state, consists (*a*) so far as its content is concerned, in the unity of objective freedom (i.e. freedom of the universal or substantial will) and subjective freedom (i.e. freedom of everyone in his knowing and in his volition of particular ends); and consequently, (*b*) so far as its form is concerned, in self-determining action on laws and principles which are thoughts and so universal. This Idea is the absolutely eternal and necessary being of mind.

Another question readily presents itself here: 'Who is to frame the constitution?' This question seems clear, but closer inspection shows at once that it is meaningless, for it presupposes that there is no constitution there, but only an agglomeration of atomic individuals. How an agglomeration of individuals could acquire a constitution, whether automatically or by someone's aid, whether as a present or by force or by thought, it would have to be allowed to settle for itself, since with an agglomeration the concept has nothing to do. But if the question presupposes an already existent constitution, then it is not about framing but only about altering the constitution, and the very presupposition of a constitution directly implies that its alteration may come about only by constitutional means. In any case, however, it is absolutely essential that the constitution should not be regarded as something made, even though it has come into being in time. It must be treated rather as something simply existent in and by itself, as divine therefore, and constant, and so as exalted above the sphere of things that are made.

The conception of the monarch is therefore of all conceptions the hardest for ratiocination, i.e. for the method of reflection employed by the Understanding. This method refuses to move beyond isolated categories and hence here again knows only *raisonnement,* finite points of view, and deductive argumentation. Consequently it exhibits the dignity of the monarch as something deduced, not only in its form, but in its essence. The truth is, however, that to be something not deduced but purely self-originating is precisely the conception of monarchy. Akin, then, to this reasoning is the idea of treating the monarch's right as grounded in the authority of God, since it is in its divinity that its unconditional character is contained. We are familiar, however, with the misunderstandings connected with this idea, and it is precisely this 'divine' element which it is the task of a philosophic treatment to comprehend.

We may speak of the 'sovereignty of the people' in the sense that any people whatever is self-subsistent vis-à-vis other peoples, and constitutes a state of its own, like the British people for instance. But the peoples of England, Scotland, or Ireland, or the peoples of Venice, Genoa, Ceylon, &c., are not sovereign peoples at all now that they have ceased to have rulers or supreme governments of their own.

We may also speak of sovereignty in home affairs residing in the people, provided that we are speaking generally about the whole state and meaning only what was shown above, namely, that it is to the state that sovereignty belongs.

The usual sense, however, in which men have recently begun to speak of the 'sovereignty of the people' is that it is something opposed to the sovereignty existent in the monarch. So opposed to the sovereignty of the monarch, the sovereignty of the people is one of the confused notions based on the wild idea of the "people." Taken without its monarch and the articulation of the whole which is the indispensable and direct concomitant of monarchy, the people is a formless mass and no longer a state. It lacks every one of those determinate characteristics—sovereignty, government, judges, magistrates, class-divisions, &c.,—which are to be found only in a whole which is inwardly organized. By the very emergence into a people's life of moments of this kind which have a bearing on an organization, on political life, a people ceases to be that indeterminate abstraction which, when represented in a quite general way, is called the 'people.'

At the stage at which constitutions are divided, as above mentioned, into democracy, aristocracy, and monarchy, the point of view taken is that of a still substantial unity, abiding in itself, without having yet embarked on its infinite differentiation and the plumbing of its own depths. At that stage, the moment of the final, self-determining, decision of the will does not come on the scene explicitly in its own proper actuality as an organic moment immanent in the state. None the less, even in those comparatively immature constitutional forms, there must always be individuals at the head. Leaders must either be available already, as they are in monarchies of that type, or, as happens in aristocracies, but more particularly in democracies, they may rise to the top, as statesmen or generals, by chance and in accordance with the particular needs of the hour. This must happen, since everything done and everything actual is inaugurated and brought to completion by the single decisive act of a leader.

To define freedom of the press as freedom to say and write whatever we please is parallel to the assertion that freedom as such means freedom to do as we please. Talk of this kind is due to wholly uneducated, crude, and superficial ideas. Moreover, it is in the very nature of the thing that abstract thinking should nowhere be so stubborn, so unintelligent, as in this matter of free speech, because what it is considering is the most fleeting, the most contingent, and the most personal side of opinion in its infinite diversity of content and tergiversation. Beyond the direct incitation to theft, murder, rebellion, &c., there lies its artfully constructed expression—an expression which seems in itself quite general and vague, while all the time it conceals a meaning anything but vague or else is compatible with inferences which are not actually expressed, and it is impossible to determine whether they rightly follow from it, or whether they were meant to be inferred from it. This vagueness of matter and form precludes laws on these topics from attaining the requisite determinacy of law, and since the trespass, wrong, and injury here are so extremely personal and subjective in form, judgment on them is reduced equally to a wholly subjective verdict. Such an injury is directed against the thoughts, opinions, and wills of others, but apart from that, these form the element in which alone it is actually anything. But this element is the sphere of the freedom of others, and it therefore depends on them whether the injurious expression of opinion is or is not actually an effective act.

Laws then may be criticized by exhibiting their indeterminacy as well as by arguing that they leave it open to the speaker or writer to devise turns of phrase or tricks of expression, and so evade the laws or claim that judicial decisions are mere subjective verdicts. Further, however, against the view that the expression of opinion is an act with injurious effects, it may be maintained that it is not an act at all, but only opining and thinking, or only talking. And so we have before us a claim that mere opining and talking is to go unpunished because it is of a purely subjective character both in form and content, because it does not mean anything and is of no importance. And yet in the same breath we have the claim that this same opining and talking should be held in high esteem and respect—the opining because it is personal property and in fact pre-eminently the property of mind; the talking because it is only this same property being expressed and used.

But the substance of the matter is and remains that traducing the honour of anyone, slander, abuse, the contemptuous caricature of government, its ministers, officials, and in particular the person of the monarch, defiance of the laws, incitement to rebellion, &c., &c., are all crimes or misdemeanours in one or other of their numerous gradations. The rather high degree of indeterminability which such actions acquire on account of the element in which they are expressed does not annul this fundamental character of theirs. Its only effect is that the subjective field in which they are committed also determines the nature and form of the reaction to the offence. It is the field in which the offence was committed which itself necessitates subjectivity of view, contingency, &c., in the reaction to the offence, whether the reaction takes the form of punishment proper or of police action to prevent crimes. Here, as always, abstract thinking sets itself to explain away the fundamental and concrete nature of the thing by concentrating on isolated aspects of its external appearance and on abstractions drawn therefrom.

The sciences, however, are not to be found anywhere in the field of opinion and subjective views, provided of course that they be sciences in other respects. Their exposition is not a matter of clever turns of phrases, allusiveness, half-utterances, and semi-reticences, but consists in the unambiguous, determinate, and open expression of their meaning and purport. It follows that they do not fall under the category of public opinion. Apart from this, however, as I said just now, the element in which views and their expression become actions in the full sense and exist effectively, consists of the intelligence, principles, and opinions of others. Hence this aspect of these actions, i.e. their effectiveness proper and their danger to individuals, society, and the state, depends on the character of the ground on which they fall, just as a spark falling on a heap of gunpowder is more dangerous than if it falls on hard ground where it vanishes without trace. Thus, just as the right of science to express itself depends on and is safeguarded by its subject-matter and content, so an illegitimate expression may also acquire a measure of security, or at least sufferance, in the scorn which it has brought upon itself. An offence of this sort is punishable on its own account too, but part of it may be accounted that kind of nemesis which inner impotence, feeling itself oppressed by the preponderating abilities and virtues of others, is impelled to vent in order to come to itself again in face of such superiority, and to restore some self-consciousness to its own nullity. It was a nemesis of a more harmless type which Roman soldiers vented against their generals when they sang scurrilous songs about them in triumphal processions in order in a way to get even with them for all the hard service and discipline they had undergone, and especially for the omission of their names from the triumphal honours. The former type of nemesis, the bad and hateful type, is deprived of its effect by being treated with scorn, and hence, like the public, which perhaps forms a circle of spectators of scurrility, it is restricted to futile malice and to the self-condemnation which it implicitly contains.

4. Individualism, Democracy, and the State *

HEINRICH VON TREITSCHKE

The individual should feel himself a member of his State, and as such have courage to take its errors upon him. There must be no question of subjects having the right to oppose a sovereignty which in their opinion is not moral. Cases may arise when the State's action touches the foundation of the moral life, namely, religious feeling. When the Huguenots in France had their religion proscribed, and were commanded to worship their God under forms which their deepest conviction held to be unchristian, conscience drove them out from their fatherland, but we must not praise the fine temper of these martyrs for religion from the standpoint of the theologian without recognizing the degree of tragic guilt which is always blended with such moral compulsion. The Huguenots who left their homes were gallant men, no doubt, but each of them had a bitter conflict to fight out within himself before he placed his love for the Heidelberg Catechism above his hereditary love for his country and his king. In modern times there have been Radical parties who have in their vanity imagined themselves faced with a similar struggle, which had in fact only a subjective existence in their own exalted imagination. This was the reason why a number of the German-Americans forsook their fatherland. It is foolish to admire them for this. We must always maintain the principle that the State is in itself an ethical force and a high moral good.

* From Heinrich von Treitschke, *Politics*. (1897–1898; translated by B. Dugdale and T. de Bille, 1916). By permission of The Macmillan Company, publishers.

A decision by the majority is only based on reason when the question at issue concerns the development of a real power, and the expression of a Will. In a Democracy supremacy is derived solely from the people, therefore its decisions must bow to the will of the people, which can only be ascertained by the voice of the majority. The presumption is that the will of the majority could be enforced by violence in the last resort, consequently the majority decides, as representing physical force. This is the true foundation of its dominion, let democratic idealists say what they like; the will of the majority is the strongest, and for this reason men give it the sanction of law. Every unprejudiced historian will admit that it is the only reasonable system by which a State can proceed upon democratic lines, but we need not delude ourselves into the idea that there is anything inherently reasonable or ideal in a set of circumstances in which the final constitutional authority is not self-derived. There can be absolutely no question of government by the majority being in itself either reasonable or just. We must envisage these matters only *in concreto*. When the Committee of Public Safety sent people to the guillotine just as they chose in the name of the majority of the French nation, they were just as much tyrants as Philip II of Spain had been. It made no difference to the victims in whose name their heads fell into the basket, for the one slavery was as good as the other.

The rule of the majority, then, which is a necessary adjunct of Democracy, is most certainly no security for political liberty. Each citizen is given the right to make his voice heard in the national decisions, but if he does not go with the majority he must just put up with it, and hope that his turn will come some day. "One half of freedom is alternately to rule and to be ruled," as Aristotle said long ago. He is here describing political liberty, and this conception of it finds no guarantee of fulfilment in government by a majority.

When we turn to the social liberty which forms the other half of freedom, we do not find a Democracy affording it any particular security either. "To live according to our own sweet will" may be possible in a Democracy, but it cannot by any means certainly be so. The idea of the State was so predominant in the Democracies of antiquity that the individual citizen was accorded absolutely no freedom of action, but was early taken under the discipline of the State, to whose brilliancy and greatness all other considerations had to give way. Sharp indeed is the contrast between this and the modern Democracy, which as we know it, seems particularly created for an economic age like our own, which thinks only of getting on by every means it can, and lives in the illusion that the heights of civilization can be reached by telephones and telegraphs. Modern Democracy sets absolutely no restraints upon the commercial intercourse between citizens. Life in the United States is a terribly hard school, in which many perish altogether, but there is absolute freedom of action in every direction, and in this lies the secret of the singular charm which this State possesses for the average man of the present day.

The political temper of a truly ruling Demos is a very remarkable study. It is clear that it must totally lack certain finer attributes of political intelligence, and more especially the gift of foresight, which is simply absent from popular government. This applies particularly to its foreign policy, a sphere in which it must always act from a very limited range of vision. *L'esprit d'escalier* is a pre-eminently democratic characteristic. Besides this there is a singular contradiction which always makes itself felt in the inner nature of a governing Demos. On the one hand we see that terrible demoniacal and base passion—envy, which plays an immeasurably important part in the life of a Democracy. No doubt if the inner heart of Germany stood revealed it would seem to have reached gigantic strength even there, as was proved by the treatment that Bismarck received. Now that he has fallen he is beginning once more to find theoretic admirers among his ancient enemies, because he has come down to their level—or so it seems. They find an intense pleasure in the thought.[1] In their institution of ostracism the Athenians had absolutely set up a public means of gratifying this passion, which they turned into a legal weapon.

The Presidents of the United States, with a few exceptions, have never been men of great ability, because these are not of the stuff to make head against the flood of slander which envy lets loose over them. There will always be natures of too rare a quality for the common herd to understand; for this reason Goethe will never be as popular an author as Schiller. In the early days of the North American Republic Alexander Hamilton was the most remarkable figure, more so in fact than Washington, yet the populace regarded him as the proverbial dog looked upon the glass of wine. He aroused the same sentiments as William Humboldt did at the Confederate Diet at Frankfurt, for he gave people the uncomfortable feeling that they did not understand him.

In strange contrast with this thoroughly democratic passion of envy, every noble-minded and independent nation will evince a capacity for hero-worship in times of excitement, until it may absolutely deify some individual great man. It becomes evident at such moments that the people really have an instinct which recognizes outstanding greatness. It is impossible to decide theoretically when it will display itself, for greatness alone is not the deciding factor. It must be admitted that Bismarck has never really been beloved by the mass of the nation, for only the educated classes have properly grasped the unique greatness of the man. Pericles, on the other hand, although his

[1] Lecture delivered in February, 1893.

character was essentially lofty, attained through his marvellous gift of eloquence to such an influence over the Athenian people that Thucydides could say of him, "He was not so much led by the people as himself their leader." For a time he ruled Athens like a king, and marvellous indeed were the home-truths which he told that Demos to their faces, for there was no trace of the flatterer in him.

This phenomenon of hero-worship appears from time to time in every Democracy. It explains the alliance of the populace with the Barcidae in Carthage and with the House of Orange in the Netherlands. We meet it again in the United States, when Washington had to thrust from him the honours which were offered him. His example did much to establish democratic institutions firmly in his country, but so great did his fame become, and so devotedly was he worshipped, that he had great difficulty in waving aside the homage that was done him. Later on General Jackson, the "Publicola," held a similar position for a brief period. He was a thoroughly coarse-natured man, but he was the conqueror of Texas, and his commercial policy was very much in accord with popular taste. Under him the State was perilously near to becoming a dictatorship, although in the end the good sense of the nation gained the upper hand. Later on, the reverence of the masses for President Lincoln rose to such a pitch that he could perfectly well have attained to kingly power among them had he so willed it. But he was of the same stamp as Washington, and he remained a convinced adherent of democratic government. In spite of all these instances the danger of a dictatorship is as constantly present in a democratic Republic as in an aristocratic one, although it is no doubt most of all to be expected in Republics without republicans, as France, with her two Napoleons, has proved to us. Thus we find Democracies swayed by curiously contradictory elements; on the one hand envy, on the other a popular delight in great heroic figures.

Where the foundation of slavery is lacking, that is to say in all modern Democracies, one may expect to find a dominant note of political mediocrity. Really striking and distinguished qualities are less comprehensible by the masses, and we may look in vain to see Art and Science encouraged by modern Democracy, which has never known a second Florence. Switzerland is a type of this form of government in our own day. There we see national schools and public health encouraged with praiseworthy eagerness, but the establishment even of polytechnics has been attended with the greatest difficulties, for the Swiss nation could not be brought to realize the usefulness of these institutions. Neither have universities ever been able to take much hold in Switzerland. They are the home of an aristocratic form of culture, and the natural inclination of a Democracy is to extend a modicum of education and prosperity over the widest possible circle, without any desire to exceed this standard.

5. German and Western Conceptions of Freedom *

ERNST TROELTSCH

The German idea of freedom possesses its own characteristic traits. Undoubtedly it has been affected by French and English ideas of liberty. Locke and Rousseau have influenced theory, whereas the English constitution and self-government and the French Revolution have been of tremendous practical impact. However, these ideas have been thoroughly transformed in the real core of German development, in the institutions which go back to Baron von Stein, Scharnhorst and Boyen, and in the philosophical, idealistic interpretation of state and history from Kant, Fichte and Hegel to the contemporary philosophical idealists. Here, too, liberty is the key word, but this liberty has its own meaning, determined by German history and the German spirit.

Liberty as creative participation in the formation of state authority means to us, not the bringing forth of governmental will out of individual wills, not control of the mandatory by the principal, but' the free, conscious and dutiful dedication of oneself to the whole, as it has been molded by history, state and nation. The whole as the expression and incarnation of collectivity is to be willed freely and always re-create anew in personal activity. Thus, prince and officials consider themselves as the first servants of the state, and citizens think of themselves as members of the state. They are all organs of the one sovereign whole which they bring forth anew in ceaseless self-devotion. Liberty consists more in duties than in rights, or, rather, in rights which are simultaneously duties. The individuals do not compose the whole, but identify themselves with it. Liberty is not equality, but service of the individual in his station organically due to him. In this, lie the dignity and active participation of the individual, but also his restraint, and all modern achievements of national unity, equality before the law, parliaments and universal military service, are molded by this spirit. This is the "state mysticism" (Staatsmystik) which our great thinkers and historians have felt in common with Plato. It has been rejected as philosophically meaningless by Bishop Welldon and his English nominalism, and it has been defined as immoral by the English ideal of independence. But Hegel saw in it the philosophy of freedom, and it has become evident, more or less consciously, more or less

* From Ernst Troeltsch, "The German Idea of Freedom" (1916), reprinted in *Deutscher Geist und Westeuropa* (J. C. B. Mohr, 1925). Translated by William Ebenstein.

coherently, in all great German creations of the century. As everything in this world, this "state mysticism" has its dangers, and can obviously degenerate in face of fear of responsibility and bureaucratic rule of officials. But where its most characteristic nerve is alive in autonomous, dutiful, self-dedication and participation combined with vigilance and responsibility, it leads to a joining of initiative with devotion, pride with discipline, creative energy with public spiritedness and sacrifice. This spirit has created all that is great in the past German century, it characterizes two expressions of life so contrary to one another as the German army and the socialist party. It has also absorbed, and digested, Bismarck's realism.

Chapter VII

THE CRY FOR THE LEADER

ONE of the two or three main tenets of antidemocratic politics is the leadership principle. The cry for the leader comes from all who refuse to grow up; it will be noticed that the voices represented in this chapter are gathered from several nations.

Few critics of nineteenth-century democracy have been so influential as Carlyle. His long life (he was born in 1795 and lived eighty-six years) may have been one factor. Like Shaw later on, Carlyle must have seemed immortal to his contemporaries. When he wrote about Martin Luther or Cromwell, some of his readers must have thought that Carlyle was writing from personal experience. A second source of influence was Carlyle's bountiful production: he published long works of four and even six volumes. The third reason for his immense influence lay in his literary style—highly personal, vituperative, brilliant, and skilfully blending truth with falsehood.

Because Carlyle attacked the "cash nexus" of capitalist civilization, he was hailed by many in his own day, as today, as a progressive thinker. Yet, as one reads his political essays, one is impressed with the fact that the anatomy of Fascism and Nazism can be unmistakably detected in his work. The essentials of the fascist mind and temper are all there: contempt for democracy which, as Carlyle puts it in *Chartism* (1840), is a self-canceling business and "gives in the long-run a net-result of zero." Democracy is, in Carlyle's eyes, less of a system of social organization than chaos and disintegration writ large and institutionalized, if emptiness and vacuity can be organized at all. He was convinced, as he put it in the *Latter-day Pamphlets* (1850), that democracy "is forever impossible." His contempt for people and his belief in aristocracy, in nature as well as in society, lead him to explain democracy as a device by which the "Sham-Noblest" are raised at the expense of "the Noble," thus perverting "the Almighty Maker's Law," according to which the Noble are in the high place, and the Ignoble in the low.

To talk of "rights of man" is, in Carlyle's view, balderdash; "it is the everlasting privilege of the foolish to be governed by the wise." This, says Carlyle, is "the first 'right of man.'" Analogously, and this, again, is good fascist doctrine, the wise and noble are duty bound to rule the foolish mass. This belief in inequality finds its strongest expression in *On Heroes, Hero-worship and the Heroic in History* (1840). "There is no act more moral between men than that of rule and obedience"—this Carlylean definition of human relationships is the exact antithesis of the democratic social morality which is founded on consent and cooperation rather than on rule and obedience. Carlyle also anticipates the fascist personal style of self-abasement and self-abnegation: "Find me the true Könning, King, or Able-man, and he *has* a divine right over me."

Carlyle's rejection of equality led him to attack, at home, all institutions of free government, from Parliament to a free press; in foreign and imperial policies his belief in inequality made him the advocate of imperialism over "inferior" races and peoples. He was not discriminating in his hatreds, and his mind seemed immensely spacious for hatreds of all sort: he hated the Irish, the Jews, the Negroes, the Latin peoples, and saw good only in the Teutonic and Anglo-Saxon peoples (of the United States he usually spoke with contempt). He conceived of the Teutons and Anglo-Saxons as the born master race destined to rule inferior breeds. As he became increasingly discouraged by the spread of suffrage and democracy in England, he looked to modern Germany as the sole remaining hope of the world. His mind had wandered to Germany, where he thought to have found his true spiritual home. In his biography of *Frederick the Great* he justified enthusiastically the conquests of the Prussian monarch, and also eulogized the trickery and wile that had accompanied them. The partition of Poland, to which Prussia was a party, elicited from Carlyle cynical approval of "Heaven's Justice."

Fearful of an expanding democracy and of social change, Carlyle was perhaps the first modern writer to develop a strategy of antidemocratic offensive, later more fully elaborated by Nazis and Fascists. Carlyle appealed to the "Captains of Industry" to become *leaders* and act like leaders, in union with the old landed aristocracy. He advised this antidemocratic group of leaders to build a well-armed, though numerically small, movement—sufficiently well armed to destroy the political institutions of an "anarchical" and disorganized majority. The "noble Few" would then establish a new order on hierarchical and militaristic lines, including the militaristic regimentation of labor.

The most interesting aspect of Carlyle's influence on social and political ideas is the fact that in England (where he had migrated from his native Scotland) it has been of little practical consequence, as viewed in the long-term perspective. His chief opponents, reformers like Bentham and Mill, changed the face of their country, whereas Carlyle always remained a lonely figure in England, admired by some and attacked by others—he did not continue a tradition in England that preceded him, nor did he establish a new school of thought which would carry on after his death. His work appeared like a meteor on the horizon in all its brilliance, but when the meteor hit the earth of England, its broken pieces were barren and lifeless. The important question, therefore, is not, was Carlyle British? The interesting question about Carlyle is not where he was born, and what language he wrote in, but where his influence was marked and widely felt. That country was Germany. In a real sense, Carlyle sent a lot of coal to Newcastle when his ideas, partly of German origin and all favorable to German ambitions for world power, were received by the Germans with real enthusiasm. A German selection from his works sold 300,000 copies in the years 1926–1932; under the Nazi regime, Carlyle was very much in vogue and widely read: his *On Heroes and Hero-worship* was compulsory reading in Nazi schools.

Friedrich Nietzsche was, like Carlyle, a man of letters whose influence was of immense political consequences. He lived to be only fifty-six when he died, after years of suffering madness, in 1900. His madness was foreshadowed in chapter headings like "Why I Am So Wise," "Why I Am So Clever," "Why I Write Such Excellent Books" (in *Ecce Homo*). His faith in the worth of his books was also evidenced by his statement "To take up one of my books is one of the rarest honors that a man can pay himself." This touch of madness, coupled with brilliant poetic imagery enriched by years of suffering and struggle, gave to his work a force and vigor that appealed to readers everywhere.

In the nineteenth century, more than any other an era of liberalism, Nietzsche was one one of the foremost leaders of "the other side." His criticism was directed, not against this or that detail of his age, but against the assumptions and values of rationalism and liberalism, in whatever form they appeared, be it politics, religion, economics, or philosophy. Like Carlyle, Nietzsche was a great hater; his hatreds always expanded and searched for new objects. He hated the human race in general, which he contemptuously called "slaves" or, in a more lenient mood, "herd" or "mass." In democracy, in particular, Nietzsche saw nothing but the triumph of the slave morality which had started with the Jews, and had been transmitted through Christianity to the modern world. Democracy is, according to Nietzsche, the destruction of the aristocratic values of Power and Beauty and Barbarism through a mass conspiracy of moralizing weaklings who erect a new, and opposed, set of values, that "the poor, the weak, the lowly, are alone the good." This contempt for democracy as the product of little "resentful" men whose "souls squint," is poured out in the pages of Nietzsche's *Genealogy of Morals* (1887), which also contains the famous, and dithyrambic, description of the kind of man whom Nietzsche, like other frustrated German *petit bourgeois,* admired as the true aristocrats: in dealing with each other, Nietzsche says, these aristocrats display consideration, loyalty, self-control, delicacy, and friendship. But outside their own country, they behave "not much better than beasts of prey which have been let loose. They enjoy there freedom from all social control, they feel that in the wilderness they can give

vent with impunity to that tension which is produced by enclosure and imprisonment in the peace of society, they *revert* to the innocence of the beast-
of-prey conscience, like jubilant monsters, who perhaps come from a ghostly
bout of murder, arson, rape, and torture, with bravado and a moral equanimity, as though merely some wild student's prank had been played, perfectly convinced that the poets have now an ample theme to sing and celebrate. It is impossible not to recognize at the core of all these aristocratic
races the beast of prey; the magnificent *blond beast,* avidly rampant for spoil
and victory." The "decline of humanity" is seen by Nietzsche in the attempt
to tame and civilize the beast of prey in man; democracy as the rule of the
slaves over the masters, the aristocrats, is the political consummation of this
disease which destroys those who "still say 'yes' to life," and elevates those
who constantly say "nay" to life, the lowly, the cunning, the weak.

Nietzsche wished that "the counting mania and the superstitious belief in
majorities were not established in Germany, as with the Latin races, and that
one could finally invent something new even in politics!" His wish was more
than granted, although the danger in Germany in 1887 was not that democracy was becoming too strong, but that it was not more than a sham in the
first place.

In his hatred of democracy and all that went with a liberal-capitalist civilization, Nietzsche put his hope, as expressed in the *Genealogy of Morals,* in
the one class in Germany which had still retained the supreme value in life,
the Will to Power: "The future of German culture rests with the sons of
Prussian officers." Of all German social groups, the Prussian officer was least
affected, Nietzsche thought, by the infiltrating poisons of Christianity, democracy, rationalism, liberalism, and socialism.

Of all the works of Nietzsche, none has probably so directly fostered the
growth of the Nazi mentality in Germany as *The Antichrist* (published
posthumously in 1902). Nietzsche's attack against Christianity was the first
in modern times to aim at the *morals* of Christianity rather than at its religion and theology—as had been done by so many opponents of Christianity.
Unlike many modern thinkers who opposed, or were indifferent to, the
religious faith in Christianity, yet accepted fully its moral teachings, Nietzsche
is relatively indifferent to the religious aspects of Christianity and concen-
trates all his hatred against Christian ethics and morals. Of all the creeds that
have sought to undermine the natural order of things (the few strong ruling
the many weak), none has had, according to Nietzsche, so disastrous effects
as Christianity. "The weak and the botched shall perish: first principle of
our humanity"—this first principle of Nietzschean humanity is utterly opposed to Christian ethics. Christianity is "more harmful than any vice" because of its "practical sympathy with all the botched and the weak." It has
waged war upon the "higher type of man," such as Nietzsche lyrically describes the blond beast, the beast of prey, the Prussian Junker. In particular,

Nietzsche singles out pity as the great disease of Christianity, because "a man loses power when he pities."

What arouses Nietzsche's ire above all is that Christianity was able to corrupt the most aristocratic of all "races," the peoples of northern Europe. Nietzsche could not forgive the Nordics that they were unable to resist Christian monotheism, "this hybrid creature of decay, nonentity, concept and contradiction, in which all the instincts of decadence, all the cowardices and languors of the soul find their sanction." Earlier, the Christians ("bloodsuckers," "parasites," "anarchists") had succeeded in demolishing another great race and empire, the Roman Empire. In both cases, Nietzsche claims, Christianity merely destroyed without showing any capacity to build anything new.

All this has been fully incorporated into the process of moral disintegration that has raged through modern Germany with constantly increasing intensity. The Nazi propagandists, under the leadership of Alfred Rosenberg, integrally accepted this Nietzschean interpretation of Christianity as a revolt of what is low and unlovely in the herd against the aristocratic virtues of power, war, and honor. Nietzsche also supplied German anti-Christianism with a new argument: that Christianity was in reality a Jewish conspiracy to dominate the world through the doctrines of monotheism, immortality of the soul, and the equality of men before God. After the Jews lost their political independence, that "priestly nation" eventually realized that "the one method of effecting satisfaction on its enemies and tyrants was by means of a radical transvaluation of values, which was at the same time an act of the *cleverest revenge.*" St. Paul attracts the wrath of Nietzsche more than any other apostle; he was the "eternal Jew" who recognized how, by the help of Christianity, a "universal conflagration could be kindled." In the Middle Ages, Jews were persecuted because they rejected Christianity. Nietzsche established in Germany the tradition of anti-Jewish hatred on the ground that the Jews had *created* Christianity. What the Nazis hated in the Jews above everything else was the fact that they were responsible for Christianity and all its values. Hating Christianity, Nietzscheans and Nazis were bound to end up hating the Jews, because, as Pope Pius XI said, Christians are all "spiritually Jews."

In *Thus Spake Zarathustra* (1883–1885), Nietzsche developed the concept of Superman as a new type of man. Without giving a very exact picture of this new breed of man who was to surpass man as hitherto known, Nietzsche made it clear that the coming of Superman would make *tabula rasa* of all the traditional values of the herd man, Christianity, pacifism, humanitarianism, democracy, socialism. This type of man would form a new *Herrenklasse,* a new class of masters which would rule over the lowly herd. Nietzsche himself did not think of a new racial superman, but of a new type of *character* which would be fulfilled in Superman. Individuality was to be most fully developed in this new *Übermensch,* as contrasted with the decay of individuality in the herd man. In this Nietzschean doctrine, as in so many of his other ideas, the question of what Nietzsche himself meant when he stated an idea is not identical with the question of how it was understood by others. The conception of Superman was meant by Nietzsche himself to indicate the need for more individuality and personality in the face of increasing standardization. There is something worth listening to in the Nietzschean idea of man who becomes supremely himself by overcoming what is weak and low in his self. Yet, to the average German, Nazi and non-Nazi, the Nietzschean vision of Superman anticipated the coming of the German master race, the new race of superior beings, to world power. Likewise, much that Nietzsche wrote about loyalty to Europe as opposed to narrow nationalism, the "German disease" of anti-Semitism, was opposed to the current pan-Germanism of his time. And yet, when the sum total is made up, the Nazis were on the right track when they elevated Nietzsche to a high position in the spiritual ancestry of Nazism: they rightly felt that what was important in Nietzsche was not an isolated passage here or there against nationalism or pan-Germanism, but his general attitude and set of values: he opposed all basic values that have been identified with the traditions of Christianity—pacifism, mercy, concern for the weak, democracy, liberalism, socialism—and upheld the values of authority, the will to power, the warrior spirit, and the leadership principle. The Nietzschean concepts of "Superman" and "transvaluation of all values" also imbued Germans, before and during the Nazi phase, with the faith that the human race could be molded into any desired shape, provided the operation was carried through with enough ruthlessness and disregard for all accepted moral considerations. In this sense, Nietzsche more than any other single German thinker helped to prepare the era of nihilism in which the code of the beast of prey was to prevail over the morality of the West. The Germans made this attempt twice since Nietzsche, and the second time the attempt almost succeeded.

The theory of the "mass" as the characteristic phenomenon of the modern age has been further elaborated by the Spanish publicist José Ortega y Gasset in *The Revolt of the Masses* (1930). Next to Miguel Unamuno, Ortega y Gasset has been the most interesting Spanish writer of the last generation. His merit consists in the fact that he examined the impact of numbers on the process of politics. The rather naïve approach of eighteenth-century rationalism and optimism saw in "the people" always the highest moral qualities, just as a twentieth-century offshoot identified "the proletariat" with all apriori perfections. The behavior of "the people" under the Nazi system in Germany demonstrated that the demonic, irrational forces of the mass can be more dangerous and savage than an individual tyrant. The problem of democracy consists in how to transform the potential "mass" or "crowd" into a "society." The novelty of Nazism and Fascism was their success in letting loose the slumbering savagery of man as a member of a "mass." Ortega y Gasset's bias is against the democratic trend which he identifies, in Nietzschean fashion, with the triumph of mediocrity over individuality and greatness; nevertheless, his book on *The Revolt of the Masses* was the first to draw attention to the dangerous fact that the expansion of popular power was accompanied, shadowlike, by potentially increasing irrationality.

The elite as the central fact of political life as it actually is, rather than as it should be, is the central doctrine of *The Ruling Class,* published in 1895 by the Italian political scientist Gaetano Mosca. Mosca claims to deal with the fauna of politics with no more bias than a zoologist deals with his. He sees in all history the rule of a minority, the ruling, or political, class (*la classe politica*) over the majority of the ruled. The methods vary, the circumstances differ, but the basic fact of the ruling class remains, regardless of the prevailing form of government, monarchy, aristocracy, or democracy. This rule by an elite is not only historically observable, but is "inevitable." The reason is that the "power of any minority is irresistible as against each single individual in the majority, who stands alone before the totality of the organized minority." Mosca clearly outlined the strategy of fascist assault on democratic institutions when he says, "A hundred men acting uniformly in concert with a common understanding, will triumph over a thousand men who are not in accord and can therefore be dealt with one by one." This recipe has been followed by totalitarians in foreign affairs as well: their preference for bilateral treaties (rather than collective agreements) and unilateral conquests was expressed handsomely by Frederick the Great, who advised that his intended victims must be eaten like an artichoke, "leaf by leaf."

Unlike blood-and-soil worshipers of the Nazi variety, Mosca denied that members of a ruling class owe their special qualities to "the blood that flows in their veins." He stressed intellectual superiority as the distinctive quality of the ruling elite, although he was aware that the factor of birth was socially important. In particular, he was impressed with the fact that members of various parliaments were the sons or grandsons, brothers or nephews of other members and ex-members.

Mosca was one of the few modern Italian writers on politics who had a rich practical experience in actual government. In 1908 he was elected to the Italian Chamber of Deputies. He soon expressed his sympathies for the Right by voting, as one of only six members of the Chamber, against universal suffrage. In 1919 he was appointed a member of the Senate, and he continued his active political life after the Fascists seized power in 1922. While not approving of every detail of Fascist doctrine or policy, he saw in it a sound and healthy movement directed against too much democracy and socialism, and reaffirming the principles of authority and nationalist imperialism.

Hitler's discussion of the leadership principle in *Mein Kampf* (1925–1927) is important, because he speaks with some authority on the subject, and also because the Germans were convinced enough by *Mein Kampf,* and disgusted enough with their Reichstag to put their fate into the hands of Adolf Hitler. His contempt for the masses extended to popular institutions like parliaments and majority decisions. Hitler hated such institutions because they seemed to him to subvert the natural order of things in which the strong ruled the weak without taking votes first. He deduced from his racialism that just as superior people have the right to rule inferior races, "the same aristocratic principle" has to guarantee "leadership and the highest influence within the respective people to the best heads." In his own mind Hitler was reasonably certain whose head was the best in Germany, and he knew what would appeal best to his fellow countrymen: "The principle which once made the Prussian army in its time into the most marvelous instrument of the German people must some day, in a transferred sense, become the principle of the construction of our whole State conception: *authority of every leader downward and responsibility upward."* The outcome of the Second World War finally convinced many Germans that, however correct Hitler's philosophy was, his leadership was not so good as that of the "decadent democracies."

---

1. Democracy Is Forever Impossible*

THOMAS CARLYLE

Alas, on this side of the Atlantic and on that, Democracy, we apprehend, is forever impossible! So much, with certainty of loud astonished contradiction from all manner of men at present, but with sure appeal to the Law of Nature and the ever-abiding Fact, may be suggested and asserted once more. The Universe itself is a Monarchy and Hierarchy; large liberty of 'voting' there, all manner of choice, utmost free-will, but with conditions inexorable and immeasurable annexed to every exercise of the same. A most free commonwealth of 'voters'; but with Eternal Justice to preside over it, Eternal Justice enforced by Almighty Power! This is the model of 'constitutions';

* From Thomas Carlyle, *Latter-Day Pamphlets* (1850).

this: nor in any Nation where there has not yet (in some supportable and withal some constantly-increasing degree) been confided to the *Noblest*, with his select series of *Nobler*, the divine everlasting duty of directing and controlling the Ignoble, has the 'Kingdom of God,' which we all pray for, 'come,' nor can 'His will' even *tend* to be 'done on Earth as it is in Heaven' till then. My Christian friends, and indeed my Sham-Christian and Anti-Christian, and all manner of men, are invited to reflect on this. They will find it to be the truth of the case. The Noble in the high place, the Ignoble in the low; that is, in all times and in all countries, the Almighty Maker's Law.

To raise the Sham-Noblest, and solemnly consecrate *him* by whatever method, new-devised, or slavishly adhered to from old wont, this, little as we may regard it, is, in all times and countries, a practical blasphemy, and Nature will in no wise forget it. Alas, there lies the origin, the fatal necessity, of modern Democracy everywhere. It is the Noblest, not the Sham-Noblest; it is God-Almighty's Noble, not the Court-Tailor's Noble, nor the Able-Editor's Noble, that must in some approximate degree, be raised to the supreme place; he and not a counterfeit,—under penalties! Penalties deep as death, and at length terrible as hell-on-earth, my constitutional friend! —Will the ballot-box raise the Noblest to the chief place; does any sane man deliberately believe such a thing? That nevertheless is the indispensable result, attain it how we may: if that is attained, all is attained; if not that, nothing. He that cannot believe the ballot-box to be attaining it, will be comparatively indifferent to the ballot-box. Excellent for keeping the ship's crew at peace under their Phantasm Captain; but unserviceable, under such, for getting round Cape Horn. Alas, that there should be human beings requiring to have these things argued of, at this late time of day!

I say, it is the everlasting privilege of the foolish to be governed by the wise; to be guided in the right path by those who know it better than they. This is the first 'right of man'; compared with which all other rights are as nothing,—mere superfluities, corollaries which will follow of their own accord out of this; if they be not contradictions to this, and less than nothing! To the wise it is not a privilege; far other indeed. Doubtless, as bringing preservation to their country, it implies preservation of themselves withal; but intrinsically it is the harshest duty a wise man, if he be indeed wise, has laid to his hand. A duty which he would fain enough shirk; which accordingly, in these sad times of doubt and cowardly sloth, he has long everywhere been endeavouring to reduce to its minimum, and has in fact in most cases nearly escaped altogether. It is an ungoverned world; a world which we flatter ourselves will henceforth need no governing. On the dust of our heroic ancestors we too sit ballot-boxing, saying to one another, It is well, it is well! By inheritance of their noble struggles, we have been permitted to sit slothful so long. By noble toil, not by shallow laughter and vain talk, they made this English Existence from a savage forest into an arable inhabitable field for us; and we, idly dreaming it would grow spontaneous crops forever, —find it now in a too questionable state; peremptorily requiring real labour and agriculture again. Real 'agriculture' is not pleasant; much pleasanter to reap and winnow (with ballot-box or otherwise) than to plough!

Who would govern that can get along without governing? He that is fittest for it, is of all men the unwillingest unless constrained. By multifarious devices we have been endeavouring to dispense with governing; and by very superficial speculations, of *laissez-faire,* supply-and-demand, &c. &c. to persuade ourselves that it is best so. The Real Captain, unless it be some Captain of mechanical Industry hired by Mammon, where is he in these days? Most likely, in silence, in sad isolation somewhere, in remote obscurity; trying if, in an evil ungoverned time, he cannot at least govern himself. The Real Captain undiscoverable; the Phantasm Captain everywhere very conspicuous:—it is thought Phantasm Captains, aided by ballot-boxes, are the true method, after all. They are much the pleasantest for the time being! And so no *Dux* or Duke of any sort, in any province of our affairs, now *leads:* the Duke's Bailiff *leads,* what little leading is required for getting-in the rents; and the Duke merely rides in the state-coach. It is everywhere so: and now at last we see a world all rushing towards strange consummations, because it is and has long been so!

2. *"Give Me a Leader"* *

THOMAS CARLYLE

Democracy, we are well aware, what is called 'self-government' of the multitude by the multitude, is in words the thing everywhere passionately clamoured for at present. Democracy makes rapid progress in these latter times, and ever more rapid, in a perilous accelerative ration; towards democracy, and that only, the progress of things is everywhere tending as to the final goal and winning-post. So think, so clamour the multitudes everywhere. And yet all men may see, whose sight is good for much, that in democracy can lie no finality; that with the completest winning of democracy there is

* From Thomas Carlyle, *Chartism* (1840).

nothing yet won,—except emptiness, and the free chance to win! Democracy is by the nature of it, a self-cancelling business: and gives in the long-run a net-result of *zero*. Where no government is wanted, save that of the parish-constable, as in America with its boundless soil, every man being able to find work and recompense for himself, democracy may subsist; not else-where, except briefly, as a swift transition towards something other and farther. Democracy never yet, that we heard of, was able to accomplish much work, beyond that same cancelling of itself. Rome and Athens are themes for the schools; unexceptionable for that purpose. In Rome and Athens, as elsewhere, if we look practically, we shall find that it was not by loud voting and debating of many, but by wise insight and ordering of a few that the work was done. So is it ever, so will it ever be. The French Convention was a Parliament elected 'by the five points,' with ballot-boxes, universal suffrages, and what not, as perfectly as Parliament can hope to be in this world; and had indeed a pretty spell of work to do and did it. The French Convention had to cease from being a free Parliament, and become more arbitrary than any Sultan Bajazet, before it could so much as subsist. It had to purge out its argumentative Girondins, elect its Supreme Committe of *Salut,* guillotine into silence and extinction all that gainsayed it, and rule and work literally by the sternest despotism ever seen in Europe, before it could rule at all. Napoleon was not president of a republic; Cromwell tried hard to rule in that way, but found that he could not. These, 'the armed soldiers of democracy,' had to chain democracy under their feet, and become despots over it, before they could work out the earnest obscure purpose of democracy itself! Democracy, take it where you will in our Europe, is found but as a regulated method of rebellion and abrogation; it abrogates the old arrangement of things; and leaves, as we say, *zero* and vacuity for the institution of a new arrangement. It is the consummation of No-government and *Laissez-faire.* It may be natural for our Europe at present; but cannot be the ultimatum of it. Not towards the impossibility, 'self-government' of a multitude by a multitude; but towards some possibility, government by the wisest, does bewildered Europe struggle. The blessedest possibility: not misgovernment, not *Laissez-faire,* but veritable government! Cannot one discern too, across all democratic turbulence, clattering of ballot-boxes and infinite sorrowful jangle, needful or not, that this at bottom is the wish and prayer of all human hearts, everywhere and at all times: "Give me a leader; a true leader, not a false sham-leader; a true leader, that he may guide me on the true way, that I may be loyal to him, that I may swear fealty to him and follow him, and feel that it is well with me!" The relation of the taught to their teacher, of the loyal subject to his guiding king, is, under one shape or another, the vital element of human Society; indispensable to it, perennial in it; without which, as a body reft of its soul, it falls down into death, and with horrid noisome dissolution passes away and disappears.

3. *Prophet of Fascism* *

THOMAS CARLYLE

We come now to the last form of Heroism; that which we call Kingship. The Commander over men; he to whose will our wills are to be subordinated, and loyally surrender themselves, and find their welfare in doing so, may be reckoned the most important of Great Men. He is practically the summary for us of *all* the various figures of Heroism; Priest, Teacher, whatsoever of earthly or of spiritual dignity we can fancy to reside in a man, embodies itself here, to *command* over us, to furnish us with constant practical teaching, to tell us for the day and hour what we are to *do*. He is called *Rex,* Regulator, *Roi:* our own name is still better; King, *Könning,* which means *Can*-ning, Able-man.

Numerous considerations, pointing towards deep, questionable, and indeed unfathomable regions, present themselves here: on the most of which we must resolutely for the present forbear to speak at all. As Burke said that perhaps fair *Trial by Jury* was the Soul of Government, and that all legislation, administration, parliamentary debating, and the rest of it, went on, in 'order to bring twelve impartial men into a jury-box';—so, by much stronger reason, may I say here, that the finding of your *Ableman* and getting him invested with the *symbols of ability,* with dignity, worship (*worth*-ship) royalty, kinghood, or whatever we call it, so that *he* may actually have room to guide according to his faculty of doing it,—is the business, well or ill accomplished, of all social procedure whatsoever in this world! Hustings-speeches, Parliamentary motions, Reform Bills, French Revolutions, all mean at heart this; or else nothing. Find in any country the Ablest Man that exists there; raise *him* to the supreme place, and loyally reverence him: you have a perfect government for that country; no ballot-box, parliamentary eloquence, voting, constitution-building, or other machinery whatsoever can improve it a whit. It is in the perfect state: an ideal country. The Ablest Man; he means also the truest-hearted, justest, the Noblest Man: what he *tells us to do* must be precisely the wisest, fittest, that we could anywhere or anyhow learn;—the thing which it will in all ways behove us, with right loyal thankfulness, and nothing doubting, to do! Our *doing* and life were then, so far as government could regulate it, well regulated; that were the ideal of constitutions.

* From Thomas Carlyle, *On Heroes, Hero-Worship and the Heroic in History* (1840).

Alas, we know very well that Ideals can never be completely embodied in practice. Ideals must ever lie a very great way off; and we will right thankfully content ourselves with any not intolerable approximation thereto! Let no man, as Schiller says, too querulously 'measure by a scale of perfection the meagre product of reality' in this poor world of ours. We will esteem him no wise man; we will esteem him a sickly, discontented, foolish man. And yet, on the other hand, it is never to be forgotten that Ideals do exist; that if they be not approximated to at all, the whole matter goes to wreck! Infallibly. No bricklayer builds a wall *perfectly* perpendicular, mathematically this is not possible; a certain degree of perpendicularity suffices him; and he, like a good bricklayer, who must have done with his job, leaves it so. And yet if he sway *too much* from the perpendicular; above all, if he throw plummet and level quite away from him, and pile brick on brick heedless, just as it comes to hand—! Such bricklayer, I think, is in a bad way. *He* has forgotten himself: but the Law of Gravitation does not forget to act on him; he and his wall rush-down into confused welter of ruin!——

This is the history of all rebellions, French Revolutions, social explosions in ancient or modern times. You have put the too *Un*able man at the head of affairs! The too ignoble, unvaliant, fatuous man. You have forgotten that there is any rule, or natural necessity whatever, of putting the Able Man there. Brick must lie on brick as it may and can. Unable Simulacrum of Ability, *quack,* in a word, must adjust himself with quack, in all manner of administration of human things;—which accordingly lie unadministered, fermenting into unmeasured masses of failure, of indigent misery: in the outward, and in the inward or spiritual, miserable millions stretch-out the hand for their due supply, and it is not there. The 'law of gravitation' acts; Nature's laws do none of them forget to act. The miserable millions burst-forth into Sansculottism, or some other sort of madness; bricks and bricklayers lie as fatal chaos!——

Much sorry stuff, written some hundred years ago or more, about the 'Divine right of Kings,' moulders unread now in the Public Libraries of this country. Far be it from us to disturb the calm process by which it is disappearing harmlessly from the earth, in those repositories! At the same time, not to let the immense rubbish go without leaving us, as it ought, some soul of it behind—I will say that it did mean something; something true, which it is important for us and all men to keep in mind. To assert that in whatever man you chose to lay hold of (by this or the other plan of clutching at him); and clapt a round piece of metal on the head of, and called King,—there straightway came to reside a divine virtue, so that *he* became a kind of God, and a Divinity inspired him with faculty and right to rule over you to all lengths: this,—what can we do with this but leave it to rot silently in the Public Libraries? But I will say withal, and that is what these Divine-right men meant, That in Kings, and in all human Authorities, and relations that men god-created can form among each other, there is verily either a Divine Right or else a Diabolic Wrong; one or the other of these two! For it is false altogether, what the last Sceptical Century taught us, that this world is a steamengine. There is a God in this world; and a God's-sanction, or else the violation of such, does look-out from all ruling and obedience, from all moral-acts of men. There is no act more moral between men than that of rule and obedience. Woe to him that claims obedience when it is not due; woe to him that refuses it when it is! God's law is in that, I say, however the Parchment-laws may run: there is a Divine Right or else a Diabolic Wrong at the heart of every claim that one man makes upon another.

It can do none of us harm to reflect on this: in all the relations of life it will concern us; in Loyalty and Royalty, the highest of these. I esteem the modern error, That all goes by self-interest, and the checking and balancing of greedy knaveries, and that, in short, there is nothing divine whatever in the association of men, a still more despicable error, natural as it is to an unbelieving century, than that of a 'divine right' in people *called* Kings. I say, Find me the true *Könning,* King, or Able-man, and he *has* a divine right over me. That we knew in some tolerable measure how to find him, and that all men were ready to acknowledge his divine right when found: this is precisely the healing which a sick world is every-where, in these ages, seeking after! The true King, as guide of the practical, has ever something of the Pontiff in him,—guide of the spiritual, from which all practice has its rise. This too is a true saying, That the *King* is head of the *Church.—* But we will leave the Polemic stuff of a dead century to lie quiet on its bookshelves.

4. *Slave Morality of Democracy* [*]

FRIEDRICH NIETZSCHE

The really great haters in the history of the world have always been priests, who are also the cleverest haters—in comparison with the cleverness of priestly revenge, every other piece of cleverness is practically negligible. Human history would be too fatuous for anything were it not for the cleverness imported into it by the weak—take at once the most important instance. All the world's efforts against the "aristocrats," the "mighty," the

[*] From Friedrich Nietzsche, *Genealogy of Morals* (1887; in Vol. XIII, *Complete Works,* ed. by Oscar Levy, 1910). By permission of The Macmillan Company, publishers.

"masters," the "holders of power," are negligible by comparison with what has been accomplished against those classes by *the Jews*—the Jews, that priestly nation which eventually realised that the one method of effecting satisfaction on its enemies and tyrants was by means of a radical transvaluation of values, which was at the same time an act of the *cleverest revenge*. Yet the method was only appropriate to a nation of priests, to a nation of the most jealously nursed priestly revengefulness. It was the Jews who, in opposition to the aristocratic equation (good = aristocratic = beautiful = happy = loved by the gods), dared with a terrifying logic to suggest the contrary equation, and indeed to maintain with the teeth of the most profound hatred (the hatred of weakness) this contrary equation, namely, "the wretched are alone the good; the poor, the weak, the lowly, are alone the good; the suffering, the needy, the sick, the loathsome, are the only ones who are pious, the only ones who are blessed, for them alone is salvation—but you, on the other hand, you aristocrats, you men of power, you are to all eternity the evil, the horrible, the covetous, the insatiate, the godless; eternally also shall you be the unblessed, the cursed, the damned!" We know who it was who reaped the heritage of this Jewish transvaluation. In the context of the monstrous and inordinately fateful initiative which the Jews have exhibited in connection with this most fundamental of all declarations of war, I remember the passage which came to my pen on another occasion (*Beyond Good and Evil,* Aph. 195)—that it was, in fact, with the Jews that the *revolt of the slaves* begins in the sphere *of morals;* that revolt which has behind it a history of two millennia, and which at the present day has only moved out of our sight, because it—has achieved victory.

While the aristocratic man lived in confidence and openness with himself the resentful man, on the other hand, is neither sincere nor naïf, nor honest and candid with himself. His soul *squints;* his mind loves hidden crannies, tortuous paths and backdoors, everything secret appeals to him as *his* world, *his* safety, *his* balm; he is past master in silence, in not forgetting, in waiting, in provisional self-depreciation and self-abasement. A race of such *resentful* men will of necessity eventually prove more *prudent* than any aristocratic race, it will honour prudence on quite a distinct scale, as, in fact, a paramount condition of existence, while prudence among aristocratic men is apt to be tinged with a delicate flavour of luxury and refinement; so among them it plays nothing like so integral a part as that complete certainty of function of the governing *unconscious* instincts, or as indeed a certain lack of prudence, such as a vehement and valiant charge, whether against danger or the enemy, or as those ecstatic bursts of rage, love, reverence, gratitude, by which at all times noble souls have recognised each other. When the resentment of the aristocratic man manifests itself, it fulfills and exhausts itself in an immediate reaction, and consequently instills no *venom:*

on the other hand, it never manifests itself at all in countless instances, when in the case of the feeble and weak it would be inevitable. An inability to take seriously for any length of time their enemies, their disasters, their *mis-deeds*—that is the sign of the full strong natures who possess a superfluity of moulding plastic force, that heals completely and produces forgetfulness: a good example of this in the modern world is Mirabeau, who had no memory for any insults and meannesses which were practised on him, and who was only incapable of forgiving because he forgot. Such a man indeed shakes off with a shrug many a worm which would have buried itself in another; it is only in characters like these that we see the possibility (supposing, of course, that there is such a possibility in the world) of the real *"love* of one's enemies." What respect for his enemies is found, forsooth, in an aristocratic man—and such a reverence is already a bridge to love! He insists on having his enemy to himself as his distinction. He tolerates no other enemy but a man in whose character there is nothing to despise and *much* to honour! On the other hand, imagine the "enemy" as the resentful man conceives him —and it is here exactly that we see his work, his creativeness; he has conceived "the evil enemy," the "evil one," and indeed that is the root idea from which he now evolves as a contrasting and corresponding figure a "good one," himself—his very self!

The method of this man is quite contrary to that of the aristocratic man, who conceives the root idea "good" spontaneously and straight away, that is to say, out of himself, and from that material then creates for himself a concept of "bad"! This "bad" of aristocratic origin and that "evil" out of the cauldron of unsatisfied hatred—the former an imitation, an "extra," an additional nuance; the latter, on the other hand, the original, the beginning, the essential act in the conception of a slave morality—these two words "bad" and "evil," how great a difference do they mark, in spite of the fact that they have an identical contrary in the idea "good." But the idea "good" is *not* the same: much rather let the question be asked, "Who is really evil according to the meaning of the morality of resentment?" In all sternness let it be answered thus:—*just* the good man of the other morality, just the aristocrat, the powerful one, the one who rules, but who is distorted by the venomous eye of resentfulness, into a new colour, a new signification, a new appearance. This particular point we would be the last to deny: the man who learnt to know those "good" ones only as enemies, learnt at the same time not to know them only as *"evil enemies,"* and the same men who *inter pares* were kept so rigorously in bounds through convention, respect, custom, and gratitude, though much more through mutual vigilance and jealousy *inter pares,* these men who in their relations with each other find so many new ways of manifesting consideration, self-control, delicacy, loyalty, pride, and friendship, these men are in reference to what is outside their circle (where the foreign element, a *foreign* country, begins), not much better than beasts of prey, which have been let loose. They enjoy there freedom from all social control, they feel that in the wilderness they can give vent with impunity to that tension which is produced by enclosure and imprisonment in the peace of society, they *revert* to the innocence of the beast-of-prey conscience, like jubilant monsters, who perhaps come from a ghostly bout of murder, arson, rape, and torture, with bravado and a moral equanimity, as though merely some wild student's prank had been played, perfectly convinced that the poets have now an ample theme to sing and celebrate. It is impossible not to recognise at the core of all these aristocratic races the beast of prey; the magnificent *blond beast,* avidly rampant for spoil and victory; this hidden core needed an outlet from time to time, the beast must get loose again, must return into the wilderness—the Roman, Arabic, German, and Japanese nobility, the Homeric heroes, the Scandinavian Vikings, are all alike in this need. It is the aristocratic races who have left the idea "Barbarian" on all the tracks in which they have marched; nay, a consciousness of this very barbarianism, and even a pride in it, manifests itself even in their highest civilisation (for example, when Pericles says to his Athenians in that celebrated funeral oration, "Our audacity has forced a way over every land and sea, rearing everywhere imperishable memorials of itself for *good* and for *evil*").

Granted the truth of the theory now believed to be true, that the very *essence of all civilisation* is to *train* out of man, the beast of prey, a tame and civilised animal, a domesticated animal, it follows indubitably that we must regard as the real *tools of civilisation* all those instincts of reaction and resentment, by the help of which the aristocratic races, together with their ideals, were finally degraded and overpowered; though that has not yet come to be synonymous with saying that the bearers of those tools also *represented* the civilisation. It is rather the contrary that is not only probable —nay, it is *palpable* to-day; these bearers of vindictive instincts that have to be bottled up, these descendants of all European and non-European slavery, especially of the pre-Aryan population—these people, I say, represent the *decline* of humanity! These "tools of civisation" are a disgrace to humanity, and constitute in reality more of an argument against civilisation, more of a reason why civilisation should be suspected. One may be perfectly justified in being always afraid of the blond beast that lies at the core of all aristocratic races, and in being on one's guard: but who would not a hundred times prefer to be afraid, when one at the same time admires, than to be immune from fear, at the cost of being perpetually obsessed with the loathsome spectacle of the distorted, the dwarfed, the stunted, the envenomed? And is that not our fate? What produces to-day our repulsion towards "man"?—for we *suffer* from "man," there is no doubt about it. It is not fear; it is rather that we have nothing more to fear from men; it is that the worm "man" is in the foreground and pullulates; it is that the "tame man," the wretched mediocre and unedifying creature, has learnt to consider himself a goal and a pinnacle, an inner meaning, an historic principle, a "higher man"; yes, it is that he has a certain right so to consider himself, in so far as he feels that in contrast to that excess of deformity, disease, exhaustion, and effeteness whose odour is beginning to pollute present-day Europe, he at any rate has achieved a relative success, he at any rate still says "yes" to life.

The future of German culture rests with the sons of Prussian officers.

Parliaments may be very useful to a strong and versatile statesman: he has something there to rely upon (every such thing must, however, be able to resist!)—upon which he can throw a great deal of responsibility. On the whole, however, I could wish that the counting mania and the superstitious belief in majorities were not established in Germany, as with the Latin races, and that one could finally invent something new even in politics! It is senseless and dangerous to let the custom of universal suffrage—which is still but a short time under cultivation, and could easily be uprooted—take a deeper root: whilst, of course, its introduction was merely an expedient to steer clear of temporary difficulties.

5. Antichrist *

FRIEDRICH NIETZSCHE

What is good? All that enhances the feeling of power, the Will to Power, and power itself in man. What is bad?—All that proceeds from weakness. What is happiness?—The feeling that power is *increasing,*—that resistance has been overcome.

Not contentment, but more power; not peace at any price, but war; not virtue, but efficiency [1] (virtue in the Renaissance sense, *virtù,* free from all moralic acid). The weak and the botched shall perish: first principle of our humanity. And they ought even to be helped to perish.

What is more harmful than any vice?—Practical sympathy with all the botched and the weak—Christianity.

We must not deck out and adorn Christianity: it has waged a deadly war

* From Friedrich Nietzsche, *The Antichrist* (1902; in Vol. XVI, *Complete Works,* ed. by Oscar Levy, 1911). By permission of The Macmillan Company, publishers.

[1] The German *"Tüchtigkeit"* has a nobler ring than our word "efficiency."—Tr.

upon this *higher* type of man, it has set a ban upon all the fundamental instincts of this type, and has distilled evil and the devil himself out of these instincts:—the strong man as the typical pariah, the villain. Christianity has sided with everything weak, low, and botched; it has made an ideal out of *antagonism* towards all the self-preservative instincts of strong life; it has corrupted even the reason of the strongest intellects, by teaching that the highest values of intellectuality are sinful, misleading and full of temptations. The most lamentable example of this was the corruption of Pascal, who believed in the perversion of his reason through original sin, whereas it had only been perverted by his Christianity.

Christianity is called the religion of *pity*.—Pity is opposed to the tonic passions which enhance the energy of the feeling of life: its action is depressing. A man loses power when he pities. By means of pity the drain on strength which suffering itself already introduces into the world is multiplied a thousandfold. Through pity, suffering itself becomes infectious; in certain circumstances it may lead to a total loss of life and vital energy, which is absurdly out of proportion to the magnitude of the cause (—the case of the death of the Nazarene). This is the first standpoint; but there is a still more important one. Supposing one measures pity according to the value of the reactions it usually stimulates, its danger to life appears in a much more telling light. On the whole, pity thwarts the law of development which is the law of selection. It preserves that which is ripe for death, it fights in favour of the disinherited and the condemned of life; thanks to the multitude of abortions of all kinds which it maintains in life, it lends life itself a sombre and questionable aspect. People have dared to call pity a virtue (—in every *noble* culture it is considered as a weakness—); people went still further, they exalted it to *the* virtue, the root and origin of all virtues,—but, of course, what must never be forgotten is the fact that this was done from the standpoint of a philosophy which was nihilistic, and on whose shield the device *The Denial of Life* was inscribed. Schopenhauer was right in this respect: by means of pity, life is denied and made *more worthy of denial,*— pity is the *praxis* of Nihilism. I repeat, this depressing and infectious instinct thwarts those instincts which aim at the preservation and enhancement of the value life: by *multiplying* misery quite as much as by preserving all that is miserable, it is the principal agent in promoting decadence,—pity exhorts people to nothing, to *nonentity!* But they do not say *"nonentity,"* they say "Beyond," or "God," or "the true life"; or Nirvana, or Salvation, or Blessedness, instead. This innocent rhetoric, which belongs to the realm of the religio-moral idiosyncrasy, immediately appears to be *very much less innocent* if one realises what the tendency is which here tries to drape itself in the mantle of sublime expressions—the tendency of hostility to life. Schopenhauer was hostile to life: that is why he elevated pity to a virtue. . . .

Aristotle, as you know, recognised in pity a morbid and dangerous state, of which it was wise to rid one's self from time to time by a purgative: he regarded tragedy as a purgative. For the sake of the instinct of life, it would certainly seem necessary to find some means of lancing any such morbid and dangerous accumulation of pity, as that which possessed Schopenhauer (and unfortunately the whole of our literary and artistic decadence as well, from St. Petersburg to Paris, from Tolstoi to Wagner), if only to make it *burst*. . . . Nothing is more unhealthy in the midst of our unhealthy modernity, than Christian pity. To be doctors *here,* to be inexorable *here,* to wield the knife effectively *here,*—all this is our business, all this is *our* kind of love to our fellows, this is what makes *us* philosophers, us hyperboreans!——

The fact that the strong races of Northern Europe did not repudiate the Christian God, certainly does not do any credit to their religious power, not to speak of their taste. They ought to have been able successfully to cope with such a morbid and decrepit offshoot of decadence. And a curse lies on their heads; because they were unable to cope with him: they made illness, decrepitude and contradiction a part of all their instincts,—since then they have not *created* any other God! Two thousand years have passed and not a single new God! But still there exists, and as if by right,—like an *ultimum* and *maximum* of god-creating power,—the *creator spiritus* in man, this miserable God of Christian monotono-theism! This hybrid creature of decay, nonentity, concept and contradiction, in which all the instincts of decadence, all the cowardices and languors of the soul find their sanction!——

In point of fact, it matters greatly to what end one lies: whether one preserves or *destroys* by means of falsehood. It is quite justifiable to bracket the *Christian* and the *Anarchist* together: their object, their instinct, is concerned only with destruction. The proof of this proposition can be read quite plainly from history: history spells it with appalling distinctness. Whereas we have just seen a religious legislation, whose object was to render the highest possible means of making life *flourish,* and of making a grand organisation of society, eternal,—Christianity found its mission in putting an end to such an organisation, *precisely because life flourishes through it.* In the one case, the net profit to the credit of reason, acquired through long ages of experiment and of insecurity, is applied usefully to the most remote ends, and the harvest, which is as large, as rich and as complete as possible, is reaped and garnered: in the other case, on the contrary, the harvest is *blighted* in a single night. That which stood there, *aere perennius,* the *imperium Romanum,* the most magnificent form of organisation, under difficult conditions, that has ever been achieved, and compared with which everything that preceded, and everything which followed it, is mere patchwork, gimcrackery, and dilettantism,—those holy anarchists made it their "piety," to destroy "the world"—that is to say, the *imperium Romanum,* until no two stones were left standing one on the other,—until even the Teutons and other clodhoppers were able to become master of it. The Christian and the anarchist are both decadents; they are both incapable of acting in any other way than disintegratingly, poisonously and witheringly, like *blood-suckers;* they are both actuated by an instinct of *mortal hatred* of everything that stands erect, that is great, that is lasting, and that is a guarantee of the future. . . . Christianity was the vampire of the *imperium Romanum*—in a night it shattered the stupendous achievement of the Romans, which was to acquire the territory for a vast civilisation which could *bide its time.*—Does no one understand this yet? The *imperium Romanum* that we know, and which the history of the Roman province teaches us to know ever more thoroughly, this most admirable work of art on a grand scale, was the beginning, its construction was calculated *to prove* its worth by millenniums,—unto this day nothing has ever again been built in this fashion, nor have men even dreamt since of building on this scale *sub specie aeterni!*—This organisation was sufficiently firm to withstand bad emperors: the accident of personalities must have nothing to do with such matters—the *first* principle of all great architecture. But it was not sufficiently firm to resist the *corruptest* form of corruption, to resist the Christians. . . . These stealthy canker-worms, which under the shadow of night, mist and duplicity, insinuated themselves into the company of every individual, and proceeded to drain him of all seriousness for *real* things, of all his instinct for *realities;* this cowardly, effeminate and sugary gang have step by step alienated all "souls" from this colossal edifice,—those valuable, virile and noble natures who felt that the cause of Rome was their own personal cause, their own personal seriousness, their own personal *pride.* The stealth of the bigot, the secrecy of the conventicle, concepts as black as hell such as the sacrifice of the innocent, the *unio mystica* in the drinking of blood, above all the slowly kindled fire of revenge, of Chandala revenge—such things became master of Rome, the same kind of religion on the pre-existent form of which Epicurus had waged war. One has only to read Lucretius in order to understand what Epicurus combated, *not* Paganism, but "Christianity," that is to say the corruption of souls through the concept of guilt, through the concept of punishment and immortality. He combated the *subterranean* cults, the whole of latent Christianity—to deny immortality was at that time a genuine *deliverance.*—And Epicurus had triumphed, every respectable thinker in the Roman Empire was an Epicurean: *then St. Paul appeared* . . . St. Paul, the Chandala hatred against Rome, against "the world," the Jew, the eternal Jew *par excellence,* become flesh and genius. . . . What he divined was, how, by the help of the small sectarian Christian movement, independent of Judaism, a universal conflagration could be kindled; how, with the symbol of the "God on the Cross," everything submerged, everything secretly insurrectionary, the whole offspring of anarchical intrigues could be gathered together to constitute an enormous power. "For salvation is of the Jews."—Christianity is the formula for the supersession, *and* epitomising of all kinds of subterranean cults, that of Osiris, of the Great Mother, of Mithras for example: St. Paul's genius consisted in his discovery of this. In this matter his instinct was so certain, that, regardless of doing violence to truth, he laid the ideas by means of which those Chandala religions fascinated, upon the very lips of the "Saviour" he had invented, and not only upon his lips,—that he *made* out of him something which even a Mithras priest could understand. . . . This was his moment of Damascus: he saw that he had *need* of the belief in immortality in order to depreciate "the world," that the notion of "hell" would become master of Rome, that with a "Beyond" this life can be killed. . . . Nihilist and Christian,—they rhyme in German, and they do not only rhyme.

I *condemn* Christianity and confront it with the most terrible accusation that an accuser has ever had in his mouth. To my mind it is the greatest of all conceivable corruptions, it has had the will to the last imaginable corruption. The Christian Church allowed nothing to escape from its corruption; it converted every value into its opposite, every truth into a lie, and every honest impulse into an ignominy of the soul. Let anyone dare to speak to me of its humanitarian blessings! To *abolish* any sort of distress was opposed to its profoundest interests; its very existence depended on states of distress; it created states of distress in order to make itself immortal. . . . The cancer germ of sin, for instance: the Church was the first to enrich mankind with this misery!—The "equality of souls before God," this falsehood, this *pretext* for the *rancunes* of all the base-minded, this anarchist bomb of a concept, which has ultimately become the revolution, the modern idea, the principle of decay of the whole of social order,—this is *Christian* dynamite. . . . The "humanitarian" blessings of Christianity! To breed a self-contradiction, an art of self-profanation, a will to lie at any price, an aversion, a contempt of all good and honest instincts out of *humanitas!* Is this what you call the blessings of Christianity?—Parasitism as the only method of the Church; sucking all the blood, all the love, all the hope of life out of mankind with anaemic and sacred ideals. A "Beyond" as the will to deny all reality; the cross as the trade-mark of the most subterranean form of conspiracy that has ever existed,—against health, beauty, well-constitutedness, bravery, intellect, kindliness of soul, *against Life itself.* . . .

This eternal accusation against Christianity I would fain write on all walls, wherever there are. walls,—I have letters with which I can make even the blind see. . . . I call Christianity the one great curse, the one enormous and innermost perversion, the one great instinct of revenge, for which no means are too venemous, too underhand, too underground and too *petty*,—I call it the one immortal blemish of mankind. . . .

And time is reckoned from the *dies nefastus* upon which this fatality came into being—from the first day of Christianity!—*why not rather from its last day?—From to-day?*—Transvaluation of all Values! . . .

6. Superman*

FRIEDRICH NIETZSCHE

I teach you the Superman. Man is something that is to be surpassed. What have ye done to surpass man?

All beings hitherto have created something beyond themselves: and ye want to be the ebb of that great tide, and would rather go back to the beast than surpass man?

What is the ape to man? A laughing-stock, a thing of shame. And just the same shall man be to the Superman: a laughing-stock, a thing of shame.

Ye have made your way from the worm to man, and much within you is still worm. Once were ye apes, and even yet man is more of an ape than any of the apes.

Even the wisest among you is only a disharmony and hybrid of plant and phantom. But do I bid you become phantoms or plants?

Lo, I teach you the Superman!

The Superman is the meaning of the earth. Let your will say: The Superman *shall be* the meaning of the earth!

I conjure you, my brethren, *remain true to the earth,* and believe not those who speak unto you of superearthly hopes! Poisoners are they, whether they know it or not.

Despisers of life are they, decaying ones and poisoned ones themselves, of whom the earth is weary: so away with them!

Once blasphemy against God was the greatest blasphemy; but God died, and therewith also those blasphemers. To blaspheme the earth is now the dreadfulest sin, and to rate the heart of the unknowable higher than the meaning of the earth!

Once the soul looked contemptuously on the body, and then that contempt was the supreme thing:—the soul wished the body meagre, ghastly, and famished. Thus it thought to escape from the body and the earth.

*From Friedrich Nietzsche, *Thus Spake Zarathustra* (1883–1885; in Vol. IV, *Complete Works,* ed. by Oscar Levy, 1911). By permission of The Macmillan Company, publishers.

Oh, that soul was itself meagre, ghastly, and famished; and cruelty was the delight of that soul!

But ye, also, my brethren, tell me: What doth your body say about your soul? Is your soul not poverty and pollution and wretched self-complacency?

Verily, a polluted stream is man. One must be a sea, to receive a polluted stream without becoming impure.

Lo, I teach you the Superman: he is that sea; in him can your great contempt be submerged.

What is the greatest thing ye can experience? It is the hour of great contempt. The hour in which even your happiness becometh loathsome unto you, and so also your reason and virtue.

The hour when ye say: "What good is my happiness! It is poverty and pollution and wretched self-complacency. But my happiness should justify existence itself!"

The hour when ye say: "What good is my reason! Doth it long for knowledge as the lion for his food? It is poverty and pollution and wretched self-complacency!"

The hour when ye say: "What good is my virtue! As yet it hath not made me passionate. How weary I am of my good and my bad! It is all poverty and pollution and wretched and self-complacency!"

The hour when ye say: "What good is my justice! I do not see that I am fervour and fuel. The just, however, are fervour and fuel!"

The hour when we say: "What good is my pity! Is not pity the cross on which he is nailed who loveth man? But my pity is not a crucifixion."

Have ye ever spoken thus? Have ye ever cried thus? Ah! would that I had heard you crying thus!

It is not your sin—is is your self-satisfaction that crieth unto heaven; your very sparingness in sin crieth unto heaven!

Where is the lightning to lick you with its tongue? Where is the frenzy with which ye should be inoculated?

Lo, I teach you the Superman: he is that lightning, he is that frenzy!——

7. Revolt of the Masses *

JOSÉ ORTEGA Y GASSET

There is one fact which, whether for good or ill, is of utmost importance in the public life of Europe at the present time. This fact is the accession of

* From José Ortega y Gasset, *The Revolt of the Masses* (W. W. Norton & Company, 1932). By permission.

the masses to complete social power. As the masses, by definition, neither should nor can direct their own personal existence, and still less rule society in general, this fact means that actually Europe is suffering from the greatest crisis that can afflict peoples, nations, and civilization. Such a crisis has occurred more than once in history. Its characteristics and its consequences are well known. So also is its name. It is called the rebellion of the masses. In order to understand this formidable fact, it is important from the start to avoid giving to the words "rebellion," "masses," and "social power" a meaning exclusively or primarily political. Public life is not solely political, but equally, and even primarily, intellectual, moral, economic, religious; it comprises all our collective habits, including our fashions both of dress and of amusement.

Perhaps the best line of approach to this historical phenomenon may be found by turning our attention to a visual experience, stressing one aspect of our epoch which is plain to our very eyes. This fact is quite simple to enunciate, though not so to analyse. I shall call it the fact of agglomeration, of "plentitude." Towns are full of people, houses full of tenants, hotels full of guests, trains full of travellers, cafés full of customers, parks full of promenaders, consulting-rooms of famous doctors full of patients, theatres full of spectators, and beaches full of bathers. What previously was, in general, no problem, now begins to be an everyday one, namely, to find room.

That is all. Can there be any fact simpler, more patent, more constant in actual life? Let us now pierce the plain surface of this observation and we shall be surprised to see how there wells forth an unexpected spring in which the white light of day, of our actual day, is broken up into its rich chromatic content. What is it that we see, and the sight of which causes us so much surprise? We see the multitude, as such, in possession of the places and the instruments created by civilization. The slightest reflection will then make us surprised at our own surprise. What about it? Is this not the ideal state of things? The theatre has seats to be occupied—in other words, so that the house may be full—and now they are overflowing; people anxious to use them are left standing outside. Though the fact be quite logical and natural, we cannot but recognise that this did not happen before and that now it does; consequently, there has been a change, an innovation, which justifies, at least for the first moment, our surprise.

To be surprised, to wonder, is to begin to understand. This is the sport, the luxury, special to the intellectual man. The gesture characteristic of his tribe consists in looking at the world with eyes wide open in wonder. Everything in the world is strange and marvellous to well-open eyes. This faculty of wonder is the delight refused to your football "fan," and, on the other hand, is the one which leads the intellectual man through life in the perpetual ecstasy of the visionary. His special attribute is the wonder of the eyes. Hence it was that the ancients gave Minerva her owl, the bird with everdazzled eyes.

Agglomeration, fullness, was not frequent before. Why then is it now? The components of the multitudes around us have not sprung from nothing. Approximately the same number of people existed fifteen years ago. Indeed, after the war it might seem natural that their number should be less. Nevertheless, it is here we come up against the first important point. The individuals who made up these multitudes existed, but not qua multitude. Scattered about the world in small groups, or solitary, they lived a life, to all appearances, divergent, dissociate, apart. Each individual or small group occupied a place, its own, in country, village, town, or quarter of the great city. Now, suddenly, they appear as an agglomeration, and looking in any direction our eyes meet with the multitudes. Not only in any direction, but precisely in the best places, the relatively refined creation of human culture, previously reserved to lesser groups, in a word, to minorities. The multitude has suddenly become visible, installing itself in the preferential positions in society. Before, if it existed, it passed unnoticed, occupying the background of the social stage; now it has advanced to the footlights and is the principal character. There are no longer protagonists; there is only the chorus.

The concept of the multitude is quantitative and visual. Without changing its nature, let us translate it into terms of sociology. We then meet with the notion of the "social mass." Society is always a dynamic unity of two component factors: minorities and masses. The minorities are individuals or groups of individuals which are specially qualified. The mass is the assemblage of persons not specially qualified. By masses, then, is not to be understood, solely or mainly, "the working masses." The mass is the average man. In this way what was mere quantity—the multitude—is converted into a qualitative determination: it becomes the common social quality, man as undifferentiated from other men, but as repeating in himself a generic type. What have we gained by this conversion of quantity into quality? Simply this: by means of the latter we understand the genesis of the former. It is evident to the verge of platitude that the normal formation of a multitude implies the coincidence of desires, ideas, ways of life in the individuals who constitute it. It will be objected that this is just what happens with every social group, however select it may strive to be. This is true; but there is an essential difference. In those groups which are characterised by not being multitude and mass, the effective coincidence of its members is based on some desire, idea, or ideal, which of itself excludes the great number. To form a minority, of whatever kind, it is necessary beforehand that each member separate himself from the multitude for special, relatively personal, reasons. Their coincidence with the others who form the minority is, then, secondary, posterior to their having each adopted an attitude of singularity, and is consequently, to a large extent, a coincidence in not coinciding. There are cases in which this singularising character of the group appears in the light of day: those English groups, which style themselves "nonconformists," where we have the grouping together of those who agree only in their disagreement in regard to the limitless multitude. This coming together of the minority precisely in order to separate themselves from the majority is a necessary ingredient in the formation of every minority. Speaking of the limited public which listened to a musician of refinement, Mallarmé wittily says that the public by its presence in small numbers stressed the absence of the multitude.

Strictly speaking, the mass, as a psychological fact, can be defined without waiting for individuals to appear in mass formation. In the presence of one individual we can decide whether he is "mass" or not. The mass is all that which sets no value on itself—good or ill—based on specific grounds, but which feels itself "just like everybody," and nevertheless is not concerned about it; is, in fact, quite happy to feel itself as one with everybody else. Imagine a humble-minded man who, having tried to estimate his own worth on specific grounds—asking himself if he has any talent for this or that, if he excels in any direction—realises that he possesses no quality of excellence. Such a man will feel that he is mediocre and commonplace, ill-gifted, but will not feel himself "mass."

When one speaks of "select minorities" it is usual for the evil-minded to twist the sense of this expression, pretending to be unaware that the select man is not the petulant person who thinks himself superior to the rest, but the man who demands more of himself than the rest, even though he may not fulfil in his person those higher exigencies. For there is no doubt that the most radical division that it is possible to make of humanity is that which splits it into two classes of creatures; those who make great demands on themselves, piling up difficulties and duties; and those who demand nothing special of themselves, but for whom to live is to be every moment what they already are, without imposing on themselves any effort towards perfection; mere buoys that float on the waves. This reminds me that orthodox Buddhism is composed of two distinct religions: one, more rigorous and difficult, the other easier and more trivial; the Mahayana—"great vehicle" or "great path"—and the Hinayana—"lesser vehicle" or "lesser path." The decisive matter is whether we attach our life to one or the other vehicle, to a maximum or a minimum of demands upon ourselves.

The division of society into masses and select minorities is, then, not a division into social classes, but into classes of men, and cannot coincide with the hierarchic separation of "upper" and "lower" classes. It is, of course, plain that in these "upper" classes, when and as long as they really are so, there is much more likelihood of finding men who adopt the "great vehicle," whereas the "lower" classes normally comprise individuals of minus quality. But, strictly speaking, within both these social classes, there are to be found mass and genuine minority. As we shall see, a characteristic of our times is the predominance, even in groups traditionally selective, of the mass and the vulgar. Thus, in the intellectual life, which of its essence requires and pre-supposes qualification, one can note the progressive triumph of the pseudo-intellectual, unqualified, unqualifiable, and, by their very mental texture, disqualified. Similarly, in the surviving groups of the "nobility," male and female. On the other hand, it is not rare to find to-day amongst working men, who before might be taken as the best example of what we are calling "mass," nobly disciplined minds.

There exist, then, in society, operations, activities, and functions of the most diverse order, which are of their very nature special, and which consequently cannot be properly carried out without special gifts. For example: certain pleasures of an artistic and refined character, or again the functions of gov-ernment and of political judgment in public affairs. Previously these special activities were exercised by qualified minorities, or at least by those who claimed such qualification. The mass asserted no right to intervene in them; they realised that if they wished to intervene they would necessarily have to acquire those special qualities and cease being mere mass. They recognised their place in a healthy dynamic social system.

If we now revert to the facts indicated at the start, they will appear clearly as the heralds of a changed attitude in the mass. They all indicate that the mass has decided to advance to the foreground of social life, to occupy the places, to use the instruments and to enjoy the pleasures hitherto reserved to the few. It is evident, for example, that the places were never intended for the multitude, for their dimensions are too limited, and the crowd is con-tinuously overflowing; thus manifesting to our eyes and in the clearest man-ner the new phenomenon: the mass, without ceasing to be mass, is supplant-ing the minorities.

No one, I believe, will regret that people are to-day enjoying themselves in greater measure and numbers than before, since they have now both the desire and the means of satisfying it. The evil lies in the fact that this decision taken by the masses to assume the activities proper to the minorities is not, and cannot be, manifested solely in the domain of pleasure, but that it is a general feature of our time. Thus—to anticipate what we shall see later—I believe that the political innovations of recent times signify nothing less than the political domination of the masses. The old democracy was tempered by a generous dose of liberalism and of enthusiasm for law. By serving these principles the individual bound himself to maintain a severe discipline over himself. Under the shelter of liberal principles and the rule of law, minor-ities could live and act. Democracy and law—life in common under the law —were synonymous. To-day we are witnessing the triumphs of a hyper-democracy in which the mass acts directly, outside the law, imposing its aspirations and its desires by means of material pressure. It is a false interpretation of the new situation to say that the mass has grown tired of politics and handed over the exercise of it to specialised persons. Quite the contrary. That was what happened previously; that was democracy. The mass took it for granted that after all, in spite of their defects and weaknesses, the minorities understood a little more of public problems than it did itself. Now, on the other hand, the mass believes that it has the right to impose and to give force of law to notions born in the café. I doubt whether there have been other periods of history in which the multitude has come to govern more directly than in our own. That is why I speak of hyperdemocracy.

The same thing is happening in other orders, particularly in the intellectual. I may be mistaken, but the present-day writer, when he takes his pen in hand to treat a subject which he has studied deeply, has to bear in mind that the average reader, who has never concerned himself with this subject, if he reads does so with the view, not of learning something from the writer, but rather, of pronouncing judgment on him when he is not in agreement with the commonplaces that the said reader carries in his head. If the individuals who make up the mass believed themselves specially qualified, it would be a case merely of personal error, not a sociological subversion. *The characteristic of the hour is that the commonplace mind, knowing itself to be commonplace, has the assurance to proclaim the rights of the commonplace and to impose them wherever it will.* As they say in the United States: "to be different is to be indecent." The mass crushes beneath it everything that is different, everything that is excellent, individual, qualified and select. Anybody who is not like everybody, who does not think like everybody, runs the risk of being eliminated. And it is clear, of course, that "everybody" is not "everybody." "Everybody" was normally the complex unity of the mass and the divergent, specialised minorities. Nowadays, "everybody" is the mass alone. Here we have the formidable fact of our times, described without any concealment of the brutality of its features.

8. *The Ruling Class**

GAETANO MOSCA

Among the constant facts and tendencies that are to be found in all political organisms, one is so obvious that it is apparent to the most casual eye.

*From Gaetano Mosca, *The Ruling Class* (1895; translated by H. D. Kahn, McGraw-Hill Book Company, 1939). By permission.

In all societies—from societies that are very meagerly developed and have barely attained the dawnings of civilization, down to the most advanced and powerful societies—two classes of people appear—a class that rules and a class that is ruled. The first class, always the less numerous, performs all political functions, monopolizes power and enjoys the advantages that power brings, whereas the second, the more numerous class, is directed and controlled by the first, in a manner that is now more or less legal, now more or less arbitrary and violent, and supplies the first, in appearance at least, with material means of subsistence and with the instrumentalities that are essential to the vitality of the political organism.

In practical life we all recognize the existence of this ruling class (or political class, as we have elsewhere chosen to define it).[1] We all know that, in our own country, whichever it may be, the management of public affairs is in the hands of a minority of influential persons, to which management, willingly or unwillingly, the majority defer. We know that the same thing goes on in neighboring countries, and in fact we should be put to it to conceive of a real world otherwise organized—a world in which all men would be directly subject to a single person without relationships of superiority or subordination, or in which all men would share equally in the direction of political affairs. If we reason otherwise in theory, that is due partly to inveterate habits that we follow in our thinking and partly to the exaggerated importance that we attach to two political facts that loom far larger in appearance than they are in reality.

The first of these facts—and one has only to open one's eyes to see it—is that in every political organism there is one individual who is chief among the leaders of the ruling class as a whole and stands, as we say, at the helm of the state. That person is not always the person who holds supreme power according to law. At times, alongside of the hereditary king or emperor there is a prime minister or a major-domo who wields an actual power that is greater than the sovereign's. At other times, in place of the elected president the influential politician who has procured the president's election will govern. Under special circumstances there may be, instead of a single person, two or three who discharge the functions of supreme control.

The second fact, too, is readily discernible. Whatever the type of political organization, pressures arising from the discontent of the masses who are governed, from the passions by which they are swayed, exert a certain amount of influence on the policies of the ruling, the political, class.

But the man who is at the head of the state would certainly not be able to govern without the support of a numerous class to enforce respect for his orders and to have them carried out; and granting that he can make one individual, or indeed many individuals, in the ruling class feel the weight of his power, he certainly cannot be at odds with the class as a whole or do

[1] Mosca, *Teorica dei governi e governo parlamentare,* Chap. I.

away with it. Even if that were possible, he would at once be forced to create another class, without the support of which action on his part would be completely paralyzed. On the other hand, granting that the discontent of the masses might succeed in deposing a ruling class, inevitably, as we shall later show, there would have to be another organized minority within the masses themselves to discharge the functions of a ruling class. Otherwise all organization, and the whole social structure, would be destroyed.

From the point of view of scientific research the real superiority of the concept of the ruling, or political, class lies in the fact that the varying structure of ruling classes has a preponderant importance in determining the political type, and also the level of civilization, of the different peoples. According to a manner of classifying forms of government that is still in vogue, Turkey and Russia were both, up to a few years ago, absolute monarchies, England and Italy were constitutional, or limited, monarchies, and France and the United States were classed as republics. The classification was based on the fact that, in the first two countries mentioned, headship in the state was hereditary and the chief was nominally omnipotent; in the second two, his office is hereditary but his powers and prerogatives are limited; in the last two, he is elected.

That classification is obviously superficial. Absolutisms though they were, there was little in common between the manners in which Russia and Turkey were managed politically, the levels of civilization in the two countries and the organization of their ruling classes being vastly different. On the same basis, the regime in Italy, a monarchy, is much more similar to the regime in France, a republic, than it is to the regime in England, also a monarchy; and there are important differences between the political organizations of the United States and France, though both countries are republics.

As we have already suggested, ingrained habits of thinking have long stood, as they still stand, in the way of scientific progress in this matter. The classification mentioned above, which divides governments into absolute monarchies, limited monarchies and republics, was devised by Montesquieu and was intended to replace the classical categories of Aristotle, who divided governments into monarchies, aristocracies and democracies. What Aristotle called a democracy was simply an aristocracy of fairly broad membership. Aristotle himself was in a position to observe that in every Greek state, whether aristocratic or democratic, there was always one person or more who had a preponderant influence. Between the day of Polybius and the day of Montesquieu, many writers perfected Aristotle's classification by introducing into it the concept of "mixed" governments. Later on the modern democratic theory, which had its source in Rousseau, took its stand upon the concept that the majority of the citizens in any state can participate, and in fact *ought* to participate, in its political life, and the doctrine of popular sovereignty still holds sway over many minds in spite of the fact that modern scholarship is making it increasingly clear that democratic, monarchical and aristocratic principles function side by side in every political organism. We shall not stop to refute this democratic theory here, since that is the task of this work as a whole. Besides, it would be hard to destroy in a few pages a whole system of ideas that has become firmly rooted in the human mind. As Las Casas aptly wrote in his life of Christopher Columbus, it is often much harder to unlearn than to learn.

We think it may be desirable, nevertheless, to reply at this point to an objection which might very readily be made to our point of view. If it is easy to understand that a single individual cannot command a group without finding within the group a minority to support him, it is rather difficult to grant, as a constant and natural fact, that minorities rule majorities, rather than majorities minorities. But that is one of the points—so numerous in all the other sciences—where the first impression one has of things is contrary to what they are in reality. In reality the dominion of an organized minority, obeying a single impulse, over the unorganized majority is inevitable. The power of any minority is irresistible as against each single individual in the majority, who stands alone before the totality of the organized minority. At the same time, the minority is organized for the very reason that it is a minority. A hundred men acting uniformly in concert, with a common understanding, will triumph over a thousand men who are not in accord and can therefore be dealt with one by one. Meanwhile it will be easier for the former to act in concert and have a mutual understanding simply because they are a hundred and not a thousand. It follows that the larger the political community, the smaller will the proportion of the governing minority to the governed majority be, and the more difficult will it be for the majority to organize for reaction against the minority.

However, in addition to the great advantage accruing to them from the fact of being organized, ruling minorities are usually so constituted that the individuals who make them up are distinguished from the mass of the governed by qualities that give them a certain material, intellectual or even moral superiority; or else they are the heirs of individuals who possessed such qualities. In other words, members of a ruling minority regularly have some attribute, real or apparent, which is highly esteemed and very influential in the society in which they live.

In some countries we find hereditary castes. In such cases the governing class is explicitly restricted to a given number of families, and birth is the one criterion that determines entry into the class or exclusion from it. Examples are exceedingly common. There is practically no country of long-standing civilization that has not had a hereditary aristocracy at one period or another in its history. We find hereditary nobilities during certain periods in China and ancient Egypt, in India, in Greece before the wars with the

Medes, in ancient Rome, among the Slavs, among the Latins and Germans of the Middle Ages, in Mexico at the time of the Discovery and in Japan down to a few years ago.

In this connection two preliminary observations are in point. In the first place, all ruling classes tend to become hereditary in fact if not in law. All political forces seem to possess a quality that in physics used to be called the force of inertia. They have a tendency, that is, to remain at the point and in the state in which they find themselves. Wealth and military valor are easily maintained in certain families by moral tradition and by heredity. Qualification for important office—the habit of, and to an extent the capacity for, dealing with affairs of consequence—is much more readily acquired when one has had a certain familiarity with them from childhood. Even when academic degrees, scientific training, special aptitudes as tested by examinations and competitions, open the way to public office, there is no eliminating that special advantage in favor of certain individuals which the French call the advantage of *positions déjà prises*. In actual fact, though examinations and competitions may theoretically be open to all, the majority never have the resources for meeting the expense of long preparation, and many others are without the connections and kinships that set an individual promptly on the right road, enabling him to avoid the gropings and blunders that are inevitable when one enters an unfamiliar environment without any guidance or support.

The democratic principle of election by broad-based suffrage would seem at first glance to be in conflict with the tendency toward stability which, according to our theory, ruling classes show. But it must be noted that candidates who are successful in democratic elections are almost always the ones who possess the political forces above enumerated, which are very often hereditary. In the English, French and Italian parliaments we frequently see the sons, grandsons, brothers, nephews and sons-in-law of members and deputies, ex-members and ex-deputies.

In the second place, when we see a hereditary caste established in a country and monopolizing political power, we may be sure that such a status de jure was preceded by a similar status de facto. Before proclaiming their exclusive and hereditary right to power the families or castes in question must have held the scepter of command in a firm grasp, completely monopolizing all the political forces of that country at that period. Otherwise such a claim on their part would only have aroused the bitterest protests and provoked the bitterest struggles.

Hereditary aristocracies often come to vaunt supernatural origins, or at least origins different from, and superior to, those of the governed classes. Such claims are explained by a highly significant social fact, namely that every governing class tends to justify its actual exercise of power by resting it on some universal moral principle. This same sort of claim has come forward in our time in scientific trappings. A number of writers, developing and amplifying Darwin's theories, contend that upper classes represent a higher level in social evolution and are therefore superior to lower classes by organic structure. Gumplowicz we have already quoted. That writer goes to the point of maintaining that the divisions of populations into trade groups and professional classes in modern civilized countries are based on ethnological heterogeneousness.[1]

Now history very definitely shows the special abilities as well as the special defects—both very marked—which have been displayed by aristocracies that have either remained absolutely closed or have made entry into their circles difficult. The ancient Roman patriciate and the English and German nobilities of modern times give a ready idea of the type we refer to. Yet in dealing with this fact, and with the theories that tend to exaggerate its significance, we can always raise the same objection—that the individuals who belong to the aristocracies in question owe their special qualities not so much to the blood that flows in their veins as to their very particular upbringing, which has brought out certain intellectual and moral tendencies in them in preference to others.

Among all the factors that figure in social superiority, intellectual superiority is the one with which heredity has least to do. The children of men of highest mentality often have very mediocre talents. That is why hereditary aristocracies have never defended their rule on the basis of intellectual superiority alone, but rather on the basis of their superiorities in character and wealth.

[1] *Der Rassenkampf.* This notion transpires from Gumplowicz's whole volume. It is explicitly formulated in Book II, Chap. XXXIII.

9. *Leader Praises Leadership Principle**

ADOLF HITLER

Is it the criterion of the statesman that he should possess the art of persuasion in as high degree as that of political intelligence in formulating great policies or decisions? Is the incapacity of a leader shown by the fact that he does not succeed in winning for a certain idea the majority of a mob thrown together by more or less savory accidents?

* From Adolf Hitler, *Mein Kampf* (1925–1927; translated by Ralph Manheim, Houghton Mifflin Company, 1943). By permission.

Indeed, has this mob ever understood an idea before success proclaimed its greatness?

Isn't every deed of genius in this world a visible protest of genius against the inertia of the mass?

And what should the statesman do, who does not succeed in gaining the favor of this mob for his plans by flattery?

Should he buy it?

Or, in view of the stupidity of his fellow citizens, should he renounce the execution of the tasks which he has recognized to be vital necessities? Should he resign or should he remain at his post?

In such a case, doesn't a man of true character find himself in a hopeless conflict between knowledge and decency, or rather honest conviction?

Where is the dividing line between his duty toward the general public and his duty toward his personal honor?

Mustn't every true leader refuse to be thus degraded to the level of a political gangster?

And, conversely, mustn't every gangster feel that he is cut out for politics, since it is never he, but some intangible mob, which has to bear the ultimate responsibility?

Mustn't our principle of parliamentary majorities lead to the demolition of any idea of leadership?

Does anyone believe that the progress of this world springs from the mind of majorities and not from the brains of individuals?

Or does anyone expect that the future will be able to dispense with this premise of human culture?

Does it not, on the contrary, today seem more indispensable than ever?

By rejecting the authority of the individual and replacing it by the numbers of some momentary mob, the parliamentary principle of majority rule sins against the basic aristocratic principle of Nature, though it must be said that this view is not necessarily embodied in the present-day decadence of our upper ten thousand.

It would be lunacy to try to estimate the value of man according to his race, thus declaring war on the Marxist idea that men are equal, unless we are determined to draw the ultimate consequences. And the ultimate consequence of recognizing the importance of blood—that is, of the racial foundation in general—is the transference of this estimation to the individual person. In general I must evaluate peoples differently on the basis of the race they belong to, and the same applies to the individual men within a national community. The realization that peoples are not equal transfers itself to the individual man within a national community, in the sense that men's minds cannot be equal, since here, too, the blood components, though equal in their broad outlines, are, in particular cases, subject to thousands of the finest differentiations.

The first consequence of this realization might at the same time be called the cruder one: an attempt to promote in the most exemplary way those elements within the national community that have been recognized as especially valuable from the racial viewpoint and to provide for their special increase.

This task is cruder because it can be recognized and solved almost mechanically. It is more difficult to recognize among the whole people the minds that are most valuable in the intellectual and ideal sense, and to gain for them that influence which not only is the due of these superior minds, but which above all is beneficial to the nation. This sifting according to capacity and ability can not be undertaken mechanically; it is a task which the struggle of daily life unceasingly performs.

A philosophy of life which endeavors to reject the democratic mass idea and give this earth to the best people—that is, the highest humanity—must logically obey the same aristocratic principle within this people and make sure that the leadership and the highest influence in this people fall to the best minds. Thus, it builds, not upon the idea of the majority, but upon the idea of personality.

The best state constitution and state form is that which, with the most unquestioned certainty, raises the best minds in the national community to leading position and leading influence.

But as, in economic life, the able men cannot be appointed from above, but must struggle through for themselves, and just as here the endless schooling, ranging from the smallest business to the largest enterprise, occurs spontaneously, with life alone giving the examinations, obviously political minds cannot be 'discovered.' Extraordinary geniuses permit of no consideration for normal mankind.

From the smallest community cell to the highest leadership of the entire Reich, the state must have the personality principle anchored in its organization.

There must be no majority decisions, but only responsible persons, and the word 'council' must be restored to its original meaning. Surely every man will have advisers by his side, but *the decisions will be made by one man.*

The principle which made the Prussian army in its time into the most wonderful instrument of the German people must some day, in a transferred sense, become the principle of the construction of our whole state conception: *authority of every leader downward and responsibility upward.*

Chapter VIII

FASCISM: GOVERNMENT BY FORCE AND LIES

FASCISM is the twentieth-century version of age-old tendencies in politics. Like democracy, it is a universal phenomenon, and, like democracy, it is firmly entrenched in the national tradition of some countries, and only an ephemeral phenomenon in others. Unlike the authoritarian absolutism of the seventeenth and eighteenth centuries, Fascism is a *post-democratic* phenomenon in politics, and it cannot be understood save as a reaction to democracy. The use of popular organizations and mass activities is one of the distinguishing features of Fascism, and it has learned from democracy the value of popular support for national policies. From socialism Fascism borrowed enough anticapitalist slogans and catchwords to attract a section of the working classes. Scientifically organized propaganda and terror was another characteristic of the fascist state. Depressing as Fascism must appear to adherents of the democratic ideal, it should be borne in mind that Fascism succeeded to power between the two world wars only in those countries in which democracy had never been firmly established, or in which it was virtually unknown. Conversely, where democracy had led a healthy life before 1914, Fascism was weak and ineffective in the nineteen twenties and thirties.

Treitschke's *Politics* (1897–1898) anticipates one of the main elements of Fascist statism by stressing the nature of the state as power. "It does not matter what you think so long as you obey"—this attitude of the state seems to Treitschke in accordance with its nature as power. Because power is all-decisive, only "the sentimentalist may bewail the overthrow of cultured Athens by Sparta or of Hellas by Rome." The admiration for power as the substance of the state leads Treitschke to the conclusion, not illogical from his initial assumption, that "the large State is the nobler type." Conversely, he saw something "ridiculous" in the nature of the small state. Fascism and Nazism took over from Treitschke this crude veneration of bigness, annihilating, if necessary, small states that stood in the way of expansion and conquest.

The spirit of German political nihilism is faithfully reflected in Carl Schmitt's article on "The Concept of 'The Political,'" published in 1927 in *Archiv für Sozialwissenschaft und Sozialpolitik*. This essay (never before translated into English) was later expanded by Schmitt into a book, and became one of the most widely read and quoted political works in Germany in the Nazi era. Schmitt was undoubtedly one of the two or three ablest German political scientists of the twentieth century. His brilliance was surpassed only by his lack of character: in 1919 Schmitt was a near Communist; later, he ran through the gamut of all major German political parties. From communism he "evolved" into a Social Democrat, Democrat, Catholic Centrist, German Nationalist, and, finally, a full-fledged Nazi. Schmitt's definition of the *friend-enemy* contrast as the peculiar and specific criterion of the realm of politics gave the German militarists and Nazis the philosophical clothing with which to cover up the vacuity of ethical nihilism. Schmitt even denies that the liberal theory of the state, which seeks to "tame" government through ethical rules and such techniques as checks and balances and separation of powers, is a political theory at all. Politics begins and ends with the possibility of an enemy—and his total annihilation. This conception of politics is extended by Schmitt from the domestic to the international scene in which states face each other all the time as implacable enemies, to be eventually destroyed.

Hitler's eulogy of the Big Lie in *Mein Kampf* is one of the most famous passages in his book. His use of the Big Lie, though advertised in advance, was amazingly effective in Germany as well as abroad. Committing, later, crimes of previously unknown magnitude, the Germans reckoned that the rest of the world would refuse to believe them because of their very magnitude, whereas it might have believed crimes on a smaller scale, which were within the range of known experience. Hitler's doctrine of the Big Lie finally boomeranged, but not before it had been instrumental in bringing about the most devastating war in history. The psychological acuteness of this theory must be distinguished from its immorality; it is a technique that demagogues will try again.

Compared with the utter nihilism of Hitler, Mussolini's political faith, as expressed in 1932 in *The Political and Social Doctrine of Fascism,* seems to remain within the orbit of Western traditions. Mussolini's ideas may have been wrong, but they were firmly based on political philosophies of a long European heritage. Compared with Abraham Lincoln or John Stuart Mill, Mussolini must appear like the devil incarnate. Compared with Hitler, Mussolini emerged as Archangel Benito. One of the main differences between the two men was this: Hitler believed in his own lies, whereas Mussolini did not.

The picture of democracy that Mussolini draws, is distorted and one-sided, as viewed from countries in which democracy has led a strong and healthy existence. As seen from countries which have known only a caricature or sham of democracy, his picture is not greatly overdrawn. Essentially, Mussolini denied that democracy was either possible or desirable—and on both scores he sought to adduce historical evidence from the general decline of the liberal-democratic ideology in the late nineteenth and early twentieth centuries. By contrast, Mussolini emphasizes the authority of the state, which he also expressed in his famous formula "Nothing outside of the state, nothing against the state, nothing above the state." More important than Mussolini's plea for a strong state is his frank rejection of the ideal of peace among nations. He holds peace impossible as well as *undesirable,* because war alone "brings up to its highest tension all human energy and puts the stamp of nobility upon the peoples who have the courage to meet it."

Probably the best ideological exposition of Italian Fascism is to be found in Alfredo Rocco's *The Political Doctrine of Fascism* (1925). Rocco's emphasis is, first, on the "organic" nature of state and society. From it Rocco deduces a relationship of group and individual which is diametrically opposed to democratic liberalism: "For Liberalism, the individual is the end and society the means; nor is it conceivable that the individual, considered in the dignity of an ultimate finality, be lowered to mere instrumentality. For Fascism, society is the end, individuals the means, and its whole life consists in using individuals as instruments for its social ends." Following Hegelian doctrines, Rocco admits rights for the state, but not the individual, whose citizenship consists essentially of duties. "In this preeminence of duty," Rocco writes, "we find the highest ethical value of Fascism." Also following Hegel, Rocco denies that the individual has any political reality *qua* citizen, and limits his citizenship to his quality as a member of a corporate group or society. This doctrine served as the theoretical basis of the corporate organization of Fascist Italy, as well as of Nazi Germany, Franco Spain, and of Portugal under Salazar. As to the problem of popular self-government, Rocco follows the old conservative doctrine that the masses are incapable of carrying on intelligently the functions of government: "Fascism therefore not only rejects the dogma of popular sovereignty and substitutes for it that of state sovereignty, but it also proclaims that the great mass of citizens is not a suitable advocate of social interests for the reason that the capacity to ignore individual private interests in favor of the higher demands of society and of history is a very rare gift and the privilege of the chosen few. Natural intelligence and cultural preparation are of great service in such tasks." Rocco does not indicate by what procedure "the chosen few" are able to impose their conception of the national interest on their fellow citizens; but the history of Italian Fascism, with its prison camps and islands of political deportation, subsequently supplied the answer.

Is Fascism a disease of particular nations, or is it a world-wide affliction? In particular, does it exist in the United States? Early in 1944, Henry A. Wallace, then Vice-President of the United States, was asked by *The New York Times* to write an article on "American Fascism" which should answer three questions: what a Fascist is; how many Fascists there are in the United States; and, finally, how dangerous American Fascists are. The least harmful Fascists in the United States are those who, like the Bundists, heil-Hitlered in public, thus obviously identifying themselves with a foreign country. The more intelligent Fascists skillfully adapt themselves to the American soil and climate, and talk the language of Americanism, if not super-Americanism. Wallace defines a Fascist as one "whose lust for money or power is combined with such an intensity of intolerance toward those of other races, parties, classes, religions, cultures, regions or nations as to make him ruthless in his use of deceit or violence to attain his ends." He thinks that there are probably several hundred thousand in the United States who meet this description. If an American Fascist be somewhat more broadly defined "as one who in case of conflict puts money and power ahead of human beings, then there are undoubtedly several million Fascists in the United States." Wallace puts particular emphasis on the part that big business has played in the fostering of fascist movements abroad as well as in the United States. Therefore he urges an expanding social, economic, and cultural democracy as the preventive cure for any fascist menace to the Americas. Writing early in 1944, when Anglo-American cooperation with Russia seemed imperturbable, Wallace warned that "Fascism in the post-war world will push steadily for Anglo-Saxon imperialism and eventually for war with Russia."

1. The State as Power *

HEINRICH VON TREITSCHKE

It is, above all, Power which makes its will to prevail; it is not the totality of the people as Hegel assumes in his deification of it. The nation is not entirely comprised in the State, but the State protects and embraces the people's life, regulating its external aspects on every side. It does not ask primarily for opinion, but demands obedience, and its laws must be obeyed, whether willingly or no.

A step forward has been taken when the mute obedience of the citizens is transformed into a rational inward assent, but it cannot be said that this is absolutely necessary. Powerful, highly-developed Empires have stood for centuries without its aid. Submission is what the State primarily requires; it insists upon acquiescence; its very essence is the accomplishment of its will. A State which can no longer carry out its purpose collapses in anarchy.

* From Heinrich von Treitschke, *Politics* (1897–1898; translated by B. Dugdale and T. de Bille, 1916). By permission of The Macmillan Company, publishers.

What a contrast to the life of the Church. We may say that power is the vital principle of the State, as faith is that of the Church, and love that of the family. The Church is an essentially spiritual force, having also an external life, but appealing first of all to conscience, insisting above all upon the willing mind, and standing high in proportion to its ability to give profound and intense expression to this its vital principle. Therefore it is said, "He that eateth and drinketh unworthily eateth and drinketh judgment to himself." But if the State were to hold this view, or, for instance, to require from its soldiers more than the fulfilment of their military duties, it would be unbearable. "It does not matter," says the State, "what you think, so long as you obey." It is for this reason that gentle characters find it so hard to understand its nature. It may be said roughly that the normal woman first obtains an insight into justice and government through men's eyes, just as the normal man has no natural aptitude for petty questions of household management. This is easily understood, for undoubtedly power is a stern idea, and its enforcement is here the highest and only aim. For this reason the ruling nations are not so much the races rich in mental endowment, but rather those whose peculiar gift is force of character. In this the thoughtful student of the world's history perceives the awful nature of justice. The sentimentalist may bewail the overthrow of cultured Athens by Sparta, or of Hellas by Rome, but the serious thinker must recognize its necessity, and understand why Florence for all her refinement could not withstand the rivalry of Venice. All these cases took their inevitable course.

The State is not an Academy of Arts. If it neglects its strength in order to promote the idealistic aspirations of man, it repudiates its own nature and perishes.   HEINRICH VON TREIT

On close examination then, it becomes clear that if the State is power, only that State which has power realizes its own idea, and this accounts for the undeniably ridiculous element which we discern in the existence of a small State. Weakness is not itself ridiculous, except when masquerading as strength. In small States that puling spirit is hatched, which judges the State by the taxes it levies, and does not perceive that if the State may not enclose and repress like an egg-shell, neither can it protect. Such thinkers fail to understand that the moral benefits for which we are indebted to the State are above all price. It is by generating this form of materialism that small States have so deleterious an effect upon their citizens.

Moreover, they are totally lacking in that capacity for justice which characterizes their greater neighbours. Any person who has plenty of relations and is not a perfect fool is soon provided for in a small country, while in a large one, although justice tends to become stereotyped, it is not possible to be so much influenced by personal and local circumstances as in the narrower sphere.

Everything considered, therefore, we reach the conclusion that the large State is the nobler type. This is more especially true of its fundamental functions such as wielding the sword in defence of the hearth and of justice. Both are better protected by a large State than a small one. The latter cannot wage war with any prospect of success.

The economic superiority of big countries is patent. A splendid security springs from the mere largeness of their scale. They can overcome economic crises far more easily. Famine, for instance, can hardly attack every part of them at once, and only in them can that truly national pride arise which is a sign of the moral stamina of a people. Their citizens' outlook upon the world will be freer and greater. The command of the sea more especially promotes it. The poet's saying is true indeed that "wide horizons liberate the mind." The time may come when no State will be counted great unless it can boast of territories beyond the seas.

Examining closely, we find that culture in general, and in the widest sense of the word, matures more happily in the broader conditions of powerful countries than within the narrow limits of a little State. When Holland was the predominant naval Power, Sir William Temple, in his book upon the United Provinces, asserted that in a small State there must be some hidden quality favourable to maritime commerce. A no less meaningless generalization is apparent in the favourite German theory that the peculiarities of our culture arise from our system of petty States. It must be obvious that the material resources favourable to Art and Science are more abundant in a large State; and if we inquire of history whether at any time the fairest fruit of human culture has ripened in a genuine petty State, the answer must be that in the normal course of a people's development the zenith of its political power coincides with that of its literary excellence.

~~~~~~

2. Politics: The Struggle with the Enemy *

CARL SCHMITT

~~~~~~

The definition of the concept of the "political" can be arrived at only through the discovery of the specifically political categories. Politics stands

* From Carl Schmitt, "The Concept of 'The Political'," *Archiv für Sozialwissenschaft und Sozialpolitik*, Vol. 58 (September, 1927). Translated by William Ebenstein.

as an independent sphere of its own, apart from other, relatively independent, spheres of human thought and action, such as morals, esthetics, economics, the complete enumeration of which is not required here. Politics must, therefore, possess its own, ultimately independent, distinguishing characteristics, to which all specifically political action can be traced back. Let us assume that, in the province of morals, these distinctions are Good and Evil; in esthetics, Beautiful and Ugly; in economics, Useful and Harmful, or Profitable and Unprofitable. The question then remains whether a specific and self-evident distinguishing characteristic exists in the realm of politics, and what it is.

The specifically political distinction to which political acts and motivations may be traced back, is the distinction of *friend* and *enemy*. It corresponds, in politics, to the relatively independent distinctions in other fields: Good and Evil in morals; Beautiful and Ugly in esthetics, etc. This distinction is independent, i.e., it cannot be deduced from any of these other distinctions, singly or combined. Just as the contrast between Good and Evil is not identical with, nor reducible to, that of Beautiful and Ugly, or of Useful and Harmful, it must not be confused or mixed up with any of these other contrasts. The distinction between friend and enemy can subsist, in theory and practice, without applying, at the same time, moral, esthetic, economic, or other distinctions. The political enemy need not be morally evil nor esthetically ugly; he need not appear as an economic competitor, and it may, in fact, be advantageous to do business with him. He is the other, the stranger, and his nature is sufficiently defined if he is, in an intense way, existentially different and strange; in case of conflict, he constitutes the negation of one's own kind of existence, and must therefore be repulsed or fought, in order to preserve one's own way of life. In psychological reality, the enemy is easily treated as evil and ugly, because politics, like any autonomous area of human life, gladly calls on the help which it can receive from the distinctions of other spheres. This does not change the independence of such specific distinctions. As a consequence, the opposite is valid, too: what is morally bad, esthetically ugly, or economically harmful, need not be the enemy; what is morally good, esthetically beautiful, and economically useful, does not become, necessarily, the friend in the specifically political meaning of the word. The basic autonomy and independence of politics is evident in the possibility of distinguishing such a specific contrast of friend and enemy from other contrasts, and to conceive of it as an independent category.

The concepts of friend and enemy are to be understood in their concrete meaning of existence, not as symbols or metaphors, nor fused with, or weakened by, economic, moral and other ideas, nor as the expression of private feelings and tendencies. They are not normative or "spiritual" contrasts. Liberalism has transformed the enemy, from the economic side, into a competitor, and from the ethical side, into a debating adversary. In the sphere of economics, it is true, there are no enemies, but only competitors, and in a world suffused with morals and ethics, there are only debating contestants. However, the enemy is something entirely different. It makes no difference whether one considers it a reprehensible and atavistic residue of barbarian ages or not, that men still separate each other as friends and enemies, or whether one entertains the hope that this distinction will disappear, one day, from the earth, or whether it is good and advisable to construe the fiction, for educational reasons, that there are no more enemies. What is at stake, are not fictions and prescriptions of what ought to be, but real existence and the real possibility of this distinction of friend and enemy. One may share those hopes and pedagogical efforts. But one cannot rationally deny that nations have been able to line up, till now, according to the distinction of friend and enemy, and that it continues as a real possibility for every politically existent nation.

The enemy is, thus, not the competitor or opponent in general. Nor is he the private opponent whom one hates. "Enemy" is only a collectivity of men who eventually, i.e., as a real possibility, will *fight* against a similar collectivity of people. Enemy is only the public enemy, because everything that relates to such a collectivity, especially a whole nation, becomes *public*.

The genuine concept of the enemy thus implies the eventual reality of a struggle. One should abstract, from this term, all accidental changes inherent in the historical evolution of the techniques of war and armaments. War is armed struggle between nations. The essential characteristic of "the weapon" is the fact that it is a means of physical killing of human beings. The word "struggle," like the term "enemy," is to be taken here in its original meaning. It does not mean competition, nor the "intellectual" struggle of discussion, nor the symbolic struggle, which, after all, every person fights, and be it only with his inertia. The terms "friend," "enemy," and "struggle" obtain their real significance from their relation to the real possibility of physical killing. War follows from enmity, because the latter is existential negation of another being. War is only the most extreme negation of enmity. As long as the concept of the enemy retains its meaning, war need not be an everyday, normal occurrence, nor need it be felt as an ideal, but must subsist as a real possibility.

The conceptual characteristics of politics imply the pluralism of states. Political unity presupposes the real possibility of an enemy and, thus, of another, co-existing political unity. Therefore, as long as there is a state, there will always be several states on earth, rather than one world "state" comprehending the whole world and all of humanity. The political world is a pluriverse, not a universe. To this extent, every theory of the state is pluralistic, though in a different sense from the pluralism of Laski. The very nature of political organization makes its universality impossible. If the various nations and human groupings of the earth were all so united as to make a struggle among them actually impossible, if the distinction between friend and enemy ceases to operate even as a mere eventuality, then all that is left is economics, morals, law, art, etc., but not politics or a state.

3. The Bigger the Lie, the Better *

ADOLF HITLER

Like the woman, whose psychic state is determined less by grounds of abstract reason than by an indefinable emotional longing for a force which will complement her nature, and who, consequently, would rather bow to a strong man than dominate a weakling, likewise the masses love a commander more than a petitioner and feel inwardly more satisfied by a doctrine, tolerating no other beside itself, than by the granting of liberalistic freedom with which, as a rule, they can do little, and are prone to feel that they have been abandoned. They are equally unaware of their shameless spiritual terrorization and the hideous abuse of their human freedom, for they absolutely fail to suspect the inner insanity of the whole doctrine. All they see is the ruthless force and brutality of its calculated manifestations, to which they always submit in the end.

All propaganda must be popular and its intellectual level must be adjusted to the most limited intelligence among those it is addressed to. Consequently, the greater the mass it is intended to reach, the lower its purely intellectual level will have to be. But if, as in propaganda for sticking out a war, the aim is to influence a whole people, we must avoid excessive intellectual demands on our public, and too much caution cannot be exerted in this direction.

The more modest its intellectual ballast, the more exclusively it takes into consideration the emotions of the masses, the more effective it will be. And this is the best proof of the soundness or unsoundness of a propaganda campaign, and not success in pleasing a few scholars or young aesthetes.

The art of propaganda lies in understanding the emotional ideas of the great masses and finding, through a psychologically correct form, the way

* From Adolf Hitler, *Mein Kampf* (1925–1927; translated by Ralph Manheim, Houghton Mifflin Company, 1943). By permission.

to the attention and thence to the heart of the broad masses. The fact that our bright boys do not understand this merely shows how mentally lazy and conceited they are.

Once we understand how necessary it is for propaganda to be adjusted to the broad mass, the following rule results:

It is a mistake to make propaganda many-sided, like scientific instruction, for instance.

The receptivity of the great masses is very limited, their intelligence is small, but their power of forgetting is enormous. In consequence of these facts, all effective propaganda must be limited to a very few points and must harp on these in slogans until the last member of the public understands what you want him to understand by your slogan. As soon as you sacrifice this slogan and try to be many-sided, the effect will piddle away, for the crowd can neither digest nor retain the material offered. In this way the result is weakened and in the end entirely cancelled out.

The magnitude of a lie always contains a certain factor of credibility, since the great masses of the people in the very bottom of their hearts tend to be corrupted rather than consciously and purposely evil, and that, therefore, in view of the primitive simplicity of their minds, they more easily fall a victim to a big lie than to a little one, since they themselves lie in little things, but would be ashamed of lies that were too big. Such a falsehood will never enter their heads, and they will not be able to believe in the possibility of such monstrous effrontery and infamous misrepresentation in others; yes, even when enlightened on the subject, they will long doubt and waver, and continue to accept at least one of these causes as true. Therefore, something of even the most insolent lie will always remain and stick—a fact which all the great lie-virtuosi and lying-clubs in this world know only too well and also make the most treacherous use of.

4. Fascism, War, Dictatorship*

BENITO MUSSOLINI

Fascism combats the whole complex system of democratic ideology, and repudiates it, whether in its theoretical premises or in its practical applica-

* From Benito Mussolini, *The Political and Social Doctrine of Fascism* (1932; English translation, The Hogarth Press, 1933). By permission.

tion. Fascism denies that the majority, by the simple fact that it is a majority, can direct human society; it denies that numbers alone can govern by means of a periodical consultation, and it affirms the immutable, beneficial, and fruitful inequality of mankind, which can never be permanently leveled through the mere operation of a mechanical process such as universal suffrage. The democratic régime may be defined as from time to time giving the people the illusion of sovereignty, while the real effective sovereignty lies in the hands of other concealed and irresponsible forces. Democracy is a régime nominally without a king, but it is ruled by many kings—more absolute, tyrannical, and ruinous than one sole king, even though a tyrant. This explains why Fascism, having first in 1922 (for reasons of expediency) assumed an attitude tending towards republicanism, renounced this point of view before the march to Rome, being convinced that the question of political form is not today of prime importance, and after having studied the examples of monarchies and republics past and present reached the conclusion that monarchy or republicanism are not to be judged, as it were, by an absolute standard; but that they represent forms in which the evolution—political, historical, traditional, or psychological—of a particular country has expressed itself. Fascism supersedes the antithesis monarchy or republicanism, while democracy still tarries beneath the domination of this idea, forever pointing out the insufficiency of the first and forever the praising of the second as the perfect régime. Today, it can be seen that there are republics innately reactionary and absolutist, and also monarchies which incorporate the most ardent social and political hopes of the future.

"Reason and science," says Renan (one of the inspired pre-Fascists) in his philosophical meditations, "are products of humanity, but to expect reason as a direct product of the people and a direct result of their action is to deceive oneself by a chimera. It is not necessary for the existence of reason that everybody should understand it. And in any case, if such a decimation of truth were necessary, it could not be achieved in a low-class democracy, which seems as though it must of its very nature extinguish any kind of noble training. The principle that society exists solely through the well-being and the personal liberty of all the individuals of which it is composed does not appear to be conformable to the plans of nature, in whose workings the race alone seems to be taken into consideration, and the individual sacrificed to it. It is greatly to be feared that the last stage of such a conception of democracy (though I must hasten to point out that the term 'democracy' may be interpreted in various ways) would end in a condition of society in which a degenerate herd would have no other preoccupation but the satisfaction of the lowest desires of common men." Thus Renan. Fascism denies, in democracy, the absurd conventional untruth of political equality dressed out in the garb of collective irresponsibility, and the myth of "happiness" and indefinite progress. But, if democracy may be conceived in diverse forms

—that is to say, taking democracy to mean a state of society in which the populace are not reduced to impotence in the State—Fascism may write itself down as "an organized, centralized, and authoritative democracy."

Fascism has taken up an attitude of complete opposition to the doctrines of Liberalism, both in the political field and the field of economics. There should be no undue exaggeration (simply with the object of immediate success in controversy) of the importance of Liberalism in the last century, nor should what was but one among many theories which appeared in that period be put forward as a religion for humanity for all time, present and to come. Liberalism only flourished for half a century. It was born in 1830 in reaction against the Holy Alliance, which had been formed with the object of diverting the destinies of Europe back to the period before 1789, and the highest point of its success was the year 1848, when even Pius IX was a Liberal. Immediately after that date it began to decay, for if the year 1848 was a year of light and hope, the following year, 1849, was a year of darkness and tragedy. The Republic of Rome was dealt a mortal blow by a sister republic—that of France—and in the same year Marx launched the gospel of the Socialist religion, the famous Communist Manifesto. In 1851 Napoleon III carried out his far from Liberal *coup d'état* and reigned in France until 1870, when he was deposed by a popular movement as the consequence of a military defeat which must be counted as one of the most decisive in history. The victor was Bismarck, who knew nothing of the religion of liberty, or the prophets by which that faith was revealed. And it is symptomatic that such a highly civilized people as the Germans were completely ignorant of the religion of liberty during the whole of the nineteenth century. It was nothing but a parenthesis, represented by that body which has been called "The ridiculous Parliament of Frankfort," which lasted only for a short period. Germany attained her national unity quite outside the doctrines of Liberalism—a doctrine which seems entirely foreign to the German mind, a mind essentially monarchic—while Liberalism is the logical and, indeed, historical forerunner of anarchy. The stages in the achievement of German unity are the three wars of '64, '66, and '70, which were guided by such "Liberals" as Von Moltke and Bismarck. As for Italian unity, its debt to Liberalism is completely inferior in contrast to that which it owes to the work of Mazzini and Garibaldi, who were not Liberals. Had it not been for the intervention of the anti-Liberal Napoleon, we should not have gained Lombardy; and without the help of the again anti-Liberal Bismarck at Sadowa and Sedan it is very probable that we should never have gained the province of Venice in '66, or been able to enter Rome in '70. From 1870 to 1914 a period began during which even the very high priests of the religion themselves had to recognize the gathering twilight of their faith—defeated as it was by the decadence of literature and atavism in practice—that is to say, Nationalism, Futurism, Fascism. The era of Liberalism, after having accumulated an infinity of Gordian knots, tried to untie them in the slaughter of the World War—and never has any religion demanded of votaries such a monstrous sacrifice. Perhaps the Liberal Gods were athirst for blood? But now, today, the Liberal faith must shut the doors of its deserted temples, deserted because the peoples of the world realize that its worship—agnostic in the field of economics and indifferent in the field of politics and morals—will lead, as it has already led, to certain ruin. In addition to this, let it be pointed out that all the political hopes of the present day are anti-Liberal, and it is therefore supremely ridiculous to try to classify this sole creed as outside the judgment of history, as though history were a hunting ground reserved for the professors of Liberalism—as though Liberalism were the final unalterable verdict of civilization.

The foundation of Fascism is the conception of the State, its character, its duty, and its aim. Fascism conceives of the State as an absolute, in comparison with which all individuals or groups are relative, only to be conceived of in their relation to the State. The conception of the Liberal State is not that of a directing force, guiding the play and development, both material and spiritual, of a collective body, but merely a force limited to the function of recording results; on the other hand, the Fascist State is itself conscious, and has itself a will and a personality—thus it may be called the "ethic" State. In 1929, at the first five-yearly assembly of the Fascist régime, I said:

"For us Fascists, the State is not merely a guardian, preoccupied solely with the duty of assuring the personal safety of the citizens; nor is it an organization with purely material aims, such as to guarantee a certain level of well-being and peaceful conditions of life; for a mere council of administration would be sufficient to realize such objects. Nor is it a purely political creation, divorced from all contact with the complex material reality which makes up the life of the individual and the life of the people as a whole. The State, as conceived of and as created by Fascism, is a spiritual and moral fact in itself, since its political, juridical, and economic organization of the nation is a concrete thing: and such an organization must be in its origins and development a manifestation of the spirit. The State is the guarantor of security both internal and external, but it is also the custodian and transmitter of the spirit of the people, as it has grown up through the centuries in language, in custom, and in faith. And the State is not only a living reality of the present, it is also linked with the past and above all with the future, and thus transcending the brief limits of individual life, it represents the immanent spirit of the nation. The forms in which States express themselves may change, but the necessity for such forms is eternal. It is the State which educates its citizens in civic virtue, gives them a consciousness of their mission and welds them into unity; harmonizing their various interests through justice, and transmitting to future generations the mental conquests of science, or art, of law and the solidarity of humanity. It leads men from primitive tribal life to that highest expression of human power which is Empire: it links up through the centuries the names of those of its members who have died for its existence and to obedience to its laws, it holds up the memory of the leaders who have increased its territory and the geniuses who have illumined it with glory as an example to be followed by future generations. When the conception of the State declines, and disunifying and contrifugal tendencies prevail, whether of individuals or of particular groups, the nations where such phenomena appear are in their decline."

From 1929 until today, evolution, both political and economic, has everywhere gone to prove the validity of these doctrinal promises. Of such gigantic importance is the State. Is it the force which alone can provide a solution to the dramatic contradictions of capitalism, and that state of affairs which we call the shade of Jules Simon, who in the dawn of Liberalism proclaimed that, "The State must labor to make itself unnecessary, and prepare the way for its own dismissal?" Or of McCulloch, who, in the second half of the last century, affirmed that the State must guard against the danger of governing too much? What would the Englishman, Bentham, say today to the continual and inevitably invoked intervention of the State in the sphere of economics, while according to his theories industry should ask no more of the State than to be left in peace? Or the German, Humboldt, according to whom the "lazy" State should be considered the best? It is true that the second wave of Liberal economists were less extreme than the first, and Adam Smith himself opened the door—if only very cautiously—which leads to State intervention in the economic field: but whoever says Liberalism implies individualism, and whoever says Fascism implies the State. Yet the Fascist State is unique, and an original creation. It is not reactionary, but revolutionary, in that it anticipates the solution of the universal political problems which elsewhere have to be settled in the political field by the rivalry of parties, the excessive power of the parliamentary régime and the irresponsibility of political assemblies; while it meets the problems of the economic field by a system of syndicalism which is continually increasing in importance, as much in the sphere of labor as of industry: and in the moral field enforces order, discipline, and obedience to that which is the determined moral code of the country. Fascism desires the State to be a strong and organic body, at the same time reposing upon broad and popular support. The Fascist State has drawn into itself even the economic activities of the nation, and, through the corporative social and educational institutions created by it, its influence reaches every aspect of the national life and includes, framed in their respective organizations, all the political, economic and spiritual forces of the nation. A State which reposes upon the support of millions of individuals who recognize its authority, are continually conscious of its power and are ready at once to serve it, is not the old tyrannical

State of the medieval lord nor has it anything in common with the absolute governments either before or after 1789. The individual in the Fascist State is not annulled but rather multiplied, just in the same way that a soldier in a regiment is not diminished but rather increased by the number of his comrades. The Fascist State organizes the nation, but leaves a sufficient margin of liberty to the individual; the latter is deprived of all useless and possibly harmful freedom, but retains what is essential; the deciding power in this question cannot be the individual, but the State alone.

Above all, Fascism, in so far as it considers the future and the development of humanity quite apart from political considerations of the moment, believes neither in the possibility nor the utility of perpetual peace. It thus repudiates the doctrine of Pacifism—born of a renunciation of the struggle and an act of cowardice in the face of sacrifice. War alone brings up to its highest tension all human energy and puts the stamp of nobility upon the peoples who have the courage to meet it. All other trials are substitutes, which never really put men into the position where they have to make the great decision—the alternative of life or death. Thus a doctrine which is founded upon this harmful postulate of peace is hostile to Fascism. And thus hostile to the spirit of Fascism, though accepted for what use they can be in dealing with particular political situations, are all the international leagues and societies which, as history will show, can be scattered to the winds when once strong national feeling is aroused by any motive—sentimental, ideal, or practical. This anti-pacifist spirit is carried by Fascism even into the life of the individual; the proud motto of the *Squadrista,* "Me ne Frego," written on the bandage of the wound, is an act of philosophy not only stoic, the summary of a doctrine not only political—it is the education to combat, the acceptance of the risks which combat implies, and a new way of life for Italy. Thus the Fascist accepts life and loves it, knowing nothing of and despising suicide: he rather conceives of life as duty and struggle and conquest, life which should be high and full, lived for oneself, but above all for others—those who are at hand and those who are far distant, contemporaries, and those who will come after.

The "demographic" policy of the régime is the result of the above premises. The Fascist, too, loves in actual fact his neighbor, but this "neighbor" is not merely a vague and undefined concept, this love for one's neighbor puts no obstacle in the way of necessary educational severity, and still less to differentiation of status and to physical distance. Fascism repudiates any universal embrace, and in order to live worthily in the community of civilized peoples watches its contemporaries with vigilant eyes, takes good note of their state of mind and, in the changing trend of their interests, does not allow itself to be deceived by temporary and fallacious appearances.

The Fascist State is an embodied will to power and government: the Roman tradition is here an ideal of force in action. According to Fascism, government is not so much a thing to be expressed in territorial or military terms as in terms of morality and the spirit. It must be thought of as an empire—that is to say, a nation which directly or indirectly rules other nations, without the need for conquering a single square yard of territory. For Fascism, the growth of empire, that is to say the expansion of the nation, is an essential manifestation of vitality, and its opposite a sign of decadence. Peoples which are rising, or rising again after a period of decadence, are always imperialist; any renunciation is a sign of decay and of death. Fascism is the doctrine best adapted to represent the tendencies and the aspirations of a people, like the people of Italy, who are rising again after many centuries of abasement and foreign servitude. But empire demands discipline, the coordination of all forces and a deeply felt sense of duty and sacrifice: this fact explains many aspects of the practical working of the régime, the character of many forces in the State, and the necessarily severe measures which must be taken against those who would oppose this spontaneous and inevitable movement of Italy in the twentieth century, and would oppose it by recalling the outworn ideology of the nineteenth century—repudiated wheresoever there has been the courage to undertake great experiments of social and political transformation; for never before has the nation stood more in need of authority, of direction, and of order. If every age has its own characteristic doctrine, there are a thousand signs which point to Fascism as the characteristic doctrine of our time. For if a doctrine must be a living thing, this is proved by the fact that Fascism has created a living faith; and that this faith is very powerful in the minds of men, is demonstrated by those who have suffered and died for it.

Fascism has henceforth in the world the universality of all those doctrines which, in realizing themselves, have represented a stage in the history of the human spirit.

~~~~~~

5. *The Political Doctrine of Fascism* *

ALFREDO ROCCO

~~~~~~

The true antithesis, not to this or that manifestation of the liberal-democratic-socialistic conception of the state but to the concept itself, is to be

* From Alfredo Rocco, "The Political Doctrine of Fascism," *International Conciliation* (October, 1926). By permission of the Carnegie Endowment for International Peace.

found in the doctrine of Fascism. For while the disagreement between Liberalism and Democracy, and between Liberalism and Socialism lies in a difference of method, as we have said, the rift between Socialism, Democracy, and Liberalism on one side and Fascism on the other is caused by a difference in concept. As a matter of fact, Fascism never raises the question of methods, using in its political praxis now liberal ways, now democratic means and at times even socialistic devices. This indifference to method often exposes Fascism to the charge of incoherence on the part of superficial observers, who do not see that what counts with us is the end and that therefore even when we employ the same means we act with a radically different spiritual attitude and strive for entirely different results. The Fascist concept then of the nation, of the scope of the state, and of the relations obtaining between society and its individual components, rejects entirely the doctrine which I said proceeded from the theories of natural law developed in the course of the XVI, XVII, and XVIII centuries and which form the basis of the liberal, democratic, and socialistic ideology.

I shall not try here to expound this doctrine but shall limit myself to a brief résumé of its fundamental concepts.

Man—the political animal—according to the definition of Aristotle, lives and must live in society. A human being outside the pale of society is an inconceivable thing—a non-man. Humankind in its entirety lives in social groups that are still, today, very numerous and diverse, varying in importance and organization from the tribes of Central Africa to the great Western Empires. These various societies are fractions of the human species each one of them endowed with a unified organization. And as there is no unique organization of the human species, there is not "one" but there are "several" human societies. Humanity therefore exists solely as a biological concept, not as a social one.

Each society on the other hand exists in the unity of both its biological and its social contents. Socially considered it is a fraction of the human species endowed with unity of organization for the attainment of the peculiar ends of the species.

This definition brings out all the elements of the social phenomenon and not merely those relating to the preservation and perpetuation of the species. For man is not solely matter; and the ends of the human species, far from being the materialistic ones we have in common with other animals, are, rather, and predominantly, the spiritual finalities which are peculiar to man and which every form of society strives to attain as well as its stage of social development allows. Thus the organization of every social group is more or less pervaded by the spiritual influxes of: unity of language, of culture, of religion, of tradition, of customs, and in general of feeling and of volition, which are as essential as the material elements: unity of economic interests, of living conditions, and of territory. The definition given above demonstrates another truth, which has been ignored by the political doctrines that for the last four centuries have been the foundations of political systems, viz., that the social concept has a biological aspect, because social groups are fractions of the human species, each one possessing a peculiar organization, a particular rank in the development of civilization with certain needs and appropriate ends, in short, a life which is really its own. If social groups are then fractions of the human species, they must possess the same fundamental traits of the human species, which means that they must be considered as a succession of generations and not as a collection of individuals.

It is evident therefore that as the human species is not the total of the living human beings of the world, so the various social groups which compose it are not the sum of the several individuals which at a given moment belong to it, but rather the infinite series of the past, present, and future generations constituting it. And as the ends of the human species are not those of the several individuals living at a certain moment, being occasionally in direct opposition to them, so the ends of the various social groups are not necessarily those of the individuals that belong to the groups but may even possibly be in conflict with such ends, as one sees clearly whenever the preservation and the development of the species demands the sacrifice of the individual, to wit, in times of war.

Fascism replaces therefore the old atomistic and mechanical state theory which was at the basis of the liberal and democratic doctrines with an organic and historic concept. When I say organic I do not wish to convey the impression that I consider society as an organism after the manner of the so-called "organic theories of the state"; but rather to indicate that the social groups as fractions of the species receive thereby a life and scope which transcend the scope and life of the individuals indentifying themselves with the history and finalities of the uninterrupted series of generations. It is irrelevant in this connection to determine whether social groups, considered as fractions of the species, constitute organisms. The important thing is to ascertain that this organic concept of the state gives to society a continuous life over and beyond the existence of the several individuals.

The relations therefore between state and citizens are completely reversed by the Fascist doctrine. Instead of the liberal-democratic formula, "society for the individual," we have, "individuals for society" with this difference however: that while the liberal doctrines eliminated society, Fascism does not submerge the individual in the social group. It subordinates him, but does not eliminate him; the individual as a part of his generation ever remaining an element of society however transient and insignificant he may be. Moreover the development of individuals in each generation, when coordinated and harmonized, conditions the development and prosperity of the entire social unit.

At this juncture the antithesis between the two theories must appear complete and absolute. Liberalism, Democracy, and Socialism look upon social groups as aggregates of living individuals; for Fascism they are the recapitulating unity of the indefinite series of generations. For Liberalism, society has no purposes other than those of the members living at a given moment. For Fascism, society has historical and immanent ends of preservation, expansion, improvement, quite distinct from those of the individuals which at a given moment compose it; so distinct in fact that they may even be in opposition. Hence the necessity, for which the older doctrines make little allowance, of sacrifice, even up to the total immolation of individuals, in behalf of society; hence the true explanation of war, eternal law of mankind, interpreted by the liberal-democratic doctrines as a degenerate absurdity or as a maddened monstrosity.

For Liberalism, society has no life distinct from the life of the individuals, or as the phrase goes: *solvitur in singularitates*. For Fascism, the life of society overlaps the existence of individuals and projects itself into the succeeding generations through centuries and millennia. Individuals come into being, grow, and die, followed by others, unceasingly; social unity remains always identical to itself. For Liberalism, the individual is the end and society the means; nor is it conceivable that the individual, considered in the dignity of an ultimate finality, be lowered to mere instrumentality. For Fascism, society is the end, individuals the means, and its whole life consists in using individuals as instruments for its social ends. The state therefore guards and protects the welfare and development of individuals not for their exclusive interest, but because of the identity of the needs of individuals with those of society as a whole. We can thus accept and explain institutions and practices, which like the death penalty, are condemned by Liberalism in the name of the preeminence of individualism.

The fundamental problem of society in the old doctrines is the question of the rights of individuals. It may be the right to freedom as the Liberals would have it; or the right to the government of the commonwealth as the Democrats claim it, or the right to economic justice as the Socialists contend; but in every case it is the right of individuals, or groups of individuals (classes). Fascism on the other hand faces squarely the problem of the right of the state and of the duty of individuals. Individual rights are only recognized in so far as they are implied in the rights of the state. In this preeminence of duty we find the highest ethical value of Fascism.

This, however, does not mean that the problems raised by the other schools are ignored by Fascism. It means simply that it faces them and solves them differently, as, for example, the problem of liberty.

There is a Liberal theory of freedom, and there is a Fascist concept of liberty. For we, too, maintain the necessity of safeguarding the conditions that make for the free development of the individual; we, too, believe that the oppression of individual personality can find no place in the modern state. We do not, however, accept a bill of rights which tends to make the individual superior to the state and to empower him to act in opposition to society. Our concept of liberty is that the individual must be allowed to develop his personality in behalf of the state, for these ephemeral and infinitesimal elements of the complex and permanent life of society determine by their normal growth the development of the state. But this individual growth must be normal. A huge and disproportionate development of the individual or of classes, would prove as fatal to society as abnormal growths are to living organisms. Freedom therefore is due to the citizen and to classes on condition that they exercise it in the interest of society as a whole and within the limits set by social exigencies, liberty being, like any other individual right, a concession of the state. What I say concerning civil liberties applies to economic freedom as well. Fascism does not look upon the doctrine of economic liberty as an absolute dogma. It does not refer economic problems to individual needs, to individual interest, to individual solutions. On the contrary it considers the economic development, and especially the production of wealth, as an eminently social concern, wealth being for society an essential element of power and prosperity. But Fascism maintains that in the ordinary run of events economic liberty serves the social purposes best; that it is profitable to entrust to individual initiative the task of economic development both as to production and as to distribution; that in the economic world individual ambition is the most effective means for obtaining the best social results with the least effort. Therefore, on the question also of economic liberty the Fascists differ fundamentally from the Liberals; the latter see in liberty a principle, the Fascists accept it as a method. By the Liberals, freedom is recognized in the interest of the citizens; the Fascists grant it in the interest of society. In other terms, Fascists make of the individual an economic instrument for the advancement of society, an instrument which they use so long as it functions and which they subordinate when no longer serviceable. In this guise Fascism solves the eternal problem of economic freedom and of state interference, considering both as mere methods which may or may not be employed in accordance with the social needs of the moment.

What I have said concerning political and economic Liberalism applies also to Democracy. The latter envisages fundamentally the problem of sovereignty; Fascism does also, but in an entirely different manner. Democracy vests sovereignty in the people, that is to say, in the mass of human beings. Fascism discovers sovereignty to be inherent in society when it is juridically organized as a state. Democracy therefore turns over the government of the state to the multitude of living men that they may use it to further their own interests; Fascism insists that the government be entrusted to men capable of rising above their own private interests and of realizing the aspirations of the social collectivity, considered in its unity and in its relation to the past and future. Fascism therefore not only rejects the dogma of popular sovereignty and substitutes for it that of state sovereignty, but it also proclaims that the great mass of citizens is not a suitable advocate of social interests for the reason that the capacity to ignore individual private interests in favor of the higher demands of society and of history is a very rare gift and the privilege of the chosen few. Natural intelligence and cultural preparation are of great service in such tasks. Still more valuable perhaps is the intuitiveness of rare great minds, their traditionalism and their inherited qualities. This must not however be construed to mean that the masses are not to be allowed to exercise any influence on the life of the state. On the contrary, among peoples with a great history and with noble traditions, even the lowest elements of society possess an instinctive discernment of what is necessary for the welfare of the race, which in moments of great historical crises reveals itself to be almost infallible. It is therefore as wise to afford to this instinct the means of declaring itself as it is judicious to entrust the normal control of the commonwealth to a selected élite.

As for Socialism, the Fascist doctrine frankly recognizes that the problem raised by it as to the relations between capital and labor is a very serious one, perhaps the central one of modern life. What Fascism does not countenance is the collectivistic solution proposed by the Socialists. The chief defect of the socialistic method has been clearly demonstrated by the experience of the last few years. It does not take into account human nature, and is therefore outside of reality, in that it will not recognize that the most powerful spring of human activities lies in individual self-interest and that therefore the elimination from the economic field of this interest results in complete paralysis. The suppression of private ownership of capital carries with it the suppression of capital itself, for capital is formed by savings and no one will want to save, but will rather consume all he makes if he knows he cannot keep and hand down to his heirs the results of his labors. The dispersion of capital means the end of production since capital, no matter who owns it, is always an indispensable tool of production. Collective organization of production is followed therefore by the paralysis of production since, by eliminating from the productive mechanism the incentive of individual interest, the product becomes rarer and more costly. Socialism then, as experience has shown, leads to increase in consumption, to the dispersion of capital and therefore to poverty. Of what avail is it, then, to build a social machine which will more justly distribute wealth if this very wealth is destroyed by the construction of this machine? Socialism committed an irreparable error when it made of private property a matter of justice while in truth it is a problem of social utility. The recognition of individual property rights, then, is a part of the Fascist doctrine not because of its individual bearing but because of its social utility.

We must reject, therefore, the socialistic solution but we cannot allow the problem raised by the Socialists to remain unsolved, not only because justice demands a solution but also because the persistence of this problem in liberal and democratic régimes has been a menace to public order and to the authority of the state. Unlimited and unrestrained class self-defense, evinced by strikes and lockouts, by boycotts and sabotage, leads inevitably to anarchy. The Fascist doctrine, enacting justice among the classes in compliance with a fundamental necessity of modern life, does away with class self-defense, which, like individual self-defense in the days of barbarism, is a source of disorder and civil war.

Having reduced the problem to these terms, only one solution is possible, the realization of justice among the classes by and through the state. Centuries ago the state, as the specific organ of justice, abolished personal self-defense in individual controversies and substituted for it state justice. The time has now come when class self-defense also must be replaced by state justice. To facilitate the change Fascism has created its own syndicalism. The suppression of class self-defense does not mean the suppression of class defense which is an inalienable necessity of modern economic life. Class organization is a fact which cannot be ignored but it must be controlled, disciplined, and subordinated by the state. The syndicate, instead of being, as formerly, an organ of extra-legal defense, must be turned into an organ of legal defense which will become judicial defense as soon as labor conflicts become a matter of judicial settlement. Fascism therefore has transformed the syndicate, that old revolutionary instrument of syndicalistic socialists, into an instrument of legal defense of the classes both within and without the law courts. This solution may encounter obstacles in its development; the obstacles of malevolence, of suspicion of the untried, of erroneous calculation, etc., but it is destined to triumph even though it must advance through progressive stages.

---

6. Fascism: The American Brand*

HENRY A. WALLACE

On returning from my trip to the West in February, I received a request from *The New York Times* to write a piece answering the following questions:

(1) *What is a Fascist?*

The New York Times (Sunday Magazine, April 19, 1944). By permission of Henry A. Wallace and *The New York Times*.

(2) *How many Fascists have we?*

(3) *How dangerous are they?*

A Fascist is one whose lust for money or power is combined with such an intensity of intolerance toward those of other races, parties, classes, religions, cultures, regions or nations as to make him ruthless in his use of deceit or violence to attain his ends. The supreme god of a Fascist to which his ends are directed may be money or power; may be a race or a class; may be a military clique or an economic group; or may be a culture, religion or a political party.

The perfect type of Fascist throughout recent centuries has been the Prussian Junker, who developed such hatred for other races and such allegiance to a military clique as to make him willing at all times to engage in any degree of deceit and violence necessary to place his culture and race astride the world. In every big nation of the world are at least a few people who have the fascist temperament. Every Jew baiter, every Catholic hater is a Fascist at heart. The hoodlums who have been desecrating churches, cathedrals and synagogues in some of our larger cities are ripe material for fascist leadership.

The obvious types of American Fascists are dealt with on the air and in the press. These demagogues and stooges are fronts for others. Dangerous as these people may be, they are not so significant as thousands of other people who have never been mentioned. The really dangerous American Fascists are not those who are hooked up directly or indirectly with the Axis. The FBI has its finger on those.

The dangerous American Fascist is the man who wants to do in the United States in an American way what Hitler did in Germany in a Prussian way. The American Fascist would prefer not to use violence. His method is to poison the channels of public information. With a Fascist the problem is never how best to present the truth to the public but how best to use the news to deceive the public into giving the Fascist and his group more money or more power.

If we define an American Fascist as one who in case of conflict puts money and power ahead of human beings, then there are undoubtedly several million Fascists in the United States. There are probably several hundred thousand if we narrow the definition to include only those who in their search for money and power are ruthless and deceitful.

Most American Fascists are enthusiastically supporting the war effort. They are doing this even in those cases where they hope to have profitable connections with German chemical firms after the war ends. They are patriotic in time of war because it is to their interest to be so, but in time of peace they follow power and the dollar wherever they may lead.

American Fascism will not be really dangerous until there is a purposeful coalition between the cartelists, the deliberate poisoners of public information and those who stand for the KKK type of demagog. Every year, however, the deliberate, systematic poisoning of the public channels of information is becoming more evident. At the moment the anti-Jewish, anti-Negro, anti-Catholic outbreaks are not too serious, but who can say what they will be if the poisoning of the public mind continues and we enter a period of serious depression?

The European brand of Fascism will probably present its most serious post-war threat to us via Latin America. The effect of the war has been to raise the cost of living in most Latin-American countries much faster than the wages of labor. The Fascists in most Latin-American countries tell the people that the reason their wages won't buy as much in the way of goods is because of Yankee imperialism.

The Fascists in Latin America learn to speak and act like natives. Our chemical and other manufacturing concerns are all too often ready to let the Germans have Latin-American markets provided the American companies can work out an arrangement which will enable them to charge high prices to the consumer inside the United States. Following this war, technology will have reached such a point that it will be possible for Germans, using South America as a base, to cause us much more difficulty in World War III than they did in World War II. The military and land-owning cliques in many South American countries will find it attractive financially to work with German Fascist concerns as well as expedient from the standpoint of temporary power politics.

Fascism is a world-wide disease. Its greatest threat to the United States will come after the war, either via Latin America or within the United States itself.

Still another danger is represented by those who, paying lip service to democracy and the common welfare, in their insatiable greed for money and the power which money gives, do not hesitate surreptitiously to evade the laws designed to safeguard the public from monopolistic extortion. American Fascists of this stamp were clandestinely aligned with their German counterparts before the war and are even now preparing to resume where they left off, after "the present unpleasantness" ceases.

To the end of facilitating the re-establishment of these international cartels, these stuffed-shirt Fascists are presently engaged—not always covertly—in a campaign to subvert the distinctively democratic public policy founded on the principle of economic freedom. They seek nothing more, of course (and, incidentally, nothing less), than a license for an even more rigorous and more remorseless application of the principle of "charging what the traffic will bear," in league with their erstwhile Axis partners, than that which glorified the "new era" of the Twenties—and prostrated the world economy in the Thirties. They have a vain delusion that in this fashion they can again bring the common man to his knees and make of him this time a groveling suppliant who will "keep to his place." The susceptibility to hal-lucinations of this kind is one of the surest signs of the fascist mentality.

The symptoms of fascist thinking are colored by environment and adapted to immediate circumstances. But always and everywhere they can be iden-tified by their appeal to prejudice and by the desire to play upon the fears and vanities of different groups in order to gain power. It is no coincidence that the growth of modern tyrants has in every case been heralded by the growth of prejudice. It may be shocking to some people in this country to realize that, without meaning to do so, they hold views in common with Hitler when they preach discrimination against other religious, racial or economic groups. Likewise, many people whose patriotism is their proudest boast play Hitler's game by retailing distrust of our Allies and by giving currency to snide suspicions without foundation in fact.

The American Fascists are most easily recognized by their deliberate per-version of truth and fact. Their newspapers and propaganda carefully culti-vate every fissure of disunity, every crack in the common front against Fascism. They use every opportunity to impugn democracy. They use isola-tionism as a slogan to conceal their own selfish imperialism.

They cultivate hate and distrust of both Britain and Russia. They claim to be super-patriots, but they would destroy every liberty guaranteed by the Constitution. They demand free enterprise, but are the spokesmen for monopoly and vested interest. Their final objective, toward which all their deceit is directed, is to capture political power so that using the power of the State and the power of the market simultaneously they may keep the com-mon man in eternal subjection.

Several leaders of industry in this country who have gained a new vision of the meaning of opportunity through co-operation with Government have warned the public openly that there are some selfish groups in industry who are willing to jeopardize the structure of American liberty to gain some temporary advantage. We all know the part that the cartels played in bring-ing Hitler to power and the rule the giant German trusts have played in Nazi conquests. Monopolists who fear competition and who distrust democ-racy because it stands for equal opportunity would like to secure their posi-tion against small and energetic enterprise. In an effort to eliminate the possibility of any rival growing up, some monopolists would sacrifice de-mocracy itself.

The sincerity of monopolists and cartelists who deny that they have any fascist tendencies is easily tested. Do they uphold, in their policies and prac-tices, the genuine principles of free enterprise, granting to the newcomer, the little business man, the inventor, a fair start in the game? To ask this ques-tion is to answer it. The monopolist wants no rivals. The cartelists want to regiment existing business, to eliminate all competition and to prevent the emergence of new enterprise. In other words, the cartelist and the monopolist don't believe in economic democracy and if necessary are willing to see political democracy die in order to maintain their grip on economic life.

Very often big business gives unwitting aid to Fascism. Many British business men would be incensed if they were branded as Fascists, yet by playing the cartel game they supported the policies that led to Munich and finally to the Duesseldorf agreement, signed the day following Hitler's seizure of Czechoslovakia. In this agreement they sanctioned the cartelization of industry in Germany and England, and stated that they intended to exert pressure on their Governments to cartelize world trade. In the United States many industrialists whose personal patriotism is unquestioned placed themselves and their corporations in ambiguous positions because they had succumbed to the false security of cartel agreements with totalitarian German concerns.

It can be pointed out to such men that many of the German industrialists who financed Hitler found they had created a Frankenstein monster who did not hesitate to destroy them economically or personally if it suited his purpose. The ghost (and this may be literal) of Thyssen should haunt every American business man so minded. Similarly, many thousands of business men who played ball with the Nazis found that the swastika stood for a double-cross, by which small industries were sold out to the giant combines, or to enrich favored members of the Nazi party.

It has been claimed at times that our modern age of technology facilitates dictatorship. What we must understand is that the industries, processes and inventions created by modern science can be used either to subjugate or liberate. The choice is up to us. The myth of fascist efficiency has deluded many people. It was Mussolini's vaunted claim that he "made the trains run on time." In the end, however, he brought to the Italian people impoverishment and defeat. It was Hitler's claim that he eliminated all unemployment in Germany. Neither is there unemployment in a prison camp.

Democracy to crush Fascism internally must demonstrate its capacity to "make the trains run on time." It must develop the ability to keep people fully employed and at the same time balance the budget. It must put human beings first and dollars second. It must appeal to reason and decency and not to violence and deceit. We must not tolerate oppressive government or industrial oligarchy in the form of monopolies and cartels. As long as scientific research and inventive ingenuity outrun our ability to devise social mechanisms to raise the living standards of the people we may expect the liberal potential of the United States to increase. If this liberal potential is properly channeled we may expect the area of freedom of the United States to increase. The problem is to speed up our rate of social invention in the service of the welfare of all the people.

So long as private economic governments stifle initiative and attempt to control technological development, it is not possible for genuine advances to be made in economic and political democracy. As long as we falter in the solution of the unemployment problem; as long as monopoly chokes off the opportunities for investment and the development of an expanding economy, the specter of Fascism will haunt our efforts to promote the general welfare.

The world-wide, age-long struggle between fascism and democracy will not stop when the fighting ends in Germany and Japan. Democracy can win the peace only if it does two things:

(1) Speeds up the rate of political and economic inventions so that both production and, especially, distribution can match in their power and practical effect on the daily life of the common man the immense and growing volume of scientific research, mechanical invention and management technique.

(2) Vivifies with the greatest intensity the spiritual processes which are both the foundation and the very essence of democracy.

The second of these two requirements is even more likely to be overlooked than the first. Our colleges, because of their preoccupation with science, history, economics and athletics, stimulate too little serious questioning in the minds of the young Wall Streeters (and young La Salle Streeters) concerning that which is the essence of both democracy and religion—the fatherhood of God and the brotherhood of man. Democracy might well be called the religion of the general welfare in action. Against the international, imperialistic aspects of Fascism and cartels it has its own type of internationalism— the Good Neighbor policy. But the Good Neighbor policy will be replaced by a new Fascism if, after this war, we do as we did after the last war—insist on higher tariffs and the punitive payment of debts which foreign nations owe us.

The moral and spiritual aspects of both personal and international relationships have a practical bearing which so-called practical men deny. This dullness of vision regarding the importance of the general welfare to the individual is the measure of the failure of our schools and churches to teach the spiritual significance of genuine democracy. Until democracy in effective enthusiastic action fills the vacuum created by the power of modern inventions we may expect the Fascists to increase in power after the war, both in the United States and in the world.

Fascism in the post-war world inevitably will push steadily for Anglo-Saxon imperialism and eventually for war with Russia. Already American Fascists are talking and writing about this conflict and using it as an excuse for their internal hatreds and intolerances toward certain races, creeds and classes.

It should also be evident from what has been said above that exhibitions of the native brand of Fascism are not confined to any single section, class or religion. Happily, it can be said that as yet Fascism has not captured a predominant place in the outlook of any American section, class or religion.

It may be encountered in Wall Street, Main Street or Tobacco Road. Some even suspect that they can detect incipient traces of it along the Potomac. It is an infectious disease and we must all be on our guard against intolerance, bigotry and the pretension of invidious distinction. But if we put our trust in the common sense of common men and "with malice toward none and charity for all" go forward on the great adventure of making political, economic and social democracy a practical reality, we shall not fail.

~~~~~~~~~~~~~~~~~~~~~~~~ Part III ~~~~~~~~~~~~~~~~~~~~~~~~

CAPITALISM, SOCIALISM, PLANNING

~~~~~~

In Defense of Private Property

Revolutionary Marxism

English Socialism

Plan or No Plan?

Economic Threats to Freedom

Chapter IX

IN DEFENSE OF PRIVATE PROPERTY

FOR one hundred years, the "economic problem" has been a leitmotiv of political conflict in the Western world. The Industrial Revolution led to a rapid growth of wealth and population; but, like other revolutions, it created new problems not sufficiently anticipated beforehand. The intimate connection between political freedom and reasonable economic opportunity has been recognized in theory everywhere—although the solutions have varied in accordance with needs as qualified by history and tradition.

The liberal capitalistic approach to political economy has been more firmly entrenched in the United States than in any other country, more, even, than in England, where it originated. Just as John Locke's doctrines of political government have influenced American ideas and institutions more strongly than those of anyone else, his economic philosophy has impinged upon American economic life with equal measure. In his *Two Treatises of Government* (1690) Locke developed a theory of property which has permeated the economic and political foundations of the American system. In fact, the aura of Locke's prestige has been so high that much economic doctrine has been attributed to him which directly contradicts his plainly stated views.

Locke's theory of property starts with the inquiry as to how private property can be justified at all. Since every man has a property in his own person, the "labor of his body and the work of his hands we may say are properly his." Labor *creates* property: the human effort that is "mixed" with natural resources is the decisive criterion which alone justifies private property. Thus Locke avoids justifying property on the ground that "the law" protects it, and instead goes back to the law behind the law, the law of nature, according to which man's property in his own body, also extends to its labor.

But labor does more than create property: it also determines the *value* of property. "It is labor indeed," Locke says, "that puts the difference of value on everything." In fact, he stresses the proportion of labor in the value of an economic good highly enough to say that "of the products of the earth useful to the life of man nine-tenths are the effects of labor." This Lockean theory of property—that labor is the title to property and the source of economic value—was later more fully elaborated by Smith and Ricardo (who defended capitalism); in the hands of the socialists, Locke's theory of value and property became the most powerful weapon of attacking capitalism. When Locke defended property on the ground of individual effort and initiative, he protected the productive capacities of a new system of commercial and industrial capitalism against the shackles and curbs imposed by restrictive traditions of an authoritarian state. By making labor the title to property and the source of value, Locke translated the rise of a new class to power into terms of a new political economy. In relation to the age that preceded him, Locke's economic philosophy—the liberation of the enterprising individual from paralyzing restrictions of force and custom—was altogether progressive. When the socialists—a century and a half after Locke—used the same theory of value to demand the socialization of the means of production, they did not prove that they were more progressive than he, but that certain economic facts had changed since Locke, especially the concentration of property and income.

Locke himself did not work out a consistently unambiguous theory as to *how much property* a person may fairly claim for himself. In general, he is inclined to acknowledge that the right to property is limited: "As much as anyone can make use of to any advantage of life before it spoils, so much he may by his labor fix a property in; whatever is beyond this, is more than his share, and belongs to others. Nothing was made by God for man to spoil or destroy." This relative equality of property, based on the individual's limited capacity to make use of, and enjoy, earthly goods, would have lasted forever, "had not the invention of money, and by tacit agreement of men to put a value on it, introduced (by consent) larger possessions and a right to them." The criterion which Locke applies is that of waste. Before money was invented, man had no moral right to hoard the products of the earth and allow them to rot and spoil. His capacity to consume perishable goods determined the amount of property he could rightfully own. In a later phase, man would exchange perishable fruit (like plums) for durable ones (like nuts). By disposing of the plums he had done his duty toward society, preventing their waste in his possession. From durable nuts to even more durable gold, or "a sparkling pebble or diamond," was only a small and logical step. And if he kept on hoarding these durable goods (like gold and diamonds and money) "all his life, he invaded not the right of others." Thus Locke arrives at defining money as "some lasting thing that men might keep without spoiling, and that, by mutual consent, men would take in exchange for the truly useful but perishable supports of life." In his doctrine of property Locke makes no serious attempt to reconcile the teaching of natural law, which seems to result in reasonable equality of property, with the inequality of property which stems, by consent among men, from the use of money.

What is the relation of property to government? Locke's answer to this question has guided the makers of the American Constitution and those who later applied and lived under it. He stresses the fact that *property precedes government,* and that the sole purpose of government, the reason why men give up the state of nature for a compact of political organization, is "for the mutual preservation of their lives, liberties, and estates, which I call by the general name, property." This broad Lockean concept of property exceeds man's purely economic interests, and encompasses almost the whole orbit of his "life, liberty, and pursuit of happiness." When he speaks of property what Locke thinks of includes economic property, but is by no means identical with it. Of the three elements he lists, economic property is probably considered by him to be the most important; but it must be remembered that Locke thought of property as liberating its owner, rather than as enslaving others.

Since consent establishes government and maintains it, and since the preservation of property is the purpose of government, it follows that the supreme power of the state "cannot take from any man any part of his property without his own consent." Even if a commonwealth is based on freely elected representative institutions, it cannot "dispose of the estates of the subjects arbitrarily." The Fourteenth Amendment to the Constitution of the United States embodies this Lockean thesis, that no State shall "deprive any person of life, liberty, or property, without due process of law."

In his passionate enthusiasm for the legislative branch of government as against the executive, Locke has bequeathed another ideological legacy which has retained stronger vitality in the United States than in England. There, the development of the cabinet system since the eighteenth century has controverted some of Locke's misgivings about the inherent evil of a strong and effective executive. Despite Locke, England has not become a despotism, although her legislature has been overshadowed by the executive. Even after England went Socialist in 1945, her Prime Minister, far from being a bloody tyrant (socialism was supposed to be the distilled essence of centralization), turned out to be more than mild. In the United States, on the other hand, the Lockean sanctification of the legislative branch as contrasted with the devil theory of the executive has by no means lost its vote-getting magic.

Locke supported property with arguments based on reason and the law of nature. Edmund Burke came to the defense of property from a diametrically opposite point of view: the historical method, combined with the conception that society was not (as Locke held) founded by a social contract, but was an organic, living being, greater and more significant than the individuals who compose it. Burke's *Reflections on the Revolution in France* (1790) is probably still the most impressive statement of conservative political thought. In England his influence has been immense, and by no means confined to one political persuasion. In the United States his ideas have nurtured whatever conservative political philosophy was consciously developed. There is no dearth of conservatives in the United States, but conservatism as an ideology is considered "Old World" and "un-American." While Burke's central interest lay in government, he was well aware of the role that property played in political institutions.

He saw society not in terms of equal individuals, but of unequal groups and historically recognized interests. Property was such an interest, founded on *prescription,* rather than on natural law or abstract reasoning. The aristocracy and monarchy were also institutions based on prescription. While property is not the only criterion of the privileged classes and interests, which Burke deems worthy to rule the nation, he is well aware of the connections between property and the established order; both he saw threatened by the progress of popular democracy in France. Whereas Locke attached to property the qualification that it was originally equal, at least, Burke frankly states the doctrine that the "characteristic essence of property, formed out of the combined principles of its acquisition and conservation, is to be *unequal."* The inequality of property that Burke defended was closely related to his conception of society in which rank and privilege played such a large part. Conversely, Burke fully realized, and approved of, political inequality as the result of economic inequality. "Hereditary property and hereditary distinction" wholly composed the House of Lords, and he was pleased that the House of Commons was also made up (in his time) of large property owners. As to the unpropertied masses, Burke wanted them to be content with "Virtual Representation" under which, as he said in a letter to Sir Hercules Langrishe (January 3, 1792), "there is a communion of interests, and a sympathy in feelings and desires between those who act in the name of any description of people and the people in whose name they act, though the trustees are not actually chosen by them. This is virtual representation. Such a representation I think to be in many cases even better than the actual." However, quite apart from Burke's direct eulogies of property and its privileges, his indirect support was possibly even more important. What mattered most was that Burke emphasized the values of prescription, inheritance, rank, and distinction, which all helped to buttress the cause of inequality of property and government.

The doctrine that of the three fundamental principles of government (the protection of life, liberty, and property), "the chief of these is property," is forcefully espoused by Mr. Justice Van Orsdel, of the Court of Appeals of the District of Columbia, in *Children's Hospital of the District of Columbia* v. *Adkins* (1922). The issue involved was whether a minimum-wage law for women, passed by Congress in September, 1918, was constitutional. The Supreme Court of the District of Columbia, like the lower court, had declared it unconstitutional in 1921; the Court of Appeal upheld this decision in 1922, and was supported by the Supreme Court of the United States in 1923, on the ground that minimum-wage laws violated the "freedom of contract." It was only in 1937 that the Supreme Court reversed itself, and held minimum-wage laws constitutional in *West Coast Hotel* v. *Parrish* (1937). The difference between 1922 and 1937 was a great depression and a New Deal.

In the seventeenth century the defense of private property was directed against absolute monarchs and restrictive legal and economic rules and customs. In the twentieth century, private property is on the defensive against the expanding force of socialism. Walter Lippmann's *The Good Society* (1937) is probably the clearest restatement of the theory of private property in an increasingly collectivist age. Lippmann disagrees with Locke's natural-law interpretation of property as being prior and superior to government: "The title to property is a construction of the law. Contracts are legal instruments. Corporations are legal creatures. It is, therefore, misleading to think of them as existing somehow outside the law and then to ask whether it is permissible to 'interfere' with them." Unlike Locke, who lived at the dawn of the capitalist system and therefore could hardly foresee its blemishes, Lippmann lives in the era of "late capitalism" ("Spätkapitalismus," as Sombart called it), which has revealed how the system can be abused.

The extreme individualism which insists on no regulation of property and private rights seems to Lippmann to be as unreal as the universal regulation of all human relations by official commands is arbitrary and unjust. Lippmann pleads for the strengthening of the rule of law as opposed to authoritarian decisions of irresponsible rulers. The function of the state is to adjust conflicts and disputes between private citizens in their dealings with each other, rather than to conduct their affairs through administrative machinery. Where Locke favored the legislative branch of the government against the executive, Lippmann is an equally strong partisan of the judiciary and the judicial method against the administrative method. The judicial method, based on the principles of the common law, is characteristic of "democratic liberalism"; the method of "arbitrary sovereign commands" expresses "authoritarian collectivism."

How is private property to be made secure in an age in which it is constantly attacked? "The real security of private property," Lippmann writes, "must rest not on a fatuous longing for a sole and despotic dominion over the necessities of all men's existence but on a reconciliation of all men's claims in a system of substantially equal rights. It is not loyalty to the cause of private property to confirm the monopolists in their privileges. To do that is to prepare the extinction of private property either by general disorder and pillage or by the establishment of an administered collectivism. The true principle is to be ready to liquidate these rights of possession which enable some men, by excluding all other men from access to land and to the resources of nature, to exact a tribute based not on their own labor but on mere legal possession." Lippmann is confident that the giant business corporations and monopolies are not a necessary development in the capitalist system, and can be reformed by remedial legislation. The sorry record of the antitrust legislation in the United States and elsewhere does not invalidate his logic. Past contrary experience does not necessarily disprove Lippmann's thesis on this point: but his argument would be more forceful if it could lean on the actual past rather than on a hypothetical future.

Lippmann differs in one fundamental point from Locke: whereas the latter saw in property only a relationship between man and *things,* Lippmann emphasizes that property is a relationship between man and *man,* and, like other human relationships, regulated by, and subject to, law. Even Marxist critics of Locke had taken over from him the doctrine that property was a relationship between man and things; Friedrich Engels claimed that in the classless society of socialism the domination of man over man would be replaced by the "administration of things." By contrast, Lippmann is aware that the essential character of property lies in the relations it establishes between men; in private giant monopolies he sees, therefore, the danger of "private corporate collectivism." The experience of large-scale business, monopoly or near monopoly, has taught the difficulty of drawing sharply defined lines of distinction between private government and public government.

Herbert Hoover's article on "The Fifth Freedom" (1943) is significant because it echoes faithfully the sentiments and temper of many millions of Americans on the subject of what is often referred to as "free enterprise." Prematurely proclaimed dead, these sentiments have shown remarkable strength in the United States after the end of the Second World War. If Hoover is a statesman rather than a political theorist, he has, nevertheless, typified a strand in the fabric of American social and political thought that is still vital and articulate.

1. The End of Government *

JOHN LOCKE

Whether we consider natural reason, which tells us that men being once born have a right to their preservation, and consequently to meat and drink and such other things as nature affords for their subsistence; or revelation, which gives us an account of those grants God made of the world to Adam,

* From John Locke, *Two Treatises of Government* (1690).

and to Noah and his sons, 'tis very clear that God, as King David says, Psalm CXV. 16, "has given the earth to the children of men," given it to mankind in common. But this being supposed, it seems to some a very great difficulty how anyone should ever come to have a property in anything. I will not content myself to answer that if it be difficult to make out property upon a supposition that God gave the world to Adam and his posterity in common, it is impossible that any man but one universal monarch should have any property upon a supposition that God gave the world to Adam and his heirs in succession, exclusive of all the rest of his posterity. But I shall endeavor to show how men might come to have a property in several parts of that which God gave to mankind in common, and that without any express compact of all the commoners.

God, who hath given the world to men in common, hath also given them reason to make use of it to the best advantage of life and convenience. The earth and all that is therein is given to men for the support and comfort of their being. And though all the fruits it naturally produces, and beasts it feeds, belong to mankind in common, as they are produced by the spontaneous hand of nature; and nobody has originally a private dominion exclusive of the rest of mankind in any of them as they are thus in their natural state; yet being given for the use of men, there must of necessity be a means to appropriate them some way or other before they can be of any use or at all beneficial to any particular man. The fruit or venison which nourishes the wild Indian, who knows no enclosure, and is still a tenant in common, must be his, and so his, i.e., a part of him, that another can no longer have any right to it, before it can do any good for the support of his life.

Though the earth and all inferior creatures be common to all men, yet every man has a property in his own person; this nobody has any right to but himself. The labor of his body and the work of his hands we may say are properly his. Whatsoever, then, he removes out of the state that nature hath provided and left it in, he hath mixed his labor with, and joined to it something that is his own, and thereby makes it his property. It being by him removed from the common state nature placed it in, it hath by this labor something annexed to it that excludes the common right of other men. For this labor being the unquestionable property of the laborer, no man but he can have a right to what that is once joined to, at least where there is enough, and as good left in common for others.

He that is nourished by the acorns he picked up under an oak, or the apples he gathered from the trees in the wood, has certainly appropriated them to himself. Nobody can deny but the nourishment is his. I ask, then, When did they begin to be his—when he digested, or when he ate, or when he boiled, or when he brought them home, or when he picked them up? And 'tis plain if the first gathering made them not his, nothing else could. That labor put a distinction between them and common; that added something to them more than nature, the common mother of all, had done, and so they became his private right. And will anyone say he had no right to those acorns or apples he thus appropriated, because he had not the consent of all mankind to make them his? Was it a robbery thus to assume to himself what belonged to all in common? If such a consent as that was necessary, man had starved, notwithstanding the plenty God had given him. We see in commons which remain so by compact that 'tis the taking any part of what is common and removing it out of the state nature leaves it in, which begins the property; without which the common is of no use. And the taking of this or that part does not depend on the express consent of all the commoners. Thus the grass my horse has bit, the turfs my servant has cut, and the ore I have dug in any place where I have a right to them in common with others, become my property without the assignation or consent of anybody. The labor that was mine removing them out of that common state they were in, hath fixed my property in them.

By making an explicit consent of every commoner necessary to anyone's appropriating to himself any part of what is given in common, children or servants could not cut the meat which their father or master had provided for them in common without assigning to everyone his peculiar part. Though the water running in the fountain be everyone's, yet who can doubt but that in the pitcher is his only who drew it out? His labor hath taken it out of the hands of Nature where it was common, and belonged equally to all her children, and hath thereby appropriated it to himself.

Thus this law of reason makes the deer that Indian's who hath killed it; it is allowed to be his goods who hath bestowed his labor upon it, though, before, it was the common right of everyone. And amongst those who are counted the civilized part of mankind, who have made and multiplied positive laws to determine property, this original law of nature for the beginning of property, in what was before common, still takes place, and by virtue thereof, what fish anyone catches in the ocean, that great and still remaining common of mankind; or what ambergris anyone takes up here is by the labor that removes it out of that common state nature left it in, made his property who takes that pains about it. And even amongst us, the hare that anyone is hunting is thought his who pursues her during the chase. For being a beast that is still looked upon as common, and no man's private possession, whoever has employed so much labor about any of that kind as to find and pursue her has thereby removed her from the state of nature wherein she was common, and hath began a property.

It will perhaps be objected to this, that if gathering the acorns, or other fruits of the earth, etc., makes a right to them, then anyone may engross as much as he will. To which I answer, Not so. The same law of nature that does by this means give us property, does also bound that property too. "God has given us all things richly" (I Tim. vi. 17), is the voice of reason confirmed by inspiration. But how far has He given it us? To enjoy. As much as anyone can make use of to any advantage of life before it spoils, so much he may by his labor fix a property in; whatever is beyond this, is more than his share, and belongs to others. Nothing was made by God for man to spoil or destroy. And thus considering the plenty of natural provisions there was a long time in the world, and the few spenders, and to how small a part of that provision the industry of one man could extend itself, and engross it to the prejudice of others—especially keeping within the bounds, set by reason, of what might serve for his use—there could be then little room for quarrels or contentions about property so established.

But the chief matter of property being now not the fruits of the earth, and the beasts that subsist on it, but the earth itself, as that which takes in and carries with it all the rest, I think it is plain that property in that, too, is acquired as the former. As much land as a man tills, plants, improves, cultivates, and can use the product of, so much is his property. He by his labor does as it were enclose it from the common. Nor will it invalidate his right to say, everybody else has an equal title to it; and therefore he cannot appropriate, he cannot enclose, without the consent of all his fellow-commoners, all mankind. God, when He gave the world in common to all mankind, commanded man also to labor, and the penury of his condition required it of him. God and his reason commanded him to subdue the earth, i.e., improve it for the benefit of life, and therein lay out something upon it that was his own, his labor. He that, in obedience to this command of God, subdued, tilled, and sowed any part of it, thereby annexed to it something that was his property, which another had no title to, nor could without injury take from him.

Nor was this appropriation of any parcel of land, by improving it, any prejudice to any other man, since there was still enough and as good left; and more than the yet unprovided could use. So that in effect there was never the less left for others because of his enclosure for himself. For he that leaves as much as another can make use of, does as good as take nothing at all. Nobody could think himself injured by the drinking of another man, though he took a good draught, who had a whole river of the same water left him to quench his thirst; and the case of land and water, where there is enough of both, is perfectly the same.

God gave the world to men in common; but since He gave it them for their benefit, and the greatest conveniences of life they were capable to draw from it, it cannot be supposed He meant it should always remain common and uncultivated. He gave it to the use of the industrious and rational (and labor was to be his title to it), not to the fancy or covetousness of the quarrelsome and contentious. He that had as good left for his improvement as was already taken up, needed not complain, ought not to meddle with what was already improved by another's labor; if he did, it is plain he desired the benefit of another's pains, which he had no right to, and not the ground which God had given him in common with others to labor on, and whereof there was as good left as that already possessed, and more than he knew what to do with, or his industry could reach to.

It is true, in land that is common in England, or any other country where there is plenty of people under Government, who have money and commerce, no one can enclose or appropriate any part without the consent of all his fellow-commoners: because this is left common by compact, i.e., by the law of the land, which is not to be violated. And though it be common in respect of some men, it is not so to all mankind; but is the joint property of this country, or this parish. Besides, the remainder, after such enclosure, would not be as good to the rest of the commoners as the whole was, when they could all make use of the whole; whereas in the beginning and first peopling of the great common of the world it was quite otherwise. The law man was under was rather for appropriating. God commanded, and his wants forced him, to labor. That was his property, which could not be taken from him wherever he had fixed it. And hence subduing or cultivating the earth, and having dominion, we see are joined together. The one gave title to the other. So that God, by commanding to subdue, gave authority so far to appropriate. And the condition of human life, which requires labor and materials to work on, necessarily introduces private possessions.

The measure of property nature has well set by the extent of men's labor and the conveniency of life. No man's labor could subdue or appropriate all, nor could his enjoyment consume more than a small part; so that it was impossible for any man, this way, to entrench upon the right of another or acquire to himself a property to the prejudice of his neighbor, who would still have room for as good and as large a possession (after the other had taken out his) as before it was appropriated. Which measure did confine every man's possession to a very moderate proportion, and such as he might appropriate to himself without injury to anybody in the first ages of the world, when men were more in danger to be lost, by wandering from their company, in the then vast wilderness of the earth than to be straitened for want of room to plant in.

The same measure may be allowed still, without prejudice to anybody, full as the world seems. For, supposing a man or family, in the state they were at first, peopling of the world by the children of Adam or Noah, let him plant in some inland vacant places of America. We shall find that the possessions he could make himself, upon the measures we have given, would not be very large, nor, even to this day, prejudice the rest of mankind or give them reason to complain or think themselves injured by this man's encroachment, though the race of men have now spread themselves to all the corners of the world, and do infinitely exceed the small number that was at the beginning. Nay, the extent of ground is of so little value without labor that I have heard it affirmed that in Spain itself a man may be permitted to plough, sow, and reap, without being disturbed, upon land he has no other title to, but only his making use of it. But, on the contrary, the inhabitants think themselves beholden to him who, by his industry on neglected, and consequently waste land, has increased the stock of corn, which they wanted. But be this as it will, which I lay no stress on, this I dare boldly affirm, that the same rule of propriety—viz., that every man should have as much as he could make use of, would hold still in the world, without straitening anybody, since there is land enough in the world to suffice double the inhabitants, had not the invention of money, and the tacit agreement of men to put a value on it, introduced (by consent) larger possessions and a right to them; which, how it has done, I shall by and by show more at large.

This is certain, that in the beginning, before the desire of having more than man needed had altered the intrinsic value of things, which depends only on their usefulness to the life of man; or had agreed that a little piece of yellow metal which would keep without wasting or decay should be worth a great piece of flesh or a whole heap of corn, though men had a right to appropriate by their labor, each one to himself, as much of the things of nature as he could use, yet this could not be much, nor to the prejudice of others, where the same plenty was still left to those who would use the same industry.

Before the appropriation of land, he who gathered as much of the wild fruit, killed, caught, or tamed as many of the beasts as he could; he that so employed his pains about any of the spontaneous products of nature as in any way to alter them from the state which nature put them in, by placing any of his labor on them, did thereby acquire a propriety in them. But if they perished in his possession without their due use; if the fruits rotted, or the venison putrefied before he could spend it, he offended against the common law of nature, and was liable to be punished; he invaded his neighbor's share, for he had no right further than his use called for any of them and they might serve to afford him conveniences of life.

The same measures governed the possessions of land, too. Whatsoever he tilled and reaped, laid up, and made use of before it spoiled, that was his peculiar right; whatsoever he enclosed and could feed and make use of, the cattle and product was also his. But if either the grass of his enclosure rotted on the ground, or the fruit of his planting perished without gathering and laying up, this part of the earth, notwithstanding his enclosure, was still to be looked on as waste, and might be the possession of any other. Thus, at the beginning, Cain might take as much ground as he could till and make it his own land, and yet leave enough for Abel's sheep to feed on; a few acres would serve for both their possessions. But as families increased, and industry enlarged their stocks, their possessions enlarged with the need of them; but yet it was commonly without any fixed property in the ground they made use of, till they incorporated, settled themselves together, and built cities; and then, by consent, they came in time to set out the bounds of their distinct territories, and agree on limits between them and their neighbors, and, by laws within themselves, settled the properties of those of the same society. For we see that in that part of the world which was first inhabited, and therefore like to be best peopled, even as low down as Abraham's time, they wandered with their flocks and their herds, which was their substance, freely up and down—and this Abraham did in a country where he was a stranger; whence it is plain that, at least, a great part of the land lay in common, that the inhabitants valued it not, nor claimed property in any more than they made use of; but when there was not room enough in the same place for their herds to feed together, they, by consent, as Abraham and Lot did (Gen. xiii. 5), separated and enlarged their pasture where it best liked them. And for the same reason, Esau went from his father and his brother, and planted in Mount Seir (Gen. xxxvi. 6).

And thus, without supposing any private dominion and property in Adam over all the world, exclusive of all other men, which can no way be proved, nor any one's property be made out from it, but supposing the world, given as it was to the children of men in common, we see how labor could make men distinct titles to several parcels of it for their private uses, wherein there could be no doubt of right, no room for quarrel.

Nor is it so strange, as perhaps before consideration it may appear, that the property of labor should be able to overbalance the community of land. For it is labor indeed that puts the difference of value on everything; and let anyone consider what the difference is between an acre of land planted with tobacco or sugar, sown with wheat or barley, and an acre of the same land lying in common without any husbandry upon it, and he will find that the improvement of labor makes the far greater part of the value. I think it will be but a very modest computation to say that of the products of the earth useful to the life of man nine-tenths are the effects of labor; nay, if we will rightly estimate things as they come to our use, and cast up the several expenses about them—what in them is purely owing to nature, and what to labor—we shall find that in most of them ninety-nine hundredths are wholly to be put on the account of labor.

There cannot be a clearer demonstration of anything than several nations of the Americans are of this, who are rich in land and poor in all the comforts of life; whom nature, having furnished as liberally as any other people with the materials of plenty—i.e., a fruitful soil, apt to produce in abundance what might serve for food, raiment, and delight; yet, for want of improving it by labor, have not one hundredth part of the conveniences we enjoy, and a king of a large and fruitful territory there feeds, lodges, and is clad worse than a day laborer in England.

To make this a little clearer, let us but trace some of the ordinary provisions of life, through their several progresses, before they come to our use, and see how much they receive of their value from human industry. Bread, wine, and cloth are things of daily use and great plenty; yet, notwithstanding, acorns, water, and leaves or skins, must be our bread, drink, and clothing, did not labor furnish us with these more useful commodities. For whatever bread is more worth than acorns, wine than water, and cloth or silk than leaves, skins, or moss, that is wholly owing to labor and industry: the one of these being the food and raiment which unassisted nature furnishes us with; the other, provisions which our industry and pains prepare for us; which how much they exceed the other in value when anyone hath computed, he will then see how much labor makes the far greatest part of the value of things we enjoy in this world. And the ground which produces the materials is scarce to be reckoned in as any, or at most but a very small, part of it; so little that even amongst us land that is left wholly to nature, that hath no improvement of pasturage, tillage, or planting, is called, as indeed it is, "waste," and we shall find the benefit of it amount to little more than nothing.

An acre of land that bears here twenty bushels of wheat, and another in America which, with the same husbandry, would do the like, are without doubt of the same natural intrinsic value; but yet the benefit mankind receives from the one in a year is worth £5, and from the other possibly not worth a penny, if all the profit an Indian received from it were to be valued and sold here; at least, I may truly say, not one-thousandth. 'Tis labor, then, which puts the greatest part of value upon land, without which it would scarcely be worth anything; 'tis to that we owe the greatest part of all its useful products, for all that the straw, bran, bread, of that acre of wheat is more worth than the product of an acre of as good land which lies waste, is all the effect of labor. For 'tis not barely the ploughman's pains, the reaper's and thresher's toil, and the baker's sweat, is to be counted into the bread we eat; the labor of those who broke the oxen, who dug and wrought the iron and stones, who felled and framed the timber employed about the plough, mill, oven, or any other utensils, which are a vast number, requisite to this corn, from its sowing, to its being made bread, must all be charged on the account of labor, and received as an effect of that. Nature and the earth furnished only the almost worthless materials as in themselves. 'Twould be a strange catalogue of things that industry provided, and made use of, about every loaf of bread before it came to our use, if we could trace them— iron, wood, leather, bark, timber, stone, bricks, coals, lime, cloth, dyeing drugs, pitch, tar, masts, ropes, and all the materials made use of in the ship that brought any of the commodities made use of by any of the workmen to any part of the work all which it would be almost impossible—at least, too long—to reckon up.

From all which it is evident that, though the things of nature are given in common, yet man, by being master of himself and proprietor of his own person and the actions of labor of it, had still in himself the great foundation of property; and that which made up the great part of what he applied to the support or comfort of his being, when invention and arts had improved the conveniences of life, was perfectly his own, and did not belong in common to others.

Thus labor, in the beginning, gave a right of property, wherever anyone was pleased to employ it upon what was common, which remained a long while the far greater part, and is yet more than mankind makes use of. Men at first, for the most part, contented themselves with what unassisted nature offered to their necessities; and though afterwards, in some parts of the world (where the increase of people and stock, with the use of money, had made land scarce, and so of some value), the several communities settled the bounds of their distinct territories, and, by laws within themselves, regulated the properties of the private men of their society, and so, by compact and agreement, settled the property which labor and industry began—and the leagues that have been made between several states and kingdoms, either expressly or tacitly disowning all claim and right to the land in the other's possession, have, by common consent, given up their pretenses to their natural common right, which originally they had to those countries; and so have, by positive agreement, settled a property amongst themselves in distinct parts of the world—yet there are still great tracts of ground to be found which, the inhabitants thereof not having joined with the rest of mankind in the consent of the use of their common money, lie waste, and are more than the people who dwell on it do or can make use of, and so still lie in common; though this can scarce happen amongst that part of mankind that have consented to the use of money.

The greatest part of things really useful to the life of man, and such as the necessity of subsisting made the first commoners of the world look after, as it doth the Americans now, are generally things of short duration, such as, if they are not consumed by use, will decay and perish of themselves: gold, silver, and diamonds are things that fancy or agreement have put the value on more than real use and the necessary support of life. Now, of those good things which nature hath provided in common, everyone hath a right, as hath been said, to as much as he could use, and had a property in all he could effect with his labor—all that his industry could extend to, to alter from the state nature had put it in, was his. He that gathered a hundred bushels of acorns or apples had thereby a property in them; they were his goods as soon as gathered. He was only to look that he used them before they spoiled, else he took more than his share, and robbed others; and, indeed, it was a foolish thing, as well as dishonest, to hoard up more than he could make use of. If he gave away a part to anybody else, so that it perished not uselessly in his possession, these he also made use of; and if he also bartered away plums that would have rotted in a week, for nuts that would last good for his eating a whole year, he did no injury; he wasted not the common stock, destroyed no part of the portion of goods that belonged to others, so long as nothing perished uselessly in his hands. Again, if he would give his nuts for a piece of metal, pleased with its color, or exchange his sheep for shells, or wool for a sparkling pebble or a diamond, and keep those by him all his life, he invaded not the right of others; he might heap up as much of these durable things as he pleased, the exceeding of the bounds of his just property not lying in the largeness of his possessions, but the perishing of anything uselessly in it.

And thus came in the use of money—some lasting thing that men might keep without spoiling, and that, by mutual consent, men would take in exchange for the truly useful but perishable supports of life.

And as different degrees of industry were apt to give men possessions in different proportions, so this invention of money gave them the opportunity to continue and enlarge them; for supposing an island, separate from all possible commerce with the rest of the world, wherein there were but a hundred families—but there were sheep, horses, and cows, with other useful animals, wholesome fruits, and land enough for corn for a hundred thousand times as many, but nothing in the island, either because of its commonness or perishableness, fit to supply the place of money—what reason could anyone have there to enlarge his possessions beyond the use of his family and a plentiful supply to its consumption, either in what their own industry produced, or they could barter for like perishable useful commodities with others? Where there is not something both lasting and scarce, and so valuable to be hoarded up, there men will not be apt to enlarge their possessions of land, were it never so rich, never so free for them to take; for I ask, what would a man value ten thousand or a hundred thousand acres of excellent land, ready cultivated, and well stocked too with cattle, in the middle of the inland parts of America, where he had no hopes of commerce with other parts of the world, to draw money to him by the sale of the product? It would not be worth the enclosing, and we should see him give up again to the wild common of nature whatever was more than would supply the conveniences of life to be had there for him and his family.

Thus in the beginning all the world was America, and more so than that is now, for no such thing as money was anywhere known. Find out something that hath the use and value of money amongst his neighbors, you shall see the same man will begin presently to enlarge his possessions.

But since gold and silver, being little useful to the life of man in proportion to food, raiment, and carriage, has its value only from the consent of men, whereof labor yet makes, in great part, the measure, it is plain that the consent of men have agreed to a disproportionate and unequal possession of the earth—I mean out of the bounds of society and compact; for in governments the laws regulate it; they having, by consent, found out and agreed in a way how a man may rightfully and without injury possess more than he himself can make use of by receiving gold and silver, which may continue long in a man's possession, without decaying for the over-plus, and agreeing those metals should have a value.

And thus, I think, it is very easy to conceive without any difficulty how labor could at first begin a title of property in the common things of nature, and how the spending it upon our uses bounded it; so that there could then be no reason of quarrelling about title, nor any doubt about the largeness of possession it gave. Right and conveniency went together; for as a man had a right to all he could employ his labor upon, so he had no temptation to labor for more than he could make use of. This left no room for controversy about the title, nor for encroachment on the right of others; what portion of man carved to himself was easily seen, and it was useless, as well as dishonest, to carve himself too much, or take more than he needed.

If man in the state of nature be so free, as has been said, if he be absolute lord of his own person or possessions, equal to the greatest, and subject to nobody, why will he part with his freedom, this empire, and subject himself to the dominion and control of any other power? To which, it is obvious to answer, that though in the state of nature he hath such a right, yet the enjoyment of it is very uncertain, and constantly exposed to the invasions of others. For all being kings as much as he, every man his equal, and the greater part no strict observers of equity and justice, the enjoyment of the property he has in this state is very unsafe, very unsecure. This makes him willing to quit this condition, which, however free, is full of fears and continual dangers; and it is not without reason that he seeks out and is willing to join in society with others, who are already united, or have a mind to unite, for the mutual preservation of their lives, liberties, and estates, which I call by the general name, property.

The great and chief end, therefore, of men's uniting into commonwealths, and putting themselves under government, is the preservation of their property; to which in the state of nature there are many things wanting.

The great end of men's entering into society being the enjoyment of their properties in peace and safety, and the great instrument and means of that being the laws established in that society: the first and fundamental positive law of all commonwealths, is the establishing of the legislative power; as the first and fundamental natural law, which is to govern even the legislative itself, is the preservation of the society, and (as far as will consist with the public good) of every person in it. This legislative is not only the supreme power of the commonwealth, but sacred and unalterable in the hands where the community have once placed it; nor can any edict of anybody else, in what form soever conceived, or by what power soever backed, have the force and obligation of a law, which has not its sanction from that legislative which the public has chosen and appointed. For without this the law could not have that, which is absolutely necessary to its being a law, the consent of the society over whom nobody can have a power to make laws; but by their own consent, and by authority received from them; and therefore all the obedience, which by the most solemn ties anyone can be obliged to pay, ultimately terminates in this supreme power, and is directed by those laws which it enacts; nor can any oaths to any foreign power whatsoever, or any domestic subordinate power discharge any member of the society from his obedience to the legislative, acting pursuant to their trust; nor oblige him to any obedience contrary to the laws so enacted, or farther than they do allow; it being ridiculous to imagine one can be tied ultimately to obey any power in the society which is not the supreme.

Though the legislative, whether placed in one or more, whether it be always in being, or only by intervals, though it be the supreme power in every commonwealth, yet,

First, It is not nor can possibly be absolutely arbitrary over the lives and fortunes of the people. For it being but the joint power of every member of the society given up to that person, or assembly, which is legislator; it can be no more than those persons had in a state of nature before they entered into society, and gave it up to the community. For nobody can transfer to another more power than he has in himself; and nobody has an absolute arbitrary power over himself, or over any other to destroy his own life, or take away the life or property of another. A man as has been proved cannot subject himself to the arbitrary power of another; and having in the state of nature no arbitrary power over the life, liberty, or possession of another, but only so much as the law of nature gave him for the preservation of himself, and the rest of mankind; this is all he doth, or can give up to the commonwealth, and by it to the legislative power, so that the legislative can have no more than this. Their power in the utmost bounds of it, is limited to the public good of society. It is a power that hath no other end but preservation, and therefore can never have a right to destroy, enslave, or designedly to impoverish the subjects. The obligations of the law of nature cease not in society, but only in many cases are drawn closer, and have by human laws known penalties annexed to them to enforce their observation. Thus the law of nature stands as an eternal rule to all men, legislators as well as others. The rules that they make for other men's actions must, as well as their own, and other men's actions, be conformable to the law of nature, i.e., to the will of God, of which that is a declaration, and the fundamental law of nature being the preservation of mankind, no human sanction can be good or valid against it.

Secondly, The legislative, or supreme authority, cannot assume to itself a power to rule by extemporary arbitrary decrees, but is bound to dispense justice, and decide the rights of the subject by promulgated standing laws, and known authorized judges. For the law of nature being unwritten, and so nowhere to be found but in the minds of men, they who through passion or interest shall miscite or misapply it, cannot so easily be convinced of their mistake where there is no established judge. And so it serves not, as it ought, to determine the rights, and fence the properties of those that live under it, especially where every one is judge, interpreter, and executioner of it too, and that in his own case; and he that has right on his side, having ordinarily but his own single strength hath not force enough to defend himself from injuries, or punish delinquents. To avoid these inconveniences, which disorder men's properties in the state of nature, men unite into societies that they many have the united strength of the whole society to secure and defend their properties, and may have standing rules to bound it, by which everyone may know what is his. To this end it is that men give up all their natural power to the society which they enter into, and the community put the legislative power into such hands as they think fit, with this trust, that they shall be governed by declared laws, or else their peace, quiet, and property, will still be at the same uncertainty as it was in the state of nature.

Absolute arbitrary power, or governing without settled standing laws, can neither of them consist with the ends of society and government, which men would not quit the freedom of the state of nature for, and tie themselves up under, were it not to preserve their lives, liberties, and fortunes; and by stated rules of right and property to secure their peace and quiet. It cannot be supposed that they should intend, had they a power so to do, to give to anyone, or more, an absolute arbitrary power over their persons and estates, and put a force into the magistrate's hand to execute his unlimited will arbitrarily upon them. This were to put themselves into a worse condition than the state of nature, wherein they had a liberty to defend their right against the injuries of others, and were upon equal terms of force to maintain it, whether invaded by a single man or many in combination. Whereas, by supposing they have given up themselves to the absolute arbitrary power and will of a legislator, they have disarmed themselves, and armed him, to make prey of them when he pleases. He being in a much worse condition that is exposed to the arbitrary power of one man who has the command of 100,000, than he that is exposed to the arbitrary power of 100,000 single men; nobody being secure that his will, who hath such a command, is better than that of other men, though his force be 100,000 times stronger. And, therefore, whatever form the commonwealth is under, the ruling power ought to govern by declared and received laws, and not by extemporary dictates and undetermined resolutions. For then mankind will be in a far worse condition than in the state of nature, if they shall have armed one, or a few men, with the joint power of a multitude to force them to obey at pleasure the exorbitant and unlimited decrees of their sudden thoughts, or unrestrained, and, till that moment, unknown wills, without having any measures set down which may guide and justify their actions. For all the power the government has, being only for the good of the society, as it ought not to be arbitrary and at pleasure, so it ought to be exercised by established and promulgated laws; that both the people may know their duty and be safe and secure within the limits of the law; and the rulers too kept within their due bounds, and not be tempted by the power they have in their hands to employ it to such purposes, and by such measures, as they would not have known, and own not willingly.

Thirdly, The supreme power cannot take from any man any part of his property without his own consent. For the preservation of property being the end of government, and that for which men enter into society, it necessarily supposes and requires that the people should have property, without which they must be supposed to lose that by entering into society, which was the end for which they entered into it, too gross an absurdity for any man to own. Men, therefore, in society having property, they have such a right to the goods which by the law of the community are theirs, that nobody hath a right to take them or any part of them from them, without their own consent; without this they have no property at all. For I have truly no property in that which another can by right take from me when he pleases, against my consent. Hence it is a mistake to think that the supreme or legislative power of any commonwealth can do what it will, and dispose of the estates of the subjects arbitrarily, or take any part of them at pleasure. This is not much to be feared in governments where the legislative consists wholly, or in part, in assemblies which are variable, whose members, upon the dissolution of the assembly, are subjects under the common laws of their country, equally with the rest. But in governments where the legislative is in one lasting assembly, always in being, or in one man, as in absolute monarchies, there is danger still, that they will think themselves to have a distinct interest from the rest of the community, and so will be apt to increase their own riches and power by taking what they think fit from the people. For a man's property is not at all secure, though there be good and equitable laws to set the bounds of it between him and his fellow subjects, if he who commands those subjects have power to take from any private man what part he pleases of his property, and use and dispose of it as he thinks good.

But government, into whosesoever hands it is put, being, as I have before shown, entrusted with this condition, and for this end, that men might have and secure their properties, the prince, or senate, however it may have power to make laws for the regulating of property between the subjects one amongst another, yet can never have a power to take to themselves the whole or any part of the subject's property without their own consent. For this would be in effect to leave them no property at all. And to let us see that even absolute power, where it is necessary, is not arbitrary by being absolute, but is still limited by that reason, and confined to those ends which required it in some cases to be absolute, we need look no farther than the common practice of martial discipline. For the preservation of the army, and in it the whole commonwealth, requires an absolute obedience to the command of every superior officer, and it is justly death to disobey or dispute the most dangerous or unreasonable of them; but yet we see that neither the sergeant, that could command a soldier to march up to the mouth of a cannon, or stand in a breach, where he is almost sure to perish, can command that soldier to give him one penny of his money; nor the general, that can condemn him to death for deserting his post, or not obeying the most desperate orders, cannot yet, with all his absolute power of life and death, dispose of one farthing of that soldier's estate, or seize one jot of his goods, whom yet he can command anything, and hang for the least disobedience. Because such a blind obedience is necessary to that end for which the commander has his power, viz., the preservation of the rest; but the disposing of his goods has nothing to do with it.

'Tis true governments cannot be supported without great charge, and it is fit everyone who enjoys a share of the protection should pay out of his estate his proportion for the maintenance of it. But still it must be with his own consent, i.e., the consent of the majority giving it either by themselves or their representatives chosen by them. For if anyone shall claim a power to lay and levy taxes on the people, by his own authority, and without such consent of the people, he thereby invades the fundamental law of property, and subverts the end of government. For what property have I in that which another may by right take when he pleases to himself?

Fourthly, The legislative cannot transfer the power of making laws to any other hands; for it being but a delegated power from the people, they who have it cannot pass it over to others. The people alone can appoint the form of the commonwealth, which is by constituting the legislative, and appointing in whose hands that shall be. And when the people have said we will submit to rules, and be governed by laws made by such men, and in such forms, nobody else can say other men shall make laws for them; nor can the people be bound by any laws but such as are enacted by those whom they have chosen and authorized to make laws for them.

These are the bounds which the trust that is put in them by the society, and the law of God and Nature, have set to the legislative power of every commonwealth, in all forms of government.

First, They are to govern by promulgated established laws, not to be varied in particular cases, but to have one rule for rich and poor, for the favorite at court and the countryman at plough.

Secondly, These laws also ought to be designed for no other end ultimately but the good of the people.

Thirdly, They must not raise taxes on the property of the people without the consent of the people, given by themselves or their deputies. And this properly concerns only such governments where the legislative is always in being, or at least where the people have not reserved any part of the legislative to deputies, to be from time to time chosen by themselves.

Fourthly, The legislative neither must nor can transfer the power of making laws to anybody else, or place it anywhere but where the people have.

2. *Representation of Property* *

EDMUND BURKE

Nothing is a due and adequate representation of a state that does not represent its ability, as well as its property. But as ability is a vigorous and active principle, and as property is sluggish, inert and timid, it never can be safe from the invasions of ability, unless it be, out of all proportion, predominant in the representation. It must be represented too in great masses of accumulation, or it is not rightly protected. The characteristic essence of property, formed out of the combined principles of its acquisition and conservation, is to be *unequal*. The great masses therefore which excite envy, and tempt rapacity, must be put out of the possibility of danger. Then they form a natural rampart about the lesser properties in all their gradations. The same quantity of property, which is by the natural course of things divided among many, has not the same operation. Its defensive power is weakened as it is diffused. In this diffusion each man's portion is less than what, in the eagerness of his desires, he may flatter himself to obtain by dissipating the accumulations of others. The plunder of the few would indeed give but a share inconceivably small in the distribution to the many. But the many are not capable of making this calculation; and those who lead them to rapine never intend this distribution.

The power of perpetuating our property in our families is one of the most

* From Edmund Burke, *Reflections on the Revolution in France* (1790).

valuable and interesting circumstances belonging to it, and that which tends the most to the perpetuation of society itself. It makes our weakness subservient to our virtue; it grafts benevolence even upon avarice. The possessors of family wealth, and of the distinction which attends hereditary possession, (as most concerned in it,) are the natural securities for this transmission. With us the House of Peers is formed upon this principle. It is wholly composed of hereditary property and hereditary distinction; and made therefore the third of the legislature; and, in the last event, the sole judge of all property in all its subdivisions. The House of Commons too, though not necessarily, yet in fact, is always so composed, in the far greater part. Let those large proprietors be what they will, and they have their chance of being among the best, they are, at the very worst, the ballast in the vessel of the commonwealth. For though hereditary wealth, and the rank which goes with it, are too much idolized by creeping sycophants, and the blind, abject admirers of power, they are too rashly slighted in shallow speculations of the petulant, assuming, short-sighted coxcombs of philosophy. Some decent, regulated pre-eminence, some preference (not exclusive appropriation), given to birth, is neither unnatural, nor unjust, nor impolitic.

It is said, that twenty-four millions ought to prevail over two hundred thousand. True; if the constitution of a kingdom be a problem of arithmetic. This sort of discourse does well enough with the lamp-post for its second: to men who *may* reason calmly, it is ridiculous. The will of the many, and their interest, must very often differ; and great will be the difference when they make an evil choice. A government of five hundred country attorneys and obscure curates is not good for twenty-four millions of men, though it were chosen by eight and forty millions; nor is it the better for being guided by a dozen of persons of quality, who have betrayed their trust in order to obtain that power. At present, you seem in everything to have strayed out of the high road of nature. The property of France does not govern it. Of course property is destroyed, and rational liberty has no existence.

When all the frauds, impostures, violences, rapines, burnings, murders, confiscations, compulsory paper currencies, and every description of tyranny and cruelty employed to bring about and to uphold this Revolution, have their natural effect, that is, to shock the moral sentiments of all virtuous and sober minds, the abettors of this philosophic system immediately strain their throats in a declamation against the old monarchical government of France. When they have rendered that deposed power sufficiently black, they then proceed in argument, as if all those who disapprove of their new abuses must of course be partisans of the old; that those who reprobate their crude and violent schemes of liberty ought to be treated as advocates for servitude. I admit that their necessities do compel them to this base and contemptible fraud. Nothing can reconcile men to their proceedings and projects but the supposition that there is no third option between them and some tyranny as odious as can be furnished by the records of history, or by the invention of poets. This prattling of theirs hardly deserves the name of sophistry. It is nothing but plain impudence. Have these gentlemen never heard, in the whole circle of the worlds of theory and practice, of anything between the despotism of the monarch and the despotism of the multitude? Have they never heard of a monarchy directed by laws, controlled and balanced by the great hereditary wealth and hereditary dignity of a nation; and both again controlled by a judicious check from the reason and feeling of the people at large, acting by a suitable and permanent organ? Is it then impossible that a man may be found who, without criminal ill intention, or pitiable absurdity, shall prefer such a mixed and tempered government to either of the extremes; and who may repute that nation to be destitute of all wisdom and of all virtue, which having in its choice to obtain such a government with ease, *or rather to confirm it when actually possessed,* thought proper to commit a thousand crimes, and to subject their country to a thousand evils, in order to avoid it? Is it then a truth so universally acknowledged, that a pure democracy is the only tolerable form into which human society can be thrown, that a man is not permitted to hesitate about its merits, without the suspicion of being a friend to tyranny, that is, of being a foe to mankind?

With the National Assembly of France, possession is nothing. I see the National Assembly openly reprobate the doctrine of prescription, which one of the greatest of their own lawyers[1] tells us, with great truth, is a part of the law of nature. He tells us that the positive ascertainment of its limits, and its security from invasion, were among the causes for which civil society itself has been instituted. If prescription be once shaken, no species of property is secure, when it once becomes an object large enough to tempt the cupidity of indigent power. I see a practice perfectly correspondent to their contempt of this great fundamental part of natural law. I see the confiscators begin with bishops, and chapters, and monasteries; but I do not see them end there. I see the princes of blood, who, by the oldest usages of that kingdom held large landed estates (hardly with the compliment of a debate), deprived of their possessions, and, in lieu of their stable, independent property, reduced to the hope of some precarious, charitable pension, at the pleasure of an assembly, which of course will pay little regard to the rights of pensioners at pleasure, when it despises those of legal proprietors. Flushed with the insolence of the first inglorious victories, and pressed by the distresses caused by the lust of unhallowed lucre, disappointed but not discouraged, they have at length ventured completely to subvert all property

[1] Domat.

of all descriptions throughout the extent of a great kingdom. They have compelled all men, in all transactions of commerce, in the disposal of lands, in civil dealing, and through the whole communion of life, to accept as perfect payment and good and lawful tender, the symbols of their speculations on a projected sale of their plunder. What vestiges of liberty or property have they left? The tenant-right of a cabbage-garden, a year's interest in a hovel, the good-will of an ale-house or a baker's shop, the very shadow of a constructive property, are more ceremoniously treated in our parliament, than with you the oldest and most valuable landed possessions, in the hands of the most respectable personages, or than the whole body of the monied and commercial interest of your country. We entertain a high opinion of the legislative authority; but we have never dreamt that parliaments had any right whatever to violate property, to over-rule prescription, or to force a currency of their own fiction in the place of that which is real, and recognized by the law of nations. But you, who began with refusing to submit to the most moderate restraints, have ended by establishing an unheard-of despotism. I find the ground upon which your confiscators go is this: that indeed their proceedings could not be supported in a court of justice; but that the rules of prescription cannot bind a legislative assembly. So that this legislative assembly of a free nation sits, not for the security, but for the destruction of property, and not of property only, but of every rule and maxim which can give it stability and of those instruments which can alone give it circulation.

In every prosperous community something more is produced than goes to the immediate support of the producer. This surplus forms the income of the landed capitalist. It will be spent by a proprietor who does not labour. But this idleness is itself the spring of labour; this repose the spur to industry. The only concern for the state is, that the capital taken in rent from the land, should be returned again to the industry from whence it came; and that its expenditure should be with the least possible detriment to the morals of those who expend it, and to those of the people to whom it is returned.

Why should the expenditure of a great landed property, which is a dispersion of the surplus product of the soil, appear intolerable to you or to me, when it takes its course through the accumulation of great libraries, which are the history of the force and weakness of the human mind; through great collections of ancient records, medals and coins, which attest and explain laws and customs; through paintings and statues that, by imitating nature, seem to extend the limits of creation; through grand monuments of the dead, which continue the regards and connexions of life beyond the grave; through collections of the specimens of nature, which become a representative assembly of all the classes and families of the world, that by disposition facilitate, and, by exciting curiosity, open the avenues to science? If, by great permanent establishments, all these objects of expense are better secured from the inconstant sport of personal caprice and personal extravagance, are they worse than if the same tastes prevailed in scattered individuals?

3. Property—The First Principle of Government*

MR. JUSTICE VAN ORSDEL

High wages do not necessarily tend to good morals, or the promotion of the general welfare. The standard of virtue and morality is no higher among the prosperous than among the poor. Their worth cannot be measured in dollars and cents, or promoted by a legal subsidy. Never have wages been so high as since the outbreak of the late war, and never in the history of the republic has crime been so universal; and this condition, it must be conceded, has made a like unfavorable impression upon the morals of the people. A wage based upon competitive ability is just, and leads to frugality and honest industry, and inspires an ambition to attain the highest possible efficiency, while the equal wage paralyzes ambition and promotes prodigality and indolence. It takes away the strongest incentive to human labor, thrift, and efficiency, and works injustice to employee and employer alike, thus affecting injuriously the whole social and industrial fabric. Experience has demonstrated that a fixed minimum wage means, in the last analysis, a fixed wage; since the employer, being compelled to advance some to a wage higher than their earning capacity, will, to equalize the cost of operation, lower the wage of the more competent to the common basis.

Any intimation that the Constitution is flexible, even in response to the police power, is unsound. Powers expressly delegated by the Constitution—such, for example, as the regulation of interstate commerce—may be extended to meet changing conditions, providing it can be accomplished without altering fundamental principles; but the principles are immutable, not elastic, or subject to change. That a state may not impair the obligations of a contract, or that no person can be deprived of his property without due process of law, are principles fundamental, and if the Legislature, in re-

* From *Children's Hospital of the District of Columbia* v. *Adkins*, 284 Fed. Rep. 613 (1922).

sponse to public clamor for an experimental social reform, may break down these constitutional guaranties by calling an act a "health law," or a "public morality law," or a "public welfare law," all guaranties of the Constitution, under the alleged exercise of the police power, may be changed, modified, or totally eliminated.

Nor is the extent of such modification a matter of judicial discretion. To hold that the courts may declare a law, violating the same principle, constitutional under one state of fact, and unconstitutional under another, is the exercise of arbitrary power—a power said to exist nowhere in our system of government. And nowhere could it be lodged with more dangerous results than in the courts.

The tendency of the times to socialize property rights under the subterfuge of police regulation is dangerous, and if continued will prove destructive of our free institutions. It should be remembered that of the three fundamental principles which underlie government, and for which government exists, the protection of life, liberty, and property, the chief of these is property; not that any amount of property is more valuable than the life or liberty of the citizen, but the history of civilization proves that, when the citizen is deprived of the free use and enjoyment of his property, anarchy and revolution follow, and life and liberty are without protection.

The highest freedom consists in obedience to law, and a strict adherence to the limitations of the Constitution. In no way can the freedom of the citizen be more effectively curtailed and ultimately destroyed than by a deprivation of those inherent rights safeguarded by our fundamental law. The security of society depends upon the extent of the protection afforded the individual citizen under the Constitution against the demands and incursions of the government. The only tyranny the citizenship of this republic need fear is from the government itself. The character and value of government is measured by the security which surrounds the individual in the use and enjoyment of his property. These rights will only remain secure so long as the Bill of Rights—the first ten amendments of the Constitution—are construed liberally in favor of the individual and strictly against the government. They were early adopted because of a widespread apprehension that the time might come when the government would assume to trespass upon those inalienable individual rights announced in the Declaration of Independence and afterwards incorporated in the Bill of Rights. Courts, therefore, should be slow to lend aid to the government in this modern tendency to invade individual property rights.

4. The Rule of Law and Regulation of Property *

WALTER LIPPMANN

I. SOCIAL CONTROL BY LAW RATHER THAN BY COMMANDS

In distinguishing between the regulation of affairs by reciprocal rights and duties on the one hand, by overhead administrative order on the other, we can, I believe, clarify what Burke called "one of the finest problems in legislation," which is "What the state ought to take upon itself to direct by the public wisdom, and what it ought to leave, with as little interference as possible, to individual discretion." [1]

This problem baffled the influential thinkers and statesmen of the nineteenth century, and their failure to elucidate it successfully caused that popular bewilderment in which men came to think that they must make an exclusive choice between the anarchy of unrestrained property owners and the management of property by public officials. They thought they had to decide between doing nothing and administering almost everything. Those who wished to let things alone called themselves individualists and said they believed in liberty. Those who wished to direct the course of affairs became collectivists and appealed to the desire for security, order, and equality.

The choice is not, I think, exclusive, and it has been posed only because of faulty observation and an insufficient analysis. There is no exclusive choice between direction by the state and noninterference with individual behavior, between state collectivism and laissez-faire as understood by the latter-day liberals. This supposed choice ignores the whole immense field occupied by the development of private rights and duties, and, therefore, it is not true that individuals must be left to do what they like or be told by officials what they must do. There is another way, the way of the common law, in which abuses are regulated and public policy is made effective by altering the private rights that are enforceable in the courts.

This becomes self-evident when we remember what the laissez-faire theorists forgot: that the individualism they are talking about exists by virtue of lawful rights that are enforced by the state.[2] The title to property is a

---

* From Walter Lippmann, *The Good Society* (1937). By permission of Little, Brown & Company and The Atlantic Monthly Press.

[1] "Thoughts and Details on Scarcity," *Works*, Vol. V, p. 107.

[2] Cf. Ernest Barker's Translator's Introduction to Gierke's *Natural Law and the Theory of Society*, LXX.

construction of the law. Contracts are legal instruments. Corporations are legal creatures. It is, therefore, misleading to think of them as existing somehow outside the law and then to ask whether it is permissible to "interfere" with them. Thus the English law governing the inheritance of real property produced a different distribution of property from that produced by the French law. For in England the oldest son had different legal rights from those he had in France. Property of any kind, contracts of any kind, corporate organization of any kind, exist only because there are certain rights and immunities which can be enforced, when they have been legally established, by enlisting the coercive authority of the state. To speak of letting things alone is, therefore, to use a meaningless and a deceptive phrase. No one who asks to be let alone really wishes to be let completely alone: what he asks is that he be enabled to enjoy the undisputed exercise of the rights which he enjoys. But he expects the state to interfere promptly and effectively if anyone disturbs him. He insists that his rights shall be enforced.

For some curious reason, the debate between individualists and collectivists has been carried on with both factions assuming that the *existing* system of private rights must either be left undisturbed or that it must be abolished; that existing rights must be maintained absolutely or extinguished absolutely; that either "property" must be what it happened to be when they were quarreling about it or the means of production must be administered by officials of the state. The dilemma is unreal and unnecessary. The system of private land tenure which happens to prevail at one moment in some country is not the only possible system of land tenure. The only possible alternative is not the nationalization of the land. The alternative may be any one of innumerable other systems of private land tenure. The only possible alternative to the existing system of private contract in industrial relations is not the replacement of private contracts by public administration. There are many alternatives, many possible ways of changing the kinds of private contracts that the law will require the courts to enforce. The only alternative to the concentrated corporate control of industry is not a concentrated government control of business corporations. It may be any one of many possible modifications of the law of corporate rights.

But in the nineteenth century individualists and collectivists alike persuaded themselves that the existing system of private rights could not be modified: that it had either to be maintained or to be superseded. Thus they created for themselves the fatal dilemma which has divided mankind into those who merely wish to preserve the status quo with all its abuses and those who wish to make a new social order by the authoritarian power of the state. Collectivists and individualists had lost sight of one of the most obvious facts in human experience, that great and salutary changes in human relations can be and usually have been effected not by commands from on high but by amending the laws under which men deal with one another.

Any student of history could have told them that laws have changed radically in the course of history. Yet it was somehow assumed that laws were absolute, and therefore incapable of serious modification. So the debate has proceeded on the assumption that the choice lies between stubborn conservatism and complete revolution, that the rights of property as they stood in the nineteenth century have either to be confirmed and protected or that property owners have to be expropriated and their possessions administered by the state. The latter-day liberals, having committed themselves to the fallacy that existing rights are absolute, have been inhibited by their own fallacy from working out any programme to relieve the evils of modern society. The collectivists, believing in the same fallacy, merely drew an opposite conclusion. They turned to the state as deus ex machina, believing that the relief which could not be obtained by a readjustment of personal rights could be obtained by authoritative commands.

The essential intellectual difficulty may be seen in Burke's statement of the problem. He assumes that the state must either "direct" or must not "interfere." But suppose I invent a new mousetrap and suppose the law says that no one may use my invention during my lifetime without paying me the royalty I choose to charge. Is this *direction* or is it *interference?* Now suppose the state amends the law, saying that I have an exclusive patent for five years only: after that anyone may copy my mousetrap without being liable to a suit for damages. That amendment of the law will radically alter the mousetrap situation. But is this act of social control to be called *direction* or is it to be called *non-interference?* From my point of view I suppose I have been interfered with. But my neighbors might say that they have been released from an undue interference on my part with their right to catch mice more successfully; that I was levying an unjust toll for an invention that was probably suggested to me, in part at least, by someone else's invention.

Is it not clear that the terms of the discussion do not really fit the facts, and that the debate could go on forever? A change in the law governing my right to patent the invention does not fit into either of Burke's categories. Yet the change in the law causes a real change in the situation. Though the state has not undertaken to direct the invention or to administer the manufacture of mousetraps, it is not letting me "alone" without social control. The change is brought by a readjustment of the rights of my neighbors and of myself. Impressive social changes may have been effected—the public health improved, a new industry brought into being, I prevented from becoming a millionaire, my neighbors relieved of a bitter grievance, good feeling promoted. But these things have been done without appointing new officials empowered to issue commands to anyone.

There are not, then, as Burke and so many after him assumed, only two realms, one in which there is no regulation of men's behavior, another in which men must obey the commands of their superiors. To state the problem in this fashion is to overlook the realm of private rights and duties where significant relations are regulated by general laws impartially applied to specific controversies, not by commands issued by some men to other men. Except where a few solitary individuals subsist in a wilderness, the actual choice is between the regulation of social affairs by adjudicating and adjusting private rights on the one hand, by arbitrary sovereign commands on the other. The one is the method of a common law; the other the method of the prerogatives of superior persons. The one is the system of democratic liberalism, the other of authoritarian collectivism.

In the light of this distinction much unnecessary confusion is dissipated. We shall not, for example, fall into the error of regarding the existing law of property, of contracts, of corporations, as marking a realm in which the state does not or should not intervene. We shall recognize it for what it is, as a structure of rights and duties, immunities and privileges, built by custom, judicial interpretation, and statute, and maintained by the coercive authority of the state. We shall not think of all this as subsisting somehow outside the law, and then become involved in an empty debate as to whether the law may interfere with it. The whole of it, all property, and everything which we include in the general name of private enterprise, is the product of a legal development and can exist only by virtue of the law. This is evident enough in periods of social disorder when for want of law observance and law enforcement the whole private economy may collapse in a day.

We shall not compound the error by thinking that the law of property contracts and corporations is immutable.

II. THE REGULATION OF PROPERTY

It was, as we have already seen, at this point that nineteenth-century liberalism came to a dead end: where it chose to treat property and the powers of the business corporation as in effect absolute and untouchable. Then it was that liberal statesmen, being unable to regulate property and corporations effectively, had to give way to the collectivists.

The latter-day liberals had a vague notion that they must regard private property as approximating, to use Blackstone's words, "that sole and despotic dominion which one man claims and exercises over the external things of the world, in total exclusion of the right of any other individual in the universe." [1]

But no such sole and despotic dominion exists or can be established, and it was a signal disservice to the maintenance of free enterprise when men attempted to claim and to exercise such a sole and despotic dominion. For the rights of property have no existence outside the law: they are simply the rights which courts of law will recognize. No man can hold or enjoy

[1] Blackstone, *Commentaries,* Bk. II, Ch. I.

property openly and securely except by virtue of the readiness of the state to enforce his lawful right. Without a lawful title, he has no property; he is merely a possessor without recourse against those who are strong enough to help themselves to his goods.

Not only is all property a right established by law and enforceable at law: all property is a complex system of rights. This system is not the same system in respect to all kinds of things. It is not the same system at all times in respect to the same things. It is not the same system in all places at the same time in respect to the same things. In other words there is no such thing as an absolute, immutable, and indefeasible system of property rights.

Thus the system of private property is not uniform for urban land and for land at the frontier. The title to urban land may, for example, be subject to zoning ordinances which completely nullify any pretension that the owner exercises a sole and despotic dominion, "in total exclusion of the right of any other individual." If, in defiance of the zoning ordinance, he attempts to establish a garage, his neighbors have rights which they can enforce. The landowner has no absolute rights in his property; he has only conditional rights which vary from place to place. He cannot put up a jerry-built structure on Broadway, but he can, if he likes, go out into the open country and build himself a house of wood and paper held together by safety pins. Moreover, he holds his property on Broadway subject not only to the existing building laws but to future changes in those laws. And the same is true of his house in the country: if, for example, it were judged to be a fire hazard, his neighbors by a change in the law might be invested with the right to protect themselves by bringing suit or entering a complaint.

The same property rights do not adhere to land which contains minerals, to land which controls water power, to land usable for bridgeheads, ferry landings, and highways, for railway tracks and conduits in city streets. The rights of property are not uniform in patents, in animals, in news gathered by reporters, in radio channels, in the air traversed by flying machines, in gold, silver, and platinum, in an author's manuscript, in all inheritances and in all gifts. Though we think of all these rights as property, in fact property consists of an extremely varied collection of rights.

What is more, the special rights which make up different kinds of property are not immutable. Before the appearance of the airplane the owner of a piece of land was held to have a title to a pyramid which had its apex at the centre of the earth and an infinitely wide base out in infinite space. Under a recent decision in an American court, his rights in the air extend no higher up than a safe distance above the roof of his house. The conditions on which the title to land can be enjoyed, acquired by sale, transmitted by gift or inheritance, have been profoundly modified again and again. Less than three hundred years ago, for example, the obligation of the English tenant to render personal services to the lord of the manor was commuted to the payment of a pecuniary rent. The right of the landlord to appropriate the monopoly rent of the land is by no means absolute, being subject to the power both of eminent domain and of taxation.

If we ask ourselves whether in this bewildering complex of rights which men call property there is any clarifying principle of order, we must, it seems to me, take as our premise the principle enunciated by Sir William Blackstone that "the earth . . . and all things therein are the general property of all mankind, exclusive of other beings, from the immediate gift of the Creator." [1] This does not mean that the earth and all things therein should be administered by a central collectivist authority or that individuals should not or cannot be made secure in the enjoyment of private rights. But it does mean that no individual can or should exercise a sole and despotic dominion over any portion of the earth or of the things therein. The earth is limited in size and its use is necessary to every man's existence. Therefore, the rights of any man upon the earth must be reconciled with the equal rights of other men, not only of living men but of the unborn generations. No one in his senses can therefore believe in an absolute right of property which would permit the transient possessors of the land to destroy its fertility, to burn down forests, to cause the streams to dry up, to squander at will the minerals under the surface. These owners did not make these resources. They are unable to re-create them. What title have they then to claim that posterity has no rights which they must respect? The true doctrine surely is that men hold property in limited and necessary natural resources, not as sovereigns, but as tenants—who have rights and also duties—of mankind.

And likewise, no one believes in an absolute right of property which gives such exclusive possession that property owners can so monopolize the land and the resources that other men can live only by paying the price they choose to exact. Men may pretend to believe in such a theory of property. In practice it is unworkable. The dispossessed and the disinherited will haunt them and terrorize them. The desperate insecurity of all private property in the modern world is due to the fact that the propertied classes, in resisting a modification of their rights, have aroused the revolutionary impulse to abolish all their rights. Modern bolshevism is the product of the attempt to make property an absolute right.

The real security of private property must rest not on a fatuous longing for a sole and despotic dominion over the necessities of all men's existence but on a reconciliation of all men's claims in a system of substantially equal rights. It is not loyalty to the cause of private property to confirm the monopolists in their privileges. To do that is to prepare the extinction of private property either by general disorder and pillage or by the establishment of an administered collectivism. The true principle is to be ready to liquidate these rights of possession which enable some men, by excluding

[1] *Op. cit.,* Bk. II, Ch. I.

all other men from access to land and to the resources of nature, to exact a tribute based not on their own labor but on mere legal possession.

If all property is a complex of legal rights, the business corporation, with its privilege of limited liability and perpetual succession, is even more obviously a legal creation. It is no exaggeration to say that without the corporate device modern capitalism could not have been evolved. Now an aggregation of individuals can, when they are incorporated, do things which they could not possibly do as separate individuals nor as an informal association of individuals. They can do these things only because of legal rights acquired in their charter. But for that charter they would have separate and unlimited liability for the acts done by their association; when one of them died or resigned, the association would have been dissolved, like a marriage or a partnership.

It is plain that a corporation enjoys great advantages as against unincorporated individuals. It can assemble the property of great masses of individuals, administer it collectively, and, though its directors or managers fall sick or die, the corporate organization goes on. Now all of these advantages are created and maintained by the law which says that under certain conditions individuals have the right to incorporate and as a corporation to enjoy certain privileges and immunities. How can such rights be regarded as inalienable and immutable? Is it not evident that in granting the privilege of incorporation the state may fix the conditions, that it may say what the rights of an incorporated body are, that it may say that the privilege of limited liability and perpetual succession shall be enjoyed only in so far as the corporation meets certain specific obligations?

Yet for reasons which it is not necessary for us to examine here, the ability to incorporate came to be regarded in the nineteenth century not as a privilege granted by law but as some sort of unquestioned right. The founders of the American Republic had no such notion and the liberals of the eighteenth century would have regarded it as preposterous.

A charter of incorporation to use property for profit is a state-created privilege, particularly when it grants to its members the partial immunity of limited liability. There is, therefore, no reason why that charter should be vague and general: it can be made as specific in its definition of what rights the corporation may exercise and what duties it must perform as the lawmakers choose to make it. In the charter and in the statutes governing corporations they can stipulate any public policy they deem desirable. They can stipulate that the members of the corporation shall not enjoy limited liability or perpetual succession if the courts find that they have violated the terms of the charter. The lawmakers can stipulate the grounds on which competitors, customers, employees, creditors, and debtors may sue for violations of the charter and the law. Moreover, the lawmakers may stipulate, if they deem it wise, how much land a corporation may own and no title in excess of that amount would be a good title. They may stipulate as to whether one corporation may own another, for how long and on what terms it may own patents, in what measure it may own natural resources, whether it shall be capitalized through the issue of bonds or equity shares, what shall be the rights of its security holders. They may stipulate the manner in which the accounts shall be kept, and what information must be made public and how often.

Thus, without overhead direction, a very comprehensive regulation of corporate activity is feasible. It can be achieved by defining in the law the respective rights of a corporation and of those with whom it transacts business. Yet such a system of regulation does not invest public officials with the authority to administer the affairs of the corporation or to issue commands and prohibitions to the corporate managers. It does not increase the power of officials over the life and labor of citizens. It merely readjusts, theoretically in any degree and in any manner, the rights of citizens with one another, and then relies upon individuals to put the law in motion when they believe they can prove in court that their rights have been violated.

But though, theoretically, the lawmakers could set any conditions they chose upon the right to incorporate, in fact they could not legislate capriciously. For as they approached the point where they were converting the privileges of incorporation into a risk and a burden, men would simply turn in their corporate charters and revert to some form of partnership. At that point the social advantages of the corporation would be lost, and the excessive rights against corporations granted to customers, employees, investors, or competitors, would have defeated their own purposes. Thus the system would have to be reasonable in order to be effective. It would have to represent a wise reconciliation of collaborating and competing interests. But that is one of the paramount virtues of the liberal method of regulating human affairs through the adjustment of private rights: that it is compelled to work, not by the compulsion of irresistible authority from on high but by conciliation, justice, and comity among persons.

It has been a great illusion to think of the modern business corporation as a kind of autonomous principality with inherent power derived from some mysterious source that is independent of the state. The power of the business corporation is entirely a power granted by the state, dependent from day to day upon the continued enforcement of the law by the state which has invested it with its privileges and immunities. It cannot be true, as so many lawyers have argued, that corporate rights are inalienable and immutable and indefeasible. Previous to about 1850 a special act of the legislature was needed in order to charter a corporation. Fifty years ago no common-law lawyer would have thought it conceivable that one corporation could own the stock of another. The business corporation, as we know it, is founded on the fact that legislatures and courts gradually invested incorporated associations with new rights, rights which did not exist a hundred years ago, rights which can, therefore, by no stretch of the imagination be regarded as anything but conditional and subject to alteration.

By the same token it is no less untrue that modern corporate capitalism is a predestined development due to some mysterious necessity of the machine process, or to some inexorable tendency to the agglomeration of wealth and power. The promoters of the giant corporation were not giants to whom ordinary men had to yield. They were ordinarily enterprising men who made the most of legal privileges with which legislatures and courts had inadvertently endowed them. The essential elements out of which the giant corporations were assembled were titles to land and natural resources and patents, limited liability for debts and damages, perpetual succession, their chartered right to set up an internal government of the corporate organization.

Any or all of these elements could have been and can at any time be redefined and subjected to new conditions. In short, their existing rights are not absolute. The development of private corporate collectivism is in no sense inevitable. The potentialities of regulation are as numerous and varied as the points at which the corporation has relations—with its customers, its employees, its competitors, its providers of raw materials and transportation, its stockholders and bondholders, its neighbors in the places where it operates, and the tax collector. The field of the business corporation is not an immunized area which is sterile to the possibility of reform and regulation. The business corporation can be reformed and regulated by a readjustment of private rights, and there is no reason whatever for the assumption, made both by individualists and by collectivists, that corporations must either be allowed to enjoy all their present rights or be taken over and administered by the state.

~~~~~~

5. The Fifth Freedom *

HERBERT HOOVER

~~~~~~

The President of the United States on January 6, 1941, stated that we seek "everywhere in the world" the four old freedoms: freedom of speech and expression, freedom of religion, freedom from fear, freedom from want.

* The Rotarian (April, 1943). Reprinted in Herbert Hoover, Addresses upon the American Road: World War II, 1941–1945 (D. Van Nostrand Company, 1946). By permission.

Soon thereafter I called attention to the fact that there is a Fifth Freedom —economic freedom—without which none of the other four freedoms will be realized.

I have stated many times over the years that to be free, men must choose their jobs and callings, bargain for their own wages and salaries, save and provide by private property for their families and old age. And they must be free to engage in enterprise so long as each does not injure his fellow-men. And that requires laws to prevent abuse. And when I use the term "Fifth Freedom," I use it in this sense only, not in the sense of laissez faire or economic exploitation. Exploitation is the negation of freedom. The Fifth Freedom does not mean going back to abuses.

Laws to prevent men doing economic injury to their fellows were universal in civilized countries long before the First World War. In the United States, for example, the State and Federal Governments had established regulation of banks, railroads, utilities, coinage; prevention of combinations to restrain trade; government support to credit in times of stress; public works; tariffs; limitations on hours of labor and in other directions.

The key of such government action to economic freedom is that government must not destroy but promote freedom. When Governments exert regulation of economic life, they must do so by definite statutory rules of conduct imposed by legislative bodies that all men may read as they run and in which they may have at all times the protection of the courts. No final judicial or legislative authority must be delegated to bureaucrats, or at once tyranny begins.

When Government violates these principles, it sooner or later weakens constitutional safeguards of personal liberty and representative government.

When Government goes into business in competition with citizens, bureaucracy always relies upon tyranny to win. And bureaucracy never develops that competence in management which comes from the mills of competition. Its conduct of business inevitably lowers the living standards of the people. Nor does bureaucracy ever discover or invent. A Millikan, Ford, or Edison never came from a bureaucracy.

And inherent in bureaucracy is the grasping spirit of more and more power. It always resents criticism and sooner or later begins directly or indirectly to limit free speech and free press. Intellectual and spiritual freedom will not long survive the passing of economic freedom. One of the illusions of our time is that we can have totalitarian economics and the personal freedoms. Ten nations on the Continent of Europe tried it and wound up with dictators and no liberty.

The first trench in the battle for the five freedoms is to maintain them in America. That rests upon fidelity not only to the letter, but to the spirit of constitutional government. Failure of Congress to assert its responsibilities or for the Executive to take steps beyond the authority of Congress is a direct destruction of the safeguards of freedom. We badly need a complete overhaul of our governmental relations to the Fifth Freedom if it is to be preserved.

The Fifth Freedom in no way inhibits social reforms and social advancement. In fact, it furnishes the increasing resources upon which such progress can be built. And itself flourishes upon the advancing social aspirations of our people. Social advancement was part of the whole American concept during the whole of our national life. The greatest of all social advances was free education. Next came concern for public health. We have always held it an obligation to prevent suffering from misfortune, to care for widows, orphans, and old age, and those upon whom disaster falls.

The methods have gradually improved from the ancient work-house, the asylum, and the county hospital to more systematic and more inclusive action. And that more inclusive action has only been possible with the growing wealth born from the Fifth Freedom. For many years in the United States our States and the nation have been gradually developing protection to children, to women, limitation of hours, and safeguards of health in industry. From these 48 laboratories we have seen the development of such actions as public health control, hospitalization, care of children, workmen's compensation, unemployment and health insurance, old-age, widows', and orphans' pensions. They are not new ideas. As we expand in these purposes, there are safeguards to liberty that can and must be preserved.

One of these safeguards is where personal insurance for any purpose is given by the Government it must be contributory. Even where subsidized by the Federal Government it should be administered by the States to limit the growth of centralized bureaucracy and political action.

Liberty has its greatest protection from local not centralized government.

Another concept in all social insurance or pensions must be that the responsibility of the people as a whole is to provide only a reasonable subsistence basis. Beyond that the citizen must look after himself if initiative and self-respect are to be maintained. Today our measures in these matters badly need vigorous overhauling to make them comport with these fundamental principles; to put them upon a "pay-as-you-go" basis; to make them inclusive of everybody; and to make them synchronize and not destroy private institutions and efforts.

A system devoted to development of individuality and personal freedom is a complicated business. It can destroy its own purposes by foolish action.

Today we are faced with the relation of personal liberty to total war. Our people must be mobilized for that immediate purpose.

We must sacrifice much economic freedom to win the war. That is economic Fascism, for Fascist economics were born of just these measures in the last war. But there are two vast differences in the application of this sort of economic system at the hands of democracies or at the hands of dictators.

First, in democracies we strive to keep free speech, free press, free worship, trial by jury, and the other personal liberties alive. And, second, we want so to design our actions that these Fascist economic measures are not frozen into life, but shall thaw out after the war.

Even the temporary suspension of economic liberty creates grave dangers because liberty rapidly atrophies from disuse. Vested interests and vested habits grow around its restrictions. It would be a vain thing to fight the war and lose our own liberties. If we would have them return, we must hold furiously to the ideals of economic liberty. We must challenge every departure from them. There are just two tests: "Is this departure necessary to win the war?" "How are we going to restore these freedoms after the war?"

We have no right to complain of necessary sacrifices. Our soldiers and sailors are deprived of all their freedoms except the right to grouse a little. But they will expect their freedoms back when they come home.

Under the stress of reconstruction after the war, our liberties will be slow in coming back, but the essential thing in this sort of question is the direction in which we travel. We must establish the direction now.

Chapter X

REVOLUTIONARY MARXISM

THE struggle between capitalism and socialism is a family affair. Elements of the socialist faith—"one world," peace, equality, social and economic justice—are as old as civilized life. But, as an effective political movement, socialism is inseparable from the Industrial Revolution and the problems it created. Without modern industry and an urban working class, there can be no socialist mass organizations. The Industrial Revolution separated man from the ownership of the tools of production: first, the self-employing artisan was replaced by the capitalist employer, who owned the machines employing hundreds and thousands of workers owning nothing but their hands. Second, as modern technology progressed, the proportion of those who owned the instruments of production shrank enormously, thus widening the gap between those who owned the tools and those who worked them. Third, as modern industry developed, the incidence of capital investments in the total process of production rose steadily: greater initial amounts of capital were needed to start out in business and manufacture. The basic capital requirement to manufacture buggies and supply horses is less than to manufacture automobiles and locomotives. Fourth, concentration of capital was accompanied by concentration of control, so that fewer and fewer persons controlled bigger and bigger aggregates of wealth, although ownership—as distinct from control—spread through the corporate form of business organization.

Where small property has survived as an efficient economic unit, as in agriculture, the socialist idea has made little headway. And where there has been little industrialization, as in Tsarist Russia, China, or Latin America, socialism has aimed not so much at nationalizing the means of production (there would not be much to nationalize, in the first place), as at the building of a modern industrial economy on the basis of public ownership. Because initial capital requirements are heavy, especially in durable goods and basic industries, the state has often been forced to operate new industries on the basis of public ownership, even where it officially persecuted the socialist movement.

Modern socialism has appeared in two main forms: revolutionary, Marxist communism aims at the overthrow of capitalism through revolutionary

363

means, and believes in the necessity of setting up a dictatorship of the proletariat (through the agency of the Communist party) until the remnants of the capitalist ideology and habits of thought are liquidated. Evolutionary, democratic socialism, on the other hand, adheres to the method of constitutional procedure all throughout: it seeks power through ballots rather than bullets; and, once in power, it maintains democratic methods of government, and subjects itself to periodic tests of approval or disapproval by the electorate.

Revolutionary Marxism visualizes the transition from capitalism to socialism as sudden and complete; there is no payment of compensation for expropriated property, because capitalist property is, morally and socially, little better than theft derived from exploitation. By contrast, democratic socialism is slow and piecemeal, evolves (like other transactions of advanced capitalism) on the installment plan, and has to prove its right to hold power by gaining, and keeping, the consent of the majority. In democracies, governments chosen by the majority of the electorate must follow the first law of democratic politics: not to exhaust all possibilities of victory, and not to outrage the defeated minority party to the point of humiliation and revolt. In a dictatorship, opponents are liquidated. In a democracy, opponents must be won over. Democratic socialism can ill afford to follow dogmas for their sake, and must prove pragmatically, through actual accomplishments, its moral right to apply the principle of public ownership to those industries which stand to gain from socialization. As to compensation, democratic socialism does not believe that legitimate expectations of citizens may be violated, and persists in the belief that expropriation of private property is permissible only after due process and proper compensation. It "just isn't done" to take away property by legislative fiat, democratic socialists believe. If the whole economic system be compared to a basket of eggs, Marxist communism burns the basket and scrambles all eggs at once—never to be unscrambled again. Democratic socialism keeps the basket, and cooks only small orders of scrambled eggs at one time, because it believes in the Aristotelian observation that "the guest will judge better of a feast than the cook."

It can thus be seen that revolutionary Marxist communism and democratic socialism have one objective in common: the transfer to public ownership of the means of production. But the journey they propose for their respective goals differs as much as any two political methods can differ. To the democratic socialist the freedom of the individual is so all-important that he puts it above everything else, including the socialization of the economy. He is a patient fellow who knows that he may have to wait a long time indeed, until he can peacefully persuade his fellow citizens that capitalism is inefficient and unjust, and that his proposals are practical and equitable. The communist tells him that it is useless to try the conquest of power by persuasion, because all mediums of communication, education, and propaganda are biased in favor of the capitalist *status quo,* and that freedom of the press means little if one desires to start a metropolitan newspaper, but lacks the four or five million dollars with which to begin. The democratic socialist can only retort that, like other believers in democracy, he has the faith that a reasonable case, reasonably presented, will eventually win the hearts of the people. This faith of the democratic socialist may often be overly optimistic, but so is the faith of all democrats.

The choice between Marxist revolutionary communism and democratic evolutionary socialism is, like other vital choices, not a matter of pure logic. Facts of history limit the range of discretion in social action. Where political democracy has fragile roots, the communist solution of the economic problem will seem the more natural. This is why the transition from monarchical autocracy to communism has been successful in Russia, or Yugoslavia, or Bulgaria. Where, however, the political tradition of democracy has been deeply embedded in the structure of national life, as in England, Scandinavia, New Zealand, and Australia, democratic socialism seems the more natural solution of fundamental economic ills. Conversely, Sidney Webb and Attlee would be as out of place in Russia or Outer Mongolia, as Lenin and Stalin would be in Westminster.

The greatest single influence in the development of revolutionary socialism has been Karl Marx. The background of Prussian politics of the first half of the nineteenth century, with political prisons and exiles as the normal facts of life, was hardly the best schooling in the practice of democracy. In one sense the political theory of Karl Marx is inverted Prussianism: before the revolution, the Junkers and capitalists sit on top, and rule with an iron hand over the masses of the people. Come the revolution, and the roles are reversed: the people control the state, through customary dictatorial methods, and the erstwhile oppressors and exploiters are put into their place. This may explain why Marxism has been so popular in Russia and Germany, and why it has been so weak where government by consent makes it difficult for individuals and groups to hate each other to the point of mutual liquidation. Where communist movements have grown in countries with strong democratic traditions, as in France and Czechoslovakia, they have been forced to abandon their revolutionary methods and adapt themselves to some of the prevailing democratic procedures.

Marx's analysis of the capitalist system has influenced the *making* of history even more than the writing of history. Regardless of what one accepts, or rejects, in the monumental work of Marx, of his social, economic, political, and philosophical ideas, it is virtually impossible simply to by-pass him. He said of himself that he was not a "Marxist," and those who insist on all or nothing in relation to his ideas betray Marx the man, as well as Marx the social scientist. He believed that, as he put it in one of his earliest writings

(*Theses on Feuerbach,* 1845), "in practice man must prove the truth," which would exclude the easier method of turning to the truth as revealed by the Authority, whether Karl Marx or any other god or prophet. The *Theses on Feuerbach* were written by Marx when he was only twenty-seven, and his whole conception of the task of philosophy is indicated by his charge that "the philosophers have only *interpreted* the world; the point however is to *change* it." This is distinctly un-Hegelian, and contrary to what respectable philosophers have been doing all along.

Marx's philosophy of history and politics has to be gathered from many incidental remarks and comments in his writings and letters. One of the few places, in which he has given a summary statement of the *economic interpretation of history,* is in the preface to *The Critique of Political Economy* (1859). This brief document contains virtually all the important ideas of Marx's analysis of historical change and of the relative significance of the various social forces and institutions: "that the anatomy of civil society is to be found in political economy." Contrary to pre-Marxian social analysis, which emphasized law and politics as the determining factors in society, Marx reverses the scale of importance, and considers the "productive relationship" of society as the basis, whereas legal relations and forms of government are the "superstructure." Marx puts it in this way: "The mode of production of the material means of existence conditions the whole process of social, political and intellectual life." One of his most famous formulations is that *men's social existence determines their consciousness,* and not, as had been generally accepted without challenge before Marx, that the "consciousness of men determines their existence." What Marx stresses here is that man's ideas are not completely accidental and haphazard, or freely left to his choice. Thus, the legal, political, religious, and cultural ideologies and institutions of a pastoral type of civilization will fundamentally differ from those of the feudal society, and both will have little in common with the social, political, legal, religious, and intellectual outlook and organization of the modern industrial society.

Turning to the question of what causes historical change, Marx abandons the study of monarchs and their relations with court ladies and fellow dynasts, and is also dissatisfied with the approach to history through a long list of battles and wars. Instead, he tries to locate the deeper cause of real social change in factors that go beyond the powers of rulers and victorious war leaders: "At a certain stage of their development the material productive forces of society come into contradiction with the existing productive relationships, or, what is but a legal expression for these, with the property relationships within which they have moved before. From forms of development of the productive forces these relationships are transformed into their fetters. Then an epoch of social revolution opens. With the change in the economic foundation the whole vast superstructure is more or less rapidly transformed." Thus, when new productive *forces* developed within the productive *relationships* of the feudal system, social revolution was, according to Marx, inevitable. What has doomed all historically known economic systems is the fact that when new productive forces develop, the existing productive relationship stands in the way of their proper utilization. Each system thus becomes eventually wasteful in terms of the potentialities which have developed in its womb, but which are not permitted to be born and grow.

The capitalist system, too, shows the same tendency, according to Marx, when the productive forces (the capacity to produce) have outstripped the productive relationships (law of property, production for private profit). The capitalist system as a system of social, economic and legal relations thus has come to stand in the way of the technological *forces* that are not permitted to be fully utilized. Only socialism will, according to Marx, bring about a new system of productive relationships (public ownership of the means of production, production for common use rather than private profit) that will match the tremendous forces of production already potentially existent and known to man. Marx predicted the failure of the capitalist system to use all available productive forces at a time when capitalism grew by leaps and bounds, and when populations increased in all industrial nations. Yet the experience of the last generation has shown that only in time of war capitalist societies produce to the full extent of their capacity. In "normal" times, millions of men are forced to be without work, and machinery rusts in idleness.

In *The Communist Manifesto*, Marx and his collaborator Friedrich Engels explain how social change through revolution actually occurs. When the forces of production begin to outstrip the methods of production (or productive relationships), the owners of the means of production do not step aside, so as to accelerate the inevitable course of history. Bound by the limitations of their ideology (which, in turn, expresses the existing modes of production), they sincerely believe that the existing system is economically the most efficient, socially the most equitable, and generally in harmony with the laws of nature and the will of whatever god they venerate. It is not a question of the greed of the individual feudal landowner (who stands in the way of the more productive capitalist system), or of the selfishness of the individual capitalist (who obstructs the coming of a socialist system of production). In each case the owners of the means of production will utilize all the instruments of the legal, political, and ideological superstructure to block the growth of those forces which represent the potentially more progressive economic system. This is why Marx and Engels state early in *The Communist Manifesto,* "The history of all hitherto existing society is the history of class struggles." In the nineteenth century, the bourgeoisie liked to think of itself as extremely law-abiding and respectable—once it had won its class struggle. Yet Marx and Engels remind it that, historically, it "has played a most revolutionary part."

The end of capitalism will be brought about, not by "subversive" conspiracies and astute political leaders, but by the same inexorable social laws that destroyed previous systems. Just as feudalism, e.g., prepared its own grave by developing those forces—the urban bourgeoisie—which eventually destroyed it, capitalism does the same thing: "The essential condition for the existence and for the sway of the bourgeois class is the formation and augmentation of capital; the condition for capital is wage-labor. Wage-labor rests exclusively on competition between the laborers. The advance of industry, whose involuntary promoter is the bourgeoisie, replaces the isolation of the laborers, due to competition, by their revolutionary combinations, due to association. The development of modern industry, therefore, cuts from under its feet the very foundation on which the bourgeoisie produces and appropriates products. What the bourgeoisie therefore produces, above all, are its own grave-diggers. Its fall and the victory of the proletariat are equally inevitable." And, as Marx and Engels look at history, they can find no instance where a major social and economic system has freely abdicated to its successor. Therefore, the Communists "openly declare that their ends can be attained only by the forcible overthrow of all existing social conditions." This is one of the crucial tenets of revolutionary Marxist communism.

After the death of Marx (1883), Engels carried on the heritage of his greater partner. In a letter to the German socialist writer Joseph Bloch (dated September 21, 1890), Engels restated the problem of the relations between the economic and noneconomic forces in history. Engels candidly admits that "Marx and I are ourselves partly to blame for the fact that younger writers sometimes lay more stress on the economic side than is due to it." Engels tries to strengthen the weight that has to be given to political, historical, and cultural factors, and in particular stresses the point that the economic (or "materialist") conception of history holds the economic factor to be *ultimately* the decisive one, but does not consider it to be the *only* determining element.

Lenin's *State and Revolution* (1917) was written in the late summer of 1917; Lenin was in hiding near the Finnish border part of the time, as the Kerensky government had issued an order for his arrest. The book consists of six chapters; as Lenin explains in a postscript (dated December 13, 1917), he planned to add a seventh chapter on the Russian revolutions of 1905 and 1917, but he was "interrupted" by the November revolution of 1917, and, as he puts it: "It is more pleasant and useful to go through the 'experience of revolution' than to write about it." In the literature of Marxism, *The State and Revolution* is of immense importance. Where Marx and Engels (in perhaps typically nineteenth-century liberal fashion) neglected the factor of *political power,* Lenin, the master strategist of one of the half dozen great revolutions in history, was keenly interested in the anatomy of the state. Lenin fully accepts the Marxist thesis that the transitional state between capitalism and the socialist society "can be only the revolutionary dictatorship of the proletariat." Lenin denies that capitalism and democracy are compatible at all, and affirms that under capitalism democracy always remains "a democracy for the minority, only for the possessing classes, only for the rich." Lenin then describes the techniques that the capitalist state employs, in order to maintain itself in power. In the words of *The Communist Manifesto,* the "executive of the modern State is but a committee for managing the common affairs of the whole bourgeoisie." Behind the formalities of capitalist political democracy, Lenin sees, in effect, the dictatorship of the bourgeoisie. He also denies that the transition from capitalism to socialism can be accomplished simply, smoothly, and directly, "as the liberal professors and petty-bourgeois opportunists would have us believe. No, development— toward communism—proceeds through the dictatorship of the proletariat; it cannot be otherwise, for the *resistance* of the capitalist exploiters cannot be *broken* by anyone else or in any other way." In the transitional stage between capitalism and the communist society, "the state" will continue to exist, because machinery for the suppression of the capitalist exploiters will still be required in the dictatorship of the proletariat. But Lenin points out that, in this phase already, the state begins to "wither away," because the task of the majority (the victorious proletariat) in suppressing the minority (the defeated capitalists) is different, in quantitative and qualitative terms, from the previous, capitalist state, in which a minority (of capitalists) suppressed the majority (of the exploited). Finally, once communism is fully established, the state becomes "absolutely unnecessary, for there is *no one* to be suppressed—'no one' in the sense of a *class,* in the sense of a systematic struggle against a definite section of the population." With the causes of exploitation of class by class removed, with the abolition of classes, the state will therefore inevitably "wither away." There will be true freedom for all, and "when freedom exists, there will be no state."

Lenin wisely adds that he leaves the question of length of time, or of "the concrete withering away, quite open." Without indicating the time it will take to transform the "lower phase" of communist society (the dictatorship of the proletariat) to the "higher phase" (when the state will wither away), Lenin describes the condition of such transformation: "The state will be able to wither away completely when society can apply the rule: 'From each according to his ability, to each according to his needs', i.e., when people have become so accustomed to observing the fundamental rules of social life and when their labor is so productive that they will voluntarily work *according to their ability."* Lenin, like Marx, denies that the vision of a society without a mechanism of force and power ("the state") is Utopian. Yet Marxism shares with Christianity (perhaps all religions), anarchy, democracy, and pacifism the faith that man is so perfectible that one day he will no longer need the corrective force of government, law, and prisons. In religion, the trouble is the Adam in man; in Marx, the Adam is capitalism.

So far, at least, the Communist state has shown little proclivity to wither away in the Soviet Union. So far, the Soviet Union still is in the first, or "lower," phase of communism, when the dictatorship of the proletariat requires the retention of a machinery of legal and political suppression. Stalin, following Lenin, has also left the question open as to how long the present "phase" will last, and has refused to hint at the probable time when the state will begin to wither away.

Returning from dreams to reality, one of the most interesting documents in revolutionary Marxist literature is Lenin's call to revolution, addressed to the members of the Central Committee of the Bolshevik party. It was written on the evening of November 6, 1917, only a few hours before the provisional government in Petrograd was overthrown by armed insurrection under Bolshevik leadership, which made Lenin himself the head of the new government.

The "New Deal" was an attempt, born in the depression of the nineteen thirties, to steer a new course of social and economic action in the United States. Its advocates have rarely thought of it as more than a mild reform, long overdue; its opponents have branded it as rank socialism, and the first step to the communist state in America. In a selection of the thought of *Karl Marx* ("Living Thoughts Library," 1940), Leon Trotsky, writing mainly for the American public, took up the general question of socialism and the United States; among other matters, he also dealt with the New Deal. To Leon Trotsky, Henry A. Wallace did not appear nearly so "radical" or "socialist" as, say, to Colonel McCormick or the *Wall Street Journal*. Contrary to those who hold that socialism will never be established in the United States because of its unique historical experience and institutions, Trotsky insists that the laws of capitalist decay and socialist reconstruction will eventually operate even in the rich American continent. As a Marxist, he does not yield his conviction that the change will be revolutionary, because the ruling "plutocracy" will be little inclined to forego its position by consent.

Why an American liberal and democrat (in fact, any liberal democrat) cannot embrace the communist creed is explained by Morris R. Cohen in his essay, "Why I Am Not a Communist" (1934). This was written during the great depression, when despair at the economic chaos produced by capitalism drove many a liberal, especially in the United States, into the fold of the communist faith. A true and lifelong liberal, Cohen gives his reasons why he could not be a liberal and Communist at the same time.

1. On Philosophy *

KARL MARX

The question whether objective truth can be attributed to human thinking is not a question of theory, but is a practical question. In practice man must prove the truth, i.e., the reality and power, the "this-sidedness" of his thinking. The dispute over the reality or non-reality of thinking which is isolated from practice is a purely scholastic question.

The materialist doctrine that men are products of circumstances and upbringing and that, therefore, changed men are products of other circumstances and changed upbringing, forgets that circumstances are changed precisely by men and that the educator must himself be educated. Hence this doctrine necessarily arrives at dividing society into two parts, of which one towers above society (in Robert Owen, for example).

The coincidence of the changing of circumstances and of human activity can only be conceived and rationally understood as revolutionising practice.

Social life is essentially *practical*. All mysteries which mislead theory to mysticism find their rational solution in human practice and in the comprehension of this practice.

The philosophers have only *interpreted* the world in various ways; the point however is to *change* it.

2. Economic Interpretation of History †

KARL MARX

My investigations led to the conclusion that legal relations as well as forms of State could not be understood from themselves, nor from the so-called

---

* From Karl Marx, *Theses on Feuerbach* (written in 1845; first published in 1888 in *Ludwig Feuerbach* by Friedrich Engels).

† From Karl Marx, *A Contribution to the Critique of Political Economy* (1859; translated by Emile Burns in *A Handbook of Marxism*, International Publishers, 1935). By permission.

general development of the human mind, but, on the contrary, are rooted in the material conditions of life, the aggregate of which Hegel, following the precedent of the English and French of the eighteenth century, grouped under the name of "civil society"; but that the anatomy of civil society is to be found in political economy. My study of the latter, begun in Paris, was continued in Brussels, whither I migrated in consequence of an expulsion order issued by M. Guizot. The general conclusion I arrived at—and once reached, it served as the guiding thread in my studies—can be briefly formulated as follows: In the social production of their means of existence men enter into definite, necessary relations which are independent of their will, productive relationships which correspond to a definite stage of development of their material productive forces. The aggregate of these productive relationships constitutes the economic structure of society, the real basis on which a juridical and political superstructure arises, and to which definite forms of social consciousness correspond. The mode of production of the material means of existence conditions the whole process of social, political and intellectual life. It is not the consciousness of men that determines their existence, but, on the contrary, it is their social existence that determines their consciousness. At a certain stage of their development the material productive forces of society come into contradiction with the existing productive relationships, or, what is but a legal expression for these, with the property relationships within which they had moved before. From forms of development of the productive forces these relationships are transformed into their fetters. Then an epoch of social revolution opens. With the change in the economic foundation the whole vast super-structure is more or less rapidly transformed. In considering such revolutions it is necessary always to distinguish between the material revolution in the economic conditions of production, which can be determined with scientific accuracy, and the juridical, political, religious, aesthetic or philosophic—in a word, ideological forms wherein men become conscious of this conflict and fight it out. Just as we cannot judge an individual on the basis of his own opinion of himself, so such a revolutionary epoch cannot be judged from its own consciousness; but on the contrary this consciousness must be explained from the contradictions of material life, from the existing conflict between social productive forces and productive relationships. A social system never perishes before all the productive forces have developed for which it is wide enough; and new, higher productive relationships never come into being before the material conditions for their existence have been brought to maturity within the womb of the old society itself. Therefore, mankind always sets itself only such problems as it can solve; for when we look closer we will always find that the problem itself only arises when the material conditions for its solution are already present or at least in the process of coming into being. In broad outline, the Asiatic, the ancient, the feudal and the modern bourgeois modes of production can be indicated as progressive epochs in the economic system of society. Bourgeois productive relationships are the last antagonistic form of the social process of production—antagonistic in the sense not of individual antagonism, but of an antagonism rising out of the conditions of the social life of individuals; but the productive forces developing within the womb of bourgeois society at the same time create the material conditions for the solution of this antagonism. With this social system, therefore, the pre-history of human society comes to a close.

~~~~~~

3. The Communist Manifesto*

KARL MARX AND FRIEDRICH ENGELS

~~~~~~

A spectre is haunting Europe—the spectre of Communism. All the powers of old Europe have entered into a holy alliance to exorcise this spectre: Pope and Tsar, Metternich and Guizot, French Radicals and German police-spies.

Where is the party in opposition that has not been decried as communistic by its opponents in power? Where is the Opposition that has not hurled back the branding reproach of Communism, against the more advanced opposition parties, as well as against its reactionary adversaries?

Two things result from this fact:

1. Communism is already acknowledged by all European powers to be itself a power.

2. It is high time that Communists should openly, in the face of the whole world, publish their views, their aims, their tendencies, and meet this nursery tale of the spectre of Communism with a manifesto of the party itself.

To this end, Communists of various nationalities have assembled in London, and sketched the following manifesto, to be published in the English, French, German, Italian, Flemish and Danish languages:

I: BOURGEOIS AND PROLETARIANS

The history of all hitherto existing society is the history of class struggles.

Freeman and slave, patrician and plebeian, lord and serf, guild-master and journeyman, in a word, oppressor and oppressed, stood in constant opposition to one another, carried on an uninterrupted, now hidden, now open fight, a

---

* From Karl Marx and Friedrich Engels, *The Communist Manifesto* (1848; English translation of 1888, edited by Friedrich Engels).

fight that each time ended, either in a revolutionary reconstitution of society at large, or in the common ruin of the contending classes.

In the earlier epochs of history, we find almost everywhere a complicated arrangement of society into various orders, a manifold gradation of social rank. In ancient Rome we have patricians, knights, plebeians, slaves; in the Middle Ages, feudal lords, vassals, guild-masters, journeymen, apprentices, serfs; in almost all of these classes, again, subordinate gradations.

The modern bourgeois society that has sprouted from the ruins of feudal society has not done away with class antagonisms. It has but established new classes, new conditions of oppression, new forms of struggle in place of the old ones.

Our epoch, the epoch of the bourgeoisie, possesses, however, this distinctive feature: it has simplified the class antagonisms. Society as a whole is more and more splitting up into two great hostile camps, into two great classes directly facing each other—bourgeoisie and proletariat.

From the serfs of the Middle Ages sprang the chartered burghers of the earliest towns. From these burgesses the first elements of the bourgeoisie were developed.

The discovery of America, the rounding of the Cape, opened up fresh ground for the rising bourgeoisie. The East-Indian and Chinese markets, the colonisation of America, trade with the colonies, the increase in the means of exchange and in commodities generally, gave to commerce, to navigation, to industry, an impulse never before known, and thereby, to the revolutionary element in the tottering feudal society, a rapid development.

The feudal system of industry, in which industrial production was monopolised by closed guilds, now no longer sufficed for the growing wants of the new markets. The manufacturing system took its place. The guild-masters were pushed aside by the manufacturing middle class; division of labour between the different corporate guilds vanished in the face of division of labour in each single workshop.

Meantime the markets kept ever growing, the demand ever rising. Even manufacture no longer sufficed. Thereupon, steam and machinery revolutionised industrial production. The place of manufacture was taken by the giant, modern industry, the place of the industrial middle class, by industrial millionaires, the leaders of whole industrial armies, the modern bourgeois.

Modern industry has established the world market, for which the discovery of America paved the way. This market has given an immense development to commerce, to navigation, to communication by land. This development has, in its turn, reacted on the extension of industry; and in proportion as industry, commerce, navigation, railways extended, in the same proportion the bourgeoisie developed, increased its capital, and pushed into the background every class handed down from the Middle Ages.

We see, therefore, how the modern bourgeoisie is itself the product of a long course of development, of a series of revolutions in the modes of production and of exchange.

Each step in the development of the bourgeoisie was accompanied by a corresponding political advance of that class. An oppressed class under the sway of the feudal nobility, an armed and self-governing association in the mediaeval commune; here independent urban republic (as in Italy and Germany), there taxable "third estate" of the monarchy (as in France); afterwards, in the period of manufacture proper, serving either the semi-feudal or the absolute monarchy as a counterpoise against the nobility, and, in fact, corner-stone of the great monarchies in general, the bourgeoisie has at last, since the establishment of Modern Industry and of the world market, conquered for itself, in the modern representative State, exclusive political sway. The executive of the modern State is but a committee for managing the common affairs of the whole bourgeoisie.

The bourgeoisie, historically, has played a most revolutionary part.

The bourgeoisie, wherever it has got the upper hand, has put an end to all feudal, patriarchal, idyllic relations. It has pitilessly torn asunder the motley feudal ties that bound man to his "natural superiors," and has left no other nexus between man and man than naked self-interest, than callous "cash payment." It has drowned the most heavenly ecstasies of religious fervour, of chivalrous enthusiasm, of philistine sentimentalism, in the icy water of egotistical calculation. It has resolved personal worth into exchange value, and in place of the numberless indefeasible chartered freedoms, has set up that single, unconscionable freedom—Free Trade. In one word, for exploitation, veiled by religious and political illusions, it has substituted naked, shameless, direct, brutal exploitation.

The bourgeoisie has stripped of its halo every occupation hitherto honoured and looked up to with reverent awe. It has converted the physician, the lawyer, the priest, the poet, the man of science, into its paid wage-labourers.

The bourgeoisie has torn away from the family its sentimental veil, and has reduced the family relation to a mere money relation.

The bourgeoisie has disclosed how it came to pass that the brutal display of vigour in the Middle Ages, which reactionaries so much admire, found its fitting complement in the most slothful indolence. It has been the first to show what man's activity can bring about. It has accomplished wonders far surpassing Egyptian pyramids, Roman aqueducts, and Gothic cathedrals; it has conducted expeditions that put in the shade all former Exoduses of nations and crusades.

The bourgeoisie cannot exist without constantly revolutionising the instruments of production, and thereby the relations of production, and with them the whole relations of society. Conservation of the old modes of production in unaltered form, was, on the contrary, the first condition of existence for all earlier industrial classes. Constant revolutionising of production, uninterrupted disturbance of all social conditions, everlasting uncertainty and agitation distinguished the bourgeois epoch from all earlier ones. All fixed, fast-frozen relations, with their train of ancient and venerable prejudices and opinions, are swept away, all new-formed ones become antiquated before they can ossify. All that is solid melts into air, all that is holy is profaned, and man is at last compelled to face with sober senses his real conditions of life and his relations with his kind.

The need of a constantly expanding market for its products chases the bourgeoisie over the whole surface of the globe. It must nestle everywhere, settle everywhere, establish connections everywhere.

The bourgeoisie has through its exploitation of the world market given a cosmopolitan character to production and consumption in every country. To the great chagrin of reactionaries, it has drawn from under the feet of industry the national ground on which it stood. All old-established national industries have been destroyed or are daily being destroyed. They are dislodged by new industries, whose introduction becomes a life and death question for all civilised nations, by industries that no longer work up indigenous raw material, but raw material drawn from the remotest zones; industries whose products are consumed, not only at home, but in every quarter of the globe. In place of the old wants, satisfied by the production of the country, we find new wants, requiring for their satisfaction the products of distant lands and climes. In place of the old local and national seclusion and self-sufficiency, we have intercourse in every direction, universal inter-dependence of nations. And as in material, so also in intellectual production. The intellectual creations of individual nations become common property. National one-sidedness and narrow-mindedness become more and more impossible, and from the numerous national and local literatures there arises a world literature.

The bourgeoisie, by the rapid improvement of all instruments of production, by the immensely facilitated means of communication, draws all, even the most barbarian, nations into civilisation. The cheap prices of its commodities are the heavy artillery with which it batters down all Chinese walls, with which it forces the barbarians' intensely obstinate hatred of foreigners to capitulate. It compels all nations, on pain of extinction, to adopt the bourgeois modes of production; it compels them to introduce what it calls civilisation into their midst, i.e., to become bourgeois themselves. In one word, it creates a world after its own image.

The bourgeoisie has subjected the country to the rule of the towns. It has created enormous cities, has greatly increased the urban population as compared with the rural, and has thus rescued a considerable part of the population from the idiocy of rural life. Just as it has made the country dependent on the towns, so it has made barbarian and semi-barbarian countries dependent on the civilised ones, nations of peasants on nations of bourgeois, the East on the West.

The bourgeoisie keeps more and more doing away with the scattered state of the population, of the means of production, and of property. It has agglomerated population, centralised means of production, and has concentrated property in a few hands. The necessary consequence of this was political centralisation. Independent, or but loosely connected provinces, with separate interests, laws, governments and systems of taxation, became lumped together into one nation, with one government, one code of laws, one national class interest, one frontier and one customs tariff.

The bourgeoisie, during its rule of scarce one hundred years, has created more massive and more colossal productive forces than have all preceding generations together. Subjection of nature's forces to man, machinery, application of chemistry to industry and agriculture, steam-navigation, railways, electric telegraphs, clearing of whole continents for cultivation, canalisation of rivers, whole populations conjured out of the ground—what earlier century had even a presentiment that such productive forces slumbered in the lap of social labour?

We see then; the means of production and of exchange, on whose foundation the bourgeoisie built itself up, were generated in feudal society. At a certain stage in the development of these means of production and of exchange, the conditions under which feudal society produced and exchanged, the feudal organisation of agriculture and manufacturing industry, in one word, the feudal relations of property became no longer compatible with the already developed productive forces; they became so many fetters. They had to be burst asunder; they were burst asunder.

Into their place stepped free competition, accompanied by a social and political constitution adapted to it, and by the economical and political sway of the bourgeois class.

A similar movement is going on before our own eyes. Modern bourgeois society with its relations of production, of exchange and of property, a society that has conjured up such gigantic means of production and of exchange, is like the sorcerer who is no longer able to control the powers of the nether world whom he has called up by his spells. For many a decade past the history of industry and commerce is but the history of the revolt of modern productive forces against modern conditions of production, against the property relations that are the conditions for the existence of the bourgeoisie and of its rule. It is enough to mention the commercial crises that by their periodical return put the existence of the entire bourgeois society on its trial, each time more threateningly. In these crises a great part not only of the existing products, but also of the previously created productive forces, are periodically destroyed. In these crises there breaks out an epidemic that, in all earlier epochs, would have seemed an absurdity—the epidemic of over-production. Society suddenly finds itself put back into a state of momentary barbarism; it appears as if a famine, a universal war of devastation had cut off the supply of every means of subsistence; industry and commerce seem to be destroyed. And why? Because there is too much civilisation, too much means of subsistence, too much industry, too much commerce. The productive forces at the disposal of society no longer tend to further the development of the conditions of bourgeois property; on the contrary, they have become too powerful for these conditions, by which they are fettered, and so soon as they overcome these fetters, they bring disorder into the whole of bourgeois society, endanger the existence of bourgeois property. The conditions of bourgeois society are too narrow to comprise the wealth created by them. And how does the bourgeoisie get over these crises? On the one hand by enforced destruction of a mass of productive forces; on the other, by the conquest of new markets, and by the more thorough exploitation of the old ones. That is to say, by paving the way for more extensive and more destructive crises, and by diminishing the means whereby crises are prevented.

The weapons with which the bourgeoisie felled feudalism to the ground are now turned against the bourgeoisie itself.

But not only has the bourgeoisie forged the weapons that bring death to itself; it has also called into existence the men who are to wield those weapons —the modern working class—the proletarians.

In proportion as the bourgeoisie, i.e., capital, is developed, in the same proportion is the proletariat, the modern working class, developed—a class of labourers, who live only so long as they find work, and who find work only so long as their labour increases capital. These labourers, who must sell themselves piecemeal, are a commodity, like every other article of commerce, and are consequently exposed to all the vicissitudes of competition, to all the fluctuations of the market.

Owing to the extensive use of machinery and to division of labour, the work of the proletarians has lost all individual character, and, consequently, all charm for the workman. He becomes an appendage of the machine, and it is only the most simple, most monotonous, and most easily acquired knack, that is required of him. Hence, the cost of production of a workman is restricted, almost entirely, to the means of subsistence that he requires for his maintenance, and for the propagation of his race. But the price of a commodity, and therefore, also of labour, is equal to its cost of production. In proportion, therefore, as the repulsiveness of the work increases, the wage decreases. Nay, more, in proportion as the use of machinery and division of labour increases, in the same porportion the burden of toil also increases, whether by prolongation of the working hours, by increase of the work exacted in a given time, or by increased speed of the machinery, etc.

Modern industry has converted the little workshop of the patriarchal master into the great factory of the industrial capitalist. Masses of labourers, crowded into the factory, are organised like soldiers. As privates of the industrial army they are placed under the command of a perfect hierarchy of officers and sergeants. Not only are they slaves of the bourgeois class, and of the bourgeois state; they are daily and hourly enslaved by the machine, by the over-looker, and, above all, by the individual bourgeois manufacturer himself. The more openly this despotism proclaims gain to be its end and aim, the more petty, the more hateful and the more embittering it is.

The less the skill and exertion of strength implied in manual labour, in other words, the more modern industry becomes developed, the more is the labour of men superseded by that of women. Differences of age and sex have no longer any distinctive social validity for the working class. All are instruments of labour, more or less expensive to use, according to their age and sex.

No sooner is the exploitation of the labourer by the manufacturer so far at an end that he receives his wages in cash than he is set upon by the other portions of the bourgeoisie, the landlord, the shopkeeper, the pawnbroker, etc.

The lower strata of the middle class—the small tradespeople, shopkeepers, and retired tradesmen generally, the handicraftsmen and peasants—all these sink gradually into the proletariat, partly because their diminutive capital does not suffice for the scale on which modern industry is carried on, and is swamped in the competition with the large capitalists, partly because their specialised skill is rendered worthless by new methods of production. Thus the proletariat is recruited from all classes of the population.

The proletariat goes through various stages of development. With its birth begins its struggle with the bourgeoisie. At first the contest is carried on by individual labourers, then by the work people of a factory, then by the operatives of one trade, in one locality, against the individual bourgeois who directly exploits them. They direct their attacks not against the bourgeois conditions of production, but against the instruments of production themselves; they destroy imported wares that compete with their labour, they smash to pieces machinery, they set factories ablaze, they seek to restore by force the vanished status of the workman of the Middle Ages.

At this stage the labourers still form an incoherent mass scattered over the whole country, and broken up by their mutual competition. If anywhere they unite to form more compact bodies, this is not yet the consequence of their own active union, but of the union of the bourgeoisie, which class, in order to attain its own political ends, is compelled to set the whole proletariat in motion, and is moreover yet, for a time, able to do so. At this stage, therefore, the proletarians do not fight their enemies, but the enemies of their enemies, the remnants of absolute monarchy, the land-owners, the non-industrial bourgeois, the petty bourgeoisie. Thus the whole historical movement is concentrated in the hands of the bourgeoisie; every victory so obtained is a victory for the bourgeoisie.

But with the development of industry the proletariat not only increases in number; it becomes concentrated in greater masses, its strength grows, and it feels that strength more. The various interests and conditions of life within the ranks of the proletariat are more and more equalised, in proportion as machinery obliterates all distinctions of labour, and nearly everywhere reduces wages to the same low level. The growing competition among the bourgeois, and the resulting commercial crises, make the wages of the workers ever more fluctuating. The unceasing improvement of machinery, ever more rapidly developing, makes their livelihood more and more precarious; the collisions between individual workmen and individual bourgeois take more and more the character of collisions between two classes. Thereupon the workers begin to form combinations (trades' unions) against the bourgeois; they club together in order to keep up the rate of wages; they found permanent associations in order to make provision beforehand for these occasional revolts. Here and there the contest breaks out into riots.

Now and then the workers are victorious, but only for a time. The real fruit of their battles lies, not in the immediate result, but in the ever expanding union of the workers. This union is helped on by the improved means of communication that are created by modern industry, and that place the workers of different localities in contact with one another. It was just this contact that was needed to centralise the numerous local struggles, all of the same character, into one national struggle between classes. But every class struggle is a political struggle. And that union, to attain which the burghers of the Middle Ages, with their miserable highways, required centuries, the modern proletarians, thanks to railways, achieve in a few years.

This organisation of the proletarians into a class, and consequently into a political party, is continually being upset again by the competition between the workers themselves. But it ever rises up again, stronger, firmer, mightier. It compels legislative recognition of particular interests of the workers, by taking advantage of the divisions among the bourgeoisie itself. Thus the ten-hours' bill in England was carried.

Altogether, collisions between the classes of the old society further in many ways the course of development of the proletariat. The bourgeoisie finds itself involved in a constant battle. At first with the aristocracy; later on, with those portions of the bourgeoisie itself, whose interests have become antagonistic to the progress of industry; at all times with the bourgeoisie of foreign countries. In all these battles it sees itself compelled to appeal to the proletariat, to ask for its help, and thus to drag it into the political arena. The bourgeoisie itself, therefore, supplies the proletariat with its own elements of political and general education, in other words, it furnishes the proletariat with weapons for fighting the bourgeoisie.

Further, as we have already seen, entire sections of the ruling classes are, by the advance of industry, precipitated into the proletariat, or are at least threatened in their conditions of existence. These also supply the proletariat with fresh elements of enlightenment and progress.

Finally, in times when the class struggle nears the decisive hour, the process of dissolution going on within the ruling class, in fact within the whole range of old society, assumes such a violent, glaring character that a small section of the ruling class cuts itself adrift and joins the revolutionary class, the class that holds the future in its hands. Just as, therefore, at an earlier period, a section of the nobility went over to the bourgeoisie, so now a portion of the bourgeoisie goes over to the proletariat, and, in particular, a portion of the bourgeois ideologists, who have raised themselves to the level of comprehending theoretically the historical movement as a whole.

Of all the classes that stand face to face with the bourgeoisie to-day, the proletariat alone is a really revolutionary class. The other classes decay and finally disappear in the face of modern industry; the proletariat is its special and essential product.

The lower middle class, the small manufacturer, the shopkeeper, the artisan, the peasant, all these fight against the bourgeoisie, to save from extinction their existence as fractions of the middle class. They are therefore not revolutionary but conservative. Nay, more, they are reactionary, for they try to roll back the wheel of history. If by chance they are revolutionary, they are so only in view of their impending transfer into the protetariat; they thus defend not their present, but their future interests; they desert their own standpoint to place themselves at that of the proletariat.

The "dangerous class," the social scum, that passively rotting mass thrown off by the lowest layers of old society, may, here and there, be swept into the movement by a proletarian revolution; its conditions of life, however, prepare it far more for the part of a bribed tool of reactionary intrigue.

In the conditions of the proletariat, those of old society at large are already virtually swamped. The proletarian is without property; his relation to his wife and children has no longer anything in common with the bourgeois family relations; modern industrial labour, modern subjection to capital, the same in England as in France, in America as in Germany, has stripped him of every trace of national character. Law, morality, religion, are to him so many bourgeois prejudices, behind which lurk in ambush just as many bourgeois interests.

All the preceding classes that got the upper hand, sought to fortify their already acquired status by subjecting society at large to their conditions of appropriation. The proletarians cannot become masters of the productive forces of society, except by abolishing their own previous mode of appropriation, and thereby also every other previous mode of appropriation. They have nothing of their own to secure and to fortify; their mission is to destroy all previous securities for, and insurances of, individual property.

All previous historical movements were movements of minorities, or in the interest of minorities. The proletarian movement is the self-conscious, independent movement of the immense majority, in the interest of the immense majority. The proletariat, the lowest stratum of our present society, cannot stir, cannot raise itself up, without the whole superincumbent strata of official society being sprung into the air.

Though not in substance, yet in form, the struggle of the proletariat with the bourgeoisie is at first a national struggle. The proletariat of each country must, of course, first of all settle matters with its own bourgeoisie.

In depicting the most general phases of the development of the proletariat, we traced the more or less veiled civil war, raging within existing society, up to the point where that war breaks out into open revolution, and where the violent overthrow of the bourgeoisie lays the foundation for the sway of the proletariat.

Hitherto, every form of society has been based, as we have already seen, on the antagonism of oppressing and oppressed classes. But in order to oppress a class, certain conditions must be assured to it under which it can, at least, continue its slavish existence. The serf, in the period of serfdom, raised himself to membership in the commune, just as the petty bourgeois, under the yoke of feudal absolutism, managed to develop into a bourgeois. The modern labourer, on the contrary, instead of rising with the progress of industry, sinks deeper and deeper below the conditions of existence of his own class. He becomes a pauper, and pauperism develops more rapidly than population and wealth. And here it becomes evident that the bourgeoisie is unfit any longer to be the ruling class in society and to impose its conditions of existence upon society as an over-riding law. It is unfit to rule because it is incompetent to assure an existence to its slave within his slavery, because it cannot help letting him sink into such a state, that it has to feed him, instead of being fed by him. Society can no longer live under this bourgeoisie; in other words, its existence is no longer compatible with society.

The essential condition for the existence and for the sway of the bourgeois class is the formation and augmentation of capital; the condition for capital is wage-labour. Wage-labour rests exclusively on competition between the labourers. The advance of industry, whose involuntary promoter is the bourgeoisie, replaces the isolation of the labourers, due to competition, by their revolutionary combination, due to association. The development of modern industry, therefore, cuts from under its feet the very foundation on which the bourgeoisie produces and appropriates products. What the bourgeoisie therefore produces, above all, are its own grave-diggers. Its fall and the victory of the proletariat are equally inevitable.

The Communists everywhere support every revolutionary movement against the existing social and political order of things.

In all these movements they bring to the front, as the leading question in each, the property question, no matter what its degree of development at the time.

Finally, they labour everywhere for the union and agreement of the democratic parties of all countries.

The Communists disdain to conceal their views and aims. They openly declare that their ends can be attained only by the forcible overthrow of all existing social conditions. Let the ruling classes tremble at a Communist revolution. The proletarians have nothing to lose but their chains. They have a world to win.

Working men of all countries, unite!

~~~~~~

4. Economic and Noneconomic Forces in History*

FRIEDRICH ENGELS

~~~~~~

According to the materialist conception of history the determining element in history is *ultimately* the production and reproduction in real life. More than this neither Marx nor I have ever asserted. If therefore somebody twists this into the statement that the economic element is the *only* determining one, he transforms it into a meaningless, abstract and absurd phrase. The economic situation is the basis, but the various elements of the superstructure—political forms of the class struggle and its consequences, constitutions established by the victorious class after a successful battle, etc.—forms of law—and then even the reflexes of all these actual struggles in the brains of the combatants: political, legal, philosophical theories, religious ideas and their further development into systems of dogma—also exercise their influence upon the course of the historical struggles and in many cases preponderate in determining their *form*. There is an interaction of all these elements, in which, amid all the endless *host* of accidents (*i.e.*, of things and events whose inner connection is so remote or so impossible to prove that we regard it as absent and can neglect it), the economic movement finally asserts itself as necessary. Otherwise the application of the theory to any period of history one chose would be easier than the solution of a simple equation of the first degree.

We make our own history, but in the first place under very definite presuppositions and conditions. Among these the economic ones are finally decisive. But the political, etc., ones, and indeed even the traditions which haunt human minds, also play a part, although not the decisive one. The Prussian

* From a letter to Joseph Bloch (September 21, 1890; reprinted in Karl Marx and Friedrich Engels, *Correspondence*, International Publishers, 1934). By permission.

State arose and developed from historical, ultimately from economic causes. But it could scarcely be maintained without pedantry that among the many small states of North Germany, Brandenburg was specifically determined by economic necessity to become the great power embodying the economic, linguistic and, after the Reformation, also the religious differences between north and south, and not by other elements as well (above all by its entanglement with Poland, owing to the possession of Prussia, and hence with international, political relations—which were indeed also decisive in the formation of the Austrian dynastic power). Without making oneself ridiculous it would be difficult to succeed in explaining in terms of economics the existence of every small state in Germany, past and present, or the origin of the High German consonant mutations, which the geographical wall of partition formed by the mountains from the Sudetic range to the Taunus extended to a regular division throughout Germany.

In the second place, however, history makes itself in such a way that the final result always arises from conflicts between many individual wills, of which each again has been made what it is by a host of particular conditions of life. Thus there are innumerable intersecting forces, an infinite series of parallelograms of forces which give rise to one resultant—the historical event. This again may itself be viewed as the product of a power which, taken as a whole, works *unconsciously* and without volition. For what each individual wills is obstructed by everyone else, and what emerges is something that no one willed. Thus past history proceeds in the manner of a natural process and is also essentially subject to the same laws of movement. But from the fact that individual wills—of which each desires what he is impelled to by his physical constitution and external, in the last resort economic, circumstances (either his own personal circumstances or those of society in general)—do not attain what they want, but are merged into a collective mean, a common resultant, it must not be concluded that their value $= 0$. On the contrary, each contributes to the resultant and is to this degree involved in it.

I would ask you to study this theory further from its original sources and not at second-hand, it is really much easier. Marx hardly wrote anything in which it did not play a part. But especially *The Eighteenth Brumaire of Louis Bonaparte* is a most excellent example of its application. There are also many allusions in *Capital*. Then I may also direct you to my writings: *Herr E. Dühring's Revolution in Science* and *Ludwig Feuerbach and the Exit of Classical German Philosophy,* in which I have given the most detailed account of historical materialism which, so far as I know, exists.

Marx and I are ourselves partly to blame for the fact that younger writers sometimes lay more stress on the economic side than is due to it. We had to emphasise this main principle in opposition to our adversaries, who denied it, and we had not always the time, the place or the opportunity to allow the other elements involved in the interaction to come into their rights. But when it was a case of presenting a section of history, that is, of a practical application, the thing was different and there no error was possible. Unfortunately, however, it happens only too often that people think they have fully understood a theory and can apply it without more ado from the moment they have mastered its main principles, and those even not always correctly. And I cannot exempt many of the more recent "Marxists" from this reproach, for the most wonderful rubbish has been produced from this quarter too.

5. The Withering Away of the State *

V. I. LENIN

The transition from capitalist society—which is developing towards communism—to a communist society is impossible without a "political transition period," and the state in this period can only be the revolutionary dictatorship of the proletariat.

What, then, is the relation of this dictatorship to democracy?

We have seen that *The Communist Manifesto* simply places the two ideas side by side: "to raise the proletariat to the position of the ruling class" and "to win the battle of democracy." On the basis of all that has been said above, it is possible to determine more precisely how democracy changes in the transition from capitalism to communism.

In capitalist society, under the conditions most favourable to its development, we have more or less complete democracy in the democratic republic. But this democracy is always restricted by the narrow framework of capitalist exploitation, and consequently always remains, in reality, a democracy for the minority, only for the possessing classes, only for the rich. Freedom in capitalist society always remains about the same as it was in the ancient Greek republics: freedom for the slave-owners. Owing to the conditions of capitalist exploitation the modern wage-slaves are also so crushed by want and poverty that "they cannot be bothered with democracy," "they cannot be bothered with politics"; in the ordinary peaceful course of events the majority of the population is debarred from participating in social and political life.

The correctness of this statement is perhaps most clearly proved by Germany, precisely because in that country constitutional legality lasted and re-

* From V. I. Lenin, *State and Revolution* (1917; in Lenin, *Selected Works*, VII, International Publishers, 1937). By permission.

mained stable for a remarkably long time—for nearly half a century (1871–1914)—and because during this period Social-Democracy was able to achieve far more in Germany than in other countries in the way of "utilising legality," and was able to organise a larger proportion of the working class into a political party than anywhere else in the world.

What is this largest proportion of politically conscious and active wage-slaves that has so far been observed in capitalist society? One million members of the Social-Democratic Party—out of fifteen million wage-workers! Three million organised in trade unions—out of fifteen million! [1]

Democracy for an insignificant minority, democracy for the rich—that is the democracy of capitalist society. If we look more closely into the mechanism of capitalist democracy, everywhere, in the "petty"—so-called petty—details of the suffrage (residential qualification, exclusion of women, etc.), and in the technique of the representative institutions, in the actual obstacles to the right of assembly (public buildings are not for "beggars"!), in the purely capitalist organisation of the daily press, etc., etc.—on all sides we see restriction after restriction upon democracy. These restrictions, exceptions, exclusions, obstacles for the poor, seem slight, especially in the eyes of one who has never known want himself and has never been in close contact with the oppressed classes in their mass life (and nine-tenths, if not ninety-nine hundredths, of the bourgeois publicists and politicians are of this category); but in their sum total these restrictions exclude and squeeze out the poor from politics, from taking an active part in democracy.

Marx grasped this *essence* of capitalist democracy splendidly, when, in analysing the experience of the Commune, he said that the oppressed were allowed, once every few years, to decide which particular representatives of the oppressing class should misrepresent them in parliament!

But from this capitalist democracy—inevitably narrow, tacitly repelling the poor, and therefore hypocritical and false to the core—development does not proceed simply, smoothly and directly to "greater and greater democracy," as the liberal professors and petty-bourgeois opportunists would have us believe. No, development—towards communism—proceeds through the dictatorship of the proletariat; it cannot do otherwise, for the *resistance* of the capitalist exploiters cannot be *broken* by anyone else or in any other way.

But the dictatorship of the proletariat, *i.e.,* the organisation of the vanguard of the oppressed as the ruling class for the purpose of crushing the oppressors, cannot result merely in an expansion of democracy. *Simultaneously* with an immense expansion of democracy which *for the first time* becomes democracy for the poor, democracy for the people, and not democracy for the rich, the dictatorship of the proletariat imposes a series of restrictions on the freedom of the oppressors, the exploiters, the capitalists. We must crush them in order to free humanity from wage-slavery; their resistance must be

[1] According to the figures for 1917.

broken by force; it is clear that where there is suppression there is also violence, there is no freedom, no democracy.

Engels expressed this splendidly in his letter to Bebel when he said, as the reader will remember, that

> "so long as the proletariat still *uses* the state it does not use it in the interests of freedom but in order to hold down its adversaries, and as soon as it becomes possible to speak of freedom the state as such ceases to exist."

Democracy for the vast majority of the people, and suppression by force, *i.e.,* exclusion from democracy, of the exploiters and oppressors of the people —this is the change democracy undergoes during the *transition* from capitalism to communism.

Only in communist society, when the resistance of the capitalists has been completely broken, when the capitalists have disappeared, when there are no classes (*i.e.,* when there is no difference between the members of society as regards their relation to the social means of production), *only then* does "the state . . . cease to exist," and it *"becomes possible to speak of freedom."* Only then will really complete democracy, democracy without any exceptions, be possible and be realised. And only then will democracy itself begin to *wither away* owing to the simple fact that, freed from capitalist slavery, from the untold horrors, savagery, absurdities and infamies of capitalist exploitation, people will gradually *become accustomed* to observing the elementary rules of social life that have been known for centuries and repeated for thousands of years in all copy-book maxims; they will become accustomed to observing them without force, without compulsion, without subordination, without the *special apparatus* for compulsion which is called the state.

The expression "the state *withers away"* is very well chosen, for it indicates both the gradual and the spontaneous nature of the process. Only habit can, and undoubtedly will, have such an effect; for we see around us millions of times how readily people become accustomed to observing the necessary rules of social life if there is no exploitation, if there is nothing that causes indignation, that calls forth protest and revolt and has to be *suppressed*.

Thus, in capitalist society we have a democracy that is curtailed, wretched, false; a democracy only for the rich, for the minority. The dictatorship of the proletariat, the period of transition to communism, will, for the first time, create democracy for the people, for the majority, in addition to the necessary suppression of the minority—the exploiters. Communism alone is capable of giving really complete democracy, and the more complete it is the more quickly will it become unnecessary and wither away of itself.

In other words: under capitalism we have a state in the proper sense of the word, that is, a special machine for the suppression of one class by another, and of the majority by the minority at that. Naturally, the successful discharge of such a task as the systematic suppression of the exploited majority by the exploiting minority calls for the greatest ferocity and savagery in the work of suppression, it calls for seas of blood through which mankind has to wade in slavery, serfdom and wage-labour.

Furthermore, during the *transition* from capitalism to communism, suppression is *still* necessary; but it is the suppression of the exploiting minority by the exploited majority. A special apparatus, a special machine for suppression, the "state," is *still* necessary, but this is now a transitory state; it is no longer a state in the proper sense; for the suppression of the minority of exploiters by the majority of the wage-slaves *of yesterday* is comparatively so easy, simple and natural a task that it will entail far less bloodshed than the suppression of the risings of slaves, serfs or wage-labourers, and it will cost mankind far less. This is compatible with the diffusion of democracy among such an overwhelming majority of the population that the need for a *special machine* of suppression will begin to disappear. The exploiters are, naturally, unable to suppress the people without a very complex machine for performing this task; but *the people* can suppress the exploiters with a very simple "machine," almost without a "machine," without a special apparatus, by the simple *organisation of the armed masses* (such as the Soviets of Workers' and Soldiers' Deputies, we may remark, running ahead a little).

Finally, only communism makes the state absolutely unnecessary, for there is *no one* to be suppressed—"no one" in the sense of a *class,* in the sense of a systematic struggle against a definite section of the population. We are not utopians, and we do not in the least deny the possibility and inevitability of excesses on the part of *individual persons,* or the need to suppress *such* excesses. But, in the first place, no special machine, no special apparatus of repression is needed for this: this will be done by the armed people itself, as simply and as readily as any crowd of civilised people, even in modern society, parts two people who are fighting, or interferes to prevent a woman from being assaulted. And, secondly, we know that the fundamental social cause of excesses, which consist in violating the rules of social life, is the exploitation of the masses, their want and their poverty. With the removal of this chief cause, excesses will inevitably begin to *"wither away."* We do not know how quickly and in what order, but we know that they will wither away. With their withering away, the state will also *wither away.*

Without dropping into utopias, Marx defined more fully what can be defined *now* regarding this future, namely the difference between the lower and higher phases (degrees, stages) of communist society.

THE FIRST PHASE OF COMMUNIST SOCIETY

In the *Critique of the Gotha Programme,* Marx goes into some detail to disprove Lassalle's idea that under socialism the worker will receive the "undiminished" or "whole proceeds of his labour." Marx shows that from the whole of the social labour of society it is necessary to deduct a reserve fund, a fund for the expansion of production, for the replacement of "worn-out" machinery, and so on; then, also, from the means of consumption must be deducted a fund for the expenses of management, for schools, hospitals, homes for the aged, and so on

Instead of Lassalle's hazy, obscure, general phrase—"the whole proceeds of his labour to the worker"—Marx makes a sober estimate of exactly how socialist society will have to manage its affairs. Marx proceeds to make a *concrete* analysis of the conditions of life of a society in which there is no capitalism, and says:

"What we have to deal with here (in analysing the programme of the Party) is a communist society not as it has *developed* on its own foundations, but on the contrary as it *emerges* from capitalist society; which is thus in every respect economically, morally and intellectually still stamped with the birth marks of the old society from whose womb it emerges." [1]

And it is this communist society—a society which has just come into the world out of the womb of capitalism and which, in every respect, bears the birth marks of the old society—that Marx terms the "first," or lower, phase of communist society.

The means of production are no longer the private property of individuals. The means of production belong to the whole of society. Every member of society, performing a certain part of socially-necessary labour, receives a certificate from society to the effect that he has done such and such an amount of work. According to this certificate, he receives from the public warehouses, where articles of consumption are stored, a corresponding quantity of products. Deducting that proportion of labour which goes to the public fund, every worker, therefore, receives from society as much as he has given it.

"Equal right" seems to reign supreme.

But when Lassalle, having such a social order in view (generally called socialism, but termed by Marx the first phase of communism), speaks of this as "equitable distribution," and says that this is "the equal right" of "all members of society" to "equal proceeds of labour," he is mistaken, and Marx exposes his error.

"Equal right," says Marx, we indeed have here; but it is *still* a "bourgeois right," which, like every right, *presupposes inequality*. Every right is an application of the *same* measure to *different* people who, in fact, are not the same and are not equal to one another; that is why "equal right" is really a violation of equality and an injustice. As a matter of fact, every man having performed as much social labour as another receives an equal share of the social product (less the above-mentioned deductions).

[1] *Critique of the Gotha Programme.*

But people are not alike: one is strong, another is weak; one is married, another is not; one has more children, another has less, and so on. And the conclusion Marx draws is:

" ... with an equal output and hence an equal share in the social consumption fund, one will in fact receive more than another, one will be richer than another and so on. To avoid all these defects, right, instead of being equal, would have to be unequal." [1]

Hence, the first phase of communism cannot produce justice and equality; differences, and unjust differences, in wealth will still exist, but the *exploitation* of man by man will have become impossible, because it will be impossible to seize the *means of production,* the factories, machines, land, etc., as private property. In smashing Lassalle's petty-bourgeois, confused phrases about "equality" and "justice" *in general,* Marx shows the *course of development* of communist society, which, at first, is compelled to abolish *only* the "injustice" of the means of production having been seized by private individuals and which *cannot* at once abolish the other injustice of the distribution of articles of consumption "according to the amount of work performed" (and not according to needs).

The vulgar economists, including the bourgeois professors and also "our" Tugan-Baranovsky, constantly reproach the Socialists with forgetting the inequality of people and with "dreaming" of abolishing this inequality. Such a reproach, as we see, only proves the extreme ignorance of Messieurs the bourgeois ideologists.

Marx not only scrupulously takes into account the inevitable inequality of men; he also takes into account the fact that the mere conversion of the means of production into the common property of the whole of society (generally called "socialism") *does not remove* the defects of distribution and the inequality of "bourgeois right" which *continue to prevail* as long as the products are divided "according to the amount of work performed." Continuing, Marx says:

"But these defects are inevitable in the first phase of communist society as it is when it has just emerged after prolonged birthpangs from capitalist society. Right can never be higher than the economic structure of society and the cultural development thereby determined." [2]

And so, in the first phase of communist society (generally called socialism) "bourgeois right" is *not* abolished in its entirety, but only in part, only in proportion to the economic transformation so far attained, *i.e.,* only in respect of the means of production. "Bourgeois right" recognises them as the private

[1] *Ibid.*
[2] *Ibid.*

property of separate individuals. Socialism converts them into *common* property. *To that extent,* and to that extent alone, "bourgeois right" disappears.

However, it continues to exist so far as its other part is concerned; it remains in the capacity of regulator (determining factor) in the distribution of products and allotment of labour among the members of society. The socialist principle: "He who does not work, neither shall he eat," is *already* realised; the other socialist principle: "An equal amount of labour for an equal quantity of products," is also *already* realised. But this is not yet communism, and it does not abolish "bourgeois right," which gives to unequal individuals, in return for an unequal (actually unequal) amount of work, an equal quantity of products.

This is a "defect," says Marx, but it is unavoidable in the first phase of communism; for if we are not to fall into utopianism, we cannot imagine that, having overthrown capitalism, people will at once learn to work for society *without any standard of right;* indeed, the abolition of capitalism *does not immediately* create the economic prerequisites for *such* a change.

And there is as yet no other standard than that of "bourgeois right." To this extent, therefore, there is still need for a state, which, while safeguarding the public ownership of the means of production, would safeguard the equality of labour and equality in the distribution of products.

The state withers away in so far as there are no longer any capitalists, any classes, and consequently, no *class* can be *suppressed*.

But the state has not yet completely withered away, since there still remains the protection of "bourgeois right" which sanctifies actual inequality. For the complete withering away of the state, complete communism is necessary.

THE HIGHER PHASE OF COMMUNIST SOCIETY

Marx continues:

"In a higher phase of communist society after the enslaving subordination of individuals under division of labour, and therewith also the antithesis between mental and physical labour, has vanished; after labour has become not merely a means to live but has become itself the primary necessity of life; after the productive forces have also increased with the all-round development of the individual, and all the springs of co-operative wealth flow more abundantly—only then can the narrow horizon of bourgeois right be fully left behind and society inscribe on its banners: from each according to his ability, to each according to his needs!" [1]

Only now can we appreciate to the full the correctness of Engels' remarks in which he mercilessly ridiculed the absurdity of combining the words

[1] *Ibid.*

"freedom" and "state." While the state exists there is no freedom. When freedom exists, there will be no state.

The economic basis for the complete withering away of the state is the high stage of development of communism in which the antithesis between mental and physical labour disappears, that is to say, when one of the principal sources of modern *social* inequality—a source, moreover, which cannot be removed immediately by the mere conversion of the means of production into public property, by the mere expropriation of the capitalists—disappears.

This expropriation will *facilitate* the enormous development of the productive forces. And seeing how capitalism is already *retarding* this development to an incredible degree, seeing how much progress could be achieved even on the basis of the present level of modern technique, we have a right to say with the fullest confidence that the expropriation of the capitalists will inevitably result in the enormous development of the productive forces of human society. But how rapidly this development will proceed, how soon it will reach the point of breaking away from the division of labour, of removing the antithesis between mental and physical labour, of transforming work into the "primary necessity of life"—we do not and *cannot* know.

That is why we have a right to speak only of the inevitable withering away of the state; we must emphasise the protracted nature of this process and its dependence upon the rapidity of development of the *higher phase* of communism; and we leave the question of length of time, or the concrete forms of the withering away, quite open, because *no material is available* to enable us to answer these questions.

The state will be able to wither away completely when society can apply the rule: "From each according to his ability, to each according to his needs," *i.e.,* when people have become so accustomed to observing the fundamental rules of social life and when their labour is so productive that they will voluntarily work *according to their ability.* "The narrow horizon of bourgeois right," which compels one to calculate with the shrewdness of a Shylock whether he has not worked half an hour more than another, whether he is not getting less pay than another—this narrow horizon will then be left behind. There will then be no need for society to make an exact calculation of the quantity of products to be distributed to each of its members; each will take freely "according to his needs."

From the bourgeois point of view, it is easy to declare such a social order to be "a pure utopia," and to sneer at the Socialists for promising everyone the right to receive from society, without any control of the labour of the individual citizen, any quantity of truffles, automobiles, pianos, etc. Even now, most bourgeois "savants" make shift with such sneers, thereby displaying at once their ignorance and their selfish defence of capitalism.

Ignorance—for it has never entered the head of any Socialist to "promise" that the higher phase of communism will arrive; and the great Socialists, in *foreseeing* its arrival, presupposed both a productivity of labour unlike the present and a person *unlike the present* man in the street who, like the seminary students in Pomyalovsky's story,[1] is capable of damaging the stores of social wealth "just for fun," and of demanding the impossible.

Until the "higher" phase of communism arrives, the Socialists demand the *strictest* control, by society *and by the state,* of the amount of labour and the amount of consumption; but this control must *start* with the expropriation of the capitalists, with the establishment of workers' control over the capitalists, and must be carried out, not by a state of bureaucrats, but by a state of *armed workers.*

The selfish defence of capitalism by the bourgeois ideologists (and their hangers-on, like Messrs. Tseretelli, Chernov and Co.) lies in their *substituting* controversies and discussions about the distant future for the essential imperative questions of *present-day* policy, *viz.,* the expropriation of the capitalists, the conversion of *all* citizens into workers and employees of *one* huge "syndicate"—the whole state—and the complete subordination of the whole of the work of this syndicate to the really democratic state of the *Soviets of Workers' and Soldiers' Deputies.*

In reality, when a learned professor, and following him some philistine, and following the latter Messrs. Tseretelli and Chernov, talk of the unreasonable utopias, of the demagogic promises of the Bolsheviks, of the impossibility of "introducing" socialism, it is the higher stage or phase of communism which they have in mind, and which no one has ever promised, or has even thought of "introducing," because, generally speaking, it cannot be "introduced."

And this brings us to the question of the scientific difference between socialism and communism which Engels touched on in his above-quoted argument about the incorrectness of the name "Social-Democrat." The political difference between the first, or lower, and the higher phase of communism will in time, no doubt, be tremendous; but it would be ridiculous to take cognisance of this difference now, under capitalism; only some isolated anarchist, perhaps, could invest it with primary importance (if there are still any people among the anarchists who have learned nothing from the "Plekhanovist" conversion of the Kropotkins, the Graveses, the Cornelisens and other "leading lights" of anarchism into social-chauvinists or "anarcho-trenchists," as Gay, one of the few anarchists who has still preserved a sense of honour and a conscience, has expressed it).

But the scientific difference between socialism and communism is clear.

---

[1] Pomyalovsky's *Seminary Sketches,* depicting the life of the students in an ecclesiastical seminary, of which drunkenness, rioting and filthy pranks were typical.

What is generally called socialism was termed by Marx the "first" or lower phase of communist society. In so far as the means of production become *common* property, the word "communism" is also applicable here, providing we do not forget that it is *not* complete communism. The great significance of Marx's explanations lies in that here, too, he consistently applies materialist dialectics, the theory of development, and regards communism as something which develops *out* of capitalism. Instead of scholastically invented, "concocted" definitions and fruitless disputes about words (what is socialism? what is communism?), Marx gives an analysis of what may be called stages in the economic ripeness of communism.

In its first phase, or first stage, communism *cannot* as yet be economically ripe and entirely free from all the traditions and all traces of capitalism. Hence the interesting phenomenon that communism in its first phase retains "the narrow horizon of *bourgeois* right." Of course, bourgeois right in regard to distribution of articles of *consumption* inevitably presupposes the existence of the *bourgeois state,* for right is nothing without an apparatus capable of *enforcing* the observance of the standards of right.

Consequently, for a certain time not only bourgeois right, but even the bourgeois state remains under communism, without the bourgeoisie!

This may sound like a paradox or simply a dialectical puzzle which Marxism is often accused of inventing by people who would not take the slightest trouble to study its extraordinarily profound content.

As a matter of fact, however, the remnants of the old surviving in the new confront us in life at every step, in nature as well as in society. Marx did not smuggle a scrap of "bourgeois" right into communism of his own accord; he indicated what is economically and politically inevitable in the society which is emerging *from the womb* of capitalism.

Democracy is of great importance for the working class in its struggle for freedom against the capitalists. But democracy is by no means a boundary that must not be overstepped; it is only one of the stages in the process of development from feudalism to capitalism, and from capitalism to communism.

Democracy means equality. The great significance of the proletariat's struggle for equality and the significance of equality as a slogan will be clear if we correctly interpret it as meaning the abolition of *classes*. But democracy means only *formal* equality. As soon as equality is obtained for all members of society *in relation to* the ownership of the means of production, that is, equality of labour and equality of wages, humanity will inevitably be confronted with the question of going beyond formal equality to real equality, *i.e.,* to applying the rule, "from each according to his ability, to each according to his needs." By what stages, by what practical measures humanity will proceed to his higher aim—we do not and cannot know. But it is important to realise how infinitely mendacious is the ordinary bourgeois conception of socialism as something lifeless, petrified, fixed once for all, whereas in reality *only* under socialism will a rapid, genuine, really mass movement, embracing first the *majority* and then the whole of the population, commence in all spheres of social and individual life.

Democracy is a form of state, one of its varieties. Consequently, like every state, it, on the one hand, represents the organised, systematic application of force against persons; but, on the other hand, it signifies the formal recognition of the equality of all citizens, the equal right of all to determine the structure and administration of the state. This, in turn, is connected with the fact that, at a certain stage in the development of democracy, it first rallies the proletariat as a revolutionary class against capitalism, and gives it the opportunity to crush, to smash to atoms, to wipe off the face of the earth the bourgeois, even the republican bourgeois, state machine, the standing army, the police and bureaucracy; to substitute for all this a *more* democratic, but still a state machine in the shape of the armed masses of workers who become transformed into a universal people's militia.

Here "quantity is transformed into quality": *such* a degree of democracy is connected with overstepping the boundaries of bourgeois society, with the beginning of its socialist reconstruction. If, indeed, *all* take part in the administration of the state, capitalism cannot retain its hold. The development of capitalism, in turn, itself creates the *prerequisites* that *enable* indeed "all" to take part in the administration of the state. Some of these prerequisites are: universal literacy, already achieved in most of the advanced capitalist countries, then the "training and disciplining" of millions of workers by the huge, complex and socialised apparatus of the post-office, the railways, the big factories, large-scale commerce, banking, etc., etc.

With such *economic* prerequisites it is quite possible, immediately, overnight, after the overthrow of the capitalists and bureaucrats, to supersede them in the *control* of production and distribution, in the work of *keeping account* of labour and its products by the armed workers, by the whole of the armed population. (The question of control and accounting must not be confused with the question of the scientifically educated staff of engineers, agronomists and so on. These gentlemen are working today and obey the capitalists; they will work even better tomorrow and obey the armed workers.)

Accounting and control—these are the *principal* things that are necessary for the "setting up" and correct functioning of the *first phase* of communist society. *All* citizens are transformed into the salaried employees of the state, which consists of the armed workers. *All* citizens become employees and workers of a *single* national state "syndicate." All that is required is that they should work equally—do their proper share of work—

and get paid equally. The accounting and control necessary for this have been so utterly *simplified* by capitalism that they have become the extraordinarily simple operations of checking, recording and issuing receipts, which anyone who can read and write and who knows the first four rules of arithmetic can perform.[1]

When the *majority* of the people themselves begin everywhere to keep such accounts and maintain such control over the capitalists (now converted into employees) and over the intellectual gentry, who preserve their capitalist habits, this control will really become universal, general, national; and there will be no way of getting away from it, there will be "nowhere to go."

The whole of society will have become a single office and a single factory with equality of work and equality of pay.

But this "factory" discipline, which the proletariat will extend to the whole of society after the defeat of the capitalists and the overthrow of the exploiters, is by no means our ideal, or our ultimate goal. It is but a necessary *step* for the purpose of thoroughly purging society of all the hideousness and foulness of capitalist exploitation, *and for the purpose of advancing further.*

From the moment all members of society, or even only the overwhelming majority, have learned to administer the state *themselves,* have taken this business into their own hands, have "set up" control over the insignificant minority of capitalists, over the gentry, who wish to preserve their capitalist habits, and over the workers who have been completely demoralised by capitalism—from this moment the need for government begins to disappear. The more complete democracy becomes, the nearer the moment approaches when it becomes unnecessary. The more democratic the "state" of the armed workers—which is "no longer a state in the proper sense of the word"—becomes, the more rapidly does *the state* begin to wither away.

For when *all* have learned the art of administration, and will indeed independently administer social production, will independently keep accounts, control the idlers, the gentlefolk, the swindlers and similar "guardians of capitalist traditions," the escape from this national accounting and control will inevitably become so increasingly difficult, such a rare exception, and will probably be accompanied by such swift and severe punishment (for the armed workers are practical men and not sentimental intellectuals, and they will scarcely allow anyone to trifle with them), that very soon the *necessity* of observing the simple, fundamental rules of human intercourse will become a *habit.*

The door will then be wide open for the transition from the first phase of communist society to its higher phase, and with it to the complete withering away of the state.

[1] When most of the functions of the state are reduced to this accounting and control by the workers themselves, it ceases to be a "political state," the "public functions will lose their political character and be transformed into . . . simple administrative functions."

6. Call to Revolution*

V. I. LENIN

COMRADES,

I am writing these lines on the evening of November 6 [October 24]. The situation is critical in the extreme. It is absolutely clear that to delay the insurrection now will veritably be fatal.

I exhort my comrades with all my heart and strength to realise that everything now hangs on a thread; that we are being confronted by problems that can be solved not by conferences or congresses (even Congresses of Soviets), but exclusively by the people, by the masses, by the struggle of the armed masses.

The bourgeois onslaught of the Kornilovists and the removal of Verkhovsky show that we must not wait. We must at all costs, this very evening, this very night, arrest the government, first disarming (defeating, if they offer resistance) the *Junkers* and so forth.

We must not wait! We may lose everything!

The gain from the seizure of power immediately will be that the people (not the Congress, but the people, the army and the peasants in the first place) will be defended from the Kornilovist government, which has driven out Verkhovsky and has hatched a second Kornilov plot.

Who must take power?

At present that is not important. Let the Revolutionary Military Committee take it, or "some other institution," declaring that it will relinquish the power only to the true representatives of the interests of the people, the interests of the army (immediate proposals for peace), the interests of the peasants (the land to be taken immediately and private property abolished), the interests of the starving.

All boroughs, all regiments, all forces must be mobilised immediately and must send their delegations to the Revolutionary Military Committee and to the Central Committee of the Bolsheviks with the insistent demand that under no circumstances shall the power be left in the hands of Kerensky and Co. until November 7 [October 25]; not under any circumstances; the matter must be decided unconditionally this very evening, or this very night.

History will not forgive revolutionaries for procrastinating when they can be victorious today (will certainly be victorious today), while they risk losing much, in fact, everything, tomorrow.

* From V. I. Lenin, *Selected Works*, VI (International Publishers, 1936). By permission.

If we seize power today, we seize it not in opposition to the Soviets but on their behalf.

The seizure of power is a matter of insurrection; its political purpose will be clear after the seizure.

It would be a disaster, or a sheer formality, to await the wavering vote of November 7 [October 25]. The people have the right and the duty to decide such questions not by a vote, but by force; in critical moments of revolution, the people have the right and the duty to give directions to their representatives, even their best representatives, and not to wait for them.

This is proved by the history of all revolutions; and it would be an infinite crime on the part of the revolutionaries were they to let the moment pass, knowing that upon them depends the *salvation of the revolution,* the proposal of peace, the saving of Petrograd, salvation from famine, the transfer of the land to the peasants.

The government is wavering. It must be *destroyed* at all costs!

To delay action will be fatal.

November 6 [October 24], 1917.

~~~~~~

7. *Marxism and the United States* *

LEON TROTSKY

~~~~~~

FASCISM AND THE NEW DEAL

Two methods for saving historically doomed capitalism are to-day vying with each other in the world arena—Fascism and the New Deal. Fascism bases its programme on the demolition of labour organizations, on the destruction of social reforms, and on the complete annihilation of democratic rights, in order to forestall a resurrection of the proletariat's class struggle. The fascist state officially legalizes the degradation of workers and the pauperization of the middle classes, in the name of saving the "nation" and the "race"—presumptuous names under which decaying capitalism figures.

The policy of the New Deal, which tries to save imperialist democracy by way of sops to the labour and farmer aristocracy, is in its broad compass accessible only to the very wealthy nations, and so in that sense it is Ameri-

* From Leon Trotsky, *Karl Marx* (The Living Thoughts Library, David McKay Co., 1939). By permission.

can policy *par excellence*. The American government has attempted to shift a part of the costs of that policy to the shoulders of the monopolists, exhorting them to raise wages and shorten the labour day and thus increase the purchasing power of the population and extend production. Léon Blum attempted to translate this sermon into elementary school French. In vain! The French capitalist, like the American, does not produce for the sake of production but for profit. He is always ready to limit production, even to destroy manufactured products, if thereby his own share of the national income will be increased.

The New Deal programme is all the more inconsistent in that, while preaching sermons to the magnates of capital about the advantages of abundance over scarcity, the government dispenses premiums for cutting down on production. Is greater confusion possible? The government confutes its critics with the challenge: can you do better? What all this means is that on the basis of capitalism the situation is hopeless.

Beginning with 1933, *i.e.,* in the course of the last six years in America, the federal government, the states, and the municipalities have handed out to the unemployed nearly fifteen billion dollars in relief, a sum quite insufficient in itself and representing merely the smaller part of lost wages, but at the same time, considering the declining national income, a colossal sum. During 1938, which was a year of comparative economic revival, the national debt of the United States increased by two billion dollars past the thirty-eight billion dollar mark, or twelve billion dollars more than the highest point at the end of the World War. Early in 1939 it passed the forty billion dollar mark. And then what? The mounting national debt is of course a burden on posterity. But the New Deal itself was possible only because of the tremendous wealth accumulated by past generations. Only a very rich nation could indulge itself in so extravagant a policy. But even such a nation cannot indefinitely go on living at the expense of past generations. The New Deal policy with its fictitious achievements and its very real increase in the national debt is unavoidably bound to culminate in ferocious capitalist reaction and a devastating explosion of imperialism. In other words, it is directed into the same channels as the policy of Fascism.

ANOMALY OR NORM?

The Secretary of the Interior of the United States, Harold L. Ickes, considers it "one of the strangest anomalies in all history" that America, democratic in form, is autocratic in substance: "America, the land of majority rule but controlled at least until 1933 (!) by monopolies that in their turn are controlled by a negligible number of their stockholders." The diagnosis is correct, with the exception of the intimation that with the advent of Roosevelt the rule of monopoly either ceased or weakened. Yet what Ickes calls "one of the strangest anomalies in all history," is as a matter of fact, the unquestionable norm of capitalism. The domination of the weak by the strong, of the many by the few, of the toilers by the exploiters is a basic law of bourgeois democracy. What distinguishes the United States from other countries is merely the greater scope and the greater heinousness in the contradictions of its capitalism. The absence of a feudal past, rich natural resources, an energetic and enterprising people, in a word, all the prerequisites that augured an uninterrupted development of democracy, have actually brought about a fantastic concentration of wealth.

Promising this time to wage the fight against monopolies to a triumphant issue, Ickes recklessly harks back to Thomas Jefferson, Andrew Jackson, Abraham Lincoln, Theodore Roosevelt, and Woodrow Wilson as the predecessors of Franklin D. Roosevelt. "Practically all of our greatest historical figures," said he on 30th December 1937, "are famous because of their persistent and courageous fight to prevent and control the overconcentration of wealth and power in a few hands." But it follows from his own words that the fruit of this "persistent and courageous fight" is the complete domination of democracy by the plutocracy.

For some inexplicable reason Ickes thinks that this time victory is assured, provided the people understand that the fight is "not between the New Deal and the average enlightened businessman, but between the New Deal and the Bourbons of the sixty families who have brought the rest of the businessmen in the United States under the terror of their domination." This authoritative spokesman does not explain just how the "Bourbons" managed to subjugate all the enlightened businessmen, notwithstanding democracy and the efforts of the "greatest historical figures." The Rockefellers, the Morgans, the Mellons, the Vanderbilts, the Guggenheims, the Fords & Co. did not invade the United States from the outside, as Cortez invaded Mexico: they grew organically out of the "people," or more precisely, out of the class of "enlightened industrialists and businessmen" and became, in line with Marx's prognosis, the natural apogee of capitalism. Since a young and strong democracy in its heyday was unable to check the concentration of wealth when the process was only at its inception, is it possible to believe even for a minute that a decaying democracy is capable of weakening class antagonisms that have attained their utmost limit? Anyway, the experience of the New Deal has produced no ground for such optimism. Refuting the charges of big business against the government, Robert H. Jackson, a person high in the councils of the administration, proved with figures that during Roosevelt's tenure the profits of the magnates of capital reached heights they themselves had ceased to dream about during the last period of Hoover's presidency, from which it follows, in any event, that Roosevelt's fight against monopolies has been crowned with no greater success than the struggle of all his predecessors.

TO BRING BACK YESTERDAY

One cannot but agree with Professor Lewis W. Douglas, the former Director of the Budget in the Roosevelt Administration, when he condemns the government for "attacking monopoly in one field while fostering monopoly in many others." Yet in the nature of the thing it cannot be otherwise. According to Marx, the government is the executive committee of the ruling class. To-day monopolists are the strongest section of the ruling class. No government is in any position to fight against monopoly in general, *i.e.,* against the class by whose will it rules. While attacking one phase of monopoly, it is obliged to seek an ally in other phases of monopoly. In union with banks and light industry it can deliver occasional blows against the trusts of heavy industry, which, by the way, do not stop earning fantastic profits because of that.

Lewis Douglas does not counterpose science to the official quackery, but merely another kind of quackery. He sees the source of monopoly not in capitalism but in protectionism and, accordingly, discovers the salvation of society not in the abolition of private ownership of the means of production but in the lowering of customs tariffs. "Unless the freedom of markets is restored," he predicts, it is "doubtful that the freedom of all institutions— enterprise, speech, education, religion—can survive." In other words, without restoring the freedom of international trade, democracy, wherever and to the extent that it has yet survived, must yield either to a revolutionary or to a fascist dictatorship. But freedom of international trade is inconceivable without freedom of internal trade, *i.e.,* without competition. And freedom of competition is inconceivable under the sway of monopoly. Unfortunately, Mr. Douglas, quite like Mr. Ickes, like Mr. Jackson, like Mr. Cummings, and like Mr. Roosevelt himself, has not gone to the trouble to initiate us into his own prescription against monopolistic capitalism and thereby— against either a revolution or a totalitarian regime.

Freedom of trade, like freedom of competition, like the prosperity of the middle class, belongs to the irrevocable past. To bring back yesterday, is now the sole prescription of the democratic reformers of capitalism: to bring back more "freedom" to small and middle-sized industrialists and businessmen, to change the money and credit system in their favour, to free the market from being bossed by the trusts, to eliminate professional speculators from the stock exchange, to restore freedom of international trade, and so forth *ad infinitum*. The reformers even dream of limiting the use of machines and placing a proscription on technique, which disturbs the social balance and causes a lot of worry.

SCIENTISTS AND MARXISM

Speaking in defence of science on 7th December 1937, Dr. Robert A. Millikan, a leading American physicist, observed: "United States statistics show that the percentage of the population 'gainfully employed' has steadily increased during the last fifty years, when science has been most rapidly applied." This defence of capitalism under the guise of defending science cannot be called a happy one. It is precisely during the last half-century that "was broken the link of times" and the interrelation of economics and technique altered sharply. The period referred to by Millikan included the beginning of capitalist decline as well as the highest point of capitalist prosperity. To hush up the beginning of that decline, which is world-wide, is to stand forth as an apologist for capitalism. Rejecting Socialism in an off-hand manner with the aid of arguments that would scarcely do honour even to Henry Ford, Dr. Millikan tells us that no system of distribution can satisfy the needs of man without raising the range of production. Undoubtedly! But it is a pity that the famous physicist did not explain to the millions of American unemployed just how they were to participate in raising the national income. Abstract preachment about the saving grace of individual initiative and high productivity of labour will certainly not provide the unemployed with jobs, nor will it fill the budgetary deficit, nor lead the nation's business out of its blind alley.

What distinguishes Marx is the universality of his genius, his ability to understand phenomena and processes of various fields in their inherent connection. Without being a specialist in natural sciences, he was one of the first to appreciate the significance of the great discoveries in that field; for example, the theory of Darwinism. Marx was assured of that pre-eminence not so much by virtue of his intellect as by virtue of his method. Bourgeois-minded scientists may think that they are above Socialism; yet Robert Millikan's case is but one more confirmation that in the sphere of sociology they continue to be hopeless quacks.

PRODUCTIVE POSSIBILITIES AND PRIVATE OWNERSHIP

In his message to Congress at the beginning of 1937 President Roosevelt expressed his desire to raise the national income to ninety or one hundred billion dollars, without however indicating just how. In itself this progamme is exceedingly modest. In 1929, when there were approximately 2,000,000 unemployed, the national income reached eighty-one billion dollars. Setting in motion the present productive forces would not only suffice to realize Roosevelt's programme but even to surpass it considerably. Machines, raw materials, workers, everything is available, not to mention the population's need for the products. If, notwithstanding that, the plan is unrealizable—and unrealizable it is—the only reason is the irreconcilable conflict that has developed between capitalist ownership and society's need for expanding production. The famous government-sponsored National Survey of Potential Productive Capacity came to the conclusion that the cost of production and services used in 1929 amounted to nearly ninety-four billion dollars, calculated on the basis of retail prices. Yet if all the actual productive possibilities were utilized, that figure would have risen to 135 billion dollars, which would have averaged $4370 a year per family, sufficient to secure a decent and comfortable living. It must be added that the calculations of the National Survey are based on the present productive organization of the United States, as it came about in consequence of capitalism's anarchic history. If the equipment itself were re-equipped on the basis of a unified socialist plan, the productive calculations could be considerably surpassed and a high comfortable standard of living, on the basis of an extremely short labour day, assured to all the people.

Therefore, to save society, it is not necessary either to check the development of technique, to shut down factories, to award premiums to farmers for sabotaging agriculture, to turn a third of the workers into paupers, or to call upon maniacs to be dictators. Not one of these measures, which are a shocking mockery of the interests of society, is necessary. What is indispensable and urgent is to separate the means of production from their present parasitic owners and to organize society in accordance with a rational plan. Then it would at once be possible really to cure society of its ills. All those able to work would find a job. The workday would gradually decrease. The wants of all members of society would secure increasing satisfaction. The words "poverty," "crisis," "exploitation," would drop out of circulation. Mankind would at last cross the threshold into true humanity.

THE INEVITABILITY OF SOCIALISM

"Along with the constantly diminishing number of magnates of capital . . ." says Marx, "grows the mass of misery, oppression, slavery, degradation, exploitation; but with this too grows the revolt of the working-class, a class always increasing in numbers, and disciplined, united, organized by the very mechanism of the process of capitalist production itself. . . . Centralization of the means of production and socialization of labour at last reach a point where they become incompatible with their capitalist integument. This integument is burst asunder. The knell of capitalist private property sounds. The expropriators are expropriated." That is the Socialist revolution. To Marx, the problem of reconstructing society did not arise from some prescription, motivated by his personal predilections; it followed, as an iron-clad historical necessity—on the one hand, from the productive forces grown to powerful maturity; on the other, from the impossibility further to foster these forces at the mercy of the law of value.

The lucubrations of certain intellectuals on the theme that, regardless of Marx's teaching, socialism is not *inevitable* but merely *possible,* are devoid of any content whatsoever. Obviously, Marx did not imply that socialism would come about without man's volition and action: any such idea is simply an absurdity. Marx foretold that out of the economic collapse in which the development of capitalism must inevitably culminate—and this collapse is before our very eyes—there can be no other way out except socialization of the means of production. The productive forces need a new organizer and a new master, and since existence determines consciousness, Marx had no doubt that the working class, at the cost of errors and defeats, will come to understand the actual situation and, sooner or later, will draw the imperative practical conclusions.

That socialization of the capitalist-created means of production is of tremendous economic benefit is to-day demonstrable not only in theory but also by the experiment of the U.S.S.R., notwithstanding the limitations of that experiment. True, capitalistic reactionaries, not without artifice, use Stalin's regime as a scarecrow against the ideas of socialism. As a matter of fact, Marx never said that socialism could be achieved in a single country, and moreover, a backward country. The continuing privations of the masses in the U.S.S.R., the omnipotence of the privileged caste, which has lifted itself above the nation and its misery, finally, the rampant club-law of the bureaucrats are not consequences of the socialist method of economy but of the isolation and backwardness of the U.S.S.R. caught in the ring of capitalist encirclement. The wonder is that under such exceptionally unfavourable conditions planned economy has managed to demonstrate its insuperable benefits.

All the saviours of capitalism, the democratic as well as the fascist kind, attempt to limit, or at least to camouflage, the power of the magnates of capital, in order to forestall "the expropriation of the expropriators." They all recognize, and many of them openly admit, that the failure of their reformist attempts must inevitably lead to socialist revolution. They have all managed to demonstrate that their methods of saving capitalism are but reactionary and helpless quackery. Marx's prognosis about the inevitability of socialism is thus fully confirmed by proof of the negative

THE INEVITABILITY OF SOCIALIST REVOLUTION

The programme of "Technocracy," which flourished in the period of the great crisis of 1929–1932, was founded on the correct premise that economy can be rationalized only through the union of technique at the height of science and government at the service of society. Such a union is possible, provided technique and government are liberated from the slavery of private ownership. That is where the great revolutionary task begins. In order to liberate technique from the cabal of private interests and place the government at the service of society, it is necessary to "expropriate the expropriators." Only a powerful class, interested in its own liberation and opposed to the monopolistic expropriators, is capable of consummating this task. Only in unison with a proletarian government can the qualified stratum of technicians build a truly scientific and a truly national, *i.e.*, a socialist economy.

It would be best, of course, to achieve this purpose in a peaceful, gradual, democratic way. But the social order that has outlived itself never yields its place to its successor without resistance. If in its day the young forceful democracy proved incapable of forestalling the seizure of wealth and power by the plutocracy, is it possible to expect that a senile and devastated democracy will prove capable of transforming a social order based on the untrammelled rule of sixty families? Theory and history teach that a succession of social regimes presupposes the highest form of the class struggle, *i.e.*, revolution. Even slavery could not be abolished in the United States without a civil war. "Force is the midwife of every old society pregnant with a new one." No one has yet been able to refute Marx on this basic tenet in the sociology of class society. Only a socialist revolution can clear the road to socialism.

MARXISM IN THE UNITED STATES

The North American republic has gone further than others in the sphere of technique and the organization of production. Not only Americans but all of mankind will build on that foundation. However, the various phases of the social process in one and the same nation have varying rhythms, depending on special historical conditions. While the United States enjoys tremendous superiority in technology, its economic thought is extremely backward in both the right and left wings. John L. Lewis has about the same views as Franklin D. Roosevelt. Considering the nature of his office, Lewis's social function is incomparably more conservative, not to say reactionary, than Roosevelt's. In certain American circles there is a tendency to repudiate this or that radical theory without the slightest scientific criticism, by simply dismissing it as "un-American." But where can you find the differentiating criterion of that? Christianity was imported into the United States along with logarithms, Shakespeare's poetry, notions on the rights of man and the citizen, and certain other not unimportant products of human thought. To-day Marxism stands in the same category.

The American Secretary of Agriculture Henry A. Wallace imputed to the author of these lines ". . . a dogmatic thinness which is bitterly un-American" and counterposed to Russian dogmatism the opportunist spirit of Jefferson, who knew how to get along with his opponents. Apparently, it has never occurred to Mr. Wallace that a policy of compromise is not a function of some immaterial national spirit, but a product of material conditions. A nation rapidly growing rich has sufficient reserves for conciliation between hostile classes and parties. When, on the other hand, social contradictions are sharpened, the ground for compromise disappears. America was free of

"dogmatic thinness" only because it had a plethora of virgin areas, in-
exhaustible resources of natural wealth and, it would seem, limitless opportunities for enrichment. True, even under these conditions the spirit of compromise did not prevent the Civil War when the hour for it struck. Anyway,
the material conditions which made up the basis of "Americanism" are to-
day increasingly relegated to the past. Hence the profound crisis of traditional American ideology.

Empiric thinking, limited to the solution of immediate tasks from time to
time, seemed adequate enough in labour as well as in bourgeois circles so
long as Marx's law of value did everybody's thinking. But to-day that very
law produces opposite effects. Instead of urging economy forward, it undermines its foundations. Conciliatory eclectic thinking, maintaining an unfavourable or disdainful attitude towards Marxism as a "dogma," and with
its philosophic apogee, pragmatism, becomes utterly inadequate, increasingly
insubstantial, reactionary and downright funny.

On the contrary, it is the traditional ideas of "Americanism" that have
become lifeless, petrified "dogma," giving rise to nothing but errors and
confusion. At the same time, the economic teaching of Marx has acquired
peculiar viability and pointedness for the United States. Although *Capital*
rests on international material, preponderantly English, in its theoretical
foundation it is an analysis of pure capitalism, capitalism in general, capitalism as such. Undoubtedly the capitalism grown on the virgin, unhistorical
soil of America comes closest to that ideal type of capitalism.

Saving Mr. Wallace's presence, America developed economically not in
accordance with the principles of Jefferson, but in accordance with the laws
of Marx. There is as little offence to national self-esteem in acknowledging
this as in recognizing that America turns around the sun in accordance with
the laws of Newton. *Capital* offers a faultless diagnosis of the malady and an
irreplaceable prognosis. In that sense the teaching of Marx is far more
permeated with new "Americanism" than the ideas of Hoover and Roosevelt, of Green and Lewis.

True, there is a widespread original literature in the United States devoted
to the crisis of American economy. In so far as conscientious economists offer
an objective picture of the destructive trends of American capitalism, their
investigations, regardless of their theoretical premises, look like direct illustrations of Marx's theory. The conservative tradition makes itself known,
however, when these authors stubbornly restrain themselves from definitive
conclusions, limiting themselves to gloomy predictions or such edifying
banalities as "the country must understand," "public opinion must earnestly
consider," and the like. These books look like a knife without a blade.

The United States had Marxists in the past, it is true, but they were a
strange type of Marxist, or rather, three strange types. In the first place, there
were the émigrés cast out of Europe, who did what they could but could not

find any response; in the second place, isolated American groups, like the De Leonists, who, in the course of events, and because of their own mistakes, turned themselves into sects; in the third place, dilettantes attracted by the October Revolution and sympathetic to Marxism as an exotic teaching that had little to do with the United States. Their day is over. Now dawns the new epoch of an independent class movement of the proletariat and at the same time of—genuine Marxism. In this, too, America will in a few jumps catch up with Europe and outdistance it. Progressive technique and a progressive social structure will pave their own way in the sphere of doctrine. The best theoreticians of Marxism will appear on American soil. Marx will become the mentor of the advanced American workers.

~~~~~~

8. Why I Am Not a Communist *

MORRIS R. COHEN

~~~~~~

Like many others who are not Communists, I hold no brief for the injustices and stupidities of the present capitalist regime. Indeed, I have never ceased to be grateful for the illumination on historic and contemporary social issues which I found in studying Marx's *Das Kapital*. It prepared me to see that the present general breakdown of capitalist economy is not an unforeseeable accident but a consequence of the private ownership of the machinery of production, whereby the processes of industry are directed for the profit of individual capitalists rather than for the satisfaction of our common needs. The old optimistic but essentially anarchistic notion that the good of all will best be promoted by "rugged individualism," by each pursuing his own selfish economic gain, is a cruel superstition which no man possessed of both reason and a decent amount of human sympathy can maintain in the face of the hideous miseries of our present disorder. When good crops turn out to be calamitous to the farmers who toil to raise them, because the city workers cannot with their needed labor buy the cereals and cotton which they need for food and clothing, the bankruptcy of capitalism is as clear as anything in human affairs can be.

But while the foregoing or essentially similar criticism of the evils of capi-

* *The Modern Monthly* (April, 1934; reprinted in *The Meaning of Marx: A Symposium*, by Bertrand Russell, John Dewey, Morris Cohen, Sidney Hook, and Sherwood Eddy, Rinehart & Company, Inc., 1934; and in Morris R. Cohen, *The Faith of a Liberal*, Henry Holt and Company, 1946. Copyright, 1934, by Farrar & Rinehart, Inc.). By permission.

talism is largely used by Communists, it is not peculiar to them. They share it not only with other Marxian socialists—whom, with self-defeating unfairness, they characterize as Fascists or social-fascists—but also with many liberal social reformers. For Marx himself freely borrowed his ideas from bourgeois historians as well as from Saint-Simon, Fourier, and their followers, whom he, with the characteristic human failing of borrowers, belittled as Utopians. (Note, for instance, how closely the *Communist Manifesto* follows Victor Considérant's *Principes du Socialisme, Manifeste de la Démocratie,* not only in ideas but also in their linguistic expression.) What distinguishes present-day Communists is not, therefore, their professed ultimate goal or their analysis of our economic ills, but their political remedy or program—to wit, the seizure of power by armed rebellion and the setting up of a dictatorship by the leaders of the Communist Party. To be sure, this dictatorship is to be in the name of the *proletariat,* just as the fascist dictatorship is in the name of *the whole nation.* But such verbal tricks cannot hide the brute facts of tyrannical suppression necessarily involved in all dictatorship. For the wielders of dictatorial power are few, they are seldom if ever themselves toilers, and they can maintain their power only by ruthlessly suppressing all expression of popular dissatisfaction with their rule. And where there is no freedom of discussion, there is no freedom of thought.

This program of civil war, dictatorship, and the illiberal or fanatically intolerant spirit which war psychology always engenders may bring more miseries than those that the Communists seek to remove; and the arguments to prove that such war is desirable or inevitable seem to be patently inadequate.

Communists ignore the historic truth that civil wars are much more destructive of all that men hold dearest than are wars between nations; and all the arguments that they use against the latter, including the late "war to end war," are much more cogent against civil wars. Wars between nations are necessarily restricted in scope and do not prevent—to a limited extent they even stimulate—co-operation within a community. But civil wars necessarily dislocate all existing social organs and leave us with little social capital or machinery to rebuild a better society.

The hatreds which fratricidal wars develop are more persistent and destructive than those developed by wars that terminate in treaties or agreements.

Having lived under the tyranny of the Czar, I cannot and do not condemn all revolutions. But the success and benefits of any revolution depend on the extent to which—like the American Revolution of 1776, the French Revolution of 1789, and the anti-Czarist Revolution of March 1917—it approximates national unanimity in the co-operation of diverse classes. When armed uprisings have been undertaken by single oppressed classes, as in the revolt of the gladiators in Rome, the various peasant revolts in England, Germany, and Russia, the French Commune of 1871, or the Moscow uprising of 1905, they have left a deplorably monotonous record of bloody massacres and oppressive reaction. The idea that armed rebellion is the only or the always effective cure for social ills seems to me no better than the old superstition of medieval medicine that blood-letting is the only and the sovereign remedy for all bodily ills.

Communists may feel that the benefits of their Revolution of 1917 outweigh all the terrific hardships which the Russian people have suffered since then. But reasonable people in America will do well to demand better evidence than has yet been offered that they can improve their lot by blindly imitating Russia. Russian breadlines, and famine without breadlines, are certainly not *prima facie* improvements over American conditions. At best a revolution is a regrettable means to bring about greater human welfare. It always unleashes the forces that thrive in disorder, the brutal executions, imprisonments, and, what is even worse, the sordid spying that undermines all feeling of personal security. These forces, once let loose, are difficult to control and they tend to perpetuate themselves. If, therefore, human well-being, rather than mere destruction, is our aim, we must be as critically-minded in considering the consequences of armed revolution as in considering the evils of the existing regime.

One of the reasons that lead Communists to ignore the terrific destruction which armed rebellion must bring about is the conviction that "the revolution" is inevitable. In this they follow Marx, who, dominated by the Hegelian dialectic, regarded the victory of the proletariat over the bourgeoisie as inevitable,[1] so that all that human effort can hope to achieve is "to shorten and lessen the birth pangs" of the new order.[2] There is, however, very little scientific value in this dialectic argument, and many Communists are quite ready to soft-pedal it and admit that some human mistake or misstep might lead to the triumph of Fascism. The truth is that the dialectic method which Marx inherited from Hegel and Schelling is an outgrowth of speculations carried on in theologic seminaries. The "system" of production takes the place of the councils or the mills of the gods. Such oriental fatalism has little support in the spirit and method of modern science. Let us therefore leave the pretended dialectic proof and examine the contention on an historical basis.

Historically, the argument is put thus: When did any class give up its power without a bloody struggle? As in most rhetorical questions, the questioner does not stop for an answer, assuming that his ignorance is conclusive as to the facts. Now, it is not difficult to give instances of ruling classes giving up their sovereignty without armed resistance. The English landed aristocracy did it in the Reform Bill of 1832; and the Russian nobility did it in 1863

[1] *Capital* (Tr. by Untermann, 1932), I, p. 837.
[2] *Ibid.*, pp. 14-15.

when they freed their serfs, though history showed clearly that in this way not only their political power but their very existence was doomed (for money income has never been so secure as direct revenue from the land, and life in cities reduced the absolute number of noble families). In our own country, the old seaboard aristocracy, which put over the United States Constitution and controlled the government up to the Jacksonian era, offered no armed resistance when the backwoods farmers outvoted them and removed church and property qualifications for office and for the franchise.

But it is not necessary to multiply such instances. It is more important to observe that history does not show that any *class* ever gained its enfranchisement through a bloody rebellion carried out by its own unaided efforts. When ruling classes are overthrown it is generally by a combination of groups that have risen to power only after a long process. For the parties to a rebellion cannot succeed unless they have more resources than the established regime. Thus the ascendancy of the French bourgeoisie was aided by the royal power which Richelieu and Colbert used in the seventeenth century to transform the landed barons into independent courtiers. Even so, the French Revolution of 1789 would have been impossible without the co-operation of the peasantry, whose opposition to their ancient seigneurs was strengthened as the latter ceased to be independent rulers of the land. This is in a measure also true of the supposedly purely Communist Revolution in Russia. For in that revolution, too, the peasantry had a much greater share than is ordinarily assumed. After all, the amount of landed communal property (that of the crown, the church, etc.) which was changed by the peasants into individual ownership may have been greater than the amount of private property made communal by the Soviet regime. Even the system of collective farms is, after all, a return to the old *mir* system, using modern machinery. The success of the Russian Revolution was largely due to the landlords' agents who, in their endeavor to restore the rule of the landlords, threw the peasantry into the arms of the Bolshevists. Indeed, the strictly Marxian economics, with its ideology of surplus-value due to the ownership of the means of production, is inherently inapplicable to the case of the peasant who cultivates his own piece of ground.

Even more important, however, is it to note that no amount of repetition can make a truth of the dogma that the capitalist class alone rules this country and like the Almighty can do what it pleases. It would be folly to deny that, as individuals or as a class, capitalists have more than their proportionate share of influence in the government, and that they have exercised it unintelligently and with dire results. But it is equally absurd to maintain that they have governed or can govern without the co-operation of the farmers and the influential middle classes. None of our recent constitutional amendments—not the income-tax amendment, not the popular election of the United States Senators, not woman suffrage, neither prohibition nor its repeal—nor any other major bit of legislation can be said to have been imposed on our country in the interests of the capitalist class. The farmers, who despite mortgages still cling to the private ownership of their land, are actually the dominant political group even in industrial states like New York, Pennsylvania, and Illinois.

The Communist division of mankind into workingmen and capitalists suffers from the fallacy of simplism. Our social structure and effective class divisions are much more complicated. As the productivity of machinery increases, the middle classes increase rather than decrease. Hence, a program based entirely on the supposed exclusive interests of the proletariat has no reasonable prospect. Any real threat of an armed uprising will only strengthen the reactionaries, who are not less intelligent than the Communist leaders, understand just as well how to reach and influence our people, and have more ample means for organization. If our working classes find it difficult to learn what their true interests are and do not know how to control their representatives in the government and in the trade unions, there is little prospect that they will be able to control things better during a rebellion or during the ensuing dictatorship.

If the history of the past is any guide at all, it indicates that real improvements in the future will come like the improvements of the past—namely, through co-operation among different groups, each of which is wise enough to see the necessity of compromising with those with whom we have to live together and whom we cannot or do not wish to exterminate.

I know that this notion of compromise or of taking counsel as the least wasteful way of adjusting differences is regarded as hopelessly antiquated and bourgeois, but I do not believe that the ideas of so-called Utopian socialists have really been refuted by those who arrogate the epithet "scientific" to themselves. The Communists seem to me to be much more Utopian and quite unscientific in their claims that the working class alone can by its own efforts completely transform our social order.

I do not have very high expectations from the efforts of sentimental benevolence. Yet I cannot help noticing that the leaders of the Communists and of other revolutionary labor movements—Engels, Marx, Lassalle, Luxemburg, Liebknecht, Lenin, and Trotsky—have not been drawn to it by economic solidarity. They were not workingmen nor even all of workingmen's families. They were driven to their role by human sympathy. Sympathy with the sufferings of our fellow men is a human motive that cannot be read out of history. It has exerted tremendous social pressure. Without it you cannot explain the course of nineteenth-century factory legislation, the freeing of serfs and slaves, or the elimination of the grosser forms of human exploitation. Though some who regard themselves as followers of Karl Marx are constantly denouncing reformers who believe in piecemeal improvement and hope rather that things will get worse so as to drive people into a revolution,

Marx himself did not always take that view. Very wisely he attached great importance to English factory legislation which restricted the number of hours per working day, for he realized that every little bit that strengthens the workers strengthens their resistance to exploitation. Those who are most oppressed and depressed, the inhabitants of the slums, do not revolt—they have not energy enough to think of it. When, therefore, Mr. Strachey and others criticize socialists for not bringing about the millennium when they get into power, I am not at all impressed. I do not believe that the socialists or the Labor Party in England have been free from shameful error. But neither have the Communists, or any other human group, been free from it. Trite though it sounds, it is nevertheless true that no human arrangement can bring about perfection on earth. And while the illusion of omniscience may offer great consolation, it brings endless inhumanity when it leads us to shut the gates of mercy. Real as are our human conflicts, our fundamental identity of interest in the face of hostile nature seems to me worthy of more serious attention than the Communists have been willing to accord it.

If liberalism were dead, I should still maintain that it deserved to live, that it had not been condemned in the court of human reason, but lynched outside of it by the passionate and uncompromisingly ruthless war spirit, common to Communists and Fascists. But I do not believe that liberalism is dead, even though it is under eclipse. There still seems to me enough reason left to which to appeal against reckless fanaticism.

It is pure fanaticism to belittle the gains that have come to mankind from the spirit of free inquiry, free discussion, and accommodation. No human individual or group of individuals can claim omniscience. Hence society can only suffer serious loss when one group suppresses the opinions and criticisms of all others. In purely abstract questions compromise may often be a sign of confusion. One cannot really believe inconsistent principles at the same time. But in the absence of perfect or even adequate knowledge in regard to human affairs and their future, we must adopt an experimental attitude and treat principles not as eternal dogmas, but as hypotheses, to be tried to the extent that they indicate the general direction of solution to specific issues. But as the scientist must be ever ready to modify his own hypothesis or to recognize wherein a contrary hypothesis has merits or deserves preference, so in practical affairs we must be prepared to learn from those who differ with us, and to recognize that however contradictory diverse views may appear in discourse they may not be so in their practical applications.

Thus, the principles of Communism and individualism may be held like theologic dogmas, eternally true and on no occasion ever to be contaminated one by the other. But in fact, when Communists get into power they do not differ so much from others. No one ever wished to make everything communal property. Nor does anyone in his senses believe that any individual will ever with impunity be permitted to use his "property" in an antisocial way when the rest of the community is aroused thereby. In actual life, the question how far Communism shall be pushed depends more upon specific analyses of actual situations—that is, upon factual knowledge. There can be no doubt that individualism à la Herbert Hoover has led millions to destruction. Nevertheless, we must not forget that a Communist regime will, after all, be run by individuals who will exercise a tremendous amount of power, no less than do our captains of industry or finance today. There is no real advantage in assuming that under Communism the laboring classes will be omniscient. We know perfectly well how labor leaders like John Lewis keep their power by bureaucratic rather than democratic methods. May it not be that the Stalins also keep their power by bureaucratic rather than democratic methods?

Indeed the ruthless suppression of dissent within the Communist Party in Russia and the systematic glorification of the national heroes and military objectives of Czarist days suggest that the Bolshevik Revolution was not so complete a break with the Russian past as most of its friends and enemies assumed in earlier days. In any event we have witnessed in the history of the Communist movement since 1917 a dramatic demonstration of the way in which the glorification of power—first as a means of destroying a ruling class, then as a means of defending a beleaguered state from surrounding enemies, and finally as a means of extending Communism to neighboring lands—comes imperceptibly to displace the ends or objectives which once formed the core of Communist thought. Thus, one by one, the worst features of capitalist society and imperialism, against which Communism cut its eye teeth in protests—extreme inequality in wages, speed-up of workers, secret diplomacy, and armed intervention as a technique of international intercourse—have been taken over by the Soviet Union, with only a set of thin verbal distinctions to distinguish the "good" techniques of Communism from the corresponding "bad" techniques used by capitalism. As is always the case, the glorification of power dulls the sense of righteousness to which any movement for bettering the basic conditions of human living must appeal.

The Communist criticism of liberalism seems to me altogether baseless and worthless. One would suppose from it that liberalism is a peculiar excrescence of capitalism. This is, however, not true. The essence of liberalism —freedom of thought and inquiry, freedom of discussion and criticism—is not the invention of the capitalist system. It is rather the mother of Greek and modern science, without which our present industrial order and the labor movement would be impossible. The plea that the denial of freedom is a temporary necessity is advanced by all militarists. It ignores the fact that, when suppression becomes a habit, it is not readily abandoned. Thus, when the Christian Church after its alliance with the Roman Empire began the policy of "compelling them to enter," it kept up the habit of intolerant persecution for many centuries. Those who believe that many of the finer fruits of civilization were thereby choked should be careful about strengthening the forces of intolerance.

When the Communists tell me that I must choose between their dictatorship and Fascism, I feel that I am offered the choice between being shot and being hanged. It would be suicide for liberal civilization to accept this as exhausting the field of human possibility. I prefer to hope that the present wave of irrationalism and of fanatical intolerance will recede and that the great human energy which manifests itself in free thought will not perish. Often before, it has emerged after being swamped by passionate superstitions. There is no reason to feel that it may not do so again.

Chapter XI

ENGLISH SOCIALISM

IN THE seventeenth century the English established themselves as the world's leaders of progressive politics by making Parliament supreme against rival claimants, especially the Crown. Since then, the idea of popular sovereignty has become an integral part of civilized government. Some nations, like France, learned from England's example. Others have not learned their lesson, and still live, politically, three or four centuries behind the times.

In the twentieth century London may again become the symbol of a world ideology—democratic socialism. That England was first in developing socialist ideas was due to the fact that she was first in starting the Industrial Revolution which created the urban working classes—without which there can be no socialist *movement*. English socialism could not but be democratic from the start, because government by consent was a part of English life. Revolutionary Marxist communism, like the revolutionary Right, Fascism, finds unfavorable soil in England. Of all free parliaments in the world, the Communists have always had the smallest representation in the United States and England. This was disputed by some in the British election of 1945, when the number of Communist M.P.s in the House of Commons rose by fully 100 per cent—from one M.P. to two, out of a total of 640.

Americans can no longer afford to look upon the various approaches to socialism with the detachment of yesteryear. As a result of the Second World War, Soviet-American relations dominate the issue of world peace. Since the foreign policy of a Great Power is related, in many respects, to its internal political and economic system, familiarity with the principles of Marxism-Leninism is indispensable to an understanding of the methods and goals of Soviet policy, domestic and international.

Important as the knowledge of the foundations of Marxist revolutionary communism is to the American citizen, whose grasp of political realities is so vital to the whole world, the main ideas of English socialism are even more important to him. "We are all socialists now," said Sir William Harcourt, a British Liberal leader, in 1884. Since then the trend, all over the world, has been toward more collective action. In the United States this tendency found expression in Woodrow Wilson's "New Freedom," and in

415

Franklin D. Roosevelt's "New Deal." What was considered intolerable interference in the United States a generation ago, in fields like labor, social security, and education has gradually been accepted as just and inevitable. If the American economic system, the last island of a sheltered capitalist civilization, is going to develop at all in the direction of more public action and responsibility, Britain, and not Russia, supplies the laboratory in which the American observer will want to see what tests are being made, and why. Attlee is not nearly the dramatic figure that Lenin was; but to an American, Sidney Webb, and Tawney, and Attlee, are of greater *practical* importance than the quarrels between Stalin and Trotsky, or Marx's call to revolution, coupled with the doctrine of the dictatorship of the proletariat. If the United States were to become socialist, it would be done slowly, as in England, and not overnight, as in Russia: it would also have to be passed by Congress, rather than be imposed by revolutionary militias. The problem in Russia was to *build* industry in a highly agrarian, and politically inexperienced, country. The problem of socialism in the United States, as in England, is to *nationalize* the existing industrial system in an industrial nation with a highly literate population, experienced over a long period of time in democratic politics. Finally, there was practically no middle class in Russia in 1917. In the United States, as in England, the problem will be to persuade a sufficient number of the key group in society, the class of managers and technicians, that they will fare better under socialism.

Marx arrived at socialism through Hegelian dialectics. William Morris became a socialist late in his life, because as an artist and poet, he suffered from the squalor, drabness, and poverty of life under industrial capitalism. Where Marx thought in cosmic terms—the development of world history according to inevitable social laws, the laws of surplus value, philosophical materialism, to name but a few—Morris saw ugly household goods and furnishings, and men and women who lacked joy and beauty in their daily lives. Even after Morris had taken to Marx in a friendly spirit, recognizing his great genius and passionate sense of justice, he did not pretend to have understood Marx altogether. When once challenged in a public meeting in Glasgow, Morris exclaimed: "I am asked if I believe in Marx's theory of value. To speak quite frankly, I do not know what Marx's theory of value is, and I'm damned if I want to know." What Morris cared about was not this or that "system," but human beings. He felt intensely that the arts must be brought again into the daily lives of men and women, and their creative impulses be given opportunity of expression in their daily life and work. In "How We Live and How We Might Live," an essay published in 1885, Morris gives an account of the ravages that capitalism has inflicted on the soul of man as well as on his material conditions—and how life could be made more just and beautiful, once profit and greed were removed as the two all-powerful masters.

In his work on *Socialism in England* (1889), Sidney Webb draws a detailed picture of socialism, not as a blueprint, but as a practical solution of practical problems; writing in 1889, eleven years before the birth of the Labor party, he is, nevertheless, able to enumerate a long list of services and activities, on the national and municipal level, which were carried on by public authorities. Even the Conservative party, Webb noted, was "constantly being 'permeated' by new ideas emanating from the other side." Webb defines socialism through three criteria: "On the economic side, Socialism implies the collective administration of rent and interest, leaving to the individual only the wages of his labor, of hand or brain. On the political side, it involves the collective control over, and ultimate administration of, all the main instruments of wealth production. On the ethical side, it expresses the general recognition of fraternity, the universal obligation of personal service, and the subordination of personal ambition to the common good." Webb finally stressed the point that in England any "organic changes" would have to be democratic, gradual, constitutional, peaceful, and would have to be accepted as morally just by the masses of the people.

The influence of the Webbs is clearly visible in the work of R. H. Tawney, especially in his *The Acquisitive Society* (1921). It is generally considered in England to be one of the great classics of English socialist thought. Tawney is one of the foremost stylists of the English language, and his books, particularly *The Acquisitive Society* and *Equality* (1931) have become part of general English literature. Avoiding unnecessary technical terms, Tawney defines industry as "nothing more mysterious than a body of men associated, in various degrees of competition and co-operation, to win their livelihood by providing the community with some service which it requires." The function of industry, therefore, is service. However, under the capitalist system of industry and wealth, "functionless" property has developed, property which yields income and power without rendering any service. The essence of property is power, a kind of "limited sovereignty." This power becomes easily tyrannical when it is not responsible to anyone but itself, and when the only question asked is, "What does it yield?" rather than "What service does it perform?" From functionless property comes the power of those "who do not work over those who do," and Tawney warns that functionless property is "the greatest enemy of legitimate property itself." Tawney states two principles which will have to be applied to industry if it is to be a function ("an activity which embodies and expresses the idea of social purpose") rather than tyranny: "The first principle is that industry should be subordinated to the community in such a way as to render the best service technically possible, that those who render that service faithfully should be honourably paid, and that those who render no service should not be paid at all, because it is of the essence of a function that it should find its meaning in the satisfaction, not of itself, but of the end which it serves. The second is that its direction and government should be in the hands of persons who are responsible to those who are directed and governed, because it is the condition of economic freedom that men should not be ruled by an authority which they cannot control."

What the Webbs and Tawney have argued has become reality in the life-work of Clement R. Attlee. In *The Labour Party in Perspective* (1937), the Leader of the Labor party and Prime Minister of the first majority Labor government in English history, gives an intimate picture of the kind of men who have built the British Labor party. It may sound startling to many European (and possibly American) socialists that "the first place in the influence that built up the Socialist movement must be given to religion." In most Continental and Latin-American countries, socialism and religion are considered two entirely different worlds, living in nonbelligerent neutrality at best, and in open warfare at worst. Pope Pius XI emphasized this strongly when he warned in his encyclical *Quadragesimo anno* (1931) that "No one can be, at the same time, a sincere Catholic and a true Socialist." England is probably the only major country in the world where religion has nurtured the socialist faith and has even been, as Attlee claims, its first influence. Likewise, when socialist orators elsewhere refer to a Bible, they may mean *The Communist Manifesto* or *The State and Revolution;* in England, Attlee says, "there are probably more texts from the Bible enunciated from Socialist platforms than from those of all other parties," and it is "possible in Britain for a parson to declare himself a Communist and for millions of faithful Catholics to support the Labour Party."

Before the Second World War, one of the main points of Nazi-Fascist propaganda in the Western nations was the inevitability of an ultimate choice between communism and Fascism, and the offer of saving the world from the threat of communism through the Berlin-Rome-Tokyo Axis. Writing in 1937, when this propaganda convinced more than a few, Attlee rejected this choice: "I do not think that Britain must follow the Moscow or the Berlin road," mainly because the totalitarian state must make use of force and intolerance. "Avoiding both Fascism and Communism," Attlee wrote, "this country, I believe, can afford to the world an example of how society can adapt itself to new conditions and base itself on new principles without breach of continuity and without violence and intolerance." Attlee also notices the fact, without which the Labor party could never gain power: it had become a "national" party, whereas in its beginnings it had been essentially a party representing organized labor. Many "individuals from the better-off classes" have joined the Labor party because of their realization of the "immoral and unjust basis of capitalism."

The spirit of British socialism is well reflected in the writings of Sidney and Beatrice Webb, Tawney, Laski, and a host of others; but the number of systematic treatises on the nature of British socialist philosophy is relatively small. One of the keenest analytical works in this field is E.F.M. Durbin's *The Politics of Democratic Socialism*. Published in the grim year of 1940, the book helped to reaffirm the faith in the democratic process, come what may. Durbin is especially well qualified, as a distinguished economist, to study the phenomenon of capitalism on the broad basis of fact and history. Although an economist, Durbin believes that the *political* factor, the issue of revolution or evolution, of dictatorship or parliamentary government, is the really decisive problem. Rejecting the totalitarianism of Marxist revolutionary communism, Durbin was confident, in 1940, that not only would Britain be able to solve her economic problems within the framework of democratic socialism, but that she would lead the world on the road to a new society of political freedom *and* economic equality.

The strength of British socialism lies in the fact, foreseen by Sidney Webb in 1889, that the conservatives were being constantly "permeated" by socialist ideas. In a letter dated August 3, 1925, to the late Justice Holmes, Sir Fredrick Pollock made an observation on socialism and the common law which is of interest to persons other than lawyers. Sir Frederick was rather conservative, but this did not prevent him from seeing that socialism contained an old principle of the common law, viz., the opposition to monopolies.

Is socialism a new method of producing and distributing material goods, or does it envisage a new way of life? What are its human and cultural ideals? Herbert Read's *The Politics of the Unpolitical* (1943) contains an essay entitled "To Hell with Culture," which discusses the relations between socialist culture, art, and the individual. Like William Morris, Read has come to socialism via art and poetry, and his socialism, again like that of Morris, is a peculiar and unclassifiable blend of intens concern for beauty, individualism, anarchy, and a profound faith that the democratic experience of the human race has only begun, and must be carried on to previously undreamed-of heights. Read himself mentions Rousseau, Jefferson, Lincoln, Proudhon, Ruskin, Marx, Morris, and Kropotkin as kindred spirits. In the best Morris tradition, Read invites the reader to take the case of the chair he is sitting on while reading, and pursue his social investigations from that point on. Men like Read will rarely found, or join, political parties. But their influence in England has always been real, because their protest against capitalism has sprung from their consciousness and suffering as artists and poets, and because they are concerned with people rather than with abstractions.

1. How We Live and How We Might Live *

WILLIAM MORRIS

The word Revolution, which we Socialists are so often forced to use, has a terrible sound in most people's ears, even when we have explained to them that it does not necessarily mean a change accompanied by riot and all kinds of violence, and cannot mean a change made mechanically and in the teeth of opinion by a group of men who have somehow managed to seize on the executive power for the moment. Even when we explain that we use the word revolution in its etymological sense, and mean by it a change in the basis of society, people are scared at the idea of such a vast change, and beg that you will speak of reform and not revolution. As, however, we Socialists do not at all mean by our word revolution what these worthy people mean by their word reform, I can't help thinking that it would be a mistake to use it, whatever projects we might conceal beneath its harmless envelope. So we will stick to our word, which means a change of the basis of society; it may frighten people, but it will at least warn them that there is something to be frightened about, which will be no less dangerous for being ignored; and also it may encourage some people, and will mean to them at least not a fear, but a hope.

Fear and Hope—those are the names of the two great passions which rule the race of man, and with which revolutionists have to deal; to give hope to the many oppressed and fear to the few oppressors, that is our business; if we do the first and give hope to the many, the few *must* be frightened by their hope; otherwise we do not want to frighten them; it is not revenge we want for poor people, but happiness; indeed, what revenge can be taken for all the thousands of years of the sufferings of the poor?

However, many of the oppressors of the poor, most of them, we will say, are not conscious of their being oppressors (we shall see why presently); they live in an orderly, quiet way themselves, as far as possible removed from the feelings of a Roman slave-owner or a Legree; they know that the poor exist, but their sufferings do not present themselves to them in a trenchant and dramatic way; they themselves have troubles to bear, and they think doubtless that to bear trouble is the lot of humanity; nor have they any means of comparing the troubles of their lives with those of people lower

* 1885. Reprinted in *Signs of Change* (1888) and included in William Morris, *Selected Writings* (ed. by G. D. H. Cole, The Nonesuch Press, 1934).

in the social scale; and if ever the thought of those heavier troubles obtrudes itself upon them, they console themselves with the maxim that people do get used to the troubles they have to bear, whatever they may be.

Indeed, as far as regards individuals at least, that is but too true, so that we have as supporters of the present state of things, however bad it may be, first those comfortable unconscious oppressors who think that they have everything to fear from any change which would involve more than the softest and most gradual of reforms, and secondly those poor people who, living hard and anxiously as they do, can hardly conceive of any change for the better happening to them, and dare not risk one tittle of their poor possessions in taking any action towards a possible bettering of their condition; so that while we can do little with the rich save inspire them with fear, it is hard indeed to give the poor any hope. It is, then, no less than reasonable that those whom we try to involve in the great struggle for a better form of life than that which we now lead should call on us to give them at least some idea of what that life may be like.

A reasonable request, but hard to satisfy, since we are living under a system that makes conscious effort towards reconstruction almost impossible: it is not unreasonable on our part to answer, "There are certain definite obstacles to the real progress of man; we can tell you what these are; take them away, and then you shall see."

However, I purpose now to offer myself as a victim for the satisfaction of those who consider that as things now go we have at least got something, and are terrified at the idea of losing their hold of that, lest they should find they are worse off than before, and have nothing. Yet in the course of my endeavour to show how we might live, I must more or less deal in negatives. I mean to say I must point out where in my opinion we fall short in our present attempt at decent life. I must ask the rich and well-to-do what sort of position it is which they are so anxious to preserve at any cost? and if, after all, it will be such a terrible loss to them to give it up? and I must point out to the poor that they, with capacities for living a dignified and generous life, are in a position which they cannot endure without continued degradation.

How do we live, then, under our present system? Let us look at it a little.

And first, please to understand that our present system of Society is based on a state of perpetual war. Do any of you think that this is as it should be? I know that you have often been told that the competition, which is at present the rule of all production, is a good thing, and stimulates the progress of the race; but the people who tell you this should call competition by its shorter name of *war* if they wish to be honest, and you would then be free to consider whether or no war stimulates progress, otherwise than as a mad bull chasing you over your own garden may do. War, or competition, whichever you please to call it, means at the best pursuing your own advantage at the cost of some one else's loss, and in the process of it you must not be sparing of destruction even of your own possessions, or you will certainly come by the worse in the struggle. You understand that perfectly as to the kind of war in which people go out to kill and be killed; that sort of war in which ships are commissioned, for instance, "to sink, burn, and destroy"; but it appears that you are not so conscious of this waste of goods when you are only carrying on that other war called *commerce;* observe, however, that the waste is there all the same.

Now let us look at this kind of war a little closer, run through some of the forms of it, that we may see how the "burn, sink, and destroy" is carried on in it.

First, you have that form of it called national rivalry, which in good truth is nowadays the cause of all gunpowder and bayonet wars which civilized nations wage. For years past we English have been rather shy of them, except on those happy occasions when we could carry them on at no sort of risk to ourselves, when the killing was all on one side, or at all events when we hoped it would be. We have been shy of gunpowder war with a respectable enemy for a long while, and I will tell you why: It is because we have had the lion's share of the world-market; we didn't want to fight for it as a nation, for we had got it; but now this is changing in a most significant, and, to a Socialist, a most cheering way; we are losing or have lost that lion's share; it is now a desperate "competition" between the great nations of civilization for the world-market, and tomorrow it may be a desperate war for that end. As a result, the furthering of war (if it be not on too large a scale) is no longer confined to the honour-and-glory kind of old Tories, who if they meant anything at all by it meant that a Tory war would be a good occasion for damping down democracy; we have changed all that, and now it is quite another kind of politician that is wont to urge us on to "patriotism" as 'tis called. The leaders of the Progressive Liberals, as they would call themselves, longheaded persons who know well enough that social movements are going on, who are not blind to the fact that the world will move with their help or without it; these have been the Jingoes of these later days. I don't mean to say they know what they are doing: politicans, as you well know, take good care to shut their eyes to everything that may happen six months ahead; but what is being done is this: that the present system, which always must include national rivalry, is pushing us into a desperate scramble for the markets on more or less equal terms with other nations, because, once more, we have lost that command of them which we once had. Desperate is not too strong a word. We shall let this impulse to snatch markets carry us whither it will, whither it must. To-day it is successful burglary and disgrace, tomorrow it may be mere defeat and disgrace.

Now this is not a digression, although in saying this I am nearer to what is generally called politics than I shall be again. I only want to show you what commercial war comes to when it has to do with foreign nations, and that even the dullest can see how mere waste must go with it. That is how we live now with foreign nations, prepared to ruin them without war if possible, with it if necessary, let alone meantime the disgraceful exploiting of savage tribes and barbarous peoples on whom we force at once our shoddy wares and our hypocrisy at the cannon's mouth.

Well, surely Socialism can offer you something in the place of all that. It can; it can offer you peace and friendship instead of war. We might live utterly without national rivalries, acknowledging that while it is best for those who feel that they naturally form a community under one name to govern themselves, yet that no community in civilization should feel that it had interests opposed to any other, their economical condition being at any rate similar; so that any citizen of one community could fall to work and live without disturbance of his life when he was in a foreign country, and would fit into his place quite naturally; so that all civilized nations would form one great community, agreeing together as to the kind and amount of production where it could be best produced; avoiding waste by all means. Please to think of the amount of waste which they would avoid, how much such a revolution would add to the wealth of the world! What creature on earth would be harmed by such a revolution? Nay, would not everybody be the better for it? And what hinders it? I will tell you presently.

Meantime let us pass from this "competition" between nations to that between "the organizers of labour," great firms, joint-stock companies; capitalists, in short, and see how competition "stimulates production" among them: indeed it does do that; but what kind of production? Well, production of something to sell at a profit, or say production of profits: and note how war commercial stimulates that: a certain market is demanding goods; there are, say, a hundred manufacturers who make that kind of goods, and every one of them would if he could keep that market to himself, and struggles desperately to get as much of it as he can, with the obvious result that presently the thing is overdone, and the market is glutted, and all that fury of manufacture has to sink into cold ashes. Doesn't that seem something like war to you? Can't you see the waste of it—waste of labour, skill, cunning, waste of life in short? Well you may say, but it cheapens the goods. In a sense it does; and yet only apparently, as wages have a tendency to sink for the ordinary worker in proportion as prices sink; and at what a cost do we gain this appearance of cheapness! Plainly speaking, at the cost of cheating the consumer and starving the real producer for the benefit of the gambler, who uses both consumer and producer as his milch cows. I needn't go at length into the subject of adulteration, for every one knows what kind of a part it plays in this sort of commerce; but remember that it is an absolutely necessary incident to the production of profit out of wares, which is the business of the so-called manufacturer; and this you must understand, that, taking him in the lump, the consumer is perfectly helpless against the gambler; the goods are forced on him by their cheapness, and with them a certain kind of life which that energetic, that aggressive cheapness determines for him: for so far-reaching is this curse of commercial war that no country is safe from its ravages; the traditions of a thousand years fall before it in a month; it overruns a weak or semi-barbarous country, and whatever romance or pleasure or art existed there, is trodden down into a mire of sordidness and ugliness; the Indian or Javanese craftsman may no longer ply his craft leisurely, working a few hours a day, in producing a maze of strange beauty on a piece of cloth; a steam-engine is set a-going at Manchester, and that victory over nature and a thousand stubborn difficulties is used for the base work of producing a sort of plaster of china-clay and shoddy, and the Asiatic worker, if he is not starved to death outright, as plentifully happens, is driven himself into a factory to lower the wages of his Manchester brother worker, and nothing of character is left him except, most like, an accumulation of fear and hatred of that to him most unaccountable evil, his English master. The South Sea Islander must leave his canoe-carving, his sweet rest, and his graceful dances, and become the slave of a slave: trousers, shoddy, rum, missionary, and fatal disease—he must swallow all this civilization in the lump, and neither himself nor we can help him now till social order displaces the hideous tyranny of gambling that has ruined him.

Let those be types of the consumer: but now for the producer; I mean the real producer, the worker; how does this scramble for the plunder of the market affect him? The manufacturer, in the eagerness of his war, has had to collect into one neighborhood a vast army of workers, he has drilled them till they are as fit as may be for his special branch of production, that is, for making a profit out of it, and with the result of their being fit for nothing else: well, when the glut comes in that market he is supplying, what happens to this army, every private in which has been depending on the steady demand in that market, and acting, as he could not choose but act, as if it were to go on forever? You know well what happens to these men: the factory door is shut on them; on a very large part of them often, and at the best on the reserve army of labour, so busily employed in the time of inflation. What becomes of them? Nay, we know that well enough just now. But what we don't know, or don't choose to know, is that this reserve army of labour is an absolute necessity for commercial war; if *our* manufacturers had not got these poor devils whom they could draft on to their machines when the demand swelled, other manufacturers in France, or Germany, or America, would step in and take the market from them.

So you see, as we live now, it is necessary that a vast part of the industrial population should be exposed to the danger of periodical semi-starvation, and that, not for the advantage of the people in another part of the world, but for their degradation and enslavement.

Just let your minds run for a moment on the kind of waste which this means, this opening up of new markets among savage and barbarous countries which is the extreme type of the force of the profit-market on the world, and you will surely see what a hideous nightmare that profit-market is: it keeps us sweating and terrified for our livelihood, unable to read a book, or look at a picture, or have pleasant fields to walk in, or to lie in the sun, or to share in the knowledge of our time, to have in short either animal or intellectual pleasure, and for what? that we may go on living the same slavish life till we die, in order to provide for a rich man what is called a life of ease and luxury; that is to say, a life so empty, unwholesome, and degraded, that perhaps, on the whole, he is worse off than we the workers are: and as to the result of all this suffering, it is luckiest when it is nothing at all, when you can say that the wares have done nobody any good; for oftenest they have done many people harm, and we have toiled and groaned and died in making poison and destruction for our fellowmen.

Well, I say all this is war, and the result of war, the war this time, not of competing nations, but of competing firms or capitalist units: and it is this war of the firms which hinders the peace between nations which you surely have agreed with me in thinking is so necessary; for you must know that war is the very breath of the nostrils of these fighting firms, and they have now, in our times, got into their hands nearly all the political power, and they band together in each country in order to make their respective governments fulfil just two functions: the first is at home to act as a strong police force, to keep the ring in which the strong are beating down the weak; the second is to act as a piratical body-guard abroad, a petard to explode the doors which lead to the markets of the world: markets at any price abroad, uninterfered-with-privilege, falsely called laissez-faire,[1] at any price at home, to provide these is the sole business of a government such as our industrial captains have been able to conceive of. I must now try to show you the reason of all this, and what it rests on, by trying to answer the question, Why have the profit-makers got all this power, or at least why are they able to keep it?

That takes us to the third form of war commercial: the last, and the one which all the rest is founded on. We have spoken first of the war of rival nations; next of that of rival firms: we have now to speak of rival men. As nations under the present system are driven to compete with one another for the markets of the world, and as firms or the captains of industry have to scramble for their share of the profits of the markets, so also have

---

[1] Falsely; because the privileged classes have at their back the force of the Executive by means of which to compel the unprivileged to accept the terms; if this is "free competition" there is no meaning in words.

the workers to compete with each other—for livelihood; and it is this constant competition or war amongst them which enables the profit-grinders to make their profits, and by means of the wealth so acquired to take all the executive power of the country into their hands. But here is the difference between the position of the workers and the profit-makers: to the latter, the profit-grinders, war is necessary; you cannot have profit-making without competition, individual, corporate, and national; but you may work for a livelihood without competing; you may combine instead of competing.

I have said war was the life-breath of the profit-makers; in like manner, combination is the life of the workers. The working-classes or proletariat cannot even exist as a class without combination of some sort. The necessity which forced the profit-grinders to collect their men first into workshops working by the division of labour, and next into great factories worked by machinery, and so gradually draw them into the great towns and centres of civilization, gave birth to a distinct working-class or proletariat: and this it was which gave them their *mechanical* existence, so to say. But note, that they are indeed combined into social groups for the production of wares, but only as yet mechanically; they do not know what they are working at, nor whom they are working for, because they are combining to produce wares of which the profit of a master forms an essential part, instead of goods for their own use: as long as they do this, and compete with each other for leave to do it, they will be, and will feel themselves to be, simply a part of those competing firms I have been speaking of; they will be in fact just a part of the machinery for the production of profit; and so long as this lasts it will be the aim of the masters or profit-makers to decrease the market value of this human part of the machinery; that is to say, since they already hold in their hands the labour of dead men in the form of capital and machinery, it is their interest, or we will say their necessity, to pay as little as they can help for the labour of living men which they have to buy from day to day: and since the workmen they employ have nothing but their labour-power, they are compelled to underbid one another for employment and wages, and so enable the capitalist to play his game.

I have said that, as things go, the workers are a part of the competing firms, an adjunct of capital. Nevertheless, they are only so by compulsion, and even without their being conscious of it, they struggle against that compulsion and its immediate results, the lowering of their wages, of their standard of life: and this they do, and must do, both as a class and individually: just as the slave of the great Roman lord, though he distinctly felt himself to be a part of the household, yet collectively was a force in reserve for its destruction, and individually stole from his lord whenever he could safely do so. So, here, you see, is another form of war necessary to the way we live now, the war of class against class, which, when it rises to its height, and it seems to be rising at present, will destroy those other forms of war we have been speaking of; will make the position of the profit-makers, of perpetual commercial war, untenable; will destroy the present system of competitive privilege, or commercial war.

Now observe, I said that to the existence of the workers it was combination, not competition, that was necessary, while to that of the profit-makers combination was impossible, and war necessary. The present position of the workers is that of the machinery of commerce, or in plainer words its slaves; when they change that position and become free, the class of profit-makers must cease to exist; and what will then be the position of the workers? Even as it is they are the one necessary part of society, the life-giving part; the other classes are but hangers-on who live on them. But what should they be, what will they be, when they, once for all, come to know their real power, and cease competing with one another for livelihood? I will tell you: they will be society, they will be the community. And being society—that is, there being no class outside them to contend with—they can then regulate their labour in accordance with their own real needs.

There is much talk about supply and demand, but the supply and demand usually meant is an artificial one; it is under the sway of the gambling market; the demand is forced, as I hinted above, before it is supplied; nor, as each producer is working against all the rest, can the producers hold their hands, till the market is glutted and the workers thrown out on the streets, hear that there has been over-production, amidst which over-plus of unsaleable goods they go ill-supplied with even necessaries, because the wealth which they themselves have created is "ill-distributed," as we call it—that is, unjustly taken away from them.

When the workers are society they will regulate their labour, so that the supply and demand shall be genuine, not gambling; the two will then be commensurate, for it is the same society which demands that also supplies; there will be no more artificial famines then, no more poverty amidst over-production, amidst too great a stock of the very things which should supply poverty and turn it into well-being. In short, there will be no waste and therefore no tyranny.

Well, now, what Socialism offers you in place of these artificial famines, with their so-called over-production, is, once more, regulation of the markets; supply and demand commensurate; no gambling, and consequently (once more) no waste; not overwork and weariness for the worker one month, and the next no work and terror of starvation, but steady work and plenty of leisure every month; not cheap market wares, that is to say, adulterated wares, with scarcely any *good* in them, mere scaffold-poles for building up profits; no labour would be spent on such things as these, which people would cease to want when they ceased to be slaves. Not these, but such goods as best fulfilled the real uses of the consumers would labour be set to make; for, profit being abolished, people could have what they wanted, instead of what the profit-grinders at home and abroad forced them to take.

For what I want you to understand is this: that in every civilized country at least there is plenty for all—is, or at any rate might be. Even with labour so misdirected as it is at present, an equitable distribution of the wealth we have would make all people comparatively comfortable; but that is nothing to the wealth we might have if labour were not misdirected.

Observe, in the early days of the history of man he was the slave of his immediate necessities; Nature was mighty and he was feeble, and he had to wage constant war with her for his daily food and such shelter as he could get. His life was bound down and limited by this constant struggle; all his morals, laws, religion, are in fact the outcome and the reflection of this ceaseless toil of earning his livelihood. Time passed, and little by little, step by step, he grew stronger, till now after all these ages he has almost completely conquered Nature, and one would think should now have leisure to turn his thoughts towards higher things than procuring tomorrow's dinner. But, alas! his progress has been broken and halting; and though he has indeed conquered Nature and has her forces under his control to do what he will with, he still has himself to conquer, he still has to think how he will best use those forces which he has mastered. At present he uses them blindly, foolishly, as one driven by mere fate. It would almost seem as if some phantom of the ceaseless pursuit of food which was once the master of the savage was still haunting the civilized man; who toils in a dream, as it were, haunted by mere dim unreal hopes, born of vague recollections of the days gone by. Out of that dream he must wake, and face things as they really are. The conquest of Nature is complete, may we not say? and now our business is and has for long been the organization of man, who wields the forces of Nature. Nor till this is attempted at least shall we ever be free of that terrible phantom of fear of starvation which, with its brother devil, desire of domination, drives us into injustice, cruelty, and dastardliness of all kinds: to cease to fear our fellows and learn to depend on them, to do away with competition and build up cooperation, is our one necessity.

Now, to get closer to details; you probably know that every man in civilization is worth, so to say, more than his skin; working, as he must work, socially, he can produce more than will keep himself alive and in fair condition; and this has been so for many centuries, from the time, in fact, when warring tribes began to make their conquered enemies slaves instead of killing them; and of course his capacity of producing these extras has gone on increasing faster and faster, till to-day one man will weave, for instance, as much cloth in a week as will clothe a whole village for years; and the real question of civilization has always been what are we to do with this extra produce of labour—a question which the phantom, fear of starvation, and its fellow, desire of domination, has driven men to answer pretty badly always, and worst of all perhaps in these present days, when the extra produce has grown with such prodigious speed. The practical answer has always been for man to struggle with his fellow for private possession of undue shares of these extras, and all kinds of devices have been employed by those who found themselves in possession of the power of taking them from others to keep those whom they had robbed in perpetual subjection; and these latter, as I have already hinted, had no chance of resisting this fleecing as long as they were few and scattered, and consequently could have little sense of their common oppression. But now that, owing to the very pursuit of these undue shares of profit, or extra earnings, men have become more dependent on each other for production, and have been driven, as I said before, to combine together for that end more completely, the power of the workers—that is to say, of the robbed or fleeced class—has enormously increased, and it only remains for them to understand that they have this power. When they do that they will be able to give the right answer to the question what is to be done with the extra products of labour over and above what will keep the labourer alive to labour: which answer is, that the worker will have all that he produces, and not be fleeced at all: and remember that he produces collectively, and therefore he will do effectively what work is required of him according to his capacity, and of the produce of that work he will have what he needs; because, you see, he cannot *use* more than he needs—he can only *waste* it.

If this arrangement seems to you preposterously ideal, as it well may, looking at our present condition, I must back it up by saying that when men are organized so that their labour is not wasted, they will be relieved from the fear of starvation and the desire of domination, and will have freedom and leisure to look round and see what they really do need.

Now something of that I can conceive for my own self, and I will lay my ideas before you, so that you may compare them with your own, asking you always to remember that the very differences in men's capacities and desires, after the common need of food and shelter is satisfied, will make it easier to deal with their desires in a communal state of things.

What is it that I need, therefore, which my surrounding circumstances can give me—my dealings with my fellowmen—setting aside inevitable accidents which co-operation and forethought cannot control, if there be such?

Well, first of all I claim good health; and I say that a vast proportion of people in civilization scarcely even know what that means. To feel mere life a pleasure; to enjoy the moving one's limbs and exercising one's bodily powers; to play, as it were, with sun and wind and rain; to rejoice in satisfying the due bodily appetites of a human animal without fear of degradation or sense of wrong-doing: yes, and therewithal to be well-formed, straight-limbed, strongly knit, expressive of countenance—to be, in a word, beautiful—that also I claim. If we cannot have this claim satisfied, we are but poor creatures after all; and I claim it in the teeth of those terrible

doctrines of asceticism, which, born of the despair of the oppressed and degraded, have been for so many ages used as instruments for the continuance
of that oppression and degradation.

And I believe that this claim for a healthy body for all of us carries with
it all other due claims: for who knows where the seeds of disease which
even rich people suffer from were first sown: from the luxury of an ancestor,
perhaps; yet often, I suspect, from his poverty. And for the poor: a distinguished physicist has said that the poor suffer always from one disease—
hunger; and at least I know this, that if a man is overworked in any degree
he cannot enjoy the sort of health I am speaking of; nor can he if he is
continually chained to one dull round of mechanical work, with no hope at
the other end of it; nor if he lives in continual sordid anxiety for his livelihood, nor if he is ill-housed, nor if he is deprived of all enjoyment of the
natural beauty of the world, nor if he has no amusement to quicken the
flow of his spirits from time to time: all these things, which touch more or
less directly on his bodily condition, are born of the claim I make to live
in good health; indeed, I suspect that these good conditions must have been
in force for several generations before a population in general will be really
healthy, as I have hinted above; but also I doubt not that in the course of
time they would, joined to other conditions, of which more hereafter, gradually breed such a population, living in enjoyment of animal life at least,
happy therefore, and beautiful according to the beauty of their race. On this
point I may note that the very variations in the races of men are caused by
the conditions under which they live, and though in these rougher parts of
the world we lack some of the advantages of climate and surroundings, yet, if
we were working for livelihood and not for profit, we might easily neutralize
many of the disadvantages of our climate, at least enough to give due scope
to the full development of our race.

Now the next thing I claim is education. And you must not say that every
English child is educated now; that sort of education will not answer my
claim, though I cheerfully admit it is something: something, and yet after
all only class education. What I claim is liberal education; opportunity, that
is, to have my share of whatever knowledge there is in the world according
to my capacity or bent of mind, historical or scientific; and also to have my
share of skill of hand which is about in the world, either in the industrial
handicrafts or in the fine arts; picture-painting, sculpture, music, acting, or
the like: I claim to be taught, if I can be taught, more than one craft to
exercise for the benefit of the community. You may think this a large claim,
but I am clear it is not too large a claim if the community is to have any
gain out of my special capacities, if we are not all to be beaten down to a
dull level of mediocrity as we are now, all but the very strongest and
toughest of us.

But also I know that this claim for education involves one for public advantages in the shape of public libraries, schools, and the like, such as no private person, not even the richest, could command: but these I claim very confidently, being sure that no reasonable community could bear to be without such helps to a decent life.

Again, the claim for education involves a claim for abundant leisure, which once more I make with confidence; because when once we have shaken off the slavery of profit, labour would be organized so unwastefully that no heavy burden would be laid on the individual citizen; every one of whom as a matter of course would have to pay his toll of some obviously useful work. At present you must note that all the amazing machinery which we have invented has served only to increase the amount of profit-bearing wares; in other words, to increase the amount of profit pouched by individuals for their own advantage, part of which profit they use as capital for the production of more profit, with ever the same waste attached to it, and part as private riches or means for luxurious living, which again is sheer waste—is in fact to be looked on as a kind of bonfire on which rich men burn up the product of the labour they have fleeced from the workers beyond what they themselves can use. So I say that, in spite of our inventions, no worker works under the present system an hour the less on account of those labour-saving machines, so-called. But under a happier state of things they would be used simply for saving labour, with the result of a vast amount of leisure gained for the community to be added to that gained by the avoidance of the waste of useless luxury, and the abolition of the service of commercial war.

And I may say that as to that leisure, as I should in no case do any harm to any one with it, so I should often do some direct good to the community with it, by practising arts or occupations for my hands or brain which would give pleasure to many of the citizens; in other words, a great deal of the best work done would be done in the leisure time of men relieved from any anxiety as to their livelihood, and eager to exercise their special talent, as all men, nay, all animals are.

Now, again this leisure would enable me to please myself and expand my mind by travelling if I had a mind to it; because, say, for instance, that I were a shoemaker; if due social order were established, it by no means follows that I should always be obliged to make shoes in one place; a due amount of easily conceivable arrangement would enable me to make shoes in Rome, say, for three months, and to come back with new ideas of building, gathered from the sight of the works of past ages, amongst other things which would perhaps be of service in London.

But now, in order that my leisure might not degenerate into idleness and aimlessness, I must set up a claim for due work to do. Nothing to my mind is more important than this demand, and I must ask your leave to say something about it. I have mentioned that I should probably use my leisure for doing a good deal of what is now called work; but it is clear that if I am a member of a Socialist Community I must do my due share of rougher work than this—my due share of what my capacity enables me to do, that is; no fitting of me to a Procrustean bed; but even that share of work necessary to the existence of the simplest social life must, in the first place, whatever else it is, be reasonable work; that is, it must be such work as a good citizen can see the necessity for; as a member of the community, I .must have agreed to do it.

To take two strong instances of the contrary, I won't submit to be dressed up in red and marched off to shoot at any French or German or Arab friend in a quarrel that I don't understand; I will rebel sooner than do that.

Nor will I submit to waste my time and energies in making some trifling toy which I know only a fool can desire; I will rebel sooner than do that.

However, you may be sure that in a state of social order I shall have no need to rebel against any such pieces of unreason; only I am forced to speak from the way we live to the way we might live.

Again, if the necessary reasonable work be of a mechanical kind, I must be helped to do it by a machine, not to cheapen my labour, but so that as little time as possible may be spent upon it, and that I may be able to think of other things while I am tending the machine. And if the work be specially rough or exhausing, you will, I am sure, agree with me in saying that I must take turns in doing it with other people; I mean I mustn't, for instance, be expected to spend my working hours always at the bottom of a coal-pit. I think such work as that ought to be largely volunteer work, and done, as I say, in spells. And what I say of very rough work I say also of nasty work. On the other hand, I should think very little of the manhood of a stout and healthy man who did not feel a pleasure in doing rough work; always supposing him to work under the conditions I have been speaking of—namely, feeling that it was useful (and consequently honoured), and that it was not continuous or hopeless, and that he was really doing it of his own free will.

The last claim I make for my work is that the places I worked in, factories or workshops, should be pleasant, just as the fields where our most necessary work is done are plèasant. Believe me there is nothing in the world to prevent this being done, save the necessity of making profits on all wares; in other words, the wares are cheapened at the expense of people being forced to work in crowded, unwholesome, squalid, noisy dens: that is to say, they are cheapened at the expense of the workman's life.

Well, so much for my claims as to my *necessary* work, my tribute to the community. I believe people would find, as they advanced in their capacity for carrying on social order, that life so lived was much less expensive than we now can have any idea of, and that, after a little, people would rather be anxious to seek work than to avoid it; that our working hours would rather be merry parties of men and maids, young men and old enjoying themselves over their work, than the grumpy weariness it mostly is now. Then would come the time for the new birth of art, so much talked of, so long deferred; people could not help showing their mirth and pleasure in their work, and would be always wishing to express it in a tangible and more or less enduring form, and the workshop would once more be a school of art, whose influence no one could escape from.

And, again, that word art leads me to my last claim, which is that the material surroundings of my life should be pleasant, generous, and beautiful; that I know is a large claim, but this I will say about it, that if it cannot be satisfied, if every civilized community cannot provide such surroundings for all its members, I do not want the world to go on; it is a mere misery that man has ever existed. I do not think it possible under the present circumstances to speak too strongly on this point. I feel sure that the time will come when people will find it difficult to believe that a rich community such as ours, having such command over external Nature, could have submitted to live such a mean, shabby, dirty life as we do.

And once for all, there is nothing in our circumstances save the hunting of profit that drives us into it. It is profit which draws men into enormous unmanageable aggregations called towns, for instance; profit which crowds them up when they are there into quarters without gardens or open spaces; profit which won't take the most ordinary precautions against wrapping a whole district in a cloud of sulphurous smoke; which turns beautiful rivers into filthy sewers; which condemns all but the rich to live in houses idiotically cramped and confined at the best, and at the worst in houses for whose wretchedness there is no name.

I say it is almost incredible that we should bear such crass stupidity as this; nor should we if we could help it. We shall not bear it when the workers get out of their heads that they are but an appendage to profit-grinding, that the more profits that are made the more employment at high wages there will be for them, and that therefore all the increditable filth, disorder, and degradation of modern civilization are signs of their prosperity. So far from that, they are signs of their slavery. When they are no longer slaves they will claim as a matter of course that every man and every family should be generously lodged; that every child should be able to play in a garden close to the place his parents live in; that the houses should by their obvious decency and order be ornaments to Nature, not disfigurements of it; for the decency and order above-mentioned when carried to the due pitch would most assuredly lead to beauty in building. All this, of course, would mean the people—that is, all society—duly organized, having in its own hands the means of production, to be *owned* by no individual, but used by all as occasion called for its use, and can only be done on those terms; on any other terms people will be driven to accumulate private wealth for themselves, and thus, as we have seen, to waste the goods of the community and perpetuate the division into classes, which means continual war and waste.

As to what extent it may be necessary or desirable for people under social order to live in common, we may differ pretty much according to our tendencies towards social life. For my part I can't see why we should think it a hardship to eat with the people we work with; I am sure that as to many things, such as valuable books, pictures, and splendour of surroundings, we shall find it better to club our means together; and I must say that often when I have been sickened by the stupidity of the mean idiotic rabbit warrens that rich men build for themselves in Bayswater and elsewhere, I console myself with visions of the noble communal hall of the future, unsparing of materials, generous in worthy ornament, alive with the noblest thoughts of our time, and the past, embodied in the best art which a free and manly people could produce; such an abode of man as no private enterprise could come anywhere near for beauty and fitness, because only collective thought and collective life could cherish the aspirations which would give birth to its beauty, or have the skill and leisure to carry them out. I for my part should think it much the reverse of a hardship if I had to read my books and meet my friends in such a place; nor do I think I am better off to live in a vulgar stuccoed house crowded with upholstery that I despise, in all respects degrading to the mind and enervating to the body to live in, simply because I call it my own, or my house.

It is not an original remark, but I make it here, that my home is where I meet people with whom I sympathise, whom I love.

Well, that is my opinion as a middle-class man. Whether a working-class man would think his family possession of his wretched little room better than his share of the palace of which I have spoken, I must leave to his opinion, and to the imaginations of the middle class, who perhaps may sometimes conceive the fact that the said worker is cramped for space and comfort —say on washing-day.

Before I leave this matter to the surroundings of life, I wish to meet a possible objection. I have spoken of machinery being used freely for releasing people from the more mechanical and repulsive part of necessary labour; and I know that to some cultivated people, people of the artistic turn of mind, machinery is particularly distasteful, and they will be apt to say you will never get your surroundings pleasant so long as you are surrounded by machinery. I don't quite admit that; it is the allowing machines to be our masters and not our servants that so injures the beauty of life nowadays. In other words, it is the token of the terrible crime we have fallen into of using our control of the powers of Nature for the purpose of enslaving people, we care less meantime of how much happiness we rob their lives of.

Yet for the consolation of the artists I will say that I believe indeed that a state of social order would probably lead at first to a great development of machinery for really useful purposes, because people will still be anxious about getting through the work necessary to holding society together; but that after a while they will find that there is not so much work to do as they expected, and that then they will have leisure to reconsider the whole subject; and if it seems to them that a certain industry would be carried on more pleasantly as regards the worker, and more effectually as regards the goods, by using hand-work rather than machinery, they will certainly get rid of their machinery, because it will be possible for them to do so. It isn't possible now; we are not at liberty to do so; we are slaves to the monsters which we have created. And I have a kind of hope that the very elaboration of machinery in a society whose purpose is not the multiplication of labour, as it now is, but the carrying on of a pleasant life, as it would be under social order—that the elaboration of machinery, I say, will lead to the simplification of life, and so once more to the limitation of machinery.

Well, I will now let my claims for decent life stand as I have made them. To sum them up in brief, they are: First, a healthy body; second, an active mind in sympathy with the past, the present, and the future; thirdly, occupation fit for a healthy body and an active mind; and fourthly, a beautiful world to live in.

These are the conditions of life which the refined man of all ages has set before him as the thing above all others to be attained. Too often he has been so foiled in their pursuit that he has turned longing eyes backward to the days before civilization, when man's sole business was getting himself food from day to day, and hope was dormant in him, or at least could not be expressed by him.

Indeed, if civilization (as many think) forbids the realization of the hope to attain such conditions of life, then civilization forbids mankind to be happy; and if that be the case, then let us stifle all aspirations towards progress—nay, all feelings of mutual good-will and affection between men—and snatch each one of us what we can from the heap of wealth that fools create for rogues to grow fat on; or better still, let us as speedily as possible find some means of dying like men, since we are forbidden to live like men.

Rather, however, take courage, and believe that we of this age, in spite of all its torment and disorder, have been born to a wonderful heritage fashioned of the work of those that have gone before us; and that the day of the organization of man is dawning. It is not we who can build up the new social order; the past ages have done the most of that work for us; but we can clear our eyes to the signs of the times, and we shall then see that the attainment of a good condition of life is being made possible for us, and that it is now our business to stretch out our hands to take it.

And how? Chiefly, I think, by educating people to a sense of their real capacities as men, so that they may be able to use to their own good the political power which is rapidly being thrust upon them; to get them to see that the old system of organizing labour *for individual profit* is becoming unmanageable, and that the whole people have now got to choose between the confusion resulting from the break up of that system and the determination to take in hand the labour now organized for profit, and use its organization for the livelihood of the community: to get people to see that individual profit-makers are not a necessity for labour but an obstruction to it, and that not only or chiefly because they are the perpetual pensioners of labour, as they are, but rather because of the waste which their existence as a class necessitates. All this we have to teach people, when we have taught ourselves; and I admit that the work is long and burdensome; as I began by saying, people have been made so timorous of change by the terror of starvation that even the unluckiest of them are stolid and hard to move. Hard as the work is, however, its reward is not doubtful. The mere fact that a body of men, however small, are banded together as Socialist missionaries shows that the change is going on. As the working classes, the real organic part of society, take in these ideas, hope will arise in them, and they will claim changes in society, many of which doubtless will not tend directly towards their emancipation, because they will be claimed without due knowledge of the one thing necessary to claim, *equality of condition;* but which indirectly will help to break up our rotten sham society, while that claim for equality of condition will be made constantly and with growing loudness till it *must* be listened to, and then at last it will only be a step over the border, and the civilised world will be socialised; and, looking back on what has been, we shall be astonished to think of how long we submitted to live as we live now.

2. *Parliamentary and Municipal Socialism* *

SIDNEY WEBB

"We are all Socialists now," avowed the Right Honorable Sir William Vernon Harcourt in the British House of Commons lately, and the Prince of Wales recently made the same confession. Whatever may be the value of these vague declarations, it is certain that the progress of Socialism is just now the most marked characteristic of English thought.[1]

* From Sidney Webb, *Socialism in England* (Publications of the American Economic Association, IV, 2, April, 1889). By permission.

[1] See the pamphlet by the present writer, *The Progress of Socialism* (Second edition, London, 1888, The Modern Press, 13 Paternoster Row).

At the same time, the influence of Socialism in English public life may very easily be overlooked by a casual observer, especially as it is still often ignored or misapprehended by public men themselves. English politics are, by tradition, so exclusively an affair of the "classes" that even the greatest movements in democratic thought are apt to escape the notice of those unaccustomed to watch the tendencies of the still largely inarticulate masses. The development of Socialistic institutions has, moreover, been so gradual, and has met with such universal acceptance, that the great majority of citizens are still quite unaware of the extent to which Individualist principles have been abandoned. The ordinary party politician, intent only upon the issues of the moment, would probably deny that Socialism, as a vital political force, has any existence in England at all.

Americans in particular find it difficult adequately to realize the rapid progress of Democracy in England, whether political or social. Those unfamiliar with English political life are almost inevitably led to mistake the surviving forms of Feudalism, with their corresponding social inequalities, for greater drawbacks and deductions from the political Democracy than they really are. It may confidently be asserted that the existence of an hereditary peerage offers less of an obstacle to genuine reform that that of the political "rings and bosses," so graphically portrayed by Mr. Bryce.[1] The English Conservative Party, moreover, by no means corresponds to the various conservative or reactionary elements in continental politics, but is itself constantly being "permeated" by new ideas emanating from the other side. A party whose leaders carried the abolition of the Corn Laws (1846), most of the Factory Acts, household suffrage in the towns (1867), and Democratic local self-government in London and the rural districts (1888), cannot be said to be a mere party of reaction. The fact that all these measures were unwilling concessions to popular pressure only emphasizes their democratic character.

Nor is it easy to realize the extent of the progress of the economic side of Democracy—that is to say, Socialism itself. Students have grown so accustomed to think of Socialism as a mere "Utopia," spun from the humanity-intoxicated brains of various Frenchmen of the beginning of the century, that they find great difficulty in recognizing it in any other aspect. But on the part of the critics this is simple ignorance. Down to the present generation the aspirant after social reform, whether Socialist or Individualist, naturally embodied his ideas in a detailed plan of a new social order, from which all contemporary evils were eliminated. Just as Plato had his "Republic," Campanella his "City of the Sun," and Sir Thomas More his "Utopia," so Babeuf had his "Charter of Equality," Cabet his "Icaria," St. Simon his "Industrial System," and Fourier his ideal "Phalanstery." Robert Owen spent a fortune in pressing upon a stiff-necked generation a "New

[1] *The American Commonwealth*, Vol. II.

Moral World"; and even Comte, superior, as he was, to many of the weaknesses of his time, must needs add a detailed "Polity" to his "Philosophy" of Positivism.

The leading feature of all these proposals (not excluding the last) was what may be called their "statical" character. The ideal society was represented as a perfectly balanced equilibrium without need or possibility of future organic alteration. Now-a-days, owing mainly to the efforts of Comte, Darwin and Spencer, we can no longer think of the future society as an unchanging state. The social ideal from being statical has become dynamic. The necessity of the constant growth and development of the social organism has become axiomatic. No philosopher now looks for anything but the gradual passing of the old order into the new, without breach of continuity or abrupt general change of social tissue. The new becomes itself old, often before it is consciously recognized as new, and history shows us nothing but constant gradual evolution.

Most Socialists have learnt this lesson [1] even better than their opponents, and find now their strongest argument therein. But the common criticism of Socialism has not yet noted the change, and continues to deal mainly with the obsolete Utopias of the pre-evolutionary age. Modern Socialists are still reproached with the domestic details of an imaginary "Phalanstery" or with the failure of "Queenwood" or "Icaria," whereas they are now advocating the conscious adoption of principles of social organization which advanced communities have already dimly and unconsciously found to be the inevitable outcome of Democracy and the Industrial Revolution.

Nor is there any special socialist method of reform. It may suit the interested defenders of the existing order, or heated journalistic imaginations, to imagine that Socialism necessarily implies a sudden and forcible overthrow of police and government in a kind of tumultuous rising of the common people. The student of Socialism knows that it is not necessarily, or even usually, bound up with anything of the sort. It is a safe maxim that the character of a revolutionary movement in this respect depends mainly upon the nature of the repressing forces.

In Russia, for instance, whatever socialist thought exists, is a portion of the so-called Nihilist movement. This is, itself, not socialist in character, (either "collectivist" or "anarchist,") but seeks merely political and administrative reforms. The violent methods used by some of the Russian Nihilists are, however, not followed in countries enjoying greater political freedom.

In Germany, in spite of considerable repression, Socialism is an exclusively

---

[1] "I am aware that there are some who suppose that our present bourgeois arrangements must be totally destroyed and others substituted almost at a blow. But, however successful a revolution might be, it is certain that mankind cannot change its whole nature all at once. Break the old shell, certainly, but never forget the fact that the new forms *must* grow out of the old." H. M. Hyndman, *Historical Basis of Socialism*, p. 305 (London, 1883, Kegan Paul & Co.)

Parliamentary force of the first magnitude. In France it is mainly a factor in Paris municipal politics. In England to-day the comparatively small avowed Socialist party obtains most of its influence by the unconscious permeation of all schools of thought. In all three countries the development of socialistic institutions is gradual, persistent and carried out by legislative enactments. Whatever may be the case in other countries, no one acquainted with English politics can reasonably fear that this feature will not continue. No student of society, whether Socialist or Individualist, can doubt that any important organic changes will necessarily be (1) Democratic, and thus acceptable to a majority of the people and prepared for in the minds of all; (2) gradual, and thus causing no dislocation, however rapid may be the rate of progress; (3) not regarded as immoral by the mass of people, and thus not subjectively demoralizing to them; and in this country, at any rate (4), constitutional and peaceful.

If Socialism is thus neither a Utopia nor a specially violent method of revolution, what, it may be asked, are its distinctive features? It is not easy to reply in a single sentence. The ideas denoted by Socialism represent the outcome of a gradual change of thought in economics, ethics and politics. The Socialist is distinguished from the Individualist, not so much by any special Shibboleth as by a complete difference as to the main principles of social organization. The essental contribution of the century to sociology has been the supersession of the Individual by the Community as the starting point of social investigations.[1] Socialism is the product of this development, arising, with it, from the contemporary industrial evolution. On the economic side, Socialism implies the collective administration of rent and interest, leaving to the individual only the wages of his labor, of hand or brain. On the political side, it involves the collective control over, and ultimate administration of, all the main instruments of wealth production. On the ethical side, it expresses the general recognition of fraternity, the universal obligation of personal service, and the subordination of personal ambition to the common good.

It is difficult to assign a beginning to English socialist legislation, even in the modern sense of the term. Before the Mediaeval conception of the State has passed away, the Elizabethan Poor Laws, culminating in the great Act of 1601, definitely asserted the right of the very poorest to participate in the results of the national industry. During the next two centuries socialistic legislation was almost confined to this form of collectivist philanthropy, while the commercial development of the country was preparing the way for the great industrial revolution and the triumph of private capitalism. At the beginning of the present century the zenith of industrial individual-

[1] A full statement of this intellectual movement will be found in the articles "Political Economy" and "Socialism" in the Encyclopaedia Britannica (ninth edition). See also T. Kirkup's *Inquiry Into Socialism* (London, 1887, Longmans).

ism seems to have been reached. Political tyranny was at its height but the fullest liberty was left to the owner of land and capital, so far, at least, as all the new industries were concerned, to use them for his utmost personal advantage, however many lives of men, women and children were destroyed in the process. The results upon the national life were so appalling that practical statesmen were compelled to intervene. The first Factory Act was passed in 1802,[1] and others followed in 1819 (59 Geo. III c. 66), 1825 (6 Geo. IV c. 63) and 1831 (1 and 2 Wm. IV c. 39). It was however left for the gradually developing humanitarian influence, led by Tory and aristocratic members, such as Mr. M. T. Sadler and Lord Shaftesbury, to make these limitations upon private property really effective, in the teeth of the most embittered opposition from the contemporary Liberals and political economists.

Since that day the progress has been rapid. Every decade has seen a notable stride taken towards genuine popular government, and every such advance has been used by the people to procure the passage of further socialist legislation.

The Reform Bill of 1832, mere middle-class enfranchisement as it was, resulted in 1833 (3 and 4 Wm. IV c. 103) in the first really effective factory act, and enabled Lord Ashley (afterwards Lord Shaftesbury) to carry his acts of 1842, 1844 and 1847, each imposing fresh restrictions on private ownership of the means of production. The same reforming impulse gave us the Mining Act of 1842 (5 and 6 Vic. c. 99) and by the Municipal Corporations Act of 1835 created several hundred energetic centres of local socialistic development. The same period saw the beginning of sanitary legislation, by which a further series of limitations were imposed on land and capital owners for the common weal. During the first 45 years of the century nearly 400 "Local Improvement Acts" were passed, conferring sanitary powers upon more than 200 local authorities.[2]

In 1847 and 1848, these scattered legislative powers were gathered up into important codes, finally consolidated in the "Public Health Act" of 1875. This legislation is wholly socialist in character. Innumerable restrictions upon the free use of private property are imposed, and the rights of ownership are thereby in the public interest considerably curtailed. The value of the inferior kinds of house property is frequently much diminished by the enforcement of these provisions. The community, by its local political organizations, has assumed the collective administration of innumerable social services and levies, mainly to the advantage of the poorer classes, a series of "rates," or assessments upon real property, which now absorbs a large percentage of its annual rental. This class of socialist legislation is constantly increasing.

[1] 42 Geo. III., c. 73. See the *History of English Factory Legislation* by E. von Plener (London, 1873, Chapman and Hall).
[2] Clifford, *History of Private Bill Legislation,* Vol. II., p. 300.

It is not only in matters of sanitation that this "municipal socialism" is progressing. Nearly half the gas consumers of the Kingdom already consume gas made by themselves as citizens collectively, in 168 different localities,[1] as many as 14 local authorities obtained power to borrow money to engage in the gas industry in a single year.[2] Water supply is rapidly coming to be universally a matter of public provision, no fewer than 71 separate governing bodies obtaining loans for this purpose in the year 1885-6 alone.[3] The prevailing tendency is for the municipalities to absorb also the tramway (horse-cars) industry, 31 localities already owning their own lines, comprising a quarter of the total mileage in the Kingdom.[4] Eight of these authorities lease their lines, but the others do not shrink from this public organization of labor and successfully administer their own property. Several of them even hire lines from neighboring owners and work them on lease. The franchises of the London Tramway Companies expire in a few years, and there is already a strong feeling in favor of the lines being worked directly by the County Council as the only practicable means of securing shorter hours and proper treatment for the employees.

Besides the numerous acts regulating factories and workshops, and similar legislation dealing with mines, printworks, fishcuring establishments, bakehouses, alkali works and many other industries, there are now extensive codes regulating merchant shipping and seamen, gasworks, railways, tramways, theatres, public houses, and in fact nearly every large trade.

Nor is there any sign of a slackening in this progress. The "Shop Hours Regulation Act" of 1887 limited the hours during which any shop employing "young persons" may be kept open; and it is already apparent that a formidable agitation will soon compel the explicit restriction of the working day for adults. The Political Economists will offer no opposition as to principle. "I see nothing," said Professor Jevons already in 1882, referring to the proposal for an "Eight Hours Bill," "to forbid the State interfering in the matter if it could be clearly shown that the existing customs are injurious to health, and that there is no other probable remedy. Neither principle, experience nor precedent, in other cases of legislation, prevents us from contemplating the idea of State interference in such circumstances."[5]

Public education will not appear a socialist measure in the United States, where the ample resources of the reserved public lands prevent its essentially collectivist character from being recognized. In England, however, the rapid progress towards free government schools is rightly cited as a marked instance of socialist progress. The increasing absorption of the incomes of the

[1] Board of Trade Return, 1889.
[2] Report of Local Government Board for 1886–7, C-5526.
[3] Report of Local Government Board for 1886–7, C-5526.
[4] House of Commons Return, H. C. 347, 1888.
[5] The State in Relation to Labor, ch. 3, p. 65.

comparatively rich, to provide for the education of their poorer brethren, makes its socialist character disagreeably obtrusive to the capitalist as well as to the private school proprietor. The movement towards the public provision of meals in the schools of poor districts is a still stronger testimony to the growth of the "collective" spirit. Many hundreds of thousands of gratuitous or cheap meals are already supplied to city children by organized charitable efforts with the cooperation of the school authorities. The London School Board has already begun to discuss the necessity of placing these private collective agencies under direct public control and supervision. "One free meal a day," to be provided by the School Board itself, out of the rates upon property, was in the programme of not a few School Board candidates last year; and Mrs. Besant, the leading socialist advocate of this measure, was triumphantly returned at the head of the poll in East London.

The necessity of providing public work for the "unemployed," now a chronic winter feature of our great cities, is becoming daily more generally recognized. The government has already been forced to issue circulars to all local authorities urging them to set on foot extra works for the sake of offering employment at low wages to those demanding it. This is now done each winter, to a small extent, in many localities, and there is now a demand for the permanent public organization of the labor of all the recipients of Poor Law relief. Plans suggested by the Rev. Herbert Mills and others, based on the Industrial Colonies of Holland and Germany, are about to be tried, as it is now universally admitted that only by such collectivist measures can the evils be dealt with.

The "Housing of the Poor" in England's great cities is another problem already beginning to be solved on essentially socialist lines. Over six million dollars have already been spent by London local authorities in subsidizing the building of cheap artisans' dwellings, and it is now strongly urged that the London County Council should take up the work with greatly increased energy. The city of Glasgow has, indeed, gone much further, the municipality (which already provides gas, water, markets, baths, wash houses, slaughterhouses, parks, botanic gardens, art galleries, museums, libraries, tramways, "houses of refuge," and industrial and other schools) having demolished vast areas of "slum" property, and itself built large blocks of dwellings for the poor, let at "moderate" rents. The municipality also maintains a number of "common lodging houses" with most successful results.[1]

This "Municipal Socialism" is being rapidly imitated by other local authorities with the effect of absorbing in "rates" a constantly increasing share of the rental of the country. Our progressive "municipalization of rent," by increase of local rates, is clearly only an unconscious form of gradual Land Nationalization. Many students, however, still have the idea that Socialism implies a rigidly centralized national administration of all the details of life. This is an

---

[1] Report of City of Glasgow Improvement Trust, 1888.

entire misapprehension of the Socialist position. Such a society would be as abhorrent to Mr. William Morris as to Mr. Auberon Herbert. Socialists have, in fact, as yet contributed nothing to the difficult problem of political science as to the proper line of division between the functions of the central government and those of local authorities. All that can be said is, that in England Socialists and Individualists alike will more probably desire to make the regulation and taxation of private industry matters of centralization, whilst actual public administration will probably be municipal. Factory Acts[1] and the Land tax will be national, but gasworks and tramways local.

Subject to this distinction, hardly anyone now objects to the extension of local government activity. The innumerable multiplicity of services now performed by the local governing authorities makes it indeed impossible to record them all and causes the English Government, in its various ramifications, to be by far the largest direct employer of labor in the country.

Besides our international relations and the army, navy, police and the courts of justice, the community now carries on for itself, in some part or another of these islands, the post-office, telegraphs, carriage of small commodities, coinage surveys, the regulation of the currency and note issue, the provision of weights and measures, the making, sweeping, lighting and repairing of the streets, roads and bridges, life insurance, the grant of annuities, ship-building, stock broking, banking, farming and money lending. It provides for many thousands of us from birth to burial, midwifery, nursery, education, board and lodging, vaccination, medical attendance, medicine, public worship, amusements and burial. It furnishes and maintains its own museums, parks, botanic gardens, art galleries, libraries, concert halls, roads, streets, bridges, markets, fire engines, light-houses, pilots, ferries, surf boats, steamtugs, lifeboats, slaughter-houses, cemeteries, public baths, wash houses, pounds, harbors, piers, wharves, hospitals, dispensaries, gas works, water works, tramways, telegraph cables, allotments, cow meadows, artisans' dwellings, common lodging houses, schools, churches, and reading rooms. It carries on and publishes its own researches in geology, meteorology, statistics, zoology, geography, and even theology. In our colonies the English Government further allows and encourages the communities to provide for themselves railways, canals, pawnbroking, theatres, forestry, cinchona farms, irrigation, leper villages, casinos, bathing establishments, and immigration; and to deal in ballast, guano, quinine, opium, salt, and what not.[2] Every one of these functions, including even the army, navy, police and courts of justice, was at one time left to private enterprise, and was a source of legitimate individual investment of capital. Step by step the community has absorbed them, wholly or partially, and the area of private exploitation has

[1] See the *Experimentum crucis* recorded by Jevons. (*The State in Relation to Labor*, Ch. III, p. 59.)

[2] See the *Colonial Office List* (London, annually, Harrison).

been lessened. Parallel with this progressive nationalization or municipalization of industry, there has gone on, outside, the elimination of the purely personal element in business management. The older economists doubted whether anything but banking and insurance could be carried on by joint stock enterprise; now every conceivable industry down to baking and milk-selling is successfully managed by the salaried officers of large corporations of idle shareholders. More than one-third of the whole business of England, measured by the capital employed, is now done by joint stock companies,[1] whose shareholders could be expropriated by the community with little more dislocation of industry than is caused by the daily purchase of shares on the Stock Exchange.

Besides all its direct supersession of private enterprise, the State now registers, inspects and controls nearly all the industrial functions which it has not yet absorbed. In addition to births, marriages, deaths, and electors, the State registers all solicitors, barristers, notaries, brokers, newspaper proprietors, playing-card makers, brewers, bankers, seamen, captains, mates, doctors, cabmen, hawkers, pawnbrokers, tobacconists, distillers, plate dealers, game dealers, all insurance companies, friendly societies, endowed schools and charities, limited companies, lands, houses, deeds, bills of sale, compositions, ships, arms, dogs, cats, omnibuses, books, plays, pamphlets, newspapers, raw cotton, trade marks, and patents; lodging houses, public houses, refreshment houses, theatres, music halls, places of worship, elementary schools, and dancing rooms.

Nor is the registration a mere form. Most of the foregoing are also inspected and criticized, as well as all railways, tramways, ships, mines, factories, canal boats, public conveyances, fisheries, slaughter houses, dairies, milk shops, bakeries, baby farms, gas meters, schools of anatomy, vivisection laboratories, explosive works, Scotch herrings and common lodging houses.

The inspection is often detailed and exhaustive. It may be said moreover, once for all, the laws of this kind are much more rigidly enforced and generally obeyed in England than in the United States. The State in most of the larger industrial operations prescribes the age of the worker, the hours of work, the amount of air, light, cubic space, heat, lavatory, accommodation, holidays, and meal times; where, when, and how wages shall be paid; how machinery, staircases, lift-holes, mines, and quarries are to be fenced and guarded; how and when the plant shall be cleaned, repaired, and worked. Even the kind of package in which some articles shall be sold is duly prescribed, so that the individual capitalist shall take no advantage of his position. On every side he is being registered, inspected, controlled, and eventually superseded by the community, and is compelled in the meantime to cede for public purposes an ever increasing share of his rent and interest.

It will be objected by many persons that this is not what they understand

[1] See Mr. Giffen's, statistics, brought up to date in *Facts for Socialists* (Fabian Tract No. 5).

by Socialism. There are doubtless still some who might be compelled to admit that they imagined that Socialists wanted to bring about a sanguinary conflict in the streets, and then the next day to compel all delicately nurtured people to work at a fixed rate of wages, in the government factories. This, however, is merely part of the obstinate survival of the "Utopian" conception of Socialism already referred to. Whether we so describe them or not, these features of modern English society are essentially "collectivist" in character, and are utterly contrary to the Individualist principles lately dominant in thought. Mr. Herbert Spencer quite properly regards the whole course of legislation during the present generation as subversive of that unrestrained individual liberty which forms his ideal of social order.[1] He also foretells its inevitable issue.

"The numerous socialist changes made by Act of Parliament joined with numerous others presently to be made, will by and by be all merged in State Socialism—swallowed in the vast wave which they have little by little raised." "It is indeed certain," the political economists now agree, "that industrial society will not permanently remain without a systematic organization. The mere conflict of private interests will never produce a well-ordered commonwealth of labor." [2]

Our unconscious acceptance of this progressive Socialism is a striking testimony to the change which has come over the country of Godwin, Malthus and James Mill. The "practical man," oblivious or contemptuous of any theory of the Social Organism or general principles of social organization, has been forced by the necessities of the time, into an ever deepening collectivist channel. Socialism, of course, he still rejects and despises. The Individualist City Councillor will walk along the municipal pavement, lit by municipal gas and cleansed by municipal brooms with municipal water, and seeing by the municipal clock in the municipal market, that he is too early to meet his children coming from the municipal school hard by the county lunatic asylum and municipal hospital, will use the national telegraph system to tell them not to walk through the municipal park but to come by the municipal tramway, to meet him in the municipal reading room, by the municipal art gallery, museum and library, where he intends to consult some of the national publications in order to prepare his next speech in the municipal town-hall, in favor of the nationalization of canals and the increase of the government control over the railway system. "Socialism, sir," he will say, "don't waste the time of a practical man by your fantastic absurdities. Self-help, sir, individual self-help, that's what's made our city what it is."

[1] *Man vs. State* (London, 1884, Williams & Norgate).
[2] Article on "Political Economy" in Encyclopaedia Britannica, ninth edition, Vol. XIX, p. 382 (1886).

3. The Tyranny of Functionless Property *

R. H. TAWNEY

"Possession," said the Egoist, "without obligation to the object possessed, approaches felicity." Functionless property appears natural to those who believe that society should be organized for the acquisition of private wealth, and attacks upon it perverse or malicious, because the question which such persons ask of any institution is, "What does it yield?" And such property yields much to those who own it. Those, however, who hold that social unity and effective work are possible only if society is organized and wealth distributed on the basis of function, will ask of an institution not, "What dividends does it pay?" but "What service does it perform?" To them the fact that much property yields income irrespective of any service which is performed or obligation which is recognized by its owners will appear, not a quality, but a vice. They will see in the social confusion which it produces, payments disproportionate to service here, and payments without any service at all there, and dissatisfaction everywhere, a convincing confirmation of their argument that to build on a foundation of rights and of rights alone is to build on a quicksand.

From this portentous exaggeration into an absolute of what once was, and still might be, a sane and social institution, most other evils follow. Its fruits are the power of those who do not work over those who do, the alternate subservience and rebelliousness of those who work towards those who do not, the starving of science and thought and creative effort for fear that expenditure upon them should impinge on the comfort of the sluggard and the *fainéant,* and the arrangement of society in most of its subsidiary activities to suit the convenience, not of those who work usefully, but of those who spend gaily; so that the most hideous, desolate, and parsimonious places in the country are those in which the greatest wealth is produced, the Clyde valley, or the cotton towns of Lancashire, or the mining villages of Scotland and Wales, and the gayest and most luxurious those in which it is consumed. From the point of view of social health and economic efficiency, society should obtain its material equipment at the cheapest price possible, and, after providing for depreciation and expansion, should distribute the whole product to its working members and their dependents. What happens at present, however, is that its workers are hired at the cheapest price which

* From R. H. Tawney, *The Acquisitive Society* (Harcourt, Brace and Company, 1921). By permission.

the market (as modified by organization) allows, and that the surplus, somewhat diminished by taxation, is distributed to the owners of property.

Profits may vary in a given year from a loss to 100 per cent. But wages are fixed at a level which will enable the marginal firm to continue producing one year with another; and the surplus, even when due partly to efficient management, goes neither to managers nor to manual workers, but to shareholders. The meaning of the process becomes startlingly apparent when, as recently in Lancashire, large blocks of capital change hands at a period of abnormal activity. The existing shareholders receive the equivalent of the capitalized expectation of future profits. The workers, as workers, do not participate in the immense increment in value. And when, in the future, they demand an advance in wages, they will be met by the answer that profits, which before the transaction would have been reckoned large, yield shareholders after it only a low rate of interest on their investment.

The truth is that, whereas in earlier ages the protection of property was normally the protection of work, the relationship between them has come in the course of the economic development of the last two centuries to be very nearly reversed. The two elements which compose civilization are active efforts and passive property, the labour of human things and the tools which human beings use. Of these two elements those who supply the first maintain and improve it, those who own the second normally dictate its character, its development, and its administration. Hence, though politically free, the mass of mankind live in effect under rules imposed to protect the interests of the small section among them whose primary concern is ownership. From this subordination of creative activity to passive property, the worker who depends upon his brains, the organizer, inventor, teacher or doctor suffers almost as much embarrassment as the craftsman. The real economic cleavage is not, as is often said, between employers and employed, but between all who do constructive work, from scientist to labourer, on the one hand, and all whose main interest is the preservation of existing proprietary rights upon the other, irrespective of whether they contribute to constructive work or not.

If, therefore, under the modern conditions which have concentrated any substantial share of property in the hands of a small minority of the population, the world is to be governed for the advantage of those who own, it is only incidentally and by accident that the results will be agreeable to those who work. In practice there is a constant collision between them. Turned into another channel, half the wealth distributed in dividends to functionless shareholders, could secure every child a good education up to 18, could re-endow English universities, and (since more efficient production is important) could equip English industries for more efficient production. Half the ingenuity now applied to the protection of property could have made most industrial diseases as rare as smallpox, and most English cities into places of health and even of beauty. What stands in the way is the doctrine that the rights of property are absolute, irrespective of any social function which its owners may perform. So the laws which are most stringently enforced are still the laws which protect property, though the protection of property is no longer likely to be equivalent to the protection of work, and the interests which govern industry and predominate in public affairs are proprietary interests.

A mill-owner may impose conditions which degrade a generation of operatives; but his brother magistrates will let him off with a caution or a nominal fine to do the same to the next. For he is an owner of property. A landowner may draw rents from slums in which young children die at the rate of 200 per 1000; but he will be none the less welcome in polite society. For property has no obligations and therefore can do no wrong. Urban land may be held from the market on the outskirts of cities in which human beings are living three to a room, and rural land may be used for sport when villagers are leaving it to overcrowd them still more. No public authority intervenes, for both are property.

Nor are these practical evils the gravest consequences which flow from the hypertrophy of property in an industrial society. Property is in its nature a kind of limited sovereignty. Its essence is a power, secured by the State to some individual or group as against all others, to dispose of the objects over which the proprietary rights are exercised. When those objects are simple and easily obtained, the property is normally harmless or beneficial. When they are such that, while they can be acquired only by the few, the mass of mankind cannot live unless it has free access to them, their proprietors, in prescribing their use, may become the irresponsible governors of thousands of other human beings.

Hence, when pushed to extremes, applied to purposes for which it was not designed, and in an environment to which it is not adapted, property in things swells into something which is, in effect, sovereignty over persons. "The main objection to a large corporation," writes Mr. Justice Brandeis, of the Supreme Court of the U. S. A., "is that it makes possible—and in many cases makes inevitable—the exercise of industrial absolutism." In England such absolutism is felt mainly in the hours of work, above all in the power to deprive the wage-earner of his livelihood by dismissing him from his employment. In America there are cities where the company owns not only the works, but halls and meeting-places, streets and pavements, where the town council and police are its nominees, and the pulpit and press its mouthpieces, where no meeting can be held to which it objects and no citizen can dwell of whom it disapproves.[1] Such property confers a private franchise or

---

[1] See the *Report on the Steel Strike of 1919,* by the Commission of Inquiry of the Interchurch World Movement, W. Z. Foster, *The Great Steel Strike,* and the Final Report of the United States Commission on Industrial Relations.

jurisdiction analogous to that which in some periods has been associated with the ownership of land. The men who endure it may possess as citizens the right to "life, liberty, and the pursuit of happiness." But they live, in effect, at the will of a lord.

To those who believe that institutions which repudiate all moral significance must sooner or later collapse, a society which confuses the protection of property with the preservation of its functionless perversions will appear as precarious as that which has left the memorials of its tasteless frivolity and more tasteless ostentation in the gardens of Versailles. Do men love peace? They will see the greatest enemy of social unity in rights which involve no obligation to co-operate for the service of society. Do they value equality? Property rights which dispense their owners from the common human necessity of labour make inequality an institution permeating every corner of society, from the distribution of material wealth to the training of intellect itself. Do they desire greater industrial efficiency? There is no more fatal obstacle to efficiency than the revelation that idleness has the same privileges as industry, and that for every additional blow with the pick or hammer an additional profit will be distributed among shareholders who wield neither.

Indeed, functionless property is the greatest enemy of legitimate property itself. It is the parasite which kills the organism that produced it. Bad money drives out good, and, as the history of the last two hundred years shows, when property for acquisition or power and property for service or for use jostle each other freely in the market, without restrictions such as some legal systems have imposed on alienation and inheritance, the latter tends normally to be absorbed by the former, because it has less resisting power. Thus functionless property grows, and as it grows it undermines the creative energy which produced the institution of property and which in earlier ages property protected. It cannot unite men, for what unites them is the bond of service to a common purpose, and that bond it repudiates, since its very essence is the maintenance of rights irrespective of service. It cannot create; it can only spend, so that the number of scientists, inventors, artists, or men of letters who have sprung in the course of the last century from hereditary riches can be numbered on one hand. It values neither culture nor beauty, but only the power which belongs to wealth and the ostentation which is the symbol of it.

So those who dread these qualities, energy and thought and the creative spirit—and they are many—will not discriminate, as we have tried to discriminate, between different types and kinds of property, in order that they may preserve those which are legitimate and abolish those which are not. They will endeavour to preserve all private property, even in its most degenerate forms. And those who value those things will try to promote them by relieving property of its perversions and thus enabling it to return to its true nature.

They will not desire to establish any visionary communism, for they will realize that the free disposal of a sufficiency of personal possessions is the condition of a healthy and self-respecting life, and will seek to distribute more widely the property rights which make them to-day the privilege of a minority. But they will refuse to submit to the naïve philosophy which would treat all proprietary rights as equal in sanctity merely because they are identical in name. They will distinguish sharply between property which is used by its owner for the conduct of his profession or the upkeep of his household, and property which is merely a claim on wealth produced by another's labour. They will insist that property is moral and healthy only when it is used as a condition, not of idleness, but of activity, and when it involves the discharge of definite personal obligations. They will endeavour in short, to base it upon the principle of function.

4. On the Road to Victory *

CLEMENT R. ATTLEE

Predominantly the parties on the Continent have been built on the writings of Karl Marx. Around his teachings the movement has grown. Different interpretations have been put upon his creed. In some countries other powerful influences have been at work, and the characters of his apostles and the circumstances of the countries to which they belong have necessarily caused differences in the method pursued by particular parties, but they have this in common—that they were formed as definite Socialist movements, inspired by the word revealed to Marx.

In Britain the history of the movement has been entirely different. Widely diffused as his influence has been, the number of those who accepted Marxism as a creed has always been small. The number of those who have entered the Socialist movement as the direct result of his teaching has been but a fraction of the whole. One must seek the inspiration of the majority of British Socialists in other directions.

Leaving aside Owen and the early pioneers, I think that the first place in

*From Clement R. Attlee, *The Labour Party in Perspective* (Victor Gollancz, 1937). by permission of Prime Minister Attlee.

the influences that built up the Socialist movement must be given to religion. England in the nineteenth century was still a nation of Bible readers. To put the Bible into the hands of an Englishman is to do a very dangerous thing. He will find there material which may send him out as a preacher of some religious, social, or economic doctrine. The large number of religious sects in this country, and the various tenets that many of them hold, illustrate this.

The Bible is full of revolutionary teaching, and it is not surprising that, in a country where thought is free, many men and women have drawn from it the support which they needed for their instinctive revolt against the inhuman conditions which Capitalism brings. I think that probably the majority of those who have built up the Socialist movement in this country have been adherents of the Christian religion—and not merely adherents, but enthusiastic members of some religious body. There are probably more texts from the Bible enunciated from Socialist platforms than from those of all other parties. Not only the adherents of dissenting bodies whose less privileged position inclined them to take a Left Wing line in politics, but also many clergy and laymen of the Established Church, found that the Capitalist system was incompatible with Christianity. It is significant that the gap between the end of Owenism and the birth of the Social Democratic Federation is filled by the Christian Socialist movement of Kingsley and Maurice. Here one sees a feature which distinguishes the British movement from most of those abroad. In no other country has Christianity become converted to Socialism to such an extent as in Britain. In no other Socialist movement has Christian thought had such a powerful leavening effect. It is possible in Britain for a parson to declare himself a Communist and for millions of faithful Catholics to support the Labour Party. It may be noted as a factor in building the British Labour movement on broad foundations that so many of the adherents of the Catholic Faith in Britain come from Ireland, where a creed of political and economic revolt has been inculcated into a Catholic population. The British Labour movement owes much to these men and women, who brought over from their own country their hatred of oppression.

The Labour Party necessarily differs from those Continental countries where Socialists found themselves faced by a Church either closely bound up with the State or with property or class interests, and inimical to liberty of thought. Where, as in many countries, the workers in the formative years of the Socialist movement were attached to a dogmatic faith which controlled every phase of their lives, it was natural that the movement of revolt should be anti-clerical. To meet the conditions there was set up a dogmatism equally narrow and exclusive. The divisions between blacks and reds extending into every activity became absolute. Neither side could influence the other any more than can two contending armies entrenched against each other. Such a division undoubtedly gives great driving-force and cohesion to a movement, but it creates such a fissure in the body politic that the result is either stalemate or revolution. Neither can advance or retreat. In Britain, on the other hand, where political and religious differences do not coincide, there is a constant broadening owing to contact.

I do not believe that the only choice before us is the acceptance of Fascism or Communism. I do not think that Britain must follow the Moscow or the Berlin road. Those two roads have certain features in common. They are straight, narrow, and artificial. They drive through the landscape of humanity with little apparent reference to its contours or to the graces of the countryside which have been derived from the past. Those who journey along them attain a very high rate of speed, and they scorn old-fashioned meandering paths. There are many casualties on that account. A high rate of speed may give great pleasure to those who control the machines, but it may mean a vast amount of discomfort to the driven. The real question is, to what place will those who complete the journey arrive? —if, indeed, they do arrive, for there is a great possibility of a terrible catastrophe on the way. One may ask, too, in what kind of condition will those who journey be like when the road has been traversed? One can give no certain answer to these questions, whether one considers the travellers on the Moscow or on the Berlin highways.

I have already set out my objections to the Totalitarian State, whether formed on the Fascist or Communist model, and I will not repeat them here. I do not think that it is desirable as an ideal or necessary as a stage in human development. In my view the Totalitarian State is not an advance in civilisation but a retrogression. It has been adopted by peoples who are politically and socially immature. They have not grasped the fact that the essential condition for an advanced civilisation is tolerance, and that a society in which men and women of differing views on many subjects can live together in peace and harmony is a higher type than one in which all must conform to a single pattern. The achievement of the Totalitarian State involves the use of force, and its continuance requires the use of the same methods. The one thing indispensable is an all-pervading police service. While this continues there is no freedom, and until it is abolished the experiment in Russia will not attract the majority of the British people.

It is, in my view, the strength, not the weakness, of Britain which allows of wide tolerance and freedom, permitting people to disagree on matters of vital importance and yet to continue to live together in friendly intercourse. To exchange this for a society in which everything is subordinated to a ruthless class warfare would be a retrograde step. Avoiding both Fascism and Communism, this country, I believe, can afford to the world an example of how society can adapt itself to new conditions and base itself on new principles without breach of continuity and without violence and intolerance. We have in the past to a great extent avoided the civil wars which have done such a vast amount of harm in other countries. It is, I think, a false reading of history to think that what has happened elsewhere must necessarily happen in this country. It has not been so in the past. It was, I think, characteristic of Britain that, on the only occasion on which there arose a military dictatorship, the dictator was a man who strove continually for tolerance and sought unceasingly to rid himself of the burden of absolute power and to return to the ways of constitutionalism. Cromwell was as English as Mussolini is Italian.

I think that nations tend to follow very closely their national traditions. Italy has frequently been the arena for faction fights and proscriptions. The Fascist methods are nothing new to the descendants of the Guelfs and Ghibellines. Military despotism has been a feature of German history. It is still a question whether or not Russia will return to the autocracy which she has so long endured. It is my faith that Britain will be true to her traditions, and that, despite the profound differences that separate the supporters of Socialism and Capitalism, the changes which are necessary will be brought about without bloodshed and violence. It is the genius of the British people to modify and adapt old institutions to new purposes. I think that the same process which has been followed in the past will be employed in the future for changing the social and economic structure of this country.

I believe that the Labour Party is the instrument whereby this change will be effected. Typically British, the Labour Party has shown its power of adaption to new conditions and new purposes. At its inception it was a party representing almost entirely organised Labour. Its programme was sectional, not national. It has since then developed into a national party, open to all, and has a policy which embraces every phase of national life. In its earlier days it would have been a fair criticism to have said that it could not aspire to power because its appeal was too narrow. It is not true to-day. Increasingly it draws its strength from men and women of all classes of society. Its achievement of power does not depend on an alteration in the quality of its adherents, but in their quantity. It has to convert to its faith many millions of workers who still cling to Capitalism. It has to persuade many members of the classes which depend in the main on their own work for their livelihood that true community of interest is based on fellowship in service, not on participation in profits.

There is, I believe, an ever-growing number of people who, although comparatively well-to-do, are yet profoundly dissatisfied with the Capitalist system. There are technicians and business managers who find that their efforts lead only to frustration. When they invent new machinery or introduce improvements into production, they more often than not find that as a result of their labours a number of workers have been thrown out of their jobs, while not infrequently the increased production which they have effected cannot be absorbed because of the mal-distribution of purchasing power.

There is also a realisation that in modern large-scale industry there is but little chance of a man becoming his own master. He is apt to be only a servant of a company. He realises that he might as well serve the community instead of a certain number of profit-takers. The uncertainty of private enterprise which was so manifest during the great depression has made more attractive the prospects of serving the State or the municipality. But I think that a more powerful motive which is bringing into the ranks of labour so many individuals from the better-off classes is a realisation of the immoral and unjust basis of Capitalism. The social conscience speaks loudly to-day. Where formerly it impelled people of goodwill to give to charity, it now leads them to examine into the system which produces injustice. Where formerly they were content to deal with results, they now seek to remove causes.

The fact is that the ranks of the supporters of the Capitalist system are constantly being thinned by the desertion of those who have lost faith in it. Many of these find their way into the ranks of Labour. There is, however, a great body of citizens who, while unable to give their former support to Capitalism, still fear to accept Socialism and all its implications. I believe that they will come to realise that there is no alternative. At present they hesitate partly through prejudice and partly through misunderstanding.

It is the task of the Labour Party to win over to its side all these elements which are still uncertain of their position. To do this involves a receptivity on the part of the Labour Party itself. It does not in my view involve watering down Labour's Socialist creed in order to attract new adherents who cannot accept the full Socialist faith. On the contrary I believe that it is only a clear and bold policy that will attract their support. It is not the preaching of a feeble kind of Liberalism that is required, but a frank statement of the full Socialist faith in terms which will be understood.

I do not believe that there is need for a great change in the constitution of the Labour Party. Its basis in organised Labour must remain. The complaint that the Labour Party is bossed by a few Trade Union officials is untrue. The constitution of the Party is democratic. Individual membership is open to all. I anticipate that in the course of the next few years there will be a rapid increase of individual membership which will give the local Labour Parties an even greater influence than that which they now possess. I hope that the Party will continue to be a party of the rank and file, and that those who enter its ranks will accept the conditions and discipline of democracy. There is not, and should not be, a royal road to influence in the Labour movement.

The Labour Party is what its members make it.

The future of the Labour Party depends on two things—its success in winning power in this country, and the way in which it uses that power when it has been obtained.

I am convinced that whenever this mandate has been given, the Labour programme must be carried out with the utmost vigour and resolution. To delay dealing with essentials would be fatal. To show irresolution or cowardice would be to invite defeat. A Labour Government should make it quite plain that it will suffer nothing to hinder it in carrying out the popular will. In all great enterprises it is the first steps that are difficult, and it is the way in which these are taken that makes the difference between success or failure. A Labour Government, not in a spirit of malice or revenge, but with the greatest regard for justice to all, must resolutely set about its task of rebuilding the life of this country on the principles of liberty, equality, and social justice, and of joining with other nations to create a world Commonwealth.

~~~~~~

5. Britain: World Leader of Democratic Socialism *

E. F. M. DURBIN

~~~~~~

The Marxist system of thought is based upon four propositions of an ascending degree of particularity—first that the governing motive in human life is that of acquisitiveness; secondly that acquisitiveness must manifest itself in the form of group struggle in so far as it produces historical change; thirdly that this group struggle must break out into civil war during any period in which power is transferred from one class to another; and fourthly that a dictatorship of the proletariat and of the Communist Party over the proletariat can achieve social justice or Socialism.

I have found it impossible to accept any one of these four propositions in an unamended form. While it is possible to concede that acquisitiveness is an important and universal motive in human behaviour—animating us all, present in every group contest, deeply influencing the whole course of history—it is not possible to accept the view that it is a sole determining cause, a solitary source of change, or the final or fundamental cause in history. The pattern of social causes is more complex, and the causes at work in it

* From E. F. M. Durbin, *The Politics of Democratic Socialism* (Routledge, 1940). By permission.

are of many kinds. Nor was it possible to accept the view that even where rational acquisitiveness is present, it must take the form of group contest. It is obvious that co-operation plays just as important a role in the economic life of society, and that changes and discoveries in the field of co-operation are every bit as significant in the determination of historical change as are movements in the technique of struggle.

But the most important doctrines for my purpose are the two political theses—that civil war is inevitable, and that social justice can be secured by the dictatorship of the Communist Party. Neither of these doctrines, however, seems to bear the light of psychological or historical evidence particularly well. It appears from the history of our own country alone that classes have been defeated without violence, and that we were brought within measurable distance of civil war in a struggle between two parties of the same class. And we have just seen that the method of government implied by a dictatorship, and the release of unbridled aggression made possible by the circumstances of a dictatorship, render it almost inconceivable that a dictatorship of any kind could create social justice, or restore political liberty without a further revolution.

It would perhaps be as well to say at this point that I do not wish for a moment to decry the importance or value of Marxist thought to the social sciences. After Marx and Engels had completed their life work, all further historical reflection and political theory has of necessity been 'post-Marxian.' They accomplished an intellectual revolution in the historical and social sciences upon which all who come after them must build. Their emphasis upon the importance of acquisitiveness in history—Mr. Cole's 'realistic interpretation' of history—their analysis of the mechanics of group struggle, their picture of society as a mechanism of institutions, are ideas that may change and develop, but can never wholly disappear. They are part of our contemporary understanding of what we are.

It is only static Marxianism that is blind, and whose political implications are wrong. All that Marx said, and Lenin said, must be amended, re-interpreted and set in proper perspective by the greater knowledge of social institutions that we have now accumulated, the further historical experience through which we have passed since they wrote, and, most important of all, by the extra-ordinary increase in our knowledge of psychological motive and emotional process. Marxism must, like every body of thought, change and grow if it is to live.

For the purpose of this book the most important conclusion that I have tried to establish is the last. I have tried to show why I so profoundly believe that we cannot proceed by the Communist road to a better social order. Strong and violent men have always believed that they could build a new heaven and a new earth, if only they were allowed to override and destroy those who disagreed with them. It is not so. The problem of social life is the problem of reconciling the conflicting ends of different persons and different groups. Justice cannot be achieved, much less happiness, by the mere crushing of one party to a conflict. Injustice remains, hatred remains, the drawn sword cannot be sheathed, the machine-gun cannot be put away. Monotonously and horribly the victims will continue to tramp down to death, their shoulders bowed by suffering, their eyes glazed with hatred and fear. It is twenty years since the Communist Party obtained undisputed political power in Russia. Still the victims tramp down to death. There is no end to the suffering, the river of blood flows on. For those of us who live in quieter and happier lands, this is not the way. To those who really seek a better social order—and are not merely seeking in political action relief from the explosive violence of their own natures—I would say with assurance: *This is not the road!*

Is there any other and better way to walk in?

I value the social tradition in which we live. The services of this country to the cause of human happiness cannot be lightly dismissed. We have, for centuries now, led the world in the arts of government and in the discovery of the springs of social peace. We first applied the principles of reason to the tasks of economic organization and industrial production. By so doing we made possible, for all men, levels of prosperity and wealth that would have appeared Utopian, even fantastic, to generations that lived before the onset of the English Industrial Revolution. We have, from the beginning, made invaluable contributions to the advancement of science and learning. To-day through the generosity and long-sighted wisdom of one group of our scientists—the practising psycho-analysts—standing in marked and honourable contrast to the behaviour of most other professions, we have gathered into our society the most distinguished group of psychologists in the world, working in the forefront of contemporary science. We shall continue, in many fields of human endeavour, to lead and not to follow the generality of mankind.

We have, in this country, much of which to be ashamed. The distribution of income is nowhere less equal. The grip of a class system that frustrates the search for comradeship between us, and wastes a monstrously high proportion of our natural talent, is extraordinarily strong, and is not the less strong, nor the less destructive, because it is so little resented. In this generation moreover, we have been guilty of the most terrible crimes of popular vandalism. We have torn down some of our finest buildings, and we have permitted the speculative builder and the profiteering landlord to drive hideous scars across our countryside; straggling in promiscuous rape over the lovely body of our ancient agricultural civilization. We have revealed ourselves to the world as ruthlessly uncultured, and our generation will go down to posterity as one of the most aesthetically destructive in our history

—a rival in the popular demonology of the future to the unforgettable excesses of the Reformation and the Civil War. Although we have reason to be proud of our social tradition we have, therefore, no occasion to be contented with its chequered pattern.

The future of the British tradition is not secure. It is threatened from within and from without. There are dictatorial parties at home and there is the ever-present threat of attack from abroad. We could no longer walk quietly in our traditional paths of liberty if either of our violent parties grew to power, or if we were on the losing side in the present European war. Even victory in it will endanger the stability of our society. Hence peace was and is one, though not the sole or the first, of our vital interests.

When the peace of Europe is restored, and in so far as we have preserved the institutions of a free government, we have still a great service to perform for ourselves and for the world.

Every generation is in part united, and in part inspired, by some conception of a better and a more just society. The conception varies from age to age, and reflects in large measure the peculiar needs and the dominant philosophy of the time in which it enlivens men to hope. There is a rough law of compensation in its form. The deeper the distress of the world in which they live, the more Utopian is likely to be the hope by which men sustain themselves in their daily labour. Despite the fear of aerial bombardment, ours is predominantly an age of quietness and comfort. The standard of living continuously rises about us, and our social life is not torn by deep religious or political conflicts, moving men to violent solutions. We can therefore afford modest dreams and practicable aspirations. We do not need the soothing vision of a perfect society to reconcile us to a bitter distress.

The conception of a better society, by which the broad trends of our policy can best be instructed, is therefore of a specific kind. We need not be content with anything less, nor need we ask for more, than a society in which property as a source of social inequality is made to wither slowly away, in which the establishment of a rational central control has restored expansion and created economic stability, in which political democracy is preserved and perfected as a method of government, and in which children may grow, free from secret fear, into a sociable and happy maturity. This is what I mean by a more just society. An important, indeed an essential, part of it is the constituent principle of Socialism. Within it the common happiness of mankind can be, for a long season, safely established.

Nor need we fear that this society is far away, or difficult to achieve. There is nothing in it that could not be established in a single generation, if we had the eyes to see, and the hearts to will, this reasonable programme of social betterment. We have only to open our eyes and stretch out our hands to pluck this precious fruit from the tree of knowledge.

I feel the conviction, ever more strongly as I grow older, that it is in this land, rather than in any other, that these hopes are likely to find their first fulfilment. We shall not be conscious of the birth in our midst of a new society, because we do not exercise our minds in self-analysis, or construct systematic social philosophies. But as I move about this island, in its quiet lanes and in its crowded streets, meeting people of all classes and persuasions, I feel the life of a strong and quiet people about me; more deeply united than they realize, more creative than they ever suspect. Here, if anywhere, the will for the common good is strong. From it and from the common friendliness we bear to one another we can continue to make, if we will, a society of which all men will be glad.

6. Socialism and the Common Law *

FREDERICK POLLOCK

The element of truth in Socialism is to my mind something the Common Law knew long before any modern Socialists were born: Monopolies are in principle odious, and when they are necessary they must be under public control: whether the control shall be central or local, direct as in the post-office, or indirect by way of regulated franchises, is a matter of means and economic expediency (thus electric supply now seems capable of centralization on a great scale and with advantage, and our numerous railway companies are now amalgamated in a few groups). Our lady the Common Law is a very wise old lady though she still has something to learn in telling what she knows.

7. Socialist Culture, Art, and the Individual †

HERBERT READ

Seventy years ago Walt Whitman wrote in his *Democratic Vistas:*
"We have frequently printed the word Democracy. Yet I cannot too often

* From *Holmes-Pollock Letters,* edited by Mark DeWolfe Howe (2 vol., Harvard University Press, 1941). By permission.
† From Herbert Read, *The Politics of the Unpolitical* (Routledge, 1943). By permission.

repeat that it is a word the real gist of which still sleeps, quite unawakened, notwithstanding the resonance and the many angry tempests out of which its syllables have come, from pen and tongue. It is a great word, whose history, I suppose, remains unwritten, because that history has yet to be enacted."

Democracy is still a great word, and in spite of many wordy prophets who have used it since Whitman's time, its gist still sleeps, its history is still unenacted. Nothing is more absurd, among all the political absurdities committed by fascists and Nazis, than their assumption that democracy is a system that has been tried and has failed. Democracy has been promulgated and its principles endlessly proclaimed; but in no country in the world has it ever, for more than the brief space of a few months, been put into practice. For democracy requires three conditions for its fulfilment, and until all three conditions are satisfied, it cannot be said to exist. It is only necessary to state these conditions to show that democracy never has existed in modern times:

The first condition of democracy is that *all production should be for use, and not for profit.*

The second condition is that *each should give according to his ability, and each receive according to his needs.*

The third condition is that *the workers in each industry should collectively own and control that industry.*

It is not my business in this particular essay to defend the conception of democracy underlying these conditions. It does not seem to be the conception of democracy held by the Labour Party, the Trade Union Congress, the Communist Party, Mr. Churchill or President Roosevelt; but nevertheless I would claim that it is the classical conception of democracy as gradually evolved by its philosophers—by Rousseau, Jefferson, Lincoln, Proudhon, Owen, Ruskin, Marx, Morris, Kropotkin, and whoever else was democratic in his heart no less than in his head. But what I intend to demonstrate here is that the higher values of life, the democratic equivalent of the civilization of Greece or of the Middle Ages, cannot be achieved unless by democracy we mean a form of society in which all these three conditions are satisfied.

I think it will be generally admitted that production for use and not for profit is the basic economic doctrine of socialism. The opponents of socialism might argue that only a lunatic would neglect to take into consideration the needs of the public. But that is to miss the whole point of the statement. Capitalists do, of course, produce for use, and even invent uses for which to produce—in their own language, they create a demand. By their intensive methods of production and their extensive methods of publicity they have keyed up the machinery of production to unimagined levels, and up to a point mankind has benefited from the resulting plethora. Unfortunately capitalism has not been able to solve the problem of supplying the consumer with sufficient purchasing power to absorb this plethora: it could only invent various methods of restricting production so as to prevent a plethora.

Capitalism can produce the goods, even if it cannot sell them. But what kind of goods? It is here that we have to introduce our aesthetic criterion—and don't let anyone be frightened by the word aesthetic. Let us first note that the quality of the goods so lavishly produced under capitalism varies enormously. Whatever you take—carpets or chairs, houses or clothes, cigarettes or sausages, you will find that there are not one but twenty or thirty grades—something very good and efficient at the top of the scale, and something very cheap and nasty at the bottom of the scale. And pyramid-like, the bottom of the scale is enormously bigger than the top.

Take the case of the chair you are sitting on as you read this book. It may be one of three things: (1) a decent well-made chair inherited from your great-great-grandmother; (2) a decent well-made chair which you bought at an expensive shop; or (3) an indifferent, uncomfortable chair; shabby after a year's use, which was the best you could afford. (There are some subsidiary categories—expensive chairs which are also uncomfortable, for example; and moderately comfortable seats in public vehicles.)

Production for profit means that, at whatever cost to the comfort, appearance and durability of the chair, the capitalist must put chairs on the market to suit every kind of person. And since the chair will be competing with other needs—carpets, clocks and sewing-machines—it must cost as little as possible even on the low scale of purchasing power at which he is aiming. Hence the capitalist must progressively lower the quality of the materials he is using: he must use cheap wood and little of it, cheap springs and cheap upholstery. He must evolve a design which is cheap to produce and easy to sell, which means that he must disguise his cheap materials with veneer and varnish and other shams. Even if he is aiming at the top market, he still has to remember his margin of profits; and as the size of the market shrinks, and mass production becomes less possible, this margin has to be increased. That is to say, the difference between the intrinsic value of the materials used and the price charged to the consumer has to be bigger; and the subterfuges necessary to disguise this difference have to be cleverer.

It is then that the capitalist has to put on, among other things, a bit of culture—a claw-and-ball foot in the manner of Chippendale, a wriggly bit of scrollwork in papier-maché, an inlay of mother-of-pearl. In extreme cases he must "distress" the piece—that is to say, employ a man to throw bolts and nails at the chair until it has been knocked about enough to look "antique."

Such is production for profit. By production for use we mean a system which will have only two considerations in mind—function and fulfilment. You want a chair to relax in—very well, we shall discover what are the best angles to allow a man's limbs to rest freely and without strain. We shall next consider which would be the most suitable materials to use in the manufacture of such a chair, bearing in mind, not only the purpose the chair has to serve, but also the other furniture with which the chair will be associated. Then, and then only, we shall design a chair to meet all these requirements. Finally we shall set about making the chair, and when it is made to our satisfaction, we shall offer it to you in exchange for the tokens which represent the good work which, all the time we were making the chair, you were doing for the community at your particular job.

That is the economic process under socialism. But I am supposed to be writing about spiritual values—about beauty and all that sort of thing, and where do they come in? We have produced a chair which is strong and comfortable, but is it a work of art?

The answer, according to my philosophy of art, is Yes. If an object is made of appropriate materials to an appropriate design and perfectly fulfils its function, then we need not worry any more about its aesthetic value: it is *automatically* a work of art. Fitness for function is the modern definition of the eternal quality we call beauty, and this fitness for function is the inevitable result of an economy directed to use and not to profit.

Incidentally, we may note that when the profit system has to place function before profit, as in the production of an aeroplane or a racing-car, it also inevitably produces a work of art. But the question to ask is: why are not all the things produced under capitalism as beautiful as its aeroplanes and racing-cars?

The second condition of democracy is expressed in the Marxian slogan: "From each according to his ability, to each according to his needs."

This condition is linked to the one we have already discussed. To take the question of ability first. A profit system of production subordinates the person to the job. In a rough-and-ready way it sorts people out according to their ability: that is to say, it continues to employ a man only so long as he is capable of doing the job efficiently, and only so long as there is a job to do. It rarely asks whether a particular man would be better at another job, and it gives that man little or no opportunity of finding out whether he could do another job better. Capitalism is concerned with labour only as a power element, the partner of steam and electricity. And since the cost of this power has to be reckoned against the possible profits, capitalism does all it can to reduce that cost.

One way of reducing the cost is to increase the quantity of work per human unit. Capitalism (and state socialism as established in Russia) introduces the time element into the calculation of results. The best riveter is the man who can fix the greatest number of rivets in a given time. The best miner is the man who can excavate the greatest quantity of coal in a given time. This time criterion is extended to all forms of production, and it is always at war with the criterion of quality. When the work is purely mechanical, the qualitative element may not be compromised, A quick riveter may also be a good riveter. But if the work requires any considerable degree of skill, care or deliberation, then the quality will decline in inverse ratio to the speed of production. This applies, not only to "artistic" work such as painting and sculpture, but also to "practical" work such as grinding the cylinders of an aero-engine or ploughing a field.

From each according to his ability can be replaced by another familiar phrase—equality of opportunity. In a natural society it should be possible for people to sort themselves out so that every man and woman is doing the job for which he or she feels naturally qualified; and if, in this respect, nature needs a little assistance, it can be provided by schools and technical colleges which will enable young people to discover themselves and their abilities.

That half of the slogan does not present much difficulty: it is obviously reasonable that the right man should have the right job, and that he should do that job to the best of his ability. But then we say: "to each according to his needs," and this is the more important half, and the essentially democratic half, of the socialist doctrine.

Let us ask: what are the needs of each one of us? Sufficient food and clothing, adequate housing—a certain minimum of these necessities should be the inalienable right of every member of the community. Until it can provide these minimum necessities, a society must be branded as inhuman and inefficient.

And that is perhaps all that early socialists like Marx and Engels meant by the phrase "to each according to his needs." But the underlying assumption of this essay is that in any civilization worth living in, the needs of man are not merely material. He hungers for other things—for beauty, for companionship, for joy. These, too, a natural society must provide.

We have already seen that by establishing a system of production for use we shall inevitably secure the first of these spiritual needs—beauty. To see how the other spiritual values will be secured we must turn to the third condition of democracy—workers' ownership of industry.

This is a controversial issue, even within the democratic ranks. Since that fatal day in 1872 when Marx scuttled the First International, the socialist movement has been split into two irreconcilable camps. The fundamental nature of the division has been hidden by a confusion of names and a multiplicity of leagues, alliances, federations and societies. But the issue is simply whether industry is to be controlled from the bottom upwards, by the workers and their elected delegates; or whether it is to be centralized and controlled from the top, by an abstraction we call the state, but which in effect means a small and exclusive class of bureaucrats.

"Letting alone" is not the same as *"laissez-faire."* A person is not left alone if he has a cupboard full of cares. He must be left alone with sufficient food and shelter to safeguard his health, and he must be left alone with sufficient material to work with. Then *"laissez-faire"*—then let him do what he likes to do.

To keep a class of people in comfort and then let them do what they please offends the sense of social equity—every dustman might then set up as an artist. But that is not exactly what I propose. I have said: To hell with culture; and to this consignment we might add another: To hell with the artist. *Art as a separate profession is merely a consequence of culture as a separate entity.* In a natural society there will be no precious or privileged beings called artists: there will only be workers. Or, if you prefer Gill's more paradoxical statement of the same truth: in a natural society there will be no despised and unprivileged beings called workers: there will only be artists. "The artist is not a special kind of man, but every man is a special kind of artist." [1]

But among workers there are various degrees of ability. And the people capable of recognizing this ability are the workers themselves in their several professions. For example, architects and engineers will know which few individuals among them design so superlatively well that they deserve, for the common good, to be exempted from routine tasks and encouraged to devote their energies to those types of work which are not so much utilitarian as "creative"—that is to say, expressive of their own inventive intuitions or perhaps of collective needs—needs which are inarticulate until the artist gives them actuality.

It is the same with every other type of artist—the painter and the sculptor no less than the architect and the engineer. The possible exception is the poet, the "divine literatus" to whom Whitman gave such a vital function in the democratic vista. There is no basic profession which stands in the same relation to poetry as building does to architecture. Writing is, of course, a profession, and in a democratic society it should have its appropriate guild or collective—as it has in Russia to-day. Once it is free from the rivalries and log-rolling which accompany writing for profit (or writing on the backs of advertisements, as Chesterton called journalism), a Writers' Guild might be entrusted with the economic organization of this particular kind of work; but genius will often elude its systematic survey. Against this eventuality there can be no social safeguard. There are certain types of genius which

[1] Gill took this paradox from the writings of another wise man, Dr. Ananda Coomaraswamy; it sums up the teachings of William Morris and the practice of the medieval guild system.

are always in advance of the general level of sensibility—even the general level of professional sensibility. In the past such men have been frustrated or have been starved. In a natural society they will at least avoid the second fate.

Production for use, mutual aid, workers' control—these are the slogans of democracy, and these are the slogans of a creative civilization. There is nothing mysterious or difficult about such a civilization; indeed, some of the primitive civilizations still existing in remote corners of the world, and many primitive civilizations of the past, including that of prehistoric man, deserve to be called creative. What they make, if it is only a plaited basket or an unpainted pot, they make with instinctive rightness and directness. It is impossible to compare such primitive communities with our own highly organized modes of living, but their social economy in its simple way answers to our slogans. Production is for use and not for profit; and all work is done without compulsion for the general benefit of the community. On their simple level of living there is ample social security, and no man sells his labour to a middleman or boss: work is either individual or communal, and in either case it is free from the dispiriting influences of slavery and manumission.

But we are not a primitive society and there is no need to become primitive in order to secure the essentials of democratic liberty. We want to retain all our scientific and industrial triumphs—electric power, machine tools, mass production and the rest. We do not propose to revert to the economy of the hand-loom and the plough—ideal as this may seem in retrospect. We propose that the workers and technicians who have *made* the modern instruments of production should *control* them—control their use and determine the flow of their production. It can be done. Russia has shown that the essential organization can be created, and we should not be blinded to the significance of that great achievement by the perversion it has suffered at the hands of bureaucrats. For a brief spell democratic Spain showed us that workers' control could be an efficient reality. Workers' control can be established in this country, and there is not much point in discussing the finer values of civilization until that essential change has been effected.

The fundamental truth about economics is that the methods and instruments of production, freely used and fairly used, are capable of giving every human being a decent standard of living. The factors which obstruct the free and fair use of the methods and instruments of production are the factors which must disappear before a natural society can be established. Whatever these factors are—an obsolete financial system, the private ownership of property, rent and usury—they are anti-democratic factors, and prevent the establishment of a natural society and consequently prevent the establishment of a creative civilization.

Economics are outside the scope of this book, but I cannot avoid them. Unless the present economic system is abolished, its roots eradicated and all its intricate branches lopped, the first conditions for a democratic alternative to the fake culture of our present civilization are not satisfied. For this reason one cannot be very specific about the features of a democratic culture. Engineers and designers can make the working drawings for a motor-car, and granted the right kind of machinery, they can be sure that the type of car they have designed will run when it is completed. But they cannot predict where that car will travel. A democratic culture is the journey a democratic society will make when once it has been established. If it is well made we know that our democratic society will travel far. And with the man for whom it was made at the wheel, we can be sure that it will travel in the right direction, discovering new countries, new prospects, new climates. We have already had brief glimpses down these democratic vistas, and presently I shall describe them more fully. But first let us take a backward glance at the dump we propose to leave behind us.

I write, not as a philistine, but as a man who could not only claim to be cultured in the accepted sense of the word, but who has actually devoted most of his life to cultural things—to the practice of the arts of the present and the elucidation of the arts of the past. My philosophy is a direct product of my aesthetic experience, and I believe that life without art would be a graceless and brutish existence. I could not live without the spiritual values of art. I know that some people are insensitive to these values, but before allowing myself to pity or despise such people, I try to imagine how they got themselves into such a poor state of mind. The more I consider such people, the more clearly I begin to perceive that though there may be a minority who have been hopelessly brutalized by their environment and upbringing, the great majority are not insensitive, but indifferent. They have sensibility, but the thing we call culture does not stir them. Architecture and sculpture, painting and poetry, are not the immediate concerns of their lives. They are therefore not sensibly moved by the baroque rhetoric of St. Paul's, or the painted ceiling of the Sistine Chapel, or any of the minor monuments of our culture. If they go into a museum or art gallery, they move about with dead eyes; they have strayed among people who do not speak their language, with whom they cannot by any means communicate.

Now the common assumption is that this strayed riveter, as we may call him, should set about it and learn the language of this strange country— that he should attend museum lectures and adult education classes in the little spare time he has, and so gradually lift himself on to the cultured level. Our whole educational system is built on that assumption, and very few democrats would be found to question it. And yet a moment's consideration should convince us that an educational system which is built on such an assumption is fundamentally wrong, and fundamentally undemocratic. Our riveter has probably strayed from a cheerless street in Birmingham, where he inhabits a mean little house furnished with such shoddy comforts as he has been able to afford out of his inadequate wage. I need not pursue the man's life in all its dreary detail: there he stands, typical of millions of workers in this country, his clumsy boots on the parquet floor, and you are asking him to appreciate a painting by Botticelli or a bust by Bernini, a Spanish textile or a fine piece of Limoges enamel. If drink is the shortest road out of Manchester, there is a possibility that art may be the shortest road out of Birmingham; but it will not be a crowded road, and only a very odd and eccentric worker will be found to respond to the aesthetic thrills that run down a cultured spine.

There are cultured people who, realizing this fact, are honest enough to abandon their democratic pretensions—they put up an impenetrable barrier between the people and art, between the worker and "culture." It is much better, they say, "that civilization should be retained in the hands of those persons to whom it professionally belongs. Until they are educated, and unless they are, it will be one worker in a million who wants to read a modern poem." [1]

Such people are right, and such people are wrong. They are right to assume that an impenetrable barrier exists between *their* culture and the worker: they are wrong to imagine that the worker has no cultural sensibility. The worker has as much latent sensibility as any human being, but that sensibility can only be awakened when meaning is restored to his daily work and he is allowed to create his own culture.

Do not let us be deceived by the argument that culture is the same for all time—that art is a unity and beauty an absolute value. If you are going to talk about abstract conceptions like beauty, then we can freely grant that they are absolute and eternal. But abstract conceptions are not works of art. Works of art are things of use—houses and their furniture, for example; and if, like sculpture and poetry, they are not things of immediate use, then they should be things consonant with the things we use—that is to say, part of our daily life, tuned to our daily habits, accessible to our daily needs. It is not until art expresses the immediate hopes and aspirations of humanity that it acquires its social relevance.

A culture begins with simple things—with the way the potter moulds the clay on his wheel, the way a weaver threads his yarns, the way the builder builds his house. Greek culture did not begin with the Parthenon: it began with a whitewashed hut on a hillside. Culture has always developed as an infinitely slow but sure refinement and elaboration of simple things—refinement and elaboration of speech, refinement and elaboration of shapes,

[1] Sacheverell Sitwell, *Sacred and Profane Love*, p. 88.

refinement and elaboration of proportions, with the original purity persisting right through. A democratic culture will begin in a *similar* way. We shall not revert to the peasant's hut or the potter's wheel. We shall begin with the elements of modern industry—electric power, metal alloys, cement, the tractor and the aeroplane. We shall consider these things as the raw materials of a civilization and we shall work out their appropriate use and appropriate forms, without reference to the lath and plaster of the past.

To-day we are bound hand and foot to the past. Because property is a sacred thing and land values a source of untold wealth, our houses must be crowded together and our streets must follow their ancient illogical meanderings. Because houses must be built at the lowest possible cost to allow the highest possible profit, they are denied the art and science of the architect. Because everything we buy for use must be sold for profit, and because there must always be this profitable margin between cost and price, our pots and our pans, our furniture and our clothes, have the same shoddy consistency, the same competitive cheapness. The whole of our capitalist culture is one immense veneer: a surface refinement hiding the cheapness and shoddiness at the heart of things.

To hell with such a culture! To the rubbish-heap and furnace with it all! Let us celebrate the democratic revolution with the biggest holocaust in the history of the world. When Hitler has finished bombing our cities, let the demolition squads complete the good work. Then let us go out into the wide open spaces and build anew.

Let us build cities that are not too big, but spacious, with traffic flowing freely through their leafy avenues, with children playing safely in their green and flowery parks, with people living happily in bright efficient houses. Let us place our factories and workshops where natural conditions of supply make their location most convenient—the necessary electric power can be laid on anywhere. Let us balance agriculture and industry, town and country —let us do all these sensible and elementary things and *then* let us talk about our culture.

A culture of pots and pans! some of my readers may cry contemptuously. I do not despise a culture of pots and pans, because, as I have already said, the best civilizations of the past may be judged by their pots and pans. But what I am now asserting, as a law of history no less than as a principle of social economy, is that until a society can produce beautiful pots and pans as naturally as it grows potatoes, it will be incapable of those higher forms of art which in the past have taken the form of temples and cathedrals, epics and dramas.

As for the past, let the past take care of itself. I know that there is such a thing as tradition, but in so far as it is valuable it is a body of technical knowledge—the mysteries of the old guilds—and can safely be entrusted to the care of the new guilds. There is a traditional way of thatching haystacks and a traditional way of writing sonnets: they can be learned by any apprentice. If I am told that this is not the profoundest meaning of the word tradition, I will not be obtuse; but I will merely suggest that the state of the world to-day is a sufficient comment on those traditional embodiments of wisdom, ecclesiastical or academic, which we are expected to honour. The cultural problem, we are told by these traditionalists, is at bottom a spiritual, even a religious one. But this is not true. At least, it is no truer of the cultural problem than of the economic problem, or any of the other problems which await solution.

Chapter XII

PLAN OR NO PLAN?

A GENERATION can hardly be called well ordered which in the span of twenty-five years has suffered from the two greatest wars in history, interrupted—to make the chaos complete—by the severest economic depression on record. The clamor for planning, for economic stability at home, and for peace in the world, has therefore expressed, knowingly and unknowingly, the yearning for salvation from chaos and disorder. Mankind has lost the cheerful faith of the late eighteenth century that we live in the best of worlds, that there is a natural harmony in society, and, therefore, the less interference the better.

In his paper on "Authority and Social Change," read at the Harvard Tercentenary Conference in 1936, John Dewey raises the question, in view of the apparent intractability of human problems, where there are "resources that have not as yet been tried out in the large field of human relations, resources that are available and that carry with them the potential promise of successful application." Dewey's answer is that the untried resource in the field of human and social relationships is "the utilization of organized intelligence, the manifold benefits and values of which we have substantial and reliable evidence in the narrower field of science." The application of scientific methods, of organized intelligence, would save humanity from the two extremes of authoritative power and unregulated individual freedom, to which "most of the sorrows and defeats of the past" may be attributed.

In *The Good Society* (1937), Walter Lippmann was probably one of the first American writers to attack planning as a dangerous tendency, leading eventually to totalitarianism and misery. He drew his main ideas from the works of Ludwig von Mises, an Austrian economist who, as early as 1922, in *Socialism,* had proved its impossibility. Lippmann's chief conclusion is that planning is intimately connected with dictatorship and war. In 1937 planning was mainly identified with the militaristic systems of the Fascist Axis, or with the totalitarian one-party regime in the Soviet Union. After the Second World War, planning greatly expanded in nations that were governed by democratic socialist administrations (England, New Zealand, Scandinavia, Australia). Whether these countries will end in oligarchies preparing for wars of aggression is more than doubtful.

The most famous anti-planning book is Friedrich A. Hayek's *The Road to Serfdom* (1944). Its excellence was immediately recognized, being digested in *The Reader's Digest,* and distributed widely by all sorts of agencies, from the Standard Oil Co. to the Book-of-the-Month Club. Hayek is an economist who is familiar with Continental thinking, having lived in Austria most of his early life, as well as with British problems, having settled in England in 1931. The tenor of his book is his anxiety that, just as socialism in Germany was followed by Nazi totalitarianism, so would the collectivist trend in England and the United States be followed by a drift toward the destruction of democracy. If the political background of Germany were about the same as that of England and the United States, Hayek's case would be incontrovertible. Hayek is persuaded that in a planned economy "the worst get to the top." Bevin may not be perfect, but he is hardly in the same class with Ribbentrop and Ciano; Prime Minister Attlee has been engaged in a great deal of far-reaching planning without the aid of an English Himmler. In fact, even an opponent is said to have called Attlee a "sheep in sheep's clothing." The Gestapo, the concentration camps, and the murder camps are, according to Hayek's argument, the result of planning necessarily ending in totalitarianism, rather than phenomena of *German politics,* based on German history. Hayek is also seriously concerned about the incompatibility of planning with the rule of law. He sees in the collectivist movement a dangerous trend of substituting bureaucratic, irresponsible orders for the impartiality of the rule of law. The experience in England and other democratic countries which are engaged in socialist planning will tell whether "intolerance and brutal suppression of dissent, deception and spying, the complete disregard of the life and happiness of the individual are essential and unavoidable" from the "collectivist standpoint." Professor Hayek himself survived tolerably well the holocaust that swept over England when Clement Attlee seized the reins of power in 1945 and settled in 10 Downing Street. As long as Hayek continues to teach his brand of antisocialist economics at the London School of Economics and Political Science, he will still be on the high road to freedom.

Of the many writers who have sought to refute the main arguments of Hayek's *Road to Serfdom,* Barbara Wootton is probably the one who has best succeeded in presenting the other side of the story. As early as 1934 she published a distinguished study *Plan or No Plan* (to which this chapter owes its title). In 1945 she published *Freedom Under Planning,* in which she sets out to demonstrate that freedom and planning are compatible. In fact, she goes further: whereas Hayek proposes that freedom is not possible with planning, she claims that it is impossible *without* planning, if it is to be the possession of all citizens rather than the privilege of the few. Mrs. Wootton makes the point that much of the discussion of planning is unreal because complete planning, or no planning at all, are assumed as the only two alternatives. In actual life, no economic system is, or can be, completely planned or completely unplanned: "Planning is a matter of degree." As a fervent believer in democracy, Mrs. Wootton is confident that "a happy and fruitful marriage between freedom and planning" can be arranged.

In his two books, *On the Agenda of Democracy* (1941) and *Systematic Politics* (1945), Charles Merriam analyzes the experience of America in the field of planning as well as its potential future. Merriam has not been merely one of the leading students of politics in the United States; all his life he has combined theory with practice. At the University of Chicago he was one of the founders of the "Chicago School" of political science, the distinguishing feature of which was the keen interest in practical problems of better government and administration in Chicago, the region, and the nation. Merriam was a Chicago alderman and (unsuccessful) Republican candidate for mayor, and for fourteen years he served on national agencies, including the National Resources Planning Board. Merriam injects into the discussion of planning a note of sanity by showing that planning was not invented by exuberant New Deal brain trusters, but has a long and honorable record in the history of the United States from its beginning. The Constitution was the first great act of planning, and the "Constitutional Convention itself was a large-scale planning board." Merriam states the important principle that "government is not the master of men, but men cannot master their problems without it." A strong believer in the possibility and desirability of a "mixed economy" of private and public enterprise, Merriam warns that "free enterprise has far more to fear from lack of planning than from its development and application to national resources." Finally, he includes in the agenda of planning the outlawry of war and the establishment of effective international peace; in most discussions of planning, the domestic scene alone is considered, and, within it, in the main, the economic problem. Merriam approaches planning as a citizen of the world.

1. Science and Society *

JOHN DEWEY

The scene which the world exhibits to the observer at the present time is so obviously one of general instability, insecurity, and increasing conflict—

* From John Dewey, "Authority and Social Change" (1936; reprinted in *John Dewey's Philosophy,* ed. by Joseph Ratner, Random House, 1939). By permission of Henry Holt and Company, holders of the copyright.

both within nations and between them—that I cannot conceive that any one will deny the *desirability* of effecting and enstating some organic union of freedom and authority. Enormous doubt will well exist, however, as to the possibility of establishing any social system in which the union is practically embodied. This question, it will be justly urged, is *the* issue that emerges even if the substantial validity of the points so far made is admitted. In fact, it may even be justly urged that this question confronts us as the controlling and decisive question just because, or to the degree that, the validity of my argument thus far is granted.

The weight of the evidence of the past is assuredly strongly against the realization of any such possibility. As far as the idea of organized authority is concerned, the pathos of the collective life of mankind on this planet is its exhibition of the dire human need for some authority; while its ever-mounting tragedy is due to the fact that the need has been repeatedly betrayed by the very institutions that claimed to satisfy it. That all is not well, on the other hand, with the principle of individualistic freedom in the form in which it has been influential up to now, is shown by more than one fact in the present scene of discord and insecurity. Above all is this manifested by the recrudescence of the principle of authority in its most extreme and primitive form—the rise of dictatorships.

As if in substantiation of the old idea that nature abhors a vacuum, it might be contended that economic competitive individualism, free from social control, had created a moral and social vacuum which recourse to dictatorships is filling. In many countries, the demand for collective and organized guidance and support has become so urgent that the very idea of individual freedom has gone into the discard and become an ideal, not to be praised, but to be despised. The regime of economic individualistic liberty is attacked by dictatorships from both the right and the left. In countries in which there are no open and acknowledged dictatorships, the conceptions of liberty and individualism seem to be losing their magic force; and security, discipline, order, and solidarity are, by social transfer, acquiring magic power in their stead. The actual concrete conditions that produce resort to dictatorships vary from country to country. But the phenomenon is so widespread it demands a generalized explanation. The most obvious one is the virtual bankruptcy and moribund state of a regime of individual initiative and enterprise conducted for private gain and subject to no control by recognized, collective authority.

Neither the past nor the present affords, then, any ground for expecting that the adjustment of authority and freedom, stability and change, will be achieved by following old paths. The idea that any solution at all can ever be attained may seem to some romantic and utopian. But the most fantastically unrealistic of all notions is the widely prevalent belief that we can attain enduring stable authority by employing or re-exhuming the institutional means tried in the past; equally fantastic is the belief that the assured freedom of individuals can be secured by pitting individuals against one another in a pitiless struggle for material possessions and economic power. The issue, in my judgment, can be narrowed down to this question: Are there resources that have not as yet been tried out in the large field of human relations, resources that are available and that carry with them the potential promise of successful application?

In raising this question I am aware that it is almost inevitable that what I have said about the human necessity for some kind of collective authority to give individuals direction in their relations with one another, and to give them the support that comes from a sense of solidarity, will appear to be a plea for a return to some kind of social control brought about through, and perpetuated by, external institutional means. If my question is so taken, then the criticism I have made of the alliance that has taken place between the principle of individual freedom and private initiative and enterprise in economic matters will necessarily also seem to be merely an argument for social control by means of a collective planned economy—put forward, of course, with some change in vocabulary. However, the argument in fact cuts in both directions. It indicates that while movements in the direction of collective, planned economy may cure evils from which we are now suffering, it will in the end go the way of all past attempts at organization of authoritative power unless some hitherto untried means are utilized on a large and systematic scale for bringing into life the desired and desirable organic coordination. Otherwise we shall finally find ourselves repeating on a different plane the old struggle between social organization and individual freedom, with the oscillation from one principle to the other that has so characteristically marked the past.

The resource that has not yet been tried on any large scale, in the broad field of human, social relationships is the utilization of organized intelligence, the manifold benefits and values of which we have substantial and reliable evidence in the narrower field of science.

Within a limited area, the collective intelligence which is exemplified in the growth and application of scientific method has already become authoritative. It is authoritative in the field of beliefs regarding the structure of nature and relevant to our understanding of physical events. To a considerable extent, the same statement holds true of beliefs about historical personages and historical events—especially with those that are sufficiently remote from the present time. When we turn to the practical side, we see that the same method is supreme in controlling and guiding our active dealings with material things and physical energies. To a large and significant extent, the Baconian prophecy that knowledge is power of control has been realized in this particular, somewhat narrowly circumscribed area. To be sure, it cannot be said that intelligence, operating by the methods that constitute science, has as yet completely won *undisputed* right and authority to control beliefs even in the restricted physical field. But organized intelligence has made an advance that is truly surprising when we consider the short time in which it has functioned and the powerful foes against which it had to make its way: the foes of inertia, of old, long-established traditions and habits—inertia, traditions, and habits all of them entrenched in forms of institutional life that are effulgent with the prestige of time, that are enveloped in the glamor of imaginative appeal, and that are crowned, severally and collectively, with an emotional halo made of the values that men most prize.

The record of the struggle that goes by the name of "conflict between science and religion," or, if you please, "conflict between theology and science," was essentially a conflict of claims to exercise social authority. It was not a conflict just between two sets of theoretical beliefs, but between two alignments of social forces—one which was old and had institutional power that it did not hesitate to use, and one which was new and striving and craving for recognition against gigantic odds.

What is pertinent, what is deeply significant to the theme of the *relation* between collective authority and freedom, is that the progress of intelligence —as exemplified in this summary story of scientific advance—exhibits their organic, effective union. Science has made its way by releasing, not by suppressing, the elements of variation, of invention and innovation, of novel creation in individuals. It is as true of the history of modern sciences as it is of the history of painting or music that its advances have been initiated by individuals who freed themselves from the bonds of tradition and custom whenever they found the latter hampering their own powers of reflection, observation, and construction.

In spite of science's dependence for its development upon the free initiative, invention, and enterprise of individual inquirers, the authority of science issues from and is based upon collective activity, cooperatively organized. Even when, temporarily, the ideas put forth in science by individuals sharply diverge from received beliefs, the method used is a public and open method which succeeds only as it tends to produce agreement, unity of belief among all who labored in the same field. Every scientific inquirer, even when he deviates most widely from current ideas, depends upon methods and conclusions that are a common possession and not of private ownership, even though all of the methods and conclusions may at some time have been initially the product of private invention. The contribution the scientific inquirer makes is collectively tested and developed and, in the measure that it is cooperatively confirmed, becomes a part of the common fund of the intellectual commonwealth.

One can most easily recognize the difference between the aim and operation of the free individual in the sphere of science and in that of current individualistic economic enterprise by stretching the fancy to the point of imagining a scientific inquirer adopting the standards of the business entrepreneur. Imagine the scientific man who should say that his conclusion was scientific and in so saying maintain that it was also the product of his private wants and efforts goading him on to seek his private advantage. The mere suggestion of such an absurdity vividly discloses the gap that divides the manifestations of individual freedom in these two areas of human activity. The suggestion brings into bold relief and in typical form the kind of individual freedom that is both supported by collective, organic authority and that in turn changes and is encouraged to change and develop, by its own operations, the authority upon which it depends.

The thesis that the operation of cooperative intelligence as displayed in science is a working model of the union of freedom and authority does not slight the fact that the method has operated up to the present in a limited and relatively technical area. On the contrary, it emphasizes that fact. If the method of intelligence had been employed in any large field in the comprehensive and basic area of the relations of human beings to one another in social life and institutions, there would be no present need for our argument. The contrast between the restricted scope of its use and the possible range of its application to human relations—political, economic, and moral—is outstanding and depressing. It is this very contrast that defines the great problem that has to be solved.

No consideration of the problem is adequate that does not take into account one fact about the development of the modern individualistic movement in industry and business. There is a suppressed premise in all the claims and reasonings of the individualistic school. All the beneficial changes that have been produced are attributed to the free play of individuals seeking primarily their own profit as isolated individuals. But in fact, the entire modern industrial development is the fruit of the technological applications of science. By and large, the economic changes of recent centuries have been parasitic upon the advances made in natural science. There is not a single process involved in the production and distribution of goods that is not dependent upon the utilization of results which are consequences of the method of collective, organic intelligence working in mathematics, physics, and chemistry. To speak baldly, it is a plain falsehood that the advances which the defenders of the existing regime point to as justification for its continuance are due to mere individualistic initiative and enterprise. Individualistic initiative and enterprise have sequestered and appropriated the fruits of collective cooperative intelligence. This they have done alone. But without the aid and support of organized intelligence they would have been impotent —perhaps even in those activities in which they have shown themselves to be socially most powerful.

In sum, the great weakness of the historic movement that has laid claim to the title of liberalism and that has proclaimed its operating purpose to be that of securing and protecting the freedom of individuals—the great weakness of this movement has been its failure to recognize that the true and final source of change has been, and now is, the corporate intelligence embodied in science. The principle, as I have already said, cuts in two directions. In so far as the attempts that are now being made in the direction of organized social control and planned economy ignore the role of scientific intelligence, in so far as these attempts depend upon and turn for support to external institutional changes affected for the most part by force, just so far are they re-enstating reliance upon the method of external authority that has always broken down in the past. For a time, while in need of security and a sense and feeling of solidarity, men will submit to authority of this kind. But if history shows anything, it shows that the variable factors in individuals cannot be permanently suppressed or completely eradicated. The principle of individual freedom expressed in the modern individualistic movement is deeply rooted in the constitution of human beings. The truth embodied in it cannot die no matter how much force is brought down upon it. The tragedy of the movement is that it misconceived and misplaced the source and seat of this principle of freedom. But the attempt to uproot and eliminate this principle on behalf of the assurance of security and attainment of solidarity by means of external authority is doomed to ultimate defeat no matter what its temporary victories.

There is no need to dwell upon the enormous obstacles that stand in the way of extending from its present limited field to the larger field of human relations the control of organized intelligence, operating through the release of individual powers and capabilities. There is the weight of past history on the side of those who are cynical or pessimistic about the possibility of achieving this humanly desirable and humanly necessary task. I do not predict that the extension will ever be effectively actualized. But I do claim that the problem of the relation of authority and freedom, of stability and change, if it can be solved, will be solved in this way. The failure of other methods and the desperateness of the present situation will be a spur to some to do their best to make the extension actual. They know that to hold in advance of trial that success is impossible is a way of condemning humanity to that futile and destructive oscillation between authoritative power and unregulated individual freedom to which we may justly attribute most of the sorrows and defeats of the past. They are aware of the slow processes of history and of the unmeasured stretch of time that lies ahead of mankind. They do not expect any speedy victory in the execution of the most difficult task human beings ever set their hearts and minds to attempt. They are, however, buoyed by the assurance that no matter how slight the immediate effect of their efforts, they are themselves, in their trials, exemplifying one of the first principles of the method of scientific intelligence. For they are projecting into events a large and comprehensive idea by experimental methods that correct and mature the method and the idea in the very process of trial. The very desperateness of the situation is, for such as these, but a spur to sustained. courageous effort.

2. *Planning versus Democracy* *

WALTER LIPPMANN

The primary factor which makes civilian planning incalculable is the freedom of the people to spend their income. Planning is theoretically possible only if consumption is rationed. For a plan of production *is* a plan of consumption. If the authority is to decide what shall be produced, it has already decided what shall be consumed. In military planning that is precisely what takes place: the authorities decide what the army shall consume and what of the national product shall be left for the civilians. No economy can, therefore, be planned for civilians unless there is such scarcity that the necessities of existence can be rationed. As productivity rises above the subsistence level, free spending becomes possible. A planned production to meet a free demand is a contradiction in terms and as meaningless as a square circle.

It follows, too, that a plan of production is incompatible with voluntary labor, with freedom to choose an occupation. A plan of production is not only a plan of consumption, but a plan of how long, at what, and where the people shall work. By no possible manipulation of wage rates could the planners attract to the various jobs precisely the right number of workers. Under voluntary labor, particularly with consumption rationed and standardized, the unpleasant jobs would be avoided and the good jobs overcrowded. Therefore the inevitable and necessary complement of the rationing of consumption is the conscription of labor, either by overt act of law or by driving workers into the undesirable jobs by offering them starvation as the alternative. This is, of course, exactly what happens in a thoroughly militarized state.

The conscription of labor and the rationing of consumption are not to be regarded as transitional or as accidental devices in a planned economy. They are the very substance of it. To make a five-year plan of what a whole nation shall produce is to determine how it shall labor and what it shall receive. It can receive only what the plan provides. It can obtain what the plan provides

* From Walter Lippmann, *The Good Society* (1937). By permission of Little, Brown & Company and The Atlantic Monthly Press.

only by doing the work which the plan calls for. It must do that work or the plan is a failure; it must accept what the plan yields in the way of goods or it must do without.

All this is perfectly understood in an army or in war time when a whole nation is in arms. The civilian planner can not avoid the rationing and the conscription, for they are the very essence of his proposal. There is no escape. If the people are free to reject the rations, the plan is frustrated; if they are free to work less or at different occupations than those prescribed, the plan cannot be executed. Therefore their labor and their standards of living have to be dictated by the planning board or by some sovereign power superior to the board. In a militarized society that sovereign power is the general staff.

But who, in a civilian society, is to decide what is to be the specific content of the abundant life? It cannot be the people deciding by referendum or through a majority of their elected representatives. For if the sovereign power to pick the plan is in the people, the power to amend it is there also at all times. Now a plan subject to change from month to month or even from year to year is not a plan; if the decision has been taken to make ten million cars at $500 and one million suburban houses at $3000, the people cannot change their minds a year later, scrap the machinery to make the cars, abandon the houses when they are partly built, and decide to produce instead skyscraper apartment houses and underground railroads.

There is, in short, no way by which the objectives of a planned economy can be made to depend upon popular decision. They must be imposed by an oligarchy of some sort,[1] and that oligarchy must, if the plan is to be carried through, be irresponsible in matters of policy. Individual oligarchs might, of course, be held accountable for breaches of the law just as generals can be court-martialed. But their policy can no more be made a matter of continuous accountability to the voters than the strategic arrangements of the generals can be determined by the rank and file. The planning board or their superiors have to determine what the life and labor of the people shall be.

Not only is it impossible for the people to control the plan, but, what is more, the planners must control the people. They must be despots who tolerate no effective challenge to their authority. Therefore civilian planning is compelled to presuppose that somehow the despots who climb to power will be benevolent—that is to say, will know and desire the supreme good of their subjects. This is the implicit premise of all the books which recommend the establishment of a planned economy in a civilian society. They paint an entrancing vision of what a benevolent despotism could do. They ask—never very clearly, to be sure—that somehow the people should surrender the planning of their existence to "engineers," "experts," and "technologists," to leaders, saviors, heroes. This is the political premise of the whole collectivist

[1] Which may, of course, let the people ratify the plan once and irrevocably by plebiscite, as in the German and Italian plebiscites.

philosophy: that the dictators will be patriotic or class-conscious, whichever term seems the more eulogistic to the orator. It is the premise, too, of the whole philosophy of regulation by the state, currently regarded as progressivism. Though it is disguised by the illusion that a bureaucracy accountable to a majority of voters, and susceptible to the pressure of organized minorities, is not exercising compulsion, it is evident that the more varied and comprehensive the regulation becomes, the more the state becomes a despotic power as against the individual. For the fragment of control over the government which he exercises through his vote is in no effective sense proportionate to the authority exercised over him by the government.

Benevolent despots might indeed be found. On the other hand they might not be. They may appear at one time; they may not appear at another. The people, unless they choose to face the machine guns on the barricades, can take no steps to see to it that benevolent despots are selected and the malevolent cashiered. They cannot select their despots. The despots must select themselves, and, no matter whether they are good or bad, they will continue in office as long as they can suppress rebellion and escape assassination.

Thus, by a kind of tragic irony, the search for security and a rational society, if it seeks salvation through political authority, ends in the most irrational form of government imaginable—in the dictatorship of casual oligarchs, who have no hereditary title, no constitutional origin or responsibility, who cannot be replaced except by violence. The reformers who are staking their hopes on good despots, because they are so eager to plan the future, leave unplanned that on which all their hopes depend. Because a planned society must be one in which the people obey their rulers, there can be no plan to find the planners: the selection of the despots who are to make society so rational and so secure has to be left to the insecurity of irrational chance.

~~~~~~

3. Road to Serfdom *

FRIEDRICH A. HAYEK

~~~~~~

Nothing distinguishes more clearly conditions in a free country from those in a country under arbitrary government than the observance in the

* From Friedrich A. Hayek, *The Road to Serfdom* (University of Chicago Press, 1944). By permission.

former of the great principles known as the Rule of Law. Stripped of all technicalities, this means that government in all its actions is bound by rules fixed and announced beforehand—rules which make it possible to foresee with fair certainty how the authority will use its coercive powers in given circumstances and to plan one's individual affairs on the basis of this knowledge.[1] Though this ideal can never be perfectly achieved, since legislators as well as those to whom the administration of the law is intrusted are fallible men, the essential point, that the discretion left to the executive organs wielding coercive power should be reduced as much as possible, is clear enough. While every law restricts individual freedom to some extent by altering the means which people may use in the pursuit of their aims, under the Rule of Law the government is prevented from stultifying individual efforts by *ad hoc* action. Within the known rules of the game the individual is free to pursue his personal ends and desires, certain that the powers of government will not be used deliberately to frustrate his efforts.

The distinction we have drawn before between the creation of a permanent framework of laws within which the productive activity is guided by individual decisions and the direction of economic activity by a central authority is thus really a particular case of the more general distinction between the Rule of Law and arbitrary government. Under the first the government confines itself to fixing rules determining the conditions under which the available resources may be used, leaving to the individuals the decision for what ends they are to be used. Under the second the government directs the use of the means of production to particular ends. The first type of rules can be made in advance, in the shape of *formal rules* which do not aim at the wants and needs of particular people. They are intended to be merely instrumental in the pursuit of people's various individual ends. And they are, or ought to be, intended for such long periods that it is impossible to know whether they will assist particular people more than others. They could almost be described as a kind of instrument of production, helping people to predict the behavior of those with whom they must collaborate, rather than as efforts toward the satisfaction of particular needs.

Economic planning of the collectivist kind necessarily involves the very opposite of this. The planning authority cannot confine itself to providing opportunities for unknown people to make whatever use of them they like. It

---

[1] According to the classical exposition by A. V. Dicey in *The Law of the Constitution* (8th ed.), p. 198, the Rule of Law "means, in the first place, the absolute supremacy or predominance of regular law as opposed to the influence of arbitrary power, and excludes the existence of arbitrariness, of prerogative, or even of wide discretionary authority on the part of government." Largely as a result of Dicey's work the term has, however, in England acquired a narrower technical meaning which does not concern us here. The wider and older meaning of the concept of the rule or reign of law, which in England had become an established tradition which was more taken for granted than discussed, has been most fully elaborated, just because it raised what were new problems there, in the early nineteenth-century discussion in Germany about the nature of the *Rechtsstaat*.

cannot tie itself down in advance to general and formal rules which prevent arbitrariness. It must provide for the actual needs of people as they arise and then choose deliberately between them. It must constantly decide questions which cannot be answered by formal principles only, and, in making these decisions, it must set up distinctions of merit between the needs of different people. When the government has to decide how many pigs are to be raised or how many busses are to be run, which coal mines are to operate, or at what prices shoes are to be sold, these decisions cannot be deduced from formal principles or settled for long periods in advance. They depend inevitably on the circumstances of the moment, and, in making such decisions, it will always be necessary to balance one against the other the interests of various persons and groups. In the end somebody's views will have to decide whose interests are more important; and these views must become part of the law of the land, a new distinction of rank which the coercive apparatus of government imposes upon the people.

The distinction we have just used between formal law or justice and substantive rules is very important and at the same time most difficult to draw precisely in practice. Yet the general principle involved is simple enough. The difference between the two kinds of rules is the same as that between laying down a Rule of the Road, as in the Highway Code, and ordering people where to go; or, better still, between providing signposts and commanding people which road to take. The formal rules tell people in advance what action the state will take in certain types of situation, defined in general terms, without reference to time and place or particular people. They refer to typical situations into which anyone may get and in which the existence of such rules will be useful for a great variety of individual purposes. The knowledge that in such situations the state will act in a definite way, or require people to behave in a certain manner, is provided as a means for people to use in making their own plans. Formal rules are thus merely instrumental in the sense that they are expected to be useful to yet unknown people, for purposes for which these people will decide to use them, and in circumstances which cannot be foreseen in detail. In fact, that we do *not* know their concrete effect, that we do *not* know what particular ends these rules will further, or which particular people they will assist, that they are merely given the form most likely on the whole to benefit all the people affected by them, is the most important criterion of formal rules in the sense in which we here use this term. They do not involve a choice between particular ends or particular people, because we just cannot know beforehand by whom and in what way they will be used.

In our age, with its passion for conscious control of everything, it may appear paradoxical to claim as a virtue that under one system we shall know less about the particular effect of the measures the state takes than would be true under most other systems and that a method of social control should be deemed superior because of our ignorance of its precise results. Yet this consideration is in fact the rationale of the great liberal principal of the Rule of Law. And the apparent paradox dissolves rapidly when we follow the argument a little further.

This argument is twofold; the first is economic and can here only briefly be stated. The state should confine itself to establishing rules applying to general types of situations and should allow the individuals freedom in everything which depends on the circumstances of time and place, because only the individuals concerned in each instance can fully know these circumstances and adapt their actions to them. If the individuals are to be able to use their knowledge effectively in making plans, they must be able to predict actions of the state which may affect these plans. But if the actions of the state are to be predictable they must be determined by rules fixed independently of the concrete circumstances which can be neither foreseen nor taken into account beforehand: and the particular effects of such actions will be unpredictable. If, on the other hand, the state were to direct the individual's actions so as to achieve particular ends, its action would have to be decided on the basis of the full circumstances of the moment and would therefore be unpredictable. Hence the familiar fact that the more the state "plans," the more difficult planning becomes for the individual.

The second, moral or political, argument is even more directly relevant to the point under discussion. If the state is precisely to foresee the incidence of its actions, it means that it can leave those affected no choice. Wherever the state can exactly foresee the effects on particular people of alternative courses of action, it is also the state which chooses between the different ends. If we want to create new opportunities open to all, to offer chances of which people can make what use they like, the precise results cannot be foreseen. General rules, genuine laws as distinguished from specific orders, must therefore be intended to operate in circumstances which cannot be foreseen in detail, and, therefore, their effect on particular ends or particular people cannot be known beforehand. It is in this sense alone that it is at all possible for the legislator to be impartial. To be impartial means to have no answer to certain questions—to the kind of questions which, if we have to decide them, we decide by tossing a coin. In a world where everything was precisely foreseen, the state could hardly do anything and remain impartial.

Where the precise effects of government policy on particular people are known, where the government aims directly at such particular effects, it cannot help knowing these effects, and therefore it cannot be impartial. It must, of necessity, take sides, impose its valuations upon people and, instead of assisting them in the advancement of their own ends, choose the ends for them. As soon as the particular effects are foreseen at the time a law is made, it ceases to be a mere instrument to be used by the people and becomes instead an instrument used by the lawgiver upon the people and for his ends. The state ceases to be a piece of utilitarian machinery intended to help individuals in the fullest development of their individual personality and becomes a "moral" institution—where "moral" is not used in contrast to immoral but describes an institution which imposes on its members its views on all moral questions, whether these views be moral or highly immoral. In this sense the Nazi or any other collectivist state is "moral," while the liberal state is not.

Perhaps it will be said that all this raises no serious problem because in the kind of questions which the economic planner would have to decide he need not and should not be guided by his individual prejudices but could rely on the general conviction of what is fair and reasonable. This contention usually receives support from those who have experience of planning in a particular industry and who find that there is no insuperable difficulty about arriving at a decision which all those immediately interested will accept as fair. The reason why this experience proves nothing is, of course, the selection of the "interests" concerned when planning is confined to a particular industry. Those most immediately interested in a particular issue are not necessarily the best judges of the interests of society as a whole. To take only the most characteristic case: when capital and labor in an industry agree on some policy of restriction and thus exploit the consumers, there is usually no difficulty about the division of the spoils in proportion to former earnings or on some similar principle. The loss which is divided between thousands or millions is usually either simply disregarded or quite inadequately considered. If we want to test the usefulness of the principle of "fairness" in deciding the kind of issues which arise in economic planning, we must apply it to some question where the gains and the losses are seen equally clearly. In such instances it is readily recognized that no general principle such as fairness can provide an answer. When we have to choose between higher wages for nurses or doctors and more extensive services for the sick, more milk for children and better wages for agricultural workers, or between employment for the unemployed or better wages for those already employed, nothing short of a complete system of values in which every want of every person or group has a definite place is necessary to provide an answer.

In fact, as planning becomes more and more extensive, it becomes regularly necessary to qualify legal provisions increasingly by reference to what is "fair" or "reasonable"; this means that it becomes necessary to leave the decision of the concrete case more and more to the discretion of the judge or authority in question. One could write a history of the decline of the Rule of Law, the disappearance of the *Rechtsstaat*, in terms of the progressive introduction of these vague formulas into legislation and jurisdiction, and of the increasing arbitrariness and uncertainty of, and the consequent disrespect for, the law and the judicature, which in these circumstances could not but become an instrument of policy. It is important to point out once more in this connection that this process of the decline of the Rule of Law had been going on steadily in Germany for some time before Hitler came into power and that a policy well advanced toward totalitarian planning had already done a great deal of the work which Hitler completed.

There can be no doubt that planning necessarily involves deliberate discrimination between particular needs of different people, and allowing one man to do what another must be prevented from doing. It must lay down by a legal rule how well off particular people shall be and what different people are to be allowed to have and do. It means in effect a return to the rule of status, a reversal of the "movement of progressive societies" which, in the famous phrase of Sir Henry Maine, "has hitherto been a movement from status to contract." Indeed, the Rule of Law, more than the rule of contract, should probably be regarded as the true opposite of the rule of status. It is the Rule of Law, in the sense of the rule of formal law, the absence of legal privileges of particular people designated by authority, which safeguards that equality before the law which is the opposite of arbitrary government.

4. Planning for Freedom *

BARBARA WOOTTON

The freedoms that matter in ordinary life are definite and concrete; and they change with the changing ways of different ages and different civilizations. Freedom today might mean, for instance, freedom to ask for your cards and sweep out of an objectionable job; freedom to say what you think of the government in language of your own choosing; freedom to join, or refuse to join, the Transport and General Workers' Union; freedom to start a rival Union on your own; freedom to be a Freemason, a Catholic or a Plymouth Brother; freedom from concentration camps, official spying and detention without trial; freedom to stand for Parliament or the Parish Council on any program that you like; freedom to strike or not to strike; freedom to wear a nightdress or pyjamas as you prefer. No one would suggest that all

* From Barbara Wootton, *Freedom under Planning* (University of North Carolina Press, 1945). By permission.

these freedoms are of equal importance; nor do these examples necessarily cover all the freedoms that we actually have, can have, or ought to have. The relative value of different freedoms, and the conditions under which they can in fact be realized are difficult and debatable matters, and are, in fact, debated in the pages that follow. But a random list of typical contemporary freedoms is useful as a reminder that free*dom* has to be perpetually reinterpreted into free*doms*. You can philosophize endlessly about freedom; but in daily life it is freedoms that you want. This book would in fact have been called *Freedoms under Planning,* had not the title been so impossibly ugly.

At the same time all freedoms have a common quality—the quality, in fact, of freedom. If the discussion is to be practical and realistic, it is necessary to have a working notion of what this particular quality is. For the purpose of this book, which is severely practical, freedom may be simply defined as ability to do what you want. Behind every word in that definition there lurks, admittedly, a mass of philosophic doubts and subtleties. In practice one must turn a blind eye to these, and build on the assumption that in ordinary life most people recognize the difference between ability to do what they want, and inability to do this. Lack of freedom, at all events, is unmistakable enough. Most of us know only too well the peculiar emotion of frustration by which denial or deprivation of freedom is accompanied.

Taking this earthly, commonsense view of the nature of freedom, we admittedly bypass the complex issues raised by the child who, on returning to a progressive school after the holidays, is said to have asked: "Mummy, shall I still have to do what I want to do?" Equally we suspend judgment on the implications of the (no doubt apocryphal) Treasury Minute [1] which declared that: "It is one thing to compel an officer to retire voluntarily, another to permit him to retire compulsorily. Please keep the two distinct, lest worse confusion befall." What is more important, we deny the validity, for all practical purposes, of any distinction between what people want to do, and what they "really" want to do. Any such distinction is extremely dangerous, and may be the cloak for some of the most wicked, because the most insidious, attacks upon freedom. For sooner or later what I "really" want to do turns out to be a polite paraphrase for what you think I ought to want to do. But freedom means freedom to do what *I* want, and not what anybody else wants me to want—or else it has no meaning at all. How my wants come to be what they are is, no doubt, the result of a complex social and personal process which had best be left to the psychologist to explore. So far as freedom is concerned, what people want to do must be taken as something to be discovered, not changed.

There is another reason for emphasizing this. Freedom for everybody to do what he wants is not necessarily the sole purpose of organized society.

[1] Quoted by Mallalieu: *Pass to You, Please,* p. 105.

There may be other admirable social ends which conflict with, or demand, limitations upon freedom. The possibility of one such conflict and the methods by which it may be resolved is indeed the theme of this book. It is, however, possible to use the word freedom in such a comprehensive way that it covers practically every conceivable social end. For instance, a full belly and an educated mind are commonly thought of today as good things in themselves; and the view is widely held that it is the business of the state to see that people are in fact in a position to enjoy these blessings. But the use of the terms "freedom from want" and "freedom from ignorance" to describe these desirable conditions is liable to confuse any serious discussion of freedom, and to obscure real problems. For in this way the term freedom is easily stretched so wide as to be emptied of distinctive meaning; and the very possibility of conflict, real enough in experience, between freedom and other praiseworthy social ends is disposed of by a verbal trick. The fact is, of course, that people's freedom—their ability to do what they want—is affected in many and complex ways by nearly every kind of organized social activity. Thus, one of the reasons for desiring a full stomach is that, if your stomach is empty, you will not be free to do anything else until you have filled it. But it is absurd to infer from this either that freedom consists in, and is identical with, a state of repletion, or that the limitation which the pangs of hunger impose on your freedom is the only reason for wishing to be rid of those pangs. A condition of well-fed, well-housed, well-clad, even well-entertained, slavery is not an imaginary impossibility. It is only too possible. But it is not freedom. Freedom should not be defined in terms which, even by implication, deny the possibility that a high degree of material well-being may be accompanied by deprivation of freedom. Prisoners would not become free men even if they were looked after as well as race horses.

Where all the terms are so highly charged with political bias it is necessary to be unusually careful about definitions. What then is meant by planning? Planning, in the sense that is relevant here, may be defined as the conscious and deliberate choice of economic priorities by some public authority. Economic activity consists essentially of choice. Shall I spend this shilling on a pint of milk or send a greetings telegram to my mother on her birthday? Shall I buy a house or rent one? Shall this field be plowed, left as pasture or built over? The first two of these choices may be said to be concerned with priorities of consumption, the third with priorities of production. There must of course always be some connection between the two kinds of choice, since it is not possible to consume that which is not produced. In the long run the pattern of consumption, apart from saving and waste (both of which, by a stretch of language not greater than is customary in the peculiar vocabulary of economics, may be included as special forms of consumption) is identical with the pattern of production. It does not, however, follow that whoever determines the general pattern of production also necessarily decides just exactly what each individual will consume.

It is this planning of production which is the heart of the matter. Since it is not possible to produce indefinite quantities of everything in a given place, as for instance in this island, there must be choice, and there must be priority. You cannot feed a cow off a suburban villa; to that extent there is on every acre a conflict between agriculture and building, in which one must eventually give way to the other. In every case, therefore, priorities of production must somehow be eventually determined. In the world as we know it there are, in principle, two ways, in one or other or both of which these questions can be settled. They can be settled consciously and deliberately as part of a plan, or they can be left to settle themselves through the higgling of the market (more politely known as the market mechanism). In the latter case, the final picture emerges as the unpremeditated result of the decisions of perhaps thousands of people, each of whom is concerned only with his own particular part (and that often a very tiny one) of the whole. Planning, on the other hand, implies that there is a known target to be aimed at. In the Soviet Union, the planned output of coal, for instance, in the third year of the second five-year plan, was 110 million tons. The output actually realized was 108.9 million tons.[1] The plan figure thus stands as a measure by which to judge the results that were in fact recorded. In this country, at about the same time, the annual output of coal was 226.5 million tons. Nobody planned that. It happened.

It will be noticed that I have confined the term planning to the determination of priorities by a public authority In this context "public authority" means a state or government (with police and military power to give effect to its decisions if necessary); or some other body which the state has itself created, or to which it has expressly devolved certain rights and duties—such as the London County Council, created by Act of Parliament in 1888, or the London Passenger Transport Board, also created by Act of Parliament, in 1933. This limitation on the meaning of planning is a matter of convenience. In ordinary speech the decision to put a shilling on a horse may well be spoken of as part of an *individual's* economic plan; and in some instances large-scale economic planning may be undertaken by other than public bodies. The total output of certain chemicals in this country, for instance, must be fairly closely planned by Imperial Chemical Industries. The policy of that firm will make a most significant difference to the total. As has been said, however, the uncoordinated small-scale plans of individuals generally add up to a result which is completely unplanned; and the large-scale planning of private monopolies raises issues which, though alarming and important enough, are different from those characteristic of what is coming to be called a "planned economic system."

[1] State Planning Commission of the U.S.S.R., *The Second Five-Year Plan*, p. XXIV.

The use of the phrase "economic system" must not be held to imply that the world is neatly divided into planned economies on the one hand, and unplanned economies on the other. Planning is a matter of degree. It is nowhere completely absent nor does it anywhere cover 100 per cent of all economic activity. Yet the span that divides the Soviet Union from New Deal America may be wide enough to justify the use, as a convenient short-hand, of the respective labels "planned" and "unplanned" "*system.*" Even in the Soviet Union, the collective farmer can grow and sell what he likes as he likes on his own modest allotment, not bothering about anybody's plans but his own. In real life a pure economy is as improbable as a pure race. Economic hybrids are scarcely less varied than biological.

It is perhaps worth adding that state planning of priorities in production, even if it covered much the greater part of our economic life, is not neces-sarily identical with socialism. Socialism is generally held to mean (among other things) public ownership and operation of industry. Now, in theory at least, it is quite possible for the state to make all major decisions about how much of what is to be produced, without itself undertaking anything approaching the whole of that production. That is indeed, near enough, what happens in war. Production and priorities are officially planned and are carried out to government order; but by no means all these orders are executed in firms in which the workers are directly government employees. In principle, therefore, the distinction between socialism and economic planning is parallel with the distinction between doing something yourself and telling, or paying, somebody else to do it. How far such planning with-out socialism would be practicable except in the special circumstances of war is a question to which experience gives as yet no clear answer. The con-vinced socialist (if he can be persuaded to proceed beyond dogmatic asser-tion that the two are inherently incompatible) will argue that government plans which are not also government-executed will either founder on the rocks of vested interest, or be wrecked by exploitation. In a world where business men are accustomed to make their own plans with an eye on their own or their firm's profit, very strong pressure may be put on the govern-ment to frame its own programs to suit the wishes at least of those private concerns which are large enough to make themselves heard. If this fails, the business world, it is said, will bring up a large armory of weapons with which to defeat the substance, while accepting the letter, of a government program; and finally the apparatus of controls (price regulation, profit limitation, quotas, perhaps concentration of industry, to name only a few complexities) which government will need to establish to prevent such tricks—will prove so formidable that in the end the conclusion that it would be more sensible to do the job yourself will become irresistible. That is, any-how, how it looks to the socialist. What people will put up with in the war, he will say, is no guide to what can be done with them in peace; and, even in war, it cannot be said that the enforcement of the controls necessary for comprehensive planning is either frictionless or easy. The amount of effort which is devoted to circumventing government regulations seems to be considerable: the amount of effort devoted to circumventing such efforts to circumvent the law is even greater. And even so there are still black markets and prosecutions. If this is what happens in war, the socialist will write off the possibilities of public planning without public production in peacetime, when the danger and the glory are past, as hopeless. Necessarily, however, this remains a question of opinion. Nor is it certain that the answer is the same for all communities at all times. Business men vary both in their predatory qualities, and in their sense of public responsibility. Until the weight of experience is conclusive one way or the other, the problems of freedom under planning must be treated as distinct from those of freedom under socialism. But the prudent will remember the possibility that the one may lead to the other.

The whole question of the relation between freedom of enterprise and planning needs to be treated as a matter more of expediency than of principle. The traditional controversies between socialists and non-socialists only obscure the practical issue which we have to face. These controversies are barren, first, because they are framed in terms not of quantitative differences, but of absolute systems. We have not seen, and we shall not see, the ideal socialist state: we have not seen, and we shall not see, unadulterated capitalism. Even the highly planned Russian economy, as has already been remarked, carries its fringe of private enterprise; and the Americans have their public utilities. Just as every economy in the world is a mixture of plan and no-plan, so is every economy in the world a mixture of the same ingredients —private enterprise, state and municipal enterprise, semi-public corporations, and producers and consumers co-operatives, compounded in varying proportions. Realistic discussion must concern itself, not with two extreme alternatives, but with the endless possible quantitative variations of the mixture.

The socialistic-capitalist controversy is barren, in the second place, because it involves a confusion of ends and means. The ultimate test of any economic or social policy or "system" is its reflection in the lives of the individuals whom it affects. The values that matter are happiness, freedom, security, and the fulfillment of individual personalities in harmony, not in conflict, with one another. It is by their ability to promote such values as these that economic "systems" must be compared: these systems are means, not ends. The assumption that happiness, freedom, security, and the harmonious fulfillment of personalities, can be realized either only where men and women are employed in the service of public authorities, or only where they are not so employed, is unsupported either by experience or by rational expectation: there is no magic virtue in public employment, no magic vice in the enterprise of the private business man; and the converse is equally true. Both public and private employment are to be judged by their fruits: and the fruits are always various. Often the way of life of individuals may have more in common with that of their opposite numbers under a different system, than with others living under the same system as themselves. The Southern farmer of capitalist America is nearer to many Soviet peasants than to the New York financier; and the Swedish farmer would both understand, and differ from, his Russian and his American counterpart. All of these enjoy, and all of them lack, certain elements of freedom, happiness and security: all enjoy and all lack certain opportunities for fulfillment of their personalities. It is by a concrete, realistic measure of these enjoyments, and not by any *a priori* theories of the inherent superiority of one system over another by which alone policy must be guided.

Even those convinced socialists who have prejudged the issue in their own minds would do well, for tactical reasons, to accept this empirical approach to their chosen goal. The smoothest path towards social ownership of industry is along the road of the demonstrated failure of private enterprise to enrich individual lives in these ultimate values. The roughest possible road, calculated to arouse the bitterest opposition and to minimize disinterested support, is a comprehensive program of socialization for its own sake. If economic planning for security and rising standards of living fails, because of the resistances and the uncooperative attitude of the business world, the case for public ownership will be strengthened beyond all measure. It is not strengthened by anticipations of such failure, unsupported by the evidence of experience.

In the end it will no doubt be the state of everybody's temper as much as anything else which will decide the issue.

There is nothing in the conscious planning of economic priorities which is inherently incompatible with the freedoms which mean most to the contemporary Englishman or American. Civil liberties are quite unaffected. We can, if we wish, deliberately plan so as to give the fullest possible scope for the pursuit by individuals and social groups of cultural ends which are in no way state-determined. The consumer can enjoy the pleasure of comparing prices and qualities, and spending money that is freely available to the limit of his income, just as and when he thinks fit. Industrial direction and industrial conscription are unnecessary. Planning need not even be the death-warrant of all private enterprise; and it is certainly not the passport of political dictatorship. It is true (and indeed obvious) that the *same* part of the economic pattern cannot both be deliberately planned, and left to emerge as the result of the uncoordinated actions of thousands of consumers. But consumer sovereignty, in any meaningful and defensible sense, seems to be quite unattainable and certainly never to have been attained outside the covers of an academic textbook; and there is the less cause for tears on this account, inasmuch as no ordinary consumer would be conscious whether he enjoyed that sovereignty or not. It is true also that the preservation of free choice of employment under planning would be impossible if wages were to be settled by a private tug-of-war between employers and employed, in which each party exploited its full economic strength. But against this must be set the fact that free choice of employment will never be a reality without planning, since legal freedom of choice is a mockery if economic pressure compels the chooser to accept the first available job. The right of effective choice of employment is the one great freedom which the pre-war Englishman, or American, or Continental European outside Russia, has never enjoyed. Planning could give it to him.

A happy and fruitful marriage between freedom and planning can, in short, be arranged. That leaves us with the problem (which we have so far taken as solved) of translating "can" into "will." This is a problem of social and political psychology. Success or failure turns on the behavior of the actual men and women who have the responsibility of planning: on the measure in which positions of power are filled by men and women who care for the freedom of others and (what is not less important) in whom this love of liberty is not subsequently stifled by the habit of authority. Here, of course, there can be no secure guarantee. All the old clichés are just as true as ever they were—power still corrupts, absolute power still corrupts absolutely, and eternal vigilance is just as much the price of liberty as ever it was. The prospect for freedom is indeed bright only where these truths are fully appreciated and constantly in mind. The practical question is how best to apply these age-long lessons of experience to the modern world.

The last and greatest defense of freedom under planning lies in the quality and attitude of the people. Much has been said and written lately about the "we" and "they" relationship between government and governed, official and public. To suppose that the distinction between "us" and "them" can be literally obliterated is, however, unrealistic. The official on one side of the counter is not the same flesh and blood as the client on the other, and language must and will express this difference. It is not the distinction between "us" and "them" that matters, but the nature of the relationship between the two parties. That relationship must be founded on a sense of partnership and not of fear.

We have all seen, if we have not ourselves been, the kind of person who regards any contact with authority as a contest, in which the scales are weighted in favor of officialdom. We have all seen, if we have not been, the timid who are helpless before any official form, who sign what they have not read, and for whom rights of appeal or opportunities which demand the smallest measure of personal initiative might as well not exist. And occasionally we have seen, if we have not been, citizens of a very different caliber —confident, alert and informed, yet still courteous, ready to understand and to utilize, both for themselves and for their neighbors, every opportunity which the democratic state has properly made available—citizens who understand laws or regulations which affect them and are not deterred by any occasions of official incompetence, irrelevance, indifference, or ill-manners. These, and these alone, are the stuff of which effective democracy can be made.

~~~~~~

5. *Planning: America's Experience**

CHARLES E. MERRIAM

~~~~~~

From the beginning of our national life various forms of planning have been in evidence. The industrial situation confronting the founders of this republic was one of widespread distress, insecurity, and depression of the most anxious type. They deliberately planned a way out, when most men held that even government could not be planned. The Constitution itself was an economico-political plan on a grand scale, not only providing a democratic frame of government, but also setting up special plans for dealing with currency, tariffs, interstate commerce, and international relations. Justice was the first term in the preamble and liberty the last, but between them came the general welfare, common defense, and domestic tranquillity. The Constitutional Convention itself was a large-scale planning board.

Alexander Hamilton's well-known *Report on Manufactures* presented in 1791 was an impressive consideration of national policy in industry and related fields of American interest. In broad terms Hamilton set out the national problems of economics and government and suggested specific lines of policy to be followed. The report on internal improvements drawn up by President Jefferson's Secretary of the Treasury, Albert Gallatin, was almost equally notable. Henry Clay developed later (1820) the famous "American system," in which tariff and internal improvements occupied a conspicuous place. It is clear that the encouragement of manufactures by a policy of

* From Charles E. Merriam, *On the Agenda of Democracy* (The Godkin Lectures, Harvard University Press, 1941). By permission.

protection began as a systematic planning procedure, though later it degenerated at times into a free-for-all scramble for favors.

The land policy of the United States was planned with similar deliberation. It began with the abolition of the system of primogeniture and entail, the basis of the British system of political and economic power. The "grand plan" of John Quincy Adams for the management of the national domain was not followed; but the later development of the American homestead policy (1862) was designed to give a homestead at a nominal cost to practically all prospective settlers.

Our public educational policy rested in large part upon the broad grants of public lands given—two sections per township—for school purposes, with additional amounts for land-grant colleges. All this was notable national planning as of that day and age, democratic in purpose and method and highly successful in producing results. Those who prefer not to call this planning may, of course, apply some other term, but that will not change the spirit and temper of the work of the first great national planners who laid broad foundations for the republic of their dreams. Down to the Civil War, no country in the world had made bolder and more successful experiments in the field of government and economics alike than the United States.

Following that war, planning centered for several decades in large-scale private industries, such as had scarcely been known theretofore. Giant enterprises began to dominate whole areas of industry, and to operate them in increasingly unified and systematic fashion, although not always in the public interest. But national planning did not cease. It was resorted to whenever the public came to believe that unrestricted business enterprise failed at some point to promote the national welfare. Examples of government action designed to protect public interests are the establishment of the Interstate Commerce Commission in 1887, the passage of the Sherman Antitrust Act of 1890, the organization of the Federal Trade Commission, and a long series of national and state measures having the same general purpose.

Another step toward national planning was the development of the conservation program designed for the protection of natural resources, under the leadership of Theodore Roosevelt. This wide-ranging movement constituted a striking example of intelligent and forward-looking national policy, designed to protect and promote our common interests through various types of controls preventive of wasteful exploitation of our basic resources. In addition to the plans of the United States Government, similar systems and arrangements were set up by several of the states in various fields.

A more dramatic development of national planning was the "economic mobilization" development during the World War through the War Industries Board, the War Trade Board, the Shipping Board, the War Labor

Board, the Food Administration, the Fuel Administration, and the Railroad Administration, with their various subsidiaries. Under the stimulus of the war objective and national unity of purpose, far-reaching plans were made for the utilization of resources, for the ordering of industry, and for the focusing of the nation's strength in military and naval pressure. Nor did plans for economic mobilization end with the war. The National Defense Act of 1921 is a plan for a national war emergency—a plan which covers the wide ranges of industrial life necessarily reorganized for war purposes.

Though the war-time controls were released promptly after the armistice, the speculative boom of 1919–20 and the severe though brief depression of 1920–21 brought home to everyone the fact that peace has her defeats no less than war. The elaborate report on *Waste in Industry,* sponsored by the American Engineering Council in 1921, was a landmark in a movement toward better economic management, and this line was followed by important developments of planning in the Department of Commerce. Trade associations began their rapid growth under the benevolent auspices of the United States Government. Attacks upon waste, demands for standardization, simplification, research in production efficiency, long-time plans for stabilization and equilibrium in industry, were pressed forward.

Another notable development was the reorganization of the budgetary procedure of the United States Government through the Budget Bureau and the Director of the Budget—a reform long advocated and finally accomplished—under President Harding. While many of these powers were already in the hands of the President, the deliberate planning of ways and means for the exercise of his authority unquestionably had an important influence in the direction of systematic scrutiny and control over public expenditures. The Federal Reserve Bank was set up to be an important agency for equilibrium in the field of banking and credit. The organization of the Federal Employment Stabilization Board through the efforts of Senator Wagner and President Hoover was an attempt to plan expenditures for public works over a period of years in relation to business cycles.

Meanwhile many forms of planning appeared. City planning agencies sprang up, reaching now the number of some one thousand. County planning boards have been established covering a quarter of our three thousand counties. Some forty-five state planning agencies have been established.[1] Regional planning committees have been set up and commissions on interstate coöperation have been organized by most of the states. Many large-scale efforts in the field of planning have been developed by the United States Government in the last ten years, beginning with the Reconstruction Finance Corporation, the Home Owners' Loan Corporation, and the Federal Em-

[1] For history of state planning, see Clifford J. Hynning, *State Conservation of Resources* (1939); R. A. Walker, *The Planning Function in Urban Government* (1941).

ployment Stabilization Office under President Hoover. President Roosevelt initiated a broad sweep of policies in the field of social legislation. No effort is made here to sum up all of the attempts made in this direction.

Wide ranges of social legislation have been directed at regulation of industrial maladjustments. Sometimes these efforts took the form of labor legislation and sometimes they were aimed at the correction of corporate and other industrial abuses.

Notwithstanding differences of judgment regarding either the policy or the administration of these undertakings, there is general agreement that many of them have been highly successful. Taken together they illustrate the importance of planning our fundamental national policy in the emergency period upon which we are now entering. Doubtless many other evidences of national planning of resources both natural and human will be seen. It becomes more and more evident that the fullest use of American national resources cannot be obtained without careful and intelligent planning—national, state, and local.

The National Resources Planning Board, created by President Roosevelt in 1933, was substantially the projection of the Advisory Council recommended by President Hoover's Committee on Recent Social Trends, 1933. This body has made many studies of our physical and our human resources. The basic data regarding land use, water use, energy resources, long-time planning of public works, have been assembled by technicians and carefully analyzed, and various indicated policies have been suggested. In each of these areas broad programs have been outlined. Elaborate analyses have been made of the structure of our national economy, of consumer expenditure, and of consumer income. Reviews of industrial trends and their relation to employment stabilization, and analyses of industrial-plant location, thoroughgoing scrutiny of our relief policy, and indications of a long-time method of procedure have been prepared and presented to responsible officials. More recently the Board has undertaken the preparation of plans for the post-emergency period on a considerable scale.

Fundamental inquiries have been made into basic factors in the national economy: scientific studies of population trends, of inventions and their social implications, of research as a national resource—research in government, in industry, in university centers. In addition to printed reports, many of the results are in the form of interoffice memoranda, and in the shape of private reports and memos submitted to the Executive. These taken together constitute an important section of the work of the planning agency on whatever level of government it may be found. An advisory agency will find that much of its advice is rejected in whole or in part, but this is one of the ways in which advisors are distinguished from the responsible policy-determiners or administrators dealing with operative activities. Advice often advances through roundabout and even underground channels. There may come a moment when the advice long since given comes back with a request for a review by the one who gave it.

~~~~~~

6. Planning: America's Hope*

CHARLES E. MERRIAM

~~~~~~

If the ends of security and order are by way of settlement, a situation not yet assured, intelligent government may direct its attention to justice, welfare, and freedom and their practical implementation. Government cannot escape its share of responsibility for the progressive improvement of human personalities in the framework of the common good but must at all times stand ready to use its friendly offices for the development of a fraternal, equalitarian, libertarian way of life.

This calls for a positive program beyond the role of neutrality or the umpire in the struggle for existence. Intelligent planning involves (1) systematic attention to the growth of the gains of civilization, the mode and range of their distribution, the principles of justice and freedom in their practical application. In addition to the body of civil rights and liberties, this involves (2) a guaranty by the government, as one of the underwriters, of security in employment, minimum standards of health, education, the "social securities," and equal access to the development of creative possibilities in the human personality. The underlying principle of the responsibility of government is more important than the particular policies or mechanisms utilized for the broad purposes in view.

Our coming problems are not adequately described by the current terms "economic collectivism" and "capitalism." They are far broader in scope. They include considerations not merely economic but scientific, technological, engineering, philosophical, ethical, territorial-racial, socio-political. They include ideal as well as material considerations, diverse value systems and ideas, and institutions of many types outside the economic and governmental.

Laissez faire and communism are oversimplifications of problems which are far too complex to be contained by these economic slogans. In one sense all community action is collectivist, but with equal truth it may be said that all communities are made up of human personalities associated for their personal life-advantage as well as for the common good.

* From Charles E. Merriam, *Systematic Politics* (University of Chicago Press, 1945). By permission.

Observation, experience, and reflection point to a program in the next stage of development in which government will underwrite, as one of the co-operating underwriters, but fully responsible in the default of others:

The fullest possible development of the productive potential of all our resources, material and human, with assurance of full employment, continuity of income, minimum standards of living, including education, health, housing, the cultural amenities of life, a balance between stability and adventure, and a fair share in the growing gains of civilization.

The fullest possible development of the human personality, in relation to the common good, in a framework of freedoms and rights, of justice, liberty, equality, and the consent of the governed.

The end of world anarchy and the organization of an effective jural order of the world, outlawing aggression and imperialism, old or new fashioned in world relations, encouraging and energizing the fullest development of resources and rights everywhere.

It is vital for the future of ourselves and for the race that we recognize the meaning of government. I make bold to say on the basis of my observation, experience, and reflection ranging over a wide area of opportunity that the capacity of government is the key to the near future. We cannot hope to flout and sneer at government and yet build a sound structure of economic and social life. Government is not the master of men, but men cannot master their problems without it.

The important question is what we propose to do regarding the future development of our resources with reference to specific programs of action directed toward the common good. The development of a dynamic economy will absorb our interests and our energies for some time to come, and this can be achieved without basic changes in our industrial or political economy. That there is an underlying harmony of interests common to groups and individuals and that there are also sharp differences in personal and group advantage goes without saying. But in a dynamic economy, with full employment and full development of national resources, the national income may be so largely increased by superior use of science, by superior forms of organization and management, by superior productivity of goods and services—all well within the bounds of possibility in a free system—that the minor differences of advantage are lost sight of in the larger gains that may accrue to all.

The fear that planning will interfere with the development of free industrial society is groundless. The very purpose of planning is to release human abilities, to broaden the field of opportunity, and to enlarge human liberty. We plan primarily for freedom; the ways and means and instruments are secondary to the main purpose. The right kind of planning—democratic planning—is a guaranty of liberty and the only real assurance in our times that men can be free to make a wide range of choices.

Among the outstanding ways in which human liberty may be expanded by careful planning are:

1. Research, invention, and technological development, which are the bases of our industrial development, would profit by careful planning. Business research, governmental research, academic research—all flourish under a system of freedom, in a climate where their progress is considered one of the main-springs of human progress and is fostered in every possible way, alike in social and in natural science. Physics, chemistry, biology, engineering, medicine, education, and management are the foundations upon which much of our material and social progress depends, and they flourish best where careful attention is given to their cultivation. In a democratic society these free channels of invention and ingenuity may be kept open to all, without discrimination against race or class.

2. The frontiers of industrial development are wide open. There is every reason to believe that human enterprise and organization are likely in the immediate future to utilize more fully undeveloped resources already known and to go beyond that in the exploration and advancement of entirely new fields of industrial activity. The amazing results following the release of human ingenuity in the present drive for large-scale production show the tremendous possibilities in our present system. Only those whose imagination is dead or dying can fail to recognize the vast peacetime potential of production, once the way is cleared. Obviously, all this is not the task of government alone, but government can keep the channels of enterprise open and can help to plan for continuing growth of essential resources, both material and human.

The 100 per cent attainment of health and education alone would transform national resources in a measure defying precise calculation, but beyond question to a point of incalculable value, even in terms of dollars and cents, to say nothing of human happiness. There is a point at which expenditure for health and education would strike the law of diminishing returns, but we have not yet even come within sight of such a situation.

Free enterprise has far more to fear from lack of planning than from its development and application to national resources. Between fascism, on the one hand, and monopoly and unregulated concentrations of economic power, on the other, the free industrial system and the open free market are hard pressed now. It is not planning that has made difficulties in the smooth working of free competition, that has fostered monopolies, cartels, racketeering, high, low, or medium, but the lack of it.

In the past few years government has brought up to date types of social legislation that were a generation late, such as social security and conservation. We still lag behind at many important points. But the dramatic possibilities of the next period are far more important than either the early planning of our public lands or the later approach to belated social and humanitarian legislation.

We can take the measure of the meaning of both public and private government, and can advance without being frightened either by the word "anarchism" or the word "collectivism" applied to every individual act of the government. We can recognize that government is one of the many agencies necessary to the happiness of mankind, a useful servant of the common good, for purposes willed by the community itself.

Private enterprise and public enterprise and mixed forms of enterprise will take their proper places in the national economy and may dwell together in harmony. There may and will be regional struggles and personal struggles and sectarian struggles and racial rivalries and class struggles, but they will play their proper roles in the broad setting of the common good—not as the lords of creation, but as servants and not as masters of the common good. In a truly free economy—one which is free politically and free economically and free religiously and free culturally—no one element will have a monopoly of decisions affecting the common good.

Many atrocities have been committed in the alleged name of the common man, but usually by special seekers of special privilege taking the name of democracy in vain for their own selfish purposes, with their tongues in their cheeks. But, when men once come really into their own in a fraternal society where the dignity of man and the consent of the governed are actually in force, the vested interests of special groups, political, economic, cultural, racial, or religious, will be relatively insignificant. They may be valued for what they really are.

In that day it will be possible to realize the destiny of modern life more fully than the prophets ever dared to dream. It will be possible to make full use of science and democracy in planning for the expansion of national production, for justice, for the fair distribution of national gains, for far higher standards of living, for liberty, for the recognition of the dignity of man, and for his right to participate fully in the civilization he has helped create.

Such a program is dictated by the growth of human intelligence and its practical application to human needs, by the insistent demands for fraternal recognition and appreciation by fellow-men. It is supported by revolutionary developments of reason, observation, experience, and experiment and made practicable by the discoveries, inventions, and organization of our time which bring vast expansion of man's conscious control over the world around him.

It is no longer utopian to place on the agenda:

The effective outlawry of war

The outlawry of race inequality and personal inequality in an emerging system of resources, rights, and recognitions

The universal organization of the consent of the governed as the basis of political association

The outlawry of social insecurity and want

The outlawry of unfair shares of the gains of civilization

And, finally, the outlawry of governments serving as tools of oppression, exploitation, and privilege, and the recognition of government in theory and practice as an agent of the common good, equipped with modern devices for accomplishing the high purposes of man.

Chapter XIII

ECONOMIC THREATS TO FREEDOM

THE contradictions between political freedom and economic dependence have been noted by students of democracy for at least a hundred years. The essence of the problem consists in this: in politics, Western democracies have successfully established the principle that the holders of power must be accountable to the public. The latter is the "boss," the former, the agent. Political power in a democracy must not be held for the benefit of the rulers, but is a trust, under which the interest of the people is to be protected. In the economic realm, on the other hand, the dogma of *laissez faire* has created a constitutional situation which violates all recognized canons of democracy: at times the owners of capital wield tremendous power over the lives of their employees without due reference to the public good, without being responsible to those whose welfare they determine through basic economic decisions. Whereas in a capitalist democracy political policies are arrived at through processes of consent which begin at the bottom and end at the top, in corporate business organizations economic decisions are made from the top down to the bottom. The structure of industrial organization is hierarchical, based on discipline and obedience; more recently, this traditional pattern has been made more democratic by collective bargaining and the influence of the labor movement.

The relationships between power and responsibility in industrial relations engaged the lifework of Mr. Justice Brandeis. Before his appointment to the Supreme Court by President Wilson, Brandeis had fought monopoly in the courts, in print and in speech, wherever the occasion demanded it. Brandeis strongly believed in the capitalist system, provided it was not perverted into its exact opposite, unregulated monopoly, and provided the political liberty of democracy was also preserved in economic relations. He was persuaded that the two realms of society, politics and the economy, could not be too contradictory in the long run, and that "either political liberty will be extinguished or industrial liberty must be restored." His concept of "industrial absolutism" opposing political freedom is most clearly elaborated in the testimony he gave in 1915 before the United States Commission on Industrial Relations. Long before, he had been one of the foremost foes of monopoly.

Brandeis' ideas influenced considerably the thinking of Woodrow Wilson prior to his election to the presidency. In *The New Freedom* (1913), President Wilson expressed the rising popular revolt against trusts and monopolies and the growing control of government by business. He opposed monopoly, not because he was against free enterprise, but because he saw free business being swallowed up by monopolistic control in industry and finance. He was so strongly in favor of business that he even enthusiastically approved of "big business," distinguishing it sharply, however, from trusts. Wilson saw that the struggle between "tyranny and freedom" was not finally settled for all time by the Declaration of Independence. The gist of Wilson's political and economic philosophy is contained in these words: "What I am interested in is having the government of the United States more concerned about human rights than about property rights. Property is an instrument of humanity; humanity isn't an instrument of property."

The greatest American critic of the modern business system was Thorstein Veblen, who was born in Wisconsin in 1857 and died in California in 1929. At a time when economic unorthodoxy was rare and dangerous, Veblen preferred loneliness and ostracism to compromise and surrender. He is sometimes called the "American Marx." Veblen shared with Marx the power of keen analysis, but lacked Marx's inclination to look for universal laws that would open up all riddles. Veblen asked less ambitious questions than Marx; but that very self-limitation enabled him to arrive at more concrete and reliable solutions, without generalizations about the whole past history of man, and without prophecies about the faraway future. Marx stood with both feet on Hegel; Veblen, on the solid ground of fact.

Veblen's particular concern in modern economic life was the growing separation between the business and financial managers on the one hand and the technical experts, the engineers, on the other. Whereas Marx speaks of capitalists and proletarians, Veblen distinguishes sharply between those who manage business and those who perform the technical work. The interest of the "captains of finance" and of the business managers is to make profit, regardless of the waste of human and physical resources. The interest of the engineers is to apply fully all their skill and knowledge: but their capacity to produce is curbed by the demands of profit of the captains of industry and their bosses, the corporation financiers. The pecuniary interest of a small group of persons who wield financial control over the industrial plant of the nation takes precedence over its needs. In *The Engineers and the Price System* (1921), Veblen describes the process of growing dissatisfaction among the engineers with the "customary right of ownership by virtue of which the vested interests continue to control the industrial system for the benefit of the kept classes." Veblen thinks that, once the engineers "put their heads together" on this issue, the "massed and rough-handed legions of the industrial rank and file" will side with the engineers. Unlike Marx, who predicts that with the establishment of a socialist classless society history will take a long vacation, Veblen is not sure what kind of society will develop, once unproductive absentee ownership is driven out of existence and the engineers and workers assume a new status in the economic order.

The same pragmatic attitude is characteristic of Lord Beveridge. The "Beveridge Report" (*Report on Social Insurance and Allied Services,* 1942) was probably the most inspiring document of social philosophy that came out during the Second World War. Here was a message that promised every Briton that he could henceforth count on adequate protection against want, unemployment, illness, and old age. The report was, for a government publication, a surprising best-seller in both Britain and the United States. Two years later, in 1944, Beveridge published his even greater work on *Full Employment in a Free Society.* The reaction to the book in England was remarkable: many declared that it was the most important work in political economy since *Das Kapital.* Others said that this was the first real attempt to solve the problem of employment—a key problem of the survival of political democracy—without "judgment on the general issue between socialism and capitalism." Spokesmen of all political parties recognized in Beveridge's work a remarkable step forward in the whole debate on how to combine political liberties with economic security and progress. By contrast, the reception of the book in the United States was more polite than enthusiastic. Hayek's *Road to Serfdom* and Beveridge's *Full Employment in a Free Society* were both published in 1944. Hayek's book was a sensational best-seller in the United States, but a moderate success in Britain; Beveridge's book was a best-seller in England, but sold moderately in the United States.

Full employment in a totalitarian state is relatively simple, because the state forces people to work for low wages and under oppressive working conditions. What Beveridge seeks to achieve with his proposals is full employment in a *free society.* The essential citizen liberties to be preserved under all circumstances are listed by him as follows: "Freedom of worship, speech, writing, study and teaching; freedom of assembly and of association for political and other purposes, including the bringing about of a peaceful change of the governing authority; freedom in choice of occupation; and freedom in the management of a personal income." The private ownership of the means of production, Beveridge remarks, may be a good economic device or not, but is "not an essential citizen liberty in Britain, because it is not and never has been enjoyed by more than a very small proportion of the British people." Still, Beveridge thinks that full employment could be attained while a community "held firmly to private enterprise." Ultimately, though, if private property in the means of production should make full employment impossible, the latter would take precedence over the former. Beveridge thus avoids any *a priori* dogmas, and insists that experience, rather than preconceptions and abstractions, should be the guide to the solution of these vital issues.

As one glances at a comparison between the assets of "billion dollar" corporations in the United States and the total assessed valuation of wealth within individual states, the concept of "private government" is filled with life and meaning. In 1937 the two richest corporations, the Metropolitan Life Insurance Company and the American Telephone and Telegraph Company, had assets which were greater than the total assessed wealth within the borders of any one of thirty-eight States of the Union. This is one of the many facts that will be found in Senator O'Mahoney's *Final Statement* (1941) of the "Temporary National Economic Committee." The committee was set up in 1938, and in its three years of inquiry on the "concentration of economic power" it accomplished one of the most comprehensive and voluminous investigations in the history of the Congress. Since the "Temporary National Economic Committee" wound up its work in 1941, the concentration of wealth and the control of industry have been greatly accelerated by the war. "In 1939 firms with over 1,000 employees accounted for 30 per cent of the total employment of all American trade and industry, and 36 per cent of the total pay roll. By 1943 these figures had risen to 44 and 53 per cent, respectively"; this is the conclusion of *Economic Concentration and World War II* (Report of the Smaller War Plants Corporation to the Special Committee to Study Problems of American Small Business, United States Senate, 1946).

Business is private government. Organized in cartels, it becomes international private government. The implications of international government by cartels for the peoples of the world, and for the United States in particular, are revealed in *Cartels and National Security* (1944), a Report of the Senate Subcommittee on War Mobilization under the chairmanship of Senator Kilgore of West Virginia. Whereas treaties made by the government of the United States have to be ratified by two-thirds of the Senate, cartel agreements affecting the military potential and economic welfare of the nation have been arranged with the sole sanction of profit, and without any accountability to the public. To permit such action, Senator Kilgore says, "would be an abdication of sovereignty on the part of national governments. It would permit the economy of nations to be subverted by groups who are responsible to no public control."

1. Industrial Absolutism versus Political Liberty *

LOUIS D. BRANDEIS

My observation leads me to believe that while there are many contributing causes to [industrial] unrest, that there is one cause which is fundamental. That is the necessary conflict—the contrast between our political liberty and our industrial absolutism. We are as free politically, perhaps, as free as it is possible for us to be. Every male has his voice and vote; and the law has endeavored to enable, and has succeeded practically, in enabling him to exercise his political franchise without fear. He therefore has his part; and certainly can secure an adequate part in the government of the country in all of its political relations; that is, in all relations which are determined directly by legislation or governmental administration.

On the other hand, in dealing with industrial problems the position of the ordinary worker is exactly the reverse. The individual employee has no effective voice or vote. And the main objection, as I see it, to the very large corporation is, that it makes possible—and in many cases makes inevitable —the exercise of industrial absolutism. It is not merely the case of the individual worker against the employer which, even if he is a reasonably sized employer, presents a serious situation calling for the interposition of a union to protect the individual. But we have the situation of an employer so potent, so well organized, with such concentrated forces and with such extraordinary powers of reserve and the ability to endure against strikes and other efforts of a union, that the relatively loosely organized masses of even strong unions are unable to cope with the situation. We are dealing here with a question, not of motive, but of condition. Now, the large corporation and the managers of the powerful corporation are probably in large part actuated by motives just the same as an employer of a tenth of their size. Neither of them, as a rule, wishes to have his liberty abridged; but the smaller concern usually comes to the conclusion that it is necessary that it should be, where an important union must be dealt with. But when a great financial power has developed—when there exists these powerful organizations, which can successfully summon forces from all parts of the country, which can afford to use tremendous amounts of money in any conflict to carry out what they deem to be their business principle, and can also afford to suffer large losses—you have necessarily a condition of inequality between

* From *Testimony before the Commission on Industrial Relations* (January 23, 1915; 64th Cong., 1st Sess., *Sen. Doc.*, Vol. 26, 1916).

the two contending forces. Such contests, though undertaken with the best motives and with strong conviction on the part of the corporate managers that they are seeking what is for the best interests not only of the company but of the community, lead to absolutism. The result, in the cases of these large corporations, may be to develop a benevolent absolutism, but it is an absolutism all the same; and it is that which makes the great corporation so dangerous. There develops within the State a state so powerful that the ordinary social and industrial forces existing are insufficient to cope with it.

2. Property Rights and Human Rights*

WOODROW WILSON

American industry is not free, as once it was free; American enterprise is not free; the man with only a little capital is finding it harder to get into the field, more and more impossible to compete with the big fellow. Why? Because the laws of this country do not prevent the strong from crushing the weak. That is the reason, and because the strong have crushed the weak and the strong dominate the industry and the economic life of this country. No man can deny that the lines of endeavor have more and more narrowed and stiffened; no man who knows anything about the development of industry in this country can have failed to observe that the larger kinds of credit are more and more difficult to obtain, unless you obtain them upon the terms of uniting your efforts with those who already control the industries of the country; and nobody can fail to observe that any man who tries to set himself up in competition with any process of manufacture which has been taken under the control of large combinations of capital will presently find himself either squeezed out or obliged to sell and allow himself to be absorbed.

One of the most alarming phenomena of the time,—or rather it would be alarming if the nation had not awakened to it and shown its determination to control it,—one of the most significant signs of the new social era is the degree to which government has become associated with business. I speak, for the moment, of the control over the government exercised by Big Business.

* From Woodrow Wilson, *The New Freedom* (Doubleday & Company, Inc., 1913). By permission of Mrs. Woodrow Wilson, holder of the copyright.

Behind the whole subject, of course, is the truth that, in the new order, government and business must be associated closely. But that association is at present of a nature absolutely intolerable; the precedence is wrong, the association is upside down. Our government has been for the past few years under the control of heads of great allied corporations with special interests. It has not controlled these interests and assigned them a proper place in the whole system of business; it has submitted itself to their control. As a result, there have grown up vicious systems and schemes of governmental favoritism (the most obvious being the extravagant tariff), far-reaching in effect upon the whole fabric of life, touching to his injury every inhabitant of the land, laying unfair and impossible handicaps upon competitors, imposing taxes in every direction, stifling everywhere the free spirit of American enterprise.

We stand in the presence of a revolution,—not a bloody revolution; America is not given to the spilling of blood,—but a silent revolution, whereby America will insist upon recovering in practice those ideals which she has always professed, upon securing a government devoted to the general interest and not to special interests.

Some citizens of this country have never got beyond the Declaration of Independence, signed in Philadelphia, July 4th, 1776. Their bosoms swell against George III, but they have no consciousness of the war for freedom that is going on to-day.

The Declaration of Independence did not mention the questions of our day. It is of no consequence to us unless we can translate its general terms into examples of the present day and substitute them in some vital way for the examples it itself gives, so concrete, so intimately involved in the circumstances of the day in which it was conceived and written. It is an eminently practical document, meant for the use of practical men; not a thesis for philosophers, but a whip for tyrants; not a theory of government, but a program of action. Unless we can translate it into the questions of our own day, we are not worthy of it. we are not the sons of the sires who acted in response to its challenge.

What form does the contest between tyranny and freedom take to-day? What is the special form of tyranny we now fight? How does it endanger the rights of the people, and what do we mean to do in order to make our contest against it effectual? What are to be the items of our new declaration of independence?

By tyranny, as we now fight it, we mean control of the law, of legislation and adjudication, by organizations which do not represent the people, by means which are private and selfish. We mean, specifically, the conduct of our affairs and the shaping of our legislation in the interest of special bodies of capital and those who organize their use. We mean the alliance, for this purpose, of political machines with selfish business. We mean the exploitation of the people by legal and political means. We have seen many of our governments under these influences cease to be representative governments, cease to be governments representative of the people, and become governments representative of special interests, controlled by machines, which in their turn are not controlled by the people.

The concern of patriotic men is to put our government again on its right basis, by substituting the popular will for the rule of guardians, the processes of common counsel for those of private arrangement. In order to do this, a first necessity is to open the doors and let in the light on all affairs which the people have a right to know about.

In the first place, it is necessary to open up all the processes of our politics. They have been too secret, too complicated, too roundabout; they have consisted too much of private conferences and secret understandings, of the control of legislation by men who were not legislators, but who stood outside and dictated, controlling oftentimes by very questionable means, which they would not have dreamed of allowing to become public. The whole process must be altered. We must take the selection of candidates for office, for example, out of the hands of small groups of men, of little coteries, out of the hands of machines working behind closed doors, and put it into the hands of the people themselves again by means of direct primaries and elections to which candidates of every sort and degree may have free access. We must substitute public for private machinery.

It is necessary, in the second place, to give society command of its own economic life again by denying to those who conduct the great modern operations of business the privacy that used to belong properly enough to men who used only their own capital and their individual energy in business. The processes of capital must be as open as the processes of politics. Those who make use of the great modern accumulations of wealth, gathered together by the dragnet process of the sale of stocks and bonds, and piling up of reserves, must be treated as under a public obligation; they must be made responsible for their business methods to the great communities which are in fact their working partners, so that the hand which makes correction shall easily reach them and a new principle of responsibility be felt throughout their structure and operation.

What are the right methods of politics? Why, the right methods are those of public discussion: the methods of leadership open and above board, not closeted with "boards of guardians" or anybody else, but brought out under the sky, where honest eyes can look upon them and honest eyes can judge of them.

A modern joint stock corporation cannot in any proper sense be said to base its rights and powers upon the principles of private property. Its powers are wholly derived from legislation. It possesses them for the convenience of business at the sufferance of the public. Its stock is widely owned, passes from hand to hand, brings multitudes of men into its shifting partnerships and connects it with the interests and the investments of whole communities. It is a segment of the public; bears no analogy to a partnership or to the processes by which private property is safeguarded and managed, and should not be suffered to afford any covert whatever to those who are managing it. Its management is of public and general concern, is in a very proper sense everybody's business. The business of many of those corporations which we call public-service corporations, and which are indispensable to our daily lives and serve us with transportation and light and water and power,— their business, for instance, is clearly public business; and, therefore, we can and must penetrate their affairs by the light of examination and discussion.

A trust is an arrangement to get rid of competition, and a big business is a business that has survived competition by conquering in the field of intelligence and economy. A trust does not bring efficiency to the aid of business; it *buys efficiency out of business*. I am for big business, and I am against the trusts. Any man who can survive by his brains, any man who can put the others out of the business by making the thing cheaper to the consumer at the same time that he is increasing its intrinsic value and quality, I take off my hat to, and I say: "You are the man who can build up the United States, and I wish there were more of you."

What I am interested in is having the government of the United States more concerned about human rights than about property rights. Property is an instrument of humanity; humanity isn't an instrument of property. And yet when you see some men riding their great industries as if they were driving a car of juggernaut, not looking to see what multitudes prostrate themselves before the car and lose their lives in the crushing effect of their industry, you wonder how long men are going to be permitted to think more of their machinery than they think of their men. Did you never think of it,—men are cheap, and machinery is dear; many a superintendent is dismissed for overdriving a delicate machine, who wouldn't be dismissed for overdriving an overtaxed man. You can discard your man and replace him; there are others ready to come into his place; but you can't without great cost discard your machine and put a new one in its place. You are less apt, therefore, to look upon your men as the essential vital foundation part of your whole business. It is time that property, as compared with humanity, should take second place, not first place. We must see to it that there is no over-crowding, that there is no bad sanitation, that there is no unnecessary spread of avoidable diseases, that the purity of food is safeguarded, that there is every precaution against accident, that women are not driven to impossible tasks, nor children permitted to spend their energy before it is fit to be spent. The hope and elasticity of the race must be preserved; men must be preserved according to their individual needs, and not according to the programs of industry merely. What is the use of having industry, if we perish in producing it? If we die in trying to feed ourselves, why should we eat? If we die trying to get a foothold in the crowd, why not let the crowd trample us sooner and be done with it? I tell you that there is beginning to beat in this nation a great pulse of irresistible sympathy which is going to transform the processes of government amongst us. The strength of America is proportioned only to the health, the energy, the hope, the elasticity, the buoyancy of the American people.

You know that one of the interesting things that Mr. Jefferson said in those early days of simplicity which marked the beginnings of our government was that the best government consisted in as little governing as possible. And there is still a sense in which that is true. It is still intolerable for the government to interfere with our individual activities except where it is necessary to interfere with them in order to free them. But I feel confident that if Jefferson were living in our day he would see what we see: that the individual is caught in a great confused nexus of all sorts of complicated circumstances, and that to let him alone is to leave him helpless as against the obstacles with which he has to contend; and that, therefore, law in our day must come to the assistance of the individual. It must come to his assistance to see that he gets fair play; that is all, but that is much. Without the watchful interference, the resolute interference, of the government, there can be no fair play between individuals and such powerful institutions as the trusts. Freedom to-day is something more than being let alone. The program of a government of freedom must in these days be positive, not negative merely.

~~~~~~

3. Profit versus Production *

THORSTEIN VEBLEN

~~~~~~

In the beginning, that is to say during the early growth of the machine industry, and particularly in that new growth of mechanical industries

* From Thorstein Veblen, *The Engineers and the Price System* (copyright, 1921, by B. W. Huebsch, Inc.; 1936, by The Viking Press). By permission.

which arose directly out of the Industrial Revolution, there was no marked division between the industrial experts and the business managers. That was before the new industrial system had gone far on the road of progressive specialization and complexity, and before business had reached an exactingly large scale; so that even the business men of that time, who were without special training in technological matters, would still be able to exercise something of an intelligent oversight of the whole, and to understand something of what was required in the mechanical conduct of the work which they financed and from which they drew their income. Not unusually the designers of industrial processes and equipment would then still take care of the financial end, at the same time that they managed the shop. But from an early point in the development there set in a progressive differentiation, such as to divide those who designed and administered the industrial processes from those others who designed and managed the commercial transactions and took care of the financial end. So there also set in a corresponding division of powers between the business management and the technological experts. It became the work of the technologists to determine, on technological grounds, what could be done in the way of productive industry, and to contrive ways and means of doing it; but the business management always continued to decide, on commercial grounds, how much work should be done and what kind of quality of goods and services should be produced; and the decision of the business management has always continued to be final, and has always set the limit beyond which production must not go.

With the continued growth of specialization the experts have necessarily had more and more to say in the affairs of industry; but always their findings as to what work is to be done and what ways and means are to be employed in production have had to wait on the findings of the business managers as to what will be expedient for the purpose of commercial gain. This division between business management and industrial management has continued to go forward, at a continually accelerated rate, because the special training and experience required for any passably efficient organization and direction of these industrial processes has continually grown more exacting, calling for special knowledge and abilities on the part of those who have this work to do and requiring their undivided interest and their undivided attention to the work in hand. But these specialists in technological knowledge, abilities, interest, and experience, who have increasingly come into the case in this way—inventors, designers, chemists, mineralogists, soil experts, crop specialists, production managers, and engineers of many kinds and denominations—have continued to be employees of the captains of industry, that is to say, of the captains of finance, whose work it has been to commercialize the knowledge and abilities of the industrial experts and turn them to account for their own gain.

It is perhaps unnecessary to add the axiomatic corollary that the captains have always turned the technologists and their knowledge to account in this way only so far as would serve their own commercial profit; not to the extent of their ability, or to the limit set by the material circumstances, or by the needs of the community. The result has been, uniformly and as a matter of course, that the production of goods and services has advisedly been stopped short of productive capacity, by curtailment of output and by derangement of the productive system. There are two main reasons for this, and both have operated together throughout the machine era to stop industrial production increasingly short of productive capacity: (a) The commercial need of maintaining a profitable price has led to an increasingly imperative curtailment of the output, as fast as the advance of the industrial arts has enhanced the productive capacity. And (b) the continued advance of the mechanical technology has called for an ever-increasing volume and diversity of special knowledge, and so has left the businesslike captains of finance continually farther in arrears, so that they have been less and less capable of comprehending what is required in the ordinary way of industrial equipment and personnel. They have therefore, in effect, maintained prices at a profitable level by curtailment of output rather than by lowering production-cost per unit of output, because they have not had such a working acquaintance with the technological facts in the case as would enable them to form a passably sound judgment of suitable ways and means for lowering production-cost; and at the same time, being shrewd business men, they have been unable to rely on the hired-man's loyalty of technologists whom they do not understand. The result has been a somewhat distrustful blindfold choice of processes and personnel and a consequent enforced incompetence in the management of industry, a curtailment of output below the needs of the community, below the productive capacity of the industrial system, and below what an intelligent control of production would have made commercially profitable.

Through the earlier decades of the machine era these limitations imposed on the work of the experts by the demands of profitable business and by the technical ignorance of the business men appears not to have been a heavy handicap, whether as a hindrance to the continued development of technological knowledge, or as an obstacle to its ordinary use in industry. That was before the mechanical industry had gone far in scope, complexity, and specialization; and it was also before the continued work of the technologists had pushed the industrial system to so high a productive capacity that it is for ever in danger of turning out a larger product than is required for a profitable business. But gradually, with the passage of time and the advance of the industrial arts to a wider scope and a larger scale, and to an increasing specialization and standardization of processes, the technological knowledge that makes up the state of the industrial arts has called for a higher degree of that training that makes industrial specialists; and at the same time and by the same shift of circumstances, the captains of finance, driven by an increasingly close application to the affairs of business, have been going farther out of touch with the ordinary realities of productive industry; and, it is to be admitted, they have also continued increasingly to distrust the technological specialists, whom they do not understand, but whom they can also not get along without. The captains have perforce continued to employ the technologists, to make money for them, but they have done so only reluctantly, tardily, sparingly, and with a shrewd circumspection; only because and so far as they have been persuaded that the use of these technologists was indispensable to the making of money.

One outcome of this persistent and pervasive tardiness and circumspection on the part of the captains has been an incredibly and increasingly uneconomical use of material resources, and an incredibly wasteful organization of equipment and man-power in those great industries where the technological advance has been most marked. In good part it was this discreditable pass, to which the leading industries had been brought by these one-eyed captains of industry, that brought the regime of the captains to an inglorious close, by shifting the initiative and discretion in this domain out of their hands into those of the investment bankers. By custom the investment bankers had occupied a position between or overlapping the duties of a broker in corporate securities and those of an underwriter of corporate flotations—such a position, in effect, as is still assigned them in the standard writings on corporation finance. The increasingly large scale of corporate enterprise, as well as the growth of a mutual understanding among these business concerns, also had its share in this new move. But about this time, too, the "consulting engineers" were coming notably into evidence in many of those lines of industry in which corporation finance has habitually been concerned.

So far as concerns the present argument the ordinary duties of these consulting engineers have been to advise the investment bankers as to the industrial and commercial soundness, past and prospective, of any enterprise that is to be underwritten. These duties have comprised a painstaking and impartial examination of the physical properties involved in any given case, as well as an equally impartial auditing of the accounts and appraisal of the commercial promise of such enterprises, for the guidance of the bankers or syndicate of bankers interested in the case as underwriters. On this ground working arrangements and a mutual understanding presently arose between the consulting engineers and those banking-houses that habitually were concerned in the underwriting of corporate enterprises.

The effect of this move has been twofold: experience has brought out the fact that corporation finance, at its best and soundest, has now become a matter of comprehensive and standardized bureaucratic routine, necessarily comprising the mutual relations between various corporate concerns, and best to be taken care of by a clerical staff of trained accountants; and the same experience has put the financial house in direct touch with the technological general staff of the industrial system, whose surveillance has become increasingly imperative to the conduct of any profitable enterprise in industry. But also, by the same token, it has appeared that the corporation financier of nineteenth-century tradition is no longer of the essence of the case in corporation finance of the larger and more responsible sort. He has, in effect, come to be no better than an idle wheel in the economic mechanism, serving only to take up some of the lubricant.

Since and so far as this shift out of the nineteenth century into the twentieth has been completed, the corporation financier has ceased to be a captain of industry and has become a lieutenant of finance; the captaincy having been taken over by the syndicated investment bankers and administered as a standardized routine of accountancy, having to do with the flotation of corporation securities and with their fluctuating values, and having also something to do with regulating the rate and volume of output in those industrial enterprises which so have passed under the hand of the investment bankers.

By and large, such is the situation of the industrial system today, and of that financial business that controls the industrial system. But this state of things is not so much an accomplished fact handed on out of the recent past; it is only that such is the culmination in which it all heads up in the immediate present, and that such is the visible drift of things into the calculable future. Only during the last few years has the state of affairs in industry been obviously falling into the shape so outlined, and it is even yet only in those larger and pace-making lines of industry which are altogether of the new technological order that the state of things has reached this finished shape. But in these larger and underlying divisions of the industrial system the present posture and drift of things is unmistakable. Meantime very much still stands over out of that regime of rule-of-thumb, competitive sabotage, and commercial log-rolling, in which the businesslike captains of the old order are so altogether well at home, and which has been the best that the captains have known how to contrive for the management of that industrial system whose captains they have been. So that wherever the production experts are now taking over the management, out of the dead hand of the self-made captains, and wherever they have occasions to inquire into the established conditions of production, they find the ground cumbered with all sorts of incredible make-shifts of waste and inefficiency—such makeshifts as would perhaps pass muster with any moderately stupid elderly laymen, but which look like blindfold guesswork to these men who know something of the advanced technology and its working-out.

Hitherto, then, the growth and conduct of this industrial system presents this singular outcome. The technology—the state of the industrial arts—which takes effect in this mechanical industry is in an eminent sense a joint stock of knowledge and experience held in common by the civilized peoples. It requires the use of trained and instructed workmen—born, bred, trained, and instructed at the cost of the people at large. So also it requires, with a continually more exacting insistence, a corps of highly trained and specially gifted experts, of divers and various kinds. These, too, are born, bred, and trained at the cost of the community at large, and they draw their requisite special knowledge from the community's joint stock of accumulated experience. These expert men, technologists, engineers, or whatever name may best suit them, make up the indispensable General Staff of the industrial system; and without their immediate and unremitting guidance and correction the industrial system will not work. It is a mechanically organized structure of technical processes designed, installed, and conducted by these production engineers. Without them and their constant attention the industrial equipment, the mechanical appliances of industry, will foot up to just so much junk. The material welfare of the community is unreservedly bound up with the due working of this industrial system, and therefore with its unreserved control by the engineers, who alone are competent to manage it. To do their work as it should be done these men of the industrial general staff must have a free hand, unhampered by commercial considerations and reservations; for the production of the goods and services needed by the community they neither need nor are they in any degree benefited by any supervision or interference from the side of the owners. Yet the absentee owners, now represented, in effect, by the syndicated investment bankers, continue to control the industrial experts and limit their discretion, arbitrarily, for their own commercial gain, regardless of the needs of the community.

Hitherto these men who so make up the general staff of the industrial system have not drawn together into anything like a self-directing working force; nor have they been vested with anything more than an occasional, haphazard, and tentative control of some disjointed sector of the industrial equipment, with no direct or decisive relation to that personnel of productive industry that may be called the officers of the line and the rank and file. It is still the unbroken privilege of the financial management and its financial agents to "hire and fire." The final disposition of all the industrial forces still remains in the hands of the business men, who still continue to dispose of these forces for other than industrial ends. And all the while it is an open secret that with a reasonably free hand the production experts would today readily increase the ordinary output of industry by severalfold—variously estimated at some 300 per cent to 1200 per cent of the current output. And what stands in the way of so increasing the ordinary output of goods and services is business-as-usual.

Right lately these technologists have begun to become uneasily "class-conscious" and to reflect that they together constitute the indispensable general staff of the industrial system. Their class-consciousness has taken the immediate form of a growing sense of waste and confusion in the management of industry by the financial agents of the absentee owners. They are beginning to take stock of that all-pervading mismanagement of industry that is inseparable from its control for commercial ends. All of which brings home a realization of their own shame and of damage to the common good. So the engineers are beginning to draw together and ask themselves, "What about it?"

This uneasy movement among the technologists set in, in an undefined and fortuitous way, in the closing years of the nineteenth century; when the consulting engineers, and then presently the "efficiency engineers," began to make scattered corrections in detail, which showed up the industrial incompetence of those elderly laymen who were doing a conservative business at the cost of industry. The consulting engineers of the standard type, both then and since then, are commercialized technologists, whose work it is to appraise the industrial value of any given enterprise with a view to its commercial exploitation. They are a cross between a technological specialist and a commercial agent, beset with the limitations of both and commonly not fully competent in either line. Their normal position is that of an employee of the investment bankers, on a stipend or a retainer, and it has ordinarily been their fortune to shift over in time from a technological footing to a frankly commercial one. The case of the efficiency engineers, or scientific-management experts, is somewhat similar. They too have set out to appraise, exhibit, and correct the commercial shortcomings of the ordinary management of those industrial establishments which they investigate, to persuade the business men in charge how they may reasonably come in for larger net earnings by a more closely shorn exploitation of the industrial forces at their disposal. During the opening years of the new century a lively interest centred on the views and expositions of these two groups of industrial experts; and not least was the interest aroused by their exhibits of current facts indicating an all-pervading lag, leak, and friction in the industrial system, due to its disjointed and one-eyed management by commercial adventurers bent on private gain.

During these few years of the opening century the members of this informal guild of engineers at large have been taking an interest in this question of habitual mismanagement by ignorance and commercial sabotage, even apart from the commercial imbecility of it all. But it is the young rather than the old among them who see industry in any other light than its commercial value. Circumstances have decided that the older generation of the craft have become pretty well commercialized. Their habitual outlook has been shaped by a long and unbroken apprenticeship to the corporation financiers and the investment bankers; so that they still habitually see the industrial system as a contrivance for the round-about process of making money. Accordingly, the established official Associations and Institutes of Engineers, which are officered and engineered by the elder engineers, old and young, also continue to show the commercial bias of their creators, in what they criticize and in what they propose. But the new generation which has been coming on during the present century are not similarly true to that tradition of commercial engineering that makes the technological man an awestruck lieutenant of the captain of finance.

By training, and perhaps also by native bent, the technologists find it easy and convincing to size up men and things in terms of tangible performance, without commercial afterthought, except so far as their apprenticeship to the captains of finance may have made commercial afterthought a second nature to them. Many of the younger generations are beginning to understand that engineering begins and ends in the domain of tangible performance, and that commercial expediency is another matter. Indeed, they are beginning to understand that commercial expediency has nothing better to contribute to the engineer's work than so much lag, leak, and friction. The four years' experience of the war has also been highly instructive on that head. So they are beginning to draw together on a common ground of understanding, as men who are concerned with the ways and means of tangible performance in the way of productive industry, according to the state of the industrial arts as they know them at their best; and there is a growing conviction among them that they together constitute the sufficient and indispensable general staff of the mechanical industries, on whose unhindered team work depends the due working of the industrial system and therefore also the material welfare of the civilized peoples. So also, to these men who are trained in the stubborn logic of technology, nothing is quite real that cannot be stated in terms of tangible performance; and they are accordingly coming to understand that the whole fabric of credit and corporation finance is a tissue of make-believe.

Credit obligations and financial transactions rest on certain principles of legal formality which have been handed down from the eighteenth century, and which therefore antedate the mechanical industry and carry no secure conviction to men trained in the logic of that industry. Within this technological system of tangible performance corporation finance and all its works and gestures are completely idle; it all comes into the working scheme of the engineers only as a gratuitous intrusion which could be barred out without deranging the work at any point, provided only that men made up their mind to that effect—that is to say, provided the make-believe of absentee ownership were discontinued. Its only obvious effect on the work which the engineers have to take care of is waste of materials and retardation of the work. So the next question which the engineers are due to ask regarding this time-worn fabric of ownership, finance, sabotage, credit, and unearned income is likely to be: Why cumbers it the ground? And they are likely to find the scriptural answer ready to their hand.

It would be hazardous to surmise how, how soon, on what provocation, and with what effect the guild of engineers are due to realize that they constitute a guild, and that the material fortunes of the civilized peoples already lie loose in their hands. But it is already sufficiently plain that the industrial conditions and the drift of conviction among the engineers are drawing together to some such end.

Hitherto it has been usual to count on the interested negotiations continually carried on and never concluded between capital and labour, between the agents of the investors and the body of workmen, to bring about whatever readjustments are to be looked for in the control of productive industry and in the distribution and use of its product. These negotiations have necessarily been, and continue to be, in the nature of business transactions, bargaining for a price, since both parties to the negotiation continue to stand on the consecrated ground of ownership, free bargain, and self-help; such as the commercial wisdom of the eighteenth century saw, approved, and certified it all, in the time before the coming of this perplexing industrial system. In the course of these endless negotiations between the owners and their workmen there has been some loose and provisional syndication of claims and forces on both sides; so that each of these two recognized parties to the industrial controversy has come to make up a loose-knit vested interest, and each speaks for its own special claims as a party in interest. Each is contending for some special gain for itself and trying to drive a profitable bargain for itself, and hitherto no disinterested spokesman for the community at large or for the industrial system as a going concern has seriously cut into this controversy between these contending vested interests. The outcome has been businesslike concession and compromise, in the nature of bargain and sale. It is true, during the war, and for the conduct of the war, there were some half-concerted measures taken by the Administration in the interest of the nation at large, as a belligerent; but it has always been tacitly agreed that these were extraordinary war measures, not to be countenanced in time of peace. In time of peace the accepted rule is still business-as-usual; that is to say, investors and workmen wrangling together on a footing of business-as-usual.

These negotiations have necessarily been inconclusive. So long as ownership of resources and industrial plants is allowed, or so long as it is allowed any degree of control or consideration in the conduct of industry, nothing more substantial can come of any readjustment than a concessive mitigation of the owners' interference with production. There is accordingly nothing subversive in these bouts of bargaining between the federated workmen and the syndicated owners. It is a game of chance and skill played between two contending vested interests for private gain, in which the industrial system as a going concern enters only as a victim of interested interference. Yet the material welfare of the community, and not least of the workmen, turns on the due working of this industrial system, without interference. Concessive mitigation of the right to interfere with production, on the part of either one of these vested interests, can evidently come to nothing more substantial than a concessive mitigation.

But owing to the peculiar technological character of this industrial system, with its specialized, standardized mechanical, and highly technical interlocking processes of production, there has gradually come into being this corps of technological production specialists, into whose keeping the due functioning of the industrial system has now drifted by force of circumstance. They are, by force of circumstance, the keepers of the community's material welfare; although they have hitherto been acting, in effect, as keepers and providers of free income for the kept classes. They are thrown into the position of responsible directors of the industrial system, and by the same move they are in a position to become arbiters of the community's material welfare. They are becoming class-conscious, and they are no longer driven by a commercial interest, in any such degree as will make them a vested interest in that commercial sense in which the syndicated owners and the federated workmen are vested interests. They are, at the same time, numerically and by habitual outlook, no such heterogeneous and unwieldy body as the federated workmen, whose numbers and scattering interest has left all their endeavours substantially nugatory. In short, the engineers are in a position to make the next move.

By comparison with the population at large, including the financial powers and the kept classes, the technological specialists which come in question here are a very inconsiderable number; yet this small number is indispensable to the continued working of the productive industries. So slight are their numbers, and so sharply defined and homogeneous is their class, that a sufficiently compact and inclusive organization of their forces should arrange itself almost as a matter of course, so soon as any appreciable proportion of them shall be moved by any common purpose. And the common purpose is not far to seek, in the all-pervading industrial confusion, obstruction, waste, and retardation which business-as-usual continually throws in their face. At the same time they are the leaders of the industrial personnel, the workmen, of the officers of the line and the rank and file; and these are coming into a frame of mind to follow their leaders in any adventure that holds a promise of advancing the common good.

To these men, soberly trained in a spirit of tangible performance and endowed with something more than an even share of the sense of workmanship, and endowed also with the common heritage of partiality for the rule of Live and Let Live, the disallowance of an outworn and obstructive right of absentee ownership is not likely to seem a shocking infraction of the sacred realities. That customary right of ownership by virtue of which the vested interests continue to control the industrial system for the benefit of the kept classes belongs to an older order of things than the mechanical industry. It has come out of a past that was made up of small things and traditional make-believe. For all the purposes of that scheme of tangible performance that goes to make up the technologist's world; it is without form and void. So that, given time for due irritation, it should by no means come as a surprise if the guild of engineers are provoked to put their heads together and, quite out of hand, disallow that large absentee ownership that goes to make the vested interests and to unmake the industrial system. And there stand behind them the massed and rough-handed legions of the industrial rank and file, ill at ease and looking for new things. The older commercialized generation among them would, of course, ask themselves: Why should we worry? What do we stand to gain? But the younger generation, not so hard-bitten by commercial experience, will be quite as likely to ask themselves: What do we stand to lose? And there is the patent fact that such a thing as a general strike of the technological specialists in industry need involve no more than a minute fraction of one per cent of the population; yet it would swiftly bring a collapse of the old order and sweep the time-worn fabric of finance and absentee sabotage into the discard for good and all.

~~~~~~

4. *Full Employment in a Free Society* *

WILLIAM BEVERIDGE

~~~~~~

THE MEANING OF FULL EMPLOYMENT

What is meant by "full employment," and what is not meant by it? Full employment does not mean literally no unemployment; that is to say, it does not mean that every man and woman in the country who is fit and free for work is employed productively on every day of his or her working life. In every country with a variable climate there will be seasons when particular forms of work are impossible or difficult. In every progressive society there will be changes in the demand for labour, qualitatively if not

* From William Beveridge, *Full Employment in a Free Society* (W. W. Norton & Company, 1945). By permission.

quantitatively; that is to say, there will be periods during which particular individuals can no longer be advantageously employed in their former occupations and may be unemployed till they find and fit themselves for fresh occupations. Some frictional unemployment there will be in a progressive society however high the demand for labour. Full employment means that unemployment is reduced to short intervals of standing by, with the certainty that very soon one will be wanted in one's old job again or will be wanted in a new job that is within one's powers.

Full employment is sometimes defined as "a state of affairs in which the number of unfilled vacancies is not appreciably below the number of unemployed persons, so that unemployment at any time is due to the normal lag between a person losing one job and finding another." [1] Full employment in this Report means more than that in two ways. It means having always more vacant jobs than unemployed men, not slightly fewer jobs. It means that the jobs are at fair wages, of such a kind, and so located that the unemployed men can reasonably be expected to take them; it means, by consequence, that the normal lag between losing one job and finding another will be very short.

The proposition that there should always be more vacant jobs than unemployed men means that the labour market should always be a seller's market rather than a buyer's market. For this, on the view of society underlying this Report—that society exists for the individual—there is a decisive reason of principle. The reason is that difficulty in selling labour has consequences of a different order of harmfulness from those associated with difficulty in buying labour. A person who has difficulty in buying the labour that he wants suffers inconvenience or reduction of profits. A person who cannot sell his labour is in effect told that he is of no use. The first difficulty causes annoyance or loss. The other is a personal catastrophe. This difference remains even if an adequate income is provided, by insurance or otherwise, during unemployment; idleness even on an income corrupts; the feeling of not being wanted demoralizes. The difference remains even if most people are unemployed only for relatively short periods. As long as there is any long-term unemployment not obviously due to personal deficiency, anybody who loses his job fears that he may be one of the unlucky ones who will not get another job quickly. The short-term unemployed do not know that they are short-term unemployed till their unemployment is over.

The human difference between failing to buy and failing to sell labour is the decisive reason for aiming to make the labour market a seller's rather than a buyer's market. There are other reasons, only slightly less important.

---

[1] This definition is taken from the Nuffield College Statement on *Employment Policy and Organization of Industry after the War.* The Statement adds that full employment in this sense "cannot be completely attained so long as there exist structural maladjustments needing to be put right."

One reason is that only if there is work for all is it fair to expect work-people, individually and collectively in trade unions, to co-operate in making the most of all productive resources, including labour, and to forgo restrictionist practices. Another reason, related to this, is that the character and duration of individual unemployment caused by structural and technical change in industry will depend on the strength of the demand for labour in the new forms required after the change. The greater the pace of the economic machine, the more rapidly will structural unemployment disappear, the less resistance of every kind will there be to progress. Yet another reason is the stimulus to technical advance that is given by shortage of labour. Where men are few, machines are used to save men for what men alone can do. Where labour is cheap it is often wasted in brainless, unassisted toil. The new lands empty of men are the homes of invention and business adventure in peace. Stimulus to labour saving of all kinds is one of the by-products of full employment in war.

The full employment that is the aim of this Report means more vacant jobs than unemployed men. It means something else as well. If there were 2 million chronically unemployed men in Britain and 2¼ million vacant jobs which they could not or would not fill, there would be more vacant jobs than unemployed men, but to call this state of affairs "full employment" would be mockery. It is not enough to say that there must be more vacant jobs than idle men—more or about as many. It is also necessary to be sure that the number unemployed, or rather the duration of unemployment in the individual case, is not excessive. Full employment, in any real sense, means that unemployment in the individual case need not last for a length of time exceeding that which can be covered by unemployment insurance without risk of demoralization. Those who lose jobs must be able to find new jobs at fair wages within their capacity, without delay. This means that the demand for labour and the supply of labour are related qualitatively as well as quantitatively. The demand must be adjusted to the kind of men available or the men must be capable of adjusting themselves to the demand. In the light of the facts of unemployment, it is clear that the qualitative and local adjustment of demand for labour and supply of labour has to be approached from both ends, that of demand and that of supply. The demands must not only be sufficient in total but must be directed with regard to the quality and the location of the labour that is available. The labour supply must be capable of following the changes of demand that are inseparable from technical advance.

THE PURPOSE OF EMPLOYMENT

Idleness is not the same as Want, but a separate evil, which men do not escape by having an income. They must also have the chance of rendering useful service and of feeling that they are doing so. This means that employment is not wanted for the sake of employment, irrespective of what it produces. The material end of all human activity is consumption. Employment is wanted as a means to more consumption or more leisure, as a means to a higher standard of life. Employment which is merely time-wasting, equivalent to digging holes and filling them again, or merely destructive, like war and preparing for war, will not serve that purpose. Nor will it be felt worth while. It must be productive and progressive. The proposals of this Report are designed to preserve all the essential springs of material progress in the community, to leave to special efforts its rewards, to leave scope for change, invention, competition and initiative.

In so far as room is left for change and for freedom of movement from job to job, room is left for some unemployment. The aim of this Report is expressed in numerical terms as a reduction of unemployment to not more than 3 per cent, as compared with the 10 to 22 per cent experienced in Britain between the wars. But though the Report assumes the continuance of some unemployment and suggests a figure of 3 per cent, it is the essence of the proposals made in the Report that this 3 per cent should be unemployed only because there is industrial friction, and not because there are no vacant jobs. For men to have value and a sense of value there must always be useful things waiting to be done, with money to pay for doing them. Jobs, rather than men, should wait.

PRESERVATION OF ESSENTIAL LIBERTIES

The labour market in the past has invariably, or all but invariably, been a buyer's market rather than a seller's market, with more unemployed men —generally many more unemployed men—than unfilled jobs. To reverse this and make the labour market always a seller's rather than a buyer's market, to remove not only unemployment but the fear of unemployment, would affect the working of many existing institutions. It would change and is meant to change fundamentally the conditions of living and working in Britain, to make Britain again a land of opportunity for all. There are some things in Britain which neither full employment nor the means of achieving it should be allowed to change.

The Report, as its title indicates, is not concerned simply with the problem of full employment. It is concerned with the necessity, possibility and methods of achieving full employment in a free society, that is to say, subject to the proviso that all essential citizen liberties are preserved. The precise effect of the proviso depends on the list of essential citizen liberties. For the purpose of this Report they are taken as freedom of worship, speech, writing, study and teaching; freedom of assembly and of association for political and other purposes, including the bringing about of a peaceful change of the governing authority; freedom in choice of occupation; and freedom in the management of a personal income. The proviso excludes the totalitarian solution of full employment in a society completely planned and regimented by an irremovable dictator. It makes the problem of full employment more complex in many ways, of which four call for special notice.

First, in a free society the governing authority is liable to be changed at short intervals by peaceful methods of political organization and voting. There must be reasonable continuity of economic policy in spite of such changes of government. The machinery of government, while responsive to general changes of opinion, must be resistant to "lobbies"—that is to say, organized sectional pressures.

Second, freedom of association for industrial purposes raises the issue of wage determination. Under conditions of full employment, can a rising spiral of wages and prices be prevented if collective bargaining, with the right to strike, remains absolutely free? Can the right to strike be limited generally in a free society in peace-time?

Third, freedom in choice of occupations makes it harder to ensure that all men at all times are occupied productively. It makes it impossible to retain men forcibly in particular work or to direct them to it with the threat of imprisonment if they refuse to go. One assumption underlying this Report is that neither the Essential Work Order nor the powers of industrial direction which have been found necessary in war should be continued when the war is over. In Britain at peace the supply of labour cannot be adjusted by decree to the demand for labour; it can only be guided by economic motives. From another angle, freedom in choice of occupation raises also the issue of industrial discipline. Under conditions of full employment, if men are free to move from one employment to another and do not fear dismissal, may not some of them at least become so irregular and undisciplined in their behaviour, as to lower appreciably the efficiency of industry?

Fourth, freedom in the management of a personal income complicates the problem of full employment from another side. If men cannot be forced to buy just what has been produced, this means that the demands for labour and its products cannot be fitted forcibly to the supply. There may be continual changes in the kinds of things on which consumers want to spend their money, that is to say, in the quality of consumers' outlay. There may be changes also in its quantity. For freedom in the management of a personal income includes freedom to decide between spending now and saving so as to have the power of spending later. A totalitarian regime, even if it used money and price and wage differentials to stimulate and guide individual activity, might abolish freedom of saving. It might retain from the national income of each year that portion which it needed for investment, i.e. for the sustenance of persons engaged in making instruments and materials of further production, and might issue to consumers money which, like ration coupons, could not be saved for spending later. In a free society individuals must be allowed to plan their spending over their lives as a whole.

None of these freedoms can be exercised irresponsibly. Perpetual instability of economic or social policy would make full employment and any other social reforms futile or impossible. Bargaining for wages must be responsible, looking not to the snatching of short sectional advantages, but to the permanent good of the community. Choice of occupation means freedom in choosing between occupations which are available; it is not possible for an individual to choose to be an Archbishop of Canterbury, if that post is already filled by another. Work means doing what is wanted, not doing just what pleases one. All liberties carry their responsibilities. This does not mean that the liberties themselves must be surrendered. They must be retained.

In all the respects named, and possibly in some others, the problem of maintaining full employment is more complicated in a free society than it would be under a totalitarian regime. From one complication of some historic importance the problem, as posed here, is free. The list of essential liberties given above does not include liberty of a private citizen to own means of production and to employ other citizens in operating them at a wage. Whether private ownership of means of production to be operated by others is a good economic device or not, it must be judged as a device. It is not an essential citizen liberty in Britain, because it is not and never has been enjoyed by more than a very small proportion of the British people. It cannot even be suggested that any considerable proportion of the people have any lively hope of gaining such ownership later.

On the view taken in this Report, full employment is in fact attainable while leaving the conduct of industry in the main to private enterprise, and the proposals made in the Report are based on this view. But if, contrary to this view, it should be shown by experience or by argument that abolition of private property in the means of production was necessary for full employment, this abolition would have to be undertaken.

THE STATE AND THE CITIZEN

Full employment cannot be won and held without a great extension of the responsibilities and powers of the State exercised through organs of the central Government. No power less than that of the State can ensure adequate total outlay at all times, or can control, in the general interest, the location of industry and the use of land. To ask for full employment while objecting to these extensions of State activity is to will the end and refuse the means. It is like shouting for victory in total war while rejecting compulsory service and rationing. In this Report, the new functions and powers of the State are emphasized because they are essential. This does not mean that the end can be reached through such powers alone. The underlying principle of the Report is to propose for the State only those things which the State alone can do or which it can do better than any local authority or than private citizens either singly or in association, and to leave to these other agencies that which if they will, they can do as well as or better than the State. The Policy for Full Employment is a policy to be carried through by democratic action, of public authorities, central and local, responsible ultimately to the voters, and of voluntary associations and private citizens consciously co-operating for a common purpose which they understand and approve. The proposals in this Report preserve absolutely all the essential liberties which are more precious than full employment itself. They respect and are designed to preserve many other liberties and institutions which, though not equally essential, are deeply rooted in Britain.

The proposals imply, for instance, no weakening of local Government, no supersession of local authorities in their present field. The State must do some new things and exercise some controls which are not now exercised by anyone. It will set up the programme of planned outlay for attack on social evils and ensure the means to meet that outlay. But a large part of the execution of the programme—in health, housing, education and other fields—and the adjusting of the programme to local conditions will be a function of local rather than of central Government.

The proposals involve, again, no general change in the control or organization of industry, either on the side of management or on that of labour. They assume an expansion of the sector of industry under direct public control, but it remains a sector. The policy outlined here is put forward as something that could work and yield full employment, even though the greater part of industry continued to be conducted by private enterprise at private risk. Undoubtedly the achieving of full employment would affect the working of many industrial institutions and raise many issues; making the labour market a seller's in place of a buyer's market is a revolution which gives a new turn to every problem. Some of the most important issues, such as industrial discipline, determination of wages, determination of prices, treatment of monopolies and price associations, are discussed in Part V among the internal implications of full employment. The general conclusion is that the degree of liberty in such matters which can be left to agencies independent of the State, without imperilling the policy of full employment, depends on the responsibility and public spirit with which those liberties are exercised. There is no reason to doubt that that responsibility and public spirit will be forthcoming.

On the general issue of public ownership as against private enterprise in industry, the provisional conclusion reached is that the necessity of socialism, in the sense of nationalization of the means of production, distribution and exchange, in order to secure full employment, has not yet been demonstrated. This implies no judgment on the general issue between socialism and capitalism, which remains for debate on other grounds. It does not mean that the problem of full employment and the problem of the control of industry are in no way connected; they are connected in many ways. It means only a judgment that it would be possible to obtain full productive employment under conditions of private enterprise. Whether it would be easier or more difficult to obtain this under conditions of national enterprise and whether there are other reasons for socialism, it is not necessary here to decide. The problem of maintaining demand on the productive resources of the country so that they are employed productively in meeting human needs arises whether industry itself is controlled by profit-seeking individuals or by public authorities. It is also to a large extent the same problem in both cases. The policy outlined in this Report is suggested as something that could and should be accepted by people who differ profoundly as to the ultimate control of industry or as to the nature of social justice.

FULL EMPLOYMENT AND PRIVATE ENTERPRISE

Can a policy of full employment be carried through and yield its full benefits under a system in which production is controlled in the main by private enterprise? The policy, as it has been set out here, is primarily one of socializing demand rather than production. It may be found convenient, as a subsidiary measure, to transfer particular industries from private to public ownership, in order to increase the power of the State directly to stabilize demand in a specified sector and in order to bring monopolies under assured control. It will certainly be necessary for the State, by inspection and supervision, to protect the community against risk of exploitation by monopolies and trade associations, in all industries. And it will be necessary for the State, in planning its own outlay, to have full continuous information as to the outlay plans of all large undertakings and to have some power of modifying those plans. But all this is far short of the nationalization of production generally. In particular it leaves the small, independent enterprise, in factory or shop or farm, unaffected. The "little man" can respond to demand under full employment, as under other conditions. So long as he remains little, he remains subject to competition and the interests of consumers need no further official safeguards.

The policy set out here is one which might be adopted by a community which held firmly to private enterprise, and accepted the principle laid down by an American economist: "Private industry can and will do the job of production. It is the responsibility of the Government to do its part to ensure a constant demand." [1] Full employment is achieved in war by State control of demand without socialization of production. There is every reason for hoping that full employment could be secured in peace by the policy outlined here, while leaving the major part of industry to private enterprise. Apart from the problems of international trade, the only significant doubt

[1] Professor Alvin Hansen, in *Post War Economic Problems*, edited by Seymour Harris, p. 14.

that arises on this is as to the possibility under such conditions of bringing about a sufficient stability of private investment, and preventing its cyclical fluctuation. It is reasonable to let that doubt be resolved by experience.

It can be argued, nevertheless, that under such conditions a policy of full employment, even if it gave full employment, would fail to yield its full benefits and might lead to dangerous consequences. It can be argued that all that is proposed here is insufficient, without the socialization of production in all its more important forms. This position may be supported by a variety of arguments. In the first place, as has been pointed out above, the smooth working of a full employment policy involves the co-operation of work-people, in enforcing industrial discipline on the unruly, in securing maximum efficiency and removal of restrictions on output, in refraining from pressing unreasonable claims that might set up a vicious spiral of wages and prices. Can that co-operation, it is asked, be secured under conditions of enterprise conducted for private profit? It is argued, in the second place, that a State policy of full employment will always be liable to sabotage by capitalists desiring to make difficulties for the State. It is argued, in the third place, that substitution of national for private ownership of the means of production is necessary to prevent the piling up of wealth which may be used to manipulate the political machine. It is argued finally, that full employment will not by itself bring about the more equal distribution of income which is essential to social justice.

These arguments raise large issues, economic, political and moral, which fall to a large extent outside the scope of this Report. The importance of these issues is obvious. They are not prejudged in what is written here. The proposals of this Report are designed for one essential practical purpose—to bring to an end the mass unemployment and the fear of unemployment which, next to war, have been the greatest evils of modern times. The proposals take us round the next corner ahead—a corner which must be turned, if we desire to preserve free institutions. The problems that lie beyond that corner will become clearer when that corner has been passed; they can, if we so desire, be left to be dealt with when they are reached.

The basic proposals of this Report are neither socialism nor an alternative to socialism; they are required and will work under capitalism and under socialism alike, and whether the sector of industry conducted by private enterprise is large or is small. A conscious control of the economic system at the highest level—a new type of budget which takes man-power as its datum—adequate sustained demand directed for the products of industry—organization of the labour market—these are required in any modern society. These things the State must provide in any case, if the citizens want full employment. What else the State may be called on to do has to be determined on other grounds, or can at need be decided later. From the point of view of full employment, the decision depends largely on how private citizens use their liberties. If trade unions under full employment press wage claims unreasonably, maintenance of a stable price level will become impossible; wage determination will perforce become a function of the State. If the private owners of business undertakings under full employment set out to exploit consumers by organizing monopolies and price rings, or abuse their economic power for political purposes, or fail, with all the help of the State and in an expanding economy, to stabilize the process of investment, the private owners cannot for long be left in their ownership. If the people of Britain generally under full employment become undisciplined in industry, that will show either that they are not sufficiently civilized to be led by anything but fear of unemployment and are unworthy of freedom, or that the control of industry must be changed. All liberties have their responsibilities. The greater the sense of citizen responsibility, the greater can be the measure of liberty and the scope that is left for agencies independent of the State.

UNEMPLOYMENT AND THE INDIVIDUAL

Statistics of unemployment mean rows of men and women, not of figures only. The three million or so [1] unemployed of 1932 means three million lives being wasted in idleness, growing despair and numbing indifference. Behind these three million individuals seeking an outlet for their energies and not finding it, are their wives and families making hopeless shift with want, losing their birth-right of healthy development, wondering whether they should have been born. Beyond the men and women actually unemployed at any moment, are the millions more in work at that moment but never knowing how long that work or any work for them may last. Unemployment in the ten years before this war meant unused resources in Britain to the extent of at least £500,000,000 per year. That was the additional wealth we might have had if we had used instead of wasting our powers. But the loss of material wealth is the least of the evils of unemployment, insignificant by comparison to the other evils. Even with that loss, Britain was still one of the richest countries of the world. If that unemployment could have been divided evenly over the whole people as leisure, we should have been as rich and altogether happier; we should have had a standard of living with which few countries could compare. The greatest evil of unemployment is not the loss of additional material wealth which we might have with full employment. There are two greater evils: first, that unemployment makes men seem useless, not wanted, without a country; second, that unemployment makes men live in fear and that from fear springs hate.

So long as chronic mass unemployment seems possible, each man appears

[1] The highest number registered as unemployed was 2,979,425 in January, 1933, but 1932 in general and particularly in its second half had higher figures than 1933. No doubt even in 1932 there was some unemployment which escaped registration.

as the enemy of his fellows in a scramble for jobs. So long as there is a scramble for jobs it is idle to deplore the inevitable growth of jealous restrictions, of demarcations, of organized or voluntary limitations of output, of resistance to technical advance. By this scramble are fostered many still uglier growths—hatred of foreigners, hatred of Jews, enmity between the sexes. Failure to use our productive powers is the source of an interminable succession of evils. When that failure has been overcome, the way will be open to progress in unity without fear.

The necessity of preventing the return of mass unemployment is a recurrent theme in nearly all that has been written on reconstruction problems in Britain after the war, from whatever angle it is written. "Unemployment such as darkened the world between the two wars, must not recur." [1] "There must be no return to the disastrous waste of man-power which characterized the period between the wars." [2] This is the issue which in the years after the war, more than any other, will make or break the reputation of any minister of any government. Yet, as Sir John Anderson remarked exactly a year ago when discussing Assumption C of the Beveridge Report, "There is no question whether we can achieve full employment; we must achieve it. It is the central factor which will undermine the pattern of national life after the war, including, perhaps, the fate of democratic institutions." [3] The same thoughts find utterance in America: "Never again will doles and subsistence levels be tolerated." [4] "The liberty of a democracy is not safe if its business system does not provide employment and produce and distribute goods in such a way as to sustain an acceptable standard of living." [5]

The necessity of preventing after this war a return to the mass unemployment between the two wars is formally admitted by all. The possibility of doing so, if we are prepared to will the means as well as the end, is not open to reasonable doubt. Depressions of trade are not like earthquakes or cyclones; they are man-made. In the course of relieving unemployment, all industrial countries, but particularly Britain, have acquired much knowledge as to its causes. Though there remain some unsolved problems, the conditions without which mass unemployment cannot be prevented are known and the main lines for remedial action are clear. Finally, the experience of the two wars has shown that it is possible to have a human

[1] *Work: The Future of British Industry* (being a Report by the Conservative Sub-Committee on Industry), para. 3.

[2] *Nuffield College Memorandum on Employment Policy and Organization of Industry after the War*, para. 4.

[3] *The Times* (Editorial), 16th February, 1944.

[4] From a leaflet by the Committee for Economic Development—an organization financed by business firms to assist and encourage industry and commerce in the United States to plan for maximum employment after the war.

[5] President Roosevelt in Message to Congress, 29th April, 1938.

society in which every man's effort is wanted and none need stand idle and unpaid.

The doubt is not as to the possibility of achieving full employment but as to the possibility of achieving it without the surrender of other things that are even more precious. Some things which are more precious than full employment, that is to say, some of the essential British liberties, are surrendered in war. But it can be shown that this surrender is required by the special nature of the war objective, and not by the full employment which is incidental to war. This surrender of essential liberties would not be required for full employment in peace and should be refused. The Policy for Full Employment set out in this Report preserves all the essential British liberties; it rejects rationing, which forbids the free spending of personal income; it rejects direction of men and women to compulsory tasks; it rejects prohibition of strikes and lock-outs. The policy preserves also other liberties which, if less essential, are deeply rooted in Britain, including collective bargaining to determine wages, and private enterprise in a large sector of industry; it preserves these lesser liberties, subject to the degree of responsibility with which they are exercised. The policy preserves possibility of change, the springs of progress and the way to rising standards of life. It is not open to the criticism that it would destroy essential liberties or lead to stagnation. Is it open to any other serious objection? It will be convenient to name some of the possible objections and give brief answers.

There are some who will say that full employment, combined with unemployment insurance, will remove the incentive of effort which depends on fear of starvation. The answer is that for civilized human beings ambition and desire for service are adequate incentives. It may be that cattle must be driven by fear. Men can and should be led by hope. The policy set out in this Report is not one of stagnation or forced equality. It does not give security for life in a particular job; it gives only the opportunity of exercising one's gifts and energies in generous rather than in ungenerous rivalry with one's fellows.

There are some who will say that the great development of State activity involved in the policy proposed here will destroy the "little man," that is to say the small, independent business. The answer is that the policy does nothing of the sort, unless risk of bankruptcy in trade depressions is essential to the existence and happiness of the "little man." The policy is simply one of setting up sufficient demand. It involves, as an implication, control of monopolies to prevent exploitation of the demand and supervision of large concerns in order to plan investment. It does not touch the "little man" at all; he can work to meet the demand like any other. He will find more scope than before, once strong demand has eliminated the slumps in which so many small businesses in the past have come to grief.

There are some who will object to the proposals of this Report on the ground that they involve an extension of the activities of Government and a consequent increase in the number of civil servants. That the proposals do involve action by Government in fields which in the past have been left wholly to private enterprise is true; the justification for this lies in the failures of the past. In certain industries men may find themselves working directly for the community in place of being the employees of a monster business corporation. In all industries, the managers of large undertakings may find themselves both regulated and assisted in keeping what they do—in investment, in the location of industry, in price policy—in accord with national interest. But there is nothing in all the proposals of this Report to involve greater interference in the private lives of the mass of the people. On the contrary, not only will all the war-time restrictions on consumption and choice of work vanish with war, but many of the previous interferences with private lives will be ended. There will be no unemployment assistance subject to a means test; the 8,000 officials of the Unemployment Assistance Board in 1938 will become unnecessary for that work. So, too, a substantial proportion of the 28,000 peace-time officials of the Ministry of Labour, that is to say, those engaged in paying or calculating unemployment benefit, will find that occupation gone, though it may be hoped that most of these will render still better service in preventing unemployment by organizing the labour market. A full employment policy involves more public control over a limited class of business undertakers, and less control over the private lives of the mass of the people. It may in the end mean fewer bureaucrats, not more.

There may be some who will say that in the emphasis laid in this Report on the need for organizing the labour market the Report treats labour as a commodity, in conflict with the opening declaration of the Charter adopted by the International Labour Conference in Philadelphia in May, 1944. There is no conflict. The Philadelphia declaration that labour is not a commodity cannot mean that men should not be free to sell their labour as men sell commodities. In a free community the right to sell or to refrain from selling one's labour by hand or brain and to bargain as to the terms on which it should be used is essential. This makes important the question of how those who desire to sell their labour and those who, whether for private profit or as representatives of a public authority, desire to buy the labour, shall be brought together. In concerning itself with these matters, the Report does not treat men themselves as a commodity; it treats them, as the Philadelphia declaration demands, as an end and not as a means; it proposes a fundamental difference to be established between the position of those who desire to sell their labour and the position of all other sellers. Only for labour should the market always be a seller's market. It should not be that always for any particular commodity.

There are some who will say that the policy of this Report subordinates the individual to the State. The answer is that this criticism directly reverses the truth. If the State is regarded as more important than the individual, it may be reasonable to sacrifice the individual in mass unemployment to the progress and prosperity of his more fortunate fellows, as he is sacrificed in war by the dictators for their power and dominion or that of the race. If, on the other hand, the State is regarded as existing for the individual, a State which fails, in respect of many millions of individuals, to ensure them any opportunity of service and earning according to their powers or the possibility of a life free from the indignities and inquisitions of relief, is a State which has failed in a primary duty. Acceptance by the State of responsibility for full employment is the final necessary demonstration that the State exists for the citizens—for all the citizens—and not for itself or for a privileged class.

There are some who will say that the policy of this Report is a mere palliative which will block the way to further reforms like socialism or communism. The answer is that the policy does not block the way to these or other reforms, if they are good in themselves. It is a policy directed against one particular evil and includes steps which must be taken under any economic system which preserves essential liberties, in order to deal with that evil. The case for socialization of the means of production must be argued in the main on other grounds, of efficiency of production or of social justice. The Policy for Full Employment is in essence that the State takes responsibility for seeing that while any human needs are unsatisfied, they are converted into effective demand. This leaves open to argument on its merits the question whether production to meet that effective demand should be undertaken under conditions of private enterprise guided by profit, or of social enterprise working directly for use, or of a combination of these methods.

There are some who will say that the introduction of this or any other policy for Britain must wait for international agreement. Undoubtedly any economic policy for Britain must take account of the world of which Britain is part. It should be inspired by recognition of community of economic interest between different nations. It must be framed in alternatives to suit the alternative policies that may be adopted by other nations; it must include means of off-setting, so far as possible, fluctuations of overseas demand. But Britain must have her own policy; she will do better for the world and herself by leading, rather than by waiting and following. The subordination of British policy to supposed international exigencies has been one of the major mistakes of the period between the wars, the period of disastrous appeasement, political and economic. Britain is in the world and cannot escape from the world or her responsibilities for world order and world prosperity, but she cannot meet those responsibilities unless she puts her own house in order.

5. Concentration of Economic Power *

JOSEPH C. O'MAHONEY

The modern industrial system produced geographical concentration of productive enterprise before it produced the concentration of economic power and wealth which this committee has been studying. As all observers know, when manufacturing was moved from the home to the factory a new era began. It was a natural and in most aspects a wholly desirable development. It was the very development which has provided the present generation with all the marvelous tools which make available the amazing conveniences and luxuries in which we take so much pride, but it almost completely robbed commerce of its local aspect and made it a national phenomenon with wholly national effects and national significance. Geographical boundaries have lost most of their importance so far as commerce is concerned.

The inevitable result has been the expansion of national law. Throughout the long periods during which this change has been taking place, Congress was reluctant to impose national regulations in the place of local regulations and it made changes but slowly. This generation needs no instruction to understand that commerce among the States is the most important element of our modern economic activity, but the Congress which confronted this problem for the first time more than 50 years ago thought of interstate commerce in terms of railroad transportation only and when it set up the Interstate Commerce Commission it had no thought of "interfering with private enterprise," as the phrase goes, except with respect to the railroads. That Commission was set up to regulate the railroads only because the railroad industry had grown to such an extent and had expanded so far beyond the powers of the States to regulate in the public interest that Congress had no other recourse. From that day to this there has been a steady growth of the Government establishment at Washington, but let no one make the

* From Senator Joseph C. O'Mahoney, "The Preservation of Economic Freedom," *Final Statement, Temporary National Economic Committee* (77th Cong., 1st Sess., *Sen. Doc.* No. 39, 1941).

mistake of assuming that this growth has taken place because "politicians" have wanted to take business over. It has grown solely because commerce must be regulated by Government in the public interest and because in this country there is no agency except the Federal Government which is capable of such regulation. The duty of regulating national commerce was imposed on Congress when the Constitution was adopted. It is a power which has been exercised throughout the history of our Government and its expansion is solely the result of the growth of business and not the result of the desire of Government to throttle private enterprise.

But private enterprise is threatened; indeed, it has been undermined to an appalling degree not by Government and not so much by business itself, for all the monopolistic practices which have so frequently been condemned, but by a general failure to comprehend the change that has taken place and a failure properly to coordinate Government and business in their relation to people. This failure, it has seemed to me, is principally due to the fact that we seem not to realize that modern business is no longer the activity of individuals, but is the activity of organizations of individuals and we have permitted these organizations to grow so large that people are actually help-less before them. We have persisted in treating these organizations as though they were clothed with natural human rights instead of having only the rights which the people, acting through their Government, see fit to bestow upon them. It will be impossible even to begin the task of adjusting Gov-ernment to business until we realize that the modern business organization has grown to such proportions that neither the people, as individuals, nor through their local governments are able to cope with it. Local business, little business, private enterprise, and local government, even the govern-ment of the States themselves, are in truth and in fact submerged by modern business organizations.

CORPORATIONS GREATER THAN STATES

Let me present here a table which compares the total assessed valuation of all the property in each of the States of the Federal Union as of 1937 with the total reported assets of the 30 "billion-dollar" corporations of 1935.

Total assessed valuation of States (1937) compared with total assets of thirty "billion-dollar" corporations (1935)

	Billion
New York	25.70
Pennsylvania	12.40
Ohio	8.80
California	7.80
Massachusetts	6.30
Michigan	6.20

Total assessed valuation of States (1937) compared with total assets of thirty "billion-dollar" corporations (1935)

	Billion
New Jersey	6.20
Illinois	5.20
Indiana	•5.10
Wisconsin	4.80
Metropolitan Life Insurance Co.	4.23
American Telephone & Telegraph Co.	3.99
Missouri	3.80
Texas	3.20
Iowa	3.20
Prudential Insurance Co.	3.12
Connecticut	2.90
Pennsylvania R. R. Co.	2.86
Kansas	2.70
Maryland	2.60
Kentucky	2.40
New York Central R. R. Co.	2.35
Chase National Bank	2.33
New York Life Insurance Co.	2.22
North Carolina	2.20
Nebraska	2.10
Minnesota	2.00
Standard Oil Co.	1.89
National City Bank of New York	1.88
Guaranty Trust Co.	1.84
Equitable Life Assurance Co.	1.82
United States Steel Corporation	1.82
District of Columbia	1.78
West Virginia	1.74
Allegheny Corporation	1.73
Southern Pacific R. R. Co.	1.67
General Motors Corporation	1.49
Tennessee	1.47
Consolidated Edison Co. of New York, Inc.	1.38
Rhode Island	1.36
Louisiana	1.34
Bank of America	1.27
Mutual Life Insurance Co. of New York	1.24
Oklahoma	1.22
Commonwealth & Southern Corporation	1.17
Great Northern Ry. Co.	1.15

Total assessed valuation of States (1937) compared with total assets of thirty "billion-dollar" corporations (1935)

	Billion
Continental Illinois National Bank & Trust Co., Ohio	1.14
Northern Pacific R. R. Co.	1.13
Associated Gas & Electric Co.	1.12
Baltimore & Ohio R. R. Co.	1.11
City Service Co.	1.11
Colorado	**1.10**
Atchison, Topeka & Santa Fe R. R. Co.	1.09
Washington	**1.08**
Northwestern Mutual Life Insurance Co.	1.07
Union Pacific R. R. Co.	1.07
Georgia	**1.06**
North American Co.	1.04
South Dakota	**1.03**
Banker's Trust Co.	1.03
Alabama	.92
Oregon	.89
Maine	.66
Florida	.60
New Hampshire	.58
Utah	.52
North Dakota	.49
Mississippi	.44
Arkansas	.43
Idaho	.38
Arizona	.36
South Carolina	.36
Montana	.33
Vermont	.32
Delaware	.31
New Mexico	.29
Wyoming	.28
Nevada	.18

SOURCE: State figures from Bureau of Foreign and Domestic Commerce; corporation figures from hearings before the Senate Judiciary Committee, U. S. Senate, 75th Cong., 3d sess., on S. 10, pt. 4, ibid., pp. 768 to 773.

It will be observed that there are only 10 sovereign States which have within their respective borders property valued at more than the assets of either the Metropolitan Life Insurance Co. or the American Telegraph & Telephone Co. Stated in another way, each of these 2 corporations is richer than any one of 38 sovereign States. At the other end of the scale there are 18 States, the taxable wealth of each of which is less than the total assets of the smallest of the 30 "billion-dollar" corporations. Of these 18 States which rank so low among the sisterhood in property value and far below the smallest of the billion-dollar giants, some have been particularly active in creating interstate corporations, large and small, to carry on this national commerce upon which the economic life of the nation depends, although none of the States has the constitutional power to regulate the activities of the artificial agencies they launch upon the sea of national commerce.

Among the great corporations listed on this chart are banks, insurance companies, and industrials. In popular discussion they are regarded as "private enterprise." But how private is such enterprise after all? The American Telegraph & Telephone Co., like Commonwealth & Southern, is a public utility and although in recent years there has been a tendency in certain circles to drop the word "public" when referring to such utilities, it is nevertheless quite clear that each of them is just as public as the thousands of municipal corporations which are likewise chartered by the several States. They are different, however, from municipal corporations in that the latter operate within the borders of the States which create them while the modern inter-state corporation operates throughout the length and breadth of the land and in the field of commerce "with foreign nations and among the States," the power to regulate which was exclusively committed by the Federal Constitution to the Congress of the United States. When one considers the number of policyholders who are the owners of mutual life-insurance companies like Metropolitan and Prudential, wholly national in their operation and effect, the number of stockholders and employees of a utility like American Telegraph & Telephone, or of an industrial like General Motors and the stockholders, employees, and natural resources of industrials like the Standard Oil of New Jersey and United States Steel it becomes immediately clear that there is no justification whatsoever for thinking of these units or of dealing with them as though they were natural persons clothed with the rights which are guaranteed to flesh-and-blood persons by the Constitution of the United States.

It also becomes clear from this comparison why during the past 50 years the local aspects of commerce have been constantly decreasing in importance and the national aspects increasing. If it be said that these 30 giants fall into an unusual category and that the corporate system as a whole should not be judged by their wealth and power, it is only necessary to point out, as was shown in the hearings of this committee, that the share of all our business which is done by corporations has been steadily increasing. It was estimated, for example, by Dr. Willard L. Thorp of the Bureau of Foreign and Domestic Commerce (pt. 1, Temporary National Economic Committee hearings, p. 96) that corporations now do from 60 to 65 percent of the total volume of business in the United States. Few of these, of course, are to be classed with the billion-dollar giants, but the fact that they do so large a proportion of the business of the country is conclusive demonstration of the all important fact that we have passed from an individual economy to a corporate economy. The position of the individual businessman in all types of American industry has been steadily growing less and less important while the position of the large corporation has been growing more and more important. The computations presented by Dr. Thorp from the Bureau of Foreign and Domestic Commerce (pt. 1, Temporary National Economic Committee, p. 96) show that communication and the manufacture and distribution of electric light, power, and gas are 100 percent corporate activities. That is to say, there is no such thing as individual private enterprise left in communication or in the utility business.

In the early days of our country mining was carried on by the pioneer and it was the prospector operating usually on a grubstake who placed the riches of the western mountains at the disposal of the people. Today, 96 percent of all mining is carried on by corporations, leaving only 4 percent for individual enterprise. In transportation, all but 11 percent of the business is carried on by corporations and in manufacturing, which produces 24 percent of the total national income, all but 8 percent is carried on by the corporate unit.

Agriculture remains today the sole industry which is still carried on for the most part by private individuals in their individual capacity. Ninety-three percent of all the agricultural business of the United States is done by individuals, only 7 percent by corporations, but the total share of agriculture in the national income amounts to only 8.9 percent. The service industry is one of which one naturally thinks as a private individual activity, yet the amazing fact is that 30 percent of this business is carried on by corporations. Thus it becomes clear that the individual has been relegated to a position of everlessening importance in the structure of our modern economy. The man has been losing out to the organization of men.

GREAT CONCENTRATION OF WEALTH

It is not surprising, therefore, to find from the cold examination of the facts that organized enterprise is obtaining an increasingly larger proportion not only of national income, but of all savings and of all wealth. It was estimated by Berle and Means in their notable volume, *The Modern Corporation and Private Property,* which though published in 1932, is still regarded as the primary authority in this field, that 78 percent of all business wealth in this country is owned by corporations. Every student of the subject paints the same picture, not only that the corporations have gained the great bulk of industrial and commercial assets and income, but that within the corporate structure itself the concentration is progressing.

It is revealed by Statistics of Income, published by the United States Treasury Department for 1937 (pt. II, pp. 9, 26-27) that 228,721 corporations, each with total assets of less than $50,000, reported less than 1½ percent of all the total assets of all reporting corporations although they constituted 55 percent of the total number. At the other end of the scale, the 394 largest corporations, although they constituted less than one-tenth of 1 percent of the total number of reporting corporations, owned almost 45 percent of all corporate assets.

So much for the assets. The picture with respect to income shows the same story of concentration. Of 477,838 corporations which submitted income-tax reports for 1937, 285,810 reported no income. Of the 192,028 corporations which had reported incomes that year, 248, or one-tenth of 1 percent, had 40 percent of the total net income that was reported by all. Each of these 248 corporations had net incomes of $5,000,000 or over. If one examines now the corporations which each reported an annual income of less than $5,000, we find that they constituted in number 65 percent of all those that reported incomes, but they received considerably less than 2 percent of the total reported income or, in other words the $5,000 income corporations, 65 percent in number, received less than 2 percent of the total income while the $5,000,000 corporations constituting one-tenth of 1 percent in number, received 40 percent of the income.

It might have been imagined that with the change from the individual to the corporate economy there would probably be a large distribution of corporate ownership among individuals. The fact, however, seems to be that this amazing concentration of the corporate ownership of wealth has been accompanied by a similar concentration of dividend distribution. The great and powerful business organizations which dominate the economic scene are owned by a numerically insignificant proportion of the total population. In the study prepared by the Securities and Exchange Commission for this committee on the Distribution of Ownership in Two Hundred Largest Non-Financial Corporations (Monograph No. 29), it is indicated that fully one-half of all corporate stock dividends are received by less than 75,000 persons of the 130,000,000 who inhabit the United States. That is to say, less than 1 percent of all American corporate stockholders are the beneficiaries of one-half of all the dividends paid in this country.

The degree of concentration is even more striking when one reviews the material assembled in Monograph No. 12 on Profits, Productive Activity and New Investment, in which it is stated that only one family out of every six pays an income tax and that of these income taxpaying families only one-quarter receive corporate dividends. In 1928, according to the Treasury Department report (Statistics of Income, 1928, pp. 11-12) 96.6 percent of all the dividends reported by taxpayers that year were received by less than one-fifth of the persons who made income-tax returns. Thus it appears that the great bulk of the wealth and income of the country is owned by corporations, that the overwhelming percentage of this is owned by comparatively few corporations, that the stock ownership of these corporations is not substantially distributed among the people of the country and, finally, that the dividends paid by these corporations go to a very small proportion of the population.

6. Cartels and National Security *

HARLEY M. KILGORE

Briefly defined, international cartels are economic arrangements among private interests of several countries for the purpose of regulating industry and trade.[1]

A study of the evidence which has been accumulated [2] discloses how the cartel system of international economic relations operated in the period

---

* From Senator Harley M. Kilgore, "Cartels and National Security," *Report from the Subcommittee on War Mobilization to the Senate Committee on Military Affairs* (77th Cong., 2d Sess., Sen. Subcomm. Rep. No. 4, 1944).

[1] This definition follows common usage and also takes into account practical developments. The word "cartel" originally meant a written agreement between conflicting interests. In economics, it was first widely used abroad, particularly in Germany, to describe an agreement or arrangement between independent firms. Applied to domestic economy, the expression is used loosely to cover arrangements as diverse under American terminology as trade associations, pools, combinations, trusts, holding companies, and monopoly agreements. International cartels have developed in a variety of situations, in a few of which national governments have directly or indirectly participated. As discussions of international cooperation for peace have intensified, there has been a tendency on the part of some people to broaden the definition of a cartel to include economic agreements or treaties between nations. In this report the term "international cartel" will be limited to arrangements which are primarily between private businesses in different countries, even though in their negotiation national governments may have participated or given their sanction. Testimony before this and other Senate committees shows that, in arrangements made between American and German firms, German firms frequently cleared international cartel commitments with their Government, particularly after Adolf Hitler came to power. In contrast, arrangements by American companies were usually kept secret, not only from the public but from the American Government. Definitely excluded from the definition are economic agreements between nations such as the "wheat agreement." In short, international cartels are economic treaties or international trade agreements made by private business concerns. The word may also be used to denote the participating group.

[2] In addition to its own body of evidence, your subcommittee has examined the extensive evidence on cartel practices gathered by other Senate investigating committees during the past 8 years, notably by the Senate Committee on Patents under the chairmanship of Mr. Homer T. Bone, of Washington, the Special Senate Committee to Investigate the National Defense Program under the chairmanship of Mr. Harry S. Truman, of Missouri, and the Temporary National Economic Committee under the chairmanship of Mr. Joseph C. O'Mahoney, of Wyoming.

between the two world wars and shows by what means our Axis enemies engaged in systematic economic warfare against the United States as a prelude to their military aggressions. These economic aspects of war and peace have received far less public notice than the political and military aspects. An understanding of them, however, is necessary to insure that the mistakes made after the last war will not be repeated, and that an effective program for world security will be realized.

The German aggressors have begun to pursue a strategy which they found successful a quarter century ago; they are already deploying their economic reserves throughout the world in preparation for a third attempt at world domination. They plan to resume the old commercial pattern which served them so well. We must insure that in the defeat of Germany the economic forces of aggression will be forever eliminated along with the military forces.

Economic aggression by the Axis Powers went hand in hand with their military preparations for the present war. Our plans for peace will succeed only if international economic collaboration by the sovereign governments goes hand in hand with political and military collaboration.

The United States must take leadership in promoting economic harmony among the nations. No plan can be effective without our active participation. Our own great industrial production cannot be isolated within our national boundaries, nor can it be sent abroad on the basis of rivalry among nations without thoroughly jeopardizing the peace.

The nations of the world, by adopting and developing the program drafted at Dumbarton Oaks, will turn their backs on the economic anarchy of the post-Versailles period. They will turn their faces toward a friendly post-war world, a post-war world of amicable international settlements and cooperation for mutual prosperity.

Through economic cooperation some nations will secure for the first time the economic benefits of industrialization. Others will make rapid recovery from the devastation of war. At the same time that we take the initiative in promoting world peace, the United States will be making provision for full use of the greatest industrial machine in the history of mankind.

If we are to have full employment after the war, it is conservatively estimated that we must produce at least one and a half times the highest pre-war industrial output. The rapidly rising productivity of our economy enables us continuously to raise our own standard of living while cooperating in the industrialization of the world. Our own internal market, already the greatest in the world, must be still further developed in order to absorb the greater part of this increase; we must raise the average standard of living by at least 50 percent. In addition to this 50-percent increase in our standard of living, we should set as a goal an export volume several times the pre-war figure to achieve an economy of full production and full employment.

In terms of traditional thinking, this would seem difficult to attain. But our traditional thinking is based on cartel economics, which is scarcity economics. The nations of the world are hungry for American products. There is almost unlimited demand. Meeting part of this demand may make the difference between profitable mass production and depression in key American industries. The sale abroad of American turbines, refrigerators, airplanes, automobiles, machine tools, may mean the difference between jobs and unemployment for American workers. Eventually, we must be prepared to buy from the world approximately as much as we sell, allowing for some lag during the immediate post-war years.

These great new business opportunities will be realized only if governmental machinery for international cooperation establishes a sound basis for developing world markets. Such machinery is essential to provide the safeguards enabling American business to make sales and investments abroad several times greater than in the past.

The subcommittee's studies particularly affirm the immediate need for adopting and furthering the International Economic and Social Council proposed by the Dumbarton Oaks Conference as part of a world security organization. This does not mean that the world security organization should intervene in the management of the domestic economy of its member nations. Its machinery, however, can be used on an international level to promote political harmony and economic development by fostering amicable commercial relations. The world organization should formulate programs for the expansion of international trade for the mutual advantage of all participating nations. Some positive steps to increase world trade are already under discussion—for example, the international monetary and credit proposals initiated at the Bretton Woods Conference.

The real cooperation of sovereign nations in the field of commerce and trade necessarily spells the end of the cartel system, which has in the past proved an insuperable barrier to international harmony. Your subcommittee believes that the outlawing of the international cartel system is a necessary first step to clear the way for a new expansionist era in foreign economic relations. On this subject President Roosevelt has written Secretary of State Hull as follows:

> The history of the use of the I. G. Farben trust by the Nazis reads like a detective story. Defeat of the Nazi armies will have to be followed by the eradication of these weapons of economic warfare. But more than elimination of the political activities of German cartels will be required. Cartel practices which restrict the free flow of goods in foreign commerce will have to be curbed. With international trade involved, this end can be achieved only through collaborative action by the United Nations.

In defining this policy, which presumably will be followed by the Executive in its international economic negotiations, the President of the United States is planning for the future security and prosperity of this country, in the free-enterprise tradition of the Sherman-Clayton antitrust laws.

The elimination of restrictions on production, high prices, and exclusive market policies from the international field will not only help to preserve the peace but will assist in refocussing domestic production on maximum output, lowest price, and highest quality. It will thus provide a sound basis for the flourishing of competitive private enterprise, not only in harmonious international trade but also in expanded domestic and foreign markets.

Since the outbreak of the war, the very concerns mentioned in this report as having participated in international cartels which Germany used for aggression have made magnificent contributions to an Allied victory. Their cartel relations forcibly disrupted, they have expanded their capacity and increased production to a point where they have overwhelmed our enemies. The war emergency has demonstrated to the Nation at large and to our industrialists in particular the extent of America's economic potential, the ingenuity of American technologists. In the post-war period, this potential can not be realized under a cartel system. New methods of conducting international trade must be devised to utilize the economic energies of our liberated American industry and to stimulate its continued growth and development.

The trend toward monopoly domination of industry in the United States, Great Britain, France, and other countries created a favorable atmosphere in which German cartel groups could conduct negotiations for the division of world markets. In the period after World War I many American firms possessed new technologies, particularly in electrical, chemical, automotive, and petroleum fields. The industrial expansion necessary to give expression to these new technologies held the prospect of expanded domestic and foreign markets, bolstered by pent-up demands for peacetime goods. Leading American firms feared, however, that competitive imports and new techniques from abroad would disturb their control. They persuaded their government to erect high tariff walls. They entered into a truce with foreign cartelists. They gave up foreign markets in exchange for protection. They sought and often attained an assured monopoly at home. In short, they compromised themselves with German cartelists.

Germany's cartel groups had the tacit consent of non-German industrialists in evading the disarmament provisions of the Treaty of Versailles. Testimony before the subcommittee leaves no doubt that violations of the treaty began almost as soon as the treaty was signed. For instance the firm of Carl Zeiss, by creating a manufacturing subsidiary in Holland, was able to evade the prohibition on the manufacture of military optical instruments, such as rangefinders and periscopes. The firm of Friedrich Krupp nullified a restriction on the manufacture of armaments by gaining control of Bofors, a Swedish armament firm. I. G. Farbenindustrie continued to produce military explosives as one of its numerous enterprises, although expressly forbidden to do so.

The greatest activity in the establishment of cartel relationships by German interests occurred from 1920 through 1930. American businessmen were induced to enter into cartel agreements by the promise of freedom from German competition. In exchange for a guaranteed domestic market, American participants accepted restrictions on their own production and sales. Such restrictions limited American productive capacity and assured German dominance in foreign markets from which American and other firms were excluded. The cartel agreements often included provisions for exclusive cross-licensing of patents and exchange of technical and sales information. The Germans thus acquired access to vital American technology and know-how instrumental in building up Germany's military strength. In return, the United States firms received a minimum of detail on German technology and know-how, and then only after German Government approval on release. These exclusive licensing terms had the effect of limiting American production capacity and the manufacture of new products. At the same time, they secured for Germany economic intelligence as to the industrial and military strength of the United States.

The rapid growth of cartels during the late 1920's and early 1930's coincided with the onset of a world-wide depression. The impact of economic crisis in Germany was severe; it led to the adoption of Nazi totalitarianism. The role which the cartels played in abetting Hitler's seizure of power has been recounted at length in testimony before Congress. Krupp, Thyssen, and other powerful figures on the German industrial scene provided the Nazis with indispensable financial and political support.

Almost immediately, as a consequence of this unholy alliance between Hitler and the cartelists, Germany's plans for economic warfare, aimed at ultimate world domination, were expanded. The German Government became a silent partner in the multitude of cartel agreements among German, American, British, French, and other concerns with which German industry had established cartel relations.

Under cover of cartel agreements, Germany penetrated the economy of other nations, including the United States. Using their cartel affiliates or subsidiaries, German industrialists built up a network which impaired the production of other nations, obtained sources of foreign exchange for Germany, gathered economic intelligence and spread Nazi propaganda.

The German industrial group has been the mainstay of the international cartel system. In their agreements with American and British companies, the German cartelists specifically provided that in the event of war cartel arrangements would be resumed when hostilities were terminated. Any efforts to retain the international cartel system will therefore help to keep in power the German militarist-industrialist clique who have already planned and launched two world wars.

We will take space here to examine a few of the most common arguments advanced in support of the cartel system. It is argued that we would be excluded from foreign markets if we did not join cartels. The opposite is true. American industry in the past has voluntarily excluded itself from foreign markets by virtue of its membership in cartels. It is argued that the good features of cartels should be saved. This argument assumes that there would be some good practices left when the restrictive aspects of cartels are removed. In truth, nothing would be left, since restriction is of the very essence of cartels. It is argued that cartel agreements would assume the character of cooperative action among nations if they were publicly registered or subjected to government scrutiny. They would not. Mere registration would not endow them with a national character. Only agreements among national governments provide the framework for genuine international cooperation.

Current proposals for the maintenance of the cartel system often seek to forestall objection by disavowing the old dangerous features of cartels and by endowing them verbally with the attributes of genuine international cooperation. Some of these proposals spell out in great detail the real advantages of international cooperation. But a careful examination shows that they envision the continuance of the old controls and relationships, so that, in effect, private monopolies would be dictating what superficially appeared to be national policy and international agreement.[1]

Any proposal which would vest in private monopolies the power to make international economic agreements must be considered the antithesis of genuine democracy and international collaboration. Such action would be an abdication of sovereignty on the part of national governments. It would permit the economy of nations to be subverted by groups who are responsible to no public control. It would advance us far along the road to economic restriction and war.

A cartel system dominated by American or British interests would eventually produce the same undesirable results as the one exploited by the Germans. It would jeopardize peace and jobs in the post-war world and soon bring us face to face with the possibility of a third even more destructive world war.

Standing athwart the achievement of international goals of world pros-

[1] A widely circulated proposal of this character is that of Sir Edgar R. Jones, who would place world trade under private monopolies and merely allow for scrutiny of private agreements by an international organization of governments.

perity and enduring peace is the international cartel system as it existed before the war and, indeed, as it still exists—underground and only partially suspended—during the war. The extensive testimony before this committee and the great mass of testimony adduced by other congressional committees, have established beyond question that the international cartel system has been subversive of political security, full production and employment, and the expansion of world trade. These effects have not been incidental to the operation of the cartel system but have arisen out of their essential character. Private restrictive economic agreements designed to maximize profits inevitably minimize political security, jobs, and world trade.

Part IV

FROM NATIONALISM TO WORLD ORDER

Nationalism: Peaceful or Aggressive?

Race: Sense and Nonsense

Conflict or Common Interest?

War: The Sovereign Assassin

The Supranational Community

Chapter XIV

NATIONALISM: PEACEFUL OR AGGRESSIVE?

NO THEORY of the relations of man and the state can be realistic,
unless it gives proper consideration to the place of the state in the
great society of the world. The anarchy which has made possible the two
bloodiest wars in history within the span of twenty-five years has confirmed
the Hobbesian description of what man's life is like when there is no established government: "solitary, poor, nasty, brutish, and short." Hobbes saw
the discrepancy between two modes of living which, though contradictory,
are accepted by men. As members of the state, men have given up the advantages of savage life for the greater advantages of organized, civilized
living through law and government. Yet the states themselves are still in the
same condition of savagery in which men were before they founded a common government, and "live in the condition of perpetual war."

Since the French Revolution at least, nationalism has been one of the
driving forces of domestic, imperial, and international politics. Complex in
its origins, it has developed along many, and often contradictory, lines. In its
name, some of the greatest acts of heroism and liberty have been committed,
but also crimes of cruelty and fanaticism. In the first half of its existence—
from the late eighteenth to the middle of the nineteenth century—nationalism was essentially inspired by humanitarian, democratic ideas; this was
the story of early French, American, Czech, Italian, Irish, and Polish nationalism. In the last eighty years, on the other hand, nationalism has tended
to ally itself with parochialism, intolerance, bigotry, persecution of minorities,
racialism, and finally, imperialism and aggression—the record of Pan-Germanism, Hungarian imperialism, Japanese militarism, and finally, Fascism.

Lord Acton was one of the few farsighted liberals of the nineteenth century who perceived the dangers of nationalism at a time when most pro-
gressive-minded people thought that nationalism was a just principle of
collective liberty and virtually the last answer to the ills of politics. In an
essay on "Nationality" (1862), Lord Acton inveighs against the current
progressive doctrine of his day, that state and nationality must be identical—
a theory which Woodrow Wilson still considered the *ne plus ultra* fifty-five
years later. Action prophetically predicted that the doctrine of the *identity of
state and nationality* would necessarily lead to *political absolutism*. Against

this doctrine, Acton propounded the conception of the "multinational state" with its diversities of all kinds—linguistic, religious, national, economic and political. "Liberty provokes diversity," Acton writes, "and diversity preserves liberty by supplying the means of organization." Acton goes so far as to claim that the coexistence of several nations under the same state is "one of the chief instruments of civilization," in addition to being the best safeguard of freedom. A profoundly religious man, Acton saw in nationalism a remnant of pagan tribalism: "Christianity rejoices at the mixture of races, as paganism identifies itself with their differences, because truth is universal, and errors various and particular. In the ancient world idolatry and nationality went together, and the same term is applied in Scripture to both." Foreseeing how nationalism would eventually destroy what it set out to defend, Acton makes the, to some, paradoxical statement that "the greatest adversary of the rights of nationality is the modern theory of nationality." States which try to neutralize, absorb, or expel nationalities that are not of the *Staatsvolk,* or ruling nationality, destroy their own vitality and lose their chief basis of self-government.

Humanitarian conceptions of nationalism are also reflected in Giuseppe Mazzini, intellectual leader of Italian unity in the nineteenth century, particularly in his "Pact of Fraternity of Young Europe" (1834). Mazzini conceived of the nation as having a mission, but not a mission of imperialistic expansion inspired by conceit and haughty arrogance, but one of fulfillment toward the common goal of a fraternally united mankind. A fervent adherent of the democratic and republican faith, Mazzini worked for a free and self-governing Italy; his ultimate aim was a republican confederation of all mankind, "governed and directed by a common Declaration of Principles and a common Pact."

Mazzini's noble ideals of nation and humanity were betrayed, in the twentieth century, by his own countrymen, but were kept alive by the first president of the republic of Czechoslovakia, Thomas Garrigue Masaryk. One of the few truly great philosophers called upon to rule a state, Masaryk proved that the Platonic vision of the philosopher-king can become true, seldom as it may be. Under the most difficult circumstances, and faced with problems of different, and hostile, nationalities (especially Hungarians and Sudeten Germans), Masaryk managed to make Czechoslovakia the only genuine democratic country in Europe east of the Rhine. Having been under Austrian rule for almost four hundred years, the Czechs under Masaryk's inspiration and leadership showed remarkable moderation and political wisdom when the roles were reversed: "Our procedure with the minorities," Masaryk told Karel Čapek (*Masaryk on Thought and Life: Conversations with Karel Čapek,* 1938), "is practically given to us by our own experience under Austria-Hungary: what we did not like to be done unto us, we shall not do unto others." Masaryk refused to accept the distorted patriotism which deduces from love of one's country the right, and duty, to hate other countries: "True love is not proved by hatred, but only by love. Mankind is a sum of nations, it is not something outside the nations, and above them." And above all, Masaryk urged to express that love by "always acting humanely."

The spirit of Masaryk lives on in Czechoslovakia, transmitted by his successor, Eduard Beneš, and his many disciples and collaborators. Hubert Ripka, a member of the Czechoslovak government and a person of broad international experience, discusses the problem of *Small and Great Nations* in a booklet, based on a lecture before the Masaryk Society in Oxford in 1943, and published in 1944. Citizens of great powers are sometimes inclined to look upon small states as a "nuisance" that has survived from a dead past, but ought to be finally buried. Ripka demonstrates the fallacies that underlie most discussions of this problem. The military argument—the incapacity of the small state to defend itself—is rejected by Ripka on the ground that Great Powers, too, face that risk, as the defeat of France in 1940 so tragically revealed. Besides, no nation, not even the strongest single power, could defend itself in war by its own strength and resources. As modern wars are always coalition wars, the decisive factor is the combined strength of each side, made up of a number of states, large and small. Ripka also denies that small states are negligible in modern warfare. He reminds us of the difference which was made by the resistance of Greece and Yugoslavia to Germany—or, conversely, when Hungary, Bulgaria, and Rumania did not resist. Ripka also stresses the great contribution made by the small states to the League of Nations, as they make it again to the United Nations. As small states cannot choose between law and force but have to rely on law alone (not possessing enough force), their leadership in international affairs has often been beyond the material resources of power at their disposal. Finally, as to the charge that small states are the cause of war, Ripka retorts that "the Great Powers alone are in a position to unleash war, though they may use the small Powers as a pretext or as a spring-board for further conquests." In particular, Ripka writes that both world wars in this century were "caused not by the existence of the small nations, but by Germany's aggressive spirit, and this is directed against the small nations just as much as it is directed against the large nations."

The problems of a small power became apparent in the case of Ireland, after she regained her national selfhood. In *The National Being* (1916), A.E. (the Irish poet George Russell) discusses the values and objectives of national freedom and independence which the Irish people were about to obtain. Russell's concept of democracy encompassed man as a whole, and for the new and free Irish polity, he was particularly anxious to heal the breach between political freedom and economic unfreedom: "Democracy in politics has in no country led to democracy in its economic life," and even religion has become a "courtier of Mammon." He felt deep confidence in the farming and working people: "Nearly all the real manhood of Dublin I found was among the obscure myriads who are paid from twenty to thirty shillings [$5 to $7.50] a week. The men who will sacrifice anything for brotherhood get rarer and rarer above that limit of wealth."

Russell realized that hatred might be one of the lasting effects of foreign rule in Ireland. This is why he warns that "race hatred is the cheapest and basest of all national passions." He is psychologically on sound premises when he states that "nations hate other nations for the evil which is in themselves." Another important point that Russell reiterates throughout his book is that "nations act toward other nations as their own citizens act toward each other"; he is convinced that the realization of "economic brotherhood" would make the Irish at peace with themselves, and, as a consequence, at peace with all other nations. In all cases the Irish ought to learn the truth that "humanity will act towards their race as their race acts toward humanity." A passionate patriot, Russell warns his countrymen against the danger of totalitarian patriotism: "There are no nations to whom the entire and loyal allegiance of man's spirit could be given. It can only go out to the empires and nationalities in the womb of time, for whose coming we pray." Russell compares the people all over the world who work now for these high ideals to "outposts, sentinels, and frontiersmen thrown out before the armies of the intellectual and spiritual races yet to come into being." Lord Acton, too, had warned (in his essay on "Nationality") of the same danger of total submission to patriotism: "The man who prefers his country before every other duty shows the same spirit as the man who surrenders every right to the State. They both deny that right is superior to authority."

Like Irish and Czech nationalism, Zionism has aimed at national freedom and democracy, and not at the conquest or suppression of other nations. As a sentiment and yearning, Zionism is as old as the exile of the Jews (at no time complete) from their ancient homeland, Palestine. As a political movement, Zionism owes its existence mainly to the leadership of Theodor Herzl, an Austrian writer and publicist. Herzl served as the Paris correspondent of *Die Neue Freie Presse,* Vienna's leading daily, when the Dreyfus affair, in 1894, galvanized France and the world. Although innocent, Captain Dreyfus was found guilty of treason in a trial that revealed the alliance of anti-Semitism with the forces of clericalism, militarism, and antirepublicanism in France. After serving five years on Devil's Island, Dreyfus was pardoned in 1899, and finally found innocent in 1906. Herzl was so shaken by the experience of the Dreyfus trial that he began to devote the remainder of his short life (he died in 1904 at the age of 44) to the cause of the establishment of a Jewish state in Palestine as the solution of the Jewish problem. In 1896 he published what later became the Bible of Zionist literature: *The Jewish State* ("Der Judenstaat"). In it Herzl started with the premise that "the Jewish question still exists," and that the liberal promise of equality for all had not materialized. Herzl denies that the Jewish question is religious or social, and insists that it is a "national question." He could not foresee that close to one-half of the world's Jews (about six to seven million) would be murdered in planned "genocide" in Germany, Austria, Poland, the Balkans, and in the extermination camps of Majdanek, Oswiecim, and Buchenwald. Writing in a civilized age, he said: "Oppression and persecution cannot exterminate us." Herzl also stresses the fact that "distress" binds the Jews together. As to the Jewish state to be restored, Herzl postulates the grant of sovereignty to the Jews "over a portion of the globe large enough to satisfy the rightful requirements of a nation." This territory should be Palestine, the "ever-memorable historic home" of the Jewish people. He realizes that Palestine is much too small to absorb all the Jews in the world; but he believes that the lot of the Jews who will remain in their native countries will be a happier one if Palestine has attracted large numbers of Jews, especially from areas of acute suffering—at that time, primarily central and eastern Europe. Also, through its political, economic, and intellectual influence, the very existence of a Jewish state in Palestine would improve the position of the Jews everywhere in the world. Just as Masaryk, speaking for the Czechs, said that he had learned toleration from Austro-Hungarian oppression, so Herzl emphasizes that the Jews have learned toleration from anti-Semitism: "Every man will be free and undisturbed in his faith or his disbelief as he is in his nationality. And if it should occur that men of other creeds and different nationalities come to live amongst us, we should accord them honorable protection and equality before the law."

Imperialism is one of the chief distortions of nationalism. Love of oneself becomes hatred of others, and enslavement of other nations is clothed in such masks as "the white man's burden," or the need for "living space." Even highly democratic nations have, at one time or another, fallen victims of the disease of imperialism. J. A. Hobson, an unorthodox British economist, published in 1902 what was destined to become the classical analysis of imperialism. His *Imperialism* is divided into two parts: "The Economics of Imperialism" and "The Politics of Imperialism." His material is chiefly drawn from British experience and British sources, as might be expected, but imperialist policies of other nations are also examined. All subsequent work on imperialism, the studies by Hilferding, Luxemburg, Lenin, and Woolf (to mention but a few), is based, in the main, on Hobson's *Imperialism*. Hobson condemned imperialism because it is rapacious and immoral, and also because it tends to destroy free government at home: "Imperialism and popular government have nothing in common: they differ in spirit, in policy, in method." In addition, Hobson charged imperialism with being a constant menace to peace, and with wasting economic and financial resources on unproductive military projects. Only the establishment of a genuine democracy, political as well as economic, could wrest control from those classes that have a private vested interest in the maintenance of imperialism. Hobson concludes his book on imperialism as follows: "It is the besetting sin of all successful States, and its penalty is unalterable in the order of nature."

It is doubtful whether Hitler ever read Hobson. The vision of German imperialism in *Mein Kampf* is not bounded by anything. The Germans, as the *crème de la crème* of the Nordics, are entitled to rule the lower "races"— who receive their true "freedom" from such rule. Japan and Germany were successful and strong when they unleashed wars of imperialist aggression in this century; whether, as Hobson predicts, the order of nature will demand the due penalty, only experience will demonstrate.

1. Nationality and Liberty*

LORD ACTON

In the old European system, the rights of nationalities were neither recognised by governments nor asserted by the people. The interest of the reigning families, not those of the nations, regulated the frontiers; and the administration was conducted generally without any reference to popular desires. Where all liberties were suppressed, the claims of national independence were necessarily ignored, and a princess, in the words of Fénelon, carried a monarchy in her wedding portion. The eighteenth century acquiesced in this oblivion of corporate rights on the Continent, for the absolutists cared only for the State, and the liberals only for the individual. The Church, the nobles, and the nation had no place in the popular theories of the age; and they devised none in their own defence, for they were not openly attacked. The aristocracy retained its privileges, and the Church her property; and the dynastic interest, which overruled the natural inclination of the nations and destroyed their independence, nevertheless maintained their integrity. The national sentiment was not wounded in its most sensitive part. To dispossess a sovereign of his hereditary crown, and to annex his dominions, would have been held to inflict an injury upon all monarchies, and to furnish their subjects with a dangerous example, by depriving royalty of its inviolable character. In time of war, as there was no national cause at

* From "Nationality," *Home and Foreign Review* (July, 1862); reprinted in Lord Acton, *History of Freedom and Other Essays* (1907). By permission of The Macmillan Company, publishers.

stake, there was no attempt to rouse national feeling. The courtesy of the rulers towards each other was proportionate to the contempt for the lower orders. Compliments passed between the commanders of hostile armies; there was no bitterness, and no excitement; battles were fought with the pomp and pride of a parade. The art of war became a slow and learned game. The monarchies were united not only by a natural community of interests, but by family alliances. A marriage contract sometimes became the signal for an interminable war, whilst family connections often set a barrier to ambition. After the wars of religion came to an end in 1648, the only wars were those which were waged for an inheritance or a dependency, or against countries whose system of government exempted them from the common law of dynastic States, and made them not only unprotected but obnoxious. These countries were England and Holland, until Holland ceased to be a republic, and until, in England, the defeat of the Jacobites terminated the struggle for the Crown. There was one country, however, which still continued to be an exception; one monarch whose place was not admitted in the comity of kings.

The old despotic policy which made the Poles its prey had two adversaries, —the spirit of English liberty, and the doctrines of that revolution which destroyed the French monarchy with its own weapons; and these two contradicted in contrary ways the theory that nations have no collective rights. At the present day, the theory of nationality is not only the most powerful auxiliary of revolution, but its actual substance in the movements of the last three years. This, however, is a recent alliance, unknown to the first French Revolution. The modern theory of nationality arose partly as a legitimate consequence, partly as a reaction against it. As the system which overlooked national division was opposed by liberalism in two forms, the French and the English, so the system which insists upon them proceeds from two distinct sources, and exhibits the character either of 1688 or of 1789. When the French people abolished the authorities under which it lived, and became its own master, France was in danger of dissolution: for the common will is difficult to ascertain, and does not readily agree. "The laws," said Vergniaud, in the debate on the sentence of the king, "are obligatory only as the presumptive will of the people, which retains the right of approving or condemning them. The instant it manifests its wish the work of the national representation, the law, must disappear." This doctrine resolved society into its natural elements, and threatened to break up the country into as many republics as there were communes. For true republicanism is the principle of self-government in the whole and in all the parts. In an extensive country, it can prevail only by the union of several independent communities in a single confederacy, as in Greece, in Switzerland, in the Netherlands, and in America; so that a large republic not founded on the federal principle must result in the government of a single city, like Rome and Paris, and, in a less degree, Athens, Berne, and Amsterdam; or, in other words, a great democracy must either sacrifice self-government to unity, or preserve it by federalism.

The France of history fell together with the French State, which was the growth of centuries. The old sovereignty was destroyed. The local authorities were looked upon with aversion and alarm. The new central authority needed to be established on a new principle of unity. The state of nature, which was the ideal of society, was made the basis of the nation; descent was put in the place of tradition, and the French people was regarded as a physical product: an ethnological, not historic, unit. It was assumed that a unity existed separate from the representation and the government, wholly independent of the past, and capable at any moment of expressing or of changing its mind. In the words of Sieyès, it was no longer France, but some unknown country to which the nation was transported. The central power possessed authority, inasmuch as it obeyed the whole, and no divergence was permitted from the universal sentiment. This power, endowed with volition, was personified in the Republic One and Indivisible. The title signified that a part could not speak or act for the whole,—that there was a power supreme over the State, distinct from, and independent of, its members; and it expressed, for the first time in history, the notion of an abstract nationality. In this manner the idea of the sovereignty of the people, uncontrolled by the past, gave birth to the idea of nationality independent of the political influence of history. It sprang from the rejection of the two authorities,—of the State and of the past. The kingdom of France was, geographically as well as politically, the product of a long series of events, and the same influences which built up the State formed the territory. The Revolution repudiated alike the agencies to which France owed her boundaries and those to which she owed her government. Every effaceable trace and relic of national history was carefully wiped away,—the system of administration, the physical divisions of the country, the classes of society, the corporations, the weights and measures, the calendar. France was no longer bounded by the limits she had received from the condemned influence of her history; she could recognise only those which were set by nature. The definition of the nation was borrowed from the material world, and, in order to avoid a loss of territory, it became not only an abstraction but a fiction.

In pursuing the outward and visible growth of the national theory we are prepared for an examination of its political character and value. The absolutism which has created it denies equally that absolute right of national unity which is a product of democracy, and that claim of national liberty which belongs to the theory of freedom. These two views of nationality, corresponding to the French and to the English systems, are connected in name only, and are in reality the opposite extremes of political thought. In one case, nationality is founded on the perpetual supremacy of the collective will, of which the unity of the nation is the necessary condition, to which every other influence must defer, and against which no obligation enjoys authority, and all resistance is tyrannical. The nation is here an ideal unit founded on the race, in defiance of the modifying action of external causes, of tradition, and of existing rights. It overrules the rights and wishes of the inhabitants, absorbing their divergent interests in a fictitious unity; sacrifices their several inclinations and duties to the higher claim of nationality, and crushes all natural rights and all established liberties for the purpose of vindicating itself.[1] Whenever a single definite object is made the supreme end of the State, be it the advantage of a class, the safety or the power of the country, the greatest happiness of the greatest number, or the support of any speculative idea, the State becomes for the time inevitably absolute. Liberty alone demands for its realisation the limitation of the public authority, for liberty is the only object which benefits all alike, and provokes no sincere opposition. In supporting the claims of national unity, governments must be subverted in whose title there is no flaw, and whose policy is beneficent and equitable, and subjects must be compelled to transfer their allegiance to an authority for which they have no attachment, and which may be practically a foreign domination. Connected with this theory in nothing except in the common enmity of the absolute state, is the theory which represents nationality as an essential, but not a supreme element in determining the forms of the State. It is distinguished from the other, because it tends to diversity and not to uniformity, to harmony and not to unity; because it aims not at an arbitrary change, but at careful respect for the existing conditions of political life, and because it obeys the laws and results of history, not the aspirations of an ideal future. While the theory of unity makes the nation a source of despotism and revolution, the theory of liberty regards it as the bulwark of self-government, and the foremost limit to the excessive power of the State. Private rights, which are sacrificed to the unity, are preserved by the union of nations. No power can so efficiently resist the tendencies of centralisation, of corruption, and of absolutism, as that community which is the vastest that can be included in a State, which imposes on its members a consistent similarity of character, interest, and opinion, and which arrests the action of the sovereign by the influence of a divided patriotism. The presence of different nations under the same sovereignty is similar in its effect to the independence of the Church in the State. It provides against the servility which flourishes under the shadow of a single authority, by balancing interests, multiplying associations, and giving to the subject the restraint and support of a

---

[1] "Le sentiment d'indépendance nationale est encore plus général et plus profondément gravé dans le coeur des peuples que l'amour d'une liberté constitutionnelle. Les nations les plus soumises au despotisme éprouvent ce sentiment avec autant de vivacité que les nations libres; les peuples les plus barbares le sentent même encore plus vivement que les nations policées" (*L'Italie au Dixneuvième Siècle*, p. 148, Paris, 1821).

combined opinion. In the same way it promotes independence by forming definite groups of public opinion, and by affording a great source and centre of political sentiments, and of notions of duty not derived from the sovereign will. Liberty provokes diversity, and diversity preserves liberty by supplying the means of organisation. All those portions of law which govern the relations of men with each other, and regulate social life, are the varying result of national custom and the creation of private society. In these things, therefore, the several nations will differ from each other; for they themselves have produced them, and they do not owe them to the State which rules them all. This diversity in the same State is a firm barrier against the intrusion of the government beyond the political sphere which is common to all into the social department which escapes legislation and is ruled by spontaneous laws. This sort of interference is characteristic of an absolute government, and is sure to provoke a reaction, and finally a remedy. That intolerance of social freedom which is natural to absolutism is sure to find a corrective in the national diversities, which no other force could so efficiently provide. The coexistence of several nations under the same State is a test, as well as the best security of its freedom. It is also one of the chief instruments of civilisation; and, as such, it is in the natural and providential order, and indicates a state of greater advancement than the national unity which is the ideal of modern liberalism.

The combination of different nations in one State is as necessary a condition of civilised life as the combination of men in society. Inferior races are raised by living in political union with races intellectually superior. Exhausted and decaying nations are revived by the contact of a younger vitality. Nations in which the elements of organisation and the capacity for government have been lost, either through the demoralising influence of despotism, or the disintegrating action of democracy, are restored and educated anew under the discipline of a stronger and less corrupted race. This fertilising and regenerating process can only be obtained by living under one government. It is in the cauldron of the State that the fusion takes place by which the vigour, the knowledge, and the capacity of one portion of mankind may be communicated to another. Where political and national boundaries coincide, society ceases to advance, and nations relapse into a condition corresponding to that of men who renounce intercourse with their fellow-men. The difference between the two unites mankind not only by the benefits it confers on those who live together, but because it connects society either by a political or a national bond, gives to every people an interest in its neighbours, either because they are under the same government or because they are of the same race, and thus promotes the interests of humanity, of civilisation, and of religion.

Christianity rejoices at the mixture of races, as paganism identifies itself with their differences, because truth is universal, and errors various and particular. In the ancient world idolatry and nationality went together, and the same term is applied in Scripture to both. It was the mission of the Church to overcome national differences. The period of her undisputed supremacy was that in which all Western Europe obeyed the same laws, all literature was contained in one language, and the political unity of Christendom was personified in a single potentate, while its intellectual unity was represented in one university. As the ancient Romans concluded their conquests by carrying away the gods of the conquered people, Charlemagne overcame the national resistance of the Saxons only by the forcible destruction of their pagan rites. Out of the mediaeval period, and the combined action of the German race and the Church, came forth a new system of nations and a new conception of nationality. Nature was overcome in the nation as well as in the individual. In pagan and uncultivated times, nations were distinguished from each other by the widest diversity, not only in religion, but in customs, language, and character. Under the new law they had many things in common; the old barriers which separated them were removed, and the new principle of self-government, which Christianity imposed, enabled them to live together under the same authority, without necessarily losing their cherished habits, their customs, or their laws. The new idea of freedom made room for different races in one State. A nation was no longer what it had been to the ancient world,—the progeny of a common ancestor, or the aboriginal product of a particular region,—a result of merely physical and material causes,—but a moral and political being; not the creation of geographical or physiological unity, but developed in the course of history by the action of the State. It is derived from the State, not supreme over it. A State may in course of time produce a nationality; but that a nationality should constitute a State is contrary to the nature of modern civilisation. The nation derives its rights and its power from the memory of a former independence.

The Church has agreed in this respect with the tendency of political progress, and discouraged wherever she could the isolation of nations; admonishing them of their duties to each other, and regarding conquest and feudal investiture as the natural means of raising barbarous or sunken nations to a higher level. But though she has never attributed to national independence an immunity from the accidental consequences of feudal law, of hereditary claims, or of testamentary arrangements, she defends national liberty against uniformity and centralisation with an energy inspired by perfect community of interests. For the same enemy threatens both; and the State which is reluctant to tolerate differences, and to do justice to the peculiar character of various races, must from the same cause interfere in the internal government of religion. The connection of religious liberty with the emancipation of Poland or Ireland is not merely the accidental result of local causes; and the failure of the Concordat to unite the subjects of Austria is the natural consequence of a policy which did not desire to protect the provinces in their diversity and autonomy, and sought to bribe the Church by favours instead of strengthening her by independence. From this influence of religion in modern history has proceeded a new definition of patriotism.

The difference between nationality and the State is exhibited in the nature of patriotic attachment. Our connection with the race is merely natural or physical, whilst our duties to the political nation are ethical. One is a community of affections and instincts infinitely important and powerful in savage life, but pertaining more to the animal than to the civilised man; the other is an authority governing by laws, imposing obligations, and giving a moral sanction and character to the natural relations of society. Patriotism is in political life what faith is in religion, and it stands to the domestic feelings and to home-sickness as faith to fanaticism and to superstition. It has one aspect derived from private life and nature, for it is an extension of the family affections, as the tribe is an extension of the family. But in its real political character, patriotism consists in the development of the instinct of self-preservation into a moral duty which may involve self-sacrifice. Self-preservation is both an instinct and a duty, natural and involuntary in one respect, and at the same time a moral obligation. By the first it produces the family; by the last the State. If the nation could exist without the State, subject only to the instinct of self-preservation, it would be incapable of denying, controlling, or sacrificing itself; it would be an end and a rule to itself. But in the political order moral purposes are realised and public ends are pursued to which private interests and even existence must be sacrificed. The great sign of true patriotism, the development of selfishness into sacrifice, is the product of political life. That sense of duty which is supplied by race is not entirely separated from its selfish and instinctive basis; and the love of country, like married love, stands at the same time on a material and a moral foundation. The patriot must distinguish between the two causes or objects of his devotion. The attachment which is given only to the country is like obedience given only to the State—a submission to physical influences. The man who prefers his country before every other duty shows the same spirit as the man who surrenders every right to the State. They both deny that right is superior to authority.

The greatest adversary of the rights of nationality is the modern theory of nationality. By making the State and the nation commensurate with each other in theory, it reduces practically to a subject condition all other nationalities that may be within the boundary. It cannot admit them to an equality with the ruling nation which constitutes the State, because the State would then cease to be national, which would be a contradiction of the principle of its existence. According, therefore, to the degree of humanity and civilisation in that dominant body which claims all the rights of the community, the inferior races are exterminated, or reduced to servitude, or out-lawed, or put in a condition of dependence.

If we take the establishment of liberty for the realisation of moral duties to be the end of civil society, we must conclude that those states are sub-stantially the most perfect which, like the British and Austrian Empires, in-clude various distinct nationalities without oppressing them. Those in which no mixture of races has occurred are imperfect; and those in which its effects have disappeared are decrepit. A State which is incompetent to satisfy differ-ent races condemns itself; a State which labours to neutralise, to absorb, or to expel them, destroys its own vitality; a State which does not include them is destitute of the chief basis of self-government. The theory of nationality, therefore, is a retrograde step in history. It is the most advanced form of the revolution, and must retain its power to the end of the revolutionary period, of which it announces the approach.

~~~~~~

2. *Humanitarian Nationalism* *

GIUSEPPE MAZZINI

~~~~~~

I.

Young Europe is an association of men believing in a future of liberty, equality, and fraternity, for all mankind; and desirous of consecrating their thoughts and actions to the realisation of that future.

GENERAL PRINCIPLES

2.

One sole God;
One sole ruler,—His Law;
One sole interpreter of that law,—Humanity.

3.

To constitute humanity in such wise as to enable it throughout a con-tinuous progress to discover and apply the law of God by which it should be governed, as speedily as possible: such is the mission of *Young Europe.*

* From "Pact of Fraternity of Young Europe" (1834); reprinted in *Life and Writings of Joseph Mazzini*, III (Smith, Elder and Co,. 1905).

4.

As our true well-being consists in living in accordance with the law of our being, the knowledge and fulfilment of the law of humanity is the sole source of good. The fulfilment of the mission of *Young Europe* will result in the general good.

5.

Every mission constitutes a pledge of duty.

Every man is bound to consecrate his every faculty to its fulfilment. He will derive his rule of action from the profound conviction of that duty.

6.

Humanity can only arrive at the knowledge of its Law of Life through the free and harmonious development of all its faculties.

Humanity can only reduce that knowledge to action through the free and harmonious development of all its faculties.

Association is the sole means of realising this development.

7.

No true association is possible save among free men and equals.

8.

By the law of God, given by Him to humanity, all men are free, are brothers, and are equals.

9.

Liberty is the right of every man to exercise his faculties without impediment or restraint, in the accomplishment of his special mission, and in the choice of the means most conducive to its accomplishment.

10.

The free exercise of the faculties of the individual may in no case violate the rights of others. The special mission of each man must be accomplished in harmony with the general mission of humanity. There is no other limit to human liberty.

11.

Equality implies the recognition of uniform rights and duties for all men— for none may escape the action of the law by which they are defined—and every man should participate, in proportion to his labour, in the enjoyment of the produce resulting from the activity of all the social forces.

12.

Fraternity is the reciprocal affection, the sentiment which inclines man to do unto others as he would that others should do unto him.

13.

All privilege is a violation of Equality.
All arbitrary rule is a violation of Liberty.
Every act of egotism is a violation of Fraternity.

14.

Wheresoever privilege, arbitrary rule, or egotism are introduced into the social constitution, it is the duty of every man who comprehends his own mission to combat them by every means in his power.

15.

That which is true of each individual with regard to the other individuals forming a part of the society to which he belongs, is equally true of every people with regard to humanity.

16.

By the law of God, given by God to humanity, all the peoples are free— are brothers and are equals.

17.

Every people has its special mission, which will co-operate towards the fulfilment of the general mission of humanity. That mission constitutes its *nationality*. Nationality is sacred.

18.

All unjust rule, all violence, every act of egotism exercised to the injury of a people, is a violation of the liberty, equality, and fraternity of the peoples. All the peoples should aid and assist each other in putting an end to it.

19.

Humanity will only be truly constituted when all the peoples of which it is composed have acquired the free exercise of their sovereignty, and shall be associated in a Republican Confederation, governed and directed by a common Declaration of Principles and a common Pact, towards the common aim—the discovery and fulfilment of the Universal Moral Law.

3. Democratic Nationalism*

THOMAS G. MASARYK

We often discuss the question of our national character. The Romantics used to speak of a dove-like nature; today we prefer to lay stress on the sober, practical features of our character. Well then, what are we really like?

It is difficult to say. I am sceptical of the current definitions as to what constitutes national character; and also of those that other nations give themselves. Was Žizka a true Czech, or Hus, Chelčický, and Komenský? Dobrovský, Palacký, and Havlíček, or Hanka, and Jungman? I have read a book by a Swiss author about a dual France. Some people complain of our lack of concord as if it were characteristically Czech, and Slav, but the Germans complain about themselves in exactly the same way. And so on. The problem becomes more involved when we ask if and how national character changes at different times, and if there are some characteristic qualities that remain unchanged. There is also the point that from the earliest times until now there has been a considerable mixing of races and nations. There is no such thing as so-called "pure blood," at least not in Europe.

And besides: how and to what extent do economic conditions—prosperity, poverty, food, and occupation, technique, culture, religion, and morality, hygiene, and so on—form the national character? On the other hand one has to consider, how economic conditions, religion, and morality: how culture in general is determined, and to what extent by national character? For instance, is mathematics influenced by the nation, have French or English mathematics some special character, and what is it? Is Catholicism intrinsically Roman, Protestantism German, and the Orthodox Church Slav?

I won't deny that nations have their characters, both physical, and spiritual, but I do not regard anthropological and ethnological notions as already so certain that one could deduce from them the history of nations, and devise the right politics.

First of all, in our history nearly three hundred years are lacking of a full and free political and spiritual life; from that I would explain the immaturity in our politics; I do not deduce our shortcomings in politics from the character of the nation.

Secondly, as a society we are without traditions; the folk tradition of the

---

*From Thomas G. Masaryk, *On Thought and Life: Conversations with Karel Čapek* (1938). By permission of The Macmillan Company, publishers.

peasantry is breaking up, and we have no other; almost every one of us has come from cottages, and we have not yet had time to get ourselves into shape.

And further: I ask you how long ago is it since the Moravians felt themselves to be something different from the Czechs, and talked of a Moravian "nation"? And now the Slovaks have been joined to us, and people speak of two nations. And it would not only be a question of the definition of the character of one nation but also of the character of the various parts of the country; what for instance is the difference between a Moravian Valach and a Hanak? Therefore I repeat: we lived in subjection, and each subjection prevents the character from developing and expanding fully according to its inner law.

That is also visible in our literature. Our poetry is good but not our novels and drama. For poetry personal life is sufficient; novels and drama presuppose the accumulated experience of generations; novels are a work of a whole century.

Yes—a small poem springing from a real strong impulse, many poets make a success of that. But that is just the expression of a peculiar personal feeling; the novel, and the drama are something different—an epical poem is too, they presuppose an artistic observation of the nation, society, classes, states, and so on. In our novels I take exception to some kind of unripeness, a restricted knowledge of one's own and foreign life, too little cosmopolitanism. We observe too little.

Foreigners say of us that we are talented, practical, industrious—well, thank God too for that. In fact our farmers, our workers, are some of the best; the urban and intellectual strata are still incomplete, but we Czechs had not begun to urbanize ourselves until sixty or eighty years ago—I can still remember what modest beginnings they were, and I can say what a fair part of the way we have gone since then.

We need fifty years of undisturbed development, and we shall be where we should like to be today. It is no blind confidence in our ability, and tenacity—our history, even if somewhat disjointed, the fact that in the great political storms we held our ground, and that during the world conflagration we managed to restore our state, that all testifies to our political ability. I do not think that I exaggerate if I say that our history is one of the most interesting—we are fine fellows, but we often make a false step. I find the German anthropologists' skull and brain indices place us among the foremost nations —we are gifted, no doubt about that, but we are somewhat unstable, not circumspect enough, and shall I say, politically green; and political inexperience is a fertile soil for demagogy, and of that we have more than enough. The discussions about the crisis of democracy, and the shortcomings of parliamentary government have to a large extent their origin in that insufficient experience; and from that also that parrot-like imitation of foreign political isms—in short, we do not think enough according to our own selves, and to what is ours. In the Austrian times we got used to the negation of the state—that was the result of the subjugation; we even made ourselves believe that we could not any longer be independent. Well, no not that, with that idea I could never become reconciled; but I knew that subject people, depressed and deformed by subjugation do not easily become free in spirit too at the wave of a hand. That is why so many people among us even today repudiate the state—by distrust, by resistance to the state administration, by their bad relations with whole strata of co-citizens—to put it frankly: there are still some who side with the thief rather than the policeman. Our people have a patriotic tradition, it is true, but on many occasions they are still too indifferent to the state, against the state, almost anarchical; they don't realize that it is the attitude of the old Austrian spirit. To de-Austrianize, that means to acquire a sense for the state, and what it stands for, for the democratic state. That we must ask not only from the bureaucracy, and the army, but also from all citizens. And not only the Czechs and the Slovaks.

Democracy must be livelier and sprightlier than the old régime—especially that one of ours. We must always bear in mind that we are a small nation in an unfavourable geographical position; in effect it imposes upon us the obligation to be more alert, to think more, to achieve more than the others; or according to Palacký: every self-respecting Czech and Slovak must do three times as much as the members of big and more favourably situated nations. Only bear in mind that every educated fellow countryman of ours needs to learn at least two foreign languages—how much time it takes, and work, but also what a gain it is not only for education but also for practical intercourse with nations! And so it is in everything: if we have to hold our own with honour we must thoroughly intensify all our political and cultural endeavour. Yes, it is a painstaking job; but who does not want to take trouble, don't let him talk of nation and patriotism.

Real love for one's nation is a very beautiful thing; with a decent and honest man it comes as a matter of course; therefore he does not talk much about it, just like a decent man does not go trumpeting abroad his love for his wife, family, and so on. A real love protects, bears sacrifices—and chiefly works. And for that work for the nation and state, a clear, sensible political, and cultural programme is necessary—mere day-dreaming and getting excited is not enough. There is, after all, a difference between patriotism and jingoism; how much already did Havlíček struggle with that market-place jingoism, but for many it is as if he had never lived!

We must express our patriotism by a conscious public spirit. No doubt the state is ours, it is ours in virtue of historical right, according to the principle of the majority, and by the title that we have built it; but we have considerable minorities, and therefore we must be conscious of the difference between a state, and a nation: a nation is a cultural organization, a state a political organization. We have duties towards the nation, and we have duties towards the state. Obviously they must not conflict. We have built that state, we must know how to manage and govern it; it is our task to win over to the idea of our democratic republic the minorities with whom we are living. Their numbers, and their civilization, impose both on them and on us a democratic concord. Our procedure with the minorities is practically given to us by our own experience under Austria-Hungary: what we did not like to be done unto us, we shall not do unto others. The programme of Palacký, the father of the nation, is valid for us, and for those to come. Our history, the policy of the Premyslids, of St. Venceslas, Charles, and George must be a model for the policy with our Germans. The fact that we are surrounded on all sides by a big German neighbour, impels a thoughtful Czech to cautious and definitely wise politics.

Isn't there sometimes a conflict between the love for one's nation and for humanity, or rather: between nationalism and the humanitarian ideals like pacifism, mutual understanding between nations, and such-like things?

Between the love for one's nation, the love for one's country, and humanity there is no disagreement; as it is, it is between modern nationalism and humanity. Already that new and foreign word indicates that patriotism as our revivalists demanded it, and lived it, is something different from the nationalism of today.

As far as our national programme is concerned, remember what I told you with regard to the development of Europe, and to our own history, that is that we must take a hand in world politics, and consequently be in lively and friendly contact with other nations. Our national revival is a child of Enlightenment and of late Romanticism, it sprang from the humanitarian ideals of the Eighteenth and Nineteenth Centuries which were broadcast in France, in Germany, everywhere. Humanity—that is indeed our national programme, the programme of Dobrovský, Havlíček, and of Komenský in his day, of our kings George, and Charles, and of St. Venceslas.

Humanity does not exclude, or weaken the love for one's nation; I can, nay, I must love my nation positively, but because of that I need not hate other nations. True love is not proved by hatred, but only by love. Mankind is a sum of nations, it is not something outside the nations, and above them. Humanity, love, not only for one's neighbours, but for mankind—how am I to imagine that mankind concretely? I see a poor child that I can help—that child is mankind to me. The community with which I share its troubles, the nation with which I am combined through speech and culture is mankind. Mankind is simply a greater, or smaller sum of people for whom we can do something positive in deed, and not only in words. Humanity does not consist in day-dreaming about the whole of mankind, but in always acting humanely. If I ask politics to serve mankind, I do not infer that they ought not to be national, but just and decent. That's all.

Not as individuals, not as nations are we here merely to fulfil our egoistic aims. A nation that wished to live only for itself would be just as miserable as a man who wanted to live only for himself. Without faith in ideas and in ideals the life of men and of nations is only stagnation.

This, of course, is the political credo of an idealist.

Not at all, my boy: of a realist, in philosophy and in politics. For me politically realism means: don't bury yourself in the recollection of a glorious past, work for a glorious present; don't put your faith only in words and slogans, for then you can improve the realities, and bring them to order; don't fly up in the clouds, but stick to your earth, it is the safest and least uncertain. Whatever you work for, stick to reality. . . .

Only reality?

Yes; but without doubt reality also means spirituality, soul, love, moral order, God, and eternity. Only with them do we live an entire life, in full and complete reality, whether it be the life of an individual, or the history of nations. That full life alone is without inner conflict, such a life alone has a true and clear meaning. . . .

and is a happy life.

Yes.

---

4. *Small and Great Nations* *

HUBERT RIPKA

Small nations are reproached chiefly because they cannot defend themselves, particularly in modern warfare, against a powerful aggressor. In support of this thesis the critics point to the way in which Germany or Italy swiftly and completely crushed a whole series of small States.

This is true. But it is just as true of the Great Powers as it is of small nations. No nation, whether great or small, can defend itself against a superior enemy when it has to fight alone. This is proved by the last war and the present war.

No country has realised more fully than Germany that even a Great Power cannot run the risk of war against a superior enemy. She would never have launched this great adventure if she had foreseen her encounter with a coalition of Powers, great and small, whose resources far outstripped her

* From Hubert Ripka, *Small and Great Nations* (Czechoslovak Ministry of Foreign Affairs, London, 1944). By permission.

own. For this reason, while rearming for the war on which she was set, it was her policy to prevent the formation of this coalition. The German leaders knew perfectly well that if their political manoeuvres did not succeed, their war-machine, though the most formidable ever known, would be useless.

Neither Austria nor Czechoslovakia, it is obvious, could defend herself against Germany. Nor could Poland who, when the present war began, had to meet the whole weight of the German armies alone. Nor could France, whose military defeat in 1940 was inevitable because Russia was not yet in the war and because the British forces which came to her aid were neither large enough nor sufficiently equipped. Even if France had made better military and political preparations and even if Great Britain had immediately and completely mobilised all her resources, these two combined Great Powers would not have been strong enough to resist the German war-machine. Thanks to the resolution and heroic courage of her people Great Britain managed to resist Germany alone for several months after the fall of France. She did this partly because she is protected by the sea, which is not an insurmountable obstacle, but chiefly because her political and military leaders foresaw that sooner or later the coalition which Germany so greatly feared would take shape and prove stronger than the Axis.

The same idea lay at the roots of General de Gaulle's historic declaration when—in June, 1940—he summoned France, whose metropolitan territory had been crushed, to continue the struggle. In this dark hour he had, like Churchill, a vision of the immense resources which France and her Allies, actual and potential, could command and which were not yet mobilised.

Every war is a clash between two forces, and the stronger prevails over the weaker. The size of the belligerent Powers is an entirely relative factor. This is particularly true of modern wars, for they are always coalition wars. And in a coalition even small countries can make useful contributions to the war efforts of their Allies. If Greece had submitted to the Axis Powers the present war would have developed in a very different manner. Her heroic resistance delayed German military operations in the Mediterranean for several months. Those were precious months, and they enabled her great Allies to prepare large-scale operations. In a similar way, Yugoslavia's resistance, though it did not last long, threw out of joint the German plans of operations in the Eastern Mediterranean and thus allowed the Allies to gain time. Not until the war is over can we appreciate at its full value the part played by the Yugoslav patriots after the enemy had occupied their country. By how many months, or even years, would the war have been shortened if Hungary, Roumania and Bulgaria, instead of playing their melancholy parts as satellites of the Reich, could have found leaders who called upon them to resist? A glance at the map will provide an answer.

Was not the tragic error of Munich due to the explicit failure to understand the war potential of a small nation? If Czechoslovakia, as she always believed and hoped, had been given the chance to go to war at the side of her Allies, what would have happened? When we consider Czechoslovakia's geographical position, her natural and strongly fortified frontiers, her war industry which was large enough to serve as an arsenal for the whole of Central Europe and her well-equipped army which was ready for the fight, we are bound to admit that her contribution to the war might well have been weighty.

These few examples are sufficient to show how much depends on the political orientation of small nations and how they are far from being *quantités négligeables* as they at times appear to certain observers—on the contrary, in modern wars which always develop into coalition wars, the small nations are important factors, and often play a decisive part.[1]

It is therefore evident that the military argument that is brought against the small nations is not valid.

According to their critics, the small nations, far from wishing to place their war-potential at the services of a coalition, often try to evade their international obligations and take refuge in a policy of neutrality. Up to a certain point this was true before the last war. But the war of 1914–1918, and particularly the present war, have struck a mortal blow at the illusions which

---

[1] *Moreover—what is the criterion by which we are to decide whether a particular nation is great or small?*

The Czechoslovak Republic with an area of 140,000 km^2 was, in area, the thirteenth among the European States, in population (with 15,160,000 inhabitants in December, 1935) the ninth, in imports and exports (with 1.67% and 1.87% of the world total of imports and exports respectively) the seventh; in 1933 it was the eleventh largest importing State with 1.40% and the ninth largest exporting State with 1.53% of the world total.

But neither the territorial area, the numbers of population or the amount of foreign trade provide a sufficient criterion on the basis of which we can decide whether a nation is great or small. I will give yet another example. If we compare the production capacity in Czechoslovakia and in Italy according to the amount of coal and ores produced, we come to the following conclusion: Coal production in Czechoslovakia was far higher than in Italy. In 1935, Czechoslovakia produced 15,100,000 tons of lignite, i.e., 997 kg. per head of population; Italy produced 545,000 tons, i.e., 13 kg. per head of population. Czechoslovakia produced 10,900,000 tons of pit coal, i.e., 719 kg. per head, while Italy produced 443,000 tons, i.e., 10 kg. per head. In 1935, Czechoslovakia produced 252,600 tons of the base metal ores (iron, copper, lead and zinc ore), i.e., 16.7 kg. per head; Italy produced 373,400 tons, i.e., 8.8 kg. per head. The smelting industry (crude iron, crude steel, copper, lead, zinc) produced 1,994,700 tons in Czechoslovakia in 1935, i.e., 131.6 kgs. per head; Italy produced 2,958,700 tons, i.e., 69.9 kgs. per head.

Arms production in our country was considerably greater than in Italy. The Skoda Works and the Zbrojovka of Brno were each larger than the Italian Ansaldo Works. Another proof of the superiority of the Czechoslovak armaments industry is certainly the fact that in foreign markets it met with the competition of many States, e.g., Britain, Switzerland, Germany, Sweden and France, but never with Italian competition.

Czechoslovakia's armaments potential was such that Czechoslovakia was in a position almost single-handed to supply all the countries of Central Europe with war material.

It is clear that the division of the nations into small and great is very relative: moreover, the classification varies, relatively quickly in accordance with the population changes and economic development within the various nations. Thus in the course of a single century there has come about a complete transformation of the power relationship between France, Germany and Britain.

could still be cherished about the advantages of a policy of neutrality. Except to a very limited degree and in special instances, such a policy is no longer tenable. In our own time neutrality is no longer a refuge, but a risk. Hitler has proved, even more effectively than the General Staff of William II that a country's smallness and neutral attitude in no way protect it against invasion and war.

Certain small nations have been slow to learn this lesson. But many, it may be said, understood it. After the last war they pursued with great fervour the new policy of collective security which the League of Nations inaugurated. They devoted themselves wholeheartedly to perfecting this new international institution. Later on some of them abandoned this policy; but this was largely because they had been discouraged by the indecision of the Great Powers and because they realised that in an hour of crisis they would receive insufficient support from those powerful members of the League whose attitude was decisive. This was true of Poland, Belgium and Yugo-slavia, all of whom observed that Hitler and Mussolini failed to meet with serious resistance from the Great Powers when they chose to fall upon small countries.

At the time of the Ethiopian crisis, it is worth noting, several small countries showed themselves ready to make sacrifices for the cause of peace. Except Austria and Hungary, who were directly subjected to German and Italian pressure, and two South American Republics who then sympathised with Italy, all the small countries voted for sanctions against Italy. They were ready to apply them even at the price of being involved in war. If the policy of sanctions and collective security failed, responsibility for its failure does not rest with the small nations. The Munich crisis, which incidentally the small Powers did not provoke, marked the summit of political de-moralisation and, so to speak, canonised of the policy of *sauve qui peut;* for the first small nation to be sacrificed by the Great Powers was the very one which had been most consistent and inflexible in its policy of collective se-curity.

Here, it is true, the small Powers had a share in the responsibility; but their share was certainly no larger than that of the Great Powers. To some degree the small nation may at least be given the benefit of mitigating cir-cumstances. A neutral policy was as much an illusion with the Great Powers as with the small ones. When small Czechoslovakia created, in 1938, the impression that she wished to oppose German aggression, Lord Runciman, as the spokesman of a Great Power, urged that for the sake of peace Czechoslovakia should pursue a neutral policy.

The theory that small nations cause wars is so ridiculous that it is scarcely necessary to refute it. The two last wars broke out because of the tension between the Great Powers and not on account of the Serbs, the Belgians or the Poles. The assassination at Sarajevo was merely a pretext for Germany who wanted to settle her accounts with France and Russia and hoped that Britain would remain neutral. Germany was not concerned, in 1938, with saving the so-called Sudeten Germans, but with crushing Czechoslovakia because she blocked her path to Central and Eastern Europe. What Hitler wanted in 1939 was not Danzig, but the destruction of Poland; and for him Poland's destruction was merely the point of departure for new conquests (and at the same time he hoped that on this occasion Russia would remain neutral).

The two great wars of the twentieth century, it is evident, were caused not by the existence of the small nations, but by Germany's aggressive spirit, and this is directed against the small nations just as much as it is directed against the large nations.

It is no less ridiculous to assume that war could be avoided if the small States could be reduced in number by grouping them into some sort of larger system. Europe, in 1914, embraced a smaller number of States than in 1939, but the smaller number in 1914 did not prevent the outbreak of war. The Austro-Hungarian monarchy then formed an immense *bloc* in Central Europe; but its existence, far from reducing the danger of war, contributed largely to its outbreak. There is no link between the danger of war and the mere number of States in Europe. The belief that the "Balkanisation" of Europe constitutes a danger is false. Because of their weakness and their restricted means of action, the small States create no danger to European peace. The Great powers alone are in a position to unleash a war, though they may use the small Powers as a pretext or as a spring-board for further conquests.

What matters is not the number of States that will form the Europe of tomorrow, but the relations which will exist between them and the international organisation on which large and small countries alike will be based.

~~~~~~

5. *The National Being**

<div align="right">A.E.</div>

~~~~~~

Race hatred is the cheapest and basest of all national passions, and it is the nature of hatred, as it is the nature of love, to change us into the likeness of that which we contemplate. We grow nobly like what we adore, and ignobly like what we hate; and no people in Ireland became so anglicized

* From A.E., *The National Being: Some Thoughts on an Irish Polity* (1916). By permission of The Macmillan Company, publishers.

in intellect and temperament, and even in the manner of expression, as those who hated our neighbours most. All hatreds long persisted in bring us to every baseness for which we hated others. The only laws which we cannot break with impunity are divine laws, and no law is more eternally sure in its workings than that which condemns us to be even as that we condemned. Hate is the high commander of so many armies that an inquiry into the origin of this passion is at least as needful as histories of other contemporary notorieties. Not emperors or parliaments alone raise armies, but this passion also. It will sustain nations in defeat. When everything seems lost this wild captain will appear and the scattered forces are reunited. They will be as oblivious of danger as if they were divinely inspired, but if they win their battle it is to become like the conquered foe. All great wars in history, all conquests, all national antagonisms, result in an exchange of characteristics. It is because I wish Ireland to be itself, to act from its own will and its own centre, that I deprecate hatred as a force in national life. It is always possible to win a cause without the aid of this base helper, who betrays us ever in the hour of victory.

When a man finds the feeling of hate for another rising vehemently in himself, he should take it as a warning that conscience is battling in his own being with that very thing he loathes. Nations hate other nations for the evil which is in themselves; but they are as little given to self-analysis as individuals, and while they are right to overcome evil, they should first try to understand the genesis of the passion in their own nature. If we understand this, many of the ironies of history will be intelligible. We will understand why it was that our countrymen in Ulster and our countrymen in the rest of Ireland, who have denounced each other so vehemently, should at last appear to have exchanged characteristics: why in the North, having passionately protested against physical force movements, no-rent manifestos, and contempt for Imperial Parliament, they should have come themselves at last to organize a physical force movement, should threaten to pay no taxes, and should refuse obedience to an Act of Parliament. We will understand also why it was their opponents came themselves to address to Ulster all the arguments and denunciations Ulster had addressed to them. I do not point this out with intent to annoy, but to illustrate by late history a law in national as well as human psychology. If this unpopular psychology I have explained was adopted everywhere as true, we would never hear expressions of hate. People would realize they were first revealing and then stabbing their own characters before the world.

Nations act towards other nations as their own citizens act towards each other. When slavery existed in a State, if that nation attacked another it was with intent to enslave. Where there is a fierce economic competition between citizen and citizen then in war with another nation, the object of the war is to destroy the trade of the enemy. If the citizens in any country could develop harmonious life among themselves they would manifest the friendliest feelings towards the people of other countries. We find that it is just among groups of people who aim at harmonious life, co-operators and socialists, that the strongest national impulses to international brotherhood arise; and wars of domination are brought about by the will of those who within a State are dominant over the fortunes of the rest. Ireland, a small country, can only maintain its national identity by moral and economic forces. Physically it must be overmastered by most other European nations. Moral forces are really more powerful than physical forces. One Christ changed the spiritual life of Europe; one Buddha affected more myriads in Asia.

The co-operative ideal of brotherhood in industry has helped to make stronger the ideal of the brotherhood of humanity, and no body of men in any of the countries in the great War of our time regarded it with more genuine sorrow than those who were already beginning to promote schemes for international co-operation. It must be mainly in movements inspired with the ideal of the brotherhood of man, that the spirit will be generated which, in the future, shall make the idea of war so detestable that statesmen will find it as impossible to think of that solution of their disputes as they would think now of resorting to private assassination of political opponents. The great tragedy of Europe was brought about, not by the German Emperor, nor by Sir Edward Grey, nor by the Czar, nor by any of the other chiefs ostensibly controlling foreign policy, but by the nations themselves. These men may have been agents, but their action would have been impossible if they did not realize that there was a vast body of national feeling behind them not opposed to war. Their citizens were in conflict with each other already, generating the moods which lead on to war. Emperors, foreign secretaries, ambassadors, cabinet ministers are not really powerful to move nations against their will. On the whole, they act with the will of the nations, which they understand. Let any one ruler try, for example, to change by edict the religion of his subjects, and a week would see him bereft of place and power. They could not do this, because the will of the nation would be against it. They resort to war and prepare for it because the will of the nation is with them, and this throws us back on the private citizens, who finally are individually and collectively responsible for the actions of the State. In the everlasting battle between good and evil, private soldiers are called upon to fight as well as the captains, and it is only through the intensive cultivation by individuals and races of the higher moral and intellectual qualities, until in intensity they outweigh the mood and passion of the rest, that war will finally become obsolete as the court of appeal. When there is a panic of fire in a crowded building men are suddenly tested as to character. Some will become frenzied madmen, fighting and trampling their way out. Others will act nobly, forgetting themselves. They have no time to think. What they are in their total make-up as human beings, overbalanced either for good or evil, appears in an instant. Even so, some time in the heroic future, some nation in a crisis will be weighed and will act nobly rather than passionately, and will be prepared to risk national extinction rather than continue existence at the price of killing myriads of other human beings, and it will oppose moral and spiritual forces to material forces, and it will over-come the world by making gentleness its might, as all great spiritual teachers have done. It comes to this, we cannot overcome hatred by hatred or war by war, but by the opposites of these. Evil is not overcome by evil but by good; and any race like the Irish, eager for national life, ought to learn this truth—that humanity will act towards their race as their race acts towards humanity. The noble and the base alike beget their kin. Empires, ere they disappear, see their own mirrored majesty arise in the looking-glass of time. Opposed to the pride and pomp of Egypt were the pride and pomp of Chaldaea. Echoing the beauty of the Greek city state were many lovely cities made in their image. Carthage evoked Rome. The British Empire, by the natural balance and opposition of things, called into being another empire with a civilization of coal and steel, and with ambitions for colonies and for naval power, and with that image of itself it must wrestle for empire. The great armadas that throng the seas, the armed millions upon the earth betray the fear in the minds of races, nay, the inner spiritual certitude the soul has, that pride and lust of power must yet be humbled by their kind. They must at last meet their equals face to face, called to them as steel to magnet by some inner affinity. This is a law of life both for individuals and races, and, when this is realized, we know nothing will put an end to race conflicts except the equally determined and heroic development of the spiritual, moral, and intellectual forces which disdain to use the force and fury of material powers.

We may be assured that the divine law is not mocked, and it cannot be deceived. As men sow so do they reap. The anger we create will rend us; the love we give will return to us. Biologically, everything breeds true to its type: moods and thoughts just as much as birds and beasts and fishes. When I hear people raging against England or Germany or Russia I know that rage will beget rage, and go on begetting it, and so the whole devilish generation of passions will be continued. There are no nations to whom the entire and loyal allegiance of man's spirit could be given. It can only go out to the ideal empires and nationalities in the womb of time, for whose coming we pray. Those countries of the future we must carve out of the humanity of to-day, and we can begin building them up within our present empires and nation-alities just as we are building up the co-operative movement in a social order antagonistic to it. The people who are trying to create these new ideals in the world are outposts, sentinels, and frontiersmen thrown out before the armies of the intellectual and spiritual races yet to come into being. We can all enlist in these armies and be comrades to the pioneers. I hope many will enlist in

Ireland. I would cry to our idealists to come out of this present-day Irish Babylon, so filled with sectarian, political, and race hatreds, and to work for the future. I believe profoundly, with the most extreme of Nationalists, in the future of Ireland, and in the vision of light seen by Bridget which she saw and confessed between hopes and tears to Patrick, and that this is the Isle of Destiny and the destiny will be glorious and not ignoble, and when our hour is come we will have something to give to the world, and we will be proud to give rather than to grasp. Throughout their history Irishmen have always wrought better for others than for themselves, and when they unite in Ireland to work for each other, they will direct into the right channel all that national capacity for devotion to causes for which they are famed. We ought not only to desire to be at peace with each other, but with the whole world, and this can only be brought about by the individual citizen at all times protesting against sectarian and national passions, and taking no part in them, coming out of such angry parties altogether, as the people of the Lord were called by the divine voice to come out of Babylon. It may seem a long way to set things right, but it is the swift way and the royal road, and there is no other; and nobody, no prophet crying before his time, will be listened to until the people are ready for him. The congregation must gather before the preacher can deliver what is in him to say. The economic brotherhood which I have put forward as an Irish ideal would, in its realization, make us at peace with ourselves, and if we are at peace with ourselves we will be at peace with our neighbours and all other nations, and will wish them the good-will we have among ourselves, and will receive from them the same good-will. I do not believe in legal and formal solutions of national antagonisms. While we generate animosities among ourselves we will always display them to other nations, and I prefer to search out how it is national hatreds are begotten, and to show how that cancer can be cut out of the body politic.

6. Zionism *

THEODOR HERZL

The Jewish question still exists. It would be foolish to deny it. It is a remnant of the Middle Ages, which civilized nations do not even yet seem

* From Theodor Herzl, *The Jewish State* (1896; English translation, Scopus Publishing Co., New York, 1943). By permission.

able to shake off, try as they will. They certainly showed a generous desire to do so when they emancipated us. The Jewish question exists wherever Jews live in perceptible numbers. Where it does not exist, it is carried by Jews in the course of their migrations. We naturally move to those places where we are not persecuted, and there our presence produces persecution. This is the case in every country, and will remain so, even in those highly civilized— for instance, France—till the Jewish question finds a solution on a political basis. The unfortunate Jews are now carrying Anti-Semitism into England; they have already introduced it into America.

I believe that I understand Anti-Semitism, which is really a highly complex movement. I consider it from a Jewish standpoint, yet without fear or hatred. I believe that I can see what elements there are in it of vulgar sport, of common trade jealousy, of inherited prejudice, of religious intolerance, and also of pretended self-defence. I think the Jewish question is no more a social than a religious one, notwithstanding that it sometimes takes these and other forms. It is a national question, which can only be solved by making it a political world-question to be discussed and settled by the civilized nations of the world in council.

We are a people—one people.

We have honestly endeavored everywhere to merge ourselves in the social life of surrounding communities and to preserve only the faith of our fathers. We are not permitted to do so. In vain are we loyal patriots, our loyalty in some places running to extremes; in vain do we make the same sacrifices of life and property as our fellow-citizens; in vain do we strive to increase the fame of our native land in science and art, or her wealth by trade and commerce. In countries where we have lived for centuries we are still cried down as strangers, and often by those whose ancestors were not yet domiciled in the land where Jews had already had experience of suffering. The majority may decide which are the strangers; for this, as indeed every point which arises in the relations between nations, is a question of might. I do not here surrender any portion of our prescriptive right, when I make this statement merely in my own name as an individual. In the world as it now is and for an indefinite period will probably remain, might precedes right. It is useless, therefore, for us to be loyal patriots, as were the Huguenots who were forced to emigrate. If we could only be left in peace. . . .

But I think we shall not be left in peace.

Oppression and persecution cannot exterminate us. No nation on earth has survived such struggles and sufferings as we have gone through. Jew-baiting has merely stripped off our weaklings; the strong among us were invariably true to their race when persecution broke out against them. This attitude was most clearly apparent in the period immediately following the emancipation of the Jews. Those Jews who were advanced intellectually and materially entirely lost the feeling of belonging to their race. Wherever our political well-being has lasted for any length of time, we have assimilated with our surroundings. I think this is not discreditable. Hence, the statesman who would wish to see a Jewish strain in his nation, would have to provide for the duration of our political well-being; and even a Bismarck could not do that.

For old prejudices against us still lie deep in the hearts of the people. He who would have proofs of this need only listen to the people where they speak with frankness and simplicity: proverb and fairy-tale are both Anti-Semitic. A nation is everywhere a great child, which can certainly be educated; but its education would, even in most favorable circumstances, occupy such a vast amount of time that we could, as already mentioned, remove our own difficulties by other means long before the process was accomplished.

Assimilation, by which I understood not only external conformity in dress, habits, customs, and language, but also identity of feeling and manner—assimilation of Jews could be effected only by intermarriage. But the need for mixed marriages would have to be felt by the majority; their mere recognition by law would certainly not suffice.

The Hungarian Liberals, who have just given legal sanction to mixed marriages, have made a remarkable mistake which one of the earliest cases clearly illustrates; a baptized Jew married a Jewess. At the same time the struggle to obtain the present form of marriage accentuated distinctions between Jews and Christians, thus hindering rather than aiding the fusion of races.

Those who really wished to see the Jews disappear through intermixture with other nations, can only hope to see it come about in one way. The Jews must previously acquire economic power sufficiently great to overcome the old social prejudice against them. The aristocracy may serve as an example of this, for in its ranks occur the proportionately largest numbers of mixed marriages. The Jewish families which regild the old nobility with their money become gradually absorbed. But what form would this phenomenon assume in the middle classes, where (the Jews being a bourgeois people) the Jewish question is mainly concentrated? A previous acquisition of power could be synonymous with that economic supremacy which Jews are already erroneously declared to possess. And if the power they now possess creates rage and indignation among the Anti-Semites, what outbreaks would not an increase of power create? Hence the first step towards absorption will never be taken, because this step would involve the subjection of the majority to a hitherto scorned minority, possessing neither military nor administrative power of its own. I think, therefore, that the absorption of Jews by means of their prosperity is unlikely to occur. In countries which now are Anti-Semitic my view will be approved. In others, where Jews now feel comfortable, it will probably be violently disputed by them. My happier co-religionists will not believe me till Jew-baiting teaches them the truth; for the longer Anti-

Semitism lies in abeyance the more fiercely will it break out. The infiltration of immigrating Jews, attracted to a land by apparent security, and the ascent in the social scale of native Jews, combine powerfully to bring about a revolution. Nothing is plainer than this rational conclusion.

Because I have drawn this conclusion with complete indifference to everything but the quest of truth, I shall probably be contradicted and opposed by Jews who are in easy circumstances. In so far as private interests alone are held by their anxious or timid possessors to be in danger, they can safely be ignored, for the concerns of the poor and oppressed are of greater importance than theirs. But I wish from the outset to prevent any misconception from arising, particularly the mistaken notion that my project, if realized, would in the least degree injure property now held by Jews. I shall therefore explain everything connected with rights of property very fully. Whereas, if my plan never becomes anything more than a piece of literature, things will merely remain as they are. It might more reasonably be objected that I am giving a handle to Anti-Semitism when I say we are a people—one people; that I am hindering the assimilation of Jews where it is about to be consummated, and endangering it where it is an accomplished fact, in so far as it is possible for a solitary writer to hinder or endanger anything.

This objection will be especially brought forward in France. It will probably also be made in other countries, but I shall answer only the French Jews beforehand, because these afford the most striking example of my point.

However much I may worship personality—powerful individual personality in statesmen, inventors, artists, philosophers, or commanders, as well as the collective personality of a historic group of human beings, which we call a nation—however much I may worship personality, I do not regret its disappearance. Whoever can, will, and must perish, let him perish. But the distinctive nationality of Jews neither can, will, nor must be destroyed. It cannot be destroyed, because external enemies consolidate it. It will not be destroyed; this is shown during two thousand years of appalling suffering. It must not be destroyed, and that, as successor to numberless Jews who refused to despair, I am trying once more to prove in this pamphlet. Whole branches of Judaism may wither and fall, but the trunk remains.

EFFECTS OF ANTI-SEMITISM

The oppression we endure does not improve us, for we are not a whit better than ordinary people. It is true that we do not love our enemies; but he alone who can conquer himself dare reproach us with that fault. Oppression naturally creates hostility against oppressors, and our hostility aggravates the pressure. It is impossible to escape from this eternal round.

"No!" Some soft-hearted visionaries will say: "No, it is possible! Possible by means of the ultimate perfection of humanity."

Is it worth while pointing out the sentimental folly of this view? He who would found his hope for improved conditions on the ultimate perfection of humanity would indeed be painting a Utopia!

I referred previously to our "assimilation": I do not for a moment wish to imply that I desire such an end. Our national character is too historically famous, and, in spite of every degradation, too fine to make its annihilation desirable. We might perhaps be able to merge ourselves entirely into surrounding races, if these were to leave us in peace for a space of two generations. But they will not leave us in peace. For a little period they manage to tolerate us, and then their hostility breaks out again and again. The world is provoked somehow by our prosperity, because it has for many centuries been accustomed to consider us as the most contemptible among the poverty-stricken. In its ignorance and narrowness of heart, it fails to observe that prosperity weakens our Judaism and extinguishes our peculiarities. It is only pressure that forces us back to the parent stem; it is only hatred encompassing us that makes us strangers once more.

Thus, whether we like it or not, we are now, and shall henceforth remain, a historic group with unmistakable characteristics common to us all.

We are one people—our enemies have made us one in our despite, as repeatedly happens in history. Distress binds us together, and, thus united, we suddenly discover our strength. Yes, we are strong enough to form a State, and, indeed, a model State. We possess all human and material resources necessary for the purpose.

This is the strictly appropriate place to give an account of what has been somewhat roughly termed our "human material." But it would not be appreciated till the broad lines of the plan, on which everything depends, had first been marked out.

THE PLAN

The whole plan is in its essence perfectly simple, as it must necessarily be if it is to come within the comprehension of all.

Let the sovereignty be granted us over a portion of the globe large enough to satisfy the rightful requirements of a nation; the rest we shall manage for ourselves.

The creation of a new State is neither ridiculous nor impossible. We have in our day witnessed the process in connection with nations which were not largely members of the middle class, but poorer, less educated, and consequently weaker than ourselves. The Governments of all countries scourged by Anti-Semitism will be keenly interested in assisting us to obtain the sovereignty we want.

The plan, simple in design, but complicated in execution, will be carried out by two agencies: The Society of Jews and the Jewish Company.

The Society of Jews will do the preparatory work in the domains of science and politics, which the Jewish Company will afterwards apply practically.

The Jewish Company will see to the realization of the business interests of departing Jews, and will organize commerce and trade in the new country.

We must not imagine the departure of the Jews to be a sudden one. It will be gradual, continuous, and will cover many decades. The poorest will go first to cultivate the soil. In accordance with a preconcerted plan, they will construct roads, bridges, railways and telegraph installations; regulate rivers; and build their own habitations; their labor will create trade, trade will create markets and markets will attract new settlers, for every man will go voluntarily, at his own expense and his own risk. The labor expended on the land will enhance its value, and the Jews will soon perceive that a new and permanent sphere of operation is opening here for that spirit of enterprise which has heretofore met only with hatred and obliquy.

If we wish to found a State today, we shall not do it in the way which would have been the only possible one a thousand years ago. It is foolish to revert to old stages of civilization, as many Zionists would like to do. Supposing, for example, we were obliged to clear a country of wild beasts, we should not set about the task in the fashion of Europeans of the fifth century. We should not take spear and lance and go out singly in pursuit of bears; we should organize a large and lively hunting party, drive the animals together, and throw a melinite bomb into their midst.

If we wish to conduct building operations, we shall not plant a mass of stakes and piles on the shore of a lake, but we shall build as men build now. Indeed, we shall build in a bolder and more stately style than was ever adopted before, for we now possess means which men never yet possessed.

The emigrants standing lowest in the economic scale will be slowly followed by those of a higher grade. Those who at this moment are living in despair will go first. They will be led by the mediocre intellects which we produce so superabundantly and which are persecuted everywhere.

This pamphlet will open a general discussion on the Jewish Question, but that does not mean that there will be any voting on it. Such a result would ruin the cause from the outset, and dissentients must remember that allegiance or opposition is entirely voluntary. He who will not come with us may remain behind.

Let all who are willing to join us, fall in behind our banner and fight for our cause with voice and pen and deed.

Those Jews who fall in with our idea of a State will attach themselves to the Society, which will thereby be authorized to confer and treat with Governments in the name of our people. The Society will thus be acknowledged in its relations with Governments as a State-creating power. This acknowledgment will practically create the State.

Should the Powers declare themselves willing to admit our sovereignty over a neutral piece of land, then the Society will enter into negotiations for the possession of this land. Here two territories come under consideration,

Palestine and Argentina. In both countries important experiments in coloni-
zation have been made, though on the mistaken principle of a gradual infiltration of Jews. An infiltration is bound to end badly. It continues till the
inevitable moment when the native population feels itself threatened, and
forces the Government to stop a further influx of Jews. Immigration is consequently futile unless based on an assured supremacy.

The Society of Jews will treat with the present masters of the land, putting
itself under the protectorate of the European Powers, if they prove friendly
to the plan. We could offer the present possessors of the land enormous advantages, take upon ourselves part of the public debt, build new roads for
traffic, which our presence in the country would render necessary, and do
many other things. The creation of our State would be beneficial to adjacent
countries, because the cultivation of a strip of land increases the value of its
surrounding districts in innumerable ways.

PALESTINE OR ARGENTINA?

Shall we choose Palestine or Argentina? We shall take what is given us,
and what is selected by Jewish public opinion. The Society will determine
both these points.

Argentina is one of the most fertile countries in the world, extends over a
vast area, has a spare population and a mild climate. The Argentine Republic would derive considerable profit from the cession of a portion of its territory to us. The present infiltration of Jews has certainly produced some discontent, and it would be necessary to enlighten the Republic on the intrinsic
difference of our new movement.

Palestine is our ever-memorable historic home. The very name of Palestine would attract our people with a force of marvellous potency. Supposing
His Majesty the Sultan were to give us Palestine, we could in return undertake to regulate the whole finances of Turkey. We should there form a
portion of a rampart of Europe against Asia, an outpost of civilization as
opposed to barbarism. We should as a neutral State remain in contact with
all Europe, which would have to guarantee our existence. The sanctuaries
of Christendom would be safeguarded by assigning to them an extra-terri-
torial status such as is well-known to the law of nations.

We should form a guard of honor about these sanctuaries, answering for
the fulfilment of this duty with our existence. This guard of honor would
be the great symbol of the solution of the Jewish Question after eighteen
centuries of Jewish suffering.

DEMAND, MEDIUM, TRADE

I said in the last chapter but one, "The Jewish Company will organize
trade and commerce in the new country." I shall here insert a few remarks
on that point.

A scheme such as mine is gravely imperilled if it is opposed by "practical" people. Now "practical" people are as a rule nothing more than men sunk into the groove of daily routine, unable to emerge from a narrow circle of antiquated ideas. At the same time, their adverse opinion carries great weight, and can do considerable harm to a new project, at any rate till this new thing is sufficiently strong to throw the "practical" people and their mouldy notions to the winds.

In the earliest period of European railway construction some "practical" people were of the opinion that it was foolish to build certain lines "because there were not even sufficient passengers to fill the mail-coaches." They did not realize the truth—which now seems obvious to us—that travellers do not produce railways, but, conversely, railways produce travellers, the latent demand being, of course, taken for granted.

The impossibility of comprehending how trade and commerce are to be created in a new country which has yet to be acquired and cultivated, may be classed with those doubts of "practical" persons concerning the need of railways. A "practical" person would express himself somewhat in this fashion:

"Granted that the present situation of the Jews is in many places unendurable, and aggravated day by day; granted that there exists a desire to emigrate; granted even that the Jews do emigrate to the new country; how will they earn their living there, and what will they earn? What are they to live on when there? The business of many people cannot be artificially organized in a day."

To this I should reply: We have not the slightest intention of organizing trade artificially, and we should certainly not attempt to do it in a day. But, though the organization of it may be impossible, the promotion of it is not. And how is commerce to be encouraged? Through the medium of a demand. The demand recognized, the medium created, and it will establish itself.

If there is a real and earnest demand among Jews for an improvement of their status; if the medium to be created—the Jewish Company—is sufficiently powerful, then commerce will extend itself copiously in the new country. This is, of course, an assumption, in the same way as the development of railway traffic was an assumption in the thirties. Railroads were built all the same, for men's ideas fortunately carried them beyond the doubts of "practical" people and their mail-coaches.

THEOCRACY

Shall we end by having a theocracy? No, indeed. Faith unites us, knowledge gives us freedom. We shall therefore prevent any theocratic tendencies from coming to the fore on the part of our priesthood. We shall keep our priests within the confines of their temples in the same way as we shall keep our professional army within the confines of their barracks. Army and priesthood shall receive honors high as their functions deserve. But they must not interfere in the administration of the State which confers distinction upon them, else they will conjure up difficulties without and within.

Every man will be free and undisturbed in his faith or his disbelief as he is in his nationality. And if it should occur that men of other creeds and different nationalities come to live amongst us, we should accord them honorable protection and equality before the law. We have learnt toleration in Europe. This is not sarcastically said; for the Anti-Semitism of today could only in a very few places be taken for old religious intolerance. It is for the most part a movement among civilized nations by which they try to chase away the spectres of their own past.

~~~~~~

7. *Imperialism—Incompatible with Free Government* *

<div align="right">

J. A. HOBSON

</div>

~~~~~~

Not only does aggressive Imperialism defeat the movement towards internationalism by fostering animosities among competing empires: its attack upon the liberties and the existence of weaker or lower races stimulates in them a corresponding excess of national self-consciousness. A nationalism that bristles with resentment and is all astrain with the passion of self-defence is only less perverted from its natural genius than the nationalism which glows with the animus of greed and self-aggrandisement at the expense of others. From this aspect aggressive Imperialism is an artificial stimulation of nationalism in peoples too foreign to be absorbed and too compact to be permanently crushed. We welded Africanderdom into just such a strong dangerous nationalism, and we joined with other nations in creating a resentful nationalism until then unknown in China. The injury to nationalism in both cases consists in converting a cohesive, pacific internal force into an exclusive, hostile force, a perversion of the true power and use of nationality. The worst and most certain result is the retardation of internationalism. The older nationalism was primarily an inclusive sentiment; its natural relation to the same sentiment in another people was lack of sympathy, not open hostility; there was no inherent antagonism to prevent nationalities from growing and thriving side by side. Such in the main was

* From J. A. Hobson, *Imperialism* (1902; third edition, 1938). By permission of The Macmillan Company, publishers.

the nationalism of the earlier nineteenth century, and the politicians of Free Trade had some foundation for their dream of a quick growth of effective, informal internationalism by peaceful, profitable intercommunication of goods and ideas among nations recognizing a just harmony of interests in free peoples.

The overflow of nationalism into imperial channels quenched all such hopes. While co-existent nationalities are capable of mutual aid involving no direct antagonism of interests, co-existent empires following each its own imperial career of territorial and industrial aggrandisement are natural necessary enemies. The full nature of this antagonism on its economic side is not intelligible without a close analysis of those conditions of modern capitalist production which compel an ever keener "fight for markets," but the political antagonism is obvious.

Imperialism and popular government have nothing in common: they differ in spirit, in policy, in method. Of policy and method I have already spoken; it remains to point out how the spirit of Imperialism poisons the springs of democracy in the mind and character of the people. As our free self-governing colonies have furnished hope, encouragement, and leading to the popular aspirations in Great Britain, not merely by practical successes in the arts of popular government, but by the wafting of a spirit of freedom and equality, so our despotically ruled dependencies have ever served to damage the character of our people by feeding the habits of snobbish subservience, the admiration of wealth and rank, the corrupt survivals of the inequalities of feudalism. This process began with the advent of the East Indian nabob and the West Indian planter into English society and politics, bringing back with his plunders of the slave trade and the gains of corrupt and extortionate officialism the acts of vulgar ostentation, domineering demeanour and corrupting largesse to dazzle and degrade the life of our people. Cobden, writing in 1860 of our Indian Empire, put this pithy question: "Is it not just possible that we may become corrupted at home by the reaction of arbitrary political maxims in the East upon our domestic politics, just as Greece and Rome were demoralised by their contact with Asia?" [1]

Not merely is the reaction possible, it is inevitable. As the despotic portion of our Empire has grown in area, a larger and larger number of men, trained in the temper and methods of autocracy as soldiers and civil officials in our Crown colonies, protectorates, and Indian Empire, reinforced by numbers of merchants, planters, engineers, and overseers, whose lives have been those of a superior caste living an artificial life removed from all the healthy restraints of ordinary European society, have returned to this country, bringing back the characters, sentiments, and ideas imposed by this foreign environment. The South and South-West of England is richly sprinkled with

[1] Morley, *Life of Cobden*, Vol. ii, p. 361.

these men, many of them wealthy, most of them endowed with leisure, men openly contemptuous of democracy, devoted to material luxury, social display, and the shallower arts of intellectual life. The wealthier among them discover political ambitions, introducing into our Houses of Parliament the coarsest and most selfish spirit of "Imperialism," using their imperial experience and connexions to push profitable companies and concessions for their private benefits, and posing as authorities so as to keep the yoke of Imperialism firmly fixed upon the shoulders of the "nigger." The South African millionaire is the brand most in evidence: his methods are the most barefaced, and his success, social and political, the most redoubtable. But the practices which are writ large in Rhodes, Beit, and their parliamentary confederates are widespread on a smaller scale; the South of England is full of men of local influence in politics and society whose character has been formed in our despotic Empire, and whose incomes are chiefly derived from the maintenance and furtherance of this despotic rule. Not a few enter our local councils, or take posts in our constabulary or our prisons: everywhere they stand for coercion and for resistance to reform. Could the incomes expended in the Home Counties and other large districts of Southern Britain be traced to their sources, it would be found that they were in large measure wrung from the enforced toil of vast multitudes of black, brown, or yellow natives, by arts not differing essentially from those which supported in idleness and luxury imperial Rome.

It is, indeed, a nemesis of Imperialism that the arts and crafts of tyranny, acquired and exercised in our unfree Empire, should be turned against our liberties at home. Those who have felt surprise at the total disregard or the open contempt displayed by the aristocracy and the plutocracy of this land for infringements of the liberties of the subject and for the abrogation of constitutional rights and usages have not taken sufficiently into account the steady reflux of this poison of irresponsible autocracy from our "unfree, intolerant, aggressive" Empire.

The political effects, actual and necessary, of the new Imperialism, as illustrated in the case of the greatest of imperialist Powers, may be thus summarised. It is a constant menace to peace, by furnishing continual temptations to further aggression upon lands occupied by lower races and by embroiling our nation with other nations of rival imperial ambitions; to the sharp peril of war it adds the chronic danger and degradation of militarism, which not merely wastes the current physical and moral resources of the nations, but checks the very course of civilization. It consumes to an illimitable and incalculable extent the financial resources of a nation by military preparation, stopping the expenditure of the current income of the State upon productive public projects and burdening posterity with heavy loads of debt. Absorbing the public money, the time, interest and energy on costly and unprofitable work of territorial aggrandisement, it thus wastes those energies of public life in the governing classes and the nations which are needed for internal reforms and for the cultivation of the arts of material and intellectual progress at home. Finally, the spirit, the policy, and the methods of Imperialism are hostile to the institutions of popular self-government, favouring forms of political tyranny and social authority which are the deadly enemies of effective liberty and equality.

Analysis of Imperialism, with its natural supports, militarism, oligarchy, bureaucracy, protection, concentration of capital and violent trade fluctuations, has marked it out as the supreme danger of modern national States. The power of the imperialist forces within the nation to use the national resources for their private gain, by operating the instrument of the State, can only be overthrown by the establishment of a genuine democracy, the direction of public policy by the people for the people through representatives over whom they exercise a real control. Whether this or any other nation is yet competent for such a democracy may well be matter of grave doubt, but until and unless the external policy of a nation is "broad-based upon a people's will" there appears little hope of remedy. The scare of a great recent war may for a brief time check the confidence of these conspirators against the commonwealth, and cause them to hold their hands, but the financial forces freshly generated will demand new outlets, and will utilize the same political alliances and the same social, religious, and philanthropic supports in their pressure for new enterprises. The circumstances of each new imperialist exploit differ from those of all preceding ones: whatever ingenuity is requisite for the perversion of the public intelligence, or the inflammation of the public sentiment, will be forthcoming.

Imperialism is only beginning to realize its full resources, and to develop into a fine art the management of nations: the broad bestowal of a franchise, wielded by a people whose education has reached the stage of an uncritical ability to read printed matter, favours immensely the designs of keen business politicians, who, by controlling the press, the schools, and where necessary the churches, impose Imperialism upon the masses under the attractive guise of sensational patriotism.

The chief economic source of Imperialism has been found in the inequality of industrial opportunities by which a favoured class accumulates superfluous elements of income which, in their search for profitable investments, press ever farther afield: the influence on State policy of these investors and their financial managers secures a national alliance of other vested interests which are threatened by movements of social reform: the adoption of Imperialism thus serves the double purpose of securing private material benefits for favoured classes of investors and traders at the public cost, while sustaining the general cause of conservatism by diverting public energy and interest from domestic agitation to external employment.

The ability of a nation to shake off this dangerous usurpation of its power, and to employ the national resources in the national interest, depends upon the education of a national intelligence and a national will, which shall make democracy a political and economic reality. To term Imperialism a national policy is an impudent falsehood: the interests of the nation are opposed to every act of this expansive policy. Every enlargement of Great Britain in the tropics is a distinct enfeeblement of true British nationalism. Indeed, Imperialism is commended in some quarters for this very reason, that by breaking the narrow bounds of nationalities it facilitates and forwards internationalism. There are even those who favour or condone the forcible suppression of small nationalities by larger ones under the impulse of Imperialism, because they imagine that this is the natural approach to a world-federation and eternal peace. A falser view of political evolution it is difficult to conceive. If there is one condition precedent to effective internationalism or to the establishment of any reliable relations between States, it is the existence of strong, secure, well-developed, and responsible nations. Internationalism can never be subserved by the suppression or forcible absorption of nations; for these practices react disastrously upon the springs of internationalism, on the one hand setting nations on their armed defence and stifling the amicable approaches between them, on the other debilitating the larger nations through excessive corpulence and indigestion. The hope of a coming internationalism enjoins above all else the maintenance and natural growth of independent nationalities, for without such there could be no gradual evolution of internationalism, but only a series of unsuccessful attempts at a chaotic and unstable cosmopolitanism. As individualism is essential to any sane form of national socialism, so nationalism is essential to internationalism: no organic conception of world-politics can be framed on any other supposition.

Just in proportion as the substitution of true national governments for the existing oligarchies or sham democracies becomes possible will the apparent conflicts of national interests disappear, and the fundamental co-operation upon which nineteenth-century Free Trade prematurely relied manifest itself. The present class government means the severance or antagonism of nations, because each ruling class can only keep and use its rule by forcing the antagonisms of foreign policy: intelligent democracies would perceive their identity of interest, and would ensure it by their amicable policy. The genuine forces of internationalism, thus liberated, would first display themselves as economic forces, securing more effective international co-operation for postal, telegraphic, railway, and other transport services, for monetary exchange and for common standards of measurement of various kinds, and for the improved intercommunication of persons, goods, and information. Related and subsidiary to these purposes would come a growth of machinery of courts and congresses, at first informal and private, but gradually taking shape in more definite and more public machinery: the common interests of the arts and sciences would everywhere be weaving an elaborate network of intellectual internationalism, and both economic and intellectual community of needs and interests would contribute to the natural growth of such political solidarity as was required to maintain this real community.

It is thus, and only thus, that the existing false antagonisms of nations, with their wastes and perils and their retardation of the general course of civilization, can be resolved. To substitute for this peaceful discovery and expression of common interests a federal policy proceeding upon directly selfish political and military interests, the idea which animates an Anglo-Saxon alliance or a Pan-Teutonic empire, is deliberately to choose a longer, more difficult, and far more hazardous road to internationalism. The economic bond is far stronger and more reliable as a basis of growing internationalism than the so-called racial bond or a political alliance constructed on some short-sighted computation of a balance of power. It is, of course, quite possible that a Pan-Slav, Pan-Teutonic, Pan-British, or Pan-Latin alliance might, if the federation were kept sufficiently voluntary and elastic, contribute to the wider course of internationalism. But the frankly military purpose commonly assigned for such alliances bodes ill for such assistance. It is far more likely that such alliances would be formed in the interests of the "imperialist" classes of the contracting nations, in order the more effectively to exploit the joint national resources.

Imperialism is a depraved choice of national life, imposed by self-seeking interests which appeal to the lusts of quantitative acquisitiveness and of forceful domination surviving in a nation from early centuries of animal struggle for existence. Its adoption as a policy implies a deliberate renunciation of that cultivation of the higher inner qualities which for a nation as for an individual constitutes the ascendency of reason over brute impulse. It is the besetting sin of all successful States, and its penalty is unalterable in the order of nature.

~~~~~~

8. The Right to Conquer*

ADOLF HITLER

~~~~~~

The National Socialist movement must strive to eliminate the disproportion between our population and our area—viewing this latter as a source of

* From Adolf Hitler, *Mein Kampf* (1925–1927; translated by Ralph Manheim, Houghton Mifflin Company, 1943). By permission.

food as well as a basis for power politics—between our historical past and the hopelessness of our present impotence. And in this it must remain aware that we, as guardians of the highest humanity on this earth, are bound by the highest obligation, and the more it strives to bring the German people to radical awareness so that, in addition to breeding dogs, horses, and cats, they will have mercy on their *own* blood, the more it will be able to meet this obligation.

The right to possess soil can become a duty if without extension of its soil a great nation seems doomed to destruction. And most especially when not some little nigger nation or other is involved, but the Germanic mother of life, which has given the present-day world its cultural picture. *Germany will either be a world power or there will be no Germany.* And for world power she needs that magnitude which will give her the position she needs in the present period, and life to her citizens.

If we speak of soil in Europe today, we can primarily have in mind only *Russia* and her vassal border states.

Here Fate itself seems desirous of giving us a sign. By handing Russia to Bolshevism, it robbed the Russian nation of that intelligentsia which previously brought about and guaranteed its existence as a state. For the organization of a Russian state formation was not the result of the political abilities of the Slavs in Russia, but only a wonderful example of the state-forming efficacy of the German element in an inferior race. Numerous mighty empires on earth have been created in this way.

A state which in this age of racial poisoning dedicates itself to the care of its best racial elements must some day become lord of the earth.

Chapter XV

RACE: SENSE AND NONSENSE

RACIALISM is one of the recent perversions of nationalism. Individual self-praise is frowned upon in most parts: the German proverb *Eigenlob stinkt* (self-praise stinks) expresses the social and aesthetic stigma that is attached to self-praise. Yet translated into collective terms, self-praise suddenly becomes a sign of patriotism and loyalty.

As a student of world history and philosophy, Hegel, in his *Philosophy of History* (1837), inquires into the progress of mankind from ancient times on. Starting with the premise that "Freedom is the sole Truth of Spirit," Hegel demonstrates that the history of the world "is none other than the progress of the consciousness of Freedom." The Oriental concept was very narrow indeed: "they only knew that one is free." In the practice of government, that meant despotism, because if only one is free, all the others are unfree. The Greeks and Romans made some advance over the Orientals, because they knew that *some* were free; their concept of liberty was tied to slavery which was the unfreedom of the many. But the fulfillment of freedom for "man, as man" came with the German nations, Hegel proves, to his own satisfaction. Thus, if the history of the world is nothing but the progress of freedom, it has reached its climax and summit in the German nations with their most consummate realization of freedom. All this was said by Hegel in his lectures at the University of Berlin at a time when France had just experienced one of the greatest popular revolutions of all history, and while Prussia had set up a police state, in reaction to the dangerous liberal ideas of the West, which outdid in severity any regime that had previously existed in Prussia. The Prussian police state as the consummation and summit of human freedom—dialectical reasoning would supply almost any answer for Hegel.

From Spirit to Beer—this is the saga of the German mind in the nineteenth century. Whereas Hegel still clothed his German superiority complex in high-sounding phrases of Freedom and Spirit, Treitschke represents the coarse era of William II; in his lectures on *Politics* (1897–1898), he feels sorry for the Germans who, having emigrated to the United States, find the temperance laws "hardest to bear." As beer drinkers, the Germans drink rather more than they should, Treitschke avows, but with them this is a harmless pleasure; whereas, "if the American once begins drinking he drinks himself blind drunk." Thus Treitschke on the evil effects of strong liquor. Treitschke is satisfied that "we Germans can draw no lessons for ourselves" from the political conditions of America, and that "dirty money-grubbing interests" dominate American politics. How could "sensitive natures" be attracted by the "dollar-hunting of American life?" Treitschke was so convinced of the superiority of German Kultur over the colonial "thinness" and emptiness of American life that he wrote (in *Deutsche Kämpfe,* 1896) that "the civilization (*Gesittung*) of Mankind suffers a loss each time a German transforms himself into a Yankee."

Of all the more recent German racialist writers, Hans F. K. Günther was the most widely read and admired in the Fatherland. His *Racial Elements of European History* (1927) purported to show that the Germans were not only good, very good, indeed, but the only people who had contributed great achievements to world culture. Günther was not satisfied with claiming all European accomplishments, including those of the Greeks and Romans, for German inspiration and leadership; his imagination roamed as far as India and Persia. As long as they were under Nordic influence, they were great civilizations; as soon as the "blood of the creative, the Nordic race," ran dry, as soon as they were cut off from the Nordics, stagnation set in, and nothing much happened thenceforth. The scientific solidity of Günther appealed to the Nazi rulers so much that he was appointed to high academic and political positions. However, Günther did not do his "research" under the Third Reich, but in the Weimar Republic. The Republic gave him his opportunity; the Nazi state, his reward.

Another fellow anthropologist, Adolf Hitler, fully concurred with Günther. *Mein Kampf* is, in effect, a loud and lengthy paraphrase of one theme: the right of the German "race" to dominate the world, because the Germans are so superior to all the other breeds. Hitler was not even complimentary to his later Axis partners: both Italy and Japan get very low marks in *Mein Kampf,* when it comes to passing the course of Kultur. In the scale of values, as devised in *Mein Kampf,* Hitler does not do so badly himself. He stresses throughout his book the idea that the racialist view "recognizes not only different values of races, but also the different values of individual men." Among the world's peoples, the Germans are the superior "race." But Hitler adds the important point that this "aristocratic" viewpoint also holds within a nation: there, too, there is a scale of values, from the lowest to the highest individual. After careful and mature reflection, Hitler felt compelled to admit that he was the superior among the superior.

Probably nowhere outside Germany and Japan has racialist fancy been embroidered with so much respectability as in the United States. Madison Grant and Lothrop Stoddard are the two leading American writers in this field, and their names are frequently mentioned in German racialist writings as evidence of the fact that Germany is not the only country which had become aware of the danger of the "inferior races." In *The Passing of the Great Race* (1916), Madison Grant founds his racialist views, logically, on opposition to political and economic democracy. He is alarmed by the high taxation of the aristocratic classes in England—which might lead to the "destruction of superior types" and the rule of "the inferior classes in modern democracies." In nationalism, patriotism, freedom, and other "high-sounding names," Grant sees but the "conquered servile classes rising against the master race." Grant is unusually candid among American racialist writers when he opposes American democracy on the ground that racial equality is inherent in the concept of democracy. He is persuaded that the democratic form of government is bound to increase the "preponderance of the lower types," because a majority "must of necessity be inferior to a picked minority." This is why he rejects the French Revolution and even the American Revolution. A definite believer in the theory that one thing leads to another, Grant sees in simplified spelling a step in the direction of the destruction of the higher racial types; he is also opposed to weakening the privilege of wealth, because wealth is "the reward of successful intelligence and industry." Like Hitler, Grant has contempt for the "sentimental belief in the sanctity of human life," and advocates the "elimination of defective infants and the sterilization of such adults as are themselves of no value to the community." Grant never considers the possibility that a misguided community, though believing in his general ideas, might err in a specific case, and decide to eliminate a person like himself as being of "no value to the community." Racialists always assume that they, the aristocrats of the species, will sit on the boards which will decide who is to be "eliminated." Grant himself suggests ten per cent as the initial proportion of who is to be thus liquidated for the sake of improving "the race."

One reason why Grant was well received by Nazi racialists may be due to his conviction that Germany (except for Scandinavia) is the only place left where the "Nordic race" has maintained "its full vigor." Grant writes off England, because of the "transfer of political power from the vigorous Nordic aristocracy and middle classes to the radical and labor elements, both largely recruited from the Mediterranean type." Since the laboring elements constitute the vast majority of the English people, Grant thus discovered that the English were actually Mediterranean.

Grant's fanaticism even carries him to the suggestion that Jesus Christ was Nordic, possibly Greek. This is not a whit different from the Nazi discovery that Jesus was not of Jewish descent, but the son of a German soldier temporarily in Roman service in Palestine.

In *The Rising Tide of Color* (1920), Lothrop Stoddard warns the United States against the menace of the lower stocks at home and abroad. Stoddard, like other racialists before and after 1920, frankly calls for a crusading war on the Soviet Union; realizing that 1920, only two years after the end of the First World War, was a bad year to preach new wars, Stoddard nevertheless insists that "if this means more war, let it mean more war." Because Bolshevism advocates race equality, because it opposes white rule over the colored peoples, it is, according to Stoddard, "the arch-enemy of civilization," the "renegade, the traitor within the gates." Hitler and Bilbo would find nothing wrong with that racialist creed.

Unless some of their ideas were accepted in the United States, racialists like Stoddard and Grant could not have found the hearing which they received. The annual immigration quotas into the United States according to countries of origin indicate the racialist doctrine which underlies American law. Since every immigrant is a prospective citizen, American immigration laws hold Germans eight times as valuable for citizenship eligibility as Frenchmen, and five times as valuable as Italians. During the Second World War, Italian citizens in the United States were exempted from the status of "enemy aliens" in the fall of 1942, because the government had found that they were intensely loyal to American democracy, and had refused to work for Italian Fascism. The Germans, on the other hand, sheltered a much higher proportion of saboteurs, spies, and fifth columnists in their communities in the United States, and German citizens were, therefore, treated as "enemy aliens" to the end of the war. In fact, hundreds of naturalized American citizens of German birth were deprived of their American citizenship because of their continued allegiance to the Fatherland and Adolf Hitler, as contrasted with only a few cases of "denaturalization" of former Italian citizens. This may prove something or nothing; but it certainly does not substantiate the underlying conception of the immigration laws that Germans, *qua* Germans, are superior to Frenchmen, Italians, Czechs, Australians, New Zealanders, Greeks, Indians, and Chinese, when it comes to the appreciation of the democratic way of life. By selecting prospective immigrants into the United States according to ethnic origin rather than personal qualifications, the United States was one of the first countries in the modern world to recognize officially in its laws that one people was superior to another.

Is there anything in the discussion of the race problem that can be scientifically corroborated? In *We Europeans* (1935), Julian S. Huxley and A. C. Haddon explain what is known and what is guesswork in this whole field. They analyze the genetic, biological aspects of the problem, as well as its political and cultural implications. The term "race" itself is examined in six meanings in which it is often employed, to the confusion of all who use it. Not even the primary races (white, black, yellow) are clearly definable, and some racialist whites will be alarmed to learn from Huxley and Haddon that "white is connected with black and also with yellow through every gradation of type, and in each case along several distinct main lines of crossing." Huxley and Haddon (a geneticist and ethnologist, respectively) arrive

at the conclusion, supported by other leading scientists, that "what seems evident is that in this field, too, it is not biological but cultural factors which are
dominant."

1. The Germans—The Climax of World History and World Spirit*

G. W. F. HEGEL

The nature of Spirit may be understood by a glance at its direct opposite—
Matter. As the essence of Matter is Gravity, so, on the other hand, we may
affirm that the substance, the essence of Spirit is Freedom. All will readily
assent to the doctrine that Spirit, among other properties, is also endowed
with Freedom; but philosophy teaches that all the qualities of Spirit exist
only through Freedom; that all are but means for attaining Freedom; that
all seek and produce this and this alone. It is a result of speculative Philosophy, that Freedom is the sole truth of Spirit. Matter possesses gravity in
virtue of its tendency towards a central point. It is essentially composite; consisting of parts that *exclude* each other. It seeks its Unity; and therefore exhibits itself as self-destructive, as verging towards its opposite (an indivisible
point). If it could attain this, it would be Matter no longer, it would have
perished. It strives after the realization of its Idea; for in Unity it exists
ideally. Spirit, on the contrary, may be defined as that which has its centre
in itself. It has not a unity outside itself, but has already found it; it exists
in and *with itself*. Matter has its essence out of itself; Spirit is *self-contained
existence* (*Bei-sich-selbst-sein*). Now this is Freedom, exactly. For if I am
dependent, my being is referred to something else which I am not; I cannot
exist independently of something external. I am free, on the contrary, when my
existence depends upon myself. This self-contained existence of Spirit is none
other than self-consciousness—consciousness of one's own being. Two things
must be distinguished in consciousness; first, the fact *that I know;* secondly,
what I know. In *self* consciousness these are merged in one; for Spirit
knows itself. It involves an appreciation of its own nature, as also an energy
enabling it to realise itself; to make itself *actually* that which it is *potentially*.
According to this abstract definition it may be said of Universal History, that

it is the exhibition of Spirit in the process of working out the knowledge of that which it is potentially. And as the germ bears in itself the whole nature of the tree, and the taste and form of its fruits, so do the first traces of Spirit virtually contain the whole of that History. The Orientals have not attained the knowledge of that Spirit—Man *as such*—is free; and because they do not know this, they are not free. They only know that *one is free*. But on this very account, the freedom of that one is only caprice; ferocity—brutal recklessness of passion, or a mildness and tameness of the desires, which is itself only an accident of Nature—mere caprice like the former.— That *one* is therefore only a Despot; not a *free man*. The consciousness of Freedom first arose among the Greeks, and therefore they were free; but they, and the Romans likewise, knew only that *some* are free,—not man as such. Even Plato and Aristotle did not know this. The Greeks, therefore, had slaves; and their whole life and the maintenance of their splendid liberty, was implicated with the institution of slavery: a fact moreover, which made that liberty on the one hand only an accidental, transient and limited growth; on the other hand, constituted it a rigorous thraldom of our common nature—of the Human. The German nations, under the influence of Christianity, were the first to attain the consciousness, that man, as man, is free: that it is the *freedom* of Spirit which constitutes its essence. This consciousness arose first in religion, the inmost region of Spirit; but to introduce the principle into the various relations of the actual world, involves a more extensive problem than its simple implantation; a problem whose solution and application require a severe and lengthened process of culture. In proof of this, we may note that slavery did not cease immediately on the reception of Christianity. Still less did liberty predominate in States; or Governments and Constitutions adopt a rational organization, or recognise freedom as their basis. That application of the principle to political relations; the thorough moulding and interpenetration of the constitution of society by it, is a process identical with history itself. I have already directed attention to the distinction here involved, between a principle as such, and its *application; i.e.* its introduction and carrying out in the actual phenomena of Spirit and Life. This is a point of fundamental importance in our science, and one which must be constantly respected as essential. And in the same way as this distinction has attracted attention in view of the *Christian* principle of self-consciousness—Freedom—it also shews itself as an essential one, in view of the principle of Freedom *generally*. The History of the world is none other than the progress of the consciousness of Freedom; a progress whose development according to the necessity of its nature, it is our business to investigate.

The general statement given above, of the various grades in the consciousness of Freedom—and which we applied in the first instance to the fact that the Eastern nations knew only that *one* is free; the Greek and Roman world only that *some* are free; whilst *we* know that all men absolutely (man *as man*) are free,—supplies us with the natural division of Universal History, and suggests the mode of its discussion.

2. *Prussian Kultur versus Dollar-Hunting U.S.A.* *

HEINRICH VON TREITSCHKE

There are, no doubt, colonies not long established where social energies find freer natural scope. In them the untrammelled power of the individual is everything. In America, for instance, society is stronger than the State. The American "self-made man" is the best example of the development of social life in young colonies. Certain natures find satisfaction in the dollar-hunting of American life, but, broadly speaking, we may assert that existence is more human and more intense in Europe, steeped in her ancient culture, than yonder among the Yankees. Bancroft, the American historian, now dead, who had a limitless love for his native land, admitted that it could offer him nothing comparable to the society he found in Berlin. The peculiar thinness of the intellectual atmosphere in young countries is repellent to sensitive natures.

The unlimited political freedom in many American States is in sharpest contrast to the terrific temperance laws which exist side by side with it, and the conditions thus created are what the German immigrants find hardest to bear.

No doubt Germans often drink rather more than they should, but upon the whole it is with us a harmless pleasure, whereas if the American once begins drinking he drinks himself blind drunk. Therefore the legislative bodies have wisely directed their attention to remedying the evil, and their efforts have been supplemented by clerical fanatics, preaching against drink in general, and putting the innocuous German beer on the same level as the fearful American spirits. Hence the horrible temperance legislation in many of the States, which would lead to a preposterous inquisition into the privacy of every home if it were to be carried into effect. It never could be in a Monarchy, for every king would feel that such an inquisition would be exceeding his powers.

* From Heinrich von Treitschke, *Politics* (1897–1898; translated by B. Dugdale and T. de Bille, 1916). By permission of The Macmillan Company, publishers.

From the political conditions of America at the stage they have already reached, we Germans can draw no lesson for ourselves, and the excellent book which our compatriot Holst has written about the Union leaves us with the impression that further study will profit nothing. As wealth increases, and the inequalities within this Democracy grow with it, the deceits and dissension in the party life which is now thoroughly corrupt must come ever more into prominence. What is the real meaning in the party cleavages in North America to-day? Real divisions existed before the Civil War, when the question of Emancipation was a binding or a sundering force, but where is now the bond between the parties who confront each other sometimes as Federalists and Republicans, and then again as Republicans and Democrats? These titles themselves are absolutely meaningless, and on both sides we see nothing but ambitious men struggling to get to the top for the sake of the spoil. History has lost its meaning, and for the student of human nature it has resolved itself into a series of mere struggles for power, and since recent years have given money so tremendous an influence, it is natural that political weapons should be used to further dirty money-grubbing interests.

3. *The Nordics Did It All**

HANS F. K. GÜNTHER

The end of Greece, as of Rome, is marked by the want of outstanding men: Nordic blood has mostly run dry. The end of Greece and Rome alike is marked by the more or less invisible domination of various financiers, by the mob-minded characterizing the more and more degenerate, more and more racially mixed people, finally by a slow dying out of whole regions. The records of antiquity speak of the ruin of formerly populous towns; the Mediterranean lands were exhausted. It was only the descendants of slaves from the farthest parts of the world that did not feel disgust. Thousands of men, and those without doubt the loftiest minded, eagerly entered the monk-hood of the growing Christianity, turned away from this decaying world, and died without offspring. The 'fall' had come.

And so the history was bound to end all Nordic-led peoples once they had in their progress taken a direction that led to the disappearance of the Nordic

* From Hans F. K. Günther, *The Racial Elements of European History* (1927; translated by G. C. Wheeler, E. P. Dutton & Co., Inc.). By permission.

element. The process was bound to be speedier in those peoples who once for all had been cut off from the original Nordic region. Hindus, Hellenes, Persians, Romans, and some of the Kelts were, owing to the area they occupied, cut off from the main body of Nordic peoples, that had to stay in the German area, near the original home. A renewal of the Nordic blood within these southern peoples was impossible.

When we survey the fall in each case of the great empires and creative cultures from India to the West, this much is always clearly to be seen: that every 'fall' of a people of Indo-European speech is brought about through the running dry of the blood of the creative, the Nordic race.

4. *Eigenlob Stinkt* [*]

ADOLF HITLER

Everything we admire on this earth today—science and art, technology and inventions—is only the creative product of a few peoples and originally perhaps of *one* race. On them depends the existence of this whole culture. If they perish, the beauty of this earth will sink into the grave with them.

The folkish philosophy finds the importance of mankind in its basic racial elements. In the state it sees on principle only a means to an end and construes its end as the preservation of the racial existence of man. Thus, it by no means believes in an equality of the races, but along with their difference it recognizes their higher or lesser value and feels itself obligated, through this knowledge, to promote the victory of the better and stronger, and demand the subordination of the inferior and weaker in accordance with the eternal will that dominates this universe. Thus, in principle, it serves the basic aristocratic idea of Nature and believes in the validity of this law down to the last individual. It sees not only the different value of the races, but also the different value of the individuals.

The German Reich as a state must embrace all Germans and has the task, not only of assembling and preserving the most valuable stocks of basic racial elements in this people, but slowly and surely of raising them to a dominant position.

[*] From Adolf Hitler, *Mein Kampf* (1925–1927; translated by Ralph Manheim, Houghton Mifflin Company, 1943). By permission.

5. *It* Has *Happened Here**

MADISON GRANT

The temporary advantage of mere numbers enjoyed by the inferior classes in modern democracies can only be made permanent by the destruction of superior types—by massacre, as in Russia, or by taxation, as in England. In the latter country the financial burdens of the war and the selfish interests of labor have imposed such a load of taxation upon the upper and middle classes that marriage and children are becoming increasingly burdensome.

The best example of complete elimination of a dominant class is in Santo Domingo. The horrors of the black revolt were followed by the slow death of the culture of the white man. This history should be studied carefully because it gives in prophetic form the sequence of events that we may expect to find in Mexico and in parts of South America where the replacement of the higher type by the resurgent native is taking place.

In the countries inhabited by a population more or less racially uniform the phenomenon of the multiplication of the inferior classes fostered and aided by the noble but fatuous philanthropy of the well-to-do everywhere appears. Nature's laws when unchecked maintain a relatively fixed ratio between the classes, which is greatly impaired in modern society by humanitarian and charitable activities. The resurgence of inferior races and classes throughout not merely Europe but the world, is evident in every despatch from Egypt, Ireland, Poland, Rumania, India and Mexico. It is called nationalism, patriotism, freedom and other high-sounding names, but it is everywhere the phenomenon of the long-suppressed, conquered servile classes rising against the master race. The late Peloponnesian War in the world at large, like the Civil War in America, has shattered the prestige of the white race and it will take several generations and perhaps wars to recover its former control, if it ever does regain it. The danger is from within and not from without. Neither the black, nor the brown, nor the yellow, nor the red will conquer the white in battle. But if the valuable elements in the Nordic race mix with inferior strains or die out through race suicide, then the citadel of civilization will fall for mere lack of defenders.

In the democratic forms of government the operation of universal suffrage tends toward the selection of the average man for public office rather than

---

* From Madison Grant, *The Passing of the Great Race* (Charles Scribner's Sons, 1916). By permission.

the man qualified by birth, education and integrity. How this scheme of administration will ultimately work out remains to be seen but from a racial point of view it will inevitably increase the preponderance of the lower types and cause a corresponding loss of efficiency in the community as a whole.

The tendency in a democracy is toward a standardization of type and a diminution of the influence of genius. A majority must of necessity be inferior to a picked minority and it always resents specializations in which it cannot share. In the French Revolution the majority, calling itself "the people," deliberately endeavored to destroy the higher type and something of the same sort was in a measure done after the American Revolution by the expulsion of the Loyalists and the confiscation of their lands, with a resultant loss to the growing nation of good race strains, which were in the next century replaced by immigrants of far lower type.

In America we have nearly succeeded in destroying the privilege of birth; that is, the intellectual and moral advantage a man of good stock brings into the world with him. We are now engaged in destroying the privilege of wealth; that is, the reward of successful intelligence and industry and in some quarters there is developing a tendency to attack the privilege of intellect and to deprive a man of the advantage gained from an early and thorough classical education. Simplified spelling is a step in this direction.

There exists to-day a widespread and fatuous belief in the power of environment, as well as of education and opportunity to alter heredity, which arises from the dogma of the brotherhood of man, derived in its turn from the loose thinkers of the French Revolution and their American mimics. Such beliefs have done much damage in the past and if allowed to go uncontradicted, may do even more serious damage in the future.

Mistaken regard for what are believed to be divine laws and a sentimental belief in the sanctity of human life tend to prevent both the elimination of defective infants and the sterilization of such adults as are themselves of no value to the community. The laws of nature require the obliteration of the unfit and human life is valuable only when it is of use to the community or race.

In mankind it would not be a matter of great difficulty to secure a general consensus of public opinion as to the least desirable, let us say, ten per cent of the community. When this unemployed and unemployable human residuum has been eliminated together with the great mass of crime, poverty, alcoholism and feeblemindedness associated therewith it would be easy to consider the advisability of further restricting the perpetuation of the then remaining least valuable types. By this method mankind might ultimately become sufficiently intelligent to choose deliberately the most vital and intellectual strains to carry on the race.

If England has deteriorated, and there are those who think they see indications of such decline, it is due to the lowering proportion of the Nordic blood and the transfer of political power from the vigorous Nordic aristocracy and middle classes to the radical and labor elements, both largely recruited from the Mediterranean type.

Only in Scandinavia and northwestern Germany does the Nordic race seem to maintain its full vigor in spite of the enormous wastage of three thousand years of the swarming forth of its best fighting men. Norway, however, after the Viking outburst has never exhibited military power and Sweden, in the centuries between the Varangian period and the rise of Gustavus Adolphus, did not enjoy a reputation for fighting efficiency. All the three Scandinavian countries after vigorously attacking Christendom a thousand years ago disappeared from history as a nursery for soldiers until the Reformation when Sweden suddenly reappears just in time to save Protestantism on the Continent. To-day all three seem to be intellectually anaemic.

Race feeling may be called prejudice by those whose careers are cramped by it but it is a natural antipathy which serves to maintain the purity of type. The unfortunate fact that nearly all species of men interbred freely leaves us no choice in the matter. Races must be kept apart by artificial devices of this sort or they ultimately amalgamate and in the offspring the more generalized or lower type prevails.

The Nordics are, all over the world, a race of soldiers, sailors, adventurers and explorers, but above all, of rulers, organizers and aristocrats in sharp contrast to the essentially peasant and democratic character of the Alpines. The Nordic race is domineering, individualistic, self-reliant and jealous of their personal freedom both in political and religious systems and as a result they are usually Protestants. Chivalry and knighthood and their still surviving but greatly impaired counterparts are peculiarly Nordic traits, and feudalism, class distinctions and race pride among Europeans are traceable for the most part to the north.

In depicting the crucifixion no artist hesitates to make the two thieves brunet in contrast to the blond Saviour. This is something more than a convention, as such quasi-authentic traditions as we have of our Lord strongly suggest his Nordic, possibly Greek, physical and moral attributes.

6. Race Crusade against Bolshevism *

LOTHROP STODDARD

Bolshevism is, in fact, as anti-racial as it is anti-social. To the Bolshevik mind, with its furious hatred of constructive ability and its fanatical determination to enforce levelling, proletarian equality, the very existence of superior biological values is a crime. Bolshevism has vowed the proletarianization of the world, beginning with the white peoples. To this end it not only foments social revolution within the white world itself, but it also seeks to enlist the colored races in its grand assault on civilization. The rulers of Soviet Russia are well aware of the profound ferment now going on in colored lands. They watch this ferment with the same terrible glee that they watched the Great War and the fiasco of Versailles—and they plot to turn it to the same profit.

Accordingly, in every quarter of the globe, in Asia, Africa, Latin America, and the United States, Bolshevik agitators whisper in the ears of discontented colored men their gospel of hatred and revenge. Every nationalist aspiration, every political grievance, every social discrimination, is fuel for Bolshevism's hellish incitement to racial as well as to class war.

And this Bolshevik propaganda has not been in vain. Its results already show in the most diverse quarters, and they are ominous for the future. China, Japan, Afghanistan, India, Java, Persia, Turkey, Egypt, Brazil, Chile, Peru, Mexico, and the "black belts" of our own United States: here is a partial list of the lands where the Bolshevik leaven in color is clearly at work.

Bolshevism thus reveals itself as the arch-enemy of civilization and the race. Bolshevism is the renegade, the traitor within the gates, who would betray the citadel, degrade the very fibre of our being, and ultimately hurl a rebarbarized, racially impoverished world into the most debased and hopeless of mongrelizations.

Therefore, Bolshevism must be crushed out with iron heels, no matter what the cost. If this means more war, let it mean more war. We know only too well war's dreadful toll, particularly on racial values. But what war-losses could compare with the losses inflicted by the living death of Bolshevism? There are some things worse than war, and Bolshevism stands foremost among those dread alternatives.

* From Lothrop Stoddard, *The Rising Tide of Color* (Charles Scribner's Sons, 1920). By permission.

7. *U.S. Race Arithmetic*

ANNUAL IMMIGRATION QUOTAS INTO THE UNITED STATES
ACCORDING TO COUNTRY OF ORIGIN *

Afghanistan	100		Lithuania	386
Albania	100		Luxemburg	100
Andorra	100		Monaco	100
Arabian Peninsula	100		Morocco	100
Australia	100		Muscat (Oman)	100
Austria	1,413		Nauru †	100
Belgium	1,304		Nepal	100
Bhutan	100		Netherlands	153
Bulgaria	100		New Guinea	100
Cameroons †	100		New Zealand	100
Cameroon ‡	100		Norway	2,377
China	209		Palestine	100
Chinese	105		Philippine Islands	50
Czechoslovakia	2,874		Poland	6,524
Danzig	100		Portugal	440
Denmark	1,181		Ruanda and Urundi	100
Egypt	100		Rumania	377
Estonia	116		Samoa, West	100
Ethiopia	100		San Marino	100
Finland	569		Saudi Arabia	100
France	3,086		Siam	100
Germany	25,957		South Africa, Union	100
Great Britain and North Ireland	65,721		South West Africa	100
Greece	307		Spain	252
Hungary	869		Sweden	3,314
Iceland	100		Switzerland	1,707
India	100		Syria, Lebanon ‡	123
Iran	100		Tanganyika †	100
Iraq	100		Togoland †	100
Ireland (Eire)	17,853		Turkey	226
Italy	5,802		Soviet Republics	2,712
Japan	100		Yap, Japanese Mandate	100
Latvia	236		Yugoslavia	845
Liberia	100			
Liechtenstein	100		Total	153,879

* From *The World Almanac*, 1947. By permission of the New York *World-Telegram*.
† British mandate.
‡ French mandate.

8. Scientists Speak*

JULIAN S. HUXLEY AND A. C. HADDON

"Racial problems" are among the urgent actualities of twentieth-century politics. But as soon as we subject the concept underlying them, that of *race,* to dispassionate analysis, it turns out to be a pseudo-scientific rather than a scientific term. In other words, its use implies an appeal to the accuracy and to the prestige of science; but on investigation it turns out to have no precise or definable meaning. Further, like other pseudo-scientific terms, it can then readily be employed to rationalize emotion, and to bolster up the appeals of prejudice, by giving it a meaning to suit the context.

The term "race" is currently used in several quite different senses. In the first place, it is used to denote one of the major divisions of mankind—black, white, yellow, and brown. Secondly, it is used to denote the actual human material of a particular country, group, or nation and its biologically trans-missible characteristics: for instance, even the most ardent upholders of the Nordic theory cannot mean by the "British race" anything more than the actual inhabitants of Great Britain and their descendants overseas. Thirdly, it is used to denote a hypothetical "pure race" which is taken to have existed in the past and later to have become contaminated by admixture with foreign elements: this, for instance, lies between the idea of the "Germanic race." Fourthly, it is sometimes used as equivalent to a recognizable or supposedly recognizable physical type, as Arab, Irish, etc. Fifthly, it is occasionally applied to a local population which by reason of isolation, or supposed isolation, has become or is supposed to have become fairly uniform and stable in physical type—for example, the "Cornish race." Sixthly, it is also sometimes used in a wholly inadmissible sense to denote the peoples who speak a certain type of language; for example, in such a phrase as the "Aryan race," the "Latin races."

On all these uses, scientific analysis, backed by the results of modern genetics, throws a pitiless light. It is probable that during the early evolution of our species, it became divided up into geographical varieties, each more or less isolated from the others, and each evolving so as to become adapted to its climatic environment. The black variety adapted to hot climates, the

* From Julian S. Huxley and A. C. Haddon, *We Europeans* (with a chapter on "Europe Overseas" by A. M. Carr-Saunders, Harper & Brothers, 1936; copyright, 1936, by Julian Sorell Huxley, Alfred Cort Haddon, and Alexander Morris Carr-Saunders). By permission.

yellow variety to dry conditions, and the white variety to north-temperate latitudes, are the most prominent examples.

Such varieties would then correspond to the "geographical races," or *sub-species* as they are now generally called, to be found in many animal species. If we wish to retain the term *race* for such groups, they should be called "primary races." However, since the term race has been largely abandoned in zoology, and since in anthropology it is used in such a confusing multiplicity of senses, we had better employ the term primary *sub-species*. But—and this cannot be too strongly emphasized—such primary human sub-species are entirely hypothetical, a matter of inference only. Man's incurable and increasing propensity to wander over the face of the globe had effected a thorough mixing between the hypothetical primary sub-species long before the dawn of the historic period, had blurred the sharpness of their outlines and in some cases made it all but impossible to deduce their original type. A typical white man is very different from a typical Chinese or a typical Negro. But white is connected with black and also with yellow through every gradation of type, and in each case along several distinct main lines of crossing. Again, the simple classifications which at first suggest themselves all break down at one or another point. For instance, the Australians, though deeply pigmented and undoubtedly primitive in many ways, show the same character of hair as Europeans. We cannot with certainty assign them to a definite original sub-species. No single scheme of classification, in point of fact, has been devised which will provide a satisfactory pigeon-holing for the various human types in existence.

It is here that genetics steps in. The modern study of heredity, based on Mendel's great discoveries, has shown that after a cross between two distinct strains, blending inheritance, such as used to be assumed by anthropologists, does not occur, but that all kinds of different combinations of the original characters of the two stocks are brought into being. This is due to the fact that hereditary transmission is by means of discrete living particles, called *genes,* which reproduce themselves, and can be recombined in the most various ways.

Accordingly, if two primary sub-species meet and mix, their characteristics may be combined in their descendants. Originally, black skin might invariably have gone with flat nose and thick lips. That, however, provides not the slightest reason why it should always do so. After a cross with a stock with light pigmentation and delicate features, the combination of dark skin and delicate features, the combination of characters has, it appears, been favoured in several instances of actual crossing, notably, for instance, in India.

Similarly yellow skin and a round head seem to have been originally associated. But the two become uncoupled with the greatest facility after crossing with strains possessing different head-form and skin-colour.

Another result of the existence of definite genes as the carriers of hereditary constitution is that after a cross the resulting population will not tend to a mere average between the two original ingredients, but will, in the absence of social or natural selection, continue to produce a great diversity of types, generation after generation. There is not the slightest tendency for the population of Britain to become all medium brown in hair-colour, nor for that of Germany to become all medium long in skull-shape. In each generation black and yellow hair, long and round heads, continue to be produced, and to be produced in about the same percentage of the population.

It will now be clear why no single scheme of classification can satisfactorily pigeon-hole all known human types, or even deduce without danger of error the number and characteristics of the original "primary races" of man. Whereas in the evolution of animals there is a constant branching, each branch being permanently isolated after a certain degree of differentiation by becoming incapable of fertile crossing with other branches, in man the branches constantly meet and unite and produce new types of shoots. The conventional ancestral tree may have some advantages for representing the descent of animal types; it is wholly unsuitable and misleading for man. Further, while, in general, animal types can be reasonably classified on the basis of using degrees of resemblance to indicate degrees of relationship, no such simple scheme will serve for man. In fact, with a species in which intercrossing of divergent types is so prevalent as our own, no simple system of classification can ever be devised to represent the realities of the situation.

Theoretically, we could give a scientific description of human groups by means of the frequency distribution of the different hereditary factors or genes which they contain and the correlations denoting the tendency for the different genes to be allocated. This, however, is at the moment a mere ideal (save for the blood-group genes) and is never likely to be fulfilled except for the genes responsible for a selected group of well-marked physical characters. In the absence of this, we are driven back on measurable physical characters: here again we must content ourselves with the frequency distributions and inter-correlations of various well-marked characters to be found in particular groups. Our picture of the human species will be like a contour-map, a region of high frequency for, say, round-headedness being separated from another similar peak by a "valley" of low frequency; the gradients in frequency will, of course, vary in different directions. Furthermore, the contour-map for one character will not necessarily resemble that for another.

These considerations rob the terms *race* or *sub-species,* as applied to existing human groups, of any significance. All existing groups must have owed a great deal to crossing. It is only when a group has been relatively isolated for long periods that it will, under the influence of selection, have achieved much stability. Such stabilized groups may be called "secondary races," but they are extremely rare, and their formation must have taken immense periods of time.

In most cases it is impossible to speak of the existing population of any region as belonging to a definite "race," since as a result of migration and crossing it includes many types and their various combinations. For existing populations, the word *race* should be banished, and the descriptive and non-committal term *ethnic group* should be substituted.

With regard to the separate types which can be distinguished within an ethnic group—for instance, the tall fair-haired Nordic type, the medium-statured, round-headed Eurasiatic type, the short, dark-haired, long-headed Mediterranean type—it has been suggested that these might perhaps be called "racial" types, and be taken to represent originally "pure" stocks which have later crossed with each other. They would then represent further geographical subdivisions of the original "primary sub-species" of man. However, such a supposition begs a number of questions. Above all it presupposes that these hypothetical stocks once existed in a state of complete or almost complete genetic purity. There is no concrete evidence for this, and indeed much evidence to show that mixture has been proceeding not merely during the historic period, but back far into prehistoric times. It is more probable that even six or seven thousand years ago, such groups only represented points of high frequency for certain characters on the ethnic contour-map, and had already suffered much crossing with other groups. Race has so many connotations—of homogeneity, of purity of descent, and so forth—that it is undesirable to use it where we are not certain of our ground. Accordingly it is better to resort to a non-committal term like "ethnic type" or "genetic type," rather than "racial type." In so far as the different types were once geographically isolated, they may be called "secondary sub-species."

A given region of Europe is thus populated by a highly mixed ethnic group in which a number of distinct ethnic types and the products of their intercrossing are to be distinguished. The ethnic types are to be found more sharply defined and in relatively high concentration in certain areas—for instance, the Nordic type in parts of Scandinavia and the Mediterranean type in parts of southern Italy. There is perhaps some reason to suppose that in earlier times they existed in higher concentration and less genetic impurity, but never wholly undiluted or free from crosses with other types. The past populations of such regions would thus represent partial geographical differentiations of the human species, of a kind rather different from anything found in animals. Their later intermixture produces wholly new combinations of characters, which may become stabilized as new "ethnic types"—a process apparently without any parallel in other organisms.

Before proceeding further, there are one or two other popular fallacies to be noted. One is the misconception that a "race" is a collection of people all descended from a single original couple. This idea seems to spring largely from the family trees beloved of genealogists, in which a family is traced back to a single founder and his wife. Such family trees in reality trace the descent of a name, and have little to do with biological heredity: they are social, not genetic documents. On the genetic plane, the idea of descent from a single couple is in any case vitiated for man by the amount of intercrossing which has taken place between groups. Our ancestry will diverge as well as converge as we trace it back. With animal evolution, in tracing back the pedigree of a group you will, it is true, find convergence of separate branches (species, genera, etc.) to a common stem. But this is not the same thing as convergence to a common ancestral pair; and as a matter of fact we can be certain that the common stem is always a large body of individuals, with a certain degree of genetic variability. Change in evolution does not take place through the sudden appearance of a new sport in a single couple, who then become the ancestors of the new species or strain; it occurs by means of the spread of mutant genes through the population. The evolving strain is the whole population of a given area.

Another and even more serious misconception is that language is any criterion of "race." There are a great many examples in history of a conquering people forcing its language on the conquered; and also a great many examples of the converse process, of the conquering invaders adopting the language of the country they have invaded. It is thus quite improper to speak of the "Celtic race." There is a group of Celtic-speaking peoples, but the fact of their all speaking Celtic is no proof of common descent or genetic affinity. Similarly there is not and cannot be such a thing as an Aryan race, since the term Aryan refers to language.

This fallacy with regard to language is a particular case of a similar fallacy with regard to social culture in general. Habits, traditions, machines, dress, art, institutions, gestures, ideas—all these as well as language are part of the social environment of human beings. They are not inborn, but have to be learnt or built up by experience. None of these can serve as any criterion of racial affinity between peoples. For instance, if we had nothing to go by but specimens of machinery and other material objects, we might conclude that the modern Japanese were much more closely related to the Europeans than to the Tibetans or other Mongol peoples: we should, however, be wrong. Culture, both material and spiritual, can spread by culture-contact, whereas physical characters can only spread by actual intercrossing.

Nor can the cultural level of a people serve as evidence of its innate ability or the reverse. The ancient Romans, perfectly correctly, regarded the inhabitants of this country and of Germany as uncivilized. They would have been considerably surprised to find them leading the way in civilization a mere fifty or sixty generations later. In ancient Greece, some very eminent philosophers went further and ascribed to the northern "barbarians" an innate incapacity to rise to the attainments of the Greeks. They were confusing cultural level with innate capacity. The rapid rise of Arab culture to a high intellectual level and its subsequent fall and stagnation is another example. We must ourselves beware of falling into the same fallacy as regards the so-called "backward peoples" of the modern world.

On *a priori* grounds we may expect differences in innate ability to exist between different peoples. But achievement by itself is no guide; and so far no satisfactory method has been devised of testing differences in innate intelligence or other psychological qualities between peoples with very different education and culture. The differences in social environment override the differences in genetic equipment.

Finally there is the fallacy which equates "race" with "nation." Here again there is confusion between a genetic and a social concept, but the case demands special treatment because of the special dangers inherent in this particular fallacy. The most obvious way of demonstrating that it is a fallacy is to consider the United States of America. There is, very definitely, an American nation, whose nationalism has indeed been growing more pronounced during the last few decades; but equally definitely, there is no possibility of speaking of an American race. Rather the popular phrase so often applied to the United States of America, *the melting-pot of race,* displays the true situation. All great nations are "melting-pots of race," but America affords the most obvious example. A nation is a group of people with a common tract of country, bound together in a common State by common history, common sentiment and traditions, common social organization, and usually (though not always, as, for example, Belgium or Switzerland) by common language. It is also bound together by being the unit to which the individual belongs, so that he regards other individuals belonging to the same unit as in some way allied with him, while individuals belonging to other similar units are "foreigners," in some way alien to him. This sense of solidarity with co-nationals and of separateness from other nationals is of the essence of nationality. The nation, however, is a particular phase in the evolution of human groups, not anything permanent or inherent in human nature. It is in essentials a product of the last three hundred years, and quite different in nature and organization from other units of the same general type, such as clan, tribe, city-state, or empire. The idea of the "blood-tie" has been used to strengthen national sentiment because of the importance of such sentiment for unity and effectiveness in war. But mass-migration and military conquest, and the adoption of foreigners into the group by legal change of citizenship and by marriage, when the wife and children follow the father's nationality, make the thesis of common descent impossible to uphold. The idea of a British, a French, a German, or an Italian "race" is a political fiction, and a dangerous one at that.

Coming down from the general to the particular, we can here deal with two so-called "race" problems which are of immediate political importance— the Nordic and the Jewish. Beginning with the latter, we find that the

Jewish problem is far less a "racial" or genetic than a cultural one. The Jews are no more a distinct sharply marked "race" than are the Germans or the English. They are originally of mixed descent. During this dispersal they have interbred with the surrounding populations, so that a number of genes derived from the immigrant Jews are scattered through the general population, and the Jewish communities have come to resemble the local population in many particulars. In this way the Jews of Africa, of eastern Europe, of Spain and Portugal, and so on, have become markedly different from each other in physical type. What they have preserved and transmitted is not "racial qualities," but religious and social traditions. The Jews do not constitute a definite race, but a society forming a pseudo-national group with a strong religious basis and with peculiar historic traditions. Biologically it is almost as illegitimate to speak of a "Jewish race" as of an "Aryan race."

The Nordic theory is in another category. Instead of ascribing racial qualities to a group which is to-day essentially held together on a cultural basis, it takes a hypothetical past "race," ascribes to it a number of valuable qualities, notably initiative and leadership, and then, whenever it finds such qualities in the mixed national groups, ascribes them to the Nordic elements in the population. It then goes further, and sets up as a national ideal a return to purity of Nordic stock.

The facts of the case are as follows. The Nordic race, like other human races, has no present existence. Its former existence, like that of all "pure races," is hypothetical. There does, however, exist a Nordic type. This occurs with only a moderate degree of mixture in parts of Scandinavia, and is also to be found, but much mixed with other types, so that all intermediates and recombinations occur, in northern Europe from Britain to Russia, with pockets here and there in other countries. On various grounds we can be reasonably sure that this distribution is the result of the invasion of Europe by a group largely composed of men of this type—perhaps in the degree of purity in which the type is now found in parts of Scandinavia. This group was the "Nordic race"—a secondary sub-species in our sense. It is not certain where it originated or when its important migration took place, but most authorities believe that it came originally from the steppes of southern Russia.

But besides these facts and deductions, there exists what one can only characterize as a Nordic myth, ascribing to this "Nordic race" most of the great advances of mankind during recorded history, and asserting that their qualities of leadership fit them to rule over other races. The Aryan and Germanic myths are variants on the same theme.

These contentions appear to be based on nothing more serious than self-interest and wish-fulfilment. In the first place, it is quite certain that the great steps in civilization, when man learned to plough, to write, to build stone houses, to transport his goods in wheeled vehicles, were first taken in the near East, by peoples who by no stretch of imagination could be called

Nordic, but who seem in point of fact to have been largely of the dark, Mediterranean type. Secondly, it is true that great advances in civilization have sometimes been observed in history when invaders of a relatively light-skinned type have irrupted into countries populated by other groups—notably in Greece, though here round-headed as well as long-headed elements were included in the invaders. But in such cases both types appear to have made their contribution, and the result can be ascribed to the vivifying effects of mixture and culture-contact with as much propriety as to the inherent qualities of one of the types concerned. Indeed, where the Nordic type is most prevalent, in northern Scandinavia, there is also found among the people a tendency to introspection, accompanied by a very high suicide-rate; this may well be an effect of the northern environment, but may equally well be a characteristic of the type or due to social conditions. Generally speaking, the greatest achievements of modern civilization have occurred in regions of the greatest mixtures of types—Italy, France, Britain, and Germany, to mention only four nations. In all these countries of "mixed races," owing to the nature of Mendelian inheritance, it is rare to find pure Nordic types. The great bulk of the population will contain genes derived from many original sources. In a nation like Britain or Germany, the pure Nordic type is irrecoverable for the country at large: the population as a whole is an inextricable mixture. The Nordic type may be held up as an ideal, but this ideal is genetically unattainable, and will not affect the biological realities of the situation.

Furthermore, when we look into the facts of history, we find it far from established that men of pure or even approximately Nordic type have been the great leaders of thought or action. The great explorers of Britain displayed initiative, but hardly one of them was physically of Nordic type: the majority of the most celebrated Germans, including Goethe, Beethoven, and Kant, were medium or round-headed, not long-headed like the typical Nordics. Napoleon, Shakespeare, Einstein—a dozen great names spring to mind which in themselves should be enough to disperse the Nordic myth. The word *myth* is used advisedly, since it frequently plays a semi-religious role, as basis for a creed of passionate racialism.

From what has been said, it will be clear that "race-mixture" has in the past been beneficial. The British contain strong Nordic and Eurasiatic elements, with a definite admixture of Mediterranean types. In the Germans there is a very large Eurasiatic element which includes the Slavonic, and genes from the Mongoloid peoples have crept in via Russia. In France, the population is largely Alpine, especially in the centre, but there is a strong Nordic admixture in the north and a slighter Mediterranean one in the south. The Jews are of mixed origin, and have steadily been growing more mixed. America is proverbially a melting-pot. The Japanese are also a mixture of several ethnic types.

In human affairs it is usually impossible to say which of a number of possible causes is decisive. A nation with a mixed population achieves great things. Is its greatness due to the genetic mixture in its people, or to the culture-contacts that have been brought about? Or is it due to neither of these things, but to favourable economic circumstances? It is never possible to be sure: it may be due to all three simultaneously. At any rate, we can assert without contradiction that genetic mixture of human types is certainly not harmful, and that it is to be found in every people which has achieved great things in history.

But this does not imply that ethnic mixture must always be good. In the above examples, we are dealing with mixture between minor subdivisions of one "primary race" or sub-species. What of mixture between the major subdivisions of mankind—between black and white, for instance, or white and yellow? In this field the most violent feelings are aroused. We need only cite the strong feeling in the United States against white intermarriage with Negroes or Chinese, and in South Africa against Bantu admixture.

When we make a comparative survey, however, we find that this prejudice does not exist universally. In Europe, the feeling against intermarriage with black or brown is far less marked among the Latin-speaking nations than in Britain. For instance, Portugal contains a considerable proportion of Negro genes, derived from intermixture with slaves since the sixteenth century. In the South American countries there is little or no social discrimination against the offspring of mixed marriages, and Indian, Negro, and white stocks are inextricably blended. The population of Mexico is predominantly one of hybrids between white and Indian. In the British West Indies there is a large and respected class of half-castes arising from Negro-white admixture. In Soviet Russia there is deliberate discouragement of all race prejudice.

We need not multiply examples. What seems evident is that in this field, too, it is not biological but cultural factors which are dominant. Where, for instance, a slave-class exists of markedly different ethnic type from their masters, it is clear that marriage with one of the slave type will be frowned upon. This will not, however, prevent the occurrence of sexual relations between the two groups, though these will be almost entirely between the men of the ruling class and the women of the slave class or type. The most obvious example is that of the relations of planters and slaves in the Old South before the Civil War. Far from there always existing a sexual repulsion between markedly different types, there is often a strong sexual attraction. The disapproval of "miscegenation" is primarily social, not biological.

Chapter XVI

CONFLICT OR COMMON INTEREST?

POLITICAL organization on the national and international scale is largely determined by man's ideas of himself, his nature and capacities. Within the state, the community of interests may be split by group and class conflicts, but in the end peaceful adjustments prevent such divergencies from breaking out into armed struggle. In the relations between nations, men have not settled, in their own minds, the primary question as to what is the "natural state of things": harmony of interests (though interrupted by occasional conflicts), or conflict of interests (though interrupted by short intervals of peace). The answer one is ready to give to this question will be, in itself, one of the factors that will determine whether conflict or community will be the normal condition in the society of nations.

The sharpest analysis of this issue, from a conservative point of view, will be found in E. H. Carr's *The Twenty Years' Crisis* (1939). Carr bases his whole theory of international relations on the distinction between *Utopian* and *realistic* thinking. According to Carr, this distinction coincides with the distinction between free will and determinism: "The utopian is necessarily voluntarist: he believes in the possibility of more or less radically rejecting reality, and substituting his utopia for it by an act of will. The realist analyses a predetermined course of development which he is powerless to change." Carr expresses this difference also in the sense that the "utopian, fixing his eyes on the future, thinks in terms of creative spontaneity: the realist, rooted in the past, in terms of causality." Secondly, Carr maintains that the distinction between Utopia and reality corresponds to that of theory and practice. The Utopian desires to make political practice conform to political theory, whereas the realist looks up political theory as a "sort of codification of political practice." Thirdly, the antithesis between Utopianism and realism is also reflected in the political contrast of Left and Right: "The radical is necessarily utopian, and the conservative realist. The intellectual, the man of theory, will gravitate toward the Left just as naturally as the bureaucrat, the man of practice, will gravitate towards the Right." Carr quotes approvingly the epigram of a Nazi philosopher, Moeller van den Bruck, that "the Left has reason (*Vernunft*), the Right has wisdom (*Verstand*)." Finally, and perhaps most fundamental of all, the dichotomy of Utopia and reality is reflected in that of ethics and politics. The Utopian seeks to make politics conform to ethical standards; the realist "cannot logically accept any standard of value save that of fact."

Carr attacks with much force the doctrine of the "harmony of interests," both within the state and between states, as a typically Utopian illusion. He calls that doctrine "an ingenious moral device invoked, in perfect sincerity, by privileged groups in order to justify and maintain their dominant position." This is true within the national community, but it is equally true in the world at large, and international peace is but "a special vested interest of dominant Powers." Carr thus rejects all the assumptions of economic and political liberalism, that the state is a community with discoverable principles of public interest, and that the society of nations, too, is a community whose common interests in peace and prosperity outweigh the interests in conflict, war, and destruction. Throughout his book Carr leans heavily on German conservative writers; although realist thinking in politics has had some influence on western Europe, it "had its home in Germany." Carr is so comprehensive in his sympathies for those who attack the liberal position, that he quotes approvingly antiliberal attacks from the Right as well as from the Left: Hegel or Marx, Bismarck or Lenin, Hitler or Stalin—Carr approves of their realism, their refusal to pay heed to the liberal illusions of the nineteenth century. In particular, Prime Minister Neville Chamberlain emerges from Carr's book as the real hero: his policy of appeasing the Axis was the true expression of realism, according to Carr, as compared with the illusionary formulas of the Utopians, such as "collective security" and "indivisibility of peace."

The best reply to Carr's argument will be found in Leonard Woolf's article on "Reality and Utopia"; he wrote it (in 1940) for *The Political Quarterly,* which he edits. Woolf has also dealt with this whole problem more fully in a book, *The War for Peace* (also published in 1940). First, Woolf charges Carr with using the term "Utopia" in two different meanings which are constantly confused. The first meaning of "Utopia" is applied to a policy based on a hope or purpose which is "incapable of fulfillment," and in this sense it can be opposed to realism. But the term "Utopian" is also used as meaning "unreal" as opposed to "reality." These two meanings are different uses of the term "Utopia," and Woolf adduces several illustrations to demonstrate how Carr actually confuses them. If Chamberlain failed in his policy of appeasement, that is still no proof, according to Carr, that the policy was Utopian, because it might conceivably have succeeded. However, in the case of the failure of the League of Nations, he says that "the first and most obvious tragedy of this utopia was its ignominious defeat." Thus Woolf denies that failure or success is necessarily the criterion of whether a policy is realistic or Utopian. The *identification of fact with value* is attacked by Woolf as one of the main weaknesses of the self-styled "realists," because it provides no guide to ordered thinking: "In 1790, 1830, 1848, 1900, and 1918, if Professor Carr had been a Frenchman, he would have talked about the 'triumph' of democracy and the democratic ideals of the 'Revolution,' but in 1800, 1828, 1851, and 1939 he would have talked about their 'ignominious collapse' and utopianism." Writing early in 1940, Woolf doubted whether one of Carr's "realists," Adolf Hitler, would succeed in his "realistic" policy of organizing Europe, not on the liberal illusion and Utopia of harmony of interests, but on the basis of force and conflicting interest: "It is highly probable that his objective will not be attained and is unattainable, and is therefore really utopian." And Woolf adds: "If the criterion of utopianism is attainability, the policies of Hitler and Mr. Chamberlain are no less utopian than the League policy."

Woolf denies one of Carr's main theses, that there is "some 'reality' in a conflicting interest which does not exist in a common interest." The fact that in most instances the pursuit of a common interest necessitates the abandonment of some immediate individual interest prevents some people from being *conscious* what their true interest is. Yet, as Woolf points out, "in private life and national politics we have learnt this by bitter experience, and no one believes that the interest of men with knives to commit murder and robbery is more 'real' than the interest of men with knives to refrain and be restrained from committing murder and robbery. International psychology is still, however, so crude that even a man like Professor Carr can believe that the interest of Germany in cutting the throat of Czechoslovakia is more real than the interest of both Germany and Czechoslovakia in living peacefully together and composing conflicting interests by compromise, merely because Herr Hitler has a very large army, a very large air force, and a very loud and rasping voice." A study of the history of human society leads Woolf to the conclusion that *"generally and in the long run* common interests are more real than conflicting interests politically." The main difficulty is psychological: as in other advances of civilization, people find it difficult to give up immediate individual interests that conflict with long-term common interests, and it requires "intelligence and restraint" to learn that the individual stands to gain from this preference of the long-range interest to the immediate one. Woolf admits that people will possibly fail to learn this lesson when it comes to the establishment of international peace. But as a believer in the liberal philosophy, he is unwilling to accept the "primitive psychology" that they cannot learn where their true interests lie.

The practical implications of utilizing common interests of nations in building a stable world order are skillfully presented by David Mitrany in his study of *A Working Peace System: An Argument for the Functional Development of International Organization* (1943). Mitrany challenges the dominant conception that security, military and political, is the primary condition of making peace, and that, if the threat of war is lifted from the world, the rest will take care of itself. Instead, he proposes to organize peace by tackling concrete and immediate problems. If nations learn to cooperate on such practical issues, the big issue of peace will be disposed of in an indirect fashion. Mitrany is opposed to one over-all social-economic international agency: "The essential principle is that activities would be selected specifically and organized separately, each according to its nature, to the conditions under which it has to operate, and to the needs of the moment." This would give ample scope to experiment and variation in the organization of the different functions. This functional organization would be supplemented by the federal principle of regional agencies within a given functional authority. All throughout his study, Mitrany stresses that the conquest of poverty, disease, and ignorance could unite peoples in practical tasks which confront them all: "Peace will not be secured if we organize the world by what divides it."

As long as government was the domain of a monarch or small ruling class, it was hopefully assumed that with the control of government by the people foreign affairs and diplomacy would be taken out of the secrecy and irresponsibility of professional diplomats. Yet, as events were to prove, while democratic government solved some problems of carrying on relations with other nations, it also created new problems inherent in its very nature. Few are better equipped to dissect the anatomy of foreign relations than Harold Nicolson, who has had wide experience in the foreign service of his country, and who was, in addition, a member of the House of Commons in the critical ten years of 1935–1945. However, he is not only a practitioner of the art of diplomacy; his works on *The Congress of Vienna* (1946) and on *Peacemaking, 1919* (1933) have secured for him a distinguished place as a diplomatic historian. In *Diplomacy* (1939), Nicolson approaches problems of diplomacy and foreign affairs from the analytical, rather than historical and descriptive, point of view. His main concern is how to make the electorate of a democracy aware of its grave responsibilities in the field of foreign relations. Nicolson considers irresponsibility, ignorance, the danger of delay, and the danger of imprecision, the four main threats that confront effective diplomacy in a democracy. There is no short-cut to an easy solution; Nicolson suggests several proposals that will help to educate a democratic public toward a better understanding and control of foreign policy. While policy should be discussed in the open, negotiations should be left to professional diplomats without the floodlights of publicity cast upon them. Nicolson also feels that in foreign, as in domestic affairs, what counts is not so much knowledge of details, as far as the broad public is concerned, but "good sense and experience." In this, he expresses the typically British view that the highest quality in politics is common sense and judgment, rather than expert knowledge of "the facts."

1. Utopia and Reality: A Conservative View *

E. H. CARR

The antithesis of utopia and reality—a balance always swinging towards and away from equilibrium and never completely attaining it—is a fundamental antithesis revealing itself in many forms of thought. The two methods of approach—the inclination to ignore what was and what is in contemplation of what should be, and the inclination to deduce what should be from what was and what is—determine opposite attitudes towards every political problem. "It is the eternal dispute," as Albert Sorel puts it, "between those who imagine the world to suit their policy, and those who arrange their policy to suit the realities of the world." [1] It may be suggestive to elaborate this antithesis before proceeding to an examination of the current crisis of international politics.

FREE WILL AND DETERMINISM

The antithesis of utopia and reality can in some aspects be identified with the antithesis of Free Will and Determinism. The utopian is necessarily voluntarist: he believes in the possibility of more or less radically rejecting reality, and substituting his utopia for it by an act of will. The realist analyses a predetermined course of development which he is powerless to change. For the realist, philosophy, in the famous words of Hegel's preface to his *Philosophy of Right,* always "comes too late" to change the world. By means of philosophy, the old order "cannot be rejuvenated, but only known." The utopian, fixing his eyes on the future, thinks in terms of creative spontaneity: the realist, rooted in the past, in terms of causality. All healthy human action, and therefore all healthy thought, must establish a balance between utopia and reality, between free will and determinism. The complete realist, unconditionally accepting the causal sequence of events, deprives himself of the possibility of changing reality. The complete utopian, by rejecting the causal sequence, deprives himself of the possibility of understanding either the reality which he is seeking to change or the processes

---

* From E. H. Carr, *The Twenty Years' Crisis* (1939). By permission of The Macmillan Company, publishers.

[1] A. Sorel, *L'Europe et la Révolution Française*, p. 474.

by which it can be changed. The characteristic vice of the utopian is naivety; of the realist, sterility.[1]

The antithesis of utopia and reality also coincides with the antithesis of theory and practice. The utopian makes political theory a norm to which political practice ought to conform. The realist regards political theory as a sort of codification of political practice. The relationship of theory and practice has come to be recognized in recent years as one of the central problems of political thought. Both the utopian and the realist distort this relationship. The utopian, purporting to recognize the interdependence of purpose and fact, treats purpose as if it were the only relevant-fact, and constantly couches optative propositions in the indicative mood. The American Declaration of Independence maintains that "all men are created Equal," Mr. Litvinov that "peace is indivisible," [2] and Sir Norman Angell that "the biological division of mankind into independent warring states" is a "scientific ineptitude." [3] Yet it is a matter of common observation that all men are not born equal even in the United States, and that the Soviet Union can remain at peace while its neighbours are at war; and we should probably think little of a zoologist who described a man-eating tiger as a "scientific ineptitude." These propositions are items in a political programme disguised as statements of fact; [4] and the utopian inhabits a dream-world of such "facts," remote from the world of reality where quite contrary facts may be observed. The realist has no difficulty in perceiving that these utopian propositions are not facts but aspirations, and belong to the optative not to the indicative mood; and he goes on to shew that, considered as aspirations, they are not *a priori* propositions, but are rooted in the world of reality in a way which the utopian altogether fails to understand. Thus for the realist, the equality of man is the ideology of the under-privileged seeking to raise themselves to the level of the privileged; the indivisibility of peace the ideology of states which, being particularly exposed to attack, are eager to establish the principle that an attack on them is a matter of concern to other states more fortunately situated; [5] the ineptitude of sovereign states the ideol-

[1] The psychologist may be interested to trace here an analogy—it would be dangerous to treat it as more—with Jung's classification of psychological types as "introverted" and "extraverted" (Jung, *Psychological Types*) or William James's pairs of opposites: Rationalist-Empiricist, Intellectualist-Sensationalist, Idealist-Materialist, Optimistic-Pessimistic, Religious-Irreligious, Free-willist-Fatalistic, Monistic-Pluralistic, Dogmatical-Sceptical (W. James, *Pragmatism*).

[2] *League of Nations: Sixteenth Assembly*, p. 72.

[3] Angell, *The Great Illusion*, p. 138.

[4] Similarly, Marx's theory of surplus value has, in the words of a sympathetic critic, "rather the significance of a political and social slogan than of an economic truth" (M. Beer, *The Life and Teaching of Karl Marx*, p. 129).

[5] Having discovered that other states were perhaps more open to attack than themselves, the Soviet authorities in May 1939 dismissed Mr. Litvinov and ceased to talk about the indivisibility of peace.

ogy of predominant Powers which find the sovereignty of other states a barrier to the enjoyment of their own predominant position. This exposure of the hidden foundations of utopian theory is a necessary preliminary to any serious political science. But the realist, in denying any *a priori* quality to political theories, and in proving them to be rooted in practice, falls easily into a determinism which argues that theory, being nothing more than a rationalisation of conditioned and predetermined purpose, is a pure excrescence and impotent to alter the course of events. While therefore the utopian treats purpose as the sole ultimate fact, the realist runs the risk of treating purpose merely as the mechanical product of other facts. If we recognize that this mechanisation of human will and human aspiration is untenable and intolerable, then we must recognise that theory, as it develops out of practice and develops into practice, plays its own transforming role in the process. The political process does not consist, as the realist believes, purely in a succession of phenomena governed by mechanical laws of causation; nor does it consist, as the utopian believes, purely in the application to practice of certain theoretical truths evolved out of their inner consciousness by wise and far-seeing people. Political science must be based on a recognition of the interdependence of theory and practice, which can be attained only through a combination of utopia and reality.

LEFT AND RIGHT

The antithesis of utopia and reality, and of theory and practice, further reproduces itself in the antithesis of radical and conservative, of Left and Right, though it would be rash to assume that parties carrying these labels always represent these underlying tendencies. The radical is necessarily utopian, and the conservative realist. The intellectual, the man of theory, will gravitate towards the Left just as naturally as the bureaucrat, the man of practice, will gravitate towards the Right. Hence the Right is weak in theory, and suffers through its inaccessibility to ideas. The characteristic weakness of the Left is failure to translate its theory into practice—a failure for which it is apt to blame the bureaucrats, but which is inherent in its utopian character. "The Left has reason (*Vernunft*), the Right has wisdom (*Verstand*)," wrote the Nazi philosopher, Moeller van den Bruck.[1] From the days of Burke onwards, English conservatives have always strongly denied the possibility of deducing political practice by a logical process from political theory. "To follow the syllogism alone is a short cut to the bottomless pit," says Lord Baldwin [2]—a phrase which may suggest that he practises as well as preaches abstention from rigorously logical modes of thought. Mr. Churchill refuses to believe that "extravagant logic in doctrine" appeals to the British elector.[3] But the clearest recent definition of the different atti-

[1] Moeller van den Bruck, *Das Dritte Reich* (3rd ed.), p. 257.
[2] Baldwin, *On England*, p. 153.
[3] Winston Churchill, *Step by Step*, p. 147.

tudes of Right and Left towards foreign policy comes from a speech made in the House of Commons by Mr. Neville Chamberlain in answer to a Labour critic:

What does the hon. Member mean by foreign policy? You can lay down sound and general propositions. You can say that your foreign policy is to maintain peace; you can say that it is to protect British interests, you can say that it is to use your influence, such as it is, on behalf of the right against the wrong, as far as you can tell the right from the wrong. You can lay down all these general principles, but that is not a policy. Surely, if you are to have a policy you must take the particular situations and consider what action or inaction is suitable for those particular situations. That is what I myself mean by policy, and it is quite clear that as the situations and conditions in foreign affairs continually change from day to day, your policy cannot be stated once and for all, if it is to be applicable to every situation that arises.[1]

The intellectual superiority of the Left is seldom in doubt. The Left alone thinks out principles of political action and evolves ideals for statesmen to aim at. But it lacks practical experience which comes from close contact with reality. In Great Britain since the War, it has been a serious misfortune that the Left, having enjoyed office for negligible periods, has had little experience of administrative realities and has become more and more a party of pure theory, while the Right, having spent so little time in opposition, has had few temptations to pit the perfection of theory against the imperfections of practice. It is significant that intellectuals have come to play a more and more predominant part in the counsels of the British Left, and that the latter was recently taunted by the Prime Minister with "repeating *clichés* and phrases and tags which once may have had some significance but have none today," and with being ready to "walk into any trap if it is only baited with a familiar catchword"[2]—the characteristic vices of the intellectual in politics. In Soviet Russia, the group in power is more and more discarding theory in favour of practice as it loses the memory of its revolutionary origin. History everywhere shews that, when Left parties or politicians are brought into contact with reality through the assumption of political office, they tend to abandon their "doctrinaire" utopianism and move towards the Right, often retaining their Left labels and thereby adding to the confusion of political terminology.

ETHICS AND POLITICS

Most fundamental of all, the antithesis of utopia and reality is rooted in a different conception of the relationship of politics and ethics. The anti-

[1] House of Commons, October 21, 1937, reprinted in N. Chamberlain, *The Struggle for Peace*, p. 33.

[2] House of Commons, February 22, and October 6, 1938, reprinted in N. Chamberlain, *The Struggle for Peace*, pp. 100, 323.

thesis between the world of value and the world of nature, already implicit in the dichotomy of purpose and fact, is deeply embedded in the human consciousness and in political thought. The utopian sets up an ethical standard which purports to be independent of politics, and seeks to make politics conform to it. The realist cannot logically accept any standard of value save that of fact. In his view, the absolute standard of the utopian is conditioned and dictated by the social order, and is therefore political. Morality can only be relative, not universal. Ethics must be interpreted in terms of politics; and the search for an ethical norm outside politics is doomed to frustration. The identification of the supreme reality with the supreme good, which Christianity achieves by a bold stroke of dogmatism, is achieved by the realist through the assumption that there is no good other than the acceptance and understanding of reality.

These implications of the opposition between utopia and reality will emerge clearly from a more detailed study of the present crisis in international politics.

THE REALIST CRITIQUE OF THE HARMONY OF INTERESTS

The doctrine of the harmony of interests yields readily to analysis in terms of this principle. It is the natural assumption of a prosperous and privileged class, whose members have a dominant voice in the community and are therefore naturally prone to identify its interest with their own. In virtue of this identification, any assailant of the interests of the dominant group is made to incur the odium of assailing the alleged common interest of the whole community, and is told that in making this assault he is attacking his own higher interests. The doctrine of the harmony of interests thus serves as an ingenious moral device invoked, in perfect sincerity, by privileged groups in order to justify and maintain their dominant position. But a further point requires notice. The supremacy within the community of the privileged group may be, and often is, so overwhelming that there is, in fact, a sense in which its interests are those of the community, since its well-being necessarily carries with it some measure of well-being for other members of the community, and its collapse would entail the collapse of the community as a whole. In so far, therefore, as the alleged natural harmony of interests has any reality, it is created by the overwhelming power of the privileged group, and is an excellent illustration of the Machiavellian maxim that morality is the product of power. A few examples will make this analysis of the doctrine of the harmony of interests clear.

In the nineteenth century, the British manufacturer or merchant, having discovered that *laissez-faire* promoted his own prosperity, was sincerely convinced that it also promoted British prosperity as a whole. Nor was this alleged harmony of interests between himself and the community entirely fictitious. The predominance of the manufacturer and the merchant was so overwhelming that there was a sense in which an identity between their prosperity and British prosperity as a whole could be correctly asserted. From this it was only a short step to argue that a worker on strike, in damaging the prosperity of the British manufacturer, was damaging British prosperity as a whole, and thereby damaging his own, so that he could be plausibly denounced by the predecessors of Professor Toynbee as immoral and by the predecessors of Professor Zimmern as muddle-headed. Moreover, there was a sense in which this argument was perfectly correct. Nevertheless, the doctrine of the harmony of interests and of solidarity between the classes must have seemed a bitter mockery to the under-privileged worker, whose inferior status and insignificant stake in "British prosperity" were consecrated by it; and presently he was strong enough to force the abandonment of *laissez-faire* and the substitution for it of the "social service state," which implicitly denies the natural harmony of interests and sets out to create a new harmony by artificial means.

The same analysis may be applied in international relations. British nineteenth-century statesmen, having discovered that free trade promoted British prosperity, were sincerely convinced that, in doing so, it also promoted the prosperity of the world as a whole. British predominance in world trade was at that time so overwhelming that there was a certain undeniable harmony between British interests and the interests of the world. British prosperity flowed over into other countries, and a British economic collapse would have meant world-wide ruin. British free traders could and did argue that protectionist countries were not only egotistically damaging the prosperity of the world as a whole, but were stupidly damaging their own, so that their behaviour was both immoral and muddle-headed. In British eyes, it was irrefutably proved that international trade was a single whole, and flourished or slumped together. Nevertheless, this alleged international harmony of interests seemed a mockery to those under-privileged nations whose inferior status and insignificant stake in international trade were consecrated by it. The revolt against it destroyed that overwhelming British preponderance which had provided a plausible basis for the theory. Economically, Great Britain in the nineteenth century was dominant enough to make a bold bid to impose on the world her own conception of international economic morality. Now that competition of all against all has replaced the domination of the world market by a single Power, conceptions of international economic morality have necessarily become chaotic.

Politically, the alleged community of interest in the maintenance of peace, whose ambiguous character has already been discussed, is capitalized in the same way by a dominant nation or group of nations. Just as the ruling class in a community prays for domestic peace, which guarantees its own security and predominance, and denounces class-war, which might threaten them, so international peace becomes a special vested interest of predominant

Powers. In the past, Roman and British imperialism were commended to the world in the guise of the *pax Romana* and the *pax Britannica*. To-day, when no single Power is strong enough to dominate the world, and supremacy is vested in a group of nations, slogans like "collective security" and "resistance to aggression" serve the same purpose of proclaiming an identity of interest between the dominant group and the world as a whole in the maintenance of peace. Moreover, as in the examples we have just considered, so long as the supremacy of the dominant group is sufficiently great, there is a sense in which this identity of interests exists. "England," wrote a German professor shortly after the War, "is the solitary Power with a national programme which, while egotistic through and through, at the same time promises to the world something which the world passionately desires: order, progress and eternal peace." [1] Even to-day, if Great Britain and France went to war with Germany and Italy, the defeat of Great Britain and France by Germany and Italy would produce a far more tremendous upheaval throughout the world than the defeat of Germany and Italy by Great Britain and France; and the sympathies of all those countries which felt that they had something to lose would, other things being equal, be instinctively ranged on the Franco-British side. When Mr. Churchill declares that "the fortunes of the British Empire and its glory are inseparably interwoven with the fortunes of the world," [2] this statement has precisely the same foundation in fact as the statement that the prosperity of British manufacturers in the nineteenth century was inseparably interwoven with British prosperity as a whole. Moreover, the purpose of the statements is precisely the same, namely to establish the principle that the defence of the British Empire, or the prosperity of the British manufacturer, is a matter of common interest to the whole community, and that anyone who attacks it is therefore either immoral or muddle-headed. It is a familiar tactic of the privileged to throw moral discredit on the under-privileged by depicting them as disturbers of the peace; and this tactic is as readily applied internationally as within the national community. "International law and order," writes Professor Toynbee of a recent crisis, "were in the true interests of the whole of mankind . . . whereas the desire to perpetuate the reign of violence in international affairs was an anti-social desire which was not even in the ultimate interests of the citizens of the handful of states that officially professed this benighted and anachronistic creed." [3] This is precisely the argument, compounded of platitude and falsehood in about equal parts, which did duty in every strike in the early days of the British and American Labour movements. It was common form for employers, supported by the whole capitalist press, to denounce the "anti-social" attitude of trade union

---

[1] Dibelius, *England*, p. 109.
[2] Winston Churchill, *Arms and the Covenant*, p. 272.
[3] Toynbee, *Survey of International Affairs*, 1935, ii. p. 46.

leaders, to accuse them of attacking law and order and of introducing "the reign of violence," and to declare that "true" and "ultimate" interests of the workers lay in peaceful co-operation with the employers.[1] In the field of social relations, the disingenuous character of this argument has long been recognised. But just as the threat of class-war by the proletarian is "a natural cynical reaction to the sentimental and dishonest efforts of the privileged classes to obscure the conflict of interest between classes by a constant emphasis on the minimum interests which they have in common," [2] so the warmongering of the dissatisfied Powers is the "natural, cynical reaction" to the sentimental and dishonest platitudinising of the satisfied Powers on the common interest in peace. When Herr Hitler refuses to believe "that God has permitted some nations first to acquire a world by force and then to defend this robbery with moralising theories," [3] we have an authentic echo of the Marxist denial of a community of interest between "haves" and "havenots," of the Marxist exposure of the interested character of *"bourgeois* morality,"* and of the Marxist demand for the expropriation of the expropriators.

The crisis of September 1938 demonstrated in a striking way the political implications of the assertion of a common interest in peace. When Briand proclaimed that "peace comes before all," or Mr. Eden that "there is no dispute which cannot be settled by peaceful means," [4] the assumption underlying these platitudes was that, so long as peace was maintained, no changes distasteful to France or Great Britain could be made in the *status quo.* In the crisis, France and Great Britain were trapped by the slogans which they themselves had used in the past to discredit the dissatisfied Powers, and Germany had become sufficiently dominant (as France and Great Britain had hitherto been) to turn the desire for peace to her own advantage. Since the Munich Agreement, a significant change has occurred in the attitude of the German and Italian dictators. Herr Hitler eagerly depicts Germany as a bulwark of peace menaced by war-mongering democracies. The League of Nations, he declared in his Reichstag speech of April 28, 1938, is a "stirrer up of trouble," and collective security means "continuous danger of war." Signor Mussolini in a recent speech at Turin borrowed the British formula about the possibility of settling all international disputes by peaceful means, and declared that "there are not in Europe at present problems so big and so active as to justify a war which from a European conflict would naturally become universal." [5] It would be a mistake to dismiss such utterances as

---

[1] "Pray earnestly that right may triumph," said the representative of the Philadelphia coal-owners in an early strike organized by the United Mine Workers, "remembering that the Lord God Omnipotent still reigns, and that His reign is one of law and order, and not of violence and crime" (H. F. Pringle, *Theodore Roosevelt,* p. 267).

[2] R. Niebuhr, *Moral Man and Immoral Society,* p. 153.

[3] Speech in the Reichstag, January 30, 1939.

[4] *League of Nations: Eighteenth Assembly,* p. 63.

[5] *The Times,* May 15, 1939.

hypocritical. They are symptoms that Germany and Italy are already looking forward to the time when, as dominant Powers, they will acquire the vested interest in peace recently enjoyed by Great Britain and France, and be able to pillory the democratic countries as enemies of peace. These developments make it easier than it would perhaps have been a few years ago for an Englishman to appreciate Halévy's subtle observation that "propaganda against war is itself a form of war propaganda." [1]

THE REALIST CRITIQUE OF INTERNATIONALISM

The concept of internationalism is a special form of the doctrine of the harmony of interests. It yields to the same analysis; and there are the same difficulties about regarding it as an absolute standard independent of the interests and policies of those who promulgate it. "Cosmopolitanism," wrote Sun Yat-sen, "is the same thing as China's theory of world empire two thousand years ago. . . . China once wanted to be sovereign lord of the earth and to stand above every other nation, so she espoused cosmopolitanism." [2] In the Egypt of the Eighteenth Dynasty, according to Dr. Freud, "imperialism was reflected in religion as universality and monotheism." [3] The doctrine of a single world-state, propagated by the Roman Empire and later by the Catholic Church, was the symbol of a claim to universal dominion. Modern internationalism has its genesis in seventeenth- and eighteenth-century France, during which French hegemony in Europe was at its height. This was the period which produced Sully's *Grand Dessin* and the Abbé Saint-Pierre's *Projet de Paix Perpétuelle* (both plans to perpetuate an international *status quo* favourable to the French monarchy), which saw the birth of the humanitarian and cosmopolitan doctrines of "the Enlightenment," and which established French as the universal language of educated people. In the next century, the leadership passed to Great Britain, which became the home of internationalism. On the eve of the Great Exhibition of 1851 which, more than any other single event, established Great Britain's title to world supremacy, the Prince Consort spoke movingly of "that great end to which . . . all history points—the realisation of the unity of mankind"; [4] and Tennyson hymned "the parliament of man, the federation of the world." France chose the moment of her greatest supremacy in post-War Europe to launch a plan of "European Union"; and Japan at the present time is developing an ambition to proclaim herself the leader of a united Asia. It is symptomatic of the growing international predominance of the United States that widespread popularity should recently have been enjoyed by the book of an American journalist advocating a world union of democracies, in which the United States would play the predominant role. [5]

---

[1] Halévy, *A History of the English People in 1895–1905* (Engl. transl.), i. Introduction, p. xi.
[2] Sun Yat-sen, *San Min Chu I* (Engl. transl.), pp. 68-9.
[3] Sigmund Freud, *Moses and Monotheism*, p. 36.
[4] T. Martin, *Life of the Prince Consort*, iii. p. 247.
[5] Clarence Streit, *Union Now*.

Just as pleas for "national solidarity" in domestic politics always come from a dominant group which can use this solidarity to strengthen its own control over the nation as a whole, so pleas for international solidarity and world union come from those dominant nations which may hope to exercise control over a unified world. Countries which are struggling to force their way into the dominant group naturally tend to invoke nationalism against the internationalism of the controlling Powers. In the sixteenth century, England opposed her nascent nationalism to the internationalism of the Papacy and the Empire. Since the beginning of the nineteenth century, Germany has opposed her nascent nationalism to the internationalism first of France, then of Great Britain. This circumstance has made her impervious to those universalist and humanitarian doctrines which were popular in eighteenth-century France and nineteenth-century Britain; and her hostility to internationalism has been further aggravated since 1919, when Great Britain and France endeavoured to create a new "international order" as a bulwark of their own predominance. "By 'international,'" wrote a recent German correspondent in *The Times*, "we have come to understand a conception that places other nations at an advantage over our own." [1] Nevertheless, there is little doubt that Germany, if she became supreme in Europe, would adopt international slogans and establish some kind of international organisation to bolster up her power. A British Labour ex-Minister recently advocated the suppression of Article 16 of the Covenant of the League of Nations on the unexpected ground that the totalitarian states might some day capture the League and invoke that article to justify the use of force by themselves.[2] Though it seems unlikely that Germany or Italy would resort to the existing machinery of the League of Nations, the anticipation was, in principle, a shrewd one. There are already signs of the development of the Anti-Comintern Pact into some form of international organisation. "The Anti-Comintern Pact," said Herr Hitler in the Reichstag on January 30, 1939, "will perhaps one day become the crystallisation point of a group of Powers whose ultimate aim is none other than to eliminate the menace to the peace and culture of the world instigated by a satanic apparition." "Either Europe must achieve solidarity," remarked an Italian journal about the same time "or the 'axis' will impose it." [3] "Europe in its entirety," says Dr. Goebbels, "is adopting a new order and a new orientation under the intellectual leadership of National Socialist Germany and Fascist Italy." [4] This is the symptom not of a change of heart, but of the fact that Germany and Italy are now approaching the time when they may become strong enough to espouse internationalism. "International order," and "international solidarity" will always be slogans of those who feel strong enough to impose them on others.

[1] Dr. FitzRandolph, *The Times*, November 5, 1938.
[2] Lord Marley in the House of Lords, November 30, 1938: *Official Report*, col. 258.
[3] *Relazioni Internazionali*, quoted in *The Times*, December 5, 1938.
[4] *Völkischer Beobachter*, April 1, 1939.

The exposure of the real basis of the professedly abstract principles commonly invoked in international politics is the most damning and most convincing part of the realist indictment of utopianism. The nature of the charge is frequently misunderstood by those who seek to refute it. The charge is not that human beings fail to live up to their principles. It matters little that Wilson, who thought that the right was more precious than peace, and Briand, who thought that peace came even before justice, and Mr. Eden, who believed in collective security, failed themselves, or failed to induce their countrymen, to apply these principles consistently. What matters is that these supposedly absolute and universal principles were not principles at all, but the unconscious reflexions of national policy based on a particular interpretation of national interest at a particular time. There is a sense in which peace and co-operation between nations or classes or individuals is a common and universal end irrespective of conflicting interests and politics. There is a sense in which a common interest exists in the maintenance of order, whether it be international order or "law and order" within the nation. But as soon as the attempt is made to apply these supposedly abstract principles to a concrete political situation, they are revealed as the transparent disguises of selfish and vested interests. The bankruptcy of utopianism resides not in its failure to live up to its principles, but in the exposure of its inability to provide any absolute and disinterested standard for the conduct of international affairs. The utopian of to-day, faced by the collapse of standards whose interested character he has failed to penetrate, takes refuge in condemnation of a reality which refuses to conform to these standards. A passage penned by the German historian Meinecke immediately after the War is the best judgment by anticipation of the role of utopianism in the international politics of the post-War period:

> The profound defect of the Western, natural-law type of thought was that, when applied to the real life of the state, it remained a dead letter, did not penetrate the consciousness of statesmen, did not hinder the modern hypertrophy of state interest, and so led either to aimless complaints and doctrinaire suppositions or else to inner falsehood and cant.[1]

These "aimless complaints," these "doctrinaire suppositions," this "inner falsehood and cant" will be familiar to all those who have studied what has been written about international politics in English-speaking countries during the past few years.

[1] Meinecke, *Staatsräson*, p. 533.

2. *Utopia and Reality: A Liberal Appraisal**

LEONARD WOOLF

We are living through a period in which the use of power, force, or violence is playing a predominant part in human society. The phenomenon is
not confined to the relations between states; it can be observed within states
in the relation between government and individuals and between individual
and individual. Societies and historical periods have differed widely in their
organization of power and in the way in which force or violence has been
applied to human relations. Until comparatively recent times it was commonly held that the communal control of power and the elimination of
force or violence from human and social relations were important elements
in civilization. It was even believed that these views were not merely utopian
aspirations, but had in many cases been translated into historical facts. In
the 19th century the potential power of a physically strong man to impose
his will upon a physically weak man had in most places been rendered inoperative by social organization. By similar methods the potential power of
the man with a club, an axe, or an automatic pistol had also been rendered
inoperative. The power of kings over their subjects, of aristocrats over commoners, of men over women, of governments over citizens, of employers
over employed had often, it seemed, been eliminated or modified. Most people
believed that it was possible not only to control or modify the use of power,
but also that of violence, and to do so effectively for an intelligent purpose.
It seemed to be undeniable that the use of torture and flogging as methods
of "doing justice" had been abolished in some places, that in others it was
no longer possible for a man to be hanged for stealing a sheep or a few
pence, and that in others the utopian idea of abolishing the death penalty
had been adopted without apparently increasing the number of murderers
or of their victims.

In the nineteenth century the control of the use of power and the efforts
to eliminate force and violence from the relations between states, governments, and individuals were closely associated with the practice and theory
of liberalism, democracy, and humanitarianism. The war of 1914–1918 for
four years reversed this process of controlling, sublimating, and eliminating
the use of power or violence. War between states is not only the logical
result of "power politics," it is power politics reduced to their simplest terms.

* *The Political Quarterly*, Vol. XI (April–June, 1940). By permission.

It also entails the adoption of force and violence as primary elements in determining a vast number of human and social relations which at other times are regulated by discussion, compromise, "law," or other non-violent methods. Few people will deny that this four year period of power and violence had a considerable effect upon European society and the minds of Europeans. The simplest and most direct effects of historical events are often soon forgotten or underestimated by historians and politicians. It is a simple fact that an enormous majority of those Europeans who were not killed in what they then called the Great War did not like it; in fact, they disliked it so intensely that enormous numbers of ordinary persons said: "Never again," by which they meant that in their humble opinion everything should be done which was possible to eliminate war from European society. Their aspiration may or may not have been utopian—we shall consider this question later—but their convictions, the state of their minds, were a political reality which was having profound effects all over Europe and which not even the most realist statesman, general, or historian could afford to neglect.

One effect of this conviction was the founding of the League of Nations. The disillusionment of ordinary men and women in 1918, their feeling that war was in the twentieth century not a tolerable way of life, or even of death, their dim doubts as to whether it had proved to be an effective method of "settling anything"—these things were not the only cause of the birth of the League of Nations, but they had a good deal to do with it. The statesmen—other than Wilson—who established the League did not believe in it; they thought themselves to be realists and the League utopia. The statesmen who "worked" the League for fifteen years or so did not believe in it; they thought themselves to be realists and the League either utopia or a convenient or inconvenient instrument—it depended upon circumstances—of national policy. The main impetus which had brought the League into being and prevented it from being completely scrapped by realists or reality was another reality, the voice of common people who had said and might perhaps still say: "Never again."

The League failed. As it failed, ordinary people could no longer be heard saying: "Never again"; you heard them saying clearly, often bitterly, always helplessly, in the streets of cities, in fields, and villages, "It is coming again." The two realities were not unconnected. The failure of the League may have been due to its having been utopian, but it was not an isolated historical incident, the casual failure of an academic dream brought up with a jolt against the hard facts of life. It was only part of a general historical process or movement which can be clearly discerned in the period between November, 1918, and September, 1939. It gradually became clear that the post-war Europe was not going to return to the nineteenth century attitude towards power, force, and violence. In many countries governments allowed private armies to fight one another in the streets of great cities. Dictatorships took the place of democracies. Pogroms became a recognized method of administration; change of government or even of the government's programme or policy were effected or prevented by "massacres," "purges," executions, or political assassinations.

Fascism in Italy—national socialism in Germany—Stalinism in the U.S.S.R. —Pilsudski or a government of generals or colonels or majors in Poland— little dictators in the little countries—Manchuria, Abyssinia, the destruction of the republican government of Spain, the destruction of the democratic republic of Czechoslovakia, the invasion and partition of Poland—thus we have reached the second great war. These facts can only be stated and interpreted in terms of power, force, and violence. They are the negation of another series of terms which had previously seemed to have some meaning to human beings: peace, law, order, common interests, compromise, liberty and democracy. Human beings are never content just to accept the facts, their miseries, savagery, and stupidities. They have an itch to explain and interpret them, to find some fig leaf of a theory or philosophy to cover the nakedness of their own folly or cruelty. Politicians and professors of politics and history are always ready to supply fig leaves, theories, and philosophies, to comfort the dead, the dying, the disappointed, and the crucified with the assurance that nothing could possibly have happened except in the way in which it did happen and is happening and that everything is for the best in the worst of all possible worlds.

So today you will find any number of people offering us fig leaves to cover fascism, communism, and war, theories which prove the inevitable failure of democracy and the League of Nations, philosophies which discover the seeds of a new world in the most ancient forms of violence and slavery. There is a family likeness in all these ex post facto consolatory explanations, they rely upon a distinction between illusions, shams, or utopias and realities. Democracy was a "sham"; dictatorship is a "reality." The common interests of nations and peace are an illusion; conflict of national interests and war are "real." The League of Nations was "utopian"; power politics are "reality." The validity of these theories and of the practical policies, based upon them, which we are exhorted to pursue must depend upon what is meant by this distinction between political or historical utopia and political or historical reality. To understand the distinction is, therefore, not an academic, but a highly practical question, for it is clearly politically imbecile to ignore realities or to pursue policies which are impossible of attainment—only we must know what is a reality and what is "impossible of attainment."

Our search for enlightenment may well start from a book by Professor E. H. Carr which has recently attracted much attention.[1] Mr. Carr is Pro-

---

[1] *The Twenty Years' Crisis,* 1919–1939. (Macmillan. 10s. 6d.). It should be read together with a smaller book which Professor Carr published about the same time: *The Foreign Policy of Britain from 1918 to Sept. 1939.* (Longmans. 6s.).

fessor of International Politics and has an intimate knowledge of his subject. His book on Bakunin proved him to be a man of intelligence with an unusual capacity for historical impartiality. His new book is an attempt to lay the foundations of a science of international relations and at the same time to "analyse the underlying and significant, rather than the immediate and personal, causes" in the history of the last twenty years which have brought us once more into war. The whole of Professor Carr's analysis is based upon a distinction between utopia and reality, and if any one should be capable of making us understand what it is it should be he. There are, as one would expect, very good things in the book, acute analysis of particular situations or processes, illuminating comments on particular events, and trenchant and often salutary criticism of things, theories, and persons with whom Professor Carr is out of sympathy or out of understanding. And yet the book fails in its purpose. It does not give us the beginnings of a science of international relations, because its method is unscientific. It attempts to interpret the events of the last twenty years by means of a distinction between what is utopian and what is real in policy. But, although the whole of his argument depends upon the difference between "utopia" and "realism," he never makes clear the distinction between them either to himself or to his reader. The reason is that he had not pushed his analysis either of terms or of events or of causes—particularly psychological causes—far enough.

Let us begin with terms. The term utopia is commonly used in two different ways. We speak of a dream or a policy being utopian in the sense that it contains a purpose or is based upon a hope or ideal which is incapable of fulfilment, and in this sense we oppose it to "realism." But it is also used in the sense of "unreal" as opposed to "reality." The two senses are not the same, but they are continually confused with disastrous results to truth and clear thinking in political controversy and in Professor Carr's book. This can best be shown by examples. Professor Carr's thesis is that the beliefs, objectives, and policies of nineteenth century liberal democrats and of the supporters of the League of Nations in the international field were utopian. He means by that that their beliefs were false and that their objectives and policies were impossible of attainment—not by any means, it will be observed, the same thing. He has a good deal to say about the falseness of their beliefs, but he never clearly demonstrates to us why their objectives and policies were impossible of attainment. He often implies that the failure of the League and of the attempt to reconstruct a peaceful Europe was "inevitable" merely because it was a failure. This attitude can be seen in the emotional colour of his adjectives in such a sentence as "The first and most obvious tragedy of this utopia was its ignominious collapse." Here you have the vulgar and false view that failure is "ignominious" and proves somehow or other that the attempt itself was discreditable and unattainable. These superficial judgments are characteristic of contemporaries: in 1790, 1830,

1848, 1900, and 1918, if Professor Carr had been a Frenchman, he would have talked about the "triumph" of democracy and the democratic ideals of the "Revolution," but in 1800, 1828, 1851, and 1939 he would have talked about their "ignominious collapse" and utopianism.

As a matter of fact, Professor Carr is himself really well aware of all this. Where he approves of a policy which has failed, as for instance Mr. Chamberlain's appeasement policy, he sees that the failure does not prove its utopianism or its ignominy, and in his other book he writes: "There is a common inclination in politics to take the deterministic view that any policy which fails was bound to fail and should, therefore, never have been tried. The charge that British Ministers were the dupes of the Axis Powers should not be too lightly made." If the collapse of the policy of appeasement does not prove that it was utopian, the collapse of the League does not prove that it was utopian, and if Mr. Chamberlain's failure was not ignominious, why should Professor Carr see ignominy in the failure of the League?

The answer to this question is that Professor Carr is unconsciously infected with the temporary social psychology of the time, the acceptance of power and force and conflict as the primary (and therefore best) elements in social organization and human relations, and that he feels the necessity to provide the fig leaf of a theory to cover the results of this psychology. He does this by assuming that policies and social objectives inconsistent with *existing* facts or with the psychology of power, violence, and conflict are utopian, and his theory or proof is based upon a confusion between the two senses of "utopian" and upon the common, but completely unscientific, assumption that power, violence, and conflict are more "real" elements in society than, e.g., beliefs, law, and co-operation for a common end or common interests.

The League was a political and social organization of states. It was established in answer to a demand, and in this sense it had an objective or ideal—the elimination of war, the resolution of international conflict, and the promotion of the common interests of states or nations. The ideal or objective was not in the League, but in the heads of those who established it or caused it to be established. The League is utopian only if those ideals or objectives are impossible of attainment. The policy of the League, which aimed at organizing the relations of states upon the basis of their common rather than their conflicting interests, is not utopian merely because it aimed at an unattained ideal or objective, as Professor Carr and many other people frequently assume. All policies, even of the most realist statesmen, aim at unattained ideals or objectives. The policy of Hitler aims at the as yet unattained ideal or objective of organizing the relations of states in Europe on the basis of force and conflicting interest, with Germany having an overwhelming superiority of power and therefore able to promote her interests at the expense of other states. In Professor Carr's sense his policy is "realist"; in fact, it is highly probable that his objective will not be attained and is unattainable, and is therefore really utopian. Again, Mr. Chamberlain's policy had as its ideal or objective peace with Hitler by abandoning any common resistance to aggression, any obligation to aid victims of aggression, and by placating Hitler and yielding to his demands. The objective was certainly not attained and was probably unattainable, and the policy was abandoned for its exact opposite. If the criterion of utopianism is attainability, the policies of Hitler and Mr. Chamberlain are no less utopian than the League policy.

Professor Carr's dealing with utopianism and reality in connection with policy is unsatisfactory because he does not carry his analysis of the psychology of political objective or ideal far enough. But it also breaks down in another important way: it accepts the vulgar delusion about the "reality" of some political concepts and the "unreality" of others, and then illicitly argues that a policy concerned with the former is "utopian" and a policy concerned with the latter "realist." For instance, Professor Carr maintains that the international policy of nineteenth-century liberalism and of the League both broke down because they were based on the promotion of the common interests of states and not on the conflict of state interests. They ignored the problem of power, which is the instrument of conflicting interests. Conflicting interests and power are "real"; harmony of interests is unreal or non-existent and political instruments of co-operation in common international interests are therefore also "unreal." Hence power politics are real and the League and the liberal policy of free trade and international co-operation "utopian."

This kind of attitude towards "interests" and "power" is very common at the present moment, but it is rooted in muddled thinking. The idea that there is some "reality" in a conflicting interest which does not exist in a common interest is an illusion. It springs from the obvious fact that most people are more *conscious* of their own immediate interests than of common interests and that the pursuit of common interests almost always entails the abandonment of some immediate individual interests. But the political reality of interests does not depend upon people's consciousness of them, but on the relative effects of different actions and different forms of social organization. In private life and national politics we have learnt this by bitter experience, and no one believes that the interest of men with knives to commit murder and robbery is more "real" than the interest of men with knives to refrain and be restrained from committing murder and robbery. International psychology is still, however, so crude that even a man like Professor Carr can believe that the interest of Germany in cutting the throat of Czechoslovakia is more real than the interest of both Germany and Czechoslovakia in living peacefully together and composing conflicting interests by compromise, merely because Herr Hitler has a very large army, a very large air force, and a very loud and rasping voice.

The question what interests are real, or to put it in another way what is really the interest of an individual, a group, a class, or a nation, cannot be settled in this cavalier way. A study of the history of human society and of international relations, not to speak of one's own life, will make one very careful not to dogmatize about real or unreal interests *in any particular case.* But it also teaches this lesson: that *generally and in the long run* common interests are more real than conflicting interests politically. Nearly every one would agree that this is true with regard to the internal organization of the national state; in the long run and generally every one gains by the pursuit of a common interest even at the expense of individual interests; even the potential murderer is better off in the end if he refrains or is restrained from cutting the rich man's throat; a class which ruthlessly pursues what it considers its own interest at the expense of other classes nine times out of ten digs its own economic grave. But there is reason for thinking that what is true of national is also true of international society. For many centuries now the relations of states have been determined by acceptance of the hypothesis that their conflicting interests are so exclusively real that they must form the basis of national policy. I cannot believe that, if Professor Carr and others who agree with him examine impartially the results, they can maintain that they are encouraging. It would be interesting to learn which of the "Great Powers" had really gained by their ruthless pursuit of conflicting interests in the years 1790, 1815, 1870, 1914, and 1939, and which had lost by pursuing utopian common interests. And *realpolitik?* If reality is to be judged by success, what is the judgment of history upon the work of such realists as Napoleon I, Napoleon III, Bismarck, Wilhelm II, the Russian Tsars, not to speak of British imperialists? The fact is that nothing is more "utopian" than the idea that you can create a stable and permanent society by power and the pursuit of conflicting interests; the ideal is unattainable because it involves an attempt to use two of the most unstable and disintegrating of all social forces, violence in the service of cupidity, as the primary ingredients in that cement which is to hold society together.

The question whether co-operation of states in common interests is possible, whether the power of individual states can be controlled internationally as the power of individuals, groups, and classes have been controlled nationally, and whether these objectives and the preservation of peace can be attained through some such international organization as the League is at the same time much simpler and more complicated than it appears in the books of those who see some peculiar reality in power and conflict and are therefore continually reading the burial service over democracy, the nineteenth century, and internationalism. It has little or nothing to do with "morality," "reality," "liberalism," or "reason." Whether the policy of organizing European states pacifically and of eliminating the *probability* of war is or is not utopian depends solely upon whether that objective is or is not attainable. It has nothing whatsoever to do with some imaginary quality of "reality" attaching to power or violence and to "conflicting interests," but not attaching to law, co-operation, and common interests. The attainability of a political objective almost always depends mainly upon three elements: facts, psychology, and the creation of social machinery or organization appropriate to the object or purpose of the policy and to the psychology. For instance, the attainability of the purpose of Zionists depends first upon such facts as the size of Palestine and the climate of its several districts. It would be utopian to ignore these facts and to put into Palestine more Jews than could exist there or to put a million Jews suddenly into a district of Palestine which is a waterless desert. Another element which has to be considered is the power of the Arabs to shoot Jewish immigrants, and yet another is the conflicting and the common interests of Jews and Arabs. Here it is partly a question of fact and partly of psychology; there is no question of some mystic element of reality attaching to some of the facts and not to others. It is a fact that the Arab has or may have the power to shoot the Jew; it is also a fact that he has or may have the power to co-operate with the Jew. It may be his immediate interest, i.e., he may gain at the moment, by shooting the Jew, but on the other hand it may be his "real" interest, i.e., he might gain more, by refraining from shooting and by co-operating with the Jew. The power to shoot is no more and no less "real" than the power to co-operate, and the conflicting interest which is served by shooting is no more and no less "real" than the common interest which is served by co-operation. Here the most important element is really psychological. The attainability of the Zionist policy will depend upon whether Arabs and Jews pursue their separate interests by conflict or whether they pursue their common interests by co-operation. Lastly, provided that facts and psychology did not make the purpose of Zionism impossible, it would still be necessary to create a form of government appropriate to the peculiar purpose, the peculiar facts, and the peculiar psychology.

This analysis applies no less to the problem of war and peace and international relations than to that of Zionism. Five hundred years of European history have proved that the "realist" system of power politics, war, and the conflict of interests is grotesquely utopian. Its purpose is to ensure stability of national power, glory, prosperity, and peace; its result has been a kaleidoscope of loud voiced jingoism and national glory alternating with war, defeat, misery, and impoverishment. The reason why power policy and the attempt to establish a stable European society upon it always fails and always must fail is that it ignores both the reality of facts and the reality of psychology. That of course does not mean that the opposite policy, which was embodied in the League idea, is attainable. Whether a pacific international system, based upon co-operation in common interests, is possible in Europe will depend primarily upon facts and upon psychology. But I am inclined to think that the main difficulty, the real cause of the League's failure, is not to be looked for in facts and in "reality," but in psychology.

The international relations of France and Britain between 1895 and 1939 throw light upon the general problem of international relations and upon the effect of psychology. In 1895 France and Britain had a large number of conflicting and a large number of common interests. In the autumn of 1903 when Lansdowne and Delcassé sat down to discuss Anglo-French relations, nothing had happened to alter the objective reality of those interests. The conflict of some and the community of other interests still persisted; both series were "real." This fact blows up the whole of Professor Carr's argument about utopianism and reality in international relations. For in 1903 a revolution in Anglo-French policy and relations took place and it was determined mainly by psychology, not by power, realism, or utopianism. Before 1903 the governments of the two countries conducted their foreign policy on the basis and hypothesis that the most important, the "real," interests of France and Britain were in conflict, and that their common interests were illusory, the utopian hallucinations of little Englanders and pacifists. What benefited France harmed Britain, and vice versa twice over. The basis of their international relations was therefore assumed to be conflict of interests, and the main instrument of policy was power. Co-operation, compromise, political machinery for composing differences or pursuing common interests were ruled out; on both sides of the channel statesmen thought of the use (or threat of using) power, economic or military, to promote the interests of their own country at the expense of the other as the proper and inevitable instrument of policy.

In 1903 the relations between the two countries were completely and permanently changed, not owing to any change in their existing interests or in their relative power, but by a decision of their governments, and this decision was caused by a psychological change. Lansdowne and Delcassé did not suddenly see that the conflicting interests had suddenly become "unreal" and the common interests "real"; they came to the conclusion that in general and in the long run the two countries would gain more by pursuing common interests and attempting to compose conflicting interests by compromise than by continuing the pursuit by each of its own interests at the expense of the other. As soon as this psychological change took place, it had a devastating effect upon the importance of power as an element in the relations between the two states. In 1895 the relative power of the two countries had been an element of primary importance in their relations and policy; after 1904 it became negligible. The reason was that once the objective of policy had been changed by the Entente, power became a negligible and inappropriate instrument of that policy. This shows the absurdity of ascribing some peculiar quality of reality to power in international relations. Power is a very real element in human society, just as are law, co-operation, ideas, beliefs, and ideals; its importance at any particular moment depends to a large extent upon the social or political objective which at that moment individuals are pursuing.

There is absolutely no reason to believe that the change which took place in 1904 in the national policies and international relations of France and Britain could not also take place in the policies and international relations of all the Great Powers, or all the states, of Europe. It is no answer to say that it was only fear of Germany which made France and Britain co-operate instead of fighting one another and that their co-operation was directed *against* another Power. To say that is to admit that psychology and not reality, power, or utopianism is the primary determinant in the international situation. If fear of Germany was sufficient to turn France and Britain away from the pursuit of their "real" conflicting interests into the pursuit of their "utopian" harmony of interests and to eliminate the probability—one might almost say possibility—of war between them for half a century there is no reason, except psychological, why fear of mutual destruction should not effect a similar change in the policies of all European states.

That is the real international problem which confronts Europe and civilization today. It is not a choice between utopia and reality, but between the psychology of conflicting interests and the organization of power politics on the one hand and the psychology of common interests and the organization of international co-operation on the other. The psychology of common interests and of co-operation and peace are there; it is, no doubt, weak, particularly among statesmen, generals, and perhaps professors, but it is there, and has widened and deepened in the last century. Its weakness is largely due to two causes. The first is the universal obstacle to civilization in all spheres of human society, the fact that pursuit of common interests almost always means the abandonment of some conflicting, individual, immediate interests. The immediate appeal of the individual, conflicting interest is immensely strong, and it requires intelligence and restraint to see or learn that in the long run the individual may gain by abandoning it on the pursuit of common interests. Secondly, the international organization of power is itself a tremendous obstacle in the growth and influence of the psychology of co-operation. It breeds fear, and fear is the greatest fomenter of conflict among human beings and the most potent destroyer of co-operation.

No sensible man will pretend that establishment of international peace is an easy thing. Whether it is possible depends upon whether the international organization of power, as it exists today, can be altered and whether the psychology of common interests and co-operation can be made an active determinant of national policies. These things may not prove possible but they are not impossible because conflict and conflicting interests are real, and co-operation and common interests are utopian. To believe that is merely to try to rationalize one's own and other people's primitive psychology.

~~~~~~

3. International Organization: The Functional Approach*

DAVID MITRANY

~~~~~~

THE TREND OF OUR TIME:
FROM "RIGHTS" TO "SERVICES"

When one examines the general shape of the tasks that are facing us one is, to begin with, led to question whether order could be brought into them by the device of formal written pacts. Why did written constitutions, Declarations of Rights, and other basic charters play such a great rôle during the nineteenth century? The task of that time was to work out a new division of the sphere of authority, to determine new relationships between the individual and the state; these relationships were meant to be fixed and final, and they had to rest on general principles, largely of a negative character. It was natural and proper that all that should be laid down in formal rules, meant to remain untouched and permanent. In much the same way the new nation-state was in world society what the new citizen was in municipal society; and international rules and a host of written pacts sought like the national constitutions to fix the formal relationship between the sovereign individual states and the collectivity which in this case also was expected to be fixed and final, with international law as a gradually emerging constitution for that political cosmos.

Viewed in this light, the Covenant of the League is seen to have continued that nineteenth-century tradition. It was concerned above all with fixing in a definite way the formal relationship of the member states, and in a measure also of non-members, and only in a very secondary way with initiating positive common activities and action. The great exception, security, was a vital action, but a negative one; its end was not to promote the active regular life of the peoples, but only to protect it against being disturbed. Broadly one might say that the Covenant was an attempt to universalize and codify the

* From David Mitrany, *A Working Peace System: An Argument for the Functional Development of International Organization* (Royal Institute of International Affairs, 1943). By permission.

rules gradually evolved through political treaties and pacts, and to give them general and permanent validity. It was neither unnatural nor unreasonable to follow up that nineteenth-century trend and try to steady international relations by bringing them within the framework of a written pact, one provided with set rules for its working. But when it came to going beyond that the League could not be more or do more than what its leading members were ready to be and do, and they were ready to do but little in a positive way. It was indeed characteristic of the post-Armistice period 1918-19 that even the victors hastened to undo their common economic and other machinery, such as the Allied Shipping Control, etc., which had grown and served them well during the war. That was at a time when within each country government action and control were spreading fast, causing many a private international activity also to be cut down or cut off. In other words, the incipient common functions, as well as many old connections, were disbanded in the international sphere at the very time when a common constitution was being laid down for it. It was that divorce between life and form that doomed the League from the outset, and not any inadequacy in its written rules.

Hence it is pertinent to ask: Would another written pact, if only more elaborate and stringent, come to grips more closely with the problems of our time? Let us by way of a preliminary answer note two things. First, the lusty disregard for constitutions and pacts, for settled rules and traditional rights, which is a striking mark of the times. In the pressure for social change no such formal ties are allowed to stand in the way, either within the several countries or between them. It is a typical revolutionary mood and attitude. If it does not always take the outward form of revolution, that is because governments themselves act as spearheads of the trend, and that not only in countries ruled by dictatorships. Those who lead in this rush for social change pride themselves indeed on their disregard for forms and formalities. The appeal which Communism, Fascism, and Nazism make to youth in particular and to the masses in general lies in no small degree in that political iconoclasm. At the turn of the nineteenth century the radical masses were demanding settled rules and rights, and Napoleon could play the trump card of constitutional nationalism against the autocratic rulers. Now the masses demand social action without regard to established "rights," and the totalitarian leaders have been playing the strong card of pragmatic socialism against constitutional democracy.

That universal pressure for social reform in the second place has utterly changed the relation of nationalism to internationalism, in a way that is promising if rightly used. In constitution-making there was a parallel between the two spheres, but nothing more, for they belonged politically to different categories. The nineteenth-century nationalism rested mainly on cultural and other differentiating factors, and the creation of the nation-state meant inevitably a breaking-up of world unity. A cosmopolitan outlook spread rapidly, but the nations at the same time baulked at international organization and control, and they could justify that refusal by seemingly good principle. At present the new nationalism rests essentially on social factors; these are not only alike in the various countries, thus paradoxically creating a bond even between totalitarian groups, but often cannot make progress in isolation. At many points the life of the nation-state is overflowing back into that common world which existed before the rise of modern nationalism; at present the lines of national and international evolution are not parallel but converging, and the two spheres now belong to the same category and differ only in dimensions.

In brief, the function of the nineteenth century was to restrain the powers of authority; that led to the creation of "political man" and likewise of the "political nation," and to the definition through constitutional pacts of their relation to the wider political group. The Covenant (and the Locarno and Kellogg Pacts) was still of that species essentially, with the characteristic predominance of rules of the "thou shalt not" kind. The function of our time is rather to develop and co-ordinate the social scope of authority, and that cannot be so defined or divided. Internationally it is no longer a question of defining relations between states but of merging them—the workaday sense of the vague talk about the need to surrender some part of sovereignty. A constitutional pact could do little more than lay down certain elementary rights and duties for the members of the new community. The community itself will acquire a living body not through a written act of faith but through active organic development. Yet there is in this no fundamental dispute as to general principles and ultimate aims. The only question is which way is the more immediately practicable and promising; whether a general framework should be provided formally in advance, on some theoretical pattern, or left to grow branch by branch from action and experience, and so find its natural bent.

THE BROAD LINES OF FUNCTIONAL ORGANIZATION

The problem of our generation, put very broadly, is how to weld together the common interests of all without interfering unduly with the particular ways of each. It is a parallel problem to that which faces us in national society, and which in both spheres challenges us to find an alternative to the totalitarian pattern. A measure of centralized planning and control, for both production and distribution, is no longer to be avoided, no matter what the form of the state or the doctrine of its constitution. Through all that variety of political forms there is a growing approximation in the workings of government, with differences merely of degree and of detail. Liberal democracy needs a redefinition of the public and private spheres of action. But as the line of separation is always shifting, under the pressure of fresh social needs and demands, it must be left free to move with those needs and demands and cannot be fixed through any constitutional re-statement. The only possible principle of democratic confirmation is that public action should be undertaken only where and when and in so far as the need for common action becomes evident and is accepted, for the sake of the common good. In that way controlled democracy could yet be made the golden mean whereby social needs might be satisfied as largely and justly as possible, while still leaving as wide a residue as possible for the free choice of the individual.

That is fully as true for the international sphere. It is indeed the only way to combine as well as may be international organization with national freedom. We have already suggested that not all interests are common to all, and that the common interests do not concern all countries in the same degree. A territorial union would bind together some interests which are not of common concern to the group, while it would inevitably cut asunder some interests of common concern to the group and those outside it. The only way to avoid that twice-arbitrary surgery is to proceed by means of a natural selection, binding together those interests which are common, where they are common, and to the extent to which they are common. That functional selection and organization of international relations would extend, and in a way resume, an international development which has been gathering strength since the latter part of the nineteenth century. The work of organizing international public services and activities was taken a step further by the League, in its health and drug control work, in its work for refugees, in the experiments with the transfer of minorities and the important innovations of the League loan system, and still more through the whole activity of the I.L.O. But, in addition, many activities and interests in the past had been organized internationally by private agencies—in finance and trade and production, etc., not to speak of scientific and cultural activities. In recent years some of these activities have in various countries been brought under public national control; indeed in totalitarian countries all of them. In a measure, therefore, the present situation represents a retrogression from the recent past: self-sufficiency has spread from economics to the things of the mind, and while flying and wireless were opening up the world, many old links forged by private effort have been forcibly severed. It is unlikely that most of them could be resumed now except through public action, and if they are to operate as freely as they did in private hands, they cannot be organized otherwise than on a non-discriminating functional basis.

What would be the broad lines of such a functional organization of international activities? The essential principle is that activities would be selected specifically and organized separately, each according to its nature, to the conditions under which it has to operate, and to the needs of the moment. It would allow, therefore, all freedom for practical variation in the organization of the several functions, as well as in the working of a particular function as needs and conditions alter. Let us take as an example the group of functions which fall under communications, on which the success of post-war reconstruction will depend greatly. What is the proper basis for the international organization of *railway* systems? Clearly, it must be European, or rather, *continental,* North-American, and so on, as that gives the logical administrative limit of co-ordination. A division of the continent into separate democratic and totalitarian unions would not achieve the practical end, as political division would obstruct that necessary co-ordination; while British and American participation would make the organization more cumbrous without any added profit to the function. As regards shipping, the line of effective organization which at once suggests itself is *international,* or intercontinental, but not universal. A European union could not solve the problem of co-ordination without the co-operation of America and of certain other overseas states. *Aviation* and *broadcasting,* a third example in the same group, could be organized effectively only on a *universal* scale, with perhaps subsidiary regional arrangements for more local services. Such subsidiary regional arrangements could in fact be inserted at any time and at any stage where that might prove useful for any part of a function; devolution according to need would be as easy and natural as centralization, whereas if the basis of organization were political every such change in dimension would involve an elaborate constitutional re-arrangement. Similarly, it could be left safely to be determined by practical considerations whether at the points where functions cross each other—as rail and river transport in Europe, or civil flying in Europe and America—the two activities should be merely co-ordinated or put under one control.

These are relatively simple examples. The functional co-ordination of production, trade and distribution evidently would be more complex, especially as they have been built up on a competitive basis. But the experience with international cartels, with the reorganization of the shipping, cotton and steel industries in England, not to speak of the even wider and more relevant experience with economic co-ordination in the two world wars, they all show that the thing can be done, and that it has always been done on such functional lines. No fixed rule is needed, and no rigid pattern is desirable for the organization of these functional strata.

A certain degree of fixity would not be out of place, however, in regard to the more *negative* functions, especially those related to "law and order," but also to any others of a more formal nature, and which are likely to remain fairly static. Security, for instance, could be organized on an interlocking regional basis; and the judicial function likewise, with a hierarchy of courts, the wider acting as courts of appeal from the more local courts. Yet even in regard to security, and in addition to regional arrangements, the elasticity inherent in functional organization may prove practicable and desirable, if only in the period of transition. Anglo-American naval co-operation for the policing of the seas may prove acceptable for a time, and it would cut across physical regions; agreement on a mineral sanction would of necessity mean common action by those countries which control the main sources; and other such combinations might be found useful for any particular task in hand. That is security only for defence; security arrangements were conceived usually on a geographical basis because they were meant to prevent violence, and that would still be the task of sanctions, etc., based on some regional devolution. But in addition there is a growing functional devolution in the field of social security—in connection with health, with the drug and white slave traffic, with subversive movements, etc. In all that important field of social policing it has been found that co-ordination and co-operation with the police of other countries on functional lines, varying with each task, was both indispensable and practicable. There is no talk and no attempt in all this to encroach upon sovereignty, but only a detached functional association which works smoothly and is already accepted without question.

However that may be, in the field of more *positive* active functions—economic, social, cultural—which are varied and ever-changing in structure and purpose, any devolution must, like the main organization, follow functional lines. Land transport on the Continent would need a different organization and agencies should the railways after a time be displaced by roads; and a Channel tunnel would draw England into an arrangement in which she does not at present belong, with a corresponding change in the governing organ.

Here we discover a cardinal virtue of the functional method—what one might call the virtue of technical self-determination. The functional *dimensions,* as we have seen, determine themselves. In a like manner the function determines its appropriate *organs*. It also reveals through practice the nature of the action required under the given conditions, and in that way the *powers* needed by the respective authority. The function, one might say, determines the executive instrument suitable for its proper activity, and by the same process provides a need for the reform of that instrument at every stage. This would allow the widest latitude for variation between functions, and also in the dimension or organizaton of the same function as needs and conditions change. Not only is there in all this no need for any fixed constitutional division of authority and power, prescribed in advance, but anything beyond the most general formal rules would embarrass the working of these arrangements.

THE QUESTION OF WIDER CO-ORDINATION

The question will be asked, however, in what manner and to what degree the various functional agencies that may thus grow up would have to be linked to each other, and articulated as parts of a more comprehensive organization. It should be clear that each agency could work by itself, but that does not exclude the possibility of some of them or all being bound in some way together, if it should be found needful or useful to do so. That indeed is the test. As the whole sense of this particular method is to let activities be organized as the need for joint action arises and is accepted, it would be out of place to lay down in advance some formal plan for the co-ordination of the several functions. Co-ordination, too, would in that sense have to come about functionally. Yet certain needs and possibilities can be foreseen already now, though some are probable and others only likely, and it may help to round off the picture if we look into this aspect briefly.

1. *Within the same group* of functions probably there would have to be co-ordination either simply for technical purposes or for wider functional ends, and this would be the first stage towards a wider integration. To take again the group concerned with communications—rail, road, and air transport in Europe would need *technical* co-ordination in regard to time-tables, connections, etc. They may need also a wider *functional* co-ordination if there is to be some distribution of passenger and freight traffic for the most economic performance—whether that is done by a superior executive agency or by some arbitral body, perhaps on the lines of the F.C.C. in America. Sea and air traffic across the Atlantic or elsewhere, though separately organized, probably would also benefit from a similar type of co-ordination. Again, various mineral controls, if they should be organized separately, would need some co-ordination; though this arbitrary grouping of "minerals" would be less to the point than the co-ordination of specific minerals and other products with possible substitutes—of crude oil with synthetic oil, of crude rubber with synthetic rubber, and so on.

2. The next degree or stage might be, if found desirable, the co-ordination of *several groups* of functional agencies. For instance, the communications agencies may not only work out some means of acting together in the distribution of orders for rolling stock, ships, etc., but they could or should work in this through any agencies that may have come into being for controlling materials and production, or through some intermediary agency as a clearing house. There is no need to prescribe any pattern in advance, or that the pattern adopted in one case should be followed in all the others.

3. The co-ordination of such working functional agencies with any *international planning* agencies would present a third stage, and one that brings out some interesting possibilities, should the ideas for an International Investment Board or an International Development Commission, as an advisory organ, come to fruition. One can see how such a Development Commission might help to guide the growth of functional agencies into the most desirable channels, and could watch their inter-relations and their repercussions. And an Investment Board could guide, for instance, the distribution of orders for ships, materials, etc., not only according to the best economic use, but also for the purpose of ironing out cyclical trends. It could use, according to its nature, its authority or its influence to make of such orders a means additional to international public works, etc., for dealing with periods or pockets of unem-

ployment. Co-ordination of such a general kind may in some cases amount almost to arbitration of differences between functional agencies; regional boards or councils like those of the Pan-American Union might be used to adjust or arbitrate regional differences.

4. Beyond this there remains the habitual assumption, as we have already said, that international action must have some over-all *political authority* above it. Besides the fact that such a comprehensive authority is not now a practical possibility, it is the central view of the functional approach that such an authority is not essential for our greatest and real immediate needs. The several functions could be organized through the agreement, given specifically in each case, of the national governments chiefly interested, with the grant of the requisite powers and resources; whereas it is clear, to emphasize the previous point, that they could not allow such organizations simply to be prescribed by some universal authority, even if it existed. For an authority which had the title to do so would in effect be hardly less than a world government; and such a strong central organism might develop a tendency to take unto itself rather more authority than that originally allotted to it, requiring in its turn the checks and balances used in federal systems, but which would be difficult to provide in any loose way. If issues should arise in the functional system which would call either for some new departure or for the interpretation of existing arrangements, that could be done only in council by all the governments concerned. In so far as it may be desired to keep alive some general view of our problems, and perhaps a general watch over the policies of the several joint agencies, some body of a representative kind, like the League Assembly or the Governing Body of the I.L.O., could meet periodically, perhaps elected by proportional representation from the assemblies of the various states. Such an assembly, in which all the states would have a voice, could discuss and ventilate general policies, as an expression of the mind and will of public opinion; but it could not actually prescribe policy, or this might turn out to be at odds with the policy of governments. Any line of policy recommended by such an assembly would have to be pressed and secured through the policy-making machinery of the various countries themselves.

These then are the several types and grades of co-ordination which might develop with the growth of functional activities. But there is, finally, in the political field also the problem of security, admittedly a crucial problem, for on its being solved effectively the successful working of the other activities will depend. At the same time, the general discussion of functional organization will have served to bring out the true place and proportion of security, as something indispensable but also as something incapable by itself of achieving the peaceful growth of an international society. It is in fact a separate function like the others, not something that stands in stern isolation, overriding all the others. Looking at it in this way, as a practical function, should also make it clear that we would not achieve much if we handled it as a one-sided limited problem—at present too often summed up in "German aggression." German aggression was a particularly vicious outgrowth of a bad general system, and only a radical and general change of the system itself will provide continuous security for all. In this case, also, it would be useful to lay down some formal pledges and principles as a guiding line, but the practical organization would have to follow functional, perhaps combined with regional, lines. That is all the more necessary as we know better now how many elements besides the purely military enter into the making of "security." The various functional agencies might, in fact, play an important role in that wider aspect of security: they could both watch over and check such things as the building of strategic railways, or the accumulation of strategic stocks in metals or grains. Possibly they could even be used, very properly and effectively, as a first line of action against threatening aggression, by their withholding services from those who are causing the trouble. They could apply such preventive sanctions more effectively than if these were to wait upon the agreement and action of a number of separate governments, and they could do so as part of their established duties, and therefore with less of the political reactions caused by political action.

Peace will not be secured if we organize the world by what divides it. But in the measure in which such peace-building activities develop and succeed one might hope that the mere prevention of conflict, crucial as that may be, would in time fall to a subordinate place in the scheme of international things, while we would turn to what are the real tasks of our common society—the conquest of poverty and of disease and of ignorance. The stays of political federation were needed when life was more local and active ties still loose. But now our social interdependence is all-pervasive and all-embracing, and if it be so organized the political side will also grow as part of it. The elements of a functional system could begin to work without a general political authority, but a political authority without active social functions would remain an empty temple. Society will develop by our living it, not by policing it. Nor would any political agreement survive long under economic competition, but economic unification would build up the foundation for political agreement, even if it did not make it superfluous. In any case, as things are the political way is too ambitious. We cannot start from an ideal plane, but must be prepared to make many attempts, from many points, and build things and mend things as we go along. The essential thing is that we should be going together, in the same direction, and that we get into step now. Action at the end of the war will fix the pattern of international relations for many years to come, and in the conditions that will prevail then it is less than likely that we could hold a peace conference of the habitual kind. Frontiers must be settled, and there may be some changes; as no change can satisfy both sides, all one

could hope is that frontiers will appear less important and more acceptable
as we organize common action across them. But for this to be possible frontiers must be fixed in advance or at least in the actual armistice, or there will
be conflict; and if plans for common action are not prepared in advance,
there will be chaos—the chaos of many competing and conflicting local actions. Could a returning Czech or Greek or Polish government tell its people
to be patient and wait till a distant conclave works out plans for reconstruction?

Co-operation for the common good is the task, both for the sake of peace
and of a better life, and for that it is essential that certain interests and activities should be taken out of the mood of competition and worked together. But
it is not essential to make that co-operation fast to a territorial authority, and
indeed it would be senseless to do so when the number of those activities is
limited, while their range is the world. "Economic areas do not always run
with political areas," wrote the *New York Times* (February 26th) in com-
menting on the Alaska Highway scheme, and such cross-country co-operation would simply make frontiers less important. "Apply this principle to
certain European areas and the possibilities are dazzling." If it be said that all
that may be possible in war but hardly in peace, that can only mean that practically the thing is possible, but that we doubt whether in normal times there
would be the political will to do it. Now, apart from everything else, the
functional method stands out as a solid touchstone in that respect. Promissory
Covenants and Charters may remain a headstone to unfulfilled good intentions, but the functional way is action itself, and therefore an inescapable test
of where we stand and how far we are willing to go in building up a new
international society. It is not a promise to act in a crisis, but itself the action
that will avoid the crisis. Every activity organized in that way would be a
layer of peaceful life; and a sufficient addition to them would create increasingly deep and wide strata of peace—not the stand-offish peace of an alliance,
but one that would suffuse the world with a fertile mingling of common endeavour and achievement.

This is not an argument against any ideal of formal union, if that should
prove the ultimate goal. It is, above all, a plea for the creation now of the
elements of an active international society. Amidst the tragedy of war there is
also the promise of a broader outlook, of a much deeper understanding of the
issue than in 1918. It is because the peoples are ready for action that they
cannot wait. We have no means and no standing to work out some new constitution and try to impose it in due course upon the world. But we do have
the standing and the means to prepare for immediate practical action. We do
not know what will be the sentiments of the peoples of Europe and of other
continents at the end of the war, but we do know what their needs will be.
Any political scheme would start a disputation; *any* working arrangement
would raise a hope and make for confidence and patience. The functional way
may seem a spiritless solution—and so it is, in the sense that it detaches from

the spirit the things which are of the body. No advantage has accrued to any one when economic and other social activities are wedded to fascist or communist or other political ideologies; their progeny has always been confusion and conflict. Let these things appear quite starkly for what they are, practical household tasks, and it will be more difficult to make them into the household idols of "national interest" and "national honour." The ideological movements of our time because of their indiscriminate zeal have sometimes been compared to religious movements. They may be that, but at their core was not a promise of life hereafter. The things which are truly of the spirit—and therefore personal to the individual and to the nation—will not be less winged for being freed in their turn from that worldly ballast. Hence the argument that opposes democracy to totalitarianism does not call the real issue. It is much too simple. Society is everywhere in travail because it is everywhere in transition. Its problem after a century of *laissez faire* philosophy is to re-sift in the light of new economic possibilities and of new social aspirations what is private from what has to be public, and in the latter sphere what is local and national from what is wider. And for that task of broad social refinement a more discriminatory instrument is needed than the old dogmatic sieve. In the words of a statement by the American National Policy Committee, "part of the daring required is the daring to find new forms and to adopt them. We are lost if we dogmatically assume that the procedures of the past constitute the only true expression of democracy."

4. Democratic Diplomacy*

HAROLD NICOLSON

Every system of government has its peculiar virtues and its peculiar faults, which in their turn affect foreign policy and the machinery by which it is executed. If we admit that one of the great achievements of democratic diplomacy is to have abolished the pernicious system of secret treaties, we must also admit that it has introduced other complications which hamper, not merely the art of negotiation, but also the amity and stability of international relations.

What, therefore, are the particular dangers or difficulties to which democratic diplomacy is exposed both in its theory and in its practice? I shall begin with theory.

* From Harold Nicolson, *Diplomacy* (Harcourt, Brace and Company, 1939). By permission.

It will be generally agreed that the most potent source of danger in democratic diplomacy is the irresponsibility of the sovereign people. By this I mean that, although the people are now the sovereign authority which ultimately controls foreign policy, yet they are almost wholly unaware of the responsibilities which this entails.

In the days of absolute monarchy the personal honour of the King was involved in the maintenance of the contracts or treaties which had been signed and ratified in his name. Monarchs were not invariably very sensitive to this obligation, but they were at least aware (and Louis XIV was constantly aware) that their own reputation for integrity was directly and personally at stake. Similarly, when the control of policy shifted from the individual monarch to a governing class, the feeling persisted that the engagements entered into by the government pledged the honour of the class as a whole. Yet now that the innumerable anonymous and unconscious electorate control foreign policy, this sense of personal, or corporate responsibility no longer exists. The sovereign people are not conscious of their sovereignty and are therefore unaware that it is they themselves who have caused these treaties to be signed.

This irresponsibility is encouraged by certain popular newspapers, which are apt to advocate the repudiation of pledges without even mentioning that such pledges have been incurred by a duly elected government, and ratified, after full discussion, by both Houses of Parliament. The same newspaper proprietor who would be profoundly shocked were an advertising firm or a newsprint manufacturer to repudiate their contracts, is perfectly prepared to preach similar repudiation to the country as a whole.

Were it to become the practice of democracies to disavow the decisions which have been come to in their name and endorsed by their representatives, then clearly the whole basis of international contract would be destroyed; anarchy would follow.

This problem is closely connected with the second great danger of democratic diplomacy, namely ignorance. By "ignorance" I do not mean ignorance of ascertainable facts; it is the duty of their rulers and experts to provide the electorate with the essential facts in digestible form. It matters little whether the electorate know where Teschen is or what is the output of the Skoda works. But it does matter greatly that in their approach to foreign affairs the democracies of the world do not all of them manifest that balance and good sense which they apply to domestic problems.

Thus, even educated electors are almost totally unaware what are to-day the treaties by which their countries are bound. These treaties have been published, debated in Parliament and discussed in the press. Yet the vast majority of the people have no conception of their existence, have forgotten all about them, and would certainly clamour about "secret diplomacy" once they were invoked. It is only when the honouring of our national engagements becomes a matter of topical concern that the public remember, or even learn of, their existence. It is at that stage, when it is too late, that the sovereign people clamour for the abrogation of contracts of which they had themselves approved.

Nor is this all. The ordinary elector is not merely ignorant, lazy and forgetful regarding the international commitments for which he has himself · assumed responsibility, but he does not apply to the general theory of foreign affairs that thought and intelligence which he devotes to domestic matters. He is unwilling to make any effort of comprehension or to try to understand the simplest elements of the problem.

In Great Britain, for instance, the ordinary man or woman has not yet realized that foreign affairs are *foreign* affairs, namely that they concern, not our own national interests only, but also the interests of other countries. They imagine that a foreign policy is framed in much the same manner as a budget or an education bill. That it is prepared by the responsible Minister, submitted to the Cabinet, approved by Parliament, and that thereafter all that remains to be done is to hand it over to the Foreign Office for execution. This confusion of thought tempts them to believe that an ideal foreign policy for Great Britain has only to be devised in order to be carried out. They ignore the fact that other countries, with equally powerful armaments, interests and prejudices, must similarly be consulted if any policy is to be effective.

The extent of this ignorance, the narcotic force of ill-considered slogans, can be well illustrated by two inquiries which I myself received. The first was, "Why does not the Government enter into an offensive alliance with the United States?" The second was, "Why does the Government not understand that what the country wants is collective security and the League of Nations; and that they will never stand for any European entanglements?" The foolishness of such enquiries leads one at moments to despair of democratic diplomacy.

More dangerous even than popular ignorance, are certain forms of popular knowledge. The professional diplomatist, having spent his life in studying the psychology and conditions of foreign countries, is very chary of basing generalizations upon hastily observed phenomena. The elector shows no such hesitation. A summer cruise to Dalmatia, a bicycling tour in the Black Forest, three happy weeks at Porto Fino, and he returns equipped with certain profound convictions regarding the Near East, the relations between Herr Hitler and his General Staff, and the effect of the Abyssinian venture upon Italian public opinion. Since his judgment is based upon feelings rather than upon thoughts, he is at the mercy of any chance encounter or any accidental conversation. The fact that some impatient policeman may have pushed or prodded Effie that day at Schaffhausen may well render Effie's parents "anti-German" for life. The fact that the hotel porter at Ragusa presented Arthur with three interesting pre-war postage stamps, may well convince Arthur's father that the Jugo-Slavs are the kindliest and most gentle race on earth. A slight controversy with the *ouvreuse* of a Paris theatre may, within the space of five minutes, turn a British citizen into a passionate Francophobe. Even such accidents as bad weather or a missed railway connection may permanently influence an elector's attitude towards foreign affairs. Such effects are not the least disturbing symptoms of democratic irresponsibility.

A third danger is the danger of delay. An absolute monarch or a dictator can frame and execute a policy within the space of a few hours. A democratic government has to wait until public opinion has digested its own conclusions. True it is that these conclusions, when reached, are generally more sensible and more stable than the somnambulist certainties of a dictator. Yet the months which must elapse before any definite public opinion can be ascertained is often fatal to efficient policy or negotiation.

This time-lag between the convictions of the experts and the assent of the ordinary elector is a disadvantage which would seem inseparable from all forms of democratic diplomacy. Let me give an instance. By January 1919 Mr. Lloyd George had been convinced by his financial experts that it would be prejudicial to our own interests to extract from Germany an indemnity so large as to render bankrupt our best customer or to cause disturbances in international exchange such as would damage our economy. Yet the British public and the House of Commons took eighteen months to reach a similar conclusion. French public opinion took five years. As a result, the whole German middle classes were reduced to ruin and hopelessness, with the consequences which we are all sadly witnessing to-day.

A fourth danger which lies in wait for democratic diplomacy is the danger of imprecision. The vagueness and fluidity of democratic policy is one of its most salient vices. Not only is there the uncertainty which arises from the irresponsible attitude adopted by sovereign democracy towards its own obligations, but there is the tendency of all democracies (and especially of Anglo-Saxon democracies) to prefer a vague and comforting formula to a precise and binding definition. The effectiveness of any diplomacy is dependent upon the amount of conviction or certainty that it inspires; yet if policy be non-committal, then its servant diplomacy must also be vague. Thus it often occurs that democratic governments, by couching their statements of policy in vague or ambiguous language, invite the very dangers which they wish to prevent.

Nor is imprecision the only temptation to which a democratic statesman or diplomatist is exposed. In order that his policy may make an appeal to the ordinary man or woman he is apt to emphasize the emotional, dramatic or moral aspects of the situation and to suppress the practical aspects. In extreme cases this leads him into actual hypocrisy, as when, in defending vital national interests, he pretends that he is defending some abstract idea. This temptation is one to which British statesmen all too readily succumb.

The above considerations have mainly centred upon those changes in diplomatic theory which have been occasioned by democratic control of foreign policy. New problems have also arisen in regard to diplomatic practice.

The first problem is that of publicity, since obviously the sovereign democracy needs to be informed. The use of the printing press as an ally to diplomacy is as old as Swift and the Treaty of Utrecht. Canning and Palmerston, as we have seen, believed fervently in an instructed public opinion, and enormous influence was exercised during the later nineteenth century by such newspapers as *The Times*. Cavour in Italy and Bismarck in Germany employed the Press for the purposes of secret rather than of open diplomacy, and Bismarck himself was not above fabricating articles and letters which served the uses of his policy.

The present problem is of a different nature. In the dictator States the controlled Press is used as a vehicle of propaganda. In democratic countries the aim is to employ it for purposes of information and education. Yet a satisfactory adjustment between the needs and rights of a popular Press and the requirements of discretion has yet to be found. In Great Britain, where the Press has a fine sense of responsibility, and an even finer sense of independence, the problem has not as yet become acute. In other countries, where the Press may be venal and is often sensational, publicity has proved the enemy rather than the friend of sensible diplomacy.

Before the war the problem of publicity was dealt with by European diplomatists in different ways. It was, and still is, customary upon the continent for the Foreign Minister or Foreign Office to favour certain special newspaper or agency; these are called, politely, "the inspired press"; or, less politely, the "reptile press." In Great Britain the custom was to differentiate rather vaguely between the "responsible" and the "irresponsible" newspapers, the latter category representing those journals which were not too friendly to the government. With the advent of democratic diplomacy this system of newspaper favouritism obviously became impossible, and even in Downing Street a Press Department was installed.

The present British system, although by no means fool-proof, works well enough. In so far as "news" is concerned a loyal attempt is made not to discriminate between any of the newspapers. In so far as "guidance" is concerned, it is obvious that certain correspondents (whether serving government or opposition papers) are more experienced, intelligent and reliable than other correspondents. It is inevitable that the former should be treated with greater confidence than the latter. Nor has the system in practice aroused serious discontent.

Far more complicated than the actual relations between the Press and the Foreign Office, is the effect of a free press upon continental opinion. Foreign governments do not really believe that the British Press is as independent of the Foreign Office as is actually the case. If *The Times* writes a leading article which appears to differ from official policy, foreign observers do not believe that Printing House Square has had a sharp brain-wave all on its own, they believe that the Foreign Office is "flying a kite." Similarly, if one or other of the great national dailies launch an attack upon the Government, foreign observers tend to imagine that the latter is "testing public opinion." This misconception leads to many disadvantages. On the one hand it tempts other governments to conclude that British opinion is more divided, or the Government more undecided than they actually are. And on the other hand it leads them to blame the Foreign Office for attacks upon foreign countries or personalities which that unfortunate department is honestly quite unable to control.

The advantages of a free Press are so immeasurably greater than its disadvantages that this particular problem of democratic diplomacy need not cause anxiety. It is little more than a minor inconvenience.

A more dangerous innovation in diplomatic practice is the tendency of democratic countries to allow their politicians to take a personal part in negotiation. Clearly there are moments when it is essential that the Prime Minister or the Foreign Minister should attend important conferences. Yet repeated personal visits on the part of the Foreign Secretary of one country to the Foreign Secretary of the other should not be encouraged. Such visits arouse public expectation, lead to misunderstandings, and create confusion. The time at the disposal of these visitors is not always sufficient to allow for patience and calm deliberation. The honours which are paid to a minister in a foreign capital may tire his physique, excite his vanity, or bewilder his judgment. His desire not to offend his host may lead him, with lamentable results, to avoid raising unpalatable questions or to be imprecise regarding acute points of controversy. Nor is he always able on his return to obtain the approval of his Cabinet colleagues to his statements ·and actions.

Such visits, naturally enough, are very dear to the heart of all politicians. They are called "the value of personal contact." Yet in truth, as I have said elsewhere, diplomacy is not the art of conversation, it is the art of negotiating agreements in precise and ratifiable form. As such, it is, on all ordinary occasions, far better left to the professional diplomatist. His visits to the Foreign Office of the government to which he is accredited arouse no public expectation, inspire no Press indiscretions, and if sterile lead to no public disappointment. He has ample time to renew his visits at regular intervals and to occupy the intervening weeks or days in informing his government, obtaining instructions, and pondering tranquilly upon the negotiation itself. He is not hampered by ceremonial, or embarrassed by excessive courtesy. And above all the stages and results of his negotiation are carefully recorded in written documents.

Such are some of the main problems in theory and practice which diplomacy under a democratic system has yet to solve. I do not wish to leave in the mind of the reader the impression that I regard democratic diplomacy as more inefficient or dangerous than its predecessors. Far from it. I consider it, even in its present confused state, infinitely preferable to any other system. Yet I confess that to my mind democratic diplomacy has not as yet discovered its own formula.

How is that formula to be found? It will only be by long processes of trial and error that we can hope to adjust this infinitely delicate piano to the sturdy fingers of a popular electorate. Yet there are certain principles of adjustment which it may be well to bear in mind.

It is in the first place important that the electorate should come to realize the distinction, on which I have dwelt so heavily, between policy and negotiation. Once they fully understand that they are safeguarded against secret policy, they may not worry themselves so acutely over the imaginary terrors of secret negotiation.

In the second place, once confidence has been re-established between diplomacy and its sovereign, it is important that the professional side of diplomacy should be fortified and its basis enlarged. It is possible in future years that we may have as foreign secretaries or prime ministers men who, owing to lack of experience, take an emotional or sentimental view of foreign policy. It is essential that such men should be able to call upon the services of a thoroughly experienced staff. Yet that staff must also be democratized and must cease to be generally, although to some extent inaccurately, regarded as the preserve of the upper bourgeoisie.

And in the third place nothing should be left undone to educate the public, not so much in regard to the details of foreign affairs, as in regard to those general principles of good sense and experience which have been evolved by generations of gifted and reasonable persons, and which, so long as men live in separate independent States, must always govern their relations between themselves.

Chapter XVII

WAR: THE SOVEREIGN ASSASSIN

ONE of the paradoxical phenomena of political philosophy is that those who demand absolute law and order within the state at the same time propound anarchy as the normal, and desirable, relationship between states. Hegel is a case in point. In his *Philosophy of Law* (1821), he advocates, as we saw in earlier chapters, the strong state—on the model of the Prussian police state of the nineteenth century. Yet, when it comes to the question of how states are to live together, Hegel is an enthusiastic anarchist. In fact, he is nihilistic enough to deny that relations between states have anything in common with morality, such as regulates dealings between individuals. There is a distinctly pagan note to Hegel's claim that "the nation state is mind in its substantive rationality and immediate actuality and is therefore the absolute power on earth." The whole Stoic-Jewish-Christian tradition, that there is a higher law than the commands of the state, a law of reason, nature, or God, is flatly rejected by Hegel. If the state is the absolute power on earth, what happens when several absolutes clash? Hegel cheerfully states: "If states disagree and their particular wills cannot be harmonized, the matter can only be settled by war." However, this consequence does not alarm Hegel. On the contrary. Wars are wholesome for a number of reasons. First, "corruption in nations would be the product of prolonged, let alone 'perpetual' peace." The trouble with peace is, says Hegel, that men stagnate in it. Their idiosyncrasies become more fixed and ossified, and war is required to keep the body politic healthy. Furthermore, Hegel stresses the impact of war on domestic conditions: "As a result of war, nations are strengthened, but peoples involved in civil strife also acquire peace at home through making war abroad." Later in the century Bismarck emphasized in his memoirs that war would be the only means to revive and maintain the loyalty of the masses who had become infected with the ideas of international socialism. By 1912 the Social Democrats had become the strongest single German party, with thirty-five per cent of the German electorate voting for it.

What Hegel expresses in somewhat restrained philosophical language, Heinrich von Treitschke can be relied upon to shout from the housetops.

Like Hegel, he does not, in his *Politics* (1897–1898), accept the *fact* of war as a regrettable evil, but positively affirms the *desirability* of war: "The great strides which civilization makes against barbarism and unreason are only made actual by the sword." Like Hegel and Bismarck, Treitschke stresses the unifying force of war, that it silences social selfishness and party hatreds: "Most undoubtedly war is the only remedy for an ailing nation." Following Hegel's conception of man's freedom being fulfilled in self-sacrifice for the state, Treitschke says that the "grandeur of war lies in the utter annihilation of puny man in the great conception of the State, and it brings out the full magnificence of the sacrifice of fellow-countrymen for one another." Treitschke also maintains that war fosters political idealism, and without war there would be no heroes to remember. This argument is logical in a country in which military leaders occupy the place which, in other nations, is held by men like Voltaire, Danton and Robespierre, the Pilgrim Fathers, Tom Paine, Jefferson, Lincoln, and Roosevelt. Treitschke rejects the demand for eternal peace as "purely reactionary," because all growth and movement would then disappear. The code of honor that Treitschke prescribes for the health of the state is a purely military one: "If the flag is insulted, the State must claim reparation; should this not be forthcoming, war must follow, however small the occasion may seem." Another reason that impels a state to go to war is its unwillingness to abide by existing treaty obligations; if it cannot persuade other states peacefully to give in to demands contrary to its obligations, it has the right, Treitschke says, to "proceed to the ordeal by battle." Thus he comes to the conclusion that "war is both justifiable and moral, and that the ideal of perpetual peace is not only impossible but immoral as well."

Small as the antimilitaristic voice was in Germany, it should not be forgotten. The trouble with German democracy and liberalism was not that they failed, but that so few tried to make them succeed. Immanuel Kant's name will always stand out as that of a man who believed that civilization can be advanced only through government based on law, within the nation as well as between nations. In *Perpetual Peace* (1795), Kant has drawn one of the most inspiring pictures of a united mankind ever conceived. The federation of free states, held together by bonds of law rather than separated by savagery and "licentious liberty," is Kant's conception of international order. Kant makes the important point that a peace treaty (*pactum pacis*) finishes only a particular war, whereas a "pacific alliance" (*foedus pacificum*) would forever terminate all wars: "This alliance does not tend to any dominion over a state, but solely to the certain maintenance of the liberty of each particular state, partaking of this association." Whereas Hegel and Treitschke both embrace international anarchy and war as desirable and moral, Kant states the rational aspects of the problem in these words: "At the tribunal of reason, there is but one means of extricating states from this turbulent situation, in which they are constantly menaced with war; namely, to renounce like individuals, the anarchic liberty of savages, in order to submit themselves to coercive laws, and thus form a society of nations (*Civitas gentium*) which would insensibly embrace all the nations of the earth."

Probably no one has so richly deserved the Nobel peace prize as Sir Norman Angell, who, for over a generation, has served the cause of peace by trying to educate the British and American public to understand some of the fundamentals of international peace and war. In *The Unseen Assassins* (1932), Sir Norman defines, first, what are the greatest evils that devastate our civilization. He holds that neither outright wickedness nor lack of knowledge are to be blamed, but our failure to apply available and often self-evident knowledge to our social relationships: "We do not *desire* to create social or economic evils, to impose injustice and bring about war, but we apply policies in which those results are inherent because we fail to see the implications of the policies. Those unperceived implications are the Unseen Assassins of our peace and welfare."

Sovereignty is one of the chief of these assassins. Angell denies that the existence of nations is in itself the cause of war: "War is due to the fact that we have attached to nationality the idea of independence and sovereignty: sovereignty and the anarchy which it necessarily implies make war." History itself has proved that sovereignty and nationality are not necessarily united: Great Britain consists of the three nations of England, Wales, and Scotland, but they do not possess sovereignty—which means, in practice, the legal right to make war upon each other. The Hispanic nations in the New World are very similar in language, religion, and tradition, yet they have fought many wars among themselves. Because they failed to stay united after achieving independence from Spain but organized themselves into sovereign states, they acquired the habit of warring against one another. Conversely, if independent nations had been formed in the territory of the present United States, they would undoubtedly have learned the custom of fighting among themselves. The fact that sovereign states insist on being the judges in their own cases makes war inevitable. Obviously, if each party to a dispute takes the position that it will be the judge, it demands a right for itself which it refuses the other. Experience points to one method of escaping from the anarchy inherent in sovereignty: "No one shall be judge in his own cause, which means that he should not be his own defender. The combined power of the whole group shall be used to ensure the defence of each member; that is to say, the enjoyment of such rights as experience has shown to make for a workable and orderly co-operation at any given stage of a society's development."

When Angell published *The Unseen Assassins* in 1932, no one could fore-see that only thirteen years later the atomic bomb would be used, revealing destructive powers of undreamed-of dimensions. Harold C. Urey, Nobel prize winner in chemistry, and one of the top scientists who worked on the development of nuclear energy, has joined those scientists who are aware of the emergency situation created by the atomic bomb. In "The Atom and Humanity," an address delivered on October 21, 1945, commemorating Al-fred Nobel's birthday, Urey discusses some of the social and political impli-cations of the atomic bomb. The lure of aggression will be greater than ever: "Whereas Hitler thought he could win his aggressive war in months, these weapons will encourage future aggressors to attempt the conquest of the world in a few days." One thousand bombs could destroy thirty-three cities the size of New York. Urey is unable to present any ready-made solu-tion as to how to solve the problem of international control of atomic energy. But he "categorically defends" the proposal that no atomic bombs must be made anywhere in the world, and that no government must be allowed to possess them: "We are inevitably led to the conclusion that the United Nations Organization should possess adequate power" to deal with atomic weapons as well as with all other weapons. The United Nations should operate through an efficient inspection service with a sufficient police force to fall back on, Urey suggests. If no such control will be set up, and if atomic bombs will be produced in several nations, "we will spend all our days in deadly fear that they will be used, and in time they undoubtedly will be."

A paradox which the militarists have never learned is that the militaristic state eventually goes down before the gathering strength of the liberal, peace-minded society. In *The Free State* (1945), D. W. Brogan discusses this prob-lem with particular reference to German militarism, as contrasted with the traditions of civilian government authority in Britain and the United States. Twice in a generation Germany challenged the Western democracies (which she despised as weak, decadent, and lacking in fighting vigor), and both times Germany was defeated by the amateurs in warfare. What must be particularly humiliating to many Germans is the fact that they proved them-selves inferior in the one business which had ceaselessly engaged their thought and effort. Nowhere in the world was war studied, researched into, written and talked about, and—above all—prepared for, as in Germany. The Germans were confident in 1914 as in 1939 that their aggressions would suc-ceed, because they knew everything about war there was to be known. They did, with one exception: how to win wars.

1. The Philosophy of International Anarchy*

G. W. F. HEGEL

In peace civil life continually expands; all its departments wall themselves in, and in the long run men stagnate. Their idiosyncrasies become continually more fixed and ossified. But for health the unity of the body is required, and if its parts harden themselves into exclusiveness, that is death. Perpetual peace is often advocated as an ideal towards which humanity should strive. With that end in view, Kant proposed a league of monarchs to adjust differences between states, and the Holy Alliance was meant to be a league of much the same kind. But the state is an individual, and individuality essentially implies negation. Hence even if a number of states makes themselves into a family, this group as an individual must engender an opposite and create an enemy. As a result of war, nations are strengthened, but peoples involved in civil strife also acquire peace at home through making wars abroad. To be sure, war produces insecurity of property, but this insecurity of things is nothing but their transience—which is inevitable. We hear plenty of sermons from the pulpit about the insecurity, vanity, and instability of temporal things, but everyone thinks, however much he is moved by what he hears, that he at least will be able to retain his own. But if this insecurity now comes on the scene in the form of hussars with shining sabres and they actualize in real earnest what the preachers have said, then the moving and edifying discourses which foretold all these events turn into curses against the invader. Be that as it may, the fact remains that wars occur when the necessity of the case requires. The seeds burgeon once more, and harangues are silenced by the solemn cycles of history.

War is the state of affairs which deals in earnest with the vanity of temporal goods and concerns—a vanity at other times a common theme of edifying sermonizing. This is what makes it the moment in which the ideality of the particular attains its right and is actualized. War has the higher significance that by its agency, as I have remarked elsewhere, "the ethical health of peoples is preserved in their indifference to the stabilization of finite institutions; just as the blowing of the winds preserves the sea from the foulness which would be the result of a prolonged calm, so also corruption in nations would be the product of prolonged, let alone 'perpetual,'

* From G. W. F. Hegel, *Philosophy of Law* (1821; translated by T. M. Knox as *Philosophy of Right*, Oxford University Press, 1942). By permission.

peace." This, however, is said to be only a philosophic idea, or, to use another common expression, a 'justification of Providence,' and it is maintained that actual wars require some other justification. On this point, see below.

The ideality which is in evidence in war, i.e. in an accidental relation of a state to a foreign state, is the same as the ideality in accordance with which the domestic powers of the state are organic moments in a whole. This fact appears in history in various forms, e.g. successful wars have checked domestic unrest and consolidated the power of the state at home. Other phenomena illustrate the same point: e.g. peoples unwilling or afraid to tolerate sovereignty at home have been subjugated from abroad, and they have struggled for their independence with less glory and success the less they have been able previously to organize the powers of the state in home affairs—their freedom has died from the fear of dying; states whose autonomy has been guaranteed not by their armed forces but in other ways (e.g. by their disproportionate smallness in comparison with their neighbours) have been able to subsist with a constitution of their own which by itself would not have assured peace in either home or foreign affairs.

States are not private persons but completely autonomous totalities in themselves, and so the relation between them differs from a moral relation and a relation involving private rights. Attempts have often been made to regard the state as a person with the rights of persons and as a moral entity. But the position with private persons is that they are under the jurisdiction of a court which gives effect to what is right in principle. Now a relation between states ought also to be right in principle, but in mundane affairs a principle ought also to have power. Now since there is no power in existence which decides in face of the state what is right in principle and actualizes this decision, it follows that so far as international relations are concerned we can never get beyond an 'ought.' The relation between states is a relation between autonomous entities which makes mutual stipulations but which at the same time are superior to these stipulations.

The nation-state is mind in its substantive rationality and immediate actuality and is therefore the absolute power on earth. It follows that every state is sovereign and autonomous against its neighbours. It is entitled in the first place and without qualification to be sovereign from their point of view, i.e. to be recognized by them as sovereign. At the same time, however, this title is purely formal, and the demand for this recognition of the state, merely on the ground that it is a state, is abstract. Whether a state is in fact something absolute depends on its content, i.e. on its constitution and general situation; and recognition, implying as it does an identity between the state and its neighbour, is similarly conditional on its neighbour's judgment and will.

If states disagree and their particular wills cannot be harmonized, the matter can only be settled by war. A state through its subjects has widespread connexions and many-sided interests, and these may be readily and considerably injured; but it remains inherently indeterminable which of these injuries is to be regarded as a specific breach of treaty or as an injury to the honour and autonomy of the state. The reason for this is that a state may regard its infinity and honour as at stake in each of its concerns, however minute, and it is all the more inclined to susceptibility to injury the more its strong individuality is impelled as a result of long domestic peace to seek and create a sphere of activity abroad.

Apart from this, the state is in essence mind and therefore cannot be prepared to stop at just taking notice of an injury *after* it has actually occurred. On the contrary, there arises in addition as a cause of strife the *idea* of such an injury as the idea of a danger *threatening* from another state, together with calculations of degrees of probability on this side and that, guessing at intentions, &c., &c.

At one time the opposition between morals and politics, and the demand that the latter should conform to the former, were much canvassed. On this point only a general remark is required here. The welfare of a state has claims to recognition totally different from those of the welfare of the individual. The ethical substance, the state, has its determinate being, i.e. its right, directly embodied in something existent, something not abstract but concrete, and the principle of its conduct and behaviour can only be this concrete existent and not one of the many universal thoughts supposed to be moral commands. When politics is alleged to clash with morals and so to be always wrong, the doctrine propounded rests on superficial ideas about morality, the nature of the state, and the state's relation to the moral point of view.

2. The Blessings of War*

HEINRICH VON TREITSCHKE

Without war no State could be. All those we know of arose through war, and the protection of their members by armed force remains their primary

* From Heinrich von Treitschke, *Politics* (1897–1898; translated by B. Dugdale and T. de Bille, 1916). By permission of The Macmillan Company, publishers.

and essential task. War, therefore, will endure to the end of history, as long as there is multiplicity of States. The laws of human thought and of human nature forbid any alternative, neither is one to be wished for. The blind worshipper of an eternal peace falls into the error of isolating the State, or dreams of one which is universal, which we have already seen to be at variance with reason.

Even as it impossible to conceive of a tribunal above the State, which we have recognized as sovereign in its very essence, so it is likewise impossible to banish the idea of war from the world. It is a favourite fashion of our time to instance England as particularly ready for peace. But England is perpetually at war; there is hardly an instant in her recent history in which she has not been obliged to be fighting somewhere. The great strides which civilization makes against barbarism and unreason are only made actual by the sword. Between civilized nations also war is the form of litigation by which States make their claims valid. The arguments brought forward in these terrible law suits of the nations compel as no argument in civil suits can ever do. Often as we have tried by theory to convince the small States that Prussia alone can be the leader in Germany, we had to produce the final proof upon the battlefields of Bohemia and the Main.

Moreover war is a uniting as well as a dividing element among nations; it does not draw them together in enmity only, for through its means they learn to know and to respect each other's peculiar qualities.

It is important not to look upon war always as a judgment from God. Its consequences are evanescent; but the life of a nation is reckoned by centuries, and the final verdict can only be pronounced after the survey of whole epochs.

Such a State as Prussia might indeed be brought near to destruction by a passing phase of degeneracy; but being by the character of its people more reasonable and more free than the French, it retained the power to call up the moral force within itself, and so to regain its ascendancy. Most undoubtedly war is the one remedy for an ailing nation. Social selfishness and party hatreds must be dumb before the call of the State when its existence is at stake. Forgetting himself, the individual must only remember that he is a part of the whole, and realize the unimportance of his own life compared with the common weal.

The grandeur of war lies in the utter annihilation of puny man in the great conception of the State, and it brings out the full magnificence of the sacrifice of fellow-countrymen for one another. In war the chaff is winnowed from the wheat. Those who have lived through 1870 cannot fail to understand Niebuhr's description of his feelings in 1813, when he speaks of how no one who has entered into the joy of being bound by a common tie to all his compatriots, gentle and simple alike, can ever forget how he was up-

lifted by the love, the friendliness, and the strength of that mutual sentiment.

It is war which fosters the political idealism which the materialist rejects.
What a disaster for civilization it would be if mankind blotted its heroes
from memory. The heroes of a nation are the figures which rejoice and
inspire the spirit of its youth, and the writers whose words ring like trumpet
blasts become the idols of our boyhood and our early manhood. He who
feels no answering thrill is unworthy to bear arms for his country. To appeal
from this judgment to Christianity would be sheer perversity, for does not
the Bible distinctly say that the ruler shall rule by the sword, and again
that greater love hath no man than to lay down his life for his friend? To
Aryan races, who are before all things courageous, the foolish preaching of
everlasting peace has always been vain. They have always been men enough
to maintain with the sword what they have attained through the spirit.

Goethe once said that the North Germans were always more civilized
than the South Germans. No doubt they were, and a glance at the history
of the Princes of Lower Saxony shows that they were for ever either attacking or defending themselves. One-sided as Goethe's verdict is, it contains a
core of truth. Our ancient Empire was great under the Saxons; under the
Swabian and the Salic Emperors it declined. Heroism, bodily strength, and
chivalrous spirit is essential to the character of a noble people.

Such matters must not be examined only by the light of the student's
lamp. The historian who moves in the world of the real Will sees at once
that the demand for eternal peace is purely reactionary. He sees that all
movement and all growth would disappear with war, and that only the
exhausted, spiritless, degenerate periods of history have toyed with the idea.
Three such periods have occurred in modern history.

The first was the dismal time after the Peace of Utrecht and the death of
Louis XIV. The world seemed to be taking breath, but Frederick the Great
pronounced acutely that this was a period of universal demoralization in
European politics. The Holy Roman Empire occupied a ridiculous position.
Prussia was unprepared and faced with the problem of expansion or destruction—yet these indefinite conditions were pronounced by the apostles of reason to be fraught with good. The elder Rousseau, the Abbé Castel de St.
Pierre, and others came forward and wrote their insensate books about the
banishment of strife.

The second period, when the nations eagerly passed round the pipe of
peace, began under like circumstances after the Congress of Vienna. Its
treaties were looked upon as *ratio scripta,* and it was held to be right and
reasonable that two great nations, the Germans and the Italians, should be
cramped for all eternity.

We are living in the third period to-day. A great war seems to have
destroyed idealism in Germany. Does not the braying laughter of the vulgar

echo loud and shameless, when any of those things which have made Germany great is thrown down and broken? The foundations of our ancient and noble culture are crumbling; everything which once made us an aristocracy among the nations is mocked and trodden under foot. Certainly this is a fitting time to rave once more of everlasting peace.

But it is not worth while to speak further of these matters, for the God above us will see to it that war shall return again, a terrible medicine for mankind diseased.

Any insult offered, even if only outwardly, to the honour of a State, casts doubt upon the nature of the State. We mistake the moral laws of politics if we reproach any State with having an over-sensitive sense of honour, for this instinct must be highly developed in each one of them if it is to be true to its own essence. The State is no violet, to bloom unseen; its power should stand proudly, for all the world to see, and it cannot allow even the symbols of it to be contested. If the flag is insulted, the State must claim reparation; should this not be forthcoming, war must follow, however small the occasion may seem; for the State has never any choice but to maintain the respect in which it is held among its fellows.

When a State recognizes that existing treaties no longer express the actual political conditions, and when it cannot persuade the other Powers to give way by peaceful negotiation, the moment has come when the nations proceed to the ordeal by battle. A State thus situated is conscious when it declares war that it is performing an inevitable duty. The combatant countries are moved by no incentives of personal greed, but they feel that the real position of power is not expressed by existing treaties and that they must be determined afresh by the judgment of the nations, since no peaceful agreement can be reached. The righteousness of war depends simply and solely upon the consciousness of a moral necessity. War is justified because the great national personalities can suffer no compelling force superior to themselves and because history must always be in constant flux; war therefore must be taken as part of the divinely appointed order.

We have already seen that war is both justifiable and moral, and that the ideal of perpetual peace is not only impossible but immoral as well. It is unworthy of man's reason to regard the impracticable as feasible, but a life of pure intellect is all too often enervating to the reasoning faculty. War cannot vanish from the earth as long as human sins and passions remain what they are. It is delightful to observe how the feeling of patriotism breaks involuntarily through the cosmopolitan phrases even of the apostles of perpetual peace.

3. Perpetual Peace*

IMMANUEL KANT

The law of nations ought to be founded upon a federation of free states.

Nations, as states, like individuals, if they live in a state of nature and without laws, by their vicinity alone commit an act of lesion. One may, in order to secure its own safety, require of another to establish within it a constitution which should guarantee to all their rights. This would be a federation of nations, without the people however forming one and the same state, the idea of a state supposing the relation of a sovereign to the people, of a superior to his inferiors. Now several nations, united into one state, would no longer form but one; which contradicts the supposition, the question here being of the reciprocal rights of nations, inasmuch as they compose a multitude of different states, which ought not to be incorporated into one and the same state.

But when we see savages in their anarchy, prefer the perpetual combats of licentious liberty to a reasonable liberty, founded upon constitutional order, can we refrain to look down with the most profound contempt on this animal degradation of humanity? Must we not blush at the contempt to which the want of civilization reduces men? And would one not rather be led to think that civilized nations, each of which form a constituted state, would hasten to extricate themselves from an order of things so ignominious? But what, on the contrary, do we behold? Every state placing its majesty (for it is absurd to talk of the majesty of the people) precisely in this independence of every constraint of any external legislation whatever.

The sovereign places his glory in the power of disposing at his pleasure (without much exposing himself) of many millions of men, ever ready to sacrifice themselves for an object that does not concern them. The only difference between the savages of America and those of Europe, is, that the former have eaten up many a hostile tribe, whereas the latter have known how to make a better use of their enemies; they preserve them to augment the number of their subjects, that is to say, of instruments destined to more extensive conquests. When we consider the perverseness of human nature, which shews itself unveiled and unrestrained in the relations of nations with each other, where it is not checked, as in a state of civilization, by the coercive power of the law, one may well be astonished that the word right

* From Immanuel Kant, *Perpetual Peace* (1795).

has not yet been totally abolished from war-politics as a pedantic word, and that a state has not yet been found bold enough openly to profess this doctrine. For hitherto Grotius, Pufendorf, Wattel, and other useless and impotent defenders of the rights of nations, have been constantly cited in justification of war; though their code, purely philosophic or diplomatic, has never had the force of law, and cannot obtain it; states not being as yet subjected to any coercive power. There is no instance where their reasonings, supported by such respectable authorities, have induced a state to desist from its pretensions. However this homage which all states render to the principle of right, if even consisting only in words, is a proof of a moral disposition, which, though still slumbering, tends nevertheless vigorously to subdue in man that evil principle, of which he cannot entirely divest himself. For otherwise states would never pronounce the word right, when going to war with each other; it were then ironically, as a Gallic prince interpreted it. "It is," said he, "the prerogative nature has given to the stronger, to make himself obeyed by the weaker."

However, the field of battle is the only tribunal before which states plead their cause; but victory, by gaining the suit, does not decide in favour of their cause. Though the treaty of peace puts an end to the present war, it does not abolish a state of war (a state where continually new pretenses for war are found); which one cannot affirm to be unjust, since being their own judges, they have no other means of terminating their differences. The law of nations cannot even force them, as the law of nature obliges individuals to get free from this state of war, since having already a legal constitution, as states, they are secure against every foreign compulsion, which might tend to establish among them a more extended constitutional order.

Since, however, from her highest tribunal of moral legislation, reason without exception condemns war as a mean of right, and makes a state of peace an absolute duty; and since this peace cannot be effected or be guaranteed without a compact among nations, they must form an alliance of a peculiar kind, which might be called a pacific alliance (*foedus pacificum*) different from a treaty of peace (*pactum pacis*) inasmuch as it would forever terminate all wars, whereas the latter only finishes one. This alliance does not tend to any dominion over a state, but solely to the certain maintenance of the liberty of each particular state, partaking of this association, without being therefore obliged to submit, like men in a state of nature, to the legal constraint of public force. It can be proved, that the idea of a federation, which should insensibly extend to all states, and thus lead them to a perpetual peace, may be realized. For if fortune should so direct, that a people as powerful as enlightened, should constitute itself into a republic (a government which in its nature inclines to a perpetual peace) from that time there would be a centre for this federative association; other states might adhere thereto, in order to guarantee their liberty according to the principles of public right; and this alliance might insensibly be extended.

That a people should say, "There shall not be war among us: we will form ourselves into a state; that is to say, we will ourselves establish a legislative, executive, and judiciary power, to decide our differences,"—can be conceived.

But if this state should say, "There shall not be war between us and other states, although we do not acknowledge a supreme power, that guarantees our reciprocal rights"; upon what then can this confidence in one's rights be founded, except it is upon this free federation, this supplement of the social compact, which reason necessarily associates with the idea of public right?

The expression of law of nations, taken in a sense of right of war, presents properly no idea to the mind; since thereby is understood a power of deciding right, not according to universal laws, which restrain within the same limits all individuals, but according to partial maxims, namely, by force. Except one would wish to insinuate by this expression, that it is right, that men who admit such principles should destroy each other, and thus find perpetual peace only in the vast grave that swallows them and their iniquities.

At the tribunal of reason, there is but one mean of extricating states from this turbulent situation, in which they are constantly menaced with war; namely, to renounce, like individuals, the anarchic liberty of savages, in order to submit themselves to coercive laws, and thus form a society of nations (*civitas gentium*) which would insensibly embrace all the nations of the earth. But as the ideas which they have of the law of nations, absolutely prevent the realization of this plan, and make them reject in practice what is true in theory, there can only be substituted, to the positive idea of an universal republic (if all is not to be lost) the negative supplement of a permanent alliance, which prevents war, insensibly spreads, and stops the torrent of those unjust and inhuman passions, which always threaten to break down this fence.

4. *The Sovereign Assassin**

NORMAN ANGELL

If Europe had not formed itself or grown into sovereign nations, it would not be riven by international war. There might be civil war, there might be

* From Norman Angell, *The Unseen Assassins* (Hamish Hamilton, 1932). By permission of Sir Norman Angell.

strife of all kinds; Europe as a unity somewhat similar to the forty-eight states of North America might have sacrificed things that have been worth all the cost of separate nationalities. That is a separate question. But if Europe constituted one sovereignty she would not face, though she might face worse evils, the particular problem with which we are dealing. To repeat the truism already enunciated, if there were no nations, nations would not go to war.

Note that the earlier part of the above proposition speaks of "sovereign" nations. As noted before, when this aspect came into the argument, Scotland and Wales are nations but they do not fight each other, nor fight England, though they did once. It is not the existence of nations, or the fact of nationality, which is the cause of war. War is due to the fact that we have attached to nationality the idea of independence and sovereignty: sovereignty and the anarchy which it necessarily implies make war. We fight each other because each has said:

> We are a nation; that is to say a corporate body, a personality, *therefore* each national person is independent, a law unto itself, shall acknowledge no code regulating its relations with other similar persons. These persons shall live together without government, without laws, without institutions for their framing, their alteration or their enforcement. For if such institutions existed those persons would not be independent or sovereign, they would be subject to rule, to law.

The "therefore" of the above statement is the supreme Unseen Assassin. It stands for a complete *non sequitur*. The nation makes, if you will, by deeply rooted psychological forces, a "herd," a corporate person. But there are other such corporate bodies too: the church, the caste, the clan; sometimes the trade union, the club. But they do not ask that they shall be sovereign and independent; the state, and the only state; that they shall enter into no effective partnership with any other human organization (if partners are completely independent of each other they are not partners), owe allegiance to no other human authority.

The plain facts of history show that there was nothing "inevitable"—except in the sense that a social intelligence and discipline are of slow growth—in thus attaching to one particular form of association the quality of complete sovereignty, in dissociating it from disciplined co-operation with other groups. It was often a pure accident of history that sovereignty became attached to some groups and not to others.

There was a period after the revolution of the thirteen American colonies of Great Britain in which it seemed exceedingly doubtful whether they would form a federation at all. There was nothing inevitable about their doing so. The Spanish-American colonies when they revolted did not; and the English-speaking colonies might not have done so save for several fortuitous circumstances: the character and influence of this or that statesman amongst them, fear of the strength of the mother country. If Britain had been in reality a decadent state the revolted colonies would almost certainly have failed to hang together in order not to hang separately.

If history had taken that turn we might as easily have had half a dozen nations (a French-speaking one, perhaps, on the St. Lawrence or in Louisiana; a Dutch-speaking one on the Hudson; Spanish-speaking in California, etc.), just as we have a round dozen separate nations south of the Mexican border. We know that if such independent nations had been formed in what is now the United States (especially with differences of language and culture) they would have fought, as the independent nations which have resulted from the Spanish-American colonies have fought, even though *they* have no differences of language and culture. (Note in passing that the national characteristics, linguistic and racial, which distinguish, say, Wales from England, and both from Scotland, are far greater than those which distinguish the Chileno and the Peruvian, or the San Salvadorian and the Guatemalan. Those Spanish nations having complete sovereignty fight each other, or face the possibility by arming against each other; the British nations, having only limited sovereignty, have ceased so to do.)

Put the illustration, as already suggested, in inverse form: Imagine that at some stage in the development of Europe—at the breakdown, say, of the Western Empire—some degree of effective authority had grouped round, say, the Church; and the nations of Europe had become federalised states, like those of the American Union.[1] Then, though there might be civil war, as there has been civil war in the American Union, the problem of international war and that chaos in the international economic field as we know it to-day, would not confront us.

Why does the claim to complete sovereignty and independence, the refusal to acknowledge allegiance to a common rule of conduct, the attempt of persons or corporate bodies, having multitudinous economic and social relations, to live without government, without appropriate social institutions, necessarily involve war? Though I am not going to suggest that the rules which govern persons should necessarily apply to nations, there are principles, like those of the multiplication table, for instance, to go no further, which must apply to both.

If someone were to propose to John Smith that in this closely packed complex modern world of ours, with its motor-cars travelling at sixty miles an hour; its inevitable difference of view as to what are the best traffic rules; as to who is responsible in this or that accident; what is suitable compensation in the event of injury; insurance laws; the necessary conflict of claims

[1] Boniface VIII by a Bull claims that "all Kings, Emperors, and other Sovereigns, whoever they may be, are subject, like all other men, to be summoned before the Apostolic Courts, for every sort of cause: for we, by the permission of God, command the whole Universe." (R. F. Wright, *Medieval Internationalism*, p. 89.)

about property, rights of way, trespass, pollution of water, measures for the preservation of public health—if anyone were to suggest to him that in this sort of world you can do without legislative bodies, courts, police, without governing institutions, that is, he would regard you as insane.

And he would not qualify the verdict at all if the proposer went on to explain that, since usually folk are fundamentally decent and can be relied upon to keep their word, the idea was to replace the complicated machinery of government by an undertaking on the part of everybody always to play fair; never to take more than they were entitled to. Smith would reply that the question of goodwill was hardly involved; that differences as to what was fair and what each was entitled to were usually quite honest differences, were just the point about which the quarrels arose, that rules (especially like those of the road with reference to driving cars) had to be kept, whatever the individual thought of them, and had to be enforced if he did not like them. Suggest to Smith that such a world can work without government, and he is sure you are insane. Suggest to him, however, that the closely interwoven life of those national persons we have been discussing, for reasons just as valid, need corresponding institutions of government, and he will equally regard you as insane.

Yet the results of anarchy, though dissimilar in the two cases, not manifested, that is, in quite the same way, are hardly less dreadful in the second; as the last twenty years have shown.

Let us note the quite simple and understandable process by which with mechanical inevitability the method of anarchy produces conflict. One of the primary impulses of man, as of any animal, is self-preservation, defence, security. And society, government, as the substitute for anarchy, has largely grown up around the organisation of that function. Let us see why.

Suppose I say:

I will be my own defender of my own rights, as against another, by being stronger than any who may challenge them. To allow others to come in and say what my rights are, means that I shall have to do the will of others, not my own, which is to deprive me of independence, freedom, sovereignty. I shall take measures therefore to see that my view of my rights shall prevail.

Very well. What is the position of that other who may disagree with my view of what my rights are?

He says:

If you make yourself judge of a dispute in which the rights of both are involved, you are judge of my rights as well as your own. Why should you be judge of my rights any more than I should be judge of yours? I prefer the latter arrangement.

Now that situation is bound to result in conflict because the "right" by which each stands involves in its very terms a denial of the other's claim. Each is demanding a right for himself which he refuses to the other.

There can be no general defence, security, "self-preservation" under such a system because the defence of one deprives the other of defence; the security of the one is the insecurity of the other; "justice" for the one means injustice for the other. Under such a system you could only make both secure if each were stronger than the other; each his own judge in a dispute where another is involved. It defies arithmetic, as it defies ethics.

You get exactly the same result whether you begin from another angle of anarchy: the assertion of neutrality by members of a group. Suppose my fellows say: "Your security is no concern of ours. We are neutral. If anyone steal your property or attempt to take your life, that is not our affair." If that is the attitude, then (speaking, say, as the feudal chief, or clan, or mere individual) I shall attempt to possess sufficient power to resist any threat to my security, that is to say, my rights (which means what I believe to be my rights). I shall try to be stronger than anyone likely to be a menace. That will make such a one weaker than me, put him at my mercy, though I refuse to be at his. In any dispute—any question of his rights as against mine— he will just have to trust to my goodwill, though I refuse to trust to his. *He* will be deprived of defence by the fact of *my* defence.

Now, as a statement of principle that is just as true whether the units you are speaking of are persons, families, clans, tribes, nations, or alliances. The multiplication table is just as valid or invalid whether you apply it to stars or cabbages. When a Cabinet Minister says that the surest way to get peace is to be stronger than your prospective enemy, he is still asking each of the two parties to be stronger than the other, and gaily defying arithmetic.

Is the suggestion that such a method *must* end in conflict borne out by the event? *Circumspice.*

Now, as against this method of anarchy—of each being his own defender, and consequently his own judge—the whole experience of man points a contrary method. Its general lines are these: No one shall be judge in his own cause, which means that he should not be his own defender. The combined power of the whole group shall be used to ensure the defence of each member; that is to say, the enjoyment of such rights as experience has shown to make for a workable and orderly co-operation at any given stage of a society's development. The first right of all is the right to third-party judgment in a dispute with another, so that that other, party to the dispute, does not become its judge. There is this contrast as between the use of force socially and anarchically. In a state of anarchy the power of each individual is used to enable him to be his own judge; under the social method the power of the community is used to *prevent* any individual being his own judge.

These are the issues as between the method of anarchy and the method of organised society whether of persons or of states. It is perfectly open to argue that the method which has proved feasible in the case of persons will not for this, that or the other reason work in the case of states. There is, alas! a strong case for the belief that in the latter case we are condemned to anarchy, and so to war because the momentum of certain traditions like the Jingo-militarist-nationalist tradition is such as to render us incapable of the necessary discipline or intelligence.

But it is *not* open to say this: "We will now have peace between nations by means of a properly organised society of nations. Each member of that society shall be neutral in any dispute between the others; the society as a whole shall have no responsibility for the defence of individual members; each shall take his own measures for defence; and each shall be independent and sovereign."

For that is mere contradiction of terms: If each is neutral, sovereign, independent, then there can be no society. But that is exactly what so many of us, most of us, *are* saying, and the most serious and tragic part of it is that we do not see the contradiction.

We know by the commonest experience of everyday life—in business, in every form of personal dispute—that we should be brought to deadlock if we began on the assumption that each party could be trusted to be his own judge. Still less could we trust that judgment if the party exercising it had unquestioned preponderance of power over the other. We are aware that the acceptance of the principle of third-party judgment, when we come to contentious matters, is the only possible basis of peace; that even that cannot operate until there is some agreement as to "what is right"; that the whole process is dependent upon a certain apparatus—law making, law interpreting, law enforcing—and that without that apparatus the mere goodwill of each party would be hopelessly inadequate. We are perfectly aware that the breakdown of the institutions would be simply equivalent to the breakdown of civilisation, of peace; that always indeed have the two things been coincident. A round score of ancient civilisations broke down, because their institutions collapsed under some strain: the one collapse involved the other.

Yet this commonplace experience of daily life is not by popular judgment applied to the field of international policies at all. We genuinely care for peace; are deeply apprehensive about the recurrence of war. But, speaking broadly, we are quite indifferent about the creation of institutions, for the simple reason that we do not see the relation between the maintenance of peace and the difficult, hazardous and easily defeated task of building up a world society.

The important thing which emerges is this: We do not apply the plain lessons of daily life to the task of that ending of war we all desire. In what has just been written there is an implied condemnation of educational method. Some of our educationalists are genuinely disturbed about what they are apt to call our lack of knowledge of foreign countries, and propose to remedy it by imparting information bearing on the lives of peoples other than our own. We are assured that international understanding would be promoted by knowing other nations better. I doubt it. The bitterest quarrels —like the religious conflicts of India and Ireland—are between communities that live in the same street, live all their lives in close contact and know each other very well indeed. It is the understanding of the necessary principles of just and peaceful human relationship that is needed. The facts which bear on that are available to us all, inherent in the commonest problems of our personal contact. We do not need to know any more facts about remote peoples, whether about Esquimaux or the Nestorians. We need to realise the meaning in social principle of the facts we already know. And the way in which education has taught us to think about human society is such that we fail to apply at points where most needed, to the solution of our gravest and most urgent problems, principles which emerge most obviously from the facts of daily life.

We have dealt so far with one perfectly understandable social principle. Let us take two others, just as simple, and closely related to it, and which reveal in popular understanding the same contradictions, the same *non sequiturs,* the same failure to apply the commonest experience of one situation to another only slightly less familiar.

No argument is so readily used by the ordinary voter as an excuse for his inertia or indifference in the matter of international institutions, for his refusal, that is, to deal with the problem of international anarchy, as he has dealt with anarchy elsewhere, as this argument: You will never get over human nature. Man, he will tell you, is, by the very law of his being, a fighting animal; pugnacious, inherently unreasonable, one-sided, passionate. . . . If I have heard this argument once, I have heard it a thousand times. It is usually presented as the final, complete, unanswerable case against international action towards peace, against such efforts as the League.

Yet this fact of man's anti-social instincts is, of course, the final and fundamental case *for* the League, not against. If human nature were perfect, if men were naturally other-minded, always ready to see the other's point of view, never likely to lose their tempers, then certainly we should not need the League, international institutions. But neither should we need most of our national institutions. They are the means by which we cope with the imperfections of human nature; that imperfection is the reason for the institutions. Yet the educated man who invokes the human nature argument *against* international institutions, daily thinks of it as the supreme argument *for* national institutions. Say to him: men are quarrelsome, avaricious, one-sided, quite incapable of judging their own case, therefore let us abolish the courts and have no laws, and he will see the inconsequence in a moment. Yet suggest that he should establish corresponding institutions for nations and he deems it an adequate reply to declare that nations are quarrelsome, avaricious, one-sided, quite incapable of being their own judge. He goes his life through without seeing that that fact which he uses for one conclusion in a familiar situation, he uses for an exactly opposite conclusion in a slightly less familiar situation, and only so turns it upside down because the second situation is less familiar.

But what shall we say of education for society which produces in the mass of men that degree of understanding of the world in which they live, that much of capacity for using known fact to frame social judgments?

Or take an equally simple instance of elementary confusion touching the principles by which society functions. Constantly one hears the argument: A nation's army or navy is its policeman; armies and navies exist for the same reason that the police force exists. A favourite plea of the plain man.

Yet it might occur to him that police forces are not organised to fight each other, and that armies are. National armies as we now know them are organised for a purpose which ultimately, and broadly is the exact reverse of the purpose for which police are organised, since, in the last analysis, armies are (as we have seen) forces behind rival litigants, and the police is the force behind the judge. The police represent the combined power of the whole community (of persons) used to ensure to each member of that community his agreed rights under the law, and as part of the process, to restrain any member from using his individual force to be his own judge. If in a dispute with my neighbour about a right of way, I break down his fence to defend what I regard as my right, and invade what he regards as his property, he will invoke the police, who will restrain me from being my own defender, since, if I had that right of defence, I should be my own judge, and deny by that fact a similar right to him. The whole ultimate purpose of the police is to restrain me from using my power in that way. The community has assumed the obligation of my defence. But the nation which says: We will retain force in the shape of an army or navy powerful enough to resist anyone likely to challenge its power; but that force shall not be part of the power of the community (of nations) pledged to defend each member, but a tool enabling us to be our own defender, which means in the last resort, our own judge—that nation has obviously repudiated the police method.

The object of an army or navy is to enable the individual to impose its individual will; the object of the police is to restrain that individual from imposing his will. The police method is to make the defence of the individual the obligation of the whole community; the method of armies and navies as they now exist rejects that in favour of each defending himself. One is a social instrument; the other is an instrument of anarchy; the one depends upon competition of power, "each being stronger than the other"; the other upon pooled power, the co-operation of the whole in the maintenance of agreed rights. The two methods are plainly mutually exclusive. Yet all my life I have heard from educated men the weary phrase about needing armies for the same reason that we need police.

Whether every stage or phase of the preceding argument touching what I have called the mechanism of society be valid or not, is not for the moment in question. The point is that, at a juncture when the maintenance of civilisation depends upon a relatively simple and logical development in the organisation of society, education has not equipped the public mind even to the extent of enabling it to grasp the elements of the argument, the simplest of the issues involved.

The implications are unfamiliar to the mass of ordinary men, to the scholars turned out by our schools. It is not that they are familiar with the arguments, have applied them to the problems in hand and rejected them as invalid. I say without any hesitation, on the basis of the rather special experience of having argued the internationalist case during thirty years, in several countries, that the mass of ordinary men who form our voters, have not been led to think about the necessary mechanism of society, or to think of society as having a necessary mechanism at all; or to think about the nature of society; or to be conscious that there is such a thing as a definitely organised society. They have learned a number of rules of conduct, and have accepted them, usually as an entirely arbitrary code; the reason for them in terms of social welfare is for the most part entirely disregarded.

If John Smith made a case for anarchy, or a case (such as that made before the war by certain political philosophers in Germany) for the establishment of order in the world by the ultimate domination of one national state, one would feel that though his education had made him a bad reasoner, it had at least turned his mind to dealing with the nature of the social universe in which he lived, and his relation thereto. But you will find the modern European asserting such principles as an absolutist nationalism because his education simply has not related that thing to the needs of organised society at all.

What, for instance, is the record of European education in this matter of nationalism?

All agree that it is—among others—an extremely dangerous tendency. All on the Allied side said that of the pre-war German nationalism; all the non-French world said it of French nationalism as manifested in the Dreyfus case; Germany, ourselves and the Americans have been saying it of certain aspects of post-war French nationalism; America and the world have said it of British nationalism (especially as revealed in claims relating to belligerent rights at sea). We have said it of American nationalism as revealed in such incidents as Cleveland's Venezuelan message, the ridiculous but not harmless Anglophobia of the Bill Thompsons and the William Randolph Hearsts. To say that the nationalist's impulse cannot become a very dangerous impulse is not only to deny all evidence, but indeed to deny what all of us are saying.

Very well. Go to the histories, the text-books, in current use in the schools of Europe and America; note the attitude towards nationalism and patriotism. Is this necessary warning as to the dangerous ways in which patriotism may develop stressed? The exactly contrary thing is done. One of the features which gives to nationalism its danger is precisely the feature which is hidden; the quality most dangerous is developed. That quality is its one-sidedness, its astigmatism; the fact that it refuses to recognise in others the rights that it claims for itself; refuses to regard those others as on the same plane as itself. "We are different." Other nations may make of their patriotism a dangerous force; but *we* can never be too patriotic.

5. The Atom and Humanity *

HAROLD C. UREY

Alfred Nobel, whose birthday we celebrate today,[1] was the inventor of dynamite and of smokeless propellant powders. At the same time that he engaged in this scientific research he was very much interested in bringing lasting peace to the world. In a conversation with one of his friends he remarked that his explosives would bring peace more quickly then peace societies. After some fifty years we now realize that Nobel was wrong in his conclusion, and we find that the peace societies were also unsuccessful. Today we are faced with far more powerful explosives than any that Nobel dreamed of, and we are still discussing wars and means of bringing peace to this planet. It is my purpose to discuss the relationship of this newest weapon, the atomic bomb, to the problem of world peace. May I say that this discussion has no relationship to any atomic bomb legislation or any diplomatic moves of the United States Government. It is intended to bring the urgency of the problem before you and to discuss some long-time views to enduring peace.

* *International Conciliation* (December, 1945). By permission of the Carnegie Endowment for International Peace.

[1] Address delivered by Dr. Harold C. Urey, Nobelist in chemistry, University of Chicago, formerly of Columbia University, at the luncheon of the American-Scandinavian Foundation, New York City, commemorating birthday of Alfred Nobel, October 21, 1945.

First of all I wish to show that the progress of every weapon that has been invented by man, proceeds through the stages of crude invention to successful improvements, and the development of counter-measures against it. The position of weapons of this kind, as we know them today, is that they are in use by major combatants, that they produce a great deal of destruction in modern war, and that no completely decisive defense against them has ever been secured. Only when a weapon is completely superseded by a more effective one does it disappear from war. Following this line of argument we may expect that our atomic bombs will be obsolete only when more terrible weapons have been developed.

Machine guns were invented in the seventeenth century. They were relatively ineffective until the first World War when they were firing six hundred or seven hundred rounds per minute, and accounted for many casualties. During the second World War machine guns of many varieties were mounted on planes, tanks, ships, and other mobile mounts. Fighter planes carried as many as eight machine guns, and the large bombers were fully armed to take care of attack from any direction. The principle has been applied to larger caliber weapons, and these have had automatic aiming devices of great efficiency attached to them. No decisive counter-defense against the machine gun other than armor has been found, and there is no indication that any government in the world thinks that it does not need machine guns in modern war.

A submarine sunk the Housatonic at Charleston during our Civil War. Submarines were steadily improved. In the 1890's they had reached a size of about two hundred tons. In the first World War they began with six hundred to eight hundred tons and rose in size to about two thousand tons. In this last World War they very nearly won the battle of the Atlantic. Many counter-measures against the submarine were devised, and were found to be more expensive than the submarines which they fought. We won the battle of the Atlantic and the submarine was temporarily out. At the present time the talk is of larger submarines, and it is believed that they can be built.

The airplane was developed in the first years of this century. During the first World War it was used for scouting, and before the end of the war carried a machine gun. At the beginning of World War II the plane had evolved into the complicated machine of metal with engines of high power using high grade gasolines as fuels and carrying many machine guns and modern size bombs. Before the end of the war they evolved into enormous machines carrying many tons of bombs and machine guns to defend them. They finally were powered with jet-propelled engines and carried rockets to attack other airplanes and other objectives. They destroyed the cities of Germany and Japan and damaged cities of England, Russia, China, and Poland. No decisive defense against the airplane is known. Many intercepting devices have been developed, and they do prevent the plane from exerting its full effect. Only superior air power was effective. Each combatant threw in every ounce of effort to manufacture more and better planes, bigger and more numerous bombs and more clever mechanisms to guide them and to detect them. And the victory came to the combatant with the greater industrial capacity. This victory came only after all combatants, with the exception of the United States, had been very seriously damaged by this weapon of modern war. In the future we may expect larger and faster military planes, and all cities of the world can be expected to crumble under the loads even of ordinary bombs which such planes will carry. Some will be intercepted, but some will get through any defenses that we are likely to devise.

I could repeat this story with tanks, plane carriers, high-caliber guns, and many other weapons great and small. Any abolition of a weapon is due to the invention of something still more effective in destructive power.

We might further mention some new weapons which were developed in this war. The V-1 or the so-called buzz bomb, caused some damage, but was rather easily intercepted because of its low speed. The V-2 was in a very different category. At the beginning of the war rockets were essentially toys, but at the end of the war this rocket travelled two hundred miles and rose nearly a hundred miles above the earth and arrived at a velocity above that of sound so that it could not be heard before it arrived. It seems that this weapon can be further improved and probably can be aimed from still greater distances and guided by radio control. It can be expected that it will follow the same course as others which we know.

Finally there is the most spectacular weapon of all—namely, the atomic bomb. This weapon stopped the war and probably saved the lives of many Allied soldiers. It also presents the people of the world with their most momentous problem. Briefly, it destroyed two cities of Japan. Four square miles of Hiroshima were utterly destroyed, and the area of devastation in the case of Nagasaki was even greater—approximately ten square miles. The total area of the city was not destroyed because of its narrow shape. The energy liberated was approximately equivalent to that released in the explosion of twenty thousand tons of TNT. These two bombs were the second and third of this type to be exploded, and the third one was definitely an improvement on the second.

In regard to the future development of this weapon, we can confidently expect that it will follow the course of other military weapons which I have discussed briefly above. We can hardly think that the atomic bomb is as primitive as the early machine guns, submarines, and airplanes, at this stage, but that great improvements are possible seems a certainty. One can be quite sure that the ingenuity of man will make possible the manufacture of such bombs on a large scale.

Due to secrecy maintained in the development of this bomb, the attacks on the Japanese cities came as a complete surprise to the enemy. A single plane carried each bomb over its target. No attempt at interception by the enemy was encountered, so that bombing conditions were favorable as compared with what they would have been had the enemy expected such an attack. The light construction of Japanese cities undoubtedly contributed to the vast destruction effected. It is hardly to be expected that steel structures would crumple so easily, though photographs of some of the industrial plants showed masses of twisted steel in the burned-out plants. In a modern city the destruction might not be so complete, but there is no doubt that the destruction would be vast and would probably set fires which would completely destroy modern buildings.

This weapon at its initial trial represents an advance over existing weapons beyond that secured by any other weapon ever devised, and considering the sort of weapons already mentioned this is indeed a remarkable statement. This weapon poses one of the most serious problems ever faced in the history of man, and beside it most other problems fade into insignificance. I am amazed that anyone can take our present day strikes, reconversion, transporting the soldiers home from abroad, and other current problems, very seriously. They will all be solved some way, and their solution, whatever it may be, will not affect any of us very greatly. But atomic bombs are a different matter entirely.

Let us consider the problem of a war of atomic bombs. X years from now we shall have a stock pile of these weapons and will have unprecedented power in our hands. If only no other countries have them we shall feel very safe and secure. Of course, the citizens of any other country in the world will feel the same way. Thus the British will feel safe if Britain has these bombs and no other country has them; the Russians will feel safe if they have them and no other country does, and so with the people of other countries. But if all of the countries of the world have them none of us will feel safe. On the contrary, we shall live in constant fear of sudden and violent death. A world of vast fear and apprehension will be our lot and that of our children. Whereas Hitler thought he could win his aggressive war in months, these weapons will encourage future aggressors to attempt the conquest of the world in a few days.

I have already mentioned what we may expect in regard to the future development of bombs, based upon the past experience with military weapons. It is unnecessary for me or you to have any special information in regard to future plans for atomic bombs to draw this conclusion. But even if no improvement in the bomb were possible, what we have learned from the newspaper accounts of the bombs already exploded, shows that they are bad enough. If one bomb will devastate an area of ten square miles, a thousand bombs of this kind if properly placed would devastate ten thousand square miles. The area of New York City covers a densely populated area of about three hundred square miles. From this it is easy to calculate that these one thousand bombs, if properly placed, would destroy thirty-three cities of the size of New York.

And what is there to prevent our assuming that with sufficient effort ten thousand bombs cannot be secured? It is wrong to assume that these weapons cannot be made in large numbers as a result of future improvements in known processes.

During World War I, a strip of country across northern France and Belgium was laid waste. In World War II the cities of Germany and Japan were almost totally destroyed, as were some of those of Russia and Poland. Extensive damage was done to the cities of England. Without considering the contribution that atomic bombs may make to the destruction of cities in future wars, is it not reasonable to expect that much more damage will be done in World War III? Is it not probable that the cities in the United States would also suffer? If atomic bombs are used in the next war it seems certain that all the principal cities of the world, including those of the United States, will be utterly destroyed, and their inhabitants killed. Perhaps some will disagree with this statement, but perhaps we can settle on half of them being destroyed, or a third, but does this make any difference in our considerations? Let us accept the fact that an atomic bomb war is bound to be much more destructive than this last war; that it is bound to extend to all of the industrial countries of the world.

We can expect that counter-measures will be devised, just as they have been in other cases. Some of these counter-measures will interfere with the delivery of the bombs. We can also expect that counter-measures to the counter-measures will be developed, and more effective methods for the delivery of bombs will be devised. It may be possible to interfere with the delivery of the bombs, but then some new device will be found by someone which will then make their delivery possible. What I wish to say is that we cannot expect that a defense will be devised which is so effective that neither the United States nor any other country will decide that it is useless to manufacture such bombs. It will again be the case of dog eat dog, and much effective indiscriminate biting will result in the process. Let us then set aside the assumption that a decisive defense will be secured. Such an assumption would be contrary to experience and would be the most foolish of wishful thinking.

But we may ask whether other countries will get these weapons. It seems unnecessary to answer this question. What weapon ever devised by man ever remained the possession of the country of origin? Did this apply to machine guns or submarines or planes or tanks or high explosives or gas, or guns of any kind? We may rest assured that other countries can secure atomic bombs and may secure them more quickly than we think.

Many people ask how long may it take other countries to secure these bombs, and various estimates have been made. General Leslie R. Groves has estimated that this will be from five to ten years. It took us three and a half years from the start of serious efforts to the time when the first bomb was exploded. Further time is needed for production of an adequate supply for a really full-scale war. We should note that the British start with nearly full knowledge of our processes, and the whole world knows our lines of attack on the problem, and that these lines led to success. This is a very great advantage. Other countries at the present time must be very much afraid of the United States, in spite of the fact that aggressive war or any kind of war is far from the minds of the people of this country. The scientists, engineers, and citizens of other countries, will feel that their respective countries are in dire peril. Just imagine our sense of fear were some other country in possession of atomic bomb plants and we were not. This sense of emergency will call forth the greatest effort on the part of other countries, and I think the lowest figure given by General Groves is the safer one for these considerations. Let us then assume that we have five years in which no other country could attack us with atomic bombs.

What shall we do under this threat in this brief respite? This is a very difficult question because the problem is a very complex one. Incidentally, the problem is not made different or more complex by the atomic bomb, for the destruction that could be made without its aid would also present a very serious problem to the world. The atomic bomb really accentuates the difficulty, and perhaps is of real value to us in bringing forcibly to our attention the grave problem ahead of us, and it may induce us to make concessions from our established ways of thinking which are necessary if destruction by this means is to be avoided. In a democracy it is necessary to have an informed people if proper decisions are to be made and executed. We must all understand that the most devastating weapon of all times is now in our hands and will soon be in the hands of other industrialized countries. We should face the facts and not engage in wishful thinking, for wishing will never remove the threat of this bomb. We should rise to our responsibilities and not merely put the matter aside because we wish so much to get back to our peacetime pursuits. We cannot pass this on to the Congress or to the President, for they cannot act effectively without the approval of the people of the United States. Also, they should not move contrary to the wishes of the citizens of this country. We must understand the magnitude of this problem, and then must be prepared to act with courage.

Let us consider some possible ways of controlling the atomic bomb. In the first place, many people suggest that we should make ourselves stronger than all other nations. This is implied in all the discussion of keeping the so-called "secret" of the bomb. In my opinion if we published all our data in detail we would not shorten the five or ten years of General Groves's estimate by very much. It takes time to build plants, and it takes time to operate them.

The whole question of the atomic bomb secret is not important in itself. What is important is the policy back of it. Do we intend to engage in an armament race with other countries of the world? If the answer is yes, we should try to inspire all our people to go to work on this problem in order to produce the greatest number of the biggest bombs that can be devised, and to devise the most effective way of delivering them to those enemies of the United States that we intend to attack or that we fear will attack us. This policy will result in an atomic-bomb war with all the destruction that I have tried to emphasize in this talk, and this is exactly what I should like to see avoided.

We may try to outlaw the atomic bombs in the future. Some people say that poison gas was not used in this war because of such agreements between sovereign nations. That is only a partial truth. It is certainly a question as to whether high explosive and incendiary bombs are not more effective, ton for ton, than is poison gas, for the former not only kill people but destroy cities, while the latter leaves the cities intact. If atomic bombs are in the possession of potential enemies of the United States we shall all be afraid that they will be launched against us by means of rockets, pilotless planes, or something else, and without warning. We must watch our borders for all stray planes that might be coming in. We must introduce a police system that will be able to detect any possible planting of these bombs in our cities where a mere alarm clock would set them off at a predetermined time. The fear and tension under which we will live will make us very nervous indeed. Every country of the world will have an itchy trigger finger if we all have the atomic bombs and merely an agreement not to use them.

I do not trust any such way of controlling the use of atomic bombs. If the nations agree not to use them and are sincere, then they should also agree not to make them. Incidentally, the Pope tried to outlaw the arbalest in the twelfth century and from that time to this no outlawing of weapons has been effective.

The suggestion is made that we turn the bombs over to the United Nations Organization to enforce peace. This suggestion is better, but it also has difficulties. Where would we store the bombs in the possession of the United Nations? Europe and Asia would object to North America, and we would object to Asia or Europe. How about Africa? You can imagine that the United Nations would have an effective small policing army powered with atomic bombs at some isolated point. Would we not all be afraid of the United Nations Organization? Would we not fear that some Hitler might gain control of those weapons and subjugate the world in a very short time? There is another difficulty. We presume that if the United Nations has a store of such bombs, it proposes to use them in emergencies. Let us assume that manufacturing the bombs in any country is a criminal offense, but that in spite of this the administration of the United States decides that it will make these bombs. The United Nations can then use the bombs to interfere with this operation. They will use them to destroy all the manufacturing facilities that might be set up. In so doing they will kill a very large number of quite innocent people, and the effect will be to unite the entire country against the United Nations. If one wishes to police any State or nation, or the world, one wants to use weapons for the police purpose that will distinguish between those who violate a law and those who do not. If one can do this the law-abiding citizens will aid you against the law-breaker, but the use of a large weapon of necessity unites all classes against the policing power. Atomic bombs are good for nothing but wars and for the destruction of large cities and their populations, and large industrial plants.

But this proposal to turn the bombs over to the United Nations leads to a further suggestion. If we turn over the most powerful weapon to the United Nations, why not also turn over all large-caliber weapons of all other kinds? For, of course, they are relatively ineffective against a superior weapon. And then we come to the next step. If we have turned all our large-caliber weapons over to the United Nations, it is unnecessary for this organization to have them either, for there is no one to oppose them. We are inevitably led to the conclusion that the United Nations organization should possess adequate power to deal with this situation. What will be needed is a most efficient inspection service which will detect and report promptly any attempt to produce atomic bombs or other heavy arms and a sufficient police force to prevent such activities. In this way neither the countries of the world nor the United Nations organization will have atomic bombs and no one will need to fear them.

I am not so naive as to think that this is a solution easily arrived at. I am not even so sanguine as to think that there is a high probability that logical action of this kind can be accomplished without the dubious advantage of a third World War. But I pass the problem to you now. Do you see any way to avoid the threat of an atomic war?

I trust the conclusions of an informed public of the United States. I believe that the considered judgment of the whole people is a reliable guide, and, after all, it is the people of the United States who face destruction and death, and they should have the privilege of making their own decisions.

There are a number of statements which I would categorically defend, and I wish to present them to you:

1. If atomic bombs are made in one country they will be made in all industrial countries of the world.

2. If atomic bombs are made in all these countries we will spend all our days in deadly fear that they will be used, and in time they undoubtedly will be.

3. By one means or another no atomic bombs must be made anywhere in the world and they must not be in the possession of any government of any kind.

4. The peacetime applications of atomic energy, or, in fact, of anything else, are of no importance whatever unless the danger of atomic bombs is banished from the earth.

In conclusion, may I repeat the hope of Alfred Nobel, that this weapon is sufficiently terrible to make possible the bringing of peace to the earth.

~~~~~~

6. *The Free State versus The Military State* *

<div align="right">

D. W. BROGAN

</div>

~~~~~~

I.

The character of a state or society is often shown in small significant things. And there is a deep meaning in the custom which ordains that a President of the United States, who is, by virtue of his office, Commander-in-Chief of the American Army and Navy, should never wear military uniform, even though he has been a soldier in the past. Many Presidents have been soldiers, three of them, Washington, Jackson, Grant, were great, victorious soldiers, but it was not as soldiers but as civil officers that they were Commanders-in-Chief. The contrast with Germany is striking. William II was not only hereditary war lord, but he so exulted in the office that while his uniforms were carefully made, his civilian tailor had to guess from the shape of the uniforms what kind of civilian clothes would fit. It was beneath the dignity of the Kaiser to be measured for civilian clothes. As a civil officer, any ready-to-wear garment was adequate. In the same way, that eminently civilian official, the Chancellor, Bethmann-Hollweg, always addressed the old imperial Reichstag in uniform; that civilian of genius, Bismarck, on all great occasions wore the uniform of a colonel of cuirassiers, and even under the Weimar Republic, the defeated general, Hindenburg, very often wore, as President of the Republic, the uniform of his army rank—which, as has been said, no American victorious soldier-President ever did.[1]

It was not a minor matter, this difference between the United States and the Second Reich, any more than it is a minor matter that the Third Reich

* From D. W. Brogan, *The Free State* (Alfred A. Knopf, Inc., 1945). By permission.

[1] In England, only one soldier has ever become Prime Minister, the Duke of Wellington. Even on the battlefield, the Duke wore a kind of semi-civil dress and his most famous lieutenant, Sir Thomas Picton, commanded in a tall hat. It was this indifference to the tailoring side of war that gives special point to the most famous story about Wellington. Leaving the palace after a levée in full field-marshal's uniform, he was accosted by a civilian who said, "Mr. Smith, I believe?" "If you believe that you will believe anything." Military men in full regalia were not as common in London as in Berlin.

has put all public officers into uniform, has imposed universal salutes and greetings and has made the difference between civil and military life, between the barracks and the home, or school, or factory, so slight, and before war had been openly made, had already imposed so many of its burdens on the German people. Hitler announcing in 1939 that he would never take off his uniform-coat till victory was won is a very different leader from Mr. Churchill, changing from one type of uniform to another as his sense of comfort, fitness or humour suggests, and conducting a war to a victorious conclusion in a siren suit of civilian character and individual design. Even when a leader of a free society enjoys dressing-up, his choice is so personal that the word uniform is out of place and when he does wear uniform, he, like General Grant, may look less military at the head of a great army than Hindenburg did in a frock-coat addressing the Reichstag of republican Germany. Field-Marshal Montgomery, in his beret, slacks and umbrella, is a soldierly figure, but one in a very different tradition from that represented by Goering or Ludendorff.

What useful political truth is illustrated by this matter of dress? The useful truth that there is a difference between a civil state, a form of government in which war is a regrettable and rare activity of the community, and one in which the state and nation are in a perpetual state of preparation for or recovery from war. In one, war is the last argument; in the other, it is almost or quite the only argument—for it does not in this case matter very much whether *all* disputes are settled by arms or some by the mere threat of arms. A military, unpolitical state is one in which all institutions take their colour, their ways of working, the republic importance from the army whose pre-eminence is never in any dispute. Such a state was the Third Reich. "Prussia," said Mirabeau, "is not a state possessing an army but an army possessing a state." Prussia is not the only example. Ancient Sparta was another; Paraguay was another; the Zulu kingdom of Chaka was another. Such was not Rome; such are not Britain or the United States. And yet Rome, Britain, the United States, suffer not at all in comparison with Sparta or Prussia or the Zulus in any comparison of military achievement, or in any stocktaking of the results of a form of society and government conceived in terms of force and war and the results of a form of society in which politics, the supremacy of the civil magistrate, the domination of the law limit the power of the soldier. The military state wins victories but not campaigns, campaigns but not wars, for the simple reason that life is far more complicated than war and war far more than a mere business of soldiering. "War," said Clemenceau, "is far too serious a matter to leave to soldiers." It is—and a society that leaves it to soldiers, not only suffers from it in war but suffers from it in peace; in order to secure what victory can bring, it sacrifices so much that makes victory worth having—and, in the long run, does not get victory.

The civilian leaders of a civil state, when it is at war, will often make grave mistakes; the technical details of war cannot be as familiar to them as they are to a professional soldier. They will often listen to the wrong experts; they will often underestimate the professional who is incapable of ready speech and overestimate the brilliant talker and writer. Yet the experience of history suggests that these are not fatal defects. They are compensated for by qualities bred by civilian experience. As war has become more and more total, as it has involved the whole population, men, women, and children, it has become more and more political. The problem of organization is only, *up to a point,* a question of coercion. No coercion can compensate for complete exhaustion, no coercion can draw on resources that are not really there; above all, coercion, as such, can impose on the enemy material surrender when all hope is gone, but it cannot win him to acquiescence and the object of war is to disarm the *will* of the enemy. The habit of seeing all problems in the terms of orders given and taken, of relying, as any army must, on automatic if intelligent obedience, becomes a handicap as the war lasts, as new and unforeseen situations arise (as they must in any long war), as soon as the simple solution of a military victory quickly won is seen to be illusory. Then subtler qualities of mind and spirit are called for, then political talents are more important than merely military talents, then the country that has reserves of loyalty and independent, *private* spiritual resources wins the last round.

But it will be usually found that they have also won the real first round, the first round that is fought before the war begins. For the foreign policy, the diplomacy of a power whose basic character is military, will reflect the strength and weakness of the military mind and the military method. And it will reflect the weakness more than the strength. For within its own military sphere, military efficiency is real; outside it, military efficiency is inefficiency. It is no accident that Germany has twice managed to mobilize against herself overwhelmingly powerful coalitions of very reluctant enemies. Germany has been twice encircled—by herself. And the encirclement has been produced by the same methods that produced the early victories. It is of no avail to lament the sterility of those victories, to speculate that if this had happened one way, or that another, there would have been a breathing spell in which to enjoy or consolidate the fruits of victory. The victories were gained by the sacrifice, in peace, of those civilian qualities of compromise, legality, caution, which, of course, make preparation for aggressive war difficult and, indeed, impossible. But that they do make aggressive war difficult and in most cases impossible, is evident to the rest of the world as well. So, too, is the fact that the sacrifice of everything that, in peace-time, stands in the way of preparation for war, makes aggressive war tempting, easy and, in a sense, habitual. The very politicians and diplomats of the military state will fall easily into military manners, will threaten instead of negotiating, will bully instead of persuading. They *will* succeed in frightening their neighbours, at first into concessions, but then into resistance. It is not only German history that illustrates this point. It was King Louis XIV who put on his cannon the threatening Latin motto, "ultima ratio regum," the "last argument of kings." And intoxicated by success, increasingly careless of the public opinion of Europe—or of France—Louis XIV began to make it the first argument too. And so, despite a union of cultural and military prestige that Germany has never known, despite an intrinsic predominance that no other country has ever had, despite great soldiers and sailors and diplomatists, the France of Louis XIV forced Europe to combine to end this nightmare. The Dutch were forced to make a revolution to resist him; the English were forced to abandon a profitable neutrality; even the Hohenzollerns were forced to pay some regard to the general interests of Germany and Europe. The overweening power of France was curbed and, on his deathbed, Louis XIV repented of his political sin of loving war too much. No doubt he repented sincerely but his repentance was undoubtedly stimulated by the fact that the Duke of Marlborough and Prince Eugene (a native of Paris) turned the King's arguments against him —as Swift said when he heard of the great captures of French guns at Blenheim.

Napoleon repeated the lesson; he too drove his enemies together, forced even Prussia to take up arms with the odds against her, made all peace treaties mere truces and, sacrificing all independence of thought and action in France to making war, found that the greatest of all soldiers could not win. He, less wise than Louis XIV, never fully understood the causes of his defeat but they were plain enough. He would not let the rulers of Europe or the peoples of Europe alone. The temptation to exploit his military supremacy overcame him again and again until the continent realized that there would be no peace with Napoleon, that you could not do business with him any more than you could do business with Hitler.

Yet the rulers of France had great advantages that Germany has not. European culture in the age of Louis XIV and Napoleon was still predominantly French. Modern democracy was either not born or a weak infant, the peoples of Europe often counted for little enough in the decisions of their rulers. The French conquests were far less resented than any foreign conquests could be to-day. Even so, European society was too conscious of its own rights, of its own pride and duty, to submit. The sections of European society that looked with a friendly eye on French power, the Republican party in seventeenth-century Holland, Beethoven or Charles Fox in the age of the French Revolution, were driven into hostility and resistance.

There never has been, in this sense, a German cultural predominance in modern Europe. Too much, far too much, was sacrificed to secure material predominance for the spectacle of the power of the Second Reich to evoke more than respect. No Frenchman or Englishman looked on the work of Bismarck with the sympathetic understanding that Goethe gave to the work of Napoleon. But Bismarck knew (as Frederick the Great learned) that too open a defiance of the interests of the other European states, too complete moral and material isolation, was fatal. To prevent that isolation, to give an appearance of moderation, Bismarck was ready to cheat, to lie, to forge. But he had the supreme political virtue of knowing when to stop, when to cease to threaten. He knew that he could not make Germany strong enough to fight all Europe—and so he took care not to force all Europe to fight Germany. He made concessions to defeated France, he refused to exploit to the full his victory over Austria. He fought only partially successful battles with the soldiers who never understood how much they owed to the man who secured for them the limited wars in which their mere technical supremacy could be exploited. What they, the Prussian experts in recipes for victory, lost when they lost Bismarck, 1914 and 1939 were to show. War in 1914, like war in 1939, was a confession of political *incompetence* by the rulers of Germany, blinded by their habits of mind, bred in corporal and general alike, by the neglect of the civilian and political truths that can only be learned in a militaristic state by a genius like Bismarck and yet, in a civil state, in a real political organization, are taught by the whole structure of society to quite mediocre politicians. And, what is more important, they are daily learned by the free peoples on whom these mediocre politicians can draw for more than bravery and obedience, for originality, for ideas, for the moral resources to stand a long war and the untried, unplanned versatility that wins long wars. The military state can only plan for and win short wars and, planning for short wars, it almost always behaves in a fashion to secure that the war will not be short and so will be lost. If the object of military efficiency is to win wars, military efficiency, in the German sense, is a contradiction in terms.

For the apparent paradox is yet the truth. Real total war is more easily attained by a free state than by a purely military state.

The reasons for the apparent paradox are not very hard to find. Both the military state and the free state, in modern war, will be called on to use all their resources. The military state can, in peace-time, call on far more of the available resources than can the free state. No people readily prefers guns to butter. It has to be conditioned by propaganda, by doses of political dope, by the simple refusal of any free choice, to accept the imposition, in time of formal peace, of the basic conditions of open war, the concentration of all the economic power of the state on providing the materials of modern war. A free people like the English, even when danger is imminent, will prepare less thoroughly than the Third Reich prepared for the dangers created by its rulers. (After all, the rulers of England and the English people could have illusions about the character and designs of the rulers of the Third

Reich that those gentlemen could not have about themselves.) A free state can prepare, more or less efficiently, more or less thoroughly. But, at the best, it will still be spending on butter some resources that the military state bent on war will spend on guns. It will still have shadow war factories while the military state has real war factories. The story current in Berlin round 1936 makes the point. The worker in a baby carriage factory decided to steal each day one part of the baby carriage, naturally, since his wife was expecting a baby and the German worker, even as early as that, had no spare resources; it was not only butter that was given up! After a time he had accumulated all the necessary parts but, as he said to his wife, "no matter what I do, it always turns out to be a machine-gun."

In the free state, no matter what the rulers do, some people will insist, in peace-time, when the danger is not overwhelmingly evident, on baby carriages and butter. Free from the need of paying attention to such people, the army state can go ahead. It can mobilize all existing resources; it can make the whole economic and social system conform to the war plan—including in the war plan the economic preparation for war. It can distort the normal economy of the country and, if the country is economically important enough, can distort the economic life of its neighbours, can make the Jugoslavs take aspirin in payment for raw materials, try to make the Americans take mouth-organs for cotton. It can accumulate stores of raw materials with *Ersatz,* till the public almost forgets the days when cloth was made of wool and coffee of coffee. It can squeeze its neighbours till they find economic as well as political reasons for wishing for an end of this nightmare; it can squeeze its own people until they almost wish for war to end the strain of preparation. Fascinated by the problem of remaking the life of the community, increasingly pleased with the virtuosity they have displayed, drunk with power and, in modern Germany at any rate, corrupted by the temptations that assail any controller of economic life who can order when others have to bargain, the planners of the war state lose sight of reality. The time comes when, like Roon in 1870, they dream of setting the whole machine in motion and closing their desk, proud that everything has been foreseen. At this stage they are bound to be far better prepared to fight the war they have planned to fight than their victims who have not planned to fight at all.

And now their disillusionment begins. Unless by a happy accident (such as that which gave Roon the political genius of Bismarck as cover) the political preparation has been perfectly done, they have to fight a kind of war they did not plan to fight. They have to fight a war that more and more states join in, for the reason I have given, because they are too frightened not to. Or the planners themselves get frightened, since their planned superiority gets less as the other nations wake up and catch up—and they make war as Hitler in 1941 invaded Russia—confident, oh so confident, that all will again go according to plan. But it will not, for the plan is made in terms of military victory and that conception is not wide enough. There will have to be improvisations, changes, appeals to further total mobilizations and then further mobilizations. The initial technical advantages grow less every day; the material margin of superiority grows narrower every day, until the long victorious army finds victory, first sterile, then impossible.

But the history of the free state is very different. Of course, if that state is so limited in natural resources, or so vulnerable, that a predatory neighbour can overrun it in a few weeks, planning for war and total victory, whether done by Roon or by Goering, may seem to pay, as it seemed to pay in 1870 and 1940. *Seemed,* for the balance sheet of 1870 did not close with the Treaty of Frankfort, it was kept open for a generation later as Europe grew more and more militarized, more and more frightened of Germany and Germany more and more frightened of Europe. 1918 is an item in that balance sheet; 1944 is an item in the balance sheet of 1940. But the free state that is not so overrun has many advantages when the first shock is overcome.

Its people do not expect miracles and do not have to be presented with a less and less plausible picture of infallible leaders whose impeccable plans somehow are not going right. A democratic state is resigned to less than total efficiency in its rulers, less than total success. Because it assumes some of the responsibility for the decisions made, it assumes, too, part of the responsibility for the mistakes made. It can criticize its rulers—and itself—without losing its faith in either. It has not been, in fact, the leaders of the democracies who have been forced to invent or survive conspiracies, to find dramatic, diabolic excuses for failures, to repeat endless rhetorical appeals, to fall to the lowest demagoguery in face of bad news or collapse in infantile exultation at good. It has been Hitler who has behaved like an ill-bred brat in 1940 and has made hysterical appeals to Providence to save him and the Third Reich (in that order) in 1944.

But even on the material plane the free states gain in a long war. No battle, said Moltke, is ever fought as it is planned. Still less is any long war. The very adequacy of the pre-war plans is a handicap for the long war. The military state has already, with brilliant short-term results, taken over the economic and social life of the whole country. It has mobilized for war purposes all the national resources of the nation. But it is not creating any new resources. It is squeezing the orange but there is only one orange.

In the free state there are in existence a score of independent pools of power, material power, moral power. The individual citizen is now pouring into the national pool new resources he and his friends and partners have been creating all the time. Under the pressure of national danger he consents to be directed as to what to do with what he created in the time of peace. As the war winds on, never quite meeting the specifications of any plan, the free states are able to improvise, to adjust, to invent. There is butter to be turned into newer types of guns. There are talents, odd, original, insubordinate talents to be called on, there is an immense amount of wasteful, spontaneous life to be drawn on for war. It is not the naïve, peaceloving free states who find the rulers of their peoples looking, after a time, for magical remedies for the refusal of victory to come or, if it comes, to stay. It is not the democracies who fall for the witch-doctors or astrologers or for the panaceas, the invincible U-boat; the equally invincible Luftwaffe; the equally invincible and omnipotent secret weapon, No. 1, No. 2, etc. In the darkness that has been imposed for years on the people of the military state, it was easy to prepare for war; it was also easy to lose the habit of rational judgment, to acquire the appetite for miracles—and the habit of cursing the witch-doctors who have not wrought the miracles, cursing at first very secretly, then more openly.

One disability the peace-loving, anti-militarist nations *do* suffer from. In a country dominated by the army, like Prussia all through its history, like France under Napoleon, the army draws easily and naturally, in peace-time, on the most energetic and talented members of the nation. A very high proportion of the ablest young men will enter the army and make their careers in it. And, in consequence, planning for war in the technical sense will be more thoroughly, more competently carried out. The army in Britain, in America, even in a country like France, where it had lost a good deal of its old prestige, will not be so impressive an institution; its leaders may be, and will certainly be made to appear, mediocre and outmoded people. Again, the military state will win in the first stages of the war.

But just because war is now total this advantage will disappear as the war lasts. Even more important than the material reserves accumulated by the free action of the free citizen, or the moral resources bred by the habit of free choice, is the technical reserve bred by the civilian habit of life. For in the United States and Britain hundreds, thousands of men of great energy and initiative exist to be called into service in a great crisis. In the old days of limited warfare, when the main business was the application of a narrow technique, of drill, gunnery, tactics, the advantages of a very large class of trained officers were great. But in modern war they are much less. There is nothing specifically *military* about most of the problems of total war. The problem of planning for the invasion of France was ninety per cent non-military planning. The scores of types of landing craft needed were made and designed by the engineers of peace-time industry; it was Detroit and the Clyde that were called on; the varied, unplanned civilian resources of peaceful societies. The problems of designing a tank, or a war plane, or counter-measures against submarines, do not call for peace-time military organization, they call for technical skill and originality. And that technical skill and originality will be not less but more, because the peace-time organization has been looser, less organized, less directed to one end. The wind of discovery often bloweth where it listeth. More than that, peace technicians are always solving *real* problems, not merely planning to solve them. The difficulty that faces any military organization of making its problems real applies to its technical side too. Manoeuvres are no substitute for war; the prototype no substitute for production for use. But peace-time industry produces for use; the jeep is the child of the flivver, the corvette of the freighter. Had Nazi preparations for war been spun out for another five years or so, had the Goering stranglehold on German industry lasted a few years longer, German industry would have been more effectually mobilized for immediate successes and even less well prepared for the long pull when the first successes did not prove to be enough. There would have been more magnetic mines, or their like; more reliance on improved submarines; more reliance on air-power. And there would have been even less material and intellectual preparation for the failure of these recipes for victory. The militarist state, facing a nation of the same or superior industrial capacity, will win the first round or the first laps. But any trainer of runners or boxers knows that it is the last lap and the last round that count. And he knows too that mere endless training in running and boxing is not enough; nor is running against the clock or shadow-boxing or boxing with sparring partners. The only way to train winners is to train them in many more things than running and boxing and more important still, the would-be winners must run real races frequently, fight real fights frequently. The champion who is not in the ring often ceases to be champion. Even the Prussian or Spartan state cannot be putting on real military contests all the time. But the civil society can be putting on innumerable real contests, civil contests, all the time; their technicians are always on their toes and the training they receive in peace is equally available in war. In a deeper sense than Milton probably meant it, "peace hath her victories no less renowned than war"—and that in war.

That the English and American nations escaped this professional distortion is not due to any special moral or intellectual virtue—at any rate, not exclusively due to it. England, as Michelet said, is an island. Much of English society owes its flavour to that fact, to the comparative immunity from immediate physical danger produced by that fact. America, for all practical purposes, is even more of an island. Both could afford to do without great standing armies. Both could afford to reduce to a minimum the intrusion of military methods into civil life. But it should be pointed out that being an island or being a remote group of settlements in an isolated continent is not, in itself, a guarantee against the follies of militarism. Japan is even more of an island than England—and Japan has turned the control of her life and polity over to militarist control as thoroughly as Prussia ever did. In some South American states, Paraguay in the past, Argentina in the present, the officers have been given a political predominance that they have never known in the United States. No, there is choice as well as fatality. And there is accident as well as choice. The accident was the happy fatality that gave the English-speaking peoples an ancestral distaste for the rule of soldiers and for the "leader principle." That fatality was the rule of Cromwell, so much misunderstood and foolishly exploited by the Nazis. For the rule of Cromwell and the New Model Army, vastly superior as were both to the rule of Hitler and his party army, yet left a legacy of great political value. An incurable dislike of military rule was bequeathed both to the English and American peoples—and a most hated name was bequeathed to the Irish.[1]

Cromwell died in his bed. In less than two years the ever-victorious, highly disciplined army that seemed to have the English state and people at its mercy, dissolved. The old monarchy was restored, resting on law and custom, not on force. The 50,000 men of the New Model Army became a mere 5,000 or so, commanded by General Monk, who had no fanaticism, who had fought on both sides, and who, inspired as Professor Clark suggests by his experience in the service of the Dutch Republic, commended to his officers the example of the Dutch service "where soldiers received and observed commands, but gave none."

Even more striking is the way in which the American soldier, however highly esteemed and flattered, has been kept in firm submission to the civil power and has accepted, without question, that authority. It is no geographical phenomenon, as the case of the Latin-American states shows.

Mr. H. G. Wells is probably right in saying that Plutarch kept the United States a republic—and Plutarch, like all cultivated men of the ancient world, regretted the eclipse of the republican ideal. But Cromwell also helped; so

---

[1] A sign of the high degree of objectivity attained by the English ruling class at the height of its fame, when it alone had withstood Napoleon from the beginning to the end, is to be found in Henry Hallam's parallel between Cromwell and Napoleon. "In civil government there can be no adequate parallel between one who had sucked only the dregs of a besotted fanaticism, and one to whom the stores of reason and philosophy were open. But it must here be added that Cromwell, far unlike his antitype, never showed any signs of a legislative mind or any desire to fix his renown on that noblest human basis, the amelioration of social institutions." (Henry Hallam, *Constitutional History of England*.) What Hallam would have said if he had been asked to draw a parallel between Napoleon and his self-styled antitype, Hitler, is difficult to conceive. If Cromwell's naïve trust in the Old Testament was proof of besotted fanaticism, what would Hallam have said of the mind revealed in *Mein Kampf*? If Cromwell's failure to reform the English legal system was proof of limitations, what would he have said of the destruction of the idea of the rule of law, of even the concept of a *Rechtsstaat*, in the Third Reich? Many an Englishman and many an American was, in fact, awakened to the pathological character of the Third Reich by the literary tone of *Mein Kampf* (how right the Führer was to try to prevent publication of full translations!) and more by the destruction of any system of organized law in Germany. The dead spoke; the dead who had condemned the Cromwellian experiment to peaceful dissolution; the dead who had set up as the ideal of the American constitution-maker, "a government of laws and not of men."

did the memory of James II, who had feebly tried to rule by an army. It was after that experience that the English Parliament passed the Mutiny Act for one year at a time only; the mere existence of the army was at the annual mercy of Parliament and, then, when the American Constitution was created, at the mercy of Congress. Both Parliament and Congress sometimes carried their fear of militarism to absurd lengths; they starved the army in peace and harassed it in war. But they had their reward. They got great soldiers who were content to be great soldiers. Even so vehement a victorious general as Andrew Jackson submitted to the humiliating sentence of the civil court in that city of New Orleans which he had just saved by a brilliant victory. General Jackson obeyed as, later, President Jackson commanded. The Duke of Wellington had his windows broken fifteen years after Waterloo by a London mob that did not like his reactionary politics. He did not like it; he thought it was a little ungrateful; but, after all, he had entered politics and had to take the rough with the smooth.

In the American Civil War the federal government began with an army of 16,000 and ended it with an army of 2,000,000. At no time in the four years of brilliant improvisation had the awkward, ungainly civilian, Lincoln, the slightest reason to fear any of the military complications and threats of political action by generals that other less well ordered societies have known. His opposite number, Jefferson Davis, had the disadvantage of having had a professional military training and of having served in a real war. But despite the more and more obvious fact that he was temperamentally unfitted for his post, in face of increasing disaster, despite the overwhelming prestige of the great Southern general, Lee, the authority of the civil power remained uncontested to the bitter end. And, as defeat was inevitable anyway, the Southern soldiers and civilians who displayed these political virtues had their reward, not only in duty done but in a saving principle observed and saved to future use.

British and American generals have not been all models of disinterestedness or of single-minded devotion to the cause. They have been recruited, necessarily, from human beings. But an examination of their record does not show that they have been inferior in these qualities to the generals produced by societies which made the producing of generals their main business. It was in the German Army, in the last war, that General Max Hoffman was forced to say that if any more officers came to him promising their Nibelung-true support, he would knock their blocks off. It is in the German Army in this war that military conspiracy has reached up to Supreme Headquarters; it matters little who was conspiring against whom, or whether the motives of the conspirators were good or bad. The fact of conspiracy was decisive condemnation of a system of war-making that exalted blind obedience to heights which destroy both mind and character.

II.

One of the great blessings conferred on the professional soldier by the firm control of the civil authority and by the moral tone of the civil society he lives in, is freedom from a professional code of honour and code of morals. Nothing is more unintelligible to the English or American soldier than the German conception of a special type of military honour. An English or American officer is content to observe the general code of a good citizen and an educated gentleman. He has, as an officer, special duties, special obligations. But these do not cut him off from his civilian friends or impose on him standards of conduct unintelligible to civilians and hostile to their standards. The officer does represent in a business society a standard different from that of the mere profit-seeker, but so does the doctor, the lawyer, the teacher, the preacher, or priest. The army and navy have their special codes, but they are inside the general code. There is no obligation on the officer to fight duels in defence of his honour. That barbaric custom died out in the army and civil life alike. There is no obligation to kick civilians out of the way in defence of army honour as was done in Saverne in 1914 or to run civilians through for not getting out of the way quick enough. Neither the British nor American armies have found it necessary to set up courts of honour to create a pathological case law for a caste. They have found adequate supplies of honour all the same in many sources—including humour. It is in the German Army, not the British or American Armies as we must recall, that it was found necessary to set up a Court of Honour to try generals for treason in war-time. Again it matters little whether the really guilty men were the judges or judged. The basic guilt was that of the system. If the military systems of America and England only lost wars, their more reasonable, flexible, less humourless view of the rule of the officer might be condemned. But they win wars as well as making peace less barbaric. So did the Roman Republic in its great days when it would allow no soldiers inside the sacred city and insisted on the pre-eminence of the civil power.

The soldier who is the servant of the free state suffers under many handicaps as a technician. He has to submit to the orders of amateurs who may have only a very imperfect understanding of his technical difficulties. He has to spend much time persuading civilians instead of giving orders; he is never sole master of his army, sole judge of what is to be done, when and how. It is easy to illustrate the dangers and delays such a relation causes. There is Marlborough having to argue with timid and ill-equipped Dutch deputies; there is McClellan alienating ill-informed American politicians in the Civil War because he failed in the art of persuasion; there is the friction between Clemenceau and Foch; there is the long story of Wellington dealing with Spaniards, with Portuguese, with the government at home, learning diplomacy and patience in the process. Patience—that, above all, the general of a free state learns; the sudden glory of lightning victory is not for him. He has to submit the mere art of arms to the greater art of politics. It is only when we look at the results, over a long period, that we begin to perceive that, even when war was a simpler, more limited thing than it can be to-day, the soldier did not really suffer from these limitations. He gained; he was trained in the general art of war (which is greater than the art of fighting) and, if he did not learn, he was saved from the worst mistakes. It is the pure technician who sacrifices everything to the battle who, in the long run, loses. The most brilliant soldier of the ancient world, Hannibal, was not ill served by the Carthaginian politicians. They provided him with all the resources they could command. The basic error was not that of the maligned Suffetes but of the brilliant soldier. It was his decision to attack Rome at the very heart of her power, in Italy, that was the basic error, the error that made Cannae a sterile technical triumph. For it was based on a false *political* calculation, that military victory would dissolve the Latin confederacy on whose unity depended the power and safety of Rome. Hannibal at the gates of Rome, Napoleon on the Channel in 1805, Hitler in Paris and on the Channel in 1940, learned that victory, decisive victory, is a more elusive thing than mere triumph in the field and that mere concentration of political and military power in one politically incompetent hand is no recipe for victory, even though from a strictly military point of view all the elements of victory seem to be there.[1]

The military servant of a free state may gain more than he loses by his limited powers; he is saved from temptation as well as denied opportunities. But even if, on balance, he loses, the state does not. For it does not exist to exploit military virtuosity or to provide opportunities for its exercise by its generals. In a free state war and victory must have desirable peace-time results. Even so war-making a people as the Romans knew that.

"Hae tibi erunt artes *pacisque imponere morem.*" To impose the habit of peace was the aim of Roman war. When that aim was forgotten, when the military servants of the Republic became its masters, the life of the republic was doomed; the Consul sank into the mere Imperator, the Feldherr, the Führer. *Nostra stultitia tu es magnus* as the Roman wit said of the greatness

---

[1] The judgment of the Duke of Wellington on his great rival is worth noting in its probably unconscious revelation of the truth. "Lady Salisbury asked which was the greatest military genius, Marlborough or Napoleon? 'Why, I don't know—it is very difficult to tell. I can hardly conceive anything greater than Napoleon at the head of any army—especially a French army. Then he had one prodigious advantage—he had no responsibility—he could do whatever he pleased; and *no man ever lost more armies than he did.* Now with me the loss of every man told. I could not risk so much; I knew that if I ever lost five hundred men without the clearest necessity, I should be brought upon my knees to the bar of the House of Commons." (Stanhope, *Conversations with Wellington.*) (Italics mine.) Wellington, like Washington, was saved from the temptations of military omnipotence. He was also saved from the risk of a Jena or a Waterloo *lost.*

of Pompey, the victorious general, the head of a party. By the political folly of the Roman people, he became great to give way, in time, to Caesar. And it was not Caesar, the Imperator *par excellence,* but that much more sedate and civilian figure, Augustus, who for two or three generations postponed the crisis of the Roman state but could not for ever avoid the consequences of the passing of all effective political power to the army.

From a great event in modern history the Germans might learn the same lesson. For it is taught them by a German leader and by the people of a state that they profess to regard as Germanic. William the Silent of Nassau was faced, as leader of the revolted Netherlands, with an almost insoluble military problem. How was he, a mediocre general with a badly organized state in the process of formation, to resist great generals like Alva and Parma at the head of technically perfect Spanish armies? All his plans were handicapped, were limited by the power of the Dutch towns and provinces; no war leader had less of a free hand or had to spend more of his time in mere persuasion, mere politics. With more unquestioned power William might have scored more military successes, might have negotiated with more confidence and decision, would have had to possess his soul far less often in patience. But not only might he, like Napoleon, have lost it in the process, the result of the war would have been very different. Victory might have come sooner but it would have been a very different and less permanent victory. Indeed, the war would not have been fought at all. If the Dutch cities and provinces on the fringe of the "Holy Roman Empire of the German People" had not been obstinate, individualistic, political, they would not have rebelled. If they had not had the good fortune to have been educated by the Burgundian dynasty into a sense of the general interest of the state without being coerced into mere automatic submission to the will of the prince, they would not have dared to face the armies of Philip II of Spain.

And if, in the course of the war, they *had* put all their trust in any one prince, had abandoned their political attitude, their victory would have been far less interesting to the world; it would have been a mere Prussian victory. But it was the free Dutch Republic that produced in the next generations Rembrandt and Grotius, Vermeer and Huygens, that provided cities of refuge for Descartes and Spinoza. That Dutch Republic was, and is, of permanent interest to the whole world; there is no German state in the seventeenth century whose history and achievement concerns anybody but Germans—and not many of them have a history that concerns even Germans. In 1940 the Dutch summoned to return to their Germanic Fatherland were secured against any temptation to do so by the memory of their great, free, proud past. No more than in 1580 were they prepared to accept the German view of the decisiveness of mere victory and mere power. It was not the Dutch Protestants or, indeed, the Dutch Catholics who had accepted the German rule that the religion of the ruler was to determine the religion of his subjects. And they had their reward in sources of dignified, not hysterical and illusion-fed national pride. Of course the Dutch were luckier than the Germans of the seventeenth century. To that luck they owe their rich culture, their rich national life, their rich empire. How could any of these, even the empire, have been built by docile obedience to the rulers as by God appointed? But the *character* of Dutch luck is ignored by the merely envious German. The real Dutch luck was the historical accident that forced them to accept responsibility, that forced them to take sides, not merely to obey the local authority, however silly, however petty. The party conflicts that harassed William the Silent, that led to the death of Oldenbarnveldt and John de Witt, to the long feud between the burgher aristocracy and the House of Orange, this was the luck of the Dutch. The German subjects of the elder line of Nassau were saved from party war; the burgher aristocracy of Emden or Frankfort were saved from the dangers and temptations of real political power and responsibility. And with them were saved great philosophers like Leibniz, great architects like Fischer, saved to be, in various ways, courtiers of genius. The Dutch refused, in the seventeenth and twentieth centuries alike, the conception of leadership as Germans have accepted it; the orders given from above, obeyed uncritically, loyally, bravely from below. The people that resisted Philip II and Louis XIV were not likely to accept the authority of Hitler or see political and national promotion in acceptance as second-class members of a Germanic race whose highest political expression was fanatical obedience to such a chief.

The nineteenth century illustrated the difference between the political and the military victory in a way that suggests the work of a great dramatist. Lincoln and Bismarck, the raw, self-educated, humorous American, the highly educated, cynical, witty Prussian. Both were sceptical, but Bismarck was sceptical of the good faith, the honesty, the good sense of the masses; Lincoln was sceptical of there being any greater dose of these good qualities in the rulers. He was also sceptical of himself. Bismarck had had his republican, his Jacobin past, but he had chosen another and more profitable way. And these men, at the same time, were making or saving the union of their peoples. The unity of the German people was made, as Bismarck boasted, not by speeches or by slogans but by "blood and iron." The American union was saved by far more blood and far more iron than was needed to unite Germany. But Lincoln, as resolute in making war as Bismarck, did not for a moment believe that all that was needed was blood and iron. He thought speeches were needed; that is why he stated the classical doctrine of American democracy on the victorious battlefield of Gettysburg. Bismarck had nothing to say at Sedan. That is why with victory in sight Lincoln pleaded, in the Second Inaugural, for a just peace and admitted the share of all Americans in the national sin of slavery. These speeches, as much as the

Union preserved in arms, are the legacy of Lincoln. The legacy of Bismarck was an evasion of the political problem of how to make the German people politically mature; the legacy of Bismarck was a political system that left fatal decisions to a dilettante like William II, to a mere military technician like Ludendorff and then to that obscene parody of Lincoln, that product of the political childishness of the German people, Hitler, the demagogue without style and without truth. Compare the permanence of Lincoln's victory with the constant strain that was imposed on even the material achievement of Bismarck. If Bismarckian unity survives at all, it will survive in a mutilated form—and it will have had to be paid for in two great lost wars, more expensive in blood and iron than the American Civil War in which the mere efficiency experts could find so much to learn—if they were capable of learning.

But Germany is in Europe, not in America; Germany has jealous neighbours. "We can't be carp because the others are pike," said Bismarck. There is truth in that. But think how much Germany has suffered by her mere military victories, by the absence of any power of *attraction* in the militarized German culture. Even when Napoleonic militarism had driven the peoples as well as the governments of Europe to detest many things called French, French culture, as Goethe said, was too much the inheritance of every civilized European for the invading armies not to be awestruck at the idea of occupying Paris. For many Europeans, Weimar and Salzburg and Vienna and Frankfort have some, though not of course anything like as much appeal as Paris or Rome or Florence. But for whom has Berlin any appeal except Berliners? For whom has modern German culture, with its self-willed return to barbarism, with its exaltation of the irrational, with its worship of force, with its disdain of argument and persuasion, any spontaneous attraction? Let the horror that filled the world in 1940 when it was thought for a moment possible that the future of Europe might be determined by the Third Reich be the answer. More striking still, let the answer be the anguish with which the desperate defence of England was watched. Where in Europe were the friends of the new Germany at the very moment of its highest material triumph? Where were the friends of the long unpopular English? Let the roll-call be made, the Quislings and Musserts and Lavals against the peoples of their betrayed countries, against the élite of the modern world. For London was one of the great makers and centres of modern civilization; great names fought on the English side; great English names, great German names. On which side stood the spirit of Leibniz or of Lessing, of Schiller or of Goethe? It was no accident that, in the dark hour, the opening bars of the Fifth Symphony were taken over by the resistance movement *against* the triumphant Germans. For could anyone doubt where was the spirit of Beethoven? It may be only a legend, but it is a suggestive legend, that makes Beethoven alter the dedication of the "Eroica" to the "memory of a great man" on receipt of the news that his hero Bonaparte has sunk into a mere Emperor. Could he have consented to the more than Byzantine flattery demanded by his fellow-Austrian? Could the Mozart of the *Magic Flute* have so surrendered? By their fruits shall ye know them. By its friends shall ye know the Third Reich; its friends in victory, its rats in defeat. But it is not only the Third Reich that has sacrificed so much to gain so little. It is the Prussian state, since the days of Frederick-William I. In discipline, in courage, in material honesty, in industry, the military and civil servants of the Prussian state have been, in many cases, models. But that state has not achieved the one thing necessary, a real political life in which these minor virtues can have their place. And so its victories have been sterile and its defeats its own private business, lamented by few. Far other has been the destiny of less organized, more hopeful, less "efficient" societies, of France, of England, of the United States, of the Netherlands.

Their friends in evil fortune,

"... are exultations, agonies,
And love, and man's unconquerable mind."

Chapter XVIII

THE SUPRANATIONAL COMMUNITY

IF THERE is any hope that the dogma of state sovereignty will be recognized as incompatible with international peace, the progress toward world order will be slow at best. World government may be attainable, but it will be the end of the evolution toward international security. The intermediary phase will see advances on two lines: first, partial surrender of state sovereignty on specific issues, such as the control of atomic energy; second, the formation of political communities which will include more than one nation, without embracing the whole world at once. The multinational state, or association of states, will be the transitional phase from world chaos based on state sovereignty to world order based on international government through law. If this development may seem too slow, it is politically, under the circumstances of habit and psychology, the only feasible one.

From this point of view, the British Commonwealth of Nations and the Soviet Union are the most exciting experiments in supranational government today. Both demonstrate that *nation and sovereignty need not be identical;* in fact, these nations have discovered, after the surrender of sovereignty, that in the wider framework of the British Commonwealth or the Soviet Union, their liberties are better protected than they were before. In *National Self-Determination* (1945), Alfred Cobban explains the principle of the multinational state in relation to the British Commonwealth of Nations. Great Britain herself is not one, but three nations; the term "British" is a purely political concept. The same principle of coexistence of several nations applies to other members of the Commonwealth, like Canada and South Africa, which are, like Great Britain, *political* and not cultural nations. India, Ceylon, and Palestine (the latter not British territory, but administered by Britain as a mandate or trusteeship) are also cases of several nations' trying to live together in one territory; experience will show how well they will succeed in that task. The development of independent nations within the British Commonwealth, freely associated in one vast political community, has not undermined the sentiment that loyalty to the whole comes before loyalty to the parts (Eire in the Second World War was an exception that proved the rule): "Inside the British Commonwealth the force of nationality, which has proved so destructive in Europe, has been in part robbed of its most dangerous schismatic tendencies by general acceptance of the idea of the multi-national state. National self-determination in the British Empire has meant not merely a process of breaking down, but also one of building up, and the recognition of national liberties has proved a sounder foundation for the co-operation of different nations inside the same state than their suppression."

Whereas the attention of the world has been focused on the social and economic policies of the Communist regime in the Soviet Union, probably the greatest single achievement of the Soviet system has been in the field of nationality relations. Before 1917 Russia was, as Lenin called it, a "prison-house of nations." The national policy of the Tsars was Russification, the attempt to Russify the non-Russian nationalities. In the sphere of religion, the Tsars sought to impose the Greek Orthodox state religion on the minority churches. All this was based on the concept of a Great Russian ruling people. The establishment of the Soviet Union completely reversed this age-old policy; it was no longer necessary to be, or become, a Russian for purposes of political, economic, and cultural equality. Stalin himself, a Georgian, never suffered from the fact that he was not a Russian. He has always been very much interested in the nationality question; in many writings, and in his capacity as People's Commissar for Nationalities, he devoted much effort to the solution of what had previously embittered millions of Russian subjects. As in the case of the British Commonwealth, the Soviet Union has solved the problem of nationality by *"dissociating statehood from both nationality and race.* In spite of the numerical dominance of the Russian race in the USSR, and its undoubted cultural pre-eminence, the idea of there being a Russian state has been definitely abandoned. The very word 'Russia' was, in 1922–1923, deliberately removed from the title of the Soviet Union." This analysis of the Soviet nationality policy will be found in Sidney and Beatrice Webb's work on *Soviet Communism: A New Civilization?* (1936; in later editions, the question mark in the title was dropped). American readers of this work may be amazed to learn that occasionally Negroes from the United States are encountered in the Soviet Union, and that they enjoy there full equality with other races and peoples. Whereas the British Commonwealth has been slow to accord full equality of status to nonwhites, the Soviet Union does not accept, as a matter of socialist principle, the theory that the white race has any inherent right to rule nonwhites.

The possibility of world government in any foreseeable future is discussed by Reinhold Niebuhr in "The Myth of World Government" (1946), and in "The World Comes of Age" (1946), a reply by Albert Guérard to Niebuhr. Niebuhr, a liberal theologian, charges the American liberals that they refuse to face the fact that "there is a tremendous difference between the problem of community on the national and global level, a difference which no constitutional magic can overcome." Niebuhr denies that the world community possesses the consciousness of "we," such as exists in na-

tional communities, even in pluralistic or multinational ones. Niebuhr also
attacks those who, in analogy to the "social contract" theory, believe in the
possibility of setting up world government by deliberate act: "If the community does not exist in fact, at least in inchoate form, constitutional instruments cannot create it." Albert Guérard accepts Niebuhr's first major thesis
that a community cannot artificially be created by legal fiat. But he strongly
rejects Niebuhr's second premise, that the world community does not exist.
Guérard adduces illustrations from history and literature to prove that the
consciousness of "we" exists in the world as a whole: "This feeling that the
world is morally one is not the privilege of an élite; it is more ardent, more
spontaneous, among the masses than among the sophisticates." Guérard
asserts that the world community exists, but that it is unorganized, because
our political institutions lag a century or more behind our political consciousness: "The world spirit is full grown, but it is unarmed. It is the fossils who have the weapons; living souls are told that they need none. This
must be reversed. Our aim is to focus the consciousness of mankind through
institutions. Let us ask the people: 'Do you want the world community,
which now lives in chaos, to be *constituted,* that is to say, to live under
law? Or do you want each nation to be judge in its own quarrels, a law
unto itself?' "

No American has expressed better than President Woodrow Wilson the
faith that peace without law is impossible. He failed politically; morally he
was more than vindicated by the events that filled the two decades following
his disavowal by the Senate and the people. His prediction "with absolute
certainty" that there would be another world war "if the nations of the
world do not concert the method by which to prevent it" came true with
tragic accuracy. His conception of an international organization for the
maintenance of peace was never static and final: "Settlements may be temporary, but the action of the nations in the interest of peace and justice must
be permanent. We can set up permanent processes. We may not be able to
set up permanent decisions." This is also the nature of democratic government within a nation: the Constitution does not indicate *what* laws will be
actually passed by the legislature, but merely prescribes *how* laws are to be
made. The growth of a sense of procedure has distinguished, historically,
political civilization from political savagery. Wilson still belonged to a
generation of Americans who were not ashamed of being idealistic, who
believed that America was dedicated to the love of justice and the service
of humanity. He warned that, "if America goes back upon mankind, mankind has no other place to turn." He also predicted that should America
do just that, the world would experience "one of those penetrating chills
of reaction, which would lead to a universal cynicism." Finally, Wilson sum-
marized his approach to the problem of world peace in these words, as valid
now as they were when first pronounced: "What we seek is the reign of

law, based upon the consent of the governed and sustained by the organized opinion of mankind."

Early in the Second World War, voices were heard in the United States, magnified by the powerful echoes of the *Time-Life-Fortune* empire, that the twentieth century was going to be the "American Century." Not Berlin, but Washington would be the capital of the world. The then Vice-President of the United States, Henry A. Wallace, took up this theme in his speech "The Price of Free World Victory," addressed to the Free World Association in New York on May 8, 1942. Wallace said: "Some have spoken of the 'American Century.' I say that the century on which we are entering— the century which will come of this war—can be and must be the century of the common man. Perhaps it will be America's opportunity to suggest the freedoms and duties by which the common man must live." Wallace thus coined the phrase "century of the common man," one of the few phrases of the Second World War which may survive.

The idea of world government is by no means the exclusive possession of poets and "Utopians." Two documents demonstrate that hard-headed politicians consider world government both necessary and possible. In 1915, the legislature of the commonwealth of Massachusetts passed a resolution requesting the Congress of the United States to invite all nations to "Unite in the Formation of a World State." In 1941, both houses of the legislature of the state of North Carolina passed a "Joint Resolution for a Declaration of the Federation of the World." So far, only these two state legislatures have gone on record requesting the Congress of the United States to initiate world government. Their name will be remembered in honor, whenever men of good will join their efforts in ridding the world of war and suffering by providing for world government based on law and the consent of the governed.

---

1. The British Commonwealth of Nations*

ALFRED COBBAN

THE PRINCIPLE OF THE MULTI-NATIONAL STATE

With the British Empire we enter a field to which the nationalist theories of Europe have singularly little relevance. This perhaps explains the wide-

* From Alfred Cobban, *National Self-Determination* (Oxford University Press, 1945). By permission.

spread misconception of the nature of that Empire, and the persistence in regarding colonies and dominions alike as a huge conglomeration of territory, overrun and ruled, through some incomprehensible dispensation, by the little English nation. The fundamental fact about the British Commonwealth, on the contrary, is—confining our attention for the moment to Great Britain and the self-governing dominions—that it is multi-national through and through, and that there is no ruling nation, in the sense in which Austrians and Magyars were ruling nations in the Hapsburg Empire.

The British state was fortunate in that it lost less of its medieval political heritage than any country in Europe. Politically speaking, in relation to the two fundamental issues of nationality and sovereignty, in spite of exceptions it might be said that the British tradition runs back with no important break to the Middle Ages. Medieval states like England, France, Bohemia, Hungary, were primarily political conceptions; their cultural nationalities developed out of heterogeneous ingredients under the aegis of medieval monarchy. The English nation-state, which was thus created, acquired during the Middle Ages non-English elements which have remained distinct to the present day, in the Channel Islands, the Isle of Man, and Wales. In the early modern period, when conceivably a tendency towards compulsory assimilation might have started, another and a stronger nationality was incorporated in the United Kingdom—Scotland, which had its own laws and distinct institutions. The Lowland Scots, who made up the majority of the population, were not so different in language and culture as to make cooperation in the same state with the English impossible, but, especially with the addition of the Highlanders, were sufficiently distinct to prevent the development of a common Anglo-Scottish nation. Finally, in Ireland the United Kingdom included an even less assimilable people. Anglicization, so far as it occurred in the British Isles, was almost entirely a natural development. Where there was some attempt at compulsory Anglicization by the state, as in Ireland, it had unfortunate consequences. It was never a deliberate and persistent policy anywhere, and the British Isles have remained the home of four nations—Irish, Scottish, Welsh, and English, as well as a number of smaller sub-nations, the Channel Islanders, Manxmen, and Ulster Orangemen.

The same principle of multiple cultural nationality in a single state has followed the British Empire throughout the world. When Canada was acquired, the Treaty of Peace promised that the French should retain their own language, laws, and religion. Although a scheme of compulsory Anglicization had its supporters, the permanent trend of British policy in Canada was laid down by its first Governor, Carleton, whose views are expressed in a letter of 1767 to the home government: 'Barring a catastrophe shocking to think of, this country must, to the end of time, be peopled by the Canadian race, who already have taken such firm root and got to so great a height that any new stock transplanted will be totally hid and imperceptible among them except in the towns of Quebec and Montreal.'[1] Pitt's Canada Act of 1791 had to make provision for the growing British population, but it did so without robbing the French Canadians of their existing rights. It is significant of the association between radical democracy and the nation-state ideal that the Durham Report should have advocated a policy of assimilation. Deserving all the credit they have been given for the big step they advocated in the direction of self-governing institutions, Durham and his advisers were too much under the influence of the French conception of the *nation une et indivisible* to envisage the possibility of a democratic state containing more than one national culture. Durham indeed only advocated the grant of responsible government on the assumption that a British majority was guaranteed in Canada.[2] The possibility of preserving 'a French Canadian nationality in the midst of Anglo-American colonies and states' seemed to him a 'vain endeavour.'[3] 'I entertain no doubts,' he wrote, 'as to the national character which must be given to Lower Canada; it must be that of the British Empire; . . . that of the great race which must, in the lapse of no long period of time, be predominant over the whole North American continent.'[4] And in Buller's appended report on the state of education in Lower Canada it was frankly declared that the great object in view was 'uniting the two races and Anglifying the Canadian.'[5]

The influence of the deeper tendencies of British polity fortunately proved stronger than these ideas, and Canada emerged into independence as a state made up of two nationalities. Moreover, while the sentimental tie of the English-speaking Canadians to Great Britain was naturally far stronger, the French Canadians, in the interests of the preservation of their own nationality, proved anxious for the retention of the British connexion. This was particularly true of the clergy, who have always been the strongest force in French Canadian society.[6]

When, after the conquest of the Boer states in the South African War, the Empire had again to face the problem of a dual nationality in a single state, it already had in Great Britain and Canada precedents for its solution. The South African Constitution, having to cater for different conditions, naturally did not follow the Canadian model. The difficulties, and the possibilities of a breakdown, were much greater, and the successful maintenance of the Union of South Africa as an active constituent member of the British Commonwealth is all the more remarkable. Australia and New Zealand, being colonized mainly from the British Isles, had no problems of nation-

[1] R. Coupland, *The Quebec Act,* 1925, p. 59.
[2] *Durham Report,* ed. C. P. Lucas, 1912, Vol. I, Introduction, p. 136.
[3] *Id.* II. 70.
[4] *Id.* II. 288.
[5] *Id.* III. 288.
[6] G. Vattier, *Essai sur la mentalité canadienne-française,* 1928, pp. 315-6, 323.

ality comparable to those of the other two dominions, but the success—after initial mistakes and worse—with which New Zealand has managed to find room for the small but growing Maori population, should be recalled in this connexion.

The same problems of the multi-national state, but of a much more complicated kind, are presented in India and Ceylon. All these experiments may not in the end succeed, but the remarkable fact is the great extent to which some of them have already succeeded. It may be said that inside the British Commonwealth the force of nationality, which has proved so destructive in Europe, has been in part robbed of its most dangerous schismatic tendencies by general acceptance of the idea of the multi-national state. National self-determination in the British Empire has meant not merely a process of breaking down, but also one of building up, and the recognition of national liberties has proved a sounder foundation for the co-operation of different nations inside the same state than their suppression.

SELF-DETERMINATION BY CONSENT

Above the association of different nations in a single state there has been the association of independent, self-governing states in a far-reaching commonwealth. When English colonies grew up, in the seventeenth and eighteenth centuries, on the Atlantic coast-line of North America, it was natural that English traditions of local self-government should go with them. New ideas of sovereignty, which had been spreading in Europe in the sixteenth century, began to exercise an influence over English policy during the next two centuries. Out of the struggle against the divine-right theories of the Stuarts emerged the conception of parliamentary sovereignty, and although this stopped short of the extreme absolutism of Hobbes, it was not reconcilable with the idea of a division of authority in the Empire. Consequently, when the American colonies increased in strength and began to grow restive under British control, Parliament, tied to its own legislative supremacy, was unable to respond to the new situation. The British Government saw no *via media* between the sovereignty of Parliament and secession, and forced the American colonies to make the choice between legislative subjection to a parliament in which they were not represented and the assertion of a right of self-determination.

It is seldom that a nation is given the chance to undo its errors and does so, or that it retraces the same ground without making the same mistakes. Britain, having lost one empire in the eighteenth century, found herself with another in the nineteenth. If British policy had been thoroughly imbued with the conception of sovereignty the loss of the American colonies would have made no difference to the treatment of the new colonies; but the persistence of the contrary current of ideas in the British political mind was strong, and despite the influence of the new unifying democratic conceptions, and the legal theory of sovereignty that found expression in the writings of Austin, the memory of the American Revolution was sufficient to tilt the balance against the insistence on British sovereignty over the colonies. The history of Canada, Australia, and New Zealand is the history of a steady accretion of the powers of self-government and a steady decline in imperial control. The culmination of this development came in the report of the Inter-Imperial Relations Committee of the Imperial Conference of 1926, which declared that the self-governing states of the Empire are 'autonomous communities within the British Empire, equal in status, in no way subordinate one to another in any aspect of their domestic or external affairs, though united by a common allegiance to the Crown, and freely associated as members of the British Commonwealth of Nations.' [1] The Statute of Westminster of 1931 gave Parliamentary recognition to this equality of status.

The process of evolution of dominion status has been, to all intents, a process of self-determination, though it differs from the European manifestation of the same principle in certain important respects. The dominions are not all culturally united nation-states. Canada and South Africa are each composed of two quite distinct cultural nationalities. They are *political,* and not cultural, nations, just as is Great Britain itself. Secondly, the self-determination of the dominions has been achieved peacefully, by agreement, and not by war or revolution. Thirdly, almost complete institutional separation —apart from the periodic Imperial Conference, and the symbol of the Crown, now, however, not one crown, but several united in the same person —has been brought about; while more intangible, but powerful, ties remain, which not only prohibit war between Great Britain and the dominions, but strongly influence them to act together in a crisis, as well as in many of the more ordinary occasions of international life.

The nature of self-determination inside the British Commonwealth cannot be understood without examining these ties. In the first place, it is important to note that the existence of a common imperial nationality is not one of them. Loyalty to the British Commonwealth of Nations, whether in Great Britain, in the dominions, or in the colonies, is something quite distinct from consciousness of nationality. Apart from the declaration on British passports, which has its uses, there is really no such thing as a British imperial nationality, in either the cultural or the political meaning of the term. The absence of a single cultural nationality is too obvious to need arguing. The term 'British,' says Professor Zimmern, is 'nationally colourless.' [2] 'The English,' he claims, 'are the people who have most completely solved the problem of nationality, because they have most completely divorced it from politics.' [3] In the political sense a British nationality may be

[1] A. B. Keith, *Speeches and Documents on the British Dominions, 1918–1931,* 1932, p. 161.
[2] A. Zimmern, *The Third British Empire,* 3rd ed., 1934, p. 180.
[3] *Id.* p. 186.

said to exist in the British Isles, excluding Eire. But there is no common political nationality covering the whole British Commonwealth or Empire. The essence of political nationality is the recognition of a single political authority, and common citizenship. Neither of these factors holds for the countries in the British Commonwealth as a whole. It is true that citizenship of the various component parts of the Commonwealth is not necessarily exclusive. On the other hand, rights of migration and residence as between these separate parts are not without definite limits. The resolution moved at the Imperial Conference of 1918 by Sir S. P. Sinha declared: 'It is an inherent function of the governments of the several communities of the British Commonwealth, including India, that each should enjoy complete control of the composition of its own population by means of restriction on immigration from any of the other communities.'[1] It is hardly possible to avoid accepting the definition of the position given by Mr. McGilligan in Dáil Eireànn in 1931: 'The essential point is that you have not a single Commonwealth nationality based upon a single law. It is not a single Commonwealth nationality at all, or even a dual nationality. The Irish Free State national will be that and nothing else so far as his nationality is concerned.'[2]

The ties which still hold the British Commonwealth of Nations together are not to be sought in any of the accepted political forms. They can be summed up under three headings: sentiment, influence, and interest. Sentiment is another word for history—the effects of a common cultural and political tradition in holding together, though with no formal ties, all those parts of the Empire populated from the British Isles. Historical tradition has also built up a considerable sentiment of common membership of a great political community in many of the smaller communities—Maltese, Gibraltans, West Indians, and so on. Even of a people with a strong consciousness of its own separate nationality, such as the French Canadians, it could be said by a French observer that they had a strong sense of personal loyalty to the British Crown.[3]

'Influence,' which by no means merely radiates from Great Britain, but which has become to-day a reciprocal process throughout the Commonwealth, is something that cannot be given institutional form, but in spite of Washington's dictum, 'Influence is not government,' as Professor Hancock rightly declares, it is not necessarily an inferior instrument of policy.[4] The third cause of the cohesion of the Commonwealth is interest, which may be analysed under the headings of economy and defence, but before we turn to discuss these aspects it is necessary to conclude our discussion of the develop-

---

[1] Quoted in W. K. Hancock, *Survey of British Commonwealth Affairs*, Vol. I, *Problems of Nationality, 1918–1936*, p. 174.

[2] Keith, p. 241.

[3] Vattier, p. 311.

[4] Hancock, I. 46.

ment from the British Empire into the British Commonwealth of Nations as a process of self-determination.

It should by now be clear to every one inside the British Commonwealth, even if the situation remains incomprehensible to those outside, that Canada, Australia, New Zealand, South Africa, and Eire are completely independent and autonomous states. How completely the right to self-determination has been accepted in the British Commonwealth can be seen if we take what has come to be regarded as the acid test, the right of secession.

As the ultimate stage in the achievement of political independence, the right of secession has naturally been the latest and the most reluctantly recognized. In the discussions leading up to the Irish Treaty, it was at this point that the British Government drew the line in the concessions it was willing to make. At the Round Table Conference on India in 1930, when Mr. Srinvasa Sastri claimed that dominion status implied the right of secession, his view was contradicted by Lord Chelmsford, who declared that the concession of responsible government must be regarded as qualified by the phrase *'within* the Empire.'[1] In South Africa General Smuts made himself the advocate of the view that there was no constitutional right of secession, but in 1929 the South African Assembly, in adopting the report of an Imperial Conference on merchant shipping, did so with the proviso that it should not be taken 'as derogating from the right of any member of the British Commonwealth of Nations to withdraw therefrom.'[2]

During the last ten years British opinion on the right of secession has matured rapidly. When General Hertzog returned from the Imperial Conference of 1930 he was able to report that it had taken notice of his claim to the right of secession.[3] In 1933, Mr. de Valera inquired whether punitive measures would be taken if the Free State were to sever the British connexion. The British Government refused to commit itself to an answer to what it called a hypothetical question. The matter was perhaps less hypothetical than it imagined, for in the course of the next few years Eire peacefully seceded from the Empire, and it can be said that the right of secession for the dominions is now a recognized fact.

On the whole, however, the British Commonwealth, in so far as concerns Great Britain and the dominions, may be said to have made a notable advance towards a reconciliation of national self-determination with the survival of an association of stable and peaceful states, possessed of a right of secession, but not exercising it, and co-operating, especially for mutual defence, in peace and war. It should be added, perhaps, that many factors which help to maintain the association between the dominions and Great

[1] W. T. Elliott, *The New British Empire*, 1932, p. 196, *n.* 1.
[2] Quoted in Hancock, I. 275.
[3] *The British Empire*, Royal Institute of International Affairs, 1937, pp. 67-8.

Britain also serve to attract them towards the United States; this is true of economic relations, defence, and the use of a common language. On the other hand, it would be a mistake to suppose that closer relations between the dominions and the United States would necessarily mean strained or even looser relations with Great Britain.

Finally, it must be repeated that the degree of success achieved by the British Commonwealth in its treatment of this problem is directly traceable to the general acceptance of two principles—the principle of the multi-national state, and the principle of the divisibility of sovereignty. Where these principles did not apply, where, as in Ireland, the nationalists insisted on the uni-national state and the British Government on its absolute rights of sovereignty, no solution was found save secession, which itself left all the major problems—partition, frontier, economic relations, and strategic requirements—unsolved. Both in its successes and its one great failure the British Commonwealth of Nations has notable lessons to offer to the student of self-determination.

2. *The Soviet Union of Nations**

SIDNEY AND BEATRICE WEBB

One of the difficult problems presented to political science by the geographical unity of the Eurasian plain has always been that of the extreme diversity of the population found upon it, in race, religion, language, degrees of civilisation and culture, habits of life, historical tradition and what not. The continuity of land surface from the Gulf of Finland to the Pacific Ocean prevented the rest of the world from recognising in the tsarist régime what was essentially a colonial empire, ruled from St. Petersburg by the upper class of a superior race—not without analogy to the colonial empire of Holland, ruling its East Indian dependencies from the Hague; or indeed to that of the Britain of the eighteenth century, ruling its heterogeneous colonies from Westminster. The systems of the Dutch and the British appealed to the Bolsheviks no more than those of the Spanish and the French. The compulsory "russification" aimed at by the Russian autocracy was not only manifestly impracticable, but also in the highest degree unpopular.

Lenin and his colleagues in the Social Democratic Party of Russia had not

* From Sidney and Beatrice Webb, *Soviet Communism: A New Civilization* (Charles Scribner's Sons, 1936; revised edition, 1938). By permission.

failed to notice, from the very beginning of the twentieth century, how strong and persistent was the popular discontent caused by the tsarist insistence on the "russification" of all the national minorities within the Empire.[1] Ignoring the indications in the Communist Manifesto of 1848, as to proletarian supremacy leading to the passing away of national differences, and resisting the growing feeling through Europe in favour of united nationalist states, Lenin insisted that the Bolsheviks should declare themselves in favour, along with the right of self-determination of even the smallest nationality, also of the concession of "cultural autonomy" to national minorities included within states. This proved to be an important factor, so far as the national minorities of tsarist Russia were concerned, in securing their participation in the revolutions of February and October 1917.

How were the insistent demands of the various nationalities to be met? The Provisional Government had left this problem, along with so many others, to the prospective Constituent Assembly. But in October 1917 Lenin and his colleagues found themselves in power, before anyone had worked out any scheme of organisation that would satisfy the national minorities without endangering the strength and unity of the central authority. This did not prevent the new government from issuing a flamboyant proclamation promising autonomy in return for support.

"Mohammedans of Russia," it began, "Tartars of the Volga and Crimea; Kirghiz and Sartes of Siberia and Turkestan; Turks and Tartars of Transcaucasia, your beliefs and customs, your national institutions and culture, are hereafter free and inviolable. You have the right to them. Know that your rights, as well as those of all the peoples of Russia, are under the powerful protection of the Revolution, and of the organs of the soviets for workers, soldiers, and peasants. Lend your support to this revolution, and to its government."[2]

The working out of the problem of national minorities was entrusted to Stalin, who, as a member of one of the innumerable tribes inhabiting the Caucasian mountains, had long had a personal interest in the subject. In 1913, indeed, he had published a pamphlet in which he endeavoured to reconcile cultural autonomy with the supremacy of the whole proletarian mass.[3] He was made People's Commissar for Nationalities, with the opportunity of concentrating his whole energy on the task.

[1] Already at the London Conference of 1903, Lenin got carried a resolution stating that "The Conference declares that it stands for the complete right of self-determination of all nations"; to which the Second Congress of the Party in August 1903 added the important words "included in any state." The Central Committee of the Party, at the meeting of September 25, 1913, emphasised the necessity of guaranteeing "the right to use freely their native language in social life and in the schools."

[2] *Soviet Rule in Russia,* by W. R. Batsell, 1929, p. 109. A French translation will be found in "Le Bolshevisme et l'Islam," by Castagne, in *Revue du monde musulman,* Paris, vol. XXXI, pp. 7-8.

[3] *Marxism and the National Question,* by Josef Stalin, 1913 (in Russian).

THE SOLUTION OF THE PROBLEM

It is, we think, owing to the whole-hearted adoption of this policy of cultural autonomy, and even more to its accompaniment of leaving the local administration to be carried on mainly by "natives," that the Soviet Union, alone among the countries of Eastern Europe, can claim, with a high degree of accuracy, that it has solved the difficult problem presented by the existence of national minorities within a strongly centralised state.[1] It has found this solution, not, as France has done, along the road of absorbing the national minorities by the creation of an overpowering unity of civilisation from end to end of its territory; nor, as tsarist Russia sought in vain to do, along that of forcibly suppressing all other national peculiarities in favour of those of the dominant race; but by the novel device of *dissociating statehood from both nationality and race.* In spite of the numerical dominance of the Russian race in the USSR, and its undoubted cultural pre-eminence, the idea of there being a Russian state has been definitely abandoned. The very word "Russia" was, in 1922–1923, deliberately removed from the title of the Soviet Union. All sections of the community—apart from those legally deprived of citizenship on grounds unconnected with either race or nationality—enjoy, throughout the USSR, according to law, equal rights and duties, equal privileges and equal opportunities. Nor is this merely a formal equality under the law and the federal constitution. Nowhere in the world do habit and custom and public opinion approach nearer to a like equality in fact. Over the whole area between the Arctic Ocean and the Black Sea and the Central Asian mountains, containing vastly differing races and nationalities; men and women, irrespective of conformation of skull or pigmentation of skin, even including the occasional African negro admitted from the United States, may associate freely with whom they please; travel in the same public vehicles and frequent the same restaurants and hotels; sit next to each other in the same colleges and places of amusement; marry wherever there is mutual liking; engage on equal terms in any craft or profession for which they are qualified; join the same churches or other societies; pay the same taxes and be elected or appointed to any office or position without exception. Above all, these men and women denizens of the USSR, to whatever race or nationality they belong, can and do participate—it is even said that the smaller nationalities do so in more than their due proportion—in the highest offices of government and in the organised vocation of leadership; alike in the sovnarkoms and central executive committees of the several constituent republics and in those of the USSR, and, most important of all, in the Central Committee of the Communist Party (and its presidium), and even in the all-powerful Politbureau itself. The Bolsheviks have thus some justification for their challenging question: Of what other area containing an analogous diversity of races and nationalities can a similar assertion be made?

[1] See, for the whole problem, *National States and National Minorities,* by W. C. Macartney, 1934.

The policy of cultural autonomy and native self-government is, indeed, carried very far. It is not confined to the more powerful national minorities, nor even to groups of magnitude. Wherever a sufficient minimum of persons of a particular race or culture are settled together, the local administration allows for their peculiar needs.[1] Hardly any of the distinct races or cultures, not even the Russians who count so large a majority, are without their local minorities, dwelling amid alien local majorities. On the other hand, some of the races are wholly dispersed, and are to be found everywhere. Hence the autonomy has to be, and is, carried so far as to secure, for even the smallest minority group, its own autonomy, as regards primary school and local officials, even against the dominant minority culture.

THE MAINTENANCE OF UNITY

Yet the state as a whole maintains its unity unimpaired, and has even, like other federal states, increased its centralisation of authority. It is only in the USSR that this centralisation involves no lessening of the cultural autonomy of the minorities, and even occurs concomitantly with the strengthening of the various regional cultures. This unbroken unity, and this increasing centralisation of authority, is ensured in ways that will become plain as our exposition proceeds. It will suffice for the present to note, first, that, legally

---

[1] "There is scarcely a people in the Soviet Union which has no members who form a minority in one, or very often in many member states or regions. The Soviet Union has accordingly enacted very elaborate minority legislation, assuring to the minorities their schools and the employment of their mother tongue; wherever minorities live together in villages or districts they have been brought together in administrative units in which their language and their national characteristics have full play" (*Nationalism in the Soviet Union*, by Hans Kohn, 1934, pp. 69-70).

"The lower steps in the ladder of soviet national (minority) political organization are the ten national (minority) circuits (or oblasts), 147 national (minority) rayons, and about 3,200 national (minority) soviets (in village or city). These units represent small national (minority) groups in the midst of larger units that are permitted to develop their own national (minority) cultural life. In fairness to the soviets, it must be said that the national minorities are given every opportunity to develop their cultural interests" (*The Soviet State*, by B. W. Maxwell, 1934, p. 26).

"For example, in the RSFSR there are ten national districts, 147 national regions and 3,200 national village soviets. In the Ukrainian SSR, among the 380 regions, there are 25 national regions: 8 Russian, 7 German, 3 Bulgarian, 3 Greek, 3 Jewish and 1 Polish. Among the great number of national village soviets of the Ukrainian SSR there are 16 Moldavian, 10 Czech, 4 White Russian and even 1 Swedish and 1 French. In the Abkhdazian SSR there is even a negro soviet" (*How the Soviet Government Solves the National Question*, by L. Perchik, Moscow, 1932, p. 27). It is currently asserted in 1935 that there are in the USSR, 5,000 national soviets.

The existence of a negro village, with a soviet of its own race, is, we imagine, unique in Europe. Persons of African descent, though relatively few in number in the USSR, are more than is usually supposed. Besides the scattered workmen in many occupations who have drifted in from the United States, and a small number of highly educated negro specialists who have been engaged to assist in cotton-growing, etc., there are, about the shores of the Black Sea, quite a number of descendants of the African slaves whom the wealthy used to buy in the slave market of Constantinople. It will be remembered that Pushkin, the first great Russian poet, was of negro descent.

and formally, the powers of the superior authorities in disallowance and cancellation are the same over the autonomous republics and autonomous areas as over other oblasts, rayons, cities and villages; the cultural autonomy, though formally established in principle by general law, being essentially a matter of administrative practice. Next, the great levelling influence of the economic relations exemplified in widespread industrialisation and collectivism, which operate irrespective of race or nationality, or any geographical boundaries, constitute a silent but continuous unifying factor. Finally, the ubiquitous guidance and persuasion of the essentially unitary Communist Party, composed of members of every race and every distinctive culture in the USSR, ensures not only unity but also all the centralisation that is necessary.

Alongside this maintenance and strengthening of the minority cultures, there has been an unmistakable rise in the level of civilisation. Note first, and perhaps as most important, a marked increase, among the national minorities, of their own self-respect. It is, indeed, the many backward populations, which had suffered so much under tsarist repression that they had nothing that could be destroyed, which have gained most from the nationalities policy of the Soviet Government. They have, to a considerable extent, already lost their "inferiority complex" and gained in confidence and courage. The women, in becoming literate, have become effectually free, alike from the veil and from the control of husband or father. The children have been almost universally got to school, and have been provided with technical institutes and colleges of university rank, using the vernacular. The health of the whole people has been improved. With hospitals and medical services, epidemics have been got under, and the death-rate has everywhere been greatly reduced. All this has been carried out by the local administration, largely in the hands of "natives," but with the constant guidance of the various commissariats of health and education, and of the Communist Party, with abundant encouragement and financial assistance from Moscow, always under conditions of "cultural autonomy." Even more influential in change has been the economic development. The nomadic tribes have, to a great extent, become settled agriculturists, grouped in collective farms; the peasants have been helped to new crops; the collective farms have been mechanised; the surplus of labour has been absorbed in extensive industrial enterprises in mining and manufacturing, largely in the various localities themselves; additional railways have been constructed; and dozens of new cities have sprung up. This has been, in the main, the outcome of the First and Second Five-Year Plans of 1929 and 1933.

A NEW BASIS FOR STATEHOOD

Fundamentally what the Bolsheviks have done, and what Stalin may be thought to have long been looking for, is something which does not seem to have occurred as a possibility to western statesmen. In devising the federal organisation that we have described, they threw over, once for all and completely, the conception that statehood had, or should have, any connection with race or nationality. Political science had, for the most part, come to see, during the nineteenth century, that statehood need have nothing to do with the colour of the skin or with the profession of a particular creed. It had even sometimes contemplated the possibility of doing without a dominant national language. But right down to the resettlement of European boundaries according to the Treaty of Versailles and its fellows in 1919, the political scientists have allowed statesmen to cling to the value, if not the necessity, of a unity of race as the basis of perfect statehood. This conception is connected with, if not consciously based upon, that of an inherent and unalterable superiority of one race—usually one's own race—over others; and with the belief, for which neither history nor biological science knows of any foundation, that what is called "purity of blood" is an attribute of the highest value. The Bolsheviks put their trust in a genuine equality of citizenship, as completely irrespective of race or language as of colour or religion.[1] They neither undervalued nor overvalued the national minority cultures. What they have sought to do is to develop every one of them, in its own vernacular and with its own peculiarities. They refused to accept the assumption that there is any necessary or inherent inferiority of one race to another. They declared that scientific anthropology knows of no race, whether white or black, of which the most promising individuals could not be immeasurably advanced by appropriate education and an improvement in economic and social environment. The Bolsheviks accordingly invented the conception of the unnational state. They abandoned the word "Russia." They formed a Union of Socialist Soviet Republics in which all races stood on one and the same equal footing. And just because it is not a national state, belonging to a superior race, the Soviet Union has set itself diligently, not merely to treat the "lesser breeds within the law" with equality, but, recognising that their backwardness was due to centuries of poverty, repression and enslavement, has made it a leading feature of its policy to spend out of common funds considerably more per head on its backward races than on the superior ones, in education and social improvements, in industrial investments and agricultural reforms. The record of the USSR in this respect during the past eighteen years stands in marked contrast with the action towards their respective lower races of the governments of Holland or France, and even of that of the United Kingdom, which has been responsible for the government of India, and many of the West Indian islands, and much of Africa, for more than a century.

[1] "Their way of dealing with Home Rule and the nationalities is a masterpiece of ingenuity and elegance. None of the able statesmen of to-day in other lands has attempted to vie with them in their method of satisfying the claims of minorities" (*Russia To-day and To-morrow*, by E. J. Dillon, 1928, p. 228).

It is interesting to notice how the absorption of such a heterogeneous population as that of the Soviet Union into a strong and in many respects centralised state has been facilitated by the system of soviets, using the expedient of indirect election, instead of a parliament directly elected by mass votes. No widespread empire has yet found it possible to establish a parliament effectively representing its whole realm;[1] just as none has yet attempted to carry on its whole production and distribution of commodities and services by a cabinet responsible to a single popularly elected parliamentary assembly. But the USSR finds it quite practicable and useful to let each village in Kamchatka or Sakhalin, or beyond the Arctic circle, elect its own selosoviet, and sends its own deputies to the rayon congress of soviets, and so to the congress of soviets of the oblast or autonomous republic, and ultimately to the All-Union Congress of Soviets at Moscow, in exactly the same way, and with exactly the same rights, as a village in the oblast of Moscow or Leningrad. Such a remote and backward village, it must be remembered, which uses its own vernacular in its own schools and its own court of justice, enjoys, likewise, the privilege of filling the local offices, even the highest of them, with its own people. And what is of even greater importance, its residents are eligible, equally with persons of any other race or residence, for the Order or Companionship undertaking the Vocation of Leadership, which their leading members are encouraged and even pressed to join, and for which they are provided gratuitously with the necessary intensive training, returning to their homes equipped for filling any of the local offices, and even for promotion to the highest places in the Union. Not without reason, therefore, is it claimed that the soviet system has, for a far-flung empire, certain advantages over that of a directly elected parliamentary assembly.

[1] No one can seriously suggest that the admission to the French Senate and Chamber of Deputies, and even, very occasionally, to minor ministerial office, of members nominally elected by the people of Martinique, Guadaloupe, Reunion, Pondicherry, Guiana, Senegal or Cochin China (omitting Algeria, Tunis, Madagascar, etc.), amounts to any solution of the problem.

~~~~~~

3. The Myth of World Government*

REINHOLD NIEBUHR

~~~~~~

The French observer André Siegfried thought several decades ago that America was coming of age. One hopes he was right; though it is worth

* *The Nation* (March 16, 1946). By permission.

noting that there are many stages of maturity and we seem hardly to have reached one commensurate with the responsibilities which have been thrust upon our very powerful if very young nation. At every turn we face decisions requiring us to use our power creatively to stabilize an inchoate community of nations in a civilization which can achieve stability only in global terms.

Our hesitancies and ambiguities reveal that we have not yet overcome our adolescent pride of power or our inner securities. It would be the rightful function of a "liberal" movement in such a situation to furnish the nation with mature counsel, assuming that liberalism, whatever else it may be, represents a measure of detachment from the shortsighted collective impulses of a community. It must be regretfully recorded, however, that the liberal movement of America has not risen to the occasion. It is, if anything, more infantile than the nation. It proves its lack of maturity by trying to solve the complex problems of our global existence in purely logical and constitutional terms. We do not yet have a world community—only halting and hesitant beginnings toward one. American liberals, however, insist that one be brought into being by legal, constitutional, and governmental means, disregarding the fact, which history attests on every page, that governments may perfect the order and justice of a community but cannot create a community—for the simple reason that the authority of government is primarily the authority of the community itself. If the community does not exist in fact, at least in inchoate form, constitutional instruments cannot create it. The authority of law as such is slight, and the fear of police power is useful only to suppress incidental recalcitrance against the will of the community. The community cannot be coerced into basic order; the basic order must come from its innate cohesion.

These obvious facts are obscured in almost all the educational propaganda on the problems of world government put out by our international organizations. They are rightfully concerned about the fact that unabridged national sovereignty is a principle of anarchy in an interdependent world. Their answer to this problem is to call for a constitutional convention of the world or to try to persuade the new United Nations Organization to pass a law which will abridge the sovereignty of nations. This solution takes legal symbols for social realities. The principle of national sovereignty is the legal expression of the fact that national communities regard themselves as morally and politically autonomous. They have become increasingly conscious of the claims of other nations upon them and of the necessity of a larger degree of mutual accord, but they will have to reach a much higher degree of implicit abridgment of their moral freedom before it will be possible to fix and extend this moral and social gain by law.

The present accord between the nations, as expressed in the United Nations Charter, contains a "veto" provision by virtue of which no great power can be voted down in the council of the nations. This fact fills our liberals with moral and political disgust. It does of course prove that the great powers are not ready to submit unreservedly to the authority of a world organization. But this merely means that in the present state of world affairs peace cannot be maintained by a majority imposing its will upon a minority. When the minority is not a group of individuals but a nation or a group of nations, it will use its social and military power to defy a decision which has not been reached with its consent. We have, therefore, no real security against war. But there is no reason to think we could gain this security by constitutional means after having failed to establish the minimum basis for it by political means.

All the great nations insisted upon the veto power, and the United Nations Charter would hardly have passed the United States Senate without this provision. Russia is more insistent upon retaining the veto than we are because it is in greater danger of being voted down in the United Nations Assembly or the Security Council. This fact does not deter our constitutional idealists from bombarding the ear of the Administration and the conscience of the nation with proposals for abolishing the veto. Here the constitutional answer to the problem of world peace obviously threatens the delicate and tentative degree of accord which has been achieved politically. We are professedly interested only in establishing a universal sovereignty, and we refuse to admit that we can afford greater devotion to the principle than Russia because we run less danger of being in the minority. This taint in our idealism is obvious enough to the Russians.

It must be observed in this connection that a great deal of enthusiasm for world government is explicitly anti-Russian—for instance, that of ex-Justice Owen Roberts and Clarence Streit. The theory is: let us set up a real world government; if the Russians fail to adhere so much the worse for them. These idealists are ready to bring on another world war in the name of world government. As consolation for the dire effects of so ironic a policy, we are assured that if we must have another world war it would be spiritually thrilling to fight it for the principle of world government. Some of the enthusiasm for world government is not explicitly anti-Russian but merely too naive to recognize that the effect of demanding a constitutionally perfect world order in the present situation must be to destroy the very tentative degree of mutual trust which has been achieved between the two great centers of power.

To say that there is no way of guaranteeing the peace of the world constitutionally is not to say that there are other ways of guaranteeing it. There are none. We are living in a very unsafe world; and it will be unsafe for a long time. To note the difficulty of bringing Russia into a world community does not imply that Russia's policies based on its fears are all justified. Some are; some are not. Some are reactions to our own policies, which are prompted by our own fears. Some seem to be derived from Marxist dog-matism. But there they are. They cannot be overcome by constitutional means unless they are first mitigated by a great deal more common counsel and common experience.

The excessive devotion to constitutional answers for world problems in America seems to be a dubious inheritance from the whole "social-contract" theory of government with which the liberal democratic movement began. According to this theory men and nations create communities by the fiat of government and law. That all human communities had a long history of organic cohesion before they ever began explicitly and consciously to alter or extend it is ignored. One reason why the idea of the social contract has special prestige in America is our belief that we created a nation by consti-tutional fiat; and we think it our special business to ask the world to do in macrocosm what we so successfully accomplished in microcosm. This anal-ogy fails to consider that the cohesion of a national community is so differ-ent from the organization of a universal community that the difference is one of kind rather than degree. It also leaves out of account an important aspect of our history. If our Constitution created a "more perfect union," the union which the Constitution perfected had already been established. The fear of a common foe, the shared experiences of the battlefield, a very considerable degree of similar culture—these and many other factors pro-vided the cohesion of the American colonies. The Constitution could not have created a unity which it had to presuppose.

Emery Reves in his "Anatomy of Peace," which has become a kind of bible of American constitutional idealism, declares that the way to "prevent wars between nations once and for all" is to integrate "the scattered con-flicting national sovereignties into one unified higher sovereignty capable of creating a legal order in which all peoples will enjoy equal security, equal obligations, and equal rights under the law." The "once and for all" gives one pause, for even our own Constitution could not prevent the Civil War. But a brilliant defender of pure constitutionalism recently explained that difficulty away. The Civil War, he declared, was caused by certain ambi-guities in our Constitution which left some doubt whether we were in fact a nation or a loose federation of states. It is now our business to profit from the experience of the past and eliminate similar ambiguities from the world constitution. Unfortunately, to assume that the tortuous processes of history can thus be controlled by the power of constitutional logic is an infantile illusion.

American liberalism refuses to face the fact that there is a tremendous difference between the problem of community on the national and global level, a difference which no constitutional magic can overcome. National and imperial communities all have ethnic, linguistic, geographic, historical, and other forces of social unity. The universal community, however, has no common language or common culture—nothing to create the consciousness of "we." Modern democratic communities may be culturally and ethnically pluralistic, but they all possess a core of common spiritual possessions which the world community lacks.

The world community does, indeed, have some compelling motives toward unity. Technical civilization has created an economic interdependence which generates insufferable frictions if it is not politically managed. There is in the culture of every nation, moreover, a religious and philosophical sense of world community waiting to be actualized, and of moral obligations extending beyond the national community. There is, finally, the fear of mutual destruction. It is the thesis of the proponents of world government that the atomic bomb has so intensified the fear of mutual destruction that hitherto impossible constitutional goals now appear possible.

Undoubtedly fear may be a creative force. The scared man can run faster from the pursuing bull than he ever thought possible. But the creative power of fear does not increase in proportion to its intensity. Fear finally becomes paralyzing. Furthermore, the fear of mutual destruction easily degenerates into the fear of a particular foe. Even now it must be regretfully recorded that fear of Russia in the West and of the West in Russia seems more potent than the common fear of destruction.

These are tragic facts, and one could wish that they were not true; but it is hardly mature to deny what is so obvious. The world community lacks, in short, the potent elements of "togetherness" which national communities boast. Neither law nor police power can supply this defect. If one trusted to police power alone, the amount required by a universal state to maintain order in a community which did not cohere naturally and organically would be so great as to amount to tyranny. This was Thomas Hobbes's answer to the problem of community; the similarity between his answer and that of many of our modern constitutional idealists is instructive. Fortunately, national communities had a more organic unity than Hobbes supposed. Unfortunately, the international community corresponds at least partly to his picture.

These simple lessons must be spelled out to American idealists, not to induce a mood of defeatism, but to get them to direct the impulses of their idealism to real rather than imaginary objectives. Many creative acts are required of America that are more difficult, though more immediate and modest, than espousal of world government. Will the British loan agreement pass? If it does not, America will have proved that it does not know how to relate its wealth to an impoverished world. Shall we find a way of transferring our dangerous knowledge of the atomic bomb to some kind of world judicatory? If not, we shall have proved that we know how to resent, but not to allay, the world's fear of our power.

These immediate steps toward achieving a higher degree of mutuality among nations may be too modest to guarantee peace. But they are in the right direction. It would be intolerable if we again presented the world with a case of American schizophrenia, allowing our idealists to dream up pure answers for difficult problems while our cynics make our name odious by the irresponsible exercise of our power.

4. The Reality of World Government *

ALBERT GUÉRARD

Reinhold Niebuhr is among those world citizens who deny the existence of the world, among those Children of Light for whom Darkness alone possesses reality. This would be puzzling if we were not familiar with his method. His system of Christian apologetics is founded upon the notion of "paradox," by which he means—paradoxically—contradiction, antinomy. If Niebuhr were ever to agree with himself, he would stand self-condemned.

All this banter, of course, is within the family. I know that Niebuhr's heart is in the right place, and I have a deep respect for his mind. A controversy between us is not a duel or even a fencing bout: it is a symposium, an attempt to focus our thought.

There are two theses in Niebuhr's essay on World Government. The first is that a community cannot be created by legal or constitutional means. The second is that the world community does not exist. In the vernacular: "First catch your hare; but there is no hare."

On the first point I am in complete agreement with Niebuhr, and with the rest of the world. It is a truism. I have yet to find a man, presumably sane, who believes that a community can be created *ex nihilo* by the magic of a constitutional formula. Even Ely Culbertson, who in my opinion relies far too much on a mechanism fearfully and wonderfully made, is aware that his plan would be futile unless it satisfied the needs and desires of living men. In the many agencies that are working on this great problem there are outstanding authorities on constitutional law. Their contribution is invaluable; they challenge both idealists and pragmatists to give the words they use a definite meaning. But they never mistake verbal niceties for principles, or abstractions for concrete facts. The law can define the conditions of peace, but the law *per se* cannot create or enforce those conditions. The task before

* *The Nation* (April 20, 1946). By permission.

us is not of the same character as that of the atomic scientists. When a mysterious force had been surmised, discovered, released, harnessed, the work was done, and could not be undone by public opinion. But the drafting of a constitution is not the working out of a mathematical equation, not the performing of a chemical experiment. There is no inevitable, no ideal constitution: under ideal circumstances no constitution would be needed. Like any other man-made law, a constitution is the acknowledgment of human infirmity. It is the co-ordinated effort of the "do-gooders" to forestall and curb the evil-doers.

So I need not be told that the Weimar constitution was both fool-proof and still-born. I know that our own Constitution, based as it is on the eternal verities, is so loose that the Nine Old Men often differ about its meaning. It failed to prevent the only severe crisis in our history, the Civil War. When borrowed by other lands, it creaked, stalled, or broke down.

On the other hand, a constitution which is an amorphous mass may function admirably if it is in harmony with the instincts, the habits, the ideals of a people: the classical example is that elusive "myth" known as the British constitution. The United Nations, during the war, achieved a remarkable degree of co-ordination. It may be asserted that the normal work of the World State will be child's play, compared with the task that the defenders of freedom had to face between 1939 and 1945. Many organs were created, but there was no overall constitution. The will must find a way, but the will is more important than the way.

Niebuhr's second, and major, point is that such a will does not exist. I beg his pardon: he did not actually say anything so absurd. He did not deny that the men he criticized had, like George Washington himself, the will to world unity. But he believes they are a contemptibly puny group. They may be right; as a Christian, he must be convinced that they are right. But they are so few and weak that they should, realistically, submit to the vaster, fiercer will of the nationalists, that is, the followers of Hitler.

Even if it were so, I should refuse to bow. But I am not striking an attitude of heroic defiance. It is as an observer, not as a prophet, that I challenge the accuracy of Niebuhr's assertion. He says: "National and imperial communities all have ethnic, linguistic, geographic, historical, and other forces of social unity. The universal community, however, has no common language or common culture—nothing to create the consciousness of *We*." This is the pure doctrine of Joseph de Maistre, against the Enlightenment, the Revolution, and the Rights of Man. "I have met Russians, Englishmen, Frenchmen: I have never met *Man*"—and De Maistre called himself a Catholic! This thesis was emphatically false 150 years ago. How does it stand today?

I shall not dwell upon the threat of the atomic bomb, "one world or none," because it is demeaning to argue on the basis of fear. I merely note that Niebuhr advocates "transferring our dangerous knowledge to some kind of world judicatory"—and if he would tell us what he means by judicatory, he would give us the gist of a world constitution. But the atomic bomb was simply the irrefutable confirmation of a fact with which we were familiar: it is impossible today for any nation to be a hermit. We tried isolationism, that is, the thoroughgoing denial of the world community. Realistically speaking, it was not a success. For better or for worse, technical progress has made the world physically one, more closely knit than two neighboring valleys in eighteenth-century England. Behind modern technique there is science, and Niebuhr knows that science ignores national boundaries. Germans, Danes, Italians worked on the atomic problem; Frenchmen, Russians, Japanese had prepared the path.

All this belongs to the material world; Niebuhr spurns it, and I cannot blame him. But he condemns also the religious and philosophical world, which ought to be his own, and which posits the unity of man. He moves in the murky mystic atmosphere of German romanticism, in which national culture is the only reality. There is a "German spirit," there is an American spirit, and never the twain shall meet; there is no human spirit.

This seems to me in manifest contradiction with the facts. In the first place, the national spirit has been grossly exaggerated. The crucial instance is that of Franco Spain. There a nationalist ("There is no world community") killed half a million pure-blooded Spaniards with the aid of Italians, Germans, and Moors. The French nationalists, ten years ago, vowed: "Rather Hitler than Blum!" Today, the nationalist Kerillis does his best to defame DeGaulle. And a "German spirit" that would integrate Heinrich and Thomas Mann, Einstein, Goebbels, and Hitler would have to be so broad that it might well be called *Welt-bürgerlich*.

On the other hand, the world unity which Niebuhr denies is plain for all eyes to see. The *Homo sum* of Terence has never lost its validity. A few random examples. We are submitting without protest to food restrictions, because we cannot face the thought of being sated in a starving world. According to Ségur, people wept for joy in the streets of St. Petersburg when the Bastille fell. Father Gratry said, "So long as Poland is martyred, we shall live in a state of mortal sin"; and today the power of Franco weighs us down with shame and remorse. The planet felt the wound when Dreyfus was unjustly condemned, and great meetings were held in Paris to plead for Sacco and Vanzetti. This feeling that the world is morally one is not the privilege of an élite; it is more ardent, more spontaneous, among the masses than among the sophisticates.

I am a student of literature. I know—and Niebuhr knows—that world literature, no less than world art and world science, is more real than any purely local manifestation. I am not thinking of the happy few who enjoy Kafka, Gide, or Unamuno better than "Forever Amber." World literature begins in the cradle, not in the graduate school. Children do not reject Aesop's "Fables," Grimm's "Fairy Tales," "Pinocchio," or "Heidi" because of their foreign origin. Adolescents used to revel in Alexandre Dumas and Jules Verne. "The Hunchback of Notre-Dame" and "Les Misérables" are better known to the average American than the valuable work of Joel Barlow. If there is but a single book in a log cabin, it will be the Bible. Culturally, the world exists more vigorously than its provinces, Germany, America, or France, just as these have more intensity of life than Baden, Nebraska, or Poitou.

It is hard to argue with Niebuhr. If we suggest to him that selfishness is wasteful, that security, law, and order are sound business propositions, he will tell us loftily: "You are thinking on a low materialistic plane; national consciousness (My country, right or wrong! *Deutschland über Alles!*) is an ideal." If we plead that the fundamental unity of mankind is deeper than all tribal superstitions, he will call us naive, wishful, starry-eyed. Our ancestors called such nimbleness of wit "running with the hare, hunting with the hounds."

The world community does exist. There is a humanity common to all men; to defend it is our "common cause." This community is unorganized because our political institutions lag a century or more behind our political consciousness. Fanatical nationalists are but a virulent minority. Fully conscious, determined world citizens, I admit, are a minority also. The masses are confused, not in their feelings, but in their minds. They hate war; they hate oppression and injustice anywhere in the world. Both our pacifists and our isolationists proved that they did not want to fight for empire or prestige. Americans could only be made to fight for a human cause—democracy, freedom. The war for them was never a tussle for wealth and power but a gigantic operation of the world police against the law-breakers. If the war had not been for the defense of the world community, it would have been the ghastliest and silliest of crimes. Ask veterans, laborers, church members, Rotarians: "Do you want world war or world law?" Their answer is unequivocal. But when it comes to translating these deep feelings into definite terms, there rises some clever, plausible, learned man: "Absurd! Utopia! Immature! Unrealistic! Perfectionist! Your common humanity is nonsense. Cherish and harden those differences that cannot be maintained except by the sword." Julien Benda denounced "la trahison des clercs": there are intellectuals, aye, and clerics too, who see the light and try to shut it out.

Niebuhr would say—did say: "Let the world spirit grow organically, unconsciously, and no constitution will be needed." The world spirit is full grown, but it is unarmed. It is the fossils who have the weapons; living souls are told that they need none. This must be reversed. Our aim is to focus the consciousness of mankind through institutions. Let us ask the people: "Do you want the world community, which now lives in chaos, to be *constituted,* that is to say, to live under law? Or do you want each nation to be a judge in its own quarrels, a law unto itself?"

The desire of the common man is clear. It can be gauged by the response to the popular books of Wendell Willkie and Emery Reves. To turn that desire into a *working* world order is not an easy task. It will not happen unconsciously, automatically, organically, according to the lazy, fatalistic philosophy of the nineteenth century. A world order is not merely an aspiration; it is an act of faith, an act of will, and a complex technical problem. Many, including mad Emperor Norton, wished for a bridge over the Golden Gate; but the bridge could not be built until it was planned for, blueprinted, voted upon and financed. All this preparation—this listing of obstacles, this definition of terms, this mooting of solutions—is indispensable, and it is the work many of us are engaged upon. Modestly, without megalomania: no Lawgiver is going to descend from Mount Sinai with new Tables of the Law. But while prophetic voices are urging that the work should be done, scientific minds are exploring how it can be done. A world constitution will not end human woes, any more than ours has cured all our ills. But it will be the symbol and instrument of unity. It will not be a static Utopia; like our Constitution, it will not be merely a check but a goal to be striven for.

To this difficult task Reinhold Niebuhr, as a Christian, as a teacher, as a humanitarian, was and remains summoned. He may choose to stand, a lost teacher, with the "prophets of the past." It would be a tragic paradox. I know what Niebuhr wants in his heart: why should he be of so little faith?

~~~~~~

5. *Peace through Law* *

WOODROW WILSON

~~~~~~

I would consider myself recreant to every mother and father, every wife and sweetheart in this country, if I consented to the ending of this war without a guarantee that there would be no other. You say, "Is it an absolute guarantee?" No; there is no absolute guarantee against human passion; but even if it were only 10 per cent of a guarantee, would not you

* From Woodrow Wilson, *War and Peace: Presidential Messages, Addresses, and Public Papers, 1917–1924* (Harper & Brothers, 1927). By permission of Mrs. Woodrow Wilson, holder of the copyright.

rather have 10 per cent guarantee against war than none? If it only creates a presumption that there will not be war, would you not rather have that presumption than live under the certainty that there will be war? For, I tell you, my fellow citizens, I can predict with absolute certainty that within another generation there will be another world war if the nations of the world do not concert the method by which to prevent it.

The chief motives which led us to enter the war will be defeated unless that Covenant is ratified and acted upon with vigor. We cannot in honor whittle it down or weaken it as the Republican leaders of the Senate have proposed to do. If we are to exercise the kind of leadership to which the founders of the Republic looked forward and which they depended upon their successors to establish, we must do this with courage and unalterable determination. They expected the United States to be always the leader in the defense of liberty and ordered peace throughout the world, and we are unworthy to call ourselves their successors unless we fulfill the great purpose they entertained and proclaimed.

If Germany had dreamed that anything like the greater part of the world would combine against her, she never would have begun the war, and she did not dare to let the opinion of mankind crystallize against her by the discussion of the purposes which she had in mind. What I want to point out to you to-night is that we are making a fundamental choice. You have either got to have the old system, of which Germany was the perfect flower, or you have got to have a new system. You cannot have a new system unless you provide a substitute, an adequate substitute, for the old, and when certain of our fellow citizens take the position that we do not want to go into any combination at all but want to take care of ourselves, all I have to say to them is that that is exactly the German position.

You have been grossly misled with regard to the treaty, and particularly with regard to the proposed character of the League of Nations, by those who have assumed the serious responsibility of opposing it. They have gone so far that those who have spent their lives, as I have spent my life, in familiarizing themselves with the history and traditions and policies of the Nation, must stand amazed at the gross ignorance and impudent audacity which have led them to attempt to invent an "Americanism" of their own, which has no foundation whatever in any of the authentic traditions of the Government.

Americanism, as they conceive it, reverses the whole process of the last few tragical years. It would substitute America for Prussia in the policy of isolation and defiant segregation. Their conception of the dignity of the Nation and its interest is that we should stand apart and watch for opportunities to advance our own interests, involve ourselves in no responsibility for the maintenance of the right in the world or for the continued vindication of any of the things for which we entered the war to fight.

The conception of the great creators of the Government was absolutely opposite to this. They thought of America as the light of the world as created to lead the world in the assertion of the rights of peoples and the rights of free nations; as destined to set a responsible example to all the world of what free Government is and can do for the maintenance of right standards, both national and international.

This light the opponents of the League would quench. They would relegate the United States to a subordinate rôle in the affairs of the world.

Why should we be afraid of responsibilities which we are qualified to sustain and which the whole of our history has constituted a promise to the world we would sustain!

This is the most momentous issue that has ever been presented to the people of the United States, and I do not doubt that the hope of the whole world will be verified by an absolute assertion by the voters of the country of the determination of the United States to live up to all the great expectations which they created by entering the war and enabling the other great nations of the world to bring it to a victorious conclusion, to the confusion of Prussianism and everything that arises out of Prussianism. Surely we shall not fail to keep the promise sealed in the death and sacrifice of our incomparable soldiers, sailors and marines who await our verdict beneath the sod of France.

The old system was, Be ready, and we can be ready. I have heard gentlemen say, "America can take care of herself." Yes, she can take care of herself. Every man would have to train to arms. We would have to have a great standing army. We would have to have accumulations of military material such as Germany used to have. We would enjoy the luxuries of taxes even higher than we pay now. We could accumulate our force, and then our force would have to be directed by some kind of sufficiently vigorous central power. You would have a military government in spirit if not in form. No use having a fighting Nation if there is not somebody to swing it! If you do not want your President to be a representative of the civil purposes of this country, you can turn him into merely a commander in chief, ready to fight the world. But if you did nobody would recognize America in those strange and altered circumstances. All the world would stand at amaze and say, "Has America forgotten everything that she ever professed?" The picture is one that every American repudiates; and I challenge any man who has that purpose at the back of his thought to avow it. If he comes and tells you that America must stand alone and take care of herself, ask him how it is going to be done, and he will not dare tell you, because you would show him the door and say, "We do not know any such America."

Yet we cannot do without force. You cannot establish land titles, as I have expressed it, and not maintain them. Suppose that the land titles of South Dakota were disturbed. Suppose the farm lines were moved, say, ten feet. You know what would happen. Along every fence line you would see farmers perching with guns on their knees. The only reason they are not perching now is that there are land deeds deposited in a particular place, and the whole majesty and force and judicial system of the State of South Dakota are behind the titles. Very well, we have got to do something like that internationally. You cannot set up Poland, whom all the world through centuries has pitied and sympathized with, as the owner of her property and not have somebody take care that her title deeds are respected. You cannot establish freedom, my fellow citizens, without force, and the only force you can substitute for an armed mankind is the concerted force of the combined action of mankind through the instrumentality of all the enlightened Governments of the world. This is the only conceivable system that you can substitute for the old order of things which brought the calamity of this war upon us and would assuredly bring the calamity of another war upon us. Your choice is between the League of Nations and Germanism. I have told you what I mean by Germanism—taking care of yourselves, being armed and ready, having a chip on your shoulder, thinking of nothing but your own rights and never thinking of the rights of anybody else, thinking that you were put into this world to see that American might was asserted and forgetting that American might ought never to be used against the weak, ought never to be used in an unjust cause, ought never to be used for aggression; ought to be used with the heart of humanity beating behind it.

Sometimes people call me an idealist. Well, that is the way I know I am an American. America, my fellow citizens—I do not say it in disparagement of any other great people—America is the only idealistic Nation in the world. When I speak practical judgments about business affairs, I can only guess whether I am speaking the voice of America or not, but when I speak the ideal purposes of history I know that I am speaking the voice of America, because I have saturated myself since I was a boy in the records of that spirit, and everywhere in them there is this authentic tone of the love of justice and the service of humanity. If by any mysterious influence of error America should not take the leading part in this new enterprise of concerted power, the world would experience one of those reversals of sentiment, one of those penetrating chills of reaction, which would lead to a universal cynicism, for if America goes back upon mankind, mankind has no other place to turn. It is the hope of Nations all over the world that America will do this great thing.

Settlements may be temporary, but the action of the nations in the interest of peace and justice must be permanent. We can set up permanent processes. We may not be able to set up permanent decisions. Therefore, it seems to me that we must take, so far as we can, a picture of the world into our minds. Is it not a startling circumstance, for one thing, that the great discoveries of science, that the quiet studies of men in laboratories, that the thoughtful developments which have taken place in quiet lecture rooms, have now been turned to the destruction of civilization? The powers of destruction have not so much multiplied as gained facility. The enemy whom we have just overcome had at his seats of learning some of the principal centers of scientific study and discovery, and he used them in order to make destruction sudden and complete; and only the watchful, continuous coöperation of men can see to it that science as well as armed men is kept within the harness of civilization.

In a sense the United States is less interested in this subject than the other nations here assembled. With her great territory and her extensive sea borders, it is less likely that the United States should suffer from the attack of enemies than that many of the other nations here should suffer; and the ardor of the United States—for it is a very deep and genuine ardor —for the society of nations is not an ardor springing out of fear or apprehension, but an ardor springing out of the ideals which have come to consciousness in this war. In coming into this war the United States never for a moment thought that she was intervening in the politics of Europe or the politics of Asia or the politics of any part of the world. Her thought was that all the world had now become conscious that there was a single cause which turned upon the issues of this war. That was the cause of justice and of liberty for men of every kind and place. Therefore, the United States should feel that its part in this war had been played in vain if there ensued upon it merely a body of European settlements. It would feel that it could not take part in guaranteeing those European settlements unless that guarantee involved the continuous superintendence of the peace of the world by the associated nations of the world.

Therefore, it seems to me that we must concert our best judgment in order to make this League of Nations a vital thing—not merely a formal thing, not an occasional thing, not a thing sometimes called into life to meet an exigency, but always functioning in watchful attendance upon the interests of the nations—and that its continuity should be a vital continuity; that it should have functions that are continuing functions and that do not permit an intermission of its watchfulness and of its labour; that it should be the eye of the nations to keep watch upon the common interest, an eye that does not slumber, an eye that is everywhere watchful and attentive.

What we seek is the reign of law, based upon the consent of the governed and sustained by the organized opinion of mankind.

~~~~~~

6. *American Century or Century of the Common Man?* *

HENRY A. WALLACE

~~~~~~

We, who in a formal or an informal way represent most of the free peoples of the world, are met here tonight in the interests of the millions in all the nations who have freedom in their souls. To my mind this meeting has just one purpose—to let those millions in other countries know that here in the United States are one hundred and thirty million men, women, and children who are in this war to the finish. Our American people are utterly resolved to go on until they can strike the relentless blows that will assure a complete victory, and with it win a new day for the lovers of freedom, everywhere on this earth.

This is a fight between a slave world and a free world. Just as the United States in 1862 could not remain half slave and half free, so in 1942 the world must make its decision for a complete victory one way or the other.

As we begin the final stages of this fight to the death between the free world and the slave world, it is worth while to refresh our minds about the march of freedom for the common man. The idea of freedom—the freedom that we in the United States know and love so well—is derived from the Bible with its extraordinary emphasis on the dignity of the individual. Democracy is the only true political expression of Christianity.

The prophets of the Old Testament were the first to preach social justice. But that which was sensed by the prophets many centuries before Christ was not given complete and powerful political expression until our nation was formed as a Federal Union a century and a half ago. Even then, the march of the common people had just begun. Most of them did not yet know how to read and write. There were no public schools to which all children could go. Men and women cannot be really free until they have plenty to eat, and time and ability to read and think and talk things over. Down the years, the people of the United States have moved

* *International Conciliation* (June, 1942). By permission of Henry A. Wallace and the Carnegie Endowment for International Peace.

steadily forward in the practice of democracy. Through universal education, they now can read and write and form opinions of their own. They have learned, and are still learning, the art of production—that is, how to make a living. They have learned, and are still learning, the art of self-government.

If we were to measure freedom by standards of nutrition, education, and self-government, we might rank the United States and certain nations of Western Europe very high. But this would not be fair to other nations where education has become widespread only in the last twenty years. In many nations, a generation ago, nine out of ten of the people could not read or write. Russia, for example, was changed from an illiterate to a literate nation within one generation and, in the process, Russia's appreciation of freedom was enormously enhanced. In China, the increase during the past thirty years in the ability of the people to read and write has been matched by their increased interest in real liberty.

Everywhere, reading and writing are accompanied by industrial progress, and industrial progress sooner or later inevitably brings a strong labor movement. From a long-time and fundamental point of view, there are no backward people which are lacking in mechanical sense. Russians, Chinese, and the Indians both of India and the Americas all learn to read and write and operate machines just as well as your children and my children. Everywhere the common people are on the march. Thousands of them are learning to read and write, learning to think together, learning to use tools. These people are learning to think and work together in labor movements, some of which may be extreme or impractical at first, but which eventually will settle down to serve effectively the interests of the common man.

When the freedom-loving people march—when the farmers have an opportunity to buy land at reasonable prices and to sell the produce of their land through their own organizations, when workers have the opportunity to form unions and bargain through them collectively, and when the children of all the people have an opportunity to attend schools which teach them truths of the real world in which they live—when these opportunities are open to everyone, then the world moves straight ahead.

But in countries where the ability to read and write has been recently acquired or where the people have had no long experience in governing themselves on the basis of their own thinking, it is easy for demagogues to arise and prostitute the mind of the common man to their own base ends. Such a demagogue may get financial help from some person of wealth who is unaware of what the end result will be. With this backing, the demagogue may dominate the minds of the people, and, from whatever degree of freedom they have, lead them backward into slavery. Herr Thyssen, the wealthy German steel man, little realized what he was doing when he gave Hitler enough money to enable him to play on the minds of the German people. The demagogue is the curse of the modern world, and of all the demagogues, the worst are those financed by well-meaning wealthy men who sincerely believe that their wealth is likely to be safer if they can hire men with political "it" to change the sign posts and lure the people back into slavery of the most degraded kind. Unfortunately for the wealthy men who finance movements of this sort, as well as for the people themselves, the successful demagogue is a powerful genie who, when once let out of his bottle, refuses to obey anyone's command. As long as his spell holds, he defies God Himself, and Satan is turned loose upon the world.

Through the leaders of the Nazi revolution, Satan now is trying to lead the common man of the whole world back into slavery and darkness. For the stark truth is that the violence preached by the Nazis is the devil's own religion of darkness. So also is the doctrine that one race or one class is by heredity superior and that all other races or classes are supposed to be slaves. The belief in one Satan-inspired Fuehrer, with his Quislings, his Lavals, and his Mussolinis—his "gauleiters" in every nation in the world —is the last and ultimate darkness. Is there any hell hotter than that of being a Quisling, unless it is that of being a Laval or a Mussolini?

In a twisted sense, there is something almost great in the figure of the Supreme Devil operating through a human form, in a Hitler who has the daring to spit straight into the eye of God and man. But the Nazi system has a heroic position for only one leader. By definition only one person is allowed to retain full sovereignty over his own soul. All the rest are stooges —they are stooges who have been mentally and politically degraded, and who feel that they can get square with the world only by mentally and politically degrading other people. These stooges are really psychopathic cases. Satan has turned loose upon us the insane.

The march of freedom of the past hundred and fifty years has been a long-drawn-out people's revolution. In this Great Revolution of the people, there were the American Revolution of 1775, the French Revolution of 1792, the Latin-American revolutions of the Bolivarian era, the German revolution of 1848, and the Russian Revolution of 1918. Each spoke for the common man in terms of blood on the battlefield. Some went to excess. But the significant thing is that the people groped their way to the light. More of them learned to think and work together.

The people's revolution aims at peace and not at violence, but if the rights of the common man are attacked, it unleashes the ferocity of a she-bear who has lost a cub. When the Nazi psychologists tell their master Hitler that we in the United States may be able to produce hundreds of thousands of planes, but that we have no will to fight, they are only fooling themselves and him. The truth is that when the rights of the American people are transgressed, as those rights have been transgressed, the American people will fight with a relentless fury which will drive the ancient

Teutonic gods back cowering into their caves. The Götterdämmerung has come for Odin and his crew.

The people are on the march toward even fuller freedom than the most fortunate peoples of the earth have hitherto enjoyed. No Nazi counter-revolution will stop it. The common man will smoke the Hitler stooges out into the open in the United States, in Latin America, and in India. He will destroy their influence. No Lavals, no Mussolinis will be tolerated in a Free World.

The people in their millennial and revolutionary march toward manifesting here on earth the dignity that is in every human soul, hold as their credo the Four Freedoms enunciated by President Roosevelt in his message to Congress on January 6, 1941. These four freedoms are the very core of the revolution for which the United Nations have taken their stand. We who live in the United States may think there is nothing very revolutionary about freedom of religion, freedom of expression, and freedom from the fear of secret police. But when we begin to think about the significance of freedom from want for the average man, then we know that the revolution of the past hundred and fifty years has not been completed, either here in the United States or in any other nation in the world. We know that this revolution cannot stop until freedom from want has actually been attained.

And now, as we move forward toward realizing the Four Freedoms of this people's revolution, I would like to speak about four duties. It is my belief that every freedom, every right, every privilege has its price, its corresponding duty without which it cannot be enjoyed. The four duties of the people's revolution, as I see them today, are these:

1. The duty to produce to the limit.
2. The duty to transport as rapidly as possible to the field of battle.
3. The duty to fight with all that is in us.
4. The duty to build a peace—just, charitable, and enduring.

The fourth duty is that which inspires the other three.

We failed in our job after World War I. We did not know how to go about it to build an enduring world-wide peace. We did not have the nerve to follow through and prevent Germany from rearming. We did not insist that she "learn war no more." We did not build a peace treaty on the fundamental doctrine of the people's revolution. We did not strive wholeheartedly to create a world where there could be freedom from want for all the peoples. But by our very errors we learned much, and after this war we shall be in position to utilize our knowledge in building a world which is economically, politically and, I hope, spiritually sound.

Modern science, which is a by-product and an essential part of the people's revolution, has made it technologically possible to see that all of the people of the world get enough to eat. Half in fun and half seriously, I said the other day to Madame Litvinoff: "The object of this war is to make sure that everybody in the world has the privilege of drinking a quart of milk a day." She replied: "Yes, even half a pint." The peace must mean a better standard of living for the common man, not merely in the United States and England, but also in India, Russia, China, and Latin America—not merely in the United Nations, but also in Germany and Italy and Japan.

Some have spoken of the "American Century." I say that the century on which we are entering—the century which will come of this war—can be and must be the century of the common man. Perhaps it will be America's opportunity to suggest the freedom and duties by which the common man must live. Everywhere the common man must learn to build his own industries with his own hands in a practical fashion. Everywhere the common man must learn to increase his productivity so that he and his children can eventually pay to the world community all that they have received. No nation will have the God-given right to exploit other nations. Older nations will have the privilege to help younger nations get started on the path to industrialization, but there must be neither military nor economic imperialism. The methods of the nineteenth century will not work in the people's century which is now about to begin. India, China, and Latin America have a tremendous stake in the people's century. As their masses learn to read and write, and as they become productive mechanics, their standard of living will double and treble. Modern science, when devoted whole-heartedly to the general welfare, has in it potentialities of which we do not yet dream.

And modern science must be released from German slavery. International cartels that serve American greed and the German will to power must go. Cartels in the peace to come must be subjected to international control for the common man, as well as being under adequate control by the respective home governments. In this way, we can prevent the Germans from again building a war machine while we sleep. With international monopoly pools under control, it will be possible for inventions to serve all the people instead of only the few.

Yes, and when the time of peace comes, the citizen will again have a duty, the supreme duty of sacrificing the lesser interest for the greater interest of the general welfare. Those who write the peace must think of the whole world. There can be no privileged peoples. We ourselves in the United States are no more a master race than the Nazis. And we cannot perpetuate economic warfare without planting the seeds of military warfare. We must use our power at the peace table to build an economic peace that is just, charitable, and enduring.

If we really believe that we are fighting for a people's peace, all the rest becomes easy. Production, yes—it will be easy to get production without either strikes or sabotage; production with the whole-hearted cooperation between willing arms and keen brains; enthusiasm, zip, energy geared to the tempo of keeping at it everlastingly day after day. Hitler knows as well as those of us who sit in on the War Production Board meetings that we here in the United States are winning the battle of production. He knows that both labor and business in the United States are doing a most remarkable job and that his only hope is to crash through to a complete victory some time during the next six months.

And then there is the task of transportation to the line of battle by truck, by railroad car, by ship. We shall joyously deny ourselves so that our transportation system is improved by at least 30 per cent.

I need say little about the duty to fight. Some people declare, and Hitler believes, that the American people have grown soft in the last generation. Hitler agents continually preach in South America that we are cowards, unable to use, like the "brave" German soldiers, the weapons of modern war. It is true that American youth hates war with a holy hatred. But because of that fact and because Hitler and the German people stand as the very symbol of war, we shall fight with a tireless enthusiasm until war and the possibility of war have been removed from this planet. We shall cleanse the plague spot of Europe, which is Hitler's Germany, and with it the hell-hole of Asia— Japan.

The American people have always had guts and always will have. You know the story of Bomber Pilot Dixon and Radioman Gene Aldrich and Ordnanceman Tony Pastula—the story which Americans will be telling their children for generations to illustrate man's ability to master any fate. These men lived for thirty-four days on the open sea in a rubber life raft, eight feet by four feet, with no food but that which they took from the sea and the air with one pocket knife and a pistol. And yet they lived it through and came at last to the beach of an island they did not know. In spite of their suffering and weakness, they stood like men, with no weapon left to protect themselves, and no shoes on their feet or clothes on their backs, and walked in military file because, they said, "If there were Japs, we didn't want to be crawling."

The American fighting men, and all the fighting men of the United Nations, will need to summon all their courage during the next few months. I am convinced that the summer and fall of 1942 will be a time of supreme crisis for us all. Hitler, like the prize-fighter who realizes he is on the verge of being knocked out, is gathering all his remaining forces for one last desperate blow. There is abject fear in the heart of the madman and a growing discontent among his people as he prepares for his last all-out offensive.

We may be sure that Hitler and Japan will cooperate to do the unexpected —perhaps an attack by Japan against Alaska and our Northwest coast at a time when German transport planes will be shuttled across from Dakar to furnish leadership and stiffening to a German uprising in Latin America. In any event, the psychological and sabotage offensive in the United States and Latin America will be timed to coincide with, or anticipate by a few weeks, the height of the military offensive.

We must be especially prepared to stifle the fifth columnists in the United States who will try to sabotage not merely our war material plants, but even more important, our minds. We must be prepared for the worst kind of fifth column work in Latin America, much of it operating through the agency of governments with which the United States at present is at peace. When I say this, I recognize that the peoples, both of Latin America and of the nations supporting the agencies through which the fifth columnists work, are overwhelmingly on the side of the democracies. We must expect the offensive against us on the military, propaganda, and sabotage fronts, both in the United States and in Latin America, to reach its apex some time during the next few months. The convulsive efforts of the dying madman will be so great that some of us may be deceived into thinking that the situation is bad at a time when it is really getting better. But in the case of most of us, the events of the next few months, disturbing though they may be, will only increase our will to bring about complete victory in this war of liberation. Prepared in spirit we cannot be surprised. Psychological terrorism will fall flat. As we nerve ourselves for the supreme effort in this hemisphere we must not forget the sublime heroism of the oppressed in Europe and Asia whether it be in the mountains of Yugoslavia, the factories of Czechoslovakia and France, the farms of Poland, Denmark, Holland, and Belgium, among the seamen of Norway, or in the occupied areas of China and the Dutch East Indies. Everywhere the soul of man is letting the tyrant know that slavery of the body does not end resistance.

There can be no half measures. North, South, East, West and Middle West—the will of the American people is for complete victory.

No compromise with Satan is possible. We shall not rest until all the victims under the Nazi yoke are freed. We shall fight for a complete peace as well as a complete victory.

The people's revolution is on the march, and the Devil and all his angels cannot prevail against it. They cannot prevail, for on the side of the people is the Lord.

> "He giveth power to the faint; to them
> that have no might He increaseth strength. . . .
> They that wait upon the Lord shall mount up
> with wings as eagles; they shall run, and
> not be weary; they shall walk and not be faint."

Strong in the strength of the Lord, we who fight in the people's cause will not stop until that cause is won.

7. *American Affirmations of World Government* *

Resolutions Requesting Congress to Invite All Nations to Unite in the Formulation of a World State, Adopted by Senate of the Commonwealth of Massachusetts, February 23, 1915, and by the House of Representatives on February 26, 1915.

HOUSE .No. 1226

Resolutions accompanying the petition of R. L. Bridgman and others for the adoption of resolutions favoring the organization of all the nations into a World State. Federal Relations. January 21.

THE COMMONWEALTH OF MASSACHUSETTS

In the Year One Thousand Nine Hundred and Fifteen

RESOLUTIONS

Requesting Congress to invite All the Nations to Unite in the Formation of a World State.

Whereas, The incalculable cost and calamity of the European war have caused a strong public sentiment for the end of all war, therefore be it
Resolved, That the general court of Massachusetts hereby respectfully requests the Congress of the United States to make a declaration in substance as follows:
The United States of America affirms the political unity of all mankind.
It affirms the supremacy of world sovereignty over national sovereignty.
It promises loyal obedience to that sovereignty.
It believes that the time has come for the organization of the world government, with legislative, judicial and executive departments.
It invites all nations to join with it in the formal establishment of the government.
Resolved, That this resolution be transmitted by the secretary of the commonwealth to the senior Senator and the senior Representative in the Congress from Massachusetts for presentation in their respective branches.

---

* *International Conciliation* (June, 1941). By permission of the Carnegie Endowment for International Peace.

Joint Resolution Providing for a Declaration of the Federation of the World Passed Unanimously by the House of Representatives of North Carolina March 11, 1941, and by a Vote of Forty-Five to Five by the Senate of North Carolina March 12, 1941, and Signed by the Speaker of the House and the Lieutenant-Governor on March 13, 1941.

H.R. 338 RESOLUTION 24

A JOINT RESOLUTION PROVIDING FOR A DECLARATION OF THE FEDERATION OF THE WORLD

Whereas, it is necessary at the present juncture of human affairs to enlarge the bases of organized society by establishing a government for the community of nations, in order to preserve civilization and enable mankind to live in peace and be free, the following principles and objectives are hereby enunciated in

THE DECLARATION OF THE FEDERATION OF THE WORLD

Man, the source of all political authority, is a manifold political being. He is a citizen of several communities: the city, the State, the nation and the world. To each of these communities he owes inalienable obligations and from each he receives enduring benefits.

Communities may exist for a time without being incorporated but, under the stress of adversity, they disintegrate unless legally organized. Slowly but purposefully through the centuries, civilization has united the world, integrating its diverse local interests and creating an international community that now embraces every region and every person on the globe. This community has no government, and communities without governments perish. Either this community must succumb to anarchy or submit to the restraints of law and order.

Governments can only be established through the deliberate efforts of men. At this hour two elemental forces are struggling to organize the international community: totalitarianism and democracy. The former, a recent version of repudiated militarism and tyranny, is predicated upon the principle of compulsion, rules through dictatorship and enslaves men; the latter, a proved bulwark of the rights of man as a human being and as a citizen, derives its authority from the consent of the governed, embodies the will of free men and renders their collective judgments supreme in human affairs. The corner stone of totalitarianism is the ethnographic State, whose restricted interests define the scope of its favors; the foundation of democracy is man whose integrity is inviolable and whose welfare is its primary concern. The motivating power of the former is violence; of the latter, freedom. One feeds upon unscrupulous ambition; the other upon an enlightened sense of obligation.

One or the other of these forces will now triumph and govern mankind.

The present conflict is irrepressible and decisive. It is the challenge of the ages to the generation of today, and represents those spiritually cosmic forces which visit the world at critical periods in human history to shape the destinies of men. This world cannot remain half-slave, half-free; half-totalitarian, half-democratic. The laws of civilized society prevent intercourse between slaves and free men from being either congenial or profitable. If totalitarianism wins this conflict, the world will be ruled by tyrants, and individuals will be slaves. If democracy wins, the nations of the earth will be united in a commonwealth of free peoples, and individuals, wherever found, will be the sovereign units of the new world order.

Man has struggled from time immemorial to endow the individual with certain fundamental rights whose very existence is now imperiled. Among those rights is man's freedom to worship, speak, write, assemble and vote without arbitrary interference. To safeguard these liberties as a heritage for the human race, governments were instituted among men, with constitutional guarantees against the despotic exercise of political authority, such as are provided by elected parliaments, trial by jury, habeas corpus and due process of law. Man must now either consolidate his historic rights or lose them for generations to come.

The ceaseless changes wrought in human society by science, industry and economics, as well as by the spiritual, social and intellectual forces which impregnate all cultures, make political and geographical isolation of nations hereafter impossible. The organic life of the human race is at last indissolubly unified and can never be severed, but it must be politically ordained and made subject to law. Only a government capable of discharging all the functions of sovereignty in the executive, legislative and judicial spheres can accomplish such a task. Civilization now requires laws, in the place of treaties, as instruments to regulate commerce between peoples. The intricate conditions of modern life have rendered treaties ineffectual and obsolete, and made laws essential and inevitable. The age of treaties is dead; the age of laws is here.

Governments, limited in their jurisdiction to local geographical areas, can no longer satisfy the needs or fulfil the obligations of the human race. Just as feudalism served its purpose in human history and was superseded by nationalism, so has nationalism reached its apogee in this generation and yielded its hegemony in the body politic to internationalism. The first duty of government is to protect life and property, and when governments cease to perform this function, they capitulate on the fundamental principle of their raison d'être. Nationalism, moreover, is no longer able to preserve the political independence or the territorial integrity of nations, as recent history so tragically confirms. Sovereignty is an ideological concept without geographical barriers. It is better for the world to be ruled by an international sovereignty of reason, social justice and peace than by diverse national sovereignties organically incapable of preventing their own dissolution by conquest. Mankind must pool its resources of defense if civilization is to endure.

History has revealed but one principle by which free peoples, inhabiting extensive territories, can unite under one government without impairing their local autonomy. That principle is federation, whose virtue preserves the whole without destroying its parts and strengthens its parts without jeopardizing the whole. Federation vitalizes all nations by endowing them with security and freedom to develop their respective cultures without menace of foreign domination. It regards as sacrosanct man's personality, his rights as an individual and as a citizen and his role as a partner with all other men in the common enterprise of building civilization for the benefit of mankind. It suppresses the crime of war by reducing to the ultimate minimum the possibility of its occurrence. It renders unnecessary the further paralyzing expenditure of wealth for belligerent activity, and cancels through the ages the mortgages of war against the fortunes and services of men. It releases the full energies, intelligence and assets of society for creative, ameliorative and redemptive work on behalf of humanity. It recognizes man's morning vision of his destiny as an authentic potentiality. It apprehends the entire human race as one family, human beings everywhere as brothers and all nations as component parts of an indivisible community.

There is no alternative to the federation of all nations except endless war. No substitute for the Federation of the World can organize the international community on the basis of freedom and permanent peace. Even if continental, regional or ideological federations were attempted, the governments of these federations, in an effort to make impregnable their separate defenses, would be obliged to maintain stupendously competitive armies and navies, thereby condemning humanity indefinitely to exhaustive taxation, compulsory military service and ultimate carnage, which history reveals to be not only criminally futile but positively avoidable through judicious foresight in federating all nations. No nation should be excluded from membership in The Federation of the World that is willing to suppress its military, naval and air forces, retaining only a constabulary sufficient to police its territory and to maintain order within its jurisdiction, provided that the eligible voters of that nation are permitted the free expression of their opinions at the polls.

It Being Our Profound and Irrevocable Conviction:

That man should be forever free and that his historic rights as an individual and as a citizen should be protected by all the safeguards sanctioned by political wisdom and experience.

That governments are essential to the existence of communities and that the absence of government is anarchy.

That there exists an international community, encompassing the entire world, which has no government and which is destined, as a consequence of the present war, either to be ruthlessly dominated and exploited by totalitarianism or to be federated by democracy upon the principle of freedom for all nations and individuals.

That all human beings are citizens of this world community, which requires laws and not treaties for its government.

That the present conflict is one whose issue involves the survival of free institutions throughout the world, and that it is morally incumbent upon all free peoples, before this war proceeds further, to write the definitive Treaty of Peace in terms of the Constitutions of The Federation of the World, in order that those who are called to give their lives and fortunes for the triumph of democracy may have positive knowledge of the incorruptible utility of their sacrifice, and in order that this conflict may not be fought to found a new world order at the conclusion of hostilities but to defend the existence of one already established by The Federation of the World.

Now, therefore, be it resolved by the House of Representatives, the Senate concurring;

SECTION 1. That the General Assembly of North Carolina does hereby solemnly declare that all peoples of the earth should now be united in a commonwealth of nations to be known as The Federation of the World, and to that end it hereby endorses The Declaration of the Federation of the World as is specifically set forth in the preamble hereof, and makes said Declaration a part of this Resolution in the same manner as if same were recited herein, and requests the Senators and Members of the House of Representatives in Congress from the State of North Carolina to introduce and secure the passage of a Resolution in the Congress of the United States, committing the United States to the acceptance of the principle of The Federation of the World and requesting the President of the United States to call an International Convention to formulate a Constitution for The Federation of the World, which shall be submitted to each nation for its ratification.

SEC. 2. That when the said International Convention is called, it be urged to select a territory for the seat of government for The Federation of the World, and that the nation in which the said territory is located be requested to withdraw its jurisdiction over this area and cede it to The Federation of the World for its Capital, with all the prerogatives and attributes of sovereignty, in order that there might be built in this area a City symbolic of world unity, adequate for the needs of the nations and worthy of the aspirations and destiny of mankind.

SEC. 3. That a copy of this Resolution be sent to each of the Senators and Members of the House of Representatives in Congress from the State of North Carolina.

SEC. 4. That this Resolution shall be in full force and effect from and after its ratification.

In the General Assembly read three times and ratified, this 13th day of March, 1941.

BIBLIOGRAPHICAL NOTES

Part I: The Foundations of Democracy

CHAPTER I. THE RIGHT TO REBEL

AARON, R. I., *John Locke* (London–New York–Toronto, 1937). An excellent volume in the "Leaders of Philosophy" series; Locke's political, moral, religious and educational views are examined in Part III (pp. 257–313). A useful bibliography is included (pp. 314–321). See also Carl Becker, *The Declaration of Independence* (New York, 1922), pp. 24–79; H. R. G. Greaves, "Locke and the Separation of Powers," *Politica,* I (February, 1934), 90–102; C. H. Driver, "John Locke," in F. J. C. Hearnshaw (ed.), *The Social and Political Ideas of Some English Thinkers of the Augustan Age* (London, 1928), pp. 69–96; Leslie Stephen, *English Thought in the Eighteenth Century,* 3rd ed. (London, 1902), II, 135–152; and George Santayana, *Some Turns of Thought in Modern Philosophy* (Cambridge, 1934, pp. 1–47.

ACTON, Lord, *Lectures on Modern History* (London, 1930). See chap. XIII (pp. 219–232), "The English Revolution," and chap. XIX (pp. 305–314), "The American Revolution."

BRINTON, CRANE, *The Anatomy of Revolution* (New York, 1938). An important beginning in a neglected field. Brinton does not deal with revolution in the abstract, but bases his work, concretely, on the English, American, French, and Russian revolutions. The following studies will also be found useful: Otto Bauer, *Die illegale Partei* (Paris, 1939); K. C. Chorley, *Armies and the Art of Revolution* (London, 1943); Emilio Lussu, *Teoria della insurrezione* (Paris, 1936); and Curzio Malaparte, *Coup d'Etat: The Technique of Revolution* (New York, 1932). For an annotated bibliography, see Brinton, *op. cit.,* pp. 303–319.

BROWN, IVOR, *English Political Theory* (London, 1920; 2nd rev. ed., 1929), pp. 52–67. Chapter V, "Divine Right Defeated," deals with the seventeenth-century predecessors of Locke, who is viewed by the author as a point of culmination and conclusion rather than of beginning: "Locke did not win many new positions: what he did was most effectually to consolidate the old" (p. 62). This little book by a well-known drama critic and (later) editor of *The Observer* is one of the wisest books on English political thought.

CARRITT, E. F., *Morals and Politics* (London, 1935), pp. 72–79. A brief chapter on Locke deals primarily with his solution of the problem of political obligation.

GOUGH, J. W., *The Social Contract* (Oxford, 1936). Traces the development of the social contract theory from the ancient times to the nineteenth century.

Chap. IX (pp. 119–136) is given to "Locke and the English Revolution," and chap. XIV (pp. 209–223) examines "The Contract in American Thought."

JOAD, C. E. M., *A Guide to the Philosophy of Politics and Morals* (London, 1938). Written in a style of unusual clarity, directness and pungency. Chap. XIX is "Theory of Democracy" (pp. 770–807).

LASKI, HAROLD J., *The Dangers of Obedience and Other Essays* (New York, 1930). The first essay is "The Dangers of Obedience" (pp. 1–30). Laski argues that "a healthy loyalty is not passive and complacent, but active and critical. If it finds grounds for attack, it must occupy that ground. For all obedience that has the right to regard itself as ethical is built upon a conscious agreement with the purpose we encounter. Anything else is a betrayal of ourselves; and when we surrender the truth we see, by that betrayal we betray also the future of civilization" (p. 30). The shortest introduction into Laski's political thought is *An Introduction to Politics* (London, 1931), an essay of less than a hundred pages. His greatest book is *A Grammar of Politics* (London, 1925). See also the following of his works: *Studies in Law and Politics* (London, 1931); *The Danger of Being a Gentleman and Other Essays* (London, 1939); and *Reflections on the Revolution in Our Time* (New York, 1943).

LASKI, HAROLD J., *Political Thought in England: From Locke to Bentham* (London, 1920), pp. 22–61. In this chapter, Laski gives a sympathetic account of Locke's relation to the Revolution of 1688 and his influence on subsequent English political thought, as well as his contribution to French and American political ideas and institutions. He stresses the fact that Locke was the first English political thinker whose argument was mainly secular, and that Locke rejected a purely legal theory as a sufficient basis of political society.

READ, CONYERS (ed.), *The Constitution Reconsidered* (New York, 1938). Contains papers by Charles H. McIlwain, Gaetano Salvemini, Charles A. Beard, Walton H. Hamilton, and others. See, in particular, R. M. MacIver, "European Doctrines and the Constitution" (pp. 51–62), which discusses the influence of Locke and others. The volume includes also several papers on the influence of the American Constitution on the rest of the world, in terms of both ideas and institutions.

STOCKS, J. L., *John Locke's Contribution to Political Theory* (London, 1933). A Tercentenary Address, delivered in October of 1932 at Christ Church, the college which Locke himself had attended at Oxford. The stress is on Locke's *Civil Government* as "the first adequate formulation of the principles of the Liberal State" (p. 7).

WELDON, T. D., *States and Morals* (London, 1946). The author of this suggestive work divides all theories of the state into two groups: "Some define it as a kind of organism, others as a kind of machine" (p. 26). Locke falls into the latter category; see pp. 122–147.

CHAPTER II. FREEDOM

ACTON, Lord, *The History of Freedom and Other Essays* (London, 1907), A collection of papers and essays, one of Lord Acton's most interesting works.

It is especially illuminating on the relation of freedom and religion, and contains chapters of rare judgment and scholarship on Protestant and Catholic theories of persecution.

BECKER, CARL, *Freedom and Responsibility in the American Way of Life* (New York, 1946). See especially chaps. I–III (pp. 1–64) on the American political tradition, freedom of speech and press, and freedom of learning and teaching.

BURY, J. B., *A History of Freedom of Thought* (London, 1913). A popular account in the "Home University Library."

CARRITT, E. F., *Morals and Politics* (London, 1935), pp. 56–71, 202–216. In these two chapters, the author analyzes the difficulties inherent in the concept of Rousseau's "General Will." Carritt rejects the theory of the "General Will" as well as the contractual nature of political obligation as unsatisfactory, and adopts Kant's position that moral obligation is the true foundation of political obligation. For his interpretation of the political and philosophical meanings of freedom, see pp. 192–198.

CHAFEE, ZECHARIAH, JR., *Free Speech in the United States* (Cambridge, Mass., 1941). The leading study of civil liberty in the United States; the time covered is mainly from World War I to 1941. The work contains all the important cases of the period, but the analysis goes beyond the purely legal realm into the political and social significance of the issues in dispute.

CRAWSHAY-WILLIAMS, RUPERT, *The Comforts of Unreason* (London, 1947). Should be read in conjunction with Erich Fromm's *Escape from Freedom,* to which it is, in many ways, a fitting supplement.

CROCE, BENEDETTO, *History as the Story of Liberty* (London, 1941). Heavy going in spots, but contains an interesting thesis worth pursuing.

DAVIDSON, WILLIAM L., *Political Thought in England: The Utilitarians from Bentham to J. S. Mill* (London, 1915), pp. 158–188, 216–234. An excellent brief survey of John Stuart Mill's life and political career and his major writings on ethics and politics, including detailed discussions of *On Liberty* and *Representative Government.* See also Hans Kohn, *Prophets and Peoples* (New York, 1946), whose first chapter is on John Stuart Mill (pp. 11–42).

DEWEY, JOHN, *Problems of Men* (New York, 1946). Most of the essays in this volume were written in the nineteen thirties and forties. See especially "Liberty and Social Control" (pp. 111–125), "Challenge to Liberal Thought" (pp. 143–159), and "The Revolt against Science" (pp. 160–163). The best general introduction into Dewey's thought is his *Intelligence in the Modern World* (edited by Joseph Ratner, New York, 1939), an anthology of over a thousand pages gathered from Dewey's writings up to 1938.

KELSEN, HANS, *General Theory of Law and State* (Cambridge, Mass., 1945), pp. 284–300. In this section of his major treatise, Kelsen deals with the development of the idea of freedom and its practical applications to political institutions. For a discussion of "rights," see pp. 75–90.

LIEF, ALFRED (ed.), *The Dissenting Opinions of Mr. Justice Holmes* (New York, 1929). Gives a profound insight into one of the richest and most subtle personalities in the history of American jurisprudence and political thought. The collection of his dissenting opinions also reconfirms how the minority view of yesterday becomes the generally accepted truth of today, and is, finally, destined to become the commonplace of tomorrow.

MARITAIN, JACQUES, *True Humanism* (London, 1938), and *Scholasticism and Politics* (London, 1940). The two works contain clear and comprehensive statements of Maritain's religious and political philosophy—in his case, the two are closely interrelated.

MILL, JOHN STUART, *Autobiography* (London, 1873). One of the great autobiographies of English literature. It reveals intimate insights into Mill as a man and political thinker; it is also significant for the explanation of the reasons that brought Mill eventually very close to socialism. Of his essay *On Liberty* Mill says that none of his writings "have been either so carefully composed, or so sedulously corrected as this," and he rightly foresaw that it was "likely to survive longer than anything else that I have written." See also Crane Brinton, *English Political Thought in the Nineteenth Century* (London, 1933), pp. 89–103, and, for general background, Sir Leslie Stephens, *The English Utilitarians* (London, 1900), and Elie Halévy, *The Growth of Philosophical Radicalism* (London, 1928).

ROBERTSON, J. M., *A History of Freethought,* 2 vols., 4th ed., revised and expanded (London, 1936). The classical history of free thought, covering the ancient period, the Middle Ages, and the modern era to the French Revolution. In 1929, Robertson published *A History of Freethought in the Nineteenth Century,* a worthy complement to his other work in this field.

ROOSEVELT, FRANKLIN DELANO, *Nothing to Fear* (Cambridge, Mass., 1946). Contains the selected addresses (1932–1945) of President Roosevelt, edited with notes and a bibliographical introduction by B. V. Zevin. The important addresses are all included in their entirety.

ROUSSEAU, J. J., *The Social Contract* (Everyman's Library ed., London, 1938). The introduction by G. D. H. Cole (pp. vii–xliv), succinct and lucid, covers the essential points. See also the following books: Alfred Cobban, *Rousseau and the Modern State* (London, 1934), one of the best general works on Rousseau's political ideas; Annie Marion Osborn, *Rousseau and Burke* (London–New York–Toronto, 1940); Ernest Hunter Wright, *The Meaning of Rousseau* (London, 1929); and J. Churton Collins, *Voltaire, Montesquieu and Rousseau in England* (London, 1908). For a brief and well-done analysis of later French political thought, consult J. P. Mayer, *Political Thought in France from Sieyès to Sorel* (London, 1943).

THOMSON, DAVID, *The Democratic Ideal in France and England* (Cambridge, 1940). A sympathetic account of the growth of democratic ideas in France and England, in their similarities and differences. The author sees one of the main differences in the triumph of the Reformation in England and its failure in France: democratic thought in France became anticlerical, whereas English democratic ideals were rooted in the equalitarian faith of the Puritans. For another stimulating comparison between French and English political thought, especially in relation to the different conceptions of Liberalism, see Guido de Ruggiero, *The History of European Liberalism* (London, 1927), pp. 93–210.

CHAPTER III. LIBERTY AND EQUALITY

BEARD, CHARLES A., *The Economic Basis of Politics* (New York, 1922). See the third chapter, "The Doctrine of Political Equality."

HADLEY, ARTHUR TWINING, *The Conflict between Liberty and Equality* (Boston, 1925). Hadley was a strong defender of the right of private property, and liberty meant, according to him, the enjoyment of that right. He denied the implications of equality beyond the purely formal and political realm. His thought is characteristic of an era in American life, in the late nineteenth and early twentieth centuries, in which the protection of property was considered the true objective of the American Constitution.

HALDANE, J. B. S., *The Inequality of Man* (London, 1932). A collection of essays, mostly on popular scientific topics.

HAMMOND, J. L., *The Growth of Common Enjoyment* (L. T. Hobhouse Memorial Trust Lectures, No. 3, London, 1933). The author inquires how the amenities of civilization can be made accessible to all, and comes to this conclusion: "We are still acting as if we gave beauty no place among the great ennobling and educating influences. What kind of a leisured society are we likely to produce if we start with this fallacy? How shall we hope to preserve the vitality of culture, the higher standards of taste, and the large atmosphere in which men find satisfaction in the deeper sources of happiness? Yet with the new gifts of science we can make a happier society today when our industrial supremacy is gone than we ever created when we boasted that we were the workshop of the world" (pp. 29–30).

HAYEK, F. A., "The London School of Economics, 1895–1945," *Economica* (New Series), XIII (February, 1946), 1–31. This article by a teacher of the London School of Economics and Political Science gives due consideration to the influence of the Webbs, beginning with their founding of the institution and continuing throughout their lives. It is the record of one of the most exciting educational ventures and experiences in modern time. One of the first eight students in 1895, Max Beer, describes, in intimate and personal terms, "The Beginnings of the London School of Economics" in his book *Fifty Years of International Socialism* (London, 1935), pp. 81–88.

HOBSON, JOHN A., *Towards Social Equality* (L. T. Hobhouse Memorial Trust Lectures, No. 1, London, 1931). Hobson discusses the cost of inequality, and the advances made toward more equality.

JOAD, C. E. M., *Liberty To-Day* (New York, 1935). The first three chapters take up the case against liberty; the latter three, the case for liberty. Throughout, Joad is aware of the problems of balancing liberty with equality.

LAIRD, JOHN, *The Device of Government* (Cambridge, 1944). See chap. VII, "Political Liberty, Equality and Fraternity" (pp. 117–135).

LASKI, HAROLD J., *Liberty in the Modern State* (London, 1930). See chap. III (pp. 176–247), "Liberty and Social Power."

PERRY, RALPH BARTON, *Puritanism and Democracy* (New York, 1944). A significant work on the origins of the American mind and social thought. In chap. XIX, "Equality and Fraternity" (pp. 551–582), Perry develops eight different approaches to the problem of equality, among which he includes moral, political, legal, and social equality.

SMITH, THOMAS V., *The American Philosophy of Equality* (Chicago, 1927). A philosophical work, greatly enriched by the author's practical experience in public affairs. For another American discussion, see Henry Alonzo Myers, *Are Men Equal? An Inquiry Into the Meaning of American Democracy* (New York, 1945).

WOOLF, LEONARD, *After the Deluge* (London, 1931). An important study of the growth of the democratic idea in the West in terms of "communal psychology," including a pertinent discussion of "Democracy and Equality" (pp. 195–218 of the 1937 edition, Pelican Books).

WOOLF, LEONARD, and OTHERS, *The Modern State* (London, 1933). Presents the Labor, Liberal, and Conservative viewpoints. In his section of the book, Woolf treats of the relations of liberty and equality (pp. 40–63).

CHAPTER IV. CHARACTER AND WISDOM IN DEMOCRATIC POLITICS

CATLIN, GEORGE, *Anglo-Saxony and Its Tradition* (New York, 1939). An inquiry into the moral, political, and psychological forces that have created and maintained the democratic way of life in the English-speaking countries.

FRANKFURTER, FELIX, *The Public and Its Government* (New Haven, 1930). Chapter IV, "Expert Administration and Democracy" (pp. 123–167), examines the position of the expert and the problems of administration in a democratic society. An indispensable book to the study of modern government.

KELSEN, HANS, *General Theory of Law and State* (Cambridge, Mass., 1945), pp. 419–433. Kelsen deals with the psychological and philosophical parallels between personality types and their corresponding political systems. Difficult in spots, but rewarding. See also his *Vom Wesen und Wert der Demokratie,* 2nd ed. (Tübingen, 1929), and *Staatsform und Weltanschauung* (Tübingen, 1933).

LINDSAY, A. D., *The Essentials of Democracy* (London, 1929). This short and highly readable volume of lectures (delivered at Swarthmore College in 1929) goes beneath the surface of democratic government to the very sources of the democratic way of life. It is particularly concerned with the kind of men and women without whom democratic life is impossible. The author rightly stresses the intimate relations between government and the so-called "non-political associations," and says that "in so far as our non-political associations are undemocratic—in so far as their members are not inspired by a common purpose but kept together by force—our membership of them, instead of being a training in a larger citizenship, will teach us to expect in politics a similar conflict of power" (p. 80). This is particularly true, Lindsay holds, of our industrial system.

MASARYK, THOMAS GARRIGUE, *The Ideals of Humanity* and *How to Work* (London, 1938). These two short books (published together in one volume) by the first President of Czechoslovakia provide an insight into the mind and character of a statesman who, though an ardent lover and servant of his own people, never forgot the ideals of humanity, and who, as a practical politician, adhered to the commands of integrity and wisdom. His work was continued by his disciple, Eduard Beneš; see, in particular, Beneš's *Democracy: Today and Tomorrow* (London, 1940).

MICKLEM, NATHANIEL, *The Theology of Politics* (London–New York–Toronto, 1941). A provocative analysis of the fundamental political ideals from a religious point of view.

MORLEY, JOHN VISCOUNT, *On Compromise* (London, 1874). A classic by a great Liberal statesman and thinker, which expresses one of the inner mainsprings of democratic life and the spirit that must inspire it, if it is to survive and grow. The author searches below the superficialities of governmental forms, and is concerned with the qualities that constitute a civilized political society.

MORRISON, HERBERT S., *Science and Administration in Modern Government* (L. T. Hobhouse Memorial Trust Lectures, No. 14, London, 1944). One of the top leaders of the British Labor Party discusses the impact of science on government in peace and war.

MURRAY, GILBERT, *Liberality and Civilization* (London, 1938). No one could better survey, in a brief volume, the qualities that make up civilized living and liberal thought and behavior than Sir Gilbert Murray, Britain's leading Greek scholar and a lifelong liberal in the truest (and more than political) sense of the word. See also his *Stoic, Christian and Humanist* (London, 1940), in which he seeks to define the qualities of adult and responsible freedom.

MURRAY, ROBERT H., *The Individual and the State* (London–New York–Melbourne, 1946). A history of the relationships between state and individual from the ancient times, through the Middle Ages, down to the modern times, especially in light of the new totalitarian regimes. Chapter IX (pp. 202–224) centers on the relations between "Private and Public Morality."

NIEBUHR, REINHOLD, *The Children of Light and the Children of Darkness* (New York, 1946). One of the few recent attempts to base a theory of democracy on a (somewhat pessimistic) theology and metaphysics. See especially chap. I (pp. 1–41), "The Children of Light and the Children of Darkness," in which Niebuhr develops his main terms and ideas.

STACE, W. T., *The Destiny of Western Man* (New York, 1942). This well-reasoned book traces the sources of Western civilization historically and philosophically. The author emphasizes the Greek tradition of rationalism and the Christian inspiration of kindliness as the two main pillars of Western life.

WALLAS, GRAHAM, *Human Nature in Politics* (London, 1908). Chap. I of Part II of this pioneering book, one of the first modern works to dissect the irrational factors in politics, is "Political Morality."

Part II: Antidemocratic Thought

CHAPTER V. THE POLITICS OF PESSIMISM

ALLEN, J. W., *A History of Political Thought in the Sixteenth Century* (London, 1928). The second chapter in Part IV (pp. 447–494) is on Machiavelli; the analysis is based on Machiavelli's *Prince* as well as on his other, less well-known works. Allen's study, the best treatise on sixteenth-century political thought, concludes the appraisal of Machiavelli with the statement that he "stood, in the long run, for the principle that there is no question that must not be asked nor assumption that must be made" (p. 494).

BURKE, EDMUND, *Works,* Vol. II (The World's Classics, London, 1906). Contains the two important House of Commons speeches on America: "Speech on American Taxation" of April 19, 1774 (pp. 89–152), and "Speech for Conciliation with the Colonies" of March 22, 1775 (pp. 167–238). On Burke, see Ernest Barker, *Essays on Government* (Oxford, 1945), chaps. VI and VII (pp. 155–235); Alfred Cobban, *Edmund Burke and the Revolt Against the Eighteenth Century* (London, 1929); Sir Philip Magnus, *Edmund Burke: A Prophet of the Eighteenth Century* (London, 1939); John Morley, *Burke* (London, 1879); Annie Marion Osborn, *Rousseau and Burke* (London–New York–Toronto, 1940); and Leslie Stephen, *English Thought in the Eighteenth Century,* 3rd ed. (London, 1902), II, 219–252.

BURNHAM, JAMES, *The Machiavellians* (New York, 1943). Part II (pp. 29–77) deals, sympathetically, with "Machiavelli: The Science of Power." Burnham sees in the Machiavellian tradition the true foundation of politics and the science of politics. In addition to Machiavelli, he also deals with Mosca, Sorel, Michels, and Pareto. He comes to the conclusion that democracy as "self-government" or "government by the people" is impossible, and that the theory of democracy as self-government "must be understood as a myth, formula, or derivation" (p. 236).

CASSIRER, ERNST, *The Myth of the State* (New Haven, 1946). Chaps. X–XII (pp. 116–162) place Machiavelli in the context of his time, and relate Machiavellian ideas to broader problems of philosophy. A penetrating work, full of suggestive insights.

CROCE, BENEDETTO, *Politics and Morals* (English trans., London, 1946). Chap. II (pp. 44–50) is a defense of Machiavelli as seen in the light of Italian politics and traditions: "The art and science of politics, of pure politics, brought to maturity by the Italians, were to him a source of pride" (p. 47). See also chap. X, "Historical Pessimism" (pp. 136–138).

DONOSO CORTÉS, JUAN, *Ensayo sobre el Catolicismo, el Liberalismo y el Socialismo* (Madrid, 1851). The bible of Spanish antiliberal, antidemocratic, and antisocialist thought. The author starts out with the interesting assumption that every great political question involves a great theological question. He then proceeds to demonstrate that modern liberalism and socialism are nothing but doctrinal "errors" from the point of view of Catholic theology. For a more recent Spanish version of antidemocratic political thought, see Ramiro de Maeztu, *Defensa de la Hispanidad* (Madrid, 1934). This book has influenced, more than any other single source, the ideology of Franco Fascism. It is anti-French, anti-American, and anti-English on ideological and political grounds, and extols the authoritarian virtues of sixteenth- and seventeenth-century Spain, including the blessings of the Inquisition. The best anthology of recent Spanish and Hispanic-American thought is José Gaos (ed.), *Antología de pensamiento de lengua española en la edad contemporanea* (Mexico City, 1945).

EDWARDS, H. W. J., *The Radical Tory: Disraeli's Political Development Illustrated from His Original Writings and Speeches* (London, 1937). After Burke, no one has influenced British conservative thought more profoundly than Benjamin Disraeli. This volume of selections provides a useful guide to his thought.

GOOCH, G. P., *Hobbes* (London, 1939). This "Annual Lecture on a Master Mind" (under the auspices of the Henriette Hertz Fund of the British Academy) presents, in brief and clear form, the main outlines of Hobbes's thought, political and philosophical. Hobbes is placed in the perspective of English history and his later influence at home and abroad. Gooch concludes that it "is one of the ironies of history that the disciples whom the author of *Leviathan* failed to find in his own country and his own time are crowding the continental stage after the lapse of three hundred years" (p. 42). See also G. E. G. Catlin, *Thomas Hobbes as Philosopher, Publicist and Man of Letters* (Oxford, 1922); John Laird, *Hobbes* (London, 1934); and E. L. Woodward, "Thomas Hobbes," in F. J. C. Hearnshaw (ed.), *Social and Political Ideas of Some Great Thinkers of the Sixteenth and Seventeenth Centuries* (London, 1926), chap. VII (pp. 153–173).

HOBBES, THOMAS, *Leviathan* (Blackwell's Political Texts, Oxford, 1946). Contains a long "Introduction" (pp. vii–lxvi) by Michael Oakeshott, which is one of the best half-dozen studies of the *Leviathan* ever published. It throws new light on that classic, and deviates substantially from the orthodox interpretations. For another unorthodox analysis, see Leo Strauss, *The Political Philosophy of Hobbes* (Oxford, 1936).

LASKI, HAROLD J., *The Dangers of Obedience and Other Essays* (New York, 1930). Chap. IX, "Machiavelli and the Present Time" (pp. 238–263), is sharply critical of Machiavelli, whose doctrine is called a "gospel of death" (p. 262).

LASKI, HAROLD J., *Political Thought in England: From Locke to Bentham* (London, 1920), pp. 165–215. In the sixth chapter, Laski gives a more than sympathetic account of Burke: "There is hardly a greater figure in the history of political thought in England" (p. 214). Similar, and even more lyrical, expressions are interesting evidence of the hold that the greatest conservative writer in England has over a liberal and socialist like Laski. This extensive study of Burke, including some important critical observations, is highly revealing of the political and intellectual climate in England.

MAINE, Sir HENRY, *Popular Government* (New York, 1886). At a time when popular government seemed to progress toward eventual acceptance everywhere, Sir Henry Maine was one of the few Englishmen to sound a note of pessimism in an atmosphere of buoyant optimism. His principal argument against democracy was that "multitudes include too much ignorance to be capable of understanding their interest" (p. 86). An incisive analysis of his ideas will be found in K. B. Smellie, "Sir Henry Maine," *Economica,* VIII (March, 1928), 64–94.

MENCKEN, HENRY L., *Notes on Democracy* (New York, 1926). Strongly Nietzschean, and full of witty pessimism and cynicism about democracy. One of Mencken's main conclusions on democracy is: "It is incomparably idiotic, and hence incomparably amusing" (p. 211).

MORLEY, JOHN Viscount, *Politics and History* (London, 1923). A collection of essays, with an interesting paper on Machiavelli (pp. 129–180), written from a Liberal point of view.

OLSCHKI, LEONARDO, *Machiavelli the Scientist* (Berkeley, 1945). A very brief and suggestive interpretation of Machiavelli in the light of the new scientific tendencies of his time. Olschki characterizes Machiavelli as "one of the greatest exponents of the laical genius of Italy that sought clarity, knowledge and wisdom as manifestations of a free human judgment and of autonomous intellectual experiences" (p. 56).

PAINE, THOMAS, *The Rights of Man* (London, 1791). Probably the most famous answer to Burke's *Reflections on the Revolution in France;* the two should be read together.

CHAPTER VI. THE IDOL STATE

BROWN, IVOR, *English Political Theory,* 2nd rev. ed. (London, 1929), pp. 136–151. In the chapter "Collectivism and the Sovereign State" Brown deals with the impact of Hegel's political philosophy on English thought, particularly his doctrine of "Real Will" or (as Rousseau called it) "General Will." Brown concludes that this doctrine is "psychologically false" and "practically vicious," because it "hands unlimited powers to the person or persons who can claim to formulate it, and creates a superior class who can logically inflict 'forcible freedom' on everybody else for their 'real good'. Plato and Hegel faced the results of their premises and stood rightly against democracy" (p. 149).

CARRITT, E. F., *Morals and Politics* (London, 1935), pp. 105–127. Incisive and critical analysis of the moral foundations of Hegelian political thought, especially of Hegel's approach to the problem of political obligation. For a discussion of the two chief exponents of Hegelian political philosophy in England, Green and Bosanquet, see pp. 128–157. The best answer to Hegel and Bosanquet is L. T. Hobhouse, *The Metaphysical Theory of the State* (London, 1918). See, especially, chap. III, "The Real Will," and Appendix I, "Hegel's Theory of the Will." John H. Muirhead, *The Platonic Tradition in Anglo-Saxon Philosophy* (New York, 1931), takes up the problem of Hegelian influences in England and America (pp. 147–218, 315–323).

KOLNAI, AUREL, *The War Against the West* (New York, 1938). Chap. III (pp. 106–176) deals with German concepts of the state, based entirely on original German sources. This is one of the most authoritative studies of German thought, thoroughly documented and fully comprehensive. The spiritual challenge of German thought to the West is the theme of both the "Introduction" (pp. 17–27) and the "Conclusion" (pp. 672–685). A very useful bibliography of social and political thought, mostly favorable to antidemocratic nationalism and militarism, will be found on pp. 687–701.

MARCUSE, HERBERT, *Reason and Revolution: Hegel and the Rise of Social Theory* (London–New York–Toronto, 1941). A sympathetic account of Hegel's thought, written with insight and learning. For a general introduction into Hegel's philosophy, see G. R. G. Mure, *An Introduction to Hegel* (Oxford, 1940). The following controversy about Hegel's "Prussianism" will be found very stimulating: T. M. Knox, "Hegel and Prussianism," *Philosophy,* XV (January, 1940), 51–63; E. F. Carritt, "Hegel and Prussianism," *ibid.* (April, 1940), 190–196; and the final rejoinders by both Knox and Carritt, "Hegel and Prussianism," *ibid.* (July, 1940), 313–320. See also Bertrand Russell, *A History of Western Philosophy* (New York, 1945) pp. 730–746.

POPPER, K. R., *The Open Society and Its Enemies,* 2 vols. (London, 1945). One of the outstanding treatises on a vital issue: the struggle, in history, between social science and social myth. In the first volume, Popper presents Plato as the founder of the unscientific, dogmatic, and irrational tradition that has done so much harm in hampering the development of rational social thought and institutions. In the second volume, Hegel and Marx are similarly dealt with, Hegel much more severely than Marx. See, in particular, chap. 12, "Hegel and the New Tribalism" (pp. 25–76).

REHFISCH, HANS J., *In Tyrannos: Four Centuries of Struggle Against Tyranny in Germany* (London, 1944). Purports to give the "other side" of German thought and history; on the whole, it admirably achieves its task, although the inclusion of Hegel seems slightly dubious.

SANTAYANA, GEORGE, *Egotism in German Philosophy* (New York, 1916). A general inquiry into the nature of German philosophy and an examination of individual German thinkers like Goethe, Kant, and Nietzsche. A useful supplement to this work, written from a different point of view, is John Dewey, *German Philosophy and Politics* (New York, 1915).

SONTAG, RAYMOND, "The Future in Retrospect: The Germany of Treitschke," *Foreign Affairs,* XVIII (October, 1939), 127–139. One of the most trenchant analyses of Treitschke's *Politics.* One of Sontag's main conclusions is that the *Politics* "is valuable today because from its pages we can learn how much of the contemporary Germany is rooted deep in the past and therefore unlikely to be easily uprooted" (p. 137).

STIRK, S. C., *The Prussian Spirit: A Survey of German Literature and Politics, 1914–1940* (London, 1941). A valuable book because it is the only account, in English, of major German writers whose influence at home has been profound, although their work is virtually unknown abroad. See also Rohan D'O. Butler, *The Roots of National Socialism, 1783–1933* (New York, 1942).

TROELTSCH, ERNST, "The Ideas of Natural Law and Humanity in World Politics" (1922), in Otto Gierke, *Natural Law and the Theory of Society, 1500 to 1800* (trans. by Ernest Barker, Cambridge, 1934), I, 201–222. This lecture by Troeltsch is a profound and penetrating comparison between German and Western thought. Troeltsch points out in what basic respects German thought is opposed to the Western tradition, and he suggests that these contrasts are not the product of the last hundred or two hundred years but go back perhaps to the Middle Ages. For a good summary of German Liberalism, see Guido de Ruggiero, *The History of European Liberalism* (London, 1927), pp. 211–274; Federico Federici, *Der deutsche Liberalismus* (Zurich, 1946), an anthology of German Liberal thought from Kant to Thomas Mann; and Rudolf Olden, *The History of Liberty in Germany* (London, 1946).

WELDON, T. D., *States and Morals* (London, 1946). The conception of the state as an organism is, according to Weldon, one of the two basic political theories (the other is the idea of the state as a machine). Starting from this interesting assumption, Weldon discusses Hegel (pp. 86–98) and some of the main criteria of German political thought (pp. 178–186).

CHAPTER VII. THE CRY FOR THE LEADER

BENTLEY, ERIC RUSSELL, *A Century of Hero-Worship* (Philadelphia–New York, 1944). In Part I (pp. 15–77), "Thomas Carlyle," the author comes to the somewhat contradictory conclusion that one side of Carlyle "prefigures the best in democratic thought" (chiefly because of his opposition to economic liberalism), and that another side of him "prefigures the highbrow Fascism of our time, the Fascism of Knut Hamsun, Léon Daudet, Lawrence Dennis, and the professors of Hitler's Germany" (p. 77).

BRINTON, CRANE, *Nietzsche* (Cambridge, Mass., 1941). This is the best general introduction into Nietzsche's thought, especially his political ideas. See also George Allen Morgan, *What Nietzsche Means* (Cambridge, Mass., 1941), and Frederick Copleston, S. J., *Friedrich Nietzsche: Philosopher of Culture.* For more sympathetic accounts, consult M. P. Nicolas, *From Nietzsche Down to Hitler* (London, 1938), and Heinrich Mann, *Nietzsche* (Living Thoughts Library, New York, 1939).

BURNHAM, JAMES, *The Machiavellians* (New York, 1943). In Part III (pp. 81–115), "Mosca: The Theory of the Ruling Class," Burnham sees in Mosca one of the great representatives of the Machiavellian tradition. Thoroughly agreeing with Mosca's analysis of the ruling class, Burnham writes as follows: "No societies are governed by the people, by a majority; all societies, including societies called democratic, are ruled by a minority" (p. 236).

GRIERSON, H. J. C., *Carlyle and Hitler* (Cambridge, 1933). In many respects sympathetic to Carlyle's social and political views. The author, a distinguished Scottish literary critic and scholar, is particularly impressed with Carlyle's revolt against *laissez faire.*

MUIRHEAD, JOHN H., *The Platonic Tradition in Anglo-Saxon Philosophy* (New York, 1931). Contains a chapter, "Carlyle's Transcendental Symbolism" (pp. 123–146), which is, on the whole, very sympathetic to him. The interpretation of Carlyle's philosophy is interesting inasmuch as it traces the German sources of some of Carlyle's main ideas and attitudes. For another sympathetic account of Carlyle, see chap. XV of *The Myth of the State,* by Ernst Cassirer (New Haven, 1946), pp. 189–223.

NIETZSCHE, FRIEDRICH, *The Philosophy of Friedrich Nietzsche* (New York, n.d.). This Modern Library "Giant" contains the following five books by Nietzsche: *Thus Spake Zarathustra, Beyond Good and Evil, The Genealogy of Morals, Ecce Homo,* and *The Birth of Tragedy.*

SCHAPIRO, J. SALWYN, "Thomas Carlyle: Prophet of Fascism," *The Journal of Modern History,* XVII (June, 1945), 97–115. The experience of Fascism and Nazism has shown Carlyle in a new light, as this important study demonstrates. For a critical appraisal of Carlyle, see also J. M. Robertson, *Modern Humanists Reconsidered* (London, 1927), chap. I (pp. 1–43), and Crane Brinton, *English Political Thought in the Nineteenth Century* (London, 1933), pp. 164–177.

STACE, W. T., *The Destiny of Western Man* (New York, 1942). The last chapter is "Nietzsche or Christ?"

CHAPTER VIII. FASCISM: GOVERNMENT BY FORCE AND LIES

BENEŠ, EDUARD, *Democracy: Today and Tomorrow* (London, 1940). See chap. V, "Modern Antidemocratic Ideologies and European Democracy." As a student of politics, as Foreign Minister and President of Czechoslovakia, Beneš has had unusual opportunities to study, firsthand, Italian Fascism and, even more thoroughly, German Nazism.

BORGESE, G. A., "The Intellectual Origins of Fascism," *Social Research,* I (November, 1934), 458–485. This article by the eminent literary historian and publicist disentangles the various strands in the fabric of European Fascism. Borgese stresses the role of the romantic movement in creating an intellectual milieu which favored the growth of Fascist ideas. A similar view of romanticism is also expressed in Peter Quennell, "The Romantic Catastrophe," *Horizon,* I (May, 1940), 328–345. By contrast, Jacques Barzun absolves the romantics from this charge in *Romanticism and the Modern Ego* (Boston, 1943).

CHAKOTIN, SERGE, *The Rape of the Masses* (London, 1940). The subtitle is "The Psychology of Totalitarian Propaganda," and the work is mainly devoted to Nazism.

COLLINGWOOD, R. G., *The New Leviathan* (Oxford, 1942). The last part is entitled "Barbarism" (pp. 342–387). In it, Collingwood defines the nature of barbarism as "hostility toward civilization" (p. 342), and then proceeds to explain barbarism through four historical illustrations. A controversial work, written in a highly peculiar and mannered style, yet rich in provocative ideas.

CROSSMAN, R. H. S., *Government and the Governed* (London, 1939). Crossman was a teacher of political philosophy at Oxford, before he entered practical politics; after he was elected as a Member of Parliament in 1945, he quickly became the unacknowledged leader of a substantial group of younger Labor M.P.s who dissented, at times, from the official party "line." Chap. IX of *Government and the Governed* is "The Fascist Revolutions" (pp. 246–297).

DENNIS, LAWRENCE, *The Coming American Fascism* (New York, 1936), and *The Dynamics of War and Revolution* (New York, 1940). Dennis is one of the two or three leading fascist writers in the United States. For an authoritative statement of the main ideas of British Fascism, see Sir Oswald Mosley, *The Greater Britain* (London, 1934). Sir Oswald, the leader of the British Fascists, was interned throughout most of World War II. Dennis was unsuccessfully indicted.

DUTT, R. PALME, *Fascism and Social Revolution* (New York, 1935). One of the most authoritative interpretations of Fascism from a Marxist-Communist point of view. Dutt stresses the thesis that Fascism is essentially a symptom of capitalism in decay.

JOAD, C. E. M., *A Guide to the Philosophy of Politics and Morals* (London, 1938). Chap. XVI (pp. 605–663), "Theory of Fascism," is a clear and fair presentation of the ethical, moral, philosophical, and political origins and characteristics of Fascism and Nazism.

MENZEL, ADOLF, *Der Staatsgedanke des Faschismus* (Leipzig–Vienna, 1935). This work by one of the leading Austrian political scientists attempts to trace the main tenets of fascist political theory to their historical origins. Menzel deals with German and Italian predecessors of fascist ideas, and makes also some interesting observations on French influences like Rousseau and Sorel, and on British writers like Hobbes and Burke. His analogies are at times somewhat far-fetched, but his book is valuable in presenting the thesis that Fascism and Nazism have deep roots in the Western world, and cannot be simply explained by the iniquities of the Versailles Treaty and high unemployment figures.

MYERS, GUSTAVUS, *History of Bigotry in the United States* (New York, 1943). This work by a great, and unorthodox, American historian is of considerable importance to the understanding of antidemocratic attitudes. Myers succeeds in establishing the fact that the antidemocratic tradition in the United States (as revealed in religious and racial bigotry) has always existed side by side with the official democratic tradition of the country, although the former has never been able to win over the majority to its doctrines. The book is also valuable for the exposure of the intimate connections between religious bigotry and native American Fascism and Nazism.

NATHAN, PETER, *The Psychology of Fascism* (London, 1943). One of the few successful psychological explanations of Fascism and the fascist type of personality, by a practicing physician. See also R. Osborn, *The Psychology of Reaction* (London, 1938), which tries to combine an oversimplified Marxist interpretation of Fascism with a Freudian analysis; David Abrahamsen, *Men, Mind and Power* (New York, 1945), studies in the psychology of Nazism and Nazi leaders, including essays on Quisling and Laval; and John Dollard and Others, *Frustration and Aggression* (New Haven, 1939), chap. VII, "Democracy, Fascism, and Communism."

RAPPARD, WILLIAM E., *The Crisis of Democracy* (Chicago, 1938). Rappard, a Swiss writer, examines the growth of modern democracy and its challenge by the totalitarian systems. Chap IV deals with the origins and background of Italian Fascism and German Nazism (pp. 133–181).

SOREL, GEORGES, *Reflections on Violence* (Paris, 1906; English trans., London, 1915). This book has been of immense importance in the formation of an intellectual cult of violence. Sorel was primarily concerned with the revolution of the proletariat, but his ideas influenced also the Fascists, especially in Italy.

SWEEZY, PAUL M., *The Theory of Capitalist Development* (New York, 1942), pp. 329–347. The chapter "Fascism" is based on fairly orthodox Marxist assumptions. The author sees in Fascism "one form which imperialism assumes in the age of wars of redivision." Adopting the view that Fascism is essentially to be understood in terms of decadent capitalism, Sweezy does not give proper weight to other factors, such as historical and political traditions that determine the degree of political maturity and civilization of a society.

VEBLEN, THORSTEIN, *Imperial Germany and the Industrial Revolution* (New York, 1915). Published over a generation ago, this is still the best book on modern Germany. As in so many other matters, Veblen was unorthodox enough to perceive that German science and technology were a superficial veneer, behind which lurked archaic and antidemocratic ways of social ideas and institutions. He was the only American of his time to see that modern Japan offered a striking analogy in this peculiar combination of scientific technology and prescientific modes of thinking and living This book is indispensable to an understanding of German political thought.

Part III: Capitalism, Socialism, Planning

CHAPTER IX. IN DEFENSE OF PRIVATE PROPERTY

BECKER, CARL, *Freedom and Responsibility in the American Way of Life* (New York, 1946). Chap. V (pp. 89–122) is a defense of private economic enterprise, although it allows that there is a definite place for public intervention. However, "the primary aim of all governmental regulation of the economic life of the community should be, not to supplant the system of private economic enterprise, but to make it work" (p. 111).

BELLOC, HILAIRE, *The Restoration of Property* (New York, 1936). A defense of private property based on the "distributivist" theory, as opposed to both socialism and (unbridled) capitalism. Belloc, a leading British Catholic writer, sees in the preindustrial economy of the Middle Ages a juster distribution of property than in the monopoly capitalism of the modern era.

CECIL, Lord HUGH, *Conservatism* (London, 1912). This volume, in the Home University Library, by a leading British Conservative has an interesting chapter, "Property and Taxation" (pp. 118–158). Lord Cecil begins his argument with these observations: "Nothing has more effective significance in Conservatism than its bearing on questions of property. Ever since Conservatism arose to resist the revolutionary movement of 1789, the defense of property has been one of its principal purposes. And it is with questions of property that the most important of political conflicts in the future will be wholly or partly concerned" (p. 118).

CROMWELL, JAMES H. R., *In Defense of Capitalism* (New York, 1937). A popular book on American capitalism. See also Eric Johnston, *America Unlimited* (New York, 1944), for a vigorous defense of the American free enterprise system, and Broderick Haskell and Others, *The American Individual Enterprise System: Its Nature, Evolution and Future,* 2 vols. (New York, 1947), prepared by the Economic Principles Commission of the National Association of Manufacturers.

HAMILTON, WALTON H., "Property—According to Locke," *Yale Law Journal,* XLI (April, 1931), 864–880. Protects Locke against his own defenders, especially the zealots who have read into Locke's theories of property more than he himself meant.

HOBHOUSE, L. T., *Liberalism* (London, 1911). Chap. IV of this Home University Library volume is "Laissez Faire," and chap. VIII, "Economic Liberalism."

KEYNES, JOHN MAYNARD, *The End of Laissez Faire* (London, 1926). In this little book of fifty pages, Keynes first draws a historical sketch of the evolution of *laissez faire,* and then inquires into the economic prospects of the future. He is persuaded that capitalism, wisely managed, "can probably be made more efficient for attaining economic ends than any alternative system yet in sight, but that in itself is in many ways extremely objectionable" (pp. 52–53). Is there any way out of this dilemma? "Europe lacks the means, America the will, to make a move" (p. 54).

LARKIN, PASCHAL, *Property in the Eighteenth Century, with Special Reference to England and Locke* (Dublin, 1930). Contains analytical summaries of Locke's ideas on property and his influence on political and economic thought.

LASKI, HAROLD J., *The Rise of European Liberalism* (London, 1936). The second chapter, "The Seventeenth Century," deals with the relationships between liberalism and early capitalism, and gives an analysis of Locke as one of the central figures on this era: "His state is nothing so much as a contract between a group of business men who form a limited liability company whose memorandum of association forbids to the directors all those practices of which the Stuarts had, until this time, been guilty" (p. 116). The treatment of Locke is highly critical in this work.

SAMUEL, HERBERT Viscount, *Belief and Action* (Indianapolis–New York, 1937). This book is by a writer who has been the leader of the British Liberal Party and, simultaneously, President of the British Institute of Philosophy. Chap. XI (pp. 148–170) discusses "Poverty and Property." Viscount Samuel is a strong defender of private property as opposed to complete socialization, and holds private enterprise to be more advantageous in terms of more efficient production of goods, more competition, and better safeguarding of the standards of culture. However, he warns the owning classes that they "could fall into no greater error than to suppose that if property is to survive, poverty must be accepted also. The opposite is more likely to be true. If poverty continues, the property system will not" (p. 170).

SIMONS, HENRY S., *A Positive Program for Laissez Faire* (Chicago, 1936). Simons clearly expressed the main tenets of economic individualism and the philosophy of liberal capitalism. For a rather extreme *laissez faire* viewpoint in England, see Sir Ernest J. P. Benn, *The Return to Laissez Faire* (London, 1928), and *The Confessions of a Capitalist* (New York, 1926).

SPENCER, HERBERT, *Social Statics* (London, 1851); *Principles of Sociology,* 3 vols. (London, 1876–1896); and *The Man versus the State* (London, 1884). These three major works by Herbert Spencer are still the best and most uncompromising expression of the social and economic doctrines of *laissez faire*.

WEBER, MAX, *The Protestant Ethic and the Spirit of Capitalism* (1922, English trans., London, 1930). The great German sociologist attacks the study of capitalism from the religious angle, and stresses the role of Calvinism and Puritanism in the growth of the capitalist spirit. A not too dissimilar thesis will be found in R. H. Tawney, *Religion and the Rise of Capitalism* (London, 1926.) Weber's view is challenged by H. M. Robertson in his *Aspects of the Rise of Economic Individualism: A Criticism of Max Weber and His School* (Cambridge, 1933). Robertson adduces evidence to prove the origins of capitalism in Catholic countries like France and Italy. The answer to Robertson will be found in the work of a Jesuit writer, *The Economic Morals of the Jesuits: An Answer to Dr. H. M. Robertson,* by J. Broderick, S. J. (London, 1934). See also Ralph Barton Perry, *Puritanism and Democracy* (New York, 1944), chap XII, "The Economic Virtues" (pp. 297–320), and A. Whitney Griswold,

"Three Puritans on Prosperity," *New England Quarterly,* VII (September, 1934), 475–493.

CHAPTER X. REVOLUTIONARY MARXISM

CARR, EDWARD H., *The Soviet Impact on the Western World* (New York, 1947). Carr is one of the not too many writers on Soviet Communism for whom Russian history did not begin in 1917. He has the knowledge and historical perspective to separate, in Soviet thought and institutions, Western from Russian influences. Specifically, his short book takes up the political, economic, social, international, and ideological impacts of Sovietism on the Western world.

CARRITT, E. F., *Morals and Politics* (London, 1935), pp. 170–177. Critical analysis of "dialectical materialism."

COLE, G. D. H., *What Marx Really Meant* (London, 1934). One of the best introductions into the general body of Marx's thought, the materialist interpretation of history, his theory of the state, and his economic analyses, including the theories of value and surplus value. Cole successfully simplifies some of the complexities of Marx's ideas without doing violence to them. In addition, he points out the social changes that have taken place since Marx, and discusses their implications for socialist movements. His discussion of the new class of white-collar workers and their political psychology is particularly noteworthy.

DOBB, MAURICE, *Marx as an Economist* (New York, 1945). A brief pamphlet on the main points of Marx's economic theory in clear and elementary terms. Dobb himself is one of the leading Marxist economists in England.

DOBB, MAURICE, *Studies in the Development of Capitalism* (London, 1946). The first chapter analyzes the concept of capitalism, and opposes the Marxist interpretation of its character to non-Marxian formulations. This chapter is, to the student of political ideas, the most interesting of the book. The others are mainly historical.

EASTMAN, MAX, *Marxism: Is it Science?* (New York, 1940). A vigorously written critique of Marxist doctrine. Eastman attacks Marxism mainly on the ground that it is unscientific.

ENGELS, FRIEDRICH, *On Historical Materialism* (New York, 1940). A brief essay, published first in 1892,—one of the most succinct statements of the meaning of historical materialism. It stresses the English roots of philosophical materialism, especially Bacon, Hobbes, and Locke, the "fathers of the brilliant French school of materialists" which made the eighteenth century a "pre-eminently French century" (p. 8).

FEDERN, KARL, *The Materialist Interpretation of History* (London, 1939). The subtitle is "A Critical Analysis."

GRAY, ALEXANDER, *The Socialist Tradition: Moses to Lenin* (London, 1946). One of the few books on the evolution of socialist thought from the ancients to the moderns; interesting on the Greek, Biblical, and medieval sources of socialist ideas. Chap. XII (pp. 297–351) analyzes "Scientific Socialism" (especially Marx and Engels), and chap. XVII (pp. 459–486) is on Lenin. Gray is highly critical of Marx as a thinker and social scientists, and sees in him essentially a prophet and visionary who "has proved the most influential figure of the nineteenth century" (p. 331). As to Lenin, Gray sees his main contribution to Marxian doctrine in his theory of the dictatorship of the proletariat. Lenin's peculiar position in the history of socialism is that "somehow he got things done" (p. 484).

HALDANE, J. B. S., *The Marxist Philosophy and the Sciences* (New York, 1939). A distinguished scientist and a Marxist, Haldane attempts to apply Marxist principles and categories of analysis to the natural sciences, such as physics and chemistry, biology and psychology, mathematics, cosmology, and, finally, sociology. An unusual book that requires, apart from some familiarity with Marx and Engels, a solid knowledge of the basic data in the physical sciences.

HOOK, SIDNEY (ed.), *The Meaning of Marx* (New York, 1934). This symposium contains "An Introduction to the Study of Marx" by Sherwood Eddy; "The Meaning of Marx" by Sidney Hook; "Why I Am Not a Communist" by Bertrand Russell, John Dewey, and Morris Cohen; and "Communism Without Dogma" by Sidney Hook. Stimulating throughout.

JOAD, C. E. M., *Modern Political Theory* (Oxford, 1924). Chaps. 3–6 discuss, in elementary language, the main ideas of Marxism, socialism, syndicalism, guild socialism, communism, and anarchism. The book also contains a selected bibliography which will be useful to beginners.

KAUTSKY, KARL, *Social Democracy versus Communism* (New York, 1945). A collection of essays by the late leader of German Social Democratic thought. Of particular interest is chap. II, "Marxism and the Dictatorship of the Proletariat" (pp. 22–47). Kautsky's hostility to Bolshevism and the Soviet Union finds expression in chaps. III–VI (pp. 48–99).

LAFARGUE, PAUL, and LIEBKNECHT, WILHELM, *Karl Marx: His Life and Work* (New York, 1943). These brief "reminiscences" by Lafargue, Marx's son-in-law, and by Liebknecht, German socialist leader, reveal some of the personal traits of Marx, mostly dealing with his life in London amid his friends and political followers.

LAIDLER, HARRY W., *Social-Economic Movements* (New York, 1944). Chaps. 13–16 (pp. 121–169) deal with Marxism, particularly with the life and doctrines of Karl Marx himself. Chaps. 24–30 (pp. 347–471) discuss Communism, with special reference to the Soviet Union.

LANGE, OSCAR, and TAYLOR, FRED M., *On the Economic Theory of Socialism* Minneapolis, 1938). The two essays in this book seek to refute the charge that a socialist economy is not practicable. Specifically, Lange and Taylor turn their attention to leading opponents of socialism among economists, such as Lionel Robbins, F. A. Hayek, and Ludwig von Mises. The main argument of the two authors is that rational allocation of resources is possible under a planned socialist economy. They also emphasize that a socialist economy is not only compatible with democracy, but a natural outcome of its basic assumptions.

LASKI, HAROLD J., *Communism: 1381–1927* (London, 1927). Laski neither accepts nor rejects Marxism-Leninism *in toto*. The materialist interpretation of history seems to him, "as general doctrine, undeniable." Yet he warns that "there is no justification for the resort to violence until the resources of reason have been exhausted" (p. 180). See, especially, chap. IV, "The Communist Theory of the State." See also Laski's two pamphlets, *Karl Marx* (London, 1921) and *Marx and Today* (London, 1943).

LERNER, MAX, *Ideas Are Weapons* (New York, 1939). A study of "Lenin's *The State and Revolution*" (pp. 326–337) arrives at the conclusion that "in the movement of Western political theory he is in his realism one of the two or three towering figures since Machiavelli" (p. 337).

LINDSAY, A. D., *Karl Marx's Capital: An Introductory Essay* (London, 1925). This short volume in the popular series, The World's Manuals, attains its objective admirably. The first chapter (pp. 15–26) gives a brief outline of Marx and Hegel, emphasizing especially the influence of Hegelian dialectic on Marx. Chaps. II–IV (pp. 27–108) provide well-balanced introductions into economic determinism, the labor theory of value, and the meaning of surplus value. The final chapter (pp. 109–125) contains suggestive comparisons between Marx and Rousseau, each the father of a great revolution.

MARX, KARL, and ENGELS, FRIEDRICH, *The German Ideology* (London, 1938). Important for an understanding of Marxian philosophy and interpretation of history, this classic contains scathing criticisms of nineteenth-century German philosophers and writers.

MARX, KARL, and ENGELS, FRIEDRICH, *Selected Correspondence* (New York, 1942). Over two hundred letters, written by Marx and Engels to each other or to leading socialist writers and publicists. These letters not only reveal Marx and Engels as human beings in their relations to their friends but also contain succinctly formulated insights that frequently make a point more clearly and convincingly than more ponderous treatments in their better-known works.

POPPER, K. R., *The Open Society and Its Enemies,* 2 vols., (London, 1945). The second volume is on Hegel and Marx; chaps. 13–22 examine some of the major assumptions of Marx's thought, especially its claim to be scientific. In the literature on Marx, these studies by Popper are noteworthy for their unusual balance of judgment and historical perspective.

RUSSELL, BERTRAND, *Proposed Roads to Freedom: Socialism, Anarchism and Syndicalism* (New York, n.d.). The first part of the book looks at the past, and analyzes Marxism, anarchism, and syndicalism. The second part takes up the major problems of a socialist society, such as work and pay, government, international relations, science and art, and, finally, a vision of "The World as It Could Be Made." Unorthodox and stimulating.

STALIN, JOSEPH, and WELLS, H. G., *Marxism vs. Liberalism: An Interview* (New York, 1945). The interview of Stalin by Wells took place on July 23, 1934. Stalin denied that "the Communists are enamored with violence. They would be pleased to drop violent methods if the ruling class agreed to give way to the working class. But the experience of history speaks against such an assumption." Stalin also conceded that of all the ruling classes, the British ruling groups, aristocratic and bourgeois, were the cleverest and most flexible in granting reforms and concessions. For an introduction into Stalin's thought, see his *Selected Writings* (New York, 1942).

STRACHEY, JOHN, *The Coming Struggle for Power* (New York, 1933). Part III ("The Decay of Capitalist Culture") is, in many ways, the most interesting section of the book, dealing with the impact of decaying capitalism on religion, science, and literature, particularly in England and the United States. This book was written during Strachey's adherence to orthodox Marxism. Since 1939, Strachey has mellowed considerably and moved toward Fabianism.

SWEEZY, PAUL, M., *The Theory of Capitalist Development* (New York, 1942). Chaps. I–XII (pp. 11–236) contain one of the most authoritative recent statements of Marxian economic theory, including such basic concepts as value, surplus value, capital accumulation, the law of the falling profit rate, and crises and depressions. Chap. XV (pp. 270–286) analyzes monopoly and its impact on the nature of capitalist enterprise.

WILSON, EDMUND, *To the Finland Station* (New York, 1940). Contains studies of Marx and Engels (pp. 112–345) and Lenin (pp. 349–476). The book is also valuable for the analysis of the origins of modern socialism (especially in France) as well as for some trenchant chapters on Trotsky.

CHAPTER XI. ENGLISH SOCIALISM

BARKER, ERNEST, *Political Thought in England: 1848–1914* (London, 1915; 2nd ed., 1928), pp. 203–247. The last chapter, "Economics and Politics," traces the beginnings of socialist ideas in Britain from the eighteen eighties on. It analyzes the British reactions to Marx, and briefly indicates the birth and growth of Fabianism.

BEER, MAX, *Fifty Years of International Socialism* (London, 1935). This autobiography of a Continental socialist, who spent about a quarter of a century in England, contains some penetrating insights into English politics in general and English socialism in particular. In chap. XXIV, "Interview with Lenin" (pp. 144–159), Beer explained to Lenin some of the effects that he observed in revolutionary socialists who had fled from the Continent to England: "Revolutionary exiles, if they live for any length of time in England, turn gradually into reformists; she acts upon them as a de-revolutionizing filter. I have met in London former revolutionists and terrorists from Germany and Austria, Communards and Anarcho-Communists from the Latin countries, who had become wise in England. With an air of superior wisdom they held forth on the virtues of 'compromise, statesmanlike attitude, sagacity, well-balanced judgment, and preference of expediency to principle,' and all those stock phrases they had heard in lecture-halls, or had read in *The Times* or *The Spectator*" (pp. 152–153).

COLE, G. D. H., *Socialism in Evolution* (London, 1938). Chap. IV (pp. 133–159), "Marxism in the Modern World," is indispensable to an understanding and modification of basic Marxian doctrines in the light of social and industrial changes since Marx's death. Cole demonstrates, in particular, the impact of the growth of the white-collar workers, the "salariat," as contrasted with the old-type "proletariat" of manual workers in the heavy industries. The failure of Continental socialist parties to attract the "salariat" led to their decline, whereas the British Labor Party succeeded in winning over the allegiance of the white-collar workers, thus ensuring for itself in 1945 a strong majority in the House of Commons. The other chapters of the book deal with problems of the labor and socialist movements in Europe, particularly western Europe, and throw a good deal of light on the psychology and strategy of English socialism. See also Cole's *Persons and Places* (London, 1938), of which the following two chapters are interesting in the study of English socialism: chap. VI, "A Study in Legal Repression," and chap. IX, "Robert Owen and Owenism."

GRAY, ALEXANDER, *The Socialist Tradition: Moses to Lenin* (London, 1946). The following portions of this learned and entertainingly written work deal with English socialism: chap. V (pp. 114–135) on William Godwin; chap. VIII (pp. 197–217) on Robert Owen; chap. XI (pp. 257–296), "Early English Socialism"; chap. XIV, first half (pp. 384–401) on Fabianism; chap. XVI (pp. 433–458), "Guild Socialism," particularly on G. D. H. Cole.

LAIDLER, HARRY W., *Social-Economic Movements* (New York, 1944). Important for the study of the antecedents of English socialism, especially chap. 6, "Social Thought through the Seventeenth Century (pp. 38–43); chap. 9, "The Forerunners of Robert Owen" (pp. 71–85); chap. 10, "Robert Owen" (pp. 86–99); chap. 17, "Forerunners of Fabianism" (pp. 173–183); chap. 18, "Fabianism" (pp. 184–222); chap. 23, "Guild Socialism" (pp. 316–343).

MENGER, ANTON, *The Right to the Whole Produce of Labour* (London, 1899). Several important chapters are on eighteenth- and nineteenth-century precursors of British socialism. The English edition of the book is notable for two features: first, it contains an "Introduction" of over one hundred pages by H. S. Foxwell, mostly on nineteenth-century English socialist thought; second, Foxwell also contributed a "Bibliography of the English Socialist School" (pp. 191–267), which is unique in the literature on English socialism.

MORRIS, WILLIAM, *Selected Writings,* ed. by G. D. H. Cole (New York, 1934). This Centenary Edition contains most of Morris' essays and tracts (pp. 475–671). See, in particular, "Useful Work versus Useless Toil," "Art and Socialism," "A Factory as It Might Be," "How I Became a Socialist," and "Communism" (pp. 603–671).

PIGOU, A. C., *Socialism versus Capitalism* (London, 1937). One of Britain's leading economists deals with such issues as distribution of wealth and income, the allocation of production resources, unemployment, profit, technical efficiency, and the problem of incentive. He is sympathetic toward the method of "gradualness" in social and economic change, including the nationalization of important industries.

RUSSELL, BERTRAND, *Political Ideals* (New York, 1917). Russell's socialism is highly individualistic: "Political ideals must be based upon ideals for the individual life." He looks for a renewing of the spirit of man and society as much as for a change of the economic system of capitalism, "wasteful on the production side, and unjust on the side of distribution." The need of liberating the creative rather than the possessive impulses is strongly urged by Russell. On the other hand, he warns against the danger of overcentralization under socialism, and is sympathetic to the guild socialists and other advocates of economic decentralization.

SCHUMPETER, JOSEPH A., *Capitalism, Socialism, and Democracy* (New York, 1942; 2nd ed., 1947). A distinguished economist discusses the probable disintegration of the capitalist system and the prospects of democratic socialism in what is likely to become a classic in the literature on socialism. Schumpeter is rather critical of Marxism, and more in sympathy with the English approach.

SHAW, BERNARD, and OTHERS, *Fabian Essays* (London, 1889). The most famous document on "Fabian Socialism." In addition to Shaw, the contributors were Sydney Webb, Graham Wallas, Sydney Olivier, William Clarke, Annie Besant, and Hubert Bland. It has sold many tens of thousands of copies since its first publication, and has never ceased to be a steady seller in the field of socialist literature. For an analysis of Fabianism, see also G. D. H. Cole, *The Fabian Society* (Fabian Tract No. 258, London, 1942); E. R. Pease, *History of the Fabian Society* (New York, 1925); the Diamond Jubilee number of the *Fabian Quarterly* (No. 41, April, 1944), a special issue devoted to the history and prospects of the Fabian Society; and Margaret Cole, "The Fabian Society," *The Political Quarterly*, XV (July–Sept., 1944), 245–256.

CHAPTER XII. PLAN OR NO PLAN?

DAVIES, ERNEST, *National Enterprise: The Development of the Public Corporation* (London, 1946). The public corporation is a new and challenging institutional device of economic planning and socialization. See also William A. Robson (ed.), *Public Enterprise* (London, 1937), and Terence H. O'Brien, *British Experiments in Public Ownership and Control* (New York, 1938).

FRANKFURTER, FELIX, *The Public and Its Government* (New Haven, 1930). The first chapter, "The Demands of Modern Society upon Government" (pp. 1–35), is a concise outline of the social needs that have inevitably called for government action. In chaps. II (pp. 36–80) and III (pp. 81–122), Frankfurter discusses the following issues: "Does Law Obstruct Government?" and "Public Services and the Public."

LILIENTHAL, DAVID E., *TVA: Democracy on the March* (New York, 1944). The Tennessee Valley Authority is one of the most notable, and successful, planning experiments in the world. Its onetime chairman describes in this book how planning can be combined with the development of natural resources, with regionalism, and, above all, with democratic administration.

MANNHEIM, KARL, *Man and Society in an Age of Reconstruction* (London, 1940). A lengthy treatise, written in an unnecessarily heavy sociological jargon, but worthy of close scrutiny. See, in particular, Parts IV–VI, "Thought at the Level of Planning," "Planning for Freedom," and "Freedom at the Level of Planning."

MISES, LUDWIG von, *Socialism* (New York, 1935; originally published as *Die Gemeinwirtschaft* in 1922). An important book, because Mises was the first to popularize a few basic arguments against planning and socialism that later gained wider currency through the books of Hayek in England and of Lippmann in the United States. The reason why socialism is impossible, according to Mises, is the lack of "economic calculations" in a socialist community. In addition, all the standard arguments against planning or socialism, from bureaucratic centralization to soulless totalitarianism, are found in Mises.

SCHWARTZ, G. L., *Why Planning?* (London, 1944). This little pamphlet by a

British economist attacks the planners; it is very amusingly written, and refutes the charge that economics is necessarily a "dismal science."

WOOTTON, BARBARA, *Plan or No Plan?* (New York, 1935). Mrs. Wootton's first book on planning, and still worth reading.

CHAPTER XIII. ECONOMIC THREATS TO FREEDOM

ARNOLD, THURMAN, *The Folklore of Capitalism* (New Haven, 1937). This book, full of wit and irony as well as of learning and scholarship, shows that "political government" is not the only, or necessarily the most oppressive, form of government; "economic government," especially as it appears in corporate business and monopolies, also expresses power relations between men. Arnold shows how the folklore and mythology of capitalism transform the realities of economic government into innocent fictions and magic rituals.

BEARD, CHARLES A., *The Economic Basis of Politics* (New York, 1922; 3rd ed., 1947). One of Beard's most famous studies; it is particularly significant for its illuminating insights into the American political experience.

BERLE, A. A., and MEANS, G. C., *The Modern Corporation and Private Property* (New York, 1932). One of the pioneering works in the field of property and its transformations in the age of corporate business. The authors point to the massive concentration of property in the corporate organization of business and industry.

BRADY, ROBERT A., *Business as a System of Power* (New York, 1943). The author exposes the influence of organized big business on national government and politics, and draws his source material mainly from the United States, Great Britain, Germany, and Italy.

BRANDEIS, LOUIS, *The Curse of Bigness* (New York, 1934). The best selection of Brandeis' papers and statements on social, economic, and political issues. It has also useful bibliographies of books and articles written by, and on, Brandeis. Some of his other important books are: *Other People's Money and How the Bankers Use It* (New York, 1914); *Business—A Profession* (Boston, 1914); *The Social and Economic View of Mr. Justice Brandeis,* ed. by Alfred Lief (New York, 1930). The two most important books on Brandeis are: *Mr. Justice Brandeis,* ed. by Felix Frankfurter (New Haven, 1932), with contributions by Charles E. Hughes, Max Lerner, Felix Frankfurter, Walton H. Hamilton, and others; and *Brandeis: A Free Man's Life,* by Alpheus T. Mason (New York, 1946). The latter is based on the personal papers of Brandeis, and promises to remain the definitive biography of Brandeis as a man, creative lawyer, and progressive social thinker.

LERNER, MAX, *Ideas Are Weapons* (New York, 1939). This collection of essays has a short paper on "Woodrow Wilson: The New Freedom and the New Deal" (pp. 113–116). Lerner maintains that, despite some differences, "there is a real historical continuity between the New Freedom and the New Deal" (p. 115).

MACIVER, ROBERT M., *The Web of Government* (New York, 1947). In chap. VI (pp. 114–143), the author probes into "Property and Status" as bases of political authority: "Every system of government sustains a corresponding system of property. To change the one is to change the other" (p. 125). MacIver therefore attacks the Lockean conception of property as a right which exists prior to law and the state. In the discussion of the possibility of economic planning in a democratic society, the author argues for a mixed economy of private and public enterprise: "In the mixed economy there is not the monopoly of power that the socialist economy inevitably entails—monopoly in the sense that now there can be no foci of power outside the political order" (p. 357). MacIver takes up this issue more fully in chap. XI, "The Transformations of Function," especially in the last section on "functions of economic control" (pp. 340–359).

MADISON, CHARLES A., *Critics and Crusaders: a Century of American Protest* (New York, 1947). A good first introduction into the thinking of the major dissenters in America. The book is divided into the following sections: the "Abolitionists," the "Utopians," the "Anarchists," the "Dissident Economists," the "Militant Liberals," and the "Socialists." There is also a useful bibliography (pp. 539–554).

MERRIAM, CHARLES E., *Public and Private Government* (New Haven, 1944). In these lectures, Merriam summarizes his political thinking and experience on the relationships of public and private government. He demonstrates how political, or public, government is only one of the forms of effective social control and domination, and suggests a broader approach to the whole problem of authority, in which the power and government of social and economic groups are recognized and adequately dealt with.

NIEBUHR, REINHOLD, *The Children of Light and the Children of Darkness* (New York, 1946). Chap. III (pp. 86–118) is on the relationships of "The Community and Property." Niebuhr rejects both Liberalism and Marxism: "Neither understands property as a form of power which can be used in either its individual or its social form as an instrument of particular interest against the general interest. Liberalism makes this mistake in regard to private property and Marxism makes it in regard to socialized property" (p. 106). Niebuhr admits that, while the logic of history is behind socialization, "a wise community will walk warily and test the effect of each new adventure before further adventures" (p. 117.)

POLANYI, KARL, *The Great Transformation* (New York, 1944). A provocative and challenging inquiry into the disintegration and collapse of the nineteenth-century liberal civilization. The author sees in the doctrine of the "self-regulating market" one of the most fateful assumptions of liberal economics and politics. His interpretation of recent changes emphasizes the rediscovery of society and the reintegration of economics and politics.

SWEEZY, PAUL M., *The Theory of Capitalist Development* (New York, 1942). An account of crises, depressions, and monopolies from the Marxist point of view (pp. 133–236, 270–286).

VEBLEN, THORSTEIN, *The Engineers and the Price System* (New York, 1921). This short book is probably the best introduction into Veblen's approach to political economy. The following of his works are of major importance: *The Theory of the Leisure Class* (New York, 1899); *The Instinct of Workmanship and the State of the Industrial Arts* (New York, 1914); *The Higher Learning*

In America (New York, 1918); *Absentee Ownership and Business Enterprise in Recent Times: The Case of America* (New York, 1923); and *Essays in Our Changing Order* (New York, 1934). *What Veblen Taught* (edited, with a long introduction, by Wesley C. Mitchell, New York, 1936) is made up of selections from Veblen's more important writings. The standard biography is *Thorstein Veblen and His America,* by Joseph Dorfman (New York, 1934). A detailed bibliography of Veblen's writings will be found on pp. 519–524. Interesting analyses of Veblen are also contained in Max Lerner, *Ideas Are Weapons* (New York, 1939), pp. 117–141, and in Charles A. Madison, *Critics and Crusaders: A Century of American Protest* (New York, 1947), pp. 308–339.

Part IV: From Nationalism to World Order

CHAPTER XIV. NATIONALISM: PEACEFUL OR AGGRESSIVE?

BROGAN, D. W., *French Personalities and Problems* (New York, 1946). A collection of essays and reviews, with first-rate studies of French nationalists like Maurras and Barrès in chaps. VII, XII, and XIII. See, in particular, chap. XIII, "Charles Maurras: the Politics of Hate," for the lucid analysis of how the prophet of "integral nationalism" was finally sentenced to life imprisonment in 1944—for treasonable collaboration with the enemies of his country. A systematic study of the intimate connections between nationalism and profascist treason, in Europe and in the Americas, remains to be written.

KOHN, HANS, *Prophets and Peoples* (New York, 1946). An authority on the intellectual origins and evolution of nationalism discusses here nineteenth-century nationalism through some of its main representatives. Chap III (pp. 77–104) is on Mazzini. See also Kohn's *The Idea of Nationalism: A Study in Its Origins and Background* (New York, 1944).

MATHEW, DAVID, *Acton* (London, 1946). The best recent study of Lord Acton. See also Crane Brinton, *English Political Thought in the Nineteenth Century* (London, 1933), pp. 198–211, and E. L. Woodward, "The Place of Lord Acton in the Liberal Movement of the Nineteenth Century," *Politica,* IV (September, 1939), 248–265.

Nationalism, A Report by a Study Group of the Royal Institute of International Affairs (London–New York–Toronto, 1939). One of the outstanding investigations into the nature of nationalism, illustrated by specific case studies. See also the following: E. H. Carr, *Nationalism and After* (London, 1945), a brief survey of the evolution of nationalism in the modern era and its prospects in the future; H. Munro Chadwick, *The Nationalities of Europe and the Growth of National Ideologies* (Cambridge, 1945), with little-known facts on some medieval origins, linguistic and historical, of nationalism; John Drinkwater, *Patriotism in Literature* (London, 1924), a popularly written volume in the Home University Library; W. Friedmann, *The Crisis of the National State* (London, 1943), a notable examination of the rise of the modern national state, and of the causes of its decline and disintegration; Carlton J. H. Hayes, *Essays on Nationalism* (New York, 1926), with a valuable "Bibliographical Note" (pp.

277–279); Friedrich O. Hertz, *Nationality in History and Politics* (London, 1944), a comprehensive and scholarly work that traces the origins and evolution of modern nationalism in England, France, Russia, Austria-Hungary, and Prussia-Germany. Hertz attains a rare degree of objectivity, balance, and historical perspective. A Marxian-Leninist approach to the problem of nationalism will be found in Joseph Stalin, *Marxism and the National Question* (New York, 1942). Stalin has had a lifelong interest in this question, and at one time was Commissar of Nationalities in the Soviet government.

STANNARD, HAROLD, *What Is a Nation?* (Looking Forward Pamphlet No. 3, Royal Institute of International Affairs, London–New York, 1945). A short introduction into the various concepts of nation and nationality, analyzed against their background in the history of political thought and institutions in Europe and America.

SWEEZY, PAUL M., *The Theory of Capitalist Development* (New York, 1942), pp. 307–328). In the chapter "Imperialism," Sweezy brings the Marxist theory of imperialism up to date, and sees in socialism the only, and inevitable, answer to imperialism. This excessively economic interpretation of imperialism fails to give due consideration to the factor of power—a political rather than economic fact.

WOOLF, LEONARD, *Imperialism and Civilization* (London, 1928). A classical indictment of imperialism, written in pungent, and often brilliant, style. See also Leonard Barnes, *Empire or Democracy?* (London, 1939).

CHAPTER XV. RACE: SENSE AND NONSENSE

BARZUN, JACQUES, *Race: A Study in Modern Superstition* (New York, 1937). Especially valuable for the historical perspective it supplies. See also the following: Ruth Benedict, *Race: Science and Politics* (New York, 1943), a study by one of America's foremost anthropologists; Franz Boas, *Race, Language and Culture* (New York, 1940); V. Gordon Childe, *Man Makes Himself* (New York, 1939); John Dollard, *Caste and Class in a Southern Town* (New Haven, 1937); John B. S. Haldane, *Heredity and Politics* (New York, 1938); Friedrich Hertz, *Race and Civilization* (London, 1928); Gunnar Myrdal, *An American Dilemma: The Negro Problem and Modern Democracy* (New York, 1944), probably the most massive study of the American Negro problem ever undertaken. The most influential racialist books are Houston S. Chamberlain, *The Foundations of the Nineteenth Century* (trans. from the German, London–New York, 1911), and Count Joseph A. de Gobineau, *The Moral and Intellectual Diversity of Races* (trans. from the French, Philadelphia, 1856).

BOAS, FRANZ, *Race and Democratic Society* (New York, 1945). This volume of various essays by one of America's most distinguished anthropologists was published posthumously. In the latter part of his life, Boas took a keen interest in the political and imperialistic abuses of the racialist theories and ideologies.

HOGBEN, LANCELOT, *Dangerous Thoughts* (New York, 1940). A collection of miscellaneous essays, mostly on scientific subjects. See chap. 3 (pp. 44–58), "Race and Prejudice." Hogben spent four years in South Africa, a fertile field for studies on racialism. The quality of his writing may be judged from the following conversation (pp. 47-48):

> *Almost any South African Graduate:* If you had lived in this country as long as I have, you would know that a native can't be taught to read or write.
> *Myself:* Have you ever visited Fort Hare Missionary College?
> *Almost any S.A.G.:* Don't talk to me about missionaries.
> *Myself:* Well, I have. I have seen a class of pure blood Bantu students from the Cis-Kei working out differential equations.
> *Almost any S.A.G.:* What would you do if a black man raped your sister?

KOHN, HANS, Prophets and Peoples (New York, 1946). Chap. IV (pp. 105-130) is a critical study of Treitschke as a patriotic historian and prophet of nationalism.

KOLNAI, AUREL, *The War Against the West* (New York, 1938). Chaps. I and II (pp. 1-105) give an insight into German conceptions of nation and community. Kolnai stresses especially the "tribal egotism versus humanity and objective standards." Chaps. VIII and IX (pp. 394-671) analyze German racialism and imperialism.

MONTAGU, M. F. ASHLEY, *Man's Most Dangerous Myth: The Fallacy of Race* (New York, 1945). A competent discussion of the problem of racialism. The author explains, after a brief historical introduction into the race concept, the genetical, biological, psychological, and political aspects of the problem. One of his conclusions is that "the term 'race' itself, as it is generally applied to man, is scientifically without justification and that as commonly used the term corresponds to nothing in reality" (p. 244). The volume contains an excellent bibliography (pp. 269-289).

CHAPTER XVI. CONFLICT OR COMMON INTEREST?

BEARD, CHARLES A., *The Idea of National Interest* (New York, 1934). The subtitle is "An Analytical Study in American Foreign Policy."

BROGAN, D. W., *Is Innocence Enough?* (London, 1941). The subtitle is "Some Reflections on Foreign Affairs." Brogan writes with his customary wit and irony, and proves that, in foreign affairs, too, the road to disaster is paved with a mixture of ignorance and good intentions.

CARR, EDWARD H., *Conditions of Peace* (New York, 1942). Continues Carr's analysis of the theory of international relations which he began in *The Twenty Years' Crisis* (London, 1939).

PRICE, JOHN, *Foreign Affairs and the Public* (Looking Forward Pamphlet No. 9, Royal Institute of International Affairs, London-New York, 1946). This instructive and thoughtfully written pamphlet stresses the role that the citizen in a democracy can, and ought to, play in the formulation and understanding of foreign policy.

RUSSELL, BERTRAND, *Power* (New York, 1938). Russell analyzes the various types of power, such as priestly, kingly, revolutionary, economic, and ideological power.

SCHWARZENBERGER, GEORG, *Power Politics* (London, 1941). A systematic treatise on a complex theme, with useful bibliographies at the end of each chapter.

WELDON, T. D., *States and Morals* (London, 1946). A sound and refreshingly written book on the nature of political theory and the main types of states in historical experience. Weldon finds that there "is no universally accepted standard of morals," and that there are "numerous States with radically different moral sentiments and radically opposed political theories based on them" (p. 287). Yet he holds that such different states (particularly the United States and the Soviet Union) can exist side by side "perfectly happily," provided each knows where the other stands, and does not try to undermine the other on "first order moral questions" under the disguise of a business deal: "Provided that the two will deal with one another on second order problems (which are economic and therefore almost always capable of solution by discussion), no insoluble problem should arise. But it is obviously essential that neither the U.S.A. nor the U.S.S.R. should have any ground for suspecting that it is being sold an unacceptable political ideology by the other whenever it makes a sensible economic compromise. If both will not accept this limitation, there is nothing for it but to bring out the atomic bombs" (p. 302).

WELLESLEY, Sir VICTOR, *Diplomacy in Fetters* (London, 1944). The author examines, on the basis of long personal experience, the conditions of diplomacy under various economic and political conditions, including the relationships of democracy and diplomacy. See also Hugh Gibson, *The Road to Foreign Policy* (New York, 1944), a treatment of similar problems by an American diplomat, and Lord D'Abernon, *Foreign Policy* (Barnett House Papers, No. 14, London, 1930).

WIGHT, MARTIN, *Power Politics* (Looking Forward Pamphlet No. 8, Royal Institute of International Affairs, London–New York, 1946). An excellent brief discussion of the power factor in international relations. The author explains such concepts as great powers and small powers, the balance of power, vital interests and prestige, and briefly analyzes the impact of the United Nations on power politics.

WOOLF, LEONARD, *The War for Peace* (London, 1940). Liberal approach to international politics. See also his earlier *International Government* (London, 1916).

ZIMMERN, ALFRED, *Learning and Leadership* (London, 1930). This slim volume of slightly over one hundred pages is weightier than many a ponderous treatise in the field. The author admirably conveys the intricate and complex character of international relations, and gives a subtle account of the qualities required for their mastery, especially in a democratic civilization.

CHAPTER XVII. WAR: THE SOVEREIGN ASSASSIN

ANGELL, NORMAN, *The Great Illusion* (London, 1908; expanded, in 1938, into *The Great Illusion—Now*). Of the many works of Sir Norman Angell, this is probably still the most famous. The futility of war from an economic point of view, the nature of modern imperialism, and the need for collective security are some of the main topics of the book.

KEETON, GEORGE W., *National Sovereignty and International Order* (London, 1939). Examines the problems of state sovereignty and international order from a legal as well as a political point of view. For a fuller discussion of the legal problems consult Hersh Lauterpacht, *The Function of Law in the International Community* (Oxford, 1933), and *An International Bill of the Rights of Man* (New York, 1945).

MARRIOTT, Sir JOHN A. R., *Commonwealth or Anarchy? A Survey of Projects of Peace from the Sixteenth to the Twentieth Century* (London, 1937). A valuable aid in sudying earlier attempts to outlaw war among nations—and why those attempts eventually failed.

MEERLO, A. M., *Aftermath of Peace: Psychological Essays* (New York, 1946). The author is a Dutch psychologist and physician, who was in charge of the psychological department of the Dutch Ministry of War in London after he had escaped from German-occupied Holland. The titles of the three parts of the book are: "Three Essays on the Influence of Total War"; "The Impact of War on Social Life"; and "Psychological Peacefare." He has some especially interesting chapters on occupation, treason, hatred, fear, and psychological warfare.

MURPHY, GARDNER (ed.), *Human Nature and Enduring Peace* (Third Yearbook of the Society for the Psychological Study of Social Issues, Boston–New York, 1945). Parts I and II are "The Impulse to War" and "The Obstacles to Peace." See also Robert Waelder, *Psychological Aspects of War and Peace* (Geneva Studies, Vol. X., No. 2, Geneva, 1939).

ROUTH, D. A., "The Philosophy of International Relations: T. H. Green *versus* Hegel," *Politica,* III (September, 1938), 223–235. Elucidates the differences of thought and background between these two thinkers. Routh arrives at the conclusion that the similarity between Hegel and the modern totalitarian state on the problem of international relations is "unmistakable."

STEED, WICKHAM, *Vital Peace* (London, 1936). This "Study of Risks" has various chapters on the "case against war," the "case for war," and the "causes of war."

TOYNBEE, ARNOLD, J., *A Study of History* (abridgment of Vols. I–VI by D. C. Somervell, New York–London, 1947). Toynbee discusses, in the light of historical experience, "The Suicidalness of Militarism" (pp. 336–349).

VAGTS, ALFRED, *A History of Militarism* (New York, 1937). Particularly valuable for the analysis of the impact of militarism on political ideas and institutions.

WRIGHT, QUINCY, *A Study of War,* 2 vols. (Chicago, 1942). This work by one of the foremost American scholars in the field of international law and organization contains a wealth of data on war, its history and development, and its impact on social and political institutions.

CHAPTER XVIII. THE SUPRANATIONAL COMMUNITY

BECKER, CARL L., *How New Will the Better World Be?* (New York, 1944). Becker warns against facile optimism, and lays bare some of the intrinsic difficulties obstructing world order.

BENTWICH, NORMAN, *The Religious Foundations of Internationalism* (London,

1933). Deals with the pagan religions of antiquity, Judaism, Christianity, Islam, and the Far Eastern religions.

BEVERIDGE, Sir WILLIAM, *The Price of Peace* (London, 1945). The author states as the target: "Rule of Law in Place of Anarchy between Nations."

CECIL, VISCOUNT, *A Great Experiment: An Autobiography by Lord Robert Cecil* (New York, 1941). This human document by a great Englishman who dedicated his life to the ideal of world order is illuminating in its interpretation of why the League of Nations finally failed.

CHISHOLM, G. B., *The Psychiatry of Enduring Peace and Social Progress* (Washington, 1946). A pamphlet by a distinguished Canadian psychiatrist with extensive war experience in both world wars, supplemented by comments of Henry A. Wallace, Watson B. Miller, and others. See also Gardner Murphy (ed.), *Human Nature and Enduring Peace* (Boston–New York, 1945), Part IV, "World Order is Attainable."

GINSBERG, MORRIS, *The Unity of Mankind* (L. T. Hobhouse Memorial Trust Lectures, No. 5, London, 1935). The author, an eminent sociologist, arrives at the following conclusion: "The rate of unification has certainly been increasing enormously in the fields of economics and politics. What is needed is a parallel growth in moral wisdom. To bring social development into closer accord with ethical development is the task of social science and of social ethics in our time. In the long run our faith in the unity of mankind must rest upon our faith in the unity of human reason" (p. 29).

KELSEN, HANS, *Law and Peace in International Relations* (Cambridge, Mass., 1942). Kelsen urges that an international court with compulsory jurisdiction, rather than international government, is the immediate road to progress because "experience teaches that states submit more easily to an international court than to an international government" (p. 169).

LASKI, H. J., *Studies in the Problem of Sovereignty* (New Haven, 1917), and *The Foundations of Sovereignty and Other Essays* (New Haven, 1921). In these two books, Laski formulated his theory of "political pluralism," as opposed to the orthodox conceptions of state sovereignty.

NIEBUHR, REINHOLD, *The Children of Light and the Children of Darkness* (New York, 1946). Niebuhr develops his ideas on "The World Community" in chap. V (pp. 153-190).

REVES, EMERY, *The Anatomy of Peace* (New York, 1945). Probably the most widely read recent popular book on world government—the only way out of the present chaos of warring state sovereignties, according to the author.

WEST, RANYARD, *Psychology and World Order* (London, 1945). This short Pelican Book is a clear and elementary analysis of the psychological issues and difficulties confronting the problem of world order. The author is a practicing physician and psychiatrist.

WHEARE, K. C., *Federal Government* (London–New York–Toronto, 1946). Based on materials drawn chiefly from the federal experience of the United States, Switzerland, Canada, and Australia. A bibliography is included (pp. 261–267). See also H. R. G. Greaves, *Federal Union in Practice* (London, 1940), and W. Ivor Jennings, *A Federation for Western Europe* (Cambridge, 1940).

INDEX